CCNP Enterprise Advanced Routing ENARSI 300-410 Official Cert Guide

Companion Website and Pearson Test Prep Access Code

Access interactive study tools on this book's companion website, including practice test software, review exercises, video training, Key Term flash card application, a study planner, and more!

To access the companion website, simply follow these steps:

1. Go to **ciscopress.com/register**.

2. Enter the **print book ISBN: 9780138217525**.

3. Answer the security question to validate your purchase.

4. Go to your account page.

5. Click on the **Registered Products** tab.

6. Under the book listing, click on the **Access Bonus Content** link.

When you register your book, your Pearson Test Prep practice test access code will automatically be populated with the book listing under the Registered Products tab. You will need this code to access the practice test that comes with this book. You can redeem the code at **PearsonTestPrep.com**. Simply choose Pearson IT Certification as your product group and log into the site with the same credentials you used to register your book. Click the **Activate New Product** button and enter the access code. More detailed instructions on how to redeem your access code for both the online and desktop versions can be found on the companion website.

If you have any issues accessing the companion website or obtaining your Pearson Test Prep practice test access code, you can contact our support team by going to **pearsonitp.echelp.org**.

T0364375

CCNP Enterprise Advanced Routing

ENARSI 300-410

Official Cert Guide, Second Edition

RAYMOND LACOSTE

BRAD EDGEWORTH, CCIE No. 31574

Cisco Press

CCNP Enterprise Advanced Routing ENARSI 300-410 Official Cert Guide, Second Edition

Raymond Lacoste, Brad Edgeworth

Copyright© 2024 Cisco Systems, Inc.

Published by:

Cisco Press

1 2023

Library of Congress Control Number: 2023911481

ISBN-13: 978-0-13-821752-5

ISBN-10: 0-13-821752-1

Warning and Disclaimer

Trademark Acknowledgments

Figure credit: Figure 7-1 Wireshark

Special Sales

For information about buying this title in bulk quantities, or for special sales opportunities (which may include electronic versions; custom cover designs; and content particular to your business, training goals, marketing focus, or branding interests), please contact our corporate sales department at corpsales@pearsoned.com or (800) 382-3419.

For government sales inquiries, please contact governmentsales@pearsoned.com.

For questions about sales outside the U.S., please contact international@pearsoned.com.

Feedback Information

At Cisco Press, our goal is to create in-depth technical books of the highest quality and value. Each book is crafted with care and precision, undergoing rigorous development that involves the unique expertise of members from the professional technical community.

Readers' feedback is a natural continuation of this process. If you have any comments regarding how we could improve the quality of this book, or otherwise alter it to better suit your needs, you can contact us through email at feedback@ciscopress.com. Please make sure to include the book title and ISBN in your message.

We greatly appreciate your assistance.

Vice President, IT Professional: Mark Taub

Alliances Manager, Cisco Press: Jaci Featherly; James Risler

Director, ITP Product Management: Brett Bartow

Managing Editor: Sandra Schroeder

Development Editor: Ellie C. Bru

Senior Project Editor: Mandie Frank

Copy Editor: Kitty Wilson

Technical Editor: Hector Mendoza, Jr

Editorial Assistant: Cindy Teeters

Designer: Chuti Prasertsith

Composition: Codemantra

Indexer: Erika Millen

Proofreader: Barbara Mack

Americas Headquarters
Cisco Systems, Inc.
San Jose, CA

Asia Pacific Headquarters
Cisco Systems (USA) Pte. Ltd.
Singapore

Europe Headquarters
Cisco Systems International BV Amsterdam,
The Netherlands

Cisco has more than 200 offices worldwide. Addresses, phone numbers, and fax numbers are listed on the Cisco Website at **www.cisco.com/go**

Pearson's Commitment to Diversity, Equity, and Inclusion

Pearson is dedicated to creating bias-free content that reflects the diversity of all learners. We embrace the many dimensions of diversity, including but not limited to race, ethnicity, gender, socioeconomic status, ability, age, sexual orientation, and religious or political beliefs.

Education is a powerful force for equity and change in our world. It has the potential to deliver opportunities that improve lives and enable economic mobility. As we work with authors to create content for every product and service, we acknowledge our responsibility to demonstrate inclusivity and incorporate diverse scholarship so that everyone can achieve their potential through learning. As the world's leading learning company, we have a duty to help drive change and live up to our purpose to help more people create a better life for themselves and to create a better world.

Our ambition is to purposefully contribute to a world where

- Everyone has an equitable and lifelong opportunity to succeed through learning

- Our educational products and services are inclusive and represent the rich diversity of learners

- Our educational content accurately reflects the histories and experiences of the learners we serve

- Our educational content prompts deeper discussions with learners and motivates them to expand their own learning (and worldview)

While we work hard to present unbiased content, we want to hear from you about any concerns or needs with this Pearson product so that we can investigate and address them.

Please contact us with concerns about any potential bias at https://www.pearson.com/report-bias.html.

About the Authors

Raymond Lacoste has dedicated his career to developing the skills of those interested in IT. In 2001, he began to mentor hundreds of IT professionals pursuing their Cisco certification dreams. This role led to teaching Cisco courses full time. Raymond is currently a master instructor for Cisco Enterprise Routing and Switching, AWS, ITIL, and CyberSecurity at StormWind Studios. Raymond treats all technologies as an escape room, working to uncover every mystery in the protocols he works with. Along this journey, Raymond has passed more than 120 exams, and his office wall includes certificates from Microsoft, Cisco, ISC2, ITIL, AWS, and CompTIA. If you were visualizing Raymond's office, you'd probably expect the usual network equipment, certifications, and awards. Those certainly take up space, but they aren't his pride and joy. Most impressive, at least to Raymond, is his gemstone and mineral collection; once he starts talking about it, he just can't stop. Who doesn't get excited by a wondrous barite specimen in a pyrite matrix? Raymond presently resides with his wife and two children in eastern Canada, where they experience many adventures together.

Brad Edgeworth, CCIE No. 31574 (R&S and SP), is an SD-WAN technical solutions architect at Cisco Systems. Brad is a distinguished speaker at Cisco Live, where he has presented on various topics. Before joining Cisco, Brad worked as a network architect and consultant for various Fortune 500 companies. Brad's expertise is based on enterprise and service provider environments, with an emphasis on architectural and operational simplicity. Brad holds a bachelor of arts degree in computer systems management from St. Edward's University in Austin, Texas. Brad can be found on Twitter as @BradEdgeworth.

About the Technical Reviewer

Hector Mendoza, Jr., CCIE No. 10687 (R&S, SP, and Security), has spent the past 14 years at Cisco Systems and is currently a solutions integration architect supporting large SP customers. Prior to this proactive role in CX, he spent nearly a decade providing reactive support in High Touch Technical Services in the Security Group, where he provided escalation support for some of the largest customers for Cisco. A four-time Cisco Live speaker and an Alpha reviewer of Cisco Security courseware, Hector is a huge advocate of continuing education and knowledge sharing. Hector has a passion for technology, enjoys solving complex problems, and loves working with customers. In his spare time, he tech reviews his esteemed colleagues' Cisco Press books.

Dedications

Raymond Lacoste:

This book (just like the first edition) is dedicated to my wife, Melanie, who has dedicated her life to making me a better person, which is the hardest job in the world. Thank you, Melanie, for being the most amazing wife and mother in the world.

Brad Edgeworth:

This book is dedicated to my daughter, Teagan. Hopefully you'll want to learn what is written inside of this text. Until then, enjoy your youth.

Acknowledgments

Raymond Lacoste:

As with the first edition of this book, a huge thank you goes out to Brad for joining me on this writing adventure. Putting our knowledge together to create this work of art was the best decision. Thank you so much for sharing this with me.

Thank you to my wife and children, for allowing me to avoid many family adventures while this book was being developed and supporting me though the entire process. Love you guys!

Finally, thank you to the entire team at Cisco Press, as well as their families and friends, who work extremely hard to produce high-quality training material.

Brad Edgeworth:

To Raymond and Brett, thanks for letting me write this book. I am privileged to be able to share my knowledge with others, and I'm grateful. To the rest of the Cisco Press team, thanks for taking my block of stone and turning it into a work of art.

To the technical editor: Hector, thank you for the time and expertise.

Many people within Cisco have shared their knowledge with me and taken a chance on me with various projects over the years. For that I'm forever indebted.

Contents at a Glance

Online Elements

Contents

Icons Used in This Book

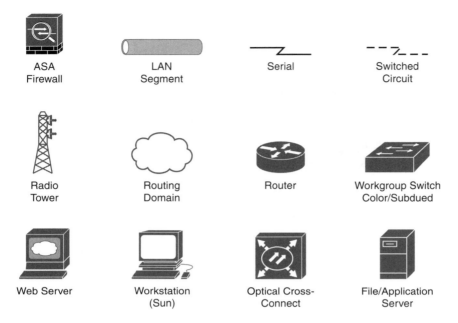

ASA
Firewall

LAN
Segment

Serial

Switched
Circuit

Radio
Tower

Routing
Domain

Router

Workgroup Switch
Color/Subdued

Web Server

Workstation
(Sun)

Optical Cross-
Connect

File/Application
Server

Command Syntax Conventions

The conventions used to present command syntax in this book are the same conventions used in the IOS Command Reference. The Command Reference describes these conventions as follows:

- **Boldface** indicates commands and keywords that are entered literally as shown. In actual configuration examples and output (not general command syntax), boldface indicates commands that are manually input by the user (such as a **show** command).

- *Italic* indicates arguments for which you supply actual values.

- Vertical bars (|) separate alternative, mutually exclusive elements.

- Square brackets ([ ]) indicate an optional element.

- Braces ({ }) indicate a required choice.

- Braces within brackets ([{ }]) indicate a required choice within an optional element.

Introduction

Congratulations! If you are reading this Introduction, then you have probably decided to obtain your Cisco CCNP Enterprise certification. Obtaining a Cisco certification will ensure that you have a solid understanding of common industry protocols along with Cisco's device architecture and configuration. Cisco has a high market share of routers and switches, with a global footprint.

Professional certifications have been an important part of the computing industry for many years and will continue to become more important. Many reasons exist for these certifications, but the most popularly cited reason is credibility. All other considerations held equal, a certified employee/consultant/job candidate is considered more valuable than one who is not certified.

Cisco provides three primary levels of certifications: Cisco Certified Network Associate (CCNA), Cisco Certified Network Professional (CCNP), and Cisco Certified Internetwork Expert (CCIE). Cisco announced changes to all three levels of certification in February 2020 and those changes still apply to the most recent exam updates. The announcement included many changes, but these are the most notable:

- The exams now include additional topics, such as programming.

- The CCNA certification is not a prerequisite for obtaining the CCNP certification. CCNA specializations are not offered anymore.

- The exams test a candidate's ability to configure and troubleshoot network devices as well as to answer multiple-choice questions.

- The CCNP is obtained by taking and passing a Core exam and a Concentration exam, such as the Implementing Cisco Enterprise Advanced Routing and Services (ENARSI).

So, if you are a CCNP Enterprise candidate you need to take and pass the CCNP and CCIE Enterprise Core ENCOR v1.1 350-401 examination. Then you need to take and pass one of the following Concentration exams to obtain your CCNP Enterprise:

- 300-410 ENARSI to obtain Implementing Cisco Enterprise Advanced Routing and Services

- 300-415 ENSDWI to obtain Implementing Cisco SD-WAN Solutions

- 300-420 ENSLD to obtain Designing Cisco Enterprise Networks

- 300-425 ENWLSD to obtain Designing Cisco Enterprise Wireless Networks

- 300-430 ENWLSI to obtain Implementing Cisco Enterprise Wireless Networks

- 300-435 ENAUTO to obtain Automating Cisco Enterprise Solutions

- 300-440 ENCC to obtain Designing and Implementing Cloud Connectivity

Goals and Methods

The most important and somewhat obvious goal of this book is to help you pass the CCNP Implementing Cisco Enterprise Advanced Routing and Services (ENARSI) 300-410 exam. In fact, if the primary objective of this book were different, then the book's title would be misleading; however, the methods used in this book to help you pass the exam are designed to also make you much more knowledgeable about how to do your job.

One key methodology used in this book is to help you discover the exam topics that you need to review in more depth, to help you fully understand and remember those details, and to help you prove to yourself that you have retained your knowledge of those topics. This book does not try to help you pass by memorization but helps you truly learn and understand the topics. The ENARSI 300-410 exam covers foundation topics in the CCNP certification, and the knowledge contained within is vitally important for a truly skilled routing/switching engineer or specialist. This book would do you a disservice if it didn't attempt to help you learn the material. To that end, the book will help you pass the exam by:

- Helping you discover which test topics you have not mastered

- Providing explanations and information to fill in your knowledge gaps

- Supplying exercises and scenarios that enhance your ability to recall and deduce the answers to test questions

- Providing practice exercises on the topics and the testing process via test questions on the companion website

Who Should Read This Book?

This book is not designed to be a general networking topics book, although it can be used for that purpose. This book is intended to tremendously increase your chances of passing the ENARSI 300-410 exam. Although other objectives can be achieved from using this book, the book is written with one goal in mind: to help you pass the exam.

So why should you want to pass the ENARSI 300-410 exam? Because it's one of the milestones toward getting the CCNP Enterprise certification, which is no small feat. What would getting the CCNP Enterprise certification mean to you? A raise, a promotion, recognition? How about enhancing your resume? Demonstrating that you are serious about continuing the learning process and that you're not content to rest on your laurels? Pleasing your reseller-employer, who needs more certified employees for a higher discount from Cisco? You might have one of these reasons for getting the CCNP Enterprise certification or one of many others.

Strategies for Exam Preparation

The strategy you use for taking the ENARSI 300-410 exam might be slightly different from strategies used by other readers, depending on the skills, knowledge, and experience you have already obtained. For instance, if you have attended the CCNP

Implementing Cisco Enterprise Advanced Routing and Services (ENARSI) 300-410 course, you might take a different approach than someone who has learned routing through on-the-job training.

Regardless of the strategy you use or the background you have, this book is designed to help you get to the point where you can pass the exam with the least amount of time required. For instance, there is no need for you to practice or read about IP addressing and subnetting if you fully understand it already. However, many people like to make sure that they truly know a topic and thus read over material that they already know. Several book features will help you gain the confidence you need to be convinced that you know some material already and to also help you know what topics you need to study more.

The Companion Website for Online Content Review

All the electronic review elements, as well as other electronic components of the book, exist on this book's companion website.

How to Access the Companion Website

To access the companion website, which gives you access to the electronic content with this book, start by establishing a login at www.ciscopress.com and registering your book. To do so, simply go to ciscopress.com/register and enter the ISBN of the print book: 9780138217525. After you have registered your book, go to your account page and click the Registered Products tab. From there, click the Access Bonus Content link to get access to the book's companion website.

Note that if you buy the Premium Edition eBook and Practice Test version of this book from Cisco Press, your book will automatically be registered on your account page. Simply go to your account page, click the Registered Products tab, and select Access Bonus Content to access the book's companion website.

How to Access the Pearson Test Prep (PTP) App

You have two options for installing and using the Pearson Test Prep application: a web app and a desktop app. To use the Pearson Test Prep application, start by finding the registration code that comes with the book. You can find the code in these ways:

- You can get your access code by registering the print ISBN (9780138217525) on ciscopress.com/register. Make sure to use the print book ISBN regardless of whether you purchased an eBook or the print book. Once you register the book, your access code will be populated on your account page under the Registered Products tab. Instructions for how to redeem the code are available on the book's companion website by clicking the Access Bonus Content link.

- Premium Edition: If you purchase the Premium Edition eBook and Practice Test directly from the Cisco Press website, the code will be populated on your account page after purchase. Just log in at ciscopress.com click Account to see details of your account, and click the digital purchases tab.

NOTE After you register your book, your code can always be found in your account under the Registered Products tab.

Once you have the access code, to find instructions about both the PTP web app and the desktop app, follow these steps:

Step 1. Open this book's companion website, as shown earlier in this Introduction under the heading "How to Access the Companion Website."

Step 2. Click the Practice Exams button.

Step 3. Follow the instructions listed there both for installing the desktop app and for using the web app.

Note that if you want to use the web app only at this point, just navigate to pearsontestprep.com, log in using the same credentials used to register your book or purchase the Premium Edition, and register this book's practice tests using the registration code you just found. The process should take only a couple of minutes.

How This Book Is Organized

Although this book could be read cover-to-cover, it is designed to be flexible and allow you to easily move between chapters and sections of chapters to cover just the material that you need more work with. If you intend to read the entire book, the order in the book is an excellent sequence to use.

The chapters cover the following topics:

■ **Chapter 1, "IPv4/IPv6 Addressing and Routing Review":** This chapter provides a review of IPv4 and IPv6 addressing, DHCP, and routing, as well as details about how to troubleshoot these topics.

■ **Chapter 2, "EIGRP":** This chapter explains the underlying mechanics of the EIGRP routing protocol, the path metric calculations, and how to configure EIGRP.

■ **Chapter 3, "Advanced EIGRP":** This chapter explains a variety of advanced concepts, such as failure detection, network summarization, router filtering, and techniques to optimize WAN sites.

■ **Chapter 4, "Troubleshooting EIGRP for IPv4":** This chapter focuses on how to troubleshoot EIGRP neighbor adjacency issues as well as EIGRP route issues.

■ **Chapter 5, "EIGRPv6":** This chapter explains how EIGRP advertises IPv6 networks and guides you through configuring, verifying, and troubleshooting EIGRPv6.

■ **Chapter 6, "OSPF":** This chapter explains the core concepts of OSPF, the exchange of routes, OSPF network types, failure detection, and OSPF authentication.

■ **Chapter 7, "Advanced OSPF":** This chapter expands on Chapter 6 by explaining the OSPF database and how it builds the topology. It also explains OSPF path selection, router summarization, and techniques to optimize an OSPF environment.

- **Chapter 8, "Troubleshooting OSPFv2":** This chapter explores how to troubleshoot OSPFv2 neighbor adjacency issues as well as route issues.

- **Chapter 9, "OSPFv3":** This chapter explains how the OSPF protocol has changed to accommodate support of the IPv6 protocol.

- **Chapter 10, "Troubleshooting OSPFv3":** This chapter explains how to troubleshoot issues that may arise with OSPFv3.

- **Chapter 11, "BGP":** This chapter explains the core concepts of BGP, its path attributes, and configuration for IPv4 and IPv6 network prefixes.

- **Chapter 12, "Advanced BGP":** This chapter expands on Chapter 11 by explaining BGP communities and configuration techniques for routers with lots of BGP peerings.

- **Chapter 13, "BGP Path Selection":** This chapter explains the BGP path selection process, how BGP identifies the best BGP path, and methods for load balancing across equal paths.

- **Chapter 14, "Troubleshooting BGP":** This chapter explores how you can identify and troubleshoot issues related to BGP neighbor adjacencies, BGP routes, and BGP path selection. It also covers MP-BGP (BGP for IPv6).

- **Chapter 15, "Route Maps and Conditional Forwarding":** This chapter explains route maps, concepts for selecting a network prefix, and how packets can be conditionally forwarded out different interfaces for certain network traffic.

- **Chapter 16, "Route Redistribution":** This chapter explains the rules of redistribution, configuration for route redistribution, and behaviors of redistribution based on the source or destination routing protocol.

- **Chapter 17, "Troubleshooting Redistribution":** This chapter focuses on how to troubleshoot issues related to redistribution, including configuration issues, suboptimal routing issues, and routing loop issues.

- **Chapter 18, "VRF, MPLS, and MPLS Layer 3 VPNs":** This chapter explores how to configure and verify VRF and introduces MPLS operations and MPLS Layer 3 VPNs.

- **Chapter 19, "DMVPN Tunnels":** This chapter covers GRE tunnels, NHRP, DMVPN, and techniques to optimize a DMVPN deployment.

- **Chapter 20, "Securing DMVPN Tunnels":** This chapter explains the importance of securing network traffic on the WAN and techniques for deploying IPsec tunnel protection for DMVPN tunnels.

- **Chapter 21, "Troubleshooting ACLs and Prefix Lists":** This chapter shows how to troubleshoot issues related to IPv4 and IPv6 access control lists and prefix lists.

- **Chapter 22, "Infrastructure Security":** This chapter covers how to troubleshoot AAA issues, uRPF issues, and CoPP issues. In addition, it introduces various IPv6 first-hop security features.

- **Chapter 23, "Device Management and Management Tools Troubleshooting":** This chapter explores how to troubleshoot issues that you might experience with local or remote access, remote transfers, syslog, SNMP, IP SLA, Object Tracking, NetFlow, and Flexible NetFlow. In addition, it introduces the troubleshooting options available with Cisco DNA Center Assurance.

- **Chapter 24, "Final Preparation":** This chapter provides tips and strategies for studying for the ENARSI 300-410 exam.

- **Chapter 25, "ENARSI 300-410 Exam Updates":** This chapter provides information about how book updates will be handled if and when Cisco decides to make changes to the ENARSI 300-410 exam.

Certification Exam Topics and This Book

The questions for each certification exam are a closely guarded secret. However, we do know which topics you must know to *successfully* complete the ENARSI 300-410 v1.1 exam. Cisco publishes them as an exam blueprint. Table I-1 lists the exam topics from the blueprint along with references to the book chapters that cover each topic. These are the same topics you should be proficient in when working with enterprise technologies in the real world.

Table I-1   Enterprise Core Topics and Chapter References

Implementing Cisco Enterprise Advanced Routing (ENARSI) (300-410) Exam Topic	Chapter(s) in Which Topic Is Covered
1.0 Layer 3 Technologies	
1.1 Troubleshoot administrative distance (all routing protocols)	1
1.2 Troubleshoot route map for any routing protocol (attributes, tagging, filtering)	17
1.3 Troubleshoot loop prevention mechanisms (filtering, tagging, split horizon, route poisoning)	17
1.4 Troubleshoot redistribution between any routing protocols or routing sources	16, 17
1.5 Troubleshoot manual and auto-summarization with any routing protocol	3, 4, 5, 7, 8, 9, 10, 12
1.6 Configure and verify policy-based routing	15
1.7 Configure and verify VRF-Lite	18
1.8 Describe Bidirectional Forwarding Detection	23
1.9 Troubleshoot EIGRP (classic and named mode; VRF and global)	4, 5
1.9.a Address families (IPv4, IPv6)	2, 3, 4, 5
1.9.b Neighbor relationship and authentication	2, 4, 5
1.9.c Loop-free path selections (RD, FD, FC, successor, feasible successor, stuck in active)	3, 4
1.9.d Stubs	4

Implementing Cisco Enterprise Advanced Routing (ENARSI) (300-410) Exam Topic	Chapter(s) in Which Topic Is Covered
1.9.e Load balancing (equal and unequal cost)	2
1.9.f Metrics	2
1.10 Troubleshoot OSPF (v2/v3)	6, 7, 8, 9, 10
1.10.a Address families (IPv4, IPv6)	8, 10
1.10.b Neighbor relationship and authentication	6, 8, 10
1.10.c Network types, area types, and router types	8, 10
1.10.c (i) Point-to-point, multipoint, broadcast, nonbroadcast	6, 8, 10
1.10.c (ii) Area type: backbone, normal, transit, stub, NSSA, totally stub	7, 8, 10
1.10.c (iii) Internal router, backbone router, ABR, ASBR	6, 8, 10
1.10.c (iv) Virtual link	7, 8
1.10.d Path preference	7
1.11 Troubleshoot BGP (Internal and External, unicast, and VRF-Lite)	11, 12, 13, 14
1.11.a Address families (IPv4, IPv6)	10, 14
1.11.b Neighbor relationship and authentication (next-hop, mulithop, 4-byte AS, private AS, route refresh, synchronization, operation, peer group, states and timers)	10, 14
1.11.c Path preference (attributes and best-path)	13, 14
1.11.d Route reflector (excluding multiple route reflectors, confederations, dynamic peer)	10
1.11.e Policies (inbound/outbound filtering, path manipulation)	11, 14
2.0 VPN Technologies	
2.1 Describe MPLS operations (LSR, LDP, label switching, LSP)	18
2.2 Describe MPLS Layer 3 VPN	18
2.3 Configure and verify DMVPN (single hub)	19, 20
2.3.a GRE/mGRE	19
2.3.b NHRP	19
2.3.c IPsec	20
2.3.d Dynamic neighbor	19
2.3.e Spoke-to-spoke	19
3.0 Infrastructure Security	
3.1 Troubleshoot device security using IOS AAA (TACACS+, RADIUS, local database)	22
3.2 Troubleshoot router security features	21,22
3.2.a IPv4 access control lists (standard, extended, time-based)	21
3.2.b IPv6 traffic filter	21
3.2.c Unicast reverse path forwarding (uRPF)	22

Implementing Cisco Enterprise Advanced Routing (ENARSI) (300-410) Exam Topic	Chapter(s) in Which Topic Is Covered
3.3 Troubleshoot control plane policing (CoPP) (Telnet, SSH, HTTP(S), SNMP, EIGRP, OSPF, BGP)	22
3.4 Describe IPv6 First Hop Security features (RA Guard, DHCP Guard, binding table, ND inspection/snooping, Source Guard)	22
4.0 Infrastructure Services	
4.1 Troubleshoot device management	23
4.1.a Console and VTY	23
4.1.b Telnet, HTTP, HTTPS, SSH, SCP	23
4.1.c (T)FTP	23
4.2 Troubleshoot SNMP (v2c, v3)	23
4.3 Troubleshoot network problems using logging (local, syslog, debugs, conditional debugs, timestamps)	23
4.4 Troubleshoot IPv4 and IPv6 DHCP (DHCP client, IOS DHCP server, DHCP relay, DHCP options)	1
4.5 Troubleshoot network performance issues using IP SLA (jitter, tracking objects, delay, connectivity)	23
4.6 Troubleshoot NetFlow (v5, v9, flexible NetFlow)	23
4.7 Troubleshoot network problems using Cisco DNA Center assurance (connectivity, monitoring, device health, network health)	23

Each version of the exam can have topics that emphasize different functions or features, and some topics can be rather broad and generalized. The goal of this book is to provide the most comprehensive coverage to ensure that you are well prepared for the exam. Although some chapters might not address specific exam topics, they provide a foundation that is necessary for a clear understanding of important topics.

It is also important to understand that this book is a "static" reference, whereas the exam topics are dynamic. Cisco can and does change the topics covered on certification exams often.

This exam guide should not be your only reference when preparing for the certification exam. You can find a wealth of information at Cisco.com that covers each topic in great detail. If you think that you need more detailed information on a specific topic, read the Cisco documentation that focuses on that topic.

Note that as technologies continue to evolve, Cisco reserves the right to change the exam topics without notice. Although you can refer to the list of exam topics in Table I-1, always check Cisco.com to verify the actual list of topics to ensure that you are prepared before taking the exam. You can view the current exam topics on any current Cisco certification exam by visiting https://www.cisco.com/c/en/us/training-events/training-certifications/next-level-certifications.html. In addition, you should keep up to date on future exam changes by using the Cisco Certification Road Map at https://learningnetwork.

cisco.com/s/cisco-certification-roadmaps. Also note that, if needed, Cisco Press might post additional preparatory content on the web page associated with this book: http://www.ciscopress.com/title/9780138217525. It's a good idea to check the website a couple weeks before taking your exam to be sure that you have up-to-date content.

Learning in a Lab Environment

This book is an excellent self-study resource for learning the technologies. However, reading is not enough, and any network engineer can tell you that you must implement a technology to fully understand it. We encourage you to re-create the topologies and technologies and follow the examples in this book.

A variety of resources are available for practicing the concepts in this book. Look online for the following:

- Cisco VIRL (Virtual Internet Routing Lab) provides a scalable, extensible network design and simulation environment. For more information about VIRL, see https://learningnetwork.cisco.com/s/virl.

- Cisco dCloud provides a huge catalog of demos, training, and sandboxes for every Cisco architecture. It offers customizable environments and is free. For more information, see https://dcloud.cisco.com.

- Cisco Devnet provides many resources on programming and programmability, along with free labs. For more information, see https://developer.cisco.com.

CHAPTER 1

IPv4/IPv6 Addressing and Routing Review

This chapter covers the following topics:

- **IPv4 Addressing:** This section provides a review of IPv4 addressing and covers issues you might face and how to troubleshoot them.

- **DHCP for IPv4:** This section reviews DHCP for IPv4 operations, explores potential DHCP issues, and examines the output of various DHCP **show** commands.

- **IPv6 Addressing:** This section provides a brief review of IPv6 addressing.

- **IPv6 SLAAC, Stateful DHCPv6, and Stateless DHCPv6:** This section explores how clients obtain IPv6 addressing information using SLAAC, stateful DHCPv6, and stateless DHCPv6.

- **Packet-Forwarding Process:** This section discusses the packet-forwarding process and the commands to verify the entries in the data structures that are used for this process. It also provides a collection of Cisco IOS Software commands that could prove useful when troubleshooting related issues.

- **Administrative Distance:** This section explains which sources of routing information are the most believable and how the routing table interacts with various data structures to populate itself with the best information.

- **Static Routes:** This section reviews how to configure and verify IPv4 and IPv6 static routes.

- **Trouble Tickets:** This section shows examples of trouble tickets that demonstrate how a structured troubleshooting process is used to solve a reported problem.

IPv6 is currently being deployed, but that deployment is occurring at a slow pace. Most networks still rely on IPv4, and many new networks and network additions are being deployed with IPv4. Therefore, you still need the skills to successfully configure, verify, and troubleshoot IPv4 addressing. Therefore, this chapter provides a review of IPv4 addressing.

Typically, when deploying IPv4 addresses, Dynamic Host Configuration Protocol (DHCP) is used so that addresses can be dynamically assigned. However, with this dynamic process, issues may arise that prevent a device from successfully obtaining an IPv4 address from a DHCP server. Therefore, this chapter reviews how DHCP operates and how to identify the issues that may prevent a client from obtaining an IP address from a DHCP server.

Sooner or later, organizations will have to switch to IPv6. There is a whole lot more to IPv6 than just having a larger address space than IPv4. This chapter reminds you how IPv6-enabled devices determine whether a destination is local or remote and explores the various options for address assignment and what to look out for when troubleshooting.

Before you dive into the advanced routing topics such as Enhanced Interior Gateway Routing Protocol (EIGRP), Open Shortest Path First (OSPF), and Border Gateway Protocol (BGP), you need to review the packet-delivery process (also known as the routing process). This is the process that a router goes through when a packet arrives at an ingress interface and needs to be switched to an egress interface. It does not matter whether the packet is an IPv4 packet or an IPv6 packet. Either way, the router goes through the same steps to successfully take a packet from an ingress interface and switch it to the egress interface. You also need to review how a router populates the routing table with "the best" routes. What classifies those routes as the best? Is an EIGRP learned route better than a static route? What about an OSPF learned route or a BGP learned route? How do they compare to the other sources of routing information? When multiple sources provide the same routing information, you need to be able to identify why the router made the decision it made.

Static routes are part of every network. However, because they are manually configured, they are prone to human error, which may lead to suboptimal routing or routing loops; therefore, this chapter reviews IPv4 and IPv6 static routing configuration and verification.

Notice that this chapter is mostly a review of IPv4/IPv6 addressing, DHCP for IPv4/IPv6, the packet-forwarding process, administrative distance, and static routing that you learned in CCNA or ENCORE. I encourage you not to skip this chapter as it will prepare you for the Implementing Cisco Enterprise Advanced Routing and Services (ENARSI) exam questions based on these topics.

"Do I Know This Already?" Quiz

The "Do I Know This Already?" quiz allows you to assess whether you should read this entire chapter thoroughly or jump to the "Exam Preparation Tasks" section. If you are in doubt about your answers to these questions or your own assessment of your knowledge of the topics, read the entire chapter. Table 1-1 lists the major headings in this chapter and their corresponding "Do I Know This Already?" quiz questions. You can find the answers in Appendix A, "Answers to the 'Do I Know This Already?' Quiz Questions."

Table 1-1 "Do I Know This Already?" Section-to-Question Mapping

Foundation Topics Section	Questions
IPv4 Addressing	1–3
DHCP for IPv4	4–6
IPv6 Addressing	7–8
IPv6 SLAAC, Stateful DHCPv6, and Stateless DHCPv6	9–12
Packet-Forwarding Process	13–15
Administrative Distance	16–19
Static Routes	20–21

> **CAUTION**   The goal of self-assessment is to gauge your mastery of the topics in this chapter. If you do not know the answer to a question or are only partially sure of the answer, you should mark that question as wrong for purposes of self-assessment. Giving yourself credit for an answer that you correctly guess skews your self-assessment results and might provide you with a false sense of security.

1. What occurs when a PC with the IP address 10.1.1.27/28 needs to communicate with a PC that has IP address 10.1.1.18? (Choose two.)
   a. It sends the frame to its default gateway.
   b. It sends the frame directly to the destination PC.
   c. It uses ARP to get the MAC address of the default gateway.
   d. It uses ARP to get the MAC address of the destination PC.

2. What occurs when a PC with the IP address 10.1.1.27/29 needs to communicate with a PC that has IP address 10.1.1.18? (Choose two.)
   a. It sends the frame to its default gateway.
   b. It sends the frame directly to the destination PC.
   c. It uses ARP to get the MAC address of the default gateway.
   d. It uses ARP to get the MAC address of the destination PC.

3. Which command enables you to verify the IP address configured on a router's interface?
   a. ipconfig
   b. show ip interface
   c. arp -a
   d. show ip arp

4. What is the correct order of operations for the DHCP for IPv4 process?
   a. Offer, Request, Ack, Discover
   b. Discover, Request, Ack, Offer
   c. Request, Offer, Discover, Ack
   d. Discover, Offer, Request, Ack

5. Which command is needed on a router interface to forward DHCP Discover messages to a DHCP server on a different subnet?
   a. ip address dhcp
   b. ip helper-address
   c. ip dhcp-forwarder
   d. ip dhcp server

6. Which command enables a router interface to obtain an IP address from a DHCP server?
   a. ip dhcp client
   b. ip dhcp server

   c.   ip address dhcp

   d.   ip helper-address

7.   What protocol is used with IPv6 to determine the MAC address of a device in the same local area network?

   a.   Address Resolution Protocol

   b.   Inverse Address Resolution Protocol

   c.   Neighbor Discovery Protocol

   d.   Neighbor Solicitation

8.   Which of the following are true when using EUI-64? (Choose two.)

   a.   The interface MAC address is used unmodified.

   b.   The interface MAC address is used with FFFE added to the middle.

   c.   The seventh bit from the left in the MAC address is flipped.

   d.   The seventh bit from the right in the MAC address is flipped.

9.   What command is used on a Cisco IOS router to enable SLAAC on an interface?

   a.   ipv6 address autoconfig

   b.   ipv6 address dhcp

   c.   ipv6 address *prefix* eui-64

   d.   ipv6 nd ra suppress

10.   Which of the following are requirements for stateless address autoconfiguration to function? (Choose three.)

   a.   The prefix must be /64.

   b.   The router must be sending and not suppressing RA messages.

   c.   The router must be enabled for IPv6 unicast routing.

   d.   The router must be sending RS messages.

11.   Which command is used to enable a router to inform clients that they need to get additional configuration information from a DHCPv6 server?

   a.   ipv6 nd ra suppress

   b.   ipv6 dhcp relay destination

   c.   ipv6 address autoconfig

   d.   ipv6 nd other-config-flag

12.   What command enables you to configure a router interface as a DHCPv6 relay agent?

   a.   ipv6 forwarder

   b.   ipv6 helper-address

   c.   ipv6 dhcp relay destination

   d.   ipv6 dhcp client

13.   Which two data structures reside at the router's data plane? (Choose two.)

   a.   IP routing table

   b.   ARP cache

   c.   Forwarding Information Base

   d.   Adjacency table

14. Which command enables you to verify routes in the FIB?

    a. show ip route

    b. show ip arp

    c. show ip cef

    d. show adjacency detail

15. Which of the following populate a routing protocol's data structure, such as the EIGRP topology table? (Choose three.)

    a. Updates from a neighbor

    b. Redistributed routes

    c. Interfaces enabled for the routing process

    d. Static routes

16. Which of the following has the lowest default administrative distance?

    a. OSPF

    b. EIGRP (internal)

    c. RIP

    d. eBGP

17. What is the default administrative distance of an OSPF intra-area route?

    a. 90

    b. 110

    c. 115

    d. 120

18. Your router has learned about the 10.0.0.0/24 network from EIGRP, OSPF, and IS-IS. What is the administrative distance of the source protocol that the router will install in the routing table to reach 10.0.0.0/24?

    a. 90

    b. 110

    c. 115

    d. 120

19. Your router has learned about the 10.0.0.0/24 network from EIGRP, OSPF, and IS-IS. You need the route learned from IS-IS installed in the routing table. What do you need to do?

    a. Nothing because IS-IS will be installed by default.

    b. Increase the administrative distance of the IS-IS route to 121.

    c. Increase the administrative distance of the EIGRP route to 116.

    d. Reduce the administrative distance of the IS-IS route to 80.

    e. Reduce the administrative distance of the IS-IS route to 109.

    f. Reduce the administrative distance of the OSPF route to 89.

20. How can you create a floating static route?

    a. Provide the static route with a metric higher than the preferred source of the route.

    b. Provide the static route with a metric lower than the preferred source of the route.

c. Provide the static route with an AD higher than the preferred source of the route.

d. Provide the static route with an AD lower than the preferred source of the route.

21. What occurs when you create an IPv4 static route with an Ethernet interface designated instead of a next-hop IP address?

a. The router uses ARP to get the MAC address of the directly connected router's IP address.

b. The router forwards the packet with the destination MAC address FFFF:FFFF:FFFF.

c. The router uses ARP to get the MAC address of the IP address in the source of the packet.

d. The router uses ARP to get the MAC address of the IP address in the destination of the packet.

Foundation Topics

IPv4 Addressing

Just as your personal street address uniquely defines where you live, an IPv4 address uniquely defines where a device resides in a network. Your street address is made of two parts—the number of your residence and the street name—and the combination of these is unique within your city/town. As a result, a pizza delivery person can bring your pizza to your house in 30 minutes, or it is free. If your house is addressed incorrectly, you may not get your pizza, and you do not want that to happen.

Similarly, with IPv4 addressing, if devices are addressed incorrectly, they may not receive the packets that are intended for them. Therefore, it is imperative that you have a solid understanding of IPv4 addressing and how to verify that devices are addressed correctly on a network. This section provides a review of IPv4 addressing and discusses issues you might face and how to troubleshoot them.

IPv4 Addressing Issues

An IPv4 address is made up of two parts: a network/subnet portion and a host portion. It is imperative that all devices in the same network/subnet share exactly the same network/subnet portion. If they are not the same, the PC could end up addressing the Layer 2 frame incorrectly and sending the packet in the wrong direction. Figure 1-1 shows a sample subnet (10.1.1.0/26) with two PCs and their default gateway, R1.

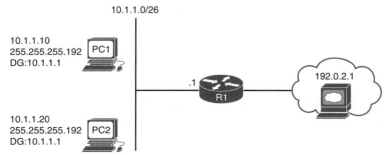

Figure 1-1 *Correct IPv4 Addressing Example*

When PC1 needs to communicate with PC2, it does a DNS lookup for the IP address of PC2. The IP address 10.1.1.20 is returned. Now PC1 needs to determine whether PC2 is located in the same subnet because this determines whether the frame has the MAC address of PC2 or the MAC address of the default gateway (DG). PC1 determines its network/subnet portion by comparing its IP address to its subnet mask in binary, as follows:

00001010.00000001.00000001.00001010	PC1's IP address in binary
11111111.11111111.11111111.11000000	PC1's subnet mask in binary
--	
00001010.00000001.00000001.00	PC1's network/subnet ID

(The 1s in the subnet mask identify the network portion.)

Now PC1 compares exactly the same binary bits to those binary bits in PC2's address, as follows:

00001010.00000001.00000001.00	PC1's network/subnet ID
00001010.00000001.00000001.00010100	PC2's IP address in binary
--	

Because the binary bits are the same, PC1 concludes that PC2 is in the same network/subnet; therefore, it communicates directly with it and does not need to send the data to its default gateway. PC1 creates a frame with its own source MAC address and the MAC address of PC2 as the destination.

Consider what occurs when PC1 needs to communicate with the web server at 192.0.2.1. It does a DNS lookup for the IP address of the web server. The IP address 192.0.2.1 is returned. Now PC1 needs to determine whether the web server is located in the same network/subnet. This determines whether the frame has the MAC address of the web server or the MAC address of the DG. PC1 determines its network/subnet portion by comparing its IP address to its subnet mask in binary, as follows:

00001010.00000001.00000001.00001010	PC1's IP address in binary
11111111.11111111.11111111.11000000	PC1's subnet mask in binary
--	
00001010.00000001.00000001.00	PC1's network/subnet ID

(The 1s in the subnet mask identify the network portion.)

Now PC1 compares exactly the same binary bits to those binary bits in the web server address, as follows:

00001010.00000001.00000001.00	PC1's network/subnet ID
11000000.00000000.00000010.00000001	Web server's IP address in binary
--	

PC1 concludes that the web server is in a different network/subnet because the bits are not the same; therefore, to communicate with the web server, it needs to send the data to its default gateway. PC1 creates a frame with its own source MAC address and the MAC address of R1 as the destination.

As you can see, accurate IP addressing is paramount for successful communication. Let's look at what happens if PC1 is configured with the wrong subnet mask (255.255.255.240), as shown in Figure 1-2.

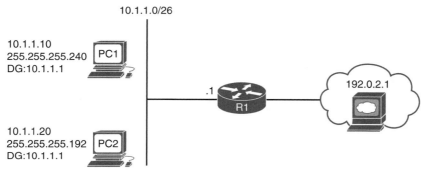

Figure 1-2 *Incorrect IPv4 Addressing Example*

PC1 determines its network/subnet portion by comparing its IP address to its subnet mask in binary, as follows:

```
00001010.00000000.00000001.00001010        PC1's IP address in binary
11111111.11111111.11111111.11110000        PC1's subnet mask in binary
-------------------------------------------
00001010.00000000.00000001.0000    PC1'snetwork/subnet ID
```

Now PC1 compares exactly the same binary bits to those binary bits in PC2's address, as follows:

```
00001010.00000000.00000001.0000    PC1's network/subnet ID
00001010.00000000.00000001.00010100        PC2's IP address in binary
-------------------------------------------
```

PC1 concludes that PC2 is not in the same network/subnet because the binary bits are not the same. Therefore, it cannot communicate directly with it and needs to send the frame to the router so that the router can route the packet to the subnet PC2 is in. However, the PCs are actually connected to the same subnet, and as a result, there is an IPv4 addressing and connectivity issue.

Not only does an *improper subnet mask* cause issues, but an *inappropriate IP address combined with the correct subnet mask* also causes issues. In addition, if the *default gateway is not configured correctly* on the PCs, packets are not forwarded to the correct device when packets need to be sent to a different subnet.

As a troubleshooter, you must quickly recognize these issues and eliminate them as possible issues. You verify the IP addressing information on a Windows PC by using the **ipconfig** command, as shown in Example 1-1. On an IOS router or IOS switch, you verify

IP addressing information by using the **show ip interface** *interface_type interface_number* command, as also shown in Example 1-1.

Example 1-1   *Verifying IP Addressing on a PC and on a Router*

```
C:\>ipconfig
Windows IP Configuration


Ethernet adapter PC1:


   Connection-specific DNS Suffix . :
   IP Address. . . . . . . . . . . .: 10.1.1.10
   Subnet Mask . . . . . . . . . . .: 255.255.255.192
   IP Address. . . . . . . . . . . .: 2001:10::10
   IP Address. . . . . . . . . . . .: fe80::4107:2cfb:df25:5124%7
   Default Gateway . . . . . . . . .: 10.1.1.1


R1# show ip interface gigabitEthernet 1/0
GigabitEthernet1/0 is up, line protocol is up
  Internet address is 10.1.1.1/26
...output omitted...
```

Determining IP Addresses Within a Subnet

This section describes a quick way to determine all the IP addresses that will be in a particular subnet. Refer to Figure 1-3 as you are exploring this method.

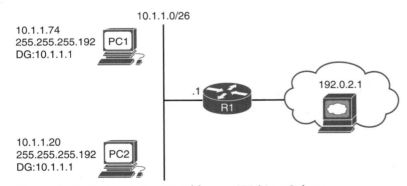

Figure 1-3   *Determining IP Addresses Within a Subnet*

To use this method, you need to find the most interesting octet in the subnet mask. In binary, it's the octet with the last binary 1. In decimal, it's the last octet that is greater than 0. In this case, for 255.255.255.192, the fourth octet is the last octet with a value greater than 0. The value of this octet is 192. If your subnet mask were 255.255.192.0, then it would be the third octet. Consider the subnet mask 255.255.255.0. Because the fourth octet is a 0, it would be the third octet, as it's the last octet with a value greater than 0.

Now, subtract 192 from 256. The result is 64. The number 64 represents the block size or the number you are counting by in that octet. The subnet in this case is 10.1.1.0/26, and because the block size is 64, this subnet begins at 10.1.1.0/26 and ends at 10.1.1.63/26. The next subnet is 10.1.1.64/26 to 10.1.1.127/26. The third subnet is 10.1.1.128/26 to 10.1.1.191/26, and so on.

Now compare the addresses of devices with the subnet ranges you just identified. In this case, PC1, PC2, and an interface on R1 are supposed to be in the same subnet. As a result, they better all be addressed correctly, or communication will not occur correctly. For example, if you are reviewing the output of **ipconfig** on PC1, as shown in Example 1-2, now that you have the ranges, you can easily see that PC1 is not in the same subnet as R1 and PC2. Although they have the same subnet mask, in this case PC1 falls in the range 10.1.1.64/26 to 10.1.1.127/26, whereas PC2 and the default gateway fall in the range 10.1.1.0/26 to 10.1.1.63/26. PC1 is in a different network/subnet, but it should be in the same subnet, according to Figure 1-3. You must fix the address on PC1 so that it is within the correct network/subnet.

Example 1-2   *Verifying IP Addressing on a PC with the* **ipconfig** *Command*

```
C:\>ipconfig
Windows IP Configuration


Ethernet adapter PC1:


Connection-specific DNS Suffix . :
IP Address. . . . . . . . . . . .: 10.1.1.74
Subnet Mask . . . . . . . . . . .: 255.255.255.192
IP Address. . . . . . . . . . . .: 2001:10::10
IP Address. . . . . . . . . . . .: fe80::4107:2cfb:df25:5124%7
Default Gateway . . . . . . . . .: 10.1.1.1
```

DHCP for IPv4

Dynamic Host Configuration Protocol (*DHCP*) is commonly used for assigning IPv4 address information to a network host. Specifically, DHCP allows a DHCP client to obtain an IP address, subnet mask, default gateway IP address, DNS server IP address, and other types of IP addressing information from a DHCP server. The DHCP server can be local within the subnet or in a remote subnet, or it can be the same device that is also the default gateway.

Because using DHCP is the most common way to deploy IPv4 addresses, you need to be well versed in the DHCP process and able to recognize issues related to DHCP. This section explains how DHCP operates and focuses on how to identify DHCP-related issues.

Reviewing DHCP Operations

If you have a cable modem, Digital Subscriber Line (DSL), or fiber connection in your home, your router most likely obtains its IP address from your service provider through DHCP. The router is also acting as a DHCP server for the devices in your home. In corporate networks, when a PC boots, that PC receives its IP address configuration information from a corporate DHCP server. Figure 1-4 illustrates the exchange of messages that occurs as a

DHCP client obtains IP addressing information from a DHCP server. This exchange is known as the *DORA process* because it involves Discover, Offer, Request, and Acknowledgment messages.

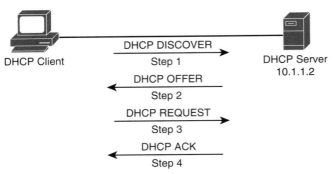

Figure 1-4 *DHCP DORA Process*

The DORA process works as follows:

Step 1. When a DHCP client initially boots, it has no IP address, default gateway, or other such configuration information. Therefore, the way a DHCP client initially communicates is by sending a broadcast message (that is, a *DHCPDISCOVER* message) to destination IP address 255.255.255.255 and destination MAC address FFFF:FFFF:FFFF in an attempt to discover a DHCP server. The source IP address is 0.0.0.0, and the source MAC address is the MAC address of the sending device.

Step 2. When a DHCP server receives a DHCPDISCOVER message, it can respond with a *DHCPOFFER* message with an unleased IP address, subnet mask, and default gateway information. Because the DHCPDISCOVER message is sent as a broadcast, more than one DHCP server might respond to this Discover message with a DHCPOFFER. However, the client typically selects the server that sent the first DHCPOFFER response it received.

Step 3. The DHCP client communicates with the selected server by sending a broadcasted *DHCPREQUEST* message indicating that it will be using the address provided in the DHCPOFFER and, as a result, wants the associated address leased to itself.

Step 4. Finally, the DHCP server responds to the client with a *DHCPACK* message indicating that the IP address is leased to the client and includes any additional DHCP options that might be needed at this point, such as the lease duration.

Notice that in step 1, the DHCPDISCOVER message is sent as a broadcast. The broadcast cannot cross a router boundary. Therefore, if a client resides on a different network from the DHCP server, you need to configure the default gateway of the client as a *DHCP relay agent* to forward the broadcast packets as unicast packets to the server. You use the **ip helper-address** *ip_address* interface configuration mode command to configure a router to relay DHCP messages to a DHCP server in the organization.

To illustrate, consider Figure 1-5 and Example 1-3. In the figure, the DHCP client belongs to the 172.16.1.0/24 network, whereas the DHCP server belongs to the 10.1.1.0/24 network. Router R1 is configured as a DHCP relay agent, using the syntax shown in Example 1-3.

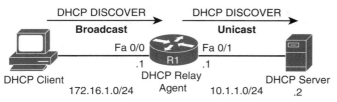

Figure 1-5   *DHCP Relay Agent*

Example 1-3   *DHCP Relay Agent Configuration*

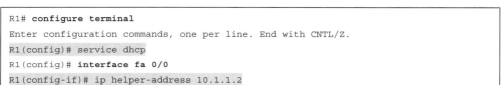

```
R1# configure terminal
Enter configuration commands, one per line. End with CNTL/Z.
R1(config)# service dhcp
R1(config)# interface fa 0/0
R1(config-if)# ip helper-address 10.1.1.2
```

In the configuration, notice the **service dhcp** command. This command enables the DHCP service on the router, which must be enabled for the DHCP service to function. This command is usually not required because the DHCP service is enabled by default; however, when troubleshooting a DHCP relay agent issue, you might want to confirm that the service is enabled. Also, the **ip helper-address 10.1.1.2** command specifies the IP address of the DHCP server. If the wrong IP address is specified, the DHCP messages are relayed to the wrong device. In addition, the **ip helper-address** command must be configured on the interface that is receiving the DHCPDISCOVER messages from the clients. If it isn't, the router cannot relay the DHCP messages.

When you configure a router to act as a DHCP relay agent, realize that it relays a few other broadcast types in addition to a DHCP message. Other protocols that are forwarded by a DHCP relay agent include the following:

- TFTP

- Domain Name System (DNS)

- Internet Time Service (ITS)

- NetBIOS name server

- NetBIOS datagram server

- BootP

- TACACS

As a reference, Table 1-2 provides a comprehensive list of DHCP message types you might encounter while troubleshooting a DHCP issue.

Table 1-2 DHCP Message Types

DHCP Message	Description
DHCPDISCOVER	A client sends this message in an attempt to locate a DHCP server. This message is sent to broadcast IP address 255.255.255.255, using UDP port 67.
DHCPOFFER	A DHCP server sends this message in response to a DHCPDISCOVER message, using UDP port 68.
DHCPREQUEST	This broadcast message is a request from the client to the DHCP server for the IP addressing information and options that were received in the DHCPOFFER message.
DHCPDECLINE	This message is sent from a client to a DHCP server to inform the server that an IP address is already in use on the network.
DHCPACK	A DHCP server sends this message to a client and includes IP configuration parameters.
DHCPNAK	A DHCP server sends this message to a client and informs the client that the DHCP server declines to provide the client with the requested IP configuration information.
DHCPRELEASE	A client sends this message to a DHCP server and informs the DHCP server that the client has released its DHCP lease, thus allowing the DHCP server to reassign the client IP address to another client.
DHCPINFORM	A client sends this message to a DHCP server and requests IP configuration parameters. Such a message might be sent from an access server requesting IP configuration information for a remote client attaching to the access server.

In addition to acting as a DHCP relay agent, a router might act as a DHCP client. Specifically, the interface of a router might obtain its IP address from a DHCP server. Figure 1-6 shows a router acting as a DHCP client, where the router's Fast Ethernet 0/1 interface obtains its IP address from a DHCP server. The following snippet provides the configuration for the router in the topology (that is, router R1). Notice that the **dhcp** option is used in the **ip address** command, instead of the usual IP address and subnet mask information.

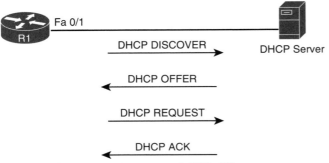

Figure 1-6 *Router Acting as a DHCP Client*

The following snippet shows a DHCP client configuration:

```
R1# configure terminal
R1(config)# int fa 0/1
R1(config-if)# ip address dhcp
```

A router and multilayer switch may also act as a DHCP server. Figure 1-7 shows a router acting as a DHCP server, and Example 1-4 shows the router configuration. The **ip dhcp excluded-address 10.8.8.1 10.8.8.10** command prevents DHCP from assigning those IP addresses to a client. Note that you do not have to include the IP address of the router interface in this exclusion because the router never hands out its own interface IP address. The **ip dhcp pool POOL-A** command creates a DHCP pool named POOL-A. This pool hands out IP addresses from the 10.8.8.0/24 network, with a default gateway of 10.8.8.1, a DNS server of 192.168.1.1, a WINS server of 192.168.1.2, and the IP address of a TFTP server with option 150. (Note that option 66 can also be used to hand out the address of a TFTP server.)

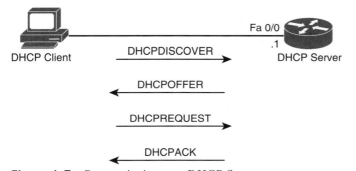

Figure 1-7   *Router Acting as a DHCP Server*

Example 1-4   *DHCP Server Configuration*

```
R1# show run
...output omitted...
ip dhcp excluded-address 10.8.8.1 10.8.8.10
!
ip dhcp pool POOL-A
 network 10.8.8.0 255.255.255.0
 default-router 10.8.8.1
 dns-server 192.168.1.1
 netbios-name-server 192.168.1.2
 option 150 10.150.150.150
...output omitted...
```

If your device is configured to receive an IP address from a DHCP server but the IP address shown on the client is an Automatic Private IP Addressing (*APIPA*) address (169.254.x.x) because of autoconfiguration, as shown in Example 1-5, you can conclude that the client could not obtain an IP address from the DHCP server. However, do not immediately assume that DHCP is the problem. It is quite possible that you have a Layer 3 routing problem, or you might have a Layer 2 problem, such as VLANs, trunks, Spanning Tree Protocol (STP), or security preventing the client's DHCPDISCOVER message from reaching the DHCP server.

Example 1-5 *Verifying a DHCP-Assigned IP Address on a PC*

```
C:\>ipconfig /all
Windows IP Configuration


...output omitted...


Ethernet adapter PC1 Lab:

  Connection-specific DNS Suffix . :
  Description . . . . . . . . . . .: AMD PCNET Family PCI Ethernet Adapter
  Physical Address. . . . . . . . .: 08-00-27-5D-06-D6
  Dhcp Enabled. . . . . . . . . . .: Yes
  Autoconfiguration Enabled . . . .: Yes
  Autoconfiguration IP Address. . .: 169.254.180.166
  Subnet Mask . . . . . . . . . . .: 255.255.0.0
  IP Address. . . . . . . . . . . .: 2001:10::10
  IP Address. . . . . . . . . . . .: fe80::a00:27ff:fe5d:6d6%4
  Default Gateway . . . . . . . . .:
```

Potential DHCP Troubleshooting Issues

When troubleshooting what you suspect might be a DHCP issue, consider the following potential issues:

■ **Router failing to forward broadcasts:** By default, a router does not forward broadcasts, including DHCPDISCOVER broadcast messages. Therefore, a router needs to be explicitly configured to act as a DHCP relay agent if the DHCP client and DHCP server are on different subnets.

■ **DHCP pool out of IP addresses:** A DHCP pool contains a finite number of addresses. Once a pool becomes depleted, new DHCP requests are rejected.

■ **Misconfiguration:** The configuration of a DHCP server might be incorrect. For example, the range of network addresses given out by a particular pool might be incorrect, or the exclusion of addresses statically assigned to routers or DNS servers might be incorrect. Even the lease could be too high or too low. For example, a lease duration that is too high may cause pool exhaustion if you have more clients than the pool can support. Consider a wireless network at an airport. Let's say there are 4096 addresses in the pool with a lease duration of 12 hours. Since users are typically not in an airport for more than 4 hours, this lease duration is too long, and the IP address will still be leased to that user until the lease expires, even if the user is no longer in the airport. Therefore, as the day progresses, more addresses are leased, until the pool is exhausted. So, setting a lower lease duration, such as 2 hours, would ensure that the lease expires sooner rather than later and helps prevent pool exhaustion.

- **Duplicate IP addresses:** A DHCP server might hand out an IP address to a client that is already statically assigned to another host on the network. These duplicate IP addresses can cause connectivity issues for both the DHCP client and the host that was statically configured for the IP address.

- **Redundant services not communicating:** Some DHCP servers coexist with other DHCP servers for redundancy. For such redundancy to function, these DHCP servers need to communicate with one another. If this interserver communication fails, the DHCP servers hand out overlapping IP addresses to their clients.

- **The "pull" nature of DHCP:** When a DHCP client wants an IP address, it requests an IP address from a DHCP server. However, the DHCP server has no ability to initiate a change in the client's IP address after the client obtains an IP address. In other words, the DHCP client pulls information from the DHCP server; the DHCP server cannot push information changes to the DHCP client.

- **Interface not configured with IP address in DHCP pool:** A router or a multilayer switch that is acting as a DHCP server must have an interface with an IP address that is part of the pool/subnet for which it is handing out IP addresses. The router only hands the addresses in the pool to clients reachable out that interface. This ensures that the router interface and the clients are in the same subnet. However, note that this is not the case if a relay agent is forwarding DHCP messages between the client and the router that is the DHCP server. In that case, the DHCP server does not have to have an IP address on an interface that is part of the pool for which it is handing out addresses.

DHCP Troubleshooting Commands

The following snippet provides sample output from the **show ip dhcp conflict** command:

```
R1# show ip dhcp conflict

IP address      Detection method    Detection time

172.16.1.3      Ping                Oct 15 2018 8:56 PM
```

The output indicates a duplicate 172.16.1.3 IP address on the network, which the router discovered via a ping. You clear the information displayed by issuing the **clear ip dhcp conflict *** command after resolving the duplicate address issue on the network.

Example 1-6 shows sample output from the **show ip dhcp binding** command. The output indicates that IP address 10.1.1.10 was assigned to a DHCP client. You can release this DHCP lease with the **clear ip dhcp binding *** command.

Example 1-6 *show ip dhcp binding Command Output*

```
R1# show ip dhcp binding
Bindings from all pools not associated with VRF:
IP address    Client-ID/           Lease expiration        Type
              Hardware address/
              User name
10.1.1.3      0100.50b6.0765.7a    Oct 17 2018 07:53 PM    Automatic
10.1.1.10     0108.0027.5d06.d6    Oct 17 2018 07:53 PM    Automatic
```

Example 1-7 shows sample output from the **debug ip dhcp server events** command. The output shows updates to the DHCP database.

Example 1-7   *debug ip dhcp server events Command Output*

```
R1# debug ip dhcp server events
DHCPD: Seeing if there is an internally specified pool class:
 DHCPD: htype 1 chaddr c001.0f1c.0000
 DHCPD: remote id 020a00000a01010101000000
 DHCPD: circuit id 00000000
DHCPD: Seeing if there is an internally specified pool class:
 DHCPD: htype 1 chaddr c001.0f1c.0000
 DHCPD: remote id 020a00000a01010101000000
 DHCPD: circuit id 00000000
DHCPD: no subnet configured for 192.168.1.238.
```

Example 1-8 shows sample output from the **debug ip dhcp server packet** command. The output shows a DHCPRELEASE message being received when a DHCP client with IP address 10.1.1.3 is shut down. You can also see the four-step process of a DHCP client obtaining IP address 10.1.1.4 with the following messages: DHCPDISCOVER, DHCPOFFER, DHCPREQUEST, and DHCPACK.

Example 1-8   *debug ip dhcp server packet Command Output*

```
R1# debug ip dhcp server packet
DHCPD: DHCPRELEASE message received from client
 0063.6973.636f.2d63.3030.312e.3066.3163.2e30.3030.302d.4661.302f.30 (10.1.1.3).
DHCPD: DHCPRELEASE message received from client
 0063.6973.636f.2d63.3030.312e.3066.3163.2e30.3030.302d.4661.302f.30 (10.1.1.3).
DHCPD: Finding a relay for client
 0063.6973.636f.2d63.3030.312e.3066.3163.2e30.3030.302d.4661.302f.30 on interface
FastEthernet0/1.
DHCPD: DHCPDISCOVER received from client
 0063.6973.636f.2d63.3030.312e.3066.3163.2e30.3030.302d.4661.302f.30 on interface
FastEthernet0/1.
DHCPD: Allocate an address without class information
 (10.1.1.0)
DHCPD: Sending DHCPOFFER to client
 0063.6973.636f.2d63.3030.312e.3066.3163.2e30.3030.302d.4661.302f.30 (10.1.1.4).
DHCPD: broadcasting BOOTREPLY to client c001.0f1c.0000.
DHCPD: DHCPREQUEST received from client
 0063.6973.636f.2d63.3030.312e.3066.3163.2e30.3030.302d.4661.302f.30.
DHCPD: No default domain to append - abort update
DHCPD: Sending DHCPACK to client
 0063.6973.636f.2d63.3030.312e.3066.3163.2e30.3030.302d.4661.302f.30 (10.1.1.4).
DHCPD: broadcasting BOOTREPLY to client c001.0f1c.0000.
```

IPv6 Addressing

Just as your personal street address uniquely defines where you live, an IPv6 address uniquely defines where a device resides. As mentioned earlier, your street address is made of two parts—the number of your residence and the street name—and the combination of these parts is unique. Similarly, an IPv6 address is made up of two parts. The first 64 bits usually represent the subnet prefix (the network you belong to), and the last 64 bits usually represent the interface ID/host ID (who you are in the network).

This section covers IPv6 addressing and assignment to give you the knowledge you need for troubleshooting IPv6 addressing issues.

IPv6 Addressing Review

As with IPv4, it is important that devices are configured with the appropriate IPv6 address based on where they reside so that packets are successfully routed to and from them. Refer to Figure 1-8, which depicts an IPv6 network. 2001:db8:a:a::/64 represents the first 64 bits of the IPv6 address, which is the network prefix. This is the IPv6 network the nodes reside in. Router R1 has interface IPv6 address 2001:db8:a:a::1, where the last 64 bits, which are ::1 in this case, represent the interface/host ID (or who R1 is in the IPv6 network). PC1 is ::10, and PC2 is ::20. All the devices in 2001:db8:a:a::/64 are configured with the default gateway address of R1's Gig0/0 interface, which is 2001:db8:a:a::1.

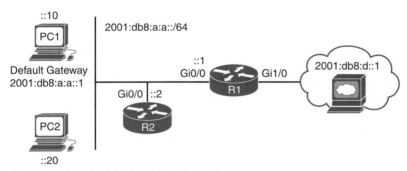

Figure 1-8   *IPv6 Addressing Example*

Just as with IPv4, when a host wants to communicate with another host, it compares its network bits to exactly the same bits in the destination IP address. If they match, both devices are in the same network; if they do not match, the devices are in different networks. If both devices are in the same network, they can communicate directly with each other, and if they are in different networks, they need to communicate through the default gateway.

For example, when PC1 in Figure 1-8 needs to communicate with the server at 2001:db8:d::1, it realizes that the web server is in a different network. Therefore, PC1 has to send the frame to the default gateway, using the default gateway's MAC address. If PC1 wants to communicate with PC2, it determines it is in the same network and communicates directly with it.

You verify the IPv6 address of a Windows PC by using the **ipconfig** command, as shown in Example 1-9. In this example, PC1 has the link-local address fe80::a00:27ff:fe5d:6d6 and the global unicast address 2001:db8:a:a::10, which was statically configured. Notice the %11 at the end of the link-local address in this case. This is the interface identification number, and it is needed so that the system knows which interface to send the packets out of; keep in mind that you can have multiple interfaces on the same device with the same link-local address assigned to them.

Example 1-9 *Using ipconfig to Verify IPv6 Addressing*

```
C:\PC1>ipconfig

Windows IP Configuration

Ethernet adapter Local Area Connection:

    Connection-specific DNS Suffix . :
    IPv6 Address. . . . . . . . . . . : 2001:db8:a:a::10
    Link-local IPv6 Address . . . . . : fe80::a00:27ff:fe5d:6d6%11
    IPv4 Address. . . . . . . . . . . : 10.1.1.10
    Subnet Mask . . . . . . . . . . . : 255.255.255.192
    Default Gateway . . . . . . . . . : 2001:db8:a:a::1
                                        10.1.1.1
```

EUI-64

Recall that an IPv6 address consists of two parts: the subnet ID and the interface/host ID. The host ID is usually 64 bits long, and as a result, it is not something you want to be configuring manually in your organization. Although you can statically define the interface ID, the best approach is to allow your end devices to automatically assign their own interface ID for global unicast and link-local addresses randomly or based on the IEEE *EUI-64* standard.

EUI-64 takes the client's MAC address, which is 48 bits, splits it in half, and adds the hex values FFFE in the middle. In addition, it takes the seventh bit from the left and flips it. So, if it is a 1, it becomes a 0, and if it is a 0, it becomes a 1. Look back at Example 1-9. Notice that the link-local address is fe80::a00:27ff:fe5d:6d6. The subnet ID is FE80::, and the interface ID is a00:27ff:fe5d:6d6. If you fill in the missing leading 0s, the address is 0a00:27ff:fe5d:06d6. This is an EUI-64 interface ID because it has FFFE in it. Let's look at how it is derived.

Example 1-10 shows the output of **ipconfig /all** on PC1. Notice that the MAC address is 08-00-27-5D-06-D6. Split it in half and add FFFE in the middle to get 08-00-27-FF-FE-5D-06-D6. Now group the hex values into groups of four and replace each dash (-) with a colon, like this: 0800:27FF:FE5D:06D6. This looks very close to what is listed in the link-local address, but it is not exactly the same. The interface ID in the link-local address starts with 0a, and ours starts with 08. This is because the seventh bit is flipped, as discussed earlier. Flip it. 08 hex in binary is 00001000. The seventh bit from left to right is a 0, so make it a 1. Now you have 00001010. Convert to hex, and you get 0a. So, your interface ID is 0A00:27FF:FE5D:06D6.

Example 1-10   *Using ipconfig /all to Verify IPv6 Addressing*

```
C:\PC1>ipconfig /all

Windows IP Configuration

  Host Name . . . . . . . . . . . .: PC1
  Primary Dns Suffix . . . . . . . :
  Node Type . . . . . . . . . . . .: Broadcast
  IP Routing Enabled. . . . . . . .: No
  WINS Proxy Enabled. . . . . . . .: No

Ethernet adapter Local Area Connection:

  Connection-specific DNS Suffix . :
  Description . . . . . . . . . . .: Intel(R) PRO/1000 MT Desktop Adapter
  Physical Address. . . . . . . . .: 08-00-27-5D-06-D6
  DHCP Enabled. . . . . . . . . . .: No
  Autoconfiguration Enabled . . . .: Yes
  IPv6 Address. . . . . . . . . . .: 2001:db8:a:a::10(Preferred)
  Link-local IPv6 Address . . . . .: fe80::a00:27ff:fe5d:6d6%11(Preferred)
  IPv4 Address. . . . . . . . . . .: 10.1.1.10(Preferred)
  Subnet Mask . . . . . . . . . . .: 255.255.255.192
  Default Gateway . . . . . . . . .: 2001:db8:a:a::1
                                      10.1.1.1
  DNS Servers . . . . . . . . . . .: fec0:0:0:ffff::1%1
                                      fec0:0:0:ffff::2%1
                                      fec0:0:0:ffff::3%1
  NetBIOS over Tcpip. . . . . . . .: Enabled
```

By default, routers use EUI-64 when generating the interface portion of the link-local address of an interface. Modern Windows PCs randomly generate the interface portion by default for the link-local address, the unique-local address, and the global unicast address when auto-configuring their IPv6 addresses. When you statically configure an IPv6 address on a PC, the interface portion is manually assigned. However, on a router, if you want to use EUI-64 for a statically configured global unicast address, use the **eui-64** keyword at the end of the **ipv6 address** command, as shown in Example 1-11.

Example 1-11   *Using EUI-64 on a Router Interface*

```
R2# config t
Enter configuration commands, one per line. End with CNTL/Z.
R2(config)# interface gigabitEthernet 0/0
R2(config-if)# ipv6 address 2001:db8:a:a::/64 eui-64
```

You verify the global unicast address and the EUI-64 interface ID assigned to an interface by using the **show ipv6 interface** command, as shown in Example 1-12. In this case, R2's Gig0/0 interface has a global unicast address that obtained the interface ID from the EUI-64 standard.

Example 1-12   *Verifying EUI-64 on a Router Interface*

```
R2# show ipv6 interface gigabitEthernet 0/0
GigabitEthernet0/0 is up, line protocol is up
 IPv6 is enabled, link-local address is FE80::C80E:15FF:FEF4:8
 No Virtual link-local address(es):
 Global unicast address(es):
 2001:DB8:A:A:C80E:15FF:FEF4:8, subnet is 2001:DB8:A:A::/64 [EUI]
 Joined group address(es):
 FF02::1
 FF02::1:FFF4:8
 MTU is 1500 bytes
 ...output omitted...
```

IPv6 SLAAC, Stateful DHCPv6, and Stateless DHCPv6

Manually assigning IP addresses (either IPv4 or IPv6) is not a scalable option. With IPv4, DHCP is a dynamic addressing option. With IPv6, you have three dynamic options to choose from: *stateless address autoconfiguration (SLAAC)*, *stateful DHCPv6*, or *stateless DHCPv6*. This section looks at the issues that might arise for each of these options and how to troubleshoot them.

SLAAC

SLAAC is designed to enable a device to configure its own IPv6 address, prefix, and default gateway without a DHCPv6 server. Windows PCs automatically have SLAAC enabled and generate their own IPv6 addresses, as shown in Example 1-13, which displays the output of **ipconfig /all** on PC1.

Example 1-13   *Using ipconfig /all to Verify That IPv6 SLAAC Is Enabled*

```
C:\PC1>ipconfig /all

Windows IP Configuration

 Host Name . . . . . . . . . . . . : PC1
 Primary Dns Suffix . . . . . . . :
 Node Type . . . . . . . . . . . . : Broadcast
 IP Routing Enabled. . . . . . . . : No
 WINS Proxy Enabled. . . . . . . . : No

Ethernet adapter Local Area Connection:
```

```
Connection-specific DNS Suffix . . : SWITCH.local
Description . . . . . . . . . . .: Intel(R) PRO/1000 MT Desktop Adapter
Physical Address. . . . . . . .: 08-00-27-5D-06-D6
DHCP Enabled. . . . . . . . . .: Yes
Autoconfiguration Enabled . . . .: Yes
IPv6 Address. . . . . . . . . .: 2001:db8::a00:27ff:fe5d:6d6(Preferred)
Link-local IPv6 Address . . . . .: fe80::a00:27ff:fe5d:6d6%11(Preferred)
IPv4 Address. . . . . . . . . . .: 10.1.1.10(Preferred)
Subnet Mask . . . . . . . . . .: 255.255.255.192
...output omitted...
```

On Cisco routers, if you want to take advantage of SLAAC, you need to enable it manually on an interface with the **ipv6 address autoconfig** command, as shown in Example 1-14.

Example 1-14   *Enabling SLAAC on a Router Interface*

```
R2# config t
Enter configuration commands, one per line. End with CNTL/Z.
R2(config)# interface gigabitEthernet 0/0
R2(config-if)# ipv6 address autoconfig
```

When a Windows PC and router interface are enabled for SLAAC, they send a *Router Solicitation* (RS) message to determine whether there are any routers connected to the local link. They then wait for a router to send a *Router Advertisement* (RA) that identifies the prefix being used by the router (the default gateway) connected to the same network they are on. They then use that prefix information to generate their own IPv6 address in the same network as the router interface that generated the RA. The router uses EUI-64 for the interface portion, and the PC randomly generates the interface portion. In addition, the PC uses the IPv6 *link-local address* of the device that sent the RA as the default gateway address.

Figure 1-9 shows the RA process. R1 sends an RA out its Gig0/0 interface. The source IPv6 address is the Gig0/0 link-local address, and the source MAC address is the MAC address of interface Gig0/0. The destination IPv6 address is the all-nodes link-local multicast IPv6 address FF02::1. The destination MAC address is the all-nodes destination MAC address 33:33:00:00:00:01, which is associated with the all-nodes link-local multicast IPv6 address FF02::1. By default, all IPv6-enabled interfaces listen for packets and frames destined for these two addresses.

When PC1 in Figure 1-9 receives the RA, it takes the prefix included in the RA, which is 2001:db8:a:a::/64, and then randomly creates the interface portion of its IPv6 address. It also takes the link-local address from the source of the RA and uses it as the default gateway address, as shown in Example 1-15, which displays the output of **ipconfig** on PC1.

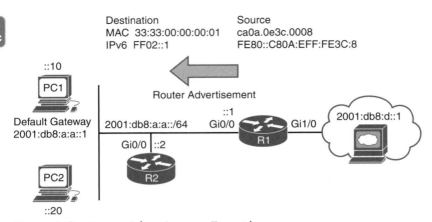

Figure 1-9 *Router Advertisement Example*

Example 1-15 *Verifying IPv6 Addresses Generated by SLAAC on a PC*

```
C:\PC1>ipconfig

Windows IP Configuration

Ethernet adapter Local Area Connection:

  Connection-specific DNS Suffix . :
  IPv6 Address. . . . . . . . . . . : 2001:db8:a:a:279:fc9b:eed4:3cd6
  Link-local IPv6 Address . . . . . : fe80::279:fc9b:eed4:3cd6%11
  IPv4 Address. . . . . . . . . . . : 10.1.1.10
  Subnet Mask . . . . . . . . . . . : 255.255.255.192
  Default Gateway . . . . . . . . . : fe80::c80a:eff:fe3c:8%11
                                      10.1.1.1
```

To verify an IPv6 address generated by SLAAC on a router interface, use the **show ipv6 interface** command. As shown in Example 1-16, the *global unicast address* was generated using SLAAC. Also notice at the bottom of the example that the default router is listed as the link-local address of R1. However, note that this occurs only if IPv6 unicast routing was not enabled on the router and, as a result, the router is acting as an end device.

Example 1-16 *Verifying IPv6 Addresses Generated by SLAAC on a Router Interface*

```
R2# show ipv6 interface gig 0/0
GigabitEthernet0/0 is up, line protocol is up
  IPv6 is enabled, link-local address is FE80::C80B:EFF:FE3C:8
  No Virtual link-local address(es):
  Stateless address autoconfig enabled
```

```
Global unicast address(es):
2001:DB8:A:A:C80B:EFF:FE3C:8, subnet is 2001:DB8:A:A::/64 [EUI/CAL/PRE]
valid lifetime 2591816 preferred lifetime 604616
Joined group address(es):
FF02::1
FF02::1:FF3C:8
...output omitted...
Default router is FE80::C80A:EFF:FE3C:8 on GigabitEthernet0/0
```

It is important to realize that RAs are generated by default on a router interface only if the router interface is enabled for IPv6, IPv6 unicast routing is enabled, and RAs are not being suppressed on the interface. Therefore, if SLAAC is not working, check the following:

- Make sure that IPv6 unicast routing is enabled on the router that should be generating RAs by using the **show run | include ipv6 unicast-routing** command, as shown in the following snippet:

  ```
  R1# show run | include ipv6 unicast-routing
  ipv6 unicast-routing
  ```

- Make sure that the appropriate interface is enabled for IPv6 by using the **show ipv6 interface** command, as shown in Example 1-17.

- Make sure that the router interface advertising RAs has a /64 prefix by using the **show ipv6 interface** command, as shown in Example 1-17. (SLAAC works only if the router is using a /64 prefix.)

- Make sure that RAs are not being suppressed on the interface by using the **show ipv6 interface** command, as shown in Example 1-18 (where they are being suppressed).

Example 1-17 *Verifying That an Interface Is Enabled for IPv6*

```
R1# show ipv6 interface gigabitEthernet 0/0
GigabitEthernet0/0 is up, line protocol is up
  IPv6 is enabled, link-local address is FE80::C80A:EFF:FE3C:8
  No Virtual link-local address(es):
  Global unicast address(es):
  2001:DB8:A:A::1, subnet is 2001:DB8:A:A::/64
  Joined group address(es):
  FF02::1
  FF02::2
  FF02::1:FF00:1
  FF02::1:FF3C:8
  ...output omitted...
```

Example 1-18 *Verifying That RAs Are Not Suppressed*

```
R1# show ipv6 interface gigabitEthernet 0/0
GigabitEthernet0/0 is up, line protocol is up
  IPv6 is enabled, link-local address is FE80::C80A:EFF:FE3C:8
  No Virtual link-local address(es):
  Global unicast address(es):
  2001:DB8:A:A::1, subnet is 2001:DB8:A:A::/64
  ...output omitted...
  ND DAD is enabled, number of DAD attempts: 1
  ND reachable time is 30000 milliseconds (using 30000)
  ND RAs are suppressed (all)
  Hosts use stateless autoconfig for addresses.
```

In addition, if you have more than one router on a subnet generating RAs, which is normal when you have redundant default gateways, the clients learn about multiple default gateways from the RAs, as shown in Example 1-19. The top default gateway is R2's link-local address, and the bottom default gateway is R1's link-local address. Now, this might seem like a benefit; however, it is a benefit only if both default gateways can reach the same networks. Refer to Figure 1-8. If PC1 uses R2 as the default gateway, the packets to the web server are dropped because R2 does not have a way to route packets to the web server, as shown in the **ping** output of Example 1-20, unless it redirects them back out the interface they arrived on, which is not a normal behavior. Therefore, if users are complaining that they cannot access resources, and they are connected to a network with multiple routers generating RAs, check the default gateways learned by SLAAC and make sure that those default gateways can route to the intended resources.

Example 1-19 *Verifying Default Gateways Configured on a PC*

```
C:\PC1># ipconfig

Windows IP Configuration

Ethernet adapter Local Area Connection:

  Connection-specific DNS Suffix . :
  IPv6 Address. . . . . . . . . . .: 2001:db8:a:a:a00:27ff:fe5d:6d6
  Link-local IPv6 Address . . . . .: fe80::a00:27ff:fe5d:6d6%11
  IPv4 Address. . . . . . . . . . .: 10.1.1.10
  Subnet Mask . . . . . . . . . . .: 255.255.255.192
  Default Gateway . . . . . . . . .: fe80::c80b:eff:fe3c:8%11
                                     fe80::c80a:eff:fe3c:8%11
                                     10.1.1.1
```

Example 1-20 *Failed Ping from PC1 to 2001:db8:d::1*

```
C:\PC1>ping 2001:db8:d::1

Pinging 2001:db8:d::1 with 32 bytes of data:
Destination net unreachable.
Destination net unreachable.
Destination net unreachable.
Destination net unreachable.


Ping statistics for 2001:db8:d::1:
 Packets: Sent = 4, Received = 0, Lost = 4 (100% loss),
```

Stateful DHCPv6

Although a device is able to determine its IPv6 address, prefix, and default gateway using SLAAC, there is not much else the devices can obtain. In a modern network, the devices may also need information such as Network Time Protocol (NTP) server information, domain name information, DNS server information, and Trivial File Transfer Protocol (TFTP) server information. To hand out the IPv6 addressing information along with all optional information, use a DHCPv6 server.

Both Cisco routers and multilayer switches may act as DHCPv6 servers. Example 1-21 provides a sample DHCPv6 configuration on R1 and the **ipv6 dhcp server** interface command necessary to enable the interface to use the DHCP pool for handing out IPv6 addressing information. If you are troubleshooting an issue where clients are not receiving IPv6 addressing information or where they are receiving wrong IPv6 addressing information from a router or multilayer switch acting as a DHCPv6 server, check the interface and make sure it was associated with the correct pool.

Example 1-21 *Sample DHCPv6 Configuration on R1*

```
R1# show run | section dhcp
ipv6 dhcp pool DHCPV6POOL
 address prefix 2001:DB8:A:A::/64
 dns-server 2001:DB8:B:B::1
 domain-name cisco.com
R1# show run interface gigabitEthernet 0/0
Building configuration...


Current configuration : 173 bytes
!
interface GigabitEthernet0/0
 no ip address
 ipv6 address 2001:DB8:A:A::1/64
 ipv6 dhcp server DHCPV6POOL
end
```

Example 1-22 provides examples of the **show ipv6 dhcp binding** command, which displays the IPv6 addresses used by clients; the **show ipv6 dhcp interface** command, which displays the interface to DHCPv6 pool associations; and the **show ipv6 dhcp pool** command, which displays the configured pools.

Example 1-22   *Verifying DHCPv6 Information on R1*

```
R1# show ipv6 dhcp binding
Client: FE80::A00:27FF:FE5D:6D6
 DUID: 000100011B101C740800275D06D6
 Username : unassigned
 VRF : default
 IA NA: IA ID 0x0E080027, T1 43200, T2 69120
 Address: 2001:DB8:A:A:D519:19AB:E903:F802
 preferred lifetime 86400, valid lifetime 172800
 expires at May 25 2018 08:37 PM (172584 seconds)

R1# show ipv6 dhcp interface
GigabitEthernet0/0 is in server mode
 Using pool: DHCPV6POOL
 Preference value: 0
 Hint from client: ignored
 Rapid-Commit: disabled

R1# show ipv6 dhcp pool
DHCPv6 pool: DHCPV6POOL
 Address allocation prefix: 2001:DB8:A:A::/64 valid 172800 preferred 86400 (1 in
use, 0 conflicts)
 DNS server: 2001:DB8:B:B::1
 Domain name: cisco.com
 Active clients: 0
```

Stateless DHCPv6

Stateless DHCPv6 is a combination of SLAAC and DHCPv6. With stateless DHCPv6, clients use a router's RA to automatically determine the IPv6 address, prefix, and default gateway. Included in the RA is a flag that tells the client to get other non-addressing information from a DHCPv6 server, such as the address of a DNS server or a TFTP server. To accomplish this, ensure that the **ipv6 nd other-config-flag** interface configuration command is enabled. This ensures that the RA informs the client that it must contact a DHCPv6 server for other information. In Example 1-23, notice this command configured under the Gigabit Ethernet 0/0 interface. Also, in Example 1-23, the output of **show ipv6 interface gigabitEthernet 0/0** states that hosts obtain IPv6 addressing from *stateless autoconfig* and other information from a *DHCP server*.

Example 1-23 *Verifying Stateless DHCPv6*

```
R1# show run int gig 0/0
Building configuration...

Current configuration : 171 bytes
!
interface GigabitEthernet0/0
 no ip address
 media-type gbic
 speed 1000
 duplex full
 negotiation auto
 ipv6 address 2001:DB8:A:A::1/64
 ipv6 nd other-config-flag
end


R1# show ipv6 interface gigabitEthernet 0/0
GigabitEthernet0/0 is up, line protocol is up
 IPv6 is enabled, link-local address is FE80::C80A:EFF:FE3C:8
 No Virtual link-local address(es):
 Global unicast address(es):
 2001:DB8:A:A::1, subnet is 2001:DB8:A:A::/64
 Joined group address(es):
 FF02::1
 FF02::2
 FF02::1:FF00:1
 FF02::1:FF3C:8
...output omitted...
 ND advertised default router preference is Medium
 Hosts use stateless autoconfig for addresses.
 Hosts use DHCP to obtain other configuration.
```

DHCPv6 Operation

DHCPv6 has a four-step negotiation process, like IPv4. However, DHCPv6 uses the following messages:

Step 1. *SOLICIT message*: A client sends this message to locate DHCPv6 servers using the multicast address FF02::1:2, which is the all-DHCPv6-servers multicast address.

Step 2. *ADVERTISE message*: Servers respond to SOLICIT messages with a unicast ADVERTISE message, offering addressing information to the client.

Step 3. *REQUEST message*: The client sends this message to the server, confirming the addresses provided and any other parameters.

Step 4. *REPLY message*: The server finalizes the process with this message.

As a reference, Table 1-3 provides a comprehensive list of DHCPv6 message types you might encounter while troubleshooting a DHCPv6 issue.

Table 1-3   DHCP Message Types

DHCP Message	Description
SOLICIT	A client sends this message in an attempt to locate a DHCPv6 server.
ADVERTISE	A DHCPv6 server sends this message in response to a SOLICIT to indicate that it is available.
REQUEST	A client sends this message to a specific DHCPv6 server to request IP configuration parameters.
CONFIRM	A client sends this message to a server to determine whether the address it was assigned is still appropriate.
RENEW	A client sends this message to the server that assigned the address in order to extend the lifetime of the addresses assigned.
REBIND	When there is no response to a RENEW, a client sends a REBIND message to a server to extend the lifetime on the address assigned.
REPLY	A server sends a client this message, which contains assigned address and configuration parameters, in response to a SOLICIT, REQUEST, RENEW, or REBIND message received from a client.
RELEASE	A client sends this message to a server to inform the server that the assigned address is no longer needed.
DECLINE	A client sends this message to a server to inform the server that the assigned address is already in use.
RECONFIGURE	A server sends this message to a client when the server has new or updated information.
INFORMATION-REQUEST	A client sends this message to a server when the client needs only additional configuration information without any IP address assignment.
RELAY-FORW	A relay agent uses this message to forward messages to a DHCP server.
RELAY-REPL	A DHCP server uses this message to reply to the relay agent.

DHCPv6 Relay Agents

All the DHCPv6 examples so far have included the DHCP server within the same local network. However, in most networks, the DHCP server is located in a different network, which creates an issue. If you review the multicast address of the SOLICIT message, notice that it is a link-local multicast address. It starts with FF02. Therefore, the multicast does not leave the local network, and the client is not able to reach the DHCPv6 server.

To relay the DHCPv6 messages to a DHCPv6 server in another network, the local router interface in the network the client belongs to needs to be configured as a *DHCPv6 relay agent*, using the **ipv6 dhcp relay destination** interface configuration command. Example 1-24 shows interface Gigabit Ethernet 0/0 configured with the command **ipv6 dhcp relay destination 2001:db8:a:b::7**, which is used to forward SOLICIT messages to a DHCPv6 server at the address listed.

Example 1-24 *Configuring R1 as a DHCPv6 Relay Agent*

```
R1# config t
Enter configuration commands, one per line. End with CNTL/Z.
R1(config)# interface gigabitethernet0/0
R1(config-if)# ipv6 dhcp relay destination 2001:db8:a:b::7
```

Packet-Forwarding Process

When troubleshooting connectivity issues for an IP-based network, the network layer (Layer 3) of the OSI reference model is often an appropriate place to begin your trouble-shooting efforts; this is referred to as the *divide-and-conquer method*. For example, if you are experiencing connectivity issues between two hosts on a network, you could check Layer 3 by pinging between the hosts. If the pings are successful, you can conclude that the issue resides at upper layers of the OSI reference model (Layers 4 through 7). However, if the pings fail, you should focus your troubleshooting efforts on Layers 1 through 3. If you ultimately determine that there is a problem at Layer 3, your efforts might be centered on a router's *packet-forwarding* process.

This section discusses the packet-forwarding process and the commands used to verify the entries in the data structures that are used for this process. It also provides you with a collection of Cisco IOS software commands that are useful when troubleshooting related issues.

Reviewing the Layer 3 Packet-Forwarding Process

To review basic routing processes, consider Figure 1-10. In this topology, PC1 needs to access HTTP resources on Server1. Notice that PC1 and Server1 are on different networks. So how does a packet from source IP address 192.168.1.2 get routed to destination IP address 192.168.3.2?

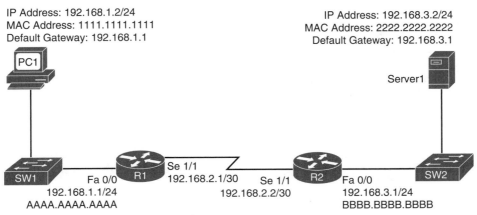

IP Address: 192.168.1.2/24
MAC Address: 1111.1111.1111
Default Gateway: 192.168.1.1

IP Address: 192.168.3.2/24
MAC Address: 2222.2222.2222
Default Gateway: 192.168.3.1

Server1

SW1   Fa 0/0   R1   Se 1/1   Se 1/1   R2   Fa 0/0   SW2
192.168.1.1/24   192.168.2.1/30   192.168.2.2/30   192.168.3.1/24
AAAA.AAAA.AAAA   BBBB.BBBB.BBBB

Figure 1-10 *Basic Routing Topology*

Consider the following step-by-step walkthrough of this process:

Step 1.   PC1 compares its IP address and subnet mask 192.168.1.2/24 with the destination IP address 192.168.3.2, as discussed earlier in the chapter. PC1 determines the network portion of its own IP address. It then compares these binary bits with the same binary bits of the destination address. If they are the same, it knows the destination is on the same subnet. If they differ, it knows the destination is on a remote subnet. PC1 concludes that the destination IP address resides on a remote subnet in this example. Therefore, PC1 needs to send the frame to its default gateway, which could have been manually configured on PC1 or dynamically learned via DHCP. In this example, PC1 has the default gateway address 192.168.1.1 (that is, router R1). To construct a proper Layer 2 frame, PC1 needs the MAC address of the frame's destination, which is PC1's default gateway in this example. If the MAC address is not in PC1's Address Resolution Protocol (*ARP*) cache, PC1 uses ARP to discover it. Once PC1 receives an ARP reply from router R1, PC1 adds router R1's MAC address to its ARP cache. PC1 then sends its data destined for Server1 in a frame addressed to R1, as shown in Figure 1-11.

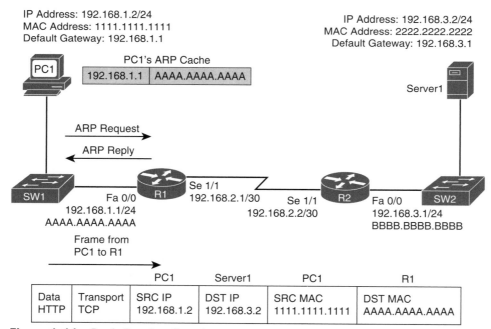

Figure 1-11   *Basic Routing, Step 1*

Step 2.   Router R1 receives the frame sent from PC1, and because the destination MAC address is R1's, R1 tears off the Layer 2 header and interrogates the IP (Layer 3) header. An IP header contains a time-to-live (*TTL*) field, which is decremented once for each router hop. Therefore, router R1 decrements the packet's TTL field. If the value in the TTL field is reduced to zero, the router discards the packet and sends a *time-exceeded* Internet Control Message Protocol (ICMP) message back to the source. If the TTL field is not decremented to zero, router R1 checks its *routing table* to determine the best path to reach the IP address 192.168.3.2. In this example, router R1's routing table has an entry stating that network 192.168.3.0/24 is accessible through interface Serial 1/1. Note that ARP is not required for serial interfaces because these interface types do not have MAC addresses. Therefore, router R1 forwards the frame out its Serial 1/1 interface, as shown in Figure 1-12, using the Point-to-Point Protocol (PPP) Layer 2 framing header.

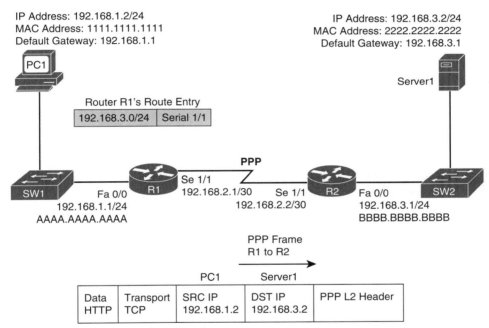

Figure 1-12   *Basic Routing, Step 2*

Step 3.   When router R2 receives the frame, it removes the PPP header and then decrements the TTL field in the IP header, just as router R1 did. Again, if the TTL field did not get decremented to zero, router R2 interrogates the IP header to determine the destination network. In this case, the destination network 192.168.3.0/24 is directly attached to router R2's Fast Ethernet 0/0 interface. Much the way PC1 sent out an ARP request to determine the MAC address of its default gateway, router R2 sends an ARP request to determine the MAC address of Server1 if it is not already known in the *ARP cache*. Once an ARP reply is received from Server1, router R2 stores the results of the ARP reply in the ARP cache and forwards the frame out its Fast Ethernet 0/0 interface to Server1, as shown in Figure 1-13.

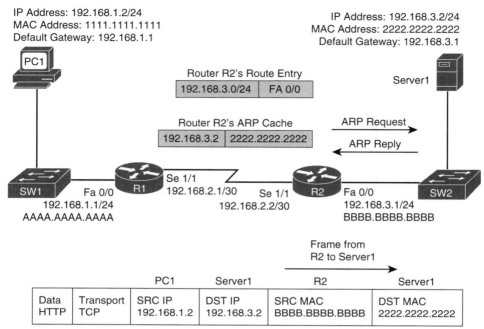

Figure 1-13   *Basic Routing, Step 3*

The previous steps identified two router data structures:

- **IP routing table:** When a router needs to route an IP packet, it consults its IP routing table to find the best match. The best match is the route that has the *longest prefix*. For example, suppose that a router has a routing entry for networks 10.0.0.0/8, 10.1.1.0/24, and 10.1.1.0/26. Also suppose that the router is trying to forward a packet with the destination IP address 10.1.1.10. The router selects the 10.1.1.0/26 route entry as the best match for 10.1.1.10 because that route entry has the longest prefix, /26 (so it matches the largest number of bits).

- **Layer 3-to-Layer 2 mapping table:** In Figure 1-13, router R2's ARP cache contains Layer 3-to-Layer 2 mapping information. Specifically, the ARP cache has a mapping that says MAC address 2222.2222.2222 corresponds to IP address 192.168.3.2. An ARP cache is the Layer 3-to-Layer 2 mapping data structure used for Ethernet-based networks, but similar data structures are used for Multipoint Frame Relay networks and Dynamic Multipoint Virtual Private Network (DMVPN) networks. However, for point-to-point links such as PPP or High-Level Data Link Control (HDLC), because there is only one other possible device connected to the other end of the link, no mapping information is needed to determine the next-hop device.

Continually querying a router's routing table and its Layer 3-to-Layer 2 mapping data structure (for example, an ARP cache) is less than efficient. Fortunately, Cisco Express Forwarding (*CEF*) gleans its information from the router's IP routing table and Layer 3-to-Layer 2 mapping tables. Then, CEF's data structures in hardware can be referenced when forwarding packets.

The two primary CEF data structures are as follows:

■ **Forwarding Information Base (FIB):** The *FIB* contains Layer 3 information, similar to the information found in an IP routing table. In addition, the FIB contains information about multicast routes and directly connected hosts.

■ **Adjacency table:** When a router is performing a route lookup using CEF, the FIB references an entry in the *adjacency table*. The adjacency table entry contains the frame header information required by the router to properly form a frame. Therefore, an egress interface and a next-hop MAC address is in an adjacency entry for a multipoint Ethernet interface, whereas a point-to-point interface requires only egress interface information.

As a reference, Figure 1-14 shows the router data structures.

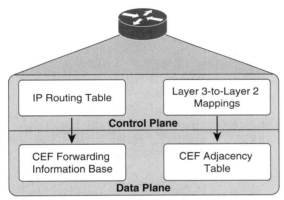

Figure 1-14   *A Router's Data Structures*

Troubleshooting the Packet-Forwarding Process

When troubleshooting packet-forwarding issues, you need to examine a router's IP routing table. If the observed behavior of the traffic is not conforming to information in the IP routing table, remember that the IP routing table is maintained by a router's *control plane* and is used to build the tables in the *data plane*. CEF is operating in the data plane and uses the FIB. You need to view the CEF data structures (that is, the FIB and the adjacency table) that contain all the information required to make packet-forwarding decisions.

Example 1-25 provides sample output from the **show ip route** *ip_address* command. The output shows that the next-hop IP address to reach IP address 192.168.1.11 is 192.168.0.11, which is accessible via interface Fast Ethernet 0/0. Because this information is coming from the control plane, it includes information about the routing protocol, which is OSPF in this case.

Example 1-25   *show ip route ip_address Command Output*

```
Router# show ip route 192.168.1.11
Routing entry for 192.168.1.0/24
Known via "ospf 1", distance 110, metric 11, type intra area
Last update from 192.168.0.11 on FastEthernet0/0, 00:06:45 ago
Routing Descriptor Blocks:
192.168.0.11, from 10.1.1.1, 00:06:45 ago, via FastEthernet0/0
Route metric is 11, traffic share count is 1
```

Example 1-26 provides sample output from the **show ip route** *ip_address subnet_mask* command. The output indicates that the entire network 192.168.1.0/24 is accessible out interface Fast Ethernet 0/0, with next-hop IP address 192.168.0.11.

Example 1-26   *show ip route ip_address subnet_mask Command Output*

```
Router# show ip route 192.168.1.0 255.255.255.0
Routing entry for 192.168.1.0/24
Known via "ospf 1", distance 110, metric 11, type intra area
Last update from 192.168.0.11 on FastEthernet0/0, 00:06:57 ago
Routing Descriptor Blocks:
192.168.0.11, from 10.1.1.1, 00:06:57 ago, via FastEthernet0/0
Route metric is 11, traffic share count is 1
```

Example 1-27 provides sample output from the **show ip route** *ip_address subnet_mask* **longer-prefixes** command, with and without the **longer-prefixes** option. Notice that the router responds that the subnet 172.16.0.0 255.255.0.0 is not in the IP routing table. However, with the **longer-prefixes** option added, two routes are displayed because these routes are subnets of the 172.16.0.0/16 network.

Example 1-27   *show ip route ip_address subnet_mask* **longer-prefixes** *Command Output*

```
Router# show ip route 172.16.0.0 255.255.0.0
% Subnet not in table
R2# show ip route 172.16.0.0 255.255.0.0 longer-prefixes
Codes: C - connected, S - static, R - RIP, M - mobile, B - BGP
D - EIGRP, EX - EIGRP external, O - OSPF, IA - OSPF inter area
N1 - OSPF NSSA external type 1, N2 - OSPF NSSA external type 2
E1 - OSPF external type 1, E2 - OSPF external type 2
i - IS-IS, su - IS-IS summary, L1 - IS-IS level-1, L2 - IS-IS level-2
ia - IS-IS inter area, * - candidate default, U - per-user static route
- ODR, P - periodic downloaded static route


Gateway of last resort is not set


172.16.0.0/30 is subnetted, 2 subnets
C 172.16.1.0 is directly connected, Serial1/0.1
C 172.16.2.0 is directly connected, Serial1/0.2
```

Example 1-28 provides sample output from the **show ip cef** *ip_address* command. The output indicates that, according to CEF, IP address 192.168.1.11 is accessible out interface Fast Ethernet 0/0, with the next-hop IP address 192.168.0.11.

Example 1-28 *show ip cef ip_address Command Output*

```
Router# show ip cef 192.168.1.11
192.168.1.0/24, version 42, epoch 0, cached adjacency 192.168.0.11
0 packets, 0 bytes
via 192.168.0.11, FastEthernet0/0, 0 dependencies
next hop 192.168.0.11, FastEthernet0/0
valid cached adjacency
```

Example 1-29 provides sample output from the **show ip cef** *ip_address subnet_mask* command. The output indicates that network 192.168.1.0/24 is accessible off interface Fast Ethernet 0/0, with the next-hop IP address 192.168.0.11.

Example 1-29 *show ip cef ip_address subnet_mask Command Output*

```
Router# show ip cef 192.168.1.0 255.255.255.0
192.168.1.0/24, version 42, epoch 0, cached adjacency 192.168.0.11
0 packets, 0 bytes
via 192.168.0.11, FastEthernet0/0, 0 dependencies
next hop 192.168.0.11, FastEthernet0/0
valid cached adjacency
```

Example 1-30 provides sample output from the **show ip cef exact-route** *source_address destination_address* command. The output indicates that a packet sourced from IP address 10.2.2.2 and destined for IP address 192.168.1.11 will be sent out interface Fast Ethernet 0/0 to next-hop IP address 192.168.0.11.

Example 1-30 *show ip cef exact-route src_ip_address dst_ip_address Command Output*

```
Router# show ip cef exact-route 10.2.2.2 192.168.1.11
10.2.2.2 -> 192.168.1.11 : FastEthernet0/0 (next hop 192.168.0.11)
```

For a multipoint interface such as Ethernet, when a router knows the next-hop address for a packet, it needs appropriate Layer 2 information to properly construct a frame. Example 1-31 provides sample output from the **show ip arp** command, which displays the ARP cache that is stored in the control plane on a router. The output shows the learned or configured MAC addresses along with their associated IP addresses.

Example 1-31 *show ip arp Command Output*

```
Router# show ip arp
Protocol Address        Age (min) Hardware Addr   Type    Interface
Internet 192.168.0.11       0      0009.b7fa.d1e1  ARPA    FastEthernet0/0
Internet 192.168.0.22       -      c001.0f70.0000  ARPA    FastEthernet0/0
```

Example 1-32 provides sample output from the **show ip nhrp** command. This command displays the Next Hop Resolution Protocol cache that is used with DMVPN networks. In this example, if a packet needs to be sent to the 192.168.255.2 next-hop IP address, the non-broadcast multi-access (NBMA) address 198.51.100.2 is used to reach it.

Example 1-32 *show ip nhrp Command Output*

```
HUBRouter# show ip nhrp
192.168.255.2/32 via 192.168.255.2
 should be entire line - Raymond
Tunnel0 created 00:02:35, expire 01:57:25
Type: dynamic, Flags: unique registered
NBMA address: 198.51.100.2
192.168.255.3/32 via 192.168.255.3
Tunnel0 created 00:02:36, expire 01:57:23
Type: dynamic, Flags: unique registered
NBMA address: 203.0.113.2
```

Example 1-33 provides sample output from the **show adjacency detail** command. The output shows the CEF information used to construct frame headers needed to reach the next-hop IP addresses through the various router interfaces. Notice the value CA1B01C4001CCA1C164000540800 for Fast Ethernet 3/0. This is the destination MAC address, the source MAC address, and the EtherType code for an Ethernet frame. The first 12 hex values are the destination MAC address, the next 12 are the source MAC address, and 0800 is the IPv4 EtherType code.

Example 1-33 *show adjacency detail Command Output*

```
Router# show adjacency detail
Protocol      Interface              Address
...output omitted...
IP            FastEthernet3/0        203.0.113.1(7)
                                     0 packets, 0 bytes
                                     epoch 0
                                     sourced in sev-epoch 1
                                     Encap length 14
                                     CA1B01C4001CCA1C164000540800
                                     L2 destination address byte offset 0
                                     L2 destination address byte length 6
                                     Link-type after encap: ip
                                     ARP
```

Administrative Distance

When designing a routed network and determining what will be the source of routing information, you have many options to choose from: connected, static, EIGRP, OSPF, and BGP, to name a few. With all these different options, you need to be able to recognize what is most trustworthy (that is, believable). This is extremely important when you are using multiple sources because only one source of information can be used to populate the routing table for any given route. As a result, it is important for a troubleshooter to understand how the best source of routing information is determined and how that source's information is placed in the routing table.

This section explains which sources of routing information are the most believable and how the routing table interacts with various data structures to populate itself with the best information.

Data Structures and the Routing Table

To better troubleshoot routing information sources, consider, generically, how the data structures of dynamic routing protocols interact with a router's IP routing table. Figure 1-15 shows the interaction between the data structures of an IP routing protocol and a router's IP routing table.

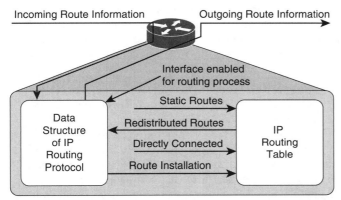

Figure 1-15   *Interaction Between the IP Routing Table and a Routing Protocol Data Structure*

As a router receives routing information from a neighboring router, the information is stored in the data structures of the IP routing protocol and analyzed by the routing protocol to determine the best path, based on metrics. An IP routing protocol's data structure can also be populated by the local router. For example, a router might be configured for route redistribution, where routing information is redistributed from the routing table into the IP routing protocol's data structure. The router might be configured to have specific interfaces participate in an IP routing protocol process. In that case, the network that the interface belongs to is placed into the routing protocol data structure as well.

But what goes in the routing table? Review Figure 1-15 again and notice that the routing protocol data structure can populate the routing table, a directly connected route can populate the routing table, and static routes can populate the routing table. These are all known as sources of routing information.

Sources of Routing Information

A router could conceivably receive routing information from the following routing sources all at the same time:

- Connected interface
- Static route

- RIP

- EIGRP

- OSPF

- BGP

If the routing information received from all these sources is for different destination networks, each one is used for its respectively learned destination networks and placed in the routing table. However, what if the route received from Routing Information Protocol (RIP) and OSPF is exactly the same? For example, say that both protocols have informed the router about the 10.1.1.0/24 network. How does the router choose which is the most believable, or the best source of routing information? It cannot use both; it must pick one and install that information in the routing table.

Routing information sources are each assigned an *administrative distance* (AD). Think of an administrative distance of a routing information source as the *believability* or *trustworthiness* of that routing source compared to the other routing information sources. Table 1-4 lists the default ADs of routing information sources. The lower the AD, the more preferred the source of information.

For instance, RIP has a default AD of 120, whereas OSPF has a default AD of 110. Therefore, if both RIP and OSPF have knowledge of a route to a specific network (for example, 10.1.1.0/24), the OSPF route is injected into the router's IP routing table because OSPF has a more believable AD. Therefore, the best route selected by an IP routing protocol's data structure is only a *candidate* to be injected into the router's IP routing table. The route is injected into the routing table only if the router concludes that it came from the best routing source. As you will see in later chapters, when you troubleshoot specific routing protocols, routes from a specific routing protocol might be missing in the routing table, or suboptimal routing may be occurring because a different routing source with a lower AD is being used.

Table 1-4   Default Administrative Distance of Route Sources

Source of Routing information	AD
Connected interface	0
Static route	1
EIGRP summary route	5
eBGP (External Border Gateway Protocol)	20
EIGRP (internal)	90
OSPF	110
IS-IS (Intermediate System to Intermediate System)	115
RIP	120
ODR (On-Demand Routing)	160
EIGRP (external)	170
iBGP (Internal Border Gateway Protocol)	200
Unknown (not believable)	255

You can verify the AD of a route in a routing table by using the **show ip route** *ip_address* command, as shown in Example 1-34. Notice in the example that the route to 10.1.1.0 has an AD of 0, and the route to 10.1.23.0 has an AD of 90.

Example 1-34   *Verifying the Administrative Distance of a Route in the Routing Table*

```
R1# show ip route 10.1.1.0
Routing entry for 10.1.1.0/26
Known via "connected", distance 0, metric 0 (connected, via interface)
Redistributing via eigrp 100
Routing Descriptor Blocks:
directly connected, via GigabitEthernet1/0
Route metric is 0, traffic share count is 1
R1# show ip route 10.1.23.0
Routing entry for 10.1.23.0/24
Known via "eigrp 100", distance 90, metric 3072, type internal
Redistributing via eigrp 100
Last update from 10.1.13.3 on GigabitEthernet2/0, 09:42:20 ago
Routing Descriptor Blocks:
10.1.13.3, from 10.1.13.3, 09:42:20 ago, via GigabitEthernet2/0
Route metric is 3072, traffic share count is 1
Total delay is 20 microseconds, minimum bandwidth is 1000000 Kbit
Reliability 255/255, minimum MTU 1500 bytes
Loading 1/255, Hops 1
```

TIP   If you ever need to make sure that the routing information or subset of routing information received from a particular source is never used, change the AD of specific routes or all routes from that source to 255, which means "do not believe."

AD is also used to manipulate path selection. For example, you might have two different paths to the same destination, learned from two different sources, such as EIGRP and a static route. In this case, the static route is preferred. However, this static route may be pointing to a backup link that is slower than the EIGRP path. Therefore, you want the EIGRP path to be installed in the routing table because the static route is causing suboptimal routing. But you are not allowed to remove the static route. To solve this issue, create a floating static route. This static route has a higher AD than the preferred route. Because you want EIGRP to be preferred, modify the static route so that it has an AD higher than EIGRP, which is 90. As a result, the EIGRP-learned route is installed in the routing table, and the static route is installed only if the EIGRP-learned route goes away.

Static Routes

Administrators manually configure static routes, and by default these routes are the second-most-trustworthy source of routing information, with an AD of 1. They allow an administrator to precisely control how to route packets for a particular destination. This section discusses the syntax of IPv4 and IPv6 static routes and explains what to look for while troubleshooting.

IPv4 Static Routes

To create an IPv4 static route, you use the **ip route** *prefix mask* {*ip_address* | *interface_ type interface_number*} [*distance*] command in global configuration mode. The following snippet displays the configuration of a static route on R1 in Figure 1-16. The static route is training R1 about the 10.1.3.0/24 network:

```
R1# config t
Enter configuration commands, one per line. End with CNTL/Z.
R1(config)# ip route 10.1.3.0 255.255.255.0 10.1.12.2 8
```

The network is reachable via the next-hop address 10.1.12.2, which is R2, and is assigned an AD of 8. (The default is 1.)

Example 1-35, which shows the output of **show ip route static** on R1, indicates that the 10.1.3.0/24 network was learned by a static route, it is reachable via the next-hop IP address 10.1.12.2, it has an AD of 8, and the metric is 0 because there is no way to know how far away the destination truly is (as there is with a dynamic routing protocol).

Example 1-35 *Verifying a Static Route on R1*

```
R1# show ip route static
Codes: L - local, C - connected, S - static, R - RIP, M - mobile, B - BGP
...output omitted...

10.0.0.0/8 is variably subnetted, 7 subnets, 2 masks
S 10.1.3.0/24 [8/0] via 10.1.12.2
```

When troubleshooting IPv4 static routes, you need to be able to recognize why a static route may not be providing the results you want. For example, are the network and mask accurate? If either of them is incorrect, your static route will not route the packets you are expecting it to route. The router might drop packets because the route used does not match the static route or any other route. It might end up forwarding packets using the default route, which may be pointing the wrong way. In addition, if the static route includes networks that it should not, you could be routing packets the wrong way.

Consider this: If you were to configure the static route **ip route 10.1.3.0 255.255.255.0 10.1.12.1** on R2 in Figure 1-16, packets destined to 10.1.3.0 would be sent to R1, which is the wrong way. However, notice in Example 1-35 that R1 points to R2 (10.1.12.2) for the network 10.1.3.0/24. Therefore, R1 and R2 simply bounce packets that are destined for 10.1.3.0/24 back and forth until the TTL expires.

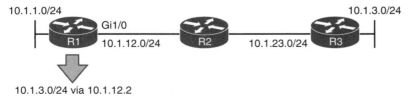

Figure 1-16 *Configuring a Static Route on R1 with the Next-Hop Option*

Notice that the next-hop IP address is a very important parameter for the static route. It tells the local router where to send the packet. For instance, in Example 1-35, the next hop is 10.1.12.2. Therefore, a packet destined to 10.1.3.0 has to go to 10.1.12.2 next. R1 now does a recursive lookup in the routing table for 10.1.12.2 to determine how to reach it, as shown in Example 1-36. This example displays the output of the **show ip route 10.1.12.2** command on R1. Notice that 10.1.12.2 is directly connected out Gigabit Ethernet 1/0.

Example 1-36   *Recursive Lookup on R1 for the Next-Hop Address*

```
R1# show ip route 10.1.12.2
Routing entry for 10.1.12.0/24
Known via "connected" distance 0, metric 0 (connected, via interface)
Routing Descriptor Blocks:
directly connected, via GigabitEthernet1/0
Route metric is 0, traffic share count is 1
```

Because the exit interface to reach 10.1.12.2 is Gigabit Ethernet 1/0, the Ethernet frame requires source and destination MAC addresses. As a result, R1 looks in its ARP cache, as shown in Example 1-37, and finds that the MAC address for 10.1.12.2 is ca08.0568.0008.

Example 1-37   *MAC Address Lookup in the ARP Cache*

```
R1# show ip arp
Protocol Address     Age (min) Hardware Addr   Type Interface
Internet 10.1.1.1       -      ca07.0568.0008  ARPA GigabitEthernet0/0
Internet 10.1.12.1      -      ca07.0568.001c  ARPA GigabitEthernet1/0
Internet 10.1.12.2      71     ca08.0568.0008  ARPA GigabitEthernet1/0
```

Notice in this case that the MAC address of the next-hop address is used for the Layer 2 frame. It is not the MAC address of the IP address in the packet. The benefit of this is that the router only has to find the MAC address of the next hop when using the ARP process, and then it can store the results in the ARP cache. Then, any packet that has to go to the next-hop address 10.1.12.2 does not require an ARP request to be sent; it needs just a lookup in the ARP cache, which makes the overall routing process more efficient.

Now that you understand the next-hop IP address, there is another option you need to know about. As you saw earlier in this chapter, in the section "IPv4 Static Routes," you can specify an exit interface instead of a next-hop IP address. There is the right time to use the exit interface; there is also a wrong time to use it. The right time is when it's a pure point-to-point interface, such as DSL or serial. Point-to-point Ethernet links are not pure point-to-point links; they are still multiaccess, and because they are Ethernet, they require source and destination MAC addresses. If you specify an Ethernet interface as the next hop, you will be making your router use ARP for the MAC address of every destination IP address in every packet. Let's look at this.

Say that you configure the following static route on R1: **ip route 10.1.3.0 255.255.255.0 gigabit Ethernet 1/0**. Example 1-38 shows how the static route appears in the routing table. It states that 10.1.3.0/24 is directly connected to Gigabit Ethernet 1/0. But is it? Refer to Figure 1-17 to know for sure. It is clear in Figure 1-17 that 10.1.3.0/24 is not directly connected. But because of the way the static route is configured, R1 thinks that it is directly connected.

Example 1-38 *Static Route with an Exit Interface Specified*

```
R1# show ip route static
...output omitted...

10.0.0.0/8 is variably subnetted, 7 subnets, 2 masks
S 10.1.3.0/24 is directly connected, GigabitEthernet1/0
```

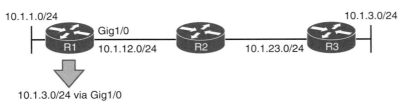

Figure 1-17 *Configuring a Static Route on R1 with an Exit Interface Option*

Imagine that users in the 10.1.1.0/24 network are trying to access resources in the 10.1.3.0/24 network. Specifically, they are accessing resources on devices with the IP addresses 10.1.3.1 through 10.1.3.8. R1 receives the packets, and it looks in the routing table and finds that the longest match is the following entry:

```
S 10.1.3.0/24 is directly connected, GigabitEthernet1/0
```

R1 believes the network is directly connected; therefore, the destination IP address in the packet is on the network connected to Gig1/0. However, you know better because Figure 1-17 shows that it is not. So, because it is an Ethernet interface, R1 uses ARP to determine the MAC address of the IP address in the destination field of the packet. (This is different from what occurred when the next-hop IP address was specified. When the next hop was specified, the MAC address of the next-hop address was used.)

Example 1-39 shows the ARP cache on R1. Notice that every destination IP address has an entry in the ARP cache. How can this be if ARP requests are not forwarded by routers? It is because of *proxy ARP*, which is on by default on the routers. Proxy ARP allows a router to respond to ARP requests with its own MAC address if it has a route in the routing table to the IP address in the ARP request. Notice that the MAC addresses listed are all the same. In addition, they match the MAC address of the 10.1.12.2 entry. Therefore, because R2 has a route to reach the IP address of the ARP request, it responds back with its MAC address.

Example 1-39 *ARP Cache on R1 with R2 Proxy ARP Enabled*

```
R1# show ip arp
Protocol Address     Age (min) Hardware Addr  Type Interface
Internet 10.1.1.1    -         ca07.0568.0008 ARPA GigabitEthernet0/0
Internet 10.1.3.1    0         ca08.0568.0008 ARPA GigabitEthernet1/0
Internet 10.1.3.2    0         ca08.0568.0008 ARPA GigabitEthernet1/0
Internet 10.1.3.3    3         ca08.0568.0008 ARPA GigabitEthernet1/0
```

```
Internet 10.1.3.4    0         ca08.0568.0008 ARPA GigabitEthernet1/0
Internet 10.1.3.5    1         ca08.0568.0008 ARPA GigabitEthernet1/
0Internet 10.1.3.6   0         ca08.0568.0008 ARPA GigabitEthernet1/
0Internet 10.1.3.7   0         ca08.0568.0008 ARPA GigabitEthernet1/
0Internet 10.1.3.8   1         ca08.0568.0008 ARPA GigabitEthernet1/0
Internet 10.1.12.1   -         ca07.0568.001c ARPA GigabitEthernet1/0
Internet 10.1.12.2   139       ca08.0568.0008 ARPA GigabitEthernet1/0
```

Example 1-40 shows how to use the **show ip interface** command to verify whether proxy ARP is enabled.

Example 1-40   *Verifying Whether Proxy ARP Is Enabled*

```
R2# show ip interface gigabitEthernet 0/0
GigabitEthernet0/0 is up, line protocol is up
Internet address is 10.1.12.2/24
Broadcast address is 255.255.255.255
Address determined by non-volatile memory
MTU is 1500 bytes
Helper address is not set
Directed broadcast forwarding is disabled
Multicast reserved groups joined: 224.0.0.5 224.0.0.6
Outgoing access list is not set
Inbound access list is not set
Proxy ARP is enabled
Local Proxy ARP is disabled
Security level is default
Split horizon is enabled
ICMP redirects are always sent
```

If proxy ARP is not enabled, the ARP cache on R1 appears as shown in Example 1-41. Notice that R1 is still sending ARP requests; however, it is not getting any ARP replies. Therefore, it cannot build the Layer 2 frame, and the result is an *encapsulation failure*, which you would be able to see if you were debugging IP packets.

Example 1-41   *ARP Cache on R1 with R2 Proxy ARP Disabled*

```
R1# show ip arp
Protocol Address     Age (min) Hardware Addr  Type Interface
Internet 10.1.1.1    -         ca07.0568.0008 ARPA GigabitEthernet0/0
Internet 10.1.3.1    0         Incomplete     ARPA
Internet 10.1.3.2    0         Incomplete     ARPA
Internet 10.1.3.3    0         Incomplete     ARPA
Internet 10.1.3.4    0         Incomplete     ARPA
Internet 10.1.3.5    0         Incomplete     ARPA
```

```
Internet 10.1.3.6  0            Incomplete   ARPA
Internet 10.1.3.7  0            Incomplete   ARPA
Internet 10.1.3.8  0            Incomplete   ARPA
Internet 10.1.12.1 -            ca07.0568.001c ARPA GigabitEthernet1/0
Internet 10.1.12.2 139          ca08.0568.0008 ARPA GigabitEthernet1/0
```

Because of the fact that R1 uses ARP to determine the MAC address of every destination IP address in every packet, you should never specify an Ethernet interface in a static route. Specifying an Ethernet interface in a static route results in excessive use of router resources, such as processor and memory, as the control plane gets involved during the forwarding process to determine the appropriate Layer 2 MAC address using ARP.

Being able to recognize misconfigured static routes and the issues that arise is an important skill to have when troubleshooting because a misconfigured static route causes traffic to be misrouted or suboptimally routed. In addition, remember that static routes have an AD of 1; therefore, they are preferred over other sources of routing information to the same destination.

IPv6 Static Routes

To create an IPv6 static route, you use the **ipv6 route** {*ipv6_prefix/prefix_length*} {*ipv6_address* | *interface_type interface_number*} [*administrative_distance*] [*next_hop_address*] command in global configuration mode.

The following snippet displays the configuration of an IPv6 static route on R1, as shown in Figure 1-18:

```
R1# config t

R1(config)# ipv6 route 2001:DB8:0:3::/64 gigabitEthernet 1/0
FE80::2 8
```

The static route is training R1 about the 2001:DB8:0:3::/64 network. The network is reachable using the next-hop address FE80::2, which is R2's link-local address, and it was assigned an AD of 8. (The default is 1.) Notice that the exit Ethernet interface is specified. This is mandatory when using the link-local address as the next hop because the same link-local address can be used on multiple router interfaces, and therefore the router has to be told which interface to use to get to this specific link-local address. However, as long as the link-local addresses are unique between the devices within the same local network, communication occurs as intended even with duplicate link-local addresses on other interfaces. If you are using a global unicast address as the next hop, you do not have to specify the exit interface.

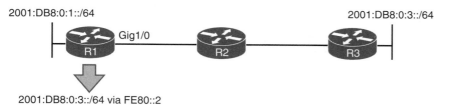

Figure 1-18 *Configuring an IPv6 Static Route on R1 with the Next-Hop Option*

Example 1-42, which shows the output of **show ipv6 route static** on R1, indicates that the 2001:DB8:0:3::/64 network was learned by a static route, it is reachable via the next-hop IP address FE80::2, it has an AD of 8, and the metric is 0 because there is no way to know how far away the destination truly is (as there is with a dynamic routing protocol).

Example 1-42   *Verifying an IPv6 Static Route on R1*

```
R1# show ipv6 route static
...output omitted...
S 2001:DB8:0:3::/64 [8/0]
via FE80::2, GigabitEthernet1/0
```

Recall that there are no broadcasts with IPv6. Therefore, IPv6 does not use ARP. It uses NDP (Neighbor Discovery Protocol), which is multicast based, to determine a neighboring device's MAC address. In this case, if R1 needs to route packets to 2001:DB8:0:3::/64, the routing table says to use the next-hop address FE80::2, which is out Gig1/0. Therefore, it consults its IPv6 neighbor table, as shown in the following snippet, to determine whether there is a MAC address for FE80::2 out Gig 1/0:

```
R1# show ipv6 neighbors

IPv6 Address        Age      Link-layer Addr    State Interface

FE80::2             0        ca08.0568.0008     REACH Gi1/0
```

It is imperative that the table have an entry that maps the link-local address and the interface. If an entry is found in the IPv6 neighbor table, it will be used. If there is no entry in the IPv6 neighbor table, a neighbor solicitation message is sent to discover the MAC address of the IPv6 address FE80::2 on Gig1/0.

As you discovered earlier with IPv4, it is not acceptable to use the interface option in a static route when the interface is an Ethernet interface because proxy ARP consumes an excessive amount of router resources. Note that proxy ARP does not exist in IPv6. Therefore, if you use the interface option with an Ethernet interface, it works only if the destination IPv6 address is directly attached to the router interface specified. This is because the destination IPv6 address in the packet is used as the next-hop address, and the MAC address needs to be discovered using NDP. If the destination is not in the directly connected network, neighbor discovery fails, and Layer 2 encapsulation ultimately fails. Consider Figure 1-18 again. On R1, if you configured the following IPv6 static route (which is called a directly attached static route), what would happen?

```
ipv6 route 2001:DB8:0:3::/64 gigabitEthernet 1/0
```

When R1 receives a packet destined for 2001:db8:0:3::3, it determines based on the static route that it is directly connected to Gig1/0 (which it is not, according to Figure 1-18). Therefore, R1 sends a Neighbor Solicitation (NS) out Gig1/0 for the MAC address associated with 2001:db8:0:3::3, using the solicited-node multicast address FF02::1:FF00:3. If no device attached to Gig1/0 is using the solicited-node multicast address FF02::1:FF00:3 and the IPv6 address 2001:db8:0:3::3, the NS goes unanswered, and Layer 2 encapsulation fails.

As you can see, being able to recognize misconfigured static routes and the issues that arise is an important skill to have when troubleshooting because a misconfigured static route causes traffic to be misrouted or suboptimally routed. In addition, remember that a static route has an AD of 1 by default; therefore, static routes are preferred over other sources of routing information to the same destination.

Trouble Tickets

This section presents various trouble tickets related to the topics discussed earlier in the chapter. The purpose of this section is to show you a process you can follow when trouble-shooting in the real world or in an exam environment.

IPv4 Addressing and Addressing Technologies Trouble Tickets

Trouble Tickets 1-1 and 1-2 are based on the topology shown in Figure 1-19.

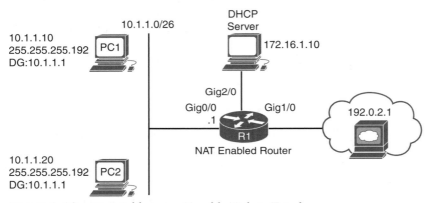

Figure 1-19   *IPv4 Addressing Trouble Tickets Topology*

Trouble Ticket 1-1

Problem: PC1 is not able to access resources on web server 192.0.2.1.

You begin troubleshooting by verifying the issue with a ping from PC1 to 192.0.2.1. As shown in Example 1-43, the ping fails.

Example 1-43   *Failed Ping from PC1 to 192.0.2.1*

```
C:\PC1>ping 192.0.2.1
Pinging 192.0.2.1 with 32 bytes of data:

Request timed out.
Request timed out.
Request timed out.
Request timed out.
Ping statistics for 192.0.2.1:
    Packets: Sent = 4, Received = 0, Lost = 4 (100% loss),
```

Next, you ping the default gateway for PC1, which is R1, at 10.1.1.1. As shown in Example 1-44, the ping is successful.

Example 1-44   *Successful Ping from PC1 to the Default Gateway*

```
C:\PC1>ping 10.1.1.1


Reply from 10.1.1.1: bytes=32 time 1ms TTL=128
Reply from 10.1.1.1: bytes=32 time 1ms TTL=128
Reply from 10.1.1.1: bytes=32 time 1ms TTL=128
Reply from 10.1.1.1: bytes=32 time 1ms TTL=128


Ping statistics for 10.1.1.1:
    Packets: Sent = 4, Received = 4, Lost = 0 (0% loss),
Approximate round trip times in milli-seconds:
    Minimum = 0ms, Maximum = 0ms, Average = 0ms
```

You decide to see whether this is an isolated incident. You access PC2 and ping 192.0.2.1, which is successful, as shown in Example 1-45.

Example 1-45   *Successful Ping from PC2 to 192.0.2.1*

```
C:\PC2>ping 192.0.2.1


Reply from 192.0.2.1: bytes=32 time 1ms TTL=128
Reply from 192.0.2.1: bytes=32 time 1ms TTL=128
Reply from 192.0.2.1: bytes=32 time 1ms TTL=128
Reply from 192.0.2.1: bytes=32 time 1ms TTL=128
Ping statistics for 192.0.2.1:
    Packets: Sent = 4, Received = 4, Lost = 0 (0% loss),
Approximate round trip times in milli-seconds:
    Minimum = 0ms, Maximum = 0ms, Average = 0ms
```

At this point, you have determined that Layer 2 and Layer 3 connectivity from PC1 and PC2 to the router are fine. You have also confirmed that PC2 can reach Internet resources even though PC1 cannot. There are many reasons this situation might exist. One of the big ones is that an access control list (ACL) on Gig0/0 or Gig1/0 is preventing PC1 from accessing resources on the Internet. Alternatively, a NAT issue could be preventing 10.1.1.10 from being translated. However, before you go down that path, review the basics. For example, what about the default gateway configured on PC1? If it is configured incorrectly, PC1 is sending packets that are destined to a remote subnet to the wrong default gateway. If you review the output of **ipconfig** on PC1, as shown in Example 1-46, you see that the default gateway is configured as 10.1.1.100, which is not the IP address of R1's interface.

Example 1-46   *ipconfig Output on PC1*

```
C:\PC1>ipconfig
Windows IP Configuration


Ethernet adapter Local Area Connection:
```

```
Connection-specific DNS Suffix . :
IP Address. . . . . . . . . . . .: 10.1.1.10
Subnet Mask . . . . . . . . . . .: 255.255.255.192
Default Gateway . . . . . . . . .: 10.1.1.100
```

After you change the default gateway on R1 to 10.1.1.1, the ping to 192.0.2.1 is successful, as shown in Example 1-47.

Example 1-47   *Successful Ping from PC1 to 192.0.2.1*

```
C:\PC1>ping 192.0.2.1

Reply from 192.0.2.1: bytes=32 time 1ms TTL=128
Reply from 192.0.2.1: bytes=32 time 1ms TTL=128
Reply from 192.0.2.1: bytes=32 time 1ms TTL=128
Reply from 192.0.2.1: bytes=32 time 1ms TTL=128


Ping statistics for 192.0.2.1:
    Packets: Sent = 4, Received = 4, Lost = 0 (0% loss),
Approximate round trip times in milli-seconds:
    Minimum = 0ms, Maximum = 0ms, Average = 0ms
```

Trouble Ticket 1-2

Problem: PC1 is not able to access resources on web server 192.0.2.1.

You begin troubleshooting by verifying the issue with a ping from PC1 to 192.0.2.1. As shown in Example 1-48, the ping fails.

Example 1-48   *Failed Ping from PC1 to 192.0.2.1*

```
C:\PC1>ping 192.0.2.1
Pinging 192.0.2.1 with 32 bytes of data:

Request timed out.
Request timed out.
Request timed out.
Request timed out.


Ping statistics for 192.0.2.1:
    Packets: Sent = 4, Received = 0, Lost = 4 (100% loss),
```

Next, you ping the default gateway for PC1, which is R1, at 10.1.1.1. As shown in Example 1-49, it fails as well.

Example 1-49 *Failed Ping from PC1 to the Default Gateway*

```
C:\PC1>ping 10.1.1.1
Pinging 10.1.1.1 with 32 bytes of data:

Request timed out.
Request timed out.
Request timed out.
Request timed out.

Ping statistics for 10.1.1.1:
    Packets: Sent = 4, Received = 0, Lost = 4 (100% loss),
```

Next, you decide to see whether this is an isolated incident by pinging from PC2 to the IP address 192.0.2.1 and to the default gateway at 10.1.1.1. As shown in Example 1-50, both of these pings fail as well, indicating that the problem is not isolated.

Example 1-50 *Failed Ping from PC2 to 192.0.2.1 and the Default Gateway*

```
C:\PC2>ping 192.0.2.1
Pinging 192.0.2.1 with 32 bytes of data:

Request timed out.
Request timed out.
Request timed out.
Request timed out.

Ping statistics for 192.0.2.1:
    Packets: Sent = 4, Received = 0, Lost = 4 (100% loss),
C:\PC2>ping 10.1.1.1
Pinging 10.1.1.1 with 32 bytes of data:

Request timed out.
Request timed out.
Request timed out.
Request timed out.

Ping statistics for 10.1.1.1:
    Packets: Sent = 4, Received = 0, Lost = 4 (100% loss),
```

At this point, you have confirmed that there is no Layer 2 or Layer 3 connectivity from PC1 or PC2 to their default gateway. This can be caused by many different factors. For example, VLANs, VLAN access control lists (VACLs), trunks, VLAN Trunking Protocol (VTP), and Spanning Tree Protocol (STP) could all possibly cause this issue to occur. However, always remember to check the basics first; in this case, start with IP addressing on the client. On PC1, you issue the **ipconfig** command, and as shown in Example 1-51, PC1 has an APIPA

(Automatic Private IP Addressing) address of 169.254.180.166/16 and no default gateway. This means that PC1 cannot contact a DHCP server and is autoconfiguring an IP address. This still does not rule out VLAN, trunks, VTP, STP, and so on as causes. However, it helps you narrow the focus.

Example 1-51 *ipconfig Output on PC1*

```
C:\PC1>ipconfig
Windows IP Configuration


Ethernet adapter Local Area Connection:

 Connection-specific DNS Suffix . :
 IP Address. . . . . . . . . . . .: 169.254.180.166
 Subnet Mask . . . . . . . . . . .: 255.255.0.0
 Default Gateway . . . . . . . . .:
```

Notice in the trouble ticket topology in Figure 1-19 that the DHCP server is located out interface Gig2/0 on R1. It is in a different subnet than the PCs. Therefore, R1 is required to forward the DHCPDISCOVER messages from the PCs to the DHCP server at 172.16.1.10. To do this, it needs the **ip helper-address** command configured on Gig0/0. You can start there to eliminate this as the issue and then focus elsewhere if needed. On R1, you issue the command **show run interface gigabitEthernet 0/0**, as shown in Example 1-52. The output indicates that the IP helper address is 172.16.1.100, which is not correct according to the network diagram.

Example 1-52 *Verifying the IP Helper Address on Gig0/0 of R1*

```
R1# show run interface gigabitEthernet 0/0
Building configuration...

Current configuration : 193 bytes
!
interface GigabitEthernet0/0
 ip address 10.1.1.1 255.255.255.192
 ip helper-address 172.16.1.100
 ip nat inside
end
```

After you fix the IP helper address with the **no ip helper-address 172.16.1.100** command and issue the **ip helper-address 172.16.1.10** command in interface configuration mode, PC1 successfully receives IP addressing information from the DHCP server, as shown in Example 1-53.

Example 1-53 *Correct IP Addressing After Fixing the **ip helper-address** Command*

```
C:\PC1>ipconfig
Windows IP Configuration

Ethernet adapter Local Area Connection:

  Connection-specific DNS Suffix . :
  IP Address. . . . . . . . . . . . : 10.1.1.10
  Subnet Mask . . . . . . . . . . . : 255.255.255.192
  Default Gateway . . . . . . . . . : 10.1.1.1
```

After you verify the addressing information on PC1, the ping to 192.0.2.1 is successful, as shown in Example 1-54.

Example 1-54 *Successful Ping from PC1 to 192.0.2.1*

```
C:\PC1>ping 192.0.2.1

Reply from 192.0.2.1: bytes=32 time 1ms TTL=128
Reply from 192.0.2.1: bytes=32 time 1ms TTL=128
Reply from 192.0.2.1: bytes=32 time 1ms TTL=128
Reply from 192.0.2.1: bytes=32 time 1ms TTL=128

Ping statistics for 192.0.2.1:
  Packets: Sent = 4, Received = 4, Lost = 0 (0% loss),
Approximate round trip times in milli-seconds:
  Minimum = 0ms, Maximum = 0ms, Average = 0ms
```

IPv6 Addressing Trouble Tickets

Trouble Tickets 1-3 and 1-4 are based on the topology shown in Figure 1-20.

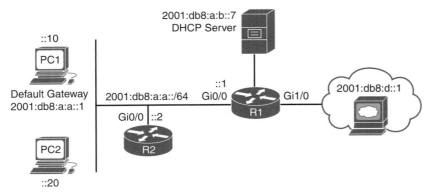

Figure 1-20 *IPv6 Addressing Trouble Tickets Topology*

Trouble Ticket 1-3

Problem: PC1 is not able to access resources on the web server 2001:db8:d::1.

Your network uses stateless address autoconfiguration for IPv6 addressing and DHCPv6 for additional options such as a domain name, TFTP server addresses, and DNS server addresses.

You begin troubleshooting by verifying the issue with a ping from PC1 to 2001:db8:d::1. As shown in Example 1-55, the ping fails.

Example 1-55   *Failed Ping from PC1 to Web Server at 2001:db8:d::1*

```
C:\PC1>ping 2001:db8:d::1

Pinging 2001:db8:d::1 with 32 bytes of data:
PING: transmit failed. General failure.
PING: transmit failed. General failure.
PING: transmit failed. General failure.
PING: transmit failed. General failure.


Ping statistics for 2001:db8:d::1:
    Packets: Sent = 4, Received = 0, Lost = 4 (100% loss),
```

You ping the default gateway at 2001:db8:a:a::1, but the ping fails, as shown in Example 1-56.

Example 1-56   *Failed Ping from PC1 to the Default Gateway at 2001:db8:a:a::1*

```
C:\PC1>ping 2001:db8:a:a::1

Pinging 2001:db8:a:a::1 with 32 bytes of data:
PING: transmit failed. General failure.
PING: transmit failed. General failure.
PING: transmit failed. General failure.
PING: transmit failed. General failure.


Ping statistics for 2001:db8:a:a::1:
    Packets: Sent = 4, Received = 0, Lost = 4 (100% loss),
```

Next, you verify the IPv6 addresses on PC1 by using the **ipconfig** command. Example 1-57 indicates that PC1 is not generating its own global unicast address using stateless address autoconfiguration or identifying a default gateway on the network.

Example 1-57   *Verifying IPv6 Addressing on PC1*

```
C:\PC1>ipconfig

Windows IP Configuration

Ethernet adapter Local Area Connection:
```

```
Connection-specific DNS Suffix .  : cisco.com
Link-local IPv6 Address . . . . . : fe80::a00:27ff:fe5d:6d6%11
IPv4 Address. . . . . . . . . . . : 10.1.1.10
Subnet Mask . . . . . . . . . . . : 255.255.255.192
Default Gateway . . . . . . . . . : 10.1.1.1
```

Your phone rings, and the user at PC2 is indicating that they cannot access any of the IPv6-enabled resources. You access PC2 and issue the **ipconfig** command, as shown in Example 1-58, and notice that it is also not generating an IPv6 address or identifying a default gateway.

Example 1-58 *Verifying IPv6 Addressing on PC2*

```
C:\PC2>ipconfig

Windows IP Configuration

Ethernet adapter Local Area Connection:

 Connection-specific DNS Suffix .  : cisco.com
 Link-local IPv6 Address . . . . . : fe80::a00:27ff:fe5d:ce47%9
 IPv4 Address. . . . . . . . . . . : 10.1.1.20
 Subnet Mask . . . . . . . . . . . : 255.255.255.192
 Default Gateway . . . . . . . . . : 10.1.1.1
```

Recall that SLAAC relies on RAs. Therefore, R1's Gig0/0 interface needs to be sending RAs on the link for PC1 and PC2 to generate their own IPv6 addresses using SLAAC. You issue the command **show ipv6 interface gigabitEthernet 0/0** on R1, as shown in Example 1-59. The output indicates that hosts use SLAAC for addresses, and DHCP is used for other configuration values. However, it also indicates that RAs are suppressed. Therefore, PC1 and PC2 do not receive RAs that provide the prefix information necessary to perform autoconfiguration.

Example 1-59 *Verifying Whether RAs Are Suppressed on R1*

```
R1# show ipv6 interface gigabitEthernet 0/0
GigabitEthernet0/0 is up, line protocol is up
  IPv6 is enabled, link-local address is FE80::C80A:EFF:FE3C:8
  No Virtual link-local address(es):
  Global unicast address(es):
  2001:DB8:A:A::1, subnet is 2001:DB8:A:A::/64
  Joined group address(es):
  FF02::1
  FF02::2
  FF02::1:2
  FF02::1:FF00:1
```

```
FF02::1:FF3C:8
MTU is 1500 bytes
ICMP error messages limited to one every 100 milliseconds
ICMP redirects are enabled
ICMP unreachables are sent
ND DAD is enabled, number of DAD attempts: 1
ND reachable time is 30000 milliseconds (using 30000)
ND RAs are suppressed (all)
Hosts use stateless autoconfig for addresses.
Hosts use DHCP to obtain other configuration.
```

You issue the command **show run interface gigabitEthernet 0/0** to verify the configuration commands on the interface. As shown in Example 1-60, the interface is configured with the command **ipv6 nd ra suppress all**, which stops R1 from sending RAs.

Example 1-60   *Verifying Interface Configuration on R1*

```
R1# show run interface gigabitEthernet 0/0
Building configuration...

Current configuration : 241 bytes
!
interface GigabitEthernet0/0
 no ip address
 ipv6 address 2001:DB8:A:A::1/64
 ipv6 nd other-config-flag
 ipv6 nd ra suppress all
 ipv6 dhcp relay destination 2001:DB8:A:B::7
end
```

After you remove this command with the **no ipv6 nd ra suppress all** command, PC1 successfully generates a global IPv6 address and identifies an IPv6 default gateway, as shown in Example 1-61.

Example 1-61   *Verifying IPv6 Addressing on PC1*

```
C:\PC1>ipconfig

Windows IP Configuration

Ethernet adapter Local Area Connection:

  Connection-specific DNS Suffix .  : cisco.com
  IPv6 Address. . . . . . . . . . . : 2001:db8:a:a:a00:27ff:fe5d:6d6
  Link-local IPv6 Address . . . . . : fe80::a00:27ff:fe5d:6d6%11
  IPv4 Address. . . . . . . . . . . : 10.1.1.10
  Subnet Mask . . . . . . . . . . . : 255.255.255.192
  Default Gateway . . . . . . . . . : fe80::c80a:eff:fe3c:8%11
                                      10.1.1.1
```

You confirm that IPv6 resources are accessible by pinging 2001:db8:d::1, as shown in Example 1-62, and it is successful. You then call the user at PC2 and confirm that he can access the resources as well. He indicates that he can.

Example 1-62   *Successful Ping from PC1 to the Web Server at 2001:db8:d::1*

```
C:\PC1>ping 2001:db8:d::1
Pinging 2001:db8:d::1 with 32 bytes of data:
Reply from 2001:db8:d::1: time=37ms
Reply from 2001:db8:d::1: time=35ms
Reply from 2001:db8:d::1: time=38ms
Reply from 2001:db8:d::1: time=38ms

Ping statistics for 2001:db8:d::1:
    Packets: Sent = 4, Received = 4, Lost = 0 (0% loss),
Approximate round trip times in milli-seconds:
   Minimum = 35ms, Maximum = 38ms, Average = 36ms
```

Trouble Ticket 1-4

Problem: PC1 is not able to access resources on the web server 2001:db8:d::1.

Your network uses stateless address autoconfiguration for IPv6 addressing and DHCPv6 for additional options such as a domain name, TFTP server addresses, and DNS server addresses.

You begin troubleshooting by verifying the issue with a ping from PC1 to 2001:db8:d::1. As shown in Example 1-63, the ping fails.

Example 1-63   *Failed Ping from PC1 to the Web Server at 2001:db8:d::1*

```
C:\PC1>ping 2001:db8:d::1

Pinging 2001:db8:d::1 with 32 bytes of data:
PING: transmit failed. General failure.
PING: transmit failed. General failure.
PING: transmit failed. General failure.
PING: transmit failed. General failure.

Ping statistics for 2001:db8:d::1:
    Packets: Sent = 4, Received = 0, Lost = 4 (100% loss),
```

You ping the default gateway at 2001:db8:a:a::1, but the ping fails, as shown in Example 1-64.

Example 1-64   *Failed Ping from PC1 to the Default Gateway at 2001:db8:a:a::1*

```
C:\PC1>ping 2001:db8:a:a::1

Pinging 2001:db8:a:a::1 with 32 bytes of data:
PING: transmit failed. General failure.
```

```
PING: transmit failed. General failure.
PING: transmit failed. General failure.
PING: transmit failed. General failure.


Ping statistics for 2001:db8:a:a::1:
    Packets: Sent = 4, Received = 0, Lost = 4 (100% loss),
```

Next, you verify the IPv6 addresses on PC1 by using the **ipconfig** command. Example 1-65 indicates that PC1 is not generating its own global unicast address using stateless address autoconfiguration; however, it is identifying a default gateway on the network at the link-local address fe80::c80a:eff:fe3c:8.

Example 1-65   *Verifying IPv6 Addressing on PC1*

```
C:\PC1>ipconfig


Windows IP Configuration


Ethernet adapter Local Area Connection:

  Connection-specific DNS Suffix .  : cisco.com
  Link-local IPv6 Address . . . . . : fe80::a00:27ff:fe5d:6d6%11
  IPv4 Address. . . . . . . . . . . : 10.1.1.10
  Subnet Mask . . . . . . . . . . . : 255.255.255.192
  Default Gateway . . . . . . . . . : fe80::c80a:eff:fe3c:8%11
                                      10.1.1.1
```

Your phone rings, and the user at PC2 is indicating that they cannot access any of the IPv6-enabled resources. You access PC2 and issue the **ipconfig** command, as shown in Example 1-66, and notice that it's experiencing the same issues as PC1.

Example 1-66   *Verifying IPv6 Addressing on PC2*

```
C:\PC2>ipconfig


Windows IP Configuration


Ethernet adapter Local Area Connection:

  Connection-specific DNS Suffix .  : cisco.com
  Link-local IPv6 Address . . . . . : fe80::a00:27ff:fe5d:ce47%9
  IPv4 Address. . . . . . . . . . . : 10.1.1.10
  Subnet Mask . . . . . . . . . . . : 255.255.255.192
  Default Gateway . . . . . . . . . : fe80::c80a:eff:fe3c:8%11
                                      10.1.1.1
```

Recall that SLAAC relies on RAs. Therefore, R1's Gig0/0 interface must send RAs on the link for PC1 and PC2 to generate their own IPv6 address using SLAAC. You issue the command **show ipv6 interface gigabitEthernet 0/0** on R1, as shown in Example 1-67. The output indicates that hosts use SLAAC for addresses, and DHCP is used for other configuration values. Also, there is no indication that RAs are being suppressed. This is also confirmed by the fact that PC1 and PC2 are identifying a default gateway. However, is it the right one? According to Examples 1-65 and 1-66, the default gateway is fe80::c80a:eff:fe3c:8. Based on Example 1-67, this is correct. If you review Example 1-67 further, can you see the issue?

Example 1-67 *Verifying Whether RAs Are Suppressed on R1*

```
R1# show ipv6 interface gigabitEthernet 0/0
GigabitEthernet0/0 is up, line protocol is up
 IPv6 is enabled, link-local address is FE80::C80A:EFF:FE3C:8
 No Virtual link-local address(es):
 Global unicast address(es):
 2001:DB8:A:A::1, subnet is 2001:DB8:A::/60
 Joined group address(es):
 FF02::1
 FF02::2
 FF02::1:2
 FF02::1:FF00:1
 FF02::1:FF3C:8
 MTU is 1500 bytes
 ICMP error messages limited to one every 100 milliseconds
 ICMP redirects are enabled
 ICMP unreachables are sent
 ND DAD is enabled, number of DAD attempts: 1
 ND reachable time is 30000 milliseconds (using 30000)
 ND advertised reachable time is 0 (unspecified)
 ND advertised retransmit interval is 0 (unspecified)
 ND router advertisements are sent every 200 seconds
 ND router advertisements live for 1800 seconds
 ND advertised default router preference is Medium
 Hosts use stateless autoconfig for addresses.
 Hosts use DHCP to obtain other configuration.
```

If you did not spot it, look at the global prefix assigned to interface Gig0/0. It is 2001:db8:a::/60. SLAAC works only if the prefix is /64.

You issue the command **show run interface gigabitEthernet 0/0** to verify the configuration commands on the interface. As shown in Example 1-68, the interface is configured with the command **ipv6 address 2001:db8:a:a::1/60**. RAs are still generated, but SLAAC does not work unless the prefix is /64.

Example 1-68   *Verifying Interface Configuration on R1*

```
R1# show run interface gigabitEthernet 0/0
Building configuration...

Current configuration : 216 bytes
!
interface GigabitEthernet0/0
 ipv6 address 2001:DB8:A:A::1/60
 ipv6 nd other-config-flag
 ipv6 dhcp relay destination 2001:DB8:A:B::7
end
```

You confirm with your network design plans that the prefix should be /64. After you remove this command with the **no ipv6 address 2001:db8:a:a::1/60** command and issue the command **ipv6 address 2001:db8:a:a::1/64**, PC1 successfully generates a global IPv6 unicast address, as shown in Example 1-69.

Example 1-69   *Verifying IPv6 Addressing on PC1*

```
C:\PC1>ipconfig

Windows IP Configuration

Ethernet adapter Local Area Connection:

 Connection-specific DNS Suffix .  : cisco.com
 IPv6 Address. . . . . . . . . . . : 2001:db8:a:a:a00:27ff:fe5d:6d6
 Link-local IPv6 Address . . . . . : fe80::a00:27ff:fe5d:6d6%11
 IPv4 Address. . . . . . . . . . . : 10.1.1.10
 Subnet Mask . . . . . . . . . . . : 255.255.255.192
 Default Gateway . . . . . . . . . : fe80::c80a:eff:fe3c:8%11
                                     10.1.1.1
```

You confirm that IPv6 resources are accessible by pinging 2001:db8:d::1, as shown in Example 1-70, and the ping is successful. In addition, you contact the user at PC2, and they indicate that everything is fine now.

Example 1-70   *Successful Ping from PC1 to the Web Server at 2001:db8:d::1*

```
C:\PC1>ping 2001:db8:d::1
Pinging 2001:db8:d::1 with 32 bytes of data:
Reply from 2001:db8:d::1: time=37ms
Reply from 2001:db8:d::1: time=35ms
Reply from 2001:db8:d::1: time=38ms
Reply from 2001:db8:d::1: time=38ms
```

```
Ping statistics for 2001:db8:d::1:
 Packets: Sent = 4, Received = 4, Lost = 0 (0% loss),
Approximate round trip times in milli-seconds:
 Minimum = 35ms, Maximum = 38ms, Average = 36ms
```

Static Routing Trouble Tickets

Trouble Tickets 1-5 and 1-6 are based on the topology shown in Figure 1-21.

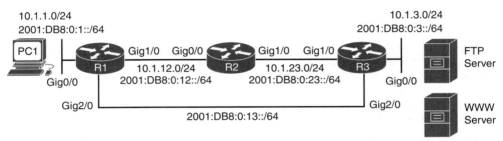

Figure 1-21   *Static Routing Trouble Tickets Topology*

Trouble Ticket 1-5

Problem: Users in the 10.1.1.0/24 network have indicated that they are not able to access resources on the FTP server in the 10.1.3.0/24 network. The FTP server uses the static IPv4 address 10.1.3.10. Users have indicated that they are able to access the web server at 10.1.3.5. (Note that this network uses only static routes.)

You start your troubleshooting efforts by verifying the problem with a ping to 10.1.3.10 from PC1 in the 10.1.1.0/24 network. As shown in Example 1-71, the ping is not successful. R1 is responding with a destination unreachable message. This indicates that R1 does not know how to route the packet destined for 10.1.3.10. In addition, you ping 10.1.3.5 from PC1, and it is successful, as shown in Example 1-71.

Example 1-71   *Failed Ping from PC1 to 10.1.3.10 and Successful Ping to 10.1.3.5*

```
C:\PC1>ping 10.1.3.10

Pinging 10.1.3.10 with 32 bytes of data;

Reply from 10.1.1.1: Destination host unreachable.
Reply from 10.1.1.1: Destination host unreachable.
Reply from 10.1.1.1: Destination host unreachable.
Reply from 10.1.1.1: Destination host unreachable.

Ping statistics for 10.1.3.10:
```

```
Packets: Sent = 4, Received = 4, lost = 0 (0% loss),
Approximate round trip times in milli-seconds:
Minimum = 0ms, Maximum = 0ms, Average = 0ms


C:\PC1>ping 10.1.3.5


Pinging 10.1.3.5 with 32 bytes of data:


Reply from 10.1.3.5: bytes=32 time 1ms TTL=128
Reply from 10.1.3.5: bytes=32 time 1ms TTL=128
Reply from 10.1.3.5: bytes=32 time 1ms TTL=128
Reply from 10.1.3.5: bytes=32 time 1ms TTL=128


Ping statistics for 10.1.3.5:
Packets: Sent = 4, Received = 4, Lost = 0 (0% loss),
Approximate round trip times in milli-seconds:
Minimum = 0ms, Maximum = 0ms, Average = 0ms
```

Next, you access R1 and issue the **show ip route** command on R1 to verify whether it knows how to route the packet to 10.1.3.10. In Example 1-72, the closest entry that matches 10.1.3.10 is the entry for 10.1.3.0/29. However, does 10.1.3.10 fall within that subnet?

Example 1-72 *Verifying Routing Table Entries*

```
R1# show ip route
...output omitted...


Gateway of last resort is not set


10.0.0.0/8 is variably subnetted, 6 subnets, 3 masks
C 10.1.1.0/24 is directly connected, GigabitEthernet0/0
L 10.1.1.1/32 is directly connected, GigabitEthernet0/0
S 10.1.3.0/29 [1/0] via 10.1.12.2
C 10.1.12.0/24 is directly connected, GigabitEthernet1/0
L 10.1.12.1/32 is directly connected, GigabitEthernet1/0
S 10.1.23.0/24 [1/0] via 10.1.12.2
```

The network 10.1.3.0/29 has a range of addresses from 10.1.3.0 to 10.1.3.7, and 10.1.3.10 does not fall within that subnet; however, 10.1.3.5 does fall within that range. This explains why the users can reach one address and not the other in the 10.1.3.0/24 network. If you execute the **show ip route 10.1.3.10** and **show ip route 10.1.3.5** commands on R1, the output verifies this further. As shown in Example 1-73, there is no match for 10.1.3.10, but there is a match for 10.1.3.5.

Example 1-73 *Verifying Specific Routes*

```
R1# show ip route 10.1.3.10
% Subnet not in table
R1# show ip route 10.1.3.5
Routing entry for 10.1.3.0/29
Known via "static", distance 1, metric 0
Routing Descriptor Blocks:
10.1.12.2
Route metric is 0, traffic share count is 1
```

Because the network in Figure 1-21 is 10.1.3.0/24, and the entry in the routing table is 10.1.3.0/29, it is possible that the static route was misconfigured. You need to verify this by examining the running configuration using the **show run | include ip route** command, as shown in the following snippet:

```
R1# show run | include ip route
ip route 10.1.3.0 255.255.255.248 10.1.12.2
ip route 10.1.23.0 255.255.255.0 10.1.12.2
```

Notice the command **ip route 10.1.3.0 255.255.255.248 10.1.12.2**. This is the command that is producing the 10.1.3.0/29 entry in the routing table. If you look closely, you will notice that the subnet mask was not configured correctly.

To solve this issue, you need to remove the static route with the command **no ip route 10.1.3.0 255.255.255.248 10.1.12.2** and create a new static route with the command **ip route 10.1.3.0 255.255.255.0 10.1.12.2**. After you do this, you issue the **show ip route** command on R1 and confirm that the entry in the routing table is 10.1.3.0/24, as shown in Example 1-74.

Example 1-74 *Verifying an Updated Static Route in the Routing Table on R1*

```
R1# show ip route
...output omitted...

Gateway of last resort is not set

10.0.0.0/8 is variably subnetted, 6 subnets, 2 masks
C 10.1.1.0/24 is directly connected, GigabitEthernet0/0
L 10.1.1.1/32 is directly connected, GigabitEthernet0/0
S 10.1.3.0/24 [1/0] via 10.1.12.2
C 10.1.12.0/24 is directly connected, GigabitEthernet1/0
L 10.1.12.1/32 is directly connected, GigabitEthernet1/0
S 10.1.23.0/24 [1/0] via 10.1.12.2
```

Next, you issue the **show ip route 10.1.3.10** command, as shown in Example 1-75, and you can see that the IP address 10.1.3.10 now matches an entry in the routing table.

Example 1-75   *Verifying That an Entry Exists for 10.1.3.10*

```
R1# show ip route 10.1.3.10
Routing entry for 10.1.3.0/24
Known via "static", distance 1, metric 0
Routing Descriptor Blocks:
10.1.12.2
Route metric is 0, traffic share count is 1
```

Finally, you ping from PC1 to the IP address 10.1.3.10, and the ping is successful, as shown in Example 1-76.

Example 1-76   *Successful Ping from PC1 to 10.1.3.10*

```
C:\PC1>ping 10.1.3.10
Pinging 10.1.3.10 with 32 bytes of data:

Reply from 10.1.3.10: bytes=32 time 1ms TTL=128
Reply from 10.1.3.10: bytes=32 time 1ms TTL=128
Reply from 10.1.3.10: bytes=32 time 1ms TTL=128
Reply from 10.1.3.10: bytes=32 time 1ms TTL=128

Ping statistics for 10.1.3.10:
Packets: Sent = 4, Received = 4, Lost = 0 (0% loss),
Approximate round trip times in milli-seconds:
Minimum = 0ms, Maximum = 0ms, Average = 0ms
```

Trouble Ticket 1-6

Problem: Your proactive traffic monitoring indicates that all traffic from 2001:DB8:0:1::/64 destined to 2001:DB8:0:3::/64 is going through R2, when it should be going directly to R3 over the Gig2/0 link. R2 should be used to forward traffic from 2001:DB8:0:1::/64 to 2001:DB8:0:3::/64 only if the Gig2/0 link fails, which it has not. You need to determine why traffic is being forwarded the wrong way and fix it. (Note that this network uses only static routes.)

You confirm the problem with a trace, as shown in Example 1-77, from PC1 to 2001:DB8:0:3::3, which is the IPv6 address of the Gig0/0 interface on R3. The trace confirms that the packets are being sent though R2.

Example 1-77   *Trace from PC1 to R3's Gig0/0 Interface*

```
C:\PC1>tracert 2001:DB8:0:3::3
Tracing route to 2001:DB8:0:3::3 over a maximum of 30 hops


1 6 ms 1 ms 2 ms 2001:DB8:0:1::1
2 5 ms 1 ms 2 ms 2001:DB8:0:12::2
3 5 ms 1 ms 2 ms 2001:DB8:0:23::3


Trace complete.
```

Next, you issue the **show ipv6 route 2001:DB8:0:3::/64** command on R1, as shown
in Example 1-78, and confirm that the next-hop IPv6 address for 2001:DB8:0:3::/64 is
2001:DB8:0:12::2, which is the IPv6 address of R2's Gig0/0 interface. The next-hop IPv6
address should be 2001:DB8:0:13::3, which is R3's Gig2/0 interface.

Example 1-78   *Verifying the IPv6 Route to 2001:DB8:0:3::/64 on R1*

```
R1# show ipv6 route 2001:DB8:0:3::/64
Routing entry for 2001:DB8:0:3::/64
Known via "static", distance 10, metric 0
Backup from "static [11]"
Route count is 1/1, share count 0
Routing paths:
2001:DB8:0:12::2
Last updated 00:09:07 ago
```

It appears that someone provided the incorrect next-hop IPv6 address in the static route.
You verify the static route configured on R1 for the 2001:DB8:0:3::/64 network by using the
show run | include ipv6 route command, as shown in Example 1-79. You notice that there
are two commands for network 2001:DB8:0:3::/64. One has a next hop of 2001:DB8:0:12::2,
and the other has a next hop of 2001:DB8:0:13::3.

Example 1-79   *Verifying the IPv6 Static Routes Configured on R1*

```
R1# show run | include ipv6 route
ipv6 route 2001:DB8:0:3::/64 2001:DB8:0:12::2 10
ipv6 route 2001:DB8:0:3::/64 2001:DB8:0:13::3 11
ipv6 route 2001:DB8:0:23::/64 2001:DB8:0:12::2
```

Why is the **ipv6 route** command with the next hop of 2001:DB8:0:12::2 being preferred over
the command with a next hop of 2001:DB8:0:13::3? If you look closely at both commands
in Example 1-80, you can see that the one with a next hop of 2001:DB8:0:12::2 is configured
with an AD of 10 and that the other, which has a next hop of 2001:DB8:0:13::3, is configured with an AD of 11. Because the lower AD is preferred, the static route with the AD of
10 is more trustworthy and is therefore the one used.

To solve this issue, you need to configure the static route with a next hop of 2001:DB8:0:13::3 with a lower AD. In this case, you change the AD to 1, which is the default for static routes, by using the **ipv6 route 2001:DB8:0:3::/64 2001:DB8:0:13::3 1** command. After the change, you revisit the routing table with the **show ipv6 route 2001:DB8:0:3::/64** command to verify that the static route with the next hop of 2001:DB8:0:13::3 is now in the routing table. Example 1-80 confirms that the change was successful.

Example 1-80   *Verifying the IPv6 Routing Table on R1*

```
R1# show ipv6 route 2001:DB8:0:3::/64
Routing entry for 2001:DB8:0:3::/64
Known via "static", distance 1, metric 0
Backup from "static [11]"
Route count is 1/1, share count 0
Routing paths:
2001:DB8:0:13::3
Last updated 00:01:14 ago
```

Next, you perform a trace from PC1 to 2001:DB8:0:3::3, as shown in Example 1-81, and it confirms that R2 is no longer being used. The traffic is now flowing across the link between R1 and R3.

Example 1-81   *Trace from PC1 to R3's Gig0/0 Interface*

```
C:\PC1>tracert 2001:DB8:0:3::3
Tracing route to 2001:DB8:0:3::3 over a maximum of 30 hops

1  6 ms  1 ms  2 ms  2001:DB8:0:1::1
2  5 ms  1 ms  2 ms  2001:DB8:0:13::3

Trace complete.
```

Exam Preparation Tasks

As mentioned in the section "How to Use This Book" in the Introduction, you have a couple choices for exam preparation: the exercises here, Chapter 24, "Final Preparation," and the exam simulation questions in the Pearson Test Prep software.

Review All Key Topics

Review the most important topics in this chapter, noted with the Key Topic icon in the outer margin of the page. Table 1-5 lists these key topics and the page number on which each is found.

Table 1-5 Key Topics for Chapter 1

Key Topic Element	Description	Page Number
Paragraph	The process used by a device to determine whether a packet will be sent to a local device or a remote device	8
Paragraph	What occurs when IPv4 addressing is not correct	9
Example 1-1	Verifying IP addressing on a PC and on a router	10
Section	Determining IP addresses within a subnet	10
List	The DHCPv4 DORA process	12
Example 1-3	DHCP relay agent configuration	13
Snippet	DHCP client configuration	15
Paragraph	How a router can be configured as a DHCP server	15
List	Items to look out for while troubleshooting DHCP-related issues	16
Section	DHCP troubleshooting commands	17
Paragraphs	The process a device uses to determine whether a packet will be sent to a local device or a remote device when using IPv6	19
Paragraph	The EUI-64 process	20
Example 1-12	Verifying EUI-64 on a router interface	22
Example 1-14	Enabling SLAAC on a router interface	23
Paragraph	The router advertisement process	24
Paragraph	Verifying SLAAC-generated IPv6 addresses	24
List	Issues that may occur while using SLAAC	25
Example 1-17	Verifying that an interface is enabled for IPv6	25
Example 1-18	Verifying that RAs are not suppressed	26
Example 1-19	Verifying default gateways configured on a PC	26
Example 1-21	Sample DHCPv6 configuration on R1	27
Example 1-22	Verifying DHCPv6 information on R1	28
Example 1-23	Verifying stateless DHCPv6	29
Step list	The four-way DHCPv6 negotiation process	29
Example 1-24	Configuring R1 as a DHCPv6 relay agent	31
List	The routing table and Layer 3-to-Layer 2 mapping table	34
List	The FIB and adjacency table	35
Example 1-25	**show ip route** *ip_address* command output	36
Example 1-28	**show ip cef** *ip_address* command output	37
Example 1-31	**show ip arp** command output	37
Table 1-4	Administrative distance of route sources	40
Example 1-34	Verifying the administrative distance of a route in the routing table	41

Key Topic Element	Description	Page Number
Paragraph	The importance of the next-hop address in an IPv4 static route	43
Paragraph	Using an Ethernet interface in an IPv4 static route	44
Paragraph	Using an Ethernet interface in an IPv6 static route	47

Define Key Terms

Define the following key terms from this chapter and check your answers in the glossary:

DHCP, DORA, DHCPDISCOVER, DHCPOFFER, DHCPREQUEST, DHCPACK, DHCP relay agent, APIPA, EUI-64, stateless address autoconfiguration (SLAAC), stateful DHCPv6, stateless DHCPv6, Router Solicitation, Router Advertisement, link-local address, global unicast address, SOLICIT message, ADVERTISE message, REQUEST message, REPLY message, DHCPv6 relay agent, packet forwarding, ARP, TTL, routing table, ARP cache, CEF, FIB, adjacency table, control plane, data plane, administrative distance, static route, proxy ARP

Use the Command Reference to Check Your Memory

The ENARSI 300-410 exam focuses on the practical, hands-on skills that networking professionals use. Therefore, you should be able to identify the commands needed to configure, verify, and troubleshoot the topics covered in this chapter.

This section includes the most important configuration and verification commands covered in this chapter. It might not be necessary to memorize the complete syntax of every command, but you should be able to remember the basic keywords that are needed.

To test your memory of the commands in Table 1-6, go to the companion website and download Appendix B, "Command Reference Exercises." Fill in the missing commands in the tables based on each command description. You can check your work by downloading Appendix C, "Command Reference Exercise Answer Key," from the companion website.

Table 1-6   Configuration and Verification Commands

Task	Command Syntax
Display the IP address, subnet mask, and default gateway of a Windows PC.	ipconfig
Display the IP address, subnet mask, and default gateway of a Windows PC, in addition to DNS servers, domain name, MAC address, and whether autoconfiguration is enabled.	ipconfig /all
Display various IP-related parameters for a router interface, including the IP address and subnet mask that have been assigned.	show ip interface *interface_type interface_number*

Task	Command Syntax
Identify any IP address conflicts a router configured as a DHCP server identifies, along with the method the router used to identify the conflicts (this is, via ping or gratuitous ARP).	**show ip dhcp conflict**
Display IP addresses that an IOS DHCP server assigns, their corresponding MAC addresses, and lease expirations.	**show ip dhcp binding**
Determine whether IPv6 is enabled on an interface, display the multicast groups the router interface is a member of, display the global and link-local unicast addresses associated with an interface, indicate whether EUI-64 or stateless autoconfiguration was used to obtain the IPv6 address for the interface, display whether RAs are suppressed for the interface, and display how devices connected to the same link as the interface will obtain IPv6 addresses and how they will obtain other options.	**show ipv6 interface** *interface_type interface_number*
Display the IPv6 addresses that are being used by each of the DHCPv6 clients.	**show ipv6 dhcp binding**
Display which DHCPv6 pool is assigned to each interface on the router.	**show ipv6 dhcp interface**
Display the configured DHCPv6 pools on the router.	**show ipv6 dhcp pool**
Display a router's best route to the specified IP address.	**show ip route** *ip_address*
Display only the static routes in a router's routing table.	**show ip route static**
Display a router's best route to the specified network if the specific route (with a matching subnet mask length) is found in the router's IP routing table.	**show ip route** *ip_address subnet_mask*
Display all routes in a router's IP routing table that are encompassed by the specified network address and subnet mask. (This command is often useful when troubleshooting route summarization issues.)	**show ip route** *ip_address subnet_ mask* **longer- prefixes**
Display information (for example, next-hop IP address and egress interface) required to forward a packet, similar to the output of the **show ip route** *ip_address* command. (The output of this command comes from CEF. Therefore, routing protocol information is not presented in the output.)	**show ip cef** *ip_address*
Display information from a router's FIB showing the information needed to route a packet to the specified network with the specified subnet mask.	**show ip cef** *ip_address subnet_mask*

Task	Command Syntax
Display the adjacency that will be used to forward a packet from the specified source IP address to the specified destination IP address. (This command is useful if the router is load balancing across multiple adjacencies, and you want to see which adjacency will be used for a certain combination of source and destination IP addresses.)	**show ip cef exact-route** *source_ address destination_address*
Display the static IPv6 routes configured on a device.	**show ipv6 route static**
Display the Layer 3 IPv6 address-to-Layer 2 MAC address mappings.	**show ipv6 neighbors**
Display a router's ARP cache, containing IPv4 address-to-MAC address mappings.	**show ip arp**

CHAPTER 2

EIGRP

This chapter covers the following topics:

- **EIGRP Fundamentals:** This section explains how EIGRP establishes a neighborship with other routers and how routes are exchanged with other routers.

- **EIGRP Configuration Modes:** This section defines the two methods of configuring EIGRP with a baseline configuration.

- **Path Metric Calculation:** This section explains how EIGRP calculates the path metric to identify the best and alternate loop-free paths.

Enhanced Interior Gateway Routing Protocol (EIGRP) is an enhanced distance vector routing protocol commonly found in enterprise networks. EIGRP is a derivative of Interior Gateway Routing Protocol (IGRP) but includes support for variable-length subnet masking (VLSM) and metrics capable of supporting higher-speed interfaces. Initially, EIGRP was a Cisco proprietary protocol, but it was released to the Internet Engineering Task Force (IETF) through RFC 7868, which was ratified in May 2016.

This chapter explains the underlying mechanics of the EIGRP routing protocol and the path metric calculations, and it demonstrates how to configure EIGRP on a router. This is the first of several chapters in the book that discuss EIGRP:

- **Chapter 2, "EIGRP":** This chapter describes the fundamental concepts of EIGRP.

- **Chapter 3, "Advanced EIGRP":** This chapter describes EIGRP's failure detection mechanisms and techniques to optimize the operations of the routing protocol. It also includes topics such as route filtering and traffic manipulation.

- **Chapter 4, "Troubleshooting EIGRP for IPv4":** This chapter reviews common problems with the routing protocols and the methodology to troubleshoot EIGRP from an IPv4 perspective.

- **Chapter 5, "EIGRPv6":** This chapter demonstrates how IPv4 EIGRP concepts carry over to IPv6 and the methods used to troubleshoot common problems.

"Do I Know This Already?" Quiz

The "Do I Know This Already?" quiz allows you to assess whether you should read this entire chapter thoroughly or jump to the "Exam Preparation Tasks" section. If you are in doubt about your answers to these questions or your own assessment of your knowledge of the topics, read the entire chapter. Table 2-1 lists the major headings in this chapter and their corresponding "Do I Know This Already?" quiz questions. You can find the answers in Appendix A, "Answers to the 'Do I Know This Already?' Quiz Questions."

Table 2-1 "Do I Know This Already?" Foundation Topics Section-to-Question Mapping

Foundation Topics Section	Questions
EIGRP Fundamentals	1–6
EIGRP Configuration Modes	7–9
Path Metric Calculation	10

CAUTION The goal of self-assessment is to gauge your mastery of the topics in this chapter. If you do not know the answer to a question or are only partially sure of the answer, you should mark that question as wrong for purposes of self-assessment. Giving yourself credit for an answer that you correctly guess skews your self-assessment results and might provide you with a false sense of security.

1. EIGRP uses protocol number _____ for inter-router communication.

   a. 87

   b. 88

   c. 89

   d. 90

2. How many packet types does EIGRP use for inter-router communication?

   a. Three

   b. Four

   c. Five

   d. Six

   e. Seven

3. Which of the following are not required to match in order to form an EIGRP adjacency?

   a. Metric K values

   b. Primary subnet

   c. Hello and hold timers

   d. Authentication parameters

4. What is an EIGRP successor?

   a. The next-hop router for the path with the lowest path metric for a destination prefix

   b. The path with the lowest metric for a destination prefix

   c. The router selected to maintain the EIGRP adjacencies for a broadcast network

   d. A route that satisfies the feasibility condition where the reported distance is less than the feasible distance

   5. What attributes does the EIGRP topology table contain? (Choose all that apply.)

   a. Destination network prefix

   b. Hop count

   c. Total path delay

   d. Maximum path bandwidth

   e. List of EIGRP neighbors

   6. What destination addresses does EIGRP use when feasible? (Choose two.)

   a. IP address 224.0.0.9

   b. IP address 224.0.0.10

   c. IP address 224.0.0.8

   d. MAC address 01:00:5E:00:00:0A

   e. MAC address 0C:15:C0:00:00:01

   7. Which of the following techniques can be used to initialize the EIGRP process? (Choose two.)

   a. Use the interface command **ip eigrp** *as-number* **ipv4 unicast**.

   b. Use the global configuration command **router eigrp** *as-number*.

   c. Use the global configuration command **router eigrp** *process-name*.

   d. Use the interface command **router eigrp** *as-number*.

   8. True or false: The EIGRP router ID (RID) must be configured for EIGRP to be able to establish neighborship.

   a. True

   b. False

   9. True or false: When using MD5 authentication between EIGRP routers, the keychain sequence numbers used on the routers can be different, as long as the password is the same.

   a. True

   b. False

   10. Which value can be modified on a router to manipulate the path taken by EIGRP but does not have an impact on other routing protocols, like OSPF?

   a. Interface bandwidth

   b. Interface MTU

   c. Interface delay

   d. Interface priority

Foundation Topics

EIGRP Fundamentals

EIGRP overcomes the deficiencies of other distance vector routing protocols, such as Routing Information Protocol (RIP), with features such as unequal-cost load balancing, support for networks 255 hops away, and rapid convergence features. EIGRP uses a *diffusing update algorithm (DUAL)* to identify network paths and provides for fast convergence using precalculated loop-free backup paths. Most distance vector routing protocols use hop count as the metric for routing decisions. However, a route-selection algorithm that uses only hop count for path selection does not take into account link speed and total delay. EIGRP adds logic to the route-selection algorithm to use factors other than hop count alone.

Autonomous Systems

A router can run multiple EIGRP processes. Each process operates under the context of an autonomous system, which represents a common routing domain. Routers within the same domain use the same metric calculation formula and exchange routes only with members of the same *autonomous system (AS)*. Do not confuse an EIGRP autonomous system with a Border Gateway Protocol (BGP) autonomous system.

In Figure 2-1, EIGRP AS 100 consists of R1, R2, R3, and R4, and EIGRP AS 200 consists of R3, R5, and R6. Each EIGRP process correlates to a specific autonomous system and maintains an independent EIGRP topology table. R1 does not have knowledge of routes from AS 200 because it is different from its own autonomous system, AS 100. R3 is able to participate in both autonomous systems and, by default, does not transfer routes learned from one autonomous system into a different autonomous system.

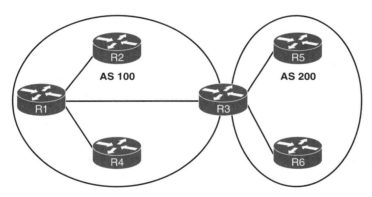

Figure 2-1   *EIGRP Autonomous Systems*

EIGRP uses *protocol-dependent modules (PDMs)* to support multiple network protocols, such as IPv4, IPv6, AppleTalk, and IPX. EIGRP is written so that the PDM is responsible for the functions to handle the route selection criteria for each communication protocol. In theory, new PDMs can be written as new communication protocols are created. Current implementations of EIGRP support only IPv4 and IPv6.

EIGRP Terminology

This section explains some of the core concepts of EIGRP, along with the path selection process. Figure 2-2 is a reference topology for this section, showing R1 calculating the best path and alternative loop-free paths to the 10.4.4.0/24 network. A value in parentheses represents the link's calculated metric for a segment based on bandwidth and delay.

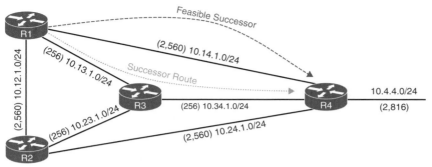

Figure 2-2   *EIGRP Reference Topology*

Table 2-2 defines important terms related to EIGRP and correlates them to Figure 2-2.

Table 2-2   EIGRP Terminology

Term	Definition
Successor route	The route with the lowest path metric to reach a destination.
	The successor route for R1 to reach 10.4.4.0/24 on R4 is R1→R3→R4.
Successor	The first next-hop router for the successor route. R1's successor for 10.4.4.0/24 is R3.
Feasible distance (FD)	The metric value for the lowest path metric to reach a destination. The feasible distance is calculated locally using the formula shown in the "Path Metric Calculation" section, later in this chapter.
	The FD calculated by R1 for the 10.4.4.0/24 destination network is 3328 (that is, 256 + 256 + 2816).
Reported distance (RD)	Distance reported by a router to reach a destination. The reported distance value is the feasible distance for the advertising router.
	R3 advertises the 10.4.4.0/24 destination network to R1 and R2 with an RD of 3072. R4 advertises the 10.4.4.0/24 destination network to R1, R2, and R3 with an RD of 2816.
Feasibility condition	For a route to be considered a backup route, the RD received for that route must be less than the FD calculated locally. This logic guarantees a loop-free path.
Feasible successor	A route that satisfies the feasibility condition is maintained as a backup route. The feasibility condition ensures that the backup route is loop free.
	The route R1→R4 is the feasible successor because the RD of 2816 is lower than the FD of 3328 for the R1→R3→R4 path.

Topology Table

EIGRP contains a *topology table*, which makes it different from a true distance vector routing protocol. EIGRP's topology table is a vital component of DUAL and contains information to identify loop-free backup routes. The topology table contains all the network prefixes advertised within an EIGRP autonomous system. Each entry in the table contains the following:

- Network prefix

- EIGRP neighbors that have advertised that prefix

- Metrics from each neighbor (reported distance and hop count)

- Values used for calculating the metric (load, reliability, total delay, and minimum bandwidth)

The command **show ip eigrp topology** [**all-links**] provides the topology table. By default, only the successor and feasible successor routes are displayed, but the optional **all-links** keyword shows the paths that did not pass the feasibility condition.

Figure 2-3 shows the topology table for R1 from Figure 2-2. This section focuses on the 10.4.4.0/24 network when explaining the topology table.

```
R1#show ip eigrp topology
EIGRP-IPv4 Topology Table for AS (100)/ID(192.168.1.1)
Codes: P - Passive, A - Active, U - Update, Q - Query, R - Reply,
    r - reply Status, s - sia Status

P 10.12.1.0/24, 1 successors, FD is 2816
    via Connected, GigabitEthernet0/3
P 10.13.1.0/24, 1 successors, FD is 2816
    via Connected, GigabitEthernet0/1
P 10.14.1.0/24, 1 successors, FD is 5120
    via Connected, GigabitEthernet0/2
P 10.23.1.0/24, 1 successors, FD is 3072
    via 10.13.1.3 (3072/2816), GigabitEthernet0/1
    via 10.12.1.2 (5376/2816), GigabitEthernet0/3
P 10.34.1.0/24, 1 successors, FD is 3072
    via 10.13.1.3 (3072/2816), GigabitEthernet0/1
    via 10.14.1.4 (5376/2816), GigabitEthernet0/2
P 10.24.1.0/24, 1 successors, FD is 5376
    via 10.12.1.2 (5376/5120), GigabitEthernet0/3
    via 10.14.1.4 (7680/5120), GigabitEthernet0/2
P 10.4.4.0/24, 1 successors, FD is 3328
    via 10.13.1.3 (3328/3072), GigabitEthernet0/1
    via 10.14.1.4 (5376/2816), GigabitEthernet0/2
```

Figure 2-3 *EIGRP Topology Output*

Examine the 10.4.4.0/24 prefix and notice that R1 calculates an FD of 3328 for the successor route. The successor (upstream router) advertises the successor route with an RD of 3072. The second path entry has a metric of 5376 and has an RD of 2816. Because 2816 is less than 3328, the second entry passes the feasibility condition, which means the second entry is classified as the feasible successor for the 10.4.4.0/24 prefix.

The 10.4.4.0/24 route is passive (P), which means the topology is stable. During a topology change, routes go into an active (A) state when computing a new path.

EIGRP Neighbors

Unlike a number of routing protocols—such as Routing Information Protocol (RIP), Open Shortest Path First (OSPF), and Intermediate System-to-Intermediate System (IS-IS)—EIGRP does not rely on periodic advertisement of all the network prefixes in an autonomous system. EIGRP neighbors exchange the entire routing table when forming an adjacency, and they advertise incremental updates only as topology changes occur within a network. The neighbor adjacency table is vital for tracking neighbor status and the updates sent to each neighbor.

Inter-Router Communication

EIGRP uses five different packet types to communicate with other routers, as shown in Table 2-3. EIGRP uses IP protocol number (88) and uses multicast packets where possible; it uses unicast packets when necessary. Communication between routers is done with multicast using the group address 224.0.0.10 or the MAC address 01:00:5e:00:00:0a when possible.

Table 2-3   EIGRP Packet Types

Opcode Value	Packet Type	Function
1	Update	Used to transmit routing and reachability information with other EIGRP neighbors
2	Request	Used to get specific information from one or more neighbors
3	Query	Sent out to search for another path during convergence
4	Reply	Sent in response to a query packet
5	Hello	Used for discovery of EIGRP neighbors and for detecting when a neighbor is no longer available

NOTE   EIGRP uses multicast packets to reduce bandwidth consumed on a link; that is, it uses one packet to reach multiple devices. While broadcast packets are used in the same general way, all nodes on a network segment process broadcast packets, whereas with multicast, only nodes listening for the particular multicast group process the multicast packets.

EIGRP uses *Reliable Transport Protocol* (*RTP*) to ensure that packets are delivered in order and to ensure that routers receive specific packets. A sequence number is included in each EIGRP packet. The sequence value zero does not require a response from the receiving EIGRP router; all other values require an ACK packet that includes the original sequence number.

Ensuring that packets are received makes the transport method reliable. All update, query, and reply packets are deemed reliable, and hello and ACK packets do not require acknowledgment and could be unreliable.

If the originating router does not receive an ACK packet from the neighbor before the retransmit timeout expires, it notifies the non-acknowledging router to stop processing its multicast packets. The originating router sends all traffic by unicast until the neighbor is fully synchronized. Upon complete synchronization, the originating router notifies the destination router to start processing multicast packets again. All unicast packets require acknowledgment. EIGRP retries up to 16 times for each packet that requires confirmation, and it resets the neighbor relationship when the neighbor reaches the retry limit of 16.

> **NOTE** In the context of EIGRP, do not confuse RTP with the Real-Time Transport Protocol (RTP), which is used for carrying audio or video over an IP network. EIGRP's RTP allows for confirmation of packets while supporting multicast. Other protocols that require reliable connection-oriented communication, such as TCP, cannot use multicast addressing.

Forming EIGRP Neighbors

Unlike other distance vector routing protocols, EIGRP requires a neighbor relationship to form before routes are processed and added to the Routing Information Base (RIB). Upon hearing an EIGRP hello packet, a router attempts to become the neighbor of the other router. The following parameters must match for the two routers to become neighbors:

- Metric formula K values
- Primary subnet matches
- Autonomous system number (ASN) matches
- Authentication parameters

Figure 2-4 shows the process EIGRP uses for forming neighbor adjacencies.

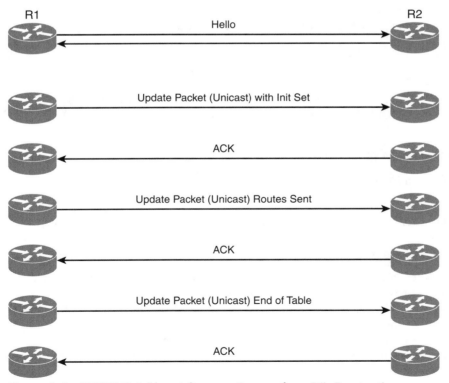

Figure 2-4 *EIGRP Neighbor Adjacency Process from R1's Perspective*

EIGRP Configuration Modes

This section describes the two methods of EIGRP configuration: classic mode and named mode.

Classic Configuration Mode

With *classic EIGRP configuration mode*, most of the configuration takes place in the EIGRP process, but some settings are configured under the interface configuration submode. This can add complexity for deployment and troubleshooting as users must scroll back and forth between the EIGRP process and individual network interfaces. Some of the settings that are set individually are hello advertisement interval, split-horizon, authentication, and summary route advertisements.

Classic configuration requires the initialization of the routing process with the global configuration command **router eigrp** *as-number* to identify the ASN and initialize the EIGRP process. The second step is to identify the network interfaces with the command **network** *ip-address* [*wildcard-mask*]. The **network** statement is explained in the following sections.

EIGRP Named Mode

EIGRP named mode configuration was released to overcome some of the difficulties network engineers have with classic EIGRP autonomous system configuration, including scattered configurations and unclear scope of commands.

EIGRP named configuration provides the following benefits:

- All the EIGRP configuration occurs in one location.

- It supports current EIGRP features and future developments.

- It supports multiple address families (including virtual routing and forwarding [VRF] instances). EIGRP named configuration is also known as *multi-address family configuration mode*.

- Commands are clear in terms of the scope of their configuration.

EIGRP named mode provides a hierarchical configuration and stores settings in three subsections:

- **Address Family:** This submode contains settings that are relevant to the global EIGRP AS operations, such as selection of network interfaces, EIGRP K values, logging settings, and stub settings.

- **Interface:** This submode contains settings that are relevant to the interface, such as hello advertisement interval, split-horizon, authentication, and summary route advertisements. In actuality, there are two methods of the EIGRP interface section's configuration. Commands can be assigned to a specific interface or to a *default* interface, in which case those settings are placed on all EIGRP-enabled interfaces. If there is a conflict between the default interface and a specific interface, the specific interface takes priority over the default interface.

- **Topology:** This submode contains settings regarding the EIGRP topology database and how routes are presented to the router's RIB. This section also contains route redistribution and administrative distance settings.

EIGRP named configuration makes it possible to run multiple instances under the same EIGRP process. The process for enabling EIGRP interfaces on a specific instance is as follows:

Step 1. Initialize the EIGRP process by using the command **router eigrp** *process-name*. (If a number is used for *process-name*, the *number* does not correlate to the autonomous system number.)

Step 2. Initialize the EIGRP instance for the appropriate address family with the command **address-family {IPv4 | IPv6} {unicast | vrf** *vrf-name*} **autonomous-system** *as-number*.

Step 3. Enable EIGRP on interfaces by using the command **network** *network wildcard-mask*.

EIGRP Network Statement

Both configuration modes use a **network** statement to identify the interfaces that EIGRP will use. The **network** statement uses a wildcard mask, which allows the configuration to be as specific or ambiguous as necessary.

> **NOTE** The two styles of EIGRP configuration are independent. Using the configuration options from classic EIGRP autonomous system configuration does not modify settings on a router running EIGRP named configuration.

The syntax for the **network** statement, which exists under the EIGRP process, is **network** *ip-address [wildcard-mask]*. The optional *wildcard-mask* can be omitted to enable interfaces that fall within the classful boundaries for that **network** statement.

A common misconception is that the **network** statement adds prefixes to the EIGRP topology table. In reality, the **network** statement identifies the interface to enable EIGRP on, and it adds the interface's connected network to the EIGRP topology table. EIGRP then advertises the topology table to other routers in the EIGRP autonomous system.

EIGRP does not add an interface's secondary connected network to the topology table. For secondary connected networks to be installed in the EIGRP routing table, they must be redistributed into the EIGRP process. Chapter 16, "Route Redistribution," provides additional coverage of route redistribution.

To help illustrate the concept of the wildcard mask, Table 2-4 provides a set of IP addresses and interfaces for a router. The following examples provide configurations to match specific scenarios.

Table 2-4   Table of Sample Interface and IP Addresses

Router Interface	IP Address
Gigabit Ethernet 0/0	10.0.0.10/24
Gigabit Ethernet 0/1	10.0.10.10/24
Gigabit Ethernet 0/2	192.0.0.10/24
Gigabit Ethernet 0/3	192.10.0.10/24

The configuration in Example 2-1 enables EIGRP only on interfaces that explicitly match the IP addresses in Table 2-4.

Example 2-1   *EIGRP Configuration with Explicit IP Addresses*

```
Router eigrp 1
    network 10.0.0.10 0.0.0.0
    network 10.0.10.10 0.0.0.0
    network 192.0.0.10 0.0.0.0
    network 192.10.0.10 0.0.0.0
```

Example 2-2 shows the EIGRP configuration using **network** statements that match the subnets used in Table 2-4. Setting the last octet of the IP address to 0 and changing the wildcard mask to 255 cause the **network** statements to match all IP addresses within the /24 network range.

Example 2-2   *EIGRP Configuration with an Explicit Subnet*

```
Router eigrp  1
    network 10.0.0.0 0.0.0.255
    network 10.0.10.0 0.0.0.255
    network 192.0.0.0 0.0.0.255
    network 192.10.0.0 0.0.0.255
```

The following snippet shows the EIGRP configuration using **network** statements for interfaces that are within the 10.0.0.0/8 or 192.0.0.0/8 network ranges:

```
router eigrp  1
    network 10.0.0.0 0.255.255.255
    network 192.0.0.0 0.255.255.255
```

The following snippet shows the configuration to enable all interfaces with EIGRP:

```
router eigrp  1
    network 0.0.0.0 255.255.255.255
```

NOTE   A key topic with wildcard **network** statements is that large ranges simplify configuration; however, they may possibly enable EIGRP on interfaces where not intended.

Sample Topology and Configuration

Figure 2-5 shows a sample topology for demonstrating EIGRP configuration in classic mode for R1 and named mode for R2.

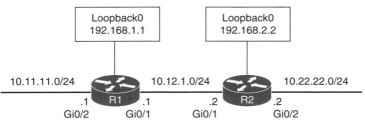

Figure 2-5 *EIGRP Sample Topology*

R1 and R2 enable EIGRP on all of their interfaces. R1 configures EIGRP using multiple specific network interface addresses, and R2 enables EIGRP on all network interfaces with one command. Example 2-3 provides the configuration that is applied to R1 and R2.

Example 2-3 *Sample EIGRP Configuration*

```
R1 (Classic Configuration)
interface Loopback0
 ip address 192.168.1.1 255.255.255.255
!
interface GigabitEthernet0/1
    ip address 10.12.1.1 255.255.255.0
!
interface GigabitEthernet0/2
    ip address 10.11.11.1 255.255.255.0
!
router eigrp 100
 network 10.11.11.1 0.0.0.0
 network 10.12.1.1 0.0.0.0
 network 192.168.1.1 0.0.0.0
```
```
R2 (Named Mode Configuration)
interface Loopback0
 ip address 192.168.2.2 255.255.255.255
!
interface GigabitEthernet0/1
    ip address 10.12.1.2 255.255.255.0
!
interface GigabitEthernet0/2
    ip address 10.22.22.2 255.255.255.0
!
router eigrp EIGRP-NAMED
 address-family ipv4 unicast autonomous-system 100
  network 0.0.0.0 255.255.255.255
```

As mentioned earlier, EIGRP named mode has three configuration submodes. The configuration in Example 2-3 uses only the EIGRP address-family submode section, which uses the **network** statement. The EIGRP topology base submode is created automatically with the command **topology base** and exited with the command **exit-af-topology**. Settings for the topology submode are listed between those two commands.

Example 2-4 demonstrates the slight difference in how the configuration is stored on the router between EIGRP classic and named mode configurations.

Example 2-4   *Comparison of EIGRP Configuration Mode Structures*

```
R1# show run | section router eigrp
router eigrp 100
 network 10.11.11.1 0.0.0.0
 network 10.12.1.1 0.0.0.0
 network 192.168.1.1 0.0.0.0

R2# show run | section router eigrp
router eigrp EIGRP-NAMED
 !
 address-family ipv4 unicast autonomous-system 100
  !
  topology base
  exit-af-topology
  network 0.0.0.0
 exit-address-family
```

NOTE   The EIGRP interface submode configurations contain the command **af-interface** *interface-id* or **af-interface default**, with any specific commands listed immediately. The EIGRP interface submode configuration is exited with the command **exit-af-interface**. This is demonstrated later in this chapter.

Confirming Interfaces

Upon configuring EIGRP, it is a good practice to verify that only the intended interfaces are running EIGRP. The command **show ip eigrp interfaces** [{*interface-id* [**detail**] | **detail**}] shows active EIGRP interfaces. Appending the optional **detail** keyword provides additional information, such as authentication, EIGRP timers, split horizon, and various packet counts.

Example 2-5 demonstrates R1's non-detailed EIGRP interface and R2's detailed information for the Gi0/1 interface.

Example 2-5   *Verifying EIGRP Interfaces*

```
R1# show ip eigrp interfaces
EIGRP-IPv4 Interfaces for AS(100)
                     Xmit Queue   PeerQ        Mean   Pacing Time  Multicast  Pending
Interface Peers  Un/Reliable  Un/Reliable  SRTT   Un/Reliable  Flow Timer Routes
Gi0/2        0       0/0          0/0         0        0/0           0          0
```

```
Gi0/1        1         0/0        0/0        10       0/0        50       0
Lo0          0         0/0        0/0         0       0/0         0       0
```

```
R2# show ip eigrp interfaces gi0/1 detail
EIGRP-IPv4 VR(EIGRP-NAMED) Address-Family Interfaces for AS(100)
                      Xmit Queue    PeerQ       Mean   Pacing Time  Multicast  Pending
Interface Peers    Un/Reliable  Un/Reliable   SRTT    Un/Reliable  Flow Timer Routes
Gi0/1        1         0/0        0/0        1583      0/0         7912        0
  Hello-interval is 5, Hold-time is 15
  Split-horizon is enabled
  Next xmit serial <none>
  Packetized sent/expedited: 2/0
  Hello's sent/expedited: 186/2
  Un/reliable mcasts: 0/2  Un/reliable ucasts: 2/2
  Mcast exceptions: 0  CR packets: 0  ACKs suppressed: 0
  Retransmissions sent: 1  Out-of-sequence rcvd: 0
  Topology-ids on interface - 0
  Authentication mode is not set
  Topologies advertised on this interface:  base
  Topologies not advertised on this interface:
```

Table 2-5 provides a brief explanation to the key fields shown with the EIGRP interfaces.

Table 2-5   EIGRP Interface Fields

Field	Description
Interface	Interfaces running EIGRP.
Peers	Number of peers detected on the interface.
Xmt Queue Un/Reliable	Number of unreliable/reliable packets remaining in the transmit queue. The value zero is an indication of a stable network.
Mean SRTT	Average time for a packet to be sent to a neighbor and a reply from that neighbor to be received, in milliseconds.
Multicast Flow Timer	Maximum time (seconds) that the router sent multicast packets.
Pending Routes	Number of routes in the transmit queue that need to be sent.

Verifying EIGRP Neighbor Adjacencies

Each EIGRP process maintains a table of neighbors to ensure that they are alive and process-ing updates properly. If EIGRP didn't keep track of neighbor states, an autonomous system could contain incorrect data and could potentially route traffic improperly. EIGRP must form a neighbor relationship before a router advertises update packets containing network prefixes.

The command **show ip eigrp neighbors** [*interface-id*] displays the EIGRP neighbors for a router. Example 2-6 shows the EIGRP neighbor information obtained using this command.

Example 2-6   *EIGRP Neighbor Confirmation*

```
R1# show ip eigrp neighbors
EIGRP-IPv4 Neighbors for AS(100)
H   Address              Interface              Hold Uptime    SRTT    RTO   Q   Seq
                                                (sec)          (ms)          Cnt Num
0   10.12.1.2            Gi0/1                  13  00:18:31   10      100   0   3
```

Table 2-6 provides a brief explanation of the key fields shown in Example 2-6.

Table 2-6   EIGRP Neighbor Columns

Field	Description
Address	IP address of the EIGRP neighbor
Interface	Interface the neighbor was detected on
Holdtime	Time left to receive a packet from this neighbor to ensure that it is still alive
SRTT	Time for a packet to be sent to a neighbor and a reply to be received from that neighbor, in milliseconds
RTO	Timeout for retransmission (waiting for ACK)
Q Cnt	Number of packets (update/query/reply) in queue for sending
Seq Num	Sequence number that was last received from this router

Displaying Installed EIGRP Routes

You can see EIGRP routes that are installed into the RIB by using the command **show ip route eigrp**. EIGRP routes that originate within the autonomous system have an administrative distance (AD) of 90 and are indicated in the routing table with a D. Routes that originate from outside the autonomous system are external EIGRP routes. External EIGRP routes have an AD of 170 and are indicated in the routing table with D EX. Placing external EIGRP routes into the RIB with a higher AD acts as a loop-prevention mechanism.

Example 2-7 displays the EIGRP routes from the sample topology in Figure 2-5. The metric for the selected route is the second number in brackets.

Example 2-7   *EIGRP Routes for R1 and R2*

```
R1# show ip route eigrp
Codes: L - local, C - connected, S - static, R - RIP, M - mobile, B - BGP
       D - EIGRP, EX - EIGRP external, O - OSPF, IA - OSPF inter area
       N1 - OSPF NSSA external type 1, N2 - OSPF NSSA external type 2
       E1 - OSPF external type 1, E2 - OSPF external type 2
       i - IS-IS, su - IS-IS summary, L1 - IS-IS level-1, L2 - IS-IS level-2
       ia - IS-IS inter area, * - candidate default, U - per-user static route
       o - ODR, P - periodic downloaded static route, H - NHRP, l - LISP
       a - application route
       + - replicated route, % - next hop override, p - overrides from PfR
```

```
Gateway of last resort is not set


      10.0.0.0/8 is variably subnetted, 5 subnets, 2 masks
D        10.22.22.0/24 [90/3072] via 10.12.1.2, 00:19:25, GigabitEthernet0/1
      192.168.2.0/32 is subnetted, 1 subnets
D        192.168.2.2 [90/2848] via 10.12.1.2, 00:19:25, GigabitEthernet0/1
```
```
R2# show ip route eigrp
! Output omitted for brevity
Gateway of last resort is not set


      10.0.0.0/8 is variably subnetted, 5 subnets, 2 masks
D        10.11.11.0/24 [90/15360] via 10.12.1.1, 00:20:34, GigabitEthernet0/1
      192.168.1.0/32 is subnetted, 1 subnets
D        192.168.1.1 [90/2570240] via 10.12.1.1, 00:20:34, GigabitEthernet0/1
```

NOTE The metrics for R2's routes are different from the metrics from R1's routes. This is because R1's classic EIGRP mode uses classic metrics, and R2's named mode uses wide metrics by default. This topic is explained in depth in the "Path Metric Calculation" section, later in this chapter.

Router ID

The router ID (RID) is a 32-bit number that uniquely identifies an EIGRP router and is used as a loop-prevention mechanism. The RID can be set dynamically, which is the default, or manually.

The algorithm for dynamically choosing the EIGRP RID uses the highest IPv4 address of any *up* loopback interfaces. If there are not any *up* loopback interfaces, the highest IPv4 address of any active *up* physical interfaces becomes the RID when the EIGRP process initializes.

IPv4 addresses are commonly used for the RID because they are 32 bits and are maintained in dotted-decimal format. You use the command **eigrp router-id** *router-id* to set the RID, as demonstrated in Example 2-8, for both classic and named mode configurations.

Example 2-8 *Static Configuration of EIGRP Router ID*

```
R1(config)# router eigrp 100
R1(config-router)# eigrp router-id 192.168.1.1
```
```
R2(config)# router eigrp EIGRP-NAMED
R2(config-router)# address-family ipv4 unicast autonomous-system 100
R2(config-router-af)# eigrp router-id 192.168.2.2
```

Passive Interfaces

Some network topologies must advertise a network segment into EIGRP but need to prevent neighbors from forming adjacencies with other routers on that segment. This might be the case, for example, when advertising access layer networks in a campus topology. In such a scenario, you need to put the EIGRP interface in a passive state. Passive EIGRP interfaces do not send out or process EIGRP hellos, which prevents EIGRP from forming adjacencies on those interfaces.

To configure an EIGRP interface as passive, you use the command **passive-interface** *interface-id* under the EIGRP process for classic configuration. Another option is to configure all interfaces as passive by default with the command **passive-interface default** and then use the command **no passive-interface** *interface-id* to allow an interface to process EIGRP packets, preempting the global *passive interface* default configuration.

Example 2-9 demonstrates making R1's Gi0/2 interface passive and also the alternative option of making all interfaces passive but setting Gi0/1 as non-passive.

Example 2-9 *Passive EIGRP Interfaces for Classic Configuration*

```
R1# configure terminal
Enter configuration commands, one per line.  End with CNTL/Z.
R1(config)# router eigrp 100
R1(config-router)# passive-interface gi0/2
```

```
R1(config)# router eigrp 100
R1(config-router)# passive-interface default
04:22:52.031: %DUAL-5-NBRCHANGE: EIGRP-IPv4 100: Neighbor 10.12.1.2
(GigabitEthernet0/1) is down: interface passive
R1(config-router)# no passive-interface gi0/1
*May 10 04:22:56.179: %DUAL-5-NBRCHANGE: EIGRP-IPv4 100: Neighbor 10.12.1.2
(GigabitEthernet0/1) is up: new adjacency
```

For a named mode configuration, you place the **passive-interface** state on **af-interface default** for all EIGRP interfaces or on a specific interface with the **af-interface** *interface-id* section. Example 2-10 shows how to set the Gi0/2 interface as passive while allowing the Gi0/1 interface to be active, using both configuration strategies.

Example 2-10 *Passive EIGRP Interfaces for Named Mode Configuration*

```
R2# configure terminal
Enter configuration commands, one per line.  End with CNTL/Z.
R2(config)# router eigrp EIGRP-NAMED
R2(config-router)# address-family ipv4 unicast autonomous-system 100
R2(config-router-af)# af-interface gi0/2
R2(config-router-af-interface)# passive-interface
```

```
R2(config)# router eigrp EIGRP-NAMED
R2(config-router)# address-family ipv4 unicast autonomous-system 100
```

```
R2(config-router-af)# af-interface default
R2(config-router-af-interface)# passive-interface
04:28:30.366: %DUAL-5-NBRCHANGE: EIGRP-IPv4 100: Neighbor 10.12.1.1
(GigabitEthernet0/1) is down: interface passiveex
R2(config-router-af-interface)# exit-af-interface
R2(config-router-af)# af-interface gi0/1
R2(config-router-af-interface)# no passive-interface
R2(config-router-af-interface)# exit-af-interface
*May 10 04:28:40.219: %DUAL-5-NBRCHANGE: EIGRP-IPv4 100: Neighbor 10.12.1.1
(GigabitEthernet0/1) is up: new adjacency
```

Example 2-11 shows what the named mode configuration looks like with some settings (that is, **passive-interface** and **no passive-interface**) placed under the **af-interface default** and **af-interface** *interface-id* settings.

Example 2-11   *Viewing the EIGRP Interface Settings with Named Mode*

```
R2# show run | section router eigrp
router eigrp EIGRP-NAMED
 !
 address-family ipv4 unicast autonomous-system 100
  !
  af-interface default
   passive-interface
  exit-af-interface
  !
  af-interface GigabitEthernet0/1
   no passive-interface
  exit-af-interface
  !
  topology base
  exit-af-topology
  network 0.0.0.0
 exit-address-family
```

A passive interface does not appear in the output of the command **show ip eigrp interfaces** even though it was enabled. Connected networks for passive interfaces are still added to the EIGRP topology table so that they are advertised to neighbors.

Example 2-12 shows that the Gi0/2 interface on R1 no longer appears; compare this to Example 2-5, where it does exist.

Example 2-12   *show ip eigrp interfaces Output*

```
R1# show ip eigrp interfaces
EIGRP-IPv4 Interfaces for AS(100)
                    Xmit Queue    PeerQ        Mean   Pacing Time   Multicast   Pending
Interface  Peers  Un/Reliable  Un/Reliable   SRTT   Un/Reliable   Flow Timer  Routes
Gi0/1       1        0/0          0/0          9        0/0            50          0
```

To accelerate troubleshooting of passive interfaces, as well as other settings, use the command **show ip protocols**, which provides a lot of valuable information about all the routing protocols. With EIGRP, it displays the EIGRP process identifier, the ASN, *K values* that are used for path calculation, RID, neighbors, AD settings, and all the passive interfaces.

Example 2-13 provides sample output for both classic and named mode instances on R1 and R2.

Example 2-13   *show ip protocols Output*

```
R1# show ip protocols
! Output omitted for brevity
Routing Protocol is "eigrp 100"
  Outgoing update filter list for all interfaces is not set
  Incoming update filter list for all interfaces is not set
  Default networks flagged in outgoing updates
  Default networks accepted from incoming updates
  EIGRP-IPv4 Protocol for AS(100)
    Metric weight K1=1, K2=0, K3=1, K4=0, K5=0
    Soft SIA disabled
    NSF-aware route hold timer is 240
    Router-ID: 192.168.1.1
    Topology : 0 (base)
      Active Timer: 3 min
      Distance: internal 90 external 170
      Maximum path: 4
      Maximum hopcount 100
      Maximum metric variance 1

  Automatic Summarization: disabled
  Maximum path: 4
  Routing for Networks:
    10.11.11.1/32
    10.12.1.1/32
    192.168.1.1/32
  Passive Interface(s):
    GigabitEthernet0/2
    Loopback0
  Routing Information Sources:
    Gateway         Distance      Last Update
    10.12.1.2             90      00:21:35
  Distance: internal 90 external 170

R2# show ip protocols
! Output omitted for brevity
Routing Protocol is "eigrp 100"
```

```
Outgoing update filter list for all interfaces is not set
Incoming update filter list for all interfaces is not set
Default networks flagged in outgoing updates
Default networks accepted from incoming updates
EIGRP-IPv4 VR(EIGRP-NAMED) Address-Family Protocol for AS(100)
  Metric weight K1=1, K2=0, K3=1, K4=0, K5=0 K6=0
  Metric rib-scale 128
  Metric version 64bit
  Soft SIA disabled
  NSF-aware route hold timer is 240
  Router-ID: 192.168.2.2
  Topology : 0 (base)
    Active Timer: 3 min
    Distance: internal 90 external 170
    Maximum path: 4
    Maximum hopcount 100
    Maximum metric variance 1
    Total Prefix Count: 5
    Total Redist Count: 0

Automatic Summarization: disabled
Maximum path: 4
Routing for Networks:
  0.0.0.0
Passive Interface(s):
  GigabitEthernet0/2
  Loopback0
Routing Information Sources:
  Gateway         Distance      Last Update
  10.12.1.1             90      00:24:26
Distance: internal 90 external 170
```

Authentication

Authentication is a mechanism for ensuring that only authorized routers are eligible to become EIGRP neighbors. It is possible for someone to add a router to a network and introduce invalid routes accidentally or maliciously. Authentication prevents such scenarios from happening. A precomputed password hash is included with all EIGRP packets, and the receiving router decrypts the hash. If the passwords do not match for a packet, the router discards the packet.

EIGRP encrypts the password by using Message Digest 5 (MD5) authentication and the keychain function. The hash consists of the key number and a password. EIGRP authentication encrypts just the password rather than the entire EIGRP packet.

> **NOTE** Keychain functionality allows a password to be valid for a specific time, so passwords can change at preconfigured times. Restricting the key sequence to a specific time is beyond the scope of this book. For more information, see Cisco.com.

To configure EIGRP authentication, you need to create a keychain and then enable EIGRP authentication on the interface. The following sections explain the steps.

Keychain Configuration

Keychain creation is accomplished with the following steps:

Step 1. Create the keychain by using the command **key chain** *key-chain-name*.

Step 2. Identify the key sequence by using the command **key** *key-number*, where *key-number* can be anything from 0 to 2147483647.

Step 3. Specify the preshared password by using the command **key-string** *password*.

> **NOTE** Be careful not to use a space after the password because the password, including any trailing space, will be used for computing the hash.

Enabling Authentication on the Interface

When using classic configuration, authentication must be enabled on the interface under the interface configuration submode. The following commands are used in the interface configuration submode:

```
ip authentication key-chain eigrp as-number key-chain-name

ip authentication mode eigrp as-number md5
```

The named mode configuration places the configurations under the EIGRP interface submode, under **af-interface default** or **af-interface** *interface-id*. Named mode configuration supports MD5 or *Hashed Message Authentication Code-Secure Hash Algorithm-256 (HMAC-SHA-256)* authentication. MD5 authentication involves the following commands:

```
authentication key-chain eigrp key-chain-name

authentication mode md5
```

HMAC-SHA-256 authentication involves the command **authentication mode hmac-sha-256** *password*.

Example 2-14 demonstrates MD5 configuration on R1 with classic EIGRP configuration and on R2 with named mode configuration. Remember that the hash is computed using the key sequence number and key string, which must match on the two nodes.

Example 2-14 *Configuring EIGRP Authentication*

```
R1(config)# key chain EIGRPKEY
R1(config-keychain)# key 2
R1(config-keychain-key)# key-string CISCO
R1(config)# interface gi0/1
R1(config-if)# ip authentication mode eigrp 100 md5
R1(config-if)# ip authentication key-chain eigrp 100 EIGRPKEY
```

```
R2(config)# key chain EIGRPKEY
R2(config-keychain)# key 2
R2(config-keychain-key)# key-string CISCO
R2(config-keychain-key)# router eigrp EIGRP-NAMED
R2(config-router)# address-family ipv4 unicast autonomous-system 100
R2(config-router-af)# af-interface default
R2(config-router-af-interface)# authentication mode md5
R2(config-router-af-interface)# authentication key-chain EIGRPKEY
```

The command **show key chain** provides verification of the keychain. Example 2-15 shows that each key sequence provides the lifetime and password.

Example 2-15 *Verifying Keychain Settings*

```
R1# show key chain
Key-chain EIGRPKEY:
    key 2 -- text "CISCO"
        accept lifetime (always valid) - (always valid) [valid now]
        send lifetime (always valid) - (always valid) [valid now]
```

The EIGRP interface detail view provides verification of EIGRP authentication on a specific interface. Example 2-16 shows detailed EIGRP interface output.

Example 2-16 *Verifying EIGRP Authentication*

```
R1# show ip eigrp interface detail
EIGRP-IPv4 Interfaces for AS(100)
                  Xmit Queue    PeerQ        Mean   Pacing Time   Multicast    Pending
Interface  Peers  Un/Reliable   Un/Reliable  SRTT   Un/Reliable   Flow Timer   Routes
Gi0/1        0      0/0           0/0          0       0/0           50           0
  Hello-interval is 5, Hold-time is 15
  Split-horizon is enabled
  Next xmit serial <none>
  Packetized sent/expedited: 10/1
  Hello's sent/expedited: 673/12
```

```
Un/reliable mcasts: 0/9  Un/reliable ucasts: 6/19

Mcast exceptions: 0  CR packets: 0  ACKs suppressed: 0

Retransmissions sent: 16  Out-of-sequence rcvd: 1

Topology-ids on interface - 0

Authentication mode is md5,  key-chain is "EIGRPKEY"
```

Path Metric Calculation

Metric calculation is a critical component for any routing protocol. EIGRP uses multiple factors to calculate the metric for a path. Metric calculation uses *bandwidth* and *delay* by default but can include interface load and reliability, too. Figure 2-6 shows the EIGRP classic metric formula.

$$\text{Metric} = 256 * [(K_1 * BW + \frac{K_2 * BW}{256 - \text{Load}} + K_3 * \text{Delay}) * \frac{K_5}{K_4 + \text{Reliability}}]$$

Figure 2-6 *EIGRP Metric Formula*

EIGRP uses K values to define which factors the formula uses and the impact associated with a factor when calculating the metric. A common misconception is that the K values directly apply to bandwidth, load, delay, or reliability; this is not accurate. For example, K_1 and K_2 both reference bandwidth (BW).

BW represents the slowest link in the path, scaled to a 10 Gbps link (10^7). Link speed correlates to the configured interface bandwidth on an interface and is measured in kilobits per second (Kbps). Delay is the total measure of delay in the path, measured in tens of microseconds (µs).

Taking these definitions into consideration, look at the formula for classic EIGRP metrics in Figure 2-7.

$$\text{Metric} = 256* [(K_1 * \frac{10^7}{\text{Min. Bandwidth}} + \frac{K_2 * \text{Min. Bandwidth}}{256 - \text{Load}} + \frac{K_3 * \text{Total Delay}}{10}) * \frac{K_5}{K_4 + \text{Reliability}}]$$

Figure 2-7 *EIGRP Classic Metric Formula with Definitions*

NOTE RFC 7868 states that if $K_5 = 0$, then the reliability quotient is defined to be 1. This is not demonstrated in Figure 2-7 but is shown in the simpler formula in Figure 2-8.

By default, K_1 and K_3 each has a value of 1, and K_2, K_4, and K_5 are all set to 0. Figure 2-8 places default K values into the formula and shows a streamlined version of the formula.

The EIGRP update packet includes path attributes associated with each prefix. The EIGRP path attributes can include hop count, cumulative delay, minimum bandwidth link speed, and RD. The attributes are updated each hop along the way, allowing each router to independently identify the shortest path.

$$\text{Metric} = 256 * [(1 * \frac{10^7}{\text{Min. Bandwidth}} + \frac{\frac{10^7}{0 * \text{Min. Bandwidth}}}{256 - \text{Load}} + \frac{1 * \text{Total Delay}}{10}) * \frac{0}{0 + \text{Reliability}}]$$

Equals

$$\text{Metric} = 256 * (\frac{10^7}{\text{Min. Bandwidth}} + \frac{\text{Total Delay}}{10})$$

Figure 2-8 *EIGRP Classic Metric Formula with Default K Values*

Figure 2-9 shows the information in the EIGRP update packets for the 10.1.1.0/24 network propagating through the autonomous system. Notice that the hop count increments, minimum bandwidth decreases, total delay increases, and the RD changes with each EIGRP update.

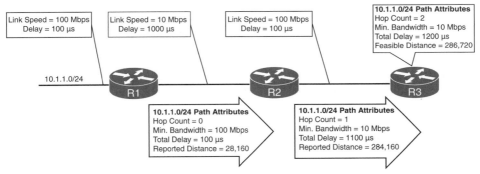

Figure 2-9 *EIGRP Attribute Propagation*

Table 2-7 shows for some common network types the link speed, delay, and EIGRP metric, based on the streamlined formula in Figure 2-8.

Table 2-7 Default EIGRP Interface Metrics for Classic Metrics

Interface Type	Link Speed (Kbps)	Delay	Metric
Serial	64	20,000 μs	40,512,000
T1	1544	20,000 μs	2,170,031
Ethernet	10,000	1000 μs	281,600
FastEthernet	100,000	100 μs	28,160
GigabitEthernet	1,000,000	10 μs	2816
TenGigabitEthernet	10,000,000	10 μs	512

Using the topology from Figure 2-2, the metrics from R1 and R2 for the 10.4.4.0/24 network are calculated using the formula in Figure 2-10. The link speed for both routers is 1 Gbps, and the total delay is 30 μs (10 μs for the 10.4.4.0/24 link, 10 μs for the 10.34.1.0/24 link, and 10 μs for the 10.13.1.0/24 link).

$$\text{Metric} = 256 * \left(\frac{10^7}{1,000,000} + \frac{30}{10} \right) = 3,328$$

Figure 2-10   *Calculating EIGRP Metrics with Default K Values*

If you are unsure of the EIGRP metrics, you can query the parameters for the formula directly from EIGRP's topology table by using the command **show ip eigrp topology** *network/prefix-length*.

Example 2-17 shows R1's topology table output for the 10.4.4.0/24 network. Notice that the output includes the successor route, any feasible successor paths, and the EIGRP state for the prefix. Each path contains the EIGRP attributes minimum bandwidth, total delay, interface reliability, load, and hop count.

Example 2-17   *EIGRP Topology for a Specific Prefix*

```
R1# show ip eigrp topology 10.4.4.0/24
! Output omitted for brevity
EIGRP-IPv4 Topology Entry for AS(100)/ID(10.14.1.1) for 10.4.4.0/24
  State is Passive, Query origin flag is 1, 1 Successor(s), FD is 3328
  Descriptor Blocks:
  10.13.1.3 (GigabitEthernet0/1), from 10.13.1.3, Send flag is 0x0
      Composite metric is (3328/3072), route is Internal
      Vector metric:
        Minimum bandwidth is 1000000 Kbit
        Total delay is 30 microseconds
        Reliability is 252/255
        Load is 1/255
        Minimum MTU is 1500
        Hop count is 2
        Originating router is 10.34.1.4
  10.14.1.4 (GigabitEthernet0/2), from 10.14.1.4, Send flag is 0x0
      Composite metric is (5376/2816), route is Internal
      Vector metric:
        Minimum bandwidth is 1000000 Kbit
        Total delay is 110 microseconds
        Reliability is 255/255
        Load is 1/255
        Minimum MTU is 1500
        Hop count is 1
        Originating router is 10.34.1.4
```

Wide Metrics

The original EIGRP specifications measured delay in 10-microsecond (μs) units and bandwidth in kilobits per second, which did not scale well with higher-speed interfaces. In

Table 2-7, notice that the delay is the same for the GigabitEthernet and TenGigabitEthernet interfaces.

Example 2-18 provides some metric calculations for common LAN interface speeds. Notice that there is not a differentiation between an 11 Gbps interface and a 20 Gbps interface. The composite metric stays at 256, despite the different bandwidth rates.

Example 2-18 *Metric Calculation for Common LAN Interface Speeds*

```
GigabitEthernet:
Scaled Bandwidth = 10,000,000 / 1,000,000
Scaled Delay = 10 / 10
Composite Metric = 10 + 1 * 256 = 2816

10 GigabitEthernet:
Scaled Bandwidth = 10,000,000 / 10,000,000
Scaled Delay = 10 / 10
Composite Metric = 1 + 1 * 256 = 512

11 GigabitEthernet:
Scaled Bandwidth = 10,000,000 / 11,000,000
Scaled Delay = 10 / 10
Composite Metric = 0 + 1 * 256 = 256

20 GigabitEthernet:
Scaled Bandwidth = 10,000,000 / 20,000,000
Scaled Delay = 10 / 10
Composite Metric = 0 + 1 * 256 = 256
```

EIGRP includes support for a second set of metrics, known as *wide metrics*, that addresses the issue of scalability with higher-capacity interfaces. Just as EIGRP scaled by 256 to accommodate IGRP, EIGRP wide metrics scale by 65,536 to accommodate higher-speed links. This provides support for interface speeds up to 655 Tbps ($65,536 \times 10^7$) without any scalability issues.

Figure 2-11 shows the explicit EIGRP wide metrics formula. Notice that an additional K value (K_6) is included that adds an extended attribute to measure jitter, energy, or other future attributes.

$$\text{Wide Metric} = 65{,}536 * \left[\left(K_1 * BW + \frac{K_2 * BW}{256 - \text{Load}} + K_3 * \text{Latency} + K_6 * \text{Extended}\right) * \frac{K_5}{K_4 + \text{Reliability}}\right]$$

Figure 2-11 *EIGRP Wide Metrics Formula*

Latency is the total interface delay measured in picoseconds (10^{12}) instead of in microseconds (10^6). Figure 2-12 shows an updated formula that takes into account the conversions in latency and scalability.

$$\text{Wide Metric} = 65{,}536 * \left[\left(\frac{K_1 * 10^7}{\text{Min. Bandwidth}} + \frac{\frac{K_2 * 10^7}{\text{Min. Bandwidth}}}{256 - \text{Load}} + \frac{K_3 * \text{Latency}}{10^6} + K_6 * \text{Extended}\right) * \frac{K_5}{K_4 + \text{Reliability}}\right]$$

Figure 2-12 *EIGRP Wide Metrics Formula with Definitions*

The interface delay varies from router to router, depending on the following logic:

- If the interface's delay was specifically set, the value is converted to picoseconds. Interface delay is always configured in tens of microseconds and is multiplied by 10^7 for picosecond conversion.

- If the interface's bandwidth was specifically set, the interface delay is configured using the classic default delay, converted to picoseconds. The configured bandwidth is not considered when determining the interface delay. If delay was configured, this step is ignored.

- If the interface supports speeds of 1 Gbps or less and does not contain bandwidth or delay configuration, the delay is the classic default delay, converted to picoseconds.

- If the interface supports speeds over 1 Gbps and does not contain bandwidth or delay configuration, the interface delay is calculated by 10^{13}/interface bandwidth.

The EIGRP classic metrics exist only with EIGRP classic configuration, and EIGRP wide metrics exist only in EIGRP named mode. The metric style used by a router is identified with the command **show ip protocols**. If a K_6 metric is present, the router is using wide-style metrics.

Example 2-19 shows the commands to verify the operational mode of EIGRP on R1 and R2. It shows that R1 does not have a K_6 metric and is using EIGRP classic metrics. R2 has a K_6 metric and is using EIGRP wide metrics.

Example 2-19 *Verifying EIGRP Metric Style*

```
R1# show ip protocols | include AS|K
  EIGRP-IPv4 Protocol for AS(100)
    Metric weight K1=1, K2=0, K3=1, K4=0, K5=0

R2# show ip protocols | include AS|K
  EIGRP-IPv4 VR(EIGRP-NAMED) Address-Family Protocol for AS(100)
    Metric weight K1=1, K2=0, K3=1, K4=0, K5=0 K6=0
```

Metric Backward Compatibility

EIGRP wide metrics were designed with backward compatibility in mind. EIGRP wide metrics set K_1 and K_3 to a value of 1 and set K_2, K_4, K_5, and K_6 to 0, which allows backward compatibility because the K value metrics match with classic metrics. As long as K_1 through K_5 are the same and K_6 is not set, the two metric styles allow adjacency between routers.

EIGRP is able to detect when peering with a router is using classic metrics, and it *unscales* the metric by using the formula in Figure 2-13.

$$\text{Unscaled Bandwidth} = \left(\frac{\text{EIGRP Bandwidth} * \text{EIGRP Classic Scale}}{\text{Scaled Bandwidth}} \right)$$

Figure 2-13 *Formula for Calculating Unscaled EIGRP Metrics*

This conversion results in loss of clarity if routes pass through a mixture of classic metric and wide metric devices. An end result of this intended behavior is that paths learned from wide metric peers always look better than paths learned from classic peers. Using a mixture of classic metric and wide metric devices could lead to suboptimal routing, so it is best to keep all devices operating with the same metric style.

Interface Delay Settings

If you do not remember the delay values from Table 2-7, you can query the values dynamically by using the command **show interface** *interface-id*. The output displays the EIGRP interface delay, in microseconds, after the DLY field. Example 2-20 provides sample output of the command on R1 and R2. The output shows that both interfaces have a delay of 10 µs.

Example 2-20 *Verifying EIGRP Interface Delay*

```
R1# show interfaces gigabitEthernet 0/1 | i DLY
  MTU 1500 bytes, BW 1000000 Kbit/sec, DLY 10 usec,

R2# show interfaces gigabitEthernet 0/1 | i DLY
  MTU 1500 bytes, BW 1000000 Kbit/sec, DLY 10 usec,
```

EIGRP delay is set on an interface-by-interface basis, allowing for manipulation of traffic patterns flowing through a specific interface on a router. Delay is configured with the interface parameter command **delay** *tens-of-microseconds* under the interface.

Example 2-21 demonstrates the modification of the delay on R1 to 100, increasing the delay to 1000 µs on the link between R1 and R2. To ensure consistent routing, modify the delay on R2's Gi0/1 interface as well. Afterward, you can verify the change.

Example 2-21 *Configuring Interface Delay*

```
R1# configure terminal
R1(config)# interface gi0/1
R1(config-if)# delay 100
R1(config-if)# do show interface Gigabit0/1 | i DLY
  MTU 1500 bytes, BW 1000000 Kbit/sec, DLY 1000 usec,
```

NOTE Bandwidth modification with the interface parameter command **bandwidth** *bandwidth* has a similar effect on the metric calculation formula but can impact other routing protocols, such as OSPF, at the same time. Modifying the interface delay only impacts EIGRP.

Custom K Values

If the default metric calculations are insufficient, you can change them to modify the path metric formula. K values for the path metric formula are set with the command **metric weights** *TOS K*1 *K*2 *K*3 *K*4 *K*5 [*K*6] under the EIGRP process. *TOS* always has a value of 0, and *K*6 is used for named mode configurations.

To ensure consistent routing logic in an EIGRP autonomous system, the K values must match between EIGRP neighbors to form an adjacency and exchange routes. The K values are included as part of the EIGRP hello packet. The K values are displayed with the **show ip protocols** command, as demonstrated with the sample topology in Example 2-13. Notice that both routers are using the default K values, with R1 using classic metrics and R2 using wide metrics.

Load Balancing

EIGRP allows multiple successor routes (with the same metric) to be installed into the RIB. Installing multiple paths into the RIB for the same prefix is called *equal-cost multipathing* (*ECMP*). At the time of this writing, the default maximum ECMP setting is four routes. You change the default ECMP setting with the command **maximum-paths** *maximum-paths* under the EIGRP process in classic mode and under the topology base submode in named mode.

Example 2-22 shows the configuration for changing the maximum paths on R1 and R2 so that classic and named mode configurations are visible.

Example 2-22   *Changing the EIGRP Maximum Paths*

```
R1# show run | section router eigrp
router eigrp 100
 maximum-paths 6
 network 0.0.0.0

R2# show run | section router eigrp
router eigrp EIGRP-NAMED
 !
 address-family ipv4 unicast autonomous-system 100
  !
  topology base
   maximum-paths 6
  exit-af-topology
  network 0.0.0.0
  eigrp router-id 192.168.2.2
 exit-address-family
```

EIGRP supports unequal-cost load balancing, which allows installation of both successor routes and feasible successors into the EIGRP RIB. To use unequal-cost load balancing with EIGRP, change EIGRP's *variance multiplier*. The EIGRP *variance value* is the feasible distance (FD) for a route multiplied by the EIGRP variance multiplier. Any feasible successor's FD with a metric below the EIGRP variance value is installed into the RIB. EIGRP installs multiple routes where the FD for the routes is less than the EIGRP variance value up to the maximum number of ECMP routes, as discussed earlier.

Dividing the feasible successor metric by the successor route metric provides the variance multiplier. The variance multiplier is a whole number, and any remainders should always round up.

Using the topology shown in Figure 2-2 and output from the EIGRP topology table in Figure 2-3, the minimum EIGRP variance multiplier can be calculated so that the direct path from R1 to R4 can be installed into the RIB. The FD for the successor route is 3328, and the FD for the feasible successor is 5376. The formula provides a value of about 1.6 and is always rounded up to the nearest whole number to provide an EIGRP variance multiplier of 2. Figure 2-14 shows the calculation.

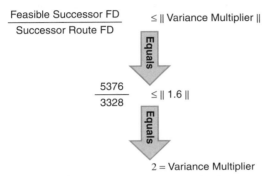

Figure 2-14   *EIGRP Variance Multiplier Formula*

The command **variance** *multiplier* configures the variance multiplier under the EIGRP process for classic configuration and under the topology base submode in named mode. Example 2-23 provides a sample configuration for each configuration mode.

Example 2-23   *Configuring EIGRP Variance*

```
R1 (Classic Configuration)
router eigrp 100
variance 2
network 0.0.0.0
```
```
R1 (Named Mode Configuration)
router eigrp EIGRP-NAMED
 !
address-family ipv4 unicast autonomous-system 100
  !
 topology base
  variance 2
 exit-af-topology
 network 0.0.0.0
 exit-address-family
```

Example 2-24 shows how to verify that both paths were installed into the RIB. Notice that the metrics for the paths are different. One path metric is 3328, and the other path metric is 5376. To see the traffic load-balancing ratios, you use the command **show ip route** *network*, as demonstrated in the second output. The load-balancing traffic share is highlighted.

Example 2-24   *Verifying Unequal-Cost Load Balancing*

```
R1# show ip route eigrp | begin Gateway
Gateway of last resort is not set


      10.0.0.0/8 is variably subnetted, 10 subnets, 2 masks
D        10.4.4.0/24 [90/5376] via 10.14.1.4, 00:00:03, GigabitEthernet0/2
                     [90/3328] via 10.13.1.3, 00:00:03, GigabitEthernet0/1
```
```
R1# show ip route 10.4.4.0
Routing entry for 10.4.4.0/24
  Known via "eigrp 100", distance 90, metric 3328, type internal
  Redistributing via eigrp 100
  Last update from 10.13.1.3 on GigabitEthernet0/1, 00:00:35 ago
  Routing Descriptor Blocks:
  * 10.14.1.4, from 10.14.1.4, 00:00:35 ago, via GigabitEthernet0/2
      Route metric is 5376, traffic share count is 149
      Total delay is 110 microseconds, minimum bandwidth is 1000000 Kbit
      Reliability 255/255, minimum MTU 1500 bytes
      Loading 1/255, Hops 1
    10.13.1.3, from 10.13.1.3, 00:00:35 ago, via GigabitEthernet0/1
      Route metric is 3328, traffic share count is 240
      Total delay is 30 microseconds, minimum bandwidth is 1000000 Kbit
      Reliability 254/255, minimum MTU 1500 bytes
      Loading 1/255, Hops 2
```

References in This Chapter

Edgeworth, Brad, Foss, Aaron, and Garza Rios, Ramiro, *IP Routing on Cisco IOS, IOS XE, and IOS XR*, Cisco Press, 2014.

RFC 7868, *Cisco's Enhanced Interior Gateway Routing Protocol (EIGRP)*, D. Savage, J. Ng, S. Moore, D. Slice, P. Paluch, and R. White. http://tools.ietf.org/html/rfc7868, May 2016.

Cisco, *Cisco IOS Software Configuration Guides*, http://www.cisco.com.

Exam Preparation Tasks

As mentioned in the section "How to Use This Book" in the Introduction, you have a couple choices for exam preparation: the exercises here, Chapter 24, "Final Preparation," and the exam simulation questions in the Pearson Test Prep software.

Review All Key Topics

Review the most important topics in this chapter, noted with the Key Topic icon in the outer margin of the page. Table 2-8 lists these key topics and the page number on which each is found.

Table 2-8   Key Topics

Key Topic Element	Description	Page Number
Paragraph	EIGRP terminology	76
Paragraph	Topology table	76
Table 2-3	EIGRP packet types	78
Paragraph	Forming EIGRP neighbors	79
Paragraph	Classic configuration mode	80
Paragraph	EIGRP named mode	80
Paragraph	Passive interfaces	88
Paragraph	Authentication	91
Paragraph	Path metric calculation	94
Paragraph	EIGRP attribute propagation	94
Figure 2-11	EIGRP wide metrics formula	97
Paragraph	Custom K values	100
Paragraph	Unequal-cost load balancing	100

Define Key Terms

Define the following key terms from this chapter and check your answers in the glossary:

autonomous system (AS), successor route, successor, feasible distance, reported distance, feasibility condition, feasible successor, topology table, classic EIGRP configuration mode, EIGRP named mode configuration, passive interface, K values, wide metrics, variance value

Use the Command Reference to Check Your Memory

The ENARSI 300-410 exam focuses on the practical, hands-on skills that networking professionals use. Therefore, you should be able to identify the commands needed to configure, verify, and troubleshoot the topics covered in this chapter.

This section includes the most important configuration and verification commands covered in this chapter. It might not be necessary to memorize the complete syntax of every command, but you should be able to remember the basic keywords that are needed.

To test your memory of the commands in Table 2-9, go to the companion website and download Appendix B, "Command Reference Exercises." Fill in the missing commands in the tables based on each command description. You can check your work by downloading Appendix C, "Command Reference Exercise Answer Key," from the companion website.

Table 2-9   Command Reference

Task	Command Syntax
Initialize EIGRP in a classic configuration.	**router eigrp** *as-number* **network** *network wildcard-mask*
Initialize EIGRP in a named mode configuration.	**router eigrp** *process-name* **address-family** {ipv4 | ipv6} {unicast | vrf *vrf-name*} **autonomous-system** *as-number* **network** *network wildcard-mask*
Define the EIGRP router ID.	**eigrp router-id** *router-id*
Configure an EIGRP-enabled interface to prevent neighbor adjacencies.	Classic: (EIGRP process) **passive-interface** *interface-id* Named mode: **af-interface** {default | *interface-id*} **passive-interface**
Configure a keychain for EIGRP MD5 authentication.	**key chain** *key-chain-name* **key** *key-number* **key-string** *password*
Configure MD5 authentication for an EIGRP interface.	Classic: (EIGRP process) **ip authentication key-chain eigrp** *as-number key-chain-name* **ip authentication mode eigrp** *as-number* **md5** Named mode: **af-interface** {default | *interface-id*} **authentication key-chain eigrp** *key-chain-name* **authentication mode md5**
Configure SHA authentication for EIGRP named mode interfaces.	Named mode: **af-interface** {default | *interface-id*} **authentication mode hmac-sha-256** *password*
Modify the interface delay for an interface.	**delay** *tens-of-microseconds*
Modify the EIGRP K values.	**metric weights** *TOS* K_1 K_2 K_3 K_4 K_5 [K_6]
Modify the default number of EIGRP maximum paths that can be installed into the RIB.	**maximum-paths** *maximum-paths*
Modify the EIGRP variance multiplier for unequal-cost load balancing.	**variance** *multiplier*
Display the EIGRP-enabled interfaces.	**show ip eigrp interface** [{*interface-id* [detail] | detail}]
Display the EIGRP topology table.	**show ip eigrp topology** [all-links]
Display the configured EIGRP keychains and passwords.	**show key chain**
Display the IP routing protocol information configured on the router.	**show ip protocols**

## CHAPTER 3

Advanced EIGRP

This chapter covers the following topics:

- **Failure Detection and Timers:** This section explains how EIGRP detects the absence of a neighbor and examines the convergence process.

- **Route Summarization:** This section explains the logic and configuration of route summarization on a router.

- **WAN Considerations:** This section reviews common design considerations related to using EIGRP in a WAN.

- **Route Manipulation:** This section explains techniques for manipulating routes.

This chapter explores the mechanisms used by EIGRP during path computations for alternate routes due to network events. It also covers design concepts for accelerating convergence and increasing the scale of an EIGRP network. The last portion of the chapter reviews techniques for manipulating routes.

"Do I Know This Already?" Quiz

The "Do I Know This Already?" quiz allows you to assess whether you should read this entire chapter thoroughly or jump to the "Exam Preparation Tasks" section. If you are in doubt about your answers to these questions or your own assessment of your knowledge of the topics, read the entire chapter. Table 3-1 lists the major headings in this chapter and their corresponding "Do I Know This Already?" quiz questions. You can find the answers in Appendix A, "Answers to the 'Do I Know This Already?' Quiz Questions."

Table 3-1 "Do I Know This Already?" Foundation Topics Section-to-Question Mapping

Foundation Topics Section	Questions
Failure Detection and Timers	1–4
Route Summarization	5–6
WAN Considerations	7
Route Manipulation	8

CAUTION   The goal of self-assessment is to gauge your mastery of the topics in this chapter. If you do not know the answer to a question or are only partially sure of the answer, you should mark that question as wrong for purposes of self-assessment. Giving yourself credit for an answer that you correctly guess skews your self-assessment results and might provide you with a false sense of security.

1. What is the default EIGRP hello timer for a high-speed interface?
   a. 1 second
   b. 5 seconds
   c. 10 seconds
   d. 20 seconds
   e. 30 seconds
   f. 60 seconds
2. What is the default EIGRP hello timer for a low-speed interface?
   a. 1 second
   b. 5 seconds
   c. 10 seconds
   d. 20 seconds
   e. 30 seconds
   f. 60 seconds
3. When a path is identified using EIGRP and in a stable fashion, the route is considered
   _____.
   a. passive
   b. dead
   c. active
   d. alive
4. How does an EIGRP router indicate that a path computation is required for a specific
   route?
   a. EIGRP sends out an EIGRP update packet with the topology change notification
      flag set.
   b. EIGRP sends out an EIGRP update packet with a metric value of zero.
   c. EIGRP sends out an EIGRP query with the delay set to infinity.
   d. EIGRP sends a route withdrawal, notifying other neighbors to remove the route
      from the topology table.
5. True or false: EIGRP summarization is performed with the command **summary-
   aggregate** *network subnet-mask* under the EIGRP process for classic mode
   configuration.
   a. True
   b. False
6. True or false: EIGRP automatic summarization is enabled by default and must be disabled to prevent issues with networks that cross classful network boundaries.
   a. True
   b. False
7. True or false: EIGRP stub site functions can be deployed at all branch sites, regardless
   of whether downstream EIGRP routers are present.
   a. True
   b. False

8. How does an EIGRP offset list manipulate a route?

    a. By completely removing a set of specific routes

    b. By reducing the total path metric to a more preferred value

    c. By adding the total path metric to a specific set of routes

    d. By adding delay to the path metric for a specific set of routes

Foundation Topics

Failure Detection and Timers

A secondary function of EIGRP *hello packets* is to ensure that EIGRP neighbors are still healthy and available. EIGRP hello packets are sent out at intervals according to the *hello timer*. The default EIGRP hello timer is 5 seconds, but EIGRP uses 60 seconds on slow-speed interfaces (T1 or lower).

EIGRP uses a second timer, called the *hold timer*, which measures the amount of time EIGRP deems the router to be reachable and functioning. The hold time value defaults to three times the hello interval. The default value is 15 seconds (or 180 seconds for slow-speed interfaces). The hold time decrements, and upon receipt of a hello packet, the hold time resets and restarts the countdown. If the hold time reaches 0, EIGRP declares the neighbor unreachable and notifies the diffusing update algorithm (DUAL) of a topology change.

The hello timer is modified with the interface parameter command **ip hello-interval eigrp** *as-number seconds*, and the hold timer is modified with the interface parameter command **ip hold-time eigrp** *as-number seconds* when using EIGRP classic configuration mode.

For named mode configurations, the commands are placed under the **af-interface default** submode or the **af-interface** *interface-id* submode. The command **hello-interval** *seconds* modifies the hello timer, and the command **hold-time** *seconds* modifies the hold timer when using named mode configuration.

Example 3-1 shows examples of changing the EIGRP hello interval to 3 seconds and the hold time to 15 seconds for R1 (in classic mode) and R2 (in named mode).

Example 3-1   *Verifying EIGRP Hello and Hold Timer Values*

```
R1 (Classic Mode Configuration)
interface GigabitEthernet0/1
 ip address 10.12.1.1 255.255.255.0
 ip hello-interval eigrp 100 3
 ip hold-time eigrp 100 15
```

```
R2 (Named Mode Configuration)
router eigrp EIGRP-NAMED
 address-family ipv4 unicast autonomous-system 100
  !
 af-interface default
```

```
    hello-interval 3
    hold-time 15
  exit-af-interface
  !
  topology base
  exit-af-topology
  network 0.0.0.0
exit-address-family
```

The EIGRP hello and hold timers are verified by viewing the EIGRP interfaces with the command **show ip eigrp interfaces detail** [*interface-id*], as demonstrated in the following snippet:

```
R1# show ip eigrp interfaces detail gi0/1 | I Hello|Hold
  Hello-interval is 3, Hold-time is 15
  Hello's sent/expedited: 18348/5
```

NOTE EIGRP neighbors can still form an adjacency if the timers do not match, but the hellos must be received before the hold time reaches zero; that is, the hello interval must be less than the hold time.

Convergence

When a link fails, and the interface protocol moves to a down state, any neighbor attached to that interface moves to a down state, too. When an EIGRP neighbor moves to a down state, path recomputation must occur for any prefix where that EIGRP neighbor was a successor (that is, an upstream router).

When EIGRP detects that it has lost its successor for a path, the feasible successor, if one exists, instantly becomes the successor route, providing a backup route. The router sends out an update packet for that path because of the new EIGRP path metrics. Downstream routers run their own DUAL algorithm for any affected prefixes to account for the new EIGRP metrics. It is possible for a change of the successor route or feasible successor to occur upon receipt of new EIGRP metrics from a successor router for a prefix.

Figure 3-1 demonstrates such a scenario, where the link between R1 and R3 fails.

When the link fails, R3 installs the feasible successor path advertised from R2 as the successor route. R3 sends an update packet with a new reported distance (RD) of 19 for the 10.1.1.0/24 prefix. R5 receives the update packet from R3 and calculates a feasible distance (FD) of 29 for the R3ÐR2ÐR1 path to 10.1.1.0/24. R5 compares that path to the one received from R4, which has a path metric of 25. R5 chooses the path through R4 as the successor route.

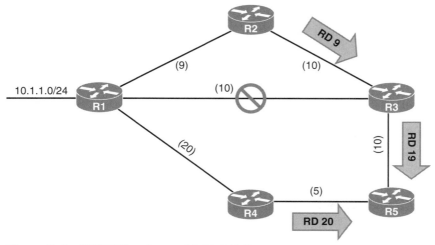

Figure 3-1 *EIGRP Topology with Link Failure*

Example 3-2 provides simulated output of R5's EIGRP topology for the 10.1.1.0/24 prefix after the R1–R3 link fails.

Example 3-2 *Simulated EIGRP Topology for the 10.1.1.0/24 Network*

```
R5# show ip eigrp topology 10.1.1.0/24
EIGRP-IPv4 Topology Entry for AS(100)/ID(192.168.5.5) for 10.1.1.0/24
  State is Passive, Query origin flag is 1, 1 Successor(s), FD is 25
  Descriptor Blocks:
 *10.45.1.4 (GigabitEthernet0/2), from 10.45.1.4, Send flag is 0x0
     Composite metric is (25/20), route is Internal
     Vector metric:
       Hop count is 2
       Originating router is 192.168.1.1
  10.35.1.3 (GigabitEthernet0/1), from 10.35.1.3, Send flag is 0x0
     Composite metric is (29/19), route is Internal
     Vector metric:
       Hop count is 3
       Originating router is 192.168.1.1
```

If a feasible successor is not available for the prefix, DUAL must perform a new route calculation. The route state changes from passive (P) to active (A) in the EIGRP topology table.

The router detecting the topology change sends out query packets to EIGRP neighbors for the route. A query packet includes the network prefix with the delay set to infinity so that other routers are aware that it is now active. When the router sends EIGRP query packets, it sets the reply status flag for each neighbor on a per-prefix basis. The router tracks the reply status for each of the EIGRP query packets on a per-prefix basis.

Upon receipt of a query packet, an EIGRP router does one of the following:

- It replies to the query that the router does not have a route to the prefix.

- If the query came from the successor for the route, the receiving router detects the delay set for infinity, sets the prefix as active in the EIGRP topology, and sends out a query packet to all downstream EIGRP neighbors for that route.

- If the query did not come from the successor for that route, it detects that the delay is set for infinity but ignores it because it did not come from the successor. The receiving router replies with the EIGRP attributes for that route.

The query process continues from router to router until a query reaches a query boundary. A query boundary is established when a router does not mark the prefix as active, meaning that it responds to a query as follows:

- It says it does not have a route to the prefix.

- It replies with EIGRP attributes because the query did not come from the successor.

When a router receives a reply for every downstream query that was sent out, it completes the DUAL, changes the route to passive, and sends a reply packet to any upstream routers that sent a query packet to it. Upon receiving the reply packet for a prefix, the router makes note of the reply packet for that neighbor and prefix. The reply process continues upstream for the queries until the first router's queries are received.

Figure 3-2 shows a topology where the link between R1 and R2 failed, and R2 has generated queries for the 10.1.1.0/24 network.

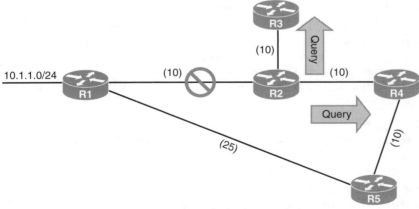

Figure 3-2 *Generation of Query Packets on R2*

For the example shown in Figure 3-2, the following steps are processed, in order, from the perspective of R2 calculating a new route to the 10.1.1.0/24 network:

Step 1.   R2 detects the link failure. R2 does not have a feasible successor for the route, sets the 10.1.1.0/24 prefix as active, and sends queries to R3 and R4.

Step 2. R3 receives the query from R2 and processes the Delay field that is set to infinity. R3 does not have any other EIGRP neighbors and sends a reply to R2, saying that a route does not exist.

R4 receives the query from R2 and processes the Delay field that is set to infinity. Because the query was received by the successor, and a feasible successor for the prefix does not exist, R4 marks the route as active and sends a query to R5.

Step 3. R5 receives the query from R4 and detects that the Delay field is set to infinity. Because the query was received by a nonsuccessor, and a successor exists on a different interface, R5 sends a reply for the 10.1.1.0/24 network to R4 with the appropriate EIGRP attributes.

Step 4. R4 receives R5's reply, acknowledges the packet, and computes a new path. Because this is the last outstanding query packet on R4, R4 sets the prefix as passive. With all queries satisfied, R4 responds to R2's query with the new EIGRP metrics.

Step 5. R2 receives R4's reply, acknowledges the packet, and computes a new path. Because this is the last outstanding query packet on R2, R2 sets the prefix as passive.

Stuck in Active

DUAL is very efficient at finding loop-free paths quickly, and it normally finds backup paths in seconds. Occasionally, an EIGRP query is delayed because of packet loss, slow neighbors, or a large hop count. EIGRP maintains a timer, known as the active timer, which has a default value of 3 minutes (180 seconds). EIGRP waits half of the active timer value (90 seconds) for a reply. If the router does not receive a response within 90 seconds, the originating router sends a *stuck in active (SIA)* query to EIGRP neighbors that did not respond.

Upon receipt of an SIA query, the router should respond within 90 seconds with an SIA reply. An SIA reply contains the route information or provides information on the query process itself. If a router fails to respond to an SIA query by the time the active timer expires, EIGRP deems the router SIA. If the SIA state is declared for a neighbor, DUAL deletes all routes from that neighbor, treating the situation as if the neighbor responded with unreachable messages for all routes.

> **NOTE**   Earlier versions of IOS terminated EIGRP neighbor sessions with routers that never replied to an SIA query.

You can troubleshoot active EIGRP prefixes only when the router is waiting for a reply. You show active queries with the command **show ip eigrp topology**.

To demonstrate the SIA process, Figure 3-3 illustrates a scenario in which the link between R1 and R2 failed. R2 sends out queries to R4 and R3. R4 sends a reply back to R2, and R3 sends a query on to R5.

A network engineer who sees the syslog message and runs the **show ip eigrp topology active** command on R2 gets the output shown in Example 3-3. The r next to the peer's IP address (10.23.1.3) indicates that R2 is still waiting on the reply from R3 and that R4 responded. The command is then executed on R3, and R3 indicates that it is waiting on a response from R5. When you execute the command on R5, you do not see any active prefixes, which implies that R5 never received a query from R3. R3's query could have been dropped on the radio tower connection.

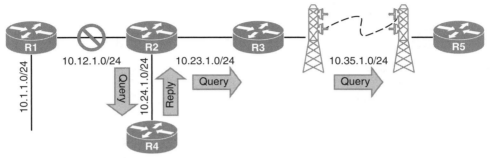

Figure 3-3 *EIGRP SIA Topology*

Example 3-3 *Output for SIA Timers*

```
R2# show ip eigrp topology active
Codes: P - Passive, A - Active, U - Update, Q - Query, R - Reply,
       r - Reply status


A 10.1.1.0/24, 0 successors, FD is 512640000, Q
    1 replies, active 00:00:01, query-origin: Local origin
        via 10.24.1.4 (Infinity/Infinity), GigabitEthernet 0/0
    1 replies, active 00:00:01, query-origin: Local origin
        via 10.23.1.3 (Infinity/Infinity), r, GigabitEthernet 0/1
    Remaining replies:
        via 10.23.1.3, r, GigabitEthernet 0/1
```

The active timer is set to 3 minutes by default. The active timer can be disabled or modified with the command **timers active-time** {**disabled** | *1-65535-minutes*} under the EIGRP process. With classic configuration mode, the command runs directly under the EIGRP process, and with named mode configuration, the command runs under the topology base. Example 3-4 demonstrates the modification of SIA to 2 minutes for R1 in classic mode and R2 in named mode.

Example 3-4 *Configuring SIA Timers*

```
R1(config)# router eigrp 100
R1(config-router)# timers active-time 2

R2(config)# router eigrp EIGRP-NAMED
R2(config-router)# address-family ipv4 unicast autonomous-system 100
R2(config-router-af)# topology base
R2(config-router-af-topology)# timers active-time 2
```

You can see the active timer by examining the IP protocols on a router with the command **show ip protocols**. Filtering with the keyword **Active** streamlines the information, as demonstrated in the following snippet, where you see that R2's SIA timer is set to 2 minutes:

```
R2# show ip protocols | include Active
    Active Timer: 2 min
```

The SIA query now occurs after 1 minute, which is half of the configured SIA timer.

Route Summarization

EIGRP works well with minimal optimization. Scalability of an EIGRP autonomous system depends on route *summarization*. As the size of an EIGRP autonomous system increases, convergence may take longer. Scaling an EIGRP topology depends on summarizing routes in a hierarchical fashion. Figure 3-4 shows summarization occurring at the access, distribution, and core layers of the network topology. In addition to shrinking the routing tables of all the routers, route summarization creates a query boundary and shrinks the query domain when a route goes active during convergence, thereby reducing SIA scenarios.

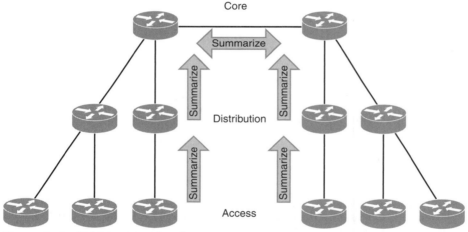

Figure 3-4   *EIGRP Hierarchical Summarization*

> **NOTE**   Route summarization on this scale requires hierarchical deployment of an IP addressing scheme.

Interface-Specific Summarization

EIGRP summarizes routes on a per-interface basis. Summarization is enabled by configuring a summary route address range under an EIGRP interface, where all the routes that fall within the summary address range are referred to as *component routes*. With summarization enabled, the component routes are suppressed (that is, not advertised), and only the summary route is advertised. The summary route is not advertised until a component route matches it. Interface-specific summarization can be performed in any portion of the network topology.

Figure 3-5 illustrates the concept of EIGRP summarization. Without summarization, R2 advertises the 172.16.1.0/24, 172.16.3.0/24, 172.16.12.0/24, and 172.16.23.0/24 routes toward R4. R2 summarizes these network prefixes to the 172.16.0.0/16 summary route so that only one advertisement is sent to R4.

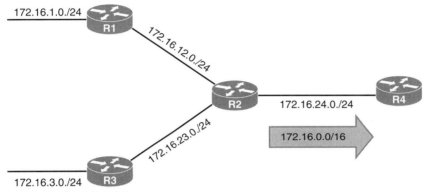

Figure 3-5 *EIGRP Summarization*

For classic EIGRP configuration mode, you use the interface parameter command **ip summary-address** *eigrp as-number network subnet-mask* [**leak-map** *route-map-name*] to place an EIGRP summary route on an interface. You perform summary route configuration for named mode under **af-interface** *interface-id*, using the command **summary-address** *network subnet-mask* [**leak-map** *route-map-name*].

The **leak-map** option allows the advertisement of the routes identified in the route map. Because suppression is avoided, the routes are considered leaked because they are advertised along with the summary aggregate. This allows for the use of longest-match routing to influence traffic patterns while suppressing most of the prefixes.

Example 3-5 shows R4's routing table before summarization is configured on R2. Notice that only /24 networks exist in the routing table.

Example 3-5 *R4's Routing Table Before Summarization*

```
R4# show ip route eigrp | begin Gateway
Gateway of last resort is not set

      172.16.0.0/16 is variably subnetted, 6 subnets, 2 masks
D        172.16.1.0/24 [90/3328] via 172.16.24.2, 1d01h, GigabitEthernet0/2
D        172.16.3.0/24 [90/3328] via 172.16.24.2, 1d01h, GigabitEthernet0/2
D        172.16.12.0/24 [90/3072] via 172.16.24.2, 1d01h, GigabitEthernet0/2
D        172.16.23.0/24 [90/3072] via 172.16.24.2, 1d01h, GigabitEthernet0/2
```

Example 3-6 shows the configuration for the 172.16.0.0/16 summary route that is advertised toward R4 out the Gi0/4 interface. Summary routes are always advertised based on the outgoing interface. The **af-interface default** option cannot be used with the **summary-address** command. It requires the use of a specific interface.

Example 3-6   *Configuring EIGRP Summarization*

```
R2 (Classic Configuration)
interface gi0/4
 ip summary-address eigrp 100 172.16.0.0/16
```
```
R2 (Named Mode Configuration)
router eigrp EIGRP-NAMED
 address-family ipv4 unicast autonomous-system 100
  af-interface GigabitEthernet0/4
   summary-address 172.16.0.0 255.255.0.0
```

Example 3-7 shows R4's routing table after summarization is enabled on R2. The number of EIGRP routes has been drastically reduced, thereby reducing consumption of CPU and memory resources. Notice that all the component routes are condensed into the 172.16.0.0/16 summary route.

Example 3-7   *R4's Routing Table After Summarization*

```
R4# show ip route eigrp | begin Gateway
Gateway of last resort is not set

     172.16.0.0/16 is variably subnetted, 3 subnets, 3 masks
D       172.16.0.0/16 [90/3072] via 172.16.24.2, 00:00:24, GigabitEthernet0/2
```

NOTE   Advertising a default route into EIGRP requires the summarization syntax described earlier in this section, except that the network and subnet-mask uses 0.0.0.0 0.0.0.0 (commonly referred to as *double quad zeros*).

Summary Discard Routes

EIGRP installs a discard route on the summarizing routers as a routing loop-prevention mechanism. A discard route is a route that matches the summary route with the destination to Null0. This prevents routing loops where portions of the summarized network range do not have a more specific entry in the Routing Information Base (RIB) on the summarizing router. The AD for the Null0 route is 5 by default.

You view the discard route by using the **show ip route** *network subnet-mask* command, as shown in Example 3-8. Notice that the AD is set to 5, and it is connected to Null0, which means that packets are discarded if a longest match is not made.

Example 3-8 *Verifying an AD Change for a Summary Route AD*

```
R2# show ip route 172.16.0.0 255.255.0.0 | include entry|distance|via
Routing entry for 172.16.0.0/16
  Known via "eigrp 100", distance 5, metric 10240, type internal
  Redistributing via eigrp 100
  * directly connected, via Null0
```

Summarization Metrics

The summarizing router uses the lowest metric of the component routes in the summary route. The path metric for the summary route is based on the path attributes of the path with the lowest metric. EIGRP path attributes such as total delay and minimum bandwidth are inserted into the summary route so that downstream routers can calculate the correct path metric for the summary route.

In Figure 3-6, R2 has a path metric of 3072 for the 172.16.1.0/24 route and a path metric of 3328 for the 172.16.3.0/24 route. The 172.16.0.0/16 summary route is advertised with the path metric 3072 and the EIGRP path attributes received by R2 from R1.

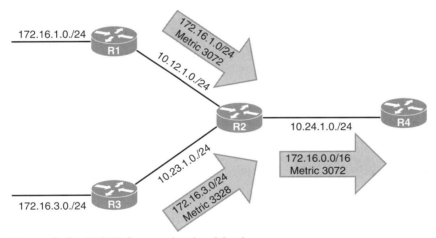

Figure 3-6 *EIGRP Summarization Metrics*

Every time a matching component route for the summary route is added or removed, EIGRP must verify that the summary route is still using the attributes from the path with the lowest metric. If it is not, a new summary route is advertised with updated EIGRP attributes, and downstream routes must run the DUAL again. The summary route hides the smaller prefixes from downstream routers, but downstream routers are still burdened with processing updates to the summary route.

The fluctuation in the path metric is resolved by statically setting the metric on the summary route with the command **summary-metric** *network {/prefix-length | subnet-mask} bandwidth delay reliability load MTU*. Bandwidth is in kilobits per second (Kbps), delay is in 10-microsecond (µs) units, reliability and load are values between 1 and 255, and the maximum transmission unit (MTU) is the MTU for the interface.

Automatic Summarization

EIGRP supports automatic summarization, automatically summarizing network advertisements when they cross a classful network boundary. Figure 3-7 shows automatic summarization for the 10.1.1.0/24 route on R2 and the 10.5.5.0/24 network on R4. R2 and R4 only advertise the classful network 10.0.0.0/8 toward R3.

Figure 3-7 *Problems with EIGRP Automatic Summarization*

Example 3-9 shows the routing table for R3. Notice that there are no routes for the 10.1.1.0/24 or 10.5.5.0/24 networks; there is only a route for 10.0.0.0/8 with next hops of R2 and R4. Traffic sent to either network could be sent out the wrong interface. This problem affects network traffic traveling across the network in addition to traffic originating from R3.

Example 3-9 *Path Selection Problems on R3 with Automatic Summarization*

```
R3# show ip route eigrp | begin Gateway
Gateway of last resort is not set

D     10.0.0.0/8 [90/3072] via 172.16.34.4, 00:08:07, GigabitEthernet0/0
                 [90/3072] via 172.16.23.2, 00:08:07, GigabitEthernet0/1
```

Example 3-10 displays similar behavior for the 172.16.23.0/24 and 172.16.34.0/24 networks, as they are advertised as 172.16.0.0/16 networks from R2 to R1. The identical advertisement occurs from R4 to R5.

Example 3-10 *Automatic Summarization on R1 and R5*

```
R1# show ip route eigrp | begin Gateway
Gateway of last resort is not set

D     172.16.0.0/16 [90/3072] via 10.12.1.2, 00:09:50, GigabitEthernet0/0
```
```
R5# show ip route eigrp | begin Gateway
Gateway of last resort is not set

D     172.16.0.0/16 [90/3072] via 10.45.1.4, 00:09:50, GigabitEthernet0/1
```

Current releases of IOS XE disable EIGRP classful network automatic summarization by default. You enable automatic summarization by using the command **auto-summary** under the EIGRP process for classic configuration mode or by using the command **topology base** for named mode configuration. To disable automatic summarization, use the command **no auto-summary**.

WAN Considerations

EIGRP does not change behavior based on the media type of an interface. Serial and Ethernet interfaces are treated the same. Some WAN topologies may require special consideration for bandwidth utilization, split horizon, or next-hop self. The following sections explain each scenario in more detail.

EIGRP Stub Router

A proper network design provides redundancy where dictated by business requirements to ensure that a remote location always maintains network connectivity. To overcome single points of failure, you can add additional routers at each site, add redundant circuits (possibly with different service providers), use different routing protocols, or use virtual private network (VPN) tunnels across the Internet for backup transport.

Figure 3-8 shows a topology with R1 and R2 providing connectivity at two key data center locations. R1 and R2 have three WAN circuits and a LAN interface. The first circuit is a 10 Gbps dedicated point-to-point circuit (10.12.1.0/24), the second circuit is a T1 (1.5 Mbps) serial link to R3, and the third circuit is an Internet connection that R1 and R2 use to maintain backup connectivity to each other through a backup VPN tunnel. EIGRP is not enabled across the VPN tunnel, and traffic should be routed across the backup VPN tunnel using a simple static route for the 10.0.0.0/8 route if the 10 Gbps circuit fails. R1 advertises the 10.1.1.0/24 prefix directly to R2 and R3, and R2 advertises the 10.2.2.0/24 prefix to R1 and R3.

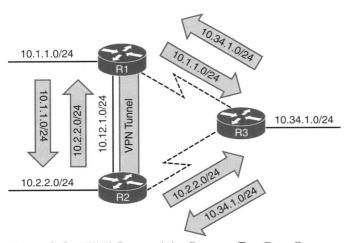

Figure 3-8 *WAN Connectivity Between Two Data Centers*

NOTE The serial WAN link network advertisements are not illustrated in Figures 3-8 to 3-12, which instead focus on advertisement of routes that are multiple hops away. In addition, the 10.1.1.0/24 and 10.2.2.0/24 network advertisements from R3 to R1 and R2 are not shown as they are less preferred to the path across the 10 Gbps circuit.

Proper network design considers traffic patterns during normal operations and throughout various failure scenarios to prevent suboptimal routing or routing loops. Figure 3-9 demonstrates the failure of the 10 Gbps network link between R1 and R2. This leaves R1 and R2 with the circuit to the Internet for the VPN tunnel and the T1 serial links to R3. R3 continues to advertise the 10.1.1.0/24 prefix to R2 even though the design wants R1's traffic to take the VPN tunnel to reach R2. This is because the 10.1.1.0/24 route learned via EIGRP is a longer match than the static route to the 10.0.0.0/8 route via the VPN tunnel. The scenario happens in the same fashion with 10.2.2.0/24 traffic transiting R3 instead of going across the VPN tunnel.

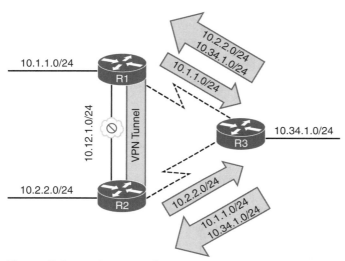

Figure 3-9 *Unintentional Transit Branch Routing*

The EIGRP stub functionality prevents scenarios like this from happening and allows an EIGRP router to conserve router resources. An *EIGRP stub router* does not advertise routes that it learns from other EIGRP peers. By default, EIGRP stubs advertise only connected and summary routes, but they can be configured so that they only receive routes or advertise any combination of redistributed routes, connected routes, or summary routes.

In Figure 3-10, R3 was configured as a stub router, and the 10 Gbps link between R1 and R2 fails. Traffic between R1 and R2 uses the backup VPN tunnel and does not traverse R3's T1 circuits because R3 is only advertising its connected networks (10.34.1.0/24).

The EIGRP stub router announces itself as a stub within the EIGRP hello packet. Neighboring routers detect the stub field and update the EIGRP neighbor table to reflect the router's stub status. If a route goes active, EIGRP does not send EIGRP queries to an EIGRP stub router. This provides faster convergence within an EIGRP autonomous system because it decreases the size of the query domain for that prefix.

You configure a stub router by placing the command **eigrp stub** {**connected** | **receive-only** | **redistributed** | **static** | **summary**} under the EIGRP process for classic configuration and under the address family for named mode configuration. Example 3-11 demonstrates the stub configuration for EIGRP classic mode and named mode.

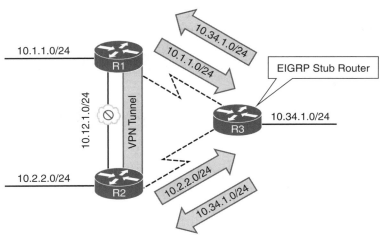

Figure 3-10 *Stopping Transit Branch Routing with an EIGRP Stub Router*

Example 3-11 *Configuring EIGRP Stub Routers*

```
R3 (Classic Configuration)
router eigrp 100
  network 0.0.0.0 255.255.255.255
  eigrp stub
```
```
R3 (Named Mode Configuration)
router eigrp EIGRP-NAMED
 address-family ipv4 unicast autonomous-system 100
  eigrp stub
```

NOTE   The **receive-only** option cannot be combined with other EIGRP stub options as it does not advertise any networks to its neighbors. The network design should be given special consideration to ensure bidirectional connectivity for any networks connected to an EIGRP router with the **receive-only** stub option to ensure that routers know how to send return traffic.

Stub Site Functions

A common problem with EIGRP stub routers is forgetting that they do not advertise EIGRP routes that they learn from another peer. Figure 3-11 expands on the previous topology and adds the R4 router to the branch network; R4 is attached to R3.

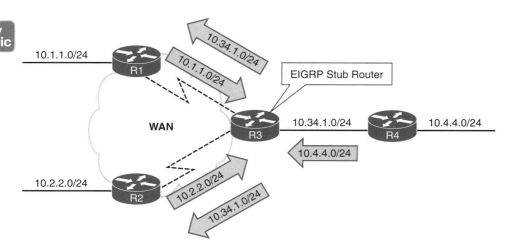

Figure 3-11   *Problems with Downstream Routing and EIGRP Stub Routers*

Say that a junior network engineer recently learned about the EIGRP stub function and configured it on R3 to prevent transient routing and reduce the size of the query domain. The users attached to R4's 10.4.4.0/24 network start to complain because they cannot access any resources attached to R1 and R2; however, they can still communicate with devices attached to R3.

Example 3-12 demonstrates the EIGRP learned routes on R1 and R4. R1 is missing the 10.4.4.0/24 prefix, and R4 is missing the 10.1.1.0/24 prefix. Both prefixes are missing because R3 is an EIGRP stub router.

Example 3-12   *Missing Routes Because of EIGRP Stub Routing*

```
R1# show ip route eigrp | begin Gateway
Gateway of last resort is not set

      10.0.0.0/8 is variably subnetted, 9 subnets, 2 masks
D        10.34.1.0/24 [90/61440] via 10.13.1.3, 00:20:26, GigabitEthernet0/5
```

```
R4# show ip route eigrp | begin Gateway
Gateway of last resort is not set

      10.0.0.0/8 is variably subnetted, 6 subnets, 2 masks
! These networks are the serial links directly attached to R3
D        10.13.1.0/24 [90/61440] via 10.34.1.3, 00:19:39, GigabitEthernet0/1
D        10.23.1.0/24 [90/61440] via 10.34.1.3, 00:19:39, GigabitEthernet0/1
```

The EIGRP stub site feature builds on EIGRP stub capabilities that allow a router to advertise itself as a stub to peers only on the specified WAN interfaces but allow it to exchange routes learned on LAN interfaces. EIGRP stub sites provide the following key benefits:

■ EIGRP neighbors on WAN links do not send EIGRP queries to the remote site when a route becomes active.

- The EIGRP stub site feature allows downstream routers to receive and advertise network prefixes across the WAN.

- The EIGRP stub site feature prevents the *EIGRP stub site route* from being a transit site.

The EIGRP stub site feature works by identifying the WAN interfaces and then setting an EIGRP stub site identifier. Routes received from a peer on the WAN interface are tagged with an EIGRP stub site identifier attribute. When EIGRP advertises network prefixes out a WAN-identified interface, it checks for an EIGRP stub site identifier. If such an identifier is found, the route is not advertised; if an EIGRP stub site identifier is not found, the route is advertised.

Figure 3-12 illustrates the concept further, with R3 being configured as a stub site router and the serial links configured as EIGRP WAN interfaces. It shows this process:

Step 1. R1 advertises the 10.1.1.0/24 route to R3, and the 10.1.1.0/24 route is received on R3's WAN interface. R3 is then able to advertise that prefix to the downstream router R4.

Step 2. R2 advertises the 10.2.2.0/24 route to R3, and the 10.2.2.0/24 route is received on R3's other WAN interface. R3 is then able to advertise that prefix to the downstream router R4.

Step 3. R4 advertises the 10.4.4.0/24 network to R3. R3 checks the 10.4.4.0/24 route for the EIGRP stub site attribute before advertising that prefix out either WAN interface. R3 is able to advertise the prefix to R1 and R2 because it does not contain an EIGRP stub site identifier attribute.

Notice that R3 does not advertise the 10.1.1.0/24 prefix to R2 and that it does not advertise the 10.2.2.0/24 prefix to R1. This is because the EIGRP stub site attribute was added upon receipt of the prefix and blocked during advertisement out the other WAN interface.

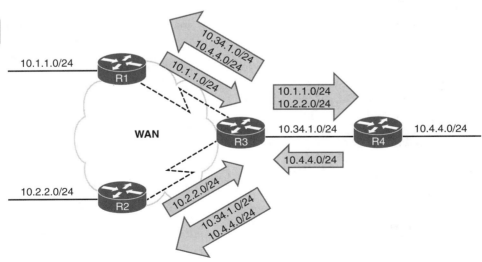

Figure 3-12 *EIGRP Stub Site Feature*

The EIGRP stub site function is available only in EIGRP named mode configuration. The WAN interfaces are identified underneath the **af-interface** *interface-id* hierarchy and use the **stub-site wan-interface** command. The stub site function and identifier are enabled with the command **eigrp stub-site** *as-number:identifier*. The *as-number:identifier* must remain the same for all devices in a site. Upon associating an interface to the EIGRP stub site, the router resets the EIGRP neighbor for that interface.

Example 3-13 provides the EIGRP stub site configuration for R3 for both serial interfaces.

Example 3-13 *EIGRP Stub Site Configuration*

```
R3
router eigrp EIGRP-NAMED
 address-family ipv4 unicast autonomous-system 100
  af-interface Serial1/0
   stub-site wan-interface
  exit-af-interface
  !
  af-interface Serial1/1
   stub-site wan-interface
  exit-af-interface
  eigrp stub-site 100:1
 exit-address-family
```

Example 3-14 shows how to verify that the 10.1.1.0/24 route learned from R3's serial interfaces is tagged with the EIGRP stub site attribute. R4 was selected for this output to demonstrate that the attribute is passed to other downstream routers.

Example 3-14 *Verifying Routes Learned from the WAN Interface*

```
R4# show ip eigrp topology 10.1.1.0/24
EIGRP-IPv4 VR(EIGRP-NAMED) Topology Entry for AS(100)/ID(192.168.4.4) for
10.1.1.0/24
  State is Passive, Query origin flag is 1, 1 Successor(s), FD is 8519680, RIB is
66560
  Descriptor Blocks:
  10.34.1.3 (GigabitEthernet0/1), from 10.34.1.3, Send flag is 0x0
      Composite metric is (8519680/7864320), route is Internal
      Vector metric:
        Minimum bandwidth is 100000 Kbit
        Total delay is 30000000 picoseconds
        Reliability is 255/255
        Load is 1/255
        Minimum MTU is 1500
        Hop count is 2
        Originating router is 192.168.1.1
      Extended Community: StubSite:100:1
```

A major benefit to the EIGRP stub site feature is that the stub functionality can be passed to a branch site that has multiple edge routers. As long as each router is configured with the EIGRP stub site feature and maintains the same stub site identifier, the site does not become a transit routing site; however, it still allows for all the routes to be easily advertised to other routers in the EIGRP autonomous system.

Example 3-15 shows how to verify that R1 recognizes R3 as an EIGRP stub router and does not send it any queries when a route becomes active.

Example 3-15 *EIGRP Stub Router Flags*

```
R1# show ip eigrp neighbors detail Serial1/0
EIGRP-IPv4 VR(EIGRP-NAMED) Address-Family Neighbors for AS(100)
H   Address              Interface          Hold Uptime   SRTT   RTO   Q    Seq
                                            (sec)         (ms)         Cnt  Num
1   10.13.1.3            Serial             11 00:04:39   13     100   0    71
    Time since Restart 00:04:35
    Version 23.0/2.0, Retrans: 0, Retries: 0, Prefixes: 3
    Topology-ids from peer - 0
    Topologies advertised to peer:    base

    Stub Peer Advertising (CONNECTED STATIC SUMMARY REDISTRIBUTED ) Routes
    Suppressing queries
Max Nbrs: 0, Current Nbrs: 0
```

NOTE   Although not required, configuring the EIGRP stub site feature on all branch routers keeps the configuration consistent and makes possible additional nondisruptive deployment of routers at that site in the future. The same *as-number:identifier* could be used for all of the site's WAN interfaces because those networks would never be advertised to other EIGRP stub sites, with the exception of tunnels or backdoor network links, which helps prevent suboptimal routing.

IP Bandwidth Percentage

Routing Information Protocol (RIP) and other routing protocols can consume all the bandwidth on slow circuits. Although the routers may have accurate routing tables, a router is worthless if no bandwidth is available for sending data packets. EIGRP overcomes this deficiency by setting the maximum available bandwidth for all circuits to 50%. This allows EIGRP to use 50% of the bandwidth and reserves 50% of the bandwidth for data packets.

The interface parameter command **ip bandwidth-percent eigrp** *as-number percentage* changes the EIGRP available bandwidth for a link on EIGRP classic configuration. The available bandwidth for EIGRP is modified under the **af-interface default** submode or the **af-interface** *interface-id* submode with the command **bandwidth-percent** *percentage* in a named mode configuration.

Example 3-16 provides the configuration for setting the bandwidth available for EIGRP on R1 for classic and named mode configurations.

Example 3-16 *EIGRP Bandwidth Percentage Configuration*

```
R1 (Classic Configuration)
interface GigabitEthernet0/0
ip address 10.34.1.4 255.255.255.0
ip bandwidth-percent eigrp 100 25

R1 (Named Mode Configuration)
router eigrp EIGRP-NAMED
 address-family ipv4 unicast autonomous-system 100
  af-interface GigabitEthernet0/0
   bandwidth-percent 25
```

You can see the EIGRP bandwidth settings by looking at the EIGRP interfaces with the **detail** option. Example 3-17 shows the EIGRP bandwidth settings.

Example 3-17 *Viewing the EIGRP Bandwidth Percentage*

```
R1# show ip eigrp interfaces detail
! Output omitted for brevity
EIGRP-IPv4 Interfaces for AS(100)
                     Xmit Queue   PeerQ       Mean  Pacing Time  Multicast   Pending
Interface Peers   Un/Reliable  Un/Reliable  SRTT  Un/Reliable  Flow Timer  Routes
Gi0/0      1          0/0         0/0         1       0/0          50         0
..
   Interface BW percentage is 25
   Authentication mode is not set
```

Split Horizon

The first distance vector routing protocols advertised network prefixes out all interfaces for all known routes. Figure 3-13 demonstrates this behavior, with three routers processing the advertisements:

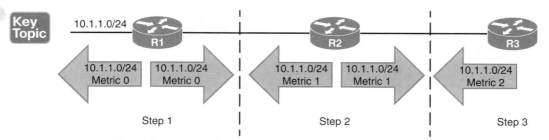

Figure 3-13 *Advertising All Routes Out All Interfaces*

Step 1. R1 advertises the 10.1.1.0/24 network out all of its interfaces.

Step 2.   R2 adds to the metric and re-advertises the network to R1 and R3. A route (in this case, 10.1.1.0/24) advertised back to the originating router (R1) is known as a *reverse route*. Reverse routes waste network resources. In this case, R1 discards the route from R2 because 10.1.1.0/24 is the connected network and has a higher AD.

Step 3.   R3 adds to the metric and advertises the reverse route to R2. R2 discards the route from R3 because it has a higher metric than the route from R1.

Figure 3-14 demonstrates a link failure between R1 and R2. R2 removes the 10.1.1.0/24 route learned from R1. It is possible that before R2 announces that the 10.1.1.0/24 network is unreachable, R3 advertises the 10.1.1.0/24 route with a metric of 2 out all interfaces.

R2 installs the route advertised from R3, which has the next-hop IP address 10.23.1.3. R3 still maintains the original route advertised from R2 with the next-hop IP address 10.23.1.2. This causes a routing loop if a packet is sent from R2 or R3 to the 10.1.1.0/24 network. Eventually, the route entries time out and end the routing loop.

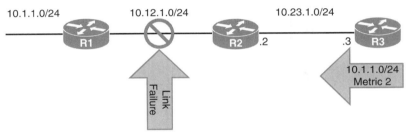

Figure 3-14   *Link Failure Between R1 and R2*

Split horizon prevents the advertisement of reverse routes and prevents scenarios like the one just described from happening. Figure 3-15 shows the same scenario as in Figure 3-14 but with split horizon enabled.

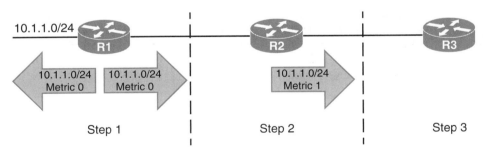

Figure 3-15   *Routing Updates with Split Horizon Enabled*

The following steps occur as R1 advertises the 10.1.10/24 prefix with split horizon enabled:

Step 1.   R1 advertises the 10.1.1.0/24 network out all of its interfaces.

Step 2.   R2 adds to the metric and re-advertises the network to R3 but does not advertise the route back to R1 because of split horizon.

Step 3.   R3 receives the route from R2 but does not advertise the route back to R2 because of split horizon.

EIGRP enables split horizon on all interfaces by default. When an interface connects to a multi-access medium that does not support full-mesh connectivity for all nodes, split horizon needs to be disabled. This scenario is commonly found with hub-and-spoke topologies such as Frame Relay, Dynamic Multipoint Virtual Private Network (DMVPN), or Layer 2 Virtual Private Network (L2VPN).

Figure 3-16 shows a hub-and-spoke topology where R1 is the hub, and R2 and R3 are spoke routers that can only communicate with the hub router. R1 uses the same interface for establishing the DMVPN tunnel, and split horizon prevents routes received from one spoke (R2) from being advertised to the other spoke (R3).

Notice that the EIGRP routing table is not complete for all the routers. R2 only has a remote route for R1's 10.1.1.0/24 network, and R3 only has a remote route for R1's 10.1.1.0/24 network. Split horizon on R1 prevents routes received from one spoke from being advertised to the other spoke.

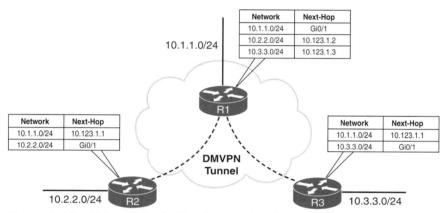

Figure 3-16 *Hub-and-Spoke Topology with Split Horizon*

You disable split horizon on a specific interface by using the interface parameter command **no ip split-horizon eigrp** *as-number* with EIGRP classic configuration. You disable split horizon on EIGRP named mode configuration under the **af-interface default** or **af-interface** *interface-id*, using the command **no split-horizon**. Example 3-18 shows a configuration to disable split horizon on the tunnel 100 interface.

Example 3-18 *Configuration to Disable Split Horizon*

```
R1 (Classic Configuration)
interface tunnel 100
  ip address 10.123.1.1 255.255.255.0
  no ip split-horizon eigrp 100
```
```
R1 (Named Mode Configuration)
router eigrp EIGRP-NAMED
 address-family ipv4 unicast autonomous-system 100
  af-interface tunnel 100
   no split-horizon
```

Figure 3-17 shows the routing table of each router after split horizon is disabled on R1. Notice that all routers have complete EIGRP routes.

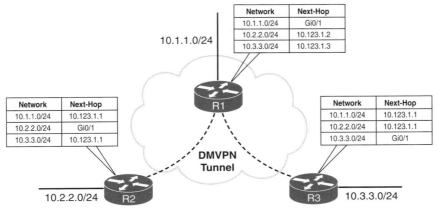

Figure 3-17   *Hub-and-Spoke Topology with Split Horizon Disabled*

Route Manipulation

Route manipulation involves selectively identifying routes that are advertised or received from neighbor routers. The routes can be modified to alter traffic patterns or removed to reduce memory utilization or to improve security. The following sections explain how routes are removed with filtering or modified with an EIGRP offset list.

Route Filtering

EIGRP supports filtering of routes as they are received or advertised from an interface. With filtering, routes can be matched against:

- Access control lists (ACLs) (named or numbered)

- IP prefix lists

- Route maps

- Gateway IP addresses

As shown in Figure 3-18, inbound filtering drops routes prior to the DUAL processing, which results in the routes not being installed into the RIB because they are not known. However, if the filtering occurs during outbound route advertisement, the routes are processed by DUAL and are installed into the local RIB of the advertising router.

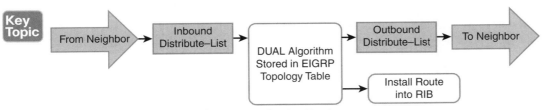

Figure 3-18   *EIGRP Distribute List Filtering Logic*

Filtering is accomplished with the command **distribute-list** {*acl-number* | *acl-name* | **prefix** *prefix-list-name* | **route-map** *route-map-name* | **gateway** *prefix-list-name*} {**in** | **out**} [*interface-id*]. EIGRP classic configuration places the command under the EIGRP process, while named mode configuration places the command under the topology base.

Prefixes that match against **deny** statements are filtered, and prefixes that match against a **permit** are passed. The **gateway** command can be used by itself or combined with a prefix list, an ACL, or a route map to restrict prefixes based on the next-hop forwarding address. Specifying an interface restricts the filtering to the interface that the route was received or advertised out of.

Figure 3-19 illustrates an EIGRP network for demonstrating inbound and outbound route filtering on R2.

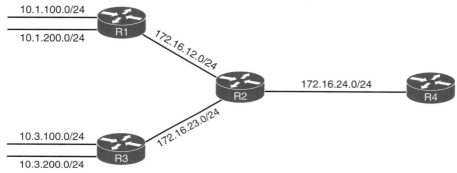

Figure 3-19   *EIGRP Distribution List Filtering Topology*

Example 3-19 shows the routing tables of R2 and R4 before the route filtering is applied. Notice that all the routes in the 10.1.0.0/16 and 10.3.0.0/16 range are present on both R2 and R4.

Example 3-19   *R2 and R4 Routing Tables*

```
R2# show ip route eigrp | begin Gateway
Gateway of last resort is not set


      10.0.0.0/24 is subnetted, 4 subnets
D        10.1.100.0 [90/15360] via 172.16.12.1, 00:05:45, GigabitEthernet0/1
D        10.1.200.0 [90/15360] via 172.16.12.1, 00:05:36, GigabitEthernet0/1
D        10.3.100.0 [90/15360] via 172.16.23.3, 00:06:26, GigabitEthernet0/3
D        10.3.200.0 [90/15360] via 172.16.23.3, 00:06:14, GigabitEthernet0/3
R4# show ip route eigrp | begin Gateway
Gateway of last resort is not set


      10.0.0.0/24 is subnetted, 4 subnets
D        10.1.100.0 [90/3328] via 172.16.24.2, 00:05:41, GigabitEthernet0/2
```

```
D          10.1.200.0 [90/3328] via 172.16.24.2, 00:05:31, GigabitEthernet0/2
D          10.3.100.0 [90/3328] via 172.16.24.2, 00:06:22, GigabitEthernet0/2
D          10.3.200.0 [90/3328] via 172.16.24.2, 00:06:10, GigabitEthernet0/2
        172.16.0.0/16 is variably subnetted, 4 subnets, 2 masks
D          172.16.12.0/24
              [90/3072] via 172.16.24.2, 00:07:04, GigabitEthernet0/2
D          172.16.23.0/24
              [90/3072] via 172.16.24.2, 00:07:04, GigabitEthernet0/2
```

Example 3-20 shows the configuration of R2 to demonstrate inbound filtering of 10.1.100.0/24 and outbound filtering of 10.3.100.0/24. The inbound filter uses a standard ACL to filter inbound routes and a prefix list to filter outbound advertisements. The **prefix** keyword must be used when referencing a prefix list.

Example 3-20 *EIGRP Route Filtering Configuration*

```
R2 (Classic Configuration)
ip access-list standard FILTER-R1-10.1.100.X
 deny 10.1.100.0
 permit any
!
ip prefix-list FILTER-R3-10.3.100.X deny 10.3.100.0/24
ip prefix-list FILTER-R3-10.3.100.X permit 0.0.0.0/0 le 32
!
router eigrp 100
 distribute-list FILTER-R1-10.1.100.X in
 distribute-list prefix FILTER-R3-10.3.100.X out

R2 (Named Mode Configuration)
ip access-list standard FILTER-R1-10.1.100.X
 deny 10.1.100.0
 permit any
!
ip prefix-list FILTER-R3-10.3.100.X deny 10.3.100.0/24
ip prefix-list FILTER-R3-10.3.100.X permit 0.0.0.0/0 le 32
!
router eigrp EIGRP-NAMED
 address-family ipv4 unicast autonomous-system 100
  topology base
    distribute-list FILTER-R1-10.1.100.X in
    distribute-list prefix FILTER-R3-10.3.100.X out
```

NOTE Conditional matching using ACLs, prefix lists, and route maps is covered in more detail in Chapter 15, "Route Maps and Conditional Forwarding."

Example 3-21 shows the routing table on R2 and R4 after EIGRP filtering is enabled on the routers. The 10.1.100.0/24 prefix is filtered upon receipt by R2, and it is not present in the EIGRP topology to advertise to R4. R2 still has the 10.3.100.0/24 prefix installed in the RIB, but the route is not advertised to R4. R4 does not have the 10.1.100.0/24 prefix or the 10.3.100.0/24 prefix in the routing table.

Example 3-21   *Verifying EIGRP Route Filtering*

```
R2# show ip route eigrp | begin Gateway
Gateway of last resort is not set


      10.0.0.0/24 is subnetted, 4 subnets
D        10.1.200.0 [90/15360] via 172.16.12.1, 00:06:58, GigabitEthernet0/1
D        10.3.100.0 [90/15360] via 172.16.23.3, 00:06:15, GigabitEthernet0/3
D        10.3.200.0 [90/15360] via 172.16.23.3, 00:06:15, GigabitEthernet0/3

R4# show ip route eigrp | begin Gateway
Gateway of last resort is not set


      10.0.0.0/24 is subnetted, 2 subnets
D        10.1.200.0 [90/3328] via 172.16.24.2, 00:00:31, GigabitEthernet0/2
D        10.3.200.0 [90/3328] via 172.16.24.2, 00:00:31, GigabitEthernet0/2
      172.16.0.0/16 is variably subnetted, 4 subnets, 2 masks
D        172.16.12.0/24
            [90/3072] via 172.16.24.2, 00:00:31, GigabitEthernet0/2
D        172.16.23.0/24
            [90/3072] via 172.16.24.2, 00:00:31, GigabitEthernet0/2
```

Traffic Steering with EIGRP Offset Lists

Modifying the EIGRP path metric provides traffic engineering in EIGRP. Modifying the delay setting for an interface modifies all routes that are received and advertised from that router's interface. *Offset lists* allow for the modification of path attributes based on the direction of the update, a specific prefix, or a combination of direction and prefix.

An offset list is configured with the command **offset-list** {*acl-number* | *acl-name*} {**in** | **out**} *offset-value* [*interface-id*] to modify the metric value of a route. Specifying an interface restricts the conditional match for the offset list to the interface that the route is received or advertised out of. EIGRP classic configuration places the command under the EIGRP process, while named mode configuration places the command under the topology base.

On the downstream neighbor, the path metric increases by the offset value specified in the offset list. The offset value is calculated from an additional delay value that was added to the existing delay in the EIGRP path attribute. Figure 3-20 shows the modified path metric formula when an offset delay is included.

Figure 3-21 shows an EIGRP topology that helps demonstrate EIGRP offset lists. R1 is advertising the 10.1.100.0/24 and 10.1.200.0/24 networks, and R3 is advertising the 10.3.100.0/24 and 10.3.200.0/24 networks.

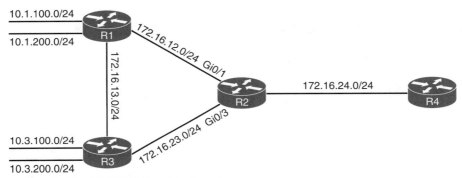

$$\text{Metric} + \text{offset} = 256 * \left(\left(\frac{10^7}{\text{Min. Bandwidth}} + \frac{\text{Total Delay}}{10} \right) + \text{Offset Delay} \right)$$

Equals

Offset = 256* Offset Delay

Figure 3-20 *EIGRP Offset Value Calculation*

Figure 3-21 *EIGRP Offset List Topology*

Example 3-22 shows the EIGRP routing tables for R2 and R4 before any path metric manipulation is performed.

Example 3-22 *R2 and R4 Routing Tables Before Offset*

```
R2# show ip route eigrp | begin Gateway
Gateway of last resort is not set


      10.0.0.0/24 is subnetted, 4 subnets
D        10.1.100.0 [90/15360] via 172.16.12.1, 00:00:35, GigabitEthernet0/1
D        10.1.200.0 [90/15360] via 172.16.12.1, 00:00:35, GigabitEthernet0/1
D        10.3.100.0 [90/15360] via 172.16.23.3, 00:00:40, GigabitEthernet0/3
D        10.3.200.0 [90/15360] via 172.16.23.3, 00:00:40, GigabitEthernet0/3
      172.16.0.0/16 is variably subnetted, 7 subnets, 2 masks
D        172.16.13.0/24
            [90/15360] via 172.16.23.3, 00:00:42, GigabitEthernet0/3
            [90/15360] via 172.16.12.1, 00:00:42, GigabitEthernet0/1
```

```
R4# show ip route eigrp | b Gateway
Gateway of last resort is not set
      10.0.0.0/24 is subnetted, 4 subnets
D        10.1.100.0 [90/3328] via 172.16.24.2, 01:22:01, GigabitEthernet0/2
D        10.1.200.0 [90/3328] via 172.16.24.2, 01:22:01, GigabitEthernet0/2
D        10.3.100.0 [90/3328] via 172.16.24.2, 01:21:57, GigabitEthernet0/2
D        10.3.200.0 [90/3328] via 172.16.24.2, 01:21:57, GigabitEthernet0/2
```

```
       172.16.0.0/16 is variably subnetted, 5 subnets, 2 masks
D         172.16.12.0/24
             [90/3072] via 172.16.24.2, 01:22:01, GigabitEthernet0/2
D         172.16.13.0/24
             [90/3328] via 172.16.24.2, 00:00:34, GigabitEthernet0/2
D         172.16.23.0/24
             [90/3072] via 172.16.24.2, 01:22:01, GigabitEthernet0/2
```

To demonstrate how an offset list is used to steer traffic, the path metric for the 10.1.100.0/24 network is incremented on R2's Gi0/1 interface so that R2 forwards packets toward R3 for that network. In addition, the 10.3.100.0/24 network is incremented on R2's Gi0/1 interface so that R2 forwards packets toward R1 for that network.

Example 3-23 displays the configuration of R2 for classic and named modes.

Example 3-23   *EIGRP Offset List Configuration*

```
R2 (Classic Configuration)
ip access-list standard R1
 permit 10.1.100.0
ip access-list standard R3
 permit 10.3.100.0
!
router eigrp 100
offset-list R1 in 200000 GigabitEthernet0/1
 offset-list R3 in 200000 GigabitEthernet0/3

R2 (Named Mode Configuration
ip access-list standard R1
 permit 10.1.100.0
ip access-list standard R3
 permit 10.3.100.0
!
router eigrp EIGRP-NAMED
 address-family ipv4 unicast autonomous-system 100
  topology base
    offset-list R1 in 200000 GigabitEthernet0/1
    offset-list R3 in 200000 GigabitEthernet0/3
```

Example 3-24 shows R2's routing table after the offset list is implemented. Notice how the path metrics and next-hop IP address changed for the 10.1.100.0/24 and 10.3.100.0/24 networks, while the metrics for the other routes remained the same.

Example 3-24 *Verifying the EIGRP Offset List*

```
R2# show ip route eigrp | begin Gateway
Gateway of last resort is not set


      10.0.0.0/24 is subnetted, 4 subnets
D        10.1.100.0 [90/20480] via 172.16.23.3, 00:05:09, GigabitEthernet0/3
D        10.1.200.0 [90/15360] via 172.16.12.1, 00:05:09, GigabitEthernet0/1
D        10.3.100.0 [90/20480] via 172.16.12.1, 00:05:09, GigabitEthernet0/1
D        10.3.200.0 [90/15360] via 172.16.23.3, 00:05:09, GigabitEthernet0/3
      172.16.0.0/16 is variably subnetted, 7 subnets, 2 masks
D        172.16.13.0/24
            [90/15360] via 172.16.23.3, 00:05:09, GigabitEthernet0/3
            [90/15360] via 172.16.12.1, 00:05:09, GigabitEthernet0/1
```

References in This Chapter

Edgeworth, Brad, Foss, Aaron, and Garza Rios, Ramiro, *IP Routing on Cisco IOS, IOS XE, and IOS XR*, Cisco Press, 2014.

RFC 7868, *Cisco's Enhanced Interior Gateway Routing Protocol (EIGRP)*, D. Savage, J. Ng, S. Moore, D. Slice, P. Paluch, and R. White, http://tools.ietf.org/html/rfc7868, May 2016.

Cisco, *Cisco IOS Software Configuration Guides*, http://www.cisco.com.

Exam Preparation Tasks

As mentioned in the section "How to Use This Book" in the Introduction, you have a couple choices for exam preparation: the exercises here, Chapter 24, "Final Preparation," and the exam simulation questions in the Pearson Test Prep software.

Review All Key Topics

Review the most important topics in this chapter, noted with the Key Topic icon in the outer margin of the page. Table 3-2 lists these key topics and the page number on which each is found.

Table 3-2 Key Topics

Key Topic Element	Description	Page Number
Section	Failure detection and timers	108
Paragraph	Convergence	109
Paragraph	Routes going active	110
Paragraph	Stuck in active	112
Paragraph	Summary routes	115
Paragraph	Summary discard routes	116
Paragraph	Summarization metrics	117

Key Topic Element	Description	Page Number
Paragraph	EIGRP stub router	119
Paragraph	EIGRP stub router configuration	120
Figure 3-11	EIGRP stub router constraints	122
Paragraph	EIGRP stub site	122
Figure 3-12	EIGRP stub site feature	123
Paragraph	IP bandwidth percentage	125
Figure 3-13	Split horizon	126
Figure 3-18	EIGRP distribution list filtering logic	129
Paragraph	EIGRP offset lists	132

Define Key Terms

Define the following key terms from this chapter, and check your answers in the glossary:

hello packets, hello timer, hold timer, stuck in active (SIA), summarization, EIGRP stub router, EIGPR stub site router, split horizon, offset list

Use the Command Reference to Check Your Memory

The ENARSI 300-410 exam focuses on the practical, hands-on skills that networking professionals use. Therefore, you should be able to identify the commands needed to configure, verify, and troubleshoot the topics covered in this chapter.

This section includes the most important configuration and verification commands covered in this chapter. It might not be necessary to memorize the complete syntax of every command, but you should be able to remember the basic keywords that are needed.

To test your memory of the commands in Table 3-3, go to the companion website and download Appendix B, "Command Reference Exercises." Fill in the missing commands in the tables based on each command description. You can check your work by downloading Appendix C, "Command Reference Exercise Answer Key," from the companion website.

Table 3-3   Command Reference

Task	Command Syntax

Modify the EIGRP hello interval and hold time per interface.	Classic: (EIGRP process)
	ip hello-interval eigrp *as-number seconds*
	ip hold-time eigrp *as-number seconds*
	
	Named mode: **af-interface** {default | *interface-id*}
	   hello-interval *seconds*
	   hold-time *seconds*

Task	Command Syntax

Configure EIGRP network summarization.	Classic: (EIGRP process)
	
	  ip summary-address eigrp *as-number network subnet-mask* [**leak-map** *route-map-name*]
	
	Named mode: (**af-interface** `interface-id`)
	
	  summary-address *network subnet-mask* [**leak-map** *route-map-name*]

Statically set the EIGRP metrics for a specific network summary aggregate.	**summary-metric** *network* {/*prefix-length* | *subnet-mask*} *bandwidth delay reliability load MTU*
Configure an EIGRP router as a stub router.	**eigrp stub** {**connected** | **receive-only** | **redistributed** | **static** | **summary**}

Configure an EIGRP router as a stub site router.	Named mode: (**af-interface** *interface-id*)
	  stub-site wan-interface
	
	And:
	  eigrp stub-site *as-number:identifier*

Disable EIGRP split horizon on an interface.	Classic: (EIGRP process)
	  no ip split-horizon eigrp *as-number*
	
	Named mode: **af-interface** {**default** | *interface-id*}
	  no split-horizon

Filter routes for an EIGRP neighbor.	**distribute-list** {*acl-number* | *acl-name* | **prefix** *prefix-list-name* | **route-map** *route-map-name* | **gateway** *prefix-list-name*} {**in** | **out**} [*interface-id*]
Modify/increase path cost for routes.	**offset-list** *offset-value* {*acl-number* | *acl-name*} {**in** | **out**} [*interface-id*]
Display the EIGRP-enabled interfaces.	**show ip eigrp interface** [{*interface-id* [**detail**] | **detail**}]
Display the EIGRP topology table.	**show ip eigrp topology** [**all-links**]
Display the IP routing protocol information configured on the router.	**show ip protocols**

## CHAPTER 4

Troubleshooting EIGRP for IPv4

This chapter covers the following topics:

- **Troubleshooting EIGRP for IPv4 Neighbor Adjacencies:** This section covers the reasons EIGRP for IPv4 neighbor relationships might not be formed and how to identify them.

- **Troubleshooting EIGRP for IPv4 Routes:** This section explores the reasons EIGRP for IPv4 routes might be missing from a router's EIGRP table or routing table and how to determine why they are missing.

- **Troubleshooting Miscellaneous EIGRP for IPv4 Issues:** This section identifies some additional issues you might face while using EIGRP, how to identify them, and how to solve them.

- **EIGRP for IPv4 Trouble Tickets:** This section provides three trouble tickets that demonstrate how to use a structured troubleshooting process to solve a reported problem.

This chapter focuses on troubleshooting EIGRP for IPv4. Chapter 5, "EIGRPv6," covers EIGRP for IPv6 and named EIGRP.

Before any routes can be exchanged between EIGRP routers on the same LAN or across a WAN, an EIGRP neighbor relationship must be formed. Neighbor relationships may not form for many reasons, and as a troubleshooter, you need to be aware of them. This chapter dives deep into these issues and gives you the tools needed to identify them and successfully solve neighbor issues.

Once neighbor relationships are formed, neighboring routers exchange EIGRP routes. In various cases, routes may end up missing, and you need to be able to determine why the routes are missing. This chapter discusses the various ways that routes could go missing and how you can identify them and solve route-related issues.

In this chapter, you will also learn how to troubleshoot issues related to load balancing, summarization, discontiguous networks, and feasible successors.

"Do I Know This Already?" Quiz

The "Do I Know This Already?" quiz allows you to assess whether you should read this entire chapter thoroughly or jump to the "Exam Preparation Tasks" section. If you are in doubt about your answers to these questions or your own assessment of your knowledge of the topics, read the entire chapter. Table 4-1 lists the major headings in this chapter and their corresponding "Do I Know This Already?" quiz questions. You can find the answers in Appendix A, "Answers to the 'Do I Know This Already?' Quiz Questions."

Table 4-1 "Do I Know This Already?" Foundation Topics Section-to-Question Mapping

Foundation Topics Section	Questions
Troubleshooting EIGRP for IPv4 Neighbor Adjacencies	1–4
Troubleshooting EIGRP for IPv4 Routes	5, 6, 8
Troubleshooting Miscellaneous EIGRP for IPv4 Issues	7, 9, 10

CAUTION   The goal of self-assessment is to gauge your mastery of the topics in this chapter. If you do not know the answer to a question or are only partially sure of the answer, you should mark that question as wrong for purposes of self-assessment. Giving yourself credit for an answer that you correctly guess skews your self-assessment results and might provide you with a false sense of security.

1. Which command enables you to verify the routers that have formed EIGRP adjacencies with the local router, how long they have been neighbors, and the current sequence numbers of EIGRP packets?

    a. show ip eigrp interfaces

    b. show ip eigrp neighbors

    c. show ip route eigrp

    d. show ip protocols

2. Which of the following are reasons EIGRP neighbor relationships might not form? (Choose three.)

    a. Different autonomous system numbers

    b. Different K values

    c. Different timers

    d. Different authentication parameters

3. Which command enables you to verify the configured EIGRP K values?

    a. show ip protocols

    b. show ip eigrp interfaces

    c. show ip eigrp neighbor

    d. show ip eigrp topology

4. Which command enables you to verify EIGRP authentication, split horizon, and configured EIGRP timers?

    a. show ip interfaces

    b. show ip protocols

    c. show ip eigrp interfaces detail

    d. show ip eigrp neighbor

5. Besides a neighbor relationship not being formed, which three of the following are reasons routes might be missing in an EIGRP autonomous system? (Choose three.)

   a. Interface not participating in the EIGRP process

   b. Filters

   c. Incorrect stub configuration

   d. Passive interface feature

6. Which command enables you to verify whether any route filters have been applied to an EIGRP-enabled interface?

   a. show ip interface brief

   b. show ip interface

   c. show ip protocols

   d. show ip eigrp interface

7. Which command enables you to verify the maximum paths configured for load balancing and whether unequal-path load balancing has been enabled?

   a. show ip protocols

   b. show ip eigrp interfaces

   c. show ip eigrp neighbors

   d. show ip interfaces

8. You have a DMVPN network that has a hub and three spokes. The spokes are not learning the routes of the other spokes. Of the following options, which is most likely the reason for this?

   a. Split horizon is enabled on the GRE interfaces of the spokes.

   b. Split horizon is enabled on the hub's mGRE interface.

   c. Split horizon is disabled on the hub's mGRE interface.

   d. Split horizon is disabled on the GRE interfaces of the spokes.

9. An EIGRP summary route is not showing up on the expected routers in the AS. Which of the following questions should you answer while troubleshooting? (Choose three.)

   a. Did you enable route summarization on the correct interface?

   b. Did you associate the summary route with the correct EIGRP autonomous system?

   c. Did you create the appropriate summary route?

   d. Did you create a route to NULL0?

10. The IP addressing scheme for your routing domain is discontiguous. What command should you use in EIGRP configuration mode to make sure that you do not have any routing issues in your EIGRP autonomous system?

   a. no auto-summary

   b. auto-summary

   c. passive-interface

   d. network *ip_address wildcard_mask*

Foundation Topics

Troubleshooting EIGRP for IPv4 Neighbor Adjacencies

EIGRP establishes neighbor relationships by sending *hello packets* to the multicast address *224.0.0.10*, out interfaces participating in the EIGRP process. To enable the EIGRP process on an interface, you use the **network** *ip_address wildcard_mask* command in router EIGRP configuration mode. For example, the command **network 10.1.1.0 0.0.0.255** enables EIGRP on all interfaces with an IP address from 10.1.1.0 through 10.1.1.255. The command **network 10.1.1.65 0.0.0.0** enables the EIGRP process on only the interface with the IP address 10.1.1.65. It seems rather simple, and it is; however, for various reasons, neighbor relationships may not form, and you need to be aware of all of them if you plan on successfully troubleshooting EIGRP-related problems. This section focuses on the reasons EIGRP neighbor relationships might not form and how you can identify them during the troubleshooting process.

To verify EIGRP neighbors, you use the **show ip eigrp neighbors** command. Example 4-1 provides sample output of the **show ip eigrp neighbors** command. It lists the IPv4 address of the neighboring device's interface that sent the hello packet, the local interface on the router used to reach that neighbor, how long the local router will consider the neighboring router to be a neighbor, how long the routers have been neighbors, the amount of time it takes for the neighbors to communicate (on average), the number of EIGRP packets in a queue waiting to be sent to a neighbor (which should always be zero since you want up-to-date routing information), and a sequence number to keep track of the EIGRP packets received from the neighbor to ensure that only newer packets are accepted and processed.

Example 4-1 *Verifying EIGRP Neighbors with show ip eigrp neighbors*

```
R2# show ip eigrp neighbors
H   Address               Interface      Hold Uptime   SRTT    RTO  Q   Seq
                                         (sec)         (ms)         Cnt Num
1   10.1.23.3             Gi1/0            14  10:01:09  72     432  0   3
0   10.1.12.1             Gi0/0            11  10:32:14  75     450  0   8
```

EIGRP neighbor relationships might not form for a variety of reasons, including the following:

- **Interface is down:** The interface must be up/up.

- **Mismatched autonomous system numbers:** Both routers need to be using the same *autonomous system number*.

- **Incorrect network statement:** The **network** statement must identify the IP address of the interface you want to include in the EIGRP process.

- **Mismatched K values:** Both routers must be using exactly the same K values.

- **Passive interface:** The *passive interface* feature suppresses the sending and receiving of hello packets while still allowing the interface's network to be advertised.

■ **Different subnets:** The exchange of hello packets must be done on the same subnet; if it isn't, the hello packets are ignored.

■ **Authentication:** If authentication is being used, the key ID and key string must match, and the key must be valid (if valid times have been configured).

■ **ACLs:** An access control list (ACL) may be denying packets to the EIGRP multicast address 224.0.0.10.

■ **Timers:** Timers do not have to match; however, if they are not configured correctly, neighbor adjacencies could flap.

When an EIGRP neighbor relationship does not form, the neighbor is not listed in the neighbor table. In such a case, you need the assistance of an accurate physical and logical network diagram and the **show cdp neighbors** command to verify who should be the neighbors.

When troubleshooting EIGRP, you need to be aware of how to verify the parameters associated with each of the reasons listed here. Let's look at them individually.

Interface Is Down

The interface must be up if you plan on forming an EIGRP neighbor adjacency. You can verify the status of an interface with the **show ip interface brief** command. The status should be listed as up, and the protocol should be listed as up.

Mismatched Autonomous System Numbers

For an EIGRP neighbor relationship to be formed, both routers need to be in the same autonomous system. You specify the autonomous system number when you issue the **router eigrp** *autonomous_system_number* command in global configuration mode. If the two routers are in different autonomous systems, they will not form an EIGRP neighbor relationship. Most EIGRP **show** commands display the autonomous system number in the output. However, the best one is **show ip protocols**, which displays an incredible amount of information for troubleshooting, as shown in Example 4-2. In this example, you can see that R1 is participating in EIGRP autonomous system 100. Using the *spot-the-difference* troubleshooting method, you can compare the autonomous system value listed to the value on a neighboring router to determine whether they differ.

Example 4-2   *Verifying the Autonomous System Number with show ip protocols*

```
R1# show ip protocols
*** IP Routing is NSF aware ***

Routing Protocol is "eigrp 100"
  Outgoing update filter list for all interfaces is not set
  Incoming update filter list for all interfaces is not set
  Default networks flagged in outgoing updates
  Default networks accepted from incoming updates
  EIGRP-IPv4 Protocol for AS(100)
    Metric weight K1=1, K2=0, K3=1, K4=0, K5=0
    NSF-aware route hold timer is 240
    Router-ID: 10.1.12.1
```

```
    Topology : 0 (base)
      Active Timer: 3 min
      Distance: internal 90 external 170
      Maximum path: 4
      Maximum hopcount 100
      Maximum metric variance 1

 Automatic Summarization: disabled
 Maximum path: 4
 Routing for Networks:
    10.1.1.1/32
    10.1.12.1/32
 Routing Information Sources:
    Gateway       Distance      Last Update
    10.1.12.2           90      09:54:36
 Distance: internal 90 external 170
```

The output of the **debug eigrp packets** command shown in Example 4-3 indicates that the router is not receiving any hello packets from the neighbors with the mismatched autonomous system number. In this example, R1 is sending hello packets out Gi0/0 and Gi1/0. However, it is not receiving any hello packets. This could be because of an autonomous system mismatch. The local router could have the wrong autonomous system number, or the remote routers could have the wrong autonomous system number.

Example 4-3 *Sample Output of* **debug eigrp packets** *When an Autonomous System Mismatch Exists*

```
R1# debug eigrp packets
 (UPDATE, REQUEST, QUERY, REPLY, HELLO, UNKNOWN, PROBE, ACK, STUB, SIAQUERY,
SIAREPLY)
EIGRP Packet debugging is on
R1#
EIGRP: Sending HELLO on Gi0/0 - paklen 20
   AS 100, Flags 0x0:(NULL), Seq 0/0 interfaceQ 0/0 iidbQ un/rely 0/0
R1#
EIGRP: Sending HELLO on Gi1/0 - paklen 20
   AS 100, Flags 0x0:(NULL), Seq 0/0 interfaceQ 0/0 iidbQ un/rely 0/0
R1#
EIGRP: Sending HELLO on Gi0/0 - paklen 20
   AS 100, Flags 0x0:(NULL), Seq 0/0 interfaceQ 0/0 iidbQ un/rely 0/0
R1# l
EIGRP: Sending HELLO on Gi1/0 - paklen 20
   AS 100, Flags 0x0:(NULL), Seq 0/0 interfaceQ 0/0 iidbQ un/rely 0/0
R1# l
EIGRP: Sending HELLO on Gi0/0 - paklen 20
   AS 100, Flags 0x0:(NULL), Seq 0/0 interfaceQ 0/0 iidbQ un/rely 0/0
R1# u all
All possible debugging has been turned off
```

Incorrect Network Statement

If the *network command* is misconfigured, EIGRP may not be enabled on the proper interfaces, and as a result, hello packets will not be sent and neighbor relationships will not be formed. You can determine which interfaces are participating in the EIGRP process with the command **show ip eigrp interfaces**. In Example 4-4, for instance, you can see that two interfaces are participating in the EIGRP process for autonomous system 100. Gi0/0 does not have an EIGRP peer, and Gi1/0 does have an EIGRP peer. This is expected because no other routers can be reached out Gi0/0 for this scenario. However, if you expect an EIGRP peer out the interface based on your documentation, you need to troubleshoot why the peering/ neighbor relationship is not forming. Shift your attention to the Pending Routes column. Notice that all interfaces are listed as 0. This is expected. Any other value in this column means that some issue on the network (such as congestion) is preventing the interface from sending the necessary updates to the neighbor.

> **NOTE** Remember that EIGRP passive interfaces do not show up in this output. Therefore, you shouldn't jump to the conclusion that the network command is incorrect or missing if the interface does not show up in this output. It is possible that the interface is passive.

Example 4-4 *Verifying EIGRP Interfaces with* **show ip eigrp interfaces**

```
R2# show ip eigrp interfaces
EIGRP-IPv4 Interfaces for AS(100)
                       Xmit Queue   Mean   Pacing Time   Multicast    Pending
Interface    Peers     Un/Reliable  SRTT   Un/Reliable   Flow Timer   Routes
Gi0/0        0            0/0        0         0/0           0            0
Gi1/0        1            0/0        78        0/0           300          0
```

The output of **show ip protocols** displays the interfaces that are running EIGRP as a result of the **network** commands. It is not obvious at first unless someone tells you. The reason it's not obvious is that it's not displayed properly. Focus on the highlighted text in Example 4-5. Notice that it states Routing for Networks. Those are *not* the networks you are routing for. Rather, you are routing for the networks associated with the interface on which EIGRP will be enabled, based on the **network** commands. In this case, **10.1.1.1/32** really means **network 10.1.1.1 0.0.0.0**, and **10.1.12.1/32** really means **network 10.1.12.1 0.0.0.0**. Therefore, a better option is to use the **show run | section router eigrp** command, as shown in Example 4-6.

Example 4-5 *Verifying Network Statements with* **show ip protocols**

```
R1# show ip protocols
*** IP Routing is NSF aware ***


Routing Protocol is "eigrp 100"
  Outgoing update filter list for all interfaces is not set
  Incoming update filter list for all interfaces is not set
  Default networks flagged in outgoing updates
```

```
Default networks accepted from incoming updates
EIGRP-IPv4 Protocol for AS(100)
  Metric weight K1=1, K2=0, K3=1, K4=0, K5=0
  NSF-aware route hold timer is 240
  Router-ID: 10.1.12.1
  Topology : 0 (base)
    Active Timer: 3 min
    Distance: internal 90 external 170
    Maximum path: 4
    Maximum hopcount 100
    Maximum metric variance 1

Automatic Summarization: disabled
Maximum path: 4
Routing for Networks:
   10.1.1.1/32
   10.1.12.1/32
Routing Information Sources:
  Gateway      Distance    Last Update
   10.1.12.2         90      09:54:36
Distance: internal 90 external 170
```

Example 4-6 *Verifying network Statements with show run | section router eigrp*

```
R1# show run | section router eigrp
router eigrp 100
network 10.1.1.1 0.0.0.0
network 10.1.12.1 0.0.0.0
```

Notice that the **network** statement is extremely important. If it is misconfigured, interfaces that should be participating in the EIGRP process might not be, and interfaces that should not be participating in the EIGRP process might be. So, you should be able to recognize issues related to the **network** statement.

When using the **debug eigrp packets** command on the router with the misconfigured or missing **network** statement, you will notice that hello packets are not being sent out the interface properly. For example, if you expect hello packets to be sent out Gig1/0, but the **debug eigrp packets** command is not indicating that this is happening, it is possible that the interface is not participating in the EIGRP process because of a bad **network** statement or the interface is passive and suppressing hello packets.

Mismatched K Values

The *K values* that are used for metric calculation must match between neighbors in order for an adjacency to form. You can verify whether K values match by using **show ip proto-cols**, as shown in Example 4-7. The default K values are highlighted in Example 4-7. Usually there is no need to change the K values. However, if they are changed, you need to make them match on every router in the autonomous system. You can use the *spot-the-difference* method when determining whether K values do not match between routers. In addition, if you are logging syslog messages with a severity level of 5, you receive a message similar to the following:

```
%DUAL-5-NBRCHANGE: EIGRP-IPv4 100: Neighbor 10.1.12.2
(GigabitEthernet1/0) is down: K-value mismatch
```

Example 4-7   *Verifying K Values with **show ip protocols***

```
R1# show ip protocols
*** IP Routing is NSF aware ***


Routing Protocol is "eigrp 100"
  Outgoing update filter list for all interfaces is not set
  Incoming update filter list for all interfaces is not set
  Default networks flagged in outgoing updates
  Default networks accepted from incoming updates
  EIGRP-IPv4 Protocol for AS(100)
    Metric weight K1=1, K2=0, K3=1, K4=0, K5=0
    NSF-aware route hold timer is 240
    Router-ID: 10.1.12.1
    Topology : 0 (base)
      Active Timer: 3 min
      Distance: internal 90 external 170
      Maximum path: 4
      Maximum hopcount 100
      Maximum metric variance 1

  Automatic Summarization: disabled
  Maximum path: 4
  Routing for Networks:
    10.1.1.1/32
    10.1.12.1/32
  Routing Information Sources:
    Gateway       Distance   Last Update
    10.1.12.2          90    09:54:36
  Distance: internal 90 external 170
```

Passive Interface

The passive interface feature is a must-have for all organizations. It does two things:

- Reduces the EIGRP-related traffic on a network

- Improves EIGRP security

The passive interface feature turns off the sending and receiving of EIGRP packets on an interface while still allowing the interface's network ID to be injected into the EIGRP process and advertised to other EIGRP neighbors. This ensures that rogue routers attached to the LAN will not be able to form an adjacency with your legitimate router on that interface because it is not sending or receiving EIGRP packets on the interface. However, if you configure the wrong interface as passive, a legitimate EIGRP neighbor relationship will not be formed. As shown in the **show ip protocols** output in Example 4-8, Gigabit Ethernet 0/0 is a passive interface. If there are no passive interfaces, the passive interface section does not appear in the **show ip protocols** output.

Example 4-8 *Verifying Passive Interfaces with **show ip protocols***

```
R1# show ip protocols
*** IP Routing is NSF aware ***

Routing Protocol is "eigrp 100"
  Outgoing update filter list for all interfaces is not set
  Incoming update filter list for all interfaces is not set
  Default networks flagged in outgoing updates
  Default networks accepted from incoming updates
  EIGRP-IPv4 Protocol for AS(100)
    Metric weight K1=1, K2=0, K3=1, K4=0, K5=0
    NSF-aware route hold timer is 240
    Router-ID: 10.1.12.1
    Topology : 0 (base)
      Active Timer: 3 min
      Distance: internal 90 external 170
      Maximum path: 4
      Maximum hopcount 100
      Maximum metric variance 1

  Automatic Summarization: disabled
  Maximum path: 4
  Routing for Networks:
    10.1.1.1/32
    10.1.12.1/32
  Passive Interface(s):
    GigabitEthernet0/0
  Routing Information Sources:
    Gateway         Distance      Last Update
    10.1.12.2             90      11:00:14
  Distance: internal 90 external 170
```

Remember that for EIGRP, passive interfaces do not appear in the EIGRP interface table. Therefore, before you jump to the conclusion that the wrong network command was used and the interface was not enabled for EIGRP, you need to check to see whether the interface is passive.

When using the **debug eigrp packets** command on the router with the passive interface, notice that hello packets are not being sent out that interface. For example, if you expect hello packets to be sent out Gig1/0 but the **debug eigrp packets** command is not indicating that this is happening, it is possible that the interface is participating in the EIGRP process but is configured as a passive interface.

Different Subnets

To form an EIGRP neighbor adjacency, the router interfaces must be on the same subnet. You can confirm this in many ways. The simplest way is to look at the interface configuration in the running configuration with the **show run interface** *interface_type interface_number* command. You can also use the **show ip interface** *interface_type interface_number* command or the **show interface** *interface_type interface_number* command. Example 4-9 shows the configuration of Gig1/0 on R1 and Gig0/0 on R2. Are they in the same subnet? Yes! Based on the IP address and the subnet mask, they are both in the 10.1.12.0/24 subnet. However, if they are not in the same subnet and you have syslog set up for a severity level of 6, you get a message similar to the following:

```
%DUAL-6-NBRINFO: EIGRP-IPv4 100: Neighbor 10.1.21.2 (Gigabit
Ethernet1/0) is blocked: not on common subnet (10.1.12.1/24)
```

Example 4-9 *Verifying IPv4 Addresses and Masks on Router Interfaces*

```
R1# show running-config interface gigabitEthernet 1/0
Building configuration...

Current configuration : 90 bytes
!
interface GigabitEthernet1/0
 ip address 10.1.12.1 255.255.255.0
 negotiation auto
end


R2# show running-config interface gigabitEthernet 0/0
Building configuration...

Current configuration : 132 bytes
!
interface GigabitEthernet0/0
 ip address 10.1.12.2 255.255.255.0
 negotiation auto
end
```

Authentication

Authentication is used to ensure that EIGRP routers form neighbor relationships only with legitimate routers and that they only accept EIGRP packets from legitimate routers. Therefore, if authentication is implemented, both routers must agree on the settings for a neighbor relationship to form. With authentication, you can use the *spot-the-difference* method. Example 4-10 shows the output of the commands **show run interface** *interface_type interface_number* and **show ip eigrp interfaces detail** *interface_type interface_number*, which identify whether EIGRP authentication is enabled on the interface. According to the highlighted output, it is. Note that the authentication must be configured on the correct interface and that it must be tied to the correct *autonomous system number*. If you put in the wrong autonomous system number, authentication will not be enabled for the correct autonomous system. In addition, make sure that you specify the correct keychain that will be used for the Message Digest 5 (MD5) authentication hash. You can verify the keychain with the command **show key chain**, as shown in Example 4-11. The keys in this example do not expire. However, if you have implemented rotating keys, the keys must be valid for authentication to be successful.

Example 4-10   *Verifying EIGRP Authentication on an Interface*

```
R1# show run interface gig 1/0
Building configuration...

Current configuration : 178 bytes
!
interface GigabitEthernet1/0
 ip address 10.1.12.1 255.255.255.0
 ip authentication mode eigrp 100 md5
 ip authentication key-chain eigrp 100 EIGRP_AUTH
 negotiation auto
end

R1# show ip eigrp interfaces detail gigabitEthernet 1/0
EIGRP-IPv4 Interfaces for AS(100)
                 Xmit Queue   PeerQ        Mean  Pacing Time  Multicast    Pending
Interface  Peers Un/Reliable  Un/Reliable  SRTT  Un/Reliable  Flow Timer   Routes
Gi1/0       1        0/0          0/0        87      0/0          376         0
  Hello-interval is 5, Hold-time is 15
  Split-horizon is enabled
  Next xmit serial <none>
  Packetized sent/expedited: 2/0
  Hello's sent/expedited: 17/2
  Un/reliable mcasts: 0/3 Un/reliable ucasts: 2/2
  Mcast exceptions: 0 CR packets: 0 ACKs suppressed: 0
  Retransmissions sent: 1 Out-of-sequence rcvd: 1
  Topology-ids on interface - 0
  Authentication mode is md5, key-chain is "EIGRP_AUTH"
```

Example 4-11   *Verifying the Keychain Used for EIGRP Authentication*

```
R1# show key chain
Key-chain EIGRP_AUTH:
    key 1 -- text "ENARSI"
        accept lifetime (always valid) - (always valid) [valid now]
        send lifetime (always valid) - (always valid) [valid now]
```

Inside the *keychain*, you find the *key ID* (1 in this case) and the *key string* (ENARSI in this case). It is mandatory that the key ID in use and the key string in use between neighbors match. Therefore, if you have multiple keys and key strings in a keychain, the same key and string must be used at the same time by both routers (meaning they must be valid and in use); otherwise, authentication will fail.

When using the **debug eigrp packets** command for troubleshooting authentication, you receive output based on the authentication issue. Example 4-12 shows the message that is generated when the neighbor is not configured for authentication. It ignores that packet and states **(missing authentication)**. When the key IDs or the key strings do not match between the neighbors, the debug output states **(invalid authentication)**, as shown in Example 4-13.

Example 4-12   *Debug Output When Authentication Is Missing on the Neighbor*

```
R1# debug eigrp packets
 (UPDATE, REQUEST, QUERY, REPLY, HELLO, UNKNOWN, PROBE, ACK, STUB, SIAQUERY,
SIAREPLY)
EIGRP Packet debugging is on
R1#
EIGRP: Sending HELLO on Gi1/0 - paklen 60
 AS 100, Flags 0x0:(NULL), Seq 0/0 interfaceQ 0/0 iidbQ un/rely 0/0
EIGRP: Gi1/0: ignored packet from 10.1.12.2, opcode = 5 (missing authentication)
EIGRP: Sending HELLO on Gi0/0 - paklen 20
 AS 100, Flags 0x0:(NULL), Seq 0/0 interfaceQ 0/0 iidbQ un/rely 0/0
R1# u all
All possible debugging has been turned off
```

Example 4-13   *Debug Output When Key IDs or Key Strings Do Not Match*

```
R1# debug eigrp packets
 (UPDATE, REQUEST, QUERY, REPLY, HELLO, UNKNOWN, PROBE, ACK, STUB, SIAQUERY,
SIAREPLY)
EIGRP Packet debugging is on
R1#
EIGRP: pkt authentication key id = 2, key not defined
EIGRP: Gi1/0: ignored packet from 10.1.12.2, opcode = 5 (invalid authentication)
EIGRP: Sending HELLO on Gi0/0 - paklen 20
 AS 100, Flags 0x0:(NULL), Seq 0/0 interfaceQ 0/0 iidbQ un/rely 0/0
EIGRP: Sending HELLO on Gi1/0 - paklen 60
 AS 100, Flags 0x0:(NULL), Seq 0/0 interfaceQ 0/0 iidbQ un/rely 0/0
R1# u all
All possible debugging has been turned off
```

ACLs

Access control lists (ACLs) are extremely powerful. How they are implemented determines what they control in a network. If there is an ACL applied to an interface and the ACL is denying EIGRP packets, or if an EIGRP packet falls victim to the implicit deny all at the end of the ACL, a neighbor relationship does not form. To determine whether an ACL is applied to an interface, use the **show ip interface** *interface_type interface_number* command, as shown in Example 4-14. Notice that ACL 100 is applied inbound on interface Gig1/0. To verify the ACL 100 entries, issue the command **show access-lists 100**, as shown in Example 4-15. In this case, you can see that ACL 100 is denying EIGRP traffic; this prevents a neighbor relationship from forming. Note that outbound ACLs do not affect EIGRP packets; only inbound ACLs do. Therefore, any outbound ACLs that deny EIGRP packets have no effect on your EIGRP troubleshooting efforts.

Example 4-14   *Verifying ACLs Applied to Interfaces*

```
R1# show ip interface gig 1/0
GigabitEthernet1/0 is up, line protocol is up
  Internet address is 10.1.12.1/24
  Broadcast address is 255.255.255.255
  Address determined by setup command
  MTU is 1500 bytes
  Helper address is not set
  Directed broadcast forwarding is disabled
  Multicast reserved groups joined: 224.0.0.10
  Outgoing access list is not set
  Inbound access list is 100
  Proxy ARP is enabled
  Local Proxy ARP is disabled
  Security level is default
  Split horizon is enabled
```

Example 4-15   *Verifying ACL Entries*

```
R1# show access-lists 100
Extended IP access list 100
    10 deny eigrp any any (62 matches)
    20 permit ip any any
```

Timers

Although EIGRP timers do not have to match, if the timers are skewed enough, an adjacency will flap. For example, suppose that R1 is using the default timers 5 and 15, while R2 is sending hello packets every 20 seconds. R1's hold time will expire before it receives another hello packet from R2; this terminates the neighbor relationship. Five seconds later, the hello packet arrives, and the neighbor relationship is formed, but it is then terminated again 15 seconds later.

Although timers do not have to match, it is important that routers send hello packets at a rate that is faster than the hold timer. You verify the configured timers with the **show ip eigrp interfaces detail** command, as shown in Example 4-10.

Troubleshooting EIGRP for IPv4 Routes

After establishing a neighbor relationship, an EIGRP router performs a full exchange of routing information with the newly established neighbor. After the full exchange, only updates to route information are exchanged with that neighbor. Routing information learned from

EIGRP neighbors is inserted into the EIGRP topology table. If the EIGRP information for a specific route happens to be the best source of information, it is installed in the routing table. There are various reasons EIGRP routes might be missing from either the topology table or the routing table, and you need to be aware of them if you plan on successfully troubleshooting EIGRP route-related problems. This section examines the reasons EIGRP routes might be missing and how to determine why they are missing.

EIGRP only learns from directly connected neighbors, which makes it easy to follow the path of routes when troubleshooting. For example, if R1 does not know about a route but its neighbor does, there is probably something wrong between the neighbors. However, if the neighbor does not know about it either, you can focus on the neighbor's neighbor and so on.

As discussed earlier, neighbor relationships are the foundation of EIGRP information sharing. If there are no neighbors, you do not learn any routes. So, besides the lack of a neighbor, what would be reasons for missing routes in an EIGRP network? The following are some common reasons EIGRP routes might be missing from either the topology table or the routing table:

- **Bad or missing network command:** The **network** command enables the EIGRP process on an interface and injects the prefix of the network the interface is part of into the EIGRP process.

- **Better source of information:** If exactly the same network prefix is learned from a more reliable source, it is used instead of the EIGRP learned information.

- **Route filtering:** A filter might be preventing a network prefix from being advertised or learned.

- **Stub configuration:** If the wrong setting is chosen during the stub router configuration, or if the wrong router is chosen as the stub router, it might prevent a network prefix from being advertised.

- **Interface is shut down:** The EIGRP-enabled interface must be up/up for the network associated with the interface to be advertised.

- **Split horizon:** A loop-prevention feature that keeps a router from advertising routes out the same interface on which they were learned might be enabled.

This section looks at each of these reasons individually and explores how to recognize them during the troubleshooting process.

Bad or Missing network Command

When you use the **network** command, the EIGRP process is enabled on the interfaces that fall within the range of IP addresses identified by the command. EIGRP then takes the network/subnet the interface is part of and injects it into the topology table so that it can be advertised to other routers in the autonomous system. Therefore, even interfaces that do not form neighbor relationships with other routers need a valid **network** statement that enables EIGRP on those interfaces so the networks the interfaces belong to are injected into the EIGRP process and advertised. If the **network** statement is missing or configured incorrectly,

EIGRP is not enabled on the interface, and the network the interface belongs to is never advertised and is therefore unreachable by other routers.

As discussed earlier in this chapter, the output of **show ip protocols** displays the **network** statements in a nonintuitive way. Focus on the highlighted text in Example 4-16. Notice that it states Routing for Networks. Those are *not* the networks you are routing for. You are routing for the networks associated with the interface on which EIGRP will be enabled, based on the **network** statement. In this case, **10.1.1.1/32** really means **network 10.1.1.1 0.0.0.0**, and **10.1.12.1/32** really means **network 10.1.12.1 0.0.0.0**.

Example 4-16   *Verifying network Statements with show ip protocols*

```
R1# show ip protocols
*** IP Routing is NSF aware ***

Routing Protocol is "eigrp 100"
  Outgoing update filter list for all interfaces is not set
  Incoming update filter list for all interfaces is not set
  Default networks flagged in outgoing updates
  Default networks accepted from incoming updates
  EIGRP-IPv4 Protocol for AS(100)
    Metric weight K1=1, K2=0, K3=1, K4=0, K5=0
    NSF-aware route hold timer is 240
    Router-ID: 10.1.12.1
    Topology : 0 (base)
      Active Timer: 3 min
      Distance: internal 90 external 170
      Maximum path: 4
      Maximum hopcount 100
      Maximum metric variance 1

  Automatic Summarization: disabled
  Maximum path: 4
  Routing for Networks:
    10.1.1.1/32
    10.1.12.1/32
  Routing Information Sources:
    Gateway         Distance    Last Update
    10.1.12.2             90     09:54:36
  Distance: internal 90 external 170
```

So what networks are you actually routing for? You are routing for the networks associated with the interfaces that are now enabled for EIGRP. In Example 4-17, you can see the output of the **show ip interface** command on R1 for Gig0/0 and Gig1/0, which was piped to include only the **Internet** address. Notice that these two interfaces are in a /24 network. As a result, the network IDs would be 10.1.1.0/24 and 10.1.12.0/24. *Those* are the networks you are routing for.

Example 4-17 *Verifying Network IDs with show ip interface*

```
R1# show ip interface gi0/0 | i Internet
 Internet address is 10.1.1.1/24
R1# show ip interface gi1/0 | i Internet
 Internet address is 10.1.12.1/24
```

Therefore, if you expect to route for the network 10.1.1.0/24 or 10.1.12.0/24, as in this case, you better have a **network** statement that enables the EIGRP process on the router interfaces in those networks.

You can confirm which interfaces are participating in the EIGRP process by using the **show ip eigrp interfaces** command, as shown earlier in Example 4-4.

Better Source of Information

For an EIGRP-learned route to be installed in the routing table, it must be the most trusted routing source. Recall that the trustworthiness of a source is based on administrative distance (AD). EIGRP's AD is 90 for internally learned routes (networks inside the autonomous system) and 170 for externally learned routes (networks outside the autonomous system). Therefore, if there is another source that is educating the same router about exactly the same network and that source has a better AD, the source with the better AD wins, and its information is installed in the routing table. Compare Example 4-18, which is an EIGRP topology table, and Example 4-19, which is the routing table displaying only the EIGRP installed routes on the router. Focus on the highlighted networks of the topology table. Do you see them listed as EIGRP routes in the routing table?

Example 4-18 *Sample show ip eigrp topology Command Output*

```
Router# show ip eigrp topology
EIGRP-IPv4 Topology Table for AS(100)/ID(192.4.4.4)
Codes: P - Passive, A - Active, U - Update, Q - Query, R - Reply,
 r - reply Status, s - sia Status

P 172.16.33.8/30, 2 successors, FD is 2681856
        via 172.16.33.6 (2681856/2169856), Serial1/0
        via 172.16.33.18 (2681856/2169856), Serial1/2
P 10.1.34.0/24, 1 successors, FD is 2816
        via Connected, GigabitEthernet2/0
P 192.7.7.7/32, 1 successors, FD is 2300416
        via 172.16.33.5 (2300416/156160), Serial1/0
        via 172.16.33.6 (2809856/2297856), Serial1/0
        via 172.16.33.18 (2809856/2297856), Serial1/2
P 192.4.4.4/32, 1 successors, FD is 128256
        via Connected, Loopback0
P 172.16.33.16/30, 1 successors, FD is 2169856
        via Connected, Serial1/2
```

```
P 172.16.32.0/25, 2 successors, FD is 2172416
        via 172.16.33.6 (2172416/28160), Serial1/0
        via 172.16.33.18 (2172416/28160), Serial1/2
P 10.1.23.0/24, 1 successors, FD is 3072
        via 10.1.34.3 (3072/2816), GigabitEthernet2/0
P 203.0.113.0/30, 1 successors, FD is 28160
        via Connected, FastEthernet3/0
P 192.5.5.5/32, 1 successors, FD is 2297856
        via 172.16.33.5 (2297856/128256), Serial1/0
P 192.3.3.3/32, 1 successors, FD is 130816
        via 10.1.34.3 (130816/128256), GigabitEthernet2/0
P 192.2.2.2/32, 1 successors, FD is 131072
        via 10.1.34.3 (131072/130816), GigabitEthernet2/0
P 10.1.13.0/24, 1 successors, FD is 3072
        via 10.1.34.3 (3072/2816), GigabitEthernet2/0
P 0.0.0.0/0, 1 successors, FD is 28160
        via Rstatic (28160/0)
P 192.1.1.1/32, 1 successors, FD is 131072
        via 10.1.34.3 (131072/130816), GigabitEthernet2/0
P 172.16.32.192/29, 1 successors, FD is 2174976
        via 172.16.33.5 (2174976/30720), Serial1/0
        via 172.16.33.6 (2684416/2172416), Serial1/0
        via 172.16.33.18 (2684416/2172416), Serial1/2
P 198.51.100.0/30, 1 successors, FD is 28416
        via 10.1.34.3 (28416/28160), GigabitEthernet2/0
P 172.16.33.12/30, 1 successors, FD is 2172416
        via 172.16.33.5 (2172416/28160), Serial1/0
P 192.6.6.6/32, 2 successors, FD is 2297856
        via 172.16.33.6 (2297856/128256), Serial1/0
        via 172.16.33.18 (2297856/128256), Serial1/2
P 172.16.33.0/29, 1 successors, FD is 2169856
        via Connected, Serial1/0
P 10.1.1.0/26, 1 successors, FD is 3328
        via 10.1.34.3 (3328/3072), GigabitEthernet2/0
P 172.16.32.128/26, 1 successors, FD is 2172416
        via 172.16.33.5 (2172416/28160), Serial1/0
```

Example 4-19 *Sample show ip route eigrp Command Output*

```
Router# show ip route eigrp
Codes: L - local, C - connected, S - static, R - RIP, M - mobile, B - BGP
  D - EIGRP, EX - EIGRP external, O - OSPF, IA - OSPF inter area
  N1 - OSPF NSSA external type 1, N2 - OSPF NSSA external type 2
```

```
     E1 - OSPF external type 1, E2 - OSPF external type 2
     i - IS-IS, su - IS-IS summary, L1 - IS-IS level-1, L2 - IS-IS level-2
     ia - IS-IS inter area, * - candidate default, U - per-user static route
     o - ODR, P - periodic downloaded static route, H - NHRP, l - LISP
     + - replicated route, % - next hop override

Gateway of last resort is 203.0.113.1 to network 0.0.0.0

     10.0.0.0/8 is variably subnetted, 5 subnets, 3 masks
D       10.1.1.0/26 [90/3328] via 10.1.34.3, 00:49:19, GigabitEthernet2/0
D       10.1.13.0/24 [90/3072] via 10.1.34.3, 00:49:22, GigabitEthernet2/0
D       10.1.23.0/24 [90/3072] via 10.1.34.3, 00:49:22, GigabitEthernet2/0
     172.16.0.0/16 is variably subnetted, 9 subnets, 5 masks
D       172.16.32.0/25 [90/2172416] via 172.16.33.18, 00:49:22, Serial1/2
                        [90/2172416] via 172.16.33.6, 00:49:22, Serial1/0
D       172.16.32.128/26 [90/2172416] via 172.16.33.5, 00:49:23, Serial1/0
D       172.16.32.192/29 [90/2174976] via 172.16.33.5, 00:49:23, Serial1/0
D       172.16.33.8/30 [90/2681856] via 172.16.33.18, 00:49:22, Serial1/2
                        [90/2681856] via 172.16.33.6, 00:49:22, Serial1/0
D       172.16.33.12/30 [90/2172416] via 172.16.33.5, 00:49:23, Serial1/0
     192.1.1.0/32 is subnetted, 1 subnets
D       192.1.1.1 [90/131072] via 10.1.34.3, 00:49:19, GigabitEthernet2/0
     192.2.2.0/32 is subnetted, 1 subnets
D       192.2.2.2 [90/131072] via 10.1.34.3, 00:49:19, GigabitEthernet2/0
     192.3.3.0/32 is subnetted, 1 subnets
D       192.3.3.3 [90/130816] via 10.1.34.3, 00:49:22, GigabitEthernet2/0
     192.5.5.0/32 is subnetted, 1 subnets
D       192.5.5.5 [90/2297856] via 172.16.33.5, 00:49:23, Serial1/0
     192.6.6.0/32 is subnetted, 1 subnets
D       192.6.6.6 [90/2297856] via 172.16.33.18, 00:49:22, Serial1/2
                   [90/2297856] via 172.16.33.6, 00:49:22, Serial1/0
     192.7.7.0/32 is subnetted, 1 subnets
D       192.7.7.7 [90/2300416] via 172.16.33.5, 00:49:23, Serial1/0
     198.51.100.0/30 is subnetted, 1 subnets
D       198.51.100.0 [90/28416] via 10.1.34.3, 00:49:22, GigabitEthernet2/0
```

None of the highlighted routes in Example 4-18 appear in the routing table as EIGRP routes. In this case, there is a better source for the same information. Example 4-20, which displays the output of the **show ip route 172.16.33.16 255.255.255.252** command, identifies that this network is directly connected and has an AD of 0. Because a directly connected network has an AD of 0, and an internal EIGRP route has an AD of 90, the directly connected source is installed in the routing table. Refer to Example 4-18 and focus on the 0.0.0.0/0 route. Notice that it says Rstatic, which means that the route was redistributed from a static route on this router. Therefore, there is a static default route on the local router with a better AD than the EIGRP default route, which would have an AD of 170. As a result, the EIGRP 0.0.0.0/0 route would not be installed in the routing table, and the static default route would be.

Example 4-20   *Sample show ip route 172.16.33.16 255.255.255.252 Command Output*

```
Router# show ip route 172.16.33.16 255.255.255.252
Routing entry for 172.16.33.16/30
  Known via "connected", distance 0, metric 0 (connected, via interface)
...output omitted...
```

Using a suboptimal source of routing information may not cause users to complain or submit a trouble ticket because they will probably still be able to access the resources they need. However, it may cause suboptimal routing in the network. Figure 4-1 shows a network running two different routing protocols. In this case, which path will be used to send traffic from PC1 to 10.1.1.0/24? If you said the longer EIGRP path, you are correct. Even though it is quicker to use the Open Shortest Path First (OSPF) path, EIGRP wins by default because it has the lower AD, and suboptimal routing occurs.

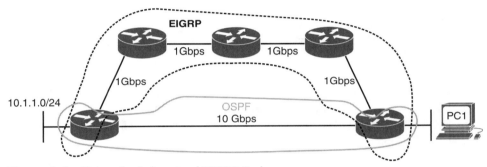

Figure 4-1   *Using the Suboptimal EIGRP Path*

Being able to recognize when a certain routing source should be used and when it should not be used is key to optimizing your network and reducing the number of troubleshooting instances related to the network being perceived as slow. In this case, you might want to consider increasing the AD of EIGRP or lowering the AD of OSPF to optimize routing.

Route Filtering

A distribute list applied to an EIGRP process controls which routes are advertised to neighbors and which routes are received from neighbors. The distribute list is applied in EIGRP configuration mode either inbound or outbound, and the routes sent or received are controlled by ACLs, prefix lists, or route maps. So, when troubleshooting route filtering, you need to consider the following:

■ Is the distribute list applied in the correct direction?

■ Is the distribute list applied to the correct interface?

■ If the distribute list is using an ACL, is the ACL correct?

■ If the distribute list is using a prefix list, is the prefix list correct?

■ If the distribute list is using a route map, is the route map correct?

The **show ip protocols** command identifies whether a distribute list is applied to all interfaces or to an individual interface, as shown in Example 4-21. This example indicates that there are no outbound filters and that there is an inbound filter on Gig1/0.

Example 4-21   *Verifying Route Filters with show ip protocols*

```
R1# show ip protocols
*** IP Routing is NSF aware ***


Routing Protocol is "eigrp 100"
Outgoing update filter list for all interfaces is not set
Incoming update filter list for all interfaces is not set
     GigabitEthernet1/0 filtered by 10 (per-user), default is not set
Default networks flagged in outgoing updates
Default networks accepted from incoming updates
EIGRP-IPv4 Protocol for AS(100)
    Metric weight K1=1, K2=0, K3=1, K4=0, K5=0
    NSF-aware route hold timer is 240
    Router-ID: 10.1.12.1
...output omitted...
```

The inbound filter in Example 4-21 on Gig1/0 is filtering with ACL 10. To verify the entries in the ACL, you must issue the **show access-lists 10** command. If a prefix list was applied, you issue the **show ip prefix-list** command. If a route map was applied, you issue the **show route-map** command.

As shown in Example 4-22, you verify the command that was used to apply the distribute list in the running configuration by reviewing the EIGRP configuration section.

Example 4-22   *Verifying the EIGRP distribute-list Command*

```
R1# show run | section router eigrp
router eigrp 100
 distribute-list 10 in GigabitEthernet1/0
 network 10.1.1.1 0.0.0.0
 network 10.1.12.1 0.0.0.0
 passive-interface GigabitEthernet0/0
```

Stub Configuration

The EIGRP *stub* feature allows you to control the scope of EIGRP queries in the network. Figure 4-2 shows the failure of network 192.168.1.0/24 on R1 that causes a query to be sent to R2 and then a query from R2 to be sent to R3 and R4. However, the query to R3 is not needed because R3 will never have alternate information about the 192.168.1.0/24 network. The query wastes resources and slows convergence. As shown in Figure 4-3, configuring the EIGRP stub feature on R3 with the **eigrp stub** command ensures that R2 never sends a query to R3.

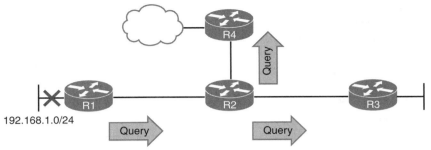

Figure 4-2 *Query Scope Without the EIGRP Stub Feature*

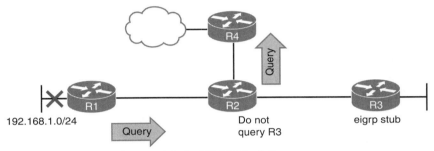

Figure 4-3 *Query Scope with the EIGRP Stub Feature*

This feature comes in handy over slow hub-and-spoke WAN links, as shown in Figure 4-4. The stub feature prevents the hub from querying the spokes, which reduces the amount of EIGRP traffic sent over the link. In addition, it reduces the chance of a route being stuck in active (SIA). SIA happens when a router does not receive a reply to a query that it sent. Over WANs, this can happen due to congestion, and it can result in the reestablishment of neighbor relationships, causing convergence and generating even more EIGRP traffic. Therefore, if you do not query the spokes, you do not have to worry about these issues.

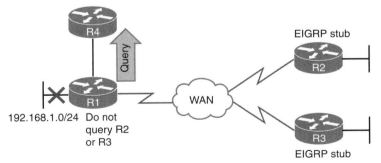

Figure 4-4 *EIGRP Stub Feature over WAN Links*

When configuring the EIGRP stub feature, you can control what routes the stub router advertises to its neighbor. By default, it advertises connected and summary routes. However, you have the option of advertising connected, summary, redistributed, or static—or a combination of these. The other option is to send no routes (called *receive only*). If the wrong option is chosen, the stub routers do not advertise the correct routes to their neighbors, resulting in missing routes on the hub and on other routers in the topology. In addition, if you configure the wrong router as the stub router (for example, R1 in Figure 4-4), R1 never fully shares all routes it knows about to R4, R2, and R3, resulting in missing routes in the topology. To verify whether a router is a stub router and determine the routes it will advertise, issue the **show ip protocols** command, as shown in Example 4-23.

Example 4-23 *show ip protocols Command Output on R2*

```
R2# show ip protocols
...output omitted...
 EIGRP-IPv4 Protocol for AS(100)
    Metric weight K1=1, K2=0, K3=1, K4=0, K5=0
    NSF-aware route hold timer is 240
    Router-ID: 192.1.1.1
    Stub, connected, summary
    Topology : 0 (base)
      Active Timer: 3 min
      Distance: internal 90 external 170
      Maximum path: 4
...output omitted...
```

To determine whether a neighbor is a stub router and the types of routes it is advertising, issue the command **show ip eigrp neighbors detail**. Example 4-24 shows the output of **show ip eigrp neighbors detail** on R1, which indicates that the neighbor is a stub router advertising connected and summary routes and suppressing queries.

Example 4-24 *Verifying Whether an EIGRP Neighbor Is a Stub Router*

```
R1# show ip eigrp neighbors detail
EIGRP-IPv4 Neighbors for AS(100)
H   Address                 Interface       Hold Uptime   SRTT   RTO  Q  Seq
                                            (sec)         (ms)       Cnt Num
0   10.1.13.1               Se1/0           14 00:00:18   99     594  0   11
   Version 11.0/2.0, Retrans: 0, Retries: 0, Prefixes: 2
   Topology-ids from peer - 0
   Stub Peer Advertising (CONNECTED SUMMARY ) Routes
   Suppressing queries
...output omitted...
```

Interface Is Shut Down

As discussed earlier, the **network** command enables the routing process on an interface. Once the EIGRP process is enabled on the interface, the network the interface is part of (that is, the directly connected entry in the routing table) is injected into the EIGRP process. If the interface is shut down, there is no directly connected entry for the network in the routing table. Therefore, the network does not exist, and there is no network that can be injected into the EIGRP process. The interface must be up/up for routes to be advertised or for neighbor relationships to be formed.

Split Horizon

The EIGRP split-horizon rule states that any routes learned inbound on an interface will not be advertised out the same interface. This rule is designed to prevent routing loops. However, this rule presents an issue in certain topologies. Figure 4-5 shows an older nonbroadcast multi-access (NBMA) Frame Relay hub-and-spoke topology or a newer Dynamic Multipoint Virtual Private Network (DMVPN) network, which both use multipoint interfaces on the hub. The multipoint interface (a single physical interface or a mGRE tunnel interface) provides connectivity to multiple routers in the same subnet out the single interface, as does Ethernet. In this figure, R2 is sending an EIGRP update to R1 on the permanent virtual circuit (PVC) or Generic Routing Encapsulation (GRE) tunnel. Because split horizon is enabled on the Se1/0 interface or the multipoint GRE tunnel interface on R1, R1 does not advertise the 10.1.2.0/24 network back out that interface. Therefore, R3 never learns about 10.1.2.0/24.

To verify whether split horizon is enabled on an interface, issue the **show ip interface** *interface_type interface_number* command, as shown in Example 4-25. In this case, you can see that split horizon is enabled.

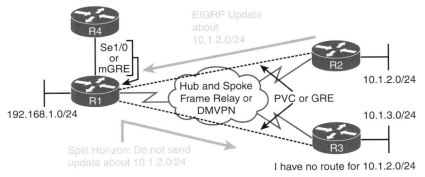

Figure 4-5 *EIGRP Split Horizon Issue*

Example 4-25 *Verifying Whether Split Horizon Is Enabled on an Interface*

```
R1# show ip interface tunnel 0
Tunnel0 is up, line protocol is up
  Internet address is 192.168.1.1/24
  Broadcast address is 255.255.255.255
  Address determined by setup command
  MTU is 1476 bytes
  Helper address is not set
  Directed broadcast forwarding is disabled
  Outgoing access list is not set
  Inbound access list is not set
  Proxy ARP is enabled
  Local Proxy ARP is disabled
  Security level is default
  Split horizon is enabled
  ICMP redirects are never sent
...output omitted...
```

To completely disable split horizon on an interface, issue the **no ip split-horizon** command in interface configuration mode. If you only want to disable it for the EIGRP process running on the interface, issue the command **no ip split-horizon eigrp** *autonomous_system_number*.

If you disable split horizon for the EIGRP process, it still shows as enabled in the output of **show ip interface** (refer to Example 4-25). To verify whether split horizon is enabled or disabled for the EIGRP process on an interface, issue the command **show ip eigrp interfaces detail** *interface_type interface_number*. Example 4-26 shows that it is disabled for EIGRP on interface tunnel 0.

Example 4-26   *Verifying Whether Split Horizon Is Enabled for EIGRP on an Interface*

```
R1# show ip eigrp interfaces detail tunnel 0
EIGRP-IPv4 Interfaces for AS(100)
                         Xmit Queue   Mean   Pacing Time   Multicast    Pending
Interface      Peers   Un/Reliable   SRTT   Un/Reliable   Flow Timer   Routes
Tu0               0       0/0          0        6/6            0          0
  Hello-interval is 5, Hold-time is 15
  Split-horizon is disabled
  Next xmit serial <none>
  Packetized sent/expedited: 0/0
  Hello's sent/expedited: 17/1
  Un/reliable mcasts: 0/0 Un/reliable ucasts: 0/0
  Mcast exceptions: 0 CR packets: 0 ACKs suppressed: 0
  Retransmissions sent: 0 Out-of-sequence rcvd: 0
  Topology-ids on interface - 0
  Authentication mode is not set
```

Troubleshooting Miscellaneous EIGRP for IPv4 Issues

So far in this chapter, the focus has been on troubleshooting EIGRP neighbor relationships and routes. In this section, the focus is on troubleshooting issues related to feasible successors, discontiguous networks and autosummarization, route summarization, and equal- and unequal-metric load balancing.

Feasible Successors

The best route (based on the lowest *feasible distance* [FD] metric) for a specific network in the EIGRP topology table becomes a candidate to be injected into the router's routing table. (The term *candidate* is used because even though it is the best EIGRP route, a better source of the same information might be used instead.) If that route is indeed injected into the routing table, that route becomes known as the *successor* (best) route. This is the route that is then advertised to neighboring routers. Example 4-27 shows a sample EIGRP topology table, which you can view by issuing the **show ip eigrp topology** command. Focus on the entry for 172.16.32.192/29. Notice that there are three paths to reach that network. However, based on the fact that it states 1 successors, only one path is being used as the best path. It is the one with the lowest FD, 2174976, which is the path through 172.16.33.5, reachable out interface Serial1/0.

Example 4-27 *Sample show ip eigrp topology Command Output*

```
R4# show ip eigrp topology
EIGRP-IPv4 Topology Table for AS(100)/ID(192.4.4.4)
Codes: P - Passive, A - Active, U - Update, Q - Query, R - Reply,
 r - reply Status, s - sia Status


...output omitted...
P 10.1.13.0/24, 1 successors, FD is 3072
        via 10.1.34.3 (3072/2816), GigabitEthernet2/0
P 0.0.0.0/0, 1 successors, FD is 28160
        via Rstatic (28160/0)
P 192.1.1.1/32, 1 successors, FD is 131072
        via 10.1.34.3 (131072/130816), GigabitEthernet2/0
P 172.16.32.192/29, 1 successors, FD is 2174976
        via 172.16.33.5 (2174976/30720), Serial1/0
        via 172.16.33.6 (2684416/2172416), Serial1/0
        via 172.16.33.18 (2684416/2172416), Serial1/2
P 198.51.100.0/30, 1 successors, FD is 28416
        via 10.1.34.3 (28416/28160), GigabitEthernet2/0
P 172.16.33.12/30, 1 successors, FD is 2172416
        via 172.16.33.5 (2172416/28160), Serial1/0
...output omitted...
```

In the brackets after the next-hop IP address is the FD followed by the *reported distance* (RD):

■ **Feasible distance:** The RD plus the metric to reach the neighbor at the next-hop address that is advertising the RD

■ **Reported distance:** The distance from the neighbor at the next-hop address to the destination network

The successor is the path with the lowest FD. However, EIGRP also pre-calculates paths that could be used if the successor disappeared. These are known as the *feasible successors*. To be a feasible successor, the RD of the path to become a feasible successor must be less than the FD of the successor. Review Example 4-27. The path through 172.16.33.5 is the successor. However, are the paths using 172.16.33.6 and 172.16.33.18 feasible successors (backups)? To determine this, take the RD of these paths (in this case, it is the same [2172416]), and compare it to the FD of the successor (2174976). Is the RD less than the FD? Yes. Therefore, they are feasible successors.

For troubleshooting, it is important to note that the output of **show ip eigrp topology** only displays the successors and feasible successors. If you need to verify the FD or RD of other paths to the same destination that are not feasible successors, you can use the **show ip eigrp topology all-links** command. Example 4-28 displays the output of **show ip eigrp topology** and **show ip eigrp topology all-links**. Focus on the entry for 10.1.34.0/24. In the output of

show ip eigrp topology, notice that there is only one path listed; in the output of show ip
eigrp topology all-links, notice that there are two paths listed. This is because the next hop
172.16.33.13 has an RD greater than the FD of the successor and therefore cannot be a feasible successor.

Example 4-28 *Sample show ip eigrp topology Comparison*

```
Router# show ip eigrp topology
EIGRP-IPv4 Topology Table for AS(100)/ID(172.16.33.14)
Codes: P - Passive, A - Active, U - Update, Q - Query, R - Reply,
       r - reply Status, s - sia Status


P 172.16.33.8/30, 1 successors, FD is 2169856
        via Connected, Serial1/0
P 10.1.34.0/24, 1 successors, FD is 2682112
        via 172.16.33.9 (2682112/2170112), Serial1/0
P 203.0.113.0/30, 1 successors, FD is 2684416
        via 172.16.33.9 (2684416/2172416), Serial1/0
P 172.16.32.192/29, 1 successors, FD is 28160
        via Connected, FastEthernet2/0
P 172.16.33.12/30, 1 successors, FD is 5511936
        via Connected, Serial1/1
P 172.16.33.0/29, 1 successors, FD is 2681856
        via 172.16.33.9 (2681856/2169856), Serial1/0


Router# show ip eigrp topology all-links
EIGRP-IPv4 Topology Table for AS(100)/ID(172.16.33.14)
Codes: P - Passive, A - Active, U - Update, Q - Query, R - Reply,
       r - reply Status, s - sia Status


P 172.16.33.8/30, 1 successors, FD is 2169856, serno 1
        via Connected, Serial1/0
P 10.1.34.0/24, 1 successors, FD is 2682112, serno 8
        via 172.16.33.9 (2682112/2170112), Serial1/0
        via 172.16.33.13 (6024192/3072256), Serial1/1
P 203.0.113.0/30, 1 successors, FD is 2684416, serno 9
        via 172.16.33.9 (2684416/2172416), Serial1/0
        via 172.16.33.13 (6026496/3074560), Serial1/1
P 172.16.32.192/29, 1 successors, FD is 28160, serno 3
        via Connected, FastEthernet2/0
P 172.16.33.12/30, 1 successors, FD is 5511936, serno 2
        via Connected, Serial1/1
P 172.16.33.0/29, 1 successors, FD is 2681856, serno 5
        via 172.16.33.9 (2681856/2169856), Serial1/0
        via 172.16.33.13 (6023936/3072000), Serial1/1
```

The EIGRP topology table contains not only the routes learned from other routers but also routes that have been redistributed into the EIGRP process and the local connected networks whose interfaces are participating in the EIGRP process, as highlighted in Example 4-29.

Example 4-29   *Verifying Connected and Redistributed Entries in the Topology Table*

```
R4# show ip eigrp topology
EIGRP-IPv4 Topology Table for AS(100)/ID(192.4.4.4)
Codes: P - Passive, A - Active, U - Update, Q - Query, R - Reply,
       r - reply Status, s - sia Status

...output omitted...
P 192.2.2.2/32, 1 successors, FD is 131072
        via 10.1.34.3 (131072/130816), GigabitEthernet2/0
P 10.1.13.0/24, 1 successors, FD is 3072
        via 10.1.34.3 (3072/2816), GigabitEthernet2/0
P 0.0.0.0/0, 1 successors, FD is 28160
        via Rstatic (28160/0)
P 192.1.1.1/32, 1 successors, FD is 131072
        via 10.1.34.3 (131072/130816), GigabitEthernet2/0
P 172.16.32.192/29, 1 successors, FD is 2174976
         via 172.16.33.5 (2174976/30720), Serial1/0
         via 172.16.33.6 (2684416/2172416), Serial1/0
         via 172.16.33.18 (2684416/2172416), Serial1/2
P 198.51.100.0/30, 1 successors, FD is 28416
         via 10.1.34.3 (28416/28160), GigabitEthernet2/0
P 172.16.33.12/30, 1 successors, FD is 2172416
         via 172.16.33.5 (2172416/28160), Serial1/0
P 192.6.6.6/32, 2 successors, FD is 2297856
         via 172.16.33.6 (2297856/128256), Serial1/0
         via 172.16.33.18 (2297856/128256), Serial1/2
P 172.16.33.0/29, 1 successors, FD is 2169856
        via Connected, Serial1/0
...output omitted...
```

Discontiguous Networks and Autosummarization

EIGRP supports variable-length subnet masking (VLSM). In earlier releases of Cisco IOS (before release 15.0), EIGRP automatically performed route summarization at *classful* network boundaries. This was an issue in networks containing *discontiguous networks*. As a result, it was necessary when configuring EIGRP to turn off automatic summarization (or *autosummarization*) by using the **no auto-summary** command in router configuration mode for an EIGRP autonomous system. However, from Cisco IOS 15.0 onward, autosummarization is off by default for EIGRP. Therefore, you do not have to worry about issuing the **no auto-summary** command anymore. However, you should be able to recognize a discontiguous network when reviewing a network topology and understand that if someone manually enabled autosummarization in your EIGRP autonomous system, routing would be broken.

Figure 4-6 provides an example of a discontiguous network. The 172.16.0.0/16 Class B classful network is considered discontiguous because it is subnetted as 172.16.1.0/24 and 172.16.2.0/24, and the subnets are separated from each other by a different classful network, which is 10.0.0.0. With automatic summarization turned on, when R3 advertises the 172.16.2.0/24 network to R2, it is summarized to 172.16.0.0/16 because it is being sent out an interface in a different classful network. So, instead of 172.16.2.0/24 being sent, 172.16.0.0/16 is sent. Likewise, the same thing happens when R1 advertises the 172.16.1.0/24 network to R2; it is advertised as 172.16.0.0/16. If you reviewed R2's routing table, you would see an entry for 172.16.0.0 with two next hops (if everything else is equal): one through R3 using Fa0/1 and the other through R1 using Fa0/0.

Now picture a packet arriving at R2 from R4 with the destination IP address 172.16.2.5. Which way does R2 send it? You see the problem? It should send it out Fa0/1, but it could send it out Fa0/0. There is a 50/50 chance it gets it correct. The moral of this story is this: If you have a discontiguous network, autosummarization has to be off, and you must take care when performing manual summarization. To verify whether automatic summarization is enabled or disabled, use the **show ip protocols** command, as shown in Example 4-30.

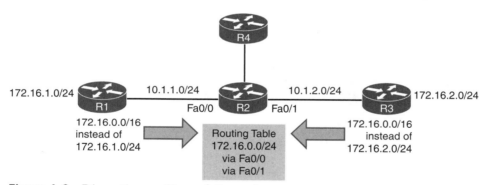

Figure 4-6 *Discontiguous Network Example*

Example 4-30 *Verifying Route Summarization with show ip protocols*

```
Router# show ip protocols
...output omitted...
 EIGRP-IPv4 Protocol for AS(100)
   Metric weight K1=1, K2=0, K3=1, K4=0, K5=0
   NSF-aware route hold timer is 240
   Router-ID: 10.1.13.1
   Topology : 0 (base)
     Active Timer: 3 min
     Distance: internal 90 external 170
     Maximum path: 4
     Maximum hopcount 100
```

```
      Maximum metric variance 1


  Automatic Summarization: disabled
  Address Summarization:
     10.1.0.0/20 for Gi2/0
        Summarizing 2 components with metric 2816
  Maximum path: 4
  Routing for Networks:
...output omitted...
```

Route Summarization

By default with IOS 15.0 and later, autosummarization is off. Therefore, you can either turn it on (which is not recommended) or perform manual route summarization (which is recommended). With EIGRP, manual route summarization is enabled on an interface-by-interface basis. Therefore, when troubleshooting route summarization, consider the following:

- Did you enable route summarization on the correct interface?

- Did you associate the summary route with the correct EIGRP autonomous system?

- Did you create the appropriate summary route?

You determine answers to all these questions by using the **show ip protocols** command, as shown in Example 4-30. In this example, autosummarization is disabled, and manual summarization is enabled for EIGRP autonomous system 100 on interface Gi2/0 for 10.1.0.0/20.

It is important that you create accurate summary routes to ensure that your router is not advertising networks in the summary route that it does not truly know how to reach. If it does, it is possible that it might receive packets to destinations that fall within the summary that it really does not know how to reach. If this is the case, it means that packets will be dropped because of the route to null 0.

When a summary route is created on a router, so is a summary route to null 0, as shown in the following snippet:

```
Router# show ip route | include Null

D 10.1.0.0/20 is a summary, 00:12:03, Null0
```

This route to null 0 is created to prevent routing loops. It is imperative that this route exists in the table to ensure that when a packet is received by the router with a destination address that falls within the summary, and a more specific route does not exist, the packet will be dropped. If the route to null 0 did not exist, and there was a default route on the router, the router would forward the packet using the default route. The next-hop router would then end up forwarding the packet back to this router because it would be using the summary route. The local router would then forward it based on the default route again, and then it would come back. This is a routing loop.

The route to null 0 has an AD of 5, as shown in the following snippet, to ensure that it is more trustworthy than most of the other sources of routing information:

```
Router# show ip route 10.1.0.0
Routing entry for 10.1.0.0/20
  Known via "eigrp 100", distance 5, metric 2816, type internal
```

Therefore, the only way this route would not be in the routing table is if you had a source with a lower AD (for example, if someone created a static route for the same summary network and pointed it to a next-hop IP address instead of null 0). This would cause a routing loop.

Load Balancing

By default, EIGRP does load balancing on four equal-metric paths. You can change this with the **maximum-paths** command in router configuration mode for EIGRP. However, EIGRP also supports load balancing across unequal-metric paths, using the *variance* feature. By default, the variance value for an EIGRP routing process is 1, which means the load balancing will occur only over equal-metric paths. You issue the **variance** *multiplier* command in router configuration mode to specify a range of metrics over which load balancing will occur. For example, suppose that a route has a metric of 200000, and you configure the **variance 2** command for the EIGRP routing process. This causes load balancing to occur over any route with a metric in the range of 200000 through 400000 (that is, 2 × 200000). As you can see, a route could have a metric as high as 400000 (that is, the variance multiplier multiplied by the best metric) and still be used.

However, even with unequal-metric load balancing, you are still governed by the **maximum-paths** command. Therefore, if you have five unequal-metric paths that you want to use, and you configure the correct variance multiplier, but **maximum-paths** is set to 2, you use only two of the five paths. To use all five, you would also need to make sure that **maximum-paths** is set to 5.

Also, remember that the feasibility condition plays a huge role in unequal-path load balancing to prevent routing loops. If the path is not a feasible successor, it cannot be used for unequal-path load balancing. There is no exception to this rule. Recall the feasibility condition: *To be a feasible successor, the RD must be less than the FD of the successor.*

To verify the configured *maximum paths* and *variance*, you use the **show ip protocols** command, as shown in Example 4-31.

Example 4-31   *Verifying Variance and Maximum Paths*

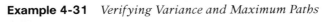

```
Router# show ip protocols
Routing Protocol is "eigrp 100"
  Outgoing update filter list for all interfaces is not set
  Incoming update filter list for all interfaces is not set
  Default networks flagged in outgoing updates
  Default networks accepted from incoming updates
  EIGRP-IPv4 Protocol for AS(100)
```

```
    Metric weight K1=1, K2=0, K3=1, K4=0, K5=0
    NSF-aware route hold timer is 240
    Router-ID: 10.1.12.1
    Topology : 0 (base)
      Active Timer: 3 min
      Distance: internal 90 external 170
      Maximum path: 4
      Maximum hopcount 100
      Maximum metric variance 1

  Automatic Summarization: disabled
  Maximum path: 4
  Routing for Networks:
    0.0.0.0
  Routing Information Sources:
    Gateway    Distance    Last Update
    10.1.12.2        90    10:26:36
  Distance: internal 90 external 170
```

EIGRP for IPv4 Trouble Tickets

This section presents various trouble tickets related to the topics discussed earlier in the chapter. The purpose of these trouble tickets is to show a process that you can follow when troubleshooting in the real world or in an exam environment. All trouble tickets in this section are based on the topology shown in Figure 4-7.

EIGRP AS 100

Figure 4-7 *EIGRP for IPv4 Trouble Tickets Topology*

Trouble Ticket 4-1

Problem: Users in the 10.1.1.0/24 network indicate that they are not able to access resources in the 10.1.3.0/24 network.

As always, the first item on the list for troubleshooting is to verify the problem. You access a PC in the 10.1.1.0/24 network and ping an IP address in the 10.1.3.0/24 network, and it is successful (0% loss), as shown in Example 4-32. However, notice that the reply is from the default gateway at 10.1.1.1, and it states Destination host unreachable. Therefore, it was technically not successful.

Example 4-32 *Destination Unreachable Result from the **ping** Command on a PC*

```
C:\>ping 10.1.3.10


Pinging 10.1.3.10 with 32 bytes of data;


Reply from 10.1.1.1: Destination host unreachable.
Reply from 10.1.1.1: Destination host unreachable.
Reply from 10.1.1.1: Destination host unreachable.
Reply from 10.1.1.1: Destination host unreachable.


Ping statistics for 10.1.3.10:
    Packets: Sent = 4, Received = 4, lost = 0 (0% loss),
Approximate round trip times in milli-seconds:
    Minimum = 0ms, Maximum = 0ms, Average = 0ms
```

The result of this ping tells you two very important things: The PC can reach the default gateway, and the default gateway does not know how to get to the 10.1.3.0/24 network. Therefore, you can focus your attention on R1 and work from there.

On R1, you issue the same ping, but it fails, as shown in Example 4-33.

Example 4-33 *Failed Ping from R1 to 10.1.3.10*

```
R1# ping 10.1.3.10
Type escape sequence to abort.
Sending 5, 100-byte ICMP Echos to 10.1.3.10, timeout is 2 seconds:
.....
Success rate is 0 percent (0/5)
```

Next, you check R1's routing table with the **show ip route** command and notice that there are only connected routes in the routing table, as shown in Example 4-34. You conclude that R1 is not learning any routes from R2.

Example 4-34 *show ip route Output on R1*

```
R1# show ip route
...output omitted...
Gateway of last resort is not set


      10.0.0.0/8 is variably subnetted, 4 subnets, 2 masks
C        10.1.1.0/24 is directly connected, GigabitEthernet0/0
L        10.1.1.1/32 is directly connected, GigabitEthernet0/0
C        10.1.12.0/24 is directly connected, GigabitEthernet1/0
L        10.1.12.1/32 is directly connected, GigabitEthernet1/0
```

According to Figure 4-7, EIGRP is the routing protocol in use. Therefore, you issue the **show ip protocols** command to verify that EIGRP is using the correct autonomous system number.

Example 4-35 displays the output of **show ip protocols**, which confirms that EIGRP 100 is in operation on R1.

Example 4-35 *show ip protocols Output on R1*

```
R1# show ip protocols
*** IP Routing is NSF aware ***


Routing Protocol is "eigrp 100"
  Outgoing update filter list for all interfaces is not set
  Incoming update filter list for all interfaces is not set
  Default networks flagged in outgoing updates
  Default networks accepted from incoming updates
  EIGRP-IPv4 Protocol for AS(100)
    Metric weight K1=1, K2=0, K3=1, K4=0, K5=0
    NSF-aware route hold timer is 240
    Router-ID: 10.1.12.1
    Topology : 0 (base)
      Active Timer: 3 min
      Distance: internal 90 external 170
      Maximum path: 4
      Maximum hopcount 100
      Maximum metric variance 1

  Automatic Summarization: disabled
  Maximum path: 4
  Routing for Networks:
    10.1.1.1/32
    10.1.12.1/32
  Routing Information Sources:
    Gateway         Distance      Last Update
    10.1.12.2             90      00:45:53
  Distance: internal 90 external 170
```

Next, you check to see whether R1 has any EIGRP neighbors. According to the topology, R2 should be a neighbor. To verify EIGRP neighbors, you issue the **show ip eigrp neighbors** command on R1, as shown in the following snippet:

```
R1# show ip eigrp neighbors
EIGRP-IPv4 Neighbors for AS(100)
```

According to the output, R1 has no neighbors.

Next, you verify whether there are any interfaces participating in the EIGRP process by using the **show ip eigrp interfaces** command. Example 4-36 indicates that there are two interfaces participating in the EIGRP process: Gi0/0 and Gi1/0.

Example 4-36 *show ip eigrp interfaces Output on R1*

```
R1# show ip eigrp interfaces
EIGRP-IPv4 Interfaces for AS(100)
                       Xmit Queue   Mean   Pacing Time   Multicast    Pending
Interface    Peers    Un/Reliable   SRTT   Un/Reliable   Flow Timer   Routes
Gi0/0          0        0/0          0       0/0           0           0
Gi1/0          0        0/0          0       0/0           304         0
```

The output of **show cdp neighbors**, as shown in Example 4-37, indicates that R1 is connected to R2 using Gig 1/0 and that R2 is using Gig 0/0. Therefore, you expect a peering between the two, using these interfaces.

Example 4-37 *show cdp neighbors Output on R1*

```
R1# show cdp neighbors
Capability Codes: R - Router, T - Trans Bridge, B - Source Route Bridge
  S - Switch, H - Host, I - IGMP, r - Repeater, P - Phone,
  D - Remote, C - CVTA, M - Two-port Mac Relay

Device ID    Local Intrfce   Holdtme   Capability   Platform    Port ID
R2           Gig 1/0         172                    R     7206VXR    Gig 0/0
```

Now is a great time to verify whether Gi0/0 on R2 is participating in the EIGRP process. On R2, you issue the **show ip eigrp interfaces** command, as shown in Example 4-38.

Example 4-38 *show ip eigrp interfaces Output on R2*

```
R2# show ip eigrp interfaces
EIGRP-IPv4 Interfaces for AS(100)
                       Xmit Queue   Mean   Pacing Time   Multicast    Pending
Interface    Peers    Un/Reliable   SRTT   Un/Reliable   Flow Timer   Routes
Gi1/0          0        0/0          0       0/0           448         0
```

Example 4-38 confirms that R2's interface Gi0/0 is not participating in the EIGRP process.

You review the output of **show run | section router eigrp** and **show ip interface brief** on R2, as shown in Example 4-39, and confirm that the wrong network statement was issued on R2. The **network** statement **network 10.1.21.2 0.0.0.0** enables the EIGRP process on the interface with that IP address. According to the output of **show ip interface brief**, the **network** statement should be **network 10.1.12.2 0.0.0.0**, based on the IP address 10.1.12.2 of interface GigabitEthernet0/0.

Example 4-39 *show run | section router eigrp Output on R2 and Verifying the Interface IP Address*

```
R2# show run | section router eigrp
router eigrp 100
 network 10.1.21.2 0.0.0.0
```

```
 network 10.1.23.2 0.0.0.0


R2# show ip interface brief
Interface          IP-Address   OK?  Method  Status  Protocol
GigabitEthernet0/0  10.1.12.2   YES  manual  up      up
GigabitEthernet1/0  10.1.23.2   YES  manual  up      up
```

To fix this issue, on R2 you execute the **no network 10.1.21.2 0.0.0.0** command and enter the **network 10.1.12.2 0.0.0.0** command in router EIGRP configuration mode instead. After you have done this, the neighbor relationship forms, as shown with the following syslog messages:

```
R1#

%DUAL-5-NBRCHANGE: EIGRP-IPv4 100: Neighbor 10.1.12.2
(GigabitEthernet1/0) is up: new adjacency

R2#

%DUAL-5-NBRCHANGE: EIGRP-IPv4 100: Neighbor 10.1.12.1
(GigabitEthernet0/0) is up: new adjacency
```

You confirm the neighbor relationship on R1 with the **show ip eigrp neighbors** command, as shown in Example 4-40.

Example 4-40   *Verifying Neighbors with the show ip eigrp neighbors Command*

```
R1# show ip eigrp neighbors
EIGRP-IPv4 Neighbors for AS(100)
H  Address               Interface      Hold Uptime   SRTT   RTO  Q  Seq
                                        (sec)         (ms)       Cnt Num
0  10.1.12.2             Gi1/0          14 00:02:10    75    450  0  12
```

You go back to the PC and ping the same IP address to confirm that the problem is solved, and you receive the same result, as shown in Example 4-41. R1 still does not know about the 10.1.3.0/24 network.

Example 4-41   *Destination Unreachable from the ping Command on a PC*

```
C:\>ping 10.1.3.10

Pinging 10.1.3.10 with 32 bytes of data;

Reply from 10.1.1.1: Destination host unreachable.
Reply from 10.1.1.1: Destination host unreachable.
Reply from 10.1.1.1: Destination host unreachable.
Reply from 10.1.1.1: Destination host unreachable.


Ping statistics for 10.1.3.10:
    Packets: Sent = 4, Received = 4, lost = 0 (0% loss),
Approximate round trip times in milli-seconds:
    Minimum = 0ms, Maximum = 0ms, Average = 0ms
```

Back on R1, you issue the **show ip route** command, as shown in Example 4-42. R1 is receiving EIGRP routes because there is now an EIGRP route in the routing table (as indicated by D). However, R1 still does not know about the 10.1.3.0/24 network.

Example 4-42   *show ip route Output After the Neighbor Relationship with R2 Is Established*

```
R1# show ip route
...output omitted...
Gateway of last resort is not set

      10.0.0.0/8 is variably subnetted, 5 subnets, 2 masks
C        10.1.1.0/24 is directly connected, GigabitEthernet0/0
L        10.1.1.1/32 is directly connected, GigabitEthernet0/0
C        10.1.12.0/24 is directly connected, GigabitEthernet1/0
L        10.1.12.1/32 is directly connected, GigabitEthernet1/0
D        10.1.23.0/24 [90/3072] via 10.1.12.2, 00:07:40, GigabitEthernet1/0
```

Does R2 know about the 10.1.3.0/24 network? Example 4-43 shows R2's routing table, which is missing 10.1.3.0/24 as well.

Example 4-43   *show ip route Output on R2*

```
R2# show ip route
...output omitted...
Gateway of last resort is not set

      10.0.0.0/8 is variably subnetted, 5 subnets, 2 masks
D        10.1.1.0/24 [90/3072] via 10.1.12.1, 00:12:11, GigabitEthernet0/0
C        10.1.12.0/24 is directly connected, GigabitEthernet0/0
L        10.1.12.2/32 is directly connected, GigabitEthernet0/0
C        10.1.23.0/24 is directly connected, GigabitEthernet1/0
L        10.1.23.2/32 is directly connected, GigabitEthernet1/0
```

For R2 to learn about the network, it has to be neighbors with R3. The R2 output of **show ip eigrp neighbors** in Example 4-44 indicates that R3 is not a neighbor; only R1 is.

Example 4-44   *show ip eigrp neighbors on R2*

```
R2# show ip eigrp neighbors
EIGRP-IPv4 Neighbors for AS(100)
H   Address              Interface    Hold   Uptime     SRTT   RTO   Q    Seq
                                      (sec)             (ms)        Cnt  Num
0   10.1.12.1            Gi0/0        11     00:17:28   65     390   0    7
```

Previously, Example 4-38 indicated that Gig1/0 on R2 is participating in the EIGRP process. Therefore, you should look at the interfaces on R3. According to the output in Example 4-45, both interfaces on R3 are participating in the EIGRP process for autonomous system 10.

Example 4-45 *show ip eigrp interfaces on R3*

```
R3# show ip eigrp interfaces
EIGRP-IPv4 Interfaces for AS(10)
                        Xmit Queue   Mean   Pacing Time   Multicast     Pending
Interface       Peers   Un/Reliable  SRTT   Un/Reliable   Flow Timer    Routes
Gi0/0             0        0/0          0       0/0            0            0
Gi1/0             0        0/0          0       0/0            0            0
```

Can you see the issue? If not, look again at Example 4-45. If you need to compare it to Example 4-44, do so.

The autonomous system numbers do not match, and to form an EIGRP neighbor relationship, the autonomous system numbers must match. To solve this issue, you must enable EIGRP autonomous system 100 on R3 and then provide the correct **network** statements to enable EIGRP on the required interfaces for autonomous system 100. You should also remove any EIGRP configurations that are not needed, such as the EIGRP autonomous system 10 configurations. Example 4-46 shows the commands needed to accomplish this.

Example 4-46 *R3 Configurations Required to Solve the Issue*

```
R3# config t
Enter configuration commands, one per line. End with CNTL/Z.
R3(config)# no router eigrp 10
R3(config)# router eigrp 100
R3(config-router)# network 10.1.3.3 0.0.0.0
R3(config-router)# network 10.1.23.3 0.0.0.0
%DUAL-5-NBRCHANGE: EIGRP-IPv4 100: Neighbor 10.1.23.2 (GigabitEthernet1/0) is up:
new adjacency
R3(config-router)#
```

Notice in Example 4-46 that the neighbor relationship with R2 is now successful. Now it is time to verify that all the issues have been solved. On R2, you issue the **show ip route** command, as shown in Example 4-47, and notice that the 10.1.3.0/24 network is present. You also issue the same command on R1 and notice that 10.1.3.0/24 is present, as shown in Example 4-48. You then ping from the PC again, and the ping is truly successful, as shown in Example 4-49.

Example 4-47 *show ip route Output on R2*

```
R2# show ip route
...output omitted...


Gateway of last resort is not set


      10.0.0.0/8 is variably subnetted, 6 subnets, 2 masks
D        10.1.1.0/24 [90/3072] via 10.1.12.1, 00:37:21, GigabitEthernet0/0
D        10.1.3.0/24 [90/3072] via 10.1.23.3, 00:06:16, GigabitEthernet1/0
```

```
C          10.1.12.0/24 is directly connected, GigabitEthernet0/0
L          10.1.12.2/32 is directly connected, GigabitEthernet0/0
C          10.1.23.0/24 is directly connected, GigabitEthernet1/0
L          10.1.23.2/32 is directly connected, GigabitEthernet1/0
```

Example 4-48 *show ip route Output on R1*

```
R1# show ip route
Codes: L - local, C - connected, S - static, R - RIP, M - mobile, B - BGP
       D - EIGRP, EX - EIGRP external, O - OSPF, IA - OSPF inter area
       N1 - OSPF NSSA external type 1, N2 - OSPF NSSA external type 2
       E1 - OSPF external type 1, E2 - OSPF external type 2
       i - IS-IS, su - IS-IS summary, L1 - IS-IS level-1, L2 - IS-IS level-2
       ia - IS-IS inter area, * - candidate default, U - per-user static route
       o - ODR, P - periodic downloaded static route, H - NHRP, l - LISP
       + - replicated route, % - next hop override

Gateway of last resort is not set
      10.0.0.0/8 is variably subnetted, 6 subnets, 2 masks
C        10.1.1.0/24 is directly connected, GigabitEthernet0/0
L        10.1.1.1/32 is directly connected, GigabitEthernet0/0
D        10.1.3.0/24 [90/3328] via 10.1.12.2, 00:07:08, GigabitEthernet1/0
C        10.1.12.0/24 is directly connected, GigabitEthernet1/0
L        10.1.12.1/32 is directly connected, GigabitEthernet1/0
D        10.1.23.0/24 [90/3072] via 10.1.12.2, 00:38:12, GigabitEthernet1/0
```

Example 4-49 *A Successful Ping from the 10.1.1.0/24 Network to the 10.1.3.0/24 Network*

```
C:\>ping 10.1.3.10

Pinging 10.1.3.10 with 32 bytes of data:

Reply from 10.1.3.10: bytes=32 time 1ms TTL=128
Reply from 10.1.3.10: bytes=32 time 1ms TTL=128
Reply from 10.1.3.10: bytes=32 time 1ms TTL=128
Reply from 10.1.3.10: bytes=32 time 1ms TTL=128

Ping statistics for 10.1.3.10:
    Packets: Sent = 4, Received = 4, Lost = 0 (0% loss),
Approximate round trip times in milli-seconds:
    Minimum = 0ms, Maximum = 0ms, Average = 0ms
```

Trouble Ticket 4-2

Problem: Users in the 10.1.1.0/24 network have indicated that they are not able to access resources in 10.1.3.0/24.

To begin, you verify the problem by pinging from a PC in the 10.1.1.0/24 network to a PC in the 10.1.3.0/24 network, as shown in Example 4-50, and it fails. Notice that the reply is from the default gateway at 10.1.1.1, and it states Destination host unreachable. Therefore, it is technically not successful.

Example 4-50 *Destination Unreachable Result from the **ping** Command on a PC*

```
C:\>ping 10.1.3.10

Pinging 10.1.3.10 with 32 bytes of data;

Reply from 10.1.1.1: Destination host unreachable.
Reply from 10.1.1.1: Destination host unreachable.
Reply from 10.1.1.1: Destination host unreachable.
Reply from 10.1.1.1: Destination host unreachable.

Ping statistics for 10.1.3.10:
    Packets: Sent = 4, Received = 4, lost = 0 (0% loss),
Approximate round trip times in milli-seconds:
    Minimum = 0ms, Maximum = 0ms, Average = 0ms
```

The result of this ping tells you two very important things: The PC can reach the default gateway, and the default gateway does not know how to get to the 10.1.3.0/24 network. Therefore, you can focus your attention on R1 and work from there.

On R1, you issue the same ping, but it fails, as shown in Example 4-51.

Example 4-51 *Failed Ping from R1 to 10.1.3.10*

```
R1# ping 10.1.3.10
Type escape sequence to abort.
Sending 5, 100-byte ICMP Echos to 10.1.3.10, timeout is 2 seconds:
.....
Success rate is 0 percent (0/5)
```

Next, you check the routing table on R1 with the **show ip route 10.1.3.0 255.255.255.0** command, as shown in the following snippet:

```
R1# show ip route 10.1.3.0 255.255.255.0
```

This is the result:

```
% Subnet not in table
```

Does R2 know about it? You go to R2 and issue the same command, as shown in the following snippet:

```
R2# show ip route 10.1.3.0 255.255.255.0
```

The result is the same as on R1:

```
% Subnet not in table
```

Next, you go to R3 and issue the same command. Notice that 10.1.3.0/24 is in the routing table as a connected route, as shown in Example 4-52.

Example 4-52   *Determining Whether a Route Is in R3's Routing Table*

```
R3# show ip route 10.1.3.0 255.255.255.0
Routing entry for 10.1.3.0/24
  Known via "connected", distance 0, metric 0 (connected, via interface)
  Redistributing via eigrp 100
  Routing Descriptor Blocks:
  * directly connected, via GigabitEthernet0/0
      Route metric is 0, traffic share count is 1
```

What prevents a connected route from being advertised using EIGRP to a neighbor? As you learned earlier, the interface not participating in the EIGRP process does this. You can check the EIGRP interface table on R3 with the **show ip eigrp interfaces** command. Example 4-53 indicates that only Gi1/0 is participating in the EIGRP process.

Example 4-53   *Determining Whether an Interface Is Participating in the EIGRP Process*

```
R3# show ip eigrp interfaces
EIGRP-IPv4 Interfaces for AS(100)
                    Xmit Queue    Mean   Pacing Time   Multicast    Pending
Interface   Peers   Un/Reliable   SRTT   Un/Reliable   Flow Timer   Routes
Gi1/0        1        0/0         821      0/0           4080         0
```

However, you should not jump to the conclusion that Gi0/0 is not participating in the EIGRP process. Remember that EIGRP passive interfaces do not appear in this output. Therefore, you should check the output of **show ip protocols** for passive interfaces. In Example 4-54, you can see that there are no passive interfaces.

Example 4-54   *Determining Whether an Interface Is Passive*

```
R3# show ip protocols
*** IP Routing is NSF aware ***

Routing Protocol is "eigrp 100"
  Outgoing update filter list for all interfaces is not set
  Incoming update filter list for all interfaces is not set
  Default networks flagged in outgoing updates
  Default networks accepted from incoming updates
  EIGRP-IPv4 Protocol for AS(100)
   Metric weight K1=1, K2=0, K3=1, K4=0, K5=0
    NSF-aware route hold timer is 240
    Router-ID: 10.1.23.3
```

```
    Topology : 0 (base)
       Active Timer: 3 min
       Distance: internal 90 external 170
       Maximum path: 4
       Maximum hopcount 100
       Maximum metric variance 1

  Automatic Summarization: disabled
  Maximum path: 4
  Routing for Networks:
     10.1.3.0/32
     10.1.23.3/32
  Routing Information Sources:
    Gateway          Distance      Last Update
    10.1.23.2              90       00:19:11
  Distance: internal 90 external 170
```

Next, you need to make sure there is a **network** statement that will enable the EIGRP process on the interface connected to the 10.1.3.0/24 network. In Example 4-54, the output of **show ip protocols** indicates that R3 is routing for the network 10.1.3.0/32. Remember from earlier in this chapter that this really means network 10.1.3.0 0.0.0.0. As a result, EIGRP is enabled on the interface with the IP address 10.1.3.0. Example 4-55, which displays the output of **show ip interface brief**, shows that there are no interfaces with that IP address. Interface GigabitEthernet0/0 has the IP address 10.1.3.3. Therefore, the **network** statement is incorrect, as shown in the output of **show run | section router eigrp** in Example 4-56.

Example 4-55   *Reviewing the Interface IP Addresses*

```
R3# show ip interface brief
Interface          IP-Address OK? Method Status Protocol
GigabitEthernet0/0 10.1.3.3    YES NVRAM  up     up
GigabitEthernet1/0 10.1.23.3   YES NVRAM  up     up
```

Example 4-56   *Reviewing the network Statements in the Running Configuration*

```
R3# show run | section router eigrp
router eigrp 100
network 10.1.3.0 0.0.0.0
network 10.1.23.3 0.0.0.0
```

After fixing the issue with the **no network 10.1.3.0 0.0.0.0** command and the **network 10.1.3.3 0.0.0.0** command, you check R1's routing table with the command **show ip route 10.1.3.0 255.255.255.0**. As shown in Example 4-57, 10.1.3.0/24 is now in the routing table and can be reached using the next hop 10.1.12.2.

Example 4-57   *Verifying That 10.1.3.0/24 Is in R1's Routing Table*

```
R1# show ip route 10.1.3.0 255.255.255.0
Routing entry for 10.1.3.0/24
  Known via "eigrp 100", distance 90, metric 3328, type internal
  Redistributing via eigrp 100
  Last update from 10.1.12.2 on GigabitEthernet1/0, 00:00:06 ago
  Routing Descriptor Blocks:
  * 10.1.12.2, from 10.1.12.2, 00:00:06 ago, via GigabitEthernet1/0
      Route metric is 3328, traffic share count is 1
      Total delay is 30 microseconds, minimum bandwidth is 1000000 Kbit
      Reliability 255/255, minimum MTU 1500 bytes
      Loading 1/255, Hops 2
```

Finally, you ping from the PC again, and the ping is successful, as shown in Example 4-58.

Example 4-58   *A Successful Ping from the 10.1.1.0/24 Network to the 10.1.3.0/24 Network*

```
C:\>ping 10.1.3.10

Pinging 10.1.3.10 with 32 bytes of data:

Reply from 10.1.3.10: bytes=32 time 1ms TTL=128
Reply from 10.1.3.10: bytes=32 time 1ms TTL=128
Reply from 10.1.3.10: bytes=32 time 1ms TTL=128
Reply from 10.1.3.10: bytes=32 time 1ms TTL=128

Ping statistics for 10.1.3.10:
    Packets: Sent = 4, Received = 4, Lost = 0 (0% loss),
Approximate round trip times in milli-seconds:
    Minimum = 0ms, Maximum = 0ms, Average = 0ms
```

Trouble Ticket 4-3

Problem: Users in the 10.1.1.0/24 network have indicated that they are not able to access resources in 10.1.3.0/24.

To begin, you verify the problem by pinging from a PC in the 10.1.1.0/24 network to a PC in the 10.1.3.0/24 network. As shown in Example 4-59, the ping fails. Notice that the reply is from the default gateway at 10.1.1.1, and it states Destination host unreachable.

Example 4-59   *Destination Unreachable Result from the ping Command on a PC*

```
C:\>ping 10.1.3.10

Pinging 10.1.3.10 with 32 bytes of data;

Reply from 10.1.1.1: Destination host unreachable.
```

```
Reply from 10.1.1.1: Destination host unreachable.
Reply from 10.1.1.1: Destination host unreachable.
Reply from 10.1.1.1: Destination host unreachable.

Ping statistics for 10.1.3.10:
    Packets: Sent = 4, Received = 4, lost = 0 (0% loss),
Approximate round trip times in milli-seconds:
    Minimum = 0ms, Maximum = 0ms, Average = 0ms
```

The result of this ping tells you two very important things: The PC can reach the default gateway, and the default gateway does not know how to get to the 10.1.3.0/24 network. Therefore, you can focus your attention on R1 and work from there.

On R1, you issue the same ping, but it fails, as shown in Example 4-60.

Example 4-60 *Failed Ping from R1 to 10.1.3.10*

```
R1# ping 10.1.3.10
Type escape sequence to abort.
Sending 5, 100-byte ICMP Echos to 10.1.3.10, timeout is 2 seconds:
.....
Success rate is 0 percent (0/5)
```

Next, you check the routing table on R1 with the **show ip route 10.1.3.0 255.255.255.0** command, as shown in the following CLI output:

```
R1# show ip route 10.1.3.0 255.255.255.0

% Subnet not in table
```

You conclude that R1 does not know about the route. However, does R2 know about the route? You go to R2 and issue the same command, as shown in Example 4-61. R2 does know about the route.

Example 4-61 *Determining Whether a Route Is in R2's Routing Table*

```
R2# show ip route 10.1.3.0 255.255.255.0
Routing entry for 10.1.3.0/24
  Known via "eigrp 100", distance 90, metric 3072, type internal
  Redistributing via eigrp 100
  Last update from 10.1.23.3 on GigabitEthernet1/0, 00:44:37 ago
  Routing Descriptor Blocks:
  * 10.1.23.3, from 10.1.23.3, 00:44:37 ago, via GigabitEthernet1/0
      Route metric is 3072, traffic share count is 1
      Total delay is 20 microseconds, minimum bandwidth is 1000000 Kbit
      Reliability 255/255, minimum MTU 1500 bytes
      Loading 1/255, Hops 1
```

Next, you go back to R1 and issue the **show ip eigrp topology** command to determine whether R1 is even learning about the 10.1.3.0/24 network. Example 4-62 indicates that it is not.

Example 4-62   *Determining Whether R1 Is Learning About 10.1.3.0/24*

```
R1# show ip eigrp topology
EIGRP-IPv4 Topology Table for AS(100)/ID(10.1.12.1)
Codes: P - Passive, A - Active, U - Update, Q - Query, R - Reply,
 r - reply Status, s - sia Status


P 10.1.12.0/24, 1 successors, FD is 2816
        via Connected, GigabitEthernet1/0
P 10.1.23.0/24, 1 successors, FD is 3072
        via 10.1.12.2 (3072/2816), GigabitEthernet1/0
P 10.1.1.0/24, 1 successors, FD is 2816
        via Connected, GigabitEthernet0/0
```

It's time to hypothesize! Why would R2 know about 10.1.3.0/24 and R1 not know about it? Consider these possibilities:

- R1 and R2 are not EIGRP neighbors.

- A route filter on R2 prevents it from advertising 10.1.3.0/24 to R1.

- A route filter on R1 prevents it from learning 10.1.3.0/24 in Gig1/0.

On R1, you issue the **show ip eigrp neighbors** command, as shown in Example 4-63, and the output shows that R2 is a neighbor. However, if you look closely at the topology table of R1, you might notice that R1 is learning about 10.1.23.0/24 from R2, meaning that they are neighbors, and routes are being learned. Therefore, you hypothesize that there must be a filter in place.

Example 4-63   *Determining Whether R2 Is a Neighbor*

```
R1# show ip eigrp neighbors
EIGRP-IPv4 Neighbors for AS(100)
H   Address                 Interface   Hold   Uptime     SRTT   RTO  Q  Seq
                                        (sec)             (ms)        Cnt Num
0   10.1.12.2               Gi1/0       12     01:20:27   72     432  0  18
```

Next, you issue the **show ip protocols** command, as shown in Example 4-64, to determine whether there are any route filters on R1. The output indicates that there is an inbound route filter on R1's GigabitEthernet 1/0 interface. The route filter is filtering based on a prefix list called DENY_10.1.3.0/24.

Example 4-64   *Determining Whether There Is a Route Filter on R1*

```
R1# show ip protocols
*** IP Routing is NSF aware ***

Routing Protocol is "eigrp 100"
  Outgoing update filter list for all interfaces is not set
  Incoming update filter list for all interfaces is not set
    GigabitEthernet1/0 filtered by (prefix-list) DENY_10.1.3.0/24 (per-user),
default is not set
  Default networks flagged in outgoing updates
  Default networks accepted from incoming updates
  EIGRP-IPv4 Protocol for AS(100)
...output omitted...
```

Next, you issue the **show ip prefix-list** command on R1, as shown in Example 4-65, and it indicates that 10.1.3.0/24 is being denied.

Example 4-65   *Reviewing the Prefix List*

```
R1# show ip prefix-list
ip prefix-list DENY_10.1.3.0/24: 2 entries
seq 5 deny 10.1.3.0/24
seq 10 permit 0.0.0.0/0 le 32
```

In this case, you can either modify the prefix list to allow 10.1.3.0/24, or you can remove the distribute list from the EIGRP process. The choice depends on the requirements of the organization or scenario. In this case, remove the distribute list from R1 with the command **no distribute-list prefix DENY_10.1.3.0/24 in GigabitEthernet1/0**. Because of this change, the neighbor relationship resets, as the following syslog message indicates:

```
%DUAL-5-NBRCHANGE: EIGRP-IPv4 100: Neighbor 10.1.12.2
(GigabitEthernet1/0) is resync: intf route configuration changed
```

After fixing the issue, you check R1's routing table with the command **show ip route 10.1.3.0 255.255.255.0**. As shown in Example 4-66, 10.1.3.0/24 is now in the routing table and can be reached through the next hop 10.1.12.2.

Example 4-66   *Verifying That 10.1.3.0/24 Is in R1's Routing Table*

```
R1# show ip route 10.1.3.0 255.255.255.0
Routing entry for 10.1.3.0/24
  Known via "eigrp 100", distance 90, metric 3328, type internal
  Redistributing via eigrp 100
  Last update from 10.1.12.2 on GigabitEthernet1/0, 00:00:06 ago
  Routing Descriptor Blocks:
  * 10.1.12.2, from 10.1.12.2, 00:00:06 ago, via GigabitEthernet1/0
      Route metric is 3328, traffic share count is 1
      Total delay is 30 microseconds, minimum bandwidth is 1000000 Kbit
      Reliability 255/255, minimum MTU 1500 bytes
      Loading 1/255, Hops 2
```

Finally, you ping from the PC again, and the ping is successful, as shown in Example 4-67.

Example 4-67　*A Successful Ping from the 10.1.1.0/24 Network to the 10.1.3.0/24 Network*

```
C:\>ping 10.1.3.10

Pinging 10.1.3.10 with 32 bytes of data:

Reply from 10.1.3.10: bytes=32 time 1ms TTL=128
Reply from 10.1.3.10: bytes=32 time 1ms TTL=128
Reply from 10.1.3.10: bytes=32 time 1ms TTL=128
Reply from 10.1.3.10: bytes=32 time 1ms TTL=128

Ping statistics for 10.1.3.10:
    Packets: Sent = 4, Received = 4, Lost = 0 (0% loss),
Approximate round trip times in milli-seconds:
    Minimum = 0ms, Maximum = 0ms, Average = 0ms
```

Exam Preparation Tasks

As mentioned in the section "How to Use This Book" in the Introduction, you have a couple choices for exam preparation: the exercises here, Chapter 24, "Final Preparation," and the exam simulation questions in the Pearson Test Prep software.

Review All Key Topics

Review the most important topics in this chapter, noted with the Key Topic icon in the outer margin of the page. Table 4-2 lists these key topics and the page number on which each is found.

Table 4-2　Key Topics

Key Topic Element	Description	Page Number
List	Possible reasons an EIGRP neighbor relationship might not form	141
Example 4-2	Verifying the autonomous system number with **show ip protocols**	142
Example 4-4	Verifying EIGRP interfaces with **show ip eigrp interfaces**	144
Example 4-7	Verifying K values with **show ip protocols**	146
Example 4-8	Verifying passive interfaces with **show ip protocols**	147
Section	Authentication	148
List	Possible reasons EIGRP for IPv4 routes may be missing from the routing table	152

Key Topic Element	Description	Page Number
Paragraph	How a better source of routing information could cause suboptimal routing	157
List	Considerations when troubleshooting route filters	157
Section	Stub configuration	158
Section	Split horizon	161
List	Considerations when troubleshooting route summarization	167
Example 4-31	Verifying variance and maximum paths	168

Define Key Terms

Define the following key terms from this chapter and check your answers in the glossary:

hello packet, 224.0.0.10, autonomous system number, passive interface, **network** command, K value, keychain, key ID, key string, split horizon, stub, feasible distance, successor, reported distance, feasible successor, classful, discontiguous network, autosummarization, classless, maximum paths, variance

Use the Command Reference to Check Your Memory

The ENARSI 300-410 exam focuses on the practical, hands-on skills that networking professionals use. Therefore, you should be able to identify the commands needed to configure, verify, and troubleshoot the topics covered in this chapter.

This section includes the most important configuration and verification commands covered in this chapter. It might not be necessary to memorize the complete syntax of every command, but you should be able to remember the basic keywords that are needed.

To test your memory of the commands in Table 4-3, go to the companion website and download Appendix B, "Command Reference Exercises." Fill in the missing commands in the tables based on each command description. You can check your work by downloading Appendix C, "Command Reference Exercise Answer Key," from the companion website.

Table 4-3   Command Reference

Task	Command Syntax
Display the IPv4 routing protocols enabled on the router; for EIGRP, display autonomous system number, outgoing and incoming filters, K values, router ID, maximum paths, variance, local stub configuration, routing for networks, routing information sources, administrative distance, and passive interfaces.	**show ip protocols**
Show a router's EIGRP neighbors.	**show ip eigrp neighbors**

Task	Command Syntax
Show detailed information about a router's EIGRP neighbors, including whether the neighbor is a stub router, along with the types of networks it is advertising as a stub.	**show ip eigrp neighbors detail**
Display all of a router's interfaces that are configured to participate in an EIGRP routing process (with the exception of passive interfaces).	**show ip eigrp interfaces**
Display the interfaces participating in the EIGRP for the IPv4 routing process, along with EIGRP hello and hold timers, whether the split horizon rule is enabled, and whether authentication is being used.	**show ip eigrp interfaces detail**
Display the EIGRP configuration in the running configuration.	**show run	section router eigrp**
Display the configuration of a specific interface in the running configuration. (This is valuable when you are trying to troubleshoot EIGRP interface commands.)	**show run interface** *interface_type interface_number*
Display the keychains and associated keys and key strings.	**show key chain**
Display IPv4 interface parameters; for EIGRP, verify whether the interface has joined the correct multicast group (224.0.0.10) and whether any ACLs applied to the interface might be preventing an EIGRP adjacency from forming.	**show ip interface** *interface_type interface_number*
Display routes known to a router's EIGRP routing process, which are contained in the EIGRP topology table. (The **all-links** keyword displays all routes learned for each network, and without the **all-links** keyword, only the successors and feasible successors are displayed for each network.)	**show ip eigrp topology [all-links]**
Show routes known to a router's IP routing table that were injected by the router's EIGRP routing process.	**show ip route eigrp**
Display all EIGRP packets exchanged with a router's EIGRP neighbors or display only specific EIGRP packet types (for example, EIGRP hello packets).	**debug eigrp packets**

## CHAPTER 5

EIGRPv6

This chapter covers the following topics:

- **EIGRPv6 Fundamentals:** This section provides an overview of EIGRPv6 and the correlation to EIGRP for routing IPv4 networks.

- **Troubleshooting EIGRPv6 Neighbor Issues:** This section discusses the reasons EIGRPv6 neighbor relationships may not be formed and how to identify them.

- **Troubleshooting EIGRPv6 Routes:** This section explores the reasons EIGRPv6 routes might be missing and how to determine why they are missing.

- **Troubleshooting Named EIGRP:** This section introduces the **show** commands that you can use to troubleshoot named EIGRP configurations.

- **EIGRPv6 and Named EIGRP Trouble Tickets:** This section provides trouble tickets that demonstrate how to use a structured troubleshooting process to solve a reported problem.

The original EIGRP routing protocol supports multiple protocol suites. Protocol-dependent modules (PDMs) provide unique neighbor and topology tables for each protocol. When the IPv6 address family is enabled, the routing protocol is commonly referred to as EIGRPv6.

This chapter reviews the fundamentals of EIGRPv6 and guides you through configuring and verification. In addition, it examines how to troubleshoot common EIGRPv6 neighbor and route issues. It also explores named EIGRP and wraps up by providing a look at two trouble tickets.

"Do I Know This Already?" Quiz

The "Do I Know This Already?" quiz allows you to assess whether you should read this entire chapter thoroughly or jump to the "Exam Preparation Tasks" section. If you are in doubt about your answers to these questions or your own assessment of your knowledge of the topics, read the entire chapter. Table 5-1 lists the major headings in this chapter and their corresponding "Do I Know This Already?" quiz questions. You can find the answers in Appendix A, "Answers to the 'Do I Know This Already?' Quiz Questions."

Table 5-1 "Do I Know This Already?" Foundation Topics Section-to-Question Mapping

Foundation Topics Section	Questions
EIGRPv6 Fundamentals	1–3
Troubleshooting EIGRPv6 Neighbor Issues	5, 9
Troubleshooting EIGRPv6 Routes	6, 7, 11
Troubleshooting Named EIGRP	8, 10

1. What address does the EIGRPv6 hello packet use for the destination address?

   a. MAC address 00:C1:00:5C:00:FF

   b. MAC address E0:00:00:06:00:AA

   c. IP address 224.0.0.8

   d. IP address 224.0.0.10

   e. IPv6 address FF02::A

   f. IPv6 address FF02::8

2. Enabling EIGRPv6 on an interface with EIGRPv6 classic configuration requires _____.

   a. the command **network** *prefix/prefix-length* under the EIGRP process

   b. the command **network** *interface-id* under the EIGRP process

   c. the command **ipv6 eigrp** *as-number* under the interface

   d. nothing; EIGRPv6 is enabled on all IPv6 interfaces upon initialization of the EIGRP process

3. Enabling EIGRPv6 on an interface with EIGRPv6 named mode configuration requires

   _____.

   a. the command **network** *prefix/prefix-length* under the EIGRP process

   b. the command **network** *interface-id* under the EIGRP process

   c. the command **ipv6 eigrp** *as-number* under the interface

   d. nothing; EIGRPv6 is enabled on all IPv6 interfaces upon initialization of the EIGRP process

4. Which EIGRPv6 command is used to verify whether any interfaces have been configured as passive interfaces?

   a. **show ipv6 protocols**

   b. **show ipv6 eigrp interfaces detail**

   c. **show ipv6 eigrp neighbors detail**

   d. **show ipv6 eigrp topology**

5. Which EIGRPv6 command enables you to verify whether the local router is a stub router?

   a. **show ipv6 protocols**

   b. **show ipv6 eigrp interfaces detail**

   c. **show ipv6 eigrp neighbors detail**

   d. **show ipv6 eigrp topology**

6. Which EIGRPv6 command enables you to verify whether a neighboring router is a stub router?

   a. show ipv6 protocols

   b. show ipv6 eigrp interfaces detail

   c. show ipv6 eigrp neighbors detail

   d. show ipv6 eigrp topology

7. Which of these commands can you use to verify which interfaces are participating in the named EIGRP IPv4 address family? (Choose two.)

   a. show ip eigrp interfaces

   b. show eigrp address-family ipv4 interfaces

   c. show ipv6 eigrp interfaces

   d. show eigrp address-family ipv6 interfaces

8. Which of the following must match to form an EIGRPv6 neighborship? (Choose two.)

   a. The subnet the interfaces belong to

   b. The autonomous system number

   c. The passive interfaces

   d. The K values

9. What must be permitted within an IPv6 ACL for an EIGRPv6 neighbor adjacency to be formed?

   a. FF02::A

   b. FF02::10

   c. The link-local address of the neighboring device

   d. The global address of the neighboring device

10. Your router is only receiving connected routes and summary routes for a neighboring EIGRP router. What are possible reasons for this? (Choose two.)

   a. A distribute list has been applied inbound on the interface connected to the neighbor and is filtering out all the routes that are not connected and all the summary routes and preventing them from being learned.

   b. The wrong interface has been configured to participate in the routing process, and a neighborship has been only partially formed.

   c. The **eigrp stub** command has been configured on your router.

   d. The interface on your router is configured as passive.

11. You have a DMVPN network using named EIGRP configuration mode to share routes between the hub (HQ) and spoke (Branch) routers. All spokes have successfully formed an EIGRP neighborship with the hub router. However, after verifying the routing tables on the spoke routers, you have concluded that the spokes are not learning any of the routes contained in each of the Branch sites; only HQ is. The spokes are only learning the routes in HQ. What is the most likely reason for this?

   a. A distribute list has been applied outbound on the spoke routers.

   b. The EIGRP split-horizon rule is enabled on the HQ router.

   c. The **eigrp stub** command has been configured on the HQ router.

   d. The interfaces on your spoke routers are configured as passive.

Foundation Topics

EIGRPv6 Fundamentals

EIGRP's functional behavior is unchanged between IPv4 and IPv6. The same administrative distance, metrics, timers, and DUAL mechanisms are in place to build the routing table. This chapter provides a detailed overview of the operation of the EIGRP protocol along with its common features. This section is devoted to discussing the components of the routing protocol that are unique to IPv6.

EIGRPv6 Inter-Router Communication

EIGRP packets are identified using the well-known protocol ID 88 for both IPv4 and IPv6. When EIGRPv6 is enabled, the routers communicate with each other using the interface's IPv6 link-local address as the source, and depending on the EIGRP packet type, the destination address may be either a unicast link-local address or the multicast link-local scoped address *FF02::A*.

Table 5-2 shows the source and destination addresses for the EIGRP packet types.

Table 5-2   EIGRPv6 Packets

EIGRP Packet	Source	Destination	Purpose
Hello	Link-local address	FF02::A	Neighbor discovery and keepalive
Acknowledgment	Link-local address	Link-local address	Acknowledges receipt of an update
Query	Link-local address	FF02::A	Request for route information during a topology change event
Reply	Link-local address	Link-local address	A response to a query message
Update	Link-local address	Link-local address	Adjacency forming
Update	Link-local address	FF02::A	Topology change

EIGRPv6 Configuration

There are two methods for configuring IPv6 for EIGRP on IOS and IOS XE routers:

- Classic AS mode

- Named mode

EIGRPv6 Classic Mode Configuration

Classic mode is the original IOS method for enabling IPv6 on EIGRP. In this mode, the routing process is configured using an *autonomous system number.*

The steps for configuring EIGRPv6 on an IOS router are as follows:

Step 1. Configure the EIGRPv6 process by using the global configuration command **ipv6 router eigrp** *as-number*.

Step 2. Assign the router ID by using the IPv6 address family command **eigrp router-id** *id*. The router ID should be manually assigned to ensure proper operation of the routing process. The default behavior for EIGRP is to locally assign a router ID based on the highest IPv4 loopback address or, if that is not available, the highest IPv4 address. The router ID does not need to map to an IPv4 address; the ID value could be any 32-bit unique dotted-decimal identifier. If an IPv4 address is not defined or if the router ID is not manually configured, the routing process does not initiate.

Step 3. Enable the process on the interface by using the interface parameter command **ipv6 eigrp** *as-number*.

Nearly all EIGRP IPv6 features are configured in the same manner in IPv4 EIGRP classic mode. The primary difference is that the **ipv6** keyword, rather than the **ip** keyword, precedes most of the commands. One noticeable exception is the familiar IPv4 **network** statement in the EIGRP routing configuration mode. The **network** statement does not exist within EIGRPv6. The protocol must be enabled directly on the interface when using the classic IPv6 EIGRP AS configuration method.

EIGRPv6 Named Mode Configuration

EIGRP named mode configuration is a newer method for configuring the protocol on IOS routers. Named mode provides support for IPv4, IPv6, and virtual routing and forwarding (VRF), all within a single EIGRP instance.

The steps for configuring EIGRP named mode are as follows:

Step 1. Configure the EIGRPv6 routing process in global configuration mode by using the command **router eigrp** *process-name*. Unlike in classic mode, you specify a name instead of an autonomous system number.

Step 2. Define the address family and autonomous system number (ASN) to the routing process by using the command **address-family ipv6 autonomous-system** *as-number*.

Step 3. Assign the router ID by using the IPv6 address family command **eigrp router-id** *router-id*.

EIGRP named mode uses a hierarchical configuration. Most of the command structure is identical to that of EIGRP IPv4 named mode; this mode simplifies configuration and improves CLI usability. All of the EIGRP-specific interface parameters are configured in the **af-interface default** or **af-interface** *interface-id* submode within the IPv6 address family of the named EIGRP process.

When the IPv6 address family is configured for the EIGRP named process, all the IPv6-enabled interfaces immediately start participating in routing. To disable the routing process on the interface, the interface needs to be shut down in **af-interface** configuration mode.

EIGRPv6 Verification

IPv6 uses the same EIGRP verification commands described in Chapter 3, "Advanced EIGRP," and Chapter 4, " Troubleshooting EIGRP for IPv4." The only modification is that the **ipv6** keyword is included in the command syntax.

Table 5-3 lists the IPv6 versions of the **show** commands that are covered in this chapter.

Table 5-3 EIGRP Display Commands

Command	Description
show ipv6 eigrp interfaces [*interface-id*] [detail]	Displays the EIGRPv6 interfaces.
show ipv6 eigrp neighbors	Displays the EIGRPv6 neighbors.
show ipv6 route eigrp	Displays only EIGRP IPv6 routes in the routing table.
show ipv6 protocols	Displays the current state of the active routing protocol processes.

Figure 5-1 illustrates a simple EIGRP topology in which EIGRPv6 AS 100 is enabled on routers R1 and R2 to provide connectivity between the networks.

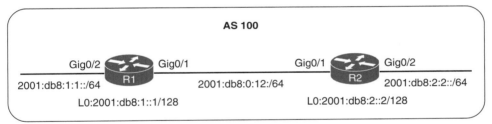

Figure 5-1 *Simple EIGRPv6 Topology*

Example 5-1 shows the full EIGRPv6 configuration for the sample topology. Both EIGRPv6 classic AS and named mode configurations are provided. Notice in IOS classic mode that the routing protocol is applied to each physical interface. In named mode, the protocol is automatically enabled on all interfaces.

Example 5-1 *EIGRPv6 Base Configuration*

```
R1 (Classic Configuration)
interface GigabitEthernet0/1
 ipv6 address 2001:DB8:0:12::1/64
 ipv6 address fe80::1 link-local
 ipv6 eigrp 100
!
interface GigabitEthernet0/2
 ipv6 address 2001:DB8:1:1::1/64
 ipv6 address fe80::1 link-local
 ipv6 eigrp 100
```

```
!
interface Loopback0
 ipv6 address 2001:DB8:1::1/128
 ipv6 eigrp 100
!
ipv6 unicast-routing
!
ipv6 router eigrp 100
 passive-interface Loopback0
 eigrp router-id 192.168.1.1
```

R2 (Named Mode Configuration)
```
interface GigabitEthernet0/1
 ipv6 address 2001:DB8:0:12::2/64
 ipv6 address fe80::2 link-local
!
interface GigabitEthernet0/2
 ipv6 address 2001:DB8:2:2::2/64
 ipv6 address fe80::2 link-local
!
interface Loopback0
 ipv6 address 2001:DB8:2::2/128
!
ipv6 unicast-routing
!
router eigrp NAMED-MODE
 address-family ipv6 unicast autonomous-system 100
  eigrp router-id 192.168.2.2
```

Example 5-2 provides verification of the EIGRPv6 neighbor adjacency. Notice that the adjacency uses link-local addressing.

Example 5-2 *EIGRPv6 Neighbor Adjacency*

```
R1# show ipv6 eigrp neighbors
EIGRP-IPv6 Neighbors for AS(100)
H    Address              Interface        Hold Uptime    SRTT   RTO   Q   Seq
                                           (sec)          (ms)         Cnt Num
0    Link-local address:  Gi0/1            13 00:01:14 1593   5000  0   7
     FE80::2
```

```
R2# show ipv6 eigrp neighbors
EIGRP-IPv6 VR(NAMED-MODE) Address-Family Neighbors for AS(100)
H    Address              Interface        Hold Uptime    SRTT   RTO   Q   Seq
                                           (sec)          (ms)         Cnt Num
0    Link-local address:  Gi0/1            11 00:01:07 21     126   0   5
     FE80::1
```

Example 5-3 shows routing table entries for R1 and R2. Notice that the IPv6 next-hop forwarding address also uses the link-local address rather than the global unicast address of the peer.

Example 5-3 *EIGRPv6 Routing Table Entries*

```
R1# show ipv6 route eigrp
! Output omitted for brevity
D    2001:DB8:2::2/128 [90/2848]
       via FE80::2, GigabitEthernet0/1
D    2001:DB8:2:2::/64 [90/3072]
     via FE80::2, GigabitEthernet0/1
R2# show ipv6 route eigrp
! Output omitted for brevity
D    2001:DB8:1:1::/64 [90/15360]
     via FE80::1, GigabitEthernet0/1
D    2001:DB8:1::1/128 [90/10752]
     via FE80::1, GigabitEthernet0/1
```

IPv6 Route Summarization

There is no concept of classful or classless routing in IPv6, and therefore, autosummarization is not possible. EIGRPv6 summarization for IPv6 is manually configured on a per-interface basis, using the same rules as for IPv4:

- The summary aggregate prefix is not advertised until a prefix matches it.

- More specific prefixes are suppressed.

- A Null0 route with an administrative distance of 5 is added to the routing table as a loop-prevention mechanism.

- A leak map can be used to advertise more specific prefixes while advertising a summary address.

Network summarization is configured at the interface level in classic mode using the command **ipv6 summary-address eigrp** *as-number ipv6-prefix/prefix-length* or in named mode with the command **summary-address** *ipv6-prefix/prefix-length* under **af-interface**.

Example 5-4 demonstrates how to configure R1 to advertise a 2001:db8:1::/48 summary route to R2 and how to configure R2 to advertise a 2001:DB8:2::/48 summary route to R1. It shows both classic and named mode summary configurations.

Example 5-4 *EIGRPv6 Summary Configuration*

```
R1 (Classic Mode Configuration)
interface GigabitEthernet0/1
 ipv6 summary-address eigrp 100 2001:DB8:1::/48
R2 (Named Mode Configuration)
router eigrp NAMED-MODE
```

5

```
address-family ipv6 unicast autonomous-system 100
 af-interface GigabitEthernet0/1
  summary-address 2001:DB8:2::/48
```

Example 5-5 shows the routing tables for R1 and R2. Notice that only the /48 summary prefix is received from the neighbor router and that the more specific /64 and /128 route entries are suppressed. A Null0 route is populated on the router for the local /48 summary route advertisement.

Example 5-5   *EIGRPv6 Routing Table Entries*

```
R1# show ipv6 route eigrp
! Output omitted for brevity
D    2001:DB8:1::/48 [5/2816]
        via Null0, directly connected
D    2001:DB8:2::/48 [90/2848]
       via FE80::2, GigabitEthernet0/1

R2# show ipv6 route eigrp
! Output omitted for brevity
D    2001:DB8:1::/48 [90/2841]
       via FE80::1, GigabitEthernet0/1
D    2001:DB8:2::/48 [5/2816]
       via Null0, directly connected
```

Default Route Advertising

You advertise a default route into the EIGRPv6 topology by placing the default prefix (::/0) as a summary address at the interface level. When you use the summary method, all prefix advertisements are suppressed by the router except for the ::/0 default route entry.

Example 5-6 demonstrates the two configuration methods for injecting a default route into EIGRPv6.

Example 5-6   *EIGRPv6 Default Route Injection*

```
R2 (Classic Configuration)
interface GigabitEthernet0/1
 ipv6 eigrp 100
 ipv6 summary-address eigrp 100 ::/0

R2 (Named Mode Configuration)
router eigrp CISCO
 address-family ipv6 unicast autonomous-system 100
  af-interface GigabitEthernet0/1
   summary-address ::/0
```

Route Filtering

In IOS and IOS XE, you use prefix lists to match IPv6 routes in route maps and distribute lists.

Example 5-7 demonstrates how to use a distribute list for filtering the default route ::/0 advertisements from an upstream neighbor connected to interface GigabitEthernet0/1. The associated prefix list BLOCK-DEFAULT with sequence 5 is a deny statement that filters the exact match for the default route prefix ::/0. Sequence 10 is a permit-any match statement that allows a prefix of any length to be received.

Example 5-7 *IOS Distribute List to Filter the Default Route*

```
R1 (Classic Configuration)
ipv6 router eigrp 100
 distribute-list prefix-list BLOCK-DEFAULT in GigabitEthernet0/1
 !
ipv6 prefix-list BLOCK-DEFAULT seq 5 deny ::/0
ipv6 prefix-list BLOCK-DEFAULT seq 10 permit ::/0 le 128

R2 (Named Mode Configuration)
router eigrp CISCO
 address-family ipv6 unicast autonomous-system 100
  topology base
   distribute-list prefix-list BLOCK-DEFAULT in GigabitEthernet0/1
  exit-af-topology
 exit-address-family
 !
ipv6 prefix-list BLOCK-DEFAULT seq 5 deny ::/0
ipv6 prefix-list BLOCK-DEFAULT seq 10 permit ::/0 le 128
```

Troubleshooting EIGRPv6 Neighbor Issues

Because EIGRPv6 is based on EIGRP for IPv4, it involves similar issues when it comes to troubleshooting, although there are a few differences for IPv6. The great news is that you do not have to learn a large amount of new information for EIGRPv6. You basically need to know the **show** commands that display the information you need to troubleshoot any given EIGRPv6-related issue.

This section explores the same issues presented in Chapter 4; however, the focus here is on the **show** commands that are used when troubleshooting EIGRPv6-related issues.

NOTE If you have not read Chapter 4, you may want to go to it first and quickly review why EIGRP neighbor relationships might not form before you continue with this chapter.

The neighbor issues with EIGRPv6 are mostly the same as with EIGRP for IPv4, except for a few differences based on the way EIGRPv6 is enabled on an interface. To verify EIGRPv6 neighbors, use the **show ipv6 eigrp neighbors** command, as shown in Example 5-8. Notice

5

that EIGRPv6 neighbors are identified by their link-local addresses. In this case, R2 is a neighbor of two different routers. One is reachable out Gi1/0, and the other is reachable out Gi0/0.

Example 5-8 *Verifying EIGRPv6 Neighbors*

```
R2# show ipv6 eigrp neighbors
EIGRP-Ipv6 Neighbors for AS(100)
H   Address                  Interface   Hold  Uptime     SRTT   RTO    Q    Seq
                                         (sec)            (ms)          Cnt  Num
1 Link-local address: .      Gi1/0       10    00:17:59   320    2880   0    4
  FE80::C823:17FF:FEEC:1C
0 Link-local address:        Gi0/0       12    00:18:01   148    888    0    3
  FE80::C820:17FF:FE04:1C
```

Interface Is Down

With EIGRPv6, to verify that an interface is up, you use the **show ipv6 interface brief** command, as shown in Example 5-9. In this example, GigabitEthernet0/0 and GigabitEthernet1/0 are up/up, and GigabitEthernet2/0 is administratively down/down. This indicates that GigabitEthernet2/0 has been configured with the **shutdown** command.

Example 5-9 *Verifying the Status of Ipv6 Interfaces*

```
R1# show ipv6 interface brief
GigabitEthernet0/0 [up/up]
  FE80::C80E:1FF:FE9C:8
  2001:DB8:0:1::1
GigabitEthernet1/0 [up/up]
  FE80::C80E:1FF:FE9C:1C
  2001:DB8:0:12::1
GigabitEthernet2/0 [administratively down/down]
  FE80::C80E:1FF:FE9C:38
  2001:DB8:0:13::1
```

Mismatched Autonomous System Numbers

With EIGRPv6, to verify the autonomous system number being used, you can use the **show ipv6 protocols** command, as shown in Example 5-10. In this example, the EIGRP autonomous system is 100.

Mismatched K Values

You verify the EIGRPv6 *K values* with the command **show ipv6 protocols**, as shown in Example 5-10. In this example, the K values are 1, 0, 1, 0, and 0, which are the defaults.

Passive Interfaces

To verify the router interfaces participating in an EIGRPv6 autonomous system that are passive, you use the **show ipv6 protocols** command, as shown in Example 5-10. In this example, GigabitEthernet 0/0 is a *passive interface*.

Example 5-10 *Verifying EIGRPv6 Configurations with show ipv6 protocols*

```
R1# show ipv6 protocols
...output omitted...
IPv6 Routing Protocol is "eigrp 100"
EIGRP-IPv6 Protocol for AS(100)
  Metric weight K1=1, K2=0, K3=1, K4=0, K5=0
  NSF-aware route hold timer is 240
  Router-ID: 10.1.12.1
  Topology : 0 (base)
    Active Timer: 3 min
    Distance: internal 90 external 170
    Maximum path: 16
    Maximum hopcount 100
    Maximum metric variance 1

  Interfaces:
    GigabitEthernet1/0
    GigabitEthernet0/0 (passive)
  Redistribution:
    None
```

Mismatched Authentication

If authentication is being used with EIGRPv6, the *key ID* and *key string* must match, and if the valid times are configured, they must match between neighbors as well. Example 5-11 shows how to verify whether an interface is enabled for EIGRPv6 authentication with the **show ipv6 eigrp interfaces detail** command and how to verify the configuration of the *keychain* that is being used with the **show key chain** command. In this example, the authentication mode is MD5, and the keychain TEST is being used.

Example 5-11 *Verifying EIGRPv6 Authentication*

```
R1# show ipv6 eigrp interfaces detail
EIGRP-IPv6 Interfaces for AS(100)
                Xmit Queue   PeerQ        Mean  Pacing Time  Multicast    Pending
Interface Peers Un/Reliable  Un/Reliable  SRTT  Un/Reliable  Flow Timer   Routes
Gi1/0      1       0/0          0/0         72       0/0         316          0
  Hello-interval is 5, Hold-time is 15
  Split-horizon is enabled
  Next xmit serial <none>
  Packetized sent/expedited: 5/0
  Hello's sent/expedited: 494/6
  Un/reliable mcasts: 0/4 Un/reliable ucasts: 4/59
  Mcast exceptions: 0 CR packets: 0 ACKs suppressed: 0
```

```
      Retransmissions sent: 54 Out-of-sequence rcvd: 3
      Topology-ids on interface - 0
      Authentication mode is md5, key-chain is "TEST"
R1# show key chain
Key-chain TEST:
    key 1 -- text "TEST"
        accept lifetime (always valid) - (always valid) [valid now]
        send lifetime (always valid) - (always valid) [valid now]
```

Timers

With EIGRPv6, timers do not have to match; however, if they are not configured appropriately, neighbor relationships might flap. You can verify timers by using the **show ipv6 eigrp interfaces detail** command, as shown in Example 5-11. In this example, the hello interval is configured as 5, and the hold interval is 15; these are the defaults.

Interface Not Participating in Routing Process

With EIGRPv6, interfaces are enabled for the routing process with the **ipv6 eigrp** *autonomous_system_number* interface configuration command. You can use two **show** commands—**show ipv6 eigrp interfaces** and **show ipv6 protocols**—to verify the interfaces that are participating in the routing process, as shown in Example 5-12. As with EIGRP for IPv4, the **show ipv6 eigrp interfaces** command does not show passive interfaces. However, **show ipv6 protocols** does.

Example 5-12   *Verifying EIGRPv6 Interfaces*

```
R1# show ipv6 eigrp interfaces
EIGRP-IPv6 Interfaces for AS(100)
                  Xmit Queue   PeerQ        Mean   Pacing Time   Multicast    Pending
Interface Peers Un/Reliable   Un/Reliable   SRTT   Un/Reliable   Flow Timer   Routes
Gi1/0       1      0/0          0/0         282       0/0          1348          0
R1# show ipv6 protocols
IPv6 Routing Protocol is "connected"
IPv6 Routing Protocol is "ND"
IPv6 Routing Protocol is "eigrp 100"
EIGRP-IPv6 Protocol for AS(100)
  Metric weight K1=1, K2=0, K3=1, K4=0, K5=0
  NSF-aware route hold timer is 240
...output omitted...
  Interfaces:
    GigabitEthernet1/0
    GigabitEthernet0/0 (passive)
  Redistribution:
  None
```

ACLs

EIGRPv6 uses the IPv6 multicast address FF02::A to form neighbor adjacencies. If an IPv6 access control list (ACL) is denying packets destined to the multicast address FF02::A, neighbor adjacencies do not form. In addition, because neighbor adjacencies are formed with link-local addresses, if the link-local address range is denied based on the source or destination IPv6 address in an interface with an IPv6 ACL, neighbor relationships do not form.

Troubleshooting EIGRPv6 Routes

The reasons a route might be missing and the steps used to troubleshoot them with EIGRPv6 are similar to those listed in Chapter 4 for EIGRP for IPv4. This section identifies some of the most common issues and the **show** commands you should use to detect them for EIGRPv6.

> **NOTE** If you have not read Chapter 4 yet, now is a good time to visit it and review reasons EIGRP routes might be missing either from the topology table or the routing table before you continue with this chapter.

Interface Not Participating in the Routing Process

For a network to be advertised by the EIGRPv6 process, the interface associated with that network must be participating in the routing process. As shown earlier in the chapter, in Example 5-12, you can use the commands **show ipv6 eigrp interfaces** and **show ipv6 protocols** to verify the interfaces participating in the process.

Better Source of Information

If exactly the same network is learned from a more reliable source, it is used instead of the EIGRPv6-learned information. To verify the AD associated with the route in the routing table, you can issue the **show ipv6 route** *ipv6_address/prefix* command. In Example 5-13, the 2001:db8:0:1::/64 network has an AD of 90, and it was learned from EIGRP autonomous system 100.

Example 5-13 *Verifying AD of IPv6 Routes*

```
R2# show ipv6 route 2001:DB8:0:1::/64
Routing entry for 2001:DB8:0:1::/64
 Known via "eigrp 100", distance 90, metric 3072, type internal
 Route count is 1/1, share count 0
 Routing paths:
   FE80::C820:17FF:FE04:1C, GigabitEthernet0/0
     Last updated 00:25:27 ago
```

Route Filtering

A filter might be preventing a route from being advertised or learned. With EIGRPv6, the **distribute-list prefix-list** command is used to configure a route filter. To verify the filter applied, use the **show run | section ipv6 router eigrp** command. In Example 5-14, a distribute list is using a prefix list called ENARSI_EIGRP to filter routes inbound on

5

GigabitEthernet1/0. To successfully troubleshoot route filtering issues, you also need to verify the IPv6 prefix list by using the **show ipv6 prefix-list** command.

Example 5-14 *Verifying EIGRPv6 Distribute List*

```
R1# show run | section ipv6 router eigrp
ipv6 router eigrp 100
 distribute-list prefix-list ENARSI_EIGRP in GigabitEthernet1/0
 passive-interface default
 no passive-interface GigabitEthernet1/0
```

Stub Configuration

If the wrong router is configured as a *stub* router, or if the wrong setting is chosen during stub router configuration, it might prevent a network from being advertised when it should be advertised. When troubleshooting EIGRPv6 stub configurations, you can use the **show ipv6 protocols** command to verify whether the local router is a stub router and the networks that it is advertising, as shown in Example 5-15. On a remote router, you can issue the **show ipv6 eigrp neighbors detail** command, as shown in Example 5-16. In this case, R1 is a stub router advertising connected and summary routes.

Example 5-15 *Verifying the EIGRP Stub Configuration on a Stub Router*

```
R1# show ipv6 protocols
IPv6 Routing Protocol is "connected"
IPv6 Routing Protocol is "ND"
IPv6 Routing Protocol is "eigrp 100"
EIGRP-IPv6 Protocol for AS(100)
  Metric weight K1=1, K2=0, K3=1, K4=0, K5=0
  NSF-aware route hold timer is 240
  Router-ID: 10.1.12.1
  Stub, connected, summary
  Topology : 0 (base)
    Active Timer: 3 min
    Distance: internal 90 external 170
    Maximum path: 16
    Maximum hopcount 100
    Maximum metric variance 1

 Interfaces:
   GigabitEthernet1/0
   GigabitEthernet0/0 (passive)
 Redistribution:
   None
```

Example 5-16 *Verifying the EIGRP Stub Configuration of a Neighbor Router*

```
R2# show ipv6 eigrp neighbors detail
EIGRP-IPv6 Neighbors for AS(100)
H   Address              Interface      Hold  Uptime    SRTT  RTO    Q    Seq
                                        (sec)           (ms)         Cnt  Num
0 Link-local address:    Gi0/0          11    00:03:35  68    408    0    10
   FE80::C820:17FF:FE04:1C
 Version 11.0/2.0, Retrans: 0, Retries: 0, Prefixes: 2
 Topology-ids from peer - 0
 Stub Peer Advertising (CONNECTED SUMMARY ) Routes
 Suppressing queries
1 Link-local address:    Gi1/0                 13    00:14:16  252  1512   0    7
   FE80::C823:17FF:FEEC:1C
 Version 11.0/2.0, Retrans: 0, Retries: 0, Prefixes: 2
 Topology-ids from peer - 0
```

Split Horizon

Split horizon is a loop-prevention feature that prevents a router from advertising routes out the same interface on which they were learned. As shown in Example 5-17, you can verify whether split horizon is enabled or disabled by using the **show ipv6 eigrp interfaces detail** command.

Example 5-17 *Verifying the EIGRP Split-Horizon Configuration*

```
R1# show ipv6 eigrp interfaces detail
EIGRP-IPv6 Interfaces for AS(100)
                 Xmit Queue    PeerQ         Mean  Pacing Time   Multicast    Pending
Interface Peers  Un/Reliable   Un/Reliable   SRTT  Un/Reliable   Flow Timer   Routes
Gi1/0      1       0/0           0/0          50      0/0           208          0
 Hello-interval is 5, Hold-time is 15
 Split-horizon is enabled
 Next xmit serial <none>
 Packetized sent/expedited: 8/0
 Hello's sent/expedited: 708/3
 Un/reliable mcasts: 0/6 Un/reliable ucasts: 11/5
 Mcast exceptions: 0 CR packets: 0 ACKs suppressed: 0
 Retransmissions sent: 1 Out-of-sequence rcvd: 0
 Topology-ids on interface - 0
 Authentication mode is md5, key-chain is "TEST"
```

As with EIGRP for IPv4, split horizon is an issue in EIGRPv6 network designs that need routes to be advertised out interfaces on which they were learned. An example of this type of network design is a Dynamic Multipoint Virtual Private Network (DMVPN), which uses a multipoint interface on the hub router. Therefore, split horizon needs to be disabled on the hub router interface of a DMVPN network so routes learned from the spoke routers can be advertised back out that interface to the other spoke routers.

Troubleshooting Named EIGRP

The purpose of EIGRP named configuration is to provide a central location on the local router to perform all EIGRP for IPv4 and IPv6 configuration. Example 5-18 provides a sample named EIGRP configuration called ENARSI_EIGRP. This named EIGRP configuration includes an IPv4 unicast address family and an IPv6 unicast address family. They are both using autonomous system 100; however, that is not mandatory and does not cause conflict as these are separate routing processes.

Example 5-18 *Sample Named EIGRP Configuration*

```
Branch# show run | section router eigrp
router eigrp ENARSI_EIGRP
 !
 address-family ipv4 unicast autonomous-system 100
  !
  af-interface default
   passive-interface
  exit-af-interface
  !
  af-interface FastEthernet1/0
   no passive-interface
  exit-af-interface
  !
  topology base
  exit-af-topology
  network 10.1.4.4 0.0.0.0
  network 10.1.14.4 0.0.0.0
  eigrp router-id 4.4.4.4
  eigrp stub connected summary
 exit-address-family
 !
 address-family ipv6 unicast autonomous-system 100
  !
  af-interface default
   passive-interface
  exit-af-interface
  !
  af-interface FastEthernet1/0
   no passive-interface
  exit-af-interface
```

```
 !
 topology base
 maximum-paths 2
 variance 3
 exit-af-topology
 eigrp router-id 44.44.44.44
 eigrp stub connected summary
exit-address-family
```

Because the configuration is the only thing that is different, all the issues already discussed for EIGRP for Ipv4 and EIGRPv6 apply here as well. However, now you need to know which **show** commands can help you successfully troubleshoot named EIGRP deployments. This section covers the **show** commands that you can use to troubleshoot named EIGRP configurations.

With *named EIGRP*, you can use all the same EIGRP **show** commands that you use for classic EIGRP for Ipv4 and classic EIGRPv6, as discussed in Chapter 4 and earlier in this chapter. However, there is also a new set of **show** commands for named EIGRP that you might want to learn.

The command **show eigrp protocols** (see Example 5-19) shows both the EIGRP for IPv4 address family and the EIGRPv6 address family, along with the autonomous system number associated with each. It also displays the K values, the router ID, whether the router is a stub router, the AD, the *maximum paths*, and the *variance*.

Example 5-19   *Output of show eigrp protocols*

```
Branch# show eigrp protocols
EIGRP-IPv4 VR(ENARSI_EIGRP) Address-Family Protocol for AS(100)
  Metric weight K1=1, K2=0, K3=1, K4=0, K5=0 K6=0
  Metric rib-scale 128
  Metric version 64bit
  NSF-aware route hold timer is 240
  Router-ID: 4.4.4.4
  Stub, connected, summary
  Topology : 0 (base)
    Active Timer: 3 min
    Distance: internal 90 external 170
    Maximum path: 4
    Maximum hopcount 100
    Maximum metric variance 1
    Total Prefix Count: 5
    Total Redist Count: 0

EIGRP-IPv6 VR(ENARSI_EIGRP) Address-Family Protocol for AS(100)
```

```
Metric weight K1=1, K2=0, K3=1, K4=0, K5=0 K6=0
Metric rib-scale 128
Metric version 64bit
NSF-aware route hold timer is 240
Router-ID: 44.44.44.44
Stub, connected, summary
Topology : 0 (base)
  Active Timer: 3 min
  Distance: internal 90 external 170
  Maximum path: 2
  Maximum hopcount 100
  Maximum metric variance 3
  Total Prefix Count: 7
  Total Redist Count: 0
```

This is similar to output of the **show ip protocols** and **show ipv6 protocols** commands. However, it is missing the interfaces that are participating in the routing process, along with the passive interfaces. Therefore, **show ip protocols** and **show ipv6 protocols** are better options than **show eigrp protocols**, at least for now.

To verify the interfaces that are participating in the routing process for each *address family*, you can issue the **show eigrp address-family ipv4 interfaces** command and the **show eigrp address-family ipv6 interfaces** command, as shown in Example 5-20. Note that passive interfaces do not show up in this output. Using the classic **show ip protocols** and **show ipv6 protocols** commands, you would be able to verify the passive interfaces.

Example 5-20 *Verifying Interfaces Participating in the Named EIGRP Process*

```
Branch# show eigrp address-family ipv4 interfaces
EIGRP-IPv4 VR(ENARSI_EIGRP) Address-Family Interfaces for AS(100)
                Xmit Queue    PeerQ       Mean   Pacing Time   Multicast    Pending
Interface Peers Un/Reliable Un/Reliable  SRTT   Un/Reliable   Flow Timer   Routes
Fa1/0       1     0/0         0/0          88      0/0            50          0
Branch# show eigrp address-family ipv6 interfaces
EIGRP-IPv6 VR(ENARSI_EIGRP) Address-Family Interfaces for AS(100)
                Xmit Queue    PeerQ       Mean   Pacing Time   Multicast    Pending
Interface Peers Un/Reliable Un/Reliable  SRTT   Un/Reliable   Flow Timer   Routes
Fa1/0       1     0/0         0/0          73      0/1            304         0
```

As shown in Example 5-21, when you add the **detail** keyword to the **show eigrp address-family ipv4 interfaces** command and the **show eigrp address-family ipv6 interfaces** command, you can verify additional interface parameters (for example, hello interval and hold time, whether split horizon is enabled, whether authentication is set, and statistics about hellos and packets).

Example 5-21   *Verifying Details of Interfaces Participating in the Named EIGRP Process*

```
Branch# show eigrp address-family ipv4 interfaces detail
EIGRP-Ipv4 VR(ENARSI_EIGRP) Address-Family Interfaces for AS(100)
                    Xmit Queue     PeerQ        Mean   Pacing Time   Multicast    Pending
Interface Peers   Un/Reliable    Un/Reliable   SRTT   Un/Reliable   Flow Timer   Routes
Fal/0       1        0/0            0/0          88       0/0            50          0
  Hello-interval is 5, Hold-time is 15
  Split-horizon is enabled
  Next xmit serial <none>
  Packetized sent/expedited: 1/0
  Hello's sent/expedited: 333/2
  Un/reliable mcasts: 0/1 Un/reliable ucasts: 2/2
  Mcast exceptions: 0 CR packets: 0 ACKs suppressed: 0
  Retransmissions sent: 1 Out-of-sequence rcvd: 1
  Topology-ids on interface - 0
  Authentication mode is not set
Branch# show eigrp address-family ipv6 interfaces detail
EIGRP-Ipv6 VR(ENARSI_EIGRP) Address-Family Interfaces for AS(100)
                    Xmit Queue     PeerQ        Mean   Pacing Time   Multicast    Pending
Interface Peers   Un/Reliable    Un/Reliable   SRTT   Un/Reliable   Flow Timer   Routes
Fal/0       1        0/0            0/0          73       0/1           304          0
  Hello-interval is 5, Hold-time is 15
  Split-horizon is enabled
  Next xmit serial <none>
  Packetized sent/expedited: 3/0
  Hello's sent/expedited: 595/3
  Un/reliable mcasts: 0/2 Un/reliable ucasts: 5/3
  Mcast exceptions: 0 CR packets: 0 ACKs suppressed: 0
  Retransmissions sent: 1 Out-of-sequence rcvd: 2
  Topology-ids on interface - 0
  Authentication mode is not set
```

You can verify neighbors with the **show eigrp address-family ipv4 neighbors** and **show eigrp address-family ipv6 neighbors** commands, as shown in Example 5-22. Just as you saw with the classic commands, if you want to verify whether a neighbor is a stub router, you can add the **detail** keyword to these commands.

5

Example 5-22   *Verifying Named EIGRP Neighbors*

```
Branch# show eigrp address-family ipv4 neighbors
EIGRP-IPv4 VR(ENARSI_EIGRP) Address-Family Neighbors for AS(100)
H   Address          Interface      Hold  Uptime     SRTT  RTO   Q    Seq
                                    (sec)            (ms)        Cnt  Num
0   10.1.14.1        Fa1/0          14    00:31:08   88    528   0    8
Branch# show eigrp address-family ipv6 neighbors
EIGRP-IPv6 VR(ENARSI_EIGRP) Address-Family Neighbors for AS(100)
H   Address          Interface      Hold  Uptime     SRTT  RTO   Q    Seq
                                    (sec)            (ms)        Cnt  Num
0 Link-local address:  Fa1/0        14    00:50:33   73    438   0    40
  FE80::C820:17FF:FE04:54
```

To display the topology table, you can use the commands **show eigrp address-family ipv4 topology** and **show eigrp address-family ipv6 topology,** as shown in Example 5-23.

Example 5-23   *Verifying Named EIGRP Topology Tables*

```
Branch# show eigrp address-family ipv4 topology
EIGRP-IPv4 VR(ENARSI_EIGRP) Topology Table for AS(100)/ID(4.4.4.4)
Codes: P - Passive, A - Active, U - Update, Q - Query, R - Reply,
 r - reply Status, s - sia Status

P 10.1.12.0/24, 1 successors, FD is 13762560
        via 10.1.14.1 (13762560/1310720), FastEthernet1/0
P 10.1.14.0/24, 1 successors, FD is 13107200
        via Connected, FastEthernet1/0
P 10.1.3.0/24, 1 successors, FD is 15073280
        via 10.1.14.1 (15073280/2621440), FastEthernet1/0
P 10.1.23.0/24, 1 successors, FD is 14417920
        via 10.1.14.1 (14417920/1966080), FastEthernet1/0
P 10.1.4.0/24, 1 successors, FD is 1310720
        via Connected, GigabitEthernet0/0
P 10.1.1.0/24, 1 successors, FD is 13762560
        via 10.1.14.1 (13762560/1310720), FastEthernet1/0


Branch# show eigrp address-family ipv6 topology
EIGRP-IPv6 VR(ENARSI_EIGRP) Topology Table for AS(100)/ID(44.44.44.44)
Codes: P - Passive, A - Active, U - Update, Q - Query, R - Reply,
 r - reply Status, s - sia Status

P 2001:DB8:0:4::/64, 1 successors, FD is 1310720
        via Connected, GigabitEthernet0/0
```

```
P 2001:DB8:0:1::/64, 1 successors, FD is 13762560
        via FE80::C820:17FF:FE04:54 (13762560/1310720), FastEthernet1/0
P 2001:DB8:0:3::/64, 1 successors, FD is 15073280
        via FE80::C820:17FF:FE04:54 (15073280/2621440), FastEthernet1/0
P ::/0, 1 successors, FD is 13762560
        via FE80::C820:17FF:FE04:54 (13762560/1310720), FastEthernet1/0
P 2001:DB8:0:14::/64, 1 successors, FD is 13107200
        via Connected, FastEthernet1/0
P 2001:DB8:0:12::/64, 1 successors, FD is 13762560
        via FE80::C820:17FF:FE04:54 (13762560/1310720), FastEthernet1/0
P 2001:DB8:0:23::/64, 1 successors, FD is 14417920
        via FE80::C820:17FF:FE04:54 (14417920/1966080), FastEthernet1/0
```

EIGRPv6 and Named EIGRP Trouble Tickets

This section presents two trouble tickets related to the topics discussed earlier in this chapter. These trouble tickets show a process that you can follow when troubleshooting in the real world or in an exam environment.

Trouble Ticket 5-1 is based on the topology shown in Figure 5-2.

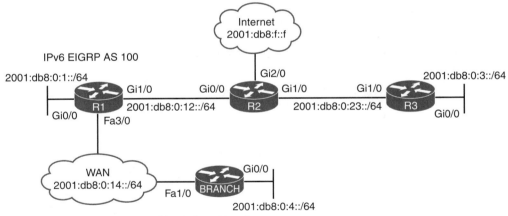

Figure 5-2 *EIGRPv6 Trouble Tickets Topology*

Trouble Ticket 5-1

Problem: Users in the Branch network 2001:db8:0:4::/64 have indicated that they are not able to access the Internet.

To verify the problem, you ping 2001:db8:f::f with the source address 2001:db8:0:4::4, as shown in Example 5-24. The ping fails.

Example 5-24   *Verifying the Issue Using an Extended IPv6 Ping*

```
Branch# ping
Protocol [ip]: ipv6
Target IPv6 address: 2001:db8:f::f
Repeat count [5]:
Datagram size [100]:
Timeout in seconds [2]:
Extended commands? [no]: y
Source address or interface: 2001:db8:0:4::4
UDP protocol? [no]:
Verbose? [no]:
Precedence [0]:
DSCP [0]:
Include hop by hop option? [no]:
Include destination option? [no]:
Sweep range of sizes? [no]:
Type escape sequence to abort.
Sending 5, 100-byte ICMP Echos to 2001:DB8:F::F, timeout is 2 seconds:
Packet sent with a source address of 2001:DB8:0:4::4
.....
Success rate is 0 percent (0/5)
```

Next, you issue the **show ipv6 route 2001:db8:f::f** command on Branch to determine whether there is a route in the IPv6 routing table to reach the address. In the following snippet, the route is not found:

```
Branch# show ipv6 route 2001:db8:f::f

% Route not found
```

Next, you visit R1 to determine whether R1 has a route to reach 2001:db8:f::f by using the command **show ipv6 route 2001:db8:f::f**. In Example 5-25, you can see that the Internet address is reachable using a default route (::/0) that was learned through EIGRP.

Example 5-25   *Verifying the Route to 2001:db8:f::f in the IPv6 Routing Table on R1*

```
R1# show ipv6 route 2001:db8:f::f
Routing entry for ::/0
  Known via "eigrp 100", distance 170, metric 2816, type external
  Route count is 1/1, share count 0
  Routing paths:
  FE80::C821:17FF:FE04:8, GigabitEthernet1/0
  Last updated 00:08:28 ago
```

You conclude from this output that Branch is not learning the default route from R1, which would be used to reach the Internet. You believe that it might be due to a neighbor relationship issue. Back on Branch, you issue the **show ipv6 eigrp neighbors** command, as shown in Example 5-26, and the output indicates that there is a neighbor relationship with a device out Fa1/0 that has the link-local address FE80::C820:17FF:FE04:54. You are pretty sure that is R1's link-local address on Fa3/0, but just to be sure, you issue the **show ipv6 interface brief** command on R1, as shown in Example 5-27. The link-local address from Example 5-26 matches the address in Example 5-27.

Example 5-26 *Verifying EIGRPv6 Neighbor Adjacencies*

```
Branch# show ipv6 eigrp neighbors
EIGRP-IPv6 Neighbors for AS(100)
H   Address             Interface   Hold  Uptime    SRTT   RTO  Q    Seq
                                    (sec)           (ms)        Cnt  Num
0 Link-local address:   Fa1/0        12   00:16:01   63    378  0    16
     FE80::C820:17FF:FE04:54
```

Example 5-27 *Verifying an IPv6 Link-Local Address*

```
R1# show ipv6 interface brief fastEthernet 3/0
FastEthernet3/0 [up/up]
 FE80::C820:17FF:FE04:54
 2001:DB8:0:14::1
```

You decide to check the EIGRPv6 topology table on Branch to see whether it is learning any IPv6 routes from R1. As shown in Example 5-28, Branch is learning routes from R1. It has learned 2001:DB8:0:1::/64 and 2001:DB8:0:12::/64. You quickly realize that those are only the connected routes on R1. You visit R1 again and issue the **show ipv6 eigrp topology** command and notice that R1 knows about other IPv6 routes, as shown in Example 5-29. However, it is not advertising them to Branch, as shown in Example 5-28.

Example 5-28 *Verifying Learned IPv6 Routes on Branch*

```
Branch# show ipv6 eigrp topology
EIGRP-IPv6 Topology Table for AS(100)/ID(4.4.4.4)
Codes: P - Passive, A - Active, U - Update, Q - Query, R - Reply,
 r - reply Status, s - sia Status

P 2001:DB8:0:4::/64, 1 successors, FD is 2816
        via Connected, GigabitEthernet0/0
P 2001:DB8:0:1::/64, 1 successors, FD is 28416
        via FE80::C820:17FF:FE04:54 (28416/2816), FastEthernet1/0
P 2001:DB8:0:14::/64, 1 successors, FD is 28160
        via Connected, FastEthernet1/0
P 2001:DB8:0:12::/64, 1 successors, FD is 28416
        via FE80::C820:17FF:FE04:54 (28416/2816), FastEthernet1/0
```

Example 5-29 *Verifying Learned IPv6 Routes on R1*

```
R1# show ipv6 eigrp topology
EIGRP-IPv6 Topology Table for AS(100)/ID(10.1.12.1)
Codes: P - Passive, A - Active, U - Update, Q - Query, R - Reply,
 r - reply Status, s - sia Status


P 2001:DB8:0:4::/64, 1 successors, FD is 28416
        via FE80::C828:DFF:FEF4:1C (28416/2816), FastEthernet3/0
P 2001:DB8:0:1::/64, 1 successors, FD is 2816
        via Connected, GigabitEthernet0/0
P 2001:DB8:0:3::/64, 1 successors, FD is 3328
        via FE80::C821:17FF:FE04:8 (3328/3072), GigabitEthernet1/0
P ::/0, 1 successors, FD is 2816
        via FE80::C821:17FF:FE04:8 (2816/256), GigabitEthernet1/0
P 2001:DB8:0:14::/64, 1 successors, FD is 28160
        via Connected, FastEthernet3/0
P 2001:DB8:0:12::/64, 1 successors, FD is 2816
        via Connected, GigabitEthernet1/0
P 2001:DB8:0:23::/64, 1 successors, FD is 3072
        via FE80::C821:17FF:FE04:8 (3072/2816), GigabitEthernet1/0
```

You believe that a route filter has been applied. Back on Branch, you issue the command
show run | section ipv6 router eigrp:

```
Branch# show run | section ipv6 router eigrp
ipv6 router eigrp 100
 eigrp router-id 4.4.4.4
```

As shown in this snippet, there is no distribute list (route filter) applied. Only the EIGRP
router ID is configured. You jump back to R1 and issue the same **show** command, as shown
in Example 5-30, and there is no distribute list (route filter) applied there either.

Example 5-30 *Verifying Route Filters on R1*

```
R1# show run | section ipv6 router eigrp
ipv6 router eigrp 100
 passive-interface default
 no passive-interface GigabitEthernet1/0
 no passive-interface FastEthernet3/0
 eigrp stub connected summary
```

However, you notice in the output in Example 5-30 that R1 is configured as an EIGRP stub
router that is advertising only connected and summary routes. This is the problem: The
wrong router was configured as a stub router. The spoke (Branch)—not the hub (R1) in HQ—
is supposed to be the stub router. To solve this issue, you remove the stub configuration

on R1 with the **no eigrp stub** command in IPv6 router EIGRP 100 configuration mode. You then issue the command **eigrp stub** on Branch in IPv6 router EIGRP 100 configuration mode.

To verify that the problem is solved, you issue the **show ipv6 route 2001:db8:f::f** command on Branch to determine whether there is an entry in the routing table now. In Example 5-31, the output shows that the default route is used.

Example 5-31 *Verifying the Route to 2001:db8:f::f in the IPv6 Routing Table on Branch*

```
Branch# show ipv6 route 2001:db8:f::f
Routing entry for ::/0
 Known via "eigrp 100", distance 170, metric 28416, type external
 Route count is 1/1, share count 0
 Routing paths:
 FE80::C820:17FF:FE04:54, FastEthernet1/0
 Last updated 00:03:09 ago
```

Next, you issue the extended IPv6 ping, as shown in Example 5-32, and it is successful.

Example 5-32 *Verifying That the Issue Is Solved by Using an Extended IPv6 Ping*

```
Branch# ping
Protocol [ip]: ipv6
Target IPv6 address: 2001:db8:f::f
Repeat count [5]:
Datagram size [100]:
Timeout in seconds [2]:
Extended commands? [no]: y
Source address or interface: 2001:db8:0:4::4
UDP protocol? [no]:
Verbose? [no]:
Precedence [0]:
DSCP [0]:
Include hop by hop option? [no]:
Include destination option? [no]:
Sweep range of sizes? [no]:
Type escape sequence to abort.
Sending 5, 100-byte ICMP Echos to 2001:DB8:F::F, timeout is 2 seconds:
Packet sent with a source address of 2001:DB8:0:4::4
!!!!!
Success rate is 100 percent (5/5)
```

Trouble Ticket 5-2

Trouble Ticket 5-2 is based on the topology shown in Figure 5-3.

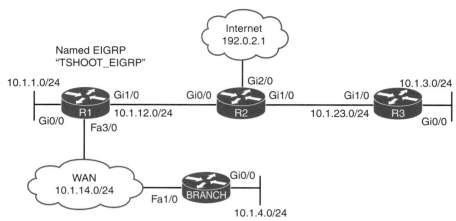

Figure 5-3 *Named EIGRP Trouble Tickets Topology*

Problem: Users in the 10.1.4.0/24 network indicate that they are not able to access resources outside their LAN.

On Branch, you verify the problem by pinging a few different IP addresses and source the packets from 10.1.4.4. As shown in Example 5-33, the pings all fail.

Example 5-33 *Verifying the Problem*

```
Branch# ping 10.1.3.3 source 10.1.4.4
Type escape sequence to abort.
Sending 5, 100-byte ICMP Echos to 10.1.3.3, timeout is 2 seconds:
Packet sent with a source address of 10.1.4.4
.....
Success rate is 0 percent (0/5)
Branch# ping 192.0.2.1 source 10.1.4.4
Type escape sequence to abort.
Sending 5, 100-byte ICMP Echos to 192.0.2.1, timeout is 2 seconds:
Packet sent with a source address of 10.1.4.4
.....
Success rate is 0 percent (0/5)
Branch# ping 10.1.1.1 source 10.1.4.4
Type escape sequence to abort.
Sending 5, 100-byte ICMP Echos to 10.1.1.1, timeout is 2 seconds:
Packet sent with a source address of 10.1.4.4
.....
Success rate is 0 percent (0/5)
```

Next, you issue the **show ip route** command to verify whether any routes are installed in the routing table. As shown in Example 5-34, only local and directly connected routes are in the routing table.

Example 5-34 *Displaying the IPv4 Routing Table on Branch*

```
Branch# show ip route
...output omitted...
Gateway of last resort is not set


 10.0.0.0/8 is variably subnetted, 4 subnets, 2 masks
C 10.1.4.0/24 is directly connected, GigabitEthernet0/0
L 10.1.4.4/32 is directly connected, GigabitEthernet0/0
C 10.1.14.0/24 is directly connected, FastEthernet1/0
L 10.1.14.4/32 is directly connected, FastEthernet1/0
```

You hypothesize that Branch is not a neighbor with R1 across the WAN. You issue the **show eigrp address-family ipv4 neighbors** command, as shown in the following snippet, and confirm that R1 is not a neighbor because the address family table is empty:

```
Branch# show eigrp address-family ipv4 neighbors

EIGRP-IPv4 VR(ENARSI_EIGRP) Address-Family Neighbors for AS(100)
```

Next, you hypothesize that FastEthernet 1/0 (the interface that will form an adjacency with R1) is not participating in the named EIGRP process. You issue the command **show eigrp address-family ipv4 interfaces**, as shown in Example 5-35, and the output confirms your hypothesis.

Example 5-35 *Displaying the Named EIGRP IPv4 Interface Table*

```
Branch# show eigrp address-family ipv4 interfaces
EIGRP-Ipv4 VR(ENARSI_EIGRP) Address-Family Interfaces for AS(100)
                    Xmit Queue    PeerQ        Mean   Pacing Time  Multicast   Pending
Interface Peers  Un/Reliable  Un/Reliable  SRTT   Un/Reliable  Flow Timer  Routes
Gi0/0     0        0/0          0/0         0      0/0          0           0
```

As shown in Example 5-36, the output of **show ip interface brief** indicates that FastEthernet 1/0 has the IPv4 address 10.1.14.4. Therefore, a **network** statement is needed to enable the EIGRP process on that interface.

Example 5-36 *Displaying the IPv4 Addresses of Interfaces*

```
Branch# show ip interface brief
Interface           IP-Address      OK? Method Status           Protocol
GigabitEthernet0/0  10.1.4.4        YES manual up               up
FastEthernet1/0     10.1.14.4       YES manual up               up
```

Armed with the information you have, you issue the **show running-config | section router eigrp** command on Branch to confirm that the network statement is missing. In Example 5-37, you see that there is a valid **network** statement for 10.1.14.4. It is **network**

10.1.14.4 0.0.0.0 and would successfully enable the EIGRP process on the interface. Therefore, you now know that your hypothesis was incorrect.

Example 5-37   *Reviewing the Named EIGRP Configuration in the Running Configuration*

```
Branch# show running-config | section router eigrp
router eigrp ENARSI_EIGRP
 !
 address-family ipv4 unicast autonomous-system 100
  !
  af-interface default
   passive-interface
  exit-af-interface
  !
  af-interface GigabitEthernet0/0
   no passive-interface
  exit-af-interface
  !
  topology base
  exit-af-topology
  network 10.1.4.4 0.0.0.0
  network 10.1.14.4 0.0.0.0
  eigrp router-id 4.4.4.4
  eigrp stub connected summary
  exit-address-family
 !
 address-family ipv6 unicast autonomous-system 100
  !
  af-interface default
   passive-interface
  exit-af-interface
  !
  af-interface FastEthernet1/0
   no passive-interface
  exit-af-interface
  !
  topology base
  maximum-paths 2
  variance 3
  exit-af-topology
  eigrp router-id 44.44.44.44
  eigrp stub connected summary
 exit-address-family
```

What could cause a neighbor relationship to fail to form? A few possibilities are authentication, passive interface, and incorrect subnet.

In Example 5-37, you notice that there are no authentication configurations. However, you do spot a passive interface configuration on GigabitEthernet0/0. The command listed in the output is the **no passive-interface** command. You also notice that *af-interface default* has the **passive-interface** command and recall that all interfaces inherit configurations under *af-interface default.* You also recall that they can be overridden with commands at the interface level. Reviewing the topology in Figure 5-3, you come to the conclusion that the wrong interface was configured with the **no passive-interface** command. It should have been FastEthernet1/0 and not GigabitEthernet0/0.

Example 5-38 presents the commands that you can use to fix this issue. Notice that once the issue is fixed, the neighbor relationship is formed with R1 at 10.1.14.1.

Example 5-38 *Modifying the Named EIGRP Configuration*

```
Branch# config t
Enter configuration commands, one per line. End with CNTL/Z.
Branch(config)# router eigrp ENARSI_EIGRP
Branch(config-router)# address-family ipv4 unicast autonomous-system 100
Branch(config-router-af)# af-interface GigabitEthernet0/0
Branch(config-router-af-interface)# passive-interface
Branch(config-router-af-interface)# exit
Branch(config-router-af)# af-interface fastEthernet1/0
Branch(config-router-af-interface)# no passive-interface
%DUAL-5-NBRCHANGE: EIGRP-IPv4 100: Neighbor 10.1.14.1 (FastEthernet1/0) is
up: new adjacency
Branch(config-router-af-interface)# end
Branch#
```

You then review the IPv4 routing table, as shown in Example 5-39, and notice all the EIGRP-learned routes.

Example 5-39 *Verifying the EIGRP-Learned Routes*

```
Branch# show ip route
...output omitted...
Gateway of last resort is 10.1.14.1 to network 0.0.0.0

D*EX 0.0.0.0/0 [170/112640] via 10.1.14.1, 00:00:34, FastEthernet1/0
     10.0.0.0/8 is variably subnetted, 8 subnets, 2 masks
D    10.1.1.0/24 [90/107520] via 10.1.14.1, 00:05:53, FastEthernet1/0
D    10.1.3.0/24 [90/117760] via 10.1.14.1, 00:05:53, FastEthernet1/0
C    10.1.4.0/24 is directly connected, GigabitEthernet0/0
L    10.1.4.4/32 is directly connected, GigabitEthernet0/0
D    10.1.12.0/24 [90/107520] via 10.1.14.1, 00:05:53, FastEthernet1/0
C    10.1.14.0/24 is directly connected, FastEthernet1/0
L    10.1.14.4/32 is directly connected, FastEthernet1/0
D    10.1.23.0/24 [90/112640] via 10.1.14.1, 00:05:53, FastEthernet1/0
```

Next, you reissue the same pings that were used to confirm the problem. As shown in Example 5-40, they are successful.

Example 5-40   *Successful Pings from Branch to Various Network IP Addresses*

```
Branch# ping 10.1.1.1 source 10.1.4.4
Type escape sequence to abort.
Sending 5, 100-byte ICMP Echos to 10.1.1.1, timeout is 2 seconds:
Packet sent with a source address of 10.1.4.4
!!!!!
Success rate is 100 percent (5/5), round-trip min/avg/max = 44/55/72 ms
Branch# ping 10.1.3.3 source 10.1.4.4
Type escape sequence to abort.
Sending 5, 100-byte ICMP Echos to 10.1.3.3, timeout is 2 seconds:
Packet sent with a source address of 10.1.4.4
!!!!!
Success rate is 100 percent (5/5), round-trip min/avg/max = 52/79/92 ms
Branch# ping 192.0.2.1 source 10.1.4.4
Type escape sequence to abort.
Sending 5, 100-byte ICMP Echos to 192.0.2.1, timeout is 2 seconds:
Packet sent with a source address of 10.1.4.4
!!!!!
Success rate is 100 percent (5/5), round-trip min/avg/max = 76/84/92 ms
```

Exam Preparation Tasks

As mentioned in the section "How to Use This Book" in the Introduction, you have a couple choices for exam preparation: the exercises here, Chapter 24, "Final Preparation," and the exam simulation questions in the Pearson Test Prep software.

Review All Key Topics

Review the most important topics in this chapter, noted with the Key Topic icon in the outer margin of the page. Table 5-4 lists these key topics and the page number on which each is found.

Table 5-4   Key Topics

Key Topic Element	Description	Page Number
Table 5-2	EIGRPv6 packets	191
Steps	EIGRPv6 classic configuration steps	192
Steps	EIGRPv6 named mode configuration steps	192
Paragraph	Disabling the routing process on an interface	192
Section	IPv6 Route Summarization	195
Section	Route filtering	197
Section	Troubleshooting EIGRPv6 neighbor issues	197

Key Topic Element	Description	Page Number
Paragraph	Two key addresses to considered when troubleshooting ACLs and EIGRPv6 neighborships	201
Paragraph	Administrative distance and the effects it has on populating the routing table with EIGRPv6 routes	201
Paragraph	Route filtering and the effects it has on populating the routing table with EIGRPv6 routes	201
Example 5-19	Output of **show eigrp protocols**	205
Example 5-21	Verifying details of interfaces participating in the named EIGRP process	207
Example 5-22	Verifying named EIGRP neighbors	208

Define Key Terms

Define the following key terms from this chapter and check your answers in the glossary:

hello packet, FF02::A, autonomous system number, K value, passive interface, key ID, key string, keychain, stub, split horizon, named EIGRP, maximum **paths**, variance, address family

Use the Command Reference to Check Your Memory

The ENARSI 300-410 exam focuses on the practical, hands-on skills that networking professionals use. Therefore, you should be able to identify the commands needed to configure, verify, and troubleshoot the topics covered in this chapter.

This section includes the most important configuration and verification commands covered in this chapter. It might not be necessary to memorize the complete syntax of every command, but you should be able to remember the basic keywords that are needed.

To test your memory of the commands in Table 5-5, go to the companion website and download Appendix B, "Command Reference Exercises." Fill in the missing commands in the tables based on each command description. You can check your work by downloading Appendix C, "Command Reference Exercise Answer Key," from the companion website.

Table 5-5 Command Reference

Task	Command Syntax

Initialize EIGRPv6 with classic configuration.	**ipv6 router eigrp** *as-number*
	  eigrp router-id *id*
	interface *interface-id*
	  ipv6 eigrp *as-number*

Initialize EIGRPv6 with named mode configuration.	**router eigrp** *process-name*
	  address-family ipv6 autonomous-system *as-number*
	  eigrp router-id *id*

Task	Command Syntax
Display all EIGRPv6 interfaces.	show ipv6 eigrp interface [*interface-id*] [detail]
Display established EIGRPv6 neighbors.	show ipv6 eigrp neighbors
Show a router's EIGRPv6 neighbors.	show ipv6 eigrp neighbors
Display the IPv6 routing protocols enabled on the router; for EIGRP, display autonomous system number, outgoing and incoming filters, K values, router ID, maximum paths, variance, local stub configuration, interfaces participating in the routing process, routing information sources, administrative distance, and passive interfaces.	show ipv6 protocols
Display all of a router's interfaces that are configured to participate in an EIGRPv6 routing process (with the exception of passive interfaces).	show ipv6 eigrp interfaces
Display the interfaces participating in the EIGRPv6 routing process, along with EIGRP hello and hold timers, whether the split horizon rule is enabled, and whether authentication is being used.	show ipv6 eigrp interfaces detail
Display the IPv6 EIGRP configuration in the running configuration.	show run | section ipv6 router eigrp
Show detailed information about a router's EIGRP neighbors, including whether the neighbor is a stub router, along with the types of networks it is advertising as a stub.	show ipv6 eigrp neighbors detail
Show routes known to a router's IP routing table that were injected by the router's EIGRP routing process.	show ipv6 route eigrp
Display detailed information about the EIGRP for IPv4 and IPv6 address families that are enabled on the router, including autonomous system number, K values, router ID, maximum paths, variance, local stub configuration, and administrative distance.	show eigrp protocols
Display the interfaces that are participating in the named EIGRP for IPv4 address family.	show eigrp address-family ipv4 interfaces
Display the interfaces that are participating in the named EIGRPv6 address family.	show eigrp address-family ipv6 interfaces

Task	Command Syntax
Display detailed information about the interfaces participating in the named EIGRP for IPv4 address family, including hello interval and hold time, whether split horizon is enabled, whether authentication is set, and statistics about hellos and packets.	show eigrp address-family ipv4 interfaces detail
Display detailed information about the interfaces participating in the named EIGRPv6 address family, including hello interval and hold time, whether split horizon is enabled, whether authentication is set, and statistics about hellos and packets.	show eigrp address-family ipv6 interfaces detail
Display the EIGRP for IPv4 neighbor relationships that have formed.	show eigrp address-family ipv4 neighbors
Display the EIGRPv6 neighbor relationships that have formed.	show eigrp address-family ipv6 neighbors
Display the EIGRP for IPv4 topology table for the address family.	show eigrp address-family ipv4 topology
Display the EIGRPv6 topology table for the address family.	show eigrp address-family ipv6 topology
Display all EIGRP packets exchanged with a router's EIGRP neighbors; however, the focus of the command can be narrowed to display only specific EIGRP packet types (for example, EIGRP hello packets).	debug eigrp packets

5

## CHAPTER 6

OSPF

This chapter covers the following topics:

- **OSPF Fundamentals:** This section provides an overview of the OSPF routing protocol.

- **OSPF Configuration:** This section explains how to configure a router with basic OSPF functionality.

- **The Designated Router and Backup Designated Router:** This section describes the function of the designated router and how it provides scalability for broadcast network segments.

- **OSPF Network Types:** This section provides an overview of the OSPF network types and their impact to OSPF's behavior.

- **Failure Detection:** This section explains how OSPF detects and verifies the health of OSPF neighbor routers.

- **Authentication:** This section explains how OSPF authentication functions and is configured.

The Open Shortest Path First (OSPF) protocol is the first link-state routing protocol covered in this book. OSPF is a nonproprietary Interior Gateway Protocol (IGP) that overcomes the deficiencies of other distance vector routing protocols. It distributes routing information within a single OSPF routing domain. OSPF introduced the concept of variable-length subnet masking (VLSM), which supports classless routing, summarization, authentication, and external route tagging. There are two main versions of OSPF in production networks today:

- **OSPFv2:** Originally defined in RFC 2328 with IPv4 support

- **OSPFv3:** Modifies the original structure to support IPv6

This chapter explains the core concepts of OSPF and the basics of establishing neighborships and exchanging routes with other OSPF routers. This chapter covers the fundamentals of OSPF and common optimizations in networks of any size. Chapter 7, "Advanced OSPF," explains the function of OSPF link-state advertisements (LSAs), OSPF stub areas, path selection, route summarization, and discontiguous networks and their repair with virtual links. Chapter 8, "Troubleshooting OSPFv2," explains how OSPF is used for routing IPv6 packets.

"Do I Know This Already?" Quiz

The "Do I Know This Already?" quiz allows you to assess whether you should read this entire chapter thoroughly or jump to the "Exam Preparation Tasks" section. If you are in doubt about your answers to these questions or your own assessment of your knowledge of the topics, read the entire chapter. Table 6-1 lists the major headings in this chapter and their corresponding "Do I Know This Already?" quiz questions. You can find the answers in Appendix A, "Answers to the 'Do I Know This Already?' Quiz Questions."

Table 6-1 "Do I Know This Already?" Foundation Topics Section-to-Question Mapping

Foundation Topics Section	Questions
OSPF Fundamentals	1–6
OSPF Configuration	7–9
The Designated Router and Backup Designated Router	10–11
OSPF Network Types	12
Failure Detection	13
Authentication	14

CAUTION The goal of self-assessment is to gauge your mastery of the topics in this chapter. If you do not know the answer to a question or are only partially sure of the answer, you should mark that question as wrong for purposes of self-assessment. Giving yourself credit for an answer that you correctly guess skews your self-assessment results and might provide you with a false sense of security.

1. What protocol number does OSPF use for inter-router communication?

   a. 87

   b. 88

   c. 89

   d. 90

2. How many packet types does OSPF use for inter-router communication?

   a. Three

   b. Four

   c. Five

   d. Six

   e. Seven

3. What destination addresses does OSPF use, when feasible? (Choose two.)

   a. IP address 224.0.0.5

   b. IP address 224.0.0.10

   c. IP address 224.0.0.8

   d. MAC address 01:00:5E:00:00:05

   e. MAC address 01:00:5E:00:00:0A

4. True or false: A router with an interface associated with Area 1 and Area 2 can inject routes learned from one area into another area.

   a. True

   b. False

5. True or false: A member router contains a complete copy of the LSDBs for every area in the routing domain.

   a. True

   b. False

6. How many states does OSPF maintain when dealing with a neighbor adjacency?

   a. Three

   b. Four

   c. Five

   d. Eight

7. True or false: The OSPF process ID must match for routers to establish a neighbor adjacency.

   a. True

   b. False

8. True or false: OSPF is only enabled on a router interface by using the command **network** *ip-address wildcard-mask* **area** *area-id* under the OSPF router process.

   a. True

   b. False

9. True or false: An advertised default route into OSPF always appears as an OSPF inter-area route.

   a. True

   b. False

10. True or false: When using a serial point-to-point link, the router with the highest IP address is the designated router.

   a. True

   b. False

11. What command is configured to prevent a router from becoming the designated router for a network segment?

   a. The interface command **ip ospf priority 0**

   b. The interface command **ip ospf priority 255**

   c. The command **dr-disable** *interface-id* under the OSPF process

   d. The command **passive-interface** *interface-id* under the OSPF process

   e. The command **dr-priority** *interface-id* **255** under the OSPF process

12. What is the advertised network for the loopback interface with IP address 10.123.4.1/30?

   a. 10.123.4.1/24

   b. 10.123.4.0/30

    c. 10.123.4.1/32

    d. 10.123.4.0/24

13. The OSPF dead interval defaults to how many times the hello interval?

    a. Two

    b. Three

    c. Four

    d. Five

14. True or false: Enabling OSPF authentication for an area consists of setting the OSFP authentication type under the OSPF process and placing the password on all area interfaces.

    a. True

    b. False

Foundation Topics

OSPF Fundamentals

OSPF sends link-state advertisements (LSAs) to neighboring routers. An LSA contains information on the link state and link metric, and OSPF advertises this information to neighboring routers exactly as the original advertising router advertised it. Received LSAs are stored in a local database called the link-state database (LSDB). This process floods the LSA throughout the OSPF routing domain just as the advertising router advertised it. All OSPF routers maintain a synchronized identical copy of the LSDB within an area.

The LSDB provides the topology of the network, in essence providing the router a complete map of the network. All OSPF routers run Dijkstra's shortest path first (SPF) algorithm to construct a loop-free topology of shortest paths. OSPF dynamically detects topology changes within the network and calculates loop-free paths in a short amount of time with minimal routing protocol traffic.

Each router sees itself as the root or top of the *SPF tree (SPT)*, and the SPT contains all network destinations within the OSPF domain. The SPT differs for each OSPF router, but the LSDB used to calculate the SPT is identical for all OSPF routers.

Figure 6-1 shows an example of a simple OSPF topology and the SPT from R1's and R4's perspective. Notice that the local router's perspective is always that of the root (or top of the tree). There is a difference in connectivity to the 10.3.3.0/24 network from R1's and R4's SPTs. From R1's perspective, the serial link between R3 and R4 is missing; from R4's perspective, the Ethernet link between R1 and R3 is missing.

The SPTs give the illusion that no redundancy exists to the networks, but remember that an SPT shows the shortest path to reach a network and is built from the LSDB, which contains all the links for an area. During a topology change, the SPT is rebuilt and may change.

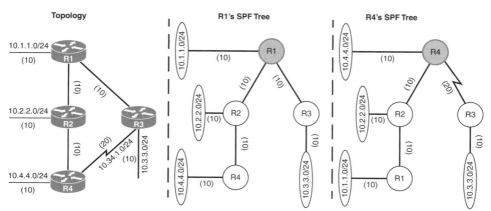

Figure 6-1 *OSPF Shortest Path First (SPF) Tree*

A router can run multiple OSPF processes. Each process maintains its own unique database, and routes learned in one OSPF process are not available to a different OSPF process without redistribution of routes between processes. The OSPF process numbers are locally significant and do not have to match among routers. If OSPF process number 1 is running on one router and OSPF process number 1234 is running on another, the two routers can become neighbors.

Areas

OSPF provides scalability for the routing table by splitting segments of the topology into multiple OSPF areas within the routing domain. An OSPF area is a logical grouping of routers or, more specifically, a logical grouping of router interfaces. Area membership is set at the interface level, and the area ID is included in the OSPF hello packet. An interface can belong to only one area. All routers within the same OSPF area maintain an identical copy of the LSDB.

An OSPF area grows in size as the number of network links and number of routers increase in the area. While using a single area simplifies the topology, there are trade-offs:

- A full SPT calculation runs when a link flaps within the area.

- With a single area, the LSDB increases in size and becomes unmanageable.

- The LSDB for the single area grows, consumes more memory, and takes longer during the SPF computation process.

- With a single area, no summarization of route information occurs.

Proper design addresses each of these issues by segmenting the OSPF routing domain into multiple OSPF areas, thereby keeping the LSDB a manageable size. Sizing and design of OSPF networks should account for the hardware constraints of the smallest router in that area.

If a router has interfaces in multiple areas, the router has multiple LSDBs (one for each area). The internal topology of one area is invisible from outside that area. If a topology change occurs (such as a link flap or an additional network added) within an area, all routers in the same OSPF area calculate the SPT again. Routers outside that area do not calculate the full

SPT again but do perform a partial SPF calculation if the metrics have changed or a prefix is removed.

In essence, an OSPF area hides the topology from another area but allows the networks to be visible in other areas within the OSPF domain. Segmenting the OSPF domain into multiple areas reduces the size of the LSDB for each area, making SPT calculations faster and decreasing LSDB flooding between routers when a link flaps.

Just because a router connects to multiple OSPF areas does not mean the routes from one area will be injected into another area. Figure 6-2 shows router R1 connected to Area 1 and Area 2. Routes from Area 1 do not advertise into Area 2 and vice versa.

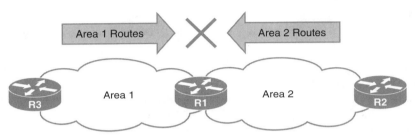

Figure 6-2 *Failed Route Advertisement Between Areas*

Area 0 is a special area called the *backbone* or *backbone area*. By design, OSPF uses a two-tier hierarchy in which all areas must connect to the upper tier, Area 0, because OSPF expects all areas to inject routing information into Area 0. Area 0 advertises the routes into other nonbackbone areas. The backbone design is crucial to preventing routing loops.

The area identifier (also known as the area ID) is a 32-bit field and can be formatted in simple decimal (0 through 4294967295) or dotted decimal (0.0.0.0 through 255.255.255.255). When configuring routers in an area, even if you use decimal format on one router and dotted-decimal format on a different router, the routers will be able to form an adjacency. OSPF advertises the area ID in the OSPF packets.

Area border routers (ABRs) are OSPF routers connected to Area 0 and another OSPF area, per Cisco definition and according to RFC 3509. ABRs are responsible for advertising routes from one area and injecting them into a different OSPF area. Every ABR needs to participate in Area 0 to allow for the advertisement of routes into another area. ABRs compute an SPT for every area that they participate in.

Figure 6-3 shows that R1 is connected to Area 0, Area 1, and Area 2. R1 is a proper ABR router because it participates in Area 0. The following occurs on R1:

■ Routes from Area 1 advertise into Area 0.

■ Routes from Area 2 advertise into Area 0.

■ Routes from Area 0 advertise into Areas 1 and 2. This includes the local Area 0 routes, in addition to the routes that were advertised into Area 0 from Area 1 and Area 2.

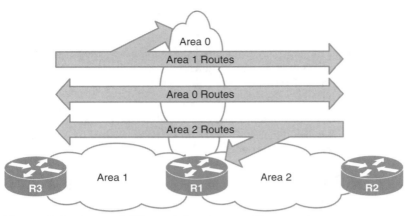

Figure 6-3 *Successful Route Advertisement Between Areas*

Inter-Router Communication

OSPF runs directly over IPv4, using protocol 89 in the IP header, which the Internet Assigned Numbers Authority (IANA) reserves for OSPF. OSPF uses multicast where possible to reduce unnecessary traffic. There are two OSPF multicast addresses:

- **AllSPFRouters:** IPv4 address 224.0.0.5 or MAC address 01:00:5E:00:00:05. All routers running OSPF should be able to receive packets with this address.

- **AllDRouters:** IPv4 address 224.0.0.6 or MAC address 01:00:5E:00:00:06. Communication with designated routers (DRs) uses this address.

Within the OSPF protocol, five types of packets are communicated. Table 6-2 briefly describes the OSPF packet types.

Table 6-2 OSPF Packet Types

Type	Packet Name	Functional Overview
1	Hello	Packets are sent out periodically on all OSPF interfaces to discover new neighbors while ensuring that other neighbors are still online.
2	Database description (DBD or DDP)	Packets are exchanged when an OSPF adjacency is first being formed. These packets are used to describe the contents of the LSDB.
3	Link-state request (LSR)	When a router thinks that part of its LSDB is stale, it may request a portion of a neighbor's database by using this packet type.
4	Link-state update (LSU)	This is an explicit LSA for a specific network link, and normally it is sent in direct response to an LSR.
5	Link-state acknowledgment	These packets are sent in response to the flooding of LSAs, thus making the flooding a reliable transport feature.

Router ID

The OSPF *router ID* (RID) is a 32-bit number that uniquely identifies an OSPF router. The OSPF RID is an essential component in building an OSPF topology. The output of some OSPF commands uses the term *neighbor ID* as a synonym for RID. The RID must be unique for each OSPF process in an OSPF domain and must be unique between OSPF processes on a router.

The RID is dynamically allocated by default, using the highest IP address of any up loopback interfaces. If there are no up loopback interfaces, the highest IP address of any active up physical interfaces becomes the RID when the OSPF process initializes. The OSPF process selects the RID when the OSPF process initializes, and it does not change until the process restarts. This means that the RID can change if a higher loopback address has been added and the process (or router) is restarted.

Setting a static RID helps with troubleshooting and reduces LSAs when an RID changes in an OSPF environment. The RID is four octets in length and is configured with the command **router-id** *router-id* under the OSPF process.

OSPF Hello Packets

OSPF *hello packets* are responsible for discovering and maintaining neighbors. In most instances, a router sends hello packets to the AllSPFRouters address (224.0.0.5). Table 6-3 lists some of the data contained within an OSPF hello packet.

Table 6-3   OSPF Hello Packet Fields

Data Field	Description
Router ID (RID)	A unique 32-bit ID within an OSPF domain that is used to build the topology.
Authentication Options	A field that allows secure communication between OSPF routers to prevent malicious activity. Options are none, plaintext, or Message Digest 5 (MD5) authentication.
Area ID	The OSPF area that the OSPF interface belongs to. It is a 32-bit number that can be written in dotted-decimal format (0.0.1.0) or decimal (256).
Interface Address Mask	The network mask for the primary IP address for the interface out which the hello is sent.
Interface Priority	The router interface priority for DR elections.
Hello Interval	The time interval, in seconds, at which a router sends out hello packets on the interface.
Dead Interval	The time interval, in seconds, that a router waits to hear a hello from a neighbor router before it declares that router down.
Designated Router and Backup Designated Router	The IP address of the DR and backup DR (BDR) for that network link.
Active Neighbor	A list of OSPF neighbors seen on that network segment. A router must have received a hello from the neighbor within the dead interval.

6

Neighbors

An OSPF neighbor is a router that shares a common OSPF-enabled network link. OSPF routers discover other neighbors through the OSPF hello packets. An adjacent OSPF neighbor is an OSPF neighbor that shares a synchronized OSPF database between the two neighbors.

Each OSPF process maintains a table for adjacent OSPF neighbors and the state of each router. Table 6-4 briefly describes the OSPF neighbor states.

Table 6-4 OSPF Neighbor States

State	Description
Down	The initial state of a neighbor relationship. It indicates that the router has not received any OSPF hello packets.
Attempt	A state that is relevant to nonbroadcast multi-access (NBMA) networks that do not support broadcast and that require explicit neighbor configuration. This state indicates that no recent information has been received, but the router is still attempting communication.
Init	A state in which a hello packet has been received from another router, but bidirectional communication has not been established.
2-Way	A state in which bidirectional communication has been established. If a DR or BDR is needed, the election occurs during this state.
ExStart	The first state in forming an adjacency. Routers identify which router will be the primary or secondary for the LSDB synchronization.
Exchange	A state during which routers are exchanging link states by using DBD packets.
Loading	A state in which LSR packets are sent to the neighbor, asking for the more recent LSAs that have been discovered (but not received) in the Exchange state.
Full	A state in which neighboring routers are fully adjacent.

Requirements for Neighbor Adjacency

The following list of requirements must be met for an OSPF neighborship to be formed:

- The RIDs must be unique between the two devices. To prevent errors, they should be unique for the entire OSPF routing domain.

- The interfaces must share a common subnet. OSPF uses the interface's primary IP address when sending out OSPF hellos. The network mask (netmask) in the hello packet is used to extract the network ID of the hello packet.

- The interface maximum transmission unit (MTU) must match because the OSPF protocol does not support fragmentation.

- The area ID must match for that segment.

- The need for a DR must match for that segment.

- OSPF hello and dead timers must match for that segment.

- The authentication type and credentials (if any) must match for that segment.

- Area type flags must be identical for that segment (stub, NSSA, and so on).

Figure 6-4 illustrates the states and packets exchanged when two routers, R1 and R2, form an OSPF adjacency.

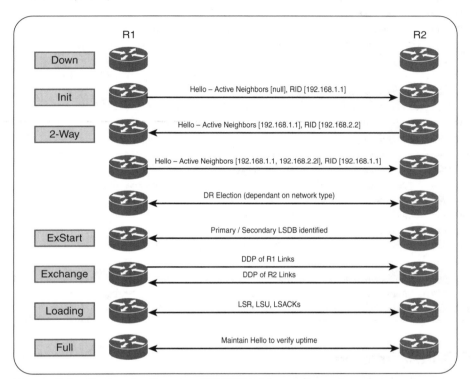

Figure 6-4   *Process for Forming OSPF Neighbor Adjacencies*

Example 6-1 shows each of the steps performed when an adjacency forms. When you enable OSPF adjacency debugging functionality, you get detailed information for all of the states.

Example 6-1   *OSPF Adjacency Debugging Output*

```
R1# debug ip ospf adj
OSPF adjacency events debugging is on

*21:10:01.735: OSPF: Build router LSA for area 0, router ID 192.168.1.1,
 seq 0x80000001, process 1
*21:10:09.203: OSPF: 2 Way Communication to 192.168.2.2 on GigabitEthernet0/0,
 state 2WAY
*21:10:39.855: OSPF: Rcv DBD from 192.168.2.2 on GigabitEthernet0/0 seq 0x1823
 opt 0x52 flag 0x7 len 32 mtu 1500 state 2WAY
```

```
*21:10:39.855: OSPF: Nbr state is 2WAY
*21:10:41.235: OSPF: end of Wait on interface GigabitEthernet0/0
*21:10:41.235: OSPF: DR/BDR election on GigabitEthernet0/0
*21:10:41.235: OSPF: Elect BDR 192.168.2.2
*21:10:41.235: OSPF: Elect DR 192.168.2.2
*21:10:41.235: DR: 192.168.2.2 (Id) BDR: 192.168.2.2 (Id)
*21:10:41.235: OSPF: GigabitEthernet0/0 Nbr 192.168.2.2: Prepare dbase exchange
*21:10:41.235: OSPF: Send DBD to 192.168.2.2 on GigabitEthernet0/0 seq 0xFA9
 opt 0x52 flag 0x7 len 32
*21:10:44.735: OSPF: Rcv DBD from 192.168.2.2 on GigabitEthernet0/0 seq 0x1823
 opt 0x52 flag 0x7 len 32 mtu 1500 state EXSTART
*21:10:44.735: OSPF: GigabitEthernet0/0 Nbr 2.2.2.2: Summary list built, size 1
*21:10:44.735: OSPF: Send DBD to 192.168.2.2 on GigabitEthernet0/0 seq 0x1823
 opt 0x52 flag 0x2 len 52
*21:10:44.743: OSPF: Rcv DBD from 192.168.2.2 on GigabitEthernet0/0 seq 0x1824
 opt 0x52 flag 0x1 len 52 mtu 1500 state EXCHANGE
*21:10:44.743: OSPF: Exchange Done with 192.168.2.2 on GigabitEthernet0/0
*21:10:44.743: OSPF: Send LS REQ to 192.168.2.2 length 12 LSA count 1
*21:10:44.743: OSPF: Send DBD to 192.168.2.2 on GigabitEthernet0/0 seq 0x1824
 opt 0x52 flag 0x0 len 32
*21:10:44.747: OSPF: Rcv LS UPD from 192.168.2.2 on GigabitEthernet0/0 length
 76 LSA count 1
*21:10:44.747: OSPF: Synchronized with 192.168.2.2 GigabitEthernet0/0, state FULL
*21:10:44.747: %OSPF-5-ADJCHG: Process 1, Nbr 192.168.2.2 on GigabitEthernet0/0
 from LOADING to FULL, Loading Done
```

OSPF Configuration

The configuration process for OSPF occurs mostly under the OSPF process, but some OSPF options go directly on the interface configuration submode. The OSPF process ID is locally significant but is generally kept the same for operational consistency. OSPF can be enabled on an interface using two methods:

- OSPF **network** statement
- Interface-specific configuration

OSPF Network Statement

The command **router ospf** *process-id* defines and initializes the OSPF process. The OSPF **network** statement identifies the interfaces that the OSPF process will use and the area that those interfaces participate in. The **network** statements match against the primary IPv4 address and netmask associated with an interface.

A common misconception is that the **network** statement advertises the networks into OSPF; in reality, though, the **network** statement selects and enables OSPF on the interface. The interface is then advertised in OSPF through the LSA. The **network** statement uses a wildcard mask, which allows the configuration to be as specific or vague as necessary. The selection of interfaces within the OSPF process is accomplished by using the command **network** *ip-address wildcard-mask* **area** *area-id*.

Interface-Specific Configuration

The second method for enabling OSPF on an interface for IOS is to configure it specifically on an interface with the command **ip ospf** *process-id* **area** *area-id* [**secondaries none**]. This method also adds secondary connected networks to the LSDB unless the **secondaries none** option is used.

This method provides explicit control for enabling OSPF; however, the configuration is not centralized, and the complexity increases as the number of interfaces on the routers increases. Interface-specific settings take precedence over the **network** statement with the assignment of the areas if a hybrid configuration exists on a router.

Passive Interfaces

Enabling an interface with OSPF is the quickest way to advertise the network segment to other OSPF routers. Making the network interface passive still adds the network segment to the LSDB but prevents the interface from forming OSPF adjacencies. A *passive interface* does not send out OSPF hellos and does not process any received OSPF packets.

The command **passive-interface** *interface-id* under the OSPF process makes the interface passive, and the command **passive-interface default** makes all interfaces passive. To allow for an interface to process OSPF packets, the command **no passive-interface** *interface-id* is used.

Sample Topology and Configuration

Figure 6-5 displays a reference topology for a basic multi-area OSPF configuration and will be referenced frequently in other sections of this chapter. In the topology:

- R1, R2, R3, and R4 belong to Area 1234.

- R4 and R5 belong to Area 0.

- R5 and R6 belong to Area 56.

- R1, R2, and R3 are member (internal) routers.

- R4 and R5 are ABRs.

- Area 1234 connects to Area 0, and Area 56 connects to Area 0.

- Routers in Area 1234 can see routes from routers in Area 0 (R4 and R5) and Area 56 (R5 and R6) and vice versa.

6

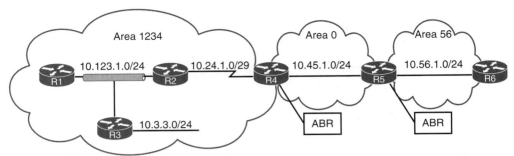

Figure 6-5 *Basic Multi-Area OSPF Topology*

To demonstrate the different methods of OSPF configuration, the routers are configured as follows:

- R1 is configured to enable OSPF on all interfaces with one **network** statement.

- R2 is configured to enable OSPF on both interfaces with two explicit **network** statements.

- R3 is configured to enable OSPF on all interfaces with one **network** statement but sets the 10.3.3.0/24 LAN interface as passive to prevent forming an OSPF adjacency on it.

- R4 is configured to enable OSPF using an interface-specific OSPF configuration.

- R5 is configured to place all interfaces in the 10.45.1.0/24 network segment into Area 0 and all other network interfaces into Area 56.

- R6 is configured to place all interfaces into Area 56 with one **network** statement.

- On R1 and R2, OSPF is enabled on all interfaces with one command, R3 uses specific network-based statements, and R4 uses interface-specific commands.

Example 6-2 provides the OSPF configurations for all six routers.

Example 6-2 *OSPF Configurations for Topology Example*

```
R1
router ospf 1
 router-id 192.168.1.1
 network 0.0.0.0 255.255.255.255 area 1234
```

```
R2
router ospf 1
 router-id 192.168.2.2
 network 10.123.1.2 0.0.0.0 area 1234
 network 10.24.1.2 0.0.0.0 area 1234
```

```
R3
router ospf 1
```

```
 router-id 192.168.3.3
 network 0.0.0.0 255.255.255.255 area 1234
 passive-interface GigabitEthernet0/1
```

```
R4
router ospf 1
 router-id 192.168.4.4
!
interface GigabitEthernet0/0
 ip ospf 1 area 0
interface Serial1/0
 ip ospf 1 area 1234
```

```
R5
router ospf 1
 router-id 192.168.5.5
 network 10.45.1.0 0.0.0.255 area 0
 network 0.0.0.0 255.255.255.255 area 56
```

```
R6
router ospf 1
 router-id 192.168.6.6
 network 0.0.0.0 255.255.255.255 area 56
```

Confirmation of Interfaces

You view OSPF-enabled interfaces by using the command **show ip ospf interface** [brief | *interface-id*]. Example 6-3 shows output from using the **show ip ospf interface** command on R4. The output lists all the OSPF-enabled interfaces, the IP address associated with each interface, the RIDs for the DR and BDR (and their associated interface IP addresses for that segment), and the OSPF timers for that interface.

Example 6-3 *Detailed OSPF Interface Output*

```
R4# show ip ospf interface
GigabitEthernet0/0 is up, line protocol is up
  Internet Address 10.45.1.4/24, Area 0, Attached via Interface Enable
  Process ID 1, Router ID 192.168.4.4, Network Type BROADCAST, Cost: 1
  Topology-MTID    Cost    Disabled    Shutdown    Topology Name
        0            1        no          no          Base
  Enabled by interface config, including secondary ip addresses
  Transmit Delay is 1 sec, State BDR, Priority 1
  Designated Router (ID) 192.168.5.5, Interface address 10.45.1.5
  Backup Designated router (ID) 192.168.4.4, Interface address 10.45.1.4
  Timer intervals configured, Hello 10, Dead 40, Wait 40, Retransmit 5
    oob-resync timeout 40
```

```
     Hello due in 00:00:02
 ..

  Neighbor Count is 1, Adjacent neighbor count is 1
     Adjacent with neighbor 192.168.5.5   (Designated Router)
  Suppress hello for 0 neighbor(s)
Serial1/0 is up, line protocol is up
  Internet Address 10.24.1.4/29, Area 1234, Attached via Interface Enable
  Process ID 1, Router ID 192.168.4.4, Network Type POINT_TO_POINT, Cost: 64
  Topology-MTID    Cost     Disabled    Shutdown     Topology Name
       0            64        no          no           Base
  Enabled by interface config, including secondary ip addresses
  Transmit Delay is 1 sec, State POINT_TO_POINT
  Timer intervals configured, Hello 10, Dead 40, Wait 40, Retransmit 5
 ..

  Neighbor Count is 1, Adjacent neighbor count is 1
     Adjacent with neighbor 192.168.2.2
  Suppress hello for 0 neighbor(s)
```

Example 6-4 shows the command with the **brief** keyword for R1, R2, R3, and R4. The State field provides useful information that helps you understand whether the interface is classified as broadcast or point-to-point, the area associated with the interface, and the process associated with the interface.

Example 6-4   *OSPF Interface Output in Brief Format*

```
R1# show ip ospf interface brief
Interface   PID   Area      IP Address/Mask      Cost   State Nbrs F/C
Gi0/0       1     1234      10.123.1.1/24        1      DROTH 2/2

R2# show ip ospf interface brief
Interface   PID   Area      IP Address/Mask      Cost   State Nbrs F/C
Se1/0       1     1234      10.24.1.1/29         64     P2P   1/1
Gi0/0       1     1234      10.123.1.2/24        1      BDR   2/2

R3# show ip ospf interface brief
Interface   PID   Area      IP Address/Mask      Cost   State Nbrs F/C
Gi0/1       1     1234      10.3.3.3/24          1      DR    0/0
Gi0/0       1     1234      10.123.1.3/24        1      DR    2/2

R4# show ip ospf interface brief
Interface   PID   Area      IP Address/Mask      Cost   State Nbrs F/C
Gi0/0       1     0         10.45.1.4/24         1      BDR   1/1
Se1/0       1     1234      10.24.1.4/29         64     P2P   1/1
```

Table 6-5 provides an overview of the fields in the output shown in Example 6-4.

Table 6-5 OSPF Interface Columns

Field	Description
Interface	Interfaces with OSPF enabled
PID	The OSPF process ID associated with this interface
Area	The area that this interface is associated with
IP Address/Mask	The IP address and subnet mask for the interface
Cost	A factor the SPF algorithm uses to calculate a metric for a path
State	The current interface state for segments with a designated router (DR, BDR, or DROTHER), P2P, LOOP, or Down
Nbrs F	The number of neighbor OSPF routers for a segment that are fully adjacent
Nbrs C	The number of neighbor OSPF routers for a segment that have been detected and are in a 2-Way state

NOTE The DROTHER is a router on the DR-enabled segment that is not the DR or the BDR; it is simply the other router. DROTHERs do not establish full adjacency with other DROTHERs.

Verification of OSPF Neighbor Adjacencies

The command **show ip ospf neighbor [detail]** provides the OSPF neighbor table. Example 6-5 displays the OSPF neighbors for R1 and R2. Notice that the state for R2's S1/0 interface does not reflect a DR status with its peering with R4 (192.168.4.4) because a DR does not exist on a point-to-point link.

Example 6-5 *OSPF Neighbor Output*

```
R1# show ip ospf neighbor
Neighbor ID     Pri    State          Dead Time    Address      Interface
192.168.2.2      1     FULL/BDR       00:00:34     10.123.1.2   GigabitEthernet0/0
192.168.3.3      1     FULL/DR        00:00:37     10.123.1.3   GigabitEthernet0/0

R2# show ip ospf neighbor
Neighbor ID     Pri    State          Dead Time    Address      Interface
192.168.4.4      0     FULL/ -        00:00:38     10.24.1.4    Serial1/0
192.168.1.1      1     FULL/DROTHER   00:00:37     10.123.1.1   GigabitEthernet0/0
192.168.3.3      1     FULL/DR        00:00:34     10.123.1.3   GigabitEthernet0/0
```

Table 6-6 provides a brief overview of the fields used in Example 6-5. The neighbor state on R1 identifies R3 as the DR and R2 as the BDR for the 10.123.1.0 network segment. R2 identifies R1 as DROTHER for that network segment.

Table 6-6 Fields from the OSPF Neighbor State Output

Field	Description
Neighbor ID	The router ID (RID) of the neighboring router.
Pri	The priority for the neighbor's interface, which is used for DR/BDR elections.
State	The first State field is the neighbor state, as described in Table 6-4. The second State field is the DR, BDR, or DROTHER role if the interface requires a DR. For non-DR network links, the second field shows just a hyphen (-).
Dead Time	The dead time left until the router is declared unreachable.
Address	The primary IP address for the OSPF neighbor.
Interface	The local interface to which the OSPF neighbor is attached.

Viewing OSPF Installed Routes

You display OSPF routes installed in the *Routing Information Base* (*RIB*) by using the command **show ip route ospf**. In the output, two sets of numbers are presented in brackets (for example, [110/2]). The first number is the administrative distance (AD), which is 110 by default for OSPF, and the second number is the metric of the path used for that network along with the next-hop IP address.

Example 6-6 provides the routing table for R1 from Figure 6-5. Notice that R1's OSPF routing table shows routes from within Area 1234 (10.24.1.0/29 and 10.3.3.0/24) as *intra-area* (O routes) and routes from Area 0 and Area 56 (10.45.1.0/24 and 10.56.1.0/24) as *inter-area* (O IA routes).

Example 6-6 shows intra-area and inter-area routes from R1's perspective in this topology.

Example 6-6 *OSPF Routes Installed in the RIB*

```
R1# show ip route ospf
! Output omitted for brevity
Codes: L - local, C - connected, S - static, R - RIP, M - mobile, B - BGP
       D - EIGRP, EX - EIGRP external, O - OSPF, IA - OSPF inter area
       N1 - OSPF NSSA external type 1, N2 - OSPF NSSA external type 2
       E1 - OSPF external type 1, E2 - OSPF external type 2
Gateway of last resort is not set


     10.0.0.0/8 is variably subnetted, 6 subnets, 3 masks
O       10.3.3.0/24 [110/2] via 10.123.1.3, 00:18:54, GigabitEthernet0/0
O       10.24.1.0/29 [110/65] via 10.123.1.2, 00:18:44, GigabitEthernet0/0
O IA    10.45.1.0/24 [110/66] via 10.123.1.2, 00:11:54, GigabitEthernet0/0
O IA    10.56.1.0/24 [110/67] via 10.123.1.2, 00:11:54, GigabitEthernet0/0
```

NOTE   The terms *path cost* and *path metric* are synonymous from OSPF's perspective.

Example 6-7 provides the routing table for R4 from Figure 6-5. Notice that R4's OSPF routing table shows the routes from within Area 1234 and Area 0 as intra-area and routes from Area 56 as inter-area because R4 does not connect to Area 56.

Notice that the metric for the 10.123.1.0/24 and 10.3.3.0/24 networks has drastically increased from the 10.56.1.0/24 network. This is because those networks are reachable across the slow serial link, which has an interface cost of 64.

Example 6-7   *OSPF Routing Tables for ABR R4*

```
R4# show ip route ospf | begin Gateway
Gateway of last resort is not set


      10.0.0.0/8 is variably subnetted, 7 subnets, 3 masks
O        10.3.3.0/24 [110/66] via 10.24.1.2, 00:03:45, Serial1/0
O IA     10.56.1.0/24 [110/2] via 10.45.1.5, 00:04:56, GigabitEthernet0/0
O        10.123.1.0/24 [110/65] via 10.24.1.2, 00:13:19, Serial1/0
```

Example 6-8 provides the routing table for R5 and R6 from Figure 6-5. R5 and R6 contain only inter-area routes in the OSPF routing table because intra-area routes are directly connected.

Example 6-8   *OSPF Routing Tables for R5 and R6*

```
R5# show ip route ospf | begin Gateway
Gateway of last resort is not set


      10.0.0.0/8 is variably subnetted, 7 subnets, 3 masks
O IA     10.3.3.0/24 [110/67] via 10.45.1.4, 00:04:13, GigabitEthernet0/0
O IA     10.24.1.0/29 [110/65] via 10.45.1.4, 00:04:13, GigabitEthernet0/0
O IA     10.123.1.0/24 [110/66] via 10.45.1.4, 00:04:13, GigabitEthernet0/0
```
```
R6# show ip route ospf | begin Gateway
Gateway of last resort is not set


      10.0.0.0/8 is variably subnetted, 6 subnets, 3 masks
O IA     10.3.3.0/24 [110/68] via 10.56.1.5, 00:07:04, GigabitEthernet0/0
O IA     10.24.1.0/29 [110/66] via 10.56.1.5, 00:08:19, GigabitEthernet0/0
O IA     10.45.1.0/24 [110/2] via 10.56.1.5, 00:08:18, GigabitEthernet0/0
O IA     10.123.1.0/24 [110/67] via 10.56.1.5, 00:08:19, GigabitEthernet0/0
```

6

External OSPF Routes

OSPF routes to networks learned from outside the OSPF domain that are injected into an OSPF domain through redistribution are known as *external OSPF routes*.

When a router redistributes prefixes into an OSPF domain, the router is called an *autonomous system boundary router (ASBR)*. An ASBR can be any OSPF router, and the ASBR function is independent of the ABR function. An OSPF domain can have an ASBR without having an ABR. An OSPF router can be an ASBR and an ABR at the same time.

External routes are classified as Type 1 or Type 2. The main differences between Type 1 and Type 2 external OSPF routes are as follows:

■ Type 1 routes are preferred over Type 2 routes.

■ The Type 1 metric equals the redistribution metric plus the total path metric to the ASBR. In other words, as the LSA propagates away from the originating ASBR, the metric increases.

■ The Type 2 metric equals only the redistribution metric. The metric is the same for the router next to the ASBR as the router 30 hops away from the originating ASBR. This is the default external metric type used by OSPF.

Figure 6-6 revisits the previous topology where R6 is redistributing two networks in to the OSPF domain. In this topology:

■ R1, R2, and R3 are member (internal) routers.

■ R4 and R5 are ABRs.

■ R6 is the ASBR.

■ 172.16.6.0/24 is being redistributed as an OSPF external Type 1 route.

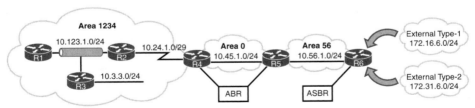

Figure 6-6 *OSPF Multi-Area Topology with External Routes*

Example 6-9 shows only the OSPF routes in the routing table from R1 and R2. The 172.16.6.0/24 network is redistributed as a Type 1 route, and the 172.31.6.0/24 network is redistributed as a Type 2 route.

External OSPF network routes are marked as O E1 and O E2 in the routing table and correlate with OSPF Type 1 and Type 2 external routes. Notice that the metric for the 172.31.6.0/24 network is the same on R1 as it is on R2, but the metric for the 172.16.6.0.0/24 network differs on the two routers because Type 1 external metrics include the path metric to the ASBR.

Example 6-9 *Examining OSPF External Route Metrics on R1 and R2*

```
R1# show ip route ospf
! Output omitted for brevity
Codes: L - local, C - connected, S - static, R - RIP, M - mobile, B - BGP
       D - EIGRP, EX - EIGRP external, O - OSPF, IA - OSPF inter area
       E1 - OSPF external type 1, E2 - OSPF external type 2
Gateway of last resort is not set

      10.0.0.0/8 is variably subnetted, 6 subnets, 3 masks
O        10.3.3.0/24 [110/2] via 10.123.1.3, 23:20:25, GigabitEthernet0/0
O        10.24.1.0/29 [110/65] via 10.123.1.2, 23:20:15, GigabitEthernet0/0
O IA     10.45.1.0/24 [110/66] via 10.123.1.2, 23:13:25, GigabitEthernet0/0
O IA     10.56.1.0/24 [110/67] via 10.123.1.2, 23:13:25, GigabitEthernet0/0
      172.16.0.0/24 is subnetted, 1 subnets
O E1     172.16.6.0 [110/87] via 10.123.1.2, 00:01:00, GigabitEthernet0/0
      172.31.0.0/24 is subnetted, 1 subnets
O E2     172.31.6.0 [110/20] via 10.123.1.2, 00:01:00, GigabitEthernet0/0
```

```
R2# show ip route ospf | begin Gateway
Gateway of last resort is not set

      10.0.0.0/8 is variably subnetted, 7 subnets, 3 masks
O        10.3.3.0/24 [110/2] via 10.123.1.3, 23:24:05, GigabitEthernet0/0
O IA     10.45.1.0/24 [110/65] via 10.24.1.4, 23:17:11, Serial1/0
O IA     10.56.1.0/24 [110/66] via 10.24.1.4, 23:17:11, Serial1/0
      172.16.0.0/24 is subnetted, 1 subnets
O E1     172.16.6.0 [110/86] via 10.24.1.4, 00:04:45, Serial1/0
      172.31.0.0/24 is subnetted, 1 subnets
O E2     172.31.6.0 [110/20] via 10.24.1.4, 00:04:45, Serial1/0
```

6

Default Route Advertisement

OSPF supports advertising the default route into the OSPF domain. The advertising router must have a default route in its routing table for the default route to be advertised. To advertise the default route, you use the command **default-information originate** [**always**] [**metric** *metric-value*] [**metric-type** *type-value*] underneath the OSPF process. The **always** optional keyword advertises the default route regardless of whether a default route exists in the RIB. In addition, the route metric can be changed with the **metric** *metric-value* option, and the metric type can be changed with the **metric-type** *type-value* option.

Figure 6-7 illustrates a common situation, where R1 has a static default route to the firewall, which is connected to the Internet. To provide connectivity to other parts of the network (that is, R2 and R3), R1 advertises a default route into OSPF.

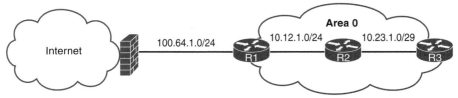

Figure 6-7   *Default Route Topology*

Example 6-10 provides the relevant configuration on R1. Notice that R1 has a static default route to the firewall (100.64.1.2) to satisfy the requirement of having the default route in the RIB.

Example 6-10   *OSPF default-information originate Configuration*

```
R1
ip route 0.0.0.0 0.0.0.0 100.64.1.2
!
router ospf 1
 network 10.0.0.0 0.255.255.255 area 0
 default-information originate
```

Example 6-11 shows the routing tables of R2 and R3. Notice that OSPF advertises the default route as an external OSPF route.

Example 6-11   *R2's and R3's Routing Tables*

```
R2# show ip route | begin Gateway
Gateway of last resort is 10.12.1.1 to network 0.0.0.0

O*E2  0.0.0.0/0 [110/1] via 10.12.1.1, 00:02:56, GigabitEthernet0/1
      10.0.0.0/8 is variably subnetted, 4 subnets, 2 masks
C        10.12.1.0/24 is directly connected, GigabitEthernet0/1
C        10.23.1.0/24 is directly connected, GigabitEthernet0/2
```

```
R3# show ip route | begin Gateway
Gateway of last resort is 10.23.1.2 to network 0.0.0.0
O*E2  0.0.0.0/0 [110/1] via 10.23.1.2, 00:01:47, GigabitEthernet0/1
      10.0.0.0/8 is variably subnetted, 3 subnets, 2 masks
O        10.12.1.0/24 [110/2] via 10.23.1.2, 00:05:20, GigabitEthernet0/1
C        10.23.1.0/24 is directly connected, GigabitEthernet0/1
```

The Designated Router and Backup Designated Router

Multi-access networks such as Ethernet (LANs) and Frame Relay networks allow more than two routers to exist on a network segment. This could cause scalability problems with OSPF as the number of routers on a segment increases. Additional routers flood more LSAs on the segment, and OSPF traffic becomes excessive as OSPF neighbor adjacencies increase. If four routers share the same multi-access network, six OSPF adjacencies form, along with six occurrences of database flooding on a network.

Using the number of edges formula, $n(n-1)/2$, where n represents the number of routers, if 5 routers were present on a segment—that is, $5(5-1)/2 = 10$—then 10 OSPF adjacencies would exist for that segment. Continuing the logic, adding 1 additional router would make 15 OSPF adjacencies on a network segment. Having so many adjacencies per segment consumes more bandwidth, more CPU processing, and more memory to maintain each of the neighbor states.

OSPF overcomes this inefficiency by creating a pseudonode (that is, a virtual router) to manage the adjacency state with all the other routers on that broadcast network segment. A router on the broadcast segment, known as the *designated router (DR)*, assumes the role of the pseudonode. The DR reduces the number of OSPF adjacencies on a multi-access network segment because routers form full OSPF adjacencies only with the DR and not with each other. The DR is then responsible for flooding the update to all OSPF routers on that segment as updates occur. Figure 6-8 demonstrates how this simplifies a four-router topology using only three neighbor adjacencies.

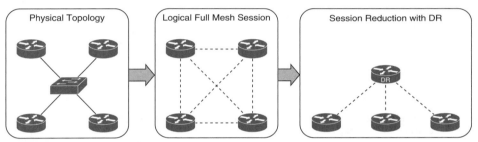

Figure 6-8   *OSPF DR Concept*

If the DR were to fail, OSPF would need to form new adjacencies, invoking all new LSAs, and could potentially cause a temporary loss of routes. In the event of DR failure, a *backup designated router (BDR)* becomes the new DR; then an election occurs to replace the BDR. To minimize transition time, the BDR also forms a full OSPF adjacency with all OSPF routers on that segment.

The DR/BDR process distributes LSAs in the following manner assuming that all OSPF routers (DR, BDR, and DROTHER) on a segment form a full OSPF adjacency with the DR and BDR:

Step 1.   As an OSPF router learns of a new route, it sends the updated LSA to the All-DRouters (224.0.0.6) address, which only the DR and BDR accept and process, as illustrated in step 1 in Figure 6-9..

Step 2.   The DR sends a unicast acknowledgment to the router that sent the initial LSA update, as illustrated in step 2 in Figure 6-9.

Step 3.   The DR floods the LSA to all the routers on the segment via the AllSPFRouters (224.0.0.5) address, as shown in step 3 in Figure 6-9.

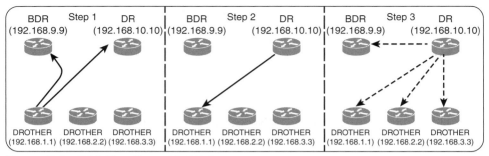

Figure 6-9 *LSA Flooding with DR Segments*

Designated Router Elections

The DR/BDR election occurs with OSPF neighborship—specifically, during the last phase of the 2-Way neighbor state and just before the ExStart state. When a router enters the 2-Way state, it has already received a hello from the neighbor. If the hello packet includes an RID other than 0.0.0.0 for the DR or BDR, the new router assumes that the current routers are the actual DR and BDR.

Any router with the OSPF priority of 1 to 255 on its OSPF interface attempts to become the DR. By default, all OSPF interfaces use a priority of 1. The routers place their RID and OSPF priority in their OSPF hellos for that segment.

Routers then receive and examine OSPF hellos from neighboring routers. If a router identifies itself as a more favorable router than the OSPF hellos it receives, it continues to send out hellos with its RID and priority listed. If the hello received is more favorable, the router updates its OSPF hello packet to use the more preferable RID in the DR field. OSPF deems a router more preferable if the priority for the interface is the highest for that segment. If the OSPF priority is the same, the higher RID is more favorable.

When all the routers have agreed on the same DR, all routers for that segment become adjacent with the DR. Then the election for the BDR takes place. The election follows the same logic as the DR election, except that the DR does not add its RID to the BDR field of the hello packet.

The OSPF DR and BDR roles cannot be preempted after the DR/BDR election. Only upon the failure (or process restart) of the DR or BDR does the election start to replace the role that is missing.

NOTE To ensure that all routers on a segment have fully initialized, OSPF initiates a wait timer when OSPF hello packets do not contain a DR/BDR router for a segment. The default value for the wait timer is the dead interval timer. When the wait timer has expired, a router participates in the DR election. The wait timer starts when OSPF first starts on an interface, so a router can still elect itself as the DR for a segment without other OSPF routers; it waits until the wait timer expires.

In Figure 6-6, the 10.123.1.0/24 network requires a DR between R1, R2, and R3. The interface role is determined by viewing the OSPF interface with the command **show ip ospf interface brief**. R3's interface Gi0/0 is elected as the DR, R2's Gi0/0 interface is elected as the BDR, and R1's Gi0/0 interface is DROTHER for the 10.123.1.0/24 network. R3's Gi0/1 interface is DR because no other router exists on that segment. R2's Serial1/0 interface is a point-to-point link and has no DR.

The neighbor's full adjacency field reflects the number of routers that have become adjacent on that network segment; the neighbor's count field is the number of other OSPF routers on that segment. The first assumption is that all routers will become adjacent with each other, but that defeats the purpose of using a DR. Only the DR and BDR become adjacent with routers on a network segment.

DR and BDR Placement

In Example 6-12, R3 wins the DR election, and R2 is elected the BDR because all the OSPF routers have the same OSPF priority, and the next decision is to use the higher RID. The RIDs match the Loopback 0 interface IP addresses, and R3's loopback address is the highest on that segment; R2's is the second highest.

Example 6-12   *OSPF Interface State*

```
R1# show ip ospf interface brief
Interface    PID    Area            IP Address/Mask      Cost   State Nbrs F/C
Lo0          1      0               192.168.1.1/32       1      LOOP  0/0
Gi0/0        1      0               10.123.1.1/24        1      DROTH 2/2

R2# show ip ospf interface brief
Interface    PID    Area            IP Address/Mask      Cost   State Nbrs F/C
Lo0          1      0               192.168.2.2/32       1      LOOP  0/0
Se1/0        1      0               10.24.1.1/29         64     P2P   1/1
Gi0/0        1      0               10.123.1.2/24        1      BDR   2/2

R3# show ip ospf interface brief
Interface    PID    Area            IP Address/Mask      Cost   State Nbrs F/C
Lo0          1      0               192.168.3.3/32       1      LOOP  0/0
Gi0/0        1      0               10.123.1.3/24        1      DR    2/2
Gi0/1        1      0               10.3.3.3/24          1      DR    0/0
```

Modifying a router's RID for DR placement is a bad design strategy. A better technique involves modifying the *interface priority* to a higher value than that of the existing DR. Changing the priority to a value higher than that of the other routers (which have a default value of 1) increases the chance of that router becoming the DR for that segment on that node. Remember that OSPF does not preempt the DR or BDR roles, and it might be necessary to restart the OSPF process on the current DR/BDR for the changes to take effect.

The priority can be set manually under the interface configuration with the command **ip ospf priority** *0-255* for IOS nodes. Setting an interface priority to 0 removes that interface from the DR/BDR election immediately. Raising the priority above the default value (1) makes that interface more favorable than interfaces with the default value.

OSPF Network Types

Different media can provide different characteristics or might limit the number of nodes allowed on a segment. Frame Relay and Ethernet are common multi-access media, and because they support more than two nodes on a network segment, there is a need for a DR. Other network circuits, such as serial links, do not require a DR and would just waste router CPU cycles.

The default OSPF network type is set based on the media used for the connection and can be changed independently of the actual media type used. Cisco's implementation of OSPF considers the various media and provides five OSPF network types, as listed in Table 6-7.

Table 6-7   OSPF Network Types

Type	Description	DR/BDR Field in OSPF Hellos	Timers
Broadcast	Default setting on OSPF-enabled Ethernet links.	Yes	Hello: 10 Wait: 40 Dead: 40
Nonbroadcast	Default setting on enabled OSPF Frame Relay main interface or Frame Relay multipoint sub-interfaces.	Yes	Hello: 30 Wait: 120 Dead: 120
Point-to-point	Default setting on enabled OSPF Frame Relay point-to-point sub-interfaces.	No	Hello: 10 Wait: 40 Dead: 40
Point-to-multipoint	Not enabled by default on any interface type. Interface is advertised as a host route (/32), and sets the next-hop address to the outbound interface. Primarily used for hub-and-spoke topologies.	No	Hello: 30 Wait: 120 Dead: 120
Loopback	Default setting on OSPF-enabled loopback interfaces. Interface is advertised as a host route (/32).	N/A	N/A

The OSPF network types are explained in more detail in the following sections.

Broadcast

Broadcast media such as Ethernet are better defined as broadcast multi-access to distinguish them from nonbroadcast multi-access (NBMA) networks. Broadcast networks are multi-access in that they are capable of connecting more than two devices, and broadcasts sent out one interface are capable of reaching all interfaces attached to that segment.

The OSPF network type is set to broadcast by default for Ethernet interfaces. A DR is required for this OSPF network type because of the possibility that multiple nodes can exist on a segment and LSA flooding needs to be controlled. The hello timer defaults to 10 seconds, as defined in RFC 2328.

The interface parameter command **ip ospf network broadcast** overrides the automatically configured setting and statically sets an interface as an OSPF broadcast network type.

Nonbroadcast

Frame Relay, ATM, and X.25 are considered NBMA in that they can connect more than two devices, and broadcasts sent out one interface might not always be capable of reaching all the interfaces attached to the segment. Dynamic virtual circuits may provide connectivity, but the topology may not be a full mesh and might only provide a hub-and-spoke topology.

Frame Relay interfaces set the OSPF network type to nonbroadcast by default. The hello protocol interval takes 30 seconds for this OSPF network type. Multiple routers can exist on a segment, so the DR functionality is used. Neighbors are statically defined with the **neighbor** *ip-address* command because multicast and broadcast functionality do not exist on this type of circuit. Configuring a static neighbor causes OSPF hellos to be sent using unicast.

The interface parameter command **ip ospf network non-broadcast** manually sets an interface as an OSPF nonbroadcast network type.

Figure 6-10 shows an example of a Frame Relay topology.

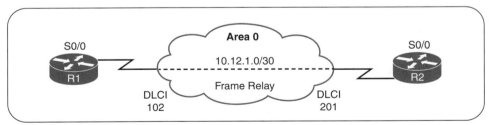

Figure 6-10   *OSPF Topology Using Frame Relay*

Example 6-13 provides the OSPF configuration over a Frame Relay interface. Notice that the static neighbor configuration is required when OSPF packets cannot be received through broadcast (multicast) discovery.

Example 6-13   *OSPF Configuration for Frame Relay Interfaces*

```
R1
interface Serial 0/0
 ip address 10.12.1.1 255.255.255.252
 encapsulation frame-relay
 no frame-relay inverse-arp
 frame-relay map ip address 10.12.1.2 102
 !
router ospf 1
 router-id 192.168.1.1
 neighbor 10.12.1.2
 network 0.0.0.0 255.255.255.255 area 0
```

The nonbroadcast network type is verified by filtering the output of the **show ip ospf interface** command with the *Type* keyword. The following snippet confirms that the interfaces operate as nonbroadcast:

```
R1# show ip ospf interface Serial 0/0 | include Type

  Process ID 1, Router ID 192.168.1.1, Network Type
NON_BROADCAST, Cost: 64
```

Point-to-Point Networks

A network circuit that allows only two devices to communicate is considered a point-to-point (P2P) network. Because of the nature of the medium, point-to-point networks do not use Address Resolution Protocol (ARP), and broadcast traffic does not become the limiting factor.

The OSPF network type is set to point-to-point by default for serial interfaces (HDLC or PPP encapsulation), Generic Routing Encapsulation (GRE) tunnels, and point-to-point Frame Relay sub-interfaces. Only two nodes can exist on this type of network medium, so OSPF does not waste CPU cycles on DR functionality. The hello timer is set to 10 seconds on OSPF point-to-point network types.

Figure 6-11 shows a serial connection between R1 and R2.

Figure 6-11   *OSPF Topology with Serial Interfaces*

Example 6-14 displays R1's and R2's relevant serial interface and OSPF configuration. Notice that there are not any special commands in the configuration.

Example 6-14 *R1 and R2 Serial and OSPF Configuration*

```
R1
interface serial 0/1
  ip address 10.12.1.1 255.255.255.252
!
router ospf 1
   router-id 192.168.1.1
   network 0.0.0.0 255.255.255.255 area 0
```

```
R2
interface serial 0/1
  ip address 10.12.1.2 255.255.255.252
!
router ospf 1
   router-id 192.168.2.2
   network 0.0.0.0 255.255.255.255 area 0
```

Example 6-15 verifies that the OSPF network type is set to POINT_TO_POINT, indicating the OSPF point-to-point network type.

Example 6-15 *Verifying OSPF P2P Interfaces*

```
R1# show ip ospf interface s0/1 | include Type
  Process ID 1, Router ID 192.168.1.1, Network Type POINT_TO_POINT, Cost: 64
```

```
R2# show ip ospf interface s0/1 | include Type
  Process ID 1, Router ID 192.168.2.2, Network Type POINT_TO_POINT, Cost: 64
```

Example 6-16 shows that point-to-point OSPF network types do not use a DR. Notice the hyphen (-) in the State field.

Example 6-16 *Verifying OSPF Neighbors on P2P Interfaces*

```
R1# show ip ospf neighbor

Neighbor ID Pri State Dead Time Address Interface
192.168.2.2 0 FULL/ - 00:00:36 10.12.1.2 Serial0/1
```

Interfaces using an OSPF P2P network type form an OSPF adjacency quickly because the DR election is bypassed, and there is no wait timer. Ethernet interfaces that are directly connected with only two OSPF speakers in the subnet could be changed to the OSPF point-to-point network type to form adjacencies more quickly and to simplify the SPF computation. The interface parameter command **ip ospf network point-to-point** manually sets an interface as an OSPF point-to-point network type.

Point-to-Multipoint Networks

The OSPF network type point-to-multipoint is not enabled by default for any medium. It requires manual configuration. A DR is not enabled for this OSPF network type, and the hello timer is set to 30 seconds. A point-to-multipoint OSPF network type supports hub-and-spoke connectivity while using the same IP subnet and is commonly found in Frame Relay and Layer 2 VPN (L2VPN) topologies.

Interfaces set for the OSPF point-to-multipoint network type add the interface's IP address to the OSPF LSDB as a /32 network. When advertising routes to OSPF peers on that interface, the next-hop address is set to the IP address of the interface even if the next-hop IP address resides on the same IP subnet.

The IOS interface parameter command **ip ospf network point-to-multipoint** manually sets an interface as an OSPF point-to-multipoint network type.

Figure 6-12 provides a topology example with R1, R2, and R3 all using Frame Relay point-to-multipoint sub-interfaces using the same subnet.

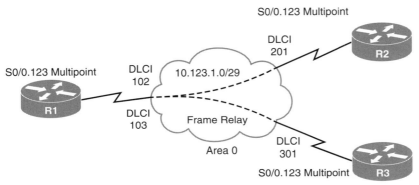

Figure 6-12 *OSPF Topology with Frame Relay Multipoint Interfaces*

Example 6-17 demonstrates the relevant configuration for all three routers.

Example 6-17 *OSPF Point-to-Multipoint Configuration*

```
R1
interface Serial 0/0
  encapsulation frame-relay
  no frame-relay inverse-arp
!
interface Serial 0/0.123 multipoint
  ip address 10.123.1.1 255.255.255.248
  frame-relay map ip 10.123.1.2 102 broadcast
  frame-relay map ip 10.123.1.3 103 broadcast
  ip ospf network point-to-multipoint
!
router ospf 1
  router-id 192.168.1.1
```

```
  network 0.0.0.0 255.255.255.255 area 0
```

```
R2
interface Serial 0/0
  encapsulation frame-relay
  no frame-relay inverse-arp
!
interface Serial 0/1/0/0.123 multipoint
  ip address 10.123.1.2 255.255.255.248
  frame-relay map ip 10.123.1.1 201 broadcast
  ip ospf network point-to-multipoint
!
router ospf 1
  router-id 192.168.2.2
  network 0.0.0.0 255.255.255.255 area 0
```

```
R3
interface Serial 0/0
  encapsulation frame-relay
  no frame-relay inverse-arp
!
interface Serial 0/0.123 multipoint
  ip address 10.123.1.3 255.255.255.248
  frame-relay map ip 10.123.1.1 301 broadcast
  ip ospf network point-to-multipoint
!
router ospf 1
  router-id 192.168.3.3
  network 0.0.0.0 255.255.255.255 area 0
```

Example 6-18 verifies that the interfaces are the OSPF point-to-multipoint network type.

Example 6-18 *Verifying OSPF Network Type Point-to-Multipoint*

```
R1# show ip ospf interface Serial 0/0.123 | include Type
   Process ID 1, Router ID 192.168.1.1, Network Type POINT_TO_MULTIPOINT, Cost: 64

R2# show ip ospf interface Serial 0/0.123 | include Type
   Process ID 1, Router ID 192.168.2.2, Network Type POINT_TO_MULTIPOINT, Cost: 64

R3# show ip ospf interface Serial 0/0.123 | include Type
   Process ID 1, Router ID 192.168.3.3, Network Type POINT_TO_MULTIPOINT, Cost: 64
```

Example 6-19 shows that OSPF does not use a DR for the OSPF point-to-multipoint network type. Notice that all three routers are on the same subnet, but R2 and R3 do not establish an adjacency with each other.

Example 6-19   *OSPF Neighbor Adjacency on a Hub-and-Spoke Topology*

```
R1# show ip ospf neighbor


Neighbor ID     Pri    State      Dead Time     Address      Interface
192.168.3.3      0    FULL/ -      00:01:33    10.123.1.3    Serial0/0.123
192.168.2.2      0    FULL/ -      00:01:40    10.123.1.2    Serial0/0.123

R2# show ip ospf neighbor


Neighbor ID     Pri    State      Dead Time     Address      Interface
192.168.1.1      0    FULL/ -      00:01:49    10.123.1.1    Serial0/0.123

R3# show ip ospf neighbor


Neighbor ID     Pri    State      Dead Time     Address      Interface
192.168.1.1      0    FULL/ -      00:01:46    10.123.1.1    Serial0/0.123
```

Example 6-20 shows that all the Serial 0/0.123 interfaces are advertised into OSPF as a /32 network and that the next-hop address is set (by R1) when advertised to the spokes nodes.

Example 6-20   *OSPF Point-to-Multipoint Routing Tables*

```
R1# show ip route ospf | begin Gateway
Gateway of last resort is not set


      10.0.0.0/8 is variably subnetted, 4 subnets, 2 masks
O        10.123.1.2/32 [110/64] via 10.123.1.2, 00:07:32, Serial0/0.123
O        10.123.1.3/32 [110/64] via 10.123.1.3, 00:03:58, Serial0/0.123
      192.168.2.0/32 is subnetted, 1 subnets
O        192.168.2.2 [110/65] via 10.123.1.2, 00:07:32, Serial0/0.123
      192.168.3.0/32 is subnetted, 1 subnets
O        192.168.3.3 [110/65] via 10.123.1.3, 00:03:58, Serial0/0.123

R2# show ip route ospf | begin Gateway
Gateway of last resort is not set


      10.0.0.0/8 is variably subnetted, 4 subnets, 2 masks
O        10.123.1.1/32 [110/64] via 10.123.1.1, 00:07:17, Serial0/0.123
O        10.123.1.3/32 [110/128] via 10.123.1.1, 00:03:39, Serial0/0.123
      192.168.1.0/32 is subnetted, 1 subnets
O        192.168.1.1 [110/65] via 10.123.1.1, 00:07:17, Serial0/0.123
      192.168.3.0/32 is subnetted, 1 subnets
O        192.168.3.3 [110/129] via 10.123.1.1, 00:03:39, Serial0/0.123
```

```
R3# show ip route ospf | begin Gateway
Gateway of last resort is not set


      10.0.0.0/8 is variably subnetted, 4 subnets, 2 masks
O        10.123.1.1/32 [110/64] via 10.123.1.1, 00:04:27, Serial0/0.123
O        10.123.1.2/32 [110/128] via 10.123.1.1, 00:04:27, Serial0/0.123
      192.168.1.0/32 is subnetted, 1 subnets
O        192.168.1.1 [110/65] via 10.123.1.1, 00:04:27, Serial0/0.123
      192.168.2.0/32 is subnetted, 1 subnets
O        192.168.2.2 [110/129] via 10.123.1.1, 00:04:27, Serial0/0.123
```

Loopback Networks

The OSPF network type loopback is enabled by default for loopback interfaces and can be used only on loopback interfaces. The OSPF loopback network type indicates that the IP address is always advertised with a /32 prefix length, even if the IP address configured on the loopback interface does not have a /32 prefix length.

You can see this behavior by looking at Figure 6-11, where the Loopback0 interface is now being advertised in to OSPF. Example 6-21 provides the updated configuration. Notice that the network type for R2's loopback interface is set to the OSPF point-to-point network type to ensure that R2's loopback interface advertises the network prefix 192.168.2.0/24 and not 192.168.2.2/32.

Example 6-21   *OSPF Loopback Network Type*

```
R1
interface Loopback0
    ip address 192.168.1.1 255.255.255.0
interface Serial 0/1
    ip address 10.12.1.1 255.255.255.252
!
router ospf 1
   router-id 192.168.1.1
   network 0.0.0.0 255.255.255.255 area 0
```

```
R2
interface Loopback0
    ip address 192.168.2.2 255.255.255.0
    ip ospf network point-to-point
interface Serial 0/0
    ip address 10.12.1.2 255.255.255.252
!
router ospf 1
   router-id 192.168.2.2
   network 0.0.0.0 255.255.255.255 area 0
```

You should check the network types for R1's and R2's loopback interface to verify that they changed and are different, as demonstrated in Example 6-22.

Example 6-22 *Displaying the OSPF Network Types for Loopback Interfaces*

```
R1# show ip ospf interface Loopback 0 | include Type
Process ID 1, Router ID 192.168.1.1, Network Type LOOPBACK, Cost: 1

R2# show ip ospf interface Loopback 0 | include Type
Process ID 1, Router ID 192.168.2.2, Network Type POINT_TO_POINT, Cost: 1
```

Example 6-23 shows the OSPF database, where you can see that R1's loopback address is a /32 network, and R2's loopback address is a /24 network. Both loopbacks were configured with a /24 network, but because R1's Lo0 is an OSPF network type of loopback, it is advertised as a /32 network.

Example 6-23 *OSPF Database Entries for OSPF Loopback Network Types*

```
R1# show ip ospf database router | I Advertising|Network|Mask
  Advertising Router: 192.168.1.1
    Link connected to: a Stub Network
      (Link ID) Network/subnet number: 192.168.1.1
      (Link Data) Network Mask: 255.255.255.255
    Link connected to: a Stub Network
      (Link ID) Network/subnet number: 10.12.1.0
      (Link Data) Network Mask: 255.255.255.0
  Advertising Router: 192.168.2.2
    Link connected to: a Stub Network
      (Link ID) Network/subnet number: 192.168.2.0
      (Link Data) Network Mask: 255.255.255.0
    Link connected to: a Stub Network
      (Link ID) Network/subnet number: 10.12.1.0
      (Link Data) Network Mask: 255.255.255.0
```

Failure Detection

A secondary function of OSPF hello packets is to ensure that adjacent OSPF neighbors are still healthy and available. OSPF sends hello packets at set intervals, according to the *hello timer*. OSPF uses a second timer called the *OSPF dead interval timer*, which defaults to four times the hello timer. Upon receipt of the hello packet from a neighboring router, the OSPF dead timer resets to the initial value, and then it starts to decrement again.

If a router does not receive a hello before the OSPF dead interval timer reaches 0, the neighbor state is changed to down. The OSPF router immediately sends out the appropriate LSA, reflecting the topology change, and the SPF algorithm processes on all routers within the area.

Hello Timer

The default OSPF hello timer interval varies based on the OSPF network type. OSPF allows modification to the hello timer interval with values between 1 and 65,535 seconds. Changing the hello timer interval modifies the default dead interval, too. The OSPF hello timer is modified with the interface configuration submode command **ip ospf hello-interval** *1-65,535*.

Dead Interval Timer

You can change the dead interval timer to a value between 1 and 65,535 seconds. You change the OSPF dead interval timer by using the command **ip ospf dead-interval** *1-65,535* under the interface configuration submode.

Verifying OSPF Timers

You view the timers for an OSPF interface by using the command **show ip ospf interface**, as demonstrated in Example 6-24. Notice the highlighted hello and dead timers in this example.

Example 6-24 *OSPF Interface Timers*

```
R1# show ip ospf interface | i Timer|line
Loopback0 is up, line protocol is up
GigabitEthernet0/2 is up, line protocol is up
 Timer intervals configured, Hello 10, Dead 40, Wait 40, Retransmit 5
GigabitEthernet0/1 is up, line protocol is up
 Timer intervals configured, Hello 10, Dead 40, Wait 40, Retransmit 5
```

Authentication

An attacker can forge OSPF packets or gain physical access to a network. After manipulating the routing table, the attacker can send traffic down links that allow for traffic interception, create a denial-of-service attack, or perform some other malicious behavior.

OSPF authentication is enabled on an interface-by-interface basis or for all interfaces in an area. You can set the password only as an interface parameter, and you must set it for every interface. If you miss an interface, the default password is set to a null value.

OSPF supports two types of authentication:

- **Plaintext:** This type of authentication provides little security, as anyone with access to the link can see the password by using a network sniffer. You enable plaintext authentication for an OSPF area with the command **area** *area-id* **authentication**, and you use the interface parameter command **ip ospf authentication** to set plaintext authentication only on that interface. You configure the plaintext password by using the interface parameter command **ip ospf authentication-key** *password*.

- **MD5 cryptographic hash:** This type of authentication uses a hash, so the password is never sent out the wire. This technique is widely accepted as being the more secure mode. You enable MD5 authentication for an OSPF area by using the command **area** *area-id* **authentication message-digest**, and you use the interface parameter command **ip ospf authentication message-digest** to set MD5 authentication for that interface.

You configure the MD5 password with the interface parameter command **ip ospf message-digest-key** *key-number* **md5** *password*.

> **NOTE** MD5 authentication is a hash of the key number and password combined. If the keys do not match, the hash differs between the nodes.

Figure 6-13 provides a simple topology to demonstrate the OSPF authentication configuration. Area 12 uses plaintext authentication, and Area 0 uses MD5 authentication. R1 and R3 use interface-based authentication, and R2 uses area-specific authentication. The password for all areas is CISCO.

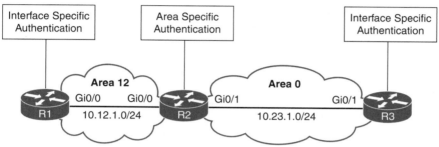

Figure 6-13 *Authentication Topology*

Example 6-25 provides the OSPF authentication configuration.

Example 6-25 *OSPF Authentication Configuration*

```
R1
interface GigabitEthernet0/0
 ip address 10.12.1.1 255.255.255.0
 ip ospf authentication
 ip ospf authentication-key CISCO
!
router ospf 1
 network 10.12.1.0 0.0.0.255 area 12

R2
interface GigabitEthernet0/0
 ip address 10.12.1.2 255.255.255.0
 ip ospf authentication-key CISCO
!
interface GigabitEthernet0/1
 ip address 10.23.1.2 255.255.255.0
 ip ospf message-digest-key 1 md5 CISCO
!
```

```
router ospf 1
 area 0 authentication message-digest
 area 12 authentication
 network 10.12.1.0 0.0.0.255 area 12
 network 10.23.1.0 0.0.0.255 area 0
```

```
R3
interface GigabitEthernet0/1
 ip address 10.23.1.3 255.255.255.0
 ip ospf authentication message-digest
 ip ospf message-digest-key 1 md5 CISCO
!
router ospf 1
 network 10.23.1.0 0.0.0.255 area 0
```

You verify the authentication settings by examining the OSPF interface *without* the **brief** option. Example 6-26 shows sample output from R1, R2, and R3, where the Gi0/0 interface uses MD5 authentication and the Gi0/1 interface uses plaintext authentication. MD5 authentication also identifies the key number that the interface uses.

Example 6-26 *Verifying IOS OSPF Authentication*

```
R1# show ip ospf interface | include line|authentication|key
GigabitEthernet0/0 is up, line protocol is up
  Simple password authentication enabled
```

```
R2# show ip ospf interface | include line|authentication|key
GigabitEthernet0/1 is up, line protocol is up
  Cryptographic authentication enabled
    Youngest key id is 1
GigabitEthernet0/0 is up, line protocol is up
  Simple password authentication enabled
```

```
R3# show ip ospf interface | include line|authentication|key
GigabitEthernet0/1 is up, line protocol is up
  Cryptographic authentication enabled
    Youngest key id is 1
```

References in This Chapter

Edgeworth, Brad, Foss, Aaron, and Garza Rios, Ramiro, *IP Routing on Cisco IOS, IOS XE, and IOS XR*, Cisco Press, 2014.

RFC 2328, *OSPF Version 2*, John Moy, IETF, http://www.ietf.org/rfc/rfc2328.txt, April 1998.

Cisco, *Cisco IOS Software Configuration Guides*, http://www.cisco.com.

Exam Preparation Tasks

As mentioned in the section "How to Use This Book" in the Introduction, you have a couple choices for exam preparation: the exercises here, Chapter 24, "Final Preparation," and the exam simulation questions in the Pearson Test Prep software.

Review All Key Topics

Review the most important topics in this chapter, noted with the Key Topic icon in the outer margin of the page. Table 6-8 lists these key topics and the page number on which each is found.

Table 6-8 Key Topics

Key Topic Element	Description	Page Number
Paragraph	OSPF areas	226
Paragraph	OSPF backbone	227
Paragraph	Area border routers	227
Table 6-2	OSPF packet types	228
Table 6-4	OSPF neighbor states	230
Paragraph	Requirements of neighbor adjacency	230
Paragraph	OSPF **network** statement	232
Paragraph	Interface-specific configuration	233
Paragraph	External OSPF routes	240
Paragraph	The designated router	243
Paragraph	Designated router elections	244
Paragraph	DR and BDR placement	245
Table 6-7	OSPF network types	246
Paragraph	Authentication	255

Define Key Terms

Define the following key terms from this chapter and check your answers in the glossary:

shortest path tree (SPT), backbone area, area border router (ABR), router ID (RID), hello packets, hello interval, dead interval, passive interface, external OSPF route, designated router (DR), backup designated router (BDR), interface priority

Use the Command Reference to Check Your Memory

The ENARSI 300-410 exam focuses on the practical, hands-on skills that networking professionals use. Therefore, you should be able to identify the commands needed to configure, verify, and troubleshoot the topics covered in this chapter.

This section includes the most important configuration and verification commands covered in this chapter. It might not be necessary to memorize the complete syntax of every command, but you should be able to remember the basic keywords that are needed.

To test your memory of the commands in Table 6-9, go to the companion website and download Appendix B, "Command Reference Exercises." Fill in the missing commands in the tables based on each command description. You can check your work by downloading Appendix C, "Command Reference Exercise Answer Key," from the companion website.

Table 6-9 Command Reference

Task	Command Syntax
Initialize the OSPF process.	**router ospf** *process-id*
Enable OSPF on network interfaces that match a specified network range for a specific OSPF area.	**network** *ip-address wildcard-mask* **area** *area-id*
Enable OSPF on an explicit specific network interface for a specific OSPF area.	**ip ospf** *process-id* **area** *area-id*
Configure a specific interface as passive.	**passive-interface** *interface-id*
Configure all interfaces as passive.	**passive-interface default**
Advertise a default route into OSPF.	**default-information originate** [**always**] [**metric** *metric-value*] [**metric-type** *type-value*]
Modify the OSPF reference bandwidth for dynamic interface metric costing.	**auto-cost reference-bandwidth** *bandwidth-in-mbps*
Configure the OSPF priority for a DR/BDR election.	**ip ospf priority** *0-255*
Statically configure an interface as a broadcast OSPF network type.	**ip ospf network broadcast**
Statically configure an interface as a nonbroadcast OSPF network type.	**ip ospf network non-broadcast**
Statically configure an interface as a point-to-point OSPF network type.	**ip ospf network point-to-point**
Statically configure an interface as a point-to-multipoint OSPF network type.	**ip ospf network point-to-multipoint**
Enable OSPF authentication for an area.	**area** *area-id* **authentication** [**message-digest**]
Define the plaintext password for an interface.	**ip ospf authentication-key** *password*
Define the MD5 password for an interface.	**ip ospf message-digest-key** *key-number* **md5** *password*
Restart the OSPF process.	**clear ip ospf process**
Display the OSPF interfaces on a router.	**show ip ospf interface** [**brief**	*interface-id*]
Display the OSPF neighbors and their current states.	**show ip ospf neighbor** [**detail**]
Display the OSPF routes that are installed in the RIB.	**show ip route ospf**

6

## CHAPTER 7

Advanced OSPF

This chapter covers the following topics:

- **Link-State Advertisements:** This section explains how Open Shortest Path First (OSPF) stores, communicates, and builds the topology from link-state advertisements (LSAs).

- **OSPF Stubby Areas:** This section explains the method OSPF provides for filtering external routes while still providing connectivity to them.

- **OSPF Path Selection:** This section explains how OSPF makes path selection choices for routes learned within the OSPF routing domain.

- **Summarization of Routes:** This section explains how network summarization works with OSPF.

- **Discontiguous Network:** This section describes discontiguous networks and explains why such a network cannot distribute routes to all areas properly.

- **Virtual Links:** This section explains how OSPF repairs a discontiguous network.

This chapter expands on Chapter 6, "OSPF," explaining the functions and features of larger enterprise networks. By the end of this chapter, you will have a solid understanding of the route advertisements within a multi-area OSPF domain, path selection, and techniques to optimize an OSPF environment.

"Do I Know This Already?" Quiz

The "Do I Know This Already?" quiz allows you to assess whether you should read this entire chapter thoroughly or jump to the "Exam Preparation Tasks" section. If you are in doubt about your answers to these questions or your own assessment of your knowledge of the topics, read the entire chapter. Table 7-1 lists the major headings in this chapter and their corresponding "Do I Know This Already?" quiz questions. You can find the answers in Appendix A, "Answers to the 'Do I Know This Already?' Quiz Questions."

Table 7-1 Do I Know This Already?" Foundation Topics Section-to-Question Mapping

Foundation Topics Section	Questions
Link-State Advertisements	1–4
OSPF Stubby Areas	5–6
OSPF Path Selection	7–8
Summarization of Routes	9–10
Discontiguous Network	11
Virtual Links	12

1. How many OSPF link-state advertisements (LSAs) are used for routing traditional IPv4 packets?

    a.   Two

    b.   Three

    c.   Five

    d.   Six

    e.   Seven

2. What is the LSA Age field in the LSDB used for?

    a.   Version control, to ensure that the most recent LSA is present

    b.   To age out old LSAs by removing an LSA when its age reaches zero

    c.   For troubleshooting, to identify exactly when the LSA was advertised

    d.   To age out old LSAs by removing an LSA when it reaches 3600 seconds

3. Which LSA type exists in all OSPF areas?

    a.   Network

    b.   Summary

    c.   Router

    d.   AS external

4. True or false: When an ABR receives a network LSA, the ABR forwards the network LSA to the other connected areas.

    a.   True

    b.   False

5. An OSPF stub area blocks which types of LSAs from being injected into the area by the ABR? (Choose two.)

    a.   Type 1 LSA

    b.   Type 3 LSA

    c.   Type 4 LSA

    d.   Type 5 LSA

6. True or false: An OSPF not-so-stubby area (NSSA) automatically creates a default route when a Type 5 LSA is blocked on the ABR from being injected into the NSSA.

    a.   True

    b.   False

7. OSPF automatically assigns a link cost to an interface based on what reference bandwidth?

   a. 100 Mbps

   b. 1 Gbps

   c. 10 Gbps

   d. 40 Gbps

8. True or false: If two different routers are redistributing the same network (such as 10.1.1.0/24) as an OSPF external Type 2 route, and they have the same metric, both paths are installed on a downstream router.

   a. True

   b. False

9. True or false: Breaking a large OSPF topology into smaller OSPF areas can be considered a form of summarization.

   a. True

   b. False

10. Summarizing external OSPF routes on an ASBR is accomplished by using the _____.

   a. interface configuration command **summary-address** *network prefix-length*

   b. OSPF process configuration command **summary-address** *network subnet-mask*

   c. OSPF process configuration command **area** *area-id* **range** *network subnet-mask*

   d. interface configuration command **area** *area-id* **summary-address** *network subnet-mask*

11. When a Type 3 LSA is received on a nonbackbone area, what does the ABR do?

   a. Discards the Type 3 LSA and does not process it

   b. Installs the Type 3 LSA for only the area for which it was received

   c. Advertises the Type 3 LSA to the backbone area and displays an error

   d. Advertises the Type 3 LSA to the backbone area

12. True or false: *Virtual link* is another term for an OSPF-enabled GRE tunnel.

   a. True

   b. False

Foundation Topics

Link-State Advertisements

An OSPF link-state advertisement (LSA) contains the link state and link metric to a neighboring router. Received LSAs are stored in a local database called the link-state database (LSDB); the LSDB advertises the link-state information to neighboring routers exactly as the original advertising router advertised it. This process floods the LSA throughout the OSPF routing domain, just as the advertising router advertised it. All OSPF routers in the same area maintain a synchronized identical copy of the LSDB for that area.

The LSDB provides the topology of the network, in essence providing the router a complete map of the network. All OSPF routers run Dijkstra's shortest path first (SPF) algorithm to construct a loop-free topology of shortest paths. OSPF dynamically detects topology changes within the routing domain and calculates loop-free paths in a short amount of time with minimal routing protocol traffic.

When OSPF neighbors become adjacent, the LSDBs synchronize between the OSPF routers. As an OSPF router adds or removes a directly connected network link to or from its database, the router floods the LSA out all active OSPF interfaces. The OSPF LSA contains a complete list of networks advertised from that router.

OSPF uses six LSA types for IPv4 routing:

- **Type 1, router:** LSAs that advertise prefixes within an area

- **Type 2, network:** LSAs that indicate the routers attached to broadcast segment within an area

- **Type 3, summary:** LSAs that advertise prefixes that originate from a different area

- **Type 4, ASBR summary:** LSA used to locate the ASBR from a different area

- **Type 5, AS external:** LSA that advertises prefixes that were redistributed in to OSPF

- **Type 7, NSSA external:** LSA for external prefixes that were redistributed in a local NSSA area

LSA Types 1, 2, and 3 are used for building the SPF tree for intra-area and inter-area route routes. LSA Types 4, 5, and 7 are related to external OSPF routes (that is, routes that were redistributed into the OSPF routing domain).

Figure 7-1 shows a packet capture of an OSPF update LSA and outlines the important components of the LSA: the LSA type, the LSA age, the sequence, and the advertising router. Because this is a Type 1 LSA, the link IDs add relevance as they list the attached networks and the associated OSPF cost for each interface.

```
Internet Protocol Version 4, Src: 10.123.4.2 (10.123.4.2), Dst: 224.0.0.6 (224.0.0.6)
Open Shortest Path First
⊞ OSPF Header
⊟ LS Update Packet
    Number of LSAs: 1 ─────────────────── LSA Type
  ⊟ LS Type: Router-LSA
      LS Age: 1 seconds ──────────── LSA Age
      Do Not Age: False
    ⊞ Options: 0x22 (DC, E)
      Link-State Advertisement Type: Router-LSA (1)
      Link State ID: 192.168.2.2
      Advertising Router: 192.168.2.2 (192.168.2.2) ──────── Advertising Router
      LS Sequence Number: 0x80000007 ─────────── LSA Sequence
      LS Checksum: 0x3653
      Length: 60
    ⊞ Flags: 0x00
      Number of Links: 3
    ⊞ Type: Stub     ID: 192.168.2.2    Data: 255.255.255.255 Metric: 1 ──────── Link IDs
    ⊞ Type: Transit  ID: 10.123.4.4     Data: 10.123.4.2      Metric: 10
    ⊞ Type: Stub     ID: 10.2.2.0       Data: 255.255.255.0   Metric: 10
```

Figure 7-1 *Packet Capture of an LSA Update for the Second Interface*

Figure 7-2 shows a sample topology to demonstrate the different LSA types. In this topology:

- R1, R2, and R3 are member (internal) routers.

- R4 and R5 are *area border routers (ABRs)*.

- R6 is the ASBR, which is redistributing the 172.16.6.0/24 network into OSPF.

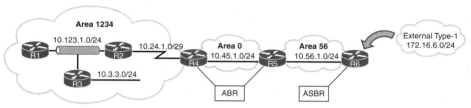

Figure 7-2 *LSA Reference Topology for LSAs*

LSA Sequences

OSPF uses the sequence number to overcome problems caused by delays in LSA propagation in a network. The LSA sequence number is a 32-bit number used to control versioning. When the originating router sends out LSAs, the LSA sequence number is incremented. If a router receives an LSA sequence that is greater than the one in the LSDB, it processes the LSA. If the LSA sequence number is lower than the one in the LSDB, the router deems the LSA old and discards it.

LSA Age and Flooding

Every OSPF LSA includes an age that is entered into the local LSDB that increments by 1 every second. When a router's OSPF LSA age exceeds 1800 seconds (that is, 30 minutes) for its prefixes, the originating router advertises a new LSA with the LSA age set to 0. As each router forwards the LSA, the LSA age is incremented with a calculated delay that reflects the link (which is minimal). If the LSA age reaches 3600, the LSA is deemed invalid and is purged from the LSDB. The repetitive flooding of LSAs is a secondary safety mechanism to ensure that all routers maintain a consistent LSDB within an area.

LSA Types

All routers within an OSPF area have an identical set of LSAs for that area. The ABRs maintain a separate set of LSAs for each OSPF area. Most LSAs in one area are different from the LSAs in another area. You can see generic router LSA output by using the command **show ip ospf database**.

LSA Type 1: Router Link

Every OSPF router advertises a Type 1 LSA (*router LSA*). Type 1 LSAs are the essential building blocks in the LSDB. A Type 1 LSA entry exists for each OSPF-enabled link (that is, an interface and its attached networks). Figure 7-3 shows that the Type 1 LSAs are not advertised outside Area 1234, thus making the underlying topology in an area invisible to other areas.

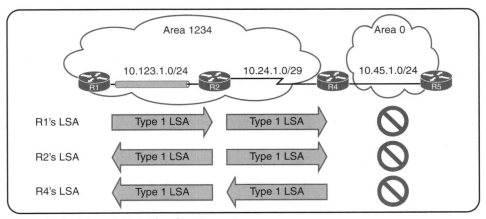

Figure 7-3 *Type 1 LSA Flooding in an Area*

For a brief summary view of the Type 1 LSAs for an area, look under the Router Link States column within the LSDB, as shown in Example 7-1.

Example 7-1 *Generic OSPF LSA Output for Type 1 LSAs*

```
R1# show ip ospf database
          OSPF Router with ID (192.168.1.1) (Process ID 1)


          Router Link States (Area 1234)


Link ID         ADV Router      Age       Seq#        Checksum Link count
192.168.1.1     192.168.1.1     14        0x80000006 0x009EA7 1
192.168.2.2     192.168.2.2     2020      0x80000006 0x00AD43 3
192.168.3.3     192.168.3.3     6         0x80000006 0x0056C4 2
192.168.4.4     192.168.4.4     61        0x80000005 0x007F8C 2
```

Table 7-2 provides an overview of the fields in the LSDB output.

Table 7-2   OSPF LSDB Fields

Field	Description
Link ID	Identifies the object that the link connects to. It can refer to the neighboring router's RID, the IP address of the DR's interface, or the IP network address.
ADV Router	The OSPF router ID for this LSA.
AGE	The age of the LSA on the router on which the command is being run. Values over 1800 are expected to refresh soon.
Seq #	The sequence number for the LSA to protect out-of-order LSAs.
Checksum	The checksum of the LSA to verify integrity during flooding.
Link Count	The number of links on this router in the Type 1 LSA.

Figure 7-4 is a reference subsection of Area 1234 taken from Figure 7-2.

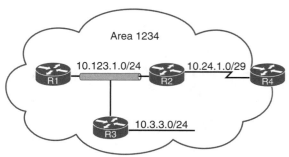

Figure 7-4   *Type 1 LSA Topology*

You can examine the Type 1 OSPF LSAs by using the command **show ip ospf database router**, as demonstrated in Example 7-2. Notice in the output that entries exist for all four routers in the area.

Example 7-2   *OSPF Type 1 LSAs for Area 1234*

```
R1# show ip ospf database router
! Output omitted for brevity
          OSPF Router with ID (192.168.1.1) (Process ID 1)

              Router Link States (Area 1234)

  LS age: 352
  Options: (No TOS-capability, DC)
  LS Type: Router Links
  Link State ID: 192.168.1.1
  Advertising Router: 192.168.1.1
  LS Seq Number: 80000014
  Length: 36
  Number of Links: 1

    Link connected to: a Transit Network
      (Link ID) Designated Router address: 10.123.1.3
      (Link Data) Router Interface address: 10.123.1.1
        TOS 0 Metrics: 1


  LS age: 381
  Options: (No TOS-capability, DC)
  LS Type: Router Links
  Link State ID: 192.168.2.2
  Advertising Router: 192.168.2.2
  LS Seq Number: 80000015
  Length: 60
  Number of Links: 3
```

```
   Link connected to: another Router (point-to-point)
     (Link ID) Neighboring Router ID: 192.168.4.4
     (Link Data) Router Interface address: 10.24.1.1
       TOS 0 Metrics: 64


   Link connected to: a Stub Network
     (Link ID) Network/subnet number: 10.24.1.0
     (Link Data) Network Mask: 255.255.255.248
       TOS 0 Metrics: 64


   Link connected to: a Transit Network
     (Link ID) Designated Router address: 10.123.1.3
     (Link Data) Router Interface address: 10.123.1.2
       TOS 0 Metrics: 1
LS age: 226
Options: (No TOS-capability, DC)
LS Type: Router Links
Link State ID: 192.168.3.3
Advertising Router: 192.168.3.3
LS Seq Number: 80000014
Length: 48
Number of Links: 2

   Link connected to: a Stub Network
     (Link ID) Network/subnet number: 10.3.3.0
     (Link Data) Network Mask: 255.255.255.0
       TOS 0 Metrics: 1


   Link connected to: a Transit Network
     (Link ID) Designated Router address: 10.123.1.3
     (Link Data) Router Interface address: 10.123.1.3
       TOS 0 Metrics: 1



LS age: 605
Options: (No TOS-capability, DC)
LS Type: Router Links
Link State ID: 192.168.4.4
Advertising Router: 192.168.4.4
LS Seq Number: 80000013
Length: 48
```

```
Area Border Router
Number of Links: 2


  Link connected to: another Router (point-to-point)
   (Link ID) Neighboring Router ID: 192.168.2.2
   (Link Data) Router Interface address: 10.24.1.4
     TOS 0 Metrics: 64


  Link connected to: a Stub Network
   (Link ID) Network/subnet number: 10.24.1.0
   (Link Data) Network Mask: 255.255.255.248
     TOS 0 Metrics: 64
```

The initial fields of each Type 1 LSA are the same as in Table 7-2. If a router is functioning as an ABR, an ASBR, or a virtual-link endpoint, the function is listed between the Length field and the Number of links field. In the output shown in Example 7-2, R4 (192.168.4.4) is an ABR.

Each OSPF-enabled interface is listed under the number of links for each router. Each network link on a router contains the following information, in this order:

■ Link type that appears after "Link connected to:". The fields can be correlated to Table 7-3.

■ Link ID, using the values based on the link type listed in Table 7-3

■ Link data (when applicable)

■ Metric for the interface

Table 7-3   OSPF Neighbor States for Type 1 LSAs

Description	Link Type	Link ID Value	Link Data
Point-to-point link (IP address assigned)	1	Neighbor RID	Interface IP address
Point-to-point link (using IP unnumbered)	1	Neighbor RID	MIB II IfIndex value
Link to transit network	2	Interface address of DR	Interface IP address
Link to stub network	3	Network address	Subnet mask
Virtual link	4	Neighbor RID	Interface IP address

During the SPF tree calculation, the network link type is one of the following:

■ **Transit:** A transit network indicates that an adjacency was formed and that a DR was elected on that link.

- **Point-to-point:** A point-to-point link indicates that an adjacency was formed on a network type that does not use a DR. Interfaces using the OSPF point-to-point network type advertise two links. One link is the point-to-point link type that identifies the OSPF neighbor RID for that segment, and the other link is a stub network link that provides the subnet mask for that network.

- **Stub:** A stub network indicates that no neighbor adjacencies were established on that link. Point-to-point and transit link types that did not become adjacent with another OSPF router are classified as a stub network link type. When an OSPF adjacency forms, the link type changes to the appropriate type: point-to-point or transit.

> **NOTE**   Secondary connected networks are always advertised as stub link types because OSPF adjacencies can never form on them.

If you correlate just Type 1 LSAs from the reference topology in Figure 7-2, then Figure 7-5 demonstrates the topology built by all routers in Area 1234, using the LSA attributes for Area 1234 from all four routers. Using only Type 1 LSAs, a connection is made between R2 and R4 because they point to each other's RID in the point-to-point LSA. Notice that the three router links on R1, R2, and R3 (10.123.1.0) have not been directly connected yet.

LSA Type 2: Network Link

A Type 2 LSA (*network LSA*) represents a multi-access network segment that uses a DR. The DR always advertises the Type 2 LSA and identifies all the routers attached to that network segment. If a DR has not been elected, a Type 2 LSA is not present in the LSDB because the corresponding Type 1 transit link type LSA is a stub. Type 2 LSAs are not flooded outside the originating OSPF area in an identical fashion to Type 1 LSAs.

A brief summary view of the Type 2 LSAs is shown in the LSDB under Net Link States. Example 7-3 provides the output for Type 2 LSAs in Area 1234 from the reference topology.

Example 7-3   *Generic OSPF LSA Output for Type 2 LSAs*

```
R1# show ip ospf database
! Output omitted for brevity
            OSPF Router with ID (192.168.1.1) (Process ID 1)
..

                Net Link States (Area 1234)

Link ID         ADV Router       Age        Seq#        Checksum
10.123.1.3      10.192.168.3.3   1752       0x80000012 0x00ADC5
```

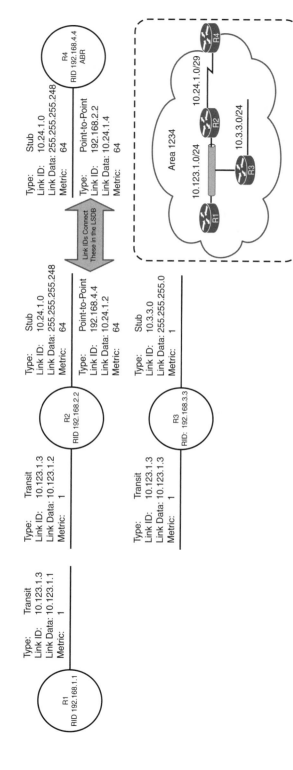

Figure 7-5 *Visualization of Type 1 LSAs*

Area 1234 has only one DR segment that connects R1, R2, and R3 because R3 has not formed an OSPF adjacency on the 10.3.3.0/24 network segment. On the 10.123.1.0/24 network segment, R3 is elected as the DR, and R2 is elected as the BDR, based on their RIDs.

To see detailed Type 2 LSA information, you use the command **show ip ospf database network**. Example 7-4 shows the Type 2 LSA that is advertised by R3 and shows that the link-state ID 10.123.1.3 attaches to R1, R2, and R3 (by listing their RIDs at the bottom). The network mask for the subnet is included in the Type 2 LSA.

Example 7-4 *Detailed Output for OSPF Type 2 LSAs*

```
R1# show ip ospf database network

            OSPF Router with ID (192.168.1.1) (Process ID 1)


                Net Link States (Area 1234)


  LS age: 356
  Options: (No TOS-capability, DC)
  LS Type: Network Links
  Link State ID: 10.123.1.3 (address of Designated Router)
  Advertising Router: 192.168.3.3
  LS Seq Number: 80000014
  Checksum: 0x4DD
  Length: 36
  Network Mask: /24
        Attached Router: 192.168.3.3
        Attached Router: 192.168.1.1
        Attached Router: 192.168.2.2
```

Now that you have the Type 2 LSA for Area 1234, all the network links are connected. Figure 7-6 provides a visualization of the Type 1 and Type 2 LSAs; it corresponds with Area 1234 perfectly.

NOTE When the DR changes for a network segment, a new Type 2 LSA is created, causing SPF to run again within the OSPF area.

LSA Type 3: Summary Link

Type 3 LSAs (*summary LSAs*) represent networks from other areas. The role of the ABRs is to participate in multiple OSPF areas and ensure that the networks associated with Type 1 LSAs are reachable in the nonoriginating OSPF areas.

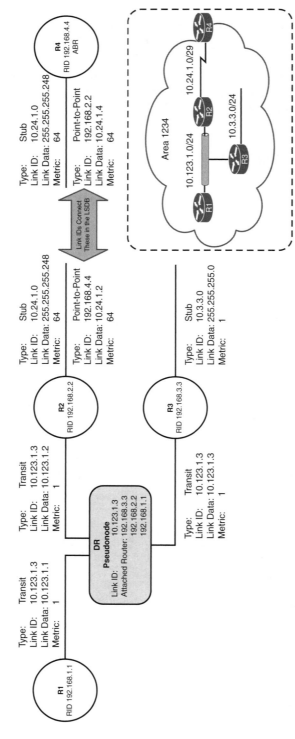

Figure 7-6 *Visualization of Area 1234 with Type 1 and Type 2 LSAs*

As explained earlier, ABRs do not forward Type 1 or Type 2 LSAs into other areas. When an ABR receives a Type 1 LSA, it creates a Type 3 LSA referencing the network in the original Type 1 LSA. (The Type 2 LSA is used to determine the network mask of the multi-access network.) The ABR then advertises the Type 3 LSA into other areas. If an ABR receives a Type 3 LSA from Area 0 (*backbone area*), it regenerates a new Type 3 LSA for the nonbackbone area and lists itself as the advertising router with the additional cost metric.

Figure 7-7 demonstrates the concept of Type 3 LSA interaction with Type 1 LSAs. Notice that the Type 1 LSAs exist only in the area of origination and convert to Type 3 when they cross the ABRs (R4 and R5).

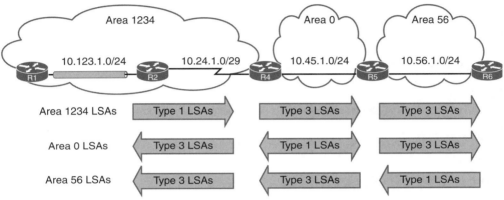

Figure 7-7 *Type 3 LSA Conceptual Diagram*

For a summary view of the Type 3 LSAs, look under Summary Net Link States, as shown in Example 7-5. The Type 3 LSAs show up under the appropriate area where they exist in the OSPF domain. For example, the 10.56.1.0 Type 3 LSA exists only in Area 0 and Area 1234 on R4. R5 contains the 10.56.1.0 Type 3 LSA only for Area 0, but not for Area 56 because Area 56 has a Type 1 LSA.

Example 7-5 *Generic OSPF LSA Output for Type 3 LSAs*

```
R4# show ip ospf database
! Output omitted for brevity
         OSPF Router with ID (192.168.4.4) (Process ID 1)
..
         Summary Net Link States (Area 0)
Link ID         ADV Router      Age       Seq#        Checksum
10.3.3.0        192.168.4.4     813       0x80000013 0x00F373
10.24.1.0       192.168.4.4     813       0x80000013 0x00CE8E
10.56.1.0       192.168.5.5     591       0x80000013 0x00F181
10.123.1.0      192.168.4.4     813       0x80000013 0x005A97
```

```
..
           Summary Net Link States (Area 1234)


Link ID         ADV Router       Age        Seq#          Checksum
10.45.1.0       192.168.4.4      813        0x80000013 0x0083FC
10.56.1.0       192.168.4.4      813        0x80000013 0x00096B
```

```
R5# show ip ospf database
! Output omitted for brevity
           OSPF Router with ID (192.168.5.5) (Process ID 1)
..
           Summary Net Link States (Area 0)


Link ID         ADV Router       Age        Seq#          Checksum
10.3.3.0        192.168.4.4      893        0x80000013 0x00F373
10.24.1.0       192.168.4.4      893        0x80000013 0x00CE8E
10.56.1.0       192.168.5.5      668        0x80000013 0x00F181
10.123.1.0      192.168.4.4      893        0x80000013 0x005A97
..
           Summary Net Link States (Area 56)


Link ID         ADV Router       Age        Seq#          Checksum
10.3.3.0        192.168.5.5      668        0x80000013 0x00F073
10.24.1.0       192.168.5.5      668        0x80000013 0x00CB8E
10.45.1.0       192.168.5.5      668        0x80000013 0x007608
10.123.1.0      192.168.5.5      668        0x80000013 0x005797
```

To see detailed Type 3 LSA information, you use the command **show ip ospf database summary**. You can restrict the output to a specific LSA by adding the prefix to the end of the command.

The advertising router for Type 3 LSAs is the last ABR that advertises the prefix. The metric in the Type 3 LSA uses the following logic:

■ If the Type 3 LSA is created from a Type 1 LSA, it is the total path metric to reach the originating router in the Type 1 LSA.

■ If the Type 3 LSA is created from a Type 3 LSA from Area 0, it is the total path metric to the ABR plus the metric in the original Type 3 LSA.

Example 7-6 shows the Type 3 LSA for the Area 56 prefix (10.56.1.0/24) from R4's LSDB. R4 is an ABR, and the information is displayed for both Area 0 and Area 1234. Notice that the metric increases in Area 1234's LSA compared to in Area 0's LSA.

Example 7-6 *Detailed Output for OSPF Type 3 LSAs*

```
R4# show ip ospf database summary 10.56.1.0
            OSPF Router with ID (192.168.4.4) (Process ID 1)


            Summary Net Link States (Area 0)


  LS age: 754
  Options: (No TOS-capability, DC, Upward)
  LS Type: Summary Links(Network)
  Link State ID: 10.56.1.0 (summary Network Number)
  Advertising Router: 192.168.5.5
  LS Seq Number: 80000013
  Checksum: 0xF181
  Length: 28
  Network Mask: /24
        MTID: 0           Metric: 1



            Summary Net Link States (Area 1234)


  LS age: 977
  Options: (No TOS-capability, DC, Upward)
  LS Type: Summary Links(Network)
  Link State ID: 10.56.1.0 (summary Network Number)
  Advertising Router: 192.168.4.4
  LS Seq Number: 80000013
  Checksum: 0x96B
  Length: 28
  Network Mask: /24
        MTID: 0           Metric: 2
```

Table 7-4 provides an explanation of the fields in a Type 3 LSA.

Table 7-4 Type 3 LSA Fields

Field	Description
Link ID	Network number
Advertising Router	RID of the router advertising the route (ABR)
Network Mask	Prefix length for the advertised network
Metric	Metric for the LSA

Key Topic

Understanding the metric in Type 3 LSAs is an important concept. Figure 7-8 provides R4's perspective of the Type 3 LSA created by ABR (R5) for the 10.56.1.0/24 network. R4 does not know if the 10.56.1.0/24 network is directly attached to the ABR (R5) or if it is multiple hops away. R4 knows that its metric to the ABR (R5) is 1 and that the Type 3 LSA already has a metric of 1, so its total path metric to reach the 10.56.1.0/24 network is 2.

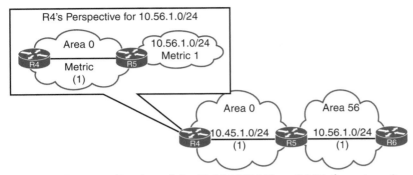

Figure 7-8 *Visualization of the 10.56.1.0/24 Type 3 LSA from Area 0*

Figure 7-9 provides R3's perspective of the Type 3 LSA created by the ABR (R4) for the 10.56.1.0/24 network. R3 does not know if the 10.56.1.0/24 network is directly attached to the ABR (R4) or if it is multiple hops away. R3 knows that its metric to the ABR (R4) is 65 and that the Type 3 LSA already has a metric of 2, so its total path metric is 67 to reach the 10.56.1.0/24 network.

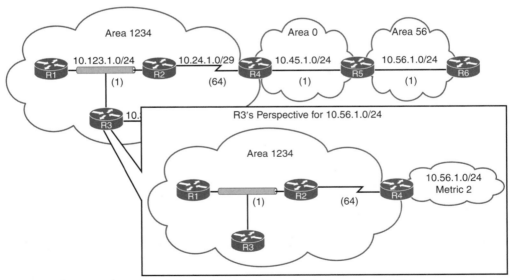

Figure 7-9 *Visualization of the 10.56.1.0/24 Type 3 LSA from Area 1234*

NOTE An ABR advertises only one Type 3 LSA for a prefix, even if it is aware of multiple paths from within its area (Type 1 LSAs) or from outside its area (Type 3 LSAs). The metric for the best path is used when the LSA is advertised into a different area.

LSA Type 5: External Routes

When a route is redistributed into OSPF, the router is known as an *autonomous system boundary router (ASBR)*. The external route is flooded throughout the entire OSPF domain as a Type 5 LSA (*external LSAs*). Type 5 LSAs are not associated with a specific area and are flooded throughout the OSPF domain. Only the LSA age is modified during flooding for Type 2 external OSPF routes.

Figure 7-10 shows R6 redistributing the 172.16.6.0/24 static route into the OSPF domain. Notice that the Type 5 LSA exists in all OSPF areas of the routing domain.

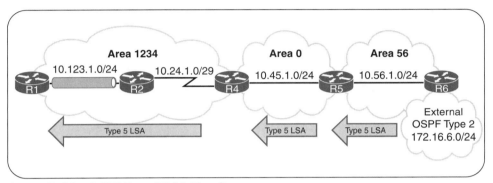

Figure 7-10   *OSPF Type 5 LSA Flooding*

Example 7-7 provides a brief summary view of the Type 5 LSAs under Type-5 AS External Link States. The link ID is the external network number, and the advertising router is the RID for the router originating the Type 5 LSA. Notice that the Type 5 LSA is not associated with a specific OSPF area. This is because Type 5 LSAs are flooded throughout the OSPF routing domain by default.

Example 7-7   *Generic OSPF LSA Output for Type 5 LSAs*

```
R6# show ip ospf database
! Output omitted for brevity

              Type-5 AS External Link States


Link ID         ADV Router      Age       Seq#        Checksum Tag
172.16.6.0      192.168.6.6     11        0x80000001 0x000866 0
```

You can see Type 5 LSAs in detail by using the command **show ip ospf database external**. ABRs only modify the LSA age as the Type 5 LSA propagates through the OSPF domain. Example 7-8 provides detailed output for the external OSPF LSAs in the OSPF domain. Notice that only the LS age is modified between the routers.

Example 7-8   *Detailed Output for OSPF Type 5 LSAs*

```
R6# show ip ospf database external
            OSPF Router with ID (192.168.6.6) (Process ID 1)


                Type-5 AS External Link States

  LS age: 720
  Options: (No TOS-capability, DC, Upward)
  LS Type: AS External Link
  Link State ID: 172.16.6.0 (External Network Number )
  Advertising Router: 192.168.6.6
  LS Seq Number: 8000000F
  Checksum: 0xA9B0
  Length: 36
  Network Mask: /24
        Metric Type: 2 (Larger than any link state path)
        MTID: 0
        Metric: 20
        Forward Address: 0.0.0.0
        External Route Tag: 0
```
```
R1# show ip ospf database external

            OSPF Router with ID (192.168.1.1) (Process ID 1)


                Type-5 AS External Link States

  LS age: 778
  Options: (No TOS-capability, DC, Upward)
  LS Type: AS External Link
  Link State ID: 172.16.6.0 (External Network Number )
  Advertising Router: 192.168.6.6
  LS Seq Number: 8000000F
  Checksum: 0xA9B0
  Length: 36
  Network Mask: /24
        Metric Type: 2 (Larger than any link state path)
        MTID: 0
        Metric: 20
        Forward Address: 0.0.0.0
        External Route Tag: 0
```

Table 7-5 provides an explanation of the fields in a Type 5 LSA.

Table 7-5   Type 5 LSA Fields

Field	Description
Link ID	External network number
Network Mask	Subnet mask for the external network
Advertising Router	RID of the router advertising the route (ASBR)
Metric Type	OSPF external metric type (Type 1 O E1 or Type 2 O E2)
Metric	Metric upon redistribution
External Route Tag	32-bit field included with an external route, which is not used by OSPF under normal operations but can be used to communicate AS boundaries or other relevant information to prevent routing loops

LSA Type 4: ASBR Summary

A Type 4 LSA (*ASBR summary LSA*) locates the ASBR for a Type 5 LSA. A Type 5 LSA is flooded through the OSPF domain, and the only mechanism to identify the ASBR is the RID. Routers examine the Type 5 LSA, check to see whether the RID is in the local area, and if the ASBR is not local, they require a mechanism to locate the ASBR.

Remember that the RID does not have to match an IP address on any OSPF router (including ASBRs). Only Type 1 or Type 2 LSAs provide a method to locate the RID within an area (refer to Figure 7-6).

Type 4 LSAs provide a way for routers to locate the ASBR when the router is in a different area from the ASBR. A Type 4 LSA is created by the first ABR, and it provides a summary route strictly for the ASBR of a Type 5 LSA. The metric for a Type 4 LSA uses the following logic:

- When the Type 5 LSA crosses the first ABR, the ABR creates a Type 4 LSA with a metric set to the total path metric to the ASBR.

- When an ABR receives a Type 4 LSA from Area 0, the ABR creates a new Type 4 LSA with a metric set to the total path metric of the first ABR plus the metric in the original Type 4 LSA.

Figure 7-11 shows how the ABRs (R4 and R5) create Type 4 LSAs for the ASBR (R6).

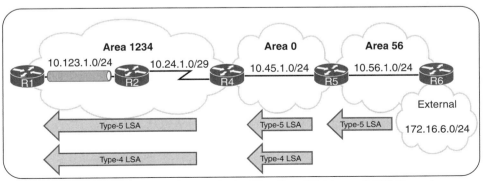

Figure 7-11   *OSPF Type 4 and Type 5 LSA Flooding Within an OSPF Domain*

Example 7-9 provides a brief summary view of the Type 4 LSAs for R4 in the LSDB under Summary ASB Link States. Notice how the advertising router changes as the LSA crosses from ABR to ABR.

Example 7-9   *Generic OSPF LSA Output for Type 4 LSAs*

```
R4# show ip ospf database
! Output omitted for brevity
        OSPF Router with ID (192.168.4.4) (Process ID 1)
..


            Summary ASB Link States (Area 0)

Link ID         ADV Router       Age       Seq#        Checksum
192.168.6.6     192.168.5.5      930       0x8000000F 0x00EB58
..

            Summary ASB Link States (Area 1234)


Link ID         ADV Router       Age       Seq#        Checksum
192.168.6.6     192.168.4.4      1153      0x8000000F 0x000342
```

To view the details of the Type 4 LSAs, you use the command **show ip ospf database asbr-summary.** Example 7-10 provides detailed output of the Type 4 LSA on R4. Notice that the metric and advertising router change between the OSPF areas.

Example 7-10   *Detailed Output for Type 4 LSAs*

```
R4# show ip ospf database asbr-summary
! Output omitted for brevity
            OSPF Router with ID (192.168.4.4) (Process ID 1)


            Summary ASB Link States (Area 0)
  LS age: 1039
  Options: (No TOS-capability, DC, Upward)
  LS Type: Summary Links(AS Boundary Router)
  Link State ID: 192.168.6.6 (AS Boundary Router address)
  Advertising Router: 192.168.5.5
  Length: 28
  Network Mask: /0
       MTID: 0         Metric: 1



            Summary ASB Link States (Area 1234)


  LS age: 1262
  Options: (No TOS-capability, DC, Upward)
```

```
LS Type: Summary Links(AS Boundary Router)
Link State ID: 192.168.6.6 (AS Boundary Router address)
Advertising Router: 192.168.4.4
Length: 28
Network Mask: /0
        MTID: 0            Metric: 2
```

NOTE An ABR advertises only one Type 4 LSA for every ASBR, even if the ASBR advertises thousands of Type 5 LSAs.

LSA Type 7: NSSA External Summary

Later in this chapter, you'll learn about using not-so-stubby areas (NSSAs) to reduce the LSDB in an area. A Type 7 LSA (*NSSA external LSA*) exists only in NSSAs where route redistribution is occurring.

An ASBR injects external routes as Type 7 LSAs in an NSSA. The ABR does not advertise Type 7 LSAs outside the originating NSSA, but it converts the Type 7 LSA into a Type 5 LSA for the other OSPF areas. If the Type 5 LSA crosses Area 0, the second ABR creates a Type 4 LSA for the Type 5 LSA.

Figure 7-12 shows Area 56 as an NSSA and R6 redistributing the 172.16.6.0/24 prefix. The Type 7 LSA exists only in Area 56. R5 injects the Type 5 LSA in Area 0, which propagates to Area 1234, and R4 creates the Type 4 LSA for Area 1234.

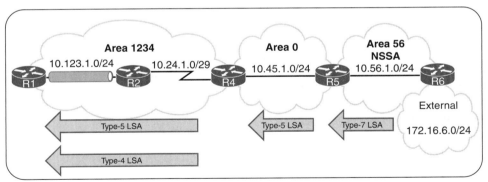

Figure 7-12 *OSPF Type 7 LSAs*

Example 7-11 provides a brief summary view of the Type 7 LSAs, under Type-7 AS External Link States. Type 7 LSAs are present only in the OSPF NSSA where redistribution is occurring. Notice that the Type 7 LSA is not present on R4; R4 contains a Type 5 LSA that was created by R5 and the Type 4 LSA (created by R4 for Area 1234).

Example 7-11 *Generic OSPF LSA Output for Type 7 LSAs*

```
R5# show ip ospf database
! Output omitted for brevity
            OSPF Router with ID (192.168.5.5) (Process ID 1)


..
Type-7 AS External Link States (Area 56)


Link ID          ADV Router       Age       Seq#          Checksum Tag
172.16.6.0       192.168.6.6      46        0x80000001 0x00A371 0

!   Notice that no Type-4 LSA has been generated. Only the Type-7 LSA for Area 56
!   and the Type-5 LSA for the other areas. R5 advertises the Type-5 LSA
            Type-5 AS External Link States


Link ID          ADV Router       Age       Seq#          Checksum Tag
172.16.6.0       192.168.5.5      38        0x80000001 0x0045DB
```

```
R4# show ip ospf database
! Output omitted for brevity
            OSPF Router with ID (192.168.4.4) (Process ID 1)

..
            Summary ASB Link States (Area 1234)


Link ID          ADV Router       Age       Seq#          Checksum
192.168.5.5      192.168.4.4      193       0x80000001 0x002A2C


            Type-5 AS External Link States


Link ID          ADV Router       Age       Seq#          Checksum Tag
172.16.6.0       192.168.5.5      176       0x80000001 0x0045DB 0
```

To see the specific Type 7 LSA details, you use the command **show ip ospf database nssa-external**. Example 7-12 shows this command executed on R5.

Example 7-12 *Detailed Output for OSPF Type 7 LSAs*

```
R5# show ip ospf database nssa-external
            OSPF Router with ID (192.168.5.5) (Process ID 1)


            Type-7 AS External Link States (Area 56)
  LS age: 122
  Options: (No TOS-capability, Type 7/5 translation, DC, Upward)
  LS Type: AS External Link
```

```
Link State ID: 172.16.6.0 (External Network Number )
Advertising Router: 192.168.6.6
LS Seq Number: 80000001
Checksum: 0xA371
Length: 36
Network Mask: /24
      Metric Type: 2 (Larger than any link state path)
      MTID: 0
      Metric: 20
      Forward Address: 10.56.1.6
      External Route Tag: 0
```

Table 7-6 provides an explanation of the fields in a Type 7 LSA.

Table 7-6   Type 7 LSA Fields

Field	Description
Link ID	External network number
Network Mask	Subnet mask for the external network
Advertising Router	RID of the router advertising the route (ASBR)
Metric Type	OSPF external metric type (Type 1 O N1 or Type 2 O N2)
Metric	Metric upon redistribution
External Route Tag	32-bit field that is included with an external route, which is not used by OSPF itself and can be used to communicate AS boundaries or other relevant information to prevent routing loops

LSA Type Summary

The OSPF LSA types might seem difficult to understand at first, but you need to understand them as they are important when troubleshooting a router's behavior for a specific prefix. Table 7-7 provides a summary of the OSPF LSAs discussed.

Table 7-7   OSPF LSA Types

LSA Type	Description
1	Router link
2	Network link
3	Summary link
4	ASBR summary
5	AS external
7	NSSA external

Figure 7-13 shows the network prefixes from the sample topology and the relevant LSAs that are present. Notice that the Type 2 LSAs are present only on the broadcast network segments that have established adjacencies with other routers (10.123.1.0/24, 10.45.1.0/24, and 10.56.1.0/24); they are not advertised outside their local area.

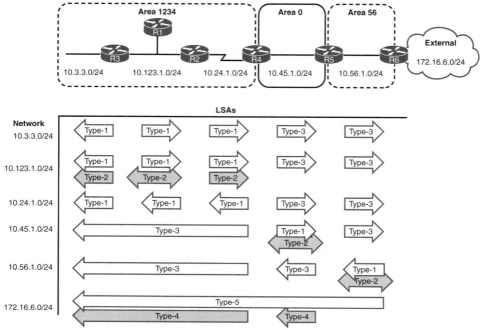

Figure 7-13 *Overview of LSA Types from the Sample Topology*

OSPF Stubby Areas

The previous section focuses on summarizing routes as they leave an area. OSPF stubby areas provide a method to filter out external routes and the option to block inter-area routes.

OSPF stubby areas are identified by the area flag in the OSPF hello packet. Every router within an OSPF stubby area needs to be configured as a stub so that the routers can establish/maintain OSPF adjacencies. The following sections explain the four types of OSPF stubby areas in more detail:

- Stub areas
- Totally stubby areas
- Not-so-stubby areas (NSSAs)
- Totally NSSAs

NOTE   Totally stubby areas and totally NSSAs are not defined in RFC 2328 but are compliant and commonly implemented by Cisco and other network vendors.

Stub Areas

OSPF stub areas prohibit Type 5 LSAs (external routes) and Type 4 LSAs (ASBR summary LSAs) from entering the area at the ABR. RFC 2328 states that when a Type 5 LSA reaches the ABR of a stub area, the ABR generates a default route for the stub via a Type 3 LSA. A Cisco ABR generates a default route when the area is configured as a stub and has an OSPF-enabled interface configured for Area 0. Figure 7-14 illustrates the concept.

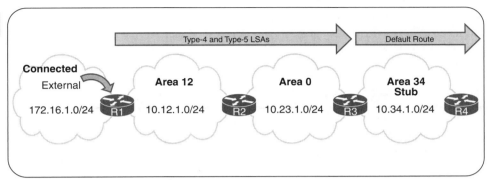

Figure 7-14 *OSPF Stub Area Concept*

Example 7-13 shows the routing tables for R3 and R4 before Area 34 is configured as a stub area. Notice the external 172.16.1.0/24 route that R1 has redistributed into the routing table and that is visible on R3 and R4.

Example 7-13 *Routing Table in Area 1 and Area 2 With Normal Areas*

```
R3# show ip route ospf | begin Gateway
! Output omitted for brevity
Gateway of last resort is not set


      10.0.0.0/8 is variably subnetted, 5 subnets, 2 masks
O IA     10.12.1.0/24 [110/2] via 10.23.1.2, 00:01:36, GigabitEthernet0/1
     172.16.0.0/24 is subnetted, 1 subnets
O E1     172.16.1.0 [110/22] via 10.23.1.2, 00:01:36, GigabitEthernet0/1
O IA     192.168.1.1 [110/3] via 10.23.1.2, 00:01:36, GigabitEthernet0/1
O        192.168.2.2 [110/2] via 10.23.1.2, 00:01:46, GigabitEthernet0/1
O        192.168.4.4 [110/2] via 10.34.1.4, 00:01:46, GigabitEthernet0/0
```

```
R4# show ip route ospf | begin Gateway
! Output omitted for brevity
Gateway of last resort is not set


      10.0.0.0/8 is variably subnetted, 4 subnets, 2 masks
O IA     10.12.1.0/24 [110/3] via 10.34.1.3, 00:00:51, GigabitEthernet0/0
O IA     10.23.1.0/24 [110/2] via 10.34.1.3, 00:00:58, GigabitEthernet0/0
     172.16.0.0/24 is subnetted, 1 subnets
O E1     172.16.1.0 [110/23] via 10.34.1.3, 00:00:46, GigabitEthernet0/0
O IA     192.168.1.1 [110/4] via 10.34.1.3, 00:00:51, GigabitEthernet0/0
O IA     192.168.2.2 [110/3] via 10.34.1.3, 00:00:58, GigabitEthernet0/0
O IA     192.168.3.3 [110/2] via 10.34.1.3, 00:00:58, GigabitEthernet0/0
```

All routers in the stub area must be configured as stubs, or an adjacency cannot form because the area type flags in the hello packets do not match. An area is configured as a stub with the OSPF process command **area** *area-id* **stub**. Example 7-14 demonstrates the configuration for R3 and R4 where Area 34 is configured as an OSPF stub area.

Example 7-14   *OSPF Stub Configuration for Area 34*

```
R3# configure terminal
Enter configuration commands, one per line.  End with CNTL/Z.
R3(config)# router ospf 1
R3(config-router)# area 34 stub

R4# configure terminal
Enter configuration commands, one per line.  End with CNTL/Z.
R4(config)# router ospf 1
R4(config-router)# area 34 stub
```

Example 7-15 shows the routing table for R3 and R4 after Area 34 is made an OSPF stub area. The routing table from R3's perspective is not modified as it receives the Type 4 and Type 5 LSAs from Area 0. When the Type 5 LSA (172.16.1.0/24) reaches the ABR (R3), the ABR generates a default route by using a Type 3 LSA. While R4 does not see the route to the 172.16.1.0/24 route in its routing table, it has connectivity to that network through the default route. Notice that inter-area routes are allowed in Area 34.

Example 7-15   *Routing Table After Stub Area Configuration*

```
R3# show ip route ospf | begin Gateway
! Output omitted for brevity
Gateway of last resort is not set

      10.0.0.0/8 is variably subnetted, 5 subnets, 2 masks
O IA     10.12.1.0/24 [110/2] via 10.23.1.2, 00:03:10, GigabitEthernet0/1
      172.16.0.0/24 is subnetted, 1 subnets
O E1     172.16.1.0 [110/22] via 10.23.1.2, 00:03:10, GigabitEthernet0/1
O IA     192.168.1.1 [110/3] via 10.23.1.2, 00:03:10, GigabitEthernet0/1
O        192.168.2.2 [110/2] via 10.23.1.2, 00:03:10, GigabitEthernet0/1
O        192.168.4.4 [110/2] via 10.34.1.4, 00:01:57, GigabitEthernet0/0

R4# show ip route ospf | begin Gateway
! Output omitted for brevity
Gateway of last resort is 10.34.1.3 to network 0.0.0.0

O*IA  0.0.0.0/0 [110/2] via 10.34.1.3, 00:02:45, GigabitEthernet0/0
      10.0.0.0/8 is variably subnetted, 4 subnets, 2 masks
O IA     10.12.1.0/24 [110/3] via 10.34.1.3, 00:02:45, GigabitEthernet0/0
O IA     10.23.1.0/24 [110/2] via 10.34.1.3, 00:02:45, GigabitEthernet0/0
O IA     192.168.1.1 [110/4] via 10.34.1.3, 00:02:45, GigabitEthernet0/0
O IA     192.168.2.2 [110/3] via 10.34.1.3, 00:02:45, GigabitEthernet0/0
O IA     192.168.3.3 [110/2] via 10.34.1.3, 00:02:45, GigabitEthernet0/0
```

> **NOTE** Default routes are Type 3 summary LSAs (inter-area summaries) because stub areas do not allow Type 5 LSAs within them. A benefit of using a Type 3 LSA is that it cannot be advertised from a nonbackbone area into a backbone area. This concept is explained later in this chapter, in the "Discontiguous Network" section.

Totally Stubby Areas

An *OSPF totally stubby area* prohibits Type 3 LSAs (inter-area), Type 4 LSAs (ASBR summary LSAs), and Type 5 LSAs (external routes) from entering the area at the ABR. When an ABR of a totally stubby area receives a Type 3 or Type 5 LSA, the ABR generates a default route for the totally stubby area.

In fact, an ABR for a totally stubby area advertises the default route into the totally stubby area the instant an interface is assigned to Area 0. Assigning the interface acts as the trigger for the Type 3 LSA that leads to the generation of the default route. Only intra-area and default routes should exist within a totally stubby area.

Figure 7-15 illustrates the totally stubby area concept.

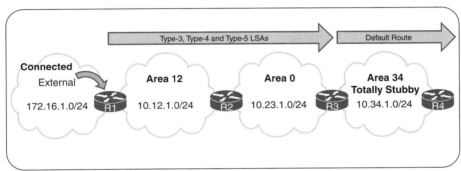

Figure 7-15 *Totally Stubby Area Concept*

Example 7-16 displays R3's and R4's routing tables before Area 34 is converted to an OSPF totally stubby area.

Example 7-16 *Routing Tables of R3 and R4 Before the Totally Stubby Area*

```
R3# show ip route ospf | begin Gateway
! Output omitted for brevity
Gateway of last resort is not set

      10.0.0.0/8 is variably subnetted, 5 subnets, 2 masks
O IA     10.12.1.0/24 [110/2] via 10.23.1.2, 00:01:36, GigabitEthernet0/1
      172.16.0.0/24 is subnetted, 1 subnets
O E1     172.16.1.0 [110/22] via 10.23.1.2, 00:01:36, GigabitEthernet0/1
O IA     192.168.1.1 [110/3] via 10.23.1.2, 00:01:36, GigabitEthernet0/1
O        192.168.2.2 [110/2] via 10.23.1.2, 00:01:46, GigabitEthernet0/1
```

```
O         192.168.4.4 [110/2] via 10.34.1.4, 00:01:46, GigabitEthernet0/0
```

```
R4# show ip route ospf | begin Gateway
! Output omitted for brevity
Gateway of last resort is not set


      10.0.0.0/8 is variably subnetted, 4 subnets, 2 masks
O IA     10.12.1.0/24 [110/3] via 10.34.1.3, 00:00:51, GigabitEthernet0/0
O IA     10.23.1.0/24 [110/2] via 10.34.1.3, 00:00:58, GigabitEthernet0/0
      172.16.0.0/24 is subnetted, 1 subnets
O E1     172.16.1.0 [110/23] via 10.34.1.3, 00:00:46, GigabitEthernet0/0
O IA     192.168.1.1 [110/4] via 10.34.1.3, 00:00:51, GigabitEthernet0/0
O IA     192.168.2.2 [110/3] via 10.34.1.3, 00:00:58, GigabitEthernet0/0
O IA     192.168.3.3 [110/2] via 10.34.1.3, 00:00:58, GigabitEthernet0/0
```

Member routers (non-ABRs) of a totally stubby area are configured the same as those in a stub area. ABRs of a totally stubby area have **no-summary** appended to the configuration. The command **area** *area-id* **stub no-summary** is configured under the OSPF process. The keyword **no-summary** does exactly what it states: It blocks all Type 3 (summary) LSAs going into the stub area, making it a totally stubby area.

Example 7-17 demonstrates the configuration of R3 and R4 for making Area 34 a totally stubby area for both routers.

Example 7-17   *Totally Stubby Area Configurations*

```
R3# configure terminal
Enter configuration commands, one per line.  End with CNTL/Z.
R3(config)# router ospf 1
R3(config-router)# area 34 stub no-summary
```

```
R4# configure terminal
Enter configuration commands, one per line.  End with CNTL/Z.
R4(config)# router ospf 1
R4(config-router)# area 34 stub
```

Example 7-18 shows the routing tables for R3 and R4 after Area 34 is converted to a totally stubby area. Notice that only the default route exists on R4. R3's loopback is a member of Area 0, but if it were a member of Area 34, it would appear as an intra-area route. The routing table on R3 has not been impacted at all.

Example 7-18   *Routing Tables After Area 34 Is Converted to a Totally Stubby Area*

```
R3# show ip route ospf | begin Gateway
! Output omitted for brevity
Gateway of last resort is not set
```

```
         10.0.0.0/8 is variably subnetted, 5 subnets, 2 masks
O IA      10.12.1.0/24 [110/2] via 10.23.1.2, 00:02:34, GigabitEthernet0/1
         172.16.0.0/24 is subnetted, 1 subnets
O E1      172.16.1.0 [110/22] via 10.23.1.2, 00:02:34, GigabitEthernet0/1
O IA      192.168.1.1 [110/3] via 10.23.1.2, 00:02:34, GigabitEthernet0/1
O         192.168.2.2 [110/2] via 10.23.1.2, 00:02:34, GigabitEthernet0/1
O         192.168.4.4 [110/2] via 10.34.1.4, 00:03:23, GigabitEthernet0/0
```

```
R4# show ip route ospf | begin Gateway
! Output omitted for brevity
Gateway of last resort is 10.34.1.3 to network 0.0.0.0

O*IA  0.0.0.0/0 [110/2] via 10.34.1.3, 00:02:24, GigabitEthernet0/0
```

Not-So-Stubby Areas

An OSPF stub area prohibits Type 5 LSAs (external routes) and Type 4 LSAs (ASBR summary LSAs) from entering the area at the ABR, and it prohibits redistribution of external routes into the stub area, too. An *OSPF not-so-stubby-area (NSSA)* prohibits Type 5 LSAs from entering at the ABR but allows for redistribution of external routes into the NSSA.

As the ASBR redistributes the route into OSPF in the NSSA, the ASBR advertises the route with a Type 7 LSA instead of a Type 5 LSA. When the Type 7 LSA reaches the ABR, the ABR converts the Type 7 LSA to a Type 5 LSA.

The ABR does not automatically advertise a default route when a Type 5 or Type 7 LSA is blocked. During configuration, an option exists to advertise a default route to provide connectivity to the blocked LSAs; in addition, other techniques can be used to ensure bidirectional connectivity.

Figure 7-16 demonstrates the concept of LSAs being processed on the ABR for the NSSA. Notice that the default route is optional and depends on the configuration.

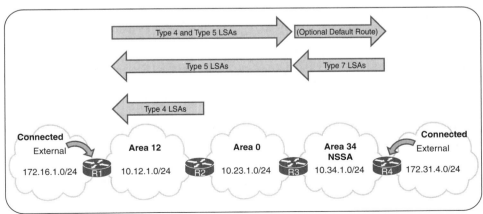

Figure 7-16   *NSSA Concept*

Example 7-19 shows the routing tables of R1, R3, and R4 before Area 34 is converted to an NSSA. Notice that R1 and R4 have received external routes from each other.

Example 7-19 *R1's, R3's, and R4's Routing Tables Before Area 34 Is Converted to an NSSA*

```
R1# show ip route ospf | section 172.31
      172.31.0.0/24 is subnetted, 1 subnets
O E1     172.31.4.0 [110/23] via 10.12.1.2, 00:00:38, GigabitEthernet0/0
```

```
R3# show ip route ospf | begin Gateway
! Output omitted for brevity
Gateway of last resort is not set

      10.0.0.0/8 is variably subnetted, 5 subnets, 2 masks
O IA     10.12.1.0/24 [110/2] via 10.23.1.2, 00:01:34, GigabitEthernet0/1
      172.16.0.0/24 is subnetted, 1 subnets
O E1     172.16.1.0 [110/22] via 10.23.1.2, 00:01:34, GigabitEthernet0/1
      172.31.0.0/24 is subnetted, 1 subnets
O E1     172.31.4.0 [110/21] via 10.34.1.4, 00:01:12, GigabitEthernet0/0
O IA     192.168.1.1 [110/3] via 10.23.1.2, 00:01:34, GigabitEthernet0/1
O        192.168.2.2 [110/2] via 10.23.1.2, 00:01:34, GigabitEthernet0/1
O        192.168.4.4 [110/2] via 10.34.1.4, 00:01:12, GigabitEthernet0/0
```

```
R4# show ip route ospf | begin Gateway
! Output omitted for brevity
Gateway of last resort is not set
      10.0.0.0/8 is variably subnetted, 4 subnets, 2 masks
O IA     10.12.1.0/24 [110/3] via 10.34.1.3, 00:02:28, GigabitEthernet0/0
O IA     10.23.1.0/24 [110/2] via 10.34.1.3, 00:02:28, GigabitEthernet0/0
      172.16.0.0/24 is subnetted, 1 subnets
O E1     172.16.1.0 [110/23] via 10.34.1.3, 00:02:28, GigabitEthernet0/0
O IA     192.168.1.1 [110/4] via 10.34.1.3, 00:02:28, GigabitEthernet0/0
O IA     192.168.2.2 [110/3] via 10.34.1.3, 00:02:28, GigabitEthernet0/0
O IA     192.168.3.3 [110/2] via 10.34.1.3, 00:02:28, GigabitEthernet0/0
```

The command **area** *area-id* **nssa** [**default-information-originate**] is placed under the OSPF process on the ABR. All routers in an NSSA must be configured with the **nssa** option, or they do not become adjacent because the area type flags must match in the OSPF hello protocol in order to become adjacent. A default route is not injected on the ABRs automatically for NSSAs, but the optional command **default-information-originate** can be appended to the configuration if a default route is needed in the NSSA.

Example 7-20 shows the OSPF configuration of R3 and R4 after making Area 34 an NSSA. R3 is configured with the optional **default-information-originate** keyword to inject the default route into Area 34. Notice that R4 is allowed to redistribute networks into the NSSA.

Example 7-20 *NSSA Configuration for Area 34 Routers*

```
R3# show run | section router ospf
router ospf 1
 router-id 192.168.3.3
 area 34 nssa default-information-originate
 network 10.23.1.0 0.0.0.255 area 0
 network 10.34.1.0 0.0.0.255 area 34
 network 192.168.3.3 0.0.0.0 area 0
```

```
R4# show run | section router ospf
router ospf 1
 router-id 192.168.4.4
 area 34 nssa
 redistribute connected metric-type 1 subnets
 network 10.34.1.0 0.0.0.255 area 34
 network 192.168.4.4 0.0.0.0 area 34
```

Example 7-21 shows the routing tables of R3 and R4 after converting Area 34 to an NSSA. On R3, the previous external route from R1 still exists as an OSPF external Type 1 (O E1) route, and R4's external route is now an OSPF external NSSA Type 1 (O N1) route. On R4, R1's external route is no longer present. R3 is configured to advertise a default route, which appears as an OSPF external NSSA Type 2 (O N2) route. The OSPF external routes are representative of a Type 7 LSA, which exists only in an NSSA.

Example 7-21 *R3 and R4 OSPF NSSA Routing Tables*

```
R3# show ip route ospf | begin Gateway
! Output omitted for brevity
Gateway of last resort is not set

      10.0.0.0/8 is variably subnetted, 5 subnets, 2 masks
O IA    10.12.1.0/24 [110/2] via 10.23.1.2, 00:04:13, GigabitEthernet0/1
      172.16.0.0/24 is subnetted, 1 subnets
O E1    172.16.1.0 [110/22] via 10.23.1.2, 00:04:13, GigabitEthernet0/1
      172.31.0.0/24 is subnetted, 1 subnets
O N1    172.31.4.0 [110/22] via 10.34.1.4, 00:03:53, GigabitEthernet0/0
O IA    192.168.1.1 [110/3] via 10.23.1.2, 00:04:13, GigabitEthernet0/1
O       192.168.2.2 [110/2] via 10.23.1.2, 00:04:13, GigabitEthernet0/1
O       192.168.4.4 [110/2] via 10.34.1.4, 00:03:53, GigabitEthernet0/0
```

```
R4# show ip route ospf | begin Gateway
! Output omitted for brevity
Gateway of last resort is 10.34.1.3 to network 0.0.0.0

O*N2  0.0.0.0/0 [110/1] via 10.34.1.3, 00:03:13, GigabitEthernet0/0
      10.0.0.0/8 is variably subnetted, 4 subnets, 2 masks
```

```
O IA    10.12.1.0/24 [110/3] via 10.34.1.3, 00:03:23, GigabitEthernet0/0
O IA    10.23.1.0/24 [110/2] via 10.34.1.3, 00:03:23, GigabitEthernet0/0
        192.168.1.0/32 is subnetted, 1 subnets
O IA    192.168.1.1 [110/4] via 10.34.1.3, 00:03:23, GigabitEthernet0/0
        192.168.2.0/32 is subnetted, 1 subnets
O IA    192.168.2.2 [110/3] via 10.34.1.3, 00:03:23, GigabitEthernet0/0
        192.168.3.0/32 is subnetted, 1 subnets
O IA    192.168.3.3 [110/2] via 10.34.1.3, 00:03:23, GigabitEthernet0/0
```

Totally NSSAs

Totally stubby areas prohibit Type 3 LSAs (inter-area), Type 4 LSAs (ASBR summary LSAs), and Type 5 LSAs (external routes) from entering the area at the ABR, and they prohibit routes from being redistributed within that area. OSPF areas that need to block Type 3 and Type 5 LSAs and still provide the capability of redistributing external networks into OSPF should use the *OSPF totally NSSA*.

When the ASBR redistributes the route into OSPF, the ASBR advertises the route with a Type 7 LSA. As the Type 7 LSA reaches the ABR, the ABR converts the Type 7 LSA to a Type 5 LSA. When an ABR for a totally NSSA receives a Type 3 LSA from the backbone, the ABR generates a default route for the totally NSSA. When an interface on the ABR is assigned to Area 0, it acts as the trigger for the Type 3 LSA that leads to the default route generation within the totally NSSA.

Figure 7-17 demonstrates how the LSAs are processed on the ABR for a totally NSSA.

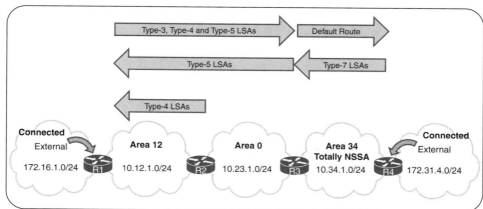

Figure 7-17 *Totally NSSA Concept*

Example 7-22 displays the routing tables of R1, R3, and R4 before Area 34 is converted into an OSPF totally NSSA.

Example 7-22 *R1's, R3s, and R4's Routing Tables Before Area 34 Is a Totally NSSA*

```
R1# show ip route ospf | section 172.31
      172.31.0.0/24 is subnetted, 1 subnets
O E1    172.31.4.0 [110/23] via 10.12.1.2, 00:00:38, GigabitEthernet0/0
R3# show ip route ospf | begin Gateway
! Output omitted for brevity
Gateway of last resort is not set


      10.0.0.0/8 is variably subnetted, 5 subnets, 2 masks
O IA    10.12.1.0/24 [110/2] via 10.23.1.2, 00:01:34, GigabitEthernet0/1
      172.16.0.0/24 is subnetted, 1 subnets
O E1    172.16.1.0 [110/22] via 10.23.1.2, 00:01:34, GigabitEthernet0/1
      172.31.0.0/24 is subnetted, 1 subnets
O E1    172.31.4.0 [110/21] via 10.34.1.4, 00:01:12, GigabitEthernet0/0
O IA    192.168.1.1 [110/3] via 10.23.1.2, 00:01:34, GigabitEthernet0/1
O       192.168.2.2 [110/2] via 10.23.1.2, 00:01:34, GigabitEthernet0/1
O       192.168.4.4 [110/2] via 10.34.1.4, 00:01:12, GigabitEthernet0/0
```

```
R4# show ip route ospf | begin Gateway
! Output omitted for brevity
Gateway of last resort is not set


      10.0.0.0/8 is variably subnetted, 4 subnets, 2 masks
O IA    10.12.1.0/24 [110/3] via 10.34.1.3, 00:02:28, GigabitEthernet0/0
O IA    10.23.1.0/24 [110/2] via 10.34.1.3, 00:02:28, GigabitEthernet0/0
      172.16.0.0/24 is subnetted, 1 subnets
O E1    172.16.1.0 [110/23] via 10.34.1.3, 00:02:28, GigabitEthernet0/0
O IA    192.168.1.1 [110/4] via 10.34.1.3, 00:02:28, GigabitEthernet0/0
O IA    192.168.2.2 [110/3] via 10.34.1.3, 00:02:28, GigabitEthernet0/0
O IA    192.168.3.3 [110/2] via 10.34.1.3, 00:02:28, GigabitEthernet0/0
```

Member routers of a totally NSSA use the same configuration as members of an NSSA. ABRs of a totally NSSA area have **no-summary** appended to the configuration. The command **area** *area-id* **nssa no-summary** is configured under the OSPF process.

Example 7-23 shows R3's and R4's OSPF configuration to convert Area 34 into a totally NSSA. Notice the **no-summary** keyword appended to R3's **nssa** command.

Example 7-23 *Totally NSSA Configuration*

```
R3# show run | section router ospf 1
router ospf 1
 router-id 192.168.3.3
 area 34 nssa no-summary
 network 10.23.1.0 0.0.0.255 area 0
```

```
network 10.34.1.0 0.0.0.255 area 34
network 192.168.3.3 0.0.0.0 area 0
```

```
R4# show run | section router ospf 1
router ospf 1
 router-id 192.168.4.4
 area 34 nssa
 redistribute connected metric-type 1 subnets
 network 10.34.1.0 0.0.0.255 area 34
 network 192.168.4.4 0.0.0.0 area 34
```

Example 7-24 shows the routing tables of R3 and R4 after Area 34 is converted into a totally NSSA. R3 detects R1's redistributed route as an O E1 (Type 5 LSA) and R4's redistributed route as an O N1 (Type 7 LSA). Notice that only the default route exists on R4. R3's loopback is a member of Area 0, but if it were a member of Area 34, it would appear as an intra-area route.

Example 7-24 *R3's and R4's Routing Tables After Area 34 Is Made a Totally NSSA*

```
R3# show ip route ospf | begin Gateway
! Output omitted for brevity
Gateway of last resort is not set


      10.0.0.0/8 is variably subnetted, 5 subnets, 2 masks
O IA    10.12.1.0/24 [110/2] via 10.23.1.2, 00:02:14, GigabitEthernet0/1
      172.16.0.0/24 is subnetted, 1 subnets
O E1    172.16.1.0 [110/22] via 10.23.1.2, 00:02:14, GigabitEthernet0/1
      172.31.0.0/24 is subnetted, 1 subnets
O N1    172.31.4.0 [110/22] via 10.34.1.4, 00:02:04, GigabitEthernet0/0
O IA    192.168.1.1 [110/3] via 10.23.1.2, 00:02:14, GigabitEthernet0/1
O       192.168.2.2 [110/2] via 10.23.1.2, 00:02:14, GigabitEthernet0/1
O       192.168.4.4 [110/2] via 10.34.1.4, 00:02:04, GigabitEthernet0/0
```

```
R4# show ip route ospf | begin Gateway
! Output omitted for brevity
Gateway of last resort is 10.34.1.3 to network 0.0.0.0

O*IA  0.0.0.0/0 [110/2] via 10.34.1.3, 00:04:21, GigabitEthernet0/0
```

OSPF Path Selection

OSPF executes Dijkstra's shortest path first (SPF) algorithm to create a loop-free topology of shortest paths. All routers use the same logic to calculate the shortest path for each network. Path selection prioritizes paths in the following order:

1. Intra-area
2. Inter-area

3. External Type 1

4. External Type 2

The following sections explain each component in detail.

Link Costs

Interface cost is an essential component for Dijkstra's SPF calculation because the shortest path metric is based on the cumulative interface cost (that is, metric) from the router to the destination. OSPF assigns the OSPF link cost (that is, metric) for an interface using the formula in Figure 7-18.

$$\text{Cost} = \frac{\text{Reference Bandwidth}}{\text{Interface Bandwidth}}$$

Figure 7-18 *OSPF Interface Cost Formula*

The default reference bandwidth is 100 Mbps. There is no differentiation in the link cost associated with a Fast Ethernet interface and a 10-Gigabit Ethernet interface. Changing the reference bandwidth to a higher value allows for differentiation of cost between higher-speed interfaces. The OSPF LSA metric field is 16-bits, and the interface cost cannot exceed 65,535.

Under the OSPF process, the command **auto-cost reference-bandwidth** *bandwidth-in-mbps* changes the reference bandwidth for all OSPF interfaces associated with that process. If the reference bandwidth is changed on one router, then the reference bandwidth should be changed on all OSPF routers to ensure that SPF uses the same logic to prevent routing loops. It is a best practice to set the same reference bandwidth for all OSPF routers.

The OSPF cost can be set manually with the command **ip ospf cost** *1-65535* under the interface. While the interface cost is limited to 65,535 because of LSA field limitations, the path metric can exceed a 16-bit value (65,535) because all the link metrics are calculated locally.

7

NOTE NX-OS uses a default reference cost of 40,000 Mbps.

Intra-area Routes

OSPF intra-area routes (Type 1 and 2 LSAs) are always preferred over inter-area routes (Type 3 LSAs). If multiple intra-area routes exist for the same network, the path with the lowest total path metric is installed in the OSPF Routing Information Base (RIB) and is then presented to the router's global RIB. If there is a tie in metric, both routes are installed into the OSPF RIB.

In Figure 7-19, R1 is calculating the route to the 10.4.4.0/24 network. Instead of taking the faster Ethernet connection (R1→R2→R4), R1 takes the path across the slower serial link to R4 (R1→R3→R4) because that is the intra-area path.

Example 7-25 shows R1's routing table entry for the 10.4.4.0/24 network. Notice that the metric is 111 and that the intra-area path selected takes the inter-area path with the lower total path metric.

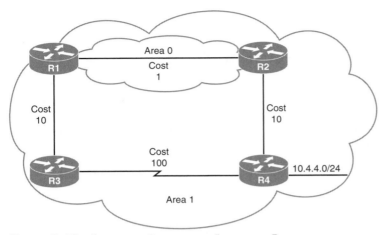

Figure 7-19 *Intra-area Routes over Inter-area Routes*

Example 7-25 *R1's Routing Table for the 10.4.4.0/24 Network*

```
R1# show ip route 10.4.4.0
Routing entry for 10.4.4.0/24
  Known via "ospf 1", distance 110, metric 111, type intra area
  Last update from 10.13.1.3 on GigabitEthernet0/1, 00:00:42 ago
  Routing Descriptor Blocks:
  * 10.13.1.3, from 10.34.1.4, 00:00:42 ago, via GigabitEthernet0/1
      Route metric is 111, traffic share count is 1
```

Inter-area Routes

The next priority for selecting a path to a network in a different area is selection of the path with the lowest total path metric to the destination. If there is a tie in metric, both paths install into the OSPF RIB. All inter-area paths for a route must go through Area 0 to be considered.

In Figure 7-20, R1 is computing the path to R6. R1 uses the path R1→R3→R5→R6 because its total path metric is 35 as compared to the metric of 40 for the R1→R2→R4→R6 path.

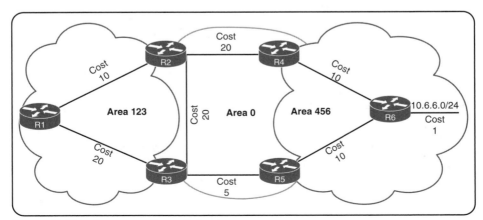

Figure 7-20 *Inter-area Route Selection*

External Route Selection

External routes are classified as Type 1 or Type 2. The main differences between Type 1 and Type 2 external OSPF routes are as follows:

- Type 1 routes are preferred over Type 2 routes.

- The Type 1 metric equals the redistribution metric plus the total path metric to the ASBR. In other words, as the LSA propagates away from the originating ASBR, the metric increases.

- The Type 2 metric equals only the redistribution metric. The metric is the same for the router next to the ASBR as for the router 30 hops away from the originating ASBR. This is the default external metric type that OSPF uses.

The following sections further explain the best-path calculation for external routes.

E1 and N1 External Routes

External OSPF Type 1 route calculation involves the redistribution metric plus the lowest path metric to reach the ASBR that advertised the network. Type 1 path metrics are lower for routers closer to the originating ASBR, whereas the path metric is higher for a router 10 hops away from the ASBR.

If there is a tie in the path metric, both routes are installed into the RIB. If the ASBR is in a different area, the path of the traffic must go through Area 0. An ABR does not install O E1 and O N1 routes into the RIB at the same time. O N1 is always given preference for a typical NSSA, and its presence prevents the O E1 from being installed on the ABR.

E2 and N2 External Routes

External OSPF Type 2 routes do not increment in metric, regardless of the path metric to the ASBR. If there is a tie in the redistribution metric, the router compares the forwarding cost. The forwarding cost is the metric to the ASBR that advertised the network, and the lower forwarding cost is preferred. If there is a tie in forwarding cost, both routes are installed into the routing table. An ABR does not install O E2 and O N2 routes into the RIB at the same time. O N2 is always given preference for a typical NSSA, and its presence prevents the O E2 from being installed on the ABR.

Figure 7-21 shows the topology for R1 computing a path to the external network (172.16.0.0/24) that is being redistributed.

The path R1→R2→R4→R6 has a metric of 20, which ties with the path R1→R3→R5→R7. The forwarding metric of the R1→R2→R4→R6 path is 31, and the forwarding metric of the R1→R3→R5→R7 path is 30. R1 installs the R1→R3→R5→R7 path into the routing table.

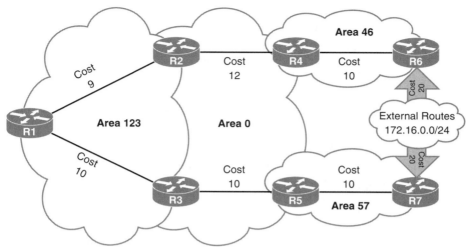

Figure 7-21   *External Type 2 Route Selection Topology*

Example 7-26 shows R1's metric and forwarding metric to the 172.16.0.0/24 network.

Example 7-26   *OSPF Forwarding Metric*

```
R1# show ip route 172.16.0.0
Routing entry for 172.16.0.0/24
  Known via "ospf 1", distance 110, metric 20, type extern 2, forward metric 30
  Last update from 10.13.1.3 on GigabitEthernet0/1, 00:12:40 ago
  Routing Descriptor Blocks:
  * 10.13.1.3, from 192.168.7.7, 00:12:40 ago, via GigabitEthernet0/1
      Route metric is 20, traffic share count is 1
```

> **NOTE**   The logic of choosing an O N*x* route (Type 7 LSA) over an O E*x* route (Type 5 LSA) is defined in RFC 3101. Choosing an O N*x* is the current default for IOS XE implementations. RFC 1583 prefers an O E*x* route (Type 5 LSA) over an O N*x* route (Type 7 LSA). RFC 1583 path selection can be enabled with the command **compatible rfc1583**.

Equal-Cost Multipathing

If OSPF identifies multiple paths in the algorithms discussed so far in this chapter, those routes are installed into the routing table using equal-cost multipathing (ECMP). The default maximum number of ECMP paths is four. The default ECMP setting can be overwritten with the command **maximum-paths** *maximum-paths* under the OSPF process to modify the default setting.

Summarization of Routes

Route scalability is a large factor for the Interior Gateway Protocols used by service providers because there can be thousands of routers running in the network. Splitting up an OSPF routing domain into multiple areas reduces the size of each area's LSDB. While the number of routers and networks remains the same within the OSPF routing domain, the detailed Type 1 and Type 2 LSAs are exchanged for simpler Type 3 LSAs.

For example, refer again to the topology for LSAs in Figure 7-6; for Area 1234, there are three Type 1 LSAs and one Type 2 LSA for the 10.123.1.0/24 network. Those four LSAs become one Type 3 LSA outside of Area 1234. Figure 7-22 illustrates the reduction of LSAs through area segmentation for the 10.123.1.0/24 network.

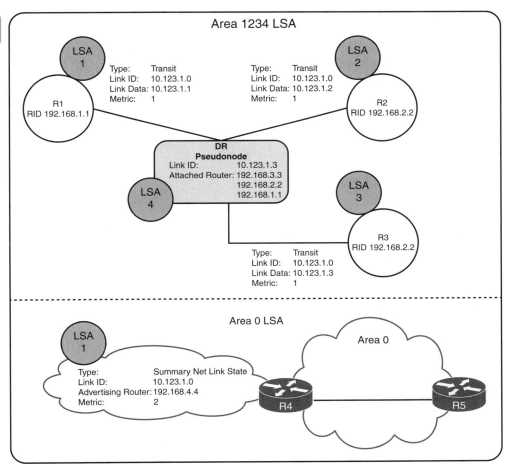

Figure 7-22 *LSA Reduction Through Area Segmentation*

Summarization Fundamentals

Another method of shrinking the LSDB involves summarizing network prefixes. Newer routers have more memory and faster processors than do older ones, but because all routers have an identical copy of the LSDB, an OSPF area needs to accommodate the smallest and slowest router in that area.

Summarization of routes also helps SPF calculations run faster. A router that has 10,000 network routes will take longer to run the SPF calculation than a router with 500 network routes. Because all routers within an area must maintain an identical copy of the LSDB, summarization occurs between areas on the ABRs.

Summarization can eliminate the SPF calculation outside the area for the summarized prefixes because the smaller prefixes are hidden. Figure 7-23 provides a simple network topology in which the serial link (between R3 and R4) significantly adds to the path metric, and all traffic uses the path through R2 to reach the 172.16.46.0/24 network. If the 10.1.12.0/24 link fails, all routers in Area 1 have to run SPF calculations. R2 identifies that the 10.1.13.0/24 and 10.1.34.0/24 networks change their next hop through the serial link. Both of the Type 3 LSAs for these networks need to be updated with new path metrics and advertised into Area 0. The routers in Area 0 run an SPF calculation only on those two prefixes.

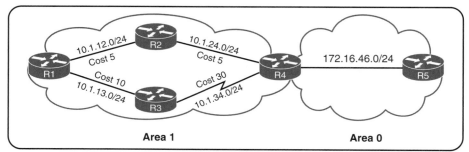

Figure 7-23   *The Impact of Summarization on SPF Topology Calculation*

Figure 7-24 shows the networks in Area 1 being summarized at the ABR into the aggregate 10.1.0.0/18 prefix. If the 10.1.12.0/24 link fails, all the routers in Area 1 still run the SPF calculation, but routers in Area 0 are not affected because the 10.1.13.0/24 and 10.1.34.0/24 networks are not known outside Area 1.

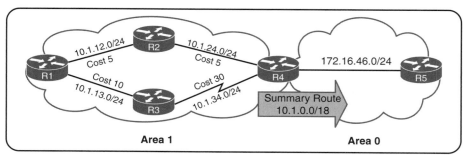

Figure 7-24   *Topology Example with Summarization*

This concept applies to networks of varying sizes but is beneficial for networks with carefully developed IP addressing schemes and proper summarization. The following sections explain summarization in more detail.

Inter-area Summarization

Inter-area summarization reduces the number of Type 3 LSAs that an ABR advertises into an area when it receives Type 1 LSAs. The network summarization range is associated with a specific source area for Type 1 LSAs.

When a Type 1 LSA in the summarization range reaches the ABR from the source area, the ABR creates a Type 3 LSA for the summarized network range. The ABR suppresses the more specific Type 3 LSAs from being generated and advertised in the neighboring areas. Inter-area summarization does not impact the Type 1 LSAs within the source area.

Figure 7-25 illustrates this concept, with the three Type 1 LSAs (172.16.1.0/24, 172.16.2.0/24, and 172.16.3.0/24) being summarized into one Type 3 LSA, as the 172.16.0.0/20 network.

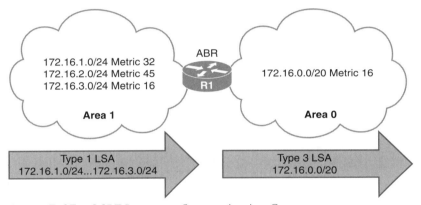

Figure 7-25   *OSPF Inter-area Summarization Concept*

Summarization works only on Type 1 LSAs and is normally configured (or designed) so that summarization occurs as routes enter the backbone from nonbackbone areas.

At the time of this writing, IOS XE routers set the default metric for the summary LSA to be the lowest metric associated with an LSA based on RFC1583 guidelines. However, the summary metric can statically be set as part of the configuration. In Figure 7-25, R1 summarizes three prefixes with various path costs. The 172.16.3.0/24 prefix has the lowest metric, so that metric will be used for the summarized route.

OSPF behaves similar to Enhanced Interior Gateway Routing Protocol (EIGRP) in that it checks every prefix in the summarization range when a matching Type 1 LSA is added or removed. If a lower metric is available, the summary LSA is advertised with the newer metric; if the lowest metric is removed, a newer and higher metric is identified, and a new summary LSA is advertised with the higher metric.

Configuration of Inter-area Summarization

You define the summarization range and associated area by using the command **area** *area-id* **range** *network subnet-mask* [**advertise** | **not-advertise**] [**cost** *metric*] under the OSPF process. The default behavior is to advertise the summary prefix, so the keyword **advertise** is not necessary. Appending **cost** *metric* to the command statically sets the metric on the summary route.

Figure 7-26 provides a topology example in which R1 is advertising the 172.16.1.0/24, 172.16.2.0/24, and 172.16.3.0/24 networks.

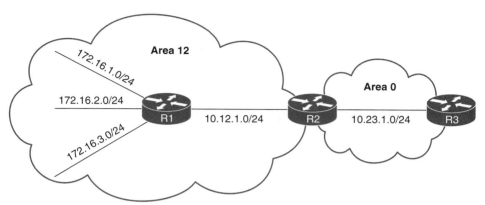

Figure 7-26   *OSPF Inter-area Summarization Example*

Example 7-27 shows the routing table on R3 before summarization. Notice that the 172.16.1.0/24, 172.16.2.0/24, and 172.16.3.0/24 routes are all present.

Example 7-27   *Routing Table Before OSPF Inter-area Route Summarization*

```
R3# show ip route ospf | begin Gateway
Gateway of last resort is not set

      10.0.0.0/8 is variably subnetted, 5 subnets, 2 masks
O IA    10.12.1.0/24 [110/2] via 10.23.1.2, 00:02:22, GigabitEthernet0/1
      172.16.0.0/24 is subnetted, 3 subnets
O IA    172.16.1.0 [110/3] via 10.23.1.2, 00:02:12, GigabitEthernet0/1
O IA    172.16.2.0 [110/3] via 10.23.1.2, 00:02:12, GigabitEthernet0/1
O IA    172.16.3.0 [110/3] via 10.23.1.2, 00:02:12, GigabitEthernet0/1
```

As the component routes 172.16.1.0/24, 172.16.2.0/24, and 172.16.3.0/24 are being advertised into Area 0, R2 summarizes them into a single summary route, 172.16.0.0/16. Example 7-28 provides R2's configuration for inter-area summarization into an aggregate route 172.16.0.0/16. A static cost of 45 is added to the summary route to reduce CPU load if any of the three networks flap.

Example 7-28   *R2's Inter-area Route Summarization Configuration*

```
router ospf 1
 router-id 192.168.2.2
 area 12 range 172.16.0.0 255.255.0.0 cost 45
 network 10.12.0.0 0.0.255.255 area 12
 network 10.23.0.0 0.0.255.255 area 0
```

Example 7-29 shows R3's routing table, which can be used to verify that the smaller component routes were suppressed while the summary route was aggregated. Notice in this output that the path metric is 46, whereas previously the metric for the 172.16.1.0/24 network was 3.

Example 7-29 *Routing Table After OSPF Inter-area Route Summarization*

```
R3# show ip route ospf | begin Gateway
Gateway of last resort is not set


     10.0.0.0/8 is variably subnetted, 3 subnets, 2 masks
O IA   10.12.1.0/24 [110/2] via 10.23.1.2, 00:02:04, GigabitEthernet0/1
O IA   172.16.0.0/16 [110/46] via 10.23.1.2, 00:00:22, GigabitEthernet0/1
```

The ABR performing inter-area summarization installs discard routes, which are routes to the Null0 interface that match the summarized network. Discard routes prevent routing loops where portions of the summarized network range do not have a more specific route in the RIB. The administrative distance (AD) for the OSPF summary discard route for internal networks is 110, and it is 254 for external networks. Example 7-30 shows the discard route to Null0 on R2.

Example 7-30 *Discard Route for Loop Prevention*

```
R2# show ip route ospf | begin Gateway
Gateway of last resort is not set


     172.16.0.0/16 is variably subnetted, 4 subnets, 2 masks
O       172.16.0.0/16 is a summary, 00:03:11, Null
O       172.16.1.0/24 [110/2] via 10.12.1.1, 00:01:26, GigabitEthernet0/0
O       172.16.2.0/24 [110/2] via 10.12.1.1, 00:01:26, GigabitEthernet0/0
O       172.16.3.0/24 [110/2] via 10.12.1.1, 00:01:26, GigabitEthernet0/0
```

External Summarization

During OSPF redistribution, external routes are redistributed into the OSPF domain as Type 5 or Type 7 LSAs (NSSA). External summarization reduces the number of external LSAs in an OSPF domain. An external summarization route is configured on the ASBR router, and a smaller component route that matches the network range does not generate a Type 5/Type 7 LSA for the specific prefix. Instead, a Type 5/Type 7 LSA with the external summary route is created, and the smaller component routes in the summary route are suppressed.

Figure 7-27 demonstrates the concept with the external network summarization range 172.16.0.0/20 configured on the ASBR (R6). The ASBR creates only one Type 5/Type 7 LSA in Area 56 when EIGRP redistributes routes into OSPF.

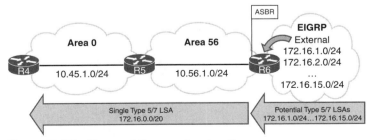

Figure 7-27 *External Summarization Concept*

Example 7-31 provides the routing table on R5 before external route summarization.

Example 7-31 *Routing Table Before External Summarization*

```
R5# show ip route ospf | begin Gateway
! Output omitted for brevity
Gateway of last resort is not set


      10.0.0.0/8 is variably subnetted, 7 subnets, 3 masks
O IA     10.3.3.0/24 [110/67] via 10.45.1.4, 00:01:58, GigabitEthernet0/0
O IA     10.24.1.0/29 [110/65] via 10.45.1.4, 00:01:58, GigabitEthernet0/0
O IA     10.123.1.0/24 [110/66] via 10.45.1.4, 00:01:58, GigabitEthernet0/0
      172.16.0.0/24 is subnetted, 15 subnets
O E2     172.16.1.0 [110/20] via 10.56.1.6, 00:01:00, GigabitEthernet0/1
O E2     172.16.2.0 [110/20] via 10.56.1.6, 00:00:43, GigabitEthernet0/1
..
O E2     172.16.14.0 [110/20] via 10.56.1.6, 00:00:19, GigabitEthernet0/1
O E2     172.16.15.0 [110/20] via 10.56.1.6, 00:00:15, GigabitEthernet0/1
```

To configure external summarization, you use the command **summary-address** *network subnet-mask* under the OSPF process. Example 7-32 demonstrates the configuration for external route summarization on R6 (the ASBR).

Example 7-32 *OSPF External Summarization Configuration*

```
R6
router ospf 1
 router-id 192.168.6.6
 summary-address 172.16.0.0 255.255.240.0
 redistribute eigrp 1 subnets
 network 10.56.1.0 0.0.0.255 area 56
```

Example 7-33 shows R5's routing table, which verifies that the component routes were summarized into the 172.16.0.0/20 summary network.

Example 7-33 *Routing Table After External Summarization*

```
R5# show ip route ospf | begin Gateway
Gateway of last resort is not set


      10.0.0.0/8 is variably subnetted, 7 subnets, 3 masks
O IA    10.3.3.0/24 [110/67] via 10.45.1.4, 00:04:55, GigabitEthernet0/0
O IA    10.24.1.0/29 [110/65] via 10.45.1.4, 00:04:55, GigabitEthernet0/0
O IA    10.123.1.0/24 [110/66] via 10.45.1.4, 00:04:55, GigabitEthernet0/0
      172.16.0.0/20 is subnetted, 1 subnets
```

```
O E2    172.16.0.0 [110/20] via 10.56.1.6, 00:00:02, GigabitEthernet0/1
```

```
R5# show ip route 172.16.0.0 255.255.240.0
Routing entry for 172.16.0.0/20
  Known via "ospf 1", distance 110, metric 20, type extern 2, forward metric 1
  Last update from 10.56.1.6 on GigabitEthernet0/1, 00:02:14 ago
  Routing Descriptor Blocks:
  * 10.56.1.6, from 192.168.6.6, 00:02:14 ago, via GigabitEthernet0/1
      Route metric is 20, traffic share count is 1
```

The summarizing ASBR installs a discard route to Null0 that matches the summary route as part of a loop-prevention mechanism. Example 7-34 shows the routing table of R6 with the external summary discard route.

Example 7-34 *R6 Discard Route Verification*

```
R6# show ip route ospf | begin Gateway
Gateway of last resort is not set

      10.0.0.0/8 is variably subnetted, 6 subnets, 3 masks
O IA    10.3.3.0/24 [110/68] via 10.56.1.5, 00:08:36, GigabitEthernet0/1
O IA    10.24.1.0/29 [110/66] via 10.56.1.5, 00:08:36, GigabitEthernet0/1
O IA    10.45.1.0/24 [110/2] via 10.56.1.5, 00:08:36, GigabitEthernet0/1
O IA    10.123.1.0/24 [110/67] via 10.56.1.5, 00:08:36, GigabitEthernet0/1
      172.16.0.0/16 is variably subnetted, 15 subnets, 3 masks
O       172.16.0.0/20 is a summary, 00:03:52, Null0
```

NOTE   ABRs for NSSAs act as ASBRs when a Type 7 LSA is converted to a Type 5 LSA. External summarization can be performed on ABRs only when they match this scenario.

Discontiguous Network

A network engineer who does not fully understand OSPF design might create a topology such as one illustrated in Figure 7-28. While R2 and R4 have OSPF interfaces in Area 0, traffic from Area 12 must cross Area 234 to reach Area 45. An OSPF network with this design is a *discontiguous network* because inter-area traffic is trying to cross a nonbackbone area.

Upon first glance at the routing tables on R2 and R4 in Figure 7-29, it seems as though routes are being advertised across Area 234; however, this is not the case. The 10.45.1.0/24 network is received by R4, injected into R4's Area 0, and then re-advertised to Area 234, where R2 installs the route.

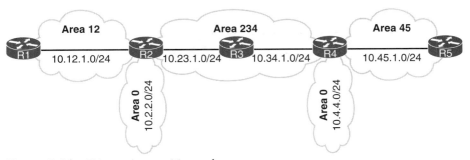

Figure 7-28 *Discontiguous Network*

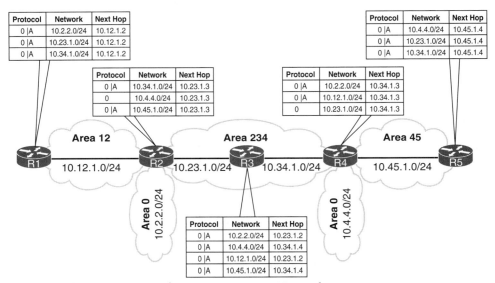

Figure 7-29 *OSPF Routes for a Discontiguous Network*

Most people would assume that R1 would learn about the route learned by Area 45 because R4 is an ABR. However, they would be wrong. ABRs follow three fundamental rules for creating Type 3 LSAs:

- Type 1 LSAs received from an area create Type 3 LSAs into backbone area and non-backbone areas.

- Type 3 LSAs received from Area 0 are created for the nonbackbone area.

- Type 3 LSAs received from a nonbackbone area are only inserted into the LSDB for the source area. An ABR does not create a Type 3 LSA for the other areas (including a segmented Area 0).

The simplest fix for a discontiguous network is to ensure that Area 0 is contiguous and convert the interfaces on R2, R3, and R4 for the 10.23.1.0/24 and 10.34.1.0/24 networks to be members of Area 0. Another option is to use a virtual link, as discussed in the following section.

Virtual Links

OSPF *virtual links* provide a method to overcome discontiguous networks. Using a virtual link is similar to running a virtual tunnel within OSPF between an ABR and another multi-area OSPF router. The tunnel belongs to the backbone (Area 0), and therefore the router terminating the virtual link becomes an ABR if it does not have an interface already associated with Area 0.

Figure 7-30 revisits the discontiguous topology from the previous section and shows a contiguous backbone between R2 and R4, with a virtual link across Area 234. With the virtual link established, the routes from Area 12 are advertised into Area 45 and vice versa.

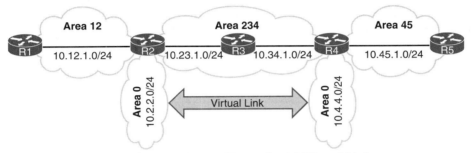

Figure 7-30 *Repair of Discontiguous Network with Virtual Links*

Virtual links are built between routers in the same area. The area in which the virtual link endpoints are established is known as the *transit area*. Each router identifies the remote router by its RID. The virtual link can be one hop away or multiple hops away from the remote device. The virtual link is built using Type 1 LSAs, where the neighbor state is Type 4, as identified earlier in the chapter, in Table 7-3.

You configure the virtual link by using the command **area** *area-id* **virtual-link** *endpoint-RID*. The configuration is performed on both endpoints of the virtual link. At least one endpoint virtual link router has to be a member of Area 0, and virtual links cannot be formed on any OSPF stubby areas. In Figure 7-30, Area 234 cannot be an OSPF stub area.

Example 7-35 demonstrates the virtual link configuration between R2 and R4. Notice that the RID is specified as the remote tunnel endpoint, even though it is not advertised into OSPF.

Example 7-35 *OSPF Virtual Link Configuration*

```
R2
router ospf 1
 router-id 192.168.2.2
 area 234 virtual-link 192.168.4.4
 network 10.2.2.2 0.0.0.0 area 0
 network 10.12.1.2 0.0.0.0 area 12
```

```
network 10.23.1.2 0.0.0.0 area 234
```

```
R4
router ospf 1
 router-id 192.168.4.4
 area 234 virtual-link 192.168.2.2
 network 10.4.4.4 0.0.0.0 area 0
 network 10.34.1.4 0.0.0.0 area 234
 network 10.45.1.4 0.0.0.0 area 45
```

To verify the virtual link status, you use the command **show ip ospf virtual-links**. Example 7-36 shows the output. Notice that the output includes the virtual link status, the outbound interface to the endpoints, and the interface cost.

Interface cost for a virtual link cannot be set or dynamically generated as the metric for the intra-area distance between the two virtual link endpoints.

Example 7-36 *OSPF Virtual Link Verification*

```
R2# show ip ospf virtual-links
Virtual Link OSPF_VL0 to router 192.168.4.4 is up
  Run as demand circuit
  DoNotAge LSA allowed.
  Transit area 234, via interface GigabitEthernet0/1
Topology-MTID    Cost    Disabled    Shutdown    Topology Name
      0            2         no          no          Base
  Transmit Delay is 1 sec, State POINT_TO_POINT,
  Timer intervals configured, Hello 10, Dead 40, Wait 40, Retransmit 5
    Hello due in 00:00:01
    Adjacency State FULL (Hello suppressed)
    Index 1/1/3, retransmission queue length 0, number of retransmission 0
    First 0x0(0)/0x0(0)/0x0(0) Next 0x0(0)/0x0(0)/0x0(0)
    Last retransmission scan length is 0, maximum is 0
    Last retransmission scan time is 0 msec, maximum is 0 msec

R4# show ip ospf virtual-links
! Output omitted for brevity
Virtual Link OSPF_VL0 to router 192.168.2.2 is up
  Run as demand circuit
  DoNotAge LSA allowed.
  Transit area 234, via interface GigabitEthernet0/0
Topology-MTID    Cost    Disabled    Shutdown    Topology Name
      0            2         no          no          Base
  Transmit Delay is 1 sec, State POINT_TO_POINT,
  Timer intervals configured, Hello 10, Dead 40, Wait 40, Retransmit 5
    Hello due in 00:00:08
    Adjacency State FULL (Hello suppressed)
```

A virtual link appears as a specific interface, as demonstrated in Example 7-37. Notice that the cost here is 2, which accounts for the metrics between R2 and R4.

Example 7-37 *OSPF Virtual Link as an OSPF Interface*

```
R4# show ip ospf interface brief
Interface    PID   Area           IP Address/Mask    Cost   State  Nbrs F/C
Gi0/2        1     0              10.4.4.4/24        1      DR     0/0
VL0          1     0              10.34.1.4/24       2      P2P    1/1
Lo0          1     34             192.168.4.4/32     1      DOWN   0/0
Gi0/1        1     45             10.45.1.4/24       1      BDR    1/1
Gi0/0        1     234            10.34.1.4/24       1      BDR    1/1
```

The virtual link routers form a point-to-point adjacency, as demonstrated in Example 7-38. Notice that R4 views R2 as a neighbor even though it is not directly connected.

Example 7-38 *A Virtual Link Displayed as an OSPF Neighbor*

```
R4# show ip ospf neighbor
Neighbor ID    Pri   State      Dead Time   Address      Interface
192.168.2.2    0     FULL/  -   -           10.23.1.2    OSPF_VL0
192.168.5.5    1     FULL/DR    00:00:34    10.45.1.5    GigabitEthernet0/1
192.168.3.3    1     FULL/DR    00:00:38    10.34.1.3    GigabitEthernet0/0
```

Example 7-39 shows the routing tables of R1 and R5 after the virtual link is established. Notice that R1 now has the 10.45.1.0/24 route in its routing table, and R5 has the 10.12.1.0/24 route in its routing table.

Example 7-39 *R1's and R5's Routing Tables After the Virtual Link Is Created*

```
R1# show ip route ospf | begin Gateway
Gateway of last resort is not set

      10.0.0.0/8 is variably subnetted, 7 subnets, 2 masks
O IA     10.2.2.0/24 [110/2] via 10.12.1.2, 00:00:10, GigabitEthernet0/0
O IA     10.4.4.0/24 [110/4] via 10.12.1.2, 00:00:05, GigabitEthernet0/0
O IA     10.23.1.0/24 [110/2] via 10.12.1.2, 00:00:10, GigabitEthernet0/0
O IA     10.34.1.0/24 [110/3] via 10.12.1.2, 00:00:10, GigabitEthernet0/0
O IA     10.45.1.0/24 [110/4] via 10.12.1.2, 00:00:05, GigabitEthernet0/0

R5# show ip route ospf | begin Gateway
Gateway of last resort is not set

      10.0.0.0/8 is variably subnetted, 7 subnets, 2 masks
O IA     10.2.2.0/24 [110/4] via 10.45.1.4, 00:00:43, GigabitEthernet0/1
O IA     10.4.4.0/24 [110/2] via 10.45.1.4, 00:01:48, GigabitEthernet0/1
O IA     10.12.1.0/24 [110/4] via 10.45.1.4, 00:00:43, GigabitEthernet0/1
O IA     10.23.1.0/24 [110/3] via 10.45.1.4, 00:01:48, GigabitEthernet0/1
O IA     10.34.1.0/24 [110/2] via 10.45.1.4, 00:01:48, GigabitEthernet0/1
```

References in This Chapter

Edgeworth, Brad, Foss, Aaron, and Garza Rios, Ramiro, *IP Routing on Cisco IOS, IOS XE, and IOS XR*, Cisco Press, 2014.

RFC 2328, *OSPF Version 2*, John Moy, IETF, http://www.ietf.org/rfc/rfc2328.txt, April 1998.

Cisco, *Cisco IOS Software Configuration Guides*, http://www.cisco.com.

Exam Preparation Tasks

As mentioned in the section "How to Use This Book" in the Introduction, you have a couple choices for exam preparation: the exercises here, Chapter 24, "Final Preparation," and the exam simulation questions in the Pearson Test Prep software.

Review All Key Topics

Review the most important topics in this chapter, noted with the Key Topic icon in the outer margin of the page. Table 7-8 lists these key topics and the page number on which each is found.

Table 7-8   Key Topics

Key Topic Element	Description	Page Number
List	Link-state advertisements	263
Paragraph	LSA Type 1: router links	264
Paragraph	LSA Type 1 link types	268
Paragraph	LSA Type 2: network link	269
Figure 7-6	Visualization of Area 1234 with Type 1 and Type 2 LSAs	271
Paragraph	LSA Type 3: summary link	271
Paragraph	LSA Type 3 metric calculations	274
Paragraph	LSA Type 3 topology	275
Paragraph	LSA Type 5: external routes	277
Figure 7-10	OSPF Type 5 LSA flooding	277
Paragraph	LSA Type 4: ASBR summary	279
Figure 7-11	OSPF Type 4 and Type 5 LSA flooding	279
Paragraph	LSA Type 7: NSSA external summary	281
Figure 7-12	OSPF Type 7 LSA advertisement	281
Figure 7-13	Overview of LSA types from a sample topology	284
Paragraph	Stub area	284
Figure 7-14	OSPF Stub area concept	285
Paragraph	Totally stubby areas	287

Key Topic Element	Description	Page Number
Figure 7-15	Totally stubby area concept	287
Paragraph	Not-so-stubby area	289
Figure 7-16	Not-so-stubby area concept	289
Paragraph	Totally not-so-stubby area	292
Figure 7-17	Totally not-so-stubby area concept	292
Paragraph	OSPF path selection	294
Paragraph	Intra-area routes	295
Paragraph	Inter-area routes	296
Paragraph	E1 and N1 external routes	297
Paragraph	E2 and N2 external routes	297
Figure 7-22	LSA reduction through area segmentation	299
Paragraph	Inter-area summarization	301
Paragraph	Summarization of Type 1 LSAs	301
Paragraph	Summarization of discard routes	303
Paragraph	External summarization	303
Paragraph	A discontiguous network	306
Paragraph	Virtual links	307
Paragraph	Locating virtual link endpoints, by RID	307

Define Key Terms

Define the following key terms from this chapter and check your answers in the glossary:

area border router (ABR), backbone area, router LSA, network LSA, summary LSA, ASBR summary LSA, autonomous system border router (ASBR), external LSA, NSSA external LSA, OSPF stub area, OSPF totally stubby area, OSPF not-so-stubby area (NSSA), OSPF totally NSSA, discontiguous network, virtual link

Use the Command Reference to Check Your Memory

The ENARSI 300-410 exam focuses on the practical, hands-on skills that networking professionals use. Therefore, you should be able to identify the commands needed to configure, verify, and troubleshoot the topics covered in this chapter.

This section includes the most important configuration and verification commands covered in this chapter. It might not be necessary to memorize the complete syntax of every command, but you should be able to remember the basic keywords that are needed.

To test your memory of the commands in Table 7-9, go to the companion website and download Appendix B, "Command Reference Exercises." Fill in the missing commands in the tables based on each command description. You can check your work by downloading Appendix C, "Command Reference Exercise Answer Key," from the companion website.

Table 7-9   Command Reference

Task	Command Syntax
Initialize the OSPF process.	**router ospf** *process-id*
Display the generic LSA listings in a router's LSDB and the type and count for each type from an advertising router.	**show ip ospf database**
Display the specific information for a Type 1, 2, 3, 4, 5, or 7 LSA.	**show ip ospf database {router	network	summary	asbr-summary	external	nssa-external}**
Configure all routers in an OSPF area as an OSPF stub area.	**area** *area-id* **stub**
Configure an ABR as a totally stubby area router ABR.	**area** *area-id* **stub no-summary**
Configure all routers in an OSPF area as an OSPF NSSA area	**area** *area-id* **nssa**
Configure an ABR for an NSSA with optional default route injection.	**area** *area-id* **nssa [default-information-originate]**
Configure an ABR as a totally NSSA router ABR.	**area** *area-id* **nssa no-summary**
Modify the OSPF reference bandwidth for dynamic interface metric costing.	**auto-cost reference-bandwidth** *bandwidth-in-mbps*
Statically set the OSPF metric for an interface.	**ip ospf cost** *1-65535*
Configure internal route summarization on the first ABR attached to the source network.	**area** *area-id* range *network subnet-mask* [*advertise	not-advertise*] [*cost metric*]
Configure external route summarization on the ASBR.	**summary-address** *network subnet-mask*
Configure an OSPF virtual link to extend Area 0.	**area** *area-id* **virtual-link** *endpoint-RID*

Troubleshooting OSPFv2

This chapter covers the following topics:

- **Troubleshooting OSPFv2 Neighbor Adjacencies:** This section covers the reasons OSPFv2 neighbor adjacencies sometimes do not form and how to identify them.

- **Troubleshooting OSPFv2 Routes:** This section covers the reasons OSPFv2 routes might be missing from the link-state database (LSDB) and routing table and how to determine why they are missing.

- **Troubleshooting Miscellaneous OSPFv2 Issues:** This section focuses on tracking link-state advertisements (LSAs) through the network, route summarization, discontiguous areas, load balancing, and default routes.

- **OSPFv2 Trouble Tickets:** This section presents three trouble tickets that demonstrate how to use a structured troubleshooting process to solve a reported problem.

The Open Shortest Path First (OSPF) dynamic routing protocol is a link-state routing protocol that uses *Dijkstra's shortest path first (SPF) algorithm*. It is an extremely scalable routing protocol because of its hierarchical design. OSPF can route for both IPv4 and IPv6 protocols. This chapter focuses on troubleshooting OSPFv2; Chapters 9, "OSPFv3," and 10, "Troubleshooting OSPFv3," focus on OSPFv3.

Before any routes are exchanged between OSPF routers on the same LAN or across a WAN, an OSPF neighbor relationship must be formed. There are many reasons a neighbor relationship may not form, and as a troubleshooter, you need to be aware of them. This chapter delves deeply into these reasons and gives you the tools needed to identify them and successfully solve neighbor issues.

Once neighbor relationships are formed, neighboring routers exchange OSPF LSAs, which contain information about routes. In various cases, routes may end up missing, and you need to be able to determine why the routes are missing. This chapter discusses the various ways that OSPF routes could go missing, how to identify the reasons they are missing, and how to solve route-related issues.

In this chapter, you will also learn how to troubleshoot issues related to load balancing, summarization, and discontiguous areas.

"Do I Know This Already?" Quiz

The "Do I Know This Already?" quiz allows you to assess whether you should read this entire chapter thoroughly or jump to the "Exam Preparation Tasks" section. If you are in doubt about your answers to these questions or your own assessment of your knowledge of the topics, read the entire chapter. Table 8-1 lists the major headings in this chapter and their corresponding "Do I Know This Already?" quiz questions. You can find the answers in Appendix A, "Answers to the 'Do I Know This Already?' Quiz Questions."

Table 8-1 "Do I Know This Already?" Foundation Topics Section-to-Question Mapping

Foundation Topics Section	Questions
Troubleshooting OSPFv2 Neighbor Adjacencies	1–5, 7
Troubleshooting OSPFv2 Routes	6, 8
Troubleshooting Miscellaneous OSPFv2 Issues	9, 10

CAUTION The goal of self-assessment is to gauge your mastery of the topics in this chapter. If you do not know the answer to a question or are only partially sure of the answer, you should mark that question as wrong for purposes of self-assessment. Giving yourself credit for an answer that you correctly guess skews your self-assessment results and might provide you with a false sense of security.

1. Which of the following prevent OSPF neighbor relationships from forming? (Choose three.)

   a. Mismatched timers

   b. Mismatched area numbers

   c. Duplicate router IDs

   d. Wrong designated router elected

2. In which OSPF states are you likely to find routers that have an MTU mismatch? (Choose two.)

   a. Init

   b. 2-Way

   c. ExStart

   d. Exchange

3. Which OSPFv2 command enables you to verify the hello interval and the dead interval?

   a. show ip protocols

   b. show ip ospf interface

   c. show ip ospf neighbor

   d. show ip ospf database

4. Which OSPFv2 **debug** command enables you to verify whether area numbers are mismatched?

   a. debug ip ospf hello

   b. debug ip ospf adj

     c. debug ip ospf packet

     d. debug ip ospf events

5. Which OSPF network type is the default on LAN interfaces?

     a. Broadcast

     b. NBMA

     c. Point-to-point

     d. Point-to-multipoint

6. Which LSA type describes routes outside the area but still within the OSPF routing domain (inter-area routes)?

     a. 1

     b. 2

     c. 3

     d. 5

7. Which of the following can prevent an OSPF neighborship from being formed?

     a. A distribute list applied inbound

     b. A distribute list applied outbound

     c. An ACL applied inbound

     d. An ACL applied outbound

8. OSPF neighborships have been successfully formed throughout the entire routing domain. Which of the following are reasons any router may be missing routes in the local LSDB or the local routing table? (Choose two.)

     a. The missing route's network interface has been configured as passive.

     b. There are duplicate router IDs in the routing domain.

     c. There is an outbound distribute list configured.

     d. The spoke is the DR in a hub-and-spoke topology.

9. Which command is used to redistribute a static default route into OSPF?

     a. redistribute static

     b. redistribute ospf 1 subnets

     c. default-information originate

     d. ip route 0.0.0.0 0.0.0.0 110

10. Which of the following are reasons a virtual link might not be forming? (Choose two.)

     a. The router's interface IP address is being used in the **virtual-link** command.

     b. The local area ID is being used in the **virtual-link** command.

     c. The router ID is being used in the **virtual-link** command.

     d. The transit area ID is being used in the **virtual-link** command.

Foundation Topics

Troubleshooting OSPFv2 Neighbor Adjacencies

OSPF establishes neighbor relationships by sending hello packets out interfaces participating in the OSPF process. To enable the OSPF process on an interface and place it in an *OSPF area*, you use the **network** *ip_address wildcard_mask* **area** *area_id* command in router OSPF configuration mode or the **ip ospf** *process_id* **area** *area_id* command in interface configuration mode. For example, the following **network** *ip_address wildcard_mask* **area** *area_id* command enables OSPF on all interfaces with an IP address from 10.1.1.0 through 10.1.1.255 and places them in Area 0: **network 10.1.1.0 0.0.0.255 area 0**. The following interface configuration command enables the OSPF process on the interface and places it in Area 51: **ip ospf 1 area 51**.

Because there are two different ways to enable OSPFv2 on an interface, you must be very careful when troubleshooting neighbor adjacencies so that you are not led down the wrong path, thinking that the OSPF process was not enabled on an interface when in fact it was. You need to check both places. This section focuses on the reasons an OSPF neighbor relationship might not form and how to identify them during the troubleshooting process.

To verify OSPFv2 neighbors, you use the **show ip ospf neighbor** command. Example 8-1 shows sample output of the **show ip ospf neighbor** command. It lists the neighbor ID, which is the router ID (RID) of the neighbor, the priority of the neighbor for the designated router/backup designated router (DR/BDR) election process, the state of the neighbor (covered shortly), and whether the neighbor is a DR, BDR, or DROTHER. In addition, it displays the dead time, which is how long the local router waits until it declares the neighbor down if it does not hear another hello packet within that time. (The default is 40 seconds on a LAN.) You can also see the neighbor's interface IP address from which the hello packet was sent and the local router interface used to reach that neighbor.

Example 8-1   *Verifying OSPF Neighbors with show ip ospf neighbor*

```
R1# show ip ospf neighbor

Neighbor ID  Pri  State      Dead Time  Address     Interface
10.1.23.2    1    FULL/BDR   00:00:37   10.1.12.2   GigabitEthernet1/0
```

When an OSPF neighbor adjacency is successfully formed, you receive a syslog message similar to the following:

```
%OSPF-5-ADJCHG: Process 1, Nbr 10.1.23.2 on GigabitEthernet1/0
from LOADING to FULL, Loading Done
```

The following are some of the reasons an OSPFv2 neighbor relationship might not form:

- **Interface is down:** The interface must be up/up.

- **Interface not running the OSPF process:** If the interface is not enabled for OSPF, it does not send hello packets or form adjacencies.

- **Mismatched timers:** Hello and dead timers must match between neighbors.

- **Mismatched area numbers:** The two ends of a link must be in the same OSPF area.

- **Mismatched area type:** In addition to a normal OSPF area type, an area type could be either a stub area or a not-so-stubby area (NSSA). The routers must agree on the type of area they are in.

- **Different subnets:** Neighbors must be in the same subnet.

- **Passive interface:** The passive interface feature suppresses the sending and receiving of hello packets while still allowing the interface's network to be advertised.

- **Mismatched authentication information:** If one OSPF interface is configured for authentication, the OSPF interface at the other end of the link must be configured with matching authentication information.

- **ACLs:** An ACL may be denying packets to the OSPF multicast address 224.0.0.5.

- **MTU mismatch:** Neighboring interfaces must have matching maximum transmission unit (MTU) values.

- **Duplicate router IDs:** Router IDs must be unique.

- **Mismatched network types:** Based on the OSPF network type characteristics and default values, two neighbors configured with a different OSPF network type might not form an adjacency.

Adjacencies are not established upon the immediate receipt of hello messages. Rather, an adjacency transitions through the various states described in Table 8-2.

Table 8-2 Adjacency States

State	Description
Down	This state indicates that no hellos have been received from a neighbor.
Attempt	This state occurs after a router sends a unicast hello (as opposed to a multicast hello) to a configured neighbor and has not yet received a hello from that neighbor.
Init	This state occurs on a router that has received a hello message from its neighbor; however, the OSPF RID of the receiving router was not contained in the hello message. If a router remains in this state for a long period, something is probably preventing that router from correctly receiving hello packets from the neighboring router.
2-Way	This state occurs when two OSPF routers have received hello messages from each other, and each router saw its own OSPF RID in the hello message it received. The 2-Way state is an acceptable state to stay in between DROTHERs on an Ethernet LAN.
ExStart	This state occurs when the routers forming a full neighbor adjacency decide who will send their routing information first. This is accomplished using the RID. The router with the higher RID becomes the primary, and the other one becomes the secondary. The primary sends the routing information first. In a multi-access network, the DR and BDR have to be determined before this state starts. However, the DR does not have to be the primary because each primary/secondary election is on a per-neighbor basis. If a router remains in this state for a long period, an MTU mismatch could exist between the neighboring routers, or a duplicate OSPF RID might exist.

Exchange	This state occurs when the two routers forming an adjacency send one another database descriptor (DBD) packets containing information about a router's link-state database. Each router compares the DBD packets received from the other router to identify missing entries in its own database. If a router remains in this state for a long period, an MTU mismatch could exist between the neighboring routers.
Loading	Based on the missing link-state database entries identified in the Exchange state, the Loading state occurs when each neighboring router requests the other router to send those missing entries. If a router remains in this state for a long period, a packet might have been corrupted, or a router might have a memory issue. Alternatively, it is possible that such a condition could result from the neighboring routers having an MTU mismatch.
Full	This state indicates that the neighboring OSPF routers have successfully exchanged their link-state information with one another, and an adjacency has been formed.

When an OSPF neighbor relationship does not form, the neighbor is not listed in the *OSPF neighbor table*. Therefore, you need the assistance of an accurate physical and logical network diagram and the **show cdp neighbors** command to verify who should be the neighbors.

When troubleshooting OSPF adjacencies, you need to be aware of how to verify the parameters associated with each of the reasons listed earlier. Let's look at them individually.

Interface Is Down

The interface must be up/up if you plan on forming an OSPF neighbor adjacency. As you learned in previous studies, such as CCNA and ENCORE, you can verify the status of an interface with the **show ip interface brief** command.

Interface Not Running the OSPF Process

If the router OSPF configuration mode **network** *ip_address wildcard_mask* **area** *area_id* command or the **ip ospf** *process_id* **area** *area_id* interface command is misconfigured, OSPF may not be enabled on the proper interfaces. As a result, hello packets are not sent, and neighbor relationships are not formed. You also must specify the OSPF area the interface belongs to. Therefore, if the command is correct except for the area ID, the interface is participating in the OSPF process but in the wrong area. This prevents a neighbor relationship from forming as well. You can verify which interfaces are participating in the OSPF process by using the command **show ip ospf interface brief**, as shown in Example 8-2. In this example, two interfaces are participating in OSPF process 1. They are both in Area 1 and are the designated router interfaces for the multi-access networks. You can also verify the IP addresses and masks of the interfaces, along with the number of full neighbor relationships formed out the interface compared to the total number of neighbors out the interface.

NOTE   Remember that OSPF passive interfaces appear in the output of the **show ip ospf interface brief** command.

Example 8-2   *Verifying OSPF Interfaces with **show ip ospf interface brief***

```
R1# show ip ospf interface brief
Interface    PID    Area          IP Address/Mask     Cost   State    Nbrs F/C
Gi0/0        1      1             10.1.1.1/24         1      DR       0/0
Gi1/0        1      1             10.1.12.1/24        1      DR       1/1
```

The output of **show ip protocols** displays the **network** *ip_address wildcard_mask* **area** *area_id* statements as well as the interfaces that were enabled for OSPF with the **ip ospf** *process_id* **area** *area_id* interface command. Take a look at Example 8-3 and focus on the highlighted text. Notice that it states *Routing for Networks*. Those are *not* the networks you are routing for. You are routing for the networks associated with the interfaces OSPF will be enabled on, based on the **network area** statement. In this case, **10.1.1.1 0.0.0.0 area 1** really means "locate the interface with this IP address and enable it for the OSPF process and place it in Area 1." In addition, you can see which interfaces were explicitly configured to participate in the OSPF process by using the **ip ospf** *process_id* **area** *area_id* interface configuration mode command. In this example, GigabitEthernet1/0 was enabled for OSPF with the **ip ospf 1 area 1** command, and GigabitEthernet0/0 was enabled for OSPF with the **network 10.1.1.1 0.0.0.0 area 1** router OSPF configuration mode command.

Example 8-3   *Verifying OSPF-Enabled Interfaces with **show ip protocols***

```
R1# show ip protocols
*** IP Routing is NSF aware ***

Routing Protocol is "ospf 1"
  Outgoing update filter list for all interfaces is not set
  Incoming update filter list for all interfaces is not set
  Router ID 10.1.12.1
  Number of areas in this router is 1. 1 normal 0 stub 0 nssa
  Maximum path: 4
  Routing for Networks:
    10.1.1.1 0.0.0.0 area 1
  Routing on Interfaces Configured Explicitly (Area 1):
    GigabitEthernet1/0
  Routing Information Sources:
    Gateway         Distance      Last Update
    10.1.23.2       110           00:24:22
  Distance: (default is 110)
```

The **network** *ip_address wildcard_mask* **area** *area_id* command is extremely important, as is the **ip ospf** *process_id* **area** *area_id* command. If either of these commands is mis-configured, interfaces that should be participating in the OSPF process might not be, and interfaces that should not be participating in the OSPF process might be. In addition, it is possible that interfaces might be participating but in the wrong area, preventing neighbor relationships from forming. Therefore, you should be able to recognize issues related to both of these commands.

> **NOTE** If an interface is enabled for OSPF with both the **network** *ip_address wildcard_mask* **area** *area_id* command and the **ip ospf** *process_id* **area** *area_id* command, the **ip ospf** *process_id* **area** *area_id* command takes precedence.

Mismatched Timers

Unlike with Enhanced Interior Gateway Routing Protocol (EIGRP), with OSPF, timers do have to match between neighbors in order for neighbor adjacencies to form. The hello timer defaults to 10 seconds for broadcast and point-to-point network types and 30 seconds for nonbroadcast and point-to-multipoint network types. The dead timer defaults to 40 seconds for broadcast and point-to-point network types and 120 seconds for nonbroadcast and point-to-multipoint network types. To verify the current timers associated with an OSPF interface, issue the **show ip ospf interface** *interface_type interface_number* command, as shown in Example 8-4. In this example, GigabitEthernet1/0 is using the default hello timer of 10 and dead timer of 40. When determining whether timers match, use the spot-the-difference method with the outputs on the two routers.

Example 8-4 *Displaying OSPF Interface Timers on R1 GigabitEthernet1/0*

```
R1# show ip ospf interface gigabitEthernet 1/0
GigabitEthernet1/0 is up, line protocol is up
 Internet Address 10.1.12.1/24, Area 1, Attached via Interface Enable
 Process ID 1, Router ID 10.1.12.1, Network Type BROADCAST, Cost: 1
 Topology-MTID Cost Disabled Shutdown Topology Name
 0 1 no no Base
 Enabled by interface config, including secondary ip addresses
 Transmit Delay is 1 sec, State DR, Priority 1
 Designated Router (ID) 10.1.12.1, Interface address 10.1.12.1
 Backup Designated router (ID) 10.1.23.2, Interface address 10.1.12.2
 Timer intervals configured, Hello 10, Dead 40, Wait 40, Retransmit 5
   oob-resync timeout 40
   Hello due in 00:00:04
 Supports Link-local Signaling (LLS)
 Cisco NSF helper support enabled
 IETF NSF helper support enabled
 Index 1/1, flood queue length 0
 Next 0x0(0)/0x0(0)
 Last flood scan length is 1, maximum is 1
 Last flood scan time is 0 msec, maximum is 4 msec
 Neighbor Count is 1, Adjacent neighbor count is 1
   Adjacent with neighbor 10.1.23.2 (Backup Designated Router)
 Suppress hello for 0 neighbor(s)
```

You can use the **debug ip ospf hello** command when troubleshooting adjacencies to reveal mismatched timers, as shown in Example 8-5. In this example, the packet received (R) has a dead timer of 44 and a hello timer of 11. The local device (C) has a dead timer of 40 and a hello timer of 10.

Example 8-5 *Using debug ip ospf hello to Identify Mismatched Timers*

```
R1# debug ip ospf hello
OSPF hello debugging is on
R1#
OSPF-1 HELLO Gi1/0: Rcv hello from 2.2.2.2 area 1 10.1.12.2
OSPF-1 HELLO Gi1/0: Mismatched hello parameters from 10.1.12.2
OSPF-1 HELLO Gi1/0: Dead R 44 C 40, Hello R 11 C 10 Mask R 255.255.255.0 C
255.255.255.0
R1#
```

 Mismatched Area Numbers

Because OSPF uses the concept of areas, it is an extremely scalable dynamic routing protocol. For OSPF routers to form neighbor adjacencies, their neighboring interfaces must be in the same area. You can verify the area an OSPF interface is part of by using the **show ip ospf interface** *interface_type interface_number* command, as shown in Example 8-6, or the **show ip ospf interface brief** command, as shown in Example 8-7. When determining whether area IDs match, you can use the spot-the-difference method with the output on the two routers.

Example 8-6 *Displaying the OSPF Interface Area by Using the show ip ospf interface interface_type interface_number Command*

```
R1# show ip ospf interface gigabitEthernet 1/0
GigabitEthernet1/0 is up, line protocol is up
 Internet Address 10.1.12.1/24, Area 1, Attached via Interface Enable
 Process ID 1, Router ID 10.1.12.1, Network Type BROADCAST, Cost: 1
 Topology-MTID Cost Disabled Shutdown Topology Name
 0 1 no no Base
 Enabled by interface config, including secondary ip addresses
 Transmit Delay is 1 sec, State DR, Priority 1
 Designated Router (ID) 10.1.12.1, Interface address 10.1.12.1
 Backup Designated router (ID) 10.1.23.2, Interface address 10.1.12.2
 Timer intervals configured, Hello 10, Dead 40, Wait 40, Retransmit 5
   oob-resync timeout 40
   Hello due in 00:00:04
 Supports Link-local Signaling (LLS)
 Cisco NSF helper support enabled
 IETF NSF helper support enabled
 Index 1/1, flood queue length 0
 Next 0x0(0)/0x0(0)
 Last flood scan length is 1, maximum is 1
 Last flood scan time is 0 msec, maximum is 4 msec
 Neighbor Count is 1, Adjacent neighbor count is 1
   Adjacent with neighbor 10.1.23.2 (Backup Designated Router)
 Suppress hello for 0 neighbor(s)
```

Example 8-7 *Displaying the OSPF Interface Area by Using the show ip ospf interface brief Command*

```
R1# show ip ospf interface brief
Interface    PID   Area          IP Address/Mask     Cost   State   Nbrs F/C
Gi1/0         1     1            10.1.12.1/24         1     DR        1/1
```

You can use the **debug ip ospf adj** command when troubleshooting adjacencies to find mismatched area numbers, as shown in Example 8-8. In this example, the packet received has an area ID of 1, and the local interface is participating in Area 2.

Example 8-8 *Using debug ip ospf adj to Identify Mismatched Area Numbers*

```
R1# debug ip ospf adj
OSPF adjacency debugging is on
R1#
OSPF-1 ADJ Gi1/0: Rcv pkt from 10.1.12.2, area 0.0.0.2, mismatched area 0.0.0.1 in
the header
R1# u all
All possible debugging has been turned off
```

Mismatched Area Type

The default OSPF area type is classified as a normal area. However, you can convert a normal area into a stub area or an NSSA area to control the types of *link-state advertisements (LSAs)* that will be sent into the area from an *area border router (ABR)*. For routers within an area to form adjacencies, they must agree on the area type. Within the hello packet, a stub area flag is designed to indicate the type of area the neighbor is in. You can verify the types of areas connected to a router by using the **show ip protocols** command. However, it does not tell you which area is which type. In Example 8-9, which displays the output of **show ip protocols**, there is only one area (Area 1); therefore, you can deduce that it is the stub area. However, for a router with multiple areas connected to it, you can verify the areas and their type by using the **show ip ospf** command, as shown in Example 8-9. In this example, any interface in Area 1 is in a stub area.

Example 8-9 *Determining the Types of OSPF Areas*

```
R1# show ip protocols
*** IP Routing is NSF aware ***

Routing Protocol is "ospf 1"
  Outgoing update filter list for all interfaces is not set
  Incoming update filter list for all interfaces is not set
  Router ID 10.1.12.1
  Number of areas in this router is 1. 0 normal 1 stub 0 nssa
  Maximum path: 4
```

8

```
Routing for Networks:
  10.1.1.1 0.0.0.0 area 1
Routing on Interfaces Configured Explicitly (Area 1):
  GigabitEthernet1/0
Routing Information Sources:
  Gateway         Distance       Last Update
  10.1.23.2       110            00:04:42
Distance: (default is 110)


R1# show ip ospf
Routing Process "ospf 1" with ID 10.1.12.1
Start time: 02:23:19.824, Time elapsed: 02:08:52.184
...output omitted...
Reference bandwidth unit is 100 mbps
 Area 1
  Number of interfaces in this area is 2
  It is a stub area
  Area has no authentication
  SPF algorithm last executed 00:05:46.800 ago
...output omitted...
```

You can use the **debug ip ospf hello** command when troubleshooting adjacencies to find mismatched area types, as shown in Example 8-10. In this example, you can see that the packet received has a mismatched Stub/Transit area option bit.

Example 8-10   *Using debug ip ospf hello to Identify Mismatched Area Types*

```
R1# debug ip ospf hello
OSPF hello debugging is on
R1#
OSPF-1 HELLO Gi1/0: Rcv hello from 2.2.2.2 area 1 10.1.12.2
OSPF-1 HELLO Gi1/0: Hello from 10.1.12.2 with mismatched Stub/Transit area option
bit
R1#
```

Different Subnets

To form an OSPF neighbor adjacency, the router interfaces must be on the same subnet. You can verify this in many ways. The simplest is to look at the interface configuration in the running configuration with the **show running-config interface** *interface_type interface_number* command. Example 8-11 shows the configuration of GigabitEthernet1/0 on R1 and GigabitEthernet0/0 on R2. Are they in the same subnet? Yes! Based on the IP address and the subnet mask, they are both in the 10.1.12.0/24 subnet.

Example 8-11   *Verifying That Neighboring Interfaces Are on the Same Subnet*

```
R1# show running-config interface gigabitEthernet 1/0
Building configuration...

Current configuration : 108 bytes
!
interface GigabitEthernet1/0
 ip address 10.1.12.1 255.255.255.0
 ip ospf 1 area 1
 negotiation auto
end

R2# show running-config interface gigabitEthernet 0/0
Building configuration...

Current configuration : 132 bytes
!
interface GigabitEthernet0/0
 ip address 10.1.12.2 255.255.255.0
 negotiation auto
end
```

Passive Interface

The passive interface feature is important for all organizations. It does two things: reduces the OSPF-related traffic on a network and improves OSPF security.

The passive interface feature turns off the sending and receiving of OSPF packets on an interface while still allowing the interface's network ID to be injected into the OSPF process and advertised to other OSPF neighbors. This ensures that rogue routers that attach to the network will not be able to form adjacencies with your legitimate router on that interface since your router is not sending or receiving OSPF packets on the interface. However, if you configure the wrong interface as passive, a legitimate OSPF neighbor relationship is not formed. As shown in the **show ip protocols** output in Example 8-12, GigabitEthernet0/0 is a passive interface. If there are no passive interfaces, this section does not appear in the output of **show ip protocols**.

Example 8-12   *Verifying Passive Interfaces with **show ip protocols***

```
R1# show ip protocols
*** IP Routing is NSF aware ***

Routing Protocol is "ospf 1"
  Outgoing update filter list for all interfaces is not set
  Incoming update filter list for all interfaces is not set
  Router ID 10.1.12.1
  Number of areas in this router is 1. 0 normal 1 stub 0 nssa
```

8

```
Maximum path: 4
Routing for Networks:
  10.1.1.1 0.0.0.0 area 1
Routing on Interfaces Configured Explicitly (Area 1):
  GigabitEthernet1/0
Passive Interface(s):
  GigabitEthernet0/0
Routing Information Sources:
  Gateway         Distance      Last Update
  10.1.23.2       110           00:00:03
Distance: (default is 110)
```

Mismatched Authentication Information

Authentication is used to ensure that your OSPF routers form neighbor relationships only with legitimate routers and that they accept OSPF packets only from legitimate routers. Therefore, if authentication is implemented, both routers must agree on the settings for a neighbor relationship to form. With authentication, you can use the spot-the-difference method when troubleshooting. OSPF supports three types of authentication:

- **Null:** Known as type 0 and means no authentication

- **Plaintext:** Known as type 1 and sends credentials in plaintext

- **MD5:** Known as type 2 and sends a hash

OSPF authentication can be enabled on an interface-by-interface basis or for all interfaces in an area at the same time. Knowing which commands to use to verify these different authentication configuration options is important. To verify whether authentication has been enabled for the entire area on a router, you use the **show ip ospf** command, as shown in Example 8-13. However, with Message Digest 5 (MD5) authentication, you still have to verify the key ID that is being used on an interface-by-interface basis by using the **show ip ospf interface** *interface_type interface_number* command, as shown in Example 8-14. In addition, you must verify the case-sensitive key string that is being used by using the **show running-config interface** *interface_type interface_number* command.

Example 8-13 *Verifying OSPF Area Authentication*

```
R1# show ip ospf
Routing Process "ospf 1" with ID 10.1.12.1
 Start time: 02:23:19.824, Time elapsed: 02:46:34.488
...output omitted...
 Reference bandwidth unit is 100 mbps
  Area 1
    Number of interfaces in this area is 2
    It is a stub area
    Area has message digest authentication
    SPF algorithm last executed 00:25:12.220 ago
...output omitted...
```

Example 8-14 *Verifying the OSPF Authentication Key*

```
R1# show ip ospf interface gigabitEthernet 1/0
GigabitEthernet1/0 is up, line protocol is up
 Internet Address 10.1.12.1/24, Area 1, Attached via Interface Enable
 ...output omitted...
 Neighbor Count is 0, Adjacent neighbor count is 0
 Suppress hello for 0 neighbor(s)
 Message digest authentication enabled
 Youngest key id is 1
```

> **NOTE** If you configure authentication on an interface-by-interface basis, the output of **show ip ospf** states *Area has no authentication*. Therefore, you need to make sure to check the output of **show ip ospf interface** as well.

You can use the **debug ip ospf adj** command, as shown in Example 8-15, when troubleshooting adjacencies to find mismatched authentication information. In this example, the packet received is using null authentication (type 0), and the local router is using plaintext authentication (type 1).

Example 8-15 *Using debug ip ospf adj to Identify Mismatched Authentication Information*

```
R1# debug ip ospf adj
OSPF adjacency debugging is on
R1#
OSPF-1 ADJ Gi1/0: Rcv pkt from 10.1.12.2 : Mismatched Authentication type. Input
packet specified type 0, we use type 1
R1#
```

ACLs

Access control lists (ACLs) are extremely powerful. How they are implemented determines what they control in a network. If an ACL is applied to an interface, and the ACL is not permitting OSPF packets, a neighbor relationship does not form. To determine whether an ACL is applied to an interface, use the **show ip interface** *interface_type interface_number* command, as shown in Example 8-16. Notice in this example that ACL 100 is applied inbound on interface GigabitEthernet1/0. To verify the ACL 100 entries, issue the command **show access-lists 100**, as shown in Example 8-17. In this case, you can see that ACL 100 is denying OSPF traffic, which prevents a neighbor relationship from forming.

Note that outbound ACLs do not affect OSPF packets. Therefore, if there is an outbound ACL configured on an interface and a neighbor adjacency is not forming, the ACL is not the problem, even though it might be denying OSPF packets, because the outbound ACL does not apply to OSPF packets generated on the local router.

8

Example 8-16   *Verifying ACLs Applied to Interfaces*

```
R1# show ip interface gig 1/0
GigabitEthernet1/0 is up, line protocol is up
 Internet address is 10.1.12.1/24
 Broadcast address is 255.255.255.255
 Address determined by setup command
 MTU is 1500 bytes
 Helper address is not set
 Directed broadcast forwarding is disabled
 Multicast reserved groups joined: 224.0.0.10
 Outgoing access list is not set
 Inbound access list is 100
 Proxy ARP is enabled
 Local Proxy ARP is disabled
 Security level is default
 Split horizon is enabled
```

Example 8-17   *Verifying ACL Entries*

```
R1# show access-lists 100
Extended IP access list 100
 10 deny ospf any any (62 matches)
 20 permit ip any any
```

MTU Mismatch

For OSPF routers to become neighbors and achieve the full adjacency state, the interface of each router forming the adjacency must have exactly the same MTU. If the MTU differs, the routers can see each other but get stuck in the ExStart/Exchange states. In Example 8-18, the output of **show ip ospf neighbor** indicates that R1 is stuck in the Exchange state and that R2 is stuck in the ExStart state.

Example 8-18   *Symptoms of an MTU Mismatch (Stuck in ExStart/Exchange)*

```
R1# show ip ospf neighbor

Neighbor ID   Pri   State         Dead Time   Address       Interface
10.1.23.2     1     EXCHANGE/DR   00:00:38    10.1.12.2     GigabitEthernet1/0

R2# show ip ospf neighbor

Neighbor ID   Pri   State         Dead Time   Address       Interface
10.1.12.1     1     EXSTART/BDR   00:00:37    10.1.12.1     GigabitEthernet0/0
```

In the output of **show ip ospf interface brief**, you can see the Nbrs F/C column without expected values. In Example 8-19, the output shows 0/1 in the Nbrs F/C column, which indicates that there is one neighbor out the interface, but there are zero full adjacencies.

Example 8-19   *Symptoms of an MTU Mismatch (Nbrs Column Values Do Not Match)*

```
R1# show ip ospf interface brief

Interface    PID    Area        IP Address/Mask     Cost   State  Nbrs  F/C
Gi1/0         1      1          10.1.12.1/24         1     BDR          0/1
Gi0/0         1      1          10.1.1.1/24          1     DR           0/0
```

To verify the MTU configured on an interface, issue the **show run interface** *interface_type interface_number* command. As shown in Example 8-20, the MTU of GigabitEthernet1/0 on R1 is 1476, and because nothing is listed in the GigabitEthernet0/0 configuration of R2, it is using the default value, 1500.

Example 8-20   *Verifying the MTU of an Interface*

```
R1# show run interface gigabitEthernet 1/0
Building configuration...

Current configuration : 195 bytes
!
interface GigabitEthernet1/0
 ip address 10.1.12.1 255.255.255.0
 ip mtu 1476
 ip ospf authentication-key CISCO
 ip ospf message-digest-key 1 md5 CISCO
 ip ospf 1 area 1
 negotiation auto
end


R2# show run interface gigabitEthernet 0/0
Building configuration...
Current configuration : 211 bytes
!
interface GigabitEthernet0/0
 ip address 10.1.12.2 255.255.255.0
 ip ospf authentication message-digest
 ip ospf message-digest-key 1 md5 CISCO
 negotiation auto
end
```

8

To solve this issue, you can either manually modify the MTU values of the interfaces so that they match, or you can use the **ip ospf mtu-ignore** interface configuration command, which stops OSPF from comparing the MTU when trying to form an adjacency.

Duplicate Router IDs

RIDs must be unique for many reasons. One of the reasons is that a neighbor relationship does not form between two routers if they have the same RID. When a duplicate RID exists, you receive a syslog message similar to the following:

```
%OSPF-4-DUP_RTRID_NBR: OSPF detected duplicate router-id 10.1.23.2
from 10.1.12.2 on interface GigabitEthernet1/0
```

To verify the RID of an OSPF router, you use the **show ip protocols** command, as shown in Example 8-21. However, almost all OSPF **show** commands display the RID in their output, so you can verify it any way you like. In Example 8-21, the output of **show ip protocols** indicates that the RID of R1 is 10.1.23.2. If you manually change the RID with the **router-id** command in router OSPF configuration mode, you must reset the OSPF process by using the **clear ip ospf process** command in order for it to take effect.

Example 8-21 *Verifying an OSPF RID*

```
R1# show ip protocols
*** IP Routing is NSF aware ***


Routing Protocol is "ospf 1"
 Outgoing update filter list for all interfaces is not set
 Incoming update filter list for all interfaces is not set
 Router ID 10.1.23.2
 Number of areas in this router is 1. 0 normal 1 stub 0 nssa
 Maximum path: 4
 Routing for Networks:
   10.1.1.1 0.0.0.0 area 1
 Routing on Interfaces Configured Explicitly (Area 1):
   GigabitEthernet1/0
 Passive Interface(s):
   Ethernet0/0
   GigabitEthernet0/0
 Routing Information Sources:
   Gateway         Distance      Last Update
   10.1.23.2       110           00:05:31
 Distance: (default is 110)
```

Mismatched Network Types

OSPF supports multiple network types. Different network types have different default values. Therefore, if two OSPF routers that are trying to form a neighbor adjacency are configured with noncompatible network types, a neighbor relationship does not form. For example, if the network type is Broadcast on R1's interface and NBMA on R2's interface, the timers do not match, and the adjacency does not form. Table 8-3 lists the OSPF network types and their characteristics.

Table 8-3   OSPF Network Types and Characteristics

Type	Default	Neighbors	DR/BDR	Timers
Broadcast	Default on LAN interfaces	Discovered automatically	DR and BDR elected automatically	Hello: 10 Dead: 40
NBMA (nonbroadcast)	Default on Frame Relay main and point-to-multipoint interfaces	Statically configured	DR must be manually configured on the hub router	Hello: 30 Dead: 120
Point-to-point	Default on point-to-point serial and point-to-point Frame Relay subinterfaces	Discovered automatically	No DR or BDR	Hello: 10 Dead: 40
Point-to-multipoint	(Not a default) Optimal for hub-and-spoke topologies (Frame Relay)	Discovered automatically	No DR or BDR	Hello: 30 Dead: 120
Point-to-multipoint nonbroadcast	(Not a default) Optimal for hub-and-spoke topologies (Frame Relay) that do not support broadcast or multicast traffic	Statically configured	No DR or BDR	Hello: 30 Dead: 120

To determine the network type associated with an OSPF-enabled interface, you can issue the command **show ip ospf interface** *interface_type interface_number*. In Example 8-22, R1's interface GigabitEthernet 1/0 is using the OSPF network type Broadcast. You can use the spot-the-difference troubleshooting method to determine whether the network types match.

Example 8-22   *Verifying OSPF Network Type*

```
R1# show ip ospf interface gigabitEthernet 1/0
GigabitEthernet1/0 is up, line protocol is up
 Internet Address 10.1.12.1/24, Area 1, Attached via Interface Enable
 Process ID 1, Router ID 10.1.12.1, Network Type BROADCAST, Cost: 1
 Topology-MTID Cost Disabled Shutdown Topology Name
 0 1 no no Base
 Enabled by interface config, including secondary ip addresses
 Transmit Delay is 1 sec, State BDR, Priority 1
 Designated Router (ID) 10.1.23.2, Interface address 10.1.12.2
 Backup Designated router (ID) 10.1.12.1, Interface address 10.1.12.1
 Timer intervals configured, Hello 10, Dead 40, Wait 40, Retransmit 5
   oob-resync timeout 40
   Hello due in 00:00:07
 Supports Link-local Signaling (LLS)
```

8

```
Cisco NSF helper support enabled
IETF NSF helper support enabled
Index 1/1, flood queue length 0
Next 0x0(0)/0x0(0)
Last flood scan length is 1, maximum is 1
Last flood scan time is 4 msec, maximum is 4 msec
Neighbor Count is 1, Adjacent neighbor count is 1
  Adjacent with neighbor 10.1.23.2 (Designated Router)
Suppress hello for 0 neighbor(s)
Message digest authentication enabled
Youngest key id is 1
```

Troubleshooting OSPFv2 Routes

OSPF routers receive LSAs from every router within the same area, meaning they learn about routes directly from the source within the same area. As a result, the LSAs must be flooded through the area. This is mandatory because every router in an area must have exactly the same *link-state database (LSDB)* for that area. This makes troubleshooting missing OSPF routes more difficult than with distance vector routing protocols because it is harder to follow the path, especially in a multi-area OSPF domain.

This section examines the reasons OSPF routes might be missing and how to determine the reason a route is missing.

As discussed earlier, neighbor relationships are the foundation of OSPF information sharing. If you have no neighbors, you will not learn any routes. So, besides the lack of a neighbor, what would be reasons for missing routes in an OSPF network?

Following is a list of some common reasons OSPF routes might be missing from either the LSDB or the routing table:

- **Interface not running the OSPF process:** If the interface is not participating in the OSPF process, the network the interface is part of is not injected into the OSPF process and is therefore not advertised to neighbors.

- **Better source of information:** If exactly the same network is learned from a more reliable source, it is used instead of the OSPF-learned information.

- **Route filtering:** A filter might be preventing a route from being installed in the routing table.

- **Stub area configuration:** If the wrong type of stub area is chosen, you might be receiving a default route instead of the actual route.

- **Interface is shut down:** The OSPF-enabled interface must be up/up for the network associated with the interface to be advertised.

- **Wrong designated router elected:** In a hub-and-spoke environment, if the wrong router is the DR, routes are not exchanged properly.

■ **Duplicate RIDs:** If there are two or more routers with the same RID, routes are missing in the topology.

The following sections examine each of these reasons individually and explain how to recognize them in the troubleshooting process.

Interface Not Running the OSPF Process

As discussed earlier, when you use the **network** *ip_address wildcard_mask* **area** *area_id* command or the **ip ospf** *process_id* **area** *area_id* interface command, the OSPF process is enabled on interfaces. OSPF then takes the network/subnet the interface is part of and injects it into the LSDB so that it can be advertised to other routers in the autonomous system. Therefore, even interfaces that do not form neighbor relationships with other routers need to be participating in the OSPF process for the interface's network ID to be advertised.

As discussed earlier in this chapter, the output of **show ip protocols** displays the **network** *ip_address wildcard_mask* **area** *area_id* command in addition to the interfaces that were explicitly configured with the **ip ospf** *process_id* **area** *area_id* interface command. Focus on the highlighted text in Example 8-23. Notice that it states *Routing for Networks*. Those are *not* the networks you are routing for. You are routing for the networks associated with the interface on which OSPF will be enabled, based on the **network** statement. So, **10.1.1.1 0.0.0.0 area 1** means to enable OSPF on the interface with the IP address 10.1.1.1 and place it in Area 1. You can then route for the network associated with that interface. Also, you can see that GigabitEthernet1/0 was explicitly configured to participate in the OSPF process; therefore, OSPF routes for the network associated with that interface as well.

Example 8-23 *Verifying OSPF-Enabled Interfaces with **show ip protocols***

```
R1# show ip protocols
*** IP Routing is NSF aware ***


Routing Protocol is "ospf 1"
  Outgoing update filter list for all interfaces is not set
  Incoming update filter list for all interfaces is not set
  Router ID 10.1.12.1
  Number of areas in this router is 1. 1 normal 0 stub 0 nssa
  Maximum path: 4
  Routing for Networks:
    10.1.1.1 0.0.0.0 area 1
  Routing on Interfaces Configured Explicitly (Area 1):
    GigabitEthernet1/0
  Passive Interface(s):
    Ethernet0/0
    GigabitEthernet0/0
  Routing Information Sources:
    Gateway         Distance      Last Update
    10.1.23.2       110           01:00:43
    10.1.23.3       110           01:00:43
  Distance: (default is 110)
```

So, what networks are you actually routing for? You're routing for the networks associated with the interfaces that are now enabled for OSPF. In Example 8-24, you can see the output of the **show ip interface** command on R1 for Gi0/0 and Gi1/0, which was piped to include only the **Internet** address. Notice that the addresses are in a /24 network. As a result, the network IDs are 10.1.1.0/24 and 10.1.12.0/24. *Those are the networks you are routing for.*

Example 8-24   *Verifying Network IDs with* **show ip interface**

```
R1# show ip interface gi0/0 | i Internet
 Internet address is 10.1.1.1/24
R1# show ip interface gi1/0 | i Internet
 Internet address is 10.1.12.1/24
```

Better Source of Information

For an OSPF-learned route to be installed in the routing table, it must be the most believable routing source. Recall that believability is based on administrative distance (AD). OSPF's AD is 110 for all learned routes: intra, inter, and external. Therefore, if there is another source that is educating the same router about exactly the same network and that source has a better AD, the source with the better AD wins, and its information is installed in the routing table. Example 8-25 shows only the OSPF-installed routes in the router. Notice that there is no OSPF entry for the networks 10.1.1.0/24 and 10.1.12.0/24.

Example 8-25   *Sample* **show ip route ospf** *Command Output*

```
R1# show ip route ospf
Codes: L - local, C - connected, S - static, R - RIP, M - mobile, B - BGP
 D - EIGRP, EX - EIGRP external, O - OSPF, IA - OSPF inter area
 N1 - OSPF NSSA external type 1, N2 - OSPF NSSA external type 2
 E1 - OSPF external type 1, E2 - OSPF external type 2
 i - IS-IS, su - IS-IS summary, L1 - IS-IS level-1, L2 - IS-IS level-2
 ia - IS-IS inter area, * - candidate default, U - per-user static route
 o - ODR, P - periodic downloaded static route, H - NHRP, l - LISP
 + - replicated route, % - next hop override

Gateway of last resort is 10.1.12.2 to network 0.0.0.0

O*E2 0.0.0.0/0 [110/1] via 10.1.12.2, 01:15:29, GigabitEthernet1/0
 10.0.0.0/8 is variably subnetted, 6 subnets, 2 masks
O IA 10.1.3.0/24 [110/3] via 10.1.12.2, 01:15:29, GigabitEthernet1/0
O IA 10.1.23.0/24 [110/2] via 10.1.12.2, 01:15:29, GigabitEthernet1/0
O IA 203.0.113.0/24 [110/3] via 10.1.12.2, 01:15:29, GigabitEthernet1/0
```

In this case, there is a better source for the 10.1.1.0/24 and 10.1.12.0/24 networks. Example 8-26 displays the output of the **show ip route 10.1.1.0 255.255.255.0** command. It identifies that this network is directly connected and has an AD of 0. Because a directly connected network has an AD of 0 and an OSPF route has an AD of 110, the directly connected source is installed in the routing table.

Example 8-26 *Sample show ip route 10.1.1.0 255.255.255.0 Command Output*

```
R1# show ip route 10.1.1.0 255.255.255.0
Routing entry for 10.1.1.0/24
 Known via "connected", distance 0, metric 0 (connected, via interface)
 Routing Descriptor Blocks:
 * directly connected, via GigabitEthernet0/0
 Route metric is 0, traffic share count is 1
```

You might be questioning whether 10.1.1.0/24 is in the LSDB because it is directly connected. Remember that when an interface is participating in the routing process, its network
is injected into the LSDB as a Type 1 (router) LSA. You can verify this with the **show ip ospf
database** command, as shown in Example 8-27. However, there is no listing for 10.1.1.0/24 in
this example. This is because you are only looking at a summary of the LSAs in the LSDB.
If you want to see the specifics of the LSA, you have to open them up. Example 8-28 shows
the output of **show ip ospf database router 10.1.12.1**. This command opens the Type 1
(router) LSA advertised by the router with the RID 10.1.12.1, which is R1. It shows that
10.1.1.0/24 is in the LSDB and therefore can be advertised in the OSPF process.

Example 8-27 *Output of show ip ospf database on R1*

```
R1# show ip ospf database

            OSPF Router with ID (10.1.12.1) (Process ID 1)

               Router Link States (Area 1)

Link ID         ADV Router      Age       Seq#          Checksum Link count
10.1.12.1       10.1.12.1       1025      0x80000009    0x006B41 2
10.1.23.2       10.1.23.2       1210      0x8000002D    0x00E7A3 1

               Net Link States (Area 1)

Link ID         ADV Router      Age       Seq#          Checksum
10.1.12.2       10.1.23.2       1210      0x80000007    0x00B307

               Summary Net Link States (Area 1)

Link ID         ADV Router      Age       Seq#          Checksum
10.1.3.0        10.1.23.2       1210      0x80000004    0x00D72E
10.1.23.0       10.1.23.2       1210      0x8000001A    0x00C418
203.0.113.0     10.1.23.2       1210      0x80000004    0x004E88

               Summary ASB Link States (Area 1)
Link ID         ADV Router      Age       Seq#          Checksum
10.1.23.3       10.1.23.2       1210      0x80000003    0x00C629
               Type-5 AS External Link States

Link ID         ADV Router      Age       Seq#          Checksum Tag
0.0.0.0         10.1.23.3       1268      0x80000003    0x00B399 1
```

Example 8-28 *Output of show ip ospf database router 10.1.12.1 on R1*

```
R1# show ip ospf database router 10.1.12.1

          OSPF Router with ID (10.1.12.1) (Process ID 1)

             Router Link States (Area 1)

  LS age: 1368
  Options: (No TOS-capability, DC)
  LS Type: Router Links
  Link State ID: 10.1.12.1
  Advertising Router: 10.1.12.1
  LS Seq Number: 80000009
  Checksum: 0x6B41
  Length: 48
  Number of Links: 2

    Link connected to: a Transit Network
     (Link ID) Designated Router address: 10.1.12.2
     (Link Data) Router Interface address: 10.1.12.1
       Number of MTID metrics: 0
        TOS 0 Metrics: 1

    Link connected to: a Stub Network
     (Link ID) Network/subnet number: 10.1.1.0
     (Link Data) Network Mask: 255.255.255.0
       Number of MTID metrics: 0
        TOS 0 Metrics: 1
```

Using a suboptimal source of routing information may not cause users to complain or submit a trouble ticket because they will probably still be able to access the resources they need. However, it might cause suboptimal routing in your network. Figure 8-1 shows a network running two different routing protocols. In this case, which path will be used to send traffic from PC1 to 10.1.1.0/24? If you said the longer EIGRP path, you are correct. Even though it is quicker to use the OSPF path, EIGRP wins by default because it has the lower AD, and suboptimal routing occurs.

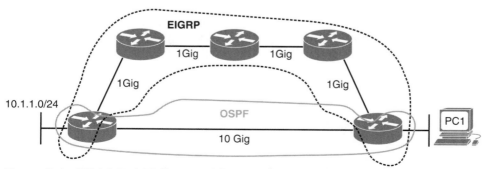

Figure 8-1 *Which Path Will Be Used from PC1 to 10.1.1.0/24?*

Being able to recognize when a certain routing source should be used and when it should not be used is key to optimizing your network and reducing the number of trouble-shooting instances related to the network being perceived as being slow. In this case, you might want to consider increasing the AD of EIGRP or lowering the AD of OSPF to optimize routing.

Route Filtering

A distribute list applied to an OSPF process controls which routes are installed into the routing table from the LSDB. Note that this differs from EIGRP, where the distribute list controls routes sent and received between neighbors. The reason this difference exists is that all OSPF routers in an area must have the same LSDB. If you were able to control the routes sent to and received from neighbors, the LSDB would not be the same among the routers in the area, which is not permitted.

To apply a route filter to OSPF, the distribute list is applied in OSPF configuration mode inbound (meaning into the routing table), and the routes installed are controlled by ACLs, prefix lists, or route maps. Therefore, when troubleshooting route filtering for OSPF, you need to consider the following:

- Is the distribute list applied in the correct direction?

- If the distribute list is using an ACL, is the ACL correct?

- If the distribute list is using a prefix list, is the prefix list correct?

- If the distribute list is using a route map, is the route map correct?

The **show ip protocols** command identifies whether a distribute list is applied to the OSPF process, as shown in Example 8-29. This example indicates that there are no outbound filters and that there is an inbound filter that is referencing the prefix list called TEST.

Example 8-29 *Verifying Route Filters with **show ip protocols***

```
R1# show ip protocols
*** IP Routing is NSF aware ***


Routing Protocol is "ospf 1"
  Outgoing update filter list for all interfaces is not set
  Incoming update filter list for all interfaces is (prefix-list) TEST
Router ID 10.1.12.1
  Number of areas in this router is 1. 1 normal 0 stub 0 nssa
  Maximum path: 4
  Routing for Networks:
    10.1.1.1 0.0.0.0 area 1
  Routing on Interfaces Configured Explicitly (Area 1):
    GigabitEthernet1/0
```

8

```
 Passive Interface(s):
   Ethernet0/0
   GigabitEthernet0/0
 Routing Information Sources:
     Gateway         Distance       Last Update
     10.1.23.2       110            00:00:20
     10.1.23.3       110            00:00:20
 Distance: (default is 110)
```

The inbound filter in Example 8-29 is filtered by prefix list TEST. To verify the entries in this prefix list, you issue the **show ip prefix-list TEST** command, as shown in Example 8-30. If an ACL is applied, you issue the **show access-list** command. If a route map is applied, you issue the **show route-map** command.

You can verify the command that was used to apply the distribute list in the running configuration as shown in Example 8-30.

Example 8-30 *Verifying the OSPF Distribute List and Prefix List*

```
R1# show ip prefix-list TEST
ip prefix-list TEST: 2 entries
 seq 5 deny 10.1.23.0/24
 seq 10 permit 0.0.0.0/0 le 32


R1# show run | section router ospf 1
router ospf 1
 area 1 authentication message-digest
 passive-interface default
 no passive-interface GigabitEthernet1/0
 network 10.1.1.1 0.0.0.0 area 1
 distribute-list prefix TEST in
```

Notice in Example 8-31 that the LSDB still has the 10.1.23.0/24 network listed, but it is not installed in the routing table because of the distribute list that is denying 10.1.23.0/24 from being installed.

Example 8-31 *Verifying OSPF Routes and LSDB After a Distribute List Is Applied*

```
R1# show ip ospf database

            OSPF Router with ID (10.1.12.1) (Process ID 1)

            Router Link States (Area 1)

Link ID         ADV Router      Age      Seq#        Checksum Link count
10.1.12.1       10.1.12.1       16       0x80000011  0x005B49 2
```

```
10.1.23.2        10.1.23.2        13         0x80000033 0x00DBA9 1


               Net Link States (Area 1)


Link ID          ADV Router       Age        Seq#        Checksum
10.1.12.2        10.1.23.2        12         0x8000000D  0x00A70D


               Summary Net Link States (Area 1)


Link ID          ADV Router       Age        Seq#        Checksum
10.1.3.0         10.1.23.2        16         0x80000002  0x00DB2C
10.1.23.0        10.1.23.2        16         0x80000002  0x00F4FF
203.0.113.0      10.1.23.2        16         0x80000002  0x005286


               Summary ASB Link States (Area 1)


Link ID          ADV Router       Age        Seq#        Checksum
10.1.23.3        10.1.23.2        18         0x80000001  0x00CA27


               Type-5 AS External Link States


Link ID          ADV Router       Age        Seq#        Checksum Tag
0.0.0.0          10.1.23.3        779        0x80000005  0x00AF9B 1


R1# show ip route
...output omitted...


Gateway of last resort is 10.1.12.2 to network 0.0.0.0


O*E2 0.0.0.0/0 [110/1] via 10.1.12.2, 00:00:02, GigabitEthernet1/0
 10.0.0.0/8 is variably subnetted, 5 subnets, 2 masks
C 10.1.1.0/24 is directly connected, GigabitEthernet0/0
L 10.1.1.1/32 is directly connected, GigabitEthernet0/0
O IA 10.1.3.0/24 [110/3] via 10.1.12.2, 00:00:02, GigabitEthernet1/0
C 10.1.12.0/24 is directly connected, GigabitEthernet1/0
L 10.1.12.1/32 is directly connected, GigabitEthernet1/0
O IA 203.0.113.0/24 [110/3] via 10.1.12.2, 00:00:02, GigabitEthernet1/0
```

Stub Area Configuration

Because all routers in an area need to have the same LSDB, you cannot manipulate the LSAs within an area; however, you can manipulate LSAs that are flowing between areas by using the stub and NSSA OSPF features.

When you create *stub areas* or *NSSAs*, you suppress Type 5 LSAs from entering an area at the ABR. With *totally stubby areas* and *totally NSSAs*, you suppress Type 5 and Type 3 LSAs from entering an area at the ABR. The routes that would have been learned from the Type 5 and Type 3 LSAs in the area are now replaced by a default route. Because there is a default route, the router has lost visibility of the overall network, and this could produce suboptimal routing if not implemented correctly in highly redundant environments.

As a result, if you are expecting a Type 5 or Type 3 LSA for a specific route, but it is not showing up in the area, you should verify whether the area is a stub area or an NSSA and determine what types of routes are being suppressed. You can verify whether the area connected to the router is a stub area or an NSSA by using the **show ip ospf** command, as shown in Example 8-32.

Example 8-32 *Determining the Types of OSPF Areas*

```
R1# show ip ospf
 Routing Process "ospf 1" with ID 10.1.12.1
 Start time: 02:23:19.824, Time elapsed: 02:08:52.184
 ...output omitted...
 Reference bandwidth unit is 100 mbps
  Area 1
   Number of interfaces in this area is 2
   It is a stub area
   Area has no authentication
   SPF algorithm last executed 00:05:46.800 ago
 ...output omitted...
```

However, remember that when implementing totally stubby areas or totally NSSAs, you are configuring the **no-summary** keyword only on the ABR. It is not needed on the other routers. Therefore, it is best to review the output of **show ip ospf** on the ABR, as shown in Example 8-33. In this example, R2 is configured to suppress Type 3 and Type 5 LSAs from entering Area 1. It replaces them with a default route with a cost of 1. So, even though R1 appears to be in a stub area, it is really in a totally stubby area, based on the configuration of R2.

Example 8-33 *Determining the Type of OSPF Area on the ABR*

```
R2# show ip ospf
 Routing Process "ospf 1" with ID 10.1.23.2
  Start time: 02:39:09.376, Time elapsed: 15:19:40.352
 ...output omitted...
  Flood list length 0
  Area 1
   Number of interfaces in this area is 1
   It is a stub area, no summary LSA in this area
   Generates stub default route with cost 1
   Area has no authentication
 ...output omitted...
```

Interface Is Shut Down

As discussed earlier, when the OSPF process is enabled on an interface, the network the interface is part of (that is, the directly connected entry in the routing table) is injected into the OSPF process. If the interface is shut down, there is no directly connected entry for the network in the routing table. Therefore, the network does not exist, and no network can be injected into the OSPF process. The interface must be up/up for routes to be advertised or for neighbor relationships to be formed.

Wrong Designated Router Elected

A multi-access network can have multiple routers residing on a common network segment. Rather than having all routers form a full mesh of adjacencies with one another, a *designated router (DR)* is elected, and all other routers on the segment form a full adjacency with the DR, as illustrated in Figure 8-2. The rest of the routers form a 2-Way adjacency with each other, and if a *backup designated router (BDR)* exists, they form a full adjacency with the BDR as well.

A DR is elected based on router priority, with larger priority values being preferable. If routers have equal priorities, the DR is elected based on the highest OSPF RID. A BDR is also elected based on the same criteria. Routers on the multi-access network form full adjacencies with the BDR in case the DR becomes unavailable.

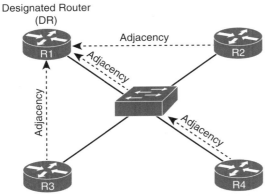

Figure 8-2 *DR Election in an Ethernet Network*

It does not matter which router is elected as the DR in a multi-access Ethernet topology or a full-mesh Frame Relay topology because every router is able to reach the DR since the Layer 2 topology lines up with the Layer 3 addressing. However, over a hub-and-spoke non-broadcast multi-access (NBMA) network such as Frame Relay or with a Dynamic Multipoint VPN (DMVPN), it does matter who the DR is because the underlying Layer 2 topology does not line up with the Layer 3 addressing.

Figure 8-3 shows a hub-and-spoke Frame Relay or DMVPN network. The multipoint interface (single physical interface or mGRE [Multipoint Generic Routing Encapsulation] tunnel interface) provides connectivity to multiple routers in the same subnet out the single interface, as Ethernet does. However, in this case, the Layer 2 topology is not the same as the Layer 3 topology. The Layer 3 topology indicates that all routers are directly reachable out the interfaces (on the same subnet). The Layer 2 topology says otherwise. You cannot directly reach R2 from R3 and vice versa. You must go through R1.

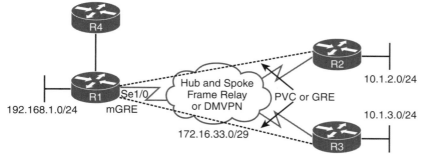

Figure 8-3 *Hub-and-Spoke Topology*

Figure 8-4 shows the wrong DR placement. The DR router needs to be reachable through a single hop because of how OSPF neighbor relationships are formed and how routers communicate with the DR. Hellos are established with the multicast address 224.0.0.5, and the DR is reachable at the multicast address 224.0.0.6. Packets destined to these two multicast addresses are not relayed by other routers. Because the DR is responsible for relaying learned routes in a multi-access network, it needs to be centrally located. Therefore, if R2 were the DR, R3 would not be able to form an adjacency with it because R1 does not relay the hello packet. Therefore, R3 cannot communicate with the DR, which means it cannot tell the DR about the 10.1.3.0 network, and as a result, no other router learns about the 10.1.3.0/24 network.

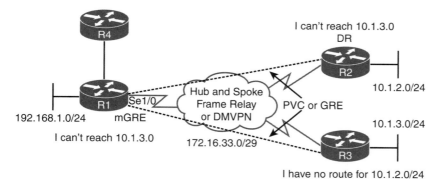

Figure 8-4 *Wrong DR Placement*

In this case, you need to control who the DR is. It must be R1 to ensure that all routers are able to send LSAs to it and receive LSAs from it, as shown in Figure 8-5.

To verify the DR placement, issue the command **show ip ospf interface** *interface_type interface_number* on each of the routers. Example 8-34 indicates that R1 considers the router with the RID 3.3.3.3 as the DR at interface 172.16.33.6. R2 considers itself the DR and R1 the BDR. R3 considers itself a DR and R1 a BDR. Therefore, there are two DRs in this hub-and-spoke environment. As a result, routes are not successfully learned by all routers in the topology.

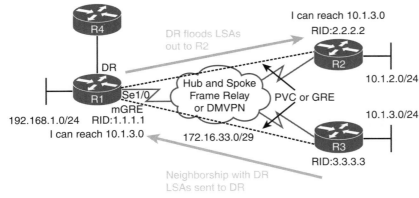

Figure 8-5 *Correct DR Placement*

Example 8-34 *Verifying the DR*

```
R1# show ip ospf interface ser 1/0
Serial1/0 is up, line protocol is up
 Internet Address 172.16.33.4/29, Area 0, Attached via Network Statement
 Process ID 1, Router ID 1.1.1.1, Network Type NON_BROADCAST, Cost: 64
 Topology-MTID Cost Disabled Shutdown Topology Name
        0         64      no      no       Base
 Transmit Delay is 1 sec, State BDR, Priority 1
 Designated Router (ID) 3.3.3.3, Interface address 172.16.33.6
 Backup Designated router (ID) 1.1.1.1, Interface address 172.16.33.4
 Timer intervals configured, Hello 30, Dead 120, Wait 120, Retransmit 5
...output omitted...


R2# show ip ospf interface ser 1/0
Serial1/0 is up, line protocol is up
 Internet Address 172.16.33.5/29, Area 0, Attached via Network Statement
 Process ID 1, Router ID 2.2.2.2, Network Type NON_BROADCAST, Cost: 64
 Topology-MTID Cost Disabled Shutdown Topology Name
        0         64      no      no       Base
 Transmit Delay is 1 sec, State DR, Priority 1
 Designated Router (ID) 2.2.2.2, Interface address 172.16.33.5
 Backup Designated router (ID) 1.1.1.1, Interface address 172.16.33.4
 Timer intervals configured, Hello 30, Dead 120, Wait 120, Retransmit 5
...output omitted...
R3# show ip ospf interface ser 1/0
Serial1/0 is up, line protocol is up
 Internet Address 172.16.33.6/29, Area 0, Attached via Network Statement
 Process ID 1, Router ID 3.3.3.3, Network Type NON_BROADCAST, Cost: 64
 Topology-MTID Cost Disabled Shutdown Topology Name
        0         64      no      no       Base
```

```
Transmit Delay is 1 sec, State DR, Priority 1
Designated Router (ID) 3.3.3.3, Interface address 172.16.33.6
Backup Designated router (ID) 1.1.1.1, Interface address 172.16.33.4
Timer intervals configured, Hello 30, Dead 120, Wait 120, Retransmit 5
...output omitted...
```

To fix this issue, you need to force R1 to be the DR by preventing R2 and R3 from ever wanting to be a DR. On R2 and R3, you go to interface configuration mode and set the OSPF priority to 0, as shown in Example 8-35.

Example 8-35   *Changing OSPF Priority on Spokes*

```
R2# config t
R2(config)# int ser 1/0
R2(config-if)# ip ospf priority 0


R3# config t
R3(config)# int ser 1/0
R3(config-if)# ip ospf priority 0
```

Now the output of **show ip ospf interface ser 1/0** on R1, as shown in Example 8-36, indicates that it is the DR and that there are no BDRs because you never want a spoke to back up the DR as it would cause the problem discussed earlier.

Example 8-36   *Verifying That the Hub Router Is the DR*

```
R1# show ip ospf interface ser 1/0
Serial1/0 is up, line protocol is up
 Internet Address 172.16.33.4/29, Area 0, Attached via Network Statement
 Process ID 1, Router ID 1.1.1.1, Network Type NON_BROADCAST, Cost: 64
 Topology-MTID Cost Disabled Shutdown Topology Name
        0       64     no       no       Base
 Transmit Delay is 1 sec, State DR, Priority 1
 Designated Router (ID) 1.1.1.1, Interface address 172.16.33.4
 No backup designated router on this network
 Old designated Router (ID) 3.3.3.3, Interface address 172.16.33.6
 ...output omitted...
```

Duplicate Router IDs

The RID uniquely identifies the routers in the OSPF domain. Because the RID is used during the formation of neighbor relationships and to determine which router is advertising a specific LSA, it is imperative that the RIDs in the domain are unique. If there are duplicate RIDs, the network issues can vary. For example, in the same area, the routers are going to see a Type 1 router LSA about networks they do not know about from an RID the same as theirs. Therefore, they think they generated the LSA, and a router does not use information contained in an LSA it receives with the same RID as theirs. However, the LSA is not from itself; it just has the same RID, and as a result, you have missing routes on various routers in the domain.

In Figure 8-6, the Type 1 router LSA from R1 is ignored by R3 because the LSA has the same RID as R3, and so R3 thinks it is its own LSA. Therefore, R3 does not learn about 10.1.1.0/24. Similarly, R1 does not learn about 10.1.3.0/24 because it is ignoring the LSA that R3 sent because it has the same RID.

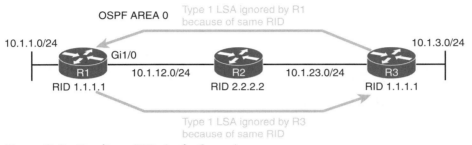

Figure 8-6 *Duplicate RIDs in the Same Area*

Having duplicate RIDs in different areas would cause the physical OSPF topology to be different from the way the SPF algorithm sees it. Figure 8-7 shows an OSPF domain with duplicate RIDs in different areas. R1 and R4 both have RID 1.1.1.1. As you can see, R2 sees the router with the RID in both Area 0 and Area 1 (which to R2 is technically the same router, but in this case, physically it is not). This can cause routing issues because some routes may not be passed between areas, causing the LSDB and the routing tables to be incomplete.

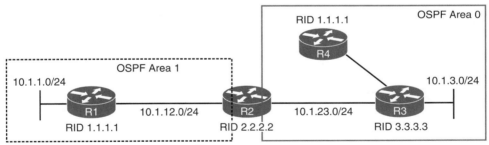

Figure 8-7 *Duplicate RIDs in Different Areas*

In both of the above examples, you may experience an OSPF flood war and receive syslog messages indicating that. A flood war occurs because the routers receive LSAs associated with their RID, but they don't "own" those networks; the other router with the duplicate RID does. Therefore, the router wants to correct this problem, and it sends out an LSA with its RID and its "owned" networks. When the other router with the duplicate RID gets the LSA, it does not agree with the information, and it sends out an LSA with its "owned" networks. This happens over and over and over again until you make the RIDs unique. If you have exhausted all possible reasons routes might not be appearing in the LSDB or the routing table, look at the RIDs of the routers by using the **show ip protocols** command, as shown in Example 8-37.

Example 8-37   *Verifying OSPF RID*

```
R1# show ip protocols
*** IP Routing is NSF aware ***

Routing Protocol is "ospf 1"
 Outgoing update filter list for all interfaces is not set
 Incoming update filter list for all interfaces is not set
 Router ID 1.1.1.1
 Number of areas in this router is 1. 0 normal 1 stub 0 nssa
 Maximum path: 4
...output omitted...
```

Troubleshooting Miscellaneous OSPFv2 Issues

So far, the focus in this chapter has been on troubleshooting issues related to OSPFv2 neighbor relationships and routes. This section looks at tracking LSAs through the network, route summarization, discontiguous areas, load balancing, and default routes.

Tracking OSPF Advertisements Through a Network

When troubleshooting an OSPF issue and trying to determine why certain entries are in a router's LSDB, tracking the path of OSPF advertisements can be valuable. For example, notice network 192.168.1.0/24 in the topology provided in Figure 8-8 and consider how this network is entered into the LSDB of the other OSPF routers.

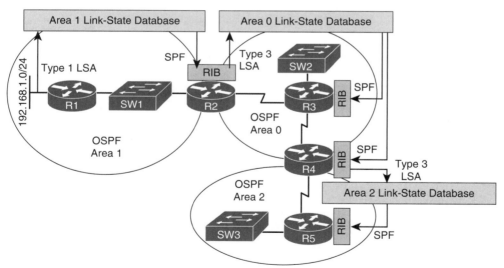

Figure 8-8   *Tracking an OSPF Advertisement*

The following steps describe how network 192.168.1.0/24, which is directly connected to router R1, is learned by the LSDBs of routers R2, R3, R4, and R5:

Step 1.   Router R1 creates a Type 1 router LSA for the 192.168.1.0/24 network in the Area 1 LSDB and floods it into Area 1.

Step 2. Router R2 receives the router LSA for 192.168.1.0/24 and places it in the Area 1 LSDB. R2 runs the shortest path first (SPF) algorithm to determine the best path through Area 1 to reach the 192.168.1.0/24 network. The best result is placed in R2's routing table (RIB).

Step 3. Router R2 informs Area 0 routers about network 192.168.1.0/24 by injecting a Type 3 LSA about the network into the LSDB of Area 0 and flooding it into Area 0. This LSA includes the cost to reach the 192.168.1.0/24 network, from the perspective of router R2.

Step 4. Each of the other Area 0 routers (that is, routers R3 and R4) receives the Type 3 LSA and adds it to its Area 0 LSDB. These routers run the SPF algorithm to determine the cost to reach router R2. This cost is then added to the cost router R2 advertised in its Type 3 LSA, and the result is stored in the RIBs for routers R3 and R4.

Step 5. Router R4 informs Area 2 routers about network 192.168.1.0/24 by injecting a Type 3 LSA about the network into the LSDB of Area 2 and flooding it into Area 2. This LSA includes the cost to reach the 192.168.1.0/24 network, from the perspective of router R4.

Step 6. Each of the routers in Area 2 receives the Type 3 LSA and adds it to its Area 2 LSDB. These routers run the SPF algorithm to determine the cost to reach router R4. This cost is then added to the cost router R4 advertised in its Type 3 LSA, and the result is stored in the RIBs of the routers.

To successfully troubleshoot OSPF-related issues, you should have a solid understanding of this process and the different types of OSPF LSAs. Table 8-4 lists the LSA types you commonly encounter when troubleshooting a Cisco-based OSPF network.

Table 8-4   OSPF LSAs

LSA Type	Description
1	All OSPF routers source Type 1 LSAs. These advertisements list information about directly connected subnets, the OSPF connection types of a router, and the known OSPF adjacencies of a router. A Type 1 LSA is not sent out its local area.
2	The designated router on a multi-access network sends a Type 2 LSA for that network if the network contains at least two routers. A Type 2 LSA contains a list of routers connected to the multi-access network and, like a Type 1 LSA, is constrained to its local area.
3	A Type 3 LSA is sourced by an ABR. Each Type 3 LSA sent into an area contains information about a network that is reachable in a different area. Note that network information is exchanged only between the backbone area and a nonbackbone area, as opposed to being exchanged between two nonbackbone areas.
4	Much like a Type 3 LSA, a Type 4 LSA is sourced by an ABR. However, instead of containing information about OSPF networks, a Type 4 LSA contains information stating how to reach an *autonomous system boundary router (ASBR)*.

8

LSA Type	Description
5	A Type 5 LSA is sourced by an ASBR and contains information about networks reachable outside the OSPF domain. A Type 5 LSA is sent to all OSPF areas except for stub areas. Note that the ABR for a stub area sends default route information into the stub area rather than sending the network-specific Type 5 LSAs.
7	A Type 7 LSA is sourced from an ASBR within an NSSA. Whereas a stub area cannot connect to an external autonomous system, an NSSA can. The Type 7 LSA exists only in the NSSA; therefore, the external routes are announced by the ABR(s) of the NSSA into Area 0 using Type 5 LSAs. In addition, as with a stub area, external routes known to another OSPF area are not forwarded into an NSSA since Type 5 LSAs are not permitted in an NSSA.

Route Summarization

OSPF is strict about where route summarization can occur. With OSPF, manual route summarization is enabled on an area-by-area basis on an ABR to summarize routes as they enter or leave an area or on an ASBR to summarize external routes being injected into an area. Therefore, when troubleshooting route summarization, you need to consider the following:

- Did you enable route summarization on the correct router?

- Did you enable route summarization for the correct area?

- Did you create the appropriate summary route?

You can find answers to all these questions by using the **show ip ospf** command, as shown in Example 8-38. In this example, R2 is an area border router, and summary address 10.1.0.0/16 for Area 1 is currently active and being advertised into Area 0.

Example 8-38   *Verifying Inter-area Route Summarization with show ip ospf*

```
R2# show ip ospf
 Routing Process "ospf 1" with ID 2.2.2.2
 ...output omitted...
 Event-log enabled, Maximum number of events: 1000, Mode: cyclic
 It is an area border router
 Router is not originating router-LSAs with maximum metric
 ...output omitted...
Reference bandwidth unit is 100 mbps
 Area BACKBONE(0)
 Number of interfaces in this area is 1
 Area has no authentication
 SPF algorithm last executed 00:03:27.000 ago
 SPF algorithm executed 14 times
 Area ranges are
 Number of LSA 6. Checksum Sum 0x033162
```

```
Number of opaque link LSA 0. Checksum Sum 0x000000
Number of DCbitless LSA 0
Number of indication LSA 0
Number of DoNotAge LSA 0
Flood list length 0
 Area 1
  Number of interfaces in this area is 1
  Area has no authentication
  SPF algorithm last executed 00:03:27.024 ago
  SPF algorithm executed 13 times
  Area ranges are
  10.1.0.0/16 Active(1) Advertise
   Number of LSA 9. Checksum Sum 0x0555F1
...output omitted...
```

Remember that inter-area summaries are created on ABRs with the **area range** command and that external summaries are created on ASBRs with the **summary-address** command.

When a summary route is created on a router, so is a summary route to Null0, as shown in the following snippet:

R2# **show ip route | include Null**

O 10.1.0.0/16 is a summary, 00:16:07, Null0

This route to Null0 is created and installed in the routing table to prevent routing loops. It is imperative that this route be in the table to ensure that if a packet is received by this router and is destined to a network that falls within the summary that the router does not really know how to reach (longer match), it is dropped. If the route to Null0 does not exist, and if there is a default route on the router, the router forwards the packet using the default route, and the next-hop router ends up forwarding it back to this router because it is using the summary route, and the local router then forwards it based on the default route, and it comes back. This is a routing loop.

It is important that you create accurate summary routes to ensure that your router is not advertising networks in the summary route that it does not truly know how to reach. If it does, it is possible that it might receive packets to destinations that fall within the summary that it really does not know how to reach. If this is the case, packets are dropped because of the route to Null0.

Unlike EIGRP, which gives the route to Null0 an AD of 5, OSPF gives the route to Null0 an AD of 110, as shown in Example 8-39. This does not ensure that it is more believable than most of the other sources of routing information. Therefore, it is possible that a better routing source could end up forwarding the traffic for networks that are included in the summary route to Null0.

8

Example 8-39   *Verifying the AD of a Local Summary Route to Null 0*

```
R2# show ip route 10.1.0.0 255.255.0.0
Routing entry for 10.1.0.0/16
 Known via "ospf 1", distance 110, metric 1, type intra area
 Routing Descriptor Blocks:
 * directly connected, via Null0
 Route metric is 1, traffic share count is 1
```

Discontiguous Areas

In a multi-area OSPF network, a backbone area (numbered *Area 0*) must exist, and all other areas must connect to Area 0. If an area is not physically adjacent to Area 0, routes are not successfully learned by all routers in the OSPF domain. To solve this issue, a *virtual link* can be configured to logically connect the nonadjacent area with Area 0. Figure 8-9 shows Area 51 not physically connected to Area 0. This results in the 10.1.4.0 network not being learned by any other router in the OSPF domain because an ABR is needed to send Type 3 LSAs into Area 0. R4 is not an ABR in this case because the requirement for an ABR is that one interface must be in Area 0 and one or more interfaces in any other area(s). In this case, R4 has no interfaces in Area 0.

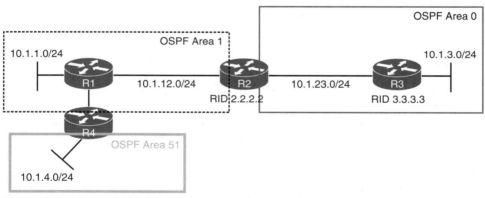

Figure 8-9   *Area 51 Not Directly Connected to Area 0*

Figure 8-10 shows a similar topology but with Area 0 discontiguous. This results in LSAs not being successfully flooded though the OSPF domain and, as a result, incomplete routing tables.

You need to be able to recognize these OSPF design issues and understand how to troubleshoot them and implement a solution. The solution is virtual links. A virtual link in both these examples is created through Area 1, which is known as the *transit area* because it transits LSAs from Area 51 to Area 0 or from Area 0 to Area 0. Note that virtual links are a temporary solution for these issues. A permanent redesign/fix should be performed as soon as possible.

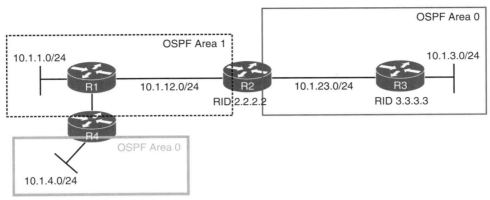

Figure 8-10 *Discontiguous Area 0*

A virtual link is created between the routers connected to the transit area by using their RIDs and the transit area number, as shown in Figure 8-11. The router OSPF configuration mode command on R2 is **area 1 virtual-link 4.4.4.4**, and the command on R4 is **area 1 virtual-link 2.2.2.2**. When the virtual link is established, R4 becomes an ABR because it has an interface (virtual interface in this case) in Area 0. Common issues related to failed virtual links include misconfigured area number or RID. If you type in the area number you are trying to connect to Area 0 instead of the transit area number, the virtual link fails to form. If you use the interface IP address rather than the RID, the virtual link fails to form.

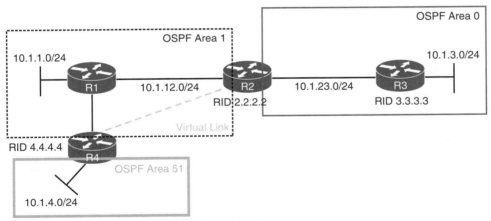

Figure 8-11 *LSA Flooding with Virtual Links*

Example 8-40 shows the output of **show ip ospf neighbor** on R2. Notice that there is a new neighbor relationship with 4.4.4.4 but that the local interface is OSPF_VL0, which refers to the virtual link interface.

Example 8-40 *Verifying a Neighbor Relationship over a Virtual Link*

```
R2# show ip ospf neighbor

Neighbor ID  Pri    State        Dead Time   Address       Interface
4.4.4.4       0     FULL/ -          -        10.1.14.4     OSPF_VL0
3.3.3.3       1     FULL/BDR     00:00:34    10.1.23.3     GigabitEthernet1/0
1.1.1.1       1     FULL/BDR     00:00:35    10.1.12.1     GigabitEthernet0/0
```

Example 8-41 shows the output of **show ip ospf virtual-links**, which provides more details about the virtual link. It is not only important to verify that the virtual link is up but that the state is full, which indicates that LSAs have been successfully exchanged.

Example 8-41 *Verifying the Virtual Link*

```
R2# show ip ospf virtual-links
Virtual Link OSPF_VL0 to router 4.4.4.4 is up
 Run as demand circuit
 DoNotAge LSA allowed.
 Transit area 1, via interface GigabitEthernet0/0
 Topology-MTID Cost Disabled Shutdown Topology Name
        0        64    no       no        Base
 Transmit Delay is 1 sec, State POINT_TO_POINT,
 Timer intervals configured, Hello 10, Dead 40, Wait 40, Retransmit 5
   Hello due in 00:00:09
   Adjacency State FULL (Hello suppressed)
   Index 2/3, retransmission queue length 0, number of retransmission 0
   First 0x0(0)/0x0(0) Next 0x0(0)/0x0(0)
   Last retransmission scan length is 0, maximum is 0
   Last retransmission scan time is 0 msec, maximum is 0 msec
```

Load Balancing

OSPF supports only equal-cost load balancing. Therefore, when troubleshooting load balancing for OSPF, your two primary points of concern are the overall end-to-end cost and the maximum number of paths permitted for load balancing. To verify the maximum number of equal-cost paths an OSPF router is currently configured to support, use the **show ip protocols** command, as shown in Example 8-42. In this example, R1 is currently using the default value of 4.

If your topology is showing multiple paths to reach certain networks in your organization but they are not all showing up in the routing table, it is likely happening because they are not equal-cost paths or the maximum paths value is configured too low.

Example 8-42 *Verifying the Maximum Number of Paths for Load Balancing*

```
R1# show ip protocols
*** IP Routing is NSF aware ***
```

```
Routing Protocol is "ospf 1"
 Outgoing update filter list for all interfaces is not set
 Incoming update filter list for all interfaces is (prefix-list) TEST
 Router ID 1.1.1.1
 Number of areas in this router is 2. 2 normal 0 stub 0 nssa
 Maximum path: 4
 Routing for Networks:
   10.1.1.1 0.0.0.0 area 1
 Routing on Interfaces Configured Explicitly (Area 1):
   GigabitEthernet1/0
...output omitted...
```

Default Route

With OSPF, a static default route is injected into the routing process using the **default-information originate** command, not the **redistribute static** command. Therefore, if you are trying to figure out why a static default route is not being advertised in the OSPF process, use the **show run | section router ospf** command to verify that the **default-information originate** command is being used.

OSPFv2 Trouble Tickets

This section presents three trouble tickets related to the topics discussed in this chapter. The purpose of these trouble tickets is to show a process that you can use when troubleshooting in the real world or in an exam environment. All the trouble tickets in this section are based on the topology shown in Figure 8-12.

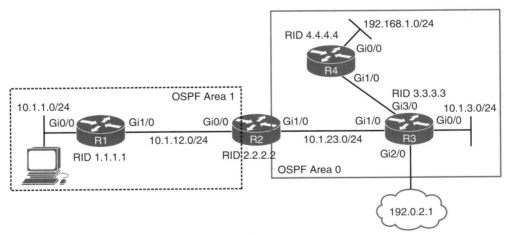

Figure 8-12 *OSPFv2 Trouble Tickets Topology*

Trouble Ticket 8-1

Problem: Users in the 10.1.1.0/24 network indicate that they are not able to access resources in the 192.168.1.0/24 network.

As always, the first item on the list for troubleshooting is to verify the problem. In this case, you access a PC in the 10.1.1.0/24 network and ping an IP address in the 192.168.1.0/24 network; the ping is successful (0% loss), as shown in Example 8-43. However, notice that the reply is from the default gateway at 10.1.1.1, and it states *Destination host unreachable*. Therefore, the ping is technically not successful.

Example 8-43   *Destination Unreachable Result from a ping Command on a PC*

```
C:\>ping 192.168.1.10

Pinging 192.168.1.10 with 32 bytes of data;

Reply from 10.1.1.1: Destination host unreachable.
Reply from 10.1.1.1: Destination host unreachable.
Reply from 10.1.1.1: Destination host unreachable.
Reply from 10.1.1.1: Destination host unreachable.


Ping statistics for 192.168.1.10:
 Packets: Sent = 4, Received = 4, lost = 0 (0% loss),
Approximate round trip times in milli-seconds:
 Minimum = 0ms, Maximum = 0ms, Average = 0ms
```

The result of this ping tells you two very important things: The PC can reach the default gateway, and the default gateway does not know how to get to the 192.168.1.0/24 network. Therefore, you can focus your attention on R1 and work from there.

On R1, you issue the same ping, but it fails, as shown in Example 8-44.

Example 8-44   *Failed Ping from R1 to 192.168.1.10*

```
R1# ping 192.168.1.10
Type escape sequence to abort.
Sending 5, 100-byte ICMP Echos to 192.168.1.10, timeout is 2 seconds:
.....
Success rate is 0 percent (0/5)
```

Next, you check R1's routing table with the **show ip route** command and notice that there are only connected routes in the routing table, as shown in Example 8-45. R1 is not learning any routes from R2.

Example 8-45   *show ip route Output on R1*

```
R1# show ip route
...output omitted...
Gateway of last resort is not set


10.0.0.0/8 is variably subnetted, 4 subnets, 2 masks
C 10.1.1.0/24 is directly connected, GigabitEthernet0/0
L 10.1.1.1/32 is directly connected, GigabitEthernet0/0
C 10.1.12.0/24 is directly connected, GigabitEthernet1/0
L 10.1.12.1/32 is directly connected, GigabitEthernet1/0
```

According to Figure 8-12, OSPF is the routing protocol in use. Therefore, you issue the **show ip protocols** command to verify that OSPF is running on R1. Example 8-46 shows output of the **show ip protocols** command and confirms that OSPF process 1 is in operation on R1.

Example 8-46 *show ip protocols Output on R1*

```
R1# show ip protocols
*** IP Routing is NSF aware ***

Routing Protocol is "ospf 1"
 Outgoing update filter list for all interfaces is not set
 Incoming update filter list for all interfaces is not set
 Router ID 1.1.1.1
 Number of areas in this router is 2. 2 normal 0 stub 0 nssa
 Maximum path: 4
 Routing for Networks:
   10.1.1.1 0.0.0.0 area 1
 Routing on Interfaces Configured Explicitly (Area 1):
   GigabitEthernet1/0
 Passive Interface(s):
   Ethernet0/0
   GigabitEthernet0/0
 Routing Information Sources:
  Gateway       Distance Last Update
  4.4.4.4       110      01:20:29
  2.2.2.2       110      00:48:38
  3.3.3.3       110      01:20:29
  10.1.23.2     110      16:56:39
  203.0.113.3 110        17:10:26
 Distance: (default is 110)
```

Next, you check to see whether R1 has any OSPF neighbors. According to the topology, R2 should be a neighbor. To verify OSPF neighbors, you issue the **show ip ospf neighbor** command on R1, as shown in Example 8-47. According to the output, R1 is a neighbor with R2.

Example 8-47 *show ip ospf neighbor Output on R1*

```
R1# show ip ospf neighbor
Neighbor ID    Pri   State    Dead Time   Address      Interface
2.2.2.2         1    FULL/DR   00:00:36    10.1.12.2    GigabitEthernet1/0
```

What is the best next step? Some would consider troubleshooting why the routes are missing on R1 by looking at various features and parameters associated with R1. However, the 192.168.1.0/24 network is in a different area. Who is responsible for telling R1 about 192.168.1.0/24? Is it R4? No. Is it R2? Yes. R2 sends a Type 3 summary LSA into Area 1, which tells Area 1 about the 192.168.1.0/24 network. Therefore, if R2 does not know about 192.168.1.0/24, you can stop troubleshooting on R1. This is a great example of how understanding the flow of different LSAs can save you time when troubleshooting.

On R2, you issue the **show ip route** command, as shown in Example 8-48, and confirm that R2 does not know about the 192.168.1.0/24 network either. In fact, it has not learned about any networks in Area 0.

Example 8-48   *show ip route Output on R2*

```
R2# show ip route
...output omitted...
Gateway of last resort is not set

 10.0.0.0/8 is variably subnetted, 6 subnets, 3 masks
O 10.1.0.0/16 is a summary, 15:15:33, Null0
O 10.1.1.0/24 [110/2] via 10.1.12.1, 01:33:14, GigabitEthernet0/0
C 10.1.12.0/24 is directly connected, GigabitEthernet0/0
L 10.1.12.2/32 is directly connected, GigabitEthernet0/0
C 10.1.23.0/24 is directly connected, GigabitEthernet1/0
L 10.1.23.2/32 is directly connected, GigabitEthernet1/0
```

Wait! Remember that with OSPF, distribute lists are used to permit or deny routes from being installed in the routing table from the LSDB. Therefore, you might be learning about them and just not installing them.

Example 8-49 shows the output of the LSDB on R2, and as you can see, there are no Area 0 Type 1 router LSAs from R3 (3.3.3.3) or R4 (4.4.4.4). Therefore, you can now officially say that R2 has not been educated about the networks that are missing.

Example 8-49   *show ip ospf database Output on R2 Confirming That Routes Are Missing*

```
R2# show ip ospf database

        OSPF Router with ID (2.2.2.2) (Process ID 1)


           Router Link States (Area 0)

Link ID      ADV Router  Age    Seq#        Checksum Link count
2.2.2.2      2.2.2.2     316    0x80000025 0x003B9F 1


           Summary Net Link States (Area 0)

Link ID      ADV Router  Age    Seq#        Checksum
10.1.0.0     2.2.2.2     1339   0x8000001C 0x00927B
           Router Link States (Area 1)


Link ID      ADV Router  Age    Seq#        Checksum Link count
1.1.1.1      1.1.1.1     1988   0x80000022 0x007843 2
2.2.2.2      2.2.2.2     316    0x80000024 0x0012BA 1
```

```
          Net Link States (Area 1)


Link ID     ADV Router  Age     Seq#         Checksum
10.1.12.2   2.2.2.2     1589    0x8000001C 0x007C75


          Summary Net Link States (Area 1)


Link ID     ADV Router  Age     Seq#         Checksum
10.1.23.0   2.2.2.2     61      0x80000020 0x008C66
```

To receive LSAs, you must have interfaces participating in the OSPF process, and you must have neighbor relationships. The output of **show cdp neighbors** indicates that R3 is a neighbor, and it is reachable out R2's local Gig 1/0 interface, as shown in Example 8-50.

Example 8-50   *Using show cdp neighbors to Verify Router Interfaces*

```
R2# show cdp neighbors
Capability Codes: R - Router, T - Trans Bridge, B - Source Route Bridge
                  S - Switch, H - Host, I - IGMP, r - Repeater, P - Phone,
                  D - Remote, C - CVTA, M - Two-port Mac Relay


Device ID    Local Intrfce    Holdtme  Capability  Platform  Port ID
R3           Gig 1/0          178          R       7206VXR   Gig 1/0
R1           Gig 0/0          179          R       7206VXR   Gig 1/0
```

The output of the commands **show ip ospf interface brief** and **show ip ospf neighbor**, as shown in Example 8-51, shows that R2's local Gi1/0 interface is participating in the OSPF process but does not have a neighbor on the interface.

Example 8-51   *Verifying OSPF-Enabled Interfaces and Neighbors*

```
R2# show ip ospf interface brief
Interface   PID   Area        IP Address/Mask    Cost  State Nbrs F/C
Gi1/0       1     0           10.1.23.2/24        1    DR    0/0
Gi0/0       1     1           10.1.12.2/24        1    DR    1/1
R2# show ip ospf neighbor


Neighbor ID    Pri   State     Dead Time    Address         Interface


1.1.1.1         1    FULL/BDR  00:00:37     10.1.12.1       GigabitEthernet0/0
```

So, you can now hypothesize that the issue is related to R2 and R3 not having a neighbor adjacency. What would cause this? As the earlier discussion in this chapter indicates, many different issues could cause this. Recall that the majority of them are interface related, and using the spot-the-difference troubleshooting method would come in handy. You can do that by examining the output of **show ip ospf interface gigabitEthernet 1/0** on R2 and R3, as shown in Example 8-52.

Example 8-52 *Comparing the OSPF Interface Parameters of R2 and R3*

```
R2# show ip ospf interface gigabitEthernet 1/0
GigabitEthernet1/0 is up, line protocol is up
 Internet Address 10.1.23.2/24, Area 0, Attached via Network Statement
 Process ID 1, Router ID 2.2.2.2, Network Type BROADCAST, Cost: 1
 Topology-MTID Cost Disabled Shutdown Topology Name
 0 1 no no Base
 Transmit Delay is 1 sec, State DR, Priority 1
 Designated Router (ID) 2.2.2.2, Interface address 10.1.23.2
 No backup designated router on this network
 Timer intervals configured, Hello 11, Dead 44, Wait 44, Retransmit 5
  oob-resync timeout 44
  Hello due in 00:00:08
 Supports Link-local Signaling (LLS)
 Cisco NSF helper support enabled
 IETF NSF helper support enabled
 Index 1/2, flood queue length 0
 Next 0x0(0)/0x0(0)
 Last flood scan length is 0, maximum is 3
 Last flood scan time is 0 msec, maximum is 4 msec
 Neighbor Count is 0, Adjacent neighbor count is 0
 Suppress hello for 0 neighbor(s)
 Message digest authentication enabled
 Youngest key id is 1


R3# show ip ospf interface gigabitEthernet 1/0
GigabitEthernet1/0 is up, line protocol is up
 Internet Address 10.1.23.3/24, Area 0, Attached via Network Statement
 Process ID 1, Router ID 3.3.3.3, Network Type BROADCAST, Cost: 1
 Topology-MTID Cost Disabled Shutdown Topology Name
 0 1 no no Base
 Transmit Delay is 1 sec, State DR, Priority 1
 Designated Router (ID) 3.3.3.3, Interface address 10.1.23.3
 No backup designated router on this network
 Timer intervals configured, Hello 10, Dead 40, Wait 40, Retransmit 5
  oob-resync timeout 40
  Hello due in 00:00:04
 Supports Link-local Signaling (LLS)
Cisco NSF helper support enabled
 IETF NSF helper support enabled
```

```
Index 2/2, flood queue length 0
Next 0x0(0)/0x0(0)
Last flood scan length is 1, maximum is 2
Last flood scan time is 0 msec, maximum is 4 msec
Neighbor Count is 0, Adjacent neighbor count is 0
Suppress hello for 0 neighbor(s)
Message digest authentication enabled
Youngest key id is 1
```

Now you can answer the following questions:

- Are the interfaces up? *Yes*

- Are the interfaces in the same subnet? *Yes*

- Are the interfaces in the same area? *Yes*

- Do the routers have unique RIDs? *Yes*

- Are the interfaces using compatible network types? *Yes*

- Do hello and dead timers match? *No* (This is a possible reason why they neighbor adjacency is not forming.)

- Do authentication parameters match? *Enabled and key match, but not sure about key string without checking the running configuration* (This is a possible reason why they neighbor adjacency is not forming.)

As you can see in Example 8-52, the hello and dead timers do not match, but they must. The output of **show run interface gigabitEthernet 1/0** on R2, as shown in Example 8-53, indicates that the command **ip ospf hello-interval 11** is configured.

Example 8-53   *Verifying Interface Configuration on R2*

```
R2# show run interface gigabitEthernet 1/0
Building configuration...

Current configuration : 196 bytes
!
interface GigabitEthernet1/0
 ip address 10.1.23.2 255.255.255.0
 ip ospf authentication message-digest
 ip ospf message-digest-key 1 md5 CISCO
 ip ospf hello-interval 11
 negotiation auto
end
```

When you run the **no ip ospf hello-interval 11** command, you receive the following syslog message on R2:

```
%OSPF-5-ADJCHG: Process 1, Nbr 3.3.3.3 on GigabitEthernet1/0 from
LOADING to FULL, Loading Done
```

This confirms that the adjacency was formed. You can also review the output of the routing table on R2 by using the **show ip route** command to confirm that the routes are learned, as shown in Example 8-54.

Example 8-54   *Verifying Routes in the Routing Table on R2*

```
R2# show ip route
...output omitted...
Gateway of last resort is 10.1.23.3 to network 0.0.0.0

O*E2 0.0.0.0/0 [110/1] via 10.1.23.3, 00:01:00, GigabitEthernet1/0
 10.0.0.0/8 is variably subnetted, 8 subnets, 3 masks
O 10.1.0.0/16 is a summary, 00:01:49, Null0
O 10.1.1.0/24 [110/2] via 10.1.12.1, 00:01:00, GigabitEthernet0/0
O 10.1.3.0/24 [110/2] via 10.1.23.3, 00:01:00, GigabitEthernet1/0
C 10.1.12.0/24 is directly connected, GigabitEthernet0/0
L 10.1.12.2/32 is directly connected, GigabitEthernet0/0
C 10.1.23.0/24 is directly connected, GigabitEthernet1/0
L 10.1.23.2/32 is directly connected, GigabitEthernet1/0
O 10.1.34.0/24 [110/2] via 10.1.23.3, 00:01:00, GigabitEthernet1/0
O 192.168.1.0/24 [110/3] via 10.1.23.3, 00:01:00, GigabitEthernet1/0
O 203.0.113.0/24 [110/2] via 10.1.23.3, 00:01:00, GigabitEthernet1/0
```

R1 also knows about the routes now, as shown in Example 8-55, which displays the output of **show ip route** on R1.

Example 8-55   *Verifying Routes in the Routing Table on R1*

```
R1# show ip route
...output omitted...
Gateway of last resort is 10.1.12.2 to network 0.0.0.0

O*E2 0.0.0.0/0 [110/1] via 10.1.12.2, 00:00:13, GigabitEthernet1/0
 10.0.0.0/8 is variably subnetted, 7 subnets, 2 masks
C 10.1.1.0/24 is directly connected, GigabitEthernet0/0
L 10.1.1.1/32 is directly connected, GigabitEthernet0/0
O IA 10.1.3.0/24 [110/3] via 10.1.12.2, 00:00:19, GigabitEthernet1/0
C 10.1.12.0/24 is directly connected, GigabitEthernet1/0
L 10.1.12.1/32 is directly connected, GigabitEthernet1/0
O IA 10.1.23.0/24 [110/2] via 10.1.12.2, 00:00:19, GigabitEthernet1/0
O IA 10.1.34.0/24 [110/3] via 10.1.12.2, 00:00:19, GigabitEthernet1/0
O IA 192.168.1.0/24 [110/4] via 10.1.12.2, 00:00:19, GigabitEthernet1/0
O IA 203.0.113.0/24 [110/3] via 10.1.12.2, 00:00:19, GigabitEthernet1/0
```

Finally, you ping from the PC again, and the ping is successful, as shown in Example 8-56.

Example 8-56   *A Successful Ping from the 10.1.1.0/24 Network to the 192.168.1.0/24 Network*

```
C:\>ping 192.168.1.10

Pinging 192.168.1.10 with 32 bytes of data:

Reply from 192.168.1.10: bytes=32 time 1ms TTL=128
Reply from 192.168.1.10: bytes=32 time 1ms TTL=128
Reply from 192.168.1.10: bytes=32 time 1ms TTL=128
Reply from 192.168.1.10: bytes=32 time 1ms TTL=128

Ping statistics for 192.168.1.10:
 Packets: Sent = 4, Received = 4, Lost = 0 (0% loss),
Approximate round trip times in milli-seconds:
 Minimum = 0ms, Maximum = 0ms, Average = 0ms
```

Trouble Ticket 8-2

Problem: Users in the 10.1.1.0/24 network indicate that they are not able to access resources in the 192.168.1.0/24 network.

As always, the first item on the list for troubleshooting is to verify the problem. You access a PC in the 10.1.1.0/24 network and ping an IP address in the 192.168.1.0/24 network, and it is successful (0% loss), as shown in Example 8-57. However, notice that the reply is from 10.1.23.2, and it states *TTL expired in transit*. Therefore, it was technically not successful.

Example 8-57   *TTL Expired in Transit Result from the ping Command on PC*

```
C:\>ping 192.168.1.10

Pinging 192.168.1.10 with 32 bytes of data:

Reply from 10.1.23.2: TTL expired in transit.
Reply from 10.1.23.2: TTL expired in transit.
Reply from 10.1.23.2: TTL expired in transit.
Reply from 10.1.23.2: TTL expired in transit.

Ping statistics for 192.168.1.10:
 Packets: sent = 4, Received = 4, Lost = 0 (0% loss),
Approximate round trip times in milli-seconds:
 Minimum = 0ms, Maximum = 0ms, Average = 0ms
```

The result of this ping tells you two very important things: The PC can reach the default gateway at 10.1.1.1, and the device at 10.1.23.2 expired the packet because the TTL reached 0, and the device sent an ICMP time exceeded message back to the PC.

Pause for a moment and think about this. If the TTL expired in transit, it means that the packet did not reach the destination before the TTL decremented to 0. Each time a router touches the packet, it decrements the TTL by 1. The operating system that created the packet will determine what the TTL is for the packet, so there is no universally default value. It could be anything that the operating system is configured to use in the range 0 to 255. So the worst-case scenario is that the packet bounced around the network and went through approximately 255 routers before the device at IP 10.1.23.2 decremented the TTL to 0 and sent the ICMP TTL expired message. Because Figure 8-12 clearly shows that there are only four routers from 10.1.1.0/24 to 192.168.1.0/24, the packet is bouncing around the network somewhere. Running a traceroute from the PC will help you identify this, as shown in Example 8-58. This example shows that R3 (10.1.23.3) and R2 (10.1.23.2) are bouncing the packet back and forth.

Example 8-58   *Traceroute Showing that R2 and R3 Are Bouncing the Packet Back and Forth*

```
C:\>tracert 192.168.1.10

Tracing route to 192.168.1.10 over a maximum of 30 hops

  1  23 ms  15 ms  10 ms  10.1.1.1
  2  36 ms  30 ms  29 ms  10.1.12.2
  3  53 ms  50 ms  39 ms  10.1.23.3
  4  61 ms  39 ms  40 ms  10.1.23.2
  5  61 ms  69 ms  59 ms  10.1.23.3
  6  68 ms  50 ms  69 ms  10.1.23.2
  7   * ms  78 ms  89 ms  10.1.23.3
  8  87 ms  69 ms   * ms  10.1.23.2
...output omitted...
 29 175 ms 169 ms 179 ms  10.1.23.3
 30 204 ms 189 ms 189 ms  10.1.23.2

Trace complete.
```

You can deduce from this that R3 is not routing the packet correctly. It is sending the packet to R2 instead of R4. If you access R3 and issue the **show ip ospf database router 4.4.4.4** command, as shown in Example 8-59, you can clearly see that R3 is learning about network 192.168.1.0/24 from R4. However, instead of using R4 as a next hop, it is using R2 because it is sending the packets to R2, as shown in the earlier trace.

Example 8-59   *Verifying Whether a Route Is in an OSPF Database*

```
R3# show ip ospf database router 4.4.4.4

            OSPF Router with ID (3.3.3.3) (Process ID 1)

               Router Link States (Area 0)
```

```
LS age: 894
Options: (No TOS-capability, DC)
LS Type: Router Links
Link State ID: 4.4.4.4
Advertising Router: 4.4.4.4
LS Seq Number: 80000004
Checksum: 0xEA47
Length: 48
Number of Links: 2
    Link connected to: a Transit Network
    (Link ID) Designated Router address: 10.1.34.4
    (Link Data) Router Interface address: 10.1.34.4
     Number of MTID metrics: 0
     TOS 0 Metrics: 1

    Link connected to: a Stub Network
    (Link ID) Network/subnet number: 192.168.1.0
    (Link Data) Network Mask: 255.255.255.0
     Number of MTID metrics: 0
      TOS 0 Metrics: 1
```

Now you can look at the routing table to see whether this network is being installed in the routing table. The output of the command **show ip route ospf** on R3, as shown in Example 8-60, indicates that this OSPF-learned route is not being installed in the routing table.

Example 8-60 *Output of show ip route ospf on R3*

```
R3# show ip route ospf
...output omitted...

Gateway of last resort is 203.0.113.1 to network 0.0.0.0

 10.0.0.0/8 is variably subnetted, 7 subnets, 3 masks
O IA 10.1.0.0/16 [110/2] via 10.1.23.2, 01:25:02, GigabitEthernet1/0
```

It's time to hypothesize! What would cause R3 to learn about the route but not install it in the routing table? Two possibilities are route filtering and a better source. If you harness your knowledge and really focus on what is happening, you can figure it out. *R3 is routing packets destined to 192.168.1.0/24, which means there must be some entry in the routing table, or policy-based routing has been enforced.*

The output of the command **show ip route 192.168.1.0 255.255.255.0** on R3 confirms that there is an entry in the routing table on R3, as shown in Example 8-61. However, it is a static entry with an AD of 1 pointing to 10.1.23.2. It looks like you found the problem. There is a better source of routing information, according to AD.

Example 8-61 *Output of show ip route 192.168.1.0 255.255.255.0 on R3*

```
R3# show ip route 192.168.1.0 255.255.255.0
Routing entry for 192.168.1.0/24
 Known via "static", distance 1, metric 0
 Routing Descriptor Blocks:
 * 10.1.23.2
  Route metric is 0, traffic share count is 1
```

The output of the command **show run | include ip route**, as shown in Example 8-62, confirms that a static route exists.

Example 8-62 *Output of show run | include ip route*

```
R3# show run | include ip route
ip route 0.0.0.0 0.0.0.0 203.0.113.1
ip route 192.168.1.0 255.255.255.0 10.1.23.2
```

After you remove this command from R3 with the **no ip route 192.168.1.0 255.255.255.0 10.1.23.2** command, a ping from the PC is successful, as shown in Example 8-63.

Example 8-63 *A Successful Ping to the 192.168.1.0/24 Network*

```
C:\>ping 192.168.1.10

Pinging 192.168.1.10 with 32 bytes of data:

Reply from 192.168.1.10: bytes=32 time 1ms TTL=128
Reply from 192.168.1.10: bytes=32 time 1ms TTL=128
Reply from 192.168.1.10: bytes=32 time 1ms TTL=128
Reply from 192.168.1.10: bytes=32 time 1ms TTL=128

Ping statistics for 192.168.1.10:
 Packets: Sent = 4, Received = 4, Lost = 0 (0% loss),
Approximate round trip times in milli-seconds:
 Minimum = 0ms, Maximum = 0ms, Average = 0ms
```

Trouble Ticket 8-3

Problem: Routers R1 and R2 are not forming a neighbor adjacency.

The first item on the list for troubleshooting is to verify the problem. You access R1 and issue the **show ip ospf neighbor** command, as shown in Example 8-64, and the output confirms that there is no neighbor relationship with R2.

Example 8-64 *Verifying R1's OSPF Neighbors*

```
R1# show ip ospf neighbor
R1#
```

You know that to have a neighbor relationship, you need interfaces participating in the OSPF process. The command **show cdp neighbors** confirms that R2 is connected to R1's local Gig 1/0 interface, as shown in Example 8-65. Therefore, you need to enable OSPF on that interface.

Example 8-65 *Verifying R1's CDP Neighbors*

```
R1# show cdp neighbors
Capability Codes: R - Router, T - Trans Bridge, B - Source Route Bridge
                  S - Switch, H - Host, I - IGMP, r - Repeater, P - Phone,
                  D - Remote, C - CVTA, M - Two-port Mac Relay
Device ID     Local Intrfce     Holdtme     Capability  Platform  Port ID
R2            Gig 1/0           142         R           7206VXR   Gig 0/0
```

The output of **show ip ospf interface brief** confirms that Gi1/0 is participating in the OSPF process, as shown in Example 8-66. However, based on Figure 8-12, it is not in the correct area. It should be in Area 1.

Example 8-66 *Verifying R1's OSPF-Enabled Interfaces*

```
R1# show ip ospf interface brief
Interface   PID   Area   IP Address/Mask   Cost  State Nbrs F/C
Gi0/0       1     1      10.1.1.1/24       1     DR    0/0
Gi1/0       1     51     10.1.12.1/24      1     DR    0/0
```

Based on Example 8-66, Gi1/0 has IP address 10.1.12.1/24. Therefore, you need a network command that includes that IP address and places the interface in Area 1. The output of **show run | section router ospf** indicates that there is a **network** command that will enable the routing process on Gi1/0 and put it in Area 1, as shown in Example 8-67.

Example 8-67 *Verifying R1's OSPF Configuration*

```
R1# show run | section router ospf
router ospf 1
 router-id 1.1.1.1
 area 1 authentication message-digest
 passive-interface default
 no passive-interface GigabitEthernet1/0
 network 10.1.1.1 0.0.0.0 area 1
 network 10.1.12.1 0.0.0.0 area 1
```

If you are scratching your head, you're not the only one at this point. The running configuration clearly shows a command that puts Gi1/0 in Area 1, yet the output of **show ip ospf interface brief** clearly shows that it is in Area 51. If you have not figured out why this happened, keep reading.

8

Recall that there are two ways to enable OSPF on an interface: with the **network area** command in router OSPF configuration mode and with the **ip ospf area** interface configuration mode command.

The **ip ospf area** command overrides the **network area** command if both commands are configured. Example 8-68 shows the GigabitEthernet1/0 interface configuration on R1, using the **show run interface gigabitEthernet 1/0** command.

Example 8-68 *Verifying R1's GigabitEthernet1/0 Configuration*

```
R1# show run interface gigabitEthernet 1/0
Building configuration...

Current configuration : 183 bytes
!
interface GigabitEthernet1/0
 ip address 10.1.12.1 255.255.255.0
 ip ospf authentication-key CISCO
 ip ospf message-digest-key 1 md5 CISCO
 ip ospf 1 area 51
 negotiation auto
end
```

Here is the issue. The **ip ospf 1 area 51** command overrides the **network 10.1.12.1 0.0.0.0 area 1** command. You either need to change the **ip ospf 1 area 51** command so that it states **area 1** or remove it completely so that the **network** command can be used.

Exam Preparation Tasks

As mentioned in the section "How to Use This Book" in the Introduction, you have a couple choices for exam preparation: the exercises here, Chapter 24, "Final Preparation," and the exam simulation questions in the Pearson Test Prep software.

Review All Key Topics

Review the most important topics in this chapter, noted with the Key Topic icon in the outer margin of the page. Table 8-5 lists these key topics and the page number on which each is found.

Table 8-5   Key Topics

Key Topic Element	Description	Page Number
Example 8-1	Verifying OSPF neighbors with **show ip ospf neighbor**	317
List	Reasons an OSPF neighbor relationship might not form	317
Table 8-2	Adjacency states	318
Example 8-2	Verifying OSPF interfaces with **show ip ospf interface brief**	320

Key Topic Element	Description	Page Number
Example 8-4	Displaying OSPF interface timers on R1 Gigabit Ethernet 1/0	321
Section	Mismatched area numbers	322
Example 8-9	Determining the type of OSPF areas	323
Paragraph	The passive interface feature and troubleshooting passive interface issues	325
Example 8-13	Verifying OSPF area authentication	326
Example 8-14	Verifying the OSPF authentication key	327
Section	MTU mismatch	328
Table 8-3	OSPF network types and characteristics	331
List	Reasons an OSPF route might be missing from either the LSDB or the routing table	332
List	Considerations when troubleshooting route filtering	337
Section	Stub area configuration	339
Paragraph	The importance of the DR election in a hub-and-spoke multi-access network	341
Table 8-4	OSPFv2 LSAs	347
List	Considerations when troubleshooting route summarization issues	348
Example 8-41	Verifying the virtual link	352

Define Key Terms

Define the following key terms from this chapter and check your answers in the glossary:

Dijkstra's shortest path first (SPF) algorithm, OSPF area, neighbor table, area border router (ABR), link-state advertisement (LSA), link-state database (LSDB), autonomous system boundary router (ASBR), stub area, totally stubby area, NSSA, totally NSSA, designated router (DR), backup designated router (BDR), virtual link

Use the Command Reference to Check Your Memory

The ENARSI 300-410 exam focuses on the practical, hands-on skills that networking professionals use. Therefore, you should be able to identify the commands needed to configure, verify, and troubleshoot the topics covered in this chapter.

This section includes the most important configuration and verification commands covered in this chapter. It might not be necessary to memorize the complete syntax of every command, but you should be able to remember the basic keywords that are needed.

To test your memory of the commands in Table 8-6, go to the companion website and download Appendix B, "Command Reference Exercises." Fill in the missing commands in the tables based on each command description. You can check your work by downloading Appendix C, "Command Reference Exercise Answer Key," from the companion website.

8

Table 8-6   Command Reference

Task	Command Syntax
Display the IPv4 routing protocols enabled on the device; for OSPFv2, display whether any route filters are applied, the RID, the number of areas the router is participating in, the types of areas, the maximum paths for load balancing, the **network area** command, the interfaces explicitly participating in the routing process, passive interfaces, routing information sources, and the AD.	**show ip protocols**
Display general OSPF parameters, including the PID, the RID, the reference bandwidth, the areas configured on the router, the types of areas (stub, totally stubby, NSSA, and totally NSSA), and area authentication.	**show ip ospf**
Display the interfaces that are participating in the OSPF process.	**show ip ospf interface brief**
Display detailed information about the interfaces participating in the OSPF process, including interface IPv4 address and mask, area ID, PID, RID, network type, cost, DR/BDR, priority, and timers.	**show ip ospf interface**
Display the OSPF devices that have formed a neighbor adjacency with the local router.	**show ip ospf neighbor**
Display the OSPF routes that have been installed in the IPv4 routing table.	**show ip route ospf**
Display the OSPF link-state database.	**show ip ospf database**
Provide information about the status of OSPF virtual links that are required for areas not physically adjacent to the backbone area (that is, Area 0).	**show ip ospf virtual-links**
Display real-time information related to the exchange of OSPF hello packets. This is useful for identifying mismatched OSPF timers and mismatched OSPF area types.	**debug ip ospf hello**
Display the transmission and reception of OSPF packets in real time.	**debug ip ospf packet**
Display real-time updates about the formation of an OSPF adjacency. This is useful for identifying mismatched area IDs and authentication information.	**debug ip ospf adj**
Display real-time information about OSPF events, including the transmission and reception of hello messages and LSAs. This might be useful on a router that appears to be ignoring hello messages received from a neighboring router.	**debug ip ospf events**

## CHAPTER 9

OSPFv3

This chapter covers the following topics:

- **OSPFv3 Fundamentals:** This section provides an overview of the OSPFv3 routing protocol, its similarities to OSPFv2, and its configuration.

- **OSPFv3 Configuration:** This section explains and demonstrates how OSPFv3 is used for exchanging IPv6 routes.

- **OSPFv3 LSA Flooding Scope:** This section provides a deeper view of the OSPFv3 link-state advertisement (LSA) structure and the comparison to OSPFv2.

Open Shortest Path First version 3 (OSPFv3) is the latest version of the OSPF protocol and includes support for both the IPv4 and IPv6 address families. The OSPFv3 protocol is not backward compatible with OSPFv2, but the protocol mechanisms described in Chapter 6, "OSPF," and Chapter 7, "Advanced OSPF," are essentially the same. This chapter expands on the previous three chapters and discusses OSPFv3 and its support of IPv6.

"Do I Know This Already?" Quiz

The "Do I Know This Already?" quiz allows you to assess whether you should read this entire chapter thoroughly or jump to the "Exam Preparation Tasks" section. If you are in doubt about your answers to these questions or your own assessment of your knowledge of the topics, read the entire chapter. Table 9-1 lists the major headings in this chapter and their corresponding "Do I Know This Already?" quiz questions. You can find the answers in Appendix A, "Answers to the 'Do I Know This Already?' Quiz Questions."

Table 9-1 Do I Know This Already?" Foundation Topics Section-to-Question Mapping

Foundation Topics Section	Questions
OSPFv3 Fundamentals	1, 2
OSPFv3 Configuration	3–5
OSPFv3 LSA Flooding Scope	6

CAUTION The goal of self-assessment is to gauge your mastery of the topics in this chapter. If you do not know the answer to a question or are only partially sure of the answer, you should mark that question as wrong for purposes of self-assessment. Giving yourself credit for an answer that you correctly guess skews your self-assessment results and might provide you with a false sense of security.

1. What protocol number does OSPFv3 use for its inter-router communication?
   a. 87
   b. 88
   c. 89
   d. 90
2. How many packet types does OSPFv3 use for inter-router communication?
   a. Three
   b. Four
   c. Five
   d. Six
   e. Seven
3. What do you need to do to enable OSPFv3 on an interface?
   a. Place the command **network** *prefix/prefix-length* under the OSPF process.
   b. Place the command **network** *interface-id* under the OSPF process.
   c. Place the command **ospfv3** *process-id* **ipv6 area** *area-id* under the interface.
   d. Nothing. OSPFv3 is enabled on all IPv6 interfaces upon initialization of the OSPF process.
4. True or false: On a brand-new router installation, OSPFv3 requires only an IPv6 link-local address to be configured and OSPFv3 to be enabled on that interface to form an OSPFv3 neighborship with another router.
   a. True
   b. False
5. True or false: OSPFv3 support for IPv4 networks only requires that an IPv4 address be assigned to the interface and that the OSPFv3 process be initialized for IPv4.
   a. True
   b. False
6. Which OSPFv3 flooding scope correlates to the links between two routers?
   a. The link-local scope
   b. The neighbor scope
   c. The process scope
   d. The autonomous system scope

Foundation Topics

OSPFv3 Fundamentals

OSPFv3 differs from OSPFv2 in several ways:

- **Support for multiple address families:** OSPFv3 supports IPv4 and IPv6 address families.
- **New LSA types:** New LSA types have been created to carry IPv6 prefixes.

- **Removal of addressing semantics:** The IP prefix information is no longer present in the OSPF packet headers. Instead, it is carried as LSA payload information, making the protocol essentially address family independent, similar to Intermediate System-to-Intermediate System (IS-IS). OSPFv3 uses the term *link* instead of *network* because the shortest path first tree (SPT) calculations are per link instead of per subnet.

- **LSA flooding:** OSPFv3 includes a new link-state type field that is used to determine the flooding scope of an LSA, as well as the handling of unknown LSA types.

- **Packet format:** OSPFv3 runs directly over IPv6, and the number of fields in the packet header has been reduced.

- **Router ID:** The router ID is used to identify neighbors, regardless of the network type in OSPFv3.

- **Authentication:** Neighbor authentication has been removed from the OSPF protocol and is now performed through IPsec extension headers in the IPv6 packet.

- **Neighbor adjacencies:** OSPFv3 inter-router communication is handled by IPv6 link-local addressing. Neighbors are not automatically detected over nonbroadcast multi-access (NBMA) interfaces. The neighbor must be manually specified using the link-local address. IPv6 allows for multiple subnets to be assigned to a single interface, and OSPFv3 allows for neighbor adjacency to form even if the two routers do not share a common subnet.

- **Multiple instances:** An OSPFv3 packet includes an instance ID field that may be used to manipulate which routers on a network segment are allowed to form adjacencies.

> **NOTE**   RFC 5340 provides in-depth coverage of all the differences between OSPFv2 and OSPFv3.

OSPFv3 Link-State Advertisement

The OSPF link-state database (LSDB) information is organized and advertised differently in version 3 than in version 2. OSPFv3 modifies the structure of the router LSA (Type 1), uses the term inter-area prefix LSA instead of network summary LSA, and uses the term inter-area router LSA instead of autonomous system boundary router (ASBR) summary LSA. The principal difference is that the router LSA is only responsible for announcing interface parameters such as the interface type (point-to-point, broadcast, NBMA, point-to-multipoint, and virtual links) and metric (cost).

IP address information is advertised independently by two new LSA types:

- Intra-area prefix LSA
- Link-local LSA

The OSPF Dijkstra's shortest path first (SPF) algorithm used to determine the SPT only examines the router and network LSAs. Advertising the IP prefix information using new LSA types eliminates the need for OSPF to perform full *shortest path first* (SPF) tree calculations every time a new IP address (prefix) is added or changed on an interface. The OSPFv3 LSDB creates a shortest path topology tree based on links instead of networks.

Table 9-2 provides a brief description of each OSPFv3 LSA type.

Table 9-2   OSPFv3 LSA Type

LSA Type	Name	Description
0x2001	Device	Every router generates router LSAs that describe the state and cost of the router's interfaces to the area.
0x2002	Network	A designated router generates network LSAs to announce all the routers attached to the link, including itself.
0x2003	Inter-area prefix	Area border routers generate inter-area prefix LSAs to describe routes to IPv6 address prefixes that belong to other areas.
0x2004	Inter-area router	Area border routers generate inter-area router LSAs to announce the addresses of autonomous system boundary routers in other areas.
0x2005	AS-external	Autonomous system boundary routers advertise AS-external LSAs to announce default routes or routes learned through redistribution from other protocols.
0x2007	NSSA	Autonomous system boundary routers that are located in a not-so-stubby area (NSSA) advertise NSSA LSAs for routes redistributed into the area.
0x0008	Link	The link LSA maps all the global unicast address prefixes associated with an interface to the link-local interface IP address of the router. The link LSA is shared only between neighbors on the same link.
0x2009	Intra-area prefix	The intra-area-prefix LSA is used to advertise one or more IPv6 prefixes that are associated with a router, stub, or transit network segment.

OSPFv3 Communication

OSPFv3 packets use protocol ID 89, and routers communicate with each other using the local interface's IPv6 link-local address as the source. Depending on the packet type, the destination address is either a unicast link-local address or the multicast link-local scoped address:

- **FF02::05:** OSPFv3 AllSPFRouters

- **FF02::06:** OSPFv3 AllDRouters

Every router uses the AllSPFRouters multicast address FF02::5 to send OSPF hello messages to routers on the same link. The hello messages are used for neighbor discovery and for detecting whether a neighbor relationship is down. The designated router (DR) and backup designated router (BDR) also use this address to send link-state update and flooding acknowledgment messages to all routers.

Non-DR/BDR routers send an update or link-state acknowledgment message to the DR and BDR using the AllDRouters address FF02::6.

9

OSPFv3 utilizes the same five packet types and logic as OSPFv2. Table 9-3 displays the name, address, and purpose of each packet.

Table 9-3 OSPFv3 Packet Types

Type	Packet Name	Source	Destination	Purpose
1	Hello	Link-local address	FF02::5 (all routers)	Discover and maintain neighbors
		Link-local address	Link-local address	Initial adjacency forming, immediate hello
2	Database description	Link-local address	Link-local address	Summarize database contents
3	Link-state request	Link-local address	Link-local address	Database information request
4	Link-state update	Link-local address	Link-local address	Initial adjacency forming, in response to link-state request
		Link-local address (from DR)	FF02::5 (all routers)	Database update
		Link-local address (from non-DR)	FF02::6 (DR/BDR)	Database update
5	Link-state acknowledgment	Link-local address	Link-local address	Initial adjacency forming, in response to link-state update
		Link-local address (from DR)	FF02::5 (all routers)	Flooding acknowledgment
		Link-local address (from non-DR)	FF02::6 (DR/BDR)	Flooding acknowledgment

OSPFv3 Configuration

The process for configuring OSPFv3 involves the following steps:

Step 1. Initialize the routing process by enabling **ipv6 unicast-routing** on the router and then configuring OSPFv3 with the command **router ospfv3** [*process-id*].

Step 2. Define the router ID (RID) by using the command **router-id**. The router ID is a 32-bit value that does not need to match an IPv4 address. It may be any number, as long as the value is unique within the OSPF domain. OSPFv3 uses the same algorithm as OSPFv2 for dynamically locating the RID. If there are not any IPv4 interfaces available, the RID is set to 0.0.0.0 and does not allow adjacencies to form.

Step 3. Initialize the address family within the routing process by using the optional command **address-family {ipv6 | ipv4} unicast**. The appropriate address family is enabled automatically when OSPFv3 is enabled on an interface.

Step 4. Use the interface command **ospfv3** *process-id* **ipv6 area** *area-id* to enable the protocol and assign the interface to an area.

Figure 9-1 shows a simple four-router topology to demonstrate OSPFv3 configuration. Area 0 consists of R1, R2, and R3, and Area 34 contains R3 and R4. R3 is the area border router (ABR).

Figure 9-1 *OSPFv3 Topology*

Example 9-1 provides the OSPFv3 and IPv6 address configurations for R1, R2, R3, and R4. IPv6 link-local addressing is configured here so that each router's interface reflects its local number (for example, R1's interfaces are set to FE80::1) in addition to traditional IPv6 addressing. The link-local addressing is statically configured to assist with any diagnostic output in this chapter. The OSPFv3 configuration is highlighted.

Example 9-1 *IPv6 Addressing and OSPFv3 Configuration*

```
R1
interface Loopback0
 ipv6 address 2001:DB8::1/128
 ospfv3 1 ipv6 area 0
!
interface GigabitEthernet0/1
 ipv6 address FE80::1 link-local
 ipv6 address 2001:DB8:0:1::1/64
 ospfv3 1 ipv6 area 0
!
interface GigabitEthernet0/2
 ipv6 address FE80::1 link-local
 ipv6 address 2001:DB8:0:12::1/64
 ospfv3 1 ipv6 area 0
!
router ospfv3 1
 router-id 192.168.1.1

R2
interface Loopback0
 ipv6 address 2001:DB8::2/128
 ospfv3 1 ipv6 area 0
!
interface GigabitEthernet0/1
ipv6 address FE80::2 link-local
 ipv6 address 2001:DB8:0:12::2/64
 ospfv3 1 ipv6 area 0
!
interface GigabitEthernet0/3
 ipv6 address 2001:DB8:0:23::2/64
 ipv6 address FE80::2 link-local
 ospfv3 1 ipv6 area 0
!
```

```
router ospfv3 1
 router-id 192.168.2.2
```

R3
```
interface Loopback0
 ipv6 address 2001:DB8::3/128
 ospfv3 1 ipv6 area 0
!
interface GigabitEthernet0/2
 ipv6 address FE80::3 link-local
 ipv6 address 2001:DB8:0:23::3/64
 ospfv3 1 ipv6 area 0
!
interface GigabitEthernet0/4
 ipv6 address FE80::3 link-local
 ipv6 address 2001:DB8:0:34::3/64
 ospfv3 1 ipv6 area 34
!
router ospfv3 1
 router-id 192.168.3.3
```

R4
```
interface Loopback0
 ipv6 address 2001:DB8::4/128
 ospfv3 1 ipv6 area 34
!
interface GigabitEthernet0/1
 ipv6 address FE80::4 link-local
 ipv6 address 2001:DB8:0:4::4/64
 ospfv3 1 ipv6 area 34
!
interface GigabitEthernet0/3
 ipv6 address FE80::4 link-local
 ipv6 address 2001:DB8:0:34::4/64
 ospfv3 1 ipv6 area 34
!
router ospfv3 1
 router-id 192.168.4.4
```

NOTE   Earlier versions of IOS used the commands **ipv6 router ospf** for initialization of the OSPF process and **ipv6 ospf** *process-id* **area** *area-id* for identification of the interface. These commands are considered legacy and should be replaced with the commands described in this chapter and the rest of this book.

OSPFv3 Verification

The commands for viewing OSPFv3 settings and statuses are very similar to those used with OSPFv2. Verifying the OSPFv3 interfaces, neighborship, and the routing table are essential to supporting OSPFv3. In essence, you replace **ip ospf** with **ospfv3**. For example, to view the neighbor adjacency for OSPFv2, you use the command **show ip ospf neighbor**, whereas you use the command **show ospfv3 ipv6 neighbor** for OSPFv3. Example 9-2 demonstrates the command executed on R3.

Example 9-2 *Identifying R3's OSPFv3 Neighbors*

```
R3# show ospfv3 ipv6 neighbor

          OSPFv3 1 address-family ipv6 (router-id 192.168.3.3)

Neighbor ID   Pri   State        Dead Time   Interface ID   Interface
192.168.2.2   1     FULL/DR      00:00:32    5              GigabitEthernet0/2
192.168.4.4   1     FULL/BDR     00:00:33    5              GigabitEthernet0/4
```

Example 9-3 shows R1's GigabitEthernet0/2 OSPFv3-enabled interface status with the command **show ospfv3 interface** [*interface-id*]. Notice how address semantics are removed compared to OSPFv2. The interface maps to the interface ID value 3 and not an IP address value, as in OSPFv2. In addition, there is some helpful topology information describing the link. The local router is the DR (192.168.1.1), and the adjacent neighbor router is the BDR (192.168.2.2).

Example 9-3 *Viewing the OSPFv3 Interface Configuration*

```
R1# show ospfv3 interface GigabitEthernet0/2
GigabitEthernet0/2 is up, line protocol is up
  Link Local Address FE80::1, Interface ID 3
  Area 0, Process ID 1, Instance ID 0, Router ID 192.168.1.1
  Network Type BROADCAST, Cost: 1
  Transmit Delay is 1 sec, State DR, Priority 1
  Designated Router (ID) 192.168.1.1, local address FE80::1
  Backup Designated router (ID) 192.168.2.2, local address FE80::2
  Timer intervals configured, Hello 10, Dead 40, Wait 40, Retransmit 5
    Hello due in 00:00:01
  Graceful restart helper support enabled
  Index 1/1/1, flood queue length 0
  Next 0x0(0)/0x0(0)/0x0(0)
  Last flood scan length is 0, maximum is 4
  Last flood scan time is 0 msec, maximum is 0 msec
  Neighbor Count is 1, Adjacent neighbor count is 1
    Adjacent with neighbor 192.168.2.2  (Backup Designated Router)
  Suppress hello for 0 neighbor(s)
```

To see a brief version of the OSPFv3 interface settings, you use the command **show ospfv3 interface brief**. The output of this command includes the associated process ID, area,

9

address family (IPv4 or IPv6), interface state, and neighbor count. Example 9-4 demonstrates this command being executed on the ABR, R3. Notice that some interfaces reside in Area 0, and others reside in Area 34.

Example 9-4   *Viewing the Brief Iteration of OSPFv3 Interfaces*

```
R3# show ospfv3 interface brief
Interface    PID    Area            AF        Cost   State Nbrs F/C
Lo0          1      0               ipv6      1      LOOP  0/0
Gi0/2        1      0               ipv6      1      BDR   1/1
Gi0/4        1      34              ipv6      1      DR    1/1
```

You can view the OSPFv3 IPv6 routing table by using the command **show ipv6 route ospf**. Intra-area routes are indicated with O, and inter-area routes are indicated with OI. Example 9-5 demonstrates this command being executed on R1. The forwarding address for the routes is the link-local address of the neighboring router.

Example 9-5   *Viewing the OSPFv3 Routes in the IPv6 Routing Table*

```
R1# show ipv6 route ospf
! Output omitted for brevity
IPv6 Routing Table - default - 11 entries
      RL - RPL, O - OSPF Intra, OI - OSPF Inter, OE1 - OSPF ext 1
      OE2 - OSPF ext 2, ON1 - OSPF NSSA ext 1, ON2 - OSPF NSSA ext 2
..
O    2001:DB8::2/128 [110/1]
     via FE80::2, GigabitEthernet0/2
O    2001:DB8::3/128 [110/2]
     via FE80::2, GigabitEthernet0/2
OI   2001:DB8::4/128 [110/3]
     via FE80::2, GigabitEthernet0/2
OI   2001:DB8:0:4::/64 [110/4]
     via FE80::2, GigabitEthernet0/2
O    2001:DB8:0:23::/64 [110/2]
     via FE80::2, GigabitEthernet0/2
OI   2001:DB8:0:34::/64 [110/3]
     via FE80::2, GigabitEthernet0/2
```

The Passive Interface

OSPFv3 supports the ability to configure an interface as passive. You configure an interface as being passive with the command **passive-interface** *interface-id* or globally with **passive-interface default**; you make an interface as active with the command **no passive-interface** *interface-id*. The command is placed under the OSPFv3 process or under the specific address family. Placing the command under the global process cascades the setting to both address families.

Example 9-6 provides an example of making the LAN interface on R1 explicitly passive and making all interfaces passive on R4 while marking the Gi0/3 interface as active.

Example 9-6 *Configuring OSPFv3 Passive Interfaces*

```
R1(config)# router ospfv3 1
R1(config-router)# passive-interface GigabitEthernet0/1
R4(config)# router ospfv3 1
R4(config-router)# passive-interface default
22:10:46.838: %OSPFv3-5-ADJCHG: Process 1, IPv6, Nbr 192.168.3.3 on GigabitEther-
net0/3 from FULL to DOWN, Neighbor Down: Interface down or detached
R4(config-router)# no passive-interface GigabitEthernet 0/3
```

The active/passive state of an interface is verified by examining the OSPFv3 interface status using the command **show ospfv3 interface** [*interface-id*] and searching for the Passive keyword. In the following snippet, R1 confirms that the Gi0/3 interface is passive:

```
R1# show ospfv3 interface gigabitEthernet 0/1 | include Passive

    No Hellos (Passive interface)
```

IPv6 Route Summarization

The ability to summarize IPv6 networks is as important as summarization routes in IPv4; it may even be more important, due to hardware scaling limitations. Referencing Figure 9-1, Example 9-7 displays the IPv6 routing table on R4 before summarization is applied on R3.

Example 9-7 *R4's IPv6 Routing Table Before Summarization*

```
R4#  show ipv6 route ospf | begin Application
     1A - LISP away, a - Application
OI   2001:DB8::1/128 [110/3]
     via FE80::3, GigabitEthernet0/3
OI   2001:DB8::2/128 [110/2]
     via FE80::3, GigabitEthernet0/3
OI   2001:DB8::3/128 [110/1]
     via FE80::3, GigabitEthernet0/3
OI   2001:DB8:0:1::/64 [110/4]
     via FE80::3, GigabitEthernet0/3
OI   2001:DB8:0:12::/64 [110/3]
     via FE80::3, GigabitEthernet0/3
OI   2001:DB8:0:23::/64 [110/2]
     via FE80::3, GigabitEthernet0/3
```

Summarizing the Area 0 router's loopback interfaces (2001:db8:0::1/128, 2001:db8:0::2/128, and 2001:db8:0::3/128) removes three routes from the routing table.

Summarization of internal OSPFv3 routes follows the same rules as for OSPFv2 and must occur on ABRs. R3 summarizes the three loopback addresses into 2001:db8:0:0::/65. Summarization commands reside under the address family in the OSPFv3 process. Summarization involves the command **area** *area-id* **range** *prefix*/*prefix-length*.

Example 9-8 shows R3's configuration for summarizing these prefixes.

9

Example 9-8 *IPv6 Summarization*

```
R3# configure terminal
Enter configuration commands, one per line. End with CNTL/Z.
R3(config)# router ospfv3 1
R3(config-router)# address-family ipv6 unicast
R3(config-router-af)# area 0 range 2001:db8:0:0::/65
```

Example 9-9 shows R4's IPv6 routing table after R3 is configured to summarize the Area 0 loopback interfaces. The summary route is highlighted.

Example 9-9 *R4's IPv6 Routing Table After Summarization*

```
R4# show ipv6 route ospf | begin Application
      1A - LISP away, a - Application
OI  2001:DB8::/65 [110/4]
     via FE80::3, GigabitEthernet0/3
OI  2001:DB8:0:1::/64 [110/4]
     via FE80::3, GigabitEthernet0/3
OI  2001:DB8:0:12::/64 [110/3]
     via FE80::3, GigabitEthernet0/3
OI  2001:DB8:0:23::/64 [110/2]
     via FE80::3, GigabitEthernet0/3
```

Network Type

OSPFv3 supports the same OSPF network types as OSPFv2. Example 9-10 shows that R2's GigabitEthernet0/3 interface is set as a broadcast OSPF network type and is confirmed as being in a DR state.

Example 9-10 *Viewing the Dynamic Configured OSPFv3 Network Type*

```
R2# show ospfv3 interface GigabitEthernet 0/3 | include Network
  Network Type BROADCAST, Cost: 1
R2# show ospfv3 interface brief
Interface    PID   Area          AF       Cost  State Nbrs F/C
Lo0          1     0             ipv6     1     LOOP  0/0
Gi0/3        1     0             ipv6     1     DR    1/1
Gi0/1        1     0             ipv6     1     BDR   1/1
```

You change the OSPFv3 network type by using the interface parameter command **ospfv3 network {point-to-point | point-to-multipoint broadcast | nonbroadcast}**. Example 9-11 demonstrates the interfaces associated to 2001:DB8:0:23::/64 being changed to point-to-point.

Example 9-11 *Changing the OSPFv3 Network Type*

```
R2# configure terminal
Enter configuration commands, one per line. End with CNTL/Z.
R2(config)# interface GigabitEthernet 0/3
R2(config-if)# ospfv3 network point-to-point
R3(config)# interface GigabitEthernet 0/2
R3(config-if)# ospfv3 network point-to-point
```

Example 9-12 shows how to verify the new settings. The network is now a point-to-point link, and the interface state is indicated as *P2P* as confirmation.

Example 9-12 *Viewing the Statically Configured OSPFv3 Network Type*

```
R2# show ospfv3 interface GigabitEthernet 0/3 | include Network
  Network Type POINT_TO_POINT, Cost: 1
R2# show ospfv3 interface brief
Interface    PID   Area          AF        Cost  State Nbrs F/C
Lo0          1     0             ipv6      1     LOOP  0/0
Gi0/3        1     0             ipv6      1     P2P   1/1
Gi0/1        1     0             ipv6      1     BDR   1/1
```

OSPFv3 Authentication

OSPFv3 does not support neighbor authentication within the protocol itself. Instead, the routing protocol utilizes IP Security (IPsec) to provide authentication. IPv6 Authentication Header (AH) or Encapsulating Security Payload (ESP) extension headers may be added to the OSPF packets to provide authentication, integrity, and confidentiality:

- **Authentication Header (AH):** Provides authentication

- **Encapsulating Security Payload (ESP):** Provides authentication and encryption

Figure 9-2 shows the IPv6 IPsec packet format.

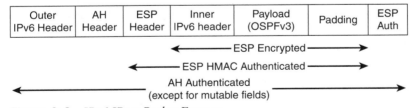

Figure 9-2 *IPv6 IPsec Packet Format*

OSPFv3 authentication supports IPsec AH authentication using the command **ospfv3 authentication** or ESP authentication and encryption with the command **ospfv3 encryption**. The configuration may be applied to an interface, a virtual link, or an entire area. Area authentication requires that every router in the area perform IPsec authentication in order to form neighbor adjacencies. Interface-level authentication settings preempt area-level settings.

Unlike with an IPsec VPN tunnel, OSPFv3 neighbor authentication does not perform Internet Key Exchange (IKE) to negotiate the IPsec security association (SA) values. Therefore, the *IPsec Security Parameter Index (SPI)* hash algorithm and key must be manually defined when configuring OSPFv3 authentication. IPsec peers cannot reuse the same SPI values. The command **show crypto ipsec sa | include spi** may be used to determine the active IPsec sessions and currently used SPI values.

The full interface command **ospfv3 encryption** {ipsec spi *spi* esp *encryption-algorithm* {*key-encryption-type key*} *authentication-algorithm* {*key-encryption-type key*} | **null**} encrypts and authenticates the OSPFv3 packet in IOS using ESP. The **null** keyword disables OSPFv3 packet payload encryption and only enables ESP header authentication.

Example 9-13 demonstrates how to configure encryption and authentication for OSPFv3 packets using ESP. The following fabricated values are included in the configuration to establish the IPsec session:

- Security policy index: = 500

- Encryption algorithm: = 3des

- Encryption key: = 012345678901234567890123456789012345678901234567

- Authentication algorithm: = sha1

- Authentication key: = 0123456789012345678901234567890123456789

NOTE The fabricated authentication and encryption key values in the example are for demonstration purposes. A real deployment should not use such predictable values.

Example 9-13 *OSPFv3 Interface Authentication and Encryption*

```
interface GigabitEthernet0/1
ospfv3 encryption ipsec spi 500 esp 3des 01234567890123456789012345678901234567
 8901234567 sha1 0123456789012345678901234567890123456789
! The ospfv3 encryption rolls over to two lines in the example, but it is only
! one single CLI command.
```

Example 9-14 demonstrates how to configure area authentication and encryption using the same IPsec settings.

Example 9-14 *OSPFv3 Area Authentication and Encryption*

```
router ospfv3 100
 area 0 encryption ipsec spi 500 esp 3des 12345678901234567890123456789012345678901234567
  8901234567 sha1 0123456789012345678901234567890123456789
! The ospfv3 encryption rolls over to two lines in the example, but it is
! entered as one long command. The running configuration will display the
! password encrypted
```

Example 9-15 displays the output of the command **show ospfv3 interface** [*interface-id*]. This **show** command can be used to verify that authentication and encryption are enabled on the interface and that a secure connection has formed with the neighbor.

Example 9-15 *OSPFv3 IPsec Verification*

```
R2# show ospfv3 interface
GigabitEthernet0/1 is up, line protocol is up
  Link Local Address FE80::2, Interface ID 3
  Area 0, Process ID 100, Instance ID 0, Router ID 100.0.0.2
  Network Type BROADCAST, Cost: 1
  3DES encryption SHA-1 auth SPI 500, secure socket UP (errors: 0)
  Transmit Delay is 1 sec, State DR, Priority 1
  Designated Router (ID) 100.0.0.2, local address FE80::2
  Backup Designated router (ID) 100.0.0.1, local address FE80::1
! Output omitted for brevity
```

OSPFv3 Link-Local Forwarding

Significant changes have occurred in how OSPF builds the area topology between OSPFv2 and OSPFv3. With OSPFv2, the interface's network addresses are used to build the adjacency and link devices. The OSPFv3 LSDB creates a shortest path topology tree based on links instead of networks. This means that transit links only require IPv6 link-local addresses for forwarding traffic. Therefore, the global IPv6 unicast addresses can be removed from the transit links between R1 and R4 from the sample topology, and R4 can still communicate R1's 2001:DB8:0:1::/64 network.

Example 9-16 demonstrates the removal of the global IPv6 unicast addresses from the transit links on R1, R2, and R3.

Example 9-16 *Removal of Global IPv6 Addresses*

```
R1# configure terminal
Enter configuration commands, one per line. End with CNTL/Z.
R1(config)# interface gi0/2
R1(config-if)# no ipv6 address 2001:DB8:0:12::1/64
```

```
R2# configure terminal
Enter configuration commands, one per line. End with CNTL/Z.
R2(config)# interface gi0/1
R2(config-if)# no ipv6 address 2001:DB8:0:12::2/64
R2(config-if)# interface Gi0/3
R2(config-if)# no ipv6 address 2001:DB8:0:23::2/64
```

```
R3# configure terminal
Enter configuration commands, one per line. End with CNTL/Z.
R3(config)# interface gigabitEthernet 0/2
R3(config-if)# no ipv6 address 2001:DB8:0:23::3/64
R3(config-if)# interface GigabitEthernet 0/4
R3(config-if)# no ipv6 address 2001:DB8:0:34::3/64
```

Example 9-17 shows the OSPFv3 learned routes from R4's perspective. Notice that the transit networks no longer appear. The loopback interface of R1, R2, and R3 still exists, along with R1's LAN interface 2001:DB8:0:1::/64.

Example 9-17 *R4's Routing Table After Removal of Global IPv6 Addresses*

```
R4# show ipv6 route ospf
IPv6 Routing Table - default - 8 entries
Codes: C - Connected, L - Local, S - Static, U - Per-user Static route
       B - BGP, HA - Home Agent, MR - Mobile Router, R - RIP
       H - NHRP, I1 - ISIS L1, I2 - ISIS L2, IA - ISIS interarea
       IS - ISIS summary, D - EIGRP, EX - EIGRP external, NM - NEMO
       ND - ND Default, NDp - ND Prefix, DCE - Destination, NDr - Redirect
       RL - RPL, O - OSPF Intra, OI - OSPF Inter, OE1 - OSPF ext 1
       OE2 - OSPF ext 2, ON1 - OSPF NSSA ext 1, ON2 - OSPF NSSA ext 2
       la - LISP alt, lr - LISP site-registrations, ld - LISP dyn-eid
       lA - LISP away, a - Application
OI  2001:DB8::1/128 [110/3]
     via FE80::3, GigabitEthernet0/3
OI  2001:DB8::2/128 [110/2]
     via FE80::3, GigabitEthernet0/3
OI  2001:DB8::3/128 [110/1]
     via FE80::3, GigabitEthernet0/3
OI  2001:DB8:0:1::/64 [110/4]
     via FE80::3, GigabitEthernet0/3
```

R4 still maintains full connectivity to those networks in Example 9-17 because the topology is built using the IPv6 link-local address. As long as the source and destination devices have routes to each other, communication can still exist. Example 9-18 demonstrates that R4 still maintains connectivity to R1's LAN interface. (This scenario is provided to demonstrate underlying mechanisms and not as a design suggestion.)

Example 9-18 *Connectivity Test with Link-Local Forwarding*

```
R4# ping 2001:DB8:0:1::1
Type escape sequence to abort.
Sending 5, 100-byte ICMP Echos to 2001:DB8:0:1::1, timeout is 2 seconds:
!!!!!
Success rate is 100 percent (5/5), round-trip min/avg/max = 4/5/6 ms
```

OSPFv3 LSA Flooding Scope

There are two LSA flooding scopes in OSPFv2: area and autonomous system. OSPFv3 allows for three flooding scopes:

- **Link-local scope:** Limited to the local link

- **Area scope:** Contains LSA flooding to the local area

- **Autonomous system scope:** Floods LSAs throughout the entire OSPF routing domain

The LS type field in OSPFv3 has been modified from 8 bits to 16 bits. Figure 9-3 shows the new LS Type field format. The 3 high-order bits of the new LS Type field allow for the encoding of flood information. The first bit, *U* (unrecognized), indicates how a router should handle an LSA if it is unrecognized. The second and third bits, both *S* (scope) bits, indicate how the LSA should be flooded. The remaining bits of the link-state field indicate the function code of the LSA. For example, a function code of 1 maps to the router LSA, which matches the original OSPFv2 LS type value 1.

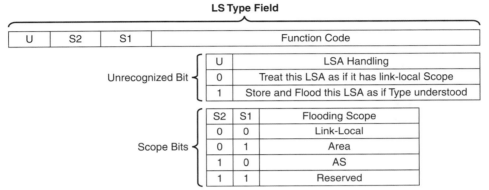

Figure 9-3 *LS Type Field*

Table 9-4 outlines all eight OSPFv3 LSA types and flooding scopes.

Table 9-4   OSPFv3 LSA Type Flooding Scope

Function Code	LS Type	LSA Name	Flooding Scope
1	0x2001	Device-LSA	Area
2	0x2002	Network-LSA	Area
3	0x2003	Inter-Area-Prefix-LSA	Area
4	0x2004	Inter-Area-Router-LSA	Area
5	0x4005	AS-External-LSA	Autonomous System
7	0x2007	NSSA-LSA	Area
8	0x0008	Link-LSA	Link-local
9	0x2009	Intra-Area-Prefix-LSA	Area

The router LSA describes the router's interface state and cost. Example 9-19 shows the output of the command **show ospfv3 database router[self-originate | adv-router *RID*]**. The optional **self-originate** keyword filters the LSAs to those created by the router on which the command is executed. The **adv-router *RID*** keyword allows for selection of the LSAs for a specific router's LSAs that exist in the local router's LSDB.

R1 is advertising a router LSA for the local GigabitEthernet0/2 interface (interface ID 4) with a cost of 1. R1 is the designated router for the segment, so it populates its own RID in the LSA.

9

Example 9-19   *Viewing the Self-Originating LSAs in the OSPFv3 Database*

```
R1# show ospfv3 database router self-originate

            OSPFv3 1 address-family ipv6 (router-id 192.168.1.1)

                    Router Link States (Area 0)

   LS age: 563
   Options: (V6-Bit, E-Bit, R-Bit, DC-Bit)
   LS Type: Router Links
   Link State ID: 0
   Advertising Router: 192.168.1.1
   LS Seq Number: 80000012
   Checksum: 0x13FB
   Length: 40
   Number of Links: 1

     Link connected to: a Transit Network
       Link Metric: 1
       Local Interface ID: 4
       Neighbor (DR) Interface ID: 4
       Neighbor (DR) Router ID: 192.168.1.1
```

OSPFv3 LSAs include an Options field that describes the router's capabilities. Table 9-5 describes the various service options.

Table 9-5   OSPFv3 Options Field Bits

Option	Description
V6	The V6 bit indicates that the router participates in IPv6 routing.
E	The E bit indicates that the router is capable of processing external LSAs. A router in a stubby area sets the E bit to clear (0). Neighboring routers do not form adjacencies if they have mismatched E bit settings.
R	The R bit indicates that the router actively participates in forwarding traffic. The R bit set to clear (0) indicates that the router is not to be used as a transit router for forwarding traffic but is still capable of exchanging route information.
DC	The DC bit is set to indicate that the router is capable of suppressing future hellos from being sent over the interface. The interface must be configured as a demand circuit for hello suppression to occur. (Demand circuits are typically used on costly low-bandwidth legacy ISDN BRI circuits, which are beyond the scope of this book.)
MC	The MC bit indicates that the router is capable of multicast extensions for OSPF (MOSPF). This bit is not used and is listed only for reference. In 2008, RFC 5340 deprecated MOSPF along with the Group-Membership-LSA.
N	The N bit indicates that the router supports Type 7 LSAs (NSSA area). Neighboring routers do not form an adjacency if they have mismatched N bit settings.

Example 9-20 shows a portion of R3's router LSAs in the LSDB. The highlighted bits indicate the functionality the router can perform in each area.

Example 9-20   *Viewing R3's LSAs in the OSPFv3 Database*

```
R1# show ospfv3 database router adv-router 192.168.3.3

          OSPFv3 1 address-family ipv6 (router-id 192.168.1.1)

              Router Link States (Area 0)

  LSA ignored in SPF calculation
  LS age: 136
  Options: (V6-Bit, E-Bit, R-Bit, DC-Bit)
  LS Type: Router Links
  Link State ID: 0
  Advertising Router: 192.168.3.3
  LS Seq Number: 80000011
  Checksum: 0x34D4
  Length: 40
  Area Border Router
  Number of Links: 1

    Link connected to: another Router (point-to-point)
      Link Metric: 1
      Local Interface ID: 4
      Neighbor Interface ID: 5
      Neighbor Router ID: 192.168.2.2
```

The network LSA describes the known routers on the broadcast interface GigabitEthernet0/2 (interface ID 4). Example 9-21 shows the output of the command **show ospfv3 database network [self-originate]**, which indicates that there are two routers present for the network: 192.168.1.1 (R1) and 192.168.2.2 (R2).

Example 9-21   *OSPFv3 Database Network*

```
R1# show ospfv3 database network self-originate

          OSPFv3 1 address-family ipv6 (router-id 192.168.1.1)

              Net Link States (Area 0)

  LS age: 1791
  Options: (V6-Bit, E-Bit, R-Bit, DC-Bit)
  LS Type: Network Links
  Link State ID: 4 (Interface ID of Designated Router)
  Advertising Router: 192.168.1.1
  LS Seq Number: 8000000B
  Checksum: 0x9F17
  Length: 32
      Attached Router: 192.168.1.1
      Attached Router: 192.168.2.2
```

9

The link LSA is responsible for providing details for the IPv6 prefixes associated with an interface. Example 9-22 shows the output of the command **show ospfv3 database link [self-originate]**. Notice that the prefix 2001:db8:0:12::/64 is associated with GigabitEthernet0/2 (interface ID 4) and can be reached using the link-local address FE80::1 and that the prefix 2001:db8:0:1::/64 is associated to GigabitEthernet0/1 (interface ID 3).

Example 9-22 *OSPFv3 Database Link*

```
R1# show ospfv3 database link self-originate
            OSPFv3 1 address-family ipv6 (router-id 192.168.1.1)

                Link (Type-8) Link States (Area 0)

  LS age: 1572
  Options: (V6-Bit, E-Bit, R-Bit, DC-Bit)
  LS Type: Link-LSA (Interface: GigabitEthernet0/2)
  Link State ID: 4 (Interface ID)
  Advertising Router: 192.168.1.1
  LS Seq Number: 8000000C
  Checksum: 0x389C
  Length: 56
  Router Priority: 1
  Link Local Address: FE80::1
  Number of Prefixes: 1
  Prefix Address: 2001:DB8:0:12::
  Prefix Length: 64, Options: None


  LS age: 1829
  Options: (V6-Bit, E-Bit, R-Bit, DC-Bit)
  LS Type: Link-LSA (Interface: GigabitEthernet0/1)
  Link State ID: 3 (Interface ID)
  Advertising Router: 192.168.1.1
  LS Seq Number: 8000000B
  Checksum: 0xBB2C
  Length: 56
  Router Priority: 1
  Link Local Address: FE80::1
  Number of Prefixes: 1
  Prefix Address: 2001:DB8:0:1::
  Prefix Length: 64, Options: None
```

R3 has backbone connectivity and is the local ABR for Area 34 in the network topology in this example. As an ABR, it is responsible for advertising inter-area prefix LSAs that describe routes that belong to other areas in the OSPF domain. The command **show ospfv3 database** displays the router's summary view OSPFv3 database.

Example 9-23 shows R3's database. Notice that R3's router LSA bits are set to B, indicating that it is an ABR router. The advertising RID for all the inter-area prefix LSAs originates from 192.168.3.3 (R3).

Example 9-23 *Summary View of an OSPFv3 LSDB*

```
R3# show ospfv3 database
! Output Omitted for brevity
            OSPFv3 1 address-family ipv6 (router-id 192.168.3.3)

                  Router Link States (Area 0)

ADV Router         Age         Seq#           Fragment ID  Link count  Bits
  192.168.1.1      416         0x80000005     0            1           None
  192.168.2.2      375         0x80000007     0            2           None
  192.168.3.3      351         0x80000005     0            1           B

                  Net Link States (Area 0)

ADV Router         Age         Seq#           Link ID   Rtr count
  192.168.2.2      375         0x80000002     3         2
  192.168.3.3      351         0x80000002     4         2

                  Inter Area Prefix Link States (Area 0)

ADV Router         Age         Seq#           Prefix
  192.168.3.3      351         0x80000002     2001:DB8:0:34::/64

                  Link (Type-8) Link States (Area 0)

ADV Router         Age         Seq#           Link ID   Interface
  192.168.2.2      375         0x80000002     5         Gi0/2
  192.168.3.3      351         0x80000002     4         Gi0/2

                  Intra Area Prefix Link States (Area 0)

ADV Router         Age         Seq#           Link ID   Ref-lstype  Ref-LSID
  192.168.1.1      416         0x80000003     0         0x2001      0
  192.168.2.2      375         0x80000002     0         0x2001      0
  192.168.2.2      375         0x80000002     3072      0x2002      3
  192.168.3.3      351         0x80000003     0         0x2001      0
  192.168.3.3      351         0x80000002     4096      0x2002      4

                  Router Link States (Area 34)

ADV Router         Age         Seq#           Fragment ID  Link count  Bits
  192.168.3.3      351         0x80000004     0            1           B
  192.168.4.4      399         0x80000005     0            1           None
```

```
                        Net Link States (Area 34)
ADV Router          Age         Seq#          Link ID     Rtr count
   192.168.4.4      399         0x80000002    5           2


                   Inter Area Prefix Link States (Area 34)


ADV Router          Age         Seq#          Prefix
   192.168.3.3      351         0x80000002    2001:DB8:0:23::/64
   192.168.3.3      351         0x80000002    2001:DB8:0:12::/64
   192.168.3.3      1572        0x80000001    2001:DB8:0:1::/64
   192.168.3.3      6           0x80000001    2001:DB8::3/128
   192.168.3.3      6           0x80000001    2001:DB8::2/128
   192.168.3.3      6           0x80000001    2001:DB8::1/128


                   Link (Type-8) Link States (Area 34)


ADV Router          Age         Seq#          Link ID     Interface
   192.168.3.3      351         0x80000002    6           Gi0/4
   192.168.4.4      399         0x80000002    5           Gi0/4


                   Intra Area Prefix Link States (Area 34)


ADV Router          Age         Seq#          Link ID     Ref-lstype   Ref-LSID
   192.168.4.4      399         0x80000002    5120        0x2002       5
```

References in This Chapter

Edgeworth, Brad, Foss, Aaron, and Garza Rios, Ramiro, *IP Routing on Cisco IOS, IOS XE, and IOS XR,*. Cisco Press, 2014.

RFC 5340, *OSPF for IPv6*, R. Coltun, D. Ferguson, J. Moy, and A. Lindem, IETF, http://www.ietf.org/rfc/rfc5340.txt, July 2008.

Cisco, Cisco IOS Software Configuration Guides, http://www.cisco.com.

Exam Preparation Tasks

As mentioned in the section "How to Use This Book" in the Introduction, you have a couple choices for exam preparation: the exercises here, Chapter 24, "Final Preparation," and the exam simulation questions in the Pearson Test Prep software.

Review All Key Topics

Review the most important topics in this chapter, noted with the Key Topic icon in the outer margin of the page. Table 9-6 lists these key topics and the page number on which each is found.

Table 9-6   Key Topics

Key Topic	Description	Page Number
Paragraph	OSPFv3 fundamentals	371
Paragraph	OSPFv3 link-state advertisement	372
Paragraph	OSPFv3 communication	373
Paragraph	OSPFv3 configuration	374
Paragraph	OSPFv3 verification	377
Paragraph	IPv6 route summarization	379
Paragraph	Network type	380
Paragraph	OSPFv3 authentication	381
Paragraph	OSPFv3 flooding scope	384

Define Key Terms

There are no key terms in this chapter.

Use the Command Reference to Check Your Memory

The ENARSI 300-410 exam focuses on the practical, hands-on skills that networking professionals use. Therefore, you should be able to identify the commands needed to configure, verify, and troubleshoot the topics covered in this chapter.

This section includes the most important configuration and verification commands covered in this chapter. It might not be necessary to memorize the complete syntax of every command, but you should be able to remember the basic keywords that are needed.

To test your memory of the commands in Table 9-7, go to the companion website and download Appendix B, "Command Reference Exercises." Fill in the missing commands in the tables based on each command description. You can check your work by downloading Appendix C, "Command Reference Exercise Answer Key," from the companion website.

Table 9-7   Command Reference

Task	Command Syntax
Configure OSPFv3 on a router and enable it on an interface.	**router ospfv3** [process-id] **interface** *interface-id* **ospfv3** *process-id* {**ipv4** | **ipv6**} **area** *area-id*
Configure a specific OSPFv3 interface as passive.	**passive-interface** *interface-id*
Configure all OSPFv3 interfaces as passive.	**passive-interface default**
Summarize an IPv6 network range on an ABR.	**area** *area-id* **range** *prefix*/*prefix-length*
Configure an OSPFv3 interface as point-to-point or broadcast network type.	**ospfv3 network** {**point-to-point** | **broadcast**}
Display OSPFv3 interface settings.	**show ospfv3 interface** [*interface-id*]
Display OSPFv3 IPv6 neighbors.	**show ospfv3 ipv6 neighbor**
Display OSPFv3 router LSAs.	**show ospfv3 database router**
Display OSPFv3 network LSAs.	**show ospfv3 database network**
Display OSPFv3 link LSAs.	**show ospfv3 database link**

9

## CHAPTER 10

Troubleshooting OSPFv3

This chapter covers the following topics:

- **Troubleshooting OSPFv3 for IPv6:** This section examines the various commands you can use to troubleshoot OSPFv3 issues.

- **OSPFv3 Trouble Tickets:** This section presents trouble tickets that demonstrate how to use a structured troubleshooting process to solve a reported problem.

- **Troubleshooting OSPFv3 Address Families:** This section describes the commands you can use to troubleshoot issues related to OSPFv3 address family configurations.

- **OSPFv3 AF Trouble Tickets:** This section presents a trouble ticket that demonstrates how to use a structured troubleshooting process to solve a reported problem.

The *Open Shortest Path First version 3 (OSPFv3)* dynamic routing protocol is a link-state routing protocol that uses *Dijkstra's shortest path first (SPF) algorithm*. It is an extremely scalable routing protocol because of its hierarchical design. OSPFv3 is designed for routing IPv6 networks. This chapter focuses on troubleshooting OSPFv3 using classic configurations and also using the OSPF address family configurations.

Before any routes can be exchanged between OSPFv3 routers on the same LAN or across a WAN, an OSPFv3 neighbor relationship must be formed. Neighbor relationships may fail to form for many reasons, and as a troubleshooter, you need to be aware of them. Chapter 8, "Troubleshooting OSPFv2," delves deeply into these reasons, and that information is not repeated in this chapter. Therefore, if you have not reviewed Chapter 8, you may want to do so before continuing with this chapter. This chapter focuses on the OSPFv3 **show** commands that can be used for troubleshooting, and it provides examples in various trouble tickets.

After neighbor relationships are formed, neighboring routers exchange OSPF *link-state advertisements (LSAs)*, which contain information about routes. In some cases, routes may end up missing, and you need to be able to determine why the routes are missing. Chapter 8 provides details related to why routes may be missing, and this chapter does not repeat that information. Rather, this chapter focuses on the OSPFv3 **show** commands that can be used for troubleshooting and provides examples in various trouble tickets.

"Do I Know This Already?" Quiz

The "Do I Know This Already?" quiz allows you to assess whether you should read this entire chapter thoroughly or jump to the "Exam Preparation Tasks" section. If you are in doubt about your answers to these questions or your own assessment of your knowledge of the topics, read the entire chapter. Table 10-1 lists the major headings in this chapter and their corresponding "Do I Know This Already?" quiz questions. You can find the answers in Appendix A, "Answers to the 'Do I Know This Already?' Quiz Questions."

Table 10-1 "Do I Know This Already?" Foundation Topics Section-to-Question Mapping

Foundation Topics Section	Questions
Troubleshooting OSPFv3 for IPv6	1–8
Troubleshooting OSPFv3 Address Families	9, 10

CAUTION The goal of self-assessment is to gauge your mastery of the topics in this chapter. If you do not know the answer to a question or are only partially sure of the answer, you should mark that question as wrong for purposes of self-assessment. Giving yourself credit for an answer that you correctly guess skews your self-assessment results and might provide you with a false sense of security.

1. What can be verified with the output of **show ipv6 protocols**? (Choose two.)
   a. The router ID
   b. Which areas are normal, stub, and not-so-stubby areas
   c. The interfaces participating in the routing process
   d. The ID of the designated router

2. Which of the following are true about the output of **show ipv6 ospf interface brief**? (Choose two.)
   a. The cost of the interface is listed.
   b. The DR/BDR state of the neighbor is listed.
   c. The area an interface is participating in is listed.
   d. The network type of the interface is listed.

3. Which IPv6 OSPFv3 command enables you to verify the configured hello interval and the dead interval?
   a. **show ipv6 protocols**
   b. **show ipv6 ospf interface**
   c. **show ipv6 ospf neighbor**
   d. **show ipv6 ospf database**

4. Which multicast addresses are used for OSPFv3? (Choose two.)
   a. FF02::A
   b. FF02::9
   c. FF02::5
   d. FF02::6

5. Which IPv6 OSPFv3 LSA is used to describe prefixes outside an area but that are still within the OSPF routing domain?
   a. Router link states
   b. Net link states
   c. Inter-area prefix link states
   d. Type 5 AS external link states

6. Which LSA type is only flooded on the local link and is not reflooded by other OSPF routers?

   a. 1
   b. 8
   c. 3
   d. 9

7. Which IPv6 OSPFv3 command enables you to verify whether an area is a stub area, totally stubby area, NSSA, or totally NSSA?

   a. show ipv6 protocols
   b. show ipv6 ospf
   c. show ipv6 ospf interface
   d. show ipv6 ospf neighbor

8. Which IPv6 OSPFv3 command enables you to verify which routers the local router has formed neighbor adjacencies with?

   a. show ipv6 protocols
   b. show ipv6 ospf
   c. show ipv6 ospf interface
   d. show ipv6 ospf neighbor

9. Which OSPFv3 address family commands are used to verify which OSPFv3 address family an interface is participating in? (Choose two.)

   a. show ospfv3
   b. show ospfv3 interface brief
   c. show ospfv3 neighbor
   d. show ospfv3 database

10. Which OSPFv3 address family **debug** command identifies whether there is a mismatched stub area configuration?

    a. debug ospfv3 hello
    b. debug ospfv3 packet
    c. debug ospfv3 adj
    d. debug ospfv3 events

Foundation Topics

Troubleshooting OSPFv3 for IPv6

Because OSPFv3 is based on OSPFv2, it presents similar issues when it comes to troubleshooting, with a few minor differences based on IPv6. This should come as a relief, as it means you do not have to learn a large amount of new information for OSPFv3. However, you do need to know the **show** commands that display the information you need to troubleshoot any given OSPFv3-related issue.

This section describes **show** commands that you can use to troubleshoot OSPFv3 neighbor adjacency issues and route issues. Chapter 8 provides complete coverage of OSPF neighbor and route issues.

OSPFv3 Troubleshooting Commands

You use the **show ipv6 protocols** command, as shown in Example 10-1, to verify which IPv6 routing protocols are running on a device. Specifically with OSPFv3, you can verify the process ID (PID), the router ID (RID), the type of router—*area border router (ABR)* or *autonomous system boundary router (ASBR)*—the number of areas the router is a member of, whether any of the areas are stub areas or NSSAs (not-so-stubby areas), the interfaces participating in the routing process and the area they belong to, and whether redistribution is occurring.

Example 10-1 *Identifying What Can Be Verified for OSPFv3 with **show ipv6 protocols***

```
R2# show ipv6 protocols
...output omitted...
IPv6 Routing Protocol is "ospf 1"
  Router ID 2.2.2.2
  Area border and autonomous system boundary router
  Number of areas: 2 normal, 0 stub, 0 nssa
  Interfaces (Area 0):
    GigabitEthernet0/0
  Interfaces (Area 23):
    GigabitEthernet1/0
  Redistribution:
    None
```

You use the **show ipv6 ospf** command, as shown in Example 10-2, to display global OSPFv3 settings. For example, you can verify the OSPFv3 PID, the RID, the type of router (ABR or ASBR), various timers and statistics, the number of areas on the router and the type of area (normal, stub, or NSSA), the reference bandwidth, and the parameters related to the different areas configured on the router (for example, whether area authentication is enabled, whether the area is a *stub area*, a *totally stubby area*, an *NSSA*, or a *totally NSSA*).

Example 10-2 *Identifying What Can Be Verified with **show ipv6 ospf***

```
R1# show ipv6 ospf
Routing Process "ospfv3 1" with ID 1.1.1.1
Supports NSSA (compatible with RFC 3101)
Event-log enabled, Maximum number of events: 1000, Mode: cyclic
It is an area border router
Router is not originating router-LSAs with maximum metric
Initial SPF schedule delay 5000 msecs
Minimum hold time between two consecutive SPFs 10000 msecs
Maximum wait time between two consecutive SPFs 10000 msecs
```

10

```
   Minimum LSA interval 5 secs
   Minimum LSA arrival 1000 msecs
   LSA group pacing timer 240 secs
   Interface flood pacing timer 33 msecs
   Retransmission pacing timer 66 msecs
   Retransmission limit dc 24 non-dc 24
 Number of external LSA 1. Checksum Sum 0x009871
 Number of areas in this router is 2. 1 normal 1 stub 0 nssa
 Graceful restart helper support enabled
 Reference bandwidth unit is 100 mbps
 RFC1583 compatibility enabled
 Area BACKBONE(0)
    Number of interfaces in this area is 2
    MD5 Authentication, SPI 257
    SPF algorithm executed 3 times
    Number of LSA 11. Checksum Sum 0x06DB20
    Number of DCbitless LSA 0
    Number of indication LSA 0
    Number of DoNotAge LSA 0
    Flood list length 0
 Area 1
    Number of interfaces in this area is 1
    It is a stub area, no summary LSA in this area
    Generates stub default route with cost 1
    SPF algorithm executed 4 times
    Number of LSA 7. Checksum Sum 0x03A033
    Number of DCbitless LSA 0
    Number of indication LSA 0
    Number of DoNotAge LSA 0
    Flood list length 0
```

The command **show ipv6 ospf interface brief**, as shown in Example 10-3, enables you to verify which interfaces are participating in the OSPFv3 process. You can also identify the PID they are attached to, the area they are participating in, the IPv6 interface ID used to represent the interface, the cost of the interface (which by default is based on the reference bandwidth divided by the interface bandwidth), the DR/BDR (*designated router/backup designated router*) state, and whether there are any neighbor adjacencies established out the interface. Notice that R1 has interfaces in Area 0 and Area 1; therefore, it is an ABR.

Example 10-3 *Identifying What Can Be Verified with show ipv6 ospf interface brief*

```
R1# show ipv6 ospf interface brief
Interface PID   Area   Intf ID   Cost   State   Nbrs F/C
Gi1/0      1      0       4        1     BDR       1/1
Gi0/0      1      0       3        1     DR        0/0
Fa3/0      1      1       6        1     BDR       1/1
```

With the **show ipv6 ospf interface** *interface_type interface_number* command, you can obtain detailed information about the interfaces participating in the OSPF process, as shown in Example 10-4. The unique information that will draw you to this command for troubleshooting includes the network type, the cost, whether authentication is enabled on the interface, the current DR/BDR state, the interface priority, the DR and BDR IDs, and the timers (hello and dead).

Example 10-4 *Identifying What Can Be Verified with **show ipv6 ospf interface** interface_type interface_number*

```
R1# show ipv6 ospf interface fastEthernet 3/0
FastEthernet3/0 is up, line protocol is up
 Link Local Address FE80::C809:13FF:FEB8:54, Interface ID 6
 Area 1, Process ID 1, Instance ID 0, Router ID 1.1.1.1
 Network Type BROADCAST, Cost: 1
 MD5 authentication SPI 256, secure socket UP (errors: 0)
 Transmit Delay is 1 sec, State BDR, Priority 1
 Designated Router (ID) 4.4.4.4, local address FE80::C808:9FF:FE30:1C
 Backup Designated router (ID) 1.1.1.1, local address FE80::C809:13FF:FEB8:54
 Timer intervals configured, Hello 10, Dead 40, Wait 40, Retransmit 5
 Hello due in 00:00:04
 Graceful restart helper support enabled
 Index 1/1/1, flood queue length 0
 Next 0x0(0)/0x0(0)/0x0(0)
 Last flood scan length is 1, maximum is 2
 Last flood scan time is 0 msec, maximum is 0 msec
 Neighbor Count is 1, Adjacent neighbor count is 1
 Adjacent with neighbor 4.4.4.4 (Designated Router)
 Suppress hello for 0 neighbor(s)
```

The **show ipv6 ospf neighbor** command enables you to verify what routers successfully formed neighbor adjacencies with the local router, as shown in Example 10-5. You can verify a neighbor by its RID, which is displayed in the Neighbor ID column, the priority of the neighbor's interface used to form the neighbor adjacency, the state of the neighbor's interface, the dead timer, the IPv6 interface ID of the neighboring device, and the local interface used to form the adjacency.

Example 10-5 *Identifying What Can Be Verified with **show ipv6 ospf neighbor***

```
R1# show ipv6 ospf neighbor

 OSPFv3 Router with ID (1.1.1.1) (Process ID 1)

Neighbor ID  Pri   State     Dead Time   Interface ID    Interface
2.2.2.2       1    FULL/DR   00:00:36        3           GigabitEthernet1/0
4.4.4.4       1    FULL/DR   00:00:39        4           FastEthernet3/0
```

10

To verify the LSAs that were collected and placed in the *link-state database (LSDB)*, you use the **show ipv6 ospf database** command, as shown in Example 10-6. In this example, R1 has information for Area 0 and Area 1 because it is an ABR.

Example 10-6   *Displaying the OSPFv3 LSDB*

```
R1# show ipv6 ospf database

        OSPFv3 Router with ID (1.1.1.1) (Process ID 1)

                Router Link States (Area 0)

ADV Router    Age Seq#        Fragment ID   Link count   Bits
  1.1.1.1     847 0x80000005      0              1         B
  2.2.2.2     748 0x80000007      0              1         B E

                Net Link States (Area 0)

ADV Router    Age Seq#        Link ID    Rtr count
  2.2.2.2     878 0x80000003      3          2

            Inter Area Prefix Link States (Area 0)

ADV Router    Age  Seq#        Prefix
  1.1.1.1    1136 0x80000001    2001:DB8:0:14::/64
  2.2.2.2    1006 0x80000002    2001:DB8:0:23::/64
  2.2.2.2    1006 0x80000002    2001:DB8:0:3::/64

            Link (Type-8) Link States (Area 0)

ADV Router    Age  Seq#        Link ID    Interface
  1.1.1.1     847  0x80000002     4        Gi1/0
  2.2.2.2    1006  0x80000002     3        Gi1/0
  1.1.1.1     847  0x80000002     3        Gi0/0

            Intra Area Prefix Link States (Area 0)

ADV Router    Age Seq#        Link ID   Ref-lstype Ref-LSID
  1.1.1.1     847 0x80000006      0       0x2001       0
  2.2.2.2     878 0x80000003    3072      0x2002       3

                Router Link States (Area 1)

ADV Router    Age  Seq#        Fragment ID Link count  Bits
  1.1.1.1    1151 0x80000004      0            1         B
```

```
4.4.4.4      1152 0x80000006           0        1           None
                  Net Link States (Area 1)


ADV Router   Age  Seq#          Link ID    Rtr count
  4.4.4.4    1147 0x80000003        4          2


          Inter Area Prefix Link States (Area 1)


ADV Router   Age Seq#            Prefix
  1.1.1.1     847 0x80000002     ::/0


          Link (Type-8) Link States (Area 1)


ADV Router   Age  Seq#          Link ID    Interface
  1.1.1.1    1105 0x80000002        6       Fa3/0
  4.4.4.4    1158 0x80000003        4       Fa3/0


          Intra Area Prefix Link States (Area 1)


ADV Router   Age  Seq#           Link ID  Ref-lstype  Ref-LSID
  4.4.4.4    1147 0x80000003       4096      0x2002        4


             Type-5 AS External Link States


ADV Router   Age Seq#            Prefix
  2.2.2.2     748 0x80000002     ::/0
```

Notice in Example 10-6 that there are two new LSA types beyond the types listed in Table 8-4 in Chapter 8: the link (Type 8) LSA and the intra-area prefix (Type 9) LSA. Table 10-2 defines these two LSAs for OSPFv3. Also notice in Example 10-6 that the OSPFv2 Type 3 LSA (summary LSA) is now called the inter-area prefix LSA.

Key Topic

Table 10-2 Additional OSPF LSAs for OSPFv3

LSA Type	Description
8	The link LSA provides information to neighbors about link-local addresses and the IPv6 addresses associated with the link. Therefore, it is only flooded on the local link and is not reflooded by other OSPF routers.
9	The intra-area prefix LSA provides information for two different scenarios. First, it provides information about IPv6 address prefixes associated with a transit network by referencing a network LSA. Second, it provides information about IPv6 address prefixes associated with a router by referencing a router LSA. Type 9 LSAs are flooded only within an area.

To verify the OSPFv3 routes that have been installed in the routing table, you use the **show ipv6 route ospf** command, as shown in Example 10-7. In this case, R1 only knows about an

10

external OSPFv3 route, which is the default route, and two inter-area routes (routes outside the area but still within the OSPFv3 domain).

Example 10-7 *Displaying the OSPFv3 Routes in the Routing Table*

```
R1# show ipv6 route ospf
IPv6 Routing Table - default - 10 entries
Codes: C - Connected, L - Local, S - Static, U - Per-user Static route
 B - BGP, R - RIP, H - NHRP, I1 - ISIS L1
 I2 - ISIS L2, IA - ISIS interarea, IS - ISIS summary, D - EIGRP
 EX - EIGRP external, ND - ND Default, NDp - ND Prefix, DCE - Destination
 NDr - Redirect, O - OSPF Intra, OI - OSPF Inter, OE1 - OSPF ext 1
 OE2 - OSPF ext 2, ON1 - OSPF NSSA ext 1, ON2 - OSPF NSSA ext 2, l - LISP
OE2 ::/0 [110/1], tag 1
      via FE80::C80A:13FF:FEB8:8, GigabitEthernet1/0
OI 2001:DB8:0:3::/64 [110/3]
      via FE80::C80A:13FF:FEB8:8, GigabitEthernet1/0
OI 2001:DB8:0:23::/64 [110/2]
      via FE80::C80A:13FF:FEB8:8, GigabitEthernet1/0
```

Use the **show ipv6 interface** *interface_type interface_id* command, as shown in Example 10-8, when troubleshooting OSPFv3 issues to verify whether the interface is listening to the multicast group addresses FF02::5 (all OSPFv3 routers) and FF02::6 (OSPFv3 DR/BDR). You can also verify the MTU and whether there are any IPv6 ACLs applied to the interface that might be blocking OSPFv3 packets or packets sourced from/destined to link-local addresses.

Example 10-8 *Displaying the IPv6 Interface Parameters*

```
R1# show ipv6 interface fastEthernet 3/0
FastEthernet3/0 is up, line protocol is up
 IPv6 is enabled, link-local address is FE80::C809:13FF:FEB8:54
 ...output omitted...
 Joined group address(es):
    FF02::1
    FF02::2
    FF02::5
    FF02::6
    FF02::1:FF00:1
    FF02::1:FFB8:54
 MTU is 1500 bytes
 ICMP error messages limited to one every 100 milliseconds
 ICMP redirects are enabled
 ICMP unreachables are sent
 Input features: Access List IPsec
 Output features: IPsec
 Inbound access list TSHOOT_ACL
 ND DAD is enabled, number of DAD attempts: 1
 ...output omitted...
```

OSPFv3 Trouble Tickets

This section presents two trouble tickets related to the topics discussed so far in this chapter. The purpose of these trouble tickets is to show a process that you can use when troubleshooting in the real world or in an exam environment. Both of the trouble tickets in this section are based on the topology shown in Figure 10-1.

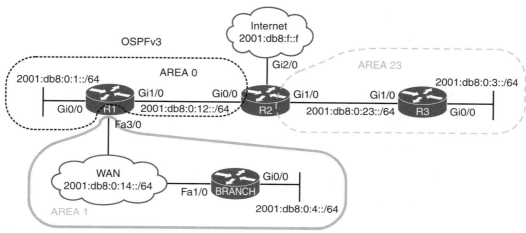

Figure 10-1   *OSPFv3 Trouble Tickets Topology*

Trouble Ticket 10-1

Problem: The network was recently updated to reduce the number of LSAs that cross the WAN link from R1 to the Branch site. The only LSA that is supposed to be permitted is a Type 3 LSA about a default route. However, reports indicate that more Type 3 LSAs are being sent from R1 to Branch.

You begin by reviewing the configuration change documents that were created when the change was implemented. You notice that the information is very vague. It only states that Area 1 was created as a totally stubby area. It does not indicate what changes were made to which devices and the commands that were used.

Your troubleshooting begins by verifying the problem with the **show ipv6 route ospf** command on Branch, as shown in Example 10-9. You confirm that there are more inter-area routes than just the default inter-area route.

Example 10-9   *Displaying the IPv6 Routing Table on Branch*

```
Branch# show ipv6 route ospf
IPv6 Routing Table - default - 10 entries
Codes: C - Connected, L - Local, S - Static, U - Per-user Static route
  B - BGP, R - RIP, H - NHRP, I1 - ISIS L1
  I2 - ISIS L2, IA - ISIS interarea, IS - ISIS summary, D - EIGRP
```

10

```
    EX - EIGRP external, ND - ND Default, NDp - ND Prefix, DCE - Destination
NDr - Redirect, O - OSPF Intra, OI - OSPF Inter, OE1 - OSPF ext 1
  OE2 - OSPF ext 2, ON1 - OSPF NSSA ext 1, ON2 - OSPF NSSA ext 2, l - LISP
OI ::/0 [110/2]
    via FE80::C801:10FF:FE20:54, FastEthernet1/0
OI 2001:DB8:0:1::/64 [110/2]
    via FE80::C801:10FF:FE20:54, FastEthernet1/0
OI 2001:DB8:0:3::/64 [110/4]
    via FE80::C801:10FF:FE20:54, FastEthernet1/0
OI 2001:DB8:0:12::/64 [110/2]
    via FE80::C801:10FF:FE20:54, FastEthernet1/0
OI 2001:DB8:0:23::/64 [110/3]
    via FE80::C801:10FF:FE20:54, FastEthernet1/0
```

Next, you want to confirm whether Branch is configured as a stub area for Area 1. You issue the command **show ipv6 ospf | include Area|stub**, as shown in Example 10-10, and confirm that it is.

Example 10-10   *Verifying Whether Area 1 Is a Stub Area on Branch*

```
Branch# show ipv6 ospf | include Area|stub
 Number of areas in this router is 1. 0 normal 1 stub 0 nssa
    Area 1
        It is a stub area
```

You then issue the same command on R1, as shown in Example 10-11. The output indicates that Area 1 is a stub area and that a default route with a cost of 1 is being injected into the area.

Example 10-11   *Verifying Whether Area 1 Is a Stub Area on R1*

```
R1# show ipv6 ospf | include Area|stub
 Number of areas in this router is 2. 1 normal 1 stub 0 nssa
    Area BACKBONE(0)
    Area 1
        It is a stub area
        Generates stub default route with cost 1
```

However, you realize that this output indicates that a stub area, not a totally stubby area, exists. If it were a totally stubby area, it would also state *no summary LSA in this area*. To confirm this, you issue the command **show run | section ipv6 router ospf** on both R1 and Branch, as shown in Example 10-12. Reviewing the output, you notice that R1 is configured with **area 1 stub**, and Branch is configured with **area 1 stub no-summary**. It appears that the commands were executed on the wrong routers.

Example 10-12 *Verifying IPv6 Router OSPF Configuration on R1 and Branch*

```
R1# show run | section ipv6 router ospf
ipv6 router ospf 1
 router-id 1.1.1.1
 area 1 stub
 passive-interface GigabitEthernet0/0


Branch# show run | section ipv6 router ospf
ipv6 router ospf 1
router-id 4.4.4.4
 area 1 stub no-summary
 passive-interface default
 no passive-interface FastEthernet1/0
```

To fix this issue, you issue the command **area 1 stub no-summary** on R1 and the commands **no area 1 stub no-summary** and **area 1 stub** on Branch. After this change has been made, you issue the command **show run | section ipv6 router ospf** on both R1 and Branch to confirm that the changes were made, as shown in Example 10-13.

Example 10-13 *Verifying IPv6 Router OSPF Configuration on R1 and Branch After Changes*

```
R1# show run | section ipv6 router ospf
ipv6 router ospf 1
 router-id 1.1.1.1
 area 1 stub no-summary
 passive-interface GigabitEthernet0/0


Branch# show run | section ipv6 router ospf
ipv6 router ospf 1
 router-id 4.4.4.4
 area 1 stub
 passive-interface default
 no passive-interface FastEthernet1/0
```

Next, you issue the command **show ipv6 ospf | include Area | stub** on R1, as shown in Example 10-14, to verify that it states *no summary LSA in this area*, which means no Type 3. It does!

Example 10-14 *Verifying Area 1 Is a Stub Area with No Summary LSAs on R1*

```
R1# show ipv6 ospf | include Area|stub
Number of areas in this router is 2. 1 normal 1 stub 0 nssa
    Area BACKBONE(0)
    Area 1
        It is a stub area, no summary LSA in this area
        Generates stub default route with cost 1
```

10

The output of **show ipv6 route ospf** on Branch contains only the default route now. The issue is solved, as shown in Example 10-15.

Example 10-15 *Verifying That Branch Is Receiving Only a Default Route*

```
Branch# show ipv6 route ospf
IPv6 Routing Table - default - 6 entries
Codes: C - Connected, L - Local, S - Static, U - Per-user Static route
 B - BGP, R - RIP, H - NHRP, I1 - ISIS L1
 I2 - ISIS L2, IA - ISIS interarea, IS - ISIS summary, D - EIGRP
 EX - EIGRP external, ND - ND Default, NDp - ND Prefix, DCE - Destination
 NDr - Redirect, O - OSPF Intra, OI - OSPF Inter, OE1 - OSPF ext 1
 OE2 - OSPF ext 2, ON1 - OSPF NSSA ext 1, ON2 - OSPF NSSA ext 2, l - LISP
OI ::/0 [110/2]
      via FE80::C801:10FF:FE20:54, FastEthernet1/0
```

Trouble Ticket 10-2

Problem: Branch users are complaining that they are unable to access any resources outside the Branch office.

You access Branch and issue the extended **ping** command, as shown in Example 10-16, to test connectivity. Connectivity fails.

Example 10-16 *Testing Connectivity from Branch to a Remote Network*

```
Branch# ping
Protocol [ip]: ipv6
Target IPv6 address: 2001:db8:0:1::1
Repeat count [5]:
Datagram size [100]:
Timeout in seconds [2]:
Extended commands? [no]: yes
Source address or interface: 2001:db8:0:4::4
UDP protocol? [no]:
Verbose? [no]:
Precedence [0]:
DSCP [0]:
Include hop by hop option? [no]:
Include destination option? [no]:
Sweep range of sizes? [no]:
Type escape sequence to abort.
Sending 5, 100-byte ICMP Echos to 2001:DB8:0:1::1, timeout is 2 seconds:
Packet sent with a source address of 2001:DB8:0:4::4
.....
Success rate is 0 percent (0/5)
```

You issue the **show ipv6 route** command on Branch and notice that there are only local and connected routes, as shown in Example 10-17.

Example 10-17   *Verifying IPv6 Routes in a Routing Table*

```
Branch# show ipv6 route
...output omitted...
C 2001:DB8:0:4::/64 [0/0]
     via GigabitEthernet0/0, directly connected
L 2001:DB8:0:4::4/128 [0/0]
     via GigabitEthernet0/0, receive
C 2001:DB8:0:14::/64 [0/0]
     via FastEthernet1/0, directly connected
L 2001:DB8:0:14::4/128 [0/0]
     via FastEthernet1/0, receive
L FF00::/8 [0/0]
     via Null0, receive
```

You conclude that no routes are being learned from R1. Therefore, there must be a neighbor issue. To confirm, you issue the command **show ipv6 ospf neighbor** on Branch, and as you suspected, the output (shown in Example 10-18) confirms that Branch is not a neighbor with R1.

Example 10-18   *Verifying IPv6 OSPF Neighbors*

```
Branch# show ipv6 ospf neighbor
Branch#
```

You suspect that the Branch interface connected to R1 is not enabled for the OSPFv3 process. You issue the **show ipv6 ospf interface brief** command to verify whether the interface is participating in the process. The output, shown in Example 10-19, indicates that Fa1/0 is participating in the OSPFv3 process.

Example 10-19   *Verifying OSPFv3-Enabled Interfaces on Branch*

```
Branch# show ipv6 ospf interface brief
Interface PID  Area Intf ID  Cost State   Nbrs F/C
Gi0/0     1    1    3        1    DR       0/0
Fa1/0     1    1    4        1    BDR      1/1
```

You decide to shift your attention to R1 and check whether the interface connected to Branch is participating in the OSPFv3 process. R1 is using Fa3/0 to connect to Branch. When you issue the command **show ipv6 ospf interface brief** on R1, as shown in Example 10-20, the output reveals that Fa3/0 is participating in the OSPF process as well.

10

Example 10-20 *Verifying OSPFv3-Enabled Interfaces on R1*

```
R1# show ipv6 ospf interface brief
Interface PID  Area  Intf ID   Cost State    Nbrs F/C
Gi1/0      1    0      4        1    BDR       1/1
Gi0/0      1    0      3        1    DR        0/0
Fa3/0      1    1      6        1    DR        0/0
```

You revisit Branch and decide to issue the **debug ipv6 ospf hello** command to gather further information. The output shown in Example 10-21 reveals that timers are mismatched from FE80::C801:10FF:FE20:54. You issue the **show cdp neighbors detail** command on Branch, as shown in Example 10-22, to confirm that R1 is using that link-local address. It is! Therefore, you conclude that the neighbor relationship is not formed because of mismatched timers.

Example 10-21 *Using debug ipv6 ospf hello to Gather Further Information*

```
Branch# debug ipv6 ospf hello
OSPFv3 hello events debugging is on for process 1, IPv6, Default vrf
Branch#
OSPFv3-1-IPv6 HELLO Fa1/0: Rcv hello from 1.1.1.1 area 1 from
FE80::C801:10FF:FE20:54 interface ID 6
OSPFv3-1-IPv6 HELLO Fa1/0: Mismatched hello parameters from FE80::C801:10FF:FE20:54
OSPFv3-1-IPv6 HELLO Fa1/0: Dead R 40 C 120, Hello R 10 C 30
Branch# u all
All possible debugging has been turned off
```

Example 10-22 *Using show cdp neighbors details to Verify the Neighbor's IPv6 Address*

```
Branch# show cdp neighbors detail
-------------------------
Device ID: R1
Entry address(es):
 IP address: 10.1.14.1
 IPv6 address: 2001:DB8:0:14::1 (global unicast)
 IPv6 address: FE80::C801:10FF:FE20:54 (link-local)
Platform: Cisco 7206VXR, Capabilities: Router
Interface: FastEthernet1/0, Port ID (outgoing port): FastEthernet3/0
...output omitted...
```

On R1, you issue the **show ipv6 ospf interface fastEthernet3/0** command, and on Branch you issue the **show ipv6 ospf interface fastEthernet1/0** command and use the spot-the-difference method, as shown in Example 10-23.

Example 10-23 *Spotting the Difference Between R1 and Branch*

```
R1# show ipv6 ospf interface fastEthernet 3/0
FastEthernet3/0 is up, line protocol is up
 Link Local Address FE80::C801:10FF:FE20:54, Interface ID 6
 Area 1, Process ID 1, Instance ID 0, Router ID 1.1.1.1
 Network Type BROADCAST, Cost: 1
 Transmit Delay is 1 sec, State DR, Priority 1
 Designated Router (ID) 1.1.1.1, local address FE80::C801:10FF:FE20:54
 No backup designated router on this network
 Timer intervals configured, Hello 10, Dead 40, Wait 40, Retransmit 5
 Hello due in 00:00:09
...output omitted...


Branch# show ipv6 ospf interface fastEthernet 1/0
FastEthernet1/0 is up, line protocol is up
 Link Local Address FE80::C800:FFF:FE7C:1C, Interface ID 4
Area 1, Process ID 1, Instance ID 0, Router ID 4.4.4.4
 Network Type NON_BROADCAST, Cost: 1
 Transmit Delay is 1 sec, State DR, Priority 1
 Designated Router (ID) 4.4.4.4, local address FE80::C800:FFF:FE7C:1C
 No backup designated router on this network
 Timer intervals configured, Hello 30, Dead 120, Wait 120, Retransmit 5
 Hello due in 00:00:25
...output omitted...
```

You immediately notice that the hello and dead timers do not match. However, you remember that you can configure them manually or manipulate them by changing the OSPF interface network type. Therefore, you check the network type in Example 10-23 and find that R1 is using BROADCAST (the default for Ethernet interfaces), and Branch is using NON_ BROADCAST (not the default for Ethernet interfaces). Therefore, someone must have manually changed the network type on Branch.

You issue the command **show run interface fastEthernet 1/0** on Branch, as shown in Example 10-24, and confirm that the network type was manually changed with the **ipv6 ospf network non-broadcast** command.

Example 10-24 *Verifying the Interface Configuration on Branch*

```
Branch# show run interface fastEthernet 1/0
Building configuration...

Current configuration : 169 bytes
!
interface FastEthernet1/0
```

10

```
ip address 10.1.14.4 255.255.255.0
duplex full
ipv6 address 2001:DB8:0:14::4/64
ipv6 ospf 1 area 1
ipv6 ospf network non-broadcast
end
```

You remove this command with the **no ipv6 ospf network non-broadcast** command, which changes the network type back to the default, BROADCAST. A syslog message then indicates that a neighbor relationship is successfully formed between R1 and Branch:

```
%OSPFv3-5-ADJCHG: Process 1, Nbr 1.1.1.1 on FastEthernet1/0 from
LOADING to FULL, Loading Done
```

You reissue the extended **ping** command on Branch, and it is successful, as shown in Example 10-25.

Example 10-25   *Testing Connectivity from Branch to a Remote Network*

```
Branch# ping
Protocol [ip]: ipv6
Target IPv6 address: 2001:db8:0:1::1
Repeat count [5]:
Datagram size [100]:
Timeout in seconds [2]:
Extended commands? [no]: yes
Source address or interface: 2001:db8:0:4::4
UDP protocol? [no]:
Verbose? [no]:
Precedence [0]:
DSCP [0]:
Include hop by hop option? [no]:
Include destination option? [no]:
Sweep range of sizes? [no]:
Type escape sequence to abort.
Sending 5, 100-byte ICMP Echos to 2001:DB8:0:1::1, timeout is 2 seconds:
Packet sent with a source address of 2001:DB8:0:4::4
!!!!!
Success rate is 100 percent (5/5), round-trip min/avg/max = 16/29/52 ms
```

Troubleshooting OSPFv3 Address Families

OSPFv3 *address families (AFs)* enable you to configure a single process to support both IPv4 and IPv6. In addition, a single database is maintained for IPv4 and IPv6. However, adjacencies are established individually for each AF, and settings can be configured on an AF-by-AF basis.

This section shows the commands you can use to troubleshoot an OSPFv3 implementation that uses address families.

Example 10-26 shows a sample OSPFv3 configuration with AFs. The OSPFv3 PID is 10 and is locally significant. Therefore, it does not have to match between neighbors. Any parameter configured under the main router OSPFv3 configuration mode applies to all address families. In this example, the **area 23 stub** command is configured under the main router OSPFv3 configuration mode; therefore, Area 23 is a stub area for both IPv4 and IPv6 address families. Note that if there are conflicts between configurations in router OSPFv3 configuration mode and AF configuration mode, AF configuration mode wins. You still enable the OSPFv3 process on an interface-by-interface basis in interface configuration mode with the **ospfv3** *process_id* {**ipv4** | **ipv6**} **area** *area_id* command. In addition, OSPFv3 interface parameters are still configured in interface configuration mode. However, remember that if you do not specify the AF (IPv4 or IPv6), the configured parameter applies to all address families. If you apply the configuration to the AF, it applies only to that AF. If a conflict exists, the AF configuration wins. In the GigabitEthernet0/0 configuration in Example 10-26, notice that the hello interval is configured without an AF specified. Therefore, it applies to both IPv4 and IPv6. However, the hello interval is also configured for the IPv6 AF. Therefore, this configuration prevails for IPv6, and a hello interval of 10 is used; IPv4 uses the hello interval 11.

Example 10-26   *Sample OSPFv3 Configuration with Address Families*

```
R2# show run | section router ospfv3
router ospfv3 10
 area 23 stub
 !
 address-family ipv4 unicast
 passive-interface default
 no passive-interface GigabitEthernet0/0
 no passive-interface GigabitEthernet1/0
 default-information originate
 router-id 2.2.2.2
 exit-address-family
 !
 address-family ipv6 unicast
 passive-interface default
 no passive-interface GigabitEthernet0/0
 no passive-interface GigabitEthernet1/0
 default-information originate
 router-id 22.22.22.22
 exit-address-family

R2# show run int gig 1/0
interface GigabitEthernet1/0
 ip address 10.1.23.2 255.255.255.0
```

10

```
 ipv6 address 2001:DB8:0:23::2/64
 ospfv3 10 ipv6 area 23
 ospfv3 10 ipv4 area 23
end


R2# show run int gig 0/0
interface GigabitEthernet0/0
 ip address 10.1.12.2 255.255.255.0
 ipv6 address 2001:DB8:0:12::2/64
 ospfv3 10 hello-interval 11
 ospfv3 10 ipv6 area 0
 ospfv3 10 ipv6 hello-interval 10
 ospfv3 10 ipv4 area 0
end
```

With OSPFv3 AFs, you can use the **show ip protocols** and **show ipv6 protocols** commands, as shown in Example 10-27, to verify the same information discussed earlier in this chapter and in Chapter 8.

Example 10-27   *Using show ip protocols and show ipv6 protocols*

```
R2# show ip protocols
*** IP Routing is NSF aware ***

Routing Protocol is "ospfv3 10"
  Outgoing update filter list for all interfaces is not set
  Incoming update filter list for all interfaces is not set
  Router ID 2.2.2.2
  Area border and autonomous system boundary router
  Number of areas: 1 normal, 1 stub, 0 nssa
  Interfaces (Area 0):
    GigabitEthernet0/0
  Interfaces (Area 23):
    GigabitEthernet1/0
  Maximum path: 4
  Routing Information Sources:
    Gateway Distance   Last Update
    2.2.2.2      110   00:12:39
    3.3.3.3      110   00:12:39
    10.1.14.1    110   00:00:57
  Distance: (default is 110)


R2# show ipv6 protocols
IPv6 Routing Protocol is "connected"
```

```
IPv6 Routing Protocol is "ND"
IPv6 Routing Protocol is "static"
IPv6 Routing Protocol is "ospf 10"
  Router ID 22.22.22.22
  Area border and autonomous system boundary router
  Number of areas: 1 normal, 1 stub, 0 nssa
  Interfaces (Area 0):
    GigabitEthernet0/0
  Interfaces (Area 23):
    GigabitEthernet1/0
  Redistribution:
  None
```

The output of **show ospfv3**, as shown in Example 10-28, displays the same information you would find with the **show ip ospf** and **show ipv6 ospf** commands. Notice that the IPv4 AF is listed first, followed by the IPv6 AF.

Key Topic

Example 10-28   *Using show ospfv3 to Verify General OSPFv3 Parameters for AFs*

```
R2# show ospfv3

OSPFv3 10 address-family ipv4
Router ID 2.2.2.2
Supports NSSA (compatible with RFC 3101)
Event-log enabled, Maximum number of events: 1000, Mode: cyclic
It is an area border and autonomous system boundary router
Redistributing External Routes from,
Originate Default Route
Router is not originating router-LSAs with maximum metric
Initial SPF schedule delay 5000 msecs
Minimum hold time between two consecutive SPFs 10000 msecs
Maximum wait time between two consecutive SPFs 10000 msecs
Minimum LSA interval 5 secs
Minimum LSA arrival 1000 msecs
LSA group pacing timer 240 secs
Interface flood pacing timer 33 msecs
Retransmission pacing timer 66 msecs
Retransmission limit dc 24 non-dc 24
Number of external LSA 1. Checksum Sum 0x0013EB
Number of areas in this router is 2. 1 normal 1 stub 0 nssa
Graceful restart helper support enabled
Reference bandwidth unit is 100 mbps
RFC1583 compatibility enabled
    Area BACKBONE(0)
        Number of interfaces in this area is 1
```

10

```
            SPF algorithm executed 13 times
            Number of LSA 11. Checksum Sum 0x05A71D
            Number of DCbitless LSA 0
            Number of indication LSA 0
            Number of DoNotAge LSA 0
            Flood list length 0
    Area 23
            Number of interfaces in this area is 1
            It is a stub area
            Generates stub default route with cost 1
            SPF algorithm executed 8 times
            Number of LSA 12. Checksum Sum 0x064322
            Number of DCbitless LSA 0
            Number of indication LSA 0
            Number of DoNotAge LSA 0
            Flood list length 0
OSPFv3 10 address-family ipv6
Router ID 22.22.22.22
Supports NSSA (compatible with RFC 3101)
Event-log enabled, Maximum number of events: 1000, Mode: cyclic
It is an area border and autonomous system boundary router
Originate Default Route
Router is not originating router-LSAs with maximum metric
Initial SPF schedule delay 5000 msecs
Minimum hold time between two consecutive SPFs 10000 msecs
Maximum wait time between two consecutive SPFs 10000 msecs
Minimum LSA interval 5 secs
Minimum LSA arrival 1000 msecs
LSA group pacing timer 240 secs
Interface flood pacing timer 33 msecs
Retransmission pacing timer 66 msecs
Retransmission limit dc 24 non-dc 24
Number of external LSA 1. Checksum Sum 0x00B8F5
Number of areas in this router is 2. 1 normal 1 stub 0 nssa
Graceful restart helper support enabled
Reference bandwidth unit is 100 mbps
RFC1583 compatibility enabled
    Area BACKBONE(0)
            Number of interfaces in this area is 1
            SPF algorithm executed 13 times
            Number of LSA 11. Checksum Sum 0x0422C7
            Number of DCbitless LSA 0
            Number of indication LSA 0
```

```
       Number of DoNotAge LSA 0
       Flood list length 0
   Area 23
       Number of interfaces in this area is 1
       It is a stub area
       Generates stub default route with cost 1
       SPF algorithm executed 11 times
       Number of LSA 12. Checksum Sum 0x0591F5
       Number of DCbitless LSA 0
       Number of indication LSA 0
       Number of DoNotAge LSA 0
       Flood list length 0
```

The output of the command **show ospfv3 interface brief** shows the interfaces participating in the OSPFv3 process for each AF. In Example 10-29, notice the added column that indicates which AF the interface is participating in.

Example 10-29 *Using show ospfv3 interface brief to Verify OSPFv3 Interfaces*

```
R2# show ospfv3 interface brief
Interface    PID     Area     AF      Cost    State    Nbrs F/C
Gi0/0        10      0        ipv4    1       BDR      1/1
Gi1/0        10      23       ipv4    1       BDR      1/1
Gi0/0        10      0        ipv6    1       BDR      1/1
Gi1/0        10      23       ipv6    1       BDR      1/1
```

The **show ospfv3 interface** command enables you to review detailed information about the interface configurations. Example 10-30 displays the IPv4 AF information at the top and the IPv6 AF information at the bottom.

Example 10-30 *Using show ospfv3 interface to Verify Details of OSPFv3 Interfaces*

```
R2# show ospfv3 interface gigabitEthernet 1/0
GigabitEthernet1/0 is up, line protocol is up
  Link Local Address FE80::C802:10FF:FE20:1C, Interface ID 4
  Internet Address 10.1.23.2/24
  Area 23, Process ID 10, Instance ID 64, Router ID 2.2.2.2
  Network Type BROADCAST, Cost: 1
  Transmit Delay is 1 sec, State BDR, Priority 1
  Designated Router (ID) 3.3.3.3, local address FE80::C804:10FF:FE74:1C
  Backup Designated router (ID) 2.2.2.2, local address FE80::C802:10FF:FE20:1C
  Timer intervals configured, Hello 10, Dead 40, Wait 40, Retransmit 5
    Hello due in 00:00:02
  Graceful restart helper support enabled
```

10

```
    Index 1/1/2, flood queue length 0
    Next 0x0(0)/0x0(0)/0x0(0)
    Last flood scan length is 4, maximum is 5
    Last flood scan time is 4 msec, maximum is 4 msec
    Neighbor Count is 1, Adjacent neighbor count is 1
      Adjacent with neighbor 3.3.3.3 (Designated Router)
    Suppress hello for 0 neighbor(s)
GigabitEthernet1/0 is up, line protocol is up
    Link Local Address FE80::C802:10FF:FE20:1C, Interface ID 4
    Area 23, Process ID 10, Instance ID 0, Router ID 22.22.22.22
    Network Type BROADCAST, Cost: 1
    Transmit Delay is 1 sec, State BDR, Priority 1
    Designated Router (ID) 33.33.33.33, local address FE80::C804:10FF:FE74:1C
    Backup Designated router (ID) 22.22.22.22, local address FE80::C802:10FF:FE20:1C
    Timer intervals configured, Hello 10, Dead 40, Wait 40, Retransmit 5
     Hello due in 00:00:03
    Graceful restart helper support enabled
    Index 1/1/2, flood queue length 0
    Next 0x0(0)/0x0(0)/0x0(0)
    Last flood scan length is 1, maximum is 4
    Last flood scan time is 0 msec, maximum is 4 msec
    Neighbor Count is 1, Adjacent neighbor count is 1
      Adjacent with neighbor 33.33.33.33 (Designated Router)
    Suppress hello for 0 neighbor(s)
```

To verify the neighbor relationships that have been formed for each AF, you issue the command **show ospfv3 neighbor**, as shown in Example 10-31. Again, the output is presenting the same information as discussed earlier in the chapter, except this time there are different sections for each AF.

Example 10-31   *Using show ospfv3 neighbor to Verify OSPFv3 Neighbors*

```
R2# show ospfv3 neighbor


          OSPFv3 10 address-family ipv4 (router-id 2.2.2.2)


Neighbor ID     Pri   State       Dead Time   Interface ID   Interface
10.1.14.1         1   FULL/DR     00:00:34    4              GigabitEthernet0/0
3.3.3.3           1   FULL/DR     00:00:36    4              GigabitEthernet1/0


          OSPFv3 10 address-family ipv6 (router-id 22.22.22.22)


Neighbor ID     Pri   State       Dead Time   Interface ID   Interface
10.1.14.1         1   FULL/DR     00:00:31    4              GigabitEthernet0/0
33.33.33.33       1   FULL/DR     00:00:34    4              GigabitEthernet1/0
```

To verify the information in the LSDB, you issue the command **show ospfv3 database**. When using AFs, the OSPFv3 database contains LSAs for both IPv4 and IPv6, as shown in Example 10-32.

Example 10-32   *Verifying the LSDB with show ospfv3 database*

```
R2# show ospfv3 database

          OSPFv3 10 address-family ipv4 (router-id 2.2.2.2)

              Router Link States (Area 0)

ADV Router       Age        Seq#         Fragment ID  Link count   Bits
2.2.2.2          1456       0x80000008   0            1            B E
10.1.14.1        1457       0x80000007   0            1            B

              Net Link States (Area 0)

ADV Router       Age        Seq#         Link ID      Rtr count
10.1.14.1        1453       0x80000003   4            2

              Inter Area Prefix Link States (Area 0)

ADV Router       Age        Seq#         Prefix
2.2.2.2          1618       0x80000003   10.1.23.0/24
2.2.2.2          94         0x80000002   10.1.3.0/24
10.1.14.1        1599       0x80000002   10.1.14.0/24
10.1.14.1        1599       0x80000002   10.1.4.0/24

              Link (Type-8) Link States (Area 0)

ADV Router       Age        Seq#         Link ID      Interface
2.2.2.2          1618       0x80000003   3            Gi0/0
10.1.14.1        1599       0x80000002   4            Gi0/0

              Intra Area Prefix Link States (Area 0)

ADV Router       Age        Seq#         Link ID      Ref-lstype Ref-LSID
10.1.14.1        1457       0x80000007   0            0x2001     0
10.1.14.1        1453       0x80000003   4096         0x2002     4

              Router Link States (Area 23)

ADV Router       Age        Seq#         Fragment ID  Link count   Bits
2.2.2.2          94         0x80000007   0            1            B
3.3.3.3          248        0x80000009   0            1            None
```

10

```
                    Net Link States (Area 23)

ADV Router        Age          Seq#          Link ID       Rtr count
  3.3.3.3         248          0x80000007    4             2


                    Inter Area Prefix Link States (Area 23)

ADV Router        Age          Seq#          Prefix
  2.2.2.2         1869         0x80000002    0.0.0.0/0
  2.2.2.2         1442         0x80000001    10.1.1.0/24
  2.2.2.2         1442         0x80000001    10.1.12.0/24
  2.2.2.2         1442         0x80000001    10.1.4.0/24
  2.2.2.2         1442         0x80000001    10.1.14.0/24


                    Link (Type-8) Link States (Area 23)

ADV Router        Age          Seq#          Link          ID Interface
  2.2.2.2         1618         0x80000004    4             Gi1/0
  3.3.3.3         1758         0x80000004    4             Gi1/0



                    Intra Area Prefix Link States (Area 23)

ADV Router        Age          Seq#          Link ID       Ref-lstype Ref-LSID
  3.3.3.3         248          0x80000008    0             0x2001     0
  3.3.3.3         248          0x80000007    4096          0x2002     4


                    Type-5 AS External Link States

ADV Router        Age          Seq#          Prefix
  2.2.2.2         1618         0x80000003    0.0.0.0/0


OSPFv3 10 address-family ipv6 (router-id 22.22.22.22)


                    Router Link States (Area 0)

ADV Router        Age          Seq#          Fragment ID   Link count    Bits
  10.1.14.1       330          0x80000007    0             1             B
  22.22.22.22     198          0x8000000A    0             1             B E
```

```
                  Net Link States (Area 0)


ADV Router        Age         Seq#          Link ID       Rtr count
  10.1.14.1       330         0x80000004    4             2


                  Inter Area Prefix Link States (Area 0)


ADV Router        Age         Seq#          Prefix
  10.1.14.1       1598        0x80000002    2001:DB8:0:14::/64
  10.1.14.1       1598        0x80000002    2001:DB8:0:4::/64
  22.22.22.22     198         0x80000002    2001:DB8:0:3::/64
  22.22.22.22     198         0x80000002    2001:DB8:0:23::/64


                  Link (Type-8) Link States (Area 0)


ADV Router        Age         Seq#          Link ID       Interface
  10.1.14.1       1598        0x80000002    4             Gi0/0
  22.22.22.22     1446        0x80000003    3             Gi0/0


                  Intra Area Prefix Link States (Area 0)


ADV Router        Age         Seq#          Link ID       Ref-lstype Ref-LSID
  10.1.14.1       330         0x80000006    0             0x2001     0
  10.1.14.1       330         0x80000004    4096          0x2002     4



                  Router Link States (Area 23)


ADV Router        Age         Seq#          Fragment ID   Link count Bits
  22.22.22.22     198         0x8000000A    0             1          B
  33.33.33.33     237         0x80000008    0             1          None



                  Net Link States (Area 23)


ADV Router        Age         Seq#          Link ID       Rtr count
  33.33.33.33     237         0x80000007    4             2


                  Inter Area Prefix Link States (Area 23)


ADV Router        Age         Seq#          Prefix
  22.22.22.22     198         0x80000005    2001:DB8:0:12::/64
  22.22.22.22     1961        0x80000002    ::/0
  22.22.22.22     198         0x80000002    2001:DB8:0:1::/64
```

10

```
    22.22.22.22      198          0x80000002  2001:DB8:0:4::/64
    22.22.22.22      198          0x80000002  2001:DB8:0:14::/64


                 Link (Type-8) Link States (Area 23)

ADV Router      Age          Seq#        Link ID     Interface
    22.22.22.22      1446         0x80000004  4           Gi1/0
    33.33.33.33      1713         0x80000004  4           Gi1/0


             Intra Area Prefix Link States (Area 23)

ADV Router      Age          Seq#        Link ID     Ref-lstype Ref-LSID
    33.33.33.33      237          0x8000000A  0           0x2001     0
    33.33.33.33      237          0x80000007  4096        0x2002     4


               Type-5 AS External Link States

ADV Router      Age          Seq#        Prefix
    22.22.22.22      1446         0x80000003  ::/0
```

Keep in mind when troubleshooting OSPFv3 AFs that both OSPF for IPv4 and OSPF for IPv6 use IPv6 to exchange routing information. Therefore, IPv6 unicast routing must be enabled on the router. Also, classic OSPFv2 and the OSPFv3 AFs are not compatible. Therefore, a router using OSPFv3 AFs for IPv4 does not peer with a router using the classic OSPFv2 configuration for IPv4 because they are not compatible.

To verify the IPv4 OSPFv3 entries in the routing table, you can use the **show ip route ospfv3** command. To verify the IPv6 OSPFv3 entries in the routing table, you can use the **show ipv6 route ospf** command.

If you need to perform any debugging for OSPFv3, you can issue the **debug ospfv3** command followed by what you want to debug, such as **events**, **packets**, **hellos**, or **adj**. This turns on debugging for all AFs. If you want to turn it on only for a specific AF, you need to include the AF in the command. For example, in the command **debug ospfv3 ipv6 hello**, **ipv6** refers to the AF.

OSPFv3 AF Trouble Ticket

This section presents a trouble ticket related to the topics discussed in the preceding section. The purpose of this trouble ticket is to show a process that you can use when troubleshooting in the real world or in an exam environment. This trouble ticket is based on the topology shown in Figure 10-2.

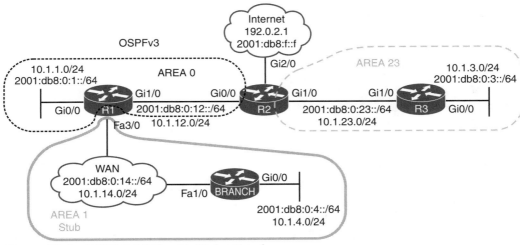

Figure 10-2 *OSPFv3 AF Trouble Ticket Topology*

Trouble Ticket 10-3

Problem: Users in Branch have indicated that they are not able to access any IPv6-enabled resources on the Internet, but they can access IPv4-enabled resources.

An extended ping issued on Branch to the destination 2001:db8:f::f confirms the issue, as shown in Example 10-33. In addition, you ping 192.0.2.1, and it is successful in confirming connectivity to IPv4-enabled resources.

Example 10-33 *Verifying Connectivity*

```
Branch# ping
Protocol [ip]: ipv6
Target IPv6 address: 2001:db8:f::f
Repeat count [5]:
Datagram size [100]:
Timeout in seconds [2]:
Extended commands? [no]: yes
Source address or interface: 2001:db8:0:4::4
UDP protocol? [no]:
Verbose? [no]:
Precedence [0]:
DSCP [0]:
Include hop by hop option? [no]:
Include destination option? [no]:
Sweep range of sizes? [no]:
Type escape sequence to abort.
Sending 5, 100-byte ICMP Echos to 2001:DB8:f::f, timeout is 2 seconds:
```

10

```
Packet sent with a source address of 2001:DB8:0:4::4
UUUUU
Success rate is 0 percent (0/5)


Branch# ping 192.0.2.1 source 10.1.4.4
Type escape sequence to abort.
Sending 5, 100-byte ICMP Echos to 192.0.2.1, timeout is 2 seconds:
Packet sent with a source address of 10.1.4.4
!!!!!
Success rate is 100 percent (5/5), round-trip min/avg/max = 80/112/152 ms
```

On the Branch router, you issue the command **show ipv6 route 2001:db8:f::f**, and Example 10-34 indicates that the Branch router has a default route that can be used to reach the IPv6 address. This explains why the ping returned UUUUU. It indicates that the destination is not reachable by some other router. But which router is returning this message?

Example 10-34 *Verifying Routes in the IPv6 Routing Table*

```
Branch# show ipv6 route 2001:db8:f::f
Routing entry for ::/0
  Known via "ospf 1", distance 110, metric 2, type inter area
  Route count is 1/1, share count 0
  Routing paths:
    FE80::C801:10FF:FE20:54, FastEthernet1/0
      Last updated 00:07:28 ago
```

To determine which router is returning the message, you issue a trace to see where it fails. Example 10-35 displays the results of the command **traceroute 2001:db8:f::f**. The trace indicates that R1 is returning the destination unreachable message.

Example 10-35 *Tracing the Path*

```
Branch# traceroute 2001:db8:f::f
Type escape sequence to abort.
Tracing the route to 2001:DB8:F::F

  1 2001:DB8:0:14::1 !U !U !U
```

You visit R1 and issue the **show ipv6 route 2001:db8:f::f** command, as shown in the following snippet, and confirm that there is no route to reach that IPv6 address:

```
R1# show ipv6 route 2001:db8:f::f
```

```
% Route not found
```

Why would Branch but not R1 have a default route? When you review the network diagram, you see that Area 1 is a stub area. Therefore, R1 is generating a default route and injecting it into the stub area. This is why the default route on Branch, as shown in the snippet, is of type inter-area and not external.

It seems that R2 might not be generating a default route when it should be. You access R2 and issue the **show ospfv3 ipv6** command, as shown in Example 10-36, and confirm that it is not an ASBR—although it should be if it is generating a default route.

Example 10-36 *Verifying OSPFv3 Parameters on R2*

```
R2# show ospfv3 ipv6
OSPFv3 10 address-family ipv6
Router ID 22.22.22.22
Supports NSSA (compatible with RFC 3101)
Event-log enabled, Maximum number of events: 1000, Mode: cyclic
It is an area border router
Router is not originating router-LSAs with maximum metric
Initial SPF schedule delay 5000 msecs
Minimum hold time between two consecutive SPFs 10000 msecs
Maximum wait time between two consecutive SPFs 10000 msecs
Minimum LSA interval 5 secs
Minimum LSA arrival 1000 msecs
LSA group pacing timer 240 secs
Interface flood pacing timer 33 msecs
Retransmission pacing timer 66 msecs
Retransmission limit dc 24 non-dc 24
Number of external LSA 0. Checksum Sum 0x000000
Number of areas in this router is 2. 1 normal 1 stub 0 nssa
Graceful restart helper support enabled
Reference bandwidth unit is 100 mbps
RFC1583 compatibility enabled
  Area BACKBONE(0)
        Number of interfaces in this area is 1
        SPF algorithm executed 14 times
        Number of LSA 11. Checksum Sum 0x04EDE6
        Number of DCbitless LSA 0
        Number of indication LSA 0
        Number of DoNotAge LSA 0
        Flood list length 0
  Area 23
        Number of interfaces in this area is 1
        It is a stub area
        Generates stub default route with cost 1
        SPF algorithm executed 11 times
        Number of LSA 12. Checksum Sum 0x06610D
        Number of DCbitless LSA 0
        Number of indication LSA 0
        Number of DoNotAge LSA 0
        Flood list length 0
```

Next, you issue the command **show run | section router ospfv3**. The output in Example 10-37 confirms that the **default-information originate** command is missing from IPv6 AF configuration mode. It is configured only under IPv4 AF configuration mode.

Example 10-37   *Verifying the OSPFv3 Configuration on R2*

```
R2# show run | section router ospfv3
router ospfv3 10
 area 23 stub
 !
 address-family ipv4 unicast
  passive-interface default
  no passive-interface GigabitEthernet0/0
  no passive-interface GigabitEthernet1/0
  default-information originate
  router-id 2.2.2.2
 exit-address-family
 !
 address-family ipv6 unicast
  passive-interface default
  no passive-interface GigabitEthernet0/0
  no passive-interface GigabitEthernet1/0
  router-id 22.22.22.22
 exit-address-family
```

You add the **default-information originate** command to IPv6 AF configuration mode and reissue the extended IPv6 ping on Branch, as shown in Example 10-38. The ping is successful.

Example 10-38   *Successful Ping to IPv6 Internet Resources*

```
Branch# ping
Protocol [ip]: ipv6
Target IPv6 address: 2001:db8:f::f
Repeat count [5]:
Datagram size [100]:
Timeout in seconds [2]:
Extended commands? [no]: yes
Source address or interface: 2001:db8:0:4::4
UDP protocol? [no]:
Verbose? [no]:
Precedence [0]:
DSCP [0]:
Include hop by hop option? [no]:
Include destination option? [no]:
```

```
Sweep range of sizes? [no]:
Type escape sequence to abort.
Sending 5, 100-byte ICMP Echos to 2001:DB8:F::F, timeout is 2 seconds:
Packet sent with a source address of 2001:DB8:0:4::4
!!!!!
Success rate is 100 percent (5/5), round-trip min/avg/max = 88/113/148 ms
```

Exam Preparation Tasks

As mentioned in the section "How to Use This Book" in the Introduction, you have a couple choices for exam preparation: the exercises here, Chapter 24, "Final Preparation," and the exam simulation questions in the Pearson Test Prep software.

Review All Key Topics

Review the most important topics in this chapter, noted with the Key Topic icon in the outer margin of the page. Table 10-3 lists these key topics and the page number on which each is found.

Table 10-3   Key Topics

Key Topic Element	Description	Page Number
Example 10-1	Identifying what can be verified for OSPFv3 with **show ipv6 protocols**	395
Example 10-2	Identifying what can be verified with **show ipv6 ospf**	395
Paragraph	Verification during the troubleshooting process with the **show ipv6 ospf interface brief** command	396
Paragraph	Verification during the troubleshooting process with the **show ipv6 ospf interface** command	397
Table 10-2	Additional OSPF LSAs for OSPFv3	399
Example 10-26	Sample OSPFv3 configuration with Afs	409
Example 10-28	Using **show ospfv3** to verify general OSPFv3 parameters for Afs	411
Example 10-29	Using **show ospfv3 interface brief** to verify OSPFv3 interfaces	413
Example 10-30	Using **show ospfv3 interface** to verify details of OSPFv3 interfaces	413

10

Define Key Terms

Define the following key terms from this chapter and check your answers in the glossary:

Open Shortest Path First version 3 (OSPFv3), Dijkstra's shortest path first (SPF) algorithm, link-state advertisement (LSA), stub area, totally stubby area, NSSA, totally NSSA, designated router, backup designated router, link-state database (LSDB), area border router (ABR), autonomous system boundary router (ASBR), address family (AF)

Use the Command Reference to Check Your Memory

The ENARSI 300-410 exam focuses on the practical, hands-on skills that networking professionals use. Therefore, you should be able to identify the commands needed to configure, verify, and troubleshoot the topics covered in this chapter.

This section includes the most important configuration and verification commands covered in this chapter. It might not be necessary to memorize the complete syntax of every command, but you should be able to remember the basic keywords that are needed.

To test your memory of the commands in Table 10-4, go to the companion website and download Appendix B, "Command Reference Exercises." Fill in the missing commands in the tables based on each command description. You can check your work by downloading Appendix C, "Command Reference Exercise Answer Key," from the companion website.

Table 10-4 Command Reference

Task	Command Syntax
Display the IPv4 routing protocols enabled on a device; for OSPFv2, display whether any route filters are applied, the RID, the number of areas the router is participating in, the types of areas, the maximum paths for load balancing, the **network area** command, the interfaces explicitly participating in the routing process, passive interfaces, routing information sources, and the AD.	**show ip protocols**
Display the IPv6 dynamic routing protocols enabled on a device; for OSPFv3, display the PID, the RID, the number of areas, the type of areas, the interfaces participating in the routing process, and redistribution information.	**show ipv6 protocols**
Display general OSPF parameters, including the PID, the RID, the reference bandwidth, the areas configured on the router, the types of areas (stub, totally stubby, NSSA, and totally NSSA), and area authentication.	**show ipv6 ospf**
Display the interfaces that are participating in the OSPF process.	**show ipv6 ospf interface brief**
Display detailed information about the interfaces participating in the OSPF process, including the interface IPv4 address and mask, area ID, PID, RID, network type, cost, DR/BDR, priority, and timers.	**show ipv6 ospf interface**

Task	Command Syntax
Display the OSPF devices that have formed a neighbor adjacency with the local router.	show ipv6 ospf neighbor
Display the OSPF routes that have been installed in the IPv4/IPv6 routing table.	show ipv6 route
Display general OSPFv3 parameters for IPv4 and IPv6 address families, including the PID, the RID, the reference bandwidth, the areas configured on the router, the types of areas (stub, totally stubby, NSSA, and totally NSSA), and area authentication.	show ospfv3
Display the interfaces that are participating in the OSPFv3 process and the AF they are participating in.	show ospfv3 interface brief
Display detailed information about the interfaces participating in the OSPFv3 address families, including interface IPv4 and IPv6 addresses, area ID, PID, RID, network type, cost, DR/BDR, priority, and timers.	show ospfv3 interface
Display the OSPFv3 neighbor adjacencies that have been formed for each AF.	show ospfv3 neighbor
Display the OSPF link-state database.	show ipv6 ospf database
Display the OSPFv3 link-state database.	show ospfv3 database
Display real-time information related to the exchange of OSPF hello packets; useful for identifying mismatched OSPF timers and mismatched OSPF area types.	debug {ip | ipv6} ospf hello debug ospfv3 {ip | ipv6} hello
Display the transmission and reception of OSPF packets in real time.	debug {ip | ipv6} ospf packet debug ospfv3 {ip | ipv6} packet
Display real-time updates about the formation of an OSPF adjacency; useful for identifying mismatched area IDs and authentication information.	debug {ip | ipv6} ospf adj debug ospfv3 {ip | ipv6} adj
Display real-time information about OSPF events, including the transmission and reception of hello messages and LSAs; might be useful on a router that appears to be ignoring hello messages received from a neighboring router.	debug {ip | ipv6} ospf events debug ospfv3 {ip | ipv6} events

## CHAPTER 11

BGP

This chapter covers the following topics:

- **BGP Fundamentals:** This section provides an overview of the fundamentals of the BGP routing protocol.

- **Basic BGP Configuration:** This section walks through the process of configuring BGP to establish a neighbor session and how routes are exchanged between peers.

- **Understanding BGP Session Types and Behaviors:** This section provides an overview of how route summarization works with BGP and some of the design considerations related to summarization.

- **Multiprotocol BGP for IPv6:** This section explains how BGP provides support for IPv6 routing and its configuration.

Border Gateway Protocol (BGP) is a standardized routing protocol that provides scalability and flexibility. BGP is the only protocol used to exchange networks on the Internet. At this writing, the Internet has more than 940,000 IPv4 network prefixes and more than 180,000 IPv6 network prefixes, and it continues to grow. BGP does not advertise incremental updates or refresh network advertisements, as do Open Shortest Path First (OSPF) and Intermediate System-to-Intermediate System (IS-IS), due to the large number of prefixes that are designed to be stored in BGP tables. BGP prefers stability within the network, as a link flap could result in route computation for thousands of routes.

This chapter explains the core concepts of BGP and the basics of advertising routes with other organizations by using BGP. Chapter 12, "Advanced BGP," explains common techniques for optimizing large-scale BGP deployments. Topics include route summarization, route filtering and manipulation, BGP communities, and BGP peer groups. Chapter 13, "BGP Path Selection," explains how a router selects a path using BGP, the BGP best-path algorithm, and BGP equal-cost multipathing. Chapter 14, "Troubleshooting BGP," explains various BGP troubleshooting techniques and concepts.

"Do I Know This Already?" Quiz

The "Do I Know This Already?" quiz allows you to assess whether you should read this entire chapter thoroughly or jump to the "Exam Preparation Tasks" section. If you are in doubt about your answers to these questions or your own assessment of your knowledge of the topics, read the entire chapter. Table 11-1 lists the major headings in this chapter and their corresponding "Do I Know This Already?" quiz questions. You can find the answers in Appendix A, "Answers to the 'Do I Know This Already?' Quiz Questions."

Table 11-1 "Do I Know This Already?" Foundation Topics Section-to-Question Mapping

Foundation Topics Section	Questions
BGP Fundamentals	1–4
Basic BGP Configuration	5–7
Understanding BGP Session Types and Behaviors	8–10
Multiprotocol BGP for IPv6	11, 12

> **CAUTION** The goal of self-assessment is to gauge your mastery of the topics in this chapter. If you do not know the answer to a question or are only partially sure of the answer, you should mark that question as wrong for purposes of self-assessment. Giving yourself credit for an answer that you correctly guess skews your self-assessment results and might provide you with a false sense of security.

1. Which of the following autonomous systems are private? (Choose two.)
   a. 64,512 through 65,534
   b. 65,000 through 65,534
   c. 4,200,000,000 through 4,294,967,294
   d. 4,265,000 through 4,265,535,016

2. Which BGP attribute must be recognized by all BGP implementations and advertised to other autonomous systems?
   a. Well-known mandatory
   b. Well-known discretionary
   c. Optional transitive
   d. Optional non-transitive

3. True or false: BGP supports dynamic neighbor discovery by both routers.
   a. True
   b. False

4. True or false: A BGP session is always one hop away from a neighbor.
   a. True
   b. False

5. True or false: The IPv4 address family must be initialized to establish a BGP session with a peer using IPv4 addressing.
   a. True
   b. False

6. Which command is used to view the BGP neighbors and their hello interval?
   a. **show bgp neighbors**
   b. **show bgp** *afi safi* **neighbors**
   c. **show bgp** *afi safi* **summary**
   d. **show** *afi* bgp **interface brief**

7. How many tables does BGP use for storing prefixes?

   a. One

   b. Two

   c. Three

   d. Four

8. True or false: A route learned from an eBGP peer is advertised to an iBGP neighbor.

   a. True

   b. False

9. True or false: A route learned from an iBGP peer is advertised to an iBGP neighbor.

   a. True

   b. False

10. Which of the following are considering iBGP scalability enhancements? (Choose two.)

   a. Route reflectors

   b. BGP route aggregation

   c. BGP confederations

   d. BGP alliances

11. True or false: The IPv6 address family must be initialized to establish a BGP session with a peer using IPv6 addressing.

   a. True

   b. False

12. True or false: IPv6 prefixes can be advertised only across a BGP session established with IPv6 addresses.

   a. True

   b. False

Foundation Topics

BGP Fundamentals

From the perspective of BGP, an *autonomous system (AS)* is a collection of routers under a single organization's control, and it uses one or more Interior Gateway Protocols (IGPs) and common metrics to route packets within the AS. If multiple IGPs or metrics are used within an AS, the AS must appear consistent to external ASs in routing policy. An IGP is not required within an AS; an AS could use BGP as the only routing protocol.

Autonomous System Numbers (ASNs)

An organization requiring connectivity to the Internet must obtain an ASN. ASNs were originally 2 bytes (in the 16-bit range), which made 65,534 ASNs possible. Due to exhaustion, RFC 4893 expanded the ASN field to accommodate 4 bytes (in the 32-bit range). This allows for 4,294,967,295 unique ASNs, providing quite an increase from the original 65,534 ASNs.

> **NOTE** RFC 1930 defined the private ASN range as 64,512 through 65,635, but RFC 6996 changed the 16-bit private ASN range to 64,512 through 65,534. RFC 7300 explains why the ASNs at the end of the 16-bit and 32-bit ASN ranges—65,535 and 4,294,967,295, respectively—should not be used.

Two blocks of private ASNs are available for any organization to use, as long as these ASNs are never exchanged publicly on the Internet. ASNs 64,512 through 65,534 are private ASNs in the 16-bit ASN range, and 4,200,000,000 through 4,294,967,294 are private ASNs in the extended 32-bit range.

> **NOTE** It is imperative to use only the ASN assigned by the IANA, the ASN assigned by your service provider, or a private ASN. Using another organization's ASN without permission could result in traffic loss and cause havoc on the Internet.

BGP Sessions

A BGP session is an established adjacency between two BGP routers. Multi-hop sessions require that the router use an underlying route installed in the Routing Information Base (RIB) (static or from any routing protocol) to establish the TCP session with the remote endpoint.

BGP sessions are categorized into two types:

- **Internal BGP (iBGP):** Sessions established with an iBGP router that are in the same AS or that participate in the same BGP confederation

- **External BGP (eBGP):** Sessions established with a BGP router that are in a different AS

Path Attributes

BGP uses *path attributes* (*PAs*) associated with each network path. The PAs provide BGP with granularity and control of routing policies in BGP. The BGP prefix PAs are classified as any of the following:

- *Well-known mandatory*

- *Well-known discretionary*

- *Optional transitive*

- *Optional non-transitive*

Well-known attributes must be recognized by all BGP implementations. Well-known mandatory attributes must be included with every prefix advertisement; well-known discretionary attributes may or may not be included with the prefix advertisement.

Optional attributes do not have to be recognized by all BGP implementations. Optional attributes can be set so that they are transitive and stay with the route advertisement from AS to AS. Other PAs are *non-transitive* and cannot be shared from AS to AS.

Loop Prevention

BGP is a *path vector routing protocol* and does not contain a complete topology of the network, as do link-state routing protocols. BGP behaves like distance vector protocols, ensuring that a path is loop free.

The BGP attribute *AS_Path* is a well-known mandatory attribute and includes a complete list of all the ASNs that the prefix advertisement has traversed from its source AS. AS_Path is used as a loop-prevention mechanism in BGP. If a BGP router receives a prefix advertisement with its AS listed in AS_Path, it discards the prefix because the router thinks the advertisement forms a loop.

Address Families

Originally, BGP was intended for routing of IPv4 prefixes between organizations, but RFC 2858 added *Multi-Protocol BGP* (*MP-BGP*) capability by adding an extension called the *address family identifier* (*AFI*). An *address family* correlates to a specific network protocol, such as IPv4 or IPv6, and additional granularity is provided through a *subsequent address family identifier* (*SAFI*), such as unicast or multicast.

In BGP, the *network layer reachability information (NLRI)* is the prefix length and the prefix. Multiprotocol BGP (MP-BGP) achieves this separation by using the BGP path attributes (PAs) MP_REACH_NLRI and MP_UNREACH_NLRI. These attributes are held inside BGP update messages and are used to carry network reachability information for different address families.

> **NOTE**   Some network engineers refer to Multiprotocol BGP as MP-BGP, and others use the term MBGP. The two terms refer to the same thing.

Every address family maintains a separate database and configuration for each protocol (address family plus sub-address family) in BGP. This allows for a routing policy in one address family to be different from a routing policy in a different address family, even though the router uses the same BGP session with the other router. BGP includes an AFI and a SAFI with every route advertisement to differentiate between the AFI and SAFI databases.

Inter-Router Communication

BGP does not use hello packets to discover neighbors, as do IGP protocols, and two BGP neighbors cannot discover each other dynamically, as is possible with OSPF. BGP was designed as an inter-autonomous routing protocol, implying that neighbor adjacencies should not change frequently and are coordinated. BGP neighbors are defined by IP address.

BGP uses TCP port 179 to communicate with other routers. TCP allows for handling of fragmentation, sequencing, and reliability (acknowledgment and retransmission) of communication packets. Most recent implementations of BGP set the do-not-fragment (DF) bit to prevent fragmentation and rely on path MTU discovery.

IGPs follow the physical topology because the sessions are formed with hellos that cannot cross network boundaries (that is, single-hop only). BGP uses TCP, which is capable of crossing network boundaries (that is, multi-hop capable). While BGP can form neighbor adjacencies that are directly connected, it can also form adjacencies that are multiple hops away.

A BGP session refers to the established adjacency between two BGP routers. Multi-hop sessions require that the router use an underlying route installed in the RIB (static or from any routing protocol) to establish the TCP session with the remote endpoint.

In Figure 11-1, R1 is able to establish a direct BGP session with R2. In addition, R2 is able to establish a BGP session with R4, even though it passes through R3. R1 and R2 use a directly connected route to locate each other. R2 uses a static route to reach the 10.34.1.0/24 network, and R4 has a static route to reach the 10.23.1.0/24 network. R3 is unaware that R2 and R4 have established a BGP session even though the packets flow through R3.

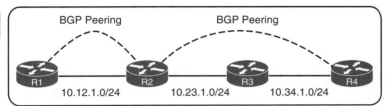

Figure 11-1 *BGP Single- and Multi-Hop Sessions*

> **NOTE** BGP neighbors connected to the same network use the ARP table to locate the IP address of the peer. Multi-hop BGP sessions require routing table information for finding the IP address of the peer. It is common to have a static route or an IGP running between iBGP neighbors for providing the topology path information to establish the BGP TCP session. A default route is not sufficient to establish a multi-hop BGP session.

BGP can be thought of as a control plane routing protocol or as an application because it allows for the exchange of routes with a peer that is multiple hops away. In Figure 11-1, R2 has established a multi-hop BGP session with R4. R3 does not require a BGP session with R2 or R4, but it does need to know all the routes to be forwarded through it.

BGP Messages

BGP communication uses four message types, as shown in Table 11-2.

Table 11-2 BGP Message Types

Type	Name	Functional Overview
1	OPEN	Sets up and establishes BGP adjacency
2	UPDATE	Advertises, updates, or withdraws routes
3	NOTIFICATION	Indicates an error condition to a BGP neighbor
4	KEEPALIVE	Ensures that BGP neighbors are still alive

OPEN

An OPEN message is used to establish a BGP adjacency. Both sides negotiate session capabilities before BGP peering is established. An OPEN message contains the BGP version number, the ASN of the originating router, the hold time, the BGP identifier, and other optional parameters that establish the session capabilities:

11

- **Hold time:** The hold time field in the OPEN messages sets the proposed *hold timer* value, in seconds, for each BGP neighbor. When establishing a BGP session, the routers use the smaller hold time value contained in the two routers' OPEN messages. The hold time value must be at least 3 seconds, or the hold time is set to 0 to disable KEEPALIVE messages. For Cisco routers, the default hold time is 180 seconds.

- **BGP identifier:** The BGP router ID (RID) is a 32-bit unique number that identifies the BGP router in the advertised prefixes. The RID can be used as a loop-prevention mechanism for routers advertised within an autonomous system. The RID can be set manually or dynamically for BGP. A nonzero value must be set in order for routers to become neighbors.

KEEPALIVE

BGP does not rely on the TCP connection state to ensure that the neighbors are still alive. KEEPALIVE messages are exchanged every one-third of the hold timer agreed upon between the two BGP routers. Cisco devices have a default hold time of 180 seconds, so the default keepalive interval is 60 seconds. If the hold time is set to 0, no KEEPALIVE messages are sent between the BGP neighbors.

UPDATE

An UPDATE message advertises any feasible routes, withdraws previously advertised routes, or can do both. The UPDATE message includes prefixes in the NLRI PA, as well as other associated BGP PAs. Prefixes that need to be withdrawn are advertised in the WWITH-DRAWN ROUTES field of the UPDATE message.

An UPDATE message can act as a keepalive to reduce unnecessary traffic. Upon receipt of an UPDATE or KEEPALIVE, the hold timer resets to the initial value. If the hold timer reaches zero, the BGP session is torn down, routes from that neighbor are removed, and an appropriate update route withdraw message is sent to other BGP neighbors for the affected prefixes. The hold time is a heartbeat mechanism for BGP neighbors to ensure that a neighbor is healthy and alive.

NOTIFICATION

A NOTIFICATION message is sent when an error is detected with the BGP session, such as a hold timer expiring, neighbor capabilities changing, or a BGP session reset being requested. This causes the BGP connection to close.

BGP Neighbor States

BGP forms a TCP session with neighbor routers called peers. BGP uses the *finite-state machine (FSM)* to maintain a table of all BGP peers and their operational status. A BGP session may report the following states:

- Idle

- Connect

- Active

- OpenSent

- OpenConfirm

- Established

Figure 11-2 shows the BGP FSM.

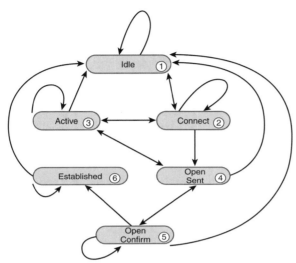

Figure 11-2 *BGP Finite-State Machine*

Idle

Idle is the first stage of the BGP FSM. BGP detects a start event and tries to initiate a TCP connection to the BGP peer and also listens for a new connection from a peer router.

If an error causes BGP to go back to the Idle state a second time, the ConnectRetry timer is set to 60 seconds and must decrement to 0 before the connection can be initiated again. Further failures to leave the Idle state result in the ConnectRetry timer doubling in length from the previous time.

Connect

In the Connect state, BGP initiates the TCP connection. If the three-way TCP handshake completes, the established BGP session resets the ConnectRetry timer, sends the OPEN message to the neighbor, and changes to the OpenSent state.

If the ConnectRetry timer depletes before this stage is complete, a new TCP connection is attempted, the ConnectRetry timer is reset, and the state stays in Connect. If the TCP connection fails, the state changes to Active. For any other event, the state is changed to Idle.

BGP routers use TCP port 179 to listen for incoming connections and as the destination port to connect to BGP peers. The router initiating the outgoing TCP connection uses a random source port and the destination port 179.

Example 11-1 shows an established BGP session with the command **show tcp brief** displaying the active TCP sessions between the routers. Notice that the TCP source port for R2 is 59884, and the destination port for R1 is 179; this means R2 initiated the connection.

Example 11-1   *Established BGP Session*

```
R1# show tcp brief
TCB        Local Address      Foreign Address      (state)
F6F84258   10.12.1.1.179      10.12.1.2.59884      ESTAB

R2# show tcp brief
TCB        Local Address      Foreign Address      (state)
EF153B88   10.12.1.2.59884    10.12.1.1.179        ESTAB
```

Active

In the Active state, BGP starts a new three-way TCP handshake. If a connection is established, an OPEN message is sent, the hold timer is set to 4 minutes, and the state moves to OpenSent. If this attempt for TCP connection fails, the state moves back to the Connect state and resets the ConnectRetry timer.

OpenSent

In the OpenSent state, an OPEN message has been sent from the originating router and is awaiting an OPEN message from the other router. When the originating router receives the OPEN message from the other router, both OPEN messages are checked for errors. The following items are checked:

- BGP versions must match.

- The source IP address of the OPEN message must match the IP address that is configured for the neighbor.

- The AS number in the OPEN message must match what is configured for the neighbor.

- BGP identifiers (RIDs) must be unique. If a RID does not exist, this condition is not met.

- Security parameters (such as password and time-to-live [TTL]) must be set appropriately.

If the OPEN messages do not have any errors, the hold time is negotiated (using the lower value), and a KEEPALIVE message is sent (assuming that it is not set to 0). The connection state is then moved to OpenConfirm. If an error is found in the OPEN message, a NOTIFICATION message is sent, and the state is moved back to Idle.

If TCP receives a disconnect message, BGP closes the connection, resets the ConnectRetry timer, and sets the state to Active. Any other event in this process results in the state moving to Idle.

OpenConfirm

In the OpenConfirm state, BGP waits for a KEEPALIVE or NOTIFICATION message. Upon receipt of a neighbor's KEEPALIVE, the state is moved to Established. If the hold timer expires, a stop event occurs, or a NOTIFICATION message is received, the state is moved to Idle.

Established

In the Established state, the BGP session is established. BGP neighbors exchange routes through UPDATE messages. As UPDATE and KEEPALIVE messages are received, the hold timer is reset. If the hold timer expires, an error is detected, and BGP moves the neighbor back to the Idle state.

Basic BGP Configuration

When configuring BGP, it is best to think of the configuration from a modular perspective. BGP router configuration requires the following components:

- **BGP session parameters:** BGP session parameters provide settings that involve establishing communication to the remote BGP neighbor. Session settings include the ASN of the BGP peer, authentication, keepalive timers, and source and destination IP address settings for the session.

- **Address family initialization:** The address family is initialized under the BGP router configuration mode. Network advertisement and summarization occur within the address family.

- **Activation of the address family on the BGP peer:** An address family must be activated for a BGP peer in order for BGP to initiate a session with that peer. The router's IP address is added to the neighbor table, and BGP attempts to establish a BGP session or accepts a BGP session initiated from the peer router.

BGP configuration involves the following steps:

Step 1. Initialize the BGP process with the global command **router bgp** *as-number*.

Step 2. Statically define the BGP router ID (RID) (optional). The dynamic RID allocation logic uses the highest IP address of any up loopback interfaces. If there is not an up loopback interface, then the highest IP address of any active up interfaces becomes the RID when the BGP process initializes.

To ensure that the RID does not change, a static RID is assigned (typically represented as an IPv4 address that resides on the router, such as a loopback address). Any IPv4 address can be used, including IP addresses not configured on the router. Statically configuring the BGP RID using the command **bgp router-id** *router-id* is a best practice. When the router ID changes, all BGP sessions reset and need to be reestablished.

Step 3. Identify the BGP neighbor's IP address and autonomous system number with the BGP router configuration command **neighbor** *ip-address* **remote-as** *as-number*.

Step 4. Specify the source interface for the BGP session (optional). It is important to understand the traffic flow of BGP packets between peers. The source IP address of the BGP packets still reflects the IP address of the outbound interface. When a BGP packet is received, the router correlates the source IP address of the packet to the IP address configured for that neighbor. If the BGP packet source does not match an entry in the neighbor table, the packet cannot be associated with a neighbor and is discarded. You specify the interface for the BGP session for a specific neighbor with the command **neighbor** *ip-address* **update-source** *interface-id*. This concept is explained further in the section "Peering Using Loopback Addresses," later in this chapter.

Step 5. Enable BGP authentication (optional). BGP supports authentication of BGP peers using a Message Digest 5 (MD5) authentication hash to prevent manipulation of BGP packets. BGP sessions that do not use authentication could potentially have spoofed updates inserted with false update messages. To enable BGP authentication, place the command **neighbor** *ip-address* **password** *password* under the neighbor session parameters.

Step 6. Modify the BGP timers (optional). BGP relies on a stable network topology due to the size of a routing table. BGP KEEPALIVE and UPDATE messages ensure that the BGP neighbor is established. The default hold timer requires that a packet be received every 3 minutes (180 seconds) to maintain the BGP session. The hold timer is negotiated when the BGP session is first established.

By default, BGP sends a KEEPALIVE message to a BGP neighbor every 60 seconds. The BGP keepalive timer and hold timer can be set at the process level or per neighbor session. Some designs may require BGP timers to be set more aggressively or adaptably, depending upon the design. The BGP timers can be modified for a session with the command **neighbor** *ip-address* **timers** *keepalive holdtime* [*minimum-holdtime*].

NOTE IOS XE activates the *IPv4 address family* by default. This simplifies the configuration in an IPv4 environment because steps 7 and 8 are optional with the default behavior enabled but may cause confusion when working with other address families. The BGP router configuration command **no bgp default ipv4-unicast** disables the automatic activation of the IPv4 AFI so that steps 7 and 8 are required.

Step 7. Initialize the address family with the BGP router configuration command **address-family** *afi safi*. Examples of AFIs are IPv4 and IPv6 and examples of SAFIs are unicast and multicast.

Step 8. Activate the address family for the BGP neighbor by using the BGP address family configuration command **neighbor** *ip-address* **activate**.

NOTE On IOS XE devices, the default SAFI for the IPv4 and IPv6 address families is unicast and is optional.

Figure 11-3 shows a topology for a simple eBGP configuration.

Example 11-2 demonstrates how to configure R1 and R2 using the IOS default and optional IPv4 AFI modifier CLI syntax. R1 is configured using the default IPv4 address family enabled, and R2 disables IOS's default IPv4 address family and manually activates it for the specific neighbor 10.12.1.1. The command **no bgp default ipv4-unicast** is not necessary on R2, and BGP will work properly for IPv4 prefixes, but using this command makes it easier to standardize behavior when working with other address families, such as IPv6. Both devices modify the optional BGP session's settings:

- Authentication is enabled with the password CISCOBGP.

- R1 sets the BGP hello timer to 10 seconds and the hold timer to 40 seconds. R2 sets the BGP hello timer to 15 seconds and the hold timer to 50 seconds.

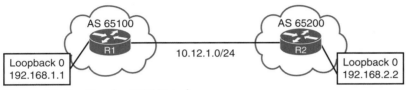

Figure 11-3 *Simple eBGP Topology*

Example 11-2 *BGP Configuration*

```
R1 (Default IPv4 Address-Family Enabled)
router bgp 65100
 neighbor 10.12.1.2 remote-as 65200
 neighbor 10.12.1.2 password CISCOBGP
 neighbor 10.12.1.2 timers 10 40

R2 (Default IPv4 Address-Family Disabled)
router bgp 65200
 no bgp default ipv4-unicast
 neighbor 10.12.1.1 remote-as 65100
 neighbor 10.12.1.1 password CISCOBGP
 neighbor 10.12.1.1 timers 15 50
 !
 address-family ipv4
 neighbor 10.12.1.1 activate
```

Verification of BGP Sessions

You verify a BGP session by using the command **show bgp** *afi safi* **summary**. Example 11-3 shows the IPv4 BGP unicast summary. Notice that the BGP RID and table version are the first components shown. The Up/Down column indicates that the BGP session is up for over 5 minutes.

11

> **NOTE**   Earlier commands, such as **show ip bgp summary**, came out before MP-BGP and do not provide a structure for the current multiprotocol capabilities in BGP. Using the AFI and SAFI syntax ensures consistency for the commands, regardless of the information exchanged by BGP. This will become more apparent as you work with address families like IPv6, VPNv4, or VPNv6.

Example 11-3   *BGP IPv4 Session Summary Verification*

```
R1# show bgp ipv4 unicast summary
BGP router identifier 192.168.1.1, local AS number 65100
BGP table version is 1, main routing table version 1

Neighbor        V     AS MsgRcvd MsgSent    TblVer  InQ OutQ Up/Down   State/PfxRcd
10.12.1.2       4  65200       8       9         1    0    0 00:05:23             0
```

Table 11-3 explains the fields of output in the BGP table.

Table 11-3   BGP Summary Fields

Field	Description
Neighbor	IP address of the BGP peer
V	BGP version used by the BGP peer
AS	Autonomous system number of the BGP peer
MsgRcvd	Count of messages received from the BGP peer
MsgSent	Count of messages sent to the BGP peer
TblVer	Last version of the BGP database sent to the peer
InQ	Number of messages received from the peer and queued to be processed
OutQ	Number of messages queued to be sent to the peer
Up/Down	Length of time the BGP session is established, or the current status if the session is not in an established state
State/PfxRcd	Current BGP peer state or the number of prefixes received from the peer

You can get BGP neighbor session state, timers, and other essential peering information by using the command **show bgp** *afi safi* **neighbors** *ip-address*, as shown in Example 11-4. Notice that the BGP hold time has negotiated to 40 based on R1's session settings.

Example 11-4   *BGP IPv4 Neighbor Output*

```
R2# show bgp ipv4 unicast neighbors 10.12.1.1
! Output omitted for brevity

! The first section provides the neighbor's IP address, remote-as, indicates if
! the neighbor is 'internal' or 'external', the neighbor's BGP version, RID,
! session state, and timers.
```

```
BGP neighbor is 10.12.1.1, remote AS65100, external link
  BGP version 4, remote router ID 192.168.1.1
  BGP state = Established, up for 00:01:04
  Last read 00:00:10, last write 00:00:09, hold is 40, keepalive is 13 seconds
  Neighbor sessions:
    1 active, is not multisession capable (disabled)
! This second section indicates the capabilities of the BGP neighbor and
! address-families configured on the neighbor.
  Neighbor capabilities:
    Route refresh: advertised and received(new)
    Four-octets ASN Capability: advertised and received
    Address family IPv4 Unicast: advertised and received
    Enhanced Refresh Capability: advertised
    Multisession Capability:
    Stateful switchover support enabled: NO for session 1
  Message statistics:
    InQ depth is 0
    OutQ depth is 0


! This section provides a list of the BGP packet types that have been received
! or sent to the neighbor router.
                     Sent        Rcvd
    Opens:              1           1
    Notifications:      0           0
    Updates:            0           0
    Keepalives:         2           2
    Route Refresh:      0           0
    Total:              4           3
  Default minimum time between advertisement runs is 0 seconds


! This section provides the BGP table version of the IPv4 Unicast address-
! family. The table version is not a 1-to-1 correlation with routes as multiple
! route change can occur during a revision change. Notice the Prefix Activity
! columns in this section.
For address family: IPv4 Unicast
  Session: 10.12.1.1
  BGP table version 1, neighbor version 1/0
  Output queue size : 0
  Index 1, Advertise bit 0
                      Sent        Rcvd
  Prefix activity:    ----        ----
    Prefixes Current:   0           0
    Prefixes Total:     0           0
```

11

```
Implicit Withdraw:              0         0
Explicit Withdraw:              0         0
Used as bestpath:              n/a        0
Used as multipath:             n/a        0


                            Outbound    Inbound
Local Policy Denied Prefixes:   --------   -------
   Total:                          0         0
Number of NLRIs in the update sent: max 0, min 0


! This section indicates that a valid route exists in the RIB to the BGP peer IP
! address, provides the number of times that the connection has established and
! time dropped, since the last reset, the reason for the reset, if path-mtu-
! discovery is enabled, and ports used for the BGP session.


 Address tracking is enabled, the RIB does have a route to 10.12.1.1
 Connections established 2; dropped 1
 Last reset 00:01:40, due to Peer closed the session
 Transport(tcp) path-mtu-discovery is enabled
Connection state is ESTAB, I/O status: 1, unread input bytes: 0
Minimum incoming TTL 0, Outgoing TTL 255
Local host: 10.12.1.2, Local port: 179
Foreign host: 10.12.1.1, Foreign port: 56824
```

Route Advertisement

BGP uses three tables for maintaining the network paths and path attributes (PAs) for a prefix. The following list briefly explains the BGP tables:

- **Adj-RIB-in:** Contains the routes in original form (that is, from before inbound route policies were processed). The table is purged after all route policies are processed to save memory.

- **Loc-RIB:** Contains all the routes that originated locally or that were received from other BGP peers. After NLRI routes pass the validity and next-hop reachability check, the BGP best-path algorithm selects the best NLRI for a specific prefix. The *Loc-RIB table* is the table used for presenting routes to the IP routing table.

- **Adj-RIB-out:** Contains the routes after outbound route policies have been processed.

You install network prefixes in the BGP Loc-RIB with the command **network** *network* **mask** *subnet-mask* [**route-map** *route-map-name*] under the appropriate BGP address family configuration. The optional **route-map** provides a method to set specific BGP PAs when the prefix installs into the Loc-RIB. Route maps are discussed in more detail in Chapter 15, "Route Maps and Conditional Forwarding."

The BGP **network** statements do not enable BGP for a specific interface. Instead, they identify a specific network prefix to be installed into the Loc-RIB table.

After you enter a BGP **network** statement, the BGP process searches the global RIB for an exact network match. The network can be a connected network, a secondary connected network, or any route from a routing protocol. After verifying that the **network** statement matches a route in the RIB, the prefix is installed into the Loc-RIB table. As the BGP prefix is installed into the Loc-RIB, the following BGP PAs are set, depending on the RIB prefix type:

- **Connected network:** The next-hop BGP attribute is set to 0.0.0.0, the BGP Origin attribute is set to i (for IGP), and the BGP weight is set to 32,768.

- **Static route or routing protocol:** The next-hop BGP attribute is set to the next-hop IP address in the RIB, the BGP Origin attribute is set to i (for IGP), the BGP weight is set to 32,768, and the multi-exit discriminator (MED) is set to the IGP metric.

Not every route in the Loc-RIB table is advertised to a BGP peer. All routes in the Loc-RIB table follow this process for advertisement to BGP peers:

Step 1. Verify that the route is valid and that the next-hop address can be resolved in the RIB. If the next-hop check fails, the route remains but does not process further.

Step 2. Process any specific outbound neighbor policies. After processing, if the route was not denied by the outbound policies, the route is maintained in the Adj-RIB-Out for later reference.

Step 3. Advertise the route to BGP peers. If the route's next-hop BGP PA is 0.0.0.0, the next-hop address is changed to the IP address of the BGP session.

Figure 11-4 illustrates the concept of installing the routes from the RIB via the **network** statement and then advertising them to BGP peers.

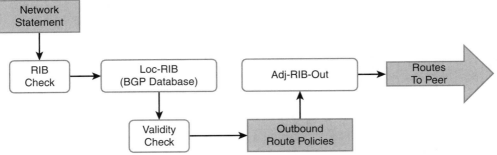

Figure 11-4 *BGP Database Processing of Local Route Advertisements*

NOTE By default, BGP only advertises the best path to other BGP peers, regardless of the number of routes (that is, NLRI routes) in the BGP Loc-RIB table.

11

Figure 11-5 expands on the previous topology, where R1 already has an eBGP session established with R2. R1 has multiple routes learned from static routes, EIGRP, and OSPF. Notice that R3's loopback was learned through EIGRP, R4's loopback is reached using a static route, and R5's loopback is learned from OSPF.

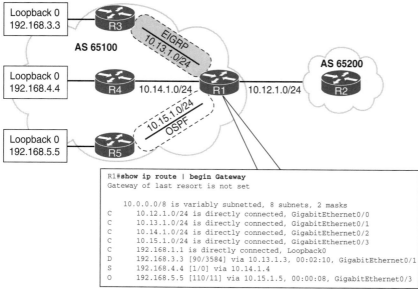

Figure 11-5   *Multiple BGP Route Sources*

All the routes in R1's routing table can be advertised into BGP, regardless of the source routing protocol. Example 11-5 demonstrates the configuration for advertising the loopback interface of R1, R3, and R4 using **network** statements on R1. Specifying every prefix that should be advertised might seem tedious, so R5's loopback interface is injected into BGP through redistribution of OSPF into BGP. R2's configuration resides under **address-family ipv4 unicast** because the default IPv4 unicast address family has been disabled.

Example 11-5   *Configuration for Advertising Non-connected Routes*

```
R1
router bgp 65100
 neighbor 10.12.1.2 remote-as 65200
 network 10.12.1.0 mask 255.255.255.0
 network 192.168.1.1 mask 255.255.255.255
 network 192.168.3.3 mask 255.255.255.255
 network 192.168.4.4 mask 255.255.255.255
 redistribute ospf 1
```
```
R2
router bgp 65200
 neighbor 10.12.1.1 remote-as 65100
```

```
address-family ipv4 unicast
 neighbor 10.12.1.1 activate
 network 10.12.1.0 mask 255.255.255.0
 network 192.168.2.2 mask 255.255.255.255
```

> **NOTE**   Redistributing routes learned from an IGP into BGP is completely safe; however, redistributing routes learned from BGP into an IGP should be done with caution. BGP is designed for large scale and can handle a routing table the size of the Internet (940,000+ prefixes), whereas IGPs could have stability problems with fewer than 20,000 routes.

Receiving and Viewing Routes

Not every prefix in the Loc-RIB table is advertised to a BGP peer or installed into the global RIB when received from a BGP peer. BGP performs the following route processing steps:

Step 1.   Store the route in the Adj-RIB-In in the original state and apply the inbound route policy, based on the neighbor on which the route was received.

Step 2.   Update the Loc-RIB with the latest entry. The Adj-RIB-In is cleared to save memory.

Step 3.   Pass a validity check to verify that the route is valid and that the next-hop address is resolvable in the RIB. If the route fails, the route remains in the Loc-RIB but is not processed further.

Step 4.   Identify the BGP best path and pass only the best path and its path attributes to step 5. The BGP best-path selection process is covered in Chapter 13, "BGP Path Selection."

Step 5.   Install the best-path route into the RIB, process the outbound route policy, store the non-discarded routes in the Adj-RIB-Out table, and advertise to BGP peers.

Figure 11-6 shows the complete BGP route processing logic. It includes the receipt of a route from a BGP peer and the BGP best-path algorithm.

The command **show bgp** *afi safi* displays the contents of the BGP database (Loc-RIB table) on the router. Every entry in the BGP Loc-RIB table contains at least one path but could contain multiple paths for the same network prefix. Example 11-6 displays the BGP table on R1, which contains locally generated routes and routes from R2.

Notice that on R1, the next hop matches the next hop learned from the RIB, AS_Path is blank, and the Origin code is IGP (for routes learned from the **network** statement) or incomplete (redistributed). The metric is carried over from R3's and R5's IGP routing protocols and is indicated as MED. R2 learns the routes strictly from eBGP and sees only MED and the Origin codes.

11

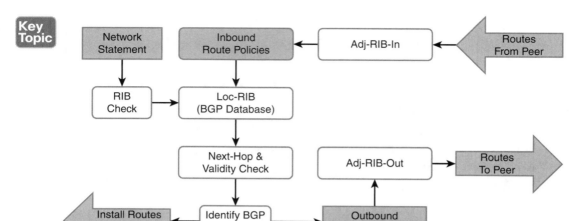

Figure 11-6 *BGP Database Processing*

Example 11-6 *BGP Table of Routes from Multiple Sources*

```
R1# show bgp ipv4 unicast
BGP table version is 9, local router ID is 192.168.1.1
Status codes: s suppressed, d damped, h history, * valid, > best, i - internal,
              r RIB-failure, S Stale, m multipath, b backup-path, f RT-Filter,
              x best-external, a additional-path, c RIB-compressed,
Origin codes: i - IGP, e - EGP, ? - incomplete
RPKI validation codes: V valid, I invalid, N Not found

     Network          Next Hop          Metric LocPrf Weight Path
 *>  10.12.1.0/24     0.0.0.0                0          32768 i
 *                    10.12.1.2              0              0 65200 i
 *>  10.15.1.0/24     0.0.0.0                0          32768 ?
 *>  192.168.1.1/32   0.0.0.0                0          32768 i
 *>  192.168.2.2/32   10.12.1.2              0              0 65200 i
 ! The following route comes from EIGRP and uses a network statement
 *>  192.168.3.3/32   10.13.1.3           3584          32768 i
 ! The following route comes from a static route and uses a network statement
 *>  192.168.4.4/32   10.14.1.4              0          32768 i
 ! The following route was redistributed from OSPF
 *>  192.168.5.5/32   10.15.1.5             11          32768 ?

R2# show bgp ipv4 unicast | begin Network
     Network          Next Hop          Metric LocPrf Weight Path
 *   10.12.1.0/24     10.12.1.1              0              0 65100 i
 *>                   0.0.0.0                0          32768 i
```

```
*>   10.15.1.0/24      10.12.1.1                    0                0 65100 ?
*>   192.168.1.1/32    10.12.1.1                    0                0 65100 i
*>   192.168.2.2/32    0.0.0.0                      0            32768 i
*>   192.168.3.3/32    10.12.1.1                 3584                0 65100 i
*>   192.168.4.4/32    10.12.1.1                    0                0 65100 i
*>   192.168.5.5/32    10.12.1.1                   11                0 65100 ?
```

Table 11-4 explains the fields of output in the BGP table.

Table 11-4   BGP Table Fields

Field	Description
Network	A list of the prefixes installed in BGP. If multiple paths exist for the same prefix, only the first prefix is listed, and other paths leave an empty space in the output. Valid paths are indicated by the *. The paths selected as the best path is indicated by an angle bracket (>).
Next Hop	A well-known mandatory BGP path attribute that defines the IP address for the next hop for that specific path.
Metric	Multiple-exit discriminator (MED), an optional non-transitive BGP path attribute used in the BGP best-path algorithm for that specific path.
LocPrf	Local preference, a well-known discretionary BGP path attribute used in the BGP best-path algorithm for that specific path.
Weight	A locally significant Cisco-defined attribute used in the BGP best-path algorithm for that specific path.
Path and Origin	AS_Path, a well-known mandatory BGP path attribute used for loop prevention and in the BGP best-path algorithm for that specific path. Origin, a well-known mandatory BGP path attribute used in the BGP best-path algorithm. The value *i* represents an IGP, *e* is for EGP, and *?* is for a route that was redistributed into BGP.

The command **show bgp** *afi safi network* displays all the paths for a specific prefix and the BGP path attributes for that prefix. Example 11-7 displays the paths for the 10.12.1.0/24 prefix. The output includes the number of paths and which path is the best path.

Example 11-7   *Viewing Explicit BGP Routes and Path Attributes*

```
R1# show bgp ipv4 unicast 10.12.1.0
BGP routing table entry for 10.12.1.0/24, version 2
Paths: (2 available, best #2, table default)
  Advertised to update-groups:
     2
  Refresh Epoch 1
```

11

```
65200
  10.12.1.2 from 10.12.1.2 (192.168.2.2)
    Origin IGP, metric 0, localpref 100, valid, external
    rx pathid: 0, tx pathid: 0
Refresh Epoch 1
Local
  0.0.0.0 from 0.0.0.0 (192.168.1.1)
    Origin IGP, metric 0, localpref 100, weight 32768, valid, sourced, local, best
    rx pathid: 0, tx pathid: 0x0
```

Table 11-5 explains the output provided in Example 11-7 and the correlation of each part of the output to BGP attributes. Some of the BGP path attributes may change, depending on the BGP features used.

Table 11-5   BGP Prefix Attributes

Output	Description
Paths: (2 available, best #2)	Provides a count of BGP paths in the BGP Loc-RIB table and identifies the path selected as the BGP best path.
	All the paths and BGP attributes are listed after this.
Advertised to update-groups	Identifies whether the path was advertised to a BGP peer.
	BGP neighbors are consolidated into BGP update groups. If a path is not advertised, *Not advertised to any peer* is displayed.
65200 (1st path) Local (2nd path)	This is the AS_Path for the path as it was received or whether the prefix was locally advertised.
10.12.1.2 from 10.12.1.2 (192.168.2.2)	The first entry lists the IP address of the next hop for the prefix. The from field lists the IP address of the advertising router. (The field could change when an external path is learned from an iBGP peer.) The number in parentheses is the BGP identifier (RID) for the node.
Origin IGP	Origin is the BGP well-known mandatory attribute that states the mechanism for advertising this path. In this instance, it is an internal path.
metric 0	Displays the optional non-transitive BGP attribute MED, also known as the BGP metric.
localpref 100	Displays the well-known discretionary BGP attribute Local Preference.
valid	Displays the validity of this path.
External (1st path) Local (2nd path)	Displays how the path was learned: internal, external, or local.

NOTE   The command **show bgp** *afi safi detail* displays the entire BGP table with all the path attributes, like those shown in Example 11-7.

The Adj-RIB-Out table is a unique table maintained for each BGP peer. It enables a network engineer to view routes advertised to a specific router. The command **show bgp** *afi safi* **neighbors** *ip-address* **advertised-routes** displays the contents of the Adj-RIB-Out table for a specific neighbor.

Example 11-8 shows the Adj-RIB-Out entries specific to each neighbor. The next-hop address reflects the local router's BGP table and is changed as the route advertises to the peer.

Example 11-8   *Neighbor-Specific View of the Adj-RIB-OUT Table*

```
R1# show bgp ipv4 unicast neighbors 10.12.1.2 advertised-routes
! Output omitted for brevity
     Network          Next Hop          Metric LocPrf Weight Path
 *>  10.12.1.0/24     0.0.0.0                0         32768 i
 *>  10.15.1.0/24     0.0.0.0                0         32768 ?
 *>  192.168.1.1/32   0.0.0.0                0         32768 i
 *>  192.168.3.3/32   10.13.1.3           3584         32768 i
 *>  192.168.4.4/32   10.14.1.4              0         32768 i
 *>  192.168.5.5/32   10.15.1.5             11         32768 ?

Total number of prefixes 6
```

```
R2# show bgp ipv4 unicast neighbors 10.12.1.1 advertised-routes
! Output omitted for brevity
     Network          Next Hop          Metric LocPrf Weight Path
 *>  10.12.1.0/24     0.0.0.0                0         32768 i
 *>  192.168.2.2/32   0.0.0.0                0         32768 i

Total number of prefixes 2
```

The **show bgp ipv4 unicast summary** command is also used to verify the exchange of routes between nodes, as shown in Example 11-9.

Example 11-9   *BGP Summary with Prefixes*

```
R1# show bgp ipv4 unicast summary
! Output omitted for brevity
Neighbor        V      AS MsgRcvd MsgSent   TblVer  InQ OutQ Up/Down   State/PfxRcd
10.12.1.2       4   65200   11      10         9    0    0 00:04:56             2
```

You display the BGP routes in the global IP routing table (RIB) by using the command **show ip route bgp**. Example 11-10 shows the BGP routes that have been installed into the routing table. The routes are from an eBGP session and have an AD of 20, and no metric is present.

11

Example 11-10 *Displaying BGP Routes in an IP Routing Table*

```
R1# show ip route bgp | begin Gateway
Gateway of last resort is not set


      192.168.2.0/32 is subnetted, 1 subnets
B        192.168.2.2 [20/0] via 10.12.1.2, 00:06:12
```

Understanding BGP Session Types and Behaviors

BGP sessions are always point-to-point between two routers and are categorized into two types:

- *Internal BGP (iBGP) session*: Sessions established with an iBGP router that are in the same AS or that participate in the same BGP confederation. iBGP sessions are considered more secure, and some of BGP's security measures are lowered compared to eBGP sessions. iBGP prefixes are assigned an *administrative distance* (AD) of 200 upon being installed into the router's RIB.

- *External BGP (eBGP) session*: Sessions established with a BGP router that are in a different AS. eBGP prefixes are assigned an AD of 20 upon being installed into the router's RIB.

There are other differences in how route advertisements operate with iBGP and eBGP sessions. These differences are explained in this section.

> **NOTE** AD is a rating of the trustworthiness of a routing information source. If a router learns about a route to a destination from more than one routing protocol, and they all have the same prefix length, AD is compared. The preference is given to the route with the lower AD.

iBGP

The need for BGP within an AS typically occurs when multiple routing policies are needed or when transit connectivity is provided between autonomous systems. In Figure 11-7, AS 65200 provides transit connectivity to AS 65100 and AS 65300. AS 65100 connects at R2, and AS 65300 connects at R4.

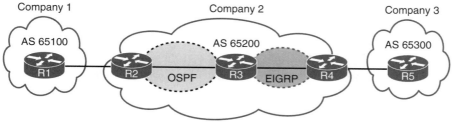

Figure 11-7 *AS 65200 Provides Transit Connectivity*

R2 could form an iBGP session directly with R4, but R3 would not know where to forward traffic to reach AS 65100 or AS 65300 when traffic from either AS reaches R3, as shown in Figure 11-8, because R3 would not have the appropriate route forwarding information for the networks in AS 65100 or AS 65300.

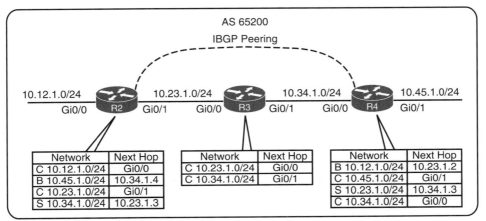

Figure 11-8 *iBGP Prefix Advertisement Behavior*

You might assume that redistributing the BGP table into an IGP overcomes the problem, but this not a viable solution for the following reasons:

- **Scalability:** At the time of this writing, the Internet has 940,000+ IPv4 network prefixes, and it continues to increase in size. IGPs cannot scale to that level of routes.

- **Custom routing:** Link-state protocols and distance vector routing protocols use metric as the primary method for route selection. IGP protocols always use this routing pattern for path selection. BGP uses multiple steps to identify the best path and allows for BGP path attributes to manipulate a prefix's path. The path could be longer, which would normally be deemed suboptimal from an IGP's perspective.

- **Path attributes:** All the BGP path attributes cannot be maintained within IGP protocols. Only BGP is capable of maintaining the path attribute as the prefix is advertised from one edge of the AS to the other edge.

Using Figure 11-8 as a reference, establishing iBGP sessions between all the same routers in a full mesh (R2, R3, and R4 in this case) allows for proper forwarding between AS 65100 and AS 65300.

NOTE Service providers provide transit connectivity. Enterprise organizations are consumers and should not provide transit connectivity between autonomous systems across the Internet.

11

> **NOTE** Routing principles and designs have changed over the years. In early iBGP deployments where the AS was used as a transit AS, network prefixes would commonly be redistributed into the IGP. To ensure full connectivity in the transit AS, BGP would use synchronization. BGP synchronization is the process of verifying that the BGP route existed in the IGP before the route could be advertised to an eBGP peer. BGP synchronization is no longer a default and is not commonly used.

iBGP Full Mesh Requirement

Earlier in this chapter, we looked at the logic of using AS_Path as a loop-detection and prevention mechanism. AS_Path can be used for detecting loops for eBGP neighbors because the ASN is prepended when advertising to another AS. However, iBGP peers do not prepend their ASN to AS_Path because the route would fail the validity check and would not install into the IP routing table.

No other method exists for detecting loops with iBGP sessions, and RFC 4271 prohibits the advertisement of a route received from an iBGP peer to another iBGP peer. RFC 4271 states that all BGP routers in a single AS must be fully meshed to provide a complete loop-free routing table and prevent traffic blackholing.

In Figure 11-9, R1, R2, and R3 are all within AS 65100. R1 has an iBGP session with R2, and R2 has an iBGP session with R3. R1 advertises the 10.1.1.0/24 prefix to R2, which is processed and inserted into R2's BGP table. R2 does not advertise the 10.1.1.0/24 route to R3 because it received the route from an iBGP peer.

To resolve this issue, R1 must form a multi-hop iBGP session so that R3 can receive the 10.1.1.0/24 route directly from R1. R1 connects to R3's 10.23.1.3 IP address, and R3 connects to R1's 10.12.1.1 IP address. R1 and R3 need a static route to the remote peering link, or R2 needs to advertise the 10.12.1.0/24 and 10.23.1.0/24 networks into BGP.

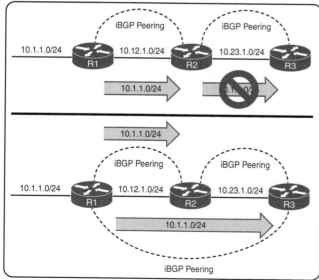

Figure 11-9 *iBGP Prefix Advertisement Behavior*

Peering Using Loopback Addresses

BGP sessions are sourced by the primary IP address of the outbound interface toward the BGP peer by default. In Figure 11-10, R1, R2, and R3 are a full mesh of iBGP sessions peered by transit links.

In the event of a link failure on the 10.13.1.0/24 network, R3's BGP session with R1 times out and terminates. R3 loses connectivity to the 10.1.1.0/24 network, even though R1 and R3 could communicate through R2 (through a multi-hop path). The loss of connectivity occurs because iBGP does not advertise routes learned from another iBGP peer, as explained in the previous section.

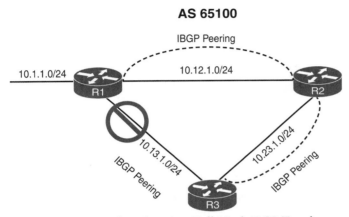

Figure 11-10 *Link Failure in a Full-Mesh iBGP Topology*

You can use two solutions to overcome the link failure:

- Add a second link between each pair of routers (so that three links become six links) and establish two BGP sessions between each pair of routers.

- Configure an IGP on the router's transit links, advertise loopback interfaces into the IGP, and then configure the BGP neighbors to establish a session to the remote router's loopback address.

The second method is more efficient and is the preferable of the two methods.

The loopback interface is virtual and always stays up. In the event of link failure, the session stays intact, and the IGP finds another path to the loopback address, in essence turning a single-hop iBGP session into a multi-hop iBGP session.

Figure 11-11 illustrates the concept of peering using loopback addresses after the 10.13.1.0/24 link fails. R1 and R3 still maintain BGP session connectivity, and routes learned from OSPF allow BGP communication traffic between the loopbacks using R2.

Updating the BGP configuration to connect the session to the IP address of the remote router's loopback address is not enough. The source IP address of the BGP packets still reflects the IP address of the outbound interface. When a BGP packet is received, the router correlates the source IP address of the packet to the BGP neighbor table. If the BGP packet source

11

does not match an entry in the neighbor table, the packet cannot be associated to a neighbor and is discarded.

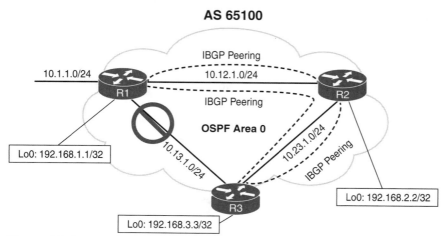

Figure 11-11 *Link Failure with iBGP Sessions on Loopback Interfaces*

The source of BGP packets can be set statically to an interface's primary IP address with the BGP session configuration command **neighbor** *ip-address* **update-source** *interface-id*.

Example 11-11 demonstrates the configuration for Figure 11-11's R1 and R2 to peer using loopback interfaces. R1 has the default IPv4 address family enabled, and R2 does not.

Example 11-11 *BGP Configuration Source from Loopback Interfaces*

```
R1 (Default IPv4 Address Family Enabled)
router ospf 1
 network 10.12.0.0 0.0.255.255 area 0
 network 10.13.0.0 0.0.255.255 area 0
 network 192.168.1.1 0.0.0.0 area 0
!
router bgp 65100
 network 10.1.1.0 mask 255.255.255.0
 neighbor remote-as 192.168.2.2 65100
 neighbor 192.168.2.2 update-source Loopback0
 neighbor remote-as 192.168.3.3 65100
 neighbor 192.168.3.3 update-source Loopback0
 !
 address-family ipv4
  neighbor 192.168.2.2 activate
  neighbor 192.168.3.3 activate

R2 (Default IPv4 Address Family Disabled)
router ospf 1
```

```
 network 10.0.0.0 0.255.255.255 area 0
 network 192.168.2.2 0.0.0.0 area 0
!
router bgp 65100
 no bgp default ipv4-unicast
 neighbor remote-as 192.168.1.1 65100
 neighbor 192.168.1.1 update-source Loopback0
 neighbor remote-as 192.168.3.3 65100
 neighbor 192.168.3.3 update-source Loopback0
 !
 address-family ipv4
  neighbor 192.168.1.1 activate
  neighbor 192.168.3.3 activate
```

Example 11-12 shows R3's BGP table after peering all three routers using loopback interfaces. Notice that the next-hop IP address is R1's loopback address (192.168.1.1). When R2 and R3 forward packets to the 10.1.1.0/24 network, a recursive lookup is performed to determine the outbound interface for the 192.168.1.1 IP address.

Example 11-12 *R3's BGP Table*

```
R3# show bgp ipv4 unicast
! Output omitted for brevity

     Network          Next Hop          Metric LocPrf Weight Path
*>  10.1.1.1/24      192.168.1.1            0    100      0 I
```

NOTE Sourcing BGP sessions from loopback interfaces eliminates the need to recompute the BGP best-path algorithm if a peering link fails, as shown in Figure 11-11. It also provides automatic load balancing if there are multiple equal-cost paths through the IGP to the loopback address.

eBGP

eBGP peerings are the core component of BGP on the Internet. eBGP involves the exchange of network prefixes between autonomous systems. The following behaviors are different on eBGP sessions than on iBGP sessions:

■ The time-to-live (TTL) on eBGP packets is set to 1. BGP packets drop in transit if a multi-hop BGP session is attempted. The TTL on iBGP packets is set to 255, which allows for multi-hop sessions.

■ The advertising router modifies the BGP next hop to the IP address sourcing the BGP connection.

- The advertising router prepends its ASN to the existing AS_Path.

- The receiving router verifies that the AS_Path does not contain an ASN that matches the local routers. BGP discards the NLRI if it fails the AS_Path loop-prevention check.

The configurations for eBGP and iBGP sessions are fundamentally the same except that the ASN in the **remote-as** statement is different from the ASN defined in the BGP process.

Figure 11-12 demonstrates the eBGP and iBGP sessions that would be needed between the routers to allow connectivity between AS 65100 and AS 65300. Notice that AS 65200 R2 establishes an iBGP session with R4 to overcome the loop-prevention behavior of iBGP learned routes, as explained earlier in this chapter.

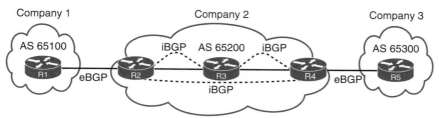

Figure 11-12 *eBGP and iBGP Sessions*

An eBGP learned path always has at least one ASN in AS_Path. If multiple ASs are listed in AS_Path, the most recent AS is always prepended (the furthest to the left). The BGP attributes for all paths to a specific network prefix can be shown with the command **show bgp ipv4 unicast** *network*.

eBGP and iBGP Topologies

Combining eBGP sessions with iBGP sessions can cause confusion in terminology and concepts. Figure 11-13 provides a reference topology for clarification of eBGP and iBGP concepts. R1 and R2 form an eBGP session, R3 and R4 form an eBGP session as well, and R2 and R3 form an iBGP session. R2 and R3 are iBGP peers and follow the rules of iBGP advertisement, even if the routes are learned from an eBGP peer.

As an eBGP prefix is advertised to an iBGP neighbor, issues may arise with the route passing the validity check and next-hop reachability check, preventing advertisements to other BGP peers. The most common issue involves the failure of the next-hop accessibility check. iBGP peers do not modify the next-hop address if the route has a next-hop address other than 0.0.0.0. The next-hop address must be resolvable in the RIB in order for it to be valid and advertised to other BGP peers.

To demonstrate this concept, only R1 and R4 have advertised their loopback interfaces into BGP: 192.168.1.1/32 and 192.168.4.4/32, respectively. Figure 11-13 displays the BGP table for all four routers. Notice that the BGP best-path symbol (>) is missing for the 192.168.4.4/32 prefix on R2 and for the 192.168.1.1/32 prefix on R3.

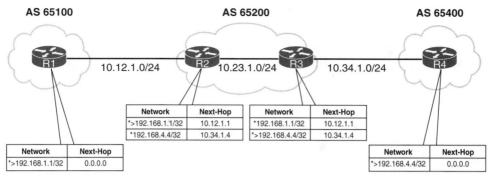

Figure 11-13 *eBGP and iBGP Topology*

R1's BGP table is missing the 192.168.4.4/32 route because the route did not pass R2's next-hop accessibility check, preventing the execution of the BGP best-path algorithm. R4 advertised the route to R3 with the next-hop address 10.34.1.4, and R3 advertised the route to R2 with the next-hop address 10.34.1.4. R2 does not have a route for the 10.34.1.4 IP address and deems the next hop inaccessible. The same logic applies to R1's 192.168.1.1/32 route when advertised toward R4.

Example 11-13 shows the BGP attributes on R3 for the 192.168.1.1/32 route. Notice that the route is not advertised to any peer because the next hop is *inaccessible*.

Example 11-13 *BGP Path Attributes for 192.168.1.1/32*

```
R3# show bgp ipv4 unicast 192.168.1.1
BGP routing table entry for 192.1681.1/32, version 2
Paths: (1 available, no best path)
  Not advertised to any peer
  Refresh Epoch 1
  65100
    10.12.1.1 (inaccessible) from 10.23.1.2 (192.168.2.2)
      Origin IGP, metric 0, localpref 100, valid, internal
```

To correct the issue, the peering links, 10.12.1.0/24 and 10.34.1.0/24, need to be in both R2's and R3's routing tables, using either of these techniques:

- IGP advertisement (Remember to use the passive interface to prevent an accidental adjacency from forming. Most IGPs do not provide the filtering capability provided by BGP.)

- Advertisement of the networks into BGP

Both techniques allow the routes to pass the next-hop accessibility test.

Figure 11-14 displays the topology with both transit links advertised into BGP. Notice that this time, all four routes are valid, with a BGP best path selected.

11

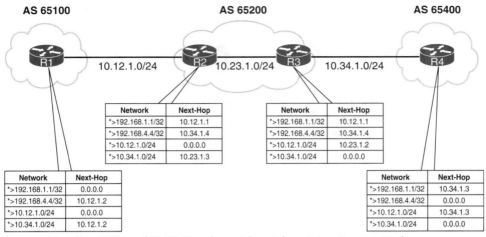

Figure 11-14 *eBGP and iBGP Topology After Advertising Peering Links*

Next-Hop Manipulation

Imagine that a service provider network has 500 routers, and every router has 200 eBGP peering links. To ensure that the next-hop address is reachable to the iBGP peers, the provider needs the advertisement of 100,000 peering networks in BGP or an IGP consuming router resources.

Another technique to ensure that the next-hop address check passes without advertising peering networks into a routing protocol involves the modification of the next-hop address. The next-hop IP address can be modified on inbound or outbound neighbor routing policies. Managing next-hop IP addresses in a routing policy can be a complicated task. You can use the **next-hop-self** feature to modify the next-hop address in the NLRI for external BGP prefixes in the IP address sourcing the BGP session.

The command **neighbor** *ip-address* **next-hop-self** [**all**] is used for each neighbor under the address family configuration. The **next-hop-self** feature does not modify the next-hop address for iBGP prefixes by default. IOS XE nodes can append the optional **all** keyword, which modifies the next-hop address on iBGP prefixes, too. Example 11-14 demonstrates the configuration for R2 and R3 so that the eBGP peer links do not need to be advertised into BGP.

Example 11-14 *BGP Configuration Source for next-hop-self*

```
R2 (Default IPv4 Address-Family Enabled)
router bgp 65200
 neighbor 10.12.1.1 remote-as 65100
 neighbor 10.23.1.3 remote-as 65200
 neighbor 10.23.1.3 next-hop-self

R3 (Default IPv4 Address-Family Disabled)
router bgp 65200
```

```
no bgp default ipv4-unicast
neighbor 10.23.1.2 remote-as 65200
neighbor 10.34.1.4 remote-as 65400
!
address-family ipv4
 neighbor 10.23.1.2 activate
 neighbor 10.23.1.2 next-hop-self
 neighbor 10.34.1.4 activate
```

Figure 11-15 shows the topology and BGP table for all four routers. With the new configuration, R1 advertises the 192.168.1.1/32 route to R2, which installs the 192.168.1.1/32 route with a next hop of the peering link (10.12.1.1). R2 advertises the eBGP route to R3 with a next-hop-self, which is the IP address R3 established with R2 (10.23.1.2). R3 now shows the route with a next hop of 10.23.1.2 and advertises the route to R4. R4 installs the route with a next hop of the peering address because it is an eBGP learned route. The same process occurs for the 192.168.4.4/32 route as it is advertised toward AS 65100.

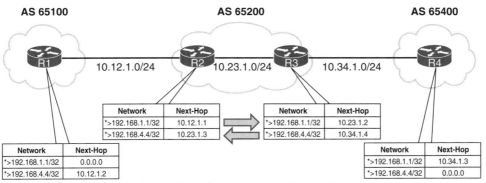

Figure 11-15 *eBGP and iBGP Topology with next-hop-self*

iBGP Scalability Enhancements

The inability of BGP to advertise a route learned from one iBGP peer to another iBGP peer can lead to scalability issues within an AS. The formula $n(n - 1)/2$ provides the number of sessions required, where n represents the number of routers. A full mesh topology of 5 routers requires 10 sessions, and a topology of 10 routers requires 45 sessions. iBGP scalability becomes an issue for large networks.

Route Reflectors

RFC 1966 introduces the idea that an iBGP peering can be configured so that it reflects routes to another iBGP peer. The router that is reflecting routes is known as a *route reflector (RR)*, and the router that is receiving reflected routes is a *route reflector client*. Route reflectors and route reflection involve three basic rules:

- **Rule 1:** If an RR receives an NLRI from a non-RR client, the RR advertises the NLRI to an RR client. It does not advertise the NLRI to a non-RR client.

11

- **Rule 2:** If an RR receives an NLRI from an RR client, it advertises the NLRI to RR clients and non-RR clients.

- **Rule 3:** If an RR receives a route from an eBGP peer, it advertises the route to RR clients and non-RR clients.

Figure 11-16 demonstrates the route reflector rules.

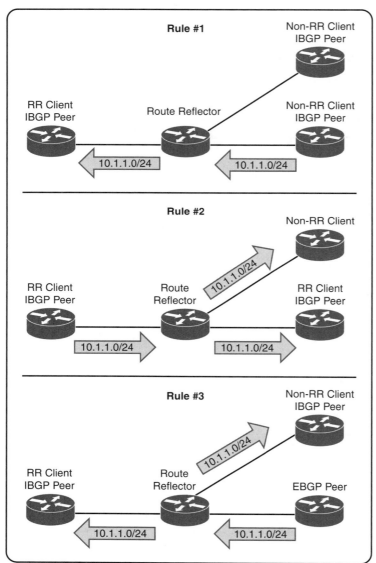

Figure 11-16   *Route Reflector Rules*

Route Reflector Configuration

Only route reflectors are aware of the change in behavior because no additional BGP configuration is performed on route reflector clients. BGP route reflection is specific to each address family. The command **neighbor** *ip-address* **route-reflector-client** is used under the neighbor address family configuration.

Figure 11-17 shows a simple iBGP topology to demonstrate the configuration of a route reflector and the route reflector clients. R1 is a route reflector client to R2, and R4 is a route reflector client to R3. R2 and R3 have a normal iBGP peering.

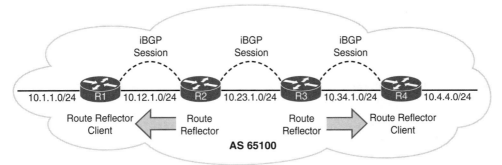

Figure 11-17 *Route Reflector Topology*

Example 11-15 shows the relevant BGP configuration for R1, R2, R3, and R4. R1 and R2 are configured with the default IPv4 address family enabled, and R3 and R4 have the default IPv4 address family disabled. Notice that the route reflector clients are configured only on R2 and R3. R1 explicitly advertises the 10.1.1.10/24 route with a **network** statement.

Example 11-15 *BGP Configuration Source from Loopback Interfaces*

```
R1 (Default IPv4 Address-Family Enabled)
router bgp 65100
 network 10.1.1.0 mask 255.255.255.0
 redistribute connected
 neighbor 10.12.1.2 remote-as 65100
```
```
R2 (Default IPv4 Address-Family Enabled)
router bgp 65100
 redistribute connected
 neighbor 10.12.1.1 remote-as 65100
 neighbor 10.12.1.1 route-reflector-client
 neighbor 10.23.1.3 remote-as 65100
```
```
R3 (Default IPv4 Address-Family Disabled)
router bgp 65100
 no bgp default ipv4-unicast
 neighbor 10.23.1.2 remote-as 65100
```

11

```
 neighbor 10.34.1.4 remote-as 65100
 !
address-family ipv4
  redistribute connected
  neighbor 10.23.1.2 activate
  neighbor 10.34.1.4 activate
  neighbor 10.34.1.4 route-reflector-client
```

```
R4 (Default IPv4 Address-Family Disabled)
router bgp 65100
 no bgp default ipv4-unicast
 neighbor 10.34.1.3 remote-as 65100
 !
 address-family ipv4
  neighbor 10.34.1.3 activate
```

Figure 11-18 shows the topology with the route reflector and route reflector client roles to demonstrate the rules of a route reflector in action. R1 advertises the 10.1.1.0/24 route to R2 as a normal iBGP advertisement. R2 receives and advertises the 10.1.1.0/24 route using the route reflector rule 2 as just explained to R3 (a non-route reflector client). R3 receives and advertises the 10.1.1.0/24 route using the route reflector rule 1 as explained to R4 (a route reflector client).

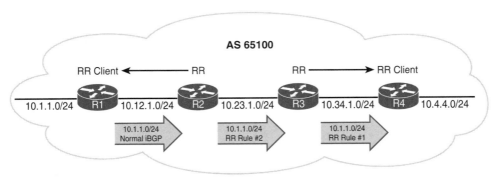

Figure 11-18 *Route Reflector Rules in a Topology*

Example 11-16 shows the BGP table for the 10.1.1.0/24 prefix. Notice that the next-hop IP address changes upon the route's installation into R2's BGP table, but it remains the same on R2, R3, and R4.

Example 11-16 *BGP Configuration Source from Loopback Interfaces*

```
R1# show bgp ipv4 unicast | i Network|10.1.1
    Network          Next Hop          Metric LocPrf Weight Path
 *>  10.1.1.0/24      0.0.0.0                0          32768 i
```

```
R2# show bgp ipv4 unicast | i Network|10.1.1
    Network          Next Hop           Metric LocPrf Weight Path
 *>i 10.1.1.0/24     10.12.1.1               0    100      0 i
```

```
R3# show bgp ipv4 unicast | i Network|10.1.1
    Network          Next Hop           Metric LocPrf Weight Path
 *>i 10.1.1.0/24     10.12.1.1               0    100      0 i
```

```
R4# show bgp ipv4 unicast | i Network|10.1.1
    Network          Next Hop           Metric LocPrf Weight Path
 *>i 10.1.1.0/24     10.12.1.1               0    100      0 i
```

NOTE Notice the i immediately after the best-path indicator (>) on R2, R3, and R4. This indicates that the prefix is learned through iBGP.

Loop Prevention in Route Reflectors

Removing the full mesh requirement in an iBGP topology introduces the potential for routing loops. When RFC 1966 was drafted, two other BGP route reflector–specific attributes were added to prevent loops:

- **Originator:** This optional non-transitive BGP attribute is created by the first route reflector and sets the value to the RID of the router that injected/advertised the prefix into the AS. If Originator is already populated on a route, it should not be overwritten. If a router receives a route with its RID in the Originator attribute, the route is discarded.

- **Cluster List:** This non-transitive BGP attribute is updated by the route reflector. This attribute is appended (not overwritten) by the route reflector with its cluster ID. By default, this is the BGP identifier. If a route reflector receives a route with its cluster ID in the Cluster List attribute, the route is discarded.

Example 11-17 shows all the BGP path attributes for the 10.1.1.0/24 route on R4. Notice that the Originator and Cluster List attributes are populated appropriately for the prefix.

Example 11-17 *Route Reflector Originator ID and Cluster List Attributes*

```
R4# show bgp ipv4 unicast 10.1.1.0/24
! Output omitted for brevity
Paths: (1 available, best #1, table default)
  Refresh Epoch 1
  Local
    10.12.1.1 from 10.34.1.3 (192.168.3.3)
      Origin IGP, metric 0, localpref 100, valid, internal, best
      Originator: 192.168.1.1, Cluster list: 192.168.3.3, 192.168.2.2
```

11

Confederations

RFC 3065 introduced the concept of *BGP confederations* as an alternative solution to the iBGP full mesh scalability issues shown earlier. A confederation consists of sub-ASs known as *member ASs* that combine into a larger AS known as an *AS confederation*. Member ASs normally use ASNs from the private ASN range (64,512 to 65,534). eBGP peers from the confederation have no knowledge that they are peering with a confederation, and they reference the *confederation identifier* in their configuration.

Figure 11-19 demonstrates a BGP confederation with the confederation identifier AS 200. The member ASs are AS 65100 and AS 65200. R3 provides route reflection in member AS 65100.

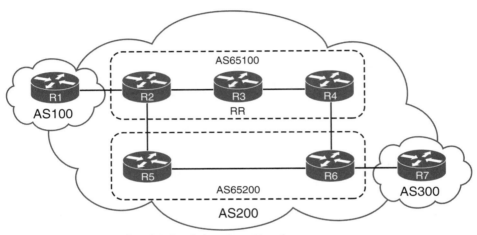

Figure 11-19   *Sample BGP Confederations Topology*

Follow these steps to configure a BGP confederation:

Step 1.   Initialize the BGP process with the global command **router bgp** *member-asn*.

Step 2.   Identify the BGP confederations with the command **bgp confederation identifier** *as-number*.

Step 3.   On routers that directly peer with another member AS, identify the peering member AS with the command **bgp confederation peers** *member-asn*.

Step 4.   Configure BGP confederation members as normal and then following the normal BGP configuration guidelines for the remaining configuration.

Example 11-18 provides the relevant BGP session configuration. R1 and R7 are not aware of the confederation and peer with R2 and R6 as though they were members of AS 200. Notice that R3 does not need the command **bgp confederation peers** because it is not peering with another member AS.

Example 11-18   *BGP Confederation Configuration*

```
R1
router bgp 100
 neighbor 10.12.1.2 remote-as 200
```

```
R2
router bgp 65100
 bgp confederation identifier 200
 bgp confederation peers 65200
 neighbor 10.12.1.1 remote-as 100
 neighbor 10.23.1.3 remote-as 65100
 neighbor 10.25.1.5 remote-as 65200
```

```
R3
router bgp 65100
 bgp confederation identifier 200
 neighbor 10.23.1.2 remote-as 65100
 neighbor 10.23.1.2 route-reflector-client
 neighbor 10.34.1.4 remote-as 65100
 neighbor 10.34.1.4 route-reflector-client
```

```
R4
router bgp 65100
 bgp confederation identifier 200
 bgp confederation peers 65200
 neighbor 10.34.1.3 remote-as 65100
 neighbor 10.46.1.6 remote-as 65200
```

```
R5
router bgp 65200
 bgp confederation identifier 200
 bgp confederation peers 65100
 neighbor 10.25.1.2 remote-as 65100
 neighbor 10.56.1.6 remote-as 65200
```

```
R6
router bgp 65200
 bgp confederation identifier 200
 bgp confederation peers 65100
 neighbor 10.46.1.4 remote-as 65100
 neighbor 10.56.1.5 remote-as 65200
 neighbor 10.67.1.7 remote-as 300
```

```
R7
router bgp 300
 neighbor 10.67.1.6 remote-as 200
```

11

Confederations share behaviors from both iBGP sessions and eBGP sessions but have the following differences:

■ The AS_Path attribute contains a subfield called AS_CONFED_SEQUENCE. AS_CONFED_SEQUENCE is displayed in parentheses before any external ASNs in AS_Path. As the route passes from member AS to member AS, AS_CONFED_SEQUENCE is appended to contain the member AS ASNs. The AS_CONFED_SEQUENCE attribute is used to prevent loops but is not used (counted) when choosing the shortest AS_Path.

■ Route reflectors can be used within the member AS as in normal iBGP peerings.

■ The BGP MED attribute is transitive to all other member ASs but does not leave the confederation.

■ The LOCAL_PREF attribute is transitive to all other member ASs but does not leave the confederation.

■ The next-hop address for external confederation routes does not change as the route is exchanged between member ASs.

■ AS_CONFED_SEQUENCE is removed from AS_Path when the route is advertised outside the confederation.

Example 11-19 shows R1's BGP table, which displays all the routes advertised in this topology. Notice that R2 removed the member AS ASNs from the route as it is advertised externally. AS 100 is not aware that AS 200 is a confederation.

Example 11-19 *AS 100's BGP Table*

```
R1-AS100# show bgp ipv4 unicast | begin Network
     Network          Next Hop          Metric LocPrf Weight Path
 *>  10.1.1.0/24      0.0.0.0                0           32768 ?
 *>  10.7.7.0/24      10.12.1.2                          0 200 300 i
 *   10.12.1.0/24     10.12.1.2              0            0 200 ?
 *>                   0.0.0.0                       0   32768 ?
 *>  10.23.1.0/24     10.12.1.2              0            0 200 ?
 *>  10.25.1.0/24     10.12.1.2              0            0 200 ?
 *>  10.46.1.0/24     10.12.1.2                          0 200 ?
 *>  10.56.1.0/24     10.12.1.2                          0 200 ?
 *>  10.67.1.0/24     10.12.1.2                          0 200 ?
 *>  10.78.1.0/24     10.12.1.2                          0 200 300 ?
```

Example 11-20 shows R2's BGP table, which participates in the member AS 65100. Notice that the next-hop IP address is not modified for the 10.7.7.0/24 prefix that was advertised by R7, even though it passed a different member AS. AS_CONFED_SEQUENCE is listed in parentheses to indicate that it passed through sub AS 65200 in the AS 200 confederation.

Example 11-20 *R2's BGP Table*

```
R2# show bgp ipv4 unicast | begin Network
     Network          Next Hop         Metric LocPrf Weight Path
 *>  10.1.1.0/24      10.12.1.1           111             0 100 ?
 *>  10.7.7.0/24      10.67.1.7             0    100      0 (65200) 300 i
 *>  10.12.1.0/24     0.0.0.0               0          32768 ?
 *                    10.12.1.1           111             0 100 ?
 *>  10.23.1.0/24     0.0.0.0               0          32768 ?
 *   10.25.1.0/24     10.25.1.5             0    100      0 (65200) ?
 *>                   0.0.0.0               0          32768 ?
 *>  10.46.1.0/24     10.56.1.6             0    100      0 (65200) ?
 *>  10.56.1.0/24     10.25.1.5             0    100      0 (65200) ?
 *>  10.67.1.0/24     10.56.1.6             0    100      0 (65200) ?
 *>  10.78.1.0/24     10.67.1.7             0    100      0 (65200) 300 ?
Processed 9 prefixes, 11 paths
```

Example 11-21 shows the full path information from the perspective of R4 for the 10.7.7.0/24 route that was advertised from R7. Notice that the path information includes the attribute *confed-internal* or *confed-external*, based on whether the route was received within the same member AS or a different one.

Example 11-21 *Confederation NLRI*

```
R4# show bgp ipv4 unicast 10.7.7.0/24
! Output omitted for brevity
BGP routing table entry for 10.7.7.0/24, version 504
Paths: (2 available, best #1, table default)
  Advertised to update-groups:
     3
  Refresh Epoch 1
  (65200) 300
    10.67.1.7 from 10.34.1.3 (192.168.3.3)
      Origin IGP, metric 0, localpref 100, valid, confed-internal, best
      Originator: 192.168.2.2, Cluster list: 192.168.3.3
      rx pathid: 0, tx pathid: 0x0
  Refresh Epoch 1
  (65200) 300
    10.67.1.7 from 10.46.1.6 (192.168.6.6)
      Origin IGP, metric 0, localpref 100, valid, confed-external
      rx pathid: 0, tx pathid: 0
```

Multiprotocol BGP for IPv6

Multiprotocol BGP (MP-BGP) enables BGP to carry NLRI for multiple protocols, such as IPv4, IPv6, and Multiprotocol Label Switching (MPLS) Layer 3 Virtual Private Network (L3VPN).

11

RFC 4760 defines the following new features:

- New address family identifier (AFI) model

- New BGPv4 optional and nontransitive attributes:

  - Multiprotocol reachable NLRI: Describes IPv6 route information

  - Multiprotocol unreachable NLRI: Withdraws the IPv6 route from service

These attributes are optional and nontransitive, so if an older router does not understand the attributes, the information can just be ignored.

All the same underlying IPv4 path vector routing protocol features and rules also apply to MP-BGP for IPv6. MP-BGP for IPv6 continues to use the same well-known TCP port 179 for session peering that BGP uses for IPv4. During the initial open message negotiation, the BGP peer routers exchange capabilities. The MP-BGP extensions include an AFI that describes the supported protocols, along with SAFI attribute fields that describe whether the prefix applies to the unicast or multicast routing table:

- **IPv4 unicast:** AFI:1, SAFI:1

- **IPv6 unicast:** AFI:2, SAFI:1

Figure 11-20 shows a simple topology with three different ASs and R2 forming an eBGP session with R1 and R3. The link-local addresses have been configured from the defined link-local range FE80::/10. All of R1's links are configured to FE80::1, all of R2's links are set to FE80::2, and all of R3's links are configured to FE80::3. This topology is used throughout this section.

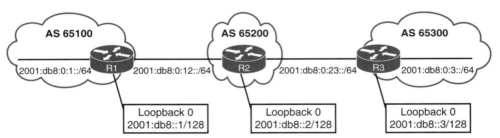

Figure 11-20 *IPv6 Sample Topology*

IPv6 Configuration

All the BGP configuration rules demonstrated earlier apply with IPv6, except that the IPv6 address family must be initialized, and the neighbor is activated. Routers with only IPv6 addressing must statically define the BGP RID to allow sessions to form.

The protocol used to establish the BGP session is independent of the AFI/SAFI route advertisements. The TCP session used by BGP is a Layer 4 protocol, and it can use either an IPv4 or IPv6 address to form a session adjacency and exchange routes.

NOTE   Unique global unicast addressing is the recommended method for BGP peering to avoid operational complexity. BGP peering using the link-local address may introduce risk if the address is not manually assigned to an interface. A hardware failure or cable move would change the MAC address, resulting in a new link-local address. This would cause the session to fail because the stateless address autoconfiguration would generate a new IP address.

Example 11-22 shows the IPv6 BGP configuration for R1, R2, and R3. The peering uses global unicast addressing to establish the session. The BGP RID has been set to the IPv4 loopback format used throughout this book. R1 advertises all its networks through redistribution, and R2 and R3 use the **network** statement to advertise all their connected networks.

Example 11-22   *Configuring IPv6 BGP*

```
R1
router bgp 65100
 bgp router-id 192.168.1.1
 no bgp default ipv4-unicast
 neighbor 2001:DB8:0:12::2 remote-as 65200
 !
address-family ipv6
  neighbor 2001:DB8:0:12::2 activate
  redistribute connected

R2
router bgp 65200
 bgp router-id 192.168.2.2
 no bgp default ipv4-unicast
 neighbor 2001:DB8:0:12::1 remote-as 65100
 neighbor 2001:DB8:0:23::3 remote-as 65300
 !
 address-family ipv6
  neighbor 2001:DB8:0:12::1 activate
  neighbor 2001:DB8:0:23::3 activate
  network 2001:DB8::2/128
  network 2001:DB8:0:12::/64
  network 2001:DB8:0:23::/64

R3
router bgp 65300
 bgp router-id 192.168.3.3
 no bgp default ipv4-unicast
 neighbor 2001:DB8:0:23::2 remote-as 65200
 !
 address-family ipv6
  neighbor 2001:DB8:0:23::2 activate
  network 2001:DB8::3/128
  network 2001:DB8:0:3::/64
  network 2001:DB8:0:23::/64
```

11

NOTE   IPv4 unicast routing capability is advertised by default in IOS XE unless the neighbor is specifically shut down within the IPv4 address family or globally within the BGP process with the command **no bgp default ipv4-unicast**.

Routers exchange AFI capabilities during the initial BGP session negotiation. The command **show bgp ipv6 unicast neighbors** *ip-address* [**detail**] displays detailed information about whether the IPv6 capabilities were negotiated successfully. Example 11-23 shows the attributes that should be examined for IPv6 session establishment and route advertisement.

Example 11-23   *Viewing BGP Neighbors for IPv6 Capabilities*

```
R1# show bgp ipv6 unicast neighbors 2001:DB8:0:12::2
! Output omitted for brevity
BGP neighbor is 2001:DB8:0:12::2,  remote AS 65200, external link
  BGP version 4, remote router ID 192.168.2.2
  BGP state = Established, up for 00:28:25
  Last read 00:00:54, last write 00:00:34, hold time is 180, keepalive interval is
60 seconds
  Neighbor sessions:
    1 active, is not multisession capable (disabled)
  Neighbor capabilities:
    Route refresh: advertised and received(new)
    Four-octets ASN Capability: advertised and received
    Address family IPv6 Unicast: advertised and received
    Enhanced Refresh Capability: advertised and received
 ..
 For address family: IPv6 Unicast
  Session: 2001:DB8:0:12::2
  BGP table version 13, neighbor version 13/0
  Output queue size : 0
  Index 1, Advertise bit 0
  1 update-group member
  Slow-peer detection is disabled
  Slow-peer split-update-group dynamic is disabled
                           Sent       Rcvd
  Prefix activity:         ----       ----
    Prefixes Current:        3          5 (Consumes 520 bytes)
    Prefixes Total:          6         10
```

The command **show bgp ipv6 unicast summary** displays a status summary of the sessions, including the number of prefixes that have been exchanged and the session uptime. Example 11-24 highlights the IPv6 AFI neighbor status for R2. Notice that the two neighbor adjacencies have been up for about 25 minutes. Neighbor 2001:db8:0:12::1 is advertising three prefixes, and neighbor 2001:db8:0:23::3 is advertising three prefixes.

Example 11-24 *Verifying the IPv6 BGP Session*

```
R2# show bgp ipv6 unicast summary
BGP router identifier 192.168.2.2, local AS number 65200
BGP table version is 19, main routing table version 19
7 network entries using 1176 bytes of memory
8 path entries using 832 bytes of memory
3/3 BGP path/bestpath attribute entries using 456 bytes of memory
2 BGP AS-PATH entries using 48 bytes of memory
0 BGP route-map cache entries using 0 bytes of memory
0 BGP filter-list cache entries using 0 bytes of memory
BGP using 2512 total bytes of memory
BGP activity 7/0 prefixes, 8/0 paths, scan interval 60 secs


Neighbor          V     AS MsgRcvd MsgSent TblVer InQ OutQ Up/Down   State/PfxRcd
2001:DB8:0:12::1  4  65100      35      37     19   0    0 00:25:08             3
2001:DB8:0:23::3  4  65300      32      37     19   0    0 00:25:11             3
```

Example 11-25 shows the IPv6 unicast BGP table for R1, R2, and R3. Notice that some of the prefixes include the unspecified address as the next hop. The unspecified address indicates that the local router is generating the prefix for the BGP table. The weight value 32,768 also indicates that the prefix is locally originated by the router.

Example 11-25 *Viewing the IPv6 BGP Table*

```
R1# show bgp ipv6 unicast
BGP table version is 13, local router ID is 192.168.1.1
Status codes: s suppressed, d damped, h history, * valid, > best, - - internal,
              r RIB-failure, S Stale, m multipath, b backup-path, f RT-Filter,
              x best-external, a additional-path, c RIB-compressed,
Origin codes: - - IGP, - - EGP, - - incomplete
RPKI validation codes: V valid, I invalid, N Not found


     Network          Next Hop        Metric LocPrf Weight Path
 *>  2001:DB8::1/128   ::                   0        32768 ?
 *>  2001:DB8::2/128   2001:DB8:0:12::2     0            0 65200 i
 *>  2001:DB8::3/128   2001:DB8:0:12::2                  0 65200 65300 i
 *>  2001:DB8:0:1::/64 ::                   0        32768 ?
 *>  2001:DB8:0:3::/64 2001:DB8:0:12::2                  0 65200 65300 i
 *   2001:DB8:0:12::/64 2001:DB8:0:12::2    0            0 65200 i
 *>                    ::                   0        32768 ?
 *>  2001:DB8:0:23::/64 2001:DB8:0:12::2                 0 65200 i
```

```
R2# show bgp ipv6 unicast | begin Network
     Network          Next Hop        Metric LocPrf Weight Path
```

```
    *>  2001:DB8::1/128     2001:DB8:0:12::1       0              0 65100 ?
    *>  2001:DB8::2/128     ::                     0          32768 i
    *>  2001:DB8::3/128     2001:DB8:0:23::3       0              0 65300 i
    *>  2001:DB8:0:1::/64   2001:DB8:0:12::1       0              0 65100 ?
    *>  2001:DB8:0:3::/64   2001:DB8:0:23::3       0              0 65300 i
    *>  2001:DB8:0:12::/64  ::                     0          32768 i
    *                       2001:DB8:0:12::1       0              0 65100 ?
    *>  2001:DB8:0:23::/64  ::                         0      32768 i
                            2001:DB8:0:23::3       0              0 65300 i

R3# show bgp ipv6 unicast | begin Network
     Network              Next Hop            Metric LocPrf Weight Path
    *>  2001:DB8::1/128     2001:DB8:0:23::2                    0 65200 65100 ?
    *>  2001:DB8::2/128     2001:DB8:0:23::2       0              0 65200 i
    *>  2001:DB8::3/128     ::                     0          32768 i
    *>  2001:DB8:0:1::/64   2001:DB8:0:23::2                    0 65200 65100 ?
    *>  2001:DB8:0:3::/64   ::                     0          32768 i
    *>  2001:DB8:0:12::/64  2001:DB8:0:23::2       0              0 65200 i
    *>  2001:DB8:0:23::/64  ::                     0          32768 i
    *>  2001:DB8:0:23::2    ::                     0          32768 i
    *                       2001:DB8:0:23::2       0              0 65200 i
```

You can view the BGP path attributes for an IPv6 prefix by using the command **show bgp
ipv6 unicast** *prefix/prefix-length*. Example 11-26 shows R3 examining R1's loopback
address. Some of the common attributes, such as those for AS_Path, Origin, and local preference, are identical to those for IPv4 prefixes.

Example 11-26 *Viewing the BGP Path Attributes for an IPv6 Prefix*

```
R3# show bgp ipv6 unicast 2001:DB8::1/128
BGP routing table entry for 2001:DB8::1/128, version 9
Paths: (1 available, best #1, table default)
  Not advertised to any peer
  Refresh Epoch 2
  65200 65100
    2001:DB8:0:23::2 (FE80::2) from 2001:DB8:0:23::2 (192.168.2.2)
      Origin incomplete, localpref 100, valid, external, best
      rx pathid: 0, tx pathid: 0x0
```

Example 11-27 shows the IPv6 BGP prefixes for R2. Notice that the next-hop address is the
link-local address for the next-hop forwarding address, which is resolved through a recursive
lookup.

Example 11-27 *Global RIB for BGP-Learned IPv6 Prefixes*

```
R2# show ipv6 route bgp
IPv6 Routing Table - default - 10 entries
Codes: C - Connected, L - Local, S - Static, U - Per-user Static route
       B - BGP, HA - Home Agent, MR - Mobile Router, R - RIP
       H - NHRP, I1 - ISIS L1, I2 - ISIS L2, IA - ISIS interarea
       IS - ISIS summary, D - EIGRP, EX - EIGRP external, NM - NEMO
       ND - ND Default, NDp - ND Prefix, DCE - Destination, NDr - Redirect
       RL - RPL, O - OSPF Intra, OI - OSPF Inter, OE1 - OSPF ext 1
       OE2 - OSPF ext 2, ON1 - OSPF NSSA ext 1, ON2 - OSPF NSSA ext 2
       la - LISP alt, lr - LISP site-registrations, ld - LISP dyn-eid
       a - Application
B    2001:DB8::1/128 [20/0]
     via FE80::1, GigabitEthernet0/0
B    2001:DB8::3/128 [20/0]
     via FE80::3, GigabitEthernet0/1
B    2001:DB8:0:1::/64 [20/0]
     via FE80::1, GigabitEthernet0/0
B    2001:DB8:0:3::/64 [20/0]
     via FE80::3, GigabitEthernet0/1
```

IPv6 over IPv4

BGP can exchange routes using either an IPv4 or IPv6 TCP session. In a typical deployment, IPv4 routes are exchanged using a dedicated IPv4 session, and IPv6 routes are exchanged with a dedicated IPv6 session. However, it is possible to share IPv6 routes over an IPv4 TCP session or IPv4 routes over an IPv6 TCP session, and it is possible to share IPv4 and IPv6 using a single BGP session.

Example 11-28 shows how to configure the exchange of IPv6 routes over IPv4 using the topology shown in Figure 11-20. Notice that the IPv6 neighbors must be activated, and the routers are injected into BGP under the IPv6 address family.

Example 11-28 *Configuring IPv6 Route Exchange over an IPv4 BGP Session*

```
R1
router bgp 65100
 bgp router-id 192.168.1.1
 no bgp default ipv4-unicast
 neighbor 10.12.1.2 remote-as 65200
 !
address-family ipv6 unicast
  redistribute connected
  neighbor 10.12.1.2 activate
```

```
R2
router bgp 65200
 bgp router-id 192.168.2.2
 no bgp default ipv4-unicast
 neighbor 10.12.1.1 remote-as 65100
 neighbor 10.23.1.3 remote-as 65300
 !
 address-family ipv6 unicast
  network 2001:DB8::2/128
  network 2001:DB8:0:12::/64
  aggregate-address 2001:DB8::/62 summary-only
  neighbor 10.12.1.1 activate
  neighbor 10.23.1.3 activate
```

```
R3
router bgp 65300
 bgp router-id 192.168.3.3
 no bgp default ipv4-unicast
 neighbor 10.23.1.2 remote-as 65200
 !
 address-family ipv6 unicast
  network 2001:DB8::3/128
  network 2001:DB8:0:3::/64
  network 2001:DB8:0:23::/64
  neighbor 10.23.1.2 activate
```

Now that BGP has been configured on all three routers, the BGP sessions can be confirmed with the command **show bgp ipv6 unicast summary**. Example 11-29 shows the verification of the IPv4 BGP session for exchanging IPv6 prefixes.

Example 11-29   *Verifying the BGP Session for IPv6 Routes*

```
R1# show bgp ipv6 unicast summary | begin Neighbor
Neighbor        V      AS MsgRcvd MsgSent  TblVer  InQ OutQ Up/Down  State/PfxRcd
10.12.1.2       4   65200   115      116      11    0    0 01:40:14            2
```

```
R2# show bgp ipv6 unicast summary | begin Neighbor
Neighbor        V      AS MsgRcvd MsgSent  TblVer  InQ OutQ Up/Down  State/PfxRcd
10.12.1.1       4   65100   114      114       8    0    0 01:39:17            3
10.23.1.3       4   65300   113      115       8    0    0 01:39:16            3
```

```
R3# show bgp ipv6 unicast summary | begin Neighbor
Neighbor        V      AS MsgRcvd MsgSent  TblVer  InQ OutQ Up/Down  State/PfxRcd
10.23.1.2       4   65200   114      112       7    0    0 01:38:49            2
```

Example 11-30 shows the IPv6 BGP table for all three routers, which verifies that the routes have been successfully advertised. The IPv6 routes advertised over an IPv4 BGP session are assigned an IPv4-mapped IPv6 address in the format (::FFFF:*xx.xx.xx.xx*) for the next hop, where *xx.xx.xx.xx* is the IPv4 address of the BGP peering. This is not a valid forwarding address, so the IPv6 route does not populate the RIB.

Example 11-30 *Viewing IPv6 Routes Exchanged over an IPv4 BGP Session*

```
R1# show bgp ipv6 unicast | begin Network
     Network            Next Hop          Metric LocPrf Weight Path
 *   2001:DB8::/62       ::FFFF:10.12.1.2       0             0 65200 i
 *>  2001:DB8::1/128     ::                     0         32768 ?
 *>  2001:DB8:0:1::/64   ::                     0         32768 ?
 *   2001:DB8:0:12::/64  ::FFFF:10.12.1.2       0             0 65200 i
 *>                      ::                     0         32768 ?


R2# show bgp ipv6 unicast | begin Network
     Network            Next Hop          Metric LocPrf Weight Path
 *>  2001:DB8::/62       ::                           32768 i
 S   2001:DB8::1/128     ::FFFF:10.12.1.1       0             0 65100 ?
 s>  2001:DB8::2/128     ::                     0         32768 i
 s   2001:DB8::3/128     ::FFFF:10.23.1.3       0             0 65300 i
 s   2001:DB8:0:1::/64   ::FFFF:10.12.1.1       0             0 65100 ?
 s   2001:DB8:0:3::/64   ::FFFF:10.23.1.3       0             0 65300 i
 *   2001:DB8:0:12::/64  ::FFFF:10.12.1.1       0             0 65100 ?
 *>                      ::                     0         32768 i
 *   2001:DB8:0:23::/64  ::FFFF:10.23.1.3       0             0 65300 i


R3# show bgp ipv6 unicast | begin Network
     Network            Next Hop          Metric LocPrf Weight Path
 *   2001:DB8::/62       ::FFFF:10.23.1.2       0             0 65200 i
 *>  2001:DB8::3/128     ::                     0         32768 i
 *>  2001:DB8:0:3::/64   ::                     0         32768 i
 *   2001:DB8:0:12::/64  ::FFFF:10.23.1.2       0             0 65200 i
 *>  2001:DB8:0:23::/64  ::                     0         32768 i
```

Example 11-31 shows a quick connectivity test between R1 and R3. The output confirms that connectivity cannot be maintained.

Example 11-31 *Checking Connectivity Between R1 and R3*

```
R1# ping 2001:DB8:0:3::3
Type escape sequence to abort.
Sending 5, 100-byte ICMP Echos to 2001:DB8:0:3::3, timeout is 2 seconds:


% No valid route for destination
Success rate is 0 percent (0/1)
```

```
R1# traceroute 2001:DB8:0:3::3
Type escape sequence to abort.
Tracing the route to 2001:DB8:0:3::3

  1   *   *   *
  2   *   *   *
  3   *   *   *
 ..
```

To correct the problem, the BGP route map needs to manually set the IPv6 next hop. Example 11-32 shows the BGP configuration for R1, R2, and R3.

Example 11-32 *Route Map to Manually Set the IPv6 Next Hop*

```
R1
route-map FromR1R2Link permit 10
 set ipv6 next-hop 2001:DB8:0:12::1
!
router bgp 65100
 address-family ipv6 unicast
  neighbor 10.12.1.2 route-map FromR1R2LINK out
```
```
R2
route-map FromR2R1LINK permit 10
 set ipv6 next-hop 2001:DB8:0:12::2
route-map FromR2R3LINK permit 10
 set ipv6 next-hop 2001:DB8:0:23::2
!
router bgp 65200
 address-family ipv6 unicast
  neighbor 10.12.1.1 route-map FromR2R1LINK out
  neighbor 10.23.1.3 route-map FromR2R3LINK out
```
```
R3
route-map FromR3R2Link permit 10
 set ipv6 next-hop 2001:DB8:0:23::3
!
router bgp 65300
 address-family ipv6 unicast
  neighbor 10.23.1.2 route-map FromR3R2Link out
```

Example 11-33 shows the BGP table after the IPv6 next-hop address is manually set on the outbound route map. The next-hop IP address is valid, and the route can now be installed into the RIB.

Example 11-33 *Viewing IPv6 Routes After Manually Setting the IPv6 Next Hop*

```
R1# show bgp ipv6 unicast | begin Network
   Network            Next Hop        Metric LocPrf Weight Path
 *> 2001:DB8::/62      2001:DB8:0:12::2       0              0 65200 i
 *> 2001:DB8::1/128    ::                     0          32768 ?
 *> 2001:DB8:0:1::/64  ::                     0          32768 ?
 *> 2001:DB8:0:12::/64 ::                     0          32768 ?
 *                     2001:DB8:0:12::2       0              0 65200 i

R2# show bgp ipv6 unicast | begin Network
   Network            Next Hop        Metric LocPrf Weight Path
 *> 2001:DB8::/62      ::                                32768 i
 s> 2001:DB8::1/128    2001:DB8:0:12::1       0              0 65100 ?
 s> 2001:DB8::2/128    ::                     0          32768 i

 s> 2001:DB8::3/128    2001:DB8:0:23::3       0              0 65300 i
 s> 2001:DB8:0:1::/64  2001:DB8:0:12::1       0              0 65100 ?
 s> 2001:DB8:0:3::/64  2001:DB8:0:23::3       0              0 65300 i
 *> 2001:DB8:0:12::/64 ::                     0          32768 i
 r> 2001:DB8:0:23::/64 2001:DB8:0:23::3       0              0 65300 i

R3# show bgp ipv6 unicast | begin Network
   Network            Next Hop        Metric LocPrf Weight Path
 *> 2001:DB8::/62      2001:DB8:0:23::2
                                             0              0 65200 i
 *> 2001:DB8::3/128    ::                     0          32768 i
 *> 2001:DB8:0:3::/64  ::                     0          32768 i
 *> 2001:DB8:0:12::/64 2001:DB8:0:23::2       0              0 65200 i
 *> 2001:DB8:0:23::/64 ::                     0          32768 i
```

References in This Chapter

Edgeworth, Brad, Foss, Aaron, and Garza Rios, Ramiro, *IP Routing on Cisco IOS, IOS XE, and IOS XR*, Cisco Press, 2014.

RFC 1966, *BGP Route Reflection*, Tony Bates and Ravi Chandra, https://www.ietf.org/rfc/rfc1966.txt, July 1996.

RFC 2858, *Multiprotocol Extensions for BGP-4*, Yakov Rekhter, Tony Bates, Ravi Chandra, and Dave Katz, https://www.ietf.org/rfc/rfc2858.txt, June 2000.

RFC 3065, *Autonomous System Confederations for BGP*, Paul Traina, Danny McPherson, Jong Scudder, https://www.ietf.org/rfc/rfc3065.txt, February 2001.

RFC 4271, *A Border Gateway Protocol 4 (BGP-4)*, Yakov Rekhter, Tony Li, and Susan Hares, https://www.ietf.org/rfc/rfc4271.txt, January 2006.

RFC 4760, *Multiprotocol Extensions for BGP-4*, Yakov Rekhter, Tony Bates, Ravi Chandra, and Dave Katz, https://www.ietf.org/rfc/rfc4760.txt, January 2007.

11

RFC 4893, *BGP Support for Four-Octet AS Number Space*, Quaizar Vohra and Enke Chen, https://www.ietf.org/rfc/rfc4893.txt, May 2007.

RFC 6996, *Autonomous System (AS) Reservation for Private Use*, J. Mitchell, https://www.ietf.org/rfc/rfc6996.txt, July 2013.

RFC 7300, *Reservation of Last Autonomous System (AS) Numbers*, J. Haas and J. Mitchell, https://www.ietf.org/rfc/rfc7300.txt, July 2014.

Exam Preparation Tasks

As mentioned in the section "How to Use This Book" in the Introduction, you have a couple choices for exam preparation: the exercises here, Chapter 24, "Final Preparation," and the exam simulation questions in the Pearson Test Prep software.

Review All Key Topics

Review the most important topics in this chapter, noted with the Key Topic icon in the outer margin of the page. Table 11-6 lists these key topics and the page number on which each is found.

Table 11-6   Key Topics

Key Topic Element	Description	Page Number
Paragraph	Autonomous system numbers (ASNs)	428
Paragraph	Path attributes	429
Paragraph	Inter-router communication	430
Figure 11-1	BGP single and multi-hop sessions	431
Paragraph	BGP messages	431
Paragraph	BGP neighbor states	432
Paragraph	Basic BGP configuration	435
Paragraph	Verification of BGP sessions	437
Table 11-3	BGP summary fields	438
List	BGP tables	440
Paragraph	BGP prefix validity check and installation	441
Figure 11-6	BGP database processing	444
Paragraph	Viewing all the paths and path attributes for a specific route	445
Paragraph	Viewing the Adj-RIB-Out table for a specific BGP peer	447
Paragraph	Understanding BGP session types and behaviors	448
Paragraph	iBGP full mesh requirement	450
Paragraph	Peering using loopback addresses	451
Paragraph	eBGP peerings	453
Paragraph	eBGP and iBGP topologies	454

Key Topic Element	Description	Page Number
Paragraph	Next-hop manipulation	456
Paragraph	Route reflectors	457
Figure 11-16	Route reflector rules	458
Paragraph	Confederations	462
Paragraph	IPv6 BGP configuration	466
Paragraph	IPv6 summarization	471
Paragraph	Advertising IPv6 prefixes over an IPv4 BGP session	471

Define Key Terms

Define the following key terms from this chapter and check your answers in the glossary:

autonomous system, well-known mandatory, well-known discretionary, optional transitive, optional non-transitive, path vector routing protocol, AS_Path, address family, eBGP session, iBGP session, route reflector, route reflector client, BGP confederation, Loc-RIB table

Use the Command Reference to Check Your Memory

The ENARSI 300-410 exam focuses on the practical, hands-on skills that networking professionals use. Therefore, you should be able to identify the commands needed to configure, verify, and troubleshoot the topics covered in this chapter.

This section includes the most important configuration and verification commands covered in this chapter. It might not be necessary to memorize the complete syntax of every command, but you should be able to remember the basic keywords that are needed.

To test your memory of the commands in Table 11-7, go to the companion website and download Appendix B, "Command Reference Exercises." Fill in the missing commands in the tables based on each command description. You can check your work by downloading Appendix C, "Command Reference Exercise Answer Key," from the companion website.

Table 11-7 Command Reference

Task	Command Syntax
Initialize the BGP router process.	**router bgp** *as-number*
Statically configure the BGP router ID.	**bgp router-id** *router-id*
Identify a BGP peer to establish a session with.	**neighbor** *ip-address* **remote-as** *as-number*
Configure the BGP session timers.	**neighbor** *ip-address* **timers** *keepalive holdtime* [*minimum-holdtime*]
Specify the source interface for BGP packets for a specific BGP peer.	**neighbor** *ip-address* **update-source** *interface-id*
Specify the ASN at which the BGP confederation should appear.	**bgp confederation identifier** *as-number*
Specify any BGP confederation member ASs that this router will peer with.	**bgp confederation peers** *member-asn*

11

Task	Command Syntax
Disable the automatic IPv4 address family configuration mode.	**no bgp default ip4-unicast**
Initialize a specific address family and sub-address family.	**address-family** *afi safi*
Activate a BGP neighbor for a specific address family.	**neighbor** *ip-address* **activate**
Advertise a network into BGP.	**network** *network* **mask** *subnet-mask* [**route-map** *route-map-name*]
Modify the next-hop IP address on prefix advertisements to match that of the IP address used for the BGP session.	**neighbor** *ip-address* **next-hop-self** [**all**]
Configure the associated BGP peer as a route reflector client.	**neighbor** *ip-address* **route-reflector-client**
Display the contents of the BGP database.	**show bgp** *afi safi* [*network*] [`detailed`]
Display a summary of the BGP table and neighbor peering sessions.	**show bgp** *afi safi* **summary**
Display the negotiated BGP settings with a specific peer and the number of prefixes exchanged with that peer.	**show bgp** *afi safi* **neighbors** *ip-address*
Display the Adj-RIB-out BGP table for a specific BGP neighbor.	**show bgp** *afi safi* **neighbor** *ip-address* **advertised routes**

## CHAPTER 12

Advanced BGP

This chapter covers the following topics:

- **Route Summarization:** This section provides an overview of the how route summarization works with Border Gateway Protocol (BGP) and some design considerations related to summarization.

- **BGP Route Filtering and Manipulation:** This section demonstrates the filtering and manipulation of routes based on network prefix, AS_Path, or other BGP path attributes.

- **BGP Communities:** This section explains BGP communities and how the well-known communities influence prefix advertisements along with how they are used for conditional prefix filtering or manipulation.

- **Maximum Prefix:** This section explains how a router can limit the number of prefixes received to ensure that the BGP table does not exceed its capacity.

- **Configuration Scalability:** This section explains the use of peer groups and peer templates to assist with BGP configurations on routers with a lot of BGP sessions.

Border Gateway Protocol (BGP) supports hundreds of thousands of network prefixes, which makes it an ideal choice for the Internet. Organizations also use BGP for its flexibility and traffic engineering properties. This chapter expands on Chapter 11, "BGP," and explains BGP's advanced features and concepts, such as BGP route summarization, route filtering, BGP communities, and techniques for optimizing a large BGP deployment.

"Do I Know This Already?" Quiz

The "Do I Know This Already?" quiz allows you to assess whether you should read this entire chapter thoroughly or jump to the "Exam Preparation Tasks" section. If you are in doubt about your answers to these questions or your own assessment of your knowledge of the topics, read the entire chapter. Table 12-1 lists the major headings in this chapter and their corresponding "Do I Know This Already?" quiz questions. You can find the answers in Appendix A, "Answers to the 'Do I Know This Already?' Quiz Questions."

Table 12-1 "Do I Know This Already?" Foundation Topics Section-to-Question Mapping

Foundation Topics Section	Questions
Route Summarization	1, 2
BGP Route Filtering and Manipulation	3–5
BGP Communities	6
Maximum Prefix	7
Configuration Scalability	8

1. Which BGP command advertises a summary route to prevent link-flap processing by downstream BGP routers?

   a. **aggregate-address** *network subnet-mask* **as-set**

   b. **aggregate-address** *network subnet-mask* **summary-only**

   c. **summary-address** *network subnet-mask*

   d. **summary-address** *network* **mask** *subnet-mask*

2. What is the BGP atomic aggregate?

   a. A BGP path attribute used to indicate that a prefix should not be advertised to a peer

   b. A BGP path attribute that indicates a loss of path attributes

   c. The amount of time that a peer's routes should not be installed due to a flapping link

   d. The BGP routes that are suppressed during summarization

3. Which extended ACL entry allows any network in the 172.16.x.x network with a /24 to /32 prefix length?

   a. **permit ip 172.16.0.0 0.0.255.255 255.255.255.0 0.0.0.255**

   b. **permit ip 172.16.0.0 255.255.0.0 0.0.255.255 0.0.0.0**

   c. **permit ip 172.16.0.0 255.255.0.0 255.255.255.0 0.0.0.255**

   d. **permit ip 172.16.0.0 0.0.255.255 0.0.255.255 0.0.0.0**

4. Which command displays only the network prefixes that originate from AS 40 or AS 45?

   a. **show bgp ipv4 unicast regexp _40|45$**

   b. **show bgp ipv4 unicast regexp ^40|45**

   c. **show bgp ipv4 unicast regexp _4(0|5)$**

   d. **show bgp ipv4 unicast regexp _[40,45]$**

5. True or false: A BGP AS_Path ACL and a prefix list can be applied to a neighbor at the same time.

   a. True

   b. False

6. Which of the following is not a well-known BGP community?

   a. No_Advertise

   b. Internet

    c. No_Export

    d. Private_Route

7. A router has been configured with the command **neighbor 10.12.1.2 maximum-prefix 100**. What happens when the BGP peer advertises 101 prefixes to it?

    a. The 101st prefix overwrites the 1st prefix in the Loc-RIB table.

    b. The 101st prefix is discarded.

    c. The BGP session is shut down.

    d. The 101st prefix is received and installed in the Loc-RIB table, and a warning message is generated.

8. What is the primary difference between a BGP peer group and a peer template?

    a. They can have different inbound routing policies.

    b. They can have different outbound routing policies.

    c. They can have different BGP authentication settings.

    d. They can have different BGP timers.

Foundation Topics

Route Summarization

Summarizing prefixes conserves router resources and accelerates best-path calculation by reducing the size of the table. Summarization, also known as route aggregation, provides the benefit of stability by hiding route flaps from downstream routers, thereby reducing routing churn. While most service providers do not accept prefixes larger than /24 for IPv4 (/25 through /32), the Internet, at the time of this writing, still has more than 940,000 routes and continues to grow. Route summarization can reduce the size of the BGP table for Internet routers.

Dynamic BGP summarization consists of the configuration of an aggregate network prefix. When viable component routes that match the aggregate network prefix enter the BGP table, the aggregate prefix is created. The originating router sets the next hop to Null0 as a discard route for the aggregated prefix for loop prevention.

Aggregate Addresses

Dynamic route summarization is accomplished with the BGP address family configuration command **aggregate-address** *network subnet-mask* [**summary-only**] [**as-set**].

Figure 12-1 shows a simple topology in which R1 established an external BGP (eBGP) session with R2, and R2 establishes an eBGP session with R3.

Example 12-1 displays the BGP tables for R1, R2, and R3 before route aggregation has been performed. R1's stub networks (172.16.1.0/24, 172.16.2.0/24, and 172.16.3.0/24) are advertised through all the autonomous systems, along with the router's loopback addresses (192.168.1.1/32, 192.168.2.2/32, and 192.168.3.3/32) and the peering links (10.12.1.0/24 and 10.23.1.0/24).

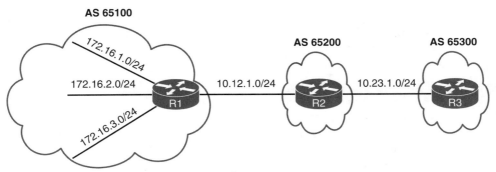

Figure 12-1 *BGP Summarization Topology*

Example 12-1 *BGP Tables for R1, R2, and R3 Without Aggregation*

```
R1# show bgp ipv4 unicast | begin Network
     Network          Next Hop          Metric LocPrf Weight Path
 *   10.12.1.0/24     10.12.1.2              0          0 65200 ?
 *>                   0.0.0.0                0      32768 ?
 *>  10.23.1.0/24     10.12.1.2              0          0 65200 ?
 *>  172.16.1.0/24    0.0.0.0                0      32768 ?
 *>  172.16.2.0/24    0.0.0.0                0      32768 ?
 *>  172.16.3.0/24    0.0.0.0                0      32768 ?
 *>  192.168.1.1/32   0.0.0.0                0      32768 ?
 *>  192.168.2.2/32   10.12.1.2              0          0 65200 ?
 *>  192.168.3.3/32   10.12.1.2                         0 65200 65300 ?

R2# show bgp ipv4 unicast | begin Network
     Network          Next Hop          Metric LocPrf Weight Path
 *   10.12.1.0/24     10.12.1.1              0          0 65100 ?
 *>                   0.0.0.0                0      32768 ?
 *   10.23.1.0/24     10.23.1.3              0          0 65300 ?
 *>                   0.0.0.0                0      32768 ?
 *>  172.16.1.0/24    10.12.1.1              0          0 65100 ?
 *>  172.16.2.0/24    10.12.1.1              0          0 65100 ?
 *>  172.16.3.0/24    10.12.1.1              0          0 65100 ?
 *>  192.168.1.1/32   10.12.1.1              0          0 65100 ?
 *>  192.168.2.2/32   0.0.0.0                0      32768 ?
 *>  192.168.3.3/32   10.23.1.3              0          0 65300 ?

R3# show bgp ipv4 unicast | begin Network
     Network          Next Hop          Metric LocPrf Weight Path
 *>  10.12.1.0/24     10.23.1.2              0          0 65200 ?
 *   10.23.1.0/24     10.23.1.2              0          0 65200 ?
 *>                   0.0.0.0                0      32768 ?
 *>  172.16.1.0/24    10.23.1.2                         0 65200 65100 ?
```

```
*>  172.16.2.0/24     10.23.1.2                              0 65200 65100 ?
*>  172.16.3.0/24     10.23.1.2                              0 65200 65100 ?
*>  192.168.1.1/32    10.23.1.2                              0 65200 65100 ?
*>  192.168.2.2/32    10.23.1.2                  0           0 65200 ?
*>  192.168.3.3/32    0.0.0.0                    0           32768 ?
```

R1 aggregates all the stub networks (172.16.1.0/24, 172.16.2.0/24, and 172.16.3.0/24) into a 172.16.0.0/20 summary route. R2 aggregates all the router's loopback addresses into a 192.168.0.0/16 summary route. Example 12-2 shows the configuration for R1 running with the default IPv4 address family and R2 running with the default IPv4 address family disabled.

Example 12-2   *Configuring BGP Route Aggregation*

```
R1# show running-config | section router bgp
router bgp 65100
 bgp log-neighbor-changes
 aggregate-address 172.16.0.0 255.255.240.0
 redistribute connected
 neighbor 10.12.1.2 remote-as 65200

R2# show running-config | section router bgp
router bgp 65200
 bgp log-neighbor-changes
 no bgp default ipv4-unicast
 neighbor 10.12.1.1 remote-as 65100
 neighbor 10.23.1.3 remote-as 65300
 !
 address-family ipv4
  aggregate-address 192.168.0.0 255.255.0.0
  redistribute connected
  neighbor 10.12.1.1 activate
  neighbor 10.23.1.3 activate
 exit-address-family
```

Example 12-3 shows the BGP tables on R1, R2, and R3 after aggregation is configured on R1 and R2.

Example 12-3   *BGP Tables for R1, R2, and R3 with Aggregation*

```
R1# show bgp ipv4 unicast | begin Network
     Network          Next Hop         Metric LocPrf Weight Path
 *   10.12.1.0/24     10.12.1.2             0           0 65200 ?
 *>                   0.0.0.0               0           32768 ?
 *>  10.23.1.0/24     10.12.1.2             0           0 65200 ?
 *>  172.16.0.0/20    0.0.0.0                           32768 i
 *>  172.16.1.0/24    0.0.0.0               0           32768 ?
```

```
 *>   172.16.2.0/24      0.0.0.0                   0          32768 ?
 *>   172.16.3.0/24      0.0.0.0                   0          32768 ?
 *>   192.168.0.0/16     10.12.1.2                 0              0 65200 i
 *>   192.168.1.1/32     0.0.0.0                   0          32768 ?
 *>   192.168.2.2/32     10.12.1.2                 0              0 65200 ?
 *>   192.168.3.3/32     10.12.1.2                                0 65200 65300 ?
```

```
R2# show bgp ipv4 unicast | begin Network
      Network           Next Hop          Metric LocPrf Weight Path
 *    10.12.1.0/24      10.12.1.1              0              0 65100 ?
 *>                     0.0.0.0                0          32768 ?
 *    10.23.1.0/24      10.23.1.3              0              0 65300 ?
 *>                     0.0.0.0                0          32768 ?
 *>   172.16.0.0/20     10.12.1.1              0              0 65100 i
 *>   172.16.1.0/24     10.12.1.1              0              0 65100 ?
 *>   172.16.2.0/24     10.12.1.1              0              0 65100 ?
 *>   172.16.3.0/24     10.12.1.1              0              0 65100 ?
 *>   192.168.0.0/16    0.0.0.0                           32768 i
 *>   192.168.1.1/32    10.12.1.1              0              0 65100 ?
 *>   192.168.2.2/32    0.0.0.0                0          32768 ?
 *>   192.168.3.3/32    10.23.1.3              0              0 65300 ?
```

```
R3# show bgp ipv4 unicast | begin Network
      Network           Next Hop          Metric LocPrf Weight Path
 *>   10.12.1.0/24      10.23.1.2              0              0 65200 ?
 *    10.23.1.0/24      10.23.1.2              0              0 65200 ?
 *>                     0.0.0.0                0          32768 ?
 *>   172.16.0.0/20     10.23.1.2                             0 65200 65100 i
 *>   172.16.1.0/24     10.23.1.2                             0 65200 65100 ?
 *>   172.16.2.0/24     10.23.1.2                             0 65200 65100 ?
 *>   172.16.3.0/24     10.23.1.2                             0 65200 65100 ?
 *>   192.168.0.0/16    10.23.1.2              0              0 65200 i
 *>   192.168.1.1/32    10.23.1.2                             0 65200 65100 ?
 *>   192.168.2.2/32    10.23.1.2              0              0 65200 ?
 *>   192.168.3.3/32    0.0.0.0                0          32768 ?
```

Notice that the 172.16.0.0/20 and 192.168.0.0/16 network prefixes are visible, but the smaller component network prefixes still exist on all the routers. The **aggregate-address** command advertises the aggregated network prefix in addition to the original component network prefixes. The optional **summary-only** keyword suppresses the component network prefixes in the summarized network prefix range. Example 12-4 demonstrates the configuration with the **summary-only** keyword.

Example 12-4 *BGP Route Summarization Configuration with Suppression*

```
R1# show running-config | section router bgp
router bgp 65100
 bgp log-neighbor-changes
 aggregate-address 172.16.0.0 255.255.240.0 summary-only
 redistribute connected
 neighbor 10.12.1.2 remote-as 65200
```

```
R2# show running-config | section router bgp
router bgp 65200
 bgp log-neighbor-changes
 no bgp default ipv4-unicast
 neighbor 10.12.1.1 remote-as 65100
 neighbor 10.23.1.3 remote-as 65300
 !
address-family ipv4
  aggregate-address 192.168.0.0 255.255.0.0 summary-only
  redistribute connected
  neighbor 10.12.1.1 activate
  neighbor 10.23.1.3 activate
 exit-address-family
```

Example 12-5 shows the BGP table for R3 after the **summary-only** keyword is added to the aggregation command. R1's component networks are aggregated in the 172.16.0.0/20 summary route, and R1's and R2's loopback addresses are aggregated into the 192.168.0.0/16 summary route. None of R1's component networks or the loopback addresses from R1 or R2 are visible on R3.

Example 12-5 *BGP Tables for R3 with Aggregation and Suppression*

```
R3# show bgp ipv4 unicast | begin Network
     Network          Next Hop         Metric LocPrf Weight Path
 *>  10.12.1.0/24     10.23.1.2             0          0 65200 ?
 *   10.23.1.0/24     10.23.1.2             0          0 65200 ?
 *>                   0.0.0.0               0      32768 ?
 *>  172.16.0.0/20    10.23.1.2                        0 65200 65100 i
 *>  192.168.0.0/16   10.23.1.2             0          0 65200 i
 *>  192.168.3.3/32   0.0.0.0               0      32768 ?
```

Example 12-6 shows the BGP table and the Routing Information Base (RIB) for R2. Notice that the component loopback networks are suppressed by BGP and are not advertised by R2. In addition, a summary discard route is installed to Null0 as a loop-prevention mechanism.

Example 12-6 *R2's BGP and RIB After Aggregation with Suppression*

```
R2# show bgp ipv4 unicast
BGP table version is 10, local router ID is 192.168.2.2
Status codes: s suppressed, d damped, h history, * valid, > best, i - internal,
              r RIB-failure, S Stale, m multipath, b backup-path, f RT-Filter,
              x best-external, a additional-path, c RIB-compressed,
Origin codes: i - IGP, e - EGP, ? - incomplete
RPKI validation codes: V valid, I invalid, N Not found

     Network          Next Hop          Metric LocPrf Weight Path
 *   10.12.1.0/24     10.12.1.1              0             0 65100 ?
 *>                   0.0.0.0                0         32768 ?
 *   10.23.1.0/24     10.23.1.3              0             0 65300 ?
 *>                   0.0.0.0                0         32768 ?
 *>  172.16.0.0/20    10.12.1.1              0             0 65100 i
 *>  192.168.0.0/16   0.0.0.0                          32768 i
 s>  192.168.1.1/32   10.12.1.1              0             0 65100 ?
 s>  192.168.2.2/32   0.0.0.0                0         32768 ?
 s>  192.168.3.3/32   10.23.1.3              0             0 65300 ?

R2# show ip route bgp | begin Gateway
Gateway of last resort is not set

      172.16.0.0/20 is subnetted, 1 subnets
B        172.16.0.0 [20/0] via 10.12.1.1, 00:06:18
B     192.168.0.0/16 [200/0], 00:05:37, Null0
      192.168.1.0/32 is subnetted, 1 subnets
B        192.168.1.1 [20/0] via 10.12.1.1, 00:02:15
      192.168.3.0/32 is subnetted, 1 subnets
B        192.168.3.3 [20/0] via 10.23.1.3, 00:02:15
```

Example 12-7 shows that R1's component networks are suppressed, and the summary discard route for 172.16.0.0/20 is installed in the RIB as well.

Example 12-7 *R1's BGP and RIB After Aggregation with Suppression*

```
R1# show bgp ipv4 unicast | begin Network
     Network          Next Hop          Metric LocPrf Weight Path
 *   10.12.1.0/24     10.12.1.2              0             0 65200 ?
 *>                   0.0.0.0                0         32768 ?
 *>  10.23.1.0/24     10.12.1.2              0             0 65200 ?
 *>  172.16.0.0/20    0.0.0.0                          32768 i
 s>  172.16.1.0/24    0.0.0.0                0         32768 ?
 s>  172.16.2.0/24    0.0.0.0                0         32768 ?
 s>  172.16.3.0/24    0.0.0.0                0         32768 ?
```

```
*>   192.168.0.0/16    10.12.1.2           0              0 65200 i
*>   192.168.1.1/32    0.0.0.0             0          32768 ?
R1# show ip route bgp | begin Gateway
Gateway of last resort is not set
     10.0.0.0/8 is variably subnetted, 3 subnets, 2 masks
B        10.23.1.0/24 [20/0] via 10.12.1.2, 00:12:50
     172.16.0.0/16 is variably subnetted, 7 subnets, 3 masks
B        172.16.0.0/20 [200/0], 00:06:51, Null0
B        192.168.0.0/16 [20/0] via 10.12.1.2, 00:06:10
```

The Atomic Aggregate Attribute

Summarized routes act like new BGP routes with a shorter prefix length. When a BGP router summarizes a route, it does not advertise the *AS_Path* information from before the route was summarized. BGP path attributes like AS_Path, multi-exit discriminator (MED), and BGP communities are not included in the new BGP aggregate prefix. The *atomic aggregate* attribute indicates that a loss of path information has occurred.

The previous BGP network prefix aggregation configuration on R1 can be removed to explain this concept. R2 can be configured to summarize the 172.16.0.0/20 and 192.168.0.0/16 routes with component route suppression. Example 12-8 shows R2's BGP configuration.

Example 12-8   *Configuration for Aggregation of 172.16.0.0/20 and 192.168.0.0/16*

```
R2# show running-config | section router bgp
router bgp 65200
 bgp log-neighbor-changes
 no bgp default ipv4-unicast
 neighbor 10.12.1.1 remote-as 65100
 neighbor 10.23.1.3 remote-as 65300
 !
 address-family ipv4
  aggregate-address 192.168.0.0 255.255.0.0 summary-only
  aggregate-address 172.16.0.0 255.255.240.0 summary-only
  redistribute connected
  neighbor 10.12.1.1 activate
  neighbor 10.23.1.3 activate
```

Example 12-9 shows R2's and R3's BGP tables. R2 is aggregating and suppressing R1's component networks (172.16.1.0/24, 172.16.2.0/24, and 172.16.3.0/24) into the 172.16.0.0/20 summary route. The component network prefixes maintain an AS_Path of 65100 on R2, and the aggregate 172.16.0.0/20 appears to be locally generated on R2.

From R3's perspective, R2 does not advertise R1's stub networks; instead, it is advertising the 172.16.0.0/20 network as its own. The AS_Path for the 172.16.0.0/20 route on R3 is simply AS 65200 and does not include AS 65100.

Example 12-9 *R2's and R3's BGP Table with Path Attribute Loss*

```
R2# show bgp ipv4 unicast | begin Network
     Network          Next Hop         Metric LocPrf Weight Path
 *   10.12.1.0/24     10.12.1.1             0              0 65100 ?
 *>                   0.0.0.0               0          32768 ?
 *   10.23.1.0/24     10.23.1.3             0              0 65300 ?
 *>                   0.0.0.0               0          32768 ?
 *>  172.16.0.0/20    0.0.0.0                          32768 i
 s>  172.16.1.0/24    10.12.1.1             0              0 65100 ?
 s>  172.16.2.0/24    10.12.1.1             0              0 65100 ?
 s>  172.16.3.0/24    10.12.1.1             0              0 65100 ?
 *>  192.168.0.0/16   0.0.0.0                          32768 i
 s>  192.168.1.1/32   10.12.1.1             0              0 65100 ?
 s>  192.168.2.2/32   0.0.0.0               0          32768 ?
 s>  192.168.3.3/32   10.23.1.3             0              0 65300 ?

R3# show bgp ipv4 unicast | begin Network
     Network          Next Hop         Metric LocPrf Weight Path
 *>  10.12.1.0/24     10.23.1.2             0              0 65200 ?
 *   10.23.1.0/24     10.23.1.2             0              0 65200 ?
 *>                   0.0.0.0               0          32768 ?
 *>  172.16.0.0/20    10.23.1.2             0              0 65200 i
 *>  192.168.0.0/16   10.23.1.2             0              0 65200 i
 *>  192.168.3.3/32   0.0.0.0               0          32768 ?
```

Example 12-10 shows R3's BGP entry for the 172.16.0.0/20 prefix. The route's information
indicates that the routes were summarized by AS 65200 by the router with the router ID
(RID) 192.168.2.2. In addition, the atomic aggregate attribute has been set to indicate a loss
of path attributes such as AS_Path in this scenario.

Example 12-10 *Examining the BGP Atomic Aggregate Attribute*

```
R3# show bgp ipv4 unicast 172.16.0.0
BGP routing table entry for 172.16.0.0/20, version 25
Paths: (1 available, best #1, table default)
  Not advertised to any peer
  Refresh Epoch 2
  65200, (aggregated by 65200 192.168.2.2)
    10.23.1.2 from 10.23.1.2 (192.168.2.2)
      Origin IGP, metric 0, localpref 100, valid, external, atomic-aggregate, best
      rx pathid: 0, tx pathid: 0x0
```

Route Aggregation with AS_SET

To keep the component route's BGP path information, the optional **as-set** keyword may be
used with the **aggregate-address** command. As the router generates the summary route, BGP
path information from the component routes are copied over to it. The AS_Path settings

from the original prefixes are stored in the AS_SET portion of AS_Path. The AS_SET, which is displayed within brackets, counts as only one AS hop, even if multiple ASs are listed.

Example 12-11 shows R2's updated BGP configuration for summarizing both prefixes with the **as-set** keyword.

Example 12-11 *Configuration for Aggregation While Preserving BGP Attributes*

```
R2# show running-config | section router bgp
router bgp 65200
 bgp log-neighbor-changes
 no bgp default ipv4-unicast
 neighbor 10.12.1.1 remote-as 65100
 neighbor 10.23.1.3 remote-as 65300
 !
address-family ipv4
 aggregate-address 192.168.0.0 255.255.0.0 as-set summary-only
 aggregate-address 172.16.0.0 255.255.240.0 as-set summary-only
 redistribute connected
 neighbor 10.12.1.1 activate
 neighbor 10.23.1.3 activate
```

Example 12-12 displays the 172.16.0.0/20 summary route again, now with the BGP path information copied into it . Notice that the AS_Path information now contains AS 65100.

Example 12-12 *Verifying That Path Attributes Are Injected into the BGP Aggregate*

```
R3# show bgp ipv4 unicast 172.16.0.0
BGP routing table entry for 172.16.0.0/20, version 30
Paths: (1 available, best #1, table default)
  Not advertised to any peer
  Refresh Epoch 2
  65200 65100, (aggregated by 65200 192.168.2.2)
    10.23.1.2 from 10.23.1.2 (192.168.2.2)
      Origin incomplete, metric 0, localpref 100, valid, external, best
      rx pathid: 0, tx pathid: 0x0

R3# show bgp ipv4 unicast | begin Network
    Network          Next Hop       Metric LocPrf Weight Path
 *>  10.12.1.0/24     10.23.1.2          0             0 65200 ?
 *   10.23.1.0/24     10.23.1.2          0             0 65200 ?
 *>                   0.0.0.0            0         32768 ?
 *>  172.16.0.0/20    10.23.1.2          0             0 65200 65100 ?
 *>  192.168.3.3/32   0.0.0.0            0         32768 ?
```

Did you notice that the 192.168.0.0/16 summary route is no longer present in R3's BGP table? The reason for this is on R2; R2 is summarizing all the loopback networks from R1 (AS 65100), R2 (AS 65200), and R3 (AS 65300). And now that R2 is copying the BGP AS_Path attributes of all the component network prefixes into the AS_SET information, the AS_Path for the 192.168.0.0/16 summary route contains AS 65300. When the aggregate is advertised to R3, R3 discards that prefix because it sees its own AS_Path in the advertisement and thinks that it is a loop.

Example 12-13 displays R2's BGP table and the path attributes for the aggregated 192.168.0.0/16 network entry.

Example 12-13 *Viewing the Aggregated Properties of 192.168.0.0/16*

```
R2# show bgp ipv4 unicast | begin Network
     Network          Next Hop         Metric LocPrf Weight Path
 *   10.12.1.0/24     10.12.1.1             0          0 65100 ?
 *>                   0.0.0.0               0      32768 ?
 *   10.23.1.0/24     10.23.1.3             0          0 65300 ?
 *>                   0.0.0.0               0      32768 ?
 *>  172.16.0.0/20    0.0.0.0                    100 32768 65100 ?
 s>  172.16.1.0/24    10.12.1.1             0          0 65100 ?
 s>  172.16.2.0/24    10.12.1.1             0          0 65100 ?
 s>  172.16.3.0/24    10.12.1.1             0          0 65100 ?
 *>  192.168.0.0/16   0.0.0.0                    100 32768 {65100,65300} ?
 s>  192.168.1.1/32   10.12.1.1             0          0 65100 ?
 s>  192.168.2.2/32   0.0.0.0               0      32768 ?
 s>  192.168.3.3/32   10.23.1.3             0          0 65300 ?

R2# show bgp ipv4 unicast 192.168.0.0
BGP routing table entry for 192.168.0.0/16, version 28
Paths: (1 available, best #1, table default)
  Advertised to update-groups:
     1
  Refresh Epoch 1
  {65100,65300}, (aggregated by 65200 192.168.2.2)
     0.0.0.0 from 0.0.0.0 (192.168.2.2)
       Origin incomplete, localpref 100, weight 32768, valid, aggregated, local, best
       rx pathid: 0, tx pathid: 0x0
```

R1 does not install the 192.168.0.0/16 summary route for the same reason that R3 does not install the 192.168.0.0/16 summary route. R1 thinks that the advertisement is a loop because it detects AS 65100 in AS_Path. You can confirm this by examining R1's BGP table, shown in Example 12-14.

Example 12-14 *R1's BGP Table, with 192.168.0.0/16 Discarded*

```
R1# show bgp ipv4 unicast | begin Network
     Network          Next Hop         Metric LocPrf Weight Path
 *   10.12.1.0/24     10.12.1.2             0          0 65200 ?
 *>                   0.0.0.0               0      32768 ?
 *>  10.23.1.0/24     10.12.1.2             0          0 65200 ?
 *>  172.16.1.0/24    0.0.0.0               0      32768 ?
 *>  172.16.2.0/24    0.0.0.0               0      32768 ?
 *>  172.16.3.0/24    0.0.0.0               0      32768 ?
 *>  192.168.1.1/32   0.0.0.0               0      32768 ?
```

IPv6 Summarization

The same process for summarizing or aggregating IPv4 prefixes occurs with IPv6 prefixes, and the format is identical except that the configuration is placed under the IPv6 address family using the command **aggregate-address** *prefix/prefix-length* [**summary-only**] [**as-set**].

Figure 12-2 provides a simple IPv6 topology to demonstrate IPv6 route aggregation.

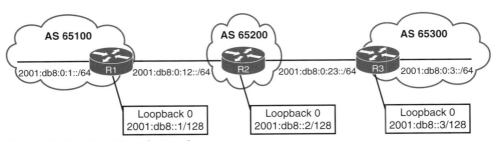

Figure 12-2   *IPv6 Sample Topology*

In our topology, we want to summarize as much of the network as possible. The summarization of the IPv6 loopback addresses (2001:db8:::1/128, 2001:db8:::2/128, and 2001:db8::3/128) and R1/R3's stub networks (2001:db8:0:1::/64 and 2001:db8:0:3/64) is fairly simple as they all fall into the base IPv6 summary range 2001:db8:0:0::/64. The fourth hextet, beginning with a decimal value of 1, 2, or 3, would consume only 2 bits; the range could be summarized easily into the 2001:db8:0:0::/62 (or 2001:db8::/62) network range.

The peering link between R2 and R3 (2001:db8:0:23::/64) requires thinking in hex first rather than in decimal values. The fourth hextet carries a decimal value of 35 (not 23), which requires 6 bits at a minimum. Table 12-2 lists the bits needed for summarization, the IPv6 summary addresses, and the component networks in each summary range.

Table 12-2   IPv6 Summarization Table

Bits Needed	Summary Address	Component Networks
2	2001:db8:0:0::/62	2001:db8:0:0::/64 through 2001:db8:0:3::/64
3	2001:db8:0:0::/61	2001:db8:0:0::/64 through 2001:db8:0:7::/64
4	2001:db8:0:0::/60	2001:db8:0:0::/64 through 2001:db8:0:F::/64
5	2001:db8:0:0::/59	2001:db8:0:0::/64 through 2001:db8:0:1F::/64
6	2001:db8:0:0::/58	2001:db8:0:0::/64 through 2001:db8:0:3F::/64

The IPv6 route summarization configuration would look as shown in Example 12-15.

Example 12-15 *Configuring IPv6 BGP Route Summarization on R2*

```
R2# show running-config | section router bgprouter bgp 65200
 bgp router-id 192.168.2.2
 bgp log-neighbor-changes
 neighbor 2001:DB8:0:12::1 remote-as 65100
 neighbor 2001:DB8:0:23::3 remote-as 65300
 !
 address-family ipv4
  no neighbor 2001:DB8:0:12::1 activate
  no neighbor 2001:DB8:0:23::3 activate
 !
 address-family ipv6
  network 2001:DB8::2/128
  network 2001:DB8:0:12::/64
  network 2001:DB8:0:23::/64
  aggregate-address 2001:DB8::/58 summary-only
  neighbor 2001:DB8:0:12::1 activate
  neighbor 2001:DB8:0:23::3 activate
```

Example 12-16 shows the BGP tables on R1 and R3. Notice that all the smaller component routes are summarized and suppressed into the 2001:db8::/58 summary route, as expected.

Example 12-16 *Verifying IPv6 Route Summarization*

```
R3# show bgp ipv6 unicast | b Network
     Network          Next Hop          Metric LocPrf Weight Path
 *>  2001:DB8::/58     2001:DB8:0:23::2       0             0 65200 i
 *>  2001:DB8::3/128   ::                     0         32768 i
 *>  2001:DB8:0:3::/64 ::                     0         32768 i
 *>  2001:DB8:0:23::/64 ::                    0         32768 i

R1# show bgp ipv6 unicast | b Network
     Network          Next Hop          Metric LocPrf Weight Path
 *>  2001:DB8::/58     2001:DB8:0:12::2       0             0 65200 i
 *>  2001:DB8::1/128   ::                     0         32768 ?
 *>  2001:DB8:0:1::/64 ::                     0         32768 ?
 *>  2001:DB8:0:12::/64 ::                    0         32768 ?
```

BGP Route Filtering and Manipulation

Conditional route selection is a method for selectively identifying prefixes that are advertised or received from peers. Selected routes can be modified or removed to manipulate traffic flows, reduce memory utilization, or improve security.

Figure 12-3 shows the complete BGP route processing logic. Notice that the route policies occur on inbound route receipt and outbound route advertisement.

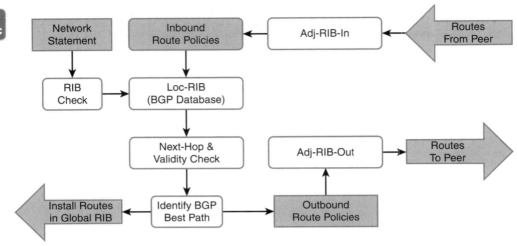

Figure 12-3 *BGP Route Policy Processing*

IOS XE provides four methods of filtering routes inbound or outbound for a specific BGP peer. Each of these methods can be used individually, or they can be used simultaneously with other methods:

- **Distribute list:** A *distribute list* filters network prefixes based on a standard or extended *access control list (ACL)*. An implicit deny is associated with any prefix that is not permitted.

- **Prefix list:** A *prefix list* is a list of prefix-matching specifications that permit or deny network prefixes in a top-down fashion, much like an ACL. An implicit deny is associated with any prefix that is not permitted.

- **AS_Path ACL/filtering:** A list of regex commands can be used to permit or deny a network prefix, based on the current AS_Path values. An implicit deny is associated with any prefix that is not permitted.

- **Route maps:** *Route maps* provide a method of conditional matching on a variety of prefix attributes and allow you to take a variety of actions. An action could be a simple permit or deny or could include the modification of BGP path attributes. An implicit deny is associated with any prefix that is not permitted.

NOTE A BGP neighbor cannot use a distribute list and prefix list at the same time in the same direction (inbound or outbound).

The following sections explain each of these filtering techniques in more detail. Imagine a simple scenario with R1 (AS 65100) that has a single eBGP peering with R2 (AS 65200), which then may peer with other autonomous systems (such as AS 65300). The relevant portion of the topology is that R1 peers with R2 and focuses on R1's BGP table, as shown in Example 12-17, with an emphasis on the network prefix and AS_Path.

Example 12-17 *Reference BGP Table*

```
R1# show bgp ipv4 unicast | begin Network
     Network          Next Hop          Metric LocPrf Weight Path
 *>  10.3.3.0/24      10.12.1.2            33             0 65200 65300 3003 ?
 *   10.12.1.0/24     10.12.1.2            22             0 65200 ?
 *>                   0.0.0.0               0         32768 ?
 *>  10.23.1.0/24     10.12.1.2           333             0 65200 ?
 *>  100.64.2.0/25    10.12.1.2            22             0 65200 ?
 *>  100.64.2.192/26  10.12.1.2            22             0 65200 ?
 *>  100.64.3.0/25    10.12.1.2            22             0 65200 65300 300 ?
 *>  192.168.1.1/32   0.0.0.0               0         32768 ?
 *>  192.168.2.2/32   10.12.1.2            22             0 65200 ?
 *>  192.168.3.3/32   10.12.1.2          3333             0 65200 65300 ?
```

Distribute List Filtering

Distribute lists allow the filtering of network prefixes on a neighbor-by-neighbor basis, using standard or extended ACLs. To configure a distribute list, you use the BGP address family configuration command **neighbor** *ip-address* **distribute-list** {*acl-number* | *acl-name*} {**in** | **out**}. Remember that extended ACLs for BGP use the source fields to match the network portion and the destination fields to match against the network mask.

Example 12-18 displays R1's BGP configuration, which demonstrates filtering with distribute lists. The configuration uses an extended ACL named ACL-ALLOW that contains two entries. The first entry allows any network that starts in the 192.168.0.0 to 192.168.255.255 range with a network length of only /32. The second entry allows networks that contain the 100.64.x.0 pattern with prefix length /25 to demonstrate the wildcard abilities of an extended ACL with BGP. The distribute list is then associated with R2's BGP session.

Example 12-18 *BGP Distribute List Configuration*

```
R1
ip access-list extended ACL-ALLOW
 permit ip 192.168.0.0 0.0.255.255 host 255.255.255.255
 permit ip 100.64.0.0 0.0.255.0 host 255.255.255.128
!
router bgp 65100
 neighbor 10.12.1.2 remote-as 65200
 address-family ipv4
 neighbor 10.12.1.2 distribute-list ACL-ALLOW in
```

Example 12-19 shows the routing table of R1. R1 injects two local routes (10.12.1.0/24 and 192.168.1.1/32) into the BGP table. The two loopback networks from R2 (AS 65200) and R3 (AS 65300) are allowed, as they are within the first ACL-ALLOW entry, and two of the networks in the 100.64.x.0 pattern (100.64.2.0/25 and 100.64.3.0/25) are accepted. The 100.64.2.192/26 network is rejected because the prefix length does not match the second ACL-ALLOW entry. (Refer to Example 12-17 to identify the routes before the BGP distribute list was applied.)

Example 12-19 *Viewing Routes Filtered by a BGP Distribute List*

```
R1# show bgp ipv4 unicast | begin Network
    Network          Next Hop          Metric LocPrf Weight Path
 *>  10.12.1.0/24     0.0.0.0                0         32768 ?
 *>  100.64.2.0/25    10.12.1.2             22             0 65200 ?
 *>  100.64.3.0/25    10.12.1.2             22             0 65200 65300 300 ?
 *>  192.168.1.1/32   0.0.0.0                0         32768 ?
 *>  192.168.2.2/32   10.12.1.2             22             0 65200 ?
 *>  192.168.3.3/32   10.12.1.2           3333             0 65200 65300 ?
```

Prefix List Filtering

Prefix lists allow the filtering of network prefixes on a neighbor-by-neighbor basis, using a prefix list. Configuring a prefix list involves using the BGP address family configuration command **neighbor** *ip-address* **prefix-list** *prefix-list-name* {**in** | **out**}.

To demonstrate the use of a prefix list, you can use the same initial BGP table from Example 12-17 and filter it to allow only routes within the RFC 1918 space. A prefix list called RFC1918 is created to permit only prefixes in the RFC1918 address space. The prefix list is then assigned as an inbound filter on R1 toward prefixes advertised from R2. Example 12-20 demonstrates the configuration of the prefix list and its application to R2.

Example 12-20 *Prefix List Filtering Configuration*

```
R1# configure terminal
Enter configuration commands, one per line. End with CNTL/Z.
R1(config)# ip prefix-list RFC1918 seq 10 permit 10.0.0.0/8 le 32
R1(config)# ip prefix-list RFC1918 seq 20 permit 172.16.0.0/12 le 32
R1(config)# ip prefix-list RFC1918 seq 30 permit 192.168.0.0/16 le 32
R1(config)# router bgp 65100
R1(config-router)# address-family ipv4 unicast
R1(config-router-af)# neighbor 10.12.1.2 prefix-list RFC1918 in
```

Now that the prefix list has been applied, the BGP table can be examined on R1, as shown in Example 12-21. Notice that the 100.64.2.0/25, 100.64.2.192/26, and 100.64.3.0/25 routes are filtered as they do not fall within the prefix list matching criteria. (Refer to Example 12-17 to identify the routes before the BGP prefix list was applied.)

Example 12-21 *Verifying Filtering with a BGP Prefix List*

```
R1# show bgp ipv4 unicast | begin Network
    Network          Next Hop          Metric LocPrf Weight Path
 *>  10.3.3.0/24      10.12.1.2             33             0 65200 65300 3003 ?
 *   10.12.1.0/24     10.12.1.2             22             0 65200 ?
 *>                   0.0.0.0                0         32768 ?
 *>  10.23.1.0/24     10.12.1.2            333             0 65200 ?
 *>  192.168.1.1/32   0.0.0.0                0         32768 ?
 *>  192.168.2.2/32   10.12.1.2             22             0 65200 ?
 *>  192.168.3.3/32   10.12.1.2           3333             0 65200 65300 ?
```

AS_Path Filtering

There may be times when conditionally matching prefixes may be too complicated, and identifying all routes from a specific organization is preferred. In such a case, path selection can be used with the BGP AS_Path. AS_Path filtering is accomplished using an AS_Path ACL, which uses *regular expressions* for matching. The following sections explain the components for this task.

Regular Expressions (Regex)

To parse through the large number of available ASNs (4,294,967,295 of them), you can use *regular expressions (regex)*. Regular expressions are based on query modifiers and used to select the appropriate content. Table 12-3 provides a brief list and description of the common regex query modifiers.

Table 12-3   Regex Query Modifiers

Modifier	Description
_ (underscore)	Matches a space
^ (caret)	Indicates the start of the string
$ (dollar sign)	Indicates the end of the string
[] (brackets)	Matches a single character or nesting within a range
- (hyphen)	Indicates a range of numbers in brackets
[^] (caret in brackets)	Excludes the characters listed in brackets
() (parentheses)	Used for nesting of search patterns
	(pipe)	Provides *or* functionality to the query
. (period)	Matches a single character, including a space
* (asterisk)	Matches zero or more characters or patterns
+ (plus sign)	Matches one or more instances of the character or pattern
? (question mark)	Matches one or no instances of the character or pattern

NOTE   The characters .^$*+()[]? are special control characters that cannot be used without using the backslash \ escape character. For example, to match on the * in the output, you would use the * syntax.

The BGP table can be parsed with regex using the command **show bgp** *afi safi* **regexp** *regex-pattern*. Figure 12-4 provides a reference topology, and Example 12-22 shows a reference BGP table to demonstrate the various regex query modifiers that can be used for a variety of common tasks.

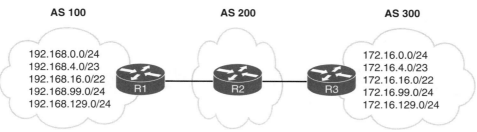

Figure 12-4   *BGP Regex Reference Topology*

Example 12-22 *BGP Table for Regex Queries*

```
R2# show bgp ipv4 unicast
! Output omitted for brevity
     Network          Next Hop    Metric LocPrf Weight Path
*>  172.16.0.0/24     172.32.23.3    0              0 300 80 90 21003 2100 i
*>  172.16.4.0/23     172.32.23.3    0              0 300 878 1190 1100 1010 i
*>  172.16.16.0/22    172.32.23.3    0              0 300 779 21234 45 i
*>  172.16.99.0/24    172.32.23.3    0              0 300 145 40 i
*>  172.16.129.0/24   172.32.23.3    0              0 300 10010 300 1010 40 50 i
*>  192.168.0.0/16    172.16.12.1    0              0 100 80 90 21003 2100 i
*>  192.168.4.0/23    172.16.12.1    0              0 100 878 1190 1100 1010 i
*>  192.168.16.0/22   172.16.12.1    0              0 100 779 21234 45 i
*>  192.168.99.0/24   172.16.12.1    0              0 100 145 40 i
*>  192.168.129.0/24  172.16.12.1    0              0 100 10010 300 1010 40 50 i
```

NOTE AS_Path for the 172.16.129.0/24 route includes AS 300 twice non-consecutively for a specific purpose. This would not be seen in real life because it indicates a routing loop.

_ (Underscore)

Query modifier function: Matches a space.

Scenario: Display prefixes with only ASs that passed through AS 100. The first assumption is that the syntax **show bgp ipv4 unicast regex 100**, as shown in Example 12-23, would be ideal. The regex query includes the following unwanted ASNs: 1100, 2100, 21003, and 10010.

Example 12-23 *BGP Regex Query for AS 100*

```
R2# show bgp ipv4 unicast regex 100
! Output omitted for brevity
     Network          Next Hop    Metric LocPrf Weight Path
*>  172.16.0.0/24     172.32.23.3    0              0 300 80 90 21003 2100 i
*>  172.16.4.0/23     172.32.23.3    0              0 300 878 1190 1100 1010 i
*>  172.16.129.0/24   172.32.23.3    0              0 300 10010 300 1010 40 50 i
*>  192.168.0.0/16    172.16.12.1    0              0 100 80 90 21003 2100 i
*>  192.168.4.0/23    172.16.12.1    0              0 100 878 1190 1100 1010 i
*>  192.168.16.0/22   172.16.12.1    0              0 100 779 21234 45 i
*>  192.168.99.0/24   172.16.12.1    0              0 100 145 40 i
*>  192.168.129.0/24  172.16.12.1    0              0 100 10010 300 1010 40 50 i
```

NOTE The shaded portion of the output indicates a portion of AS_Path that would match the query and make it visible to help you understand regex better.

Example 12-24 shows how to use the underscore (_) to imply a space left of the ASN (100) to remove the unwanted ASNs. The regex query includes the following unwanted ASN: 10010.

Example 12-24 *BGP Regex Query for AS _100*

```
R2# show bgp ipv4 unicast regexp _100
! Output omitted for brevity
     Network          Next Hop      Metric LocPrf Weight Path
*> 172.16.129.0/24   172.32.23.3       0            0 300 10010 300 1010 40 50 i
*> 192.168.0.0/16    172.16.12.1       0            0 100 80 90 21003 2100 i
*> 192.168.4.0/23    172.16.12.1       0            0 100 878 1190 1100 1010 i
*> 192.168.16.0/22   172.16.12.1       0            0 100 779 21234 45 i
*> 192.168.99.0/24   172.16.12.1       0            0 100 145 40 i
*> 192.168.129.0/24  172.16.12.1       0            0 100 10010 300 1010 40 i
```

Example 12-25 provides the final query, which uses an underscore (_) before and after the ASN (100) to finalize the query for routes that pass through AS 100.

Example 12-25 *BGP Regex Query for AS 100*

```
R2# show bgp ipv4 unicast regexp _100_
! Output omitted for brevity
     Network          Next Hop      Metric LocPrf Weight Path
*> 192.168.0.0/16    172.16.12.1       0            0 100 80 90 21003 2100 i
*> 192.168.4.0/23    172.16.12.1       0            0 100 878 1190 1100 1010 i
*> 192.168.16.0/22   172.16.12.1       0            0 100 779 21234 45 i
*> 192.168.99.0/24   172.16.12.1       0            0 100 145 40 i
*> 192.168.129.0/24  172.16.12.1       0            0 100 10010 300 1010 40 50 i
```

^ (Caret)

Query modifier function: Indicates the start of the string.

Scenario: Display only prefixes that were advertised from AS 300. At first glance, the command **show bgp ipv4 unicast regex _300_** might be acceptable for use, but in Example 12-26, the 192.168.129.0/24 prefix is also included. Notice that there are two matches in the 172.16.129.0/24 prefix.

Example 12-26 *BGP Regex Query for AS 300*

```
R2# show bgp ipv4 unicast regexp _300_
! Output omitted for brevity
     Network          Next Hop      Metric LocPrf  Weight Path
*> 172.16.0.0/24     172.32.23.3       0             0 300 80 90 21003 2100 i
*> 172.16.4.0/23     172.32.23.3       0             0 300 878 1190 1100 1010 i
*> 172.16.16.0/22    172.32.23.3       0             0 300 779 21234 45 i
*> 172.16.99.0/24    172.32.23.3       0             0 300 145 40 i
*> 172.16.129.0/24   172.32.23.3       0             0 300 10010 300 1010 40 50 i
*> 192.168.129.0/24  172.16.12.1       0             0 100 10010 300 1010 40 50 i
```

Because AS 300 is directly connected, it is more efficient to ensure that AS 300 is the first AS listed. Example 12-27 shows the caret (^) in the regex pattern.

Example 12-27   *BGP Regex Query with Caret*

```
R2# show bgp ipv4 unicast regexp ^300_
! Output omitted for brevity
     Network         Next Hop        Metric LocPrf Weight Path
*> 172.16.0.0/24    172.32.23.3         0             0 300 80 90 21003 2100 i
*> 172.16.4.0/23    172.32.23.3         0             0 300 878 1190 1100 1010 i
*> 172.16.16.0/22   172.32.23.3         0             0 300 779 21234 45 i
*> 172.16.99.0/24   172.32.23.3         0             0 300 145 40 i
*> 172.16.129.0/24  172.32.23.3         0             0 300 10010 300 1010 40 50 i
```

$ (Dollar Sign)

Query modifier function: Indicates the end of the string.

Scenario: Display only prefixes that originated in AS 40. In Example 12-28, the regex pattern _40_ is used. Unfortunately, this also includes routes that originated in AS 50.

Example 12-28   *BGP Regex Query with AS 40*

```
R2# show bgp ipv4 unicast regexp _40_
! Output omitted for brevity
   Network          Next Hop       Metric  LocPrf Weight Path
*> 172.16.99.0/24   172.32.23.3        0            0 300 145 40 i
*> 172.16.129.0/24  172.32.23.3        0            0 300 10010 300 1010 40 50 i
*> 192.168.99.0/24  172.16.12.1        0            0 100 145 40 i
*> 192.168.129.0/24 172.16.12.1        0            0 100 10010 300 1010 40 50 i
```

Example 12-29 provides a solution using the dollar sign ($) for the regex pattern _40$.

Example 12-29   *BGP Regex Query with Dollar Sign*

```
R2# show bgp ipv4 unicast regexp _40$
! Output omitted for brevity
     Network         Next Hop        Metric LocPrf Weight Path
*> 172.16.99.0/24   172.32.23.3         0             0 300 145 40 i
*> 192.168.99.0/24  172.16.12.1         0    100      0 100 145 40 i
```

[ ] (Brackets)

Query modifier function: Matches a single character or nesting within a range.

Scenario: Display only prefixes with an AS that contains 11 or 14 in it. Example 12-30 shows the regex filter 1[14].

Example 12-30 *BGP Regex Query with Brackets*

```
R2# show bgp ipv4 unicast regexp 1[14]
! Output omitted for brevity
    Network         Next Hop  Metric LocPrf   Weight Path
*>  172.16.4.0/23   172.32.23.3     0              0 300 878 1190 1100 1010 i
*>  172.16.99.0/24  172.32.23.3     0              0 300 145 40 i
*>  192.168.4.0/23  172.16.12.1     0              0 100 878 1190 1100 1010 i
*>  192.168.99.0/24 172.16.12.1     0              0 100 145 40 i
```

- (Hyphen)

Query modifier function: Indicates a range of numbers in brackets.

Scenario: Display only prefixes with the last two digits of the AS (40, 50, 60, 70, or 80). Example 12-31 shows the output of the regex query [4-8]0_.

Example 12-31 *BGP Regex Query with Hyphen*

```
R2# show bgp ipv4 unicast regexp [4-8]0_
! Output omitted for brevity
    Network          Next Hop    Metric LocPrf Weight Path
*>  172.16.0.0/24    172.32.23.3      0            0 300 80 90 21003 2100 i
*>  172.16.99.0/24   172.32.23.3      0            0 300 145 40 i
*>  172.16.129.0/24  172.32.23.3      0            0 300 10010 300 1010 40 50 i
*>  192.168.0.0/16   172.16.12.1      0            0 100 80 90 21003 2100 i
*>  192.168.99.0/24  172.16.12.1      0            0 100 145 40 i
*>  192.168.129.0/24 172.16.12.1      0            0 100 10010 300 1010 40 50 i
```

[^] (Caret in Brackets)

Query modifier function: Excludes the character listed in brackets.

Scenario: Display only prefixes where the second AS from AS 100 or AS 300 does not start with 3, 4, 5, 6, 7, or 8. The first component of the regex query restricts the AS to AS 100 or AS 300 with the regex query ^[13]00_, and the second component filters out ASs starting with 3 through 8 with the regex filter _[^3-8]. The complete regex query is ^[13]00_[^3-8], as shown in Example 12-32.

Example 12-32 *BGP Regex Query with Caret in Brackets*

```
R2# show bgp ipv4 unicast regexp ^[13]00_[^3-8]
! Output omitted for brevity
    Network          Next Hop    Metric LocPrf Weight Path
*>  172.16.99.0/24   172.32.23.3      0            0 300 145 40 i
*>  172.16.129.0/24  172.32.23.3      0            0 300 10010 300 1010 40 50 i
*>  192.168.99.0/24  172.16.12.1      0            0 100 145 40 i
*>  192.168.129.0/24 172.16.12.1      0            0 100 10010 300 1010 40 50 i
```

( ) and I (Parentheses and Pipe)

Query modifier function: Nests search patterns and provides *or* functionality.

Scenario: Display only filters where AS_Path ends with AS 40 or 45 in it. Example 12-33 shows the regex filter _4(5|0)$.

Example 12-33 *BGP Regex Query with Parentheses*

```
R2# show bgp ipv4 unicast regexp _4(5|0)$
! Output omitted for brevity
     Network          Next Hop        Metric LocPrf Weight Path
*>  172.16.16.0/22   172.32.23.3        0            0 300 779 21234 45 i
*>  172.16.99.0/24   172.32.23.3        0            0 300 145 40 i
*>  192.168.16.0/22  172.16.12.1        0            0 100 779 21234 45 i
*>  192.168.99.0/24  172.16.12.1        0            0 100 145 40 i
```

. (Period)

Query modifier function: Matches a single character, including a space.

Scenario: Display only prefixes with the originating AS 1 through 99. In Example 12-34, the regex query _..$ requires a space and then any character after that (including other spaces).

Example 12-34 *BGP Regex Query with Period*

```
R2# show bgp ipv4 unicast regexp _..$
! Output omitted for brevity
     Network          Next Hop        Metric LocPrf Weight Path
*>  172.16.16.0/22   172.32.23.3        0            0 300 779 21234 45 i
*>  172.16.99.0/24   172.32.23.3        0            0 300 145 40 i
*>  172.16.129.0/24  172.32.23.3        0            0 300 10010 300 1010 40 50 i
*>  192.168.16.0/22  172.16.12.1        0            0 100 779 21234 45 i
*>  192.168.99.0/24  172.16.12.1        0            0 100 145 40 i
*>  192.168.129.0/24 172.16.12.1        0            0 100 10010 300 1010 40 50 i
```

+ (Plus Sign)

Query modifier function: Matches one or more instances of the character or pattern.

Scenario: Display only prefixes that contain at least one 10 in the AS path but where the pattern 100 should not be used in matching. In this regex, the first portion builds the matching pattern (10)+, and the second portion adds the restriction [^(100)]. The combined regex pattern is (10)+[^(100)], as shown in Example 12-35.

Example 12-35 *BGP Regex Query with Plus Sign*

```
R2# show bgp ipv4 unicast regexp (10)+[^(100)]
! Output omitted for brevity
     Network          Next Hop        Metric LocPrf Weight Path
*>  172.16.4.0/23    172.32.23.3        0            0 300 878 1190 1100 1010 i
*>  172.16.129.0/24  172.32.23.3        0            0 300 10010 300 1010 40 50 i
*>  192.168.4.0/23   172.16.12.1        0            0 100 878 1190 1100 1010 i
*>  192.168.129.0/24 172.16.12.1        0            0 100 10010 300 1010 40 50 i
```

? (Question Mark)

Query modifier function: Matches one or no instances of the character or pattern.

Scenario: Display only prefixes from the neighboring AS or its directly connected AS (that is, restrict to two ASs away). This query is more complicated and requires you to define an initial query for identifying the AS: [0-9]+. The second component includes the space and an optional second AS. The ? limits the AS match to one or two ASs, as shown in Example 12-36.

> **NOTE** You must use the Ctrl+V escape sequence before entering the ?.

Example 12-36 *BGP Regex Query with Dollar Sign*

```
R1# show bgp ipv4 unicast regexp ^[0-9]+ ([0-9]+)?$
! Output omitted for brevity
     Network         Next Hop      Metric LocPrf Weight Path
*>  172.16.99.0/24  172.32.23.3        0              0 300 40 i
*>  192.168.99.0/24 172.16.12.1        0    100       0 100 40 i
```

* (Asterisk)

Query modifier function: Matches zero or more characters or patterns.

Scenario: Display all prefixes from any AS. This may seem like a useless task, but it might be a valid requirement when using AS_Path access lists, which are explained in the following section. Example 12-37 shows the regex query.

Example 12-37 *BGP Regex Query with Asterisk*

```
R1# show bgp ipv4 unicast regexp .*
! Output omitted for brevity
     Network          Next Hop     Metric LocPrf Weight Path
*>  172.16.0.0/24     172.32.23.3       0              0 300 80 90 21003 2100 i
*>  172.16.4.0/23     172.32.23.3       0              0 300 1080 1090 1100 1110 i
*>  172.16.16.0/22    172.32.23.3       0              0 300 11234 21234 31234 i
*>  172.16.99.0/24    172.32.23.3       0              0 300 40 i
*>  172.16.129.0/24   172.32.23.3       0              0 300 10010 300 30010 30050 i
*>  192.168.0.0/16    172.16.12.1       0    100       0 100 80 90 21003 2100 i
*>  192.168.4.0/23    172.16.12.1       0    100       0 100 1080 1090 1100 1110 i
*>  192.168.16.0/22   172.16.12.1       0    100       0 100 11234 21234 31234 i
*>  192.168.99.0/24   172.16.12.1       0    100       0 100 40 i
*>  192.168.129.0/24  172.16.12.1       0    100       0 100 10010 300 30010 30050 i
```

AS_Path ACLs

Selecting routes from a BGP neighbor by using AS_Path requires the definition of an *AS_Path access control list (AS_Path ACL)*. The AS_Path ACL processing is performed in a sequential top-down order, and the first qualifying match processes against the appropriate **permit** or **deny** action. An implicit deny exists at the end of the AS path ACL.

IOS XE supports up to 500 AS path ACLs, and you use the command **ip as-path access-list** *acl-number* {**deny** | **permit**} *regex-query* to create the AS_Path access list. The ACL is then applied with the command **neighbor** *ip-address* **filter-list** *acl-number* {**in** | **out**}.

Example 12-38 shows the routes that R2 (AS 65200) is advertising toward R1 (AS 65100).

Example 12-38   *Reference BGP Table Before Applying an AS_Path Access List*

```
R2# show bgp ipv4 unicast neighbors 10.12.1.1 advertised-routes | begin Network
     Network          Next Hop         Metric LocPrf Weight Path
 *>  10.3.3.0/24      10.23.1.3            33            0 65300 3003 ?
 *>  10.12.1.0/24     0.0.0.0               0        32768 ?
 *>  10.23.1.0/24     0.0.0.0               0        32768 ?
 *>  100.64.2.0/25    0.0.0.0               0        32768 ?
 *>  100.64.2.192/26  0.0.0.0               0        32768 ?
 *>  100.64.3.0/25    10.23.1.3             3            0 65300 300 ?
 *>  192.168.2.2/32   0.0.0.0               0        32768 ?
 *>  192.168.3.3/32   10.23.1.3           333            0 65300 ?

Total number of prefixes 8
```

R2 is advertising the routes learned from R3 (AS 65300) to R1. In essence, R2 provides transit connectivity between the autonomous systems. If this is an Internet connection and R2 is an enterprise, R2 does not want to advertise routes learned from other ASs. Using an AS_Path ACL to restrict the advertisement of only AS 65200 routes is recommended.

Example 12-39 shows the configuration on R2 using an AS_Path ACL to restrict traffic to only locally originated traffic using the regex pattern ^$. To ensure completeness, the AS_Path ACL is applied on all eBGP neighborships.

Example 12-39   *AS_Path Access List Configuration*

```
R2
ip as-path access-list 1 permit ^$
!
router bgp 65200
 address-family ipv4 unicast
  neighbor 10.12.1.1 filter-list 1 out
  neighbor 10.23.1.3 filter-list 1 out
```

Now that the AS_Path ACL has been applied, the advertised routes can be checked again. Example 12-40 displays the routes being advertised to R1. Notice that the routes do not all have AS_Paths confirming that only locally originating routes are being advertised externally. (Refer to Example 12-38 to identify the routes before the BGP AS_Path ACL was applied.)

Example 12-40 *Verifying Local Route Advertisements with an AS_Path ACL*

```
R2# show bgp ipv4 unicast neighbors 10.12.1.1 advertised-routes | begin Network
     Network           Next Hop        Metric LocPrf Weight Path
 *>  10.12.1.0/24      0.0.0.0              0        32768 ?
 *>  10.23.1.0/24      0.0.0.0              0        32768 ?
 *>  100.64.2.0/25     0.0.0.0              0        32768 ?
 *>  100.64.2.192/26   0.0.0.0              0        32768 ?
 *>  192.168.2.2/32    0.0.0.0              0        32768 ?


Total number of prefixes 5
```

Route Maps

Route maps provide more functionality than pure filtering; they provide a method to manipulate BGP path attributes as well. Route maps are applied on a BGP neighbor basis for routes that are advertised or received. A different route map can be used for each direction. The route map is associated to the BGP neighbor with the command **neighbor** *ip-address* **route-map** *route-map-name* {**in** | **out**} under the specific address family.

Example 12-41 shows the BGP routing table of R1, which is used to demonstrate the power of a route map.

Example 12-41 *BGP Table Before Applying a Route Map*

```
R1# show bgp ipv4 unicast | begin Network
     Network           Next Hop        Metric LocPrf Weight Path
 *>  10.1.1.0/24       0.0.0.0              0        32768 ?
 *>  10.3.3.0/24       10.12.1.2           33            0 65200 65300 3003 ?
 *   10.12.1.0/24      10.12.1.2           22            0 65200 ?
 *>                    0.0.0.0              0        32768 ?
 *>  10.23.1.0/24      10.12.1.2          333            0 65200 ?
 *>  100.64.2.0/25     10.12.1.2           22            0 65200 ?
 *>  100.64.2.192/26   10.12.1.2           22            0 65200 ?
 *>  100.64.3.0/25     10.12.1.2           22            0 65200 65300 300 ?
 *>  192.168.1.1/32    0.0.0.0              0        32768 ?
 *>  192.168.2.2/32    10.12.1.2           22            0 65200 ?
 *>  192.168.3.3/32    10.12.1.2         3333            0 65200 65300 ?
```

Route maps allow for multiple steps in processing as well. To demonstrate this concept, this route map includes four steps:

Step 1. Deny any routes that are in the 192.168.0.0/16 network by using a prefix list.

Step 2. Match any routes originating from AS 65200 that are within the 100.64.0.0/10 network range and set the BGP local preference to 222.

Step 3. Match any routes originating from AS 65200 that did not match step 2 and set the BGP weight to 65200.

Step 4. Permit all other routes to process.

Example 12-42 shows R1's configuration, where multiple prefix lists are referenced along with an AS_Path ACL.

Example 12-42   *R1's Route Map Configuration for Inbound AS 65200 Routes*

```
R1
ip prefix-list FIRST-RFC1918 permit  192.168.0.0/16 le 32
ip as-path access-list 1 permit _65200$
ip prefix-list SECOND-CGNAT permit 100.64.0.0/10 le 32
!
route-map AS65200IN deny 10
 description Deny any RFC1918 networks via Prefix List Matching
 match ip address prefix-list FIRST-RFC1918
route-map AS65200IN permit 20
 description Change local preference for AS65200 originate route in 100.64.x.x/10
 match ip address prefix-list SECOND-CGNAT
 match as-path 1
 set local-preference 222
route-map AS65200IN permit 30
 description Change the weight for AS65200 originate routes
 match as-path 1
 set weight 65200
route-map AS65200IN permit 40
 description Permit all other routes un-modified
!
router bgp 65100
 neighbor 10.12.1.2 remote-as 65200
 address-family ipv4 unicast
 neighbor 10.12.1.2 route-map AS65200IN in
```

Example 12-43 displays R1's BGP routing table, which shows that the following actions occurred:

■ The 192.168.2.2/32 and 192.168.3.3/32 routes were discarded. The 192.168.1.1/32 route is a locally generated route.

■ The 100.64.2.0/25 and 100.64.2.192/26 networks had the local preference modified to 222 because they originate from AS 65200 and are within the 100.64.0.0/10 network range.

■ The 10.12.1.0/24 and 10.23.1.0/24 routes from R2 have been assigned the locally significant BGP attribute weight 65,200.

■ All other routes were received and not modified.

Example 12-43 *Verifying Changes from R1's Route Map to AS 65200*

```
R1# show bgp ipv4 unicast | b Network
     Network           Next Hop         Metric LocPrf Weight Path
 *>  10.1.1.0/24       0.0.0.0               0         32768 ?
 *>  10.3.3.0/24       10.12.1.2            33             0 65200 65300 3003 ?
 r>  10.12.1.0/24      10.12.1.2            22         65200 65200 ?
 r                     0.0.0.0               0         32768 ?
 *>  10.23.1.0/24      10.12.1.2           333         65200 65200 ?
 *>  100.64.2.0/25     10.12.1.2            22    222      0 65200 ?
 *>  100.64.2.192/26   10.12.1.2            22    222      0 65200 ?
 *>  100.64.3.0/25     10.12.1.2            22             0 65200 65300 300 ?
 *>  192.168.1.1/32    0.0.0.0               0         32768 ?
```

> **NOTE** It is considered a best practice to use a different route-map for inbound and
> outbound prefixes for each BGP neighbor.

Clearing BGP Connections

Depending on the change to the BGP route manipulation technique, the BGP session may
need to be refreshed to take effect. BGP supports two methods of clearing a BGP session.
The first method is a hard reset, which tears down the BGP session, removes BGP routes
from the peer, and is the most disruptive. The second method is a soft reset, which invali-
dates the BGP cache and requests a full advertisement from its BGP peer.

You can initiate a hard reset on a router with the command **clear ip bgp** *ip-address* and a
soft reset by adding the optional **soft** keyword. You can clear all the router's BGP sessions
by using an asterisk (*) in lieu of the peer's IP address.

When a BGP policy changes, the BGP table must be processed again so that the neighbors
can be notified accordingly. Routes received by a BGP peer must be processed again. If a
BGP session supports *route refresh* capability, the peer re-advertises (refreshes) the prefixes
to the requesting router, allowing for the inbound policy to process using the new policy
changes. The route refresh capability is negotiated for each address family when the session
is established.

Performing a soft reset on sessions that support route refresh capability actually initiates a
route refresh. You can perform a soft reset for a specific address family with the command
clear bgp *afi safi* {*ip-address* | *}** soft** [**in** | **out**]. A soft reset reduces the number of routes
that must be exchanged if multiple address families are configured with a single BGP peer.
Changes to the outbound routing policies use the optional **out** keyword, and changes to
inbound routing policies use the optional **in** keyword. You can use * in lieu of specifying a
peer's IP address to perform that action for all BGP peers.

BGP Communities

BGP communities provide additional capability for tagging routes and for modifying BGP
routing policy on upstream and downstream routers. BGP communities can be appended,
removed, or modified selectively on each attribute from router to router.

A BGP community is an optional transitive BGP attribute that can traverse from AS to AS. A BGP community is a 32-bit number that can be included with a route. A BGP community can be displayed as a full 32-bit number (0 through 4,294,967,295) or as two 16-bit numbers (0 through 65535):(0 through 65535), commonly referred to as *new format*.

By convention, with private BGP communities, the first 16 bits represent the AS of the community origination, and the second 16 bits represent a pattern defined by the originating AS. The private BGP community pattern can vary from organization to organization and does not need to be registered. The pattern could signify geographic locations for one AS while signifying a method of route advertisement in another AS. Some organizations publish their private BGP community patterns on websites such as http://www.onesc.net/communities/.

In 2006, RFC 4360 expanded the capabilities of BGP communities by providing an extended format. *Extended BGP communities* provide structure for various classes of information and are commonly used for VPN services.

Enabling BGP Community Support

IOS XE routers do not advertise BGP communities to peers by default. Communities are enabled on a neighbor-by-neighbor basis with the BGP address family configuration command **neighbor** *ip-address* **send-community** [**standard** | **extended** | **both**] under the neighbor's address family configuration. If a keyword is not specified, standard communities are sent by default.

IOS XE nodes can display communities in new format, and they are easier to read if you use the global configuration command **ip bgp-community new-format**. Example 12-44 shows the BGP community in decimal format on top and then in new format.

Example 12-44 *BGP Community Formats*

```
! DECIMAL FORMAT
R3# show bgp 192.168.1.1
! Output omitted for brevity
BGP routing table entry for 192.168.1.1/32, version 6
Community: 6553602 6577023

! New-Format
R3# show bgp 192.168.1.1
! Output omitted for brevity
BGP routing table entry for 192.168.1.1/32, version 6
Community: 100:2 100:23423
```

Well-Known Communities

RFC 1997 defined a set of global communities (known as *well-known communities*) that use the community range 4,294,901,760 (0xFFFF0000) to 4,294,967,295 (0xFFFFFFFF). All routers that are capable of sending/receiving BGP communities must implement well-known communities. The following are the common well-known communities:

- Internet
- No_Advertise

- No_Export

- Local AS

The No_Advertise BGP Community

For the *No_Advertise community* (0xFFFFFF02 or 4,294,967,042), routes should not be advertised to any BGP peer. The No_Advertise BGP community can be advertised from an upstream BGP peer or locally with an inbound BGP policy. In either method, the No_Advertise community is set in the BGP Loc-RIB table that affects outbound route advertisement. The No_Advertise community is set with the command **set community no-advertise** within a route map.

Figure 12-5 demonstrates that R1 is advertising the 10.1.1.0/24 route to R2. R2 sets the BGP No_Advertise community on the prefix on an inbound route map associated with R1. R2 does not advertise the 10.1.1.0/24 route to R3.

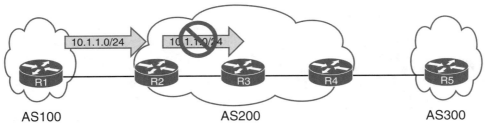

Figure 12-5 *BGP No_Advertise Community Topology*

Example 12-45 shows R2's BGP path information for the 10.1.1.0/24 route. Notice that the route was "not advertised to any peer" and has the BGP community No_Advertise set.

Example 12-45 *BGP Attributes for No_Advertise Routes*

```
R2# show bgp 10.1.1.0/24
! Output omitted for brevity
BGP routing table entry for 10.1.1.0/24, version 18
Paths: (1 available, best #1, table default, not advertised to any peer)
  Not advertised to any peer
  Refresh Epoch 1
  100, (received & used)
    10.1.12.1 from 10.1.12.1 (192.168.1.1)
      Origin IGP, metric 0, localpref 100, valid, external, best
      Community: no-advertise
```

You can quickly see BGP routes that are set with the No_Advertise community by using the command **show bgp** *afi safi* **community no-advertise**, as shown in Example 12-46.

Example 12-46 *Displaying Prefixes with the No_Advertise Community*

```
R2# show bgp ipv4 unicast community no-advertise
! Output omitted for brevity
     Network          Next Hop           Metric LocPrf Weight Path
 *>   10.1.1.0/24      10.1.12.1               0          0 100 i
```

The No_Export BGP Community

When a route is received with the *No_Export community* (0xFFFFFF01 or 4,294,967,041), the route is not advertised to any eBGP peer. If the router receiving the No_Export route is a confederation member, the route can be advertised to other sub-ASs in the confederation. The No_Export community is set with the command **set community no-export** within a route map.

Figure 12-6 shows a topology with three ASs. AS 200 is a BGP confederation composed of member AS 65100 and AS 65200. R1 is advertising the 10.1.1.0/24 route to R2, and R2 sets the No_Export community on an inbound route map associated with R1. R2 advertises the prefix to R3, and R3 advertises the prefix to R4. R4 does not advertise the prefix to R5 because it is an eBGP session, and the prefix has the No_Export BGP community.

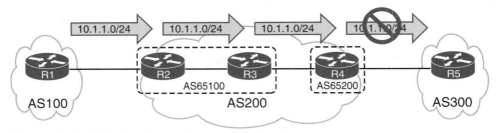

Figure 12-6 *BGP No_Export Community Topology*

Example 12-47 shows the BGP path attributes (Pas) for 10.1.1.0/24 on R3 and R4. Notice that R3 and R4 display *not advertised to EBGP peer*. R3 can advertise the 10.1.1.0/24 route to R4 because R3 and R4 are members of the same confederation, even though their autonomous system numbers (ASNs) are different.

Example 12-47 *BGP Attributes for No_Export Routes*

```
R3# show bgp ipv4 unicast 10.1.1.0/24
BGP routing table entry for 10.1.1.0/24, version 6
Paths: (1 available, best #1, table default, not advertised to EBGP peer)
  Advertised to update-groups:
    3
  Refresh Epoch 1
  100, (Received from a RR-client), (received & used)
    10.1.23.2 from 10.1.23.2 (192.168.2.2)
      Origin IGP, metric 0, localpref 100, valid, confed-internal, best
    Community: no-export
```

```
R4# show bgp ipv4 unicast 10.1.1.0/24
! Output omitted for brevity
BGP routing table entry for 10.1.1.0/24, version 4
Paths: (1 available, best #1, table default, not advertised to EBGP peer)
  Not advertised to any peer
  Refresh Epoch 1
  (65100) 100, (received & used)
    10.1.23.2 (metric 20) from 10.1.34.3 (192.168.3.3)
      Origin IGP, metric 0, localpref 100, valid, confed-external, best
      Community: no-export
```

You can see all the BGP prefixes that contain the No_Export community by using the command **show bgp** *afi safi* **community no-export**, as demonstrated in Example 12-48. Because the route contained the No_Export community, R4 did not advertise the route to R5, which is outside the BGP confederation and in a different AS.

Example 12-48 *Viewing BGP Routes with the No_Export Community*

```
R4# show bgp ipv4 unicast community no-export | b Network
     Network          Next Hop          Metric LocPrf Weight Path
 *>  10.1.1.0/24      10.1.23.2              0    100      0 (65100) 100 i

R2# show bgp ipv4 unicast community no-export | b Network
     Network          Next Hop          Metric LocPrf Weight Path
 *>  10.1.1.0/24      10.1.12.1              0             0 100 i
```

The Local AS (No_Export_SubConfed) BGP Community

With the No_Export_SubConfed community (0xFFFFFF03 or 4,294,967,043), known as the *local AS community*, a route is not advertised outside the local AS. If the router receiving a route with the local AS community is a confederation member, the route can be advertised only within the sub-AS (member AS) and is not advertised between member ASs. The local AS community is set with the command **set community local-as** within a route map.

Figure 12-7 shows a topology with three ASs. AS 200 is a BGP confederation composed of members AS 65100 and AS 65200. R1 is advertising the 10.1.1.0/24 network to R2, and R2 sets the local AS community on an inbound route map associated with R1. R2 advertises the prefix to R3, but R3 does not advertise the prefix to R4 because the prefix contains the local AS community.

Example 12-49 confirms that the prefix is *not advertised outside local AS* and that the prefix is not advertised to any peer.

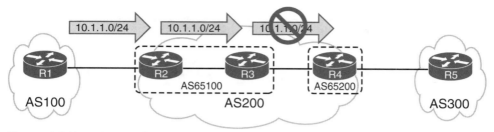

Figure 12-7 *BGP Local AS Community Topology*

Example 12-49 *BGP Attributes for Local AS Routes*

```
R3# show bgp ipv4 unicast 10.1.1.0/24
BGP routing table entry for 10.1.1.0/24, version 8
Paths: (1 available, best #1, table default, not advertised outside local AS)
  Not advertised to any peer
  Refresh Epoch 1
  100, (Received from a RR-client), (received & used)
    10.1.23.2 from 10.1.23.2 (192.168.2.2)
      Origin IGP, metric 0, localpref 100, valid, confed-internal, best
      Community: local-AS
```

You can see all the BGP prefixes that contain the local AS community by using the command **show bgp** *afi safi* **community local-as**, as demonstrated in Example 12-50.

Example 12-50 *Viewing BGP Routes with the Local AS Community*

```
R3# show bgp ipv4 unicast community local-AS | b Network
     Network          Next Hop          Metric LocPrf Weight Path
 *>i 10.1.1.0/24      10.1.23.2              0    100      0 100 i

R2# show bgp ipv4 unicast community local-AS | b Network
     Network          Next Hop          Metric LocPrf Weight Path
 *>  10.1.1.0/24      10.1.12.1              0             0 100 i
```

Conditionally Matching BGP Communities

Conditionally matching BGP communities allows for selection of prefixes based on the BGP communities within the prefixes' path attributes so that selective processing can occur in route maps. Example 12-51 shows the BGP table for R1, which has received multiple routes from R2 (AS 65200).

Example 12-51 *BGP Routes from R2 (AS 65200)*

```
R1# show bgp ipv4 unicast | begin Network
     Network          Next Hop          Metric LocPrf Weight Path
 *>  10.1.1.0/24      0.0.0.0                0          32768 ?
 *   10.12.1.0/24     10.12.1.2             22              0 65200 ?
```

```
 *>                      0.0.0.0            0       32768 ?
 *>   10.23.1.0/24       10.12.1.2        333           0 65200 ?
 *>   192.168.1.1/32     0.0.0.0            0       32768 ?
 *>   192.168.2.2/32     10.12.1.2         22           0 65200 ?
 *>   192.168.3.3/32     10.12.1.2       3333           0 65200 65300 ?
```

In this example, you want to conditionally match for a specific community. You display the entire BGP table by using the command **show bgp** *afi safi* **detail** and then manually select a route with a specific community. However, if the BGP community is known, you can display all the routes by using the command **show bgp** *afi safi* **community** *community*, as shown in the following snippet:

```
R1# show bgp ipv4 unicast community 333:333 | begin Network

        Network          Next Hop           Metric LocPrf Weight Path

 *>   10.23.1.0/24       10.12.1.2           333           0 65200 ?
```

Example 12-52 shows the explicit path entry for the 10.23.1.0/24 route and all the BGP path attributes. Notice that two BGP communities (333:333 and 65300:333) are added to the path.

Example 12-52   *Viewing BGP Path Attributes for the 10.23.1.0/24 Network*

```
R1# show ip bgp 10.23.1.0/24
BGP routing table entry for 10.23.1.0/24, version 15
Paths: (1 available, best #1, table default)
  Not advertised to any peer
  Refresh Epoch 3
  65200
    10.12.1.2 from 10.12.1.2 (192.168.2.2)
      Origin incomplete, metric 333, localpref 100, valid, external, best
      Community: 333:333 65300:333
      rx pathid: 0, tx pathid: 0x0
```

Conditionally matching requires the creation of a community list that shares a structure similar to that of an ACL, can be standard or expanded, and can be referenced by number or name. Standard community lists are numbered 1 to 99 and match either well-known communities or a private community number (*as-number:16-bit-number*). Expanded community lists are numbered 100 to 500 and use regex patterns.

The configuration syntax for a community list is **ip community-list** {*1-500* | **standard** *-list-name* | **expanded** *list-name*} {**permit** | **deny**} *community-pattern*. The community list is referenced in a route map with the command **match community** *1-500*.

NOTE   When multiple communities are on the same **ip community list** statement, all communities for that statement must exist in that route's community list. If only one out of many communities is required, you can use multiple **ip community list** statements.

Example 12-53 demonstrates the creation of a BGP community list that matches on the community 333:333. The BGP community list is then used in the first sequence of route map COMMUNITY-CHECK, which denies any routes with that community. The second route map sequence allows for all other BGP routes and sets the BGP weight (locally significant) to 111. The route map is then applied on routes advertised from R2 toward R1.

Example 12-53   *Conditionally Matching BGP Communities*

```
R1
ip community-list 100 permit 333:333
!
route-map COMMUNITY-CHECK deny 10
 description Block Routes with Community 333:333 in it
 match community 100
route-map COMMUNITY-CHECK permit 20
 description Allow routes with either community in it
 set weight 111
!
router bgp 65100
 neighbor 10.12.1.2 remote-as 65200
 address-family ipv4 unicast
 neighbor 10.12.1.2 route-map COMMUNITY-CHECK in
```

Example 12-54 shows the BGP table after the route map has been applied to the neighbor. The 10.23.1.0/24 prefix is discarded, and all the other prefixes learned from AS 65200 have the BGP weight set to 111.

Example 12-54   *R1's BGP Table After Application of the Route Map*

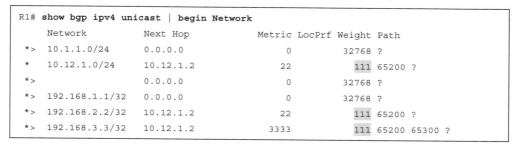

```
R1# show bgp ipv4 unicast | begin Network
     Network          Next Hop          Metric LocPrf Weight Path
 *>  10.1.1.0/24      0.0.0.0                0        32768 ?
 *   10.12.1.0/24     10.12.1.2             22         111 65200 ?
 *>                   0.0.0.0                0        32768 ?
 *>  192.168.1.1/32   0.0.0.0                0        32768 ?
 *>  192.168.2.2/32   10.12.1.2             22         111 65200 ?
 *>  192.168.3.3/32   10.12.1.2           3333         111 65200 65300 ?
```

Setting Private BGP Communities

You set a private BGP community in a route map by using the command **set community** *bgp-community* [**additive**]. By default, when you set a community, any existing communities are overwritten, but you can preserve them by using the optional **additive** keyword.

Example 12-55 shows the BGP table entries for the 10.23.1.0/24 route, which has the 333:333 and 65300:333 BGP communities. The 10.3.3.0/24 route has the 65300:300 community.

Example 12-55 *Viewing the BGP Communities for Two Network Prefixes*

```
R1# show bgp ipv4 unicast 10.23.1.0/24
! Output omitted for brevity
BGP routing table entry for 10.23.1.0/24, version 15
  65200
    10.12.1.2 from 10.12.1.2 (192.168.2.2)
      Origin incomplete, metric 333, localpref 100, valid, external, best
      Community: 333:333 65300:333
```

```
R1# show bgp ipv4 unicast 10.3.3.0/24
! Output omitted for brevity
BGP routing table entry for 10.3.3.0/24, version 12
  65200 65300 3003
    10.12.1.2 from 10.12.1.2 (192.168.2.2)
      Origin incomplete, metric 33, localpref 100, valid, external, best
      Community: 65300:300
```

Example 12-56 shows the configuration where the BGP community is set on the 10.23.1.0/24 route. The additive keyword is not used, so the previous community values of 333:333 and 65300:333 are overwritten with the 10:23 community. The 10.3.3.0/24 route has the communities 3:0, 3:3, and 10:10 added to the existing communities because that route map sequence contains the **additive** keyword. The route map is then associated with R2 (AS 65200).

Example 12-56 *Private BGP Community Configuration*

```
ip prefix-list PREFIX10.23.1.0 seq 5 permit 10.23.1.0/24
ip prefix-list PREFIX10.3.3.0 seq 5 permit 10.3.3.0/24
!
route-map SET-COMMUNITY permit 10
 match ip address prefix-list PREFIX10.23.1.0
 set community 10:23
route-map SET-COMMUNITY permit 20
 match ip address prefix-list PREFIX10.3.3.0
 set community 3:0 3:3 10:10 additive
route-map SET-COMMUNITY permit 30
!
router bgp 65100
 address-family ipv4
 neighbor 10.12.1.2 route-map SET-COMMUNITY in
```

After the route map has been applied and the routes have been refreshed, the path attributes can be examined, as demonstrated in Example 12-57. As anticipated, the previous BGP communities are removed for the 10.23.1.0/24 route, but they are maintained with the 10.3.3.0/24 route.

Example 12-57　*Verifying BGP Community Changes*

```
R1# show bgp ipv4 unicast 10.23.1.0/24
! Output omitted for brevity
BGP routing table entry for 10.23.1.0/24, version 22
  65200
    10.12.1.2 from 10.12.1.2 (192.168.2.2)
      Origin incomplete, metric 333, localpref 100, valid, external, best
      Community: 10:23
```
```
R1# show bgp ipv4 unicast 10.3.3.0/24
BGP routing table entry for 10.3.3.0/24, version 20
  65200 65300 3003
    10.12.1.2 from 10.12.1.2 (192.168.2.2)
      Origin incomplete, metric 33, localpref 100, valid, external, best
      Community: 3:0 3:3 10:10 65300:300
```

Maximum Prefix

Multiple Internet outages have occurred because routers have received more routes than they can handle. The *BGP maximum prefix* feature restricts the number of routes that are received from a BGP peer. This feature ensures that the BGP table does not overwhelm the router by exceeding its memory or processing capability. Prefix limits are typically set for BGP peers on low-end routers as a safety mechanism to ensure that they do not become overloaded.

You can have routers place prefix restrictions on a BGP neighbor by using the BGP address family configuration command **neighbor** *ip-address* **maximum-prefix** *prefix-count* [*warning-percentage*] [**restart** *time*] [**warning-only**].

When a peer advertises more routes than the maximum prefix count, the peer moves the neighbor to the *Idle (PfxCt)* state in the finite-state machine (FSM), closes the BGP session, and sends out the appropriate syslog message. The BGP session is not automatically reestablished by default. This behavior prevents a continuous cycle of loading routes, resetting the session, and reloading the routes. If you want to restart the BGP session after a certain amount of time, you can use the optional keyword **restart** *time*.

A warning is not generated before the prefix limit is reached. By adding a *warning percentage* (set to 1 to 100) after the maximum prefix count, you can have a warning message sent when the percentage is exceeded. The command for a maximum of 100 prefixes with a warning threshold of 75 is **maximum-prefix 100 75**. When the threshold is reached, the router reports the following warning message:

```
%ROUTING-BGP-5-MAXPFX : No. of IPv4 Unicast prefixes received from
192.168.1.1 has reached 75, max 100
```

You can change the maximum prefix behavior of closing the BGP session by using the optional keyword **warning-only** so that a warning message is generated instead. When the threshold has been reached, additional prefixes are discarded.

Example 12-58 shows the maximum prefix configuration that limits a router to receiving only seven prefixes.

Example 12-58 *Maximum Prefix Configuration*

```
router bgp 65100
 neighbor 10.12.1.2 remote-as 65200
 !
 address-family ipv4
  neighbor 10.12.1.2 activate
  neighbor 10.12.1.2 maximum-prefix 7
```

Example 12-59 shows that the 10.12.1.2 neighbor has exceeded the maximum prefix threshold and shut down the BGP session.

Example 12-59 *Maximum Prefix Violation*

```
R1# show bgp ipv4 unicast summary | begin Neighbor
Neighbor      V     AS MsgRcvd MsgSent   TblVer  InQ OutQ Up/Down  State/PfxRcd
10.12.1.2     4  65200      0       0        1    0    0 00:01:14 Idle (PfxCt)

R1# show log | include BGP
05:10:04.989: %BGP-5-ADJCHANGE: neighbor 10.12.1.2 Up
05:10:04.990: %BGP-4-MAXPFX: Number of prefixes received from 10.12.1.2 (afi 0)
 reaches 6, max 7
05:10:04.990: %BGP-3-MAXPFXEXCEED: Number of prefixes received from 10.12.1.2
 (afi 0): 8 exceeds limit 7
05:10:04.990: %BGP-3-NOTIFICATION: sent to neighbor 10.12.1.2 6/1
 (Maximum Number of Prefixes Reached) 7 bytes 00010100 000007
05:10:04.990: %BGP-5-NBR_RESET: Neighbor 10.12.1.2 reset
 (Peer over prefix limit)
05:10:04.990: %BGP-5-ADJCHANGE: neighbor 10.12.1.2 Down Peer over prefix limit
```

Configuration Scalability

BGP configurations can become fairly large as features are configured or BGP sessions increase. IOS-based operating systems provide methods to apply a similar configuration to multiple neighbors. This simplifies the configuration from a deployment standpoint and makes the configuration easier to read.

IOS XE Peer Groups

IOS XE *peer groups* simplify BGP configuration and reduce system resource use (CPU and memory) by grouping BGP peers together into BGP update groups. BGP update groups enable a router to perform the outbound routing policy processing one time and then replicate the update to all the members (as opposed to performing the outbound routing policy processing for every router). Because all members in the BGP update group share the same outbound policy, router resources are conserved during outbound route processing.

The routers in a BGP peer group contain the same outbound routing policy. In addition to enhancing router performance, BGP peer groups simplify the BGP configuration when there are multiple routers assigned to a peer group. All peer group settings use the *peer-group-name* field in lieu of the *ip-address* field in the **neighbor** *ip-address* commands. All routers in the peer group are in the same update group and therefore must be of the same session type: internal (iBGP) or external (eBGP).

> **NOTE** Members of a peer group can have a unique inbound routing policy.

You define a peer group by using the command **neighbor** *group-name* **peer-group** in the global BGP configuration. All BGP parameters are configured using **peer-group** *group-name* in lieu of **neighbor** *ip-address*. You link BGP peer IP addresses to the peer group by using the command **neighbor** *ip-address* **peer-group** *group-name*. BGP neighbors cannot be activated by peer group name and must be activated for each address family by IP address.

Example 12-60 shows R1's BGP configuration for peering with R2, R3, and R4. The configuration establishes an iBGP session using loopback interfaces (R2: 192.168.2.2, R3: 192.168.3.3, and R4: 192.168.4.4) and modifies the next-hop address to be set to the IP address used to establish the BGP session.

Example 12-60 *Peer Group Sample Configuration*

```
router bgp 100
 no bgp default ipv4-unicast
 neighbor AS100 peer-group
 neighbor AS100 remote-as 100
 neighbor AS100 update-source Loopback0
 neighbor 192.168.2.2 peer-group AS100
 neighbor 192.168.3.3 peer-group AS100
 neighbor 192.168.4.4 peer-group AS100
 !
 address-family ipv4
  neighbor AS100 next-hop-self
  neighbor 192.168.2.2 activate
  neighbor 192.168.3.3 activate
  neighbor 192.168.4.4 activate
```

IOS XE Peer Templates

A restriction for BGP peer groups is that they require all neighbors to have the same outbound routing policy. BGP *peer templates* allow for a reusable pattern of settings that can be applied as needed in a hierarchical format through inheritance and nesting of templates. If a conflict exists between an inherited configuration and the invoking peer template, the invoking template preempts the inherited value. There are two types of BGP peer templates:

- **Peer session:** This type of template involves configuration settings specifically for the BGP session. You define peer session template settings with the BGP configuration command **template peer-session** *template-name* and then enter any BGP session-related configuration commands.

- **Peer policy:** This type of template involves configuration settings specifically for the address family policy. You define peer policy template settings with the BGP configuration command **template peer-policy** *template-name* and then enter any BGP address family–related configuration commands.

To nest session templates, you use the command **inherit peer-session** *template-name sequence*, and to nest policy templates, you use the command **inherit peer-policy** *template-name sequence*.

Example 12-61 demonstrates the configuration of BGP peer templates. The BGP neighbor 10.12.1.2 invokes TEMPLATE-PARENT-POLICY for address family policy settings. TEMPLATE-PARENT-POLICY sets the inbound route map to FILTERROUTES and invokes TEMPLATE-CHILD-POLICY, which sets the maximum prefix limit to 10.

Example 12-61   *Peer Template Sample Configuration*

```
router bgp 100
 template peer-policy TEMPLATE-PARENT-POLICY
  route-map FILTERROUTES in
  inherit peer-policy TEMPLATE-CHILD-POLICY 20
 exit-peer-policy
 !
 template peer-policy TEMPLATE-CHILD-POLICY
  maximum-prefix 10
 exit-peer-policy
 !
 bgp log-neighbor-changes
 neighbor 10.12.1.2 remote-as 200
 !
 address-family ipv4
  neighbor 10.12.1.2 activate
  neighbor 10.12.1.2 inherit peer-policy TEMPLATE-PARENT-POLICY
```

> **NOTE**   A BGP peer can be associated with either a peer group or a template but not both.

References in This Chapter

Edgeworth, Brad, Foss, Aaron, and Garza Rios, Ramiro, *IP Routing on Cisco IOS, IOS XE, and IOS XR*, Cisco Press, 2014.

RFC 1997, *BGP Communities Attribute*, Paul Traina and Ravi Chandra, https://www.ietf.org/rfc/rfc1997.txt, August 1996.

RFC 4360, *BGP Extended Communities Attribute*, Srihari R. Sangli, Dan Tappan, and Yakov Rekhter, https://www.ietf.org/rfc/rfc4360.txt, February 2006.

Exam Preparation Tasks

As mentioned in the section "How to Use This Book" in the Introduction, you have a couple choices for exam preparation: the exercises here, Chapter 24, "Final Preparation," and the exam simulation questions in the Pearson Test Prep software.

Review All Key Topics

Review the most important topics in this chapter, noted with the Key Topic icon in the outer margin of the page. Table 12-4 lists these key topics and the page number on which each is found.

Table 12-4   Key Topics

Key Topic Element	Description	Page Number
Paragraph	Aggregate addresses	482
Paragraph	Route aggregation with suppression	485
Paragraph	The atomic aggregate attribute	488
Paragraph	Route aggregation with AS_SET	489
Paragraph	IPv6 summarization	492
Figure 12-3	BGP route policy processing	494
Paragraph	BGP filtering methods	494
Paragraph	Distribution list filtering	495
Paragraph	Prefix list filtering	496
Paragraph	Regular expressions (regex)	497
Paragraph	AS_Path ACLs	503
Paragraph	Route maps	505
Paragraph	Clearing BGP connections	507
Paragraph	Enabling BGP community support	508
Paragraph	The No_Advertise BGP community	509
Paragraph	The No_Export BGP community	510
Paragraph	The local AS (No_Export_SubConfed_BGP) community	511
Paragraph	Community list configuration	513
Paragraph	Setting private BGP communities	514
Paragraph	Maximum prefix	516
Paragraph	IOS peer groups	517
Paragraph	IOS peer templates	518

Define Key Terms

Define the following key terms from this chapter and check your answers in the glossary:

AS_Path, atomic aggregate, access control list (ACL), distribute list, prefix list, route map, regular expressions, BGP community (37), No_Advertise community, No_Export community, local AS community, peer group, peer template

Use the Command Reference to Check Your Memory

The ENARSI 300-410 exam focuses on the practical, hands-on skills that networking professionals use. Therefore, you should be able to identify the commands needed to configure, verify, and troubleshoot the topics covered in this chapter.

This section includes the most important configuration and verification commands covered in this chapter. It might not be necessary to memorize the complete syntax of every command, but you should be able to remember the basic keywords that are needed.

To test your memory of the commands in Table 12-5, go to the companion website and download Appendix B, "Command Reference Exercises." Fill in the missing commands in the tables based on each command description. You can check your work by downloading Appendix C, "Command Reference Exercise Answer Key," from the companion website.

Table 12-5 Command Reference

Task	Command Syntax
Configure a BGP aggregate IPv4 prefix.	**aggregate-address** *network subnet-mask* [**summary-only**] [**as-set**]
Configure a BGP aggregate IPv6 prefix.	**aggregate-address** *prefix/prefix-length* [**summary-only**] [**as-set**]
Configure a prefix list.	{**ip** l **ipv6**} **prefix-list** *prefix-list-name* [**seq** *sequence-number*] {**permit** l **deny**} *high-order-bit-pattern/high-order-bit-count* [**ge** *ge-value*] [**le** *le-value*]
Create a route map entry.	**route-map** *route-map-name* [**permit** l **deny**] [*sequence-number*]
Conditionally match in a route map using AS_Path.	**match as-path** *acl-number*
Conditionally match in a route map using an ACL.	**match ip address** {*acl-number* l *acl-name*}
Conditionally match in a route map using a prefix list.	**match ip address** **prefix-list** *prefix-list-name*
Conditionally match in a route map using local preference.	**match local-preference** *local-preference*
Filter routes to a BGP neighbor using an ACL.	**neighbor** *ip-address* **distribute-list** {*acl-number* l *acl-name*} {**in** l **out**}
Filter routes to a BGP neighbor using a prefix list.	**neighbor** *ip-address* **prefix-list** *prefix-list-name* {**in** l **out**}
Create an ACL based on the BGP AS_Path.	**ip as-path access-list** *acl-number* {**deny** l **permit**} *regex-query*
Filter routes to a BGP neighbor using an AS_Path ACL.	**neighbor** *ip-address* **filter-list** *acl-number* {**in** l **out**}
Associate an inbound or outbound route map to a specific BGP neighbor.	**neighbor** *ip-address* **route-map** *route-map-name* {**in** l **out**}

Task	Command Syntax
Configure IOS-based routers to display the community in new format for easier readability of BGP communities.	**ip bgp-community new-format**
Create a BGP community list for conditional route matching.	**ip community-list** {*1-500* | **standard** *list-name* | **expanded** *list-name*} {**permit** | **deny**} *community-pattern*
Set BGP communities in a route map.	**set community** *bgp-community* [**additive**]
Configure the maximum number of BGP prefixes that a neighbor can receive.	**neighbor** *ip-address* **maximum-prefix** *prefix-count* [*warning-percentage*] [**restart** *time*] [**warning-only**]
Define a BGP peer group.	**neighbor** *group-name* **peer-group**
Initiate a route refresh for a specific BGP peer.	**clear bgp** *afi safi* {*ip-address* | ***} **soft** [**in** | **out**]
Display the current BGP table, based on routes that meet a specified AS_Path regex pattern.	**show bgp** *afi safi* **regexp** *regex-pattern*
Display the current BGP table, based on routes that meet a specified BGP community.	**show bgp** *afi safi* **community** *community*

## CHAPTER 13

BGP Path Selection

This chapter covers the following topics:

- **Understanding BGP Path Selection:** This section reviews the first step of path selection, which involves selecting the longest prefix length.

- **BGP Best Path:** This section describes the logic BGP uses to identify the best path when multiple routes are installed in the BGP table.

- **BGP Equal-Cost Multipathing:** This section explains how additional paths are presented to the Routing Information Base (RIB) for installation into the routing table.

With Border Gateway Protocol (BGP), route advertisements consist of the network layer reachability information (NLRI) and the path attributes (PAs). The NLRI consists of the network prefix and prefix length; BGP attributes such as AS_Path and Origin are stored in the PAs. A BGP route may contain multiple paths to the same destination network. Every path's attributes impact the desirability of the route when a router selects the best path. A BGP router advertises only the best path to the neighboring routers.

Inside the BGP Loc-RIB table, all the routes and their path attributes are maintained with the best path calculated. The best path is then presented to the RIB for installation into the routing table of the router. If the best path is no longer available, the router uses the existing paths to quickly identify a new best path. BGP recalculates the best path for a prefix upon four possible events:

- BGP next-hop reachability change

- Failure of an interface connected to an External BGP (eBGP) peer

- Redistribution change

- Reception of new or removed paths for a route

The BGP best-path selection algorithm influences how traffic enters or leaves an autonomous system. Some router configurations modify the BGP attributes to influence inbound traffic, outbound traffic, or inbound and outbound traffic, depending on the network design requirements.

"Do I Know This Already?" Quiz

The "Do I Know This Already?" quiz allows you to assess whether you should read this entire chapter thoroughly or jump to the "Exam Preparation Tasks" section. If you are in doubt about your answers to these questions or your own assessment of your knowledge of the topics, read the entire chapter. Table 13-1 lists the major headings in this chapter and their corresponding "Do I Know This Already?" quiz questions. You can find the answers in Appendix A, "Answers to the 'Do I Know This Already?' Quiz Questions."

Table 13-1 "Do I Know This Already?" Foundation Topics Section-to-Question Mapping

Foundations Topic Section	Questions
Understanding BGP Path Selection	1
BGP Best Path	2–7
BGP Equal-Cost Multipathing	8

CAUTION The goal of self-assessment is to gauge your mastery of the topics in this chapter. If you do not know the answer to a question or are only partially sure of the answer, you should mark that question as wrong for purposes of self-assessment. Giving yourself credit for an answer that you correctly guess skews your self-assessment results and might provide you with a false sense of security.

1. True or false: BGP summarization provides a mechanism for load balancing traffic between service providers.
   a. True
   b. False

2. True or false: A BGP router advertises every path for a prefix so that every neighbor can build its own topology table.
   a. True
   b. False

3. Which of the following techniques is the second selection criterion for the BGP best path?
   a. Weight
   b. Local preference
   c. Origin
   d. MED

4. True or false: A router deletes a path from the Loc-RIB table after detecting that the current best path is inferior to a new superior path for a network prefix.
   a. True
   b. False

5. In the BGP best-path algorithm, what attribute does BGP use after network origination (local, aggregation, received by peer) to select the best path?
   a. Local preference
   b. AS_Path
   c. Accumulated Interior Gateway Protocol (AIGP)
   d. MED

6. Which of the following attributes is locally significant to the BGP best-path algorithm?

   a. Weight

   b. Local preference

   c. AS_Path

   d. MED

7. True or false: MED can only be compared between three or more different ASs.

   a. True

   b. False

8. True or false: When BGP multipathing is enabled, a router can select multiple paths as the best path so that they can all be installed into the RIB.

   a. True

   b. False

Foundation Topics

Understanding BGP Path Selection

The BGP best-path selection algorithm influences how traffic enters or leaves an *autonomous system* (*AS*). Some router configurations modify the BGP attributes to influence inbound traffic, outbound traffic, or inbound and outbound traffic, depending on the network design requirements. Many network engineers do not understand the BGP best-path selection, which can often result in suboptimal routing. This section explains the logic used by a router that uses BGP when forwarding packets.

A router always selects the path a packet should take by examining the prefix length of a network entry. The path selected for a packet depends on the prefix length, where the *longest prefix length* is always preferred. For example, /28 is preferred over /26, and /26 is preferred over /24. This logic is used to influence path selection in BGP.

Say that an organization owns the 100.64.0.0/16 network range but needs to advertise only two subnets (100.64.1.0/24 and 100.64.2.0/24) and must still provide resiliency in the event of a router failure. It could advertise both prefixes (100.64.1.0/24 and 100.64.2.0/24) from both of its routers (R1 and R2), but how can the company distribute the network traffic for each subnet if all traffic comes in on one router (that is, R1) because of the BGP best-path algorithm? Various BGP path attributes (PAs) could be modified as they are advertised externally, but a service provider (SP) could have a BGP routing policy that ignores those path attributes, resulting in random receipt of network traffic.

A more elegant way that guarantees that paths are selected deterministically outside the organization is to advertise a summary prefix (100.64.0.0/16) out both routers. Then advertise a longer matching prefix out the router for one prefix, and then advertise a longer matching prefix out the other router for the second prefix. This allows for traffic to enter a network in a deterministic manner while still providing a backup path to the other network in the event that the first router fails. Figure 13-1 shows this concept, with R1 advertising the 100.64.1.0/24 prefix, R2 advertising the 100.64.2.0/24 prefix, and both routers advertising the 100.64.0.0/16 summary network prefix.

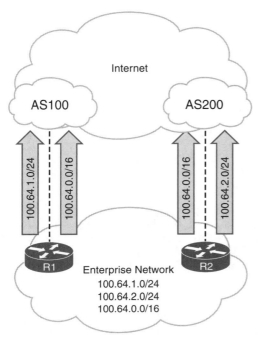

Figure 13-1 *BGP Path Selection Using the Longest Match*

Regardless of an SP's routing policy, the more specific prefixes are advertised out only one router. Redundancy is provided by advertising the summary address. If R1 crashes, devices use R2's route advertisement of 100.64.0.016 to reach the 100.64.1.0/24 network.

> **NOTE**   Ensure that the network summaries that are being advertised from your organization are within only your network range. In addition, service providers typically do not accept IPv4 routes longer than /24 (such as /25 or /26) or IPv6 routes longer than /48. Routes are restricted to control the size of the Internet routing table.

BGP Best Path

BGP automatically installs the first received path as the best path. When additional paths are received for the same network prefix length, the newer paths are compared against the current best path. If there is a tie, processing continues until a best path winner is identified.

The following list provides the attributes that the BGP best-path algorithm uses for the process of selecting the best route. These attributes are processed in the order listed:

1. Prefer the highest *weight*

2. Prefer the highest *local preference*

3. Prefer the route *originated* by the local router

4. Prefer the path with the shorter Accumulated Interior Gateway Protocol (AIGP) metric attribute

5. Prefer the shortest *AS_Path*

6. Prefer the best *Origin* code

7. Prefer the lowest multi-exit discriminator (*MED*)

8. Prefer an *external* path over an *internal* path

9. Prefer the path through the *closest IGP neighbor*

10. Prefer the path from the *oldest eBGP session*

11. Prefer the path with the *lowest neighbor BGP RID*

12. Prefer the path with the *minimum cluster list length*

13. Prefer the path with the *lowest neighbor IP address*

> **NOTE**   All BGP prefixes must pass the route validity check, and the next-hop IP address must be resolvable for the route to be eligible as a best path. Some vendors and publications consider this the first step.

The BGP routing policy can vary from organization to organization, based on the manipulation of the BGP PAs. Because some PAs are transitive and carry from one AS to another AS, those changes could impact downstream routing for other SPs, too. Other PAs are non-transitive and influence the routing policy only within the organization. Network prefixes are conditionally matched on a variety of factors, such as AS_Path length, specific ASN, and BGP communities.

BGP path attribute classifications are explained in Chapter 11, "BGP." Table 13-2 shows which BGP attributes must be supported by all BGP implementations and which BGP attributes are advertised between ASs.

Table 13-2   BGP Path Attribute Classifications

Name	Supported by All BGP Implementations	Advertised Between Autonomous Systems
Well-known mandatory	Yes	Yes
Well-known discretionary	Yes	No
Optional transitive	No	Yes
Optional nontransitive	No	No

The following sections explain the components of the best-path algorithm.

Weight

BGP weight is a Cisco-defined attribute and the first step in selecting the BGP best path. Weight is a 16-bit value (0 through 65,535) assigned locally on the router; it is not advertised to other routers. The path with the higher weight is preferred. Weight can be set for specific routes with an inbound route map or for all routes learned from a specific neighbor. Weight is not advertised to peers and only influences outbound traffic from a router or an AS.

Because it is the first step in the best-path algorithm, it should be used when other attributes should not influence the best path for a specific network prefix.

The command **set weight** *weight* in a route map sets the weight value for a matching prefix. The weight is set for all prefixes received by a neighbor using the BGP address family configuration command **neighbor** *ip-address* **weight** *weight*.

Figure 13-2 demonstrates the weight attribute and its influence on the BGP best-path algorithm:

- R4, R5, and R6 are in AS 400, with iBGP full mesh peering using loopback interfaces. AS 200 and AS 300 provide transit connectivity to AS 100.

- R4 is an edge router for AS 400 and sets the weight to 222 for the 172.16.0.0/24 prefix received from R2. This ensures that R4 uses R2 for outbound traffic to this prefix.

- R6 is an edge router for AS 400 and sets the weight to 333 for the 172.24.0.0/24 prefix received from R3. This ensures that R6 uses R3 for outbound traffic to this prefix.

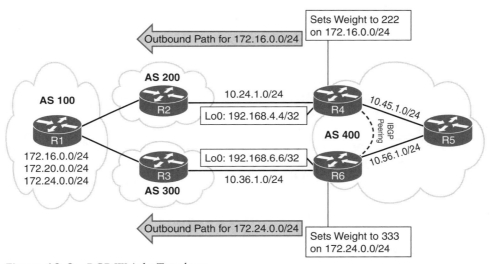

Figure 13-2 *BGP Weight Topology*

Example 13-1 demonstrates the BGP configuration for manipulating the weight on R4 and R6. R4 uses the default IPv4 address family; R6 does not use the default IPv4 address family but does use BGP peer groups.

Example 13-1 *Weight Manipulation Configuration*

```
R4
ip prefix-list PRE172 permit 172.16.0.0/24
!
route-map AS200 permit 10
 match ip address prefix-list PRE172
 set weight 222
```

```
route-map AS200 permit 20
!
router bgp 400
 neighbor 10.24.1.2 remote-as 200
 neighbor 10.24.1.2 route-map AS200 in
 neighbor 192.168.5.5 remote-as 400
 neighbor 192.168.5.5 update-source Loopback0
 neighbor 192.168.5.5 next-hop-self
 neighbor 192.168.6.6 remote-as 400
 neighbor 192.168.6.6 update-source Loopback0
 neighbor 192.168.6.6 next-hop-self
```

```
R6
ip prefix-list PRE172 permit 172.24.0.0/24
!
route-map AS300 permit 10
 match ip address prefix-list PRE172
 set weight 333
route-map AS300 permit 20
!
router bgp 400
 no bgp default ipv4-unicast
 neighbor AS400 peer-group
 neighbor AS400 remote-as 400
 neighbor AS400 update-source Loopback0
 neighbor 10.36.1.3 remote-as 300
 neighbor 192.168.4.4 peer-group AS400
 neighbor 192.168.5.5 peer-group AS400
 !
 address-family ipv4
  neighbor AS400 next-hop-self
  neighbor 10.36.1.3 activate
  neighbor 10.36.1.3 route-map AS300 in
  neighbor 192.168.4.4 activate
  neighbor 192.168.5.5 activate
```

Example 13-2 shows the BGP table for R4, R5, and R6. Notice that the weight is only set locally on R4 and R6. The weight was not advertised to any of the AS 400 routers and is set to 0 for all other prefixes. The > indicates the best path.

BGP weight is locally significant. R4, R5, and R6 use other factors later in the best-path algorithm to select the best path for the prefixes that did not have the weight modified locally.

Example 13-2   *BGP Table After Weight Manipulation*

```
R4# show bgp ipv4 unicast | begin Network
     Network          Next Hop        Metric LocPrf Weight Path
 * i 172.16.0.0/24    192.168.6.6          0    100      0 300 100 i
 *>                   10.24.1.2                         222 200 100 i
 * i 172.20.0.0/24    192.168.6.6          0    100      0 300 100 i
 *>                   10.24.1.2                           0 200 100 i
 * i 172.24.0.0/24    192.168.6.6          0    100      0 300 100 i
 *>                   10.24.1.2                           0 200 100 i

R5# show bgp ipv4 unicast | begin Network
     Network          Next Hop        Metric LocPrf Weight Path
 *>i 172.16.0.0/24    192.168.4.4          0    100      0 200 100 i
 * i                  192.168.6.6          0    100      0 300 100 i
 *>i 172.20.0.0/24    192.168.4.4          0    100      0 200 100 i
 * i                  192.168.6.6          0    100      0 300 100 i
 *>i 172.24.0.0/24    192.168.4.4          0    100      0 200 100 i
 * i                  192.168.6.6          0    100      0 300 100 i

R6# show bgp ipv4 unicast | begin Network
     Network          Next Hop        Metric LocPrf Weight Path
 * i 172.16.0.0/24    192.168.4.4          0    100      0 200 100 i
 *>                   10.36.1.3                           0 300 100 i
 * i 172.20.0.0/24    192.168.4.4          0    100      0 200 100 i
 *>                   10.36.1.3                           0 300 100 i
 * i 172.24.0.0/24    192.168.4.4          0    100      0 200 100 i
 *>                   10.36.1.3                         333 300 100 i
```

The **show bgp** *afi safi network* [**bestpath** | **best-path-reason**] command is extremely help-ful for viewing and comparing BGP path attributes. Newer versions of IOS XE contain the optional keywords **bestpath** and **best-path-reason**. Use the **bestpath** keyword to display only the path that is identified as the best path. Use the **best-path-reason** keyword to display all the paths, along with the reason a path was not identified as the best path.

Example 13-3 displays R4's path information for the 172.16.0.0/24 network prefix, using all three iterations of the command to look at a specific BGP prefix. Notice that there are multiple paths and that the best path is through R2 because the weight is set to 222.

Example 13-3   *Viewing the BGP Prefix for Best-Path Selection*

```
R4# show bgp ipv4 unicast 172.16.0.0/24
! Output omitted for brevity
BGP routing table entry for 172.16.0.0/24, version 11
Paths: (2 available, best #2, table default)
! Note:  This is Path #1
  300 100
    192.168.6.6 (metric 131072) from 192.168.6.6 (192.168.6.6)
```

```
        Origin IGP, metric 0, localpref 100, valid, internal
! Note:  This is Path #2
  200 100
    10.24.1.2 from 10.24.1.2 (192.168.2.2)
      Origin IGP, localpref 100, weight 222, valid, external, best
```

```
R4# show bgp ipv4 unicast 172.16.0.0/24 bestpath
! Output omitted for brevity
BGP routing table entry for 172.16.0.0/24, version 11
Paths: (2 available, best #2, table default)
  200 100
    10.24.1.2 from 10.24.1.2 (192.168.2.2)
      Origin IGP, localpref 100, weight 222, valid, external, best
```

```
R4# show bgp ipv4 unicast 172.16.0.0/24 best-path-reason
! Output omitted for brevity
BGP routing table entry for 172.16.0.0/24, version 11
Paths: (2 available, best #2, table default)
  300 100
    192.168.6.6 (metric 131072) from 192.168.6.6 (192.168.6.6)
      Origin IGP, metric 0, localpref 100, valid, internal
      Best Path Evaluation: Lower weight
  200 100
    10.24.1.2 from 10.24.1.2 (192.168.2.2)
      Origin IGP, localpref 100, weight 222, valid, external, best
      Best Path Evaluation: Overall best path
```

Local Preference

Local preference (LOCAL_PREF) is a well-known discretionary path attribute and is included with path advertisements throughout an AS. The local preference attribute is a 32-bit value (0 through 4,294,967,295) that indicates the preference for exiting the AS to the destination network prefix. The local preference is not advertised between eBGP peers and is typically used to influence the next-hop address for outbound traffic (that is, leaving an autonomous system). Local preference can be set for specific routes by using a route map or for all routes received from a specific neighbor.

A higher value is preferred over a lower value. If an edge BGP router does not define the local preference upon receipt of a prefix using an inbound route map, the default local preference value of 100 is used during best-path calculation and is included in advertisements to other iBGP peers. You can change the default local preference value from 100 to a different value by using the command **bgp default local-preference** *default-local-preference*.

Setting the local preference for specific routes is accomplished by using a route map or route policy with the action **set local-preference** *preference*. Modifying the local preference can influence the path selection on other iBGP peers without impacting eBGP peers because local preference is not advertised outside the autonomous system.

Figure 13-3 demonstrates modification of the local preference to influence the traffic flow for prefixes 172.24.0.0/24 and 172.16.0.0/24:

■ R4, R5, and R6 are in AS 400, with iBGP full mesh peering using loopback interfaces. AS 200 and AS 300 provide transit connectivity to AS 100.

■ R4 is an edge router for AS 400 and sets the local preference to 222 for the 172.16.0.0/24 prefix received from R2, making it the preferred path for AS 400.

■ R6 is an edge router for AS 400 and sets the local preference to 333 for the 172.24.0.0/24 prefix received from R3, making it the preferred path for AS 400.

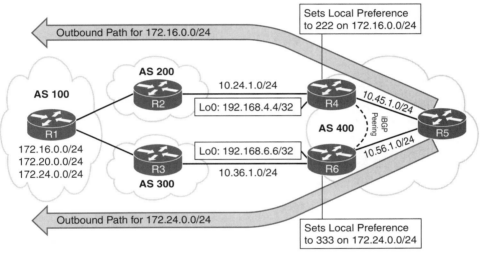

Figure 13-3 *BGP Local Preference Topology*

Example 13-4 demonstrates the BGP configuration for modifying the local preference on R4 and R6.

Example 13-4 *BGP Local Preference Configuration*

```
R4
ip prefix-list PRE172 permit 172.16.0.0/24
!
route-map AS200 permit 10
 match ip address prefix-list PRE172
 set local-preference 222
route-map AS200 permit 20
!
router bgp 400
 neighbor 10.24.1.2 remote-as 200
 neighbor 10.24.1.2 route-map AS200 in
 neighbor 192.168.5.5 remote-as 400
```

```
neighbor 192.168.5.5 update-source Loopback0
neighbor 192.168.5.5 next-hop-self
neighbor 192.168.6.6 remote-as 400
neighbor 192.168.6.6 update-source Loopback0
neighbor 192.168.6.6 next-hop-self
```

```
R6
ip prefix-list PRE172 permit 172.24.0.0/24
!
route-map AS300 permit 10
 match ip address prefix-list PRE172
 set local-preference 333
route-map AS300 permit 20
!
router bgp 400
 no bgp default ipv4-unicast
 neighbor AS400 peer-group
 neighbor AS400 remote-as 400
 neighbor AS400 update-source Loopback0
 neighbor 10.36.1.3 remote-as 300
 neighbor 192.168.4.4 peer-group AS400
 neighbor 192.168.5.5 peer-group AS400
 !
 address-family ipv4
  neighbor AS400 next-hop-self
  neighbor 10.36.1.3 activate
  neighbor 10.36.1.3 route-map AS300 in
  neighbor 192.168.4.4 activate
  neighbor 192.168.5.5 activate
```

Example 13-5 shows the BGP table for R4, R5, and R6. All three AS 400 routers send traffic toward the 172.16.0.0/24 network through R4's link to R2 (AS 200), and all three AS 400 routers send traffic toward the 172.24.0.0/24 network through R6's link to R3 (AS 300). Finding the best path for the 172.20.0.0/24 prefix requires logic in a later step of the BGP best-path algorithm. Notice that the default local preference 100 is advertised to the iBGP routers for the other prefixes.

R4 has only one path for the 172.16.0.0/24 prefix, R6 has only one path for the 172.24.0.0/24 prefix, and R5 has only one path for the 172.16.0.0/24 prefix and only one path for the 172.24.0.0/24 prefix.

Example 13-5 *R4, R5, and R6 BGP Tables After Local Preference Modification*

```
R4# show bgp ipv4 unicast | begin Network
     Network          Next Hop         Metric LocPrf Weight Path
 *>  172.16.0.0/24    10.24.1.2                 222        0 200 100 i
 * i 172.20.0.0/24  192.168.6.6          0     100        0 300 100 i
 *>                   10.24.1.2                            0 200 100 i
```

```
*>i 172.24.0.0/24   192.168.6.6              0    333      0 300 100 i
*                    10.24.1.2                              0 200 100 i
```

```
R5# show bgp ipv4 unicast | begin Network
     Network          Next Hop        Metric LocPrf Weight Path
*>i 172.16.0.0/24    192.168.4.4          0    222      0 200 100 i
*  i 172.20.0.0/24    192.168.6.6          0    100      0 300 100 i
*>i                  192.168.4.4          0    100      0 200 100 i
*>i 172.24.0.0/24    192.168.6.6          0    333      0 300 100 i
```

```
R6# show bgp ipv4 unicast | begin Network
     Network          Next Hop        Metric LocPrf Weight Path
*>i 172.16.0.0/24    192.168.4.4          0    222      0 200 100 i
*                    10.36.1.3                            0 300 100 i
*  i 172.20.0.0/24    192.168.4.4          0    100      0 200 100 i
*>                   10.36.1.3                            0 300 100 i
*>  172.24.0.0/24    10.36.1.3                 333      0 300 100 i
```

In Example 13-5, a network engineer might see that only one path exists on R4 for the 172.16.0.0/24 network prefix and think R4 deleted the path through AS 300 because it was inferior to the path through AS 200. However, that is not what has happened in this example. A router does not discard a path that is not chosen as the best path. The path is always maintained in the BGP Loc-RIB database and could be used later, in the event that the best path is no longer available. If a router identifies a different best path from the one advertised, it withdraws its previous best-path advertisement to other routers and advertises the new best path.

To fully understand what has happened, the following sections review the processing logic that occurs on each router during three phases (time cycles).

Phase I: Initial BGP Edge Route Processing

Phase I is the phase when routes are initially processed by the BGP edge routers R4 and R6.

This is what happens with R4:

- R4 receives the 172.16.0.0/24 prefix from R2 and sets the local preference to 222.

- R4 receives the 172.20.0.0/24 and 172.24.0.0/24 prefixes from R2.

- No other paths exist for these prefixes, so all paths are marked as best paths.

- R4 advertises these paths to R5 and R6. (Routes without local preference set are advertised with the local preference 100.)

This is what happens with R6:

- R6 receives the 172.24.0.0/24 prefix from R3 and sets the local preference to 333.

- R6 receives the 172.16.0.0/24 and 172.20.0.0/24 prefixes from R3.

- No other paths exist for these prefixes, so all paths are marked as best paths.

■ R6 advertises these paths to R4 and R5. (Routes without local preference set are advertised with the local preference 100.)

Example 13-6 shows simulated BGP tables on R4 and R6 during this phase. Notice the local preference for 172.16.0.0/24 on R4 and for 172.24.0.0/24 on R6. No other entries have values populated for local preference.

Example 13-6   *BGP Table After Phase I Processing*

```
R4# show bgp ipv4 unicast | begin Network
     Network            Next Hop          Metric LocPrf Weight Path
 *>  172.16.0.0/24      10.24.1.2                   222     0 200 100 i
 *>  172.20.0.0/24      10.24.1.2                           0 200 100 i
 *>  172.24.0.0/24      10.24.1.2                           0 200 100 i
R6# show bgp ipv4 unicast | begin Network
     Network            Next Hop          Metric LocPrf Weight Path
 *>  172.16.0.0/24      10.36.1.3                           0 300 100 i
 *>  172.20.0.0/24      10.36.1.3                           0 300 100 i
 *>  172.24.0.0/24      10.36.1.3                   333     0 300 100 i
```

Phase II: BGP Edge Evaluation of Multiple Paths

Phase II is the phase when R4 and R6 have received each other's routes and compare each path for a prefix. Ultimately, R6 advertises a route withdrawal for the 172.16.0.0/24 prefix, and R4 advertises a route withdrawal for the 172.24.0.0/24 prefix. R5 receives prefixes from R4 and R6 at the same time, resulting in both paths being present in the BGP Adj-RIB table.

This is what happens with R4:

■ R4 receives R6's paths for all the prefixes from R3.

■ R4 detects that the 172.16.0.0/24 path from R2 (AS 200) has a higher local preference than the path from R6 (AS 300). R4 keeps the path from R2 as the best path for the prefix.

■ R4 detects that the 172.20.0.0/24 path from R3 has the same local preference as the path from R2. (Routes without local preference use the default value 100.) Because of the tie, the best path is selected using steps after local preference in the best-path algorithm.

■ R4 detects that the 172.24.0.0/24 path from R6 (AS 300) has a higher local preference than the path from R2 (AS 200). R4 marks the path from R6 as the best path for the prefix and sends route withdrawals to R5 and R6 for the path from R2.

This is what happens with R5:

■ R5 receives paths for all network prefixes from R4 and R6.

■ R5 detects that the 172.16.0.0/24 path from R4 (AS 200) has a higher local preference than the path from R6 (AS 300). R5 marks the path from R4 as the best path for the prefix. Both paths exist in the BGP table.

- R5 detects that the 172.20.0.0/24 paths from R4 and R6 have identical local preference values and uses steps after local preference in the best-path algorithm. Both paths exist in the BGP table.

- R5 detects that the 172.24.0.0/24 path from R6 (AS 300) has a higher local preference than the path from R2 (AS 200). R5 selects the path from R6 as the best path for the prefix. Both paths exist in the BGP table.

This is what happens with R6:

- R6 receives R4's route advertisement for all the prefixes from R2.

- R6 detects that the 172.16.0.0/24 path from R4 (AS 200) has a higher local preference than the path from R3 (AS 300). R6 selects the path from R4 as the best path for the prefix and sends route withdrawals to R4 and R5 for the paths from R3.

- R6 detects that the 172.20.0.0/24 path from R3 has the same local preference as the path from R4. (Routes without local preference use the default value 100.) Because of the tie, the best path is selected using steps after local preference in the best-path algorithm.

- R6 detects that the 172.24.0.0/24 path from R3 (AS 300) has a higher local preference than the path from R4 (AS 200). R6 keeps the path from R3 as the best path for the prefix.

Example 13-7 shows the BGP tables for R4, R5, and R6 after Phase II processing.

Example 13-7   *BGP Table After Phase II Processing*

```
R4# show bgp ipv4 unicast | begin Network
     Network          Next Hop          Metric LocPrf Weight Path
 *>  172.16.0.0/24    10.24.1.2                   222      0 200 100 i
 * i                  192.168.6.6            0    100      0 300 100 i
 *>  172.20.0.0/24    10.24.1.2                            0 200 100 i
 * i                  192.168.6.6            0    100      0 300 100 i
 *   172.24.0.0/24    10.24.1.2                            0 200 100 i
 *>i                  192.168.6.6            0    333      0 300 100 i

R5# show bgp ipv4 unicast | begin Network
     Network          Next Hop          Metric LocPrf Weight Path
 *>i 172.16.0.0/24    192.168.4.4            0    222      0 200 100 i
 * i                  192.168.4.4            0    100      0 200 100 i
 * i 172.20.0.0/24    192.168.6.6            0    100      0 300 100 i
 *>i                  192.168.6.6            0    100      0 300 100 i
 *>i 172.24.0.0/24    192.168.6.6            0    333      0 300 100 i
 * i                  192.168.4.4            0    100      0 200 100 i

R6# show bgp ipv4 unicast | begin Network
     Network          Next Hop          Metric LocPrf Weight Path
 *   172.16.0.0/24    10.36.1.3                            0 300 100 i
```

```
*>i                    192.168.4.4        0   222   0 200 100 i
*>  172.20.0.0/24      10.36.1.3                    0 300 100 i
*  i                   192.168.4.4        0   100   0 200 100 i
*>  172.24.0.0/24      10.36.1.3              333   0 300 100 i
*  i                   192.168.4.4        0   100   0 200 100 i
```

Phase III: Final BGP Processing State

Phase III is the last processing phase. In this topology, R4, R5, and R6 process all the route withdrawals. In this phase:

- R4 and R5 receive R6's withdrawal for the 172.16.0.0/24 network prefix and remove it from the BGP table.

- R5 and R6 receive R4's withdrawal for the 172.24.0.0/24 network prefix and remove it from the BGP table.

Example 13-8 shows the BGP tables for R4, R5, and R6 after Phase III processing.

Example 13-8 *BGP Table After Phase III Processing*

```
R4# show bgp ipv4 unicast | begin Network
     Network          Next Hop          Metric LocPrf Weight Path
*>   172.16.0.0/24    10.24.1.2                  222    0 200 100 i
*  i 172.20.0.0/24    192.168.6.6         0     100    0 300 100 i
*>                    10.24.1.2                         0 200 100 i
*>i 172.24.0.0/24     192.168.6.6         0     333    0 300 100 i
*                     10.24.1.2                         0 200 100 i

R5# show bgp ipv4 unicast | begin Network
     Network          Next Hop          Metric LocPrf Weight Path
*>i 172.16.0.0/24     192.168.4.4         0     222    0 200 100 i
*  i 172.20.0.0/24    192.168.6.6         0     100    0 300 100 i
*>i                   192.168.4.4         0     100    0 200 100 i
*>i 172.24.0.0/24     192.168.6.6         0     333    0 300 100 i

R6# show bgp ipv4 unicast | begin Network
     Network          Next Hop          Metric LocPrf Weight Path
*>i 172.16.0.0/24     192.168.4.4         0     222    0 200 100 i
*                     10.36.1.3                        0 300 100 i
*  i 172.20.0.0/24    192.168.4.4         0     100    0 200 100 i
*>                    10.36.1.3                        0 300 100 i
*>   172.24.0.0/24    10.36.1.3                 333    0 300 100 i
```

Locally Originated in the Network or Aggregate Advertisement

The third decision point in the best-path algorithm is to determine whether the route originated locally. Preference is given in the following order:

1. Routes that were advertised locally
2. Networks that have been aggregated locally
3. Routes received by BGP peers

Accumulated Interior Gateway Protocol (AIGP)

Accumulated Interior Gateway Protocol (AIGP) is an optional nontransitive path attribute that is included with advertisements throughout an AS. Interior Gateway Protocols typically use the lowest-path metric to identify the shortest path to a destination but cannot provide the scalability of BGP. BGP uses an AS to identify a single domain of control for a routing policy. BGP does not use the path metric due to scalability issues combined with the notion that each AS may use a different routing policy to calculate metrics.

AIGP provides the ability for BGP to maintain and calculate a conceptual path metric in environments that use multiple ASs with unique IGP routing domains in each AS. The ability for BGP to make routing decisions based on a path metric is a viable option because all the ASs are under the control of a single domain, with consistent routing policies for BGP and IGPs.

In Figure 13-4, AS 100, AS 200, and AS 300 are all under the control of the same service provider. AIGP has been enabled on the BGP sessions between all the routers, and the IGPs are redistributed into BGP. The AIGP metric is advertised between AS 100, AS 200, and AS 300, allowing BGP to use the AIGP metric for best-path calculations between the ASs.

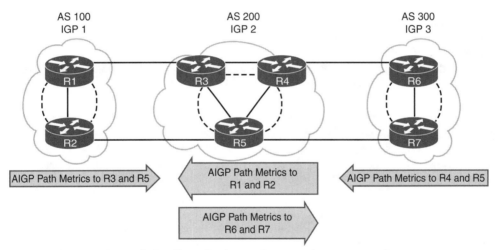

Figure 13-4 *AIGP Path Attribute Exchange Between Autonomous Systems*

AIGP PA exchanges must be agreed upon between the BGP peers, and AIGP metrics are only included in prefix advertisements between AIGP-enabled peers. AIGP metrics are enabled for a BGP neighbor with the BGP address family configuration command **neighbor** *ip-address* **aigp**.

The AIGP metric is a 32-bit (0 to 4,294,967,295) value that can be set during redistribution or during receipt of a prefix with a route map. Route maps use the configuration command **set aigp-metric** {**igp-metric** | *metric*}. The **igp-metric** keyword sets the value to the IGP path metric on the redistributing router for the specific route. Static routes and network advertisements populate the AIGP metric with the path metric to the next-hop address of the route.

The following guidelines apply to AIGP metrics:

- A path with an AIGP metric is preferred to a path without an AIGP metric.

- If the next-hop address requires a recursive lookup, the AIGP path needs to calculate a derived metric to include the distance to the next-hop address. This ensures that the cost to the BGP edge router is included. The formula is:

   Derived AIGP Metric = (Original AIGP Metric + Next-Hop AIGRP Metric)

  - If multiple AIGP paths exist and one next-hop address contains an AIGP metric and the other does not, the non-AIGP path is not used.

  - The next-hop AIGP metric is recursively added if multiple lookups are performed.

- AIGP paths are compared based on the derived AIGP metric (with recursive next hops) or the actual AIGP metric (nonrecursive next hop). The path with the lower AIGP metric is preferred.

- When router R2 advertises an AIGP-enabled path that was learned from R1, if the next-hop address changes to an R2 address, R2 increments the AIGP metric to reflect the distance (the IGP path metric) between R1 and R2.

Shortest AS_Path

The next decision factor for the BGP best-path algorithm is the AS_Path length, which typically correlates to the AS hop count. A shorter AS_Path is preferred over a longer AS_Path.

> **NOTE** When working with confederations, AS_CONFED_SEQUENCE (confederation AS_Path) is not counted, and for aggregated addresses with multiple autonomous system numbers (ASNs) under the AS_SET portion of AS_Path, the AS_SET counts for only one AS_Path entry.

Prepending ASNs to AS_Path makes the AS_Path longer, thereby making that path less desirable compared with other paths. You prepend paths by using the command **set as-path prepend** *as-number* on a route map. Typically, the AS_Path is prepended by the network owner, and the owner's own ASN is used for the prepending.

In general, a path that has had AS_Path prepended is not selected as the BGP best path because AS_Path is longer than the non-prepended path advertisement. Inbound traffic is influenced by prepending AS_Path length in advertisements sent to other ASs, and outbound traffic is influenced by prepending advertisements received from other ASs.

Figure 13-5 demonstrates how AS_Path prepending influences the outbound traffic pattern:

- R4, R5, and R6 are in AS 400, with iBGP full mesh peering using loopback interfaces. AS 200 and AS 300 provide transit connectivity to AS 100.

- R4 prepends AS 222 210 for the 172.24.0.0/24 path received from R2, making it the least preferred path for AS 400.

■ R6 prepends AS 333 321 for the 172.16.0.0/24 path received from R3, making it the least preferred path for AS 400.

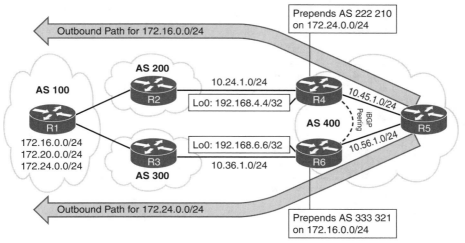

Figure 13-5 *Configuration for Modifying BGP AS_Path*

Example 13-9 shows R4's and R6's configuration for prepending AS_Path on R4 and R6.

Example 13-9 *BGP AS_Path Prepending Configuration*

```
R4
ip prefix-list PRE172 permit 172.24.0.0/24
!
route-map AS200 permit 10
 match ip address prefix-list PRE172
 set as-path prepend 222 210
route-map AS200 permit 20
!
router bgp 400
 neighbor 10.24.1.2 remote-as 200
 neighbor 10.24.1.2 route-map AS200 in
R6
ip prefix-list PRE172 permit 172.16.0.0/24
!
route-map AS300 permit 10
 match ip address prefix-list PRE172
 set as-path prepend 333 321
route-map AS300 permit 20
!
router bgp 400
 neighbor 10.36.1.3 remote-as 300
 neighbor 10.36.1.3 route-map AS300 in
```

Example 13-10 shows the BGP tables for R4, R5, and R6. All three routers have selected the path through R2 (AS 200) as the best path for the 172.16.0.0/24 network prefix because it has an AS_Path length of 2, whereas the path through R3 (AS 300) has an AS_Path length of 4. All three routers have selected the path through R3 (AS 300) as the best path for the 172.24.0.0/24 network prefix because it has the shortest AS_Path length.

Example 13-10   *BGP Tables After AS_Path Prepending*

```
R4# show bgp ipv4 unicast | begin Network
      Network          Next Hop          Metric LocPrf Weight Path
 *>   172.16.0.0/24    10.24.1.2                         0 200 100 i
 *>   172.20.0.0/24    10.24.1.2                         0 200 100 i
 * i                   192.168.6.6           0    100    0 300 100 i
 *    172.24.0.0/24    10.24.1.2                         0 222 210 200 100 i
 *>i                   192.168.6.6           0    100    0 300 100 i

R5# show bgp ipv4 unicast | begin Network
      Network          Next Hop          Metric LocPrf Weight Path
 *>i 172.16.0.0/24     192.168.4.4           0    100    0 200 100 i
 * i 172.20.0.0/24     192.168.4.4           0    100    0 200 100 i
 *>i                   192.168.6.6           0    100    0 300 100 i
 *>i 172.24.0.0/24     192.168.6.6           0    100    0 300 100 i

R6# show bgp ipv4 unicast | begin Network
      Network          Next Hop          Metric LocPrf Weight Path
 *>i 172.16.0.0/24     192.168.4.4           0    100    0 200 100 i
 *                     10.36.1.3                         0 333 321 300 100 i
 * i 172.20.0.0/24     192.168.4.4           0    100    0 200 100 i
 *>                    10.36.1.3                         0 300 100 i
 *>   172.24.0.0/24    10.36.1.3                         0 300 100 i
```

NOTE   Remember that BGP routers do not remove inferior routes. The routes must be withdrawn from a neighbor in order to be removed. The same phased approach for route advertisements that was explained earlier in this chapter, in the "Local Preference" section, applies here, too.

Origin Type

The next BGP best-path decision factor is the well-known mandatory BGP attribute named Origin. By default, networks that are advertised on Cisco routers using the network statement are set with the i (for IGP) Origin, and redistributed networks are assigned the ? (incomplete) Origin attribute. The origin preference order is as follows:

1. IGP Origin (Most)
2. Exterior Gateway Protocol (EGP) Origin
3. Incomplete Origin (Least)

You can modify a prefix's Origin attribute by using the command **set origin {igp | incomplete}** on a route map. The EGP Origin cannot be manually set on IOS XE routers.

Figure 13-6 demonstrates the modification of the origin attribute:

- R4, R5, and R6 are in AS 400, and AS 200 and AS 300 are providing transient connectivity to AS 100. AS 100 is advertising 172.16.0.0/24, 172.20.0.0/24, and 172.24.0.0/24 with the IGP Origin.

- R4 sets the Origin to incomplete for the 172.24.0.0/24 path received from R2, making it the least preferred path for R4, R5, and R6.

- R6 sets the Origin to incomplete for the 172.16.0.0/24 path received from R3, making it the least preferred path for R4, R5, and R6.

Example 13-11 shows R4's and R6's configuration for modifying the BGP Origin attribute on R4 and R6.

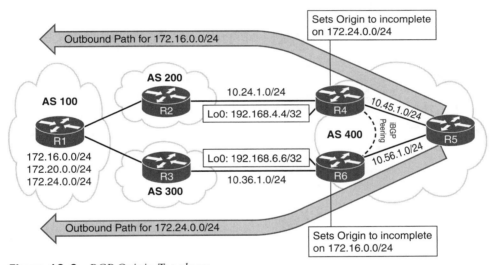

Figure 13-6 *BGP Origin Topology*

Example 13-11 *BGP Origin Manipulation Configuration*

```
R4
ip prefix-list PRE172 permit 172.24.0.0/24
!
route-map AS200 permit 10
 match ip address prefix-list PRE172
 set origin incomplete
route-map AS200 permit 20
!
router bgp 400
```

```
 neighbor 10.24.1.2 remote-as 200
 neighbor 10.24.1.2 route-map AS200 in
```

```
R6
ip prefix-list PRE172 permit 172.16.0.0/24
!
route-map AS300 permit 10
 match ip address prefix-list PRE172
 set origin incomplete
route-map AS300 permit 20
!
router bgp 400
 neighbor 10.36.1.3 remote-as 300
 neighbor 10.36.1.3 route-map AS300 in
```

Example 13-12 shows the BGP tables for R4, R5, and R6. A path with an incomplete Origin is not selected as the best path because the IGP Origin is preferred over the incomplete Origin. Notice the Origin codes (i and ?) on the far right, after the AS_Path information.

Example 13-12   *BGP Table After Origin Manipulation*

```
R4# show bgp ipv4 unicast
BGP table version is 21, local router ID is 192.168.4.4
Status codes: s suppressed, d damped, h history, * valid, > best, i - internal,
              r RIB-failure, S Stale, m multipath, b backup-path, f RT-Filter,
              x best-external, a additional-path, c RIB-compressed,
              t secondary path, L long-lived-stale,
Origin codes: i - IGP, e - EGP, ? - incomplete
RPKI validation codes: V valid, I invalid, N Not found

     Network          Next Hop         Metric LocPrf Weight Path
 *>  172.16.0.0/24    10.24.1.2                        0 200 100 i
 * i 172.20.0.0/24    192.168.6.6          0    100    0 300 100 i
 *>                   10.24.1.2                        0 200 100 i
 *>i 172.24.0.0/24    192.168.6.6          0    100    0 300 100 i
 *                    10.24.1.2                        0 200 100 ?
```
```
R5# show bgp ipv4 unicast | begin Network
     Network          Next Hop         Metric LocPrf Weight Path
 *>i 172.16.0.0/24    192.168.4.4          0    100    0 200 100 i
 * i 172.20.0.0/24    192.168.4.4          0    100    0 200 100 i
 *>i                  192.168.6.6          0    100    0 300 100 i
 *>i 172.24.0.0/24    192.168.6.6          0    100    0 300 100 i
```
```
R6# show bgp ipv4 unicast | begin Network
```

```
        Network            Next Hop         Metric LocPrf Weight Path
 *>i 172.16.0.0/24    192.168.4.4              0    100      0 200 100 i
 *                    10.36.1.3                             0 300 100 ?
 * i 172.20.0.0/24    192.168.4.4              0    100      0 200 100 i
 *>                   10.36.1.3                             0 300 100 i
 *>  172.24.0.0/24    10.36.1.3                             0 300 100 i
```

Multi-Exit Discriminator

The next BGP best-path decision factor is the non-transitive BGP *multi-exit discriminator* (*MED*) attribute. The MED uses a 32-bit value (0 to 4,294,967,295) called a *metric*. BGP sets the MED automatically to the IGP path metric during network advertisement or redistribution. If the MED is received from an eBGP session, it can be advertised to other iBGP peers, but it should not be sent outside the AS that received it. The MED's purpose is to influence traffic flows inbound from a different AS. A lower MED is preferred over a higher MED.

> **NOTE** In order for the MED to be an effective decision factor, the paths being decided upon must come from the same ASN.

RFC 4451 guidelines state that a prefix without a MED value should be given priority and, in essence, should be compared with the value 0. Some organizations require that a MED be set to a specific value for all the prefixes and declare that paths without the MED should be treated as the least preferred. By default, if the MED is missing from a prefix learned from an eBGP peer, devices use a MED of 0 for the best-path calculation. IOS routers advertise a MED of 0 to iBGP peers.

Figure 13-7 demonstrates the concept in a simple topology. AS 100 advertises the 172.16.0.0/24 and 172.20.0.0/24 network prefixes with different MED values at each edge router (R1 and R2). AS 200 sends traffic out R3 to the 172.16.0.0/24 network prefix because R1's MED (40) is lower than R2's MED (60). AS 200 sends traffic out R4 to the 172.20.0.0/24 network prefix because R2's MED (30) is lower than R1's MED (70).

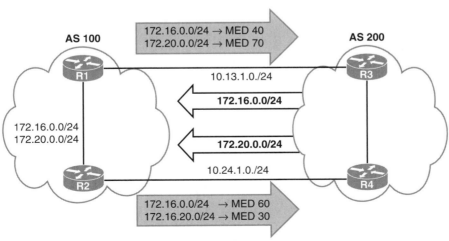

Figure 13-7 *MED Influencing Outbound Traffic*

You can use an inbound route map to set the MED with the command **set metric** *metric*. Figure 13-8 revisits the best-path selection topology but now places R2 and R3 both in AS 200, which is essential for MED to work properly. In this topology:

- R4, R5, and R6 are in AS 400, with iBGP full mesh peering using loopback interfaces. AS 200 provides transit connectivity to AS 100.

- R4 sets the MED to 40 for 172.16.0.0/24, 50 for 172.20.0.0/24, and 90 for 172.24.0.0/24.

- R6 sets the MED to 80 for 172.16.0.0/24 and 10 for 172.24.0.0/24.

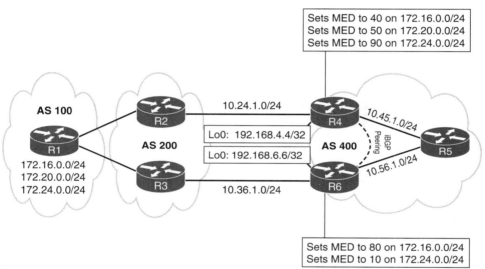

Figure 13-8 *BGP MED Manipulation*

Example 13-13 shows the configuration for manipulating the MED on R4 and R6, based on the guidelines in Figure 13-8.

Example 13-13 *Inbound Route-Map to Modify MED on Received Prefixes*

```
R4
ip prefix-list PRE172-01 permit 172.16.0.0/24
ip prefix-list PRE172-02 permit 172.20.0.0/24
ip prefix-list PRE172-03 permit 172.24.0.0/24
!
route-map AS200-R2 permit 10
 match ip address prefix-list PRE172-01
 set metric 40
route-map AS200-R2 permit 20
 match ip address prefix-list PRE172-02
 set metric 50
```

```
route-map AS200-R2 permit 30
 match ip address prefix-list PRE172-03
 set metric 90
route-map AS200-R2 permit 40
 !
router bgp 400
 neighbor 10.24.1.2 remote-as 200
 neighbor 10.24.1.2 route-map AS200-R2 in
```

```
R6
ip prefix-list PRE172-01 permit 172.16.0.0/24
ip prefix-list PRE172-03 permit 172.24.0.0/24
 !
route-map AS200-R3 permit 10
 match ip address prefix-list PRE172-01
 set metric 80
route-map AS200-R3 permit 20
 match ip address prefix-list PRE172-03
 set metric 10
route-map AS200-R3 permit 30
 !
router bgp 400
 neighbor 10.36.1.3 remote-as 200
 neighbor 10.36.1.3 route-map AS200-R3 in
```

Example 13-14 shows the BGP tables for R4, R5, and R6. All three AS 400 routers send traffic toward the 172.16.0.0/24 network prefix through R4's link to R2 because 40 is lower than 80, and all three AS 400 routers send traffic toward the 172.24.0.0/24 network prefix through R6's link to R3 because 10 is lower than 90.

Example 13-14 *R4, R5, and R6 BGP Tables After MED Modification*

```
R4# show bgp ipv4 unicast | begin Network
     Network          Next Hop         Metric LocPrf Weight Path
 *>  172.16.0.0/24    10.24.1.2            40            0 200 100 i
 *>i 172.20.0.0/24    192.168.6.6           0    100     0 200 100 i
 *                    10.24.1.2            50            0 200 100 i
 *>i 172.24.0.0/24    192.168.6.6          10    100     0 200 100 i
 *                    10.24.1.2            90            0 200 100 i
R5# show bgp ipv4 unicast | begin Network
     Network          Next Hop         Metric LocPrf Weight Path
 *>i 172.16.0.0/24    192.168.4.4          40    100     0 200 100 i
```

```
  *>i 172.20.0.0/24    192.168.6.6             0    100      0 200 100 i
  *>i 172.24.0.0/24    192.168.6.6            10    100      0 200 100 i

R6# show bgp ipv4 unicast | begin Network
      Network           Next Hop           Metric LocPrf Weight Path
  *>i 172.16.0.0/24    192.168.4.4            40    100      0 200 100 i
  *                    10.36.1.3             80             0 200 100 i
  *>  172.20.0.0/24    10.36.1.3                            0 200 100 i
  *>  172.24.0.0/24    10.36.1.3             10             0 200 100 i
```

Missing MED Behavior

An organization may expect its different SPs to advertise a MED value for every prefix. If a MED is missing, the path without a MED is preferred over a path that contains a MED. An organization can modify the default behavior so that prefixes without a MED are always selected last.

In Example 13-13, R6's route map is configured to not set the MED on the 172.20.0.0/24 prefix when received by R3. When the MED is not advertised, the value is assumed to be zero (0). All three routers in AS 400 evaluate the MED of 0 (from R3) versus 50 (from R2). The routers select the path through R3 as the preferred path.

Scenarios like this could lead to some unintended routing behavior. The command **bgp bestpath med missing-as-worst** under the BGP router process sets the MED to infinity (4,294,967,295) if the MED is missing from a path. The command should be placed on all nodes in an AS to keep the best-path algorithm configuration settings the same on all routers in the autonomous system.

The command **bgp bestpath med missing-as-worst** is applied to R4, R5, and R6. Example 13-15 shows their BGP tables after the change is made. Notice that R6 sets the MED to 4,294,967,295 for the 172.20.0.0/24 route learned from R3.

Example 13-15   *R4, R5, and R6 BGP Tables with* **med missing-as-worst**

```
R4# show bgp ipv4 unicast | begin Network
      Network           Next Hop           Metric LocPrf Weight Path
  *>  172.16.0.0/24    10.24.1.2             40             0 200 100 i
  *>  172.20.0.0/24    10.24.1.2             50             0 200 100 i
  *>i 172.24.0.0/24    192.168.6.6           10    100      0 200 100 i
  *                    10.24.1.2             90             0 200 100 i

R5# show bgp ipv4 unicast | begin Network
      Network           Next Hop           Metric LocPrf Weight Path
  *>i 172.16.0.0/24    192.168.4.4           40    100      0 200 100 i
  *>i 172.20.0.0/24    192.168.4.4           50    100      0 200 100 i
  *>i 172.24.0.0/24    192.168.6.6           10    100      0 200 100 i

R6# show bgp ipv4 unicast | begin Network
      Network           Next Hop           Metric LocPrf Weight Path
```

```
 *>i  172.16.0.0/24    192.168.4.4              40    100      0 200 100 i
 *                     10.36.1.3                80             0 200 100 i
 *>i  172.20.0.0/24    192.168.4.4              50    100      0 200 100 i
 *                     10.36.1.3        4294967295             0 200 100 i
 *>   172.24.0.0/24    10.36.1.3                10             0 200 100 i
```

NOTE The BGP configuration command **default-metric** *metric* sets the metric to the value specified when a path is received without a MED. This allows routers to calculate the BGP best path for prefixes without requiring that the MED attribute be set manually or be set to infinity.

Always Compare MED

The default MED comparison mechanism requires the AS_Path values to be identical because the policies used to set the MED could vary from AS to AS. This means that the MED can influence traffic only when multiple links are from the same service provider. Typically, organizations use different service providers for redundancy. In these situations, the default BGP rules for MED comparison need to be relaxed to compare MEDs between different service providers.

The **always-compare-med** feature allows for the comparison of MED regardless of the AS_Path. You enable this feature by using the BGP configuration command **bgp always-compare-med**.

NOTE Enable this feature on all BGP routers in the AS, or routing loops can occur.

BGP Deterministic MED

The best-path algorithm compares a route update to the existing best path and processes the paths in the order in which they are stored in the *Loc-RIB table*. The paths are stored in the order in which they are received in the BGP table. If **always-compare-med** is not enabled, the path MED is only compared against the existing best path and not against all the paths in the Loc-RIB table, which can cause variations in the MED best-path comparison process.

Figure 13-9 demonstrates a topology in which the MED is not compared due to the order of the path advertisement:

- R4 advertises the 172.16.0.0/24 prefix with a MED of 200, and R5 selects R4's path as the best path because no other paths exist.

- R3 advertises the 172.16.0.0/24 prefix with a MED of 100. The AS_Path is from a different autonomous system compared to R4's, so the MED is not considered in the BGP best-path calculation. R4's path remains the best path because it is the oldest eBGP-learned route.

■ R2 advertises the 172.16.0.0/24 prefix with a MED of 150. The AS_Path differs from R4's, so MED is not considered in the BGP best-path calculation. R4's path remains the best path because it is the oldest eBGP-learned route.

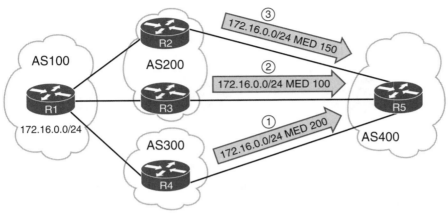

Figure 13-9 *Problems with MED Comparison*

BGP deterministic MED corrects the problem by grouping together paths with identical AS_ Path values as part of the best-path identification process. Each group's MED is compared against the other group's MED.

With BGP deterministic MED enabled, the best-path selection outcome is different. R2's and R3's paths are grouped together because they have an identical AS_Path value (200 100). R4 is placed into a separate group, by itself, because of its AS_Path (300 100). R3 is the best path for AS_Path group 200 100, and R4 is the best path for AS_Path group 300 100. The two AS_Path groups are then compared against each other, and because R3's MED is lower than R4's, R3's path is chosen as the best path, regardless of the order in which the routes are advertised.

BGP deterministic MED is enabled with the BGP configuration command **bgp deterministic-med** and is recommended for all BGP deployments in the same AS.

eBGP over iBGP

The next BGP best-path decision factor is whether the route comes from an iBGP, eBGP, or confederation member AS (Sub-AS) peering. The best-path selection order is as follows:

1. eBGP peers (most desirable)

2. Confederation member AS peers

3. iBGP peers (least desirable)

NOTE BGP confederations, which are briefly introduced in Chapter 11, are beyond the scope of the ENARSI 300-410 exam.

Lowest IGP Metric

The next decision step is to use the lowest IGP cost to the BGP next-hop address. Figure 13-10 illustrates a topology in which R2, R3, R4, and R5 are in AS 400, and the focus is on R3 and R5. AS 400 peers in a full mesh and establishes BGP sessions using Loopback 0 interfaces. R2 and R4 advertise network prefixes with the next-hop-self feature. R1 advertises the 172.16.0.0/24 network prefix to R2 and R4.

R3 prefers the path from R2 compared to the iBGP path from R4 because the metric to reach the next-hop address is lower. R5 prefers the path from R4 compared to the iBGP path from R2 because the metric to reach the next-hop address is lower.

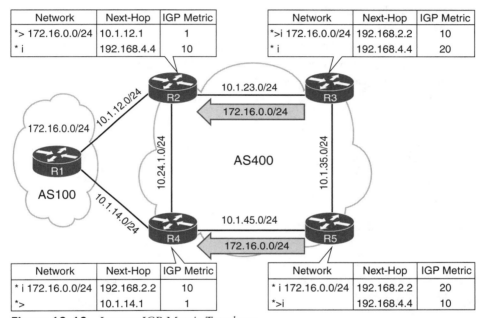

Figure 13-10 *Lowest IGP Metric Topology*

Prefer the Oldest EBGP Session

BGP can maintain large routing tables, and unstable sessions result in the BGP best-path calculation executing frequently. BGP maintains stability in a network by preferring the path from the oldest (established) BGP session. The downfall of this technique is that it does not lead to a deterministic method of identifying the BGP best path from a design perspective.

Router ID

The next step for the BGP best-path algorithm is to select the best path using the lowest router ID of the advertising EBGP router. If the route was received by a route reflector, then the originator ID is substituted for the router ID.

Minimum Cluster List Length

The next step in the BGP best-path algorithm is to select the best path using the lowest *cluster list* length. The cluster list is a non-transitive BGP attribute that is appended (not overwritten) by a route reflector with its cluster ID. Route reflectors use the **cluster-id** attribute as a loop-prevention mechanism. The cluster ID is not advertised between ASs and is locally significant. In simplest terms, this step locates the path that has traveled the smallest number of iBGP advertisement hops.

Figure 13-11 demonstrates how the minimum cluster list length is used as part of the BGP best-path calculation:

1. R3 advertises the 172.16.0.0/24 network prefix to RR1 and RR2 with only the originator ID.

2. RR1 reflects the advertisement to RR2 after appending its RID to the cluster list.

3. RR2 selects the path advertisement directly from R3. R3's cluster list length is 0, which is more desirable than RR1's cluster list length of 1.

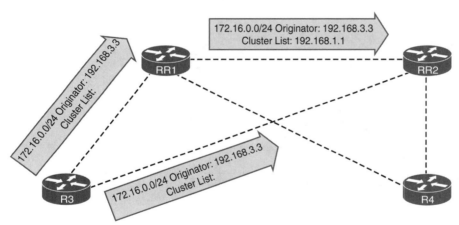

Figure 13-11   *Minimum Cluster List Length*

Lowest Neighbor Address

The last step of the BGP best-path algorithm involves selecting the path that comes from the lowest BGP neighbor address. This step is limited to iBGP peerings because eBGP peerings use the oldest received path as the tie breaker.

Figure 13-12 demonstrates the concept of choosing the router with the lowest neighbor address. R1 is advertising the 172.16.0.0/24 network prefix to R2. R1 and R2 have established two BGP sessions using the 10.12.1.0/24 and 10.12.2.0/24 network prefixes. R2 selects the path advertised from 10.12.1.1 as it is the lower IP address.

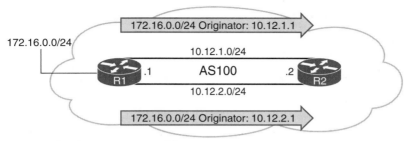

Figure 13-12 *Lowest IP Address*

BGP Multipath

All the IGP routing protocols explained in this book support equal-cost multipathing (ECMP). ECMP provides load balancing by installing multiple paths into the RIB for that protocol. BGP selects only one best path, but it allows for the installation of multiple routes into the RIB. *BGP multipath* has three different variants, only the first two of which are discussed in this book:

- eBGP multipath

- iBGP multipath

- eBGP and iBGP (eiBGP) multipath

Enabling BGP multipath does not alter the best-path algorithm or change the behavior of paths advertisement to other BGP peers. Only the BGP best path is advertised to peers.

When you configure BGP multipath, the additional paths need to match the following best-path BGP path attributes:

- Weight

- Local preference

- AS_Path length

- AS_Path content (although confederations can contain a different AS_CONFED_SEQ path)

- Origin

- MED

- Advertisement method (iBGP or eBGP) (If the prefix is learned from an iBGP advertisement, the IGP cost must match for iBGP and eBGP to be considered equal.)

You enable eBGP multipath by using the BGP configuration command **maximum-paths** *number-paths*. The number of paths indicates the allowed number of eBGP paths to install in the RIB. The command **maximum-paths ibgp** *number-paths* sets the number of iBGP routes to install in the RIB. The commands are placed under the appropriate address family.

Exam Preparation Tasks

As mentioned in the section "How to Use This Book" in the Introduction, you have a couple choices for exam preparation: the exercises here, Chapter 24, "Final Preparation," and the exam simulation questions in the Pearson Test Prep software.

Review All Key Topics

Review the most important topics in this chapter, noted with the Key Topic icon in the outer margin of the page. Table 13-3 lists these key topics and the page number on which each is found.

Table 13-3 Key Topics

Key Topic Element	Description	Page Number
Paragraph	BGP preference for the longest prefix length	526
Paragraph	Use of summarization to direct traffic flows	526
Paragraph	BGP best path	527
Table 13-2	BGP path attribute classifications	528
Paragraph	Weight	528
Paragraph	Local preference	532
Paragraph	Path removal with multiple paths	535
Paragraph	Local route origination	538
Paragraph	Accumulated Interior Gateway Protocol (AIGP)	539
Paragraph	Shortest AS_Path	540
Paragraph	Origin type	542
Paragraph	Multi-exit discriminator	545
Paragraph	Missing MED behavior	548
Paragraph	MED comparison	549
Paragraph	BGP deterministic MED	549
Paragraph	eBGP over iBGP	550
Paragraph	Lowest IGP metric	551
Paragraph	BGP equal-cost multipathing	553
Paragraph	Multipathing requirements	553

Define Key Terms

Define the following key terms from this chapter and check your answers in the glossary:

optional transitive, optional non-transitive, well-known mandatory, well-known discretionary, Loc-RIB table, BGP multipath

Use the Command Reference to Check Your Memory

The ENARSI 300-410 exam focuses on the practical, hands-on skills that networking professionals use. Therefore, you should be able to identify the commands needed to configure, verify, and troubleshoot the topics covered in this chapter.

This section includes the most important configuration and verification commands covered in this chapter. It might not be necessary to memorize the complete syntax of every command, but you should be able to remember the basic keywords that are needed.

To test your memory of the commands in Table 13-4, go to the companion website and download Appendix B, "Command Reference Exercises." Fill in the missing commands in the tables based on each command description. You can check your work by downloading Appendix C, "Command Reference Exercise Answer Key," from the companion website.

13

Table 13-4   Command Reference

Task	Command Syntax
Set the weight in a route map.	**set weight** *weight*
Set the weight for all routes learned from this neighbor.	**neighbor** *ip-address* **weight** *weight*
Set the local preference in a route map.	**set local-preference** *preference*
Set the local preference for all routes learned from this neighbor.	**neighbor** *ip-address* **local-preference** *preference*
Enable the advertise of AIGP path attributes.	**neighbor** *ip-address* **aigp**
Set the AIGP metric in a route map.	**set aigp-metric** {**igp-metric**	*metric*}
Set AS_Path prepending in a route map.	**set as-path prepend** *as-number*
Set the Origin using a route map.	**set origin** {**igp**	**incomplete**}
Set the MED using a route map.	**set metric** *metric*
Set the MED to infinity when the MED is not present.	**bgp bestpath med missing-as-worst**
Set the MED to the default value when the MED is not present.	**default-metric** *metric*
Ensure that MED is always compared, regardless of AS_Path.	**bgp always-compare-med**
Group together paths with identical AS_Path values as part of the best-path identification process.	**bgp deterministic-med**
Configure eBGP multipathing.	**maximum-paths** *number-paths*
Configure iBGP multipathing.	**maximum-paths ibgp** *number-paths*

## CHAPTER 14

Troubleshooting BGP

This chapter covers the following topics:

■ **Troubleshooting BGP Neighbor Adjacencies:** This section examines issues that may prevent a BGP neighbor relationship from forming and how to recognize and trouble-shoot these issues. Although this section focuses primarily on IPv4 unicast BGP, the same issues arise with IPv6 unicast BGP neighbor relationships.

■ **Troubleshooting BGP Routes:** This section focuses on issues that may prevent BGP routes from being learned or advertised and how to recognize and troubleshoot these issues. Although this section focuses mostly on IPv4 unicast BGP, the same issues arise with IPv6 unicast BGP routes as well.

■ **Troubleshooting BGP Path Selection:** This section explains how BGP determines the best path to reach a destination network and the importance of understanding how this process works for troubleshooting purposes.

■ **Troubleshooting BGP for IPv6:** This section discusses the methods used to success-fully troubleshoot additional issues related to BGP for IPv6 that are not seen with BGP for IPv4.

■ **BGP Trouble Tickets:** This section presents trouble tickets that demonstrate how to use a structured troubleshooting process to solve a reported problem.

■ **MP-BGP Trouble Tickets:** This section presents a trouble ticket that demonstrates how to use a structured troubleshooting process to solve a reported problem.

Border Gateway Protocol (*BGP*) is the protocol of the Internet. It is designed to exchange routing information between autonomous systems (that is, networks under different adminis-trative control). That is why it is classified as an Exterior Gateway Protocol (*EGP*). It makes best-path decisions based on attributes such as local preference, length of autonomous sys-tem path, and even BGP router ID (RID) instead of bandwidth like Open Shortest Path First (OSPF), bandwidth and delay like Enhanced Interior Gateway Routing Protocol (EIGRP), or router hops like Routing Information Protocol (RIP). BGP is the most scalable, robust, con-trollable protocol. However, with that comes a price: mistakes that lead to issues that you have to troubleshoot.

This chapter describes the various issues that you may face when trying to establish an IPv4 and IPv6 external Border Gateway Protocol (*eBGP*) and internal Border Gateway Protocol (*iBGP*) neighbor adjacency and how you can identify and troubleshoot these issues. The chapter also covers issues that may arise when exchanging IPv4 and IPv6 eBGP and iBGP routes and how you can recognize and troubleshoot them successfully. Because BGP is classified as a path vector protocol and its decisions are based on attributes, to be an efficient troubleshooter, you need to be very familiar with the decision-making process that BGP uses. Therefore, you will spend time exploring this process in the chapter as well.

"Do I Know This Already?" Quiz

The "Do I Know This Already?" quiz allows you to assess whether you should read this entire chapter thoroughly or jump to the "Exam Preparation Tasks" section. If you are in doubt about your answers to these questions or your own assessment of your knowledge of the topics, read the entire chapter. Table 14-1 lists the major headings in this chapter and their corresponding "Do I Know This Already?" quiz questions. You can find the answers in Appendix A, "Answers to the 'Do I Know This Already?' Quiz Questions."

Table 14-1 "Do I Know This Already?" Foundation Topics Section-to-Question Mapping

Foundation Topics Section	Questions
Troubleshooting BGP Neighbor Adjacencies	1–5
Troubleshooting BGP Routes	6–10
Troubleshooting BGP Path Selection	11
Troubleshooting BGP for IPv6	12, 13

CAUTION The goal of self-assessment is to gauge your mastery of the topics in this chapter. If you do not know the answer to a question or are only partially sure of the answer, you should mark that question as wrong for purposes of self-assessment. Giving yourself credit for an answer that you correctly guess skews your self-assessment results and might provide you with a false sense of security.

1. Which commands enable you to identify the IPv4 unicast BGP neighbor adjacencies that have been formed? (Choose two.)
   a. show ip route bgp
   b. show bgp ipv4 unicast
   c. show bgp ipv4 unicast summary
   d. show bgp ipv4 unicast neighbors

2. In the output of **show bgp ipv4 unicast summary**, how can you determine whether a neighbor relationship is successfully established?
   a. The neighbor is listed in the output.
   b. The Version column has a 4 in it.
   c. The State/PfxRcd column has a number in it.
   d. The State/PfxRcd column has the word Active in it.

3. Which of the following are reasons a BGP neighbor relationship might not form? (Choose two.)

   a. The BGP timers are mismatched.

   b. The BGP packets are sourced from the wrong IP address.

   c. The neighbor is reachable using a default route.

   d. The **network** command is misconfigured.

4. Which TCP port number is used to form BGP sessions?

   a. 110

   b. 123

   c. 179

   d. 443

5. What is the BGP state of a neighbor if a TCP session cannot be formed?

   a. Open

   b. Idle

   c. Active

   d. Established

6. What could prevent a route from being advertised to another BGP router? (Choose three.)

   a. Mismatched timers

   b. Split-horizon rule

   c. Missing **network mask** command

   d. Route filtering

7. Which command enables you to verify the IPv4 BGP routes that have been learned from all BGP neighbors?

   a. **show ip route bgp**

   b. **show bgp ipv4 unicast**

   c. **show bgp ipv4 unicast summary**

   d. **show bgp ipv4 unicast neighbors**

8. What occurs when the next hop of a BGP-learned route is not reachable?

   a. The route is discarded.

   b. The route is placed in the BGP table and advertised to other neighbors.

   c. The route is placed in the BGP table and not marked as valid.

   d. The route is placed in the BGP table and in the routing table.

9. Which of the following describes the BGP split-horizon rule?

   a. A BGP router that receives a BGP route from an iBGP peering shall not advertise that route to another router that is an iBGP peer.

   b. A BGP router that receives a BGP route from an eBGP peering shall not advertise that route to another router that is an iBGP peer.

   c. A BGP router that receives a BGP route from an eBGP peering shall not advertise that route to another router that is an eBGP peer.

   d. A BGP router that receives a BGP route from an iBGP peering shall discard the route.

10. Which of the following administrative distances are correct? (Choose two.)

    a. 20 for eBGP

    b. 20 for iBGP

    c. 200 for eBGP

    d. 200 for iBGP

11. Which of the following correctly identifies the order of BGP attributes for the best-path decision process?

    a. Weight, local preference, route origin, AS_Path, origin code, MED

    b. AS_Path, origin code, MED, weight, local preference, route origin

    c. Local preference, weight, route origin, AS_Path, origin code, MED

    d. Weight, local preference, route origin, AS_Path, MED, origin code

12. What do you need to do when using MP-BGP? (Choose two.)

    a. Activate the IPv6 neighbors in address family configuration mode.

    b. Activate the IPv6 neighbors in router configuration mode.

    c. Define the IPv6 neighbors in router configuration mode.

    d. Define the IPv6 neighbors in address family configuration mode.

13. Which command enables you to verify the IPv6 unicast BGP routes that have been learned?

    a. **show bgp ipv6 unicast**

    b. **show bgp ipv6 unicast summary**

    c. **show bgp ipv6 unicast neighbor**

    d. **show ipv6 route bgp**

Foundation Topics

Troubleshooting BGP Neighbor Adjacencies

With BGP, you need to establish neighbor adjacencies manually. This is unlike EIGRP and OSPF, where you enable the process on an interface, and neighbor adjacencies are formed dynamically. As a result, BGP configuration is more prone to human error, which means greater effort is often needed during the troubleshooting process. In addition, there are two flavors of BGP: internal BGP (iBGP) and external BGP (eBGP). Understanding the differences between the two and recognizing issues related to each of them is important for troubleshooting.

This section covers how BGP neighbor relationships are formed and how to recognize issues that prevent neighbor relationships from forming.

To verify IPv4 unicast BGP neighbors, you can use two **show** commands: **show bgp ipv4 unicast summary** (which works the same way as the old **show ip bgp summary** command), and **show bgp ipv4 unicast neighbors** (which works the same way as the old **show ip bgp neighbors** command). For initial verification of neighbors, it is best to use **show bgp ipv4 unicast summary** because it provides condensed output. The output of **show bgp ipv4 unicast neighbors** is very verbose and is not needed for initial neighbor verification.

Example 14-1, which shows sample output of the **show bgp ipv4 unicast summary** command, indicates that R1 has two BGP neighbors. One is at IP address 10.1.12.2, and the other is at 10.1.13.3. They are both eBGP neighbors because their autonomous system numbers (ASNs) do not match the local ASNs. Focus your attention on the State/PfxRcd column. If there is a number in this column (as there is in Example 14-1), it means you have successfully established a BGP neighbor relationship. If you see Idle or Active, there is a problem in the formation of the neighbor relationship.

Example 14-1 *Verifying BGP Neighbors with show bgp ipv4 unicast summary*

```
R1# show bgp ipv4 unicast summary
BGP router identifier 10.1.13.1, local AS number 65501
BGP table version is 1, main routing table version 1


Neighbor       V    AS     MsgRcvd MsgSent   TblVer  InQ OutQ Up/Down   State/PfxRcd
10.1.12.2      4   65502      16      16        1     0    0 00:11:25       0
10.1.13.3      4   65502      15      12        1     0    0 00:09:51       0
```

In addition, when a neighbor relationship is formed, a syslog message similar to the following is generated:

```
%BGP-5-ADJCHANGE: neighbor 10.1.12.2 Up
```

The following are some of the reasons a BGP neighbor relationship might not form:

- **Interface is down:** The interface must be up/up.

- **Layer 3 connectivity is broken:** You need to be able to reach the IP address you are trying to form the adjacency with.

- **Path to the neighbor is through the default route:** You must be able to reach the neighbor using a route other than the default route.

- **Neighbor does not have a route to the local router:** The two routers forming a BGP peering must have routes to each other.

- **Incorrect neighbor statement:** The IP address and ASN in the **neighbor** *ip_address* **remote-as** *as_number* statement must be accurate.

- **ACLs:** An access control list (ACL) or a firewall may be blocking TCP (Transmission Control Protocol) port 179.

- **BGP packets sourced from the wrong IP address:** The source IP (Internet Protocol) address of an inbound BGP packet must match the local neighbor statement.

- **The TTL (time-to-live) of the BGP packet expires:** The peer may be further away than is permitted.

- **Mismatched authentication:** The two routers must agree on the authentication parameters.

- **Misconfigured peer group:** Peer groups simplify repetitive BGP configurations; however, if not carefully implemented, they can prevent neighbor relationships from forming or routes from being learned.

- **Timers:** Timers do not have to match; however, if the *minimum holddown from neighbor* option is set, it could prevent a neighbor adjacency.

When troubleshooting BGP neighbor adjacencies, you need to be able to identify these issues and understand why they occur. Let's look at them individually.

Interface Is Down

The interface with the IP address that is being used to form BGP neighbor relationships must be up/up. This could be a physical or logical interface. Remember that you can use a loopback interface to source BGP packets. This practice is popular when you have redundant paths between neighbors. In such a case, if one path fails—for example, if a local physical interface goes down—the neighbor relationship is still available using another local physical interface since a loopback interface is the source and destination of the packets. Therefore, if you are sourcing BGP packets with the IP address of Loopback 0, the loopback interface must be up/up, and so must any physical interface that can get you to the IP address you are trying to form the neighbor relationship with.

As you have seen numerous times in this book, you can verify the status of an interface by using the **show ip interface brief** command.

Layer 3 Connectivity Is Broken

You do not have to be directly connected or in the same subnet to form a BGP neighbor relationship; however, you do need to have Layer 3 connectivity. To verify Layer 3 connectivity, you use the **ping** command. If the ping is successful, you have Layer 3 connectivity. Note that for a router to have Layer 3 connectivity, it needs to have a route in the routing table that points it in the right direction. If no route to the neighbor exists, a neighbor relationship cannot form.

When reviewing the output of **show bgp ipv4 unicast summary** in Example 14-2, notice that the State/PfxRcd field says Idle. This state occurs when the local router is not able to make a TCP connection with the neighbor. In this example, the neighbor is the router at 2.2.2.2 with which R5 is trying to form an adjacency. Reviewing the routing table on R5 with the **show ip route 2.2.2.2 255.255.255.255** command and pinging 2.2.2.2 from R5, as shown in Example 14-3, proves that Layer 3 connectivity does not exist. It is a good idea to specify the source when pinging. The source is the IP address of the local device you plan on making the BGP peering with.

Example 14-2 *Verifying BGP State with show bgp ipv4 unicast summary*

```
R5# show bgp ipv4 unicast summary
BGP router identifier 10.1.45.5, local AS number 65502
BGP table version is 1, main routing table version 1


Neighbor    V   AS      MsgRcvd MsgSent   TblVer  InQ OutQ  Up/Down  State/PfxRcd
2.2.2.2     4   65502      0       0         1      0   0    never    Idle
```

Example 14-3   *Verifying Whether a Route Exists to the Neighbor and Whether a Ping Is Successful*

```
R5# show ip route 2.2.2.2 255.255.255.255
% Network not in table


R5# ping 2.2.2.2 source 5.5.5.5
Type escape sequence to abort.
Sending 5, 100-byte ICMP Echos to 2.2.2.2, timeout is 2 seconds:
.....
Success rate is 0 percent (0/5)
```

Path to the Neighbor Is Through the Default Route

Continuing with the previous discussion on Layer 3 connectivity being broken, Example 14-4 shows that no route to 2.2.2.2 exists; however, a ping to 2.2.2.2 is successful. This is because there is a default route in the routing table on R5, as shown in Example 14-5.

Example 14-4   *No Route to Neighbor, but Ping Is Successful*

```
R5# show ip route 2.2.2.2 255.255.255.255
% Network not in table


R5# ping 2.2.2.2 source 5.5.5.5
Type escape sequence to abort.
Sending 5, 100-byte ICMP Echos to 2.2.2.2, timeout is 2 seconds:
Packet sent with a source address of 5.5.5.5
!!!!!
Success rate is 100 percent (5/5), round-trip min/avg/max = 84/91/104 ms
```

Example 14-5   *Verifying That the Default Route Exists in the Routing Table*

```
R5# show ip route
...output omitted...


Gateway of last resort is 10.1.45.4 to network 0.0.0.0

D*EX  0.0.0.0/0 [170/3328] via 10.1.45.4, 00:08:37, GigabitEthernet1/0
      3.0.0.0/32 is subnetted, 1 subnets
D        3.3.3.3 [90/131072] via 10.1.45.4, 00:53:34, GigabitEthernet1/0
      4.0.0.0/32 is subnetted, 1 subnets
D        4.4.4.4 [90/130816] via 10.1.45.4, 00:53:19, GigabitEthernet1/0
...output omitted...
```

Even though you can reach the neighbor by using the default route, BGP does not consider it a valid route for forming an adjacency. Look at the output of **show bgp ipv4 unicast**

summary on R5 in Example 14-6 and notice that the state is Idle, which indicates that you cannot form a TCP session.

Example 14-6 *Verifying the BGP State on R5 with show bgp ipv4 unicast summary*

```
R5# show bgp ipv4 unicast summary
BGP router identifier 10.1.45.5, local AS number 65502
BGP table version is 1, main routing table version 1


Neighbor     V    AS   MsgRcvd MsgSent   TblVer  InQ OutQ  Up/Down  State/PfxRcd
2.2.2.2      4  65502        0       0        1    0    0  never    Idle
```

Neighbor Does Not Have a Route to the Local Router

You have seen that the local router displays the state Idle when it does not have a route to the IP address it is trying to peer with. However, Idle also appears on a router when the neighbor does not have a route back to the local router. In Example 14-7, you can see that R2, which is trying to form a BGP peering with R5, also displays the state Idle even though it has a route to 5.5.5.5, as shown in Example 14-7. The Idle state appears because the routers cannot form the TCP session.

Example 14-7 *Verifying BGP State on R2 and the Route to 5.5.5.5*

```
R2# show bgp ipv4 unicast summary
BGP router identifier 2.2.2.2, local AS number 65502
BGP table version is 1, main routing table version 1


Neighbor     V    AS   MsgRcvd MsgSent   TblVer  InQ OutQ Up/Down  State/PfxRcd
5.5.5.5      4  65502        0       0        1    0    0 00:00:13  Idle
10.1.12.1    4  65501        2       2        1    0    0 00:00:12         0


R2# show ip route 5.5.5.5 255.255.255.255
Routing entry for 5.5.5.5/32
  Known via "eigrp 100", distance 90, metric 131072, type internal
  Redistributing via eigrp 100
  Last update from 10.1.24.4 on GigabitEthernet2/0, 00:23:58 ago
  Routing Descriptor Blocks:
  * 10.1.24.4, from 10.1.24.4, 00:23:58 ago, via GigabitEthernet2/0
      Route metric is 131072, traffic share count is 1
      Total delay is 5020 microseconds, minimum bandwidth is 1000000 Kbit
      Reliability 255/255, minimum MTU 1500 bytes
      Loading 1/255, Hops 2
```

Incorrect neighbor Statement

To form a BGP peering, you use the **neighbor** *ip_address* **remote-as** *as_number* command in BGP configuration mode. Example 14-8 displays two **neighbor remote-as** commands on R2. The **neighbor 5.5.5.5 remote-as 65502** command forms an iBGP peering, and neighbor **10.1.12.1 remote-as 65501** forms an eBGP peering. The iBGP peering is established because *remote-as 65502* matches the local ASN used to create the BGP process (*router bgp 65502*). The eBGP peering is established because *remote-as 65501* is different from the local ASN used to create the BGP process (*router bgp 65502*).

Example 14-8   *Verifying **neighbor remote-as** Commands on R2*

```
R2# show run | s router bgp
router bgp 65502
 bgp log-neighbor-changes
 neighbor 5.5.5.5 remote-as 65502
 neighbor 5.5.5.5 update-source Loopback0
 neighbor 10.1.12.1 remote-as 65501
```

There are two very important parts to this command: the address of the peer with which you form the peering and the autonomous system that the peer is in. If you make a mistake with either of these, you see either the Active or Idle state.

As discussed earlier, if there is no route for the IP address you specify, the state is Idle. However, if a route is found and a three-way TCP handshake is complete, an open message is sent. If there is no response to the open message, the state is Active.

If the ASN specified does not match the peer's ASN, the state toggles between Idle and Active.

You can verify the state of the TCP session on the routers by using the **show tcp brief all** command. In Example 14-9, notice that R2 has an established TCP session with a device at 5.5.5.5 and another device at 10.1.12.1.

Example 14-9   *Verifying the State of TCP Sessions*

```
R2# show tcp brief all
TCB        Local Address          Foreign Address          (state)
68DD357C   10.1.12.2.179          10.1.12.1.35780          ESTAB
68DD24DC   2.2.2.2.179            5.5.5.5.45723            ESTAB
```

BGP Packets Sourced from the Wrong IP Address

In a redundant topology, a BGP router has multiple active IP addresses configured across its various interfaces. Figure 14-1 shows two BGP autonomous systems. Notice that R2, R3, and R4 could form a BGP peering with each other, using any physical interface, because of the multiple paths. For example, R2 could form a peering with R4 over the direct connection or through the connection through R3.

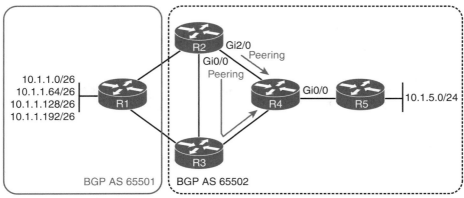

Figure 14-1 *Sample BGP Autonomous System with Redundancy*

When you issue the **neighbor** *ip_address* **remote-as** *as_number* command on a router, the *ip_address* specified is used by the router to determine whether the BGP open message came from a router it should establish a BGP peering with. The BGP open message has a source IP address, and the source IP address is compared with the address in the local **neighbor** *ip_address* **remote-as** *as_number* command. If they match, a BGP peering is formed; if not, no BGP peering is formed. By default, the source address is based on the exit interface of the router sending the BGP open message. Therefore, if R2 sends the BGP open message from Gi2/0 to R4, R4 needs to have a **neighbor** statement with R2's Gi2/0 IP address. Now, if the link between R2 and R4 fails, R2 and R4 can still peer using the links through R3. However, now R2 sends the BGP open message with the source IP address of Gi0/0, but R4's **neighbor remote-as** statement is using the Gi2/0 IP address of R2 still, and as a result, no BGP peering is formed because the BGP packets are sourced from the wrong IP address.

To control the IP address that is used when sending BGP messages, you use the **neighbor** *ip_address* **update-source** *interface_type interface_number* command. Example 14-10 shows the output of **show run | section router bgp** on R2. Notice that the peering with R4 is using the address 4.4.4.4 (which is a loopback interface on R4), and all BGP messages sent to 4.4.4.4 use the IP address of Loopback 0, which is 2.2.2.2, as shown in Example 14-10 as well.

Example 14-10 *Verifying the Neighbor Statements and Loopback IP Address on R2*

```
R2# show run | section router bgp
router bgp 65502
 bgp log-neighbor-changes
 neighbor 4.4.4.4 remote-as 65502
 neighbor 4.4.4.4 update-source Loopback0
 neighbor 10.1.12.1 remote-as 65501

R2# show ip interface brief | include Loopback
Loopback0       2.2.2.2        YES       manual up       up
```

It is imperative that R4 be configured appropriately. In this case, R4 needs to have a **neighbor remote-as** statement using R2's address 2.2.2.2 in addition to a **neighbor** statement with the **update-source** option that allows it to control the source address of BGP messages sent to R2. Example 14-11 shows the appropriate configuration on R4 to ensure that a BGP peering is successful.

Example 14-11   *Verifying That R4's BGP Configuration Mirrors That of R2*

```
R4# show run | section router bgp
router bgp 65502
 bgp log-neighbor-changes
 neighbor 2.2.2.2 remote-as 65502
 neighbor 2.2.2.2 update-source Loopback0

R4# show ip interface brief | include Loopback
Loopback0       4.4.4.4         YES     manual up          up
```

ACLs

BGP uses TCP port 179 to establish TCP sessions. A TCP session is then used to form a BGP peering. If an access control list (ACL) is blocking TCP port 179 anywhere in the path between the routers attempting to form a BGP peering, the peering does not happen. In Example 14-12, R4 (refer to Figure 14-1) has ACL 100 attached to interface Gig0/0, which denies packets sourced or destined to port 179 (BGP). As a result, a BGP peering between R2 and R5 is not possible as the packets related to BGP port 179 are being denied. At the bottom of Example 14-12, the state is Idle on R5 because the TCP session cannot be established with the neighbor at 2.2.2.2 because R4 is denying TCP traffic related to port 179.

Example 14-12   *Verifying ACLs Blocking BGP Packets and the State of R5's Neighbor Relationship*

```
R4# show access-lists
Extended IP access list 100
    10 deny tcp any any eq bgp
    20 deny tcp any eq bgp any
    30 permit ip any any

R4# show ip interface gigabitEthernet 0/0 | include access list
 Outgoing access list is 100
  Inbound access list is not set

R5# show bgp ipv4 unicast summary
BGP router identifier 10.1.45.5, local AS number 65502
BGP table version is 1, main routing table version 1


Neighbor     V    AS  MsgRcvd MsgSent   TblVer  InQ OutQ  Up/Down   State/PfxRcd
2.2.2.2      4  65502       0       0        1    0    0  00:02:24  Idle
```

In Example 14-12, the access list is denying BGP packets sourced from or destined to port 179. However, what if the ACL were only blocking BGP port 179 packets in one direction? For example, what if the entry were **deny tcp any any eq bgp** only while still being applied to Gig0/0 outbound? This means that only packets destined to port 179 outbound on Gig0/0 would be blocked. What if they were sourced from 179 going outbound instead? They would no longer be blocked. So, in this case, if you could control who the server and clients are for the BGP TCP sessions, you could still form the BGP TCP session.

That's right: BGP sessions are server/client relationships. One router is using port 179 (server), and the other router is using an ephemeral port (client). By default, both routers try to establish a TCP session using the three-way handshake because both routers send a TCP syn packet sourced from an ephemeral port and destined to port 179. They both respond with a syn/ack sourced from 179 destined to the ephemeral port, and then both send an ack sourced from the ephemeral port destined to port 179. This causes two BGP sessions between the devices when there can be only one. This situation is called a *BGP connection collision*, and BGP sorts it out automatically. In a nutshell, the router with the higher BGP RID becomes the server.

If you want to avoid BGP connection collisions, you can control who the server and client are right from the start by using the **neighbor** *ip_address* **transport connection-mode {active | passive}** command. By specifying **active**, you indicate that you want the router to actively initiate the TCP session; therefore, **active** means client. By specifying **passive**, you are indicating that you want the router to passively wait for another router to initiate the TCP session; therefore, **passive** means server.

The output of the command **show bgp ipv4 unicast neighbors** shows the local and remote port numbers that are being used. If the local port is port 179 and the remote port is an ephemeral port, the local router is the server. If the remote port is 179 and the local port is an ephemeral port, the local router is the client. In Example 14-13, the command **show bgp ipv4 unicast neighbors | i ^BGP neighbor|Local port|Foreign port** is used to just display R2's neighbors along with the local port number and the foreign port number. Notice that R2 is the client for the TCP sessions with R1 (1.1.1.1), R4 (4.4.4.4), and R5 (5.5.5.5) because the local port is a random port number. R2 is the server for the TCP session with R3 because the local port is the BGP port number 179.

Example 14-13 *Verifying Local and Foreign BGP Port Numbers*

```
R2# show bgp ipv4 unicast neighbors | i ^BGP neighbor|Local port|Foreign port
BGP neighbor is 1.1.1.1, remote AS 65501, external link
Local host: 2.2.2.2, Local port: 23938
Foreign host: 1.1.1.1, Foreign port: 179
BGP neighbor is 3.3.3.3, remote AS 65502, internal link
Local host: 2.2.2.2, Local port: 179
Foreign host: 3.3.3.3, Foreign port: 45936
BGP neighbor is 4.4.4.4, remote AS 65502, internal link
Local host: 2.2.2.2, Local port: 34532
Foreign host: 4.4.4.4, Foreign port: 179
BGP neighbor is 5.5.5.5, remote AS 65502, internal link
Local host: 2.2.2.2, Local port: 49564
Foreign host: 5.5.5.5, Foreign port: 179
```

The TTL of the BGP Packet Expires

By default, an eBGP peering occurs between directly connected routers. This means the routers forming the eBGP peering are expected to be within 1 router hop of each other. With an iBGP peering, the routers can be up to 255 router hops from each other and still form a peering. Example 14-14 shows the output of **show bgp ipv4 unicast neighbors | include BGP neighbor|TTL**, which indicates that the eBGP neighbor at 10.1.12.1 must be reachable in 1 router hop, and the iBGP neighbor at 5.5.5.5 can be up to 255 hops away. If the neighbor is not reachable in the number of hops listed, the BGP packet expires, and no neighbor relationship is formed.

Example 14-14   *Verifying the TTLs of eBGP and iBGP Packets*

```
R2# show bgp ipv4 unicast neighbors | include BGP neighbor|TTL
BGP neighbor is 5.5.5.5, remote AS 65502, internal link
Minimum incoming TTL 0, Outgoing TTL 255
BGP neighbor is 10.1.12.1, remote AS 65501, external link
Minimum incoming TTL 0, Outgoing TTL 1
```

If the TTL is not large enough to support the distance required to form a BGP peering, the packet is discarded. As an example, try to form an eBGP peering between R1 and R2 in Figure 14-2 using their loopback interfaces. R1 has a loopback interface of 1.1.1.1, and R2 has a loopback interface of 2.2.2.2. Layer 3 connectivity has been tested with a ping, and it is successful. It is also not over a default route.

Example 14-15 shows the configuration of R1 and R2. Notice that R1 is peering with R2, using the neighbor address 2.2.2.2 (R2 loopback) and the source address of Loopback 0 (1.1.1.1). R2 is peering with R1 using the neighbor address 1.1.1.1 (R1 loopback) and source address of Loopback 0 (2.2.2.2). Note that these loopback interfaces are not directly connected (one hop away), and because it is an eBGP neighbor relationship, you can expect the peering to fail.

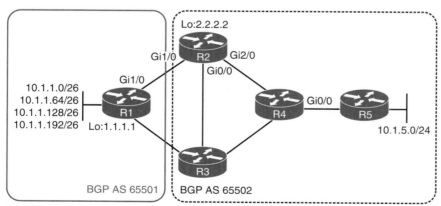

Figure 14-2   *Forming BGP Peering Between R1 and R2 Using Loopback Interfaces*

Example 14-15   *Verifying the BGP Configurations on R1 and R2*

```
R1# show run | s router bgp
router bgp 65501
 bgp log-neighbor-changes
 neighbor 2.2.2.2 remote-as 65502
 neighbor 2.2.2.2 update-source Loopback0
 neighbor 10.1.13.3 remote-as 65502


R2# show run | s router bgp
router bgp 65502
 bgp log-neighbor-changes
 neighbor 1.1.1.1 remote-as 65501
 neighbor 1.1.1.1 update-source Loopback0
 neighbor 5.5.5.5 remote-as 65502
 neighbor 5.5.5.5 update-source Loopback0
```

The output of **show bgp ipv4 unicast summary**, as shown in Example 14-16, clearly indicates that the peering is not forming as both routers are in the Idle state. This is a result of the eBGP peers' addresses not being directly connected (one router hop).

Example 14-16   *Verifying BGP States on R1 and R2*

```
R1# show bgp ipv4 unicast summary
BGP router identifier 10.1.13.1, local AS number 65501
BGP table version is 1, main routing table version 1


Neighbor      V     AS  MsgRcvd MsgSent   TblVer  InQ OutQ  Up/Down   State/PfxRcd
2.2.2.2       4  65502        0       0        1    0    0  never     Idle
10.1.13.3     4  65502       36      35        1    0    0  00:29:49             0


R2# show bgp ipv4 unicast summary
BGP router identifier 2.2.2.2, local AS number 65502
BGP table version is 1, main routing table version 1


Neighbor      V     AS  MsgRcvd MsgSent   TblVer  InQ OutQ  Up/Down   State/PfxRcd
1.1.1.1       4  65501        0       0        1    0    0  never     Idle
5.5.5.5       4  65502       27      26        1    0    0  00:20:52             0
```

To solve this issue with eBGP neighbors, you can modify the *TTL* of eBGP packets by using the **neighbor** *ip_address* **ebgp-multihop** [*TTL*] command. In this case, 2 would be enough to solve the issue. Therefore, on R1, you can type **neighbor 2.2.2.2 ebgp-multihop 2**, and on R2, you can type **neighbor 1.1.1.1 ebgp-multihop 2**. As you can see in Example 14-17, the output now states on R2 that neighbor 1.1.1.1 can be up to two hops away, and the peering is established, as shown in the output of **show bgp ipv4 unicast summary**. A trick to finding the number of hops is to use **traceroute** (as long as it's not being blocked by ACLs).

Example 14-17 *Verifying Modified TTLs of eBGP Packets*

```
R2# show bgp ipv4 unicast neighbors | include BGP neighbor|TTL
BGP neighbor is 1.1.1.1, remote AS 65501, external link
 External BGP neighbor may be up to 2 hops away.
BGP neighbor is 5.5.5.5, remote AS 65502, internal link
Minimum incoming TTL 0, Outgoing TTL 255


R2# show bgp ipv4 unicast summary
BGP router identifier 2.2.2.2, local AS number 65502
BGP table version is 1, main routing table version 1


Neighbor    V    AS    MsgRcvd MsgSent   TblVer  InQ  OutQ   Up/Down   State/PfxRcd
1.1.1.1     4    65501      2       4         1    0     0   00:00:04            0
5.5.5.5     4    65502     38      37         1    0     0   00:30:57            0
```

Mismatched Authentication

BGP supports Message Digest 5 (MD5) authentication between peers. As is typical with authentication, if any of the parameters do not match, a peering does not form. If you have syslog messaging turned on, a BGP authentication mismatch generates a syslog message like the following from the TCP facility:

```
%TCP-6-BADAUTH: No MD5 digest from 2.2.2.2(179) to 1.1.1.1(45577)
tableid - 0
```

In addition, the BGP state is Idle, as shown in Example 14-18.

Example 14-18 *Verifying Neighbor State with Mismatched Authentication*

```
R1# show bgp ipv4 unicast summary
BGP router identifier 1.1.1.1, local AS number 65501
BGP table version is 1, main routing table version 1


Neighbor    V    AS    MsgRcvd MsgSent   TblVer  InQ  OutQ   Up/Down   State/PfxRcd
2.2.2.2     4    65502      0       0         1    0     0   00:02:49   Idle
10.1.13.3   4    65502      7       5         1    0     0   00:02:48            0
```

Misconfigured Peer Groups

When a BGP-enabled router needs to send updates, it builds a separate update for each of its neighbors. When a router has a large number of BGP neighbors, this can have a significant impact on the router's CPU. To conserve processing power, you can implement BGP *peer groups*. With BGP peer groups, the router only has to run the BGP update for the entire group instead of on a neighbor-by-neighbor basis. However, even though the update is run only once, the TCP transmission must occur on a per-neighbor basis. In addition to saving CPU cycles, peer groups allow you to type or copy and paste less. Example 14-19 shows a sample peer group configuration.

When troubleshooting peer group issues, you need to look for the following possible culprits:

- **You forgot to associate the neighbor IP address with the peer group:** After the peer group is created, you need to use the **neighbor** *ip_address* **peer-group** *peer_group_ name* command to associate the neighbor with the configurations in the peer group. If you forget to do this, the neighbor IP address is not using the configurations in the peer group. It instead uses the BGP configurations outside the peer group, which could prevent a neighbor relationship from forming.

- **The peer group is not configured correctly:** It is possible that you overlooked the fact that what works for one neighbor might not work for the other. For example, using an update source of Loopback 0 may work well for the iBGP peer but not for the eBGP peer.

- **The route filter applied to the group is not appropriate for all the peers:** The filter applied using a route map or any other means may not provide the result you expect on all the routers. Be careful with filters and make sure they produce the desired results for all neighbors in the peer group.

- **Order of operations produces undesired results:** If there are conflicting entries between the peer group and a specific **neighbor** statement, the **neighbor** statement wins. In Example 14-19, the peer group states that the update source is Loopback 0. However, for neighbor 3.3.3.3, it states specifically that Loopback 1 is to be used, with the command **neighbor 3.3.3.3 update-source Loopback1**. This specific **neighbor** statement overrides the peer group.

Example 14-19 *Peer Group Configuration Example*

```
R2# show run | section router bgp
router bgp 65502
 bgp log-neighbor-changes
 network 10.1.5.0 mask 255.255.255.0
 neighbor ENARSI_IBGP_NEIGHBORS peer-group
 neighbor ENARSI_IBGP_NEIGHBORS transport connection-mode passive
 neighbor ENARSI_IBGP_NEIGHBORS update-source Loopback0
 neighbor ENARSI_IBGP_NEIGHBORS next-hop-self
 neighbor ENARSI_IBGP_NEIGHBORS route-map ENARSI_BGP_FILTER out
 neighbor 1.1.1.1 remote-as 65501
 neighbor 1.1.1.1 password CISCO
 neighbor 1.1.1.1 ebgp-multihop 2
 neighbor 1.1.1.1 update-source Loopback0
 neighbor 3.3.3.3 remote-as 65502
 neighbor 3.3.3.3 peer-group ENARSI_IBGP_NEIGHBORS
 neighbor 3.3.3.3 update-source Loopback1
 neighbor 4.4.4.4 remote-as 65502
 neighbor 4.4.4.4 peer-group ENARSI_IBGP_NEIGHBORS
 neighbor 5.5.5.5 remote-as 65502
 neighbor 5.5.5.5 peer-group ENARSI_IBGP_NEIGHBORS
```

14

Timers

To be clear, BGP timers do not have to match. This is because BGP uses the lowest timers set between the two neighbors. For example, if R1 is configured with a default hello of 60 and hold time of 180 and R3 is configured with a hello of 30 and hold time of 90, a hello of 30 and hold time of 90 will be used between the two neighbors, as shown in Example 14-20.

Notice in Example 14-20 that R3 is configured with a *minimum hold time* of 90 seconds; this ensures that if a neighbor is using aggressive timers, those timers will not be used. However, the situation is far worse than the timers simply not being used. The neighbor relationship does not form at all. Refer to Example 14-21. In this case, R1 has a hello interval set to 10 and hold time set to 30. R3 has the minimum hold time set to 90 seconds. Therefore, R3 does not agree with the 30-second hold time set by R1, and the neighbor relationship fails. You can see in the output that a BGP notification states that the hold time is not acceptable.

Example 14-20   *Verifying BGP Timers*

```
R1# show bgp ipv4 unicast neighbors 10.1.13.3 | include hold time|holdtime
  Last read 00:00:02, last write 00:00:29, hold time is 90, keepalive interval is 30
seconds
R3# show bgp ipv4 unicast neighbors 10.1.13.1 | include hold time|holdtime
  Last read 00:00:10, last write 00:00:23, hold time is 90, keepalive interval is 30
seconds
  Configured hold time is 90, keepalive interval is 30 seconds
  Minimum holdtime from neighbor is 90 seconds
```

Example 14-21   *Modifying BGP Timers to Values That Are Not Acceptable on R1*

```
R1# config t
Enter configuration commands, one per line. End with CNTL/Z.
R1(config)# router bgp 65501
R1(config-router)# neighbor 10.1.13.3 timers 10 30
R1(config-router)# do clear ip bgp 10.1.13.3
R1(config-router)#
%BGP-5-ADJCHANGE: neighbor 10.1.13.3 Down User reset
%BGP_SESSION-5-ADJCHANGE: neighbor 10.1.13.3 IPv4 Unicast topology base removed from
session User reset
%BGP-3-NOTIFICATION: received from neighbor 10.1.13.3 active 2/6 (unacceptable hold
time) 0 bytes
R1(config-router)#
%BGP-5-NBR_RESET: Neighbor 10.1.13.3 active reset (BGP Notification received)
%BGP-5-ADJCHANGE: neighbor 10.1.13.3 active Down BGP Notification received
%BGP_SESSION-5-ADJCHANGE: neighbor 10.1.13.3 IPv4 Unicast topology base removed from
session BGP Notification received
R1(config-router)#
%BGP-3-NOTIFICATION: received from neighbor 10.1.13.3 active 2/6 (unacceptable hold
time) 0 bytes
R1#
```

To summarize, timers do not have to match, but if the minimum hold time is set, the lowest timers must not be less than the minimum; if the lowest timers are less than the minimum, a neighbor relationship does not form.

Troubleshooting BGP Routes

After a BGP adjacency is formed, BGP routers exchange their BGP routes with each other. However, for various reasons, BGP routes might be missing from either the BGP table or the routing table. This section explains those reasons and how to identify and troubleshoot them.

As discussed earlier in this chapter, peers are the foundation of BGP information sharing. If you have no peers, you will not learn BGP routes. So, besides the lack of peers, what would be reasons for missing routes in a BGP network? Following is a listing of some common reasons BGP routes might be missing from either the BGP table or the routing table:

- **Missing or bad network mask command:** An accurate **network** command is needed to advertise routes.

- **Next-hop router not reachable:** To use a BGP route, the next hop must be reachable.

- **BGP split-horizon rule:** A router that learns BGP routes through an iBGP peering does not share those routes with another iBGP peer.

- **Better source of information:** If exactly the same network is learned from a more reliable source, it is used instead of the BGP-learned information.

- **Route filtering:** A filter might be preventing a route from being shared with neighbors or learned from neighbors.

To verify the IPv4 unicast BGP-learned routes or routes locally injected into the BGP table, you use the **show bgp ipv4 unicast** command (which is the same as the old **show ip bgp** command), as shown in Example 14-22. Routes appear in this table for the following reasons:

- Another BGP router advertises them to the local router.

- The **network mask** command matches a route in the local routing table.

- A **redistribute** command is used to import the route from another local source.

- The **aggregate-address** command is used to create a summary route.

It is not easy to determine the exact sources for all of the networks by looking only at the BGP table. By reviewing the commands in the running configuration along with the output of the BGP table, you can get the most accurate information. However, in the BGP table, a network with a next hop other than 0.0.0.0 indicates that the router learned it from a peer. If the next hop is 0.0.0.0, it means that the local router originated the route. If the Path column ends in ?, you can conclude that it was redistributed into the BGP process at some point. If the Path column ends in i, it means that the route was injected with the **aggregate-address** command or the **network mask** command.

Example 14-22 *Examining the BGP Table*

```
R1# show bgp ipv4 unicast
BGP table version is 10, local router ID is 1.1.1.1
Status codes: s suppressed, d damped, h history, * valid, > best, i - internal,
              r RIB-failure, S Stale, m multipath, b backup-path, f RT-Filter,
              x best-external, a additional-path, c RIB-compressed,
Origin codes: i - IGP, e - EGP, ? - incomplete
RPKI validation codes: V valid, I invalid, N Not found

     Network          Next Hop          Metric LocPrf Weight Path
*>   1.1.1.1/32       0.0.0.0                0          32768 ?
*>   10.1.1.0/26      0.0.0.0                0          32768 i
*>   10.1.1.0/24      0.0.0.0                           32768 i
*>   10.1.1.64/26     0.0.0.0                0          32768 i
*>   10.1.1.128/26    0.0.0.0                0          32768 i
*>   10.1.1.192/26    0.0.0.0                0          32768 i
*    10.1.5.0/24      10.1.13.3           3328              0 65502 i
*>                    2.2.2.2             3328              0 65502 i
*>   10.1.12.0/24     0.0.0.0                0          32768 ?
*>   10.1.13.0/24     0.0.0.0                0          32768 ?
```

To display the routing table, you use the **show ip route** command. To view only the BGP routes, you issue the command **show ip route bgp**, as shown in Example 14-23. All BGP routes appear with the code B at the beginning of each entry.

Example 14-23 *Examining the BGP Routes in the Routing Table*

```
R2# show ip route bgp
...output omitted...

Gateway of last resort is 10.1.12.1 to network 0.0.0.0

      10.0.0.0/8 is variably subnetted, 15 subnets, 3 masks
B         10.1.1.0/24 [20/0] via 1.1.1.1, 00:19:11
B         10.1.1.0/26 [20/0] via 1.1.1.1, 00:41:04
B         10.1.1.64/26 [20/0] via 1.1.1.1, 00:36:45
B         10.1.1.128/26 [20/0] via 1.1.1.1, 00:36:15
B         10.1.1.192/26 [20/0] via 1.1.1.1, 00:36:15
B         10.1.13.0/24 [20/0] via 1.1.1.1, 00:20:23
```

The following sections look at each of the possible reasons individually and describe how to recognize them during the troubleshooting process.

Missing or Bad network mask Command

The **network mask** command is used to advertise routes into BGP. If you only remember one thing about this command, remember that it is extremely picky:

- The network/prefix you want to advertise with BGP must be in the routing table from some other source (connected, static, or some other routing protocol).

- The **network mask** command must be a perfect match to the network/prefix listed in the routing table.

If these two requirements are not met, the prefix/network is not advertised. To practice identifying these requirements, review Example 14-24 and determine whether the 10.1.1.0/26 network is advertised.

Example 14-24 *Determining Whether the 10.1.1.0/26 Network Is Advertised*

```
R1# config t
Enter configuration commands, one per line. End with CNTL/Z.
R1(config)# router bgp 65501
R1(config-router)# network 10.1.1.0 mask 255.255.255.192
R1(config-router)# end
R1# show ip route
...output omitted...


Gateway of last resort is not set

      1.0.0.0/32 is subnetted, 1 subnets
C        1.1.1.1 is directly connected, Loopback0
      2.0.0.0/32 is subnetted, 1 subnets
S        2.2.2.2 [1/0] via 10.1.12.2
      10.0.0.0/8 is variably subnetted, 12 subnets, 3 masks
C        10.1.1.0/26 is directly connected, GigabitEthernet0/0.1
L        10.1.1.1/32 is directly connected, GigabitEthernet0/0.1
C        10.1.1.64/26 is directly connected, GigabitEthernet0/0.2
L        10.1.1.65/32 is directly connected, GigabitEthernet0/0.2
C        10.1.1.128/26 is directly connected, GigabitEthernet0/0.3
L        10.1.1.129/32 is directly connected, GigabitEthernet0/0.3
C        10.1.1.192/26 is directly connected, GigabitEthernet0/0.4
L        10.1.1.193/32 is directly connected, GigabitEthernet0/0.4
C        10.1.12.0/24 is directly connected, GigabitEthernet1/0
L        10.1.12.1/32 is directly connected, GigabitEthernet1/0
C        10.1.13.0/24 is directly connected, GigabitEthernet2/0
L        10.1.13.1/32 is directly connected, GigabitEthernet2/0
```

14

In Example 14-24, the 10.1.1.0/26 network is advertised because there is an exact match of the **network mask** command in the routing table.

Now review Example 14-25. Does the **network mask** command successfully advertise the route indicated here?

Example 14-25 *Determining Whether the Network Is Advertised*

```
R1# config t
Enter configuration commands, one per line. End with CNTL/Z.
R1(config)# router bgp 65501
R1(config-router)# network 10.1.1.0 mask 255.255.255.0
R1(config-router)# end
R1# show ip route
...output omitted...


Gateway of last resort is not set

      1.0.0.0/32 is subnetted, 1 subnets
C        1.1.1.1 is directly connected, Loopback0
      2.0.0.0/32 is subnetted, 1 subnets
S        2.2.2.2 [1/0] via 10.1.12.2
      10.0.0.0/8 is variably subnetted, 12 subnets, 3 masks
C        10.1.1.0/26 is directly connected, GigabitEthernet0/0.1
L        10.1.1.1/32 is directly connected, GigabitEthernet0/0.1
C        10.1.1.64/26 is directly connected, GigabitEthernet0/0.2
L        10.1.1.65/32 is directly connected, GigabitEthernet0/0.2
C        10.1.1.128/26 is directly connected, GigabitEthernet0/0.3
L        10.1.1.129/32 is directly connected, GigabitEthernet0/0.3
C        10.1.1.192/26 is directly connected, GigabitEthernet0/0.4
L        10.1.1.193/32 is directly connected, GigabitEthernet0/0.4
C        10.1.12.0/24 is directly connected, GigabitEthernet1/0
L        10.1.12.1/32 is directly connected, GigabitEthernet1/0
C        10.1.13.0/24 is directly connected, GigabitEthernet2/0
L        10.1.13.1/32 is directly connected, GigabitEthernet2/0
```

The **network mask** command in this case is 10.1.1.0/24. Although 10.1.1.0/24 as a summary would include 10.1.1.0/26, 10.1.1.64/26, 10.1.1.128/26, and 10.1.1.192/26, the **network mask** command states advertise this network (10.1.1.0/24). Because 10.1.1.0/24 is not in the routing table, nothing is advertised.

It is important that you be able to recognize a bad or missing **network mask** command as being the reason for missing routes. If a router is not learning a BGP route that it should be learning, and you trace it all the way back to the source, review the running configuration to see whether there is a **network mask** command advertising the network and whether there is a matching route in the routing table.

Next-Hop Router Not Reachable

If you are seeing BGP routes in the BGP table, but they are not appearing in the routing table, the router might not be able to reach the next hop. For a BGP router to install a BGP route in the routing table, it must be able to reach the next-hop address listed for the network. Example 14-26 shows the output of **show bgp ipv4 unicast** on R5. Focus on network 10.1.1.0/26. Notice that there is no > symbol after the *. The * > symbols indicate a valid best path to reach the network that has been installed in the routing table. In this case, the path is valid but not the best, and as a result, it is not placed in the routing table.

Example 14-26 *Identifying BGP Next-Hop Issues*

```
R5# show bgp ipv4 unicast
BGP table version is 2, local router ID is 5.5.5.5
Status codes: s suppressed, d damped, h history, * valid, > best, i - internal,
              r RIB-failure, S Stale, m multipath, b backup-path, f RT-Filter,
              x best-external, a additional-path, c RIB-compressed,
Origin codes: i - IGP, e - EGP, ? - incomplete
RPKI validation codes: V valid, I invalid, N Not found

     Network          Next Hop            Metric LocPrf Weight Path
 * i 1.1.1.1/32       1.1.1.1                  0    100      0 65501 ?
 * i 10.1.1.0/26      1.1.1.1                  0    100      0 65501 i
 * i 10.1.1.0/24      1.1.1.1                  0    100      0 65501 i
 * i 10.1.1.64/26     1.1.1.1                  0    100      0 65501 i
 * i 10.1.1.128/26    1.1.1.1                  0    100      0 65501 i
 * i 10.1.1.192/26    1.1.1.1                  0    100      0 65501 i
 r>i 10.1.5.0/24      10.1.24.4             3328    100      0 i
 * i 10.1.12.0/24     1.1.1.1                  0    100      0 65501 ?
 * i 10.1.13.0/24     1.1.1.1                  0    100      0 65501 ?
```

The reason the path in Example 14-26 is not being used is that the next-hop address is not reachable. In Example 14-27, the **ping 1.1.1.1** command fails, proving that the next hop is not reachable.

Example 14-27 *Verifying Next-Hop Reachability*

```
R5# ping 1.1.1.1
Type escape sequence to abort.
Sending 5, 100-byte ICMP Echos to 1.1.1.1, timeout is 2 seconds:
.....
Success rate is 0 percent (0/5)
```

In Figure 14-3, notice where the next-hop address 1.1.1.1 is compared to R5. The next hop for BGP routes outside an autonomous system (AS) is the IP address of the router advertising the route to the local autonomous system. The router receiving the advertisement (R2 in this case) does not change the next hop by default because BGP is based on AS-by-AS hops, not on router-by-router hops. Therefore, the next hop is the IP address of the router advertising the network from the next-hop AS.

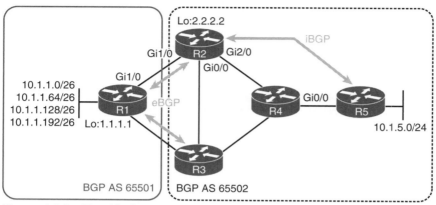

Figure 14-3 *Troubleshooting Next-Hop Address Behavior*

There are many different ways to solve this problem. The key is to train R5 about how to get to the next hop. The following are a few examples:

- Create a static default route on R2 and R3 and advertise it into the Interior Gateway Protocol (IGP) routing protocol.

- Create a static default route on R5.

- Create a static route on R5.

- Advertise the next-hop address into the IGP routing protocol.

In addition, BGP has a built-in option you can take advantage of. It is the **neighbor** *ip_ address* **next-hop-self** command. This command allows, for example, R2 to change the next-hop address to its own address before advertising the route to the peer. In Example 14-28, R2 is configured with the **neighbor 5.5.5.5 next-hop-self** command, which changes the next hop to 2.2.2.2 when R2 advertises routes to R5. Example 14-29 shows the BGP table on R5, which now has 2.2.2.2 as the next hop for 10.1.1.0/26, and it now has a > symbol, so it is the best path and is installed in the routing table.

Example 14-28 *Modifying the Next-Hop Address*

```
R2# config t
Enter configuration commands, one per line. End with CNTL/Z.
R2(config)# router bgp 65502
R2(config-router)# neighbor 5.5.5.5 next-hop-self
```

Example 14-29   *Verifying the Next-Hop Address in the BGP Table*

```
R5# show bgp ipv4 unicast
BGP table version is 10, local router ID is 5.5.5.5
Status codes: s suppressed, d damped, h history, * valid, > best, i - internal,
              r RIB-failure, S Stale, m multipath, b backup-path, f RT-Filter,
              x best-external, a additional-path, c RIB-compressed,
Origin codes: i - IGP, e - EGP, ? - incomplete
RPKI validation codes: V valid, I invalid, N Not found

     Network          Next Hop            Metric LocPrf Weight Path
*>i 10.1.1.0/26       2.2.2.2                  0    100      0 65501 i
*>i 10.1.1.0/24       2.2.2.2                  0    100      0 65501 i
*>i 10.1.1.64/26      2.2.2.2                  0    100      0 65501 i
*>i 10.1.1.128/26     2.2.2.2                  0    100      0 65501 i
*>i 10.1.1.192/26     2.2.2.2                  0    100      0 65501 i
r>i 10.1.5.0/24       2.2.2.2               3328    100      0 i
r>i 10.1.12.0/24      2.2.2.2                  0    100      0 65501 ?
r>i 10.1.13.0/24      2.2.2.2                  0    100      0 65501 ?
```

BGP Split-Horizon Rule

The BGP *split-horizon rule* states that a BGP router that receives a BGP route from an iBGP peering shall not advertise that route to another router that is an iBGP peer. It is important that you commit this rule to memory. By doing so, you will be able to recognize when this is the reason for missing routes.

Figure 14-4 shows the current BGP peerings. Notice that R2 has an iBGP peering with R4 and that R4 has an iBGP peering with R5. When R2 advertises the 10.1.1.0/26 network (as an example) to R4, it is from an iBGP peering. Because R4 and R5 are iBGP peers, R4 does not advertise the 10.1.1.0/26 network to R5 because of the BGP split-horizon rule.

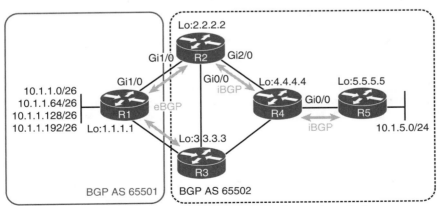

Figure 14-4   *BGP Peerings Enforcing the BGP Split-Horizon Rule*

For R5 to learn about the 10.1.1.0/26 network, it has to be an iBGP peer with the router that learned about the route from an eBGP peer or it has to be a peer with a route reflector. Figure 14-5 indicates what the iBGP peerings should be to ensure that both R4 and R5 learn about 10.1.1.0/26 (as well as the other networks). This setup also ensures that redundancy is optimized in the BGP AS.

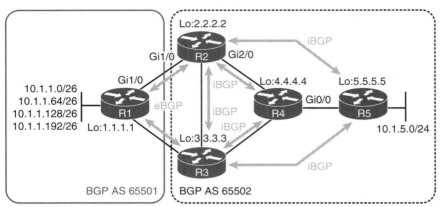

Figure 14-5 *Proper BGP Peerings to Avoid the BGP Split-Horizon Rule*

Using **show bgp ipv4 unicast summary** on all the routers to identify peerings and then drawing your peerings on paper can give you an idea of whether the BGP split-horizon rule is causing the missing routes, as long as you remember this: *A BGP router that receives a BGP route from an iBGP peering shall not advertise that route to another router that is an iBGP peer.*

Better Source of Information

Routes learned from eBGP peers have an administrative distance (AD) of 20, and routes learned from iBGP peers have an AD of 200. Why the huge difference? BGP is designed to share routes between different ASs. Therefore, if you learn a route from another AS through eBGP, iBGP, or EIGRP sources, you want the eBGP-learned route to be the best source of information over all the other dynamic routing protocols. For example, refer to Figure 14-5. R1 advertises 10.1.1.0/26 to R2 using eBGP and to R3 using eBGP. R3, because it has an iBGP peering with R2, advertises it to R2 using iBGP. In addition, let's say that on R3 you redistribute the 10.1.1.0/26 eBGP-learned route into EIGRP and that R2 learns it from an EIGRP update. Now, R2 knows about the same network from three different sources: eBGP (with an AD of 20), iBGP (with an AD of 200), and EIGRP (with an AD of 170). The eBGP path is chosen because it has the lowest AD. If it were not for eBGP having the lowest AD, you would end up with suboptimal routing as a different source would be used, and traffic would have to go to R3 first before leaving the network instead of going directly from R2 to R1.

Example 14-30 shows the output of the IPv4 unicast BGP table on R5, using the **show bgp ipv4 unicast** command. In the table, notice that the 10.1.5.0/24, 10.1.12.0/24, and 10.1.13.0/24 networks are *best* (installed in routing table), as indicated by the > symbol; however, they are not *valid*. They are listed as having a Routing Information Base (RIB) failure, as indicated by the *r*. A RIB failure means that the BGP route was not able to be installed in the routing table; however, you can clearly see that the route is in the routing table because of the > symbol. However, in this case, the route in the routing table is from a better source.

Example 14-30   *Verifying BGP Routes*

```
R5# show bgp ipv4 unicast
BGP table version is 10, local router ID is 5.5.5.5
Status codes: s suppressed, d damped, h history, * valid, > best, i - internal,
              r RIB-failure, S Stale, m multipath, b backup-path, f RT-Filter,
              x best-external, a additional-path, c RIB-compressed,
Origin codes: i - IGP, e - EGP, ? - incomplete
RPKI validation codes: V valid, I invalid, N Not found

     Network          Next Hop          Metric LocPrf Weight Path
 *  i 1.1.1.1/32      3.3.3.3                0    100      0 65501 ?
 *>i                  2.2.2.2                0    100      0 65501 ?
 *  i 10.1.1.0/26     3.3.3.3                0    100      0 65501 i
 *>i                  2.2.2.2                0    100      0 65501 i
 *  i 10.1.1.0/24     3.3.3.3                0    100      0 65501 i
 *>i                  2.2.2.2                0    100      0 65501 i
 *  i 10.1.1.64/26    3.3.3.3                0    100      0 65501 i
 *>i                  2.2.2.2                0    100      0 65501 i
 *  i 10.1.1.128/26   3.3.3.3                0    100      0 65501 i
 *>i                  2.2.2.2                0    100      0 65501 i
 *  i 10.1.1.192/26   3.3.3.3                0    100      0 65501 i
 *>i                  2.2.2.2                0    100      0 65501 i
 r  i 10.1.5.0/24     3.3.3.3             3328    100      0 i
 r>i                  2.2.2.2             3328    100      0 i
 r  i 10.1.12.0/24    3.3.3.3                0    100      0 65501 ?
 r>i                  2.2.2.2                0    100      0 65501 ?
 r  i 10.1.13.0/24    3.3.3.3                0    100      0 65501 ?
 r>i                  2.2.2.2                0    100      0 65501 ?
```

The output of the command **show ip route 10.1.5.0 255.255.255.0**, as shown in Example 14-31, indicates that 10.1.5.0/24 is learned from a connected source. In the same example, you can also see the output of **show ip route 10.1.12.0 255.255.255.0**, which indicates that it was learned from EIGRP. A connected source is always the most trustworthy; therefore, it is always used over other routing information. With regard to the 10.1.12.0/24 network, the output of **show bgp ipv4 unicast 10.1.12.0** in Example 14-32 indicates that it was learned from R2 and R3 using iBGP (*internal*), which has an AD of 200—much higher than EIGRP's AD.

Example 14-31   *Verifying the AD of Routes in the Routing Table*

```
R5# show ip route 10.1.5.0 255.255.255.0
Routing entry for 10.1.5.0/24
 Known via "connected", distance 0, metric 0 (connected, via interface)
...output omitted...


R5# show ip route 10.1.12.0 255.255.255.0
Routing entry for 10.1.12.0/24
 Known via "eigrp 100", distance 90, metric 3328, type internal
...output omitted...
```

Example 14-32   *Verifying Details of the BGP Routes*

```
R5# show bgp ipv4 unicast 10.1.12.0
BGP routing table entry for 10.1.12.0/24, version 50
Paths: (2 available, best #2, table default, RIB-failure(17))
  Not advertised to any peer
  Refresh Epoch 2
  65501
    3.3.3.3 (metric 131072) from 3.3.3.3 (3.3.3.3)
      Origin incomplete, metric 0, localpref 100, valid, internal
      rx pathid: 0, tx pathid: 0
  Refresh Epoch 2
  65501
    2.2.2.2 (metric 131072) from 2.2.2.2 (2.2.2.2)
      Origin incomplete, metric 0, localpref 100, valid, internal, best
      rx pathid: 0, tx pathid: 0x0
```

You can verify why a route is experiencing a RIB failure by using the **show bgp ipv4 unicast rib-failure** command, as shown in Example 14-33. In this example, all three RIB failures are due to the BGP route having a higher AD.

Example 14-33   *Verifying RIB Failures*

```
R5# show bgp ipv4 unicast rib-failure
  Network          Next Hop                 RIB-failure       RIB-NH Matches
  10.1.5.0/24      2.2.2.2          Higher admin distance               n/a
  10.1.12.0/24     2.2.2.2          Higher admin distance               n/a
  10.1.13.0/24     2.2.2.2          Higher admin distance               n/a
```

Route Filtering

The amount of control you have over routes in BGP is incredible, as you saw in Chapter 12, "Advanced BGP," and Chapter 13, "BGP Path Selection." When troubleshooting missing routes, you want to be able to determine whether a route filter is applied and whether it is the cause of the missing routes. Example 14-34 shows the BGP table on R5 in the output of the **show bgp ipv4 unicast** command. Notice that there is no entry for 10.1.13.0/24.

Example 14-34 *Verifying Missing Routes on R5*

```
R5# show bgp ipv4 unicast
BGP table version is 10, local router ID is 5.5.5.5
Status codes: s suppressed, d damped, h history, * valid, > best, i - internal,
              r RIB-failure, S Stale, m multipath, b backup-path, f RT-Filter,
              x best-external, a additional-path, c RIB-compressed,
Origin codes: i - IGP, e - EGP, ? - incomplete
RPKI validation codes: V valid, I invalid, N Not found

     Network          Next Hop        Metric LocPrf Weight  Path
 * i 1.1.1.1/32       3.3.3.3              0    100      0   65501 ?
 *>i                  2.2.2.2              0    100      0   65501 ?
 * i 10.1.1.0/26      3.3.3.3              0    100      0   65501 i
 *>i                  2.2.2.2              0    100      0   65501 i
 * i 10.1.1.0/24      3.3.3.3              0    100      0   65501 i
 *>i                  2.2.2.2              0    100      0   65501 i
 * i 10.1.1.64/26     3.3.3.3              0    100      0   65501 i
 *>i                  2.2.2.2              0    100      0   65501 i
 * i 10.1.1.128/26    3.3.3.3              0    100      0   65501 i
 *>i                  2.2.2.2              0    100      0   65501 i
 * i 10.1.1.192/26    3.3.3.3              0    100      0   65501 i
 *>i                  2.2.2.2              0    100      0   65501 i
 r i 10.1.5.0/24      3.3.3.3           3328    100      0   i
 r>i                  2.2.2.2           3328    100      0   i
 r i 10.1.12.0/24     3.3.3.3              0    100      0   65501 ?
 r>i                  2.2.2.2              0    100      0   65501 ?
```

You can see whether you are receiving the route from R2 or R3 by using the **show bgp ipv4 unicast neighbors** *ip_address* **routes** command, as shown in Example 14-35. The output clearly shows that you are not learning 10.1.13.0/24. But wait, this command displays routes learned after local filters have been applied. Therefore, you should check to see whether R2 or R3 is advertising the 10.1.13.0/24 route before filters are applied. As shown in Example 14-36, which displays the output of the **show bgp ipv4 unicast neighbors** *ip_address* **advertised-routes** command, R2 and R3 are advertising the 10.1.13.0/24 network to R5.

Example 14-35 *Verifying Whether Routes Are Being Received on R5*

```
R5# show bgp ipv4 unicast neighbors 2.2.2.2 routes
BGP table version is 9, local router ID is 5.5.5.5
Status codes: s suppressed, d damped, h history, * valid, > best, i - internal,
              r RIB-failure, S Stale, m multipath, b backup-path, f RT-Filter,
              x best-external, a additional-path, c RIB-compressed,
Origin codes: i - IGP, e - EGP, ? - incomplete
RPKI validation codes: V valid, I invalid, N Not found
```

```
       Network            Next Hop          Metric LocPrf Weight Path
 *>i 1.1.1.1/32           2.2.2.2                0    100      0  65501 ?
 *>i 10.1.1.0/26          2.2.2.2                0    100      0  65501 i
 *>i 10.1.1.0/24          2.2.2.2                0    100      0  65501 i
 *>i 10.1.1.64/26         2.2.2.2                0    100      0  65501 i
 *>i 10.1.1.128/26        2.2.2.2                0    100      0  65501 i
 *>i 10.1.1.192/26        2.2.2.2                0    100      0  65501 i
 r>i 10.1.5.0/24          2.2.2.2             3328    100      0  i
 r>i 10.1.12.0/24         2.2.2.2                0    100      0  65501 ?


Total number of prefixes 8
R5# show bgp ipv4 unicast neighbors 3.3.3.3 routes
BGP table version is 9, local router ID is 5.5.5.5
Status codes: s suppressed, d damped, h history, * valid, > best, i - internal,
              r RIB-failure, S Stale, m multipath, b backup-path, f RT-Filter,
              x best-external, a additional-path, c RIB-compressed,
Origin codes: i - IGP, e - EGP, ? - incomplete
RPKI validation codes: V valid, I invalid, N Not found


       Network            Next Hop          Metric LocPrf Weight    Path
 *  i 1.1.1.1/32          3.3.3.3                0    100      0     65501 ?
 *  i 10.1.1.0/26         3.3.3.3                0    100      0     65501 i
 *  i 10.1.1.0/24         3.3.3.3                0    100      0     65501 i
 *  i 10.1.1.64/26        3.3.3.3                0    100      0     65501 i
 *  i 10.1.1.128/26       3.3.3.3                0    100      0     65501 i
 *  i 10.1.1.192/26       3.3.3.3                0    100      0     65501 i
 r  i 10.1.5.0/24         3.3.3.3             3328    100      0     i
 r  i 10.1.12.0/24        3.3.3.3                0    100      0     65501 ?


Total number of prefixes 8
```

Example 14-36 *Verifying Whether Routes Are Being Sent to R5*

```
R2# show bgp ipv4 unicast neighbors 5.5.5.5 advertised-routes
BGP table version is 10, local router ID is 2.2.2.2
Status codes: s suppressed, d damped, h history, * valid, > best, i - internal,
              r RIB-failure, S Stale, m multipath, b backup-path, f RT-Filter,
              x best-external, a additional-path, c RIB-compressed,
Origin codes: i - IGP, e - EGP, ? - incomplete
RPKI validation codes: V valid, I invalid, N Not found


       Network            Next Hop          Metric LocPrf Weight    Path
 r> 1.1.1.1/32            1.1.1.1                0             0     65501 ?
```

```
  *> 10.1.1.0/26         1.1.1.1                 0               0     65501 i
  *> 10.1.1.0/24         1.1.1.1                 0               0     65501 i
  *> 10.1.1.64/26        1.1.1.1                 0               0     65501 i
  *> 10.1.1.128/26       1.1.1.1                 0               0     65501 i
  *> 10.1.1.192/26       1.1.1.1                 0               0     65501 i
  *> 10.1.5.0/24         10.1.24.4            3328           32768     i
  r> 10.1.12.0/24        1.1.1.1                 0               0     65501 ?
  *> 10.1.13.0/24        1.1.1.1                 0               0     65501 ?

Total number of prefixes 9


R3# show bgp ipv4 unicast neighbors 5.5.5.5 advertised-routes
BGP table version is 10, local router ID is 3.3.3.3
Status codes: s suppressed, d damped, h history, * valid, > best, i - internal,
              r RIB-failure, S Stale, m multipath, b backup-path, f RT-Filter,
              x best-external, a additional-path, c RIB-compressed,
Origin codes: i - IGP, e - EGP, ? - incomplete
RPKI validation codes: V valid, I invalid, N Not found


     Network           Next Hop          Metric LocPrf Weight   Path
  *> 1.1.1.1/32         10.1.13.1               0               0     65501 ?
  *> 10.1.1.0/26        10.1.13.1               0               0     65501 i
  *> 10.1.1.0/24        10.1.13.1               0               0     65501 i
  *> 10.1.1.64/26       10.1.13.1               0               0     65501 i
  *> 10.1.1.128/26      10.1.13.1               0               0     65501 i
  *> 10.1.1.192/26      10.1.13.1               0               0     65501 i
  *> 10.1.5.0/24        10.1.34.4            3328           32768     i
  *> 10.1.12.0/24       10.1.13.1               0               0     65501 ?
  r> 10.1.13.0/24       10.1.13.1               0               0     65501 ?

Total number of prefixes 9
```

The **show ip protocols** command, as shown in Example 14-37, displays the incoming filter applied to the BGP autonomous system. It is a distribute list using the prefix list called FILTER_10.1.13.0/24, as shown in Example 14-37. As also shown in Example 14-37, the prefix list is denying 10.1.13.0/24 and permitting all other routes.

Example 14-37 *Verifying Whether Filters Are Applied to R5*

```
R5# show ip protocols
...output omitted...

Routing Protocol is "bgp 65502"
  Outgoing update filter list for all interfaces is not set
  Incoming update filter list for all interfaces is (prefix-list) FILTER_10.1.13.0/24
```

```
IGP synchronization is disabled
Automatic route summarization is disabled
Neighbor(s):
  Address FiltIn FiltOut DistIn DistOut Weight RouteMap
  2.2.2.2
  3.3.3.3
Maximum path: 1
Routing Information Sources:...output omitted...


R5# show ip prefix-list
ip prefix-list FILTER_10.1.13.0/24: 2 entries
 seq 5 deny 10.1.13.0/24
 seq 10 permit 0.0.0.0/0 le 32


R5# show run | include bgp 65502|distribute-list
router bgp 65502
 distribute-list prefix FILTER_10.1.13.0/24 in
```

This example focuses on a filter that applies to the entire BGP process. Therefore, no matter which router you receive the route 10.1.13.0/24 from, it is denied. However, you can apply a filter directly to a neighbor by using any of the following commands:

- neighbor *ip_address* distribute-list *access_list_number* {in | out}

- neighbor *ip_address* prefix-list *prefix_list_name* {in | out}

- neighbor *ip_address* route-map *map_name* {in | out}

- neighbor *ip_address* filter-list *access_list_number* {in | out}

How do you verify whether a route filter is applied specifically to a neighbor? You can verify the route filters with the same **show** commands as before. Now, however, you look in a different spot in the output. In Example 14-38, an inbound distribute list is applied directly to the neighbor 2.2.2.2, as shown in the **show ip protocols** output. Notice that only the first six characters of the ACL are identified. If you then review the running configuration, you see that the distribute list is using the ACL named FILTER_10.1.13.0/24. The output of the **show ip access-list** command confirms that the router is denying the 10.1.13.0/24 network from 2.2.2.2 but allowing all other networks.

Example 14-38 *Verifying a Distribute List Applied to a Neighbor*

```
R5# show ip protocols
...output omitted...


Routing Protocol is "bgp 65502"
 Outgoing update filter list for all interfaces is not set
 Incoming update filter list for all interfaces is not set
```

```
   IGP synchronization is disabled
   Automatic route summarization is disabled
   Neighbor(s):
     Address FiltIn FiltOut DistIn DistOut Weight RouteMap
     2.2.2.2                 FILTER
     3.3.3.3
   Maximum path: 1
   Routing Information Sources:
   ...output omitted...


R5# show run | include bgp 65502|distribute-list
router bgp 65502
  neighbor 2.2.2.2 distribute-list FILTER_10.1.13.0/24 in

R5# show ip access-lists
Standard IP access list FILTER_10.1.13.0/24
  10 deny 10.1.13.0, wildcard bits 0.0.0.255
  20 permit any
```

As noted earlier, you can apply a route map, a prefix list, and a filter list directly to the **neighbor** command. The filter list appears under the FiltIn and FiltOut columns in the output of **show ip protocols**, and the route map appears under the RouteMap column in the **show ip protocols** output. If the prefix list is applied directly to a **neighbor** statement, it does not appear in the output of **show ip protocols**. You need to review the output of **show bgp ipv4 unicast neighbors**. However, recall that it is provides extremely verbose output. Therefore, you might want to use this shortcut for troubleshooting route filters:

```
show bgp ipv4 unicast neighbors ip_address | include prefix|filter|Route map
```

Example 14-39 shows a sample of what would appear in the output of **show bgp ipv4 unicast neighbors** on R5, based on different filters applied to and from neighbors R2 and R3. In the output, you can see that there is an inbound prefix list called FILTER_10.1.13.0/24 applied directly to neighbor 3.3.3.3; there is also an outbound route map called FIL-TER_10.1.5.0/24 for routes sent to neighbor 3.3.3.3. With regard to neighbor 2.2.2.2, there is an inbound network filter (that is, distribute list) applied to the **neighbor** statement that is using the ACL called FILTER_10.1.13.0/24, and there is also an inbound autonomous system path ACL called 25.

Example 14-39 *Verifying Filters Applied to the neighbor Statements*

```
R5# show bgp ipv4 unicast neighbors 3.3.3.3 | include prefix|filter|Route map
  Incoming update prefix filter list is FILTER_10.1.13.0/24
  Route map for outgoing advertisements is FILTER_10.1.5.0/24
R5# show bgp ipv4 unicast neighbors 2.2.2.2 | include prefix|filter|Route map
  Incoming update network filter list is FILTER_10.1.13.0/24
  Incoming update AS path filter list is 25
```

Troubleshooting BGP Path Selection

Unlike OSPF and EIGRP, BGP does not consider a link's bandwidth when making a route decision. Instead, BGP uses various attributes when deciding which path is the best. When troubleshooting BGP paths, you need to have a solid understanding of all the attributes to fully comprehend why BGP has made a particular decision. This section discusses the BGP best-path decision-making process. In addition, it examines private ASNs.

Understanding the Best-Path Decision-Making Process

Cisco routers review BGP attributes in the following order when deciding which path is the best:

1. Prefer the highest *weight*.
2. Prefer the highest *local preference*.
3. Prefer the route *originated* by the local router.
4. Prefer the path with the shorter Accumulated Interior Gateway Protocol (AIGP) metric attribute.
5. Prefer the shortest *AS_Path*.
6. Prefer the lowest *origin* code.
7. Prefer the lowest multi-exit discriminator (*MED*).
8. Prefer an *external* path over an *internal* path.
9. Prefer the path through the *closest IGP neighbor*.
10. Prefer the path from the oldest eBGP session.
11. Prefer the path with the lowest *neighbor BGP RID*.
12. Prefer the path with the lowest *neighbor IP address*.

As you go through the BGP best-path decision-making process, refer to Figure 14-6 and the output of **show bgp ipv4 unicast 10.1.1.0** on R5 in Example 14-40.

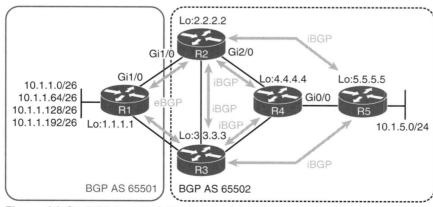

Figure 14-6 *BGP Best-Path Decision-Making Process Topology*

Example 14-40 *Verifying the BGP Table on Router R5 for Network 10.1.1.0*

```
R5# show bgp ipv4 unicast 10.1.1.0
BGP routing table entry for 10.1.1.0/26, version 46
Paths: (2 available, best #1, table default)
  Not advertised to any peer
  Refresh Epoch 4
  65501
    2.2.2.2 (metric 131072) from 2.2.2.2 (2.2.2.2)
      Origin IGP, metric 0, localpref 100, valid, internal, best
      rx pathid: 0, tx pathid: 0x0
  Refresh Epoch 1
  65501
    3.3.3.3 (metric 131072) from 3.3.3.3 (3.3.3.3)
      Origin IGP, metric 0, localpref 100, valid, internal
      rx pathid: 0, tx pathid: 0
```

When BGP finds a match, it stops and uses that attribute as the reason for choosing the path as the best—and it looks no further. In addition, if the next-hop IP address is not reachable, the router does not even go through the following process because it considers the next hop inaccessible:

Step 1. BGP first looks at weight. Higher is better. In Example 14-40, no weight is listed because both paths are using the default value 0. Therefore, weight is tied, and the next attribute is checked.

Step 2. Local preference is checked next. Higher is better. In Example 14-40, localpref is 100 (the default) for both paths; therefore, local preference is tied, and the next attribute is checked.

Step 3. The router checks whether it generated the BGP route (that is, has a next hop of 0.0.0.0). If it did, it is preferred. In Example 14-40, the next hops are 2.2.2.2 and 3.3.3.3 on the far left of the output. Therefore, R5 did not generate any of the routes, and the next attribute is checked.

Step 4. AIGP is checked next only if it's configured to be used. In this case, it is not configured as there is no AIGP metric listed in the output of Example 14-40. Therefore, the next attribute is checked.

Step 5. AS_Path is checked next. The shortest path is preferred. In Example 14-40, AS_Path is 65501 for both routes. Therefore, the AS_Path is tied, and the next attribute is checked.

Step 6. The origin code is checked next. IGP is better than EGP, which is better than incomplete. Note that this is not related to iBGP versus eBGP, which is covered later. IGP means the route was generated with the **network mask** or **summary-address** command, and incomplete means the route was redistributed into BGP. EGP means it was generated from EGP, the predecessor to BGP. In Example 14-40, the origin is IGP for both routes, which means the next attribute is checked.

Step 7.   MED (metric) is next. Lower is better. In Example 14-40, the MED (metric) is the same for both (0). Therefore, the next attribute has to be checked.

Step 8.   Now eBGP is preferred over iBGP. In Example 14-40, they are both learned via iBGP (internal). Therefore, this attribute is tied as well, and the next has to be checked.

Step 9.   The IGP path to the neighbor is compared now. In Example 14-40, the IGP path to 2.2.2.2 has a metric of 131072, and the IGP path to 3.3.3.3 has a metric of 131072. They are tied. Therefore, the next attribute has to be checked.

Step 10. If they are eBGP paths, the ages of the routes are checked. In Example 14-40, both paths are iBGP paths. Therefore, you skip this attribute and move on to the next attribute.

Step 11. The BGP RIDs are now compared. Lower is better. In Example 14-40, neighbor 2.2.2.2 has a RID of 2.2.2.2 (as displayed in the brackets), and neighbor 3.3.3.3 has a RID of 3.3.3.3 (as displayed in the brackets). Which RID is lower? 2.2.2.2 Therefore, the route provided by the neighbor with the RID of 2.2.2.2 is considered the best path. If the RID happens to be tied, the neighbor IP address is used to break the tie, and the path through the neighbor with the lowest neighbor IP address wins.

Now it is your turn! Try the following on your own, and then let's walk through it. Based on Figure 14-7 and Example 14-41, determine which attribute R2 is using to choose the best path to reach 10.1.1.128.

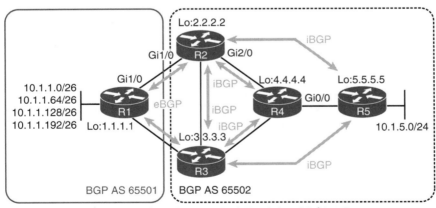

Figure 14-7   *Practicing the BGP Best-Path Decision-Making Process*

Example 14-41   *Practicing the BGP Best-Path Decision-Making Process*

```
R2# show bgp ipv4 unicast 10.1.1.128
BGP routing table entry for 10.1.1.128/26, version 6
Paths: (2 available, best #2, table default)
  Advertised to update-groups:
    2
```

```
Refresh Epoch 2
65501
   3.3.3.3 (metric 131072) from 3.3.3.3 (3.3.3.3)
   Origin IGP, metric 0, localpref 100, valid, internal
   rx pathid: 0, tx pathid: 0
Refresh Epoch 3
65501
   1.1.1.1 from 1.1.1.1 (1.1.1.1)
   Origin IGP, metric 0, localpref 100, valid, external, best
   rx pathid: 0, tx pathid: 0x0
```

Here's an examination of the process in this example:

1. The weight is tied, so continue evaluating.

2. The local preference is tied, so continue evaluating.

3. No route was originated by the local router, so continue evaluating.

4. The AIGP metric is not being used, so continue evaluating.

5. AS_Path is the same, at 65501, so continue evaluating.

6. The origin code is the same, so continue evaluating.

7. The MED metric is tied at 0, so continue evaluating.

8. The path learned from neighbor 1.1.1.1 is external (eBGP), and the path learned from neighbor 3.3.3.3 is internal (iBGP). Therefore, the path learned from neighbor 1.1.1.1 is preferred because external is preferred over internal.

If you are not getting desired paths, or if you are not getting the paths you expect to be used as *best*, you need to be able to walk through this troubleshooting process to figure out why the current best path was chosen as such. There may have been an attribute that was modified locally or remotely at some point that is influencing the decision being made. You need to be able to recognize this and then manipulate the paths in your favor by modifying the necessary attributes.

Private Autonomous System Numbers

Like IPv4 addresses, BGP ASNs also have a private range. The 2-byte AS range is 64,512 to 65,534, and the 4-byte AS range is 4,200,000,000 to 4,294,967,294. These ASNs can be used for networks that are single-homed or dual-homed to the same *ISP*, thereby preserving the public ASNs for networks that are multihomed to multiple ISPs.

Although the private ASNs can be used in a customer's network, it is imperative that the ASN not be in the AS_Path attribute when the routes are advertised to the Internet (in the global BGP table) because multiple ASs could be using the same private ASN, which would cause issues on the Internet.

If private ASNs are being sent into the global BGP table, they need to be stopped. You can accomplish this by using the **neighbor** *ip_address* **remove-private-as** command.

Using debug Commands

The majority of changes that occur with BGP generate syslog messages in real time. Therefore, you are notified through syslog if any neighbor issues occur. So, unless you really need to, you should avoid using the large number of debugs that are available because they place a lot of pressure on the routers' resources. Only use as a last resort! This section presents a few **debug** commands that might be useful. However, you can use all the **show** commands covered so far and your knowledge to determine the same thing.

Example 14-42 provides sample output from the **debug ip routing** command. The output from this command shows updates to a router's IP routing table. In this example, the Loopback 0 interface (with IP address 10.3.3.3) of a neighboring router was administratively shut down and then administratively brought back up. As the 10.3.3.3/32 network became unavailable and then once again became available, you can see that the 10.3.3.3/32 route was deleted and then added to this router's IP routing table. Notice that this output is not specific to BGP. You can use the **debug ip routing** command with routing processes other than BGP.

Example 14-42   *debug ip routing Command Output*

```
R2# debug ip routing
IP routing debugging is on
RT: 10.3.3.3/32 gateway changed from 172.16.1.1 to 172.16.2.2
RT: NET-RED 10.3.3.3/32
RT: del 10.3.3.3/32 via 172.16.2.2, bgp metric [20/0]
RT: delete subnet route to 10.3.3.3/32
RT: NET-RED 10.3.3.3/32
RT: SET_LAST_RDB for 10.3.3.3/32
 NEW rdb: via 172.16.1.1

RT: add 10.3.3.3/32 via 172.16.1.1, bgp metric [20/0]
RT: NET-RED 10.3.3.3/32
```

Example 14-43 provides sample output from the **debug ip bgp** command. The output of this command does not show the contents of BGP updates; however, this command can be useful in watching real-time state changes for IPv4 BGP peering relationships. In this example, you can see a peering session being closed for the neighbor with IP address 172.16.1.1.

Example 14-43   *debug ip bgp Command Output*

```
R2# debug ip bgp
BGP debugging is on for address family: IPv4 Unicast
*Mar 1 00:23:26.535: BGP: 172.16.1.1 remote close, state CLOSEWAIT
*Mar 1 00:23:26.535: BGP: 172.16.1.1 -reset the session
*Mar 1 00:23:26.543: BGPNSF state: 172.16.1.1 went from nsf_not_active to
 nsf_not_active
*Mar 1 00:23:26.547: BGP: 172.16.1.1 went from Established to Idle
```

```
*Mar 1 00:23:26.547: %BGP-5-ADJCHANGE: neighbor 172.16.1.1 Down Peer closed the
 session
*Mar 1 00:23:26.547: BGP: 172.16.1.1 closing
*Mar 1 00:23:26.651: BGP: 172.16.1.1 went from Idle to Active
*Mar 1 00:23:26.663: BGP: 172.16.1.1 open active delayed 30162ms (35000ms max,
 28% jitter)
```

Example 14-44 provides sample output from the **debug ip bgp updates** command. This command produces more detailed output than the **debug ip bgp** command. Specifically, you can see the content of IPv4 BGP updates. In this example, you see a route of 10.3.3.3/32 being added to a router's IP routing table.

Example 14-44   *debug ip bgp updates Command Output*

```
R2# debug ip bgp updates
BGP updates debugging is on for address family: IPv4 Unicast
*Mar 1 00:24:27.455: BGP(0): 172.16.1.1 NEXT_HOP part 1 net 10.3.3.3/32, next
 172.16.1.1
*Mar 1 00:24:27.455: BGP(0): 172.16.1.1 send UPDATE (format) 10.3.3.3/32, next
 172.16.1.1, metric 0, path 65002
*Mar 1 00:24:27.507: BGP(0): 172.16.1.1 rcv UPDATE about 10.3.3.3/32 — withdrawn
*Mar 1 00:24:27.515: BGP(0): Revise route installing 1 of 1 routes for
 10.3.3.3/32 -> 172.16.2.2(main) to main IP table
*Mar 1 00:24:27.519: BGP(0): updgrp 1 - 172.16.1.1 updates replicated for
 neighbors: 172.16.2.2
*Mar 1 00:24:27.523: BGP(0): 172.16.1.1 send UPDATE (format) 10.3.3.3/32, next
 172.16.1.2, metric 0, path 65003 65002
*Mar 1 00:24:27.547: BGP(0): 172.16.2.2 rcvd UPDATE w/ attr: nexthop 172.16.2.2,
 origin i, path 65003 65002
*Mar 1 00:24:27.551: BGP(0): 172.16.2.2 rcvd 10.3.3.3/32...duplicate ignored
*Mar 1 00:24:27.555: BGP(0): updgrp 1 - 172.16.1.1 updates replicated for
 neighbors: 172.16.2.2
*Mar 1 00:24:27.675: BGP(0): 172.16.2.2 rcv UPDATE w/ attr: nexthop 172.16.2.2,
 origin i, originator 0.0.0.0, path 65003 65001 65002, community, extended
community
*Mar 1 00:24:27.683: BGP(0): 172.16.2.2 rcv UPDATE about 10.3.3.3/32 — DENIED
 due to: AS-PATH contains our own AS;
...OUTPUT OMITTED...
```

Troubleshooting BGP for IPv6

BGP for IPv4 and BGP for IPv6 are configured in the same BGP autonomous system configuration mode, known as Multiprotocol BGP (*MP-BGP*). Implementing BGP for IPv4 and IPv6 on the same router requires the use of *address families* and the activation of neighbors for those address families. This section examines the additional issues (on top of what has been covered so far in the chapter) that you might encounter when using MP-BGP with IPv4 and IPv6 unicast routes. Refer to Figure 14-8 while reviewing this section.

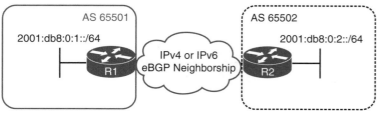

Figure 14-8 *MP-BGP Topology*

There are two different ways to exchange IPv6 routes with BGP: You can exchange them over IPv4 TCP sessions or over IPv6 TCP sessions. Example 14-45 shows a sample BGP configuration in which IPv6 routes are exchanged over an IPv4 TCP session.

Notice that there are two address families: one for IPv4 unicast, and one for IPv6 unicast. The neighbors and remote ASNs are identified outside the address family (AF) configuration. You then activate the neighbor within the AF with the **neighbor** *ip_address* **activate** command. In this example, the IPv6 AF is using an IPv4 neighbor address to establish the TCP session. Therefore, the TCP session is IPv4 based. The output of **show bgp ipv6 unicast summary**, as shown in Example 14-46, indicates that an IPv6 unicast AF neighbor adjacency has been formed with router 2.2.2.2. Notice that the adjacency has been formed with an IPv4 unicast address. This output also shows that one IPv6 prefix has been learned from the neighbor.

Example 14-45 *MP-BGP Configuration for IPv6 Routes over an IPv4 TCP Session*

```
R1# show run | s router bgp
router bgp 65501
 bgp log-neighbor-changes
 neighbor 2.2.2.2 remote-as 65502
 neighbor 2.2.2.2 ebgp-multihop 2
 neighbor 2.2.2.2 password CISCO
 neighbor 2.2.2.2 update-source Loopback0
 !
 address-family ipv4
  network 10.1.1.0 mask 255.255.255.192
  network 10.1.1.64 mask 255.255.255.192
  network 10.1.1.128 mask 255.255.255.192
  network 10.1.1.192 mask 255.255.255.192
  aggregate-address 10.1.1.0 255.255.255.0
  redistribute connected
  neighbor 2.2.2.2 activate
 exit-address-family
 !
 address-family ipv6
  network 2001:DB8:1::/64
  neighbor 2.2.2.2 activate
 exit-address-family
```

Example 14-46 *Verifying MP-BGP IPv6 Unicast Neighbor Adjacencies*

```
R1# show bgp ipv6 unicast summary
BGP router identifier 1.1.1.1, local AS number 65501
BGP table version is 2, main routing table version 2
2 network entries using 336 bytes of memory
2 path entries using 208 bytes of memory
2/1 BGP path/bestpath attribute entries using 272 bytes of memory
1 BGP AS-PATH entries using 24 bytes of memory
0 BGP route-map cache entries using 0 bytes of memory
0 BGP filter-list cache entries using 0 bytes of memory
BGP using 840 total bytes of memory
BGP activity 11/0 prefixes, 18/6 paths, scan interval 60 secs

Neighbor        V    AS   MsgRcvd MsgSent   TblVer  InQ OutQ  Up/Down  State/PfxRcd
2.2.2.2         4  65502      25      25        2    0    0  00:12:02             1
```

To verify the IPv6 unicast routes that have been learned from all neighbors, you can issue the **show bgp ipv6 unicast** command, as shown in Example 14-47. Its output displays the IPv6 BGP table. The route 2001:db8:1::/64 is locally originated because of the next hop ::, and it is in the routing table, as indicated by the *> at the beginning of the entry. Examine the 2001:db8:2::/64 route. This is the route that was learned from R2 (the 2.2.2.2 neighbor). It is not installed in the routing table, as indicated by the absence of the *>. It is not installed because the next hop is not reachable. The address ::FFFF:2.2.2.2 is a dynamically generated next hop that was created to replace the original next hop of 2.2.2.2. This occurs because an IPv6 route cannot have an IPv4 next-hop address. Why is the next hop an IPv4 address? It is because the adjacency is an IPv4 adjacency for the IPv6 AF.

Example 14-47 *Verifying MP-BGP IPv6 Unicast Routes in the IPv6 BGP Table*

```
R1# show bgp ipv6 unicast
BGP table version is 2, local router ID is 1.1.1.1
Status codes: s suppressed, d damped, h history, * valid, > best, i - internal,
              r RIB-failure, S Stale, m multipath, b backup-path, f RT-Filter,
              x best-external, a additional-path, c RIB-compressed,
Origin codes: i - IGP, e - EGP, ? - incomplete
RPKI validation codes: V valid, I invalid, N Not found

     Network          Next Hop            Metric LocPrf Weight Path
 *>  2001:DB8:1::/64  ::                        0        32768 i
 *   2001:DB8:2::/64  ::FFFF:2.2.2.2            0           0 65502 i
```

To solve this issue, you need to create a route map that changes the next hop to a valid IPv6 address and attach it to the **neighbor** statement. Now, be very careful with this. It has to be *done on the router advertising the route*, not on the router receiving the route. In Example 14-48, a route map configured on R2 changes the next-hop address to 2001:db8:12::2. The route map is then attached to the neighbor 1.1.1.1 outbound.

Example 14-48 *Modifying the BGP Next Hop*

```
R2# config t
Enter configuration commands, one per line. End with CNTL/Z.
R2(config)# route-map CHANGE_NH permit 10
R2(config-route-map)# set ipv6 next-hop 2001:db8:12::2
R2(config-route-map)# exit
R2(config)# router bgp 65502
R2(config-router)# address-family ipv6 unicast
R2(config-router-af)# neighbor 1.1.1.1 route-map CHANGE_NH out
```

When you examine the output of **show bgp ipv6 unicast** again in Example 14-49, the next hop is now a valid hop, and the route is installed in the table.

Example 14-49 *Verifying the BGP Next Hop*

```
R1# show bgp ipv6 unicast
BGP table version is 3, local router ID is 1.1.1.1
Status codes: s suppressed, d damped, h history, * valid, > best, i - internal,
              r RIB-failure, S Stale, m multipath, b backup-path, f RT-Filter,
              x best-external, a additional-path, c RIB-compressed,
Origin codes: i - IGP, e - EGP, ? - incomplete
RPKI validation codes: V valid, I invalid, N Not found


    Network          Next Hop           Metric LocPrf Weight Path
 *> 2001:DB8:1::/64  ::                      0          32768 i
 *> 2001:DB8:2::/64  2001:DB8:12::2          0              0 65502 i
```

When forming IPv6 TCP sessions and neighbor relationships, you do not have to worry about the issue just described. However, you have to make sure that you define the IPv6 neighbor and activate it. Take a look at Example 14-50. To form the IPv6 TCP session, you define the neighbor by using the **neighbor** *ipv6_address* **remote-as** *autonomous_system_number* command outside the AF configuration, and then you activate the neighbor in the IPv6 AF configuration by using the **neighbor** *ipv6_address* **activate** command.

Example 14-50 *MP-BGP Configuration for IPv6 Routes over an IPv6 TCP Session*

```
R1# show run | section router bgp
router bgp 65501
 bgp log-neighbor-changes
  neighbor 2.2.2.2 remote-as 65502
  neighbor 2.2.2.2 ebgp-multihop 2
  neighbor 2.2.2.2 password CISCO
  neighbor 2.2.2.2 update-source Loopback0
  neighbor 10.1.13.3 remote-as 65502
  neighbor 2001:DB8:12::2 remote-as 65502
  !
 address-family ipv4
```

```
   network 10.1.1.0 mask 255.255.255.192

   network 10.1.1.64 mask 255.255.255.192

   network 10.1.1.128 mask 255.255.255.192

   network 10.1.1.192 mask 255.255.255.192

   aggregate-address 10.1.1.0 255.255.255.0

   redistribute connected

   neighbor 2.2.2.2 activate

   neighbor 10.1.13.3 activate

   no neighbor 2001:DB8:12::2 activate

 exit-address-family

 !

 address-family ipv6

   network 2001:DB8:1::/64

   neighbor 2001:DB8:12::2 activate

 exit-address-family
```

The output of **show bgp ipv6 unicast summary**, as shown in Example 14-51, indicates that R1 has formed an IPv6 BGP neighbor adjacency with the device at 2001:db8:12::2 using an IPv6 TCP session, and one prefix has been received. The IPv6 BGP table, as displayed in the output of the **show bgp ipv6 unicast** command in Example 14-52, indicates that 2001:DB8:2::/64 can be reached with a next hop of 2001:DB8:12::2 and that it is installed in the routing table, as indicated by the *>.

Example 14-51   *MP-BGP Adjacencies with IPv6 TCP Sessions*

```
R1# show bgp ipv6 unicast summary
BGP router identifier 1.1.1.1, local AS number 65501
BGP table version is 5, main routing table version 5
2 network entries using 336 bytes of memory
2 path entries using 208 bytes of memory
2/2 BGP path/bestpath attribute entries using 272 bytes of memory
1 BGP AS-PATH entries using 24 bytes of memory
0 BGP route-map cache entries using 0 bytes of memory
0 BGP filter-list cache entries using 0 bytes of memory
BGP using 840 total bytes of memory
BGP activity 12/1 prefixes, 22/10 paths, scan interval 60 secs


Neighbor        V    AS   MsgRcvd MsgSent   TblVer   InQ OutQ  Up/Down  State/PfxRcd
2001:DB8:12::2 4 65502       5       5        4       0   0   00:00:05            1
```

Example 14-52   *Verifying the IPv6 BGP Table*

```
R1# show bgp ipv6 unicast
BGP table version is 5, local router ID is 1.1.1.1
Status codes: s suppressed, d damped, h history, * valid, > best, i - internal,
              r RIB-failure, S Stale, m multipath, b backup-path, f RT-Filter,
              x best-external, a additional-path, c RIB-compressed,
```

```
Origin codes: i - IGP, e - EGP, ? - incomplete
RPKI validation codes: V valid, I invalid, N Not found


     Network          Next Hop          Metric LocPrf Weight  Path
 *>  2001:DB8:1::/64  ::                     0         32768   i
 *>  2001:DB8:2::/64  2001:DB8:12::2         0             0   65502 i
```

BGP Trouble Tickets

This section presents trouble tickets related to the topics discussed earlier in this chapter. The purpose of these trouble tickets is to show a process that you can use when troubleshooting in the real world or in an exam environment. All the trouble tickets in this section are based on the topology shown in Figure 14-9.

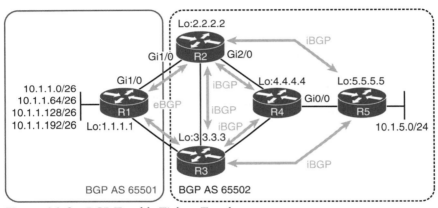

Figure 14-9 *BGP Trouble Tickets Topology*

Trouble Ticket 14-1

Problem: You are the administrator for BGP AS 65502. While you were away on vacation, the link between R1 and R2 failed. When the link between R1 and R2 fails, the link between R1 and R3 is supposed to forward traffic to BGP AS 65501. However, that did not occur while you were away. Your co-worker had to restore connectivity between R1 and R2, and complaints kept flowing in from the users in 10.1.5.0/24 about connectivity to the 10.1.1.0/24 networks being down.

At this point, connectivity is fine. You confirm this by pinging from a PC in 10.1.5.0/24 to 10.1.1.10. As Example 14-53 shows, the ping is successful. Because it is the middle of the day, you cannot bring down the link between R1 and R2 to re-create the issue because doing so would disrupt the network users. Therefore, you need to be creative with your troubleshooting efforts.

Example 14-53 *Verifying Connectivity*

```
C:\>ping 10.1.1.10

Pinging 10.1.1.10 with 32 bytes of data:

Reply from 10.1.1.10: bytes=32 time 1ms TTL=128
Reply from 10.1.1.10: bytes=32 time 1ms TTL=128
Reply from 10.1.1.10: bytes=32 time 1ms TTL=128
Reply from 10.1.1.10: bytes=32 time 1ms TTL=128

Ping statistics for 10.1.1.10:
Packets: Sent = 4, Received = 4, Lost = 0 (0% loss),
Approximate round trip times in milli-seconds:
Minimum = 0ms, Maximum = 0ms, Average = 0ms
```

For router R5 to know about the networks in AS 65501, those networks have to be advertised to R5. The best place to see whether R5 is learning about the routes is R5's BGP table. Based on the network topology, R5 should be learning about the networks from R2 and R3. Example 14-54 shows the output of **show bgp ipv4 unicast**. As you can see from the Next Hop column, all valid routes to the 10.1.1.x/26 networks are through the next hop 2.2.2.2, which is R2. There are no entries for R3 at 3.3.3.3 that are valid for those networks.

Example 14-54 *Examining R5's BGP Table*

```
R5# show bgp ipv4 unicast
BGP table version is 56, local router ID is 5.5.5.5
Status codes: s suppressed, d damped, h history, * valid, > best, i - internal,
              r RIB-failure, S Stale, m multipath, b backup-path, f RT-Filter,
              x best-external, a additional-path, c RIB-compressed,
Origin codes: i - IGP, e - EGP, ? - incomplete
RPKI validation codes: V valid, I invalid, N Not found

     Network          Next Hop         Metric LocPrf Weight  Path
 *>i 1.1.1.1/32       2.2.2.2               0    100      0  65501 ?
 *>i 10.1.1.0/26      2.2.2.2               0    100      0  65501 i
 *>i 10.1.1.64/26     2.2.2.2               0    100      0  65501 i
 *>i 10.1.1.128/26    2.2.2.2               0    100      0  65501 i
 *>i 10.1.1.192/26    2.2.2.2               0    100      0  65501 i
 r>i 10.1.5.0/24      2.2.2.2            3328    100      0  i
 r i                  3.3.3.3            3328    100      0  i
 r>i 10.1.12.0/24     2.2.2.2               0    100      0  65501 ?
 r>i 10.1.13.0/24     2.2.2.2               0    100      0  65501 ?
```

Next, you want to confirm whether R5 is even receiving the routes from R3. Therefore, you issue the commands **show bgp ipv4 unicast neighbors 2.2.2.2 routes** and **show bgp ipv4 unicast neighbors 3.3.3.3 routes** to determine which routes are being received and to compare what is being advertised from R2 against what is being advertised from R3. The output in Example 14-55 clearly shows that R5 is not receiving any routes about the 10.1.1.x/26 networks from R3. This is the reason network connectivity was lost when the link between R1 and R2 went down: R5 does not have any route information from R3.

Example 14-55 *Examining Routes Received from R2 and R3*

```
R5# show bgp ipv4 unicast neighbors 2.2.2.2 routes
BGP table version is 56, local router ID is 5.5.5.5
Status codes: s suppressed, d damped, h history, * valid, > best, i - internal,
              r RIB-failure, S Stale, m multipath, b backup-path, f RT-Filter,
              x best-external, a additional-path, c RIB-compressed,
Origin codes: i - IGP, e - EGP, ? - incomplete
RPKI validation codes: V valid, I invalid, N Not found

     Network          Next Hop          Metric LocPrf Weight Path
 *>i 1.1.1.1/32       2.2.2.2                0    100      0  65501 ?
 *>i 10.1.1.0/26      2.2.2.2                0    100      0  65501 i
 *>i 10.1.1.64/26     2.2.2.2                0    100      0  65501 i
 *>i 10.1.1.128/26    2.2.2.2                0    100      0  65501 i
 *>i 10.1.1.192/26    2.2.2.2                0    100      0  65501 i
 r>i 10.1.5.0/24      2.2.2.2             3328    100      0  i
 r>i 10.1.12.0/24     2.2.2.2                0    100      0  65501 ?
 r>i 10.1.13.0/24     2.2.2.2                0    100      0  65501 ?

Total number of prefixes 8
R5# show bgp ipv4 unicast neighbors 3.3.3.3 routes
BGP table version is 56, local router ID is 5.5.5.5
Status codes: s suppressed, d damped, h history, * valid, > best, i - internal,
              r RIB-failure, S Stale, m multipath, b backup-path, f RT-Filter,
              x best-external, a additional-path, c RIB-compressed,
Origin codes: i - IGP, e - EGP, ? - incomplete
RPKI validation codes: V valid, I invalid, N Not found

     Network          Next Hop          Metric LocPrf Weight Path
 r i 10.1.5.0/24      3.3.3.3             3328    100      0  i

Total number of prefixes 1
```

You access R3 and issue the command **show bgp ipv4 unicast neighbors 5.5.5.5 advertised-routes** to determine which routes, if any, R3 is sending to R5. In Example 14-56, you can see that no routes related to the 10.1.1.x/26 networks are being advertised to R5. So does R3 even know about the networks?

Example 14-56 *Examining Routes Sent from R3 to R5*

```
R3# show bgp ipv4 unicast neighbors 5.5.5.5 advertised-routes
BGP table version is 108, local router ID is 3.3.3.3
Status codes: s suppressed, d damped, h history, * valid, > best, i - internal,
              r RIB-failure, S Stale, m multipath, b backup-path, f RT-Filter,
              x best-external, a additional-path, c RIB-compressed,
Origin codes: i - IGP, e - EGP, ? - incomplete
RPKI validation codes: V valid, I invalid, N Not found

     Network          Next Hop          Metric LocPrf Weight Path
 *>  10.1.5.0/24      10.1.34.4          3328          32768  i

Total number of prefixes 1
```

On R3, you issue the command **show ip route 10.1.1.0 255.255.255.0 longer-prefixes**, as shown in Example 14-57, and confirm that the networks are learned from BGP. However, you also notice something else that is strange: The AD is 200, which is the value associated with iBGP-learned routes, and the next hop is through 2.2.2.2, which is R2. The AD should be 20 for eBGP, and the next hop should be R1's IP address in this case.

Example 14-57 *Examining BGP Routes in R3's Routing Table*

```
R3# show ip route 10.1.1.0 255.255.255.0 longer-prefixes
Codes: L - local, C - connected, S - static, R - RIP, M - mobile, B - BGP
 D - EIGRP, EX - EIGRP external, O - OSPF, IA - OSPF inter area
 N1 - OSPF NSSA external type 1, N2 - OSPF NSSA external type 2
 E1 - OSPF external type 1, E2 - OSPF external type 2
 i - IS-IS, su - IS-IS summary, L1 - IS-IS level-1, L2 - IS-IS level-2
 ia - IS-IS inter area, * - candidate default, U - per-user static route
 o - ODR, P - periodic downloaded static route, H - NHRP, l - LISP
 + - replicated route, % - next hop override

Gateway of last resort is not set

      10.0.0.0/8 is variably subnetted, 14 subnets, 3 masks
B        10.1.1.0/26 [200/0] via 2.2.2.2, 00:09:07
B        10.1.1.64/26 [200/0] via 2.2.2.2, 00:09:07
B        10.1.1.128/26 [200/0] via 2.2.2.2, 00:09:07
B        10.1.1.192/26 [200/0] via 2.2.2.2, 00:09:07
```

You issue the command **show bgp ipv4 unicast** on R3 to check the BGP table. Based on the output, as shown in Example 14-58, only R2 and R4 are next hops for routes. R1 is not a next hop for any of them.

Example 14-58 *Examining BGP Routes in R3's BGP Table*

```
R3# show bgp ipv4 unicast
BGP table version is 108, local router ID is 3.3.3.3
Status codes: s suppressed, d damped, h history, * valid, > best, i - internal,
              r RIB-failure, S Stale, m multipath, b backup-path, f RT-Filter,
              x best-external, a additional-path, c RIB-compressed,
Origin codes: i - IGP, e - EGP, ? - incomplete
RPKI validation codes: V valid, I invalid, N Not found

     Network           Next Hop         Metric LocPrf Weight Path
 *>i 1.1.1.1/32        2.2.2.2               0    100      0 65501 ?
 *>i 10.1.1.0/26       2.2.2.2               0    100      0 65501 i
 *>i 10.1.1.0/24       2.2.2.2               0    100      0 65501 i
 *>i 10.1.1.64/26      2.2.2.2               0    100      0 65501 i
 *>i 10.1.1.128/26     2.2.2.2               0    100      0 65501 i
 *>i 10.1.1.192/26     2.2.2.2               0    100      0 65501 i
 *  i 10.1.5.0/24      2.2.2.2            3328    100      0 i
 *>                    10.1.34.4          3328         32768 i
 r>i 10.1.12.0/24      2.2.2.2               0    100      0 65501 ?
 r>i 10.1.13.0/24      2.2.2.2               0    100      0 65501 ?
```

The output of the **show bgp ipv4 unicast neighbors 10.1.13.1 routes** command on R3 confirms that no routes are being received from R1, as shown in Example 14-59.

Example 14-59 *Verifying Routes Learned from R1*

```
R3# show bgp ipv4 unicast neighbors 10.1.13.1 routes

Total number of prefixes 0
```

Because R1 is not in your AS, you cannot access it for troubleshooting purposes. Therefore, you need to call the admin in AS 65501. However, you should not do that just yet. You can check many more items on R3. For example, to learn BGP routes, you need a BGP adjacency. To confirm that R3 is a neighbor with R1, you issue the **show bgp ipv4 unicast summary** command, as shown in Example 14-60. Based on the output, R1 and R3 are not neighbors because the state is listed as Idle. You think you have found the issue.

Example 14-60 *Verifying Neighbor Adjacency Between R1 and R3*

```
R3# show bgp ipv4 unicast summary
BGP router identifier 3.3.3.3, local AS number 65502
BGP table version is 108, main routing table version 108
9 network entries using 1296 bytes of memory
10 path entries using 800 bytes of memory
5/4 BGP path/bestpath attribute entries using 680 bytes of memory
1 BGP AS-PATH entries using 24 bytes of memory
```

```
0 BGP route-map cache entries using 0 bytes of memory
0 BGP filter-list cache entries using 0 bytes of memory
BGP using 2800 total bytes of memory
BGP activity 17/8 prefixes, 71/61 paths, scan interval 60 secs


Neighbor      V      AS  MsgRcvd MsgSent   TblVer   InQ  OutQ  Up/Down   State/PfxRcd
2.2.2.2       4   65502     34       34       108    0     0   00:24:29          9
4.4.4.4       4   65502     47       48       108    0     0   00:39:00          0
5.5.5.5       4   65502      5        6       108    0     0   00:00:18          0
10.1.13.1     4   65510      0        0         1    0     0   never     Idle
```

Comparing the output in Example 14-60 to your network documentation (refer to Figure 14-9), you notice that the ASN is incorrect for 10.1.13.1. It is listed as 65510, but it should be 65501. To fix the issue, you remove the current **neighbor remote-as** statement and add the correct one, as shown in Example 14-61. After the changes are made, the neighbor relationship is up.

Example 14-61   *Modifying the **neighbor remote-as** Statement*

```
R3# config t
Enter configuration commands, one per line. End with CNTL/Z.
R3(config)# router bgp 65502
R3(config-router)# no neighbor 10.1.13.1 remote-as 65510
R3(config-router)# neighbor 10.1.13.1 remote-as 65501
%BGP-5-ADJCHANGE: neighbor 10.1.13.1 Up
R3(config-router)#
```

To confirm that everything is fine, you access R5 and issue the **show bgp ipv4 unicast** command and confirm that routes from R2 and R3 are now listed in the BGP table, as shown in Example 14-62. Issue solved. Afterhours, you will bring down the link between R1 and R2 and confirm that traffic successfully flows between R3 and R1.

Example 14-62   *Confirming That R5 Knows Routes from R2 and R3*

```
R5# show bgp ipv4 unicast
BGP table version is 56, local router ID is 5.5.5.5
Status codes: s suppressed, d damped, h history, * valid, > best, i - internal,
              r RIB-failure, S Stale, m multipath, b backup-path, f RT-Filter,
              x best-external, a additional-path, c RIB-compressed,
Origin codes: i - IGP, e - EGP, ? - incomplete
RPKI validation codes: V valid, I invalid, N Not found


     Network          Next Hop        Metric LocPrf Weight Path
 * i 1.1.1.1/32       3.3.3.3              0    100      0 65501 ?
 *>i                  2.2.2.2              0    100      0 65501 ?
 * i 10.1.1.0/26      3.3.3.3              0    100      0 65501 i
```

*>i	2.2.2.2	0	100	0 65501 i
* i 10.1.1.64/26	3.3.3.3	0	100	0 65501 i
*>i	2.2.2.2	0	100	0 65501 i
* i 10.1.1.128/26	3.3.3.3	0	100	0 65501 i
*>i	2.2.2.2	0	100	0 65501 i
* i 10.1.1.192/26	3.3.3.3	0	100	0 65501 i
*>i	2.2.2.2	0	100	0 65501 i
r i 10.1.5.0/24	3.3.3.3	3328	100	0 i
r>i	2.2.2.2	3328	100	0 i
r i 10.1.12.0/24	3.3.3.3	0	100	0 65501 ?
r>i	2.2.2.2	0	100	0 65501 ?
r i 10.1.13.0/24	3.3.3.3	0	100	0 65501 ?
r>i	2.2.2.2	0	100	0 65501 ?

With a little bit of spare time on your hands, you decide to check the old log files from R3. You notice the following BGP message listed many times:

```
%BGP-3-NOTIFICATION: sent to neighbor 10.1.13.1 passive 2/2 (peer
in wrong AS) 2 bytes FFDD
```

The syslog message clearly states that the peer is in the wrong AS. Never forget to check your log files as part of troubleshooting. It can save you valuable time.

Trouble Ticket 14-2

Problem: You are the administrator for BGP AS 65501. Users in the 10.1.1.0/26 and 10.1.1.64/26 networks have indicated that they are not able to access resources located at 10.1.5.5. However, they can access resources locally.

You begin troubleshooting by issuing two pings on R1 to 10.1.5.5 and sourcing them from 10.1.1.1 and 10.1.1.65. As shown in Example 14-63, the pings fail.

Example 14-63 *Verifying the Issue with Pings*

```
R1# ping 10.1.5.5 source 10.1.1.1
Type escape sequence to abort.
Sending 5, 100-byte ICMP Echos to 10.1.5.5, timeout is 2 seconds:
Packet sent with a source address of 10.1.1.1
.....
Success rate is 0 percent (0/5)
R1# ping 10.1.5.5 source 10.1.1.65
Type escape sequence to abort.
Sending 5, 100-byte ICMP Echos to 10.1.5.5, timeout is 2 seconds:
Packet sent with a source address of 10.1.1.65
.....
Success rate is 0 percent (0/5)
```

You confirm with the command **show ip route 10.1.5.5** on R1, as shown in Example 14-64, that there is a route to 10.1.5.5 through R2 that is learned from BGP.

Example 14-64   *Confirming That R1 Has a Route to 10.1.5.5*

```
R1# show ip route 10.1.5.5
Routing entry for 10.1.5.0/24
  Known via "bgp 65501", distance 20, metric 3328
  Tag 65502, type external
  Last update from 2.2.2.2 00:12:35 ago
  Routing Descriptor Blocks:
  * 2.2.2.2, from 2.2.2.2, 00:12:35 ago
      Route metric is 3328, traffic share count is 1
      AS Hops 1
      Route tag 65502
      MPLS label: none
```

You would like to see how far the packets are traveling to get a rough idea of where they might be failing. Therefore, you decide to issue an extended **traceroute** in an attempt to gather some additional information. In Example 14-65, you can see that the trace is failing at the next-hop router (R2).

Example 14-65   *Identifying How Far Packets Are Traveling Before They Fail*

```
R1# traceroute 10.1.5.5 source 10.1.1.1
Type escape sequence to abort.
Tracing the route to 10.1.5.5
VRF info: (vrf in name/id, vrf out name/id)
  1 10.1.12.2 40 msec 44 msec 28 msec
  2 * * *
  3 * * *
  4 * * *
...output omitted...
R1# traceroute 10.1.5.5 source 10.1.1.65
Type escape sequence to abort.
Tracing the route to 10.1.5.5
VRF info: (vrf in name/id, vrf out name/id)
  1 10.1.12.2 44 msec 48 msec 36 msec
  2 * * *
  3 * * *
  4 * * *
...output omitted...
```

You are a bit confused, so you sit back and review what you know. You have confirmed that R1 knows about 10.1.5.5 from R2. Therefore, R1 can route packets toward that address. However, the trace that was executed is failing at R2. Is it possible that R2 does not know how to reach 10.1.1.0/26 or 10.1.1.64/26 to respond to the trace? Is it possible that 10.1.5.5 does not know about the networks either and cannot respond to the ping? You decide to focus on your thoughts about R2. R2 needs to know about the routes 10.1.1.0/26 and 10.1.1.64/26 to successfully respond to the trace. Therefore, R1 needs to be advertising the networks with the BGP **network mask** command. On R1, you issue the command **show bgp ipv4 unicast** to verify whether 10.1.1.0/26 and 10.1.1.64/26 are in the BGP table. As shown in Example 14-66, they are. Because they are in the BGP table and they are listed as valid and best, they can be advertised to the neighbors.

Example 14-66 *Verifying R1's BGP Table*

```
R1# show bgp ipv4 unicast
BGP table version is 10, local router ID is 1.1.1.1
Status codes: s suppressed, d damped, h history, * valid, > best, i - internal,
              r RIB-failure, S Stale, m multipath, b backup-path, f RT-Filter,
              x best-external, a additional-path, c RIB-compressed,
Origin codes: i - IGP, e - EGP, ? - incomplete
RPKI validation codes: V valid, I invalid, N Not found

     Network          Next Hop            Metric LocPrf Weight Path
 *>  1.1.1.1/32       0.0.0.0                  0         32768 ?
 *>  10.1.1.0/26      0.0.0.0                  0         32768 i
 *>  10.1.1.64/26     0.0.0.0                  0         32768 i
 *>  10.1.1.128/26    0.0.0.0                  0         32768 i
 *>  10.1.1.192/26    0.0.0.0                  0         32768 i
 *   10.1.5.0/24      10.1.13.3             3328             0 65502 i
 *>                   2.2.2.2               3328             0 65502 i
 *>  10.1.12.0/24     0.0.0.0                  0         32768 ?
 *>  10.1.13.0/24     0.0.0.0                  0         32768 ?
```

You issue the command **show bgp ipv4 unicast summary** to verify the BGP neighbors. Based on the output in Example 14-67, you confirm that both R2 and R3 are BGP neighbors because there is a number in the PfxRcd column.

Example 14-67 *Verifying R1's BGP Neighbors*

```
R1# show bgp ipv4 unicast summary
BGP router identifier 1.1.1.1, local AS number 65501
BGP table version is 10, main routing table version 10
9 network entries using 1296 bytes of memory
10 path entries using 800 bytes of memory
4/4 BGP path/bestpath attribute entries using 544 bytes of memory
1 BGP AS-PATH entries using 24 bytes of memory
0 BGP route-map cache entries using 0 bytes of memory
0 BGP filter-list cache entries using 0 bytes of memory
BGP using 2664 total bytes of memory
BGP activity 19/10 prefixes, 54/44 paths, scan interval 60 secs

Neighbor    V    AS MsgRcvd MsgSent   TblVer  InQ OutQ Up/Down   State/PfxRcd
2.2.2.2     4 65502      38      39       10    0    0 00:30:05             1
10.1.13.3   4 65502       7       6       10    0    0 00:02:06             1
```

Next, you issue the **show bgp ipv4 unicast neighbors 2.2.2.2 advertised-routes** command and the **show bgp ipv4 unicast neighbors 10.1.13.3 advertised-routes** command to verify which routes are being advertised to R2 and R3. As verified in Example 14-68, no routes are being advertised to the neighbors.

Example 14-68   *Verifying R1's Advertised Routes*

```
R1# show bgp ipv4 unicast neighbors 2.2.2.2 advertised-routes

Total number of prefixes 0
R1# show bgp ipv4 unicast neighbors 10.1.13.3 advertised-routes

Total number of prefixes 0
```

What could prevent a route that is valid and best in the BGP table from being advertised to an eBGP neighbor? A filter? You decide to check the output of **show ip protocols** to determine whether a filter is applied to the BGP AS. As shown in Example 14-69, no filter is applied.

Example 14-69   *Verifying Whether R1 Has Any BGP Filters*

```
R1# show ip protocols
*** IP Routing is NSF aware ***

Routing Protocol is "bgp 65501"
  Outgoing update filter list for all interfaces is not set
  Incoming update filter list for all interfaces is not set
  IGP synchronization is disabled
  Automatic route summarization is disabled
  Redistributing: connected
  Unicast Aggregate Generation:
    10.1.1.0/24
  Neighbor(s):
    Address         FiltIn FiltOut DistIn DistOut Weight RouteMap
    2.2.2.2
    10.1.13.3
  Maximum path: 1
  Routing Information Sources:
    Gateway    Distance  Last Update
    2.2.2.2          20  00:37:02
    10.1.13.3        20  21:12:13
  Distance: external 20 internal 200 local 200
```

But wait, you remember from your ENARSI studies (earlier in this chapter) that a prefix list filter does not show up in the output of **show ip protocols**. It shows up only in the BGP neighbor output. Therefore, you issue the command **show bgp ipv4 unicast neighbors | i prefix** to see whether there is any prefix list applied at all. In the output in

Example 14-70, you can see the same prefix list called BGP_FILTER applied twice in the outbound direction.

Example 14-70 *Verifying Whether R1 Has Any BGP Prefix List Filters*

```
R1# show bgp ipv4 unicast neighbors | i prefix
Outgoing update prefix filter list is BGP_FILTER
  prefix-list                          27           0
Outgoing update prefix filter list is BGP_FILTER
  prefix-list                          27           0
```

Now you feel like you are on the right track. Therefore, you issue the **show run | section router bgp** command, as shown in Example 14-71, to examine the BGP configuration on R1 and look for the culprit. You immediately notice that the prefix list BGP_FILTER is applied to neighbor 2.2.2.2 and 10.1.13.3 in the outbound direction.

Example 14-71 *Verifying the BGP Configuration on R1*

```
R1# show run | section router bgp
router bgp 65501
 bgp log-neighbor-changes
 network 10.1.1.0 mask 255.255.255.192
 network 10.1.1.64 mask 255.255.255.192
 network 10.1.1.128 mask 255.255.255.192
 network 10.1.1.192 mask 255.255.255.192
 aggregate-address 10.1.1.0 255.255.255.0
 redistribute connected
 neighbor 2.2.2.2 remote-as 65502
 neighbor 2.2.2.2 password CISCO
 neighbor 2.2.2.2 ebgp-multihop 2
 neighbor 2.2.2.2 update-source Loopback0
 neighbor 2.2.2.2 prefix-list BGP_FILTER out
 neighbor 10.1.13.3 remote-as 65502
 neighbor 10.1.13.3 prefix-list BGP_FILTER out
```

Now you want to examine the prefix list, so you issue the command **show ip prefix-list BGP_FILTER**, as shown in Example 14-72. You immediately notice that 10.1.1.128/26 and 10.1.1.192/26 are being denied. Therefore, they are not being advertised to R2 or R3. You check your documentation, and it states that 10.1.1.128/26 and 10.1.1.192/26 should not be advertised to BGP AS 65502, which this prefix list accomplishes.

Example 14-72 *Verifying a Prefix List on R1*

```
R1# show ip prefix-list BGP_FILTER
ip prefix-list BGP_FILTER: 2 entries
  seq 5 deny 10.1.1.128/26
  seq 10 deny 10.1.1.192/26
```

You think about this issue a bit more, and then it hits you: The implicit deny all at the end of the prefix list is denying all other routes. You propose that by adding the entry **ip prefix-list BGP_FILTER permit 0.0.0.0/0 le 32** to R1, as shown in Example 14-73, you can permit all other routes, which in this case are 10.1.1.0/26 and 10.1.1.64/26. You issue the command **show ip prefix-list BGP_FILTER** to confirm that it has been added.

Example 14-73   *Modifying a Prefix List on R1*

```
R1# config t
Enter configuration commands, one per line. End with CNTL/Z.
R1(config)# ip prefix-list BGP_FILTER permit 0.0.0.0/0 le 32
R1(config)# end
%SYS-5-CONFIG_I: Configured from console by console
R1# show ip prefix-list BGP_FILTER
ip prefix-list BGP_FILTER: 3 entries
 seq 5 deny 10.1.1.128/26
 seq 10 deny 10.1.1.192/26
 seq 15 permit 0.0.0.0/0 le 32
```

To force a refresh of the BGP information being sent to R1's neighbors, you issue the **clear bgp ipv4 unicast * soft out** command. You then issue the commands **show bgp ipv4 unicast neighbors 2.2.2.2 advertised-routes** and **show bgp ipv4 unicast neighbors 10.1.13.3 advertised-routes** to confirm that routes are now being advertised to R1's neighbors. The output shown in Example 14-74 confirms that 10.1.1.0/26 and 10.1.1.64/26 are now being advertised.

Example 14-74   *Verifying Routes Advertised to R1's Neighbors*

```
R1# show bgp ipv4 unicast neighbors 2.2.2.2 advertised-routes
BGP table version is 10, local router ID is 1.1.1.1
Status codes: s suppressed, d damped, h history, * valid, > best, i - internal,
              r RIB-failure, S Stale, m multipath, b backup-path, f RT-Filter,
              x best-external, a additional-path, c RIB-compressed,
Origin codes: i - IGP, e - EGP, ? - incomplete
RPKI validation codes: V valid, I invalid, N Not found

     Network          Next Hop            Metric LocPrf Weight Path
 *>  1.1.1.1/32       0.0.0.0                  0         32768 ?
 *>  10.1.1.0/26      0.0.0.0                  0         32768 i
 *>  10.1.1.64/26     0.0.0.0                  0         32768 i
 ...output omitted...
R1# show bgp ipv4 unicast neighbors 10.1.13.3 advertised-routes
BGP table version is 10, local router ID is 1.1.1.1
Status codes: s suppressed, d damped, h history, * valid, > best, i - internal,
              r RIB-failure, S Stale, m multipath, b backup-path, f RT-Filter,
              x best-external, a additional-path, c RIB-compressed,
Origin codes: i - IGP, e - EGP, ? - incomplete
RPKI validation codes: V valid, I invalid, N Not found
```

```
      Network           Next Hop           Metric LocPrf Weight Path
 *>   1.1.1.1/32        0.0.0.0                 0         32768  ?
 *>   10.1.1.0/26       0.0.0.0                 0         32768  i
 *>   10.1.1.64/26      0.0.0.0                 0         32768  i
...output omitted...
```

However, you still want to confirm that the problem is solved. Can users in 10.1.1.0/26 and
10.1.1.64/26 reach 10.1.5.5? To confirm that the problem is solved, you ping 10.1.5.5 from
10.1.1.1 and 10.1.1.65 again. As shown in Example 14-75, the problem is solved.

Example 14-75 *Verifying That the Problem Is Solved*

```
R1# ping 10.1.5.5 source 10.1.1.1
Type escape sequence to abort.
Sending 5, 100-byte ICMP Echos to 10.1.5.5, timeout is 2 seconds:
Packet sent with a source address of 10.1.1.1
!!!!!
Success rate is 100 percent (5/5), round-trip min/avg/max = 44/58/68 ms
R1# ping 10.1.5.5 source 10.1.1.65
Type escape sequence to abort.
Sending 5, 100-byte ICMP Echos to 10.1.5.5, timeout is 2 seconds:
Packet sent with a source address of 10.1.1.65
!!!!!
Success rate is 100 percent (5/5), round-trip min/avg/max = 20/48/80 ms
```

Trouble Ticket 14-3

Problem: You are the administrator for BGP AS 65502. Traffic reports indicate that all traffic out of the autonomous system is flowing through R3 and across the backup link. This is
undesirable unless the link between R2 and R1 fails.

To verify the issue, you use **traceroute** from R5. As shown in Example 14-76, the trace to
10.1.1.1 and 10.1.1.65 goes through R3 to get to AS 65501.

Example 14-76 *Verifying the Issue*

```
R5# traceroute 10.1.1.1 source 10.1.5.5
Type escape sequence to abort.
Tracing the route to 10.1.1.1
VRF info: (vrf in name/id, vrf out name/id)
 1 10.1.45.4 48 msec 40 msec 28 msec
 2 10.1.34.3 64 msec 32 msec 60 msec
 3 10.1.13.1 [AS 65501] 72 msec 52 msec 48 msec
R5# traceroute 10.1.1.65 source 10.1.5.5
Type escape sequence to abort.
Tracing the route to 10.1.1.65
VRF info: (vrf in name/id, vrf out name/id)
 1 10.1.45.4 48 msec 40 msec 28 msec
 2 10.1.34.3 64 msec 32 msec 60 msec
 3 10.1.13.1 [AS 65501] 72 msec 52 msec 48 msec
```

On R5, you issue the **show ip route 10.1.1.1** command and the **show ip route 10.1.1.65** command to verify the routes. As shown in Example 14-77, the routes are learned via iBGP and are reachable through 3.3.3.3, which is R3.

Example 14-77   *Verifying the Routes on R5*

```
R5# show ip route 10.1.1.1
Routing entry for 10.1.1.0/26
  Known via "bgp 65502", distance 200, metric 0
  Tag 65501, type internal
  Last update from 3.3.3.3 00:01:09 ago
  Routing Descriptor Blocks:
  * 3.3.3.3, from 3.3.3.3, 00:01:09 ago
      Route metric is 0, traffic share count is 1
      AS Hops 1
      Route tag 65501
      MPLS label: none
R5# show ip route 10.1.1.65
Routing entry for 10.1.1.64/26
  Known via "bgp 65502", distance 200, metric 0
 Tag 65501, type internal
  Last update from 3.3.3.3 00:02:10 ago
  Routing Descriptor Blocks:
  * 3.3.3.3, from 3.3.3.3, 00:02:10 ago
      Route metric is 0, traffic share count is 1
      AS Hops 1
      Route tag 65501
      MPLS label: none
```

Are the routes being learned from R2? You issue the **show bgp ipv4 unicast** command to examine the BGP table. According to the BGP table in Example 14-78, 10.1.1.0/26 and 10.1.1.64/26 are both learned from R2 as well. So, why is R5 preferring R3 as the best path? You must now examine the BGP path selection process between the next hops 2.2.2.2 and 3.3.3.3.

First of all, can R5 reach 2.2.2.2 and 3.3.3.3? Obviously, 3.3.3.3 is reachable because R5 is using it at the moment. However, the output of the command **show ip route 2.2.2.2**, as shown in Example 14-79, confirms that 2.2.2.2 is reachable as well. This is important because a path can never be used if the next hop is not reachable.

Next, you examine weight, as shown in Example 14-78. It is 0 for both the path using 2.2.2.2 and the path using 3.3.3.3. A tie means you need to check the next attribute, which is local preference. In this case, the path using 2.2.2.2 is 50, and the path using 3.3.3.3 is 100. Local preference has a default value of 100, and higher is better. That is why 3.3.3.3 is preferred: It has the higher local preference. It appears that the path using 2.2.2.2 had its local preference modified either when it was advertised by R2 or when it was received by R5.

Example 14-78 *Examining R5's BGP Table*

```
R5# show bgp ipv4 unicast
BGP table version is 613, local router ID is 5.5.5.5
Status codes: s suppressed, d damped, h history, * valid, > best, i - internal,
              r RIB-failure, S Stale, m multipath, b backup-path, f RT-Filter,
              x best-external, a additional-path, c RIB-compressed,
Origin codes: i - IGP, e - EGP, ? - incomplete
RPKI validation codes: V valid, I invalid, N Not found

     Network          Next Hop         Metric LocPrf Weight Path
 *>i 1.1.1.1/32       3.3.3.3               0    100      0 65501 ?
 *  i                 2.2.2.2               0     50      0 65501 ?
 *>i 10.1.1.0/26      3.3.3.3               0    100      0 65501 i
 *  i                 2.2.2.2               0     50      0 65501 i
 *>i 10.1.1.64/26     3.3.3.3               0    100      0 65501 i
 *  i                 2.2.2.2               0     50      0 65501 i
 r>i 10.1.5.0/24      3.3.3.3            3328    100      0 i
 r  i                 2.2.2.2            3328     50      0 i
 r>i 10.1.12.0/24     3.3.3.3               0    100      0 65501 ?
 r  i                 2.2.2.2               0     50      0 65501 ?
 r>i 10.1.13.0/24     3.3.3.3               0    100      0 65501 ?
 r  i                 2.2.2.2               0     50      0 65501 ?
```

Example 14-79 *Confirming That 2.2.2.2 Is Reachable*

```
R5# show ip route 2.2.2.2
Routing entry for 2.2.2.2/32
  Known via "eigrp 100", distance 90, metric 131072, type internal
  Redistributing via eigrp 100
  Last update from 10.1.45.4 on GigabitEthernet1/0, 22:33:44 ago
  Routing Descriptor Blocks:
  * 10.1.45.4, from 10.1.45.4, 22:33:44 ago, via GigabitEthernet1/0
    Route metric is 131072, traffic share count is 1
    Total delay is 5020 microseconds, minimum bandwidth is 1000000 Kbit
    Reliability 255/255, minimum MTU 1500 bytes
    Loading 1/255, Hops 2
```

You examine R5's BGP configuration with the **show run | section router bgp** command.
As shown in Example 14-80, there is no indication that the local preference is being modified. If there were, you would see a route map applied to the **neighbor** statement of 2.2.2.2.

Example 14-80 *Examining R5's BGP Configuration*

```
R5# show run | section router bgp
router bgp 65502
 bgp log-neighbor-changes
 neighbor 2.2.2.2 remote-as 65502
 neighbor 2.2.2.2 update-source Loopback0
 neighbor 3.3.3.3 remote-as 65502
 neighbor 3.3.3.3 update-source Loopback0
```

Next, you move to R2 and issue the **show run | section router bgp** command. Immediately you notice a route map called ENARSI_BGP_FILTER applied in the outbound direction for the peer group called ENARSI_IBGP_NEIGHBORS, as shown in Example 14-81. You also notice that R5 is part of the peer group. Therefore, the route map applies to R5. You need to dig into the route map now, so you issue the command **show route-map ENARSI_BGP_FIL-TER**. As shown in Example 14-82, the route map is setting the local preference to 50. You examine the network documentation, and it states that the local preference should be 150.

Example 14-81 *Examining R2's BGP Configuration*

```
R2# show run | section router bgp
router bgp 65502
 bgp log-neighbor-changes
 network 10.1.5.0 mask 255.255.255.0
 neighbor ENARSI_IBGP_NEIGHBORS peer-group
 neighbor ENARSI_IBGP_NEIGHBORS transport connection-mode passive
 neighbor ENARSI_IBGP_NEIGHBORS update-source Loopback0
 neighbor ENARSI_IBGP_NEIGHBORS next-hop-self
 neighbor ENARSI_IBGP_NEIGHBORS route-map ENARSI_BGP_FILTER out
 neighbor 1.1.1.1 remote-as 65501
 neighbor 1.1.1.1 password CISCO
 neighbor 1.1.1.1 ebgp-multihop 2
 neighbor 1.1.1.1 update-source Loopback0
 neighbor 3.3.3.3 remote-as 65502
 neighbor 3.3.3.3 peer-group ENARSI_IBGP_NEIGHBORS
 neighbor 4.4.4.4 remote-as 65502
 neighbor 4.4.4.4 peer-group ENARSI_IBGP_NEIGHBORS
 neighbor 5.5.5.5 remote-as 65502
 neighbor 5.5.5.5 peer-group ENARSI_IBGP_NEIGHBORS
```

Example 14-82 *Examining R2's Route Map*

```
R2# show route-map ENARSI_BGP_FILTER
route-map ENARSI_BGP_FILTER, permit, sequence 10
  Match clauses:
  Set clauses:
  local-preference 50
  Policy routing matches: 0 packets, 0 bytes
```

You modify the route map on R2, as shown in Example 14-83, to solve the issue. You confirm that the changes were applied by using the command **show route-map ENARSI_BGP_FILTER**. The local preference has been successfully modified to 150. To speed up the BGP changes, you issue the command **clear bgp ipv4 unicast * soft out**.

Example 14-83 *Modifying the Local Preference Value in the Route Map*

```
R2# config t
Enter configuration commands, one per line. End with CNTL/Z.
R2(config)# route-map ENARSI_BGP_FILTER 10
R2(config-route-map)# set local-preference 150
R2(config-route-map)# end
%SYS-5-CONFIG_I: Configured from console by console
R2# show route-map ENARSI_BGP_FILTER
route-map ENARSI_BGP_FILTER, permit, sequence 10
 Match clauses:
 Set clauses:
 local-preference 150
 Policy routing matches: 0 packets, 0 bytes
```

You go back to R5 and issue a trace and confirm that the path through R2 is now being used, as shown in Example 14-84.

Example 14-84 *Confirming That the Issue Is Solved*

```
R5# traceroute 10.1.1.1 source 10.1.5.5
Type escape sequence to abort.
Tracing the route to 10.1.1.1
VRF info: (vrf in name/id, vrf out name/id)
 1 10.1.45.4 28 msec 44 msec 8 msec
 2 10.1.24.2 40 msec 40 msec 40 msec
 3 10.1.12.1 [AS 65501] 64 msec 56 msec 100 msec
R5# traceroute 10.1.1.65 source 10.1.5.5
Type escape sequence to abort.
Tracing the route to 10.1.1.65
VRF info: (vrf in name/id, vrf out name/id)
 1 10.1.45.4 28 msec 44 msec 24 msec
 2 10.1.24.2 32 msec 56 msec 48 msec
 3 10.1.12.1 [AS 65501] 68 msec 36 msec 56 msec
```

MP-BGP Trouble Ticket

This section presents a trouble ticket related to the topics discussed earlier in this chapter. The purpose of this trouble ticket is to show a process that you can use when troubleshooting in the real world or in an exam environment. The trouble ticket in this section is based on the topology shown in Figure 14-10.

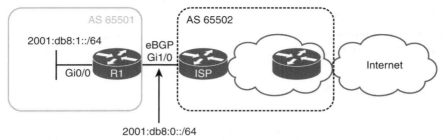

Figure 14-10 *MP-BGP Trouble Ticket Topology*

Trouble Ticket 14-4

Problem: You are an administrator of BGP AS 65501. Another administrator in your AS has asked you for help. The default route from your ISP is not being learned by your router (R1) using BGP. As a result, no one in your AS is able to reach the Internet.

You start by confirming the issue by using the **show ipv6 route** command on R1. In Example 14-85, you can see that no default route is present. The default route is supposed to be learned from the ISP router through MP-eBGP.

Example 14-85 *Verifying the Problem*

```
R1# show ipv6 route
IPv6 Routing Table - default - 5 entries
Codes: C - Connected, L - Local, S - Static, U - Per-user Static route
       B - BGP, R - RIP, H - NHRP, I1 - ISIS L1
       I2 - ISIS L2, IA - ISIS interarea, IS - ISIS summary, D - EIGRP
       EX - EIGRP external, ND - ND Default, NDp - ND Prefix, DCE - Destination
       NDr - Redirect, O - OSPF Intra, OI - OSPF Inter, OE1 - OSPF ext 1
       OE2 - OSPF ext 2, ON1 - OSPF NSSA ext 1, ON2 - OSPF NSSA ext 2, l - LISP
C   2001:DB8::/64 [0/0]
     via GigabitEthernet1/0, directly connected
L   2001:DB8::1/128 [0/0]
     via GigabitEthernet1/0, receive
C   2001:DB8:1::/64 [0/0]
     via GigabitEthernet0/0, directly connected
L   2001:DB8:1::1/128 [0/0]
     via GigabitEthernet0/0, receive
L   FF00::/8 [0/0]
     via Null0, receive
```

You issue the command **show bgp ipv6 unicast** to verify the contents of the IPv6 BGP table, as shown in the following snippet:

```
R1# show bgp ipv6 unicast

R1#
```

There is nothing in the IPv6 BGP table.

Next, you verify whether there are any IPv6 unicast BGP neighbors on R1. The output of **show bgp ipv6 unicast summary** indicates that there are no neighbors, as shown in the following snippet:

```
R1# show bgp ipv6 unicast summary

R1#
```

You have a feeling that there is an error in the BGP configuration on R1. Therefore, you issue the **show run | section router bgp** command to verify R1's BGP configuration. As shown in Example 14-86, the **neighbor 2001:DB8::2 remote-as 65502** command is specified. The address is correct, and the remote AS is correct. However, you notice the command **no neighbor 2001:DB8::2 activate**, which means that the neighbor is not activated in the AF. However, be careful here. This is the IPv4 AF, and you are dealing with IPv6. Therefore, you need to activate the neighbor in the IPv6 AF. If you look closely, you see that there is no IPv6 AF specified, and as a result, the neighbor 2001:DB8::2 is not activated.

Example 14-86 *Viewing the BGP Configuration on R1*

```
R1# show run | section router bgp
router bgp 65501
 bgp router-id 1.1.1.1
 bgp log-neighbor-changes
 neighbor 2001:DB8::2 remote-as 65502
 !
 address-family ipv4
  no neighbor 2001:DB8::2 activate
 exit-address-family
```

To solve this issue, you need to activate the neighbor with the **neighbor 2001:DB8::2 activate** command in IPv6 AF configuration mode, as shown in Example 14-87. After you activate the neighbor, the adjacency comes up.

Example 14-87 *Activating the Neighbor in Address Family Configuration Mode*

```
R1# config t
Enter configuration commands, one per line. End with CNTL/Z.
R1(config)# router bgp 65501
R1(config-router)# address-family ipv6 unicast
R1(config-router-af)# neighbor 2001:db8::2 activate
R1(config-router-af)#
%BGP-5-ADJCHANGE: neighbor 2001:DB8::2 Up
```

You examine the IPv6 BGP table on R1 again by using the **show bgp ipv6 unicast** command and notice that the default route is now listed, as shown in Example 14-88. The routing table, as shown in Example 14-89, also indicates the default route. Problem solved!

Example 14-88 *Verifying That the Default Route Is in the IPv6 BGP Table on R1*

```
R1# show bgp ipv6 unicast
BGP table version is 4, local router ID is 1.1.1.1
Status codes: s suppressed, d damped, h history, * valid, > best, i - internal,
              r RIB-failure, S Stale, m multipath, b backup-path, f RT-Filter,
              x best-external, a additional-path, c RIB-compressed,
Origin codes: i - IGP, e - EGP, ? - incomplete
RPKI validation codes: V valid, I invalid, N Not found


     Network          Next Hop            Metric LocPrf Weight Path
 *>  ::/0             2001:DB8::2              0            0 65502 i
```

14

Example 14-89 *Verifying That the Default Route Is in the IPv6 Routing Table on R1*

```
R1# show ipv6 route
IPv6 Routing Table - default - 6 entries
Codes: C - Connected, L - Local, S - Static, U - Per-user Static route
       B - BGP, R - RIP, H - NHRP, I1 - ISIS L1
       I2 - ISIS L2, IA - ISIS interarea, IS - ISIS summary, D - EIGRP
       EX - EIGRP external, ND - ND Default, NDp - ND Prefix, DCE - Destination
       NDr - Redirect, O - OSPF Intra, OI - OSPF Inter, OE1 - OSPF ext 1
       OE2 - OSPF ext 2, ON1 - OSPF NSSA ext 1, ON2 - OSPF NSSA ext 2, l - LISP
B   ::/0 [20/0]
     via FE80::C836:17FF:FEE8:1C, GigabitEthernet1/0
C   2001:DB8::/64 [0/0]
     via GigabitEthernet1/0, directly connected
L   2001:DB8::1/128 [0/0]
     via GigabitEthernet1/0, receive
C   2001:DB8:1::/64 [0/0]
     via GigabitEthernet0/0, directly connected
L   2001:DB8:1::1/128 [0/0]
     via GigabitEthernet0/0, receive
L   FF00::/8 [0/0]
     via Null0, receive
```

Exam Preparation Tasks

As mentioned in the section "How to Use This Book" in the Introduction, you have a couple choices for exam preparation: the exercises here, Chapter 24, "Final Preparation," and the exam simulation questions in the Pearson Test Prep software.

Review All Key Topics

Review the most important topics in this chapter, noted with the Key Topic icon in the outer margin of the page. Table 14-2 lists these key topics and the page number on which each is found.

Table 14-2   Key Topics

Key Topic Element	Description	Page Number
Example 14-1	Verifying BGP neighbors with **show bgp ipv4 unicast summary**	560
List	Considerations when troubleshooting BGP neighbor relationships	560
Section	The path to the neighbor through the default route	562
Section	Incorrect **neighbor** statement	564
Paragraph	How to control the source addresses of BGP packets	565
Paragraph	How BGP TCP sessions are formed and how you can control the server and client for the TCP session	567
Paragraph	Manipulating the TTL of an eBGP packet	569
Paragraph	How the minimum hold time parameter can prevent BGP neighbor relationships	572
List	The reasons a BGP route might be missing from the BGP table or the routing table	573
Example 14-22	Examining the BGP table	574
List	The requirements of the BGP **network mask** command	575
Paragraph	The BGP next-hop issue	577
Paragraph	Identifying BGP split-horizon issues	580
Paragraph	Troubleshooting filters that may be preventing BGP routes from being advertised or learned	585
Steps	The steps that BGP uses to successfully determine the best path to reach a given network	588
Paragraph	The next-hop issue that occurs when exchanging IPv6 BGP routes over IPv4 BGP TCP sessions	595
Paragraph	Solving the next-hop issue that occurs when exchanging IPv6 BGP routes over IPv4 BGP TCP sessions	595

Define Key Terms

Define the following key terms from this chapter and check your answers in the glossary:

BGP, EGP, eBGP, iBGP, TTL, peer group, split-horizon rule (iBGP), weight, local preference, AS_Path, MED, ISP, MP-BGP, address family

Use the Command Reference to Check Your Memory

The ENARSI 300-410 exam focuses on the practical, hands-on skills that networking professionals use. Therefore, you should be able to identify the commands needed to configure, verify, and troubleshoot the topics covered in this chapter.

This section includes the most important configuration and verification commands covered in this chapter. It might not be necessary to memorize the complete syntax of every command, but you should be able to remember the basic keywords that are needed.

To test your memory of the commands in Table 14-3, go to the companion website and download Appendix B, "Command Reference Exercises." Fill in the missing commands in the tables based on each command description. You can check your work by downloading Appendix C, "Command Reference Exercise Answer Key," from the companion website.

Table 14-3   Command Reference

Task	Command Syntax
Display a router's BGP RID, ASN, information about the BGP's memory usage, and summary information about IPv4/IPv6 unicast BGP neighbors.	**show bgp {ipv4 | ipv6} unicast summary**
Display detailed information about all the IPv4/IPv6 BGP neighbors of a router.	**show bgp {ipv4 | ipv6} unicast neighbors**
Display the IPv4/IPv6 network prefixes present in the IPv4/IPv6 BGP table.	**show bgp {ipv4 | ipv6} unicast**
Show routes known to a router's IPv4/IPv6 routing table that were learned from BGP.	**show {ipv4 | ipv6} route bgp**
Show real-time information about BGP events, such as the establishment of a peering relationship.	**debug ip bgp**
Show real-time information about BGP updates sent and received by a BGP router.	**debug ip bgp updates**
Display updates that occur in a router's IP routing table. (This command is not specific to BGP.)	**debug ip routing**

14

NOTE   The command **show ip bgp** displays the same output as **show bgp ipv4 unicast**. The command **show ip bgp summary** displays the same output as **show bgp ipv4 unicast summary**. The command **show ip bgp neighbors** displays the same output as **show bgp ipv4 unicast neighbors**.

## CHAPTER 15

Route Maps and Conditional Forwarding

This chapter covers the following topics:

- **Conditional Matching:** This section provides an overview of how network prefixes can be conditionally matched with ACLs or prefix lists.

- **Route Maps:** This section explains the structure of a route map and how conditional matching and conditional actions can be combined to filter or manipulate routes.

- **Conditional Forwarding of Packets:** This section explains how a router forwards packets down different paths based on the network traffic.

- **Trouble Tickets:** This section presents three trouble tickets that demonstrate how a structured troubleshooting process can be used to solve a reported problem.

This chapter explores a router's ability to select routes based on a variety of characteristics and then alter its own behavior. Means of altering a router's behavior include route manipulation, route filtering, and modifying the path taken based on the type of traffic flowing through a router.

"Do I Know This Already?" Quiz

The "Do I Know This Already?" quiz allows you to assess whether you should read this entire chapter thoroughly or jump to the "Exam Preparation Tasks" section. If you are in doubt about your answers to these questions or your own assessment of your knowledge of the topics, read the entire chapter. Table 15-1 lists the major headings in this chapter and their corresponding "Do I Know This Already?" quiz questions. You can find the answers in Appendix A, "Answers to the 'Do I Know This Already?' Quiz Questions."

Table 15-1 "Do I Know This Already?" Foundation Topics Section-to-Question Mapping

Foundation Topics Section	Questions
Conditional Matching	1, 2
Route Maps	3–5
Conditional Forwarding of Packets	6

CAUTION The goal of self-assessment is to gauge your mastery of the topics in this chapter. If you do not know the answer to a question or are only partially sure of the answer, you should mark that question as wrong for purposes of self-assessment. Giving yourself credit for an answer that you correctly guess skews your self-assessment results and might provide you with a false sense of security.

1. True or false: An extended ACL that is used to match routes changes behavior if the routing protocol is an IGP rather than BGP.
   a. True
   b. False

2. Which network prefixes match the prefix match pattern 10.168.0.0/13 ge 24? (Choose two.)
   a. 10.168.0.0/13
   b. 10.168.0.0/24
   c. 10.173.1.0/28
   d. 10.104.0.0/24

3. What happens when the route map **route-map QUESTION deny 30** does not contain a conditional match statement?
   a. Any remaining routes are discarded.
   b. Any remaining routes are accepted.
   c. All routes are discarded.
   d. All routes are accepted.

4. What happens to a route that does not match the PrefixRFC1918 prefix list when using the following route map?
   ```
   route-map QUESTION deny 10
     match ip address prefix-list PrefixRFC1918
   route-map QUESTION permit 20
     set metric 200
   ```
   a. The route is allowed, and the metric is set to 200.
   b. The route is denied.
   c. The route is allowed.
   d. The route is allowed, and the default metric is set to 100.

5. True or false: When there are multiple conditional matches of the same type, only one must be met for the prefix to match.
   a. True
   b. False

6. True or false: Policy-based routing will modify a router's routing table.
   a. True
   b. False

Foundation Topics

Conditional Matching

Applying bulk changes to routes does not easily allow for tuning of a network. This section reviews two of the techniques commonly used to conditionally matching a route: using access control lists (ACLs) and using prefix lists.

Access Control Lists (ACLs)

Originally, *access control lists* (*ACLs*) were intended to provide filtering of packets flowing into or out of a network interface, providing much the same functionality as a basic firewall. Today, ACLs provide packet classification for a variety of features, such as *quality of service* (*QoS*), or for identifying networks within routing protocols.

ACLs are composed of *access control entries* (*ACEs*), which are entries in the ACL that identify the action to be taken (**permit** or **deny**) and the relevant packet classification. Packet classification starts at the top (lowest sequence) and proceeds down (higher sequence) until a matching pattern is identified. Once a match is found, the appropriate action (**permit** or **deny**) is taken, and processing stops. At the end of every ACL is an implicit deny ACE, which denies all packets that did not match earlier in the ACL.

> **NOTE** ACE placement within an ACL is important, and unintended consequences may result from ACEs being out of order.

ACLs are classified into two categories:

■ **Standard ACLs:** Define packets based solely on the source network.

■ **Extended ACLs:** Define packets based on the source, destination, protocol, port, or a combination of other packet attributes. This book is concerned with routing and limits the scope of ACLs to source, destination, and protocol.

A standard ACL uses numbered entries 1–99 or 1300–1999 or a named ACL. An extended ACL uses numbered entries 100–199 or 2000–2699 or a named ACL. Named ACLs provide relevance to the functionality of an ACL, can be used with standard or extended ACLs, and are generally preferred over numbered entries.

Standard ACLs

The process for defining a standard ACL is as follows:

Step 1. Define the ACL by using the command **ip access-list standard** {*acl-number* | *acl-name*} and placing the CLI in ACL configuration mode.

Step 2. Configure the specific ACE entry with the command [*sequence*] {**permit** | **deny**} *source source-wildcard*. In lieu of using *source source-wildcard*, the keyword **any** replaces *0.0.0.0 255.255.255.255*, and use of the **host** keyword refers to a /32 IP address so that the *source-wildcard* can be omitted.

NOTE   Some network engineers consider the command **access-list** *acl-number* {**permit**|**deny**} *source source-wildcard* to be a legacy command because it does not allow for the deletion of a specific ACE. Any iteration of this command prefixed with the **no** keyword results in a deletion of the entire ACL and could lead to loss of access to the router if applied to an interface or other unforeseen conditions.

Table 15-2 provides sample ACL entries from within the ACL configuration mode and specifies the networks that would match with a standard ACL.

Table 15-2   Standard ACL-to-Network Entries

ACE Entry	Networks
permit any	Permits all networks
permit 172.16.0.0 0.0.255.255	Permits all networks in the 172.16.0.0 range (that is, 172.16.0.0 to 172.16.255.255)
permit host 192.168.1.1	Permits only the 192.168.1.1/32 network

NOTE   If a sequence is not provided, the sequence number auto-increments by 10 based on the highest sequence number. The first entry is 10. Sequencing allows the deletion of a specific ACE or the insertion of an ACE after the ACL is in use. Increasing ACE entries in increments of 5 or 10 is a good practice as it makes possible the later addition of entries.

Extended ACLs

The process for defining an extended ACL is as follows:

Step 1.   Define the ACL by using the command **ip access-list extended** {*acl-number* | *acl-name*} and placing the CLI in ACL configuration mode.

Step 2.   Configure the specific ACE entry with the command [**sequence**] {*permit* | *deny*} *protocol source source-wildcard destination destination-wildcard*.

The behavior for selecting a network prefix with an extended ACL varies depending on whether the protocol is an interior gateway protocol (IGP; EIGRP, OSPF, or IS-IS) or BGP.

BGP Network Selection

Key Topic

Extended ACLs react differently when matching BGP routes than when matching IGP routes. The source fields match against the network portion of the route, and the destination fields match against the network mask, as shown in Figure 15-1. Until the introduction of prefix lists, extended ACLs were the only match criteria used with BGP.

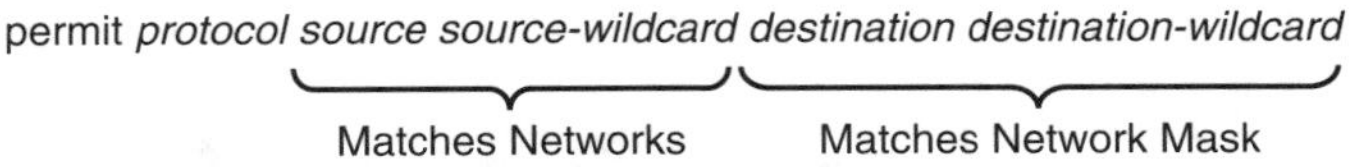

permit *protocol source source-wildcard destination destination-wildcard*
                 Matches Networks   Matches Network Mask

Figure 15-1   *BGP Extended ACL Matches*

Table 15-3 demonstrates the concept of the wildcard for the network mask and subnet mask.

Table 15-3   Extended ACL for BGP Route Selection

Extended ACL	Matches These Networks
permit ip 10.0.0.0 0.0.0.0 255.255.0.0 0.0.0.0	Permits only the 10.0.0.0/16 network
permit ip 10.0.0.0 0.0.255.0 255.255.255.0 0.0.0.0	Permits any 10.0.x.0 network with a /24 prefix length
permit ip 172.16.0.0 0.0.255.255 255.255.255.0 0.0.0.255	Permits any 172.16.x.x network with a /24 through /32 prefix length
permit ip 172.16.0.0 0.0.255.255 255.255.255.128 0.0.0.127	Permits any 172.16.x.x network with a /25 through /32 prefix length

Prefix Matching

In addition to ACLs, prefix lists provide another method of identifying networks in a routing protocol. A prefix list identifies a specific IP address, network, or network range and allows for the selection of multiple networks with a variety of prefix lengths, using a *prefix match specification*. Many network engineers prefer using a prefix list over the ACL network selection method.

A prefix match specification contains two parts: a high-order bit pattern and a high-order bit count, which determines the high-order bits in the bit pattern that are to be matched. Some documentation refers to the *high-order bit pattern* as the *address* or *network* and the *high-order bit count* as the *length* or *mask length*.

In Figure 15-2, the prefix match specification has the high-order bit pattern 192.168.0.0 and the high-order bit count 16. The high-order bit pattern has been converted to binary to demonstrate where the high-order bit count lies. Because there are not additional matching length parameters included, the high-order bit count is an exact match.

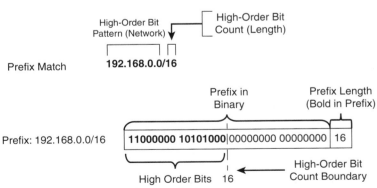

Figure 15-2   *Basic Prefix Match Pattern*

At this point, the prefix match specification logic looks identical to the functionality of an access list. The true power and flexibility come from using matching length parameters to identify multiple networks with specific prefix lengths with one statement. These are the matching length parameter options:

- **le:** Less than or equal to, <=

- **ge:** Greater than or equal to, >=

- **both:** le and ge can also be used together.

Figure 15-3 demonstrates the prefix match specification with a high-order bit pattern of 10.168.0.0 and high-order bit count of 13, where the matching length of the prefix must be greater than or equal to 24.

The 10.168.0.0/13 prefix does not meet the matching length parameter because the prefix length is less than the minimum of 24 bits, whereas the 10.168.0.0/24 prefix does meet the matching length parameter. The 10.173.1.0/28 prefix qualifies because the first 13 bits match the high-order bit pattern, and the prefix length is within the matching length parameter. The 10.104.0.0/24 prefix does not qualify because the high-order bit pattern does not match within the high-order bit count.

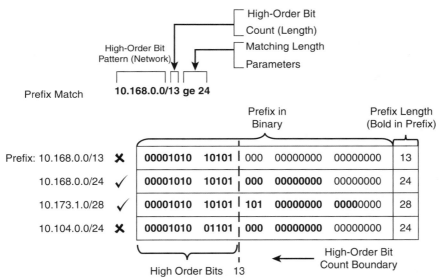

Figure 15-3 *Prefix Match Pattern with Matching Length Parameters*

Figure 15-4 demonstrates a prefix match specification with a high-order bit pattern of 10.0.0.0 and high-order bit count of 8, where the matching length must be between 22 and 26.

The 10.0.0.0/8 prefix does not match because the prefix length is too short. The 10.0.0.0/24 prefix qualifies because the bit pattern matches and the prefix length is between 22 and 26. The 10.0.0.0/30 prefix does not match because the bit pattern is too long. Any prefix that starts with 10 in the first octet and has a prefix length between 22 and 26 matches.

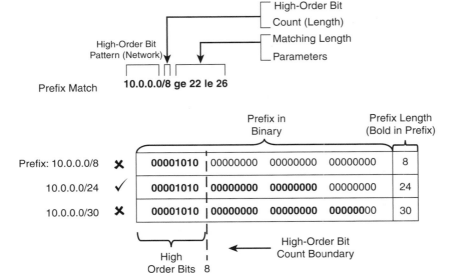

Figure 15-4 *Prefix Match with Ineligible Matched Prefixes*

> **NOTE**   Matching to a specific prefix length that is higher than the high-order bit count requires that *ge-value* and *le-value* match.

Prefix Lists

A *prefix list* can contain multiple prefix-matching specification entries that contain **permit** or **deny** actions. Prefix lists process in sequential order in a top-down fashion, and the first prefix match processes with the appropriate permit or deny action.

Prefix lists are configured with the following global configuration command syntax:

```
ip prefix-list prefix-list-name [seq sequence-number]
{permit | deny} high-order-bit-pattern/high-order-bit-count
[ge ge-value] [le le-value]
```

If a sequence is not provided, the sequence number auto-increments by 5, based on the highest sequence number. The first entry is 5. Sequencing enables the deletion of a specific entry. Because prefix lists cannot be resequenced, it is advisable to leave enough space for insertion of sequence numbers at a later time.

IOS and IOS XE require that *ge-value* be greater than the *high-order bit count* and that *le-value* be greater than or equal to the *ge-value*:

High-order bit count < ge-value <= le-value

Example 15-1 provides a sample prefix list named RFC1918 for all the networks in the RFC 1918 address range. The prefix list only allows /32 prefixes to exist in the 192.168.0.0 network range, not in any other network range in the prefix list.

Notice that sequence 5 permits all /32 prefixes in the 192.168.0.0/16 bit pattern, sequence 10 denies all /32 prefixes in any bit pattern, and sequences 15, 20, and 25 permit routes in the appropriate network ranges. The sequence order is important for the first two entries to ensure that only /32 prefixes exist in the 192.168.0.0 network in the prefix list.

Example 15-1 *Sample Prefix List*

```
ip prefix-list RFC1918 seq 5 permit 192.168.0.0/16 ge 32
ip prefix-list RFC1918 seq 10 deny 0.0.0.0/0 ge 32
ip prefix-list RFC1918 seq 15 permit 10.0.0.0/8 le 32
ip prefix-list RFC1918 seq 20 permit 172.16.0.0/12 le 32
ip prefix-list RFC1918 seq 25 permit 192.168.0.0/16 le 32
```

IPv6 Prefix Lists

The prefix matching logic works exactly the same for IPv6 networks as for IPv4 networks. The most important thing to remember is that IPv6 networks are notated in hex and not in decimal when identifying ranges. Ultimately, however, everything functions at the binary level.

IPv6 prefix lists are configured with the following global configuration command syntax:

ipv6 prefix-list *prefix-list-name* [**seq** *sequence-number*]
{**permit** | **deny**} *high-order-bit-pattern/high-order-bit-count*
[**ge** *ge-value*] [**le** *le-value*]

Example 15-2 provides a sample prefix list named PRIVATE-IPV6 for all the networks in the documentation and benchmarking IPv6 space.

Example 15-2 *Sample IPv6 Prefix List*

```
ipv6 prefix-list PRIVATE-IPV6 seq 5 permit 2001:2::/48 le 128
ipv6 prefix-list PRIVATE-IPV6 seq 10 permit 2001:db8::/32 le 128
```

Route Maps

Route maps provide many different features to a variety of routing protocols. At the simplest level, route maps can filter networks much the same way as ACLs, but they also provide additional capability through the addition or modification of network attributes. To influence a routing protocol, a route map must be referenced from the routing protocol. Route maps are critical to BGP because they are the main component in modifying a unique routing policy on a neighbor-by-neighbor basis.

Route maps have four components:

- **Sequence number:** Dictates the processing order of the route map.

- **Conditional matching criterion:** Identifies prefix characteristics (network, BGP path attribute, next hop, and so on) for a specific sequence.

- **Processing action:** Permits or denies the prefix.

- **Optional action:** Allows for manipulations dependent on how the route map is referenced on the router. Actions can include modification, addition, or removal of route characteristics.

A route map uses the following command syntax:

route-map *route-map-name* [**permit** | **deny**] [*sequence-number*]

The following rules apply to **route-map** statements:

- If a processing action is not provided, the default value **permit** is used.

- If a sequence number is not provided, the sequence number increments by 10 automatically.

- If a matching statement is not included, an implied *all prefixes* is associated with the statement.

- Processing within a route map stops after all optional actions have been processed (if configured) after matching a matching criterion.

- An implicit deny or drop is associated for prefixes that are not associated with a **permit** action.

Example 15-3 provides a sample route map to demonstrate the four components of a route map. The conditional matching criterion is based on network ranges specified in an ACL. Comments have been added to explain the behavior of the route map in each sequence.

Example 15-3   *Sample Route Map*

```
route-map EXAMPLE permit 10
 match ip address ACL-ONE
! Prefixes that match ACL-ONE are permitted. Route-map completes processing upon a
match

route-map EXAMPLE deny 20
 match ip address ACL-TWO
! Prefixes that match ACL-TWO are denied. Route-map completes processing upon a
match

route-map EXAMPLE permit 30
 match ip address ACL-THREE
 set metric 20
! Prefixes that match ACL-THREE are permitted and modify the metric. Route-map
completes
! processing upon a match

route-map EXAMPLE permit 40
! Because a matching criteria was not specified, all other prefixes are permitted
! If this sequence was not configured, all other prefixes would drop because of the
! implicit deny  for all route-maps
```

NOTE   When deleting a specific **route-map** statement, include the sequence number to avoid deleting the entire route map.

Conditional Matching

Now that the components and processing order of a route map have been explained, this section expands on how a route is matched. Table 15-4 provides the command syntax for the most common methods for conditionally matching prefixes and describes their usage. As you can see, there are a number of options available.

Table 15-4   Conditional Match Options

Match Command	Description
match as-path *acl-number*	Selects prefixes based on a regex query to isolate the ASN in the BGP *path attribute (PA)* AS_Path. (Allows for multiple match variables.)
match community community-list	Selects prefixes based on the BGP community attribute.
match interface interface-id	Matches the network or traffic based on the association or inbound interface that is identified.
match ip address {*acl-number* | *acl-name*}	Selects prefixes based on network selection criteria defined in the ACL. (Allows for multiple match variables.)
match {ip | ipv6} **address prefix-list** *prefix-list-name*	Selects prefixes based on prefix selection criteria. (Allows for multiple match variables.)
match local-preference	Selects prefixes based on the BGP attribute *Local Preference*. (Allows for multiple match variables.)
match metric {*1-4294967295* | **external** *1-4294967295*}[*+- deviation*]	Selects prefixes based on the metric, which can be exact, a range, or within acceptable deviation.
match source-protocol {bgp *asn* | connected | eigrp *asn* | ospf *process-id* | static}	Selects prefixes based on the source routing protocol and specific routing process (where applicable).
match tag *tag-value*	Selects prefixes based on a numeric tag (0 to 4294967295) that was set by another router. (Allows for multiple match variables.)

Multiple Conditional Match Conditions

If multiple variables (ACLs, prefix lists, tags, and so on) are configured for a specific route map sequence, only one variable must match for the prefix to qualify. The Boolean logic uses an *or* operator for this configuration.

In Example 15-4, sequence 10 requires that a prefix pass ACL-ONE or ACL-TWO. Notice that sequence 20 does not have a **match** statement, so all prefixes that are not passed in sequence 10 qualify and are denied.

Example 15-4   *Multiple Match Variables Sample Route Map*

```
route-map EXAMPLE permit 10
 match ip address ACL-ONE ACL-TWO
!
route-map EXAMPLE deny 20
```

15

> **NOTE**   Sequence 20 is redundant because of the implicit deny for any prefixes that are not matched in sequence 10.

If multiple match options are configured for a specific route map sequence, both match options must be met for the prefix to qualify for that sequence. The Boolean logic uses an *and* operator for this configuration.

In the following snippet, sequence 10 requires that the prefix match ACL ACL-ONE and that the metric be a value between 500 and 600:

```
route-map EXAMPLE permit 10
 match ip address ACL-ONE
 match metric 550 +- 50
```

If the prefix does not qualify for both match options, the prefix does not qualify for sequence 10 and is denied because there is not another sequence with a permit action.

Complex Matching

Some network engineers find route maps too complex if the conditional matching criteria use an ACL, an AS_Path ACL, or a prefix list that contains a **deny** statement. Example 15-5 shows a configuration in which the ACL uses a **deny** statement for the 172.16.1.0/24 network range.

Reading configurations like this should follow the sequence order first and conditional matching criteria second, and only after a match occurs should the processing action and optional action be used. Matching a **deny** statement in the conditional match criteria excludes the route from that sequence in the route map.

The prefix 172.16.1.0/24 is denied by ACL-ONE, which means there is not a match in sequences 10 and 20; therefore, the processing action (**permit** or **deny**) is not needed. Sequence 30 does not contain a match clause, so any remaining routes are permitted. The prefix 172.16.1.0/24 would pass on sequence 30 with the metric set to 20. The prefix 172.16.2.0/24 would match ACL-ONE and would pass in sequence 10.

Example 15-5   *Complex Matching Route Maps*

```
ip access-list standard ACL-ONE
 deny   172.16.1.0 0.0.0.255
 permit 172.16.0.0 0.0.255.255

route-map EXAMPLE permit 10
 match ip address ACL-ONE
!
route-map EXAMPLE deny 20
 match ip address ACL-ONE
!
route-map EXAMPLE permit 30
 set metric 20
```

> **NOTE** Route maps process in this order: Evaluate the sequence, the conditional match criteria, the processing action, and the optional action. Any **deny** statements in the match component are isolated from the route map sequence action.

Optional Actions

In addition to permitting a prefix to pass, a route map can modify route attributes. Table 15-5 provides a brief overview of the most popular attribute modifications.

Table 15-5 Route Map Set Actions

Set Action	Description
set as-path prepend {*as-number-pattern* | **last-as** *1-10*}	Prepends the AS_Path for the network prefix with the pattern specified or the ASN from the neighboring AS for one or multiple times
set ip next-hop {*ip-address* | **peer-address** | **self**}	Sets the next-hop IP address for any matching prefix. BGP dynamic manipulation uses the **peer-address** or **self** keywords
set local-preference *0-4294967295*	Sets the BGP PA local preference
set metric {**+***value* | **-***value* | *value*}	Modifies the existing metric or sets the metric for a route, with value parameters in the range 0 to 4294967295
set origin {**igp** | **incomplete**}	Sets the BGP PA origin
set tag *tag-value*	Sets a numeric tag (0 to 4294967295) for identification of networks by other routers
set weight *0-65535*	Sets the BGP PA weight

Continue

Default route map behavior is to process the route map sequences in order, and upon the first match, execute the processing action, perform any optional action (if feasible), and stop processing. This prevents multiple route map sequences from processing.

Adding the keyword **continue** to a route map allows the route map to continue processing other route map sequences. Example 15-6 provides a basic configuration. The network prefix 192.168.1.1 matches in sequences 10, 20, and 30. Because the keyword **continue** was added to sequence 10, sequence 20 processes, but sequence 30 does not process because a **continue** command was not present in sequence 20. The 192.168.1.1 prefix is permitted, and it is modified so that the metric is 20, with the next-hop address 10.12.1.1.

Example 15-6 *Route Map Configuration with the **continue** Keyword*

```
ip access-list standard ACL-ONE
 permit 192.168.1.1 0.0.0.0
 permit 172.16.0.0 0.0.255.255
 !
ip access-list standard ACL-TWO
 permit 192.168.1.1 0.0.0.0
 permit 172.31.0.0 0.0.255.255
 !
```

15

```
route-map EXAMPLE permit 10
 match ip address ACL-ONE
set metric 20
 continue
!
route-map EXAMPLE permit 20
 match ip address ACL-TWO
 set ip next-hop 10.12.1.1
!
route-map EXAMPLE permit 30
 set ip next-hop 10.13.1.3
```

NOTE The use of the **continue** command is not common and adds complexity when troubleshooting route maps.

Conditional Forwarding of Packets

A router makes forwarding decisions based on the destination address's IP packets. Some scenarios accommodate other factors, such as packet length or source address, when deciding where the router should forward a packet.

Policy-based routing (*PBR*) allows for conditional forwarding of packets based on packet characteristics besides the destination IP address.

PBR provides the following capabilities:

- Routing by protocol type (ICMP, TCP, UDP, and so on)
- Routing by source IP address, destination IP address, or both
- Manual assignment of different network paths to the same destination, based on tolerance for latency, link speed, or utilization for specific transient traffic

Some of the drawbacks of conditional routing include the following:

- Administrative burden in scalability
- Lack of network intelligence
- Troubleshooting complexity

Packets are examined for PBR processing as they are received on the router interface. Local PBR policies can also identify traffic originating from the router.

PBR verifies the existence of the next-hop IP address and then forwards packets using the specified next-hop address. Additional next-hop addresses can be configured so that if the first next-hop address is not in the Routing Information Base (RIB), the secondary next-hop addresses can be used. If none of the specified next-hop addresses exist in the routing table, the packets are not conditionally forwarded.

> **NOTE**   PBR policies do not modify the RIB because the policies are not universal for all packets. This can often complicate troubleshooting because the routing table displays the next-hop address learned from the routing protocol but does not display a different next-hop address for the conditional traffic.

PBR Configuration

PBR configuration uses a route map with **match** and **set** statements that are attached to the inbound interface. It involves the following steps:

Step 1.   Configure the route map by using the command **route-map** *route-map-name* [**permit** | **deny**] [*sequence-number*].

Step 2.   Identify the conditional match criteria. The conditional match criteria can be based on packet length with the command **match length** *minimum-length maximum-length* or can be based on the packet IP address fields with an ACL using the command **match ip address** {*access-list-number* | *acl-name*}.

Step 3.   Use the command **set ip** [**default**] **next-hop** *ip-address* [*... ip-address*] to specify one or more next hops for packets that match the criteria. The optional **default** keyword changes the behavior so that the next-hop address specified by the route map is used only if the destination address does not exist in the RIB. If a viable route exists in the RIB, then that is the next-hop address that is used for forwarding the packet.

Step 4.   Apply the route map to the inbound interface by using the interface parameter command **ip policy route-map** *route-map-name*.

Figure 15-5 provides a sample topology for illustrating PBR concepts. R1, R2, R3, R4, and R5 are all configured with OSPF. Traffic between R2 and R5 flows across the 10.24.1.0/24 network because sending traffic to R3 adds an additional cost for the second link.

Figure 15-5   *PBR Next-Hop Topology*

Example 15-7 shows the normal traffic path using **traceroute** between the 10.1.1.0/24 and 10.5.5.0/24 networks without PBR configured.

Example 15-7 *traceroute for Normal Traffic Flow*

```
R1# traceroute 10.5.5.5 source 10.1.1.1
Type escape sequence to abort.
Tracing the route to 10.5.5.5
  1 10.12.1.2 5 msec 7 msec 3 msec
  2 10.24.1.4 3 msec 5 msec 13 msec
  3 10.45.1.5 5 msec *  4 msec
```

Example 15-8 shows the PBR configuration on R2 for network traffic from 10.1.1.0/24 destined for the 10.5.5.0/24 network to route traffic to 10.23.1.3 (R3).

Example 15-8 *Configuring Policy-Based Routing*

```
R2
ip access-list extended ACL-PBR
 permit ip 10.1.1.0 0.0.0.255 10.5.5.0 0.0.0.255
!
route-map PBR-TRANSIT permit 10
 match ip address ACL-PBR
 set ip next-hop 10.23.1.3
!
interface GigabitEthernet0/1
 ip address 10.12.1.2 255.255.255.0
 ip policy route-map PBR-TRANSIT
```

NOTE   Notice in Example 15-8 that the route map does not require a second statement for traffic that is supposed to follow the RIB programming.

Example 15-9 shows the traffic path between the 10.1.1.0/24 and 10.5.5.0/24 networks after the conditional route forwarding policies are applied. Notice that the path does not use the 10.24.1.0/24 network, as shown earlier, but takes the path through R3, which is longer.

Example 15-9 *R1 to R5 Paths Demonstrating PBR*

```
R1# trace 10.5.5.5 source 10.1.1.1
Type escape sequence to abort.
Tracing the route to 10.5.5.5
  1 10.12.1.2 3 msec 3 msec 7 msec
  2 10.23.1.3 4 msec 6 msec 14 msec
  3 10.34.1.4 4 msec 1 msec 4 msec
  4 10.45.1.5 11 msec *  6 msec
```

Example 15-10 shows that applying a PBR configuration does not modify the routing table. Conditional packet forwarding is outside the view of the RIB and does not appear when you use the command **show ip route**.

Example 15-10   *R2 Routing Table for the 10.5.5.0/24 Network*

```
R2# show ip route 10.5.5.5
Routing entry for 10.5.5.0/24
  Known via "ospf 1", distance 110, metric 3, type intra area
  Last update from 10.24.1.4 on GigabitEthernet0/2, 00:12:37 ago
  Routing Descriptor Blocks:
  * 10.24.1.4, from 10.45.1.5, 00:12:37 ago, via GigabitEthernet0/2
        Route metric is 3, traffic share count is 1
```

Local PBR

Packets originated by the router are not policy routed. There is a feature for policy routing of locally generated traffic through *local PBR*. Local PBR policies are applied to the router with the global configuration command **ip local policy** *route-map-name*.

15

Figure 15-6 demonstrates a scenario where R1 is managed by an interface specifically for out-of-band management on the 172.16.14.0/24 network. OSPF has been enabled on all the routers and their interfaces except for R1's Gi0/2 interface. ACLs have been placed throughout the network to ensure that traffic destined for the 172.16.14.0/24 network only flows across the 172.16.14.0/24 network. Management traffic should never use the 10.12.1.0/24 network or the 10.23.1.0/24 network.

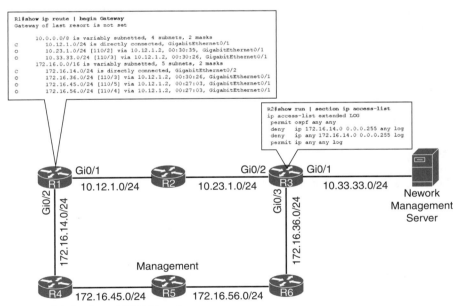

Figure 15-6   *Local PBR Topology*

As part of the problem, routers like R3 try to cross R2 to reach the 172.16.14.0/24 network. R1 does not have OSPF enabled on the 172.16.14.0/24 interface, R1 does not advertise that network into the OSPF routing domain. R4 has enabled its 172.16.14.0/24 network interface, and all traffic is directed toward the correct inbound interface.

Outbound traffic from R1's GigabitEthernet 0/2 interface still uses R1's GigabitEthernet 0/1 interface for forwarding all traffic because R1 learns about routes only through the GigabitEthernet 0/1 interface. It does not learn about the routes from R1's GigabitEthernet 0/2 interface. Even if a static route were used, it is possible that traffic could be forwarded across the out-of-band networks (172.16.0.0/16) for transit traffic, which is not desired.

Example 15-11 demonstrates that R1 forwards traffic from its GigabitEthernet 0/2 interface through 10.12.1.0/24 to the network management system on the 10.33.33.0/24 network. The traffic is blocked by an ACL that is configured on R2, as shown in Figure 15-6.

Example 15-11 *Traffic Is Not Sent Out the Interface on Which It Was Received*

```
R1# traceroute 10.33.33.3 source 172.16.14.1
Type escape sequence to abort.
Tracing the route to 10.33.33.3
VRF info: (vrf in name/id, vrf out name/id)
  1 10.12.1.2 !A  *  !A

R2# 04:40:16.194: %SEC-6-IPACCESSLOGP: list LOG denied udp
172.16.14.1(0) > 10.33.33.3(0), 1 packet
```

If you configure a local PBR on R1, it will only modify the next-hop IP address on traffic that is sourced locally from the 172.16.14.0/24 network by modifying the next-hop IP address to 172.16.14.4. Example 15-12 shows the local PBR configuration for R1.

Example 15-12 *Local PBR Configuration*

```
R1
ip access-list extended ACL-MANAGEMENT-LOCAL-PBR
 permit permit ip 172.16.14.0 0.0.0.255 any
!
route-map LOCAL-PBR permit 10
 match ip address ACL-LOCAL-PBR
 set ip next-hop 172.16.14.4
!
ip local policy route-map LOCAL-PBR
```

With the local PBR policy placed on R1, Example 15-13 verifies that network traffic between 172.16.14.1 and 10.33.33.0/24 will use the out-of-band networks (172.16.0.0/16).

Example 15-13 *Local PBR Verification*

```
R1# traceroute 10.33.33.3 source 172.16.14.1
Type escape sequence to abort.
Tracing the route to 10.33.33.3
VRF info: (vrf in name/id, vrf out name/id)
  1 172.16.14.4 3 msec 3 msec 2 msec
  2 172.16.45.5 6 msec 5 msec 6 msec
  3 172.16.56.6 7 msec 8 msec 6 msec
  4 172.16.36.3 9 msec  *   7 msec
```

You can view policy-based decisions by enabling debugging functionality on policy-based routing with the command **debug ip policy**. Example 15-14 shows the use of the **debug** command and the initiation of traffic that matches the PBR to display the output.

Example 15-14 *PBR Debugging*

```
R1# debug ip policy
Policy routing debugging is on

R1# ping  10.33.33.3 source 172.16.14.1
! Output omitted for brevity
Type escape sequence to abort.
Sending 5, 100-byte ICMP Echos to 10.33.33.3, timeout is 2 seconds:
Packet sent with a source address of 172.16.14.1
!!!!!
Success rate is 100 percent (5/5), round-trip min/avg/max = 7/7/7 ms
R1#
01:47:14.986: IP: s=172.16.14.1 (local), d=10.33.33.3, len 100, policy match
01:47:14.987: IP: route map LOCAL-PBR, item 10, permit
01:47:14.987: IP: s=172.16.14.1 (local), d=10.33.33.3 (GigabitEthernet0/2), len 100,
policy routed
01:47:14.988: IP: local to GigabitEthernet0/2 172.16.14.4
01:47:14.993: IP: s=172.16.14.1 (local), d=10.33.33.3, len 100, policy match
01:47:14.994: IP: route map LOCAL-PBR, item 10, permit
01:47:14.994: IP: s=172.16.14.1 (local), d=10.33.33.3 (GigabitEthernet0/2), len 100,
policy routed
..
```

Trouble Tickets

This section presents various trouble tickets related to the topics discussed in this chapter. The purpose of these trouble tickets is to show a process that you can follow when trouble-shooting in the real world or in an exam environment. All trouble tickets in this section are based on the topology shown in Figure 15-7.

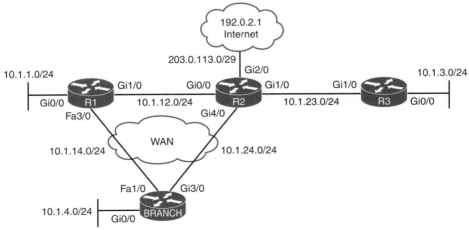

Figure 15-7 *PBR Trouble Tickets Topology*

Trouble Ticket 15-1

Problem: Traffic from 10.1.4.0/24 to 10.1.1.0/24 is routed through R2 using Gi3/0, but it should be routed directly to R1 using Fa1/0.

You begin troubleshooting by verifying the problem with a trace from a PC in 10.1.4.0/24 with the destination 10.1.1.1. As shown in Example 15-15, the path to R2 is based on the hop 10.1.24.2.

Example 15-15 *Verifying the Problem with a Trace to 10.1.1.1*

```
C:\>tracert 10.1.1.1
Tracing route to 10.1.1.1 over a maximum of 30 hops

  1      6 ms     1 ms     2 ms    10.1.4.4
  2      8 ms     3 ms     4 ms    10.1.24.2
  3     12 ms     5 ms     8 ms    10.1.12.1
Trace complete.
```

You access Branch and issue the **show ip route** command. As shown in Example 15-16, the 10.1.1.0/24 network is reachable via the next-hop address 10.1.24.2. However, as shown in Example 15-17, the Enhanced Interior Gateway Protocol (EIGRP) topology table indicates that another path can be used: a path through 10.1.14.1. EIGRP is not using this path because it does not have the best feasible distance (metric). Therefore, you have confirmed that both paths exist, and EIGRP is making the best decision. To force the traffic from 10.1.4.0 to 10.1.1.0 to use the Fast Ethernet link, PBR is used. Therefore, you shift your attention to the PBR configuration.

Example 15-16 *Verifying Routing Table Entries*

```
Branch# show ip route
Codes: L  local, C  connected, S  static, R  RIP, M  mobile, B  BGP
       D  EIGRP, EX  EIGRP external, O  OSPF, IA  OSPF inter area
       N1  OSPF NSSA external type 1, N2  OSPF NSSA external type 2
       E1  OSPF external type 1, E2  OSPF external type 2
       i  IS-IS, su  IS-IS summary, L1  IS-IS level-1, L2  IS-IS level-2
       ia  IS-IS inter area, *  candidate default, U  per-user static route
       o  ODR, P  periodic downloaded static route, H  NHRP, l  LISP
       +  replicated route, %  next hop override

Gateway of last resort is 10.1.24.2 to network 0.0.0.0

D*EX  0.0.0.0/0 [170/15360] via 10.1.24.2, 01:10:05, GigabitEthernet3/0
      10.0.0.0/8 is variably subnetted, 10 subnets, 2 masks
D        10.1.1.0/24 [90/20480] via 10.1.24.2, 01:10:05, GigabitEthernet3/0
D        10.1.3.0/24 [90/20480] via 10.1.24.2, 01:10:05, GigabitEthernet3/0
C        10.1.4.0/24 is directly connected, GigabitEthernet0/0
L        10.1.4.4/32 is directly connected, GigabitEthernet0/0
D        10.1.12.0/24 [90/15360] via 10.1.24.2, 01:10:05, GigabitEthernet3/0
```

```
C        10.1.14.0/24 is directly connected, FastEthernet1/0
L        10.1.14.4/32 is directly connected, FastEthernet1/0
D        10.1.23.0/24 [90/15360] via 10.1.24.2, 01:10:05, GigabitEthernet3/0
C        10.1.24.0/24 is directly connected, GigabitEthernet3/0
L        10.1.24.4/32 is directly connected, GigabitEthernet3/0
      192.0.2.0/32 is subnetted, 1 subnets
D EX     192.0.2.1 [170/573440] via 10.1.24.2, 00:00:06, GigabitEthernet3/0
      203.0.113.0/29 is subnetted, 1 subnets
D        203.0.113.0 [90/15360] via 10.1.24.2, 01:10:05, GigabitEthernet3/0
```

Example 15-17   *Verifying All EIGRP Routes*

```
Branch# show ip eigrp topology
EIGRP-IPv4 VR(TSHOOT) Topology Table for AS(100)/ID(10.1.24.4)
Codes: P  Passive, A  Active, U  Update, Q  Query, R  Reply,
       r  reply Status, s  sia Status

P 10.1.12.0/24, 1 successors, FD is 1966080
      via 10.1.24.2 (1966080/1310720), GigabitEthernet3/0
      via 10.1.14.1 (13762560/1310720), FastEthernet1/0
P 10.1.14.0/24, 1 successors, FD is 13107200
      via Connected, FastEthernet1/0
P 10.1.3.0/24, 1 successors, FD is 2621440
      via 10.1.24.2 (2621440/1966080), GigabitEthernet3/0
P 10.1.23.0/24, 1 successors, FD is 1966080
      via 10.1.24.2 (1966080/1310720), GigabitEthernet3/0
P 203.0.113.0/29, 1 successors, FD is 1966080
      via 10.1.24.2 (1966080/1310720), GigabitEthernet3/0
P 10.1.4.0/24, 1 successors, FD is 1310720
      via Connected, GigabitEthernet0/0
P 10.1.24.0/24, 1 successors, FD is 1310720
      via Connected, GigabitEthernet3/0
P 0.0.0.0/0, 1 successors, FD is 1966080
      via 10.1.24.2 (1966080/1310720), GigabitEthernet3/0
P 192.0.2.1/32, 1 successors, FD is 73400320, U
      via 10.1.24.2 (73400320/72744960), GigabitEthernet3/0
      via 10.1.14.1 (78643200/72089600), FastEthernet1/0
P 10.1.1.0/24, 1 successors, FD is 2621440
      via 10.1.24.2 (2621440/1966080), GigabitEthernet3/0
      via 10.1.14.1 (13762560/1310720), FastEthernet1/0
```

Because PBR is applied to ingress traffic, you use the **show ip policy** command to verify that Gig0/0 on Branch has a PBR route map attached. As shown in Example 15-18, the route map named PBR_EXAMPLE has been applied.

Example 15-18   *Verifying That a PBR Route Map Is Applied to the Correct Interface*

```
Branch# show ip policy
Interface      Route map
Gi0/0          PBR_EXAMPLE
```

Next, you issue the **show route-map** command to verify the route map, as shown in Example 15-19. There is only a single sequence, and it is a permit sequence that states that any traffic matching the addresses in ACL 100 will be policy routed to the next-hop address 10.1.14.1 *if and only if there is no specific route in the routing table*. Read that sentence again. Why does this happen *if and only if there is no specific route in the routing table*? Because the **ip default next-hop** command is used, PBR examines the routing table, and if there is a specific route in the routing table, it is used. If there is no specific route in the routing table, the packet is routed using policy-based routing.

Example 15-19   *Verifying the Route Map Configuration*

```
Branch# show route-map
route-map PBR_EXAMPLE, permit, sequence 10
  Match clauses:
    ip address (access-lists): 100
  Set clauses:
    ip default next-hop 10.1.14.1
  Policy routing matches: 0 packets, 0 bytes
```

Based on Example 15-19, you know there is a specific route in the routing table to reach 10.1.1.0/24. Therefore, the packets are not routed using policy-based routing. To solve this problem, you need to change the **ip default next-hop** command to **ip next-hop**. Example 15-20 provides the configuration needed to solve this issue.

Example 15-20   *Modifying Route Map Configuration*

```
Branch# config t
Enter configuration commands, one per line. End with CNTL/Z.
Branch(config)# route-map PBR_EXAMPLE permit 10
Branch(config-route-map)# no set ip default next-hop 10.1.14.1
Branch(config-route-map)# set ip next-hop 10.1.14.1
Branch(config-route-map)# end
```

After the configuration has been modified, you verify the changes with the **show route-map** command, as shown in Example 15-21. Now it states *ip next-hop 10.1.14.1*.

Example 15-21   *Verifying the New Route Map Configuration*

```
Branch# show route-map
route-map PBR_EXAMPLE, permit, sequence 10
  Match clauses:
    ip address (access-lists): 100
  Set clauses:
    ip next-hop 10.1.14.1
  Policy routing matches: 0 packets, 0 bytes
```

You issue the same trace from the client PC that you did at the start, and the trace confirms that packets are going across the Fast Ethernet link because of the hop with the IP address 10.1.14.1, as shown in Example 15-22. To further confirm, you issue the command **show route-map** again on Branch, as shown in Example 15-23, and notice that packets have been successfully routed using policy-based routing. Issue solved!

Example 15-22   *Confirming That Packets Are Taking the Correct Path*

```
C:\>tracert 10.1.1.1
Tracing route to 10.1.1.1 over a maximum of 30 hops


1      6 ms     1 ms     2 ms    10.1.4.4
2      8 ms     3 ms     4 ms    10.1.14.1
Trace complete.
```

Example 15-23   *Verifying Policy Matches*

```
Branch# show route-map
route-map PBR_EXAMPLE, permit, sequence 10
  Match clauses:
    ip address (access-lists): 100
  Set clauses:
    ip next-hop 10.1.14.1
  Policy routing matches: 6 packets, 360 bytes
```

Trouble Ticket 15-2

Problem: Traffic from 10.1.4.0/24 to 10.1.1.0/24 is routed though R2 using Gi3/0, but it should be routed directly to R1 using Fa1/0.

You begin troubleshooting by verifying the problem with a trace from a PC in 10.1.4.0/24 (Branch) with the destination 10.1.1.1. As shown in Example 15-24, the path to R2 is used, based on the hop 10.1.24.2.

Example 15-24   *Verifying the Problem with a Trace to 10.1.1.1*

```
C:\>tracert 10.1.1.1
Tracing route to 10.1.1.1 over a maximum of 30 hops


1      6 ms     1 ms     2 ms    10.1.4.4
2      8 ms     3 ms     4 ms    10.1.24.2
3     12 ms     5 ms     8 ms    10.1.12.1
Trace complete.
```

Because the traffic is supposed to be routed using policy-based routing, you access Branch and issue the **debug ip policy** command. You then perform the traceroute on the client again and observe the output of the **debug** commands on Branch. As shown in Example 15-25, there is a policy match for the deny sequence 10 in the PBR_EXAMPLE route map. The **debug** then states that the policy is rejected, and the packet is routed based on the routing table.

So, even though there is a match, the packet is being routed normally. This is because it is a deny sequence that is matched. A deny sequence means *do not use policy-based routing; route normally* instead.

Example 15-25   *Observing debug ip policy output*

```
Branch# debug ip policy
Policy routing debugging is on
Branch#
IP: s=10.1.4.1 (GigabitEthernet0/0), d=10.1.1.1, len 28, policy match
IP: route map PBR_EXAMPLE, item 10, deny
IP: s=10.1.4.1 (GigabitEthernet0/0), d=10.1.1.1, len 28, policy rejected - normal
forwarding
Branch#
```

Next, you issue the **show route-map** command to verify the route map, as shown in Example 15-26. There is only a single sequence, and it is a deny sequence that states any traffic matching the addresses in ACL 100 will be routed normally, regardless of any set clauses, because it is a deny sequence.

Example 15-26   *Verifying Route Map Configuration*

```
Branch# show route-map
route-map PBR_EXAMPLE, deny, sequence 10
  Match clauses:
    ip address (access-lists): 100
  Set clauses:
    ip next-hop 10.1.14.1
Nexthop tracking current: 0.0.0.0
10.1.14.1, fib_nh:0,oce:0,status:0

  Policy routing matches: 0 packets, 0 bytes
```

To solve this problem, you need to change sequence 10 so that it is *permit* instead of *deny*. Example 15-27 shows the configuration needed to solve this issue.

Example 15-27   *Modifying Route Map Configuration*

```
Branch# config t
Enter configuration commands, one per line. End with CNTL/Z.
Branch(config)# route-map PBR_EXAMPLE permit 10
Branch(config-route-map)# end
```

After modifying the configuration, you verify the changes with the **show route-map** command, as shown in Example 15-28. Now sequence 10 is a permit sequence.

Example 15-28 *Verifying the New Route Map Configuration*

```
Branch# show route-map
route-map PBR_EXAMPLE, permit, sequence 10
  Match clauses:
    ip address (access-lists): 100
  Set clauses:
    ip next-hop 10.1.14.1
  Policy routing matches: 0 packets, 0 bytes
```

You issue the same trace from the client PC that you did at the start, and the trace confirms that packets are going across the Fast Ethernet link because of the hop with the IP address 10.1.14.1, as shown in Example 15-29. To further confirm, you observe the **debug** commands on Branch, as shown in Example 15-30, and the output states that the traffic is being routed using policy-based routing. Issue solved!

Example 15-29 *Confirming That Packets Are Taking the Correct Path*

```
C:\>tracert 10.1.1.1
Tracing route to 10.1.1.1 over a maximum of 30 hops

  1      6 ms     1 ms     2 ms   10.1.4.4
  2      8 ms     3 ms     4 ms   10.1.14.1
Trace complete.
```

Example 15-30 *Verifying PBR with debug Commands*

```
Branch# debug ip policy
IP: s=10.1.4.1 (GigabitEthernet0/0), d=10.1.1.1, len 28, policy match
IP: route map PBR_EXAMPLE, item 10, permit
IP: s=10.1.4.1 (GigabitEthernet0/0), d=10.1.1.1 (FastEthernet1/0), len 28, policy
routed
IP: GigabitEthernet0/0 to FastEthernet1/0 10.1.14.1
```

Trouble Ticket 15-3

Problem: Traffic from 10.1.4.0/24 to 10.1.1.0/24 is routed though R2 using Gi3/0, but it should be routed directly to R1 using Fa1/0.

You begin troubleshooting by verifying the problem with a trace from a PC in 10.1.4.0/24 with the destination 10.1.1.1. As shown in Example 15-31, the path to R2 is taken based on the hop 10.1.24.2. This traffic should have been routed using policy-based routing to the next-hop IP address 10.1.14.1.

Example 15-31 *Verifying the Problem with a Trace to 10.1.1.1*

```
C:\>tracert 10.1.1.1
Tracing route to 10.1.1.1 over a maximum of 30 hops

  1      6 ms     1 ms     2 ms    10.1.4.4
  2      8 ms     3 ms     4 ms    10.1.24.2
  3     12 ms     5 ms     8 ms    10.1.12.1
Trace complete.
```

Because PBR is applied to ingress traffic, you start verifying that Gig0/0 on Branch has a PBR route map attached by using the **show ip policy** command. As shown in Example 15-32, the route map named PBR_EXAMPLE has been applied to interface Fa1/0. There is no route map applied to Gig0/0 for PBR.

Example 15-32 *Verifying That the PBR Route Map Is Applied to the Correct Interface*

```
Branch# show ip policy
Interface       Route map
Fa1/0           PBR_EXAMPLE
```

However, before you conclude that the route map PBR_EXAMPLE was applied to the wrong interface, make sure that it is the route map that is needed to accomplish the goal. It would be problematic if you removed this route map from Fa1/0 and applied it to Gig0/0 when that is not the true solution to the problem.

Next, you issue the **show route-map PBR_EXAMPLE** command to verify the route map, as shown in Example 15-33. There is only a single sequence, and it is a permit sequence that states any traffic matching the addresses in ACL 100 will be routed using policy-based routing to next-hop address 10.1.14.1.

Example 15-33 *Verifying Route Map Configuration*

```
Branch# show route-map PBR_EXAMPLE
route-map PBR_EXAMPLE, permit, sequence 10
  Match clauses:
    ip address (access-lists): 100
  Set clauses:
    ip next-hop 10.1.14.1
  Policy routing matches: 0 packets, 0 bytes
```

Now it is time to verify ACL 100 with the **show access-list 100** command. As shown in Example 15-34, ACL 100 is matching traffic sourced with any address from 10.1.4.0 to 10.1.4.255 and destined to any address from 10.1.1.0 to 10.1.1.255. You have verified that this is the correct ACL, and the route map is correct as well. Therefore, the route map has been applied to the wrong interface.

Example 15-34 *Verifying ACL 100 Configuration*

```
Branch# show access-lists 100
Extended IP access list 100
    10 permit ip 10.1.4.0 0.0.0.255 10.1.1.0 0.0.0.255
```

To solve this problem, you need to remove the **ip policy route-map** command from Fa1/0 and apply it to interface Gig0/0 instead. Example 15-35 provides the configuration needed to solve this issue.

Example 15-35 *Modifying the ip policy route-map Configuration*

```
Branch# config t
Enter configuration commands, one per line. End with CNTL/Z.
Branch(config)# int fa1/0
Branch(config-if)# no ip policy route-map PBR_EXAMPLE
Branch(config-if)# int gig 0/0
Branch(config-if)# ip policy route-map PBR_EXAMPLE
```

After modifying the configuration, you verify the changes with the **show ip policy** command. As shown in Example 15-36, the route map PBR_EXAMPLE is applied to Gig0/0.

Example 15-36 *Verifying That the Route Map Is Applied to the Correct Interface*

```
Branch# show ip policy
Interface       Route map
Gi0/0           PBR_EXAMPLE
```

You issue the same trace from the client PC that you did at the start, and the trace confirms that packets are going across the Fast Ethernet link because of the hop with the IP address 10.1.14.1, as shown in Example 15-37. Issued solved!

Example 15-37 *Confirming That Packets Are Taking the Correct Path*

```
C:\>tracert 10.1.1.1
Tracing route to 10.1.1.1 over a maximum of 30 hops

  1     6 ms     1 ms     2 ms    10.1.4.4
  2     8 ms     3 ms     4 ms    10.1.14.1
Trace complete.
```

Exam Preparation Tasks

As mentioned in the section "How to Use This Book" in the Introduction, you have a couple choices for exam preparation: the exercises here, Chapter 24, "Final Preparation," and the exam simulation questions in the Pearson Test Prep software.

Review All Key Topics

Review the most important topics in this chapter, noted with the Key Topic icon in the outer margin of the page. Table 15-6 lists these key topics and the page number on which each is found.

Table 15-6   Key Topics

Key Topic Element	Description	Page Number
Paragraph	Access control lists (ACLs)	622
Paragraph	BGP Network Selection	623
Paragraph	Prefix matching specification	624
Paragraph	Prefix match high-order bit pattern	624
Paragraph	Prefix match with length parameters	624
Paragraph	Prefix lists	626
Paragraph	IPv6 prefix lists	627
Paragraph	Route maps	627
Paragraph	Conditional matching	629
Paragraph	Multiple conditional match conditions	629
Paragraph	Complex matching	630
Paragraph	Optional actions	631
Paragraph	Policy-based routing (PBR)	632
Paragraph	Local PBR	635

Define Key Terms

Define the following key terms from this chapter and check your answers in the glossary:

prefix list, route map, policy-based routing

Use the Command Reference to Check Your Memory

The ENARSI 300-410 exam focuses on the practical, hands-on skills that networking professionals use. Therefore, you should be able to identify the commands needed to configure, verify, and troubleshoot the topics covered in this chapter.

This section includes the most important configuration and verification commands covered in this chapter. It might not be necessary to memorize the complete syntax of every command, but you should be able to remember the basic keywords that are needed.

To test your memory of the commands in Table 15-7, go to the companion website and download Appendix B, "Command Reference Exercises." Fill in the missing commands in the tables based on each command description. You can check your work by downloading Appendix C, "Command Reference Exercise Answer Key," from the companion website.

Table 15-7   Command Reference

Task	Command Syntax
Configure a prefix list.	{ip | ipv6} prefix-list *prefix-list-name* [seq *sequence-number*] {permit | deny} *high-order-bit-pattern/high-order-bit-count* [ge *ge-value*] [le *le-value*]
Create a route map entry.	route-map *route-map-name* [permit | deny] [*sequence-number*]
Conditionally match in a route map using AS_Path.	match as-path *acl-number*
Conditionally match in a route map using an ACL.	match ip address {*acl-number* | *acl-name*}
Conditionally match in a route map using a prefix list.	match ip address prefix-list *prefix-list-name*
Conditionally match in a route map using local preference.	match local-preference *local-preference*
Prepend the AS_Path for the network prefix with the pattern specified or from multiple iterations from neighboring autonomous systems.	set as-path prepend {*as-number-pattern* | last-as *1-10*}
Set the next-hop IP address for any matching prefix.	set ip next-hop *ip-address*
Set the BGP PA local preference.	set local-preference *0-4294967295*
Set a numeric tag (0 through 4294967295) for identification of networks by other routers.	set tag *tag-value*

15

## CHAPTER 16

Route Redistribution

This chapter covers the following topics:

- **Redistribution Overview:** This section provides an overview of redistribution fundamentals and rules of redistribution of routes between routing protocols.

- **Protocol-Specific Configuration:** This section explains protocol-specific behaviors and provides configuration examples for redistribution of routes between routing protocols.

This chapter explains the concepts involved with taking the routes from one routing protocol process and injecting them into a different routing protocol process to provide full connectivity.

"Do I Know This Already?" Quiz

The "Do I Know This Already?" quiz allows you to assess whether you should read this entire chapter thoroughly or jump to the "Exam Preparation Tasks" section. If you are in doubt about your answers to these questions or your own assessment of your knowledge of the topics, read the entire chapter. Table 16-1 lists the major headings in this chapter and their corresponding "Do I Know This Already?" quiz questions. You can find the answers in Appendix A, "Answers to the 'Do I Know This Already?' Quiz Questions."

Table 16-1 "Do I Know This Already?" Foundation Topics Section-to-Question Mapping

Foundation Topics Section	Questions
Redistribution Overview	1–6
Protocol-Specific Configuration	7, 8

CAUTION The goal of self-assessment is to gauge your mastery of the topics in this chapter. If you do not know the answer to a question or are only partially sure of the answer, you should mark that question as wrong for purposes of self-assessment. Giving yourself credit for an answer that you correctly guess skews your self-assessment results and might provide you with a false sense of security.

1. R1 learns the 10.11.11.0/24 prefix from EIGRP. EIGRP is redistributed into OSPF on R1, and OSPF is redistributed into BGP on R1. R1 advertises all the BGP network prefixes to R3. Does R3 receive the 10.11.11.0/24 prefix?

   a. Yes

   b. No

2. What is the administrative distance for external EIGRP routes?

   a. 90

   b. 110

   c. 170

   d. 200

3. What is the default seed metric for OSPF?

   a. 20

   b. 100

   c. 32,768

   d. Infinity

4. R1 learns the 10.11.11.0/24 prefix from EIGRP. EIGRP is redistributed into OSPF on R1. R1 has an OSPF adjacency with R2. R2 redistributes OSPF into BGP. R2 advertises all BGP network prefixes to R3. Does R3 receive the 10.11.11.0/24 prefix?

   a. Yes

   b. No

5. What is the administrative distance for external OSPF routes?

   a. 150

   b. 110

   c. 180

   d. 200

6. What is the default seed metric for EIGRP?

   a. 20

   b. 100

   c. 32,768

   d. Infinity

7. Which additional command is needed to redistribute external OSPF routes into EIGRP?

   a. ospf-external-prefixes redistributable

   b. eigrp receive external source networks

   c. ospf redistribute-internal

   d. None

8. Which additional command is needed to redistribute external OSPF routes in to BGP?

   a. ospf-external-prefixes redistributable

   b. match external

   c. bgp redistribute-internal

   d. none

Foundation Topics

Redistribution Overview

An organization might use multiple routing protocols, split up the routing domain between multiple instances (processes) of the same routing protocol, or need to merge networks with another organization that uses a different routing protocol. In all these scenarios, the routes from one routing protocol process need to be exchanged with a different routing protocol process to provide full connectivity. Redistribution is used to inject routes from one routing protocol into another routing protocol.

Figure 16-1 illustrates a network that has multiple routing protocols that are not working together. R1, R2, and R3 exchange routes using Enhanced Interior Gateway Routing Protocol (EIGRP), and R3, R4, and R5 exchange routes with Open Shortest Path First (OSPF). R1 and R5 advertise their Loopback 0 interfaces (192.168.1.1/32 and 192.168.5.5/32) into their appropriate routing protocol, but they cannot establish connectivity to each other. Only R3 can connect to R1 and R5 because it is the only router that participates with both routing protocols and has a complete view of the network.

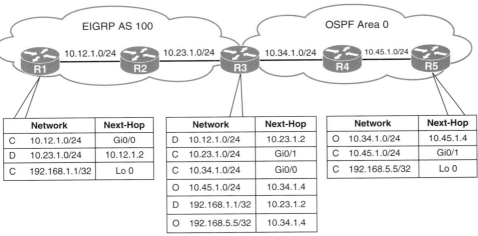

Figure 16-1 *Topology with Multiple Routing Protocols*

Even though R3 has all the routes to EIGRP and OSPF, the routes are not automatically redistributed between the routing protocols. Redistribution must be configured so that EIGRP routes are injected into OSPF and OSPF routes are injected into EIGRP. *Mutual redistribution* is a process in which both routing protocols redistribute into each other in both directions on the same router.

In Figure 16-2, the R3 router is performing mutual redistribution. The OSPF routes are present in EIGRP as external routes, and the EIGRP routes are present in the OSPF routing domain as external routes (Type 5 link-state advertisements [LSAs]). R1 and R5 can establish connectivity between their loopback interfaces because the appropriate routes are present in the routing table.

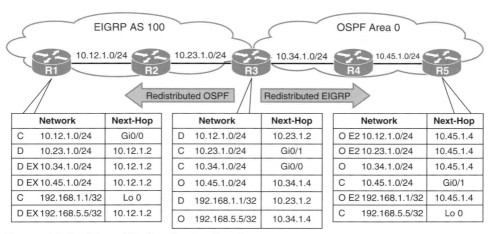

Figure 16-2 *Mutual Redistribution Topology*

Redistribution always encompasses two routing protocols: a source protocol and a destination protocol. The *source protocol* provides the network prefixes that are to be redistributed, and the *destination protocol* receives the injected network prefixes. The redistribution configuration exists under the destination protocol and identifies the source protocol. Using a route map allows for the filtering or modification of route attributes during the injection into the destination protocol. Table 16-2 provides a list of source protocols for redistribution.

Table 16-2 Redistribution Source Protocols

Route Source	Description
Static	Any static route that is present in the Routing Information Base (RIB). A static route can only be a source protocol.
Connected	Any interface in an up state that is not associated with the destination protocol. A connected route can only be a source protocol.
EIGRP	Any routes in EIGRP, including EIGRP-enabled connected networks.
OSPF	Any routes in the OSPF link-state database (LSDB), including OSPF-enabled interfaces.
BGP	Any routes in the Border Gateway Protocol (BGP) Loc-RIB table learned externally. Internal BGP (iBGP) routes require the command **bgp redistribute-internal** for redistribution into Interior Gateway Protocol (IGP) routing protocols.

Redistribution Is Not Transitive

When redistributing between two or more routing protocols on a single router, redistribution is not transitive. In other words, when a router redistributes protocol 1 into protocol 2, and protocol 2 redistributes into protocol 3, the routes from protocol 1 are not redistributed into protocol 3.

Example 16-1 provides sample logic for EIGRP mutually redistributing into OSPF and OSPF mutually redistributing into BGP.

Example 16-1   *Problematic Multiprotocol Redistribution Logic*

```
router eigrp
  redistribute ospf
router ospf
  redistribute eigrp
  redistribute bgp
router bgp
  redistribute ospf
```

Figure 16-3 illustrates redistribution on the router. The EIGRP route 172.16.1.0/24 redistributes into OSPF but does not redistribute into BGP. The BGP route 172.16.3.0/24 redistributes into OSPF but does not redistribute into EIGRP. The prefix 172.16.2.0/24 redistributes into both EIGRP and BGP.

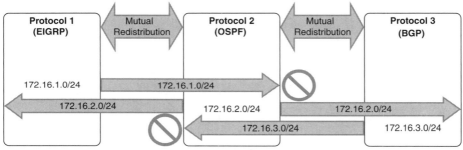

Figure 16-3   *Nontransitive Redistribution Logic*

For routes to be exchanged between all three routing protocols, mutual redistribution must be configured between all three protocols, as shown in Example 16-2.

Example 16-2   *Multiprotocol Redistribution Logic*

```
router eigrp
  redistribute ospf
  redistribute bgp
router ospf
  redistribute eigrp
  redistribute bgp
router bgp
  redistribute ospf
  redistribute eigrp
```

Now that all three routing protocols are mutually redistributed, EIGRP's 172.16.1.0/24 network exists in OSPF and BGP, OSPF's 172.1.6.2.0/24 network exists in EIGRP and BGP, and BGP's 172.16.3.0/24 network exists in OSPF and EIGRP. Figure 16-4 illustrates the router processing for all three network prefixes.

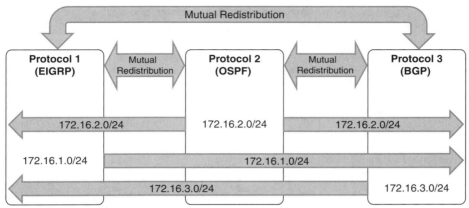

Figure 16-4 *Multiprotocol Mutual Redistribution*

Sequential Protocol Redistribution

Sequential protocol redistribution is redistribution between multiple protocols over a series of routers. For example, in Figure 16-5, R2 redistributes the EIGRP 192.168.1.1/32 prefix into BGP, and R4 redistributes the BGP 192.168.1.1/32 prefix into OSPF. All three routing protocols contain the 192.168.1.1/32 prefix.

16

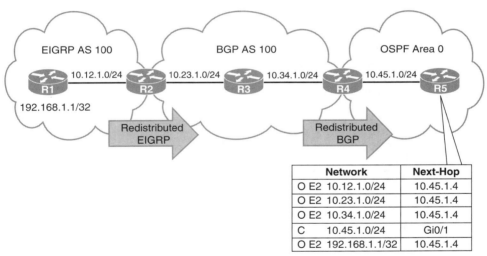

Figure 16-5 *Sequential Protocol Redistribution on Different Routers*

Routes Must Exist in the RIB

A route must exist in the RIB in order for it to be redistributed into the destination protocol. In essence, this provides a safety mechanism by ensuring that the route is deemed reachable by the redistributing router.

In addition to the route being in the RIB, the source protocol that redistributes into the destination protocol must be the source for the route in the RIB. This ensures that the router redistributes only the route it deems the best for the destination protocol. The only exception for this logic is for directly connected interfaces participating in the source protocol because they have an administrative distance (AD) of 0.

In Figure 16-6, R1 and R3 both advertise the 10.13.1.0/24 network, and R5 is redistributing RIP and OSPF routes into EIGRP. RIP has an administrative distance of 120, and OSPF has an administrative distance of 110.

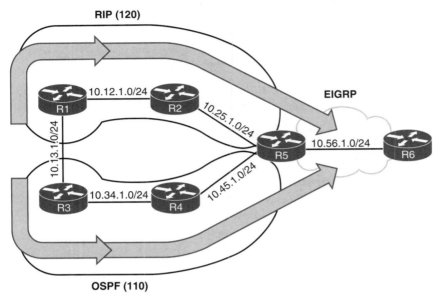

Figure 16-6   *Identification of Source Protocol Topology*

R5 receives route information for 10.13.1.0/24 from both RIP and OSPF routing protocols. Example 16-3 provides verification that R5 contains an entry for the 10.13.1.0/24 network in RIP's database and OSPF's LSDB.

Example 16-3   *Verifying the Network in the Link-State Databases*

```
R5# show ip rip database 10.13.1.0 255.255.255.0 10.13.1.0/24
    [2] via 10.25.1.2, 00:00:30, GigabitEthernet0/0

R5# show ip ospf database router 192.168.3.3
! Output omitted for brevity
          OSPF Router with ID (192.168.5.5) (Process ID 1)
  Link State ID: 192.168.3.3
  Advertising Router: 192.168.3.3
..
  Link connected to: a Stub Network
   (Link ID) Network/subnet number: 10.13.1.0
   (Link Data) Network Mask: 255.255.255.0
```

R5 determines that the most desirable path to reach 10.13.1.0/24 is the OSPF route because it has a lower AD than RIP. Example 16-4 displays R5's routing table. The 10.13.1.0/24 OSPF route is inserted into the RIB.

Example 16-4 *R5's Routing Table*

```
R5# show ip route
! Output omitted for brevity
R       10.12.1.0/24 [120/1] via 10.25.1.2, 22:46:01, GigabitEthernet0/1
O       10.13.1.0/24 [110/3] via 10.45.1.4, 00:04:27, GigabitEthernet0/0
C       10.25.1.0/24 is directly connected, GigabitEthernet0/1
O       10.34.1.0/24 [110/2] via 10.45.1.4, 22:48:24, GigabitEthernet0/0
C       10.45.1.0/24 is directly connected, GigabitEthernet0/0
C       10.56.1.0/24 is directly connected, GigabitEthernet0/2
```

Example 16-5 shows the EIGRP topology table for the 10.13.1.0/24 network. During redistribution, R5 checks the Routing Information Base (RIB) for the 10.13.1.0/24 network and verifies its existence in the RIB and confirms that the source protocol is the protocol that installed the route. EIGRP identifies the source protocol as OSPF, with a path metric of 3.

Example 16-5 *EIGRP Topology Table for the 10.13.1.0/24 Network*

```
R5# show ip eigrp topology 10.13.1.0/24
! Output omitted for brevity
EIGRP-IPv4 Topology Entry for AS(100)/ID(10.56.1.5) for 10.13.1.0/24
   State is Passive, Query origin flag is 1, 1 Successor(s), FD is 2560000256
   Descriptor Blocks:
   10.45.1.4, from Redistributed, Send flag is 0x0
      External data:
      AS number of route is 1
      External protocol is OSPF, external metric is 3
```

> **NOTE** When redistributing from a source protocol with a higher AD into a destination protocol with a lower AD, the route shown in the routing table is always that of the source protocol.

Seed Metrics

Every routing protocol uses a different methodology for calculating the best path for a route. For example, EIGRP can use bandwidth, delay, load, and reliability for calculating its best path, whereas OSPF primarily uses the path metric for calculating the shortest path first (SPF) tree (SPT). OSPF cannot calculate the SPT using EIGRP path attributes, and EIGRP cannot run a diffusing update algorithm (DUAL) using only the total path metric. The source protocol must provide relevant metrics to the destination protocols so that the destination protocol can calculate the best path for the redistributed routes.

Every protocol provides a *seed metric* at the time of redistribution that allows the destination protocol to calculate a best path. The seed metric is a baseline and may reflect a loss of information during redistribution when redistribution occurs between two different protocol types (such as EIGRP and OSPF). A route map modifies the seed metric for a route during redistribution. Table 16-3 provides a list of seed metrics for the destination routing protocol.

16

Table 16-3   Redistribution Source Protocols

Protocol	Default Seed Metric
EIGRP	Infinity. Routes set with infinity are not installed into the EIGRP topology table.
OSPF	All routes are Type 2 external. Routes sourced from BGP use a seed metric of 1, and all other protocols uses a seed metric of 20.
BGP	Origin is set to incomplete, the multi-exit discriminator (MED) is set to the IGP metric, and the weight is set to 32,768.

Protocol-Specific Configuration

Every routing protocol has a unique redistribution behavior. IOS and IOS XE routers use the following command syntax in the destination protocol to identify the source routing protocol:

redistribute {**connected** | **static** | **eigrp** *as-number* | **ospf** *process-id* [**match** {**internal** | **external** [**1**|**2**]}] | **bgp** *as-number*} [*destination-protocol- options*] [**route-map** *route-map-name*].

Redistribution commonly involves the use of route maps to manipulate or filter routes on the redistributing router. Table 16-4 lists additional conditional matching commands for route selection during redistribution.

Table 16-4   **Route Map** match **Command Options**

match Command	Description
match interface *interface-type interface-number*	Selects prefixes based on the outbound interface for the selection of routes
match route-type {**external** [**type-1**	**type-2**]	**internal**	**local**	**nssa-external** [**type-1**	**type-2**]}	Selects prefixes based on routing protocol characteristics: ■ **external:** External BGP, EIGRP, or OSPF ■ **internal:** Internal EIGRP or intra-area/inter-area OSPF routes ■ **local:** Locally generated BGP routes ■ **nssa-external:** NSSA external (Type 7 LSAs)

Table 16-5 lists the route map **set** actions that modify a route as it is redistributed into the destination protocol.

Table 16-5   **Route Map** set **Actions**

set Action	Description
set as-path prepend {*as-number- pattern*	**last-as** 1-10}	Prepends the AS_Path for the network prefix with the pattern specified or uses multiple iterations from the neighboring autonomous system.
set ip next-hop {*ip-address*	**peer- address**	**self**}	Sets the next-hop IP address for any matching prefix. BGP dynamic manipulation requires the **peer-address** or **self** keywords.
set local-preference *0-4294967295*	Sets the BGP PA local preference.

set Action	Description
set metric {**+***value* | **-***value* | *value*} * *value* parameters are 0–4294967295	Modifies the existing metric or sets the metric for a route.
set origin {**igp** | **incomplete**}	Sets the BGP PA origin.
set weight *0-65535*	Sets the BGP PA weight.

Source-Specific Behaviors

The following sections explain specific behaviors for each protocol from a source perspective.

Connected Networks

A common scenario in service provider networks involves the need for external Border Gateway Protocol (eBGP) peering networks to exist in the routing table by other internal BGP (iBGP) routers within the autonomous system. Instead of enabling the routing protocol on the interface so that the network is installed into the routing topology, the networks could be redistributed into the Interior Gateway Protocol (IGP). Choosing not to enable a routing protocol on that link removes security concerns within the IGP.

Connected networks are networks associated with primary and secondary IP addresses for any up interfaces that are not participating with the destination protocol. At times during redistribution, only select interfaces need to be redistributed. This is accomplished using a route map that selects only the desired interfaces.

Example 16-6 provides a reference route map for selecting the specific connected network 192.168.1.1/32 on the Loopback 0 interface.

Example 16-6 *Selective Connected Network Redistribution*

```
router bgp 65100
 address-family ipv4
  redistribute connected route-map RM-LOOPBACK0
!
route-map RM-LOOPBACK0 permit 10
 match interface Loopback0
```

BGP

By default, BGP redistributes only eBGP routes into IGP protocols. In Figure 16-7, R3 advertises the 192.168.3.3/32 network, and R4 advertises the 192.168.4.4/32 network into BGP. R2 is redistributing BGP into OSPF, but only the 192.168.4.4/32 address is redistributed because it is an eBGP route. The iBGP route from R3 was not included because of BGP loop-prevention rules. It is assumed that the IGP routing topology already has a path to reach R3's network 192.168.3.3/32 because it is in the same autonomous system. BGP's default behavior requires that a route have an AS_Path to redistribute into an IGP.

> **NOTE**   BGP is designed to handle a large routing table, whereas IGPs are not. To redistribute BGP into an IGP on a router with a larger BGP table (for example, the Internet table with 800,000+ routes), you use selective route redistribution. Otherwise, the IGP can become unstable in the routing domain, which can lead to packet loss.

You can change BGP behavior so that all BGP routes are redistributed by using the BGP configuration command **bgp redistribute-internal**. To enable the iBGP route 192.168.3.3/32 to redistribute into OSPF, the **bgp redistribute-internal** command is required on R2.

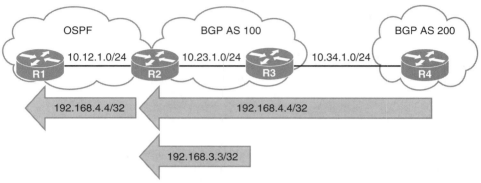

Figure 16-7 *Visualizing the Redistribution of BGP Routes*

> **NOTE** Redistributing iBGP routes into an IGP could result in routing loops. A more logical solution is to advertise the network into the IGP.

Destination-Specific Behaviors

The following sections explain specific behaviors for each protocol from a destination perspective. Routes can be redistributed between different processes of the same routing protocol, or they can be redistributed into a different routing protocol.

EIGRP

External EIGRP routes are given an AD of 170 and use a default seed metric of infinity, which prevents the installation of the routes into the EIGRP topology table. However, if an EIGRP autonomous system redistributes into another EIGRP autonomous system, all the path metrics are included during redistribution.

The default path metric can be changed from infinity to specific values for bandwidth, load, delay, reliability, and maximum transmission unit (MTU), thereby allowing for the installation into the EIGRP topology table. Routers can set the default metric with the address family configuration command **default-metric** *bandwidth delay reliability load mtu*. Delay is entered in tens of microseconds (µs).

The metric can also be set within a route map or at the time of redistribution with the command **redistribute** *source-protocol* [*metric bandwidth delay reliability load mtu*] [**route-map** *route-map-name*].

> **NOTE** Named mode EIGRP configuration occurs in the topology base configuration.

Figure 16-8 provides a topology example in which R2 mutually redistributes OSPF into EIGRP and R3 mutually redistributes BGP into EIGRP. R1 is advertising the Loopback 0 address 192.168.1.1/32, and R4 is advertising the Loopback 0 address 192.168.4.4/32.

Figure 16-8 *EIGRP Redistribution Topology*

Example 16-7 shows the relevant EIGRP configuration. R2 uses the **default-metric** configuration command and is displayed with classic and named mode configurations. Notice where the default metrics are placed with EIGRP named mode configuration. R3's configuration specifies the seed metrics with the redistribution command.

Example 16-7 *EIGRP Redistribution Configuration*

```
R2 (AS Classic Configuration)
router eigrp 100
 default-metric 1000000 1 255 1 1500
 network 10.23.1.0 0.0.0.255
 redistribute ospf 1

R2 (Named Mode Configuration)
router eigrp EIGRP-NAMED
 address-family ipv4 unicast autonomous-system 100
  topology base
   default-metric 1000000 1 255 1 1500
   redistribute ospf 1
  exit-af-topology
  network 10.23.1.0 0.0.0.255

R3 (Named Mode Configuration)
router eigrp EIGRP-NAMED
 address-family ipv4 unicast autonomous-system 100
  topology base
   redistribute bgp 65100 metric 1000000 1 255 1 1500
  exit-af-topology
  network 10.23.1.0 0.0.0.255
 exit-address-family
```

You can overwrite EIGRP seed metrics by setting K values with the route map command **set metric** *bandwidth delay reliability load mtu*. Setting the metric on a prefix-by-prefix basis during redistribution provides a method of traffic engineering. Example 16-8 shows the configuration without the use of the **default-metric** command but by setting the EIGRP metric using a route map.

Example 16-8 *EIGRP Redistribution with Route Map Configuration*

```
R2
router eigrp 100
 network 10.23.1.0 0.0.0.255
 redistribute ospf 1 route-map OSPF-2-EIGRP
!
route-map OSPF-2-EIGRP permit 10
 set metric 1000000 1 255 1 1500
```

Example 16-9 shows the EIGRP topology table with the locally redistributed routes highlighted. The routes that were redistributed by R3 (10.34.1.0/24 and 192.168.4.4/32) have an increased path metric because the delay for the R2–R3 link is added to the initial seed metrics.

Example 16-9 *EIGRP Topology Table of Redistributed Routes*

```
R2# show ip eigrp topology
EIGRP-IPv4 Topology Table for AS(100)/ID(192.168.2.2)
Codes: P - Passive, A - Active, U - Update, Q - Query, R - Reply,
       r - reply Status, s - sia Status

P 10.34.1.0/24, 1 successors, FD is 3072
         via 10.23.1.3 (3072/2816), GigabitEthernet0/1
P 192.168.4.4/32, 1 successors, FD is 3072, tag is 65200
         via 10.23.1.3 (3072/2816), GigabitEthernet0/1
P 10.12.1.0/24, 1 successors, FD is 2816
         via Redistributed (2816/0)
P 192.168.1.1/32, 1 successors, FD is 2816
         via Redistributed (2816/0)
P 10.23.1.0/24, 1 successors, FD is 2816
         via Connected, GigabitEthernet0/1
```

The redistributed routes are shown in the routing table with D EX and an AD of 170, as shown in Example 16-10.

Example 16-10 *Verifying External EIGRP Routes*

```
R2# show ip route | begin Gateway
! Output omitted for brevity
Gateway of last resort is not set
      10.0.0.0/8 is variably subnetted, 5 subnets, 2 masks
C        10.12.1.0/24 is directly connected, GigabitEthernet0/0
C        10.23.1.0/24 is directly connected, GigabitEthernet0/1
D EX     10.34.1.0/24 [170/3072] via 10.23.1.3, 00:07:43, GigabitEthernet0/1
O        192.168.1.1 [110/2] via 10.12.1.1, 00:29:22, GigabitEthernet0/0
D EX     192.168.4.4 [170/3072] via 10.23.1.3, 00:08:49, GigabitEthernet0/1
```

```
R3# show ip route | begin Gateway
! Output omitted for brevity

D EX    10.12.1.0/24 [170/15360] via 10.23.1.2, 00:22:27, GigabitEthernet0/1
C       10.23.1.0/24 is directly connected, GigabitEthernet0/1
C       10.34.1.0/24 is directly connected, GigabitEthernet0/0
D EX    192.168.1.1 [170/15360] via 10.23.1.2, 00:22:27, GigabitEthernet0/1
B       192.168.4.4 [20/0] via 10.34.1.4, 00:13:21
```

EIGRP-to-EIGRP Redistribution

Redistributing routes between EIGRP autonomous systems preserves the path metrics during redistribution. Figure 16-9 shows a topology that includes multiple EIGRP autonomous systems. R2 mutually redistributes routes between AS 10 and AS 20, and R3 mutually redistributes routes between AS 20 and AS 30. R1 advertises the Loopback 0 interface (192.168.1.1/32) into EIGRP AS 10, and R4 advertises the Loopback 0 interface (192.168.4.4/32) into EIGRP AS 30.

Figure 16-9 *Mutual EIGRP Redistribution Topology*

Example 16-11 shows the configurations for R2 and R3. The default seed metrics do not need to be set because they are maintained between EIGRP ASs. R2 is using classic configuration mode, and R3 is using EIGRP named configuration mode.

Example 16-11 *EIGRP Mutual Redistribution Configuration*

```
R2
router eigrp 10
 network 10.12.1.0 0.0.0.255
 redistribute eigrp 20
router eigrp 20
 network 10.23.1.0 0.0.0.255
 redistribute eigrp 10

R3
router eigrp EIGRP-NAMED-20
 address-family ipv4 unicast autonomous-system 20
  topology base
   redistribute eigrp 30
  exit-af-topology
  network 10.23.1.0 0.0.0.255
```

```
!
router eigrp EIGRP-NAMED-30
 address-family ipv4 unicast autonomous-system 30
  topology base
   redistribute eigrp 20
  exit-af-topology
  network 10.34.1.0 0.0.0.255
exit-address-family
```

Example 16-12 provides verification that R1 has routes learned from AS 20 and AS 30, and R4 has learned routes from AS 10 and AS 20.

Example 16-12   *Verifying Routes*

```
R1# show ip route eigrp | begin Gateway
Gateway of last resort is not set

      10.0.0.0/8 is variably subnetted, 4 subnets, 2 masks
D EX    10.23.1.0/24 [170/3072] via 10.12.1.2, 00:09:07, GigabitEthernet0/0
D EX    10.34.1.0/24 [170/3328] via 10.12.1.2, 00:05:48, GigabitEthernet0/0
      192.168.4.0/32 is subnetted, 1 subnets
D EX    192.168.4.4 [170/131328] via 10.12.1.2, 00:05:48, GigabitEthernet0/0

R4# show ip route eigrp | begin Gateway
Gateway of last resort is not set

      10.0.0.0/8 is variably subnetted, 4 subnets, 2 masks
D EX    10.12.1.0/24 [170/3328] via 10.34.1.3, 00:07:31, GigabitEthernet0/0
D EX    10.23.1.0/24 [170/3072] via 10.34.1.3, 00:07:31, GigabitEthernet0/0
      192.168.1.0/32 is subnetted, 1 subnets
D EX    192.168.1.1 [170/131328] via 10.34.1.3, 00:07:31, GigabitEthernet0/0
```

Example 16-13 shows the EIGRP topology table for the route 192.168.4.4/32 in AS 10 and AS 20. The EIGRP path metrics for bandwidth, reliability, load, and delay are the same between the autonomous systems. Notice that the feasible distance (131,072) is the same for both autonomous systems, but the reported distance (RD) is 0 for AS 10 and 130,816 for AS 20. The RD was reset when it was redistributed into AS 10.

Example 16-13   *Topology Table for 192.168.4.4/32*

```
R2# show ip eigrp topology 192.168.4.4/32
! Output omitted for brevity
EIGRP-IPv4 Topology Entry for AS(10)/ID(192.168.2.2) for 192.168.4.4/32
  State is Passive, Query origin flag is 1, 1 Successor(s), FD is 131072
  Descriptor Blocks:
  10.23.1.3, from Redistributed, Send flag is 0x0
      Composite metric is (131072/0), route is External
```

```
        Vector metric:
          Minimum bandwidth is 1000000 Kbit
          Total delay is 5020 microseconds
          Reliability is 255/255
          Load is 1/255
          Minimum MTU is 1500
          Hop count is 2
          Originating router is 192.168.2.2
        External data:
          AS number of route is 20
          External protocol is EIGRP, external metric is 131072
          Administrator tag is 0 (0x00000000)
EIGRP-IPv4 Topology Entry for AS(20)/ID(192.168.2.2) for 192.168.4.4/32
  State is Passive, Query origin flag is 1, 1 Successor(s), FD is 131072
  Descriptor Blocks:
  10.23.1.3 (GigabitEthernet0/1), from 10.23.1.3, Send flag is 0x0
      Composite metric is (131072/130816), route is External
      Vector metric:
          Minimum bandwidth is 1000000 Kbit
          Total delay is 5020 microseconds
          Reliability is 255/255
          Load is 1/255
          Minimum MTU is 1500
          Hop count is 2
          Originating router is 192.168.3.3
        External data:
          AS number of route is 30
          External protocol is EIGRP, external metric is 2570240
```

OSPF

The AD is set to 110 for intra-area, inter-area, and external OSPF routes. External OSPF routes are classified as Type 1 or Type 2, with Type 2 as the default setting. The seed metric is 1 for BGP-sourced routes and 20 for all other protocols. The exception is that if OSPF redistributes from another OSPF process, the path metric is transferred. The main differences between Type 1 and Type 2 external OSPF routes follow:

- Type 1 routes are preferred over Type 2 routes.

- The Type 1 metric equals the redistribution metric plus the total path metric to the autonomous system boundary router (ASBR). In other words, as the LSA propagates away from the originating ASBR, the metric increases.

- The Type 2 metric equals only the redistribution metric. The metric is the same for the router next to the ASBR as for the router 30 hops away from the originating ASBR. If two Type 2 paths have exactly the same metric, the lower forwarding cost is preferred. This is the default external metric type used by OSPF.

For redistribution into OSPF, you use the command **redistribute** *source-protocol* [**subnets**] [**metric** *metric*] [**metric-type** {**1** | **2**}] [**tag** *0-4294967295*] [**route-map** *route-map-name*].

If the optional **subnets** keyword is not included, only the classful networks are redistributed. The optional **tag** keyword allows for a 32-bit route tag to be included on each redistributed route. The **metric** and **metric-type** keywords can be set during redistribution.

Figure 16-10 provides a topology example in which R2 mutually redistributes EIGRP into OSPF, and R3 mutually redistributes RIP into OSPF. R1 is advertising the Loopback 0 interface 192.168.1.1/32, and R4 is advertising the Loopback 0 interface 192.168.4.4/32.

Figure 16-10   *OSPF Redistribution Topology*

Example 16-14 shows the relevant OSPF configuration. Notice that R2 and R3 use different OSPF process numbers but are still able to form an adjacency. The OSPF process numbers are locally significant in linking the OSPF-enabled interfaces to a process, as shown later in this section.

Example 16-14   *OSPF Redistribution Configuration*

```
R2
router ospf 2
 router-id 192.168.2.2
 network 10.23.1.0 0.0.0.255 area 0
 redistribute eigrp 100 subnets

R3
router ospf 3
 router-id 192.168.3.3
 redistribute rip subnets
 network 10.23.1.3 0.0.0.0 area 0
```

Example 16-15 shows the Type 5 LSAs for the external networks in the OSPF domain. This example shows that the routes 10.12.1.0/24, 10.34.1.0/24, 192.168.1.1/32, and 192.168.4.4/32 successfully redistributed into OSPF. The redistributed networks are Type 2 with a metric of 20.

Example 16-15   *OSPF LSDB from R3*

```
R3# show ip ospf database external
! Output omitted for brevity

        OSPF Router with ID (192.168.3.3) (Process ID 2)
```

```
            Type-5 AS External Link States


  Link State ID: 10.12.1.0 (External Network Number )
  Advertising Router: 192.168.2.2
  Network Mask: /24
        Metric Type: 2 (Larger than any link state path)
        Metric: 20


  Link State ID: 10.34.1.0 (External Network Number )
  Advertising Router: 192.168.3.3
  Network Mask: /24
        Metric Type: 2 (Larger than any link state path)
        Metric: 20


  Link State ID: 192.168.1.1 (External Network Number )
  Advertising Router: 10.23.1.2
  Network Mask: /32
        Metric Type: 2 (Larger than any link state path)
        Metric: 20


  Link State ID: 192.168.4.4 (External Network Number )
  Advertising Router: 192.168.3.3
  Network Mask: /32
        Metric Type: 2 (Larger than any link state path)
        Metric: 20
```

The redistributed routes appear in the routing table with O E2 for Type 2 and O E1 for Type 1 external routes. In Example 16-16, the routers do not explicitly set a metric type, and all the redistributed routes from the topology are type E2.

Example 16-16   *Verifying OSPF Route Redistribution*

```
R2# show ip route | begin Gateway
Gateway of last resort is not set


      10.0.0.0/8 is variably subnetted, 5 subnets, 2 masks
C        10.12.1.0/24 is directly connected, GigabitEthernet0/0
C        10.23.1.0/24 is directly connected, GigabitEthernet0/1
O E2     10.34.1.0/24 [110/20] via 10.23.1.3, 00:04:44, GigabitEthernet0/1
      192.168.1.0/32 is subnetted, 1 subnets
D        192.168.1.1 [90/130816] via 10.12.1.1, 00:03:56, GigabitEthernet0/0
      192.168.2.0/32 is subnetted, 1 subnets
C        192.168.2.2 is directly connected, Loopback0
O E2  192.168.4.0/24 [110/20] via 10.23.1.3, 00:04:42, GigabitEthernet0/1

R3# show ip route | begin Gateway
Gateway of last resort is not set
```

```
       10.0.0.0/8 is variably subnetted, 5 subnets, 2 masks
O E2    10.12.1.0/24 [110/20] via 10.23.1.2, 00:05:41, GigabitEthernet0/1
C       10.23.1.0/24 is directly connected, GigabitEthernet0/1
C       10.34.1.0/24 is directly connected, GigabitEthernet0/0
       192.168.1.0/32 is subnetted, 1 subnets
O E2    192.168.1.1 [110/20] via 10.23.1.2, 00:05:41, GigabitEthernet0/1
       192.168.3.0/32 is subnetted, 1 subnets
C       192.168.3.3 is directly connected, Loopback0
R       192.168.4.0/24 [120/1] via 10.34.1.4, 00:00:00, GigabitEthernet0/0
```

OSPF-to-OSPF Redistribution

Redistributing routes between OSPF processes preserves the path metric during redistribution, independent of the metric type. Figure 16-11 shows a topology with multiple OSPF processes and areas. R2 redistributes routes between OSPF process 1 and OSPF process 2, and R3 redistributes between OSPF process 2 and OSPF process 3. R2 and R3 set the metric type to 1 during redistribution so that the path metric increments. R1 advertises the Loopback 0 interface 192.168.1.1/32 into OSPF process 1, and R4 advertises the Loopback 0 interface 192.168.4.4/32 into OSPF process 3.

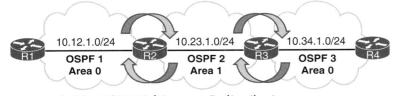

Figure 16-11 *OSPF Multiprocess Redistribution*

> **NOTE** Although the topology in Figure 16-11 looks discontiguous, OSPF is redistributing the routes between processes. This technique can be used to advertise routes over discontiguous OSPF networks, but it results in the loss of path information as the Type 1, Type 2, and Type 3 LSAs are not propagated through route redistribution.

Example 16-17 shows the relevant configurations for R2 and R3. Notice that the metric type is set at the time of redistribution into the destination protocol so that you can see the metric increase as the route travels between the OSPF processes.

Example 16-17 *OSPF Multiprocess Redistribution*

```
R2# show running-config | section router ospf
router ospf 1
 redistribute ospf 2 subnets metric-type 1
 network 10.12.1.0 0.0.0.255 area 0
router ospf 2
 redistribute ospf 1 subnets metric-type 1
 network 10.23.1.0 0.0.0.255 area 1
```

```
R3# show running-config | section router ospf
router ospf 2
 redistribute ospf 3 subnets metric-type 1
 network 10.23.1.0 0.0.0.255 area 1
router ospf 3
 redistribute ospf 2 subnets metric-type 1
 network 10.34.1.0 0.0.0.255 area 0
```

Example 16-18 provides verification that R1 has routes learned from OSPF process 3 (R3 and R4) and that R4 has routes learned from OSPF process 1 (R1 and R2). Notice that the metrics have carried over through the redistribution.

Example 16-18 *Verifying OSPF Redistribution*

```
R1# show ip route ospf | begin Gateway
Gateway of last resort is not set

      10.0.0.0/8 is variably subnetted, 4 subnets, 2 masks
O E1    10.23.1.0/24 [110/2] via 10.12.1.2, 00:00:21, GigabitEthernet0/0
O E1    10.34.1.0/24 [110/3] via 10.12.1.2, 00:00:21, GigabitEthernet0/0
      192.168.4.0/32 is subnetted, 1 subnets
O E1    192.168.4.4 [110/4] via 10.12.1.2, 00:00:21, GigabitEthernet0/0

R4# show ip route ospf | begin Gateway
Gateway of last resort is not set

      10.0.0.0/8 is variably subnetted, 4 subnets, 2 masks
O E1    10.12.1.0/24 [110/3] via 10.34.1.3, 00:01:36, GigabitEthernet0/0
O E1    10.23.1.0/24 [110/2] via 10.34.1.3, 00:01:46, GigabitEthernet0/0
      192.168.1.0/32 is subnetted, 1 subnets
O E1    192.168.1.1 [110/4] via 10.34.1.3, 02:38:49, GigabitEthernet0/0
```

OSPF Forwarding Address

OSPF Type 5 LSAs include a field known as the *forwarding address* that optimizes forwarding traffic when the source uses a shared network segment. The scenario defined in RFC 2328 is not common but is shown in Figure 16-12. OSPF is enabled on all the links in Area 0 except for network 10.123.1.0/24. R1 forms an eBGP session with R2 (the ASBR), which then redistributes the AS 100 route 192.168.1.1/32 into the OSPF domain. R3 has direct connectivity to R1 but does not establish a BGP session with R1.

Example 16-19 shows the Type 5 LSA for the AS 100 route for 192.168.1.1/32. The ASBR is identified as 10.123.1.2, which is the IP address that all OSPF routers forward packets to in order to reach the 192.168.1.1/32 network. Notice that the forwarding address is the default value 0.0.0.0.

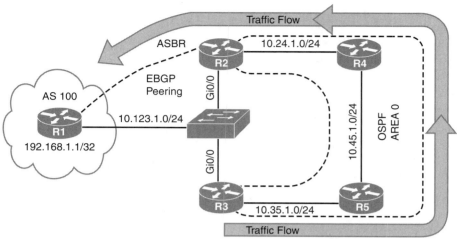

Figure 16-12   *OSPF Forwarding Address Set to the Default*

Example 16-19   *OSPF External LSA with Forwarding Address 0.0.0.0*

```
R3# show ip ospf database external
! Output omitted for brevity
                Type-5 AS External Link States

  Routing Bit Set on this LSA in topology Base with MTID 0
  LS Type: AS External Link
  Link State ID: 192.168.1.1 (External Network Number )
  Advertising Router: 10.123.1.2
  Network Mask: /32
      Metric Type: 2 (Larger than any link state path)
      Metric: 1
      Forward Address: 0.0.0.0
```

Network traffic from R3 (and R5) takes the suboptimal route R3→R5→R4→R2→R1, as shown in Example 16-20. The optimal route would use the directly connected 10.123.1.0/24 network.

Example 16-20   *Verifying Suboptimal Routing*

```
R3# trace 192.168.1.1
Tracing the route to 192.168.1.1
  1 10.35.1.5  0 msec 0 msec 1 msec
  2 10.45.1.4  0 msec 0 msec 0 msec
  3 10.24.1.2  1 msec 0 msec 0 msec
  4 10.123.1.1 1 msec *  0 msec

R5# trace 192.168.1.1
Tracing the route to 192.168.1.1
  1 10.45.1.4  0 msec 0 msec 0 msec
  2 10.24.1.2  1 msec 0 msec 0 msec
  3 10.123.1.1 1 msec *  0 msec
```

The forwarding address in OSPF Type 5 LSAs is specified in RFC 2328 for scenarios such as this. When the forwarding address is 0.0.0.0, all routers forward packets to the ASBR, introducing the potential for suboptimal routing.

The OSPF forwarding address changes from 0.0.0.0 to the next-hop IP address in the source routing protocol when:

- OSPF is enabled on the ASBR's interface that points to the next-hop IP address.

- That interface is not set to passive.

- That interface is a broadcast or nonbroadcast OSPF network type.

When the forwarding address is set to a value besides 0.0.0.0, the OSPF routers forward traffic only to the forwarding address. OSPF has been enabled on R2's and R3's Ethernet interface connected to the 10.123.1.0/24 network, as shown in Figure 16-13. The interface is Ethernet, which defaults to the broadcast OSPF network type, and all conditions have been met.

Example 16-21 provides the Type 5 LSA for the 192.168.1.1/32 network. Now that OSPF has been enabled on R2's 10.123.1.2 interface and the interface is a broadcast network type, the forwarding address has changed from 0.0.0.0 to 10.123.1.1.

16

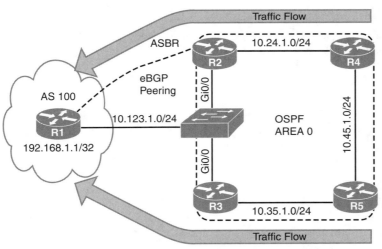

Figure 16-13 *OSPF Forwarding Address Set to Nondefault*

Example 16-21 *OSPF External LSA with Forwarding Address 10.123.1.1*

```
R3# show ip ospf database external
! Output omitted for brevity
              Type-5 AS External Link States1

  Options: (No TOS-capability, DC)
  LS Type: AS External Link
```

```
Link State ID: 192.168.1.1 (External Network Number )
Advertising Router: 10.123.1.2
Network Mask: /32
        Metric Type: 2 (Larger than any link state path)
        Metric: 1

        Forward Address: 10.123.1.1
```

Example 16-22 verifies that connectivity from R3 and R5 now takes the optimal path to R1 because the forwarding address has changed to 10.123.1.1.

Example 16-22   *Verifying Optimal Routing*

```
R3# trace 192.168.1.1
Tracing the route to 192.168.1.1
  1 10.123.1.1 0 msec *  1 msec
```

```
R5# trace 192.168.1.1
Tracing the route to 192.168.1.1
  1 10.35.1.3  0 msec 0 msec 1 msec
  2 10.123.1.1 0 msec *  1 msec
```

If the Type 5 LSA forwarding address is not a default value, the address must be an intra-area or inter-area OSPF route. If the route does not exist, the LSA is ignored and is not installed into the RIB. This ensures that there are at least two routes directly connected to the external next-hop address. Otherwise, there is no reason to include the forwarding address in the LSA.

NOTE   The OSPF forwarding address optimizes forwarding toward the destination network, but return traffic is unaffected. In Figure 16-13, outbound traffic from R3 or R5 still exits at R3's Gi0/0 interface, but return traffic is sent directly to R2.

BGP

Redistributing routes into BGP does not require a seed metric because BGP is a path vector protocol. Redistributed routes have the following BGP attributes set:

- The origin is set to incomplete.

- The next-hop address is set to the IP address of the source protocol.

- The weight is set to 32,768.

- The MED is set to the path metric of the source protocol.

Figure 16-14 shows a topology in which R2 mutually redistributes between OSPF and BGP, and R3 mutually redistributes between EIGRP AS 100 and BGP. R1 is advertising the Loopback 0 interface 192.168.1.1/32, and R4 is advertising the Loopback 0 interface 192.168.4.4/32 into the appropriate protocols.

Figure 16-14 *BGP Redistribution Topology*

Example 16-23 shows R2's BGP configuration for redistributing OSPF into BGP on R2 and R3's configuration for redistributing EIGRP into BGP. R3 has disabled the default IPv4 address family configuration. Notice that R2 and R3 have used the command **bgp redistribute-internal**, which allows for any iBGP learned prefixes to be redistributed into OSPF or EIGRP.

Example 16-23 *BGP Redistribution Configuration*

```
R2 (Default IPv4 Address Family Enabled)
router bgp 65100
 bgp redistribute-internal
 network 10.23.1.0 mask 255.255.255.0
 redistribute ospf 1
 neighbor 10.23.1.3 remote-as 65100

R3 (Default IPv4 Address Family Disabled)
router bgp 65100
 no bgp default ipv4-unicast
 neighbor 10.23.1.2 remote-as 65100
 !
 address-family ipv4
  bgp redistribute-internal
  network 10.23.1.0 mask 255.255.255.0
  redistribute eigrp 100
  neighbor 10.23.1.2 activate
 exit-address-family
```

Example 16-24 shows the BGP table for AS 65100. Notice that the 192.168.1.1/32 and 192.168.4.4/32 networks have been installed into the BGP table. The metric is carried over from the IGP metric during redistribution.

Example 16-24 *BGP Route Table*

```
R2# show bgp ipv4 unicast | begin Network
     Network          Next Hop         Metric LocPrf Weight Path
 *>  10.12.1.0/24     0.0.0.0               0          32768 ?
 * i 10.23.1.0/24     10.23.1.3             0    100      0 i
 *>                   0.0.0.0               0          32768 i
 *>i 10.34.1.0/24     10.23.1.3             0    100      0 ?
 *>  192.168.1.1/32   10.12.1.1             2          32768 ?
 *>i 192.168.4.4/32   10.34.1.4        130816    100      0 ?
```

Example 16-25 shows detailed BGP path information for the redistributed routes. The origin is incomplete, and the BGP metric matches the IGP metric at the time of redistribution.

Example 16-25   *Verifying BGP Routes*

```
R2# show bgp ipv4 unicast 192.168.1.1
! Output omitted for brevity

BGP routing table entry for 192.168.1.1/32, version 3
Paths: (1 available, best #1, table default)
  Local
    10.12.1.1 from 0.0.0.0 (192.168.2.2)
      Origin incomplete, metric 2, localpref 100, weight 32768, valid, sourced, best

R3# show bgp ipv4 unicast 192.168.4.4
BGP routing table entry for 192.168.4.4/32, version 3
Paths: (1 available, best #1, table default)
  Local
    10.34.1.4 from 0.0.0.0 (10.34.1.3)
      Origin incomplete, metric 130816, localpref 100, weight 32768, valid, sourced,
best
```

NOTE   Redistribution of routes from OSPF to BGP does not include OSPF external routes by default. **match external [1 | 2]** is required to redistribute OSPF external routes.

Highly available network designs use multiple points of redistribution to ensure redundancy, which increases the probability of route feedback. Route feedback can cause suboptimal routing or routing loops, but it can be resolved with the techniques explained in this chapter and in Chapter 12, "Advanced BGP."

Reference in This Chapter

RFC 2328, *OSPF Version 2*, John Moy, http://www.ietf.org/rfc/rfc2328.txt, April 1998.

Exam Preparation Tasks

As mentioned in the section "How to Use This Book" in the Introduction, you have a couple choices for exam preparation: the exercises here, Chapter 24, "Final Preparation," and the exam simulation questions in the Pearson Test Prep software.

Review All Key Topics

Review the most important topics in this chapter, noted with the Key Topic icon in the outer margin of the page. Table 16-6 lists these key topics and the page number on which each is found.

Table 16-6   Key Topics

Key Topic Element	Description	Page Number
Paragraph	Redistribution terminology	651
Paragraph	Redistribution is not transitive	651
Paragraph	Sequential protocol redistribution	653
Paragraph	Routes must exist in the RIB	653

Key Topic Element	Description	Page Number
Paragraph	Seed metrics	655
Table 16-3	Redistribution source protocols	656
Paragraph	Source protocol: connected networks	657
Paragraph	Source protocol: BGP	657
Paragraph	Destination protocol: EIGRP	658
Paragraph	EIGRP seed metrics	659
Paragraph	EIGRP-to-EIGRP redistribution	661
Paragraph	Destination protocol: OSPF	663
Paragraph	OSPF classful and classless redistribution	664
Paragraph	OSPF-to-OSPF redistribution	666
Paragraph	OSPF forwarding address	667
Paragraph	Destination protocol: BGP	670

Define Key Terms

Define the following key terms from this chapter and check your answers in the glossary:

mutual redistribution, source protocol, destination protocol, sequential protocol redistribution, seed metric

Use the Command Reference to Check Your Memory

The ENARSI 300-410 exam focuses on the practical, hands-on skills that networking professionals use. Therefore, you should be able to identify the commands needed to configure, verify, and troubleshoot the topics covered in this chapter.

This section includes the most important configuration and verification commands covered in this chapter. It might not be necessary to memorize the complete syntax of every command, but you should be able to remember the basic keywords that are needed.

To test your memory of the commands in Table 16-7, go to the companion website and download Appendix B, "Command Reference Exercises." Fill in the missing commands in the tables based on each command description. You can check your work by downloading Appendix C, "Command Reference Exercise Answer Key," from the companion website.

Table 16-7   Command Reference

Task	Command Syntax
Redistribute the source routing protocol into a destination routing protocol.	`redistribute {connected	static	eigrp` *as-number* `| ospf` *process-id* `[match {internal	external [1|2]}]	bgp` *as-number* `} [`*destination-protocol-options*`] [route-map` *route-map-name*`]`
Set the default EIGRP seed metric for redistributed prefixes.	`default-metric` *bandwidth delay reliability load mtu*
Allow for the redistribution of iBGP learned prefixes into an IGP.	`bgp redistribute-internal`

## CHAPTER 17

Troubleshooting Redistribution

This chapter covers the following topics:

- **Troubleshooting Advanced Redistribution Issues:** This section explains how suboptimal routing and routing loops may occur when redistributing at multiple points in the network. In addition, you will discover how to recognize these redistribution issues and solve them.

- **Troubleshooting IPv4 and IPv6 Redistribution:** This section examines the issues that you should look out for when troubleshooting redistribution for IPv4 and IPv6 routing protocols such as EIGRP, OSPF, and BGP.

- **Redistribution Trouble Tickets:** This section provides trouble tickets that demonstrate how to use a structured troubleshooting process to solve a reported problem.

There are many reasons you might need *redistribution*. It could be because you are performing a migration from one protocol to another, it might be because there are services or applications that need a specific routing protocol, it could be because you are in a mixed-vendor environment and only certain protocols are supported on the various devices, and it might even be because of political issues or country-specific requirements. Regardless of the reason, when you are using multiple routing protocols, you will more than likely be redistributing between them so that all networks can be reached by all users in the network. As a result, you are likely to experience issues that will require you to troubleshoot.

This chapter explores issues you might face when redistributing at multiple points between two protocols and examines the differences between redistributing into Enhanced Interior Gateway Routing Protocol (EIGRP), Open Shortest Path First (OSPF), and Border Gateway Protocol (BGP) for both IPv4 and IPv6. You will learn what to look out for so that you can quickly solve any issues related to redistribution. To wrap up the chapter, you will examine four redistribution trouble tickets.

"Do I Know This Already?" Quiz

The "Do I Know This Already?" quiz allows you to assess whether you should read this entire chapter thoroughly or jump to the "Exam Preparation Tasks" section. If you are in doubt about your answers to these questions or your own assessment of your knowledge of the topics, read the entire chapter. Table 17-1 lists the major headings in this chapter and their corresponding "Do I Know This Already?" quiz questions. You can find the answers in Appendix A, "Answers to the 'Do I Know This Already?' Quiz Questions."

Table 17-1 "Do I Know This Already?" Foundation Topics Section-to-Question Mapping

Foundation Topics Section	Questions
Troubleshooting Advanced Redistribution Issues	1–5
Troubleshooting IPv4 and IPv6 Redistribution	6–14

> **CAUTION** The goal of self-assessment is to gauge your mastery of the topics in this chapter. If you do not know the answer to a question or are only partially sure of the answer, you should mark that question as wrong for purposes of self-assessment. Giving yourself credit for an answer that you correctly guess skews your self-assessment results and might provide you with a false sense of security.

1. Which of the following are methods that can be used to solve routing issues caused by multipoint redistribution? (Choose all that apply.)

    a. Modify the seed metrics of the redistributed routes.

    b. Modify the administrative distances of redistributed routes.

    c. Tag routes as they are redistributed and then deny them from being redistributed back into the originating routing source.

    d. Modify the metric used to reach the boundary routers.

2. Which of the following methods can be used to solve suboptimal routing issues caused by redistribution?

    a. Modify the seed metrics of the redistributed routes.

    b. Modify the administrative distances of redistributed routes.

    c. Redistribute only classless networks.

    d. Modify the metrics of the routes before redistribution.

3. Which of the following is true?

    a. The EIGRP command **distance 165 10.1.1.1 0.0.0.0** changes the AD to 165 for all EIGRP routes learned from neighbor 10.1.1.1.

    b. The EIGRP command **distance 165 10.1.1.1 0.0.0.0** changes the AD to 165 for the EIGRP learned route 10.1.1.0/24.

    c. The EIGRP command **distance 165 10.1.1.1 0.0.0.0** changes the AD to 165 for internal EIGRP routes learned from neighbor 10.1.1.1.

    d. The EIGRP command **distance 165 10.1.1.1 0.0.0.0** changes the AD to 165 for external EIGRP routes learned from neighbor 10.1.1.1.

4. You have redistributed the 10.0.0.0/24 network from RIP into EIGRP and then from EIGRP into OSPF. What will be the administrative distance and source routing protocol code for the 10.0.0.0/24 network in the routing table of an EIGRP router in the EIGRP AS?

    a. Administrative distance will be 170, and code will be D EX.

    b. Administrative distance will be 90, and code will be D.

    c. Administrative distance will be 110, and code will be O.

    d. Administrative distance will be 110, and code will be O E2.

    e. Administrative distance will be 120, and code will be R.

5. You have redistributed the 10.0.0.0/24 network from RIP into EIGRP and then from EIGRP into OSPF. What will be the administrative distance and source routing protocol code for the 10.0.0.0/24 network in the routing table of an OSPF router in the OSPF routing domain?

    a. Administrative distance will be 170, and code will be D EX.

    b. Administrative distance will be 90, and code will be D.

    c. Administrative distance will be 110, and code will be O.

    d. Administrative distance will be 110, and code will be O E2.

    e. Administrative distance will be 120, and code will be R.

6. What must be true for a route from one routing source to be redistributed into a different routing source?

    a. The routing sources must have similar metrics.

    b. The routing sources must have similar administrative distances.

    c. The route must be in the routing table on the router performing redistribution.

    d. The route must be a directly connected route on the router performing redistribution.

7. Which of the following routing protocols have a default seed metric of unreachable? (Choose two.)

    a. RIP

    b. EIGRP

    c. OSPF

    d. BGP

8. Which of the following routing protocols has a default seed metric of 20?

    a. RIPng

    b. EIGRP for IPv6

    c. OSPFv3

    d. eBGP

9. When redistributing, you have four options for the seed metric: accepting the default value, specifying it with the **default-metric** command, using the **metric** option with the **redistribute** command, and using a route map. If all four of these are configured with different values, which will be preferred?

    a. Default values

    b. **default-metric** command

    c. **metric** option with the **redistribute** command

    d. Route map attached to the **redistribute** command

10. Which option is mandatory when redistributing OSPF routes into EIGRP?

    a. metric

    b. metric type

    c. subnets

    d. match

11. Which option is mandatory when redistributing classless networks into OSPFv2?

    a. metric

    b. metric type

    c. subnets

    d. match

12. Which of the following is not included when redistributing from one IPv6 routing protocol into another IPv6 routing protocol?

    a. A prefix

    b. A seed metric

    c. A directly connected route participating in the routing process

    d. An administrative distance

13. During redistribution that uses route maps, what occurs to a route that matches a deny entry in the route map?

    a. It is redistributed with default values.

    b. It is redistributed with the values in the set clause.

    c. It is redistributed only if there is a routing table entry for it.

    d. It is not redistributed.

14. You have redistributed the 10.0.10.64/26 network from RIP into EIGRP into OSPFv2. The 10.0.10.64/26 network is not appearing in the routing tables on any of the OSPFv2 routers. Based on the options provided, which is the most likely reason this is occurring?

    a. A metric was not provided.

    b. A metric type was not provided.

    c. The **subnets** keyword was not provided.

    d. You can't redistribute a route more than once.

Foundation Topics

Troubleshooting Advanced Redistribution Issues

Highly available network designs remove single points of failure through redundancy. When redistributing routes between protocols, there must be at least two points of redistribution in the network (as you will see in Figure 17-1) to ensure that connectivity is maintained during a failure. When performing *multipoint redistribution* between two protocols, the following issues may arise:

- Suboptimal routing

- Routing loops

These issues can lead to loss of connectivity or slow connectivity for end users. This chapter explores how to recognize these issues and the options available to fix them.

Troubleshooting Suboptimal Routing Caused by Redistribution

When redistributing routes from one routing source into another routing source, the original routing source's information is lost when the *seed metric* is injected at the redistribution point. Therefore, overall network visibility is lost or hidden from the destination routing source. This is not an issue when there is only one point of redistribution between two sources. However, if there are multiple points of redistribution between two sources, as shown in Figure 17-1, the suboptimal path may be chosen to reach networks.

In Figure 17-1, focus on R1 and R2. The optimal path to reach 192.168.2.0/24 is from R2 because the 1 Gbps link is much faster than the 10 Mbps link. When you perform redistribution on R1 and R2 into EIGRP, EIGRP does not know that the 10 Mbps link or the 1 Gbps link exists in the OSPF domain. Therefore, if an inappropriate seed metric is used during redistribution on R1 and R2, the traffic from 10.1.1.0/24 destined for 192.168.2.0/24 may take the suboptimal path through R1.

In Figure 17-1, according to the EIGRP AS, R1 is the best path because all it would see is the seed metric from redistribution and the 1 Gbps and 100 Mbps links in the EIGRP autonomous system. Therefore, if the seed metrics you define are the same on R1 and R2 when you redistribute into EIGRP, the 1 Gbps link in the EIGRP autonomous system is preferred, and traffic goes to R1. Then R1 sends it across the OSPF 10 Mbps link to 192.168.2.0/24, which is suboptimal. It works, but it is suboptimal.

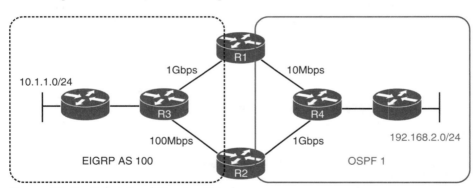

Figure 17-1 *Suboptimal Routing Topology*

You can recognize this issue in a topological diagram and also by using the **traceroute** command. In Figure 17-1, if the result of the traceroute from 10.1.1.0/24 to 192.168.2.0/24 goes through R1, you know that suboptimal routing is occurring because of redistribution.

You can solve this issue by providing different seed metrics on the *boundary routers* (R1 and R2 in this case) to ensure that a certain path is preferred because it has a lower overall *metric*. So, R2's EIGRP seed metric must be significantly better than R1's EIGRP seed metric to ensure that R3 chooses the path through R2, even though the link between R3 and R2 is slower than the link between R3 and R1. The key is to make sure the traffic avoids the 10 Mbps link.

Going in reverse, when redistributing from EIGRP into OSPF, the redistributed routes have a default seed metric of 20 and are classified as E2 routes; therefore, the metric remains as 20 throughout the OSPF domain. At first, you might think that load balancing will occur from R4 to R1 and R2 when sending traffic from 192.168.2.0/24 to 10.1.1.0/24. You would be correct only if the forwarding metrics to reach the autonomous system boundary routers (*ASBRs*) are equal and the E2 seed metrics are equal as well. In this case, the forward metrics are not equal. The 10 Mbps link has a much higher cost than the 1 Gbps link. Therefore, all the traffic from 192.168.2.0/24 to 10.1.1.0/24 goes through R2 across the 1 Gbps link, a lower metric to reach the ASBR in the OSPF domain. However, if the seed metric is set higher than 20 on R2 and is left at 20 on R1, R1 is used as the path because it now has the lower seed metric, but in this case it is the suboptimal path. Therefore, if the metric type is E2, you can simply make the preferred ASBR advertise the lowest seed metric to ensure that optimal routing is achieved. If you are using metric type E1, the cost of the links within the network is added to the cost of the seed metric to come up with the overall cost to reach the destination network. Therefore, if suboptimal routing is occurring, you need to determine which seed metrics are most appropriate with E2 to ensure that the optimal path is chosen, or you can use metric type E1 so that internal costs are used with the seed metric to determine the overall cost.

When troubleshooting suboptimal routing caused by redistribution, keep in mind the following:

- Based on the topology, you need to be able to recognize that mutual redistribution is occurring at multiple points in the network.

- Based on the connections, you need to be able to recognize the different speeds of the links.

- Based on the routing protocols in use, you need to be able to identify how the seed metric is determined and how it behaves for the different protocols.

- Based on the business requirements, you need to know how to fix the suboptimal routing by manipulating the metrics on the boundary routers with the **default-metric** command or the **metric** parameter in the **redistribute** command or within a route map.

Troubleshooting Routing Loops Caused by Redistribution

Examine Figure 17-2. The 10.1.1.0/24 network is redistributed into the EIGRP autonomous system, and then it is redistributed into the OSPF domain on R1 and R2. This does not appear to be an issue; however, it is an issue because of *administrative distance* (AD). Let's explore what happens.

When the 10.1.1.0/24 network is redistributed from RIPv2 into EIGRP autonomous system 100, it is classified as an external route in the EIGRP autonomous system. R1 and R2 place the route in the routing table with the code D EX and an AD of 170, as shown in Figure 17-3.

When R1 and R2 redistribute the 10.1.1.0/24 network in the OSPF domain, by default, the *Type 5 link-state advertisement* (LSA) is advertising 10.1.1.0/24 as an O E2 route, with an AD of 110, as shown in Figure 17-4. Don't forget that it's flooded through the area. Therefore, R1 will receive R2's LSA, and R2 will receive R1's LSA, which creates the problem.

17

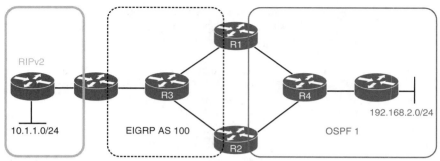

Figure 17-2 *Routing Loop Routing Topology*

Look closely at R1's two options for 10.1.1.0/24. Which one will be preferred? It is the OSPF route because it has a lower AD. Therefore, R1 points to R2 through the OSPF domain to reach 10.1.1.0/24. Look closely at R2's two options for 10.1.1.0/24. Which one is preferred? It is the OSPF route because it has a lower AD. Therefore, R2 points to R1 through the OSPF domain to reach 10.1.1.0/24.

Now when traffic is sent from 192.168.2.0/24 to 10.1.1.0/24, it bounces back and forth between R1 and R2, and this is classified as a *routing loop*.

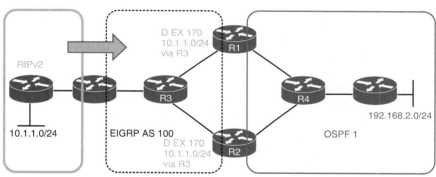

Figure 17-3 *Redistributing 10.1.1.0/24 into the EIGRP Autonomous System*

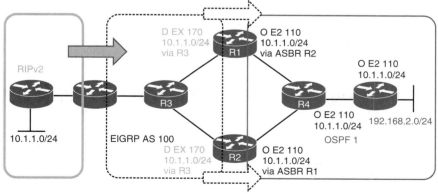

Figure 17-4 *Redistributing 10.1.1.0/24 into the OSPF Domain on R1 and R2*

However, this scenario gets worse because of how redistribution works. Remember that to redistribute a route from one routing source to another (EIGRP into OSPF, for example), that route must be in the routing table as an entry for the routing source that you are redistributing the route from.

With all this in mind, consider Figure 17-4 again. When R1 and R2 originally learned about the network 10.1.1.0/24 from R3, it was an EIGRP external route. There was no other source of information in the routing table at the time for 10.1.1.0/24; therefore, it was considered the best source and installed in the routing table as an EIGRP route. Because redistribution is occurring from EIGRP into OSPF, the 10.1.1.0/24 network is redistributed from the routing table into the OSPF process and advertised. Now, when R1 and R2 learn about the OSPF 10.1.1.0/24 route from each other, they notice that it is a better source of information because the AD is lower (110) than the one for EIGRP (170) that is currently in the routing table. Therefore, the OSPF route replaces the EIGRP route.

What happens now? Well, because the EIGRP route is still in the topology table but not in the routing table, it is no longer available for redistribution into OSPF, and therefore, there are no more Type 5 LSAs to advertise in the OSPF domain. As a result, R1 and R2 have to notify the routers in the OSPF domain that 10.1.1.0/24 no longer exists. When this happens, R1 and R2 no longer have the 10.1.1.0/24 network that they learned through OSPF from each other in the routing table. What does this cause? The EIGRP external route 10.1.1.0/24 is reinstalled in the routing table, and because redistribution from EIGRP into OSPF is occurring, the issue repeats all over again.

As you can see, the routing table is not stable because routes are inserted and removed and inserted and removed over and over again. You can see this happening with the **debug ip routing** command, which displays changes as they occur to the routing table.

Let's take this example even further. Examine Figure 17-5, which shows the 10.1.1.0/24 network being redistributed back into the EIGRP autonomous system on R1 and R2 when the OSPF route is in the routing table on R1 and R2. This is known as route feedback. Now R3 thinks that 10.1.1.0/24 is reachable through the boundary router (R5) between the RIPv2 domain and the EIGRP autonomous system, as well as through R1 and R2 between EIGRP and OSPF. Depending on the metric for each of the learned paths to 10.1.1.0/24, R3 may choose the correct path to the RIP domain or the path through R1 or R2, which would eventually blackhole the traffic.

17

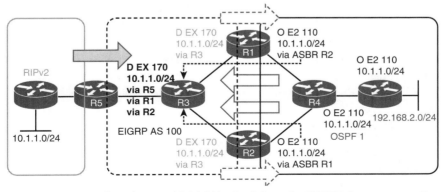

Figure 17-5   *Redistributing 10.1.1.0/24 Back into the EIGRP Autonomous System from OSPF*

This is definitely a bad situation. You can recognize this type of situation by analyzing a diagram and understanding the protocols in use. You don't even need to use any **show** commands. In addition, the symptoms are wide ranging. For example, a user might have a connection from 192.168.2.0/24 to 10.1.1.0/24 for one moment and then the connection is lost, then it is back, then lost, all because the routes are being added and removed over and over again, causing a loop, and then no loop, and so on. Therefore, you need to be able to look at the topology and identify where this type of issue might occur and implement the necessary measures to stop it from happening. Or, if it is happening, you need to identify why it is happening and propose how to fix it.

Remember that this issue was caused by AD; 110 is better than 170. Therefore, you need to either lower the AD of the EIGRP external routes on R1 and R2 for 10.1.1.0/24 or increase the AD of the OSPF Type 5 learned routes on R1 and R2 for 10.1.1.0/24. Your goal is to make sure the EIGRP learned route is the preferred route. Regardless of what you choose to do, you need to use the **distance** command on R1 and R2 and specify what the AD will be for the 10.1.1.0/24 network. If you lower the EIGRP AD, it needs to be 109 or lower, and if you decide to increase the OSPF AD, it needs to be 171 or higher.

EIGRP already differentiates between routes learned from within the autonomous system and routes learned from outside the autonomous system by assigning different administrative distance:

- **Internal EIGRP:** 90

- **External EIGRP:** 170

To modify the default administrative distance on IOS routers, use the EIGRP configuration command **distance eigrp** *ad-internal ad-external*. Valid values for the AD are between 1 and 255; a value of 255 stops the installation of the route into the Routing Information Base (RIB).

Cisco IOS routers also allow selective AD modification for specific internal networks with this command:

distance *ad source-ip source-ip-wildcard* [*acl-number* |
acl-name]

The *source-ip source-ip-wildcard* option restricts the modification of routes in the EIGRP table to those that were learned from a specific router, and the optional *acl* options identify the specific network prefix from that source. Note that EIGRP does not allow the selective AD modification based on prefixes for external EIGRP routes.

Example 17-1 demonstrates how to configure R1 and R2 in Figure 17-5 so they have an AD set to 109 for all learned external EIGRP routes, which is lower than the AD for the OSPF learned routes. Therefore, the EIGRP routes will be installed in the routing tables of R1 and R2.

Example 17-1   *EIGRP AD Manipulation Configuration*

```
R1(config)# router eigrp 100
R1(config-rtr)# distance eigrp 90 109
R1(config-rtr)# end
```

```
R2(config)# router eigrp 100
R2(config-rtr)# distance eigrp 90 109
R2(config-rtr)# end
```

OSPF uses the same default AD 110 value for routes learned within the OSPF routing domain and routes learned outside the OSPF routing domain. On IOS routers, you modify the default AD with this OSPF configuration command:

```
distance ospf {external | inter-area | intra-area} ad
```

Note that this command allows you to set a different AD for each OSPF LSA type.

In addition, IOS routers allow selective AD modification for specific networks with this command:

```
distance ad source-ip source-ip-wildcard [acl-number | acl-name]
```

The *source-ip* option restricts the modification to routes in the OSPF link-state database (LSDB) learned from the advertising router of the LSA. The *source-ip-wildcard* address field matches the router ID (RID) for the advertising route. The optional *acl* options identify the specific network prefix from that source.

Example 17-2 demonstrates how to modify R1 and R2 so that OSPF external routes are set with an AD of 171, which is higher than the default AD of external EIGRP routes (170). This ensures that the EIGRP routes are preferred over the OSPF routes for 10.0.0.0/24 in Figure 17-5 and installed in the routing tables of R1 and R2.

Example 17-2 *OSPF Customized AD Configuration*

```
R1(config)# router ospf 1
R1(config-rtr)# distance ospf external 171
R1(config-rtr)#


R2(config)# router ospf 1
R2(config-rtr)# distance ospf external 171
R2(config-rtr)#
```

BGP differentiates between routes learned from internal BGP (iBGP) peers, routes learned from external BGP (eBGP) peers, and routes learned locally. On IOS routers, you use the BGP configuration command **distance bgp** *external-ad internal-ad local-routes* to set the AD for each BGP network type and the address family command **distance** *ad source-ip source-wildcard [acl-number | acl-name]* to modify AD for routes received from a specific neighbor.

For example, the BGP command **distance 44 55 66** sets the AD for eBGP routes to 44, the AD for iBGP routes to 55, and the AD for locally learned routes to 66.

There is another way to solve the issue presented in Figure 17-5. You could attach a distribute list to the OSPF process on R1 and R2. When a distribute list is used with OSPF, it can control what routes are installed in the routing table from the OSPF database. Therefore, if you deny the 10.1.1.0/24 route in the OSPF database with an AD of 110 from being installed in the routing table with a distribute list on R1 and R2, the EIGRP route with an AD of 170 is installed in the routing table instead.

Example 17-3 shows how you can configure R1 and R2 to accomplish this.

Example 17-3   *Using a Distribute List to Control OSPF Routes Installed in the Routing Table*

```
R1(config)# ip prefix-list PREFER_EIGRP seq 10 deny 10.1.1.0/24
R1(config)# ip prefix-list PREFER_EIGRP seq 20 permit 0.0.0.0/0 le 32
R1(config)# router ospf 1
R1(config-rtr)# distribute-list prefix PREFER_EIGRP in
R1(config-rtr)#


R2(config)# ip prefix-list PREFER_EIGRP seq 10 deny 10.1.1.0/24
R2(config)# ip prefix-list PREFER_EIGRP seq 20 permit 0.0.0.0/0 le 32
R2(config)# router ospf 1
R2(config-rtr)# distribute-list prefix PREFER_EIGRP in
R2(config-rtr)#
```

Finally, you do not want the routes that are redistributed from EIGRP into OSPF to be redistributed back into the EIGRP autonomous system or vice versa. Such redistribution can cause routing issues such as loops, which prevent packets from being correctly delivered to their destination (in addition to wasting CPU and memory resources on various devices in the network). The most robust way to deal with this is to use *route tags*. Figure 17-6 shows how R1 and R2 can add a tag (which is just an arbitrary value that can be used to identify the route) when the route is redistributed. This is accomplished with route maps. In this example, when R1 redistributes the 10.1.1.0/24 route into the OSPF domain, it adds the tag 10. When R2 redistributes the 10.1.1.0/24 route into the OSPF domain, it adds the tag 20.

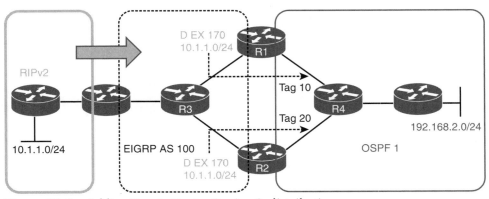

Figure 17-6   *Adding Tags to Routes During Redistribution*

Example 17-4 shows the commands that you could use to tag the 10.1.1.0/24 routes as they are redistributed on R1 and R2. First, you must define the routes you want to tag with an ACL or a prefix list. Then you create a route map that has a sequence that matches the ACL or prefix list created and that will set the desired tag when there is a match. In this case, R1 sets a tag of 10, and R2 sets a tag of 20. Do not forget about all the other routes you want to redistribute without a tag. That is what sequence 20 is for in the route map. If you forget it, all other routes are denied and not redistributed because of the implicit deny sequence at the end of a route map. You then attach the route map to the redistribution command.

Example 17-4   *Tagging Routes as They Are Being Redistributed*

```
R1#
ip prefix-list TAG_10.1.1.0/24 seq 5 permit 10.1.1.0/24
!
route-map REDIS_EIGRP_TO_OSPF permit 10
 match ip address prefix-list TAG_10.1.1.0/24
 set tag 10
route-map REDIS_EIGRP_TO_OSPF permit 20
!
router ospf 1
 redistribute eigrp 100 subnets route-map REDIS_EIGRP_TO_OSPF


R2#
ip prefix-list TAG_10.1.1.0/24 seq 5 permit 10.1.1.0/24
!
route-map REDIS_EIGRP_TO_OSPF permit 10
 match ip address prefix-list TAG_10.1.1.0/24
 set tag 20
route-map REDIS_EIGRP_TO_OSPF permit 20
!
router ospf 1
 redistribute eigrp 100 subnets route-map REDIS_EIGRP_TO_OSPF
```

You are not done yet. To prevent R1 and R2 from redistributing the OSPF-learned 10.1.1.0/24 routes with their tags back into EIGRP, you deny the routes based on their tags. As shown in Figure 17-7, on R1 you deny the routes with the tag 20 from being redistributed into the EIGRP autonomous system, and on R2 you deny the routes with the tag 10 from being redistributed into the EIGRP autonomous system.

Example 17-5 shows the commands that can be used to ensure that R1 and R2 do not redistribute the 10.1.1.0/24 networks back into the EIGRP autonomous system. Notice the very first sequence in this route map. In this case, it is deny, and when deny is used with redistribution, it indicates that matches are not redistributed. Therefore, R1 does not redistribute from OSPF into EIGRP any routes that have the tag 20, as shown in sequence 10, and sequence 20 allows all other routes to be redistributed. R2 does not redistribute any routes with the tag 10 from OSPF into EIGRP based on sequence 10, and all other routes are redistributed based on sequence 20.

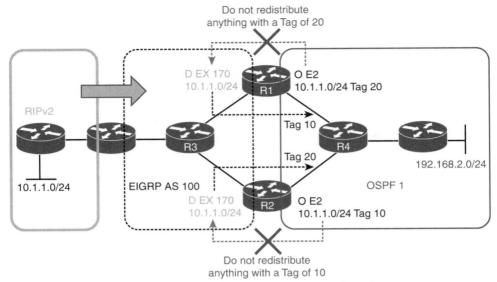

Figure 17-7   *Denying Routes with Certain Tags During Redistribution*

Example 17-5   *Using Route Tags to Prevent Routes from Being Reinjected*

```
R1#
route-map REDIS_OSPF_INTO_EIGRP deny 10
 match tag 20
route-map REDIS_OSPF_INTO_EIGRP permit 20
!
router eigrp 100
 redistribute ospf 1 metric 100000 100 255 1 1500 route-map REDIS_OSPF_INTO_EIGRP

R2#
route-map REDIS_OSPF_INTO_EIGRP deny 10
 match tag 10
route-map REDIS_OSPF_INTO_EIGRP permit 20
!
router eigrp 100
 redistribute ospf 1 metric 100000 100 255 1 1500 route-map REDIS_OSPF_INTO_EIGRP
```

So, to wrap up the coverage on advanced redistribution scenarios, keep these points in mind:

- Internal prefix information should always be preferred over external prefix information.

- Prefixes should never be redistributed back into a routing domain from which they were originally redistributed.

- A topological diagram is mandatory if you expect to solve the issues quickly and efficiently.

Troubleshooting IPv4 and IPv6 Redistribution

Route redistribution allows routes learned through one source (for example, statically configured routes, locally connected routes, or routes learned through a routing protocol) to be injected into a routing protocol. If two routing protocols are mutually redistributed, the routes learned through each routing protocol are injected into the other routing protocol.

This section reviews route redistribution and explains how to troubleshoot redistribution issues.

Route Redistribution Review

A router that connects two or more routing domains and that will be the point of redistribution is known as a *boundary router* (see Figure 17-8). A boundary router can redistribute static routes, connected routes, and routes learned through one routing protocol into another routing protocol.

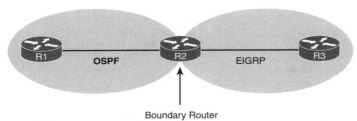

Figure 17-8   *Boundary Router*

Redistribution occurs from the routing table into a routing protocol's data structure (such as the EIGRP topology table or the OSPF LSDB), as shown in Figure 17-9. This is a key concept for troubleshooting purposes because if the route is not in the routing table, it cannot be redistributed. Keep in mind that if it is not in the routing table, you need to troubleshoot some other underlying issue in order to get redistribution to work. For example, if you are redistributing EIGRP into OSPF, and the EIGRP route is not in the routing table, that is not a redistribution problem; it is an EIGRP problem, and it must be solved first.

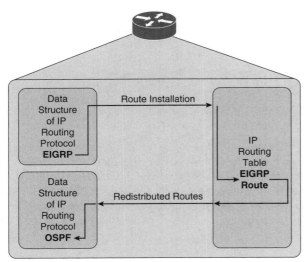

Figure 17-9   *Redistribution Occurs from the Routing Table into a Routing Protocol's Data Structure*

Different routing protocols use different types of metrics, as illustrated in Figure 17-10. Therefore, when a route is redistributed into a routing protocol, a metric used by the destination routing protocol needs to be associated with the route being redistributed.

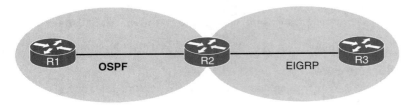

Cost   Bandwidth, Delay

Figure 17-10   *Differing Metrics Between Routing Protocols*

The metric assigned to a route being redistributed into another routing process is called a *seed metric*. The seed metric is needed to communicate relative levels of reachability between dissimilar routing protocols. A seed metric can be defined in one of three ways:

- By using the **default-metric** command

- By using the **metric** parameter with the **redistribute** command

- By applying a route map configuration to the **redistribute** command

If multiple seed metrics are defined with the commands, the order of preference is (1) metric defined in the route map that was applied to the **redistribute** command, (2) metric parameter defined with the **redistribute** command, and then (3) metric defined with the **default-metric** command.

If a seed metric is not specified, a default seed metric is used. Keep in mind that EIGRP has a default seed metric that is considered unreachable. Therefore, if you do not manually configure a seed metric when redistributing routes into EIGRP, the redistributed route is not reachable and is therefore not advertised to other routers in the routing domain. OSPF has a default seed metric of 20, unless it is a BGP route being redistributed, in which case it has a seed metric of 1. When redistributing into BGP, BGP preserves and uses the exact metric of the Interior Gateway Protocol (IGP).

> **NOTE**   For EIGRP you do not need to specify a metric when redistributing static or connected routes. In addition, for EIGRP you do not have to specify a metric when redistributing from another EIGRP autonomous system because the original metric is preserved.

Some routing protocols (for example, EIGRP and OSPF) can tag routes as either internal (that is, routes locally configured or connected) or external (that is, routes learned from another routing process) and can give priority to internal routes over external routes. The capability to distinguish between internal and external routes can help prevent a potential routing loop, where two routing protocols continually redistribute the same routes into one another at multiple redistribution points.

Keep in mind that two prerequisites must be met for the routes of one IP routing protocol to be redistributed into another IP routing protocol:

- The route needs to be installed in the IP routing table of the border router (the router performing redistribution) by the protocol being redistributed.

- The destination IP routing protocol needs a reachable metric to assign to the redistributed routes.

Based on these two prerequisites, Table 17-2 lists various redistribution troubleshooting targets and recommendations for dealing with them.

Table 17-2   Troubleshooting Targets for Route Redistribution

Troubleshooting Target	Troubleshooting Recommendation
Source routing protocol	Verify that a route to be redistributed from a routing protocol has been learned by that routing protocol. Issue appropriate **show** commands for the data structures of the source routing protocol to ensure that the source routing protocol has learned the route in question.
Route selection	Because a route must be in a router's IP routing table to be redistributed, ensure that the routes of the source routing protocol are indeed being injected into the router's IP routing table.
Redistribution configuration	If a route has been injected into a router's IP routing table from a source routing protocol but not redistributed into the destination routing protocol, check the redistribution configuration. This involves checking the metric applied to routes as they are redistributed into the destination routing protocol, checking for any route filtering that might be preventing redistribution, and checking the redistribution syntax to confirm that the correct routing process ID or autonomous system number is specified.
Destination routing protocol	If a route has been successfully redistributed into a destination routing protocol but the route has not been successfully learned by neighboring routers, you should investigate the destination routing protocol. You could use traditional methods of troubleshooting a destination routing protocol; however, keep in mind that the redistributed route might be marked as an external route. Therefore, check the characteristics of the destination routing protocol to determine whether it treats external routes differently from internal ones.

Troubleshooting Redistribution into EIGRP

When redistributing into EIGRP for IPv4, you can apply a metric with the **metric** keyword or a route map with the **route-map** keyword. If you are redistributing OSPF into EIGRP, as shown in Example 17-6, you also have the option to specify the **match** option, which allows you to match just **internal** routes, just **external** routes, just **nssa-external** routes, or a combination of them.

The most common issue you will run into when redistributing into EIGRP for IPv4 is related to the metric. Remember that the seed metric is, by default, set to infinity (unreachable).

17

Therefore, if you fail to manually set the metric using any of the options listed earlier in the chapter, routes will not be advertised to the other routers in the EIGRP autonomous system. Keep in mind that you must consider whether the metrics you specify will cause suboptimal routing if you have multiple redistribution points in the routing domain.

Also, if the wrong route map is applied, or if there is an error in the route map, routes will not be redistributed properly.

Example 17-6   *EIGRP for IPv4 Redistribution Options*

```
R1(config)# router eigrp 1
R1(config-router)# redistribute ospf 1 ?
 match Redistribution of OSPF routes
 metric Metric for redistributed routes
 route-map Route map reference
 <cr>
```

With EIGRP for IPv6, you have the same **match**, **metric**, and **route-map** keywords, as well as the **include-connected** keyword. By default, with EIGRP for IPv4, the networks associated with the local interfaces participating in the redistributed routing process are redistributed as well. However, with EIGRP for IPv6, the networks associated with the local interfaces participating in the redistributed routing process are not redistributed. Therefore, if you want to include the networks associated with the local interfaces participating in the routing process that is being redistributed, you need to use the **include-connected** keyword, as shown in Example 17-7.

Example 17-7   *EIGRP for IPv6 Redistribution Options*

```
R1(config)# ipv6 router eigrp 1
R1(config-rtr)# redistribute ospf 1 ?
 include-connected Include connected
 match Redistribution of OSPF routes
 metric Metric for redistributed routes
 route-map Route map reference
 <cr>
```

On the boundary router, you can verify which protocols are being redistributed into EIGRP for IPv4 with the **show ip protocols** command. Example 17-8 shows that OSPF routes are being redistributed into EIGRP for IPv4.

Example 17-8   *Verifying Protocols That Are Being Redistributed into EIGRP for IPv4*

```
R2# show ip protocols
*** IP Routing is NSF aware ***

Routing Protocol is "eigrp 100"
 Outgoing update filter list for all interfaces is not set
 Incoming update filter list for all interfaces is not set
 Default networks flagged in outgoing updates
 Default networks accepted from incoming updates
```

```
Redistributing: ospf
EIGRP-IPv4 Protocol for AS(100)
Metric weight K1=1, K2=0, K3=1, K4=0, K5=0
...output omitted...
```

When reviewing the EIGRP for IPv4 topology table with the **show ip eigrp topology** command, you can identify the routes that have been injected into the EIGRP process via redistribution because the output states *via Redistributed*, as shown in Example 17-9.

Example 17-9   *Verifying Routes Redistributed into EIGRP for IPv4 (Topology Table*

```
R2# show ip eigrp topology
EIGRP-IPv4 Topology Table for AS(100)/ID(203.0.113.1)
      Codes: P - Passive, A - Active, U - Update, Q - Query, R - Reply,
             r - reply Status, s - sia Status

P 10.1.12.0/24, 1 successors, FD is 2560000256
     via Redistributed (2560000256/0)
P 10.1.14.0/24, 1 successors, FD is 2560000256
     via Redistributed (2560000256/0)
P 10.1.3.0/24, 1 successors, FD is 3072
     via 10.1.23.3 (3072/2816), GigabitEthernet1/0
P 10.1.23.0/24, 1 successors, FD is 2816
     via Connected, GigabitEthernet1/0
P 10.1.1.0/24, 1 successors, FD is 2560000256
     via Redistributed (2560000256/0)
```

When examining a redistributed route in the routing table on the boundary router, as shown in Example 17-10, with the **show ip route** *ip-address* command, the output indicates how the route is known, how it is being redistributed, and the EIGRP metric values that are being used at the redistribution point.

Example 17-10   *Verifying Routes Redistributed into EIGRP for IPv4 (Routing Table)*

```
R2# show ip route 10.1.1.0
Routing entry for 10.1.1.0/24
 Known via "ospf", distance 110, metric 1
 Redistributing via eigrp 100, ospf
 Advertised by eigrp 100 metric 1 1 1 1 1
 Last update from 10.1.12.1 on GigabitEthernet0/0, 00:00:19 ago
 Routing Descriptor Blocks:
 * 10.1.12.1, from 10.1.12.1, 00:00:19 ago, via GigabitEthernet0/0
 Route metric is 1, traffic share count is 1
```

When examining the routing tables on other routers (not the boundary router) in the EIGRP for IPv4 autonomous system, the redistributed routes have an AD of 170 by default and the code D EX, as shown in Example 17-11.

Example 17-11 *Examining EIGRP for IPv4 Redistributed Routes in a Routing Table*

```
R3# show ip route
Codes: L - local, C - connected, S - static, R - RIP, M - mobile, B - BGP
       D - EIGRP, EX - EIGRP external, O - OSPF, IA - OSPF inter area
       N1 - OSPF NSSA external type 1, N2 - OSPF NSSA external type 2
       E1 - OSPF external type 1, E2 - OSPF external type 2
       i - IS-IS, su - IS-IS summary, L1 - IS-IS level-1, L2 - IS-IS level-2
       ia - IS-IS inter area, * - candidate default, U - per-user static route
       o - ODR, P - periodic downloaded static route, H - NHRP, l - LISP
       + - replicated route, % - next hop override

Gateway of last resort is not set

 10.0.0.0/8 is variably subnetted, 7 subnets, 2 masks
D EX 10.1.1.0/24
        [170/2560000512] via 10.1.23.2, 00:04:38, GigabitEthernet1/0
C 10.1.3.0/24 is directly connected, GigabitEthernet0/0
L 10.1.3.3/32 is directly connected, GigabitEthernet0/0
D EX 10.1.12.0/24
        [170/2560000512] via 10.1.23.2, 00:04:38, GigabitEthernet1/0
D EX 10.1.14.0/24
        [170/2560000512] via 10.1.23.2, 00:04:38, GigabitEthernet1/0
C 10.1.23.0/24 is directly connected, GigabitEthernet1/0
L 10.1.23.3/32 is directly connected, GigabitEthernet1/0
```

For EIGRP for IPv6, the **show ipv6 protocols** output is more detailed for redistribution, as shown in Example 17-12. Notice that it states the protocol, the seed metric, and whether connected networks are included.

Example 17-12 *Verifying EIGRP for IPv6 Redistribution with show ipv6 protocols*

```
R2# show ipv6 protocols
...output omitted...
IPv6 Routing Protocol is "eigrp 100"
EIGRP-IPv6 Protocol for AS(100)
 Metric weight K1=1, K2=0, K3=1, K4=0, K5=0
 NSF-aware route hold timer is 240
 Router-ID: 203.0.113.1
 Topology : 0 (base)
 Active Timer: 3 min
 Distance: internal 90 external 170
 Maximum path: 16
Maximum hopcount 100
 Maximum metric variance 1
```

```
Interfaces:
  GigabitEthernet1/0
Redistribution:
  Redistributing protocol OSPF 1 with metric 1 1 1 1 1 include-connected
```

The output of **show ipv6 eigrp topology** on the boundary router also indicates which routes are redistributed, as shown in Example 17-13.

Example 17-13   *Verifying EIGRP for IPv6 Redistribution with* **show ipv6 eigrp** *topology*

```
R2# show ipv6 eigrp topology
EIGRP-IPv6 Topology Table for AS(100)/ID(203.0.113.1)
Codes: P - Passive, A - Active, U - Update, Q - Query, R - Reply,
  r - reply Status, s - sia Status

P 2001:DB8:0:1::/64, 1 successors, FD is 2560000256
        via Redistributed (2560000256/0)
P 2001:DB8:0:3::/64, 1 successors, FD is 3072
        via FE80::C804:10FF:FE2C:1C (3072/2816), GigabitEthernet1/0
P 2001:DB8:0:12::/64, 1 successors, FD is 2560000256
        via Redistributed (2560000256/0)
P 2001:DB8:0:23::/64, 1 successors, FD is 2816
        via Connected, GigabitEthernet1/0
```

When examining the routing tables on other routers besides the boundary router in the EIGRP for IPv6 autonomous system, the redistributed routes have an administrative distance of 170 by default and the code EX, as shown in Example 17-14.

Example 17-14   *Verifying EIGRP for IPv6 Redistributed Routes*

```
R3# show ipv6 route
IPv6 Routing Table - default - 7 entries
Codes: C - Connected, L - Local, S - Static, U - Per-user Static route
  B - BGP, R - RIP, H - NHRP, I1 - ISIS L1
  I2 - ISIS L2, IA - ISIS interarea, IS - ISIS summary, D - EIGRP
  EX - EIGRP external, ND - ND Default, NDp - ND Prefix, DCE - Destination
  NDr - Redirect, O - OSPF Intra, OI - OSPF Inter, OE1 - OSPF ext 1
  OE2 - OSPF ext 2, ON1 - OSPF NSSA ext 1, ON2 - OSPF NSSA ext 2, l - LISP
EX 2001:DB8:0:1::/64 [170/2560000512]
      via FE80::C802:AFF:FE88:1C, GigabitEthernet1/0
C 2001:DB8:0:3::/64 [0/0]
     via GigabitEthernet0/0, directly connected
L 2001:DB8:0:3::3/128 [0/0]
     via GigabitEthernet0/0, receive
```

```
EX 2001:DB8:0:12::/64 [170/2560000512]
     via FE80::C802:AFF:FE88:1C, GigabitEthernet1/0
C 2001:DB8:0:23::/64 [0/0]
     via GigabitEthernet1/0, directly connected
L 2001:DB8:0:23::3/128 [0/0]
     via GigabitEthernet1/0, receive
L FF00::/8 [0/0]
     via Null0, receive
```

Troubleshooting Redistribution into OSPF

When redistributing into OSPF, you have more options than you have with other routing protocols, as shown in Example 17-15. The **metric** option allows you to provide a seed metric at the redistribution point. The default seed metric is 20 with OSPF; therefore, providing a metric is not mandatory. If you forget to provide a metric, redistributed routes are still advertised to other routers in the OSPF domain. The **metric-type** option is used to define the type of OSPF external route the redistributed route will be. By default, it will be Type 2, which is represented as E2 in the routing table. With E2, each router preserves the seed metric for the external routes. Type 1, which is represented as E1 in the routing table, allows each router to add to the seed metric all the other link costs to reach the redistribution point in the domain. Therefore, each router has a metric that is a combination of the seed metric and the total cost to reach the redistribution router.

With the **nssa-only** option, you can limit redistributed routes to the not-so-stubby area (NSSA) only, and with the **route-map** option, you can reference a route map that provides more granular control over the routes that are being redistributed.

The *subnets keyword* is an extremely important option. Without the **subnets** keyword, only classful networks are redistributed (for example, a Class A address with a /8 mask, a Class B address with a /16 mask, and a Class C address with a /24 mask). With the **subnets** keyword, all classless and classful networks are redistributed. Therefore, if you have any subnets that you want to redistribute, the **subnets** keyword is mandatory. The **tag** keyword can be used to add a numeric ID (tag) to the route so the route can be referenced by the tag at a later point for filtering or manipulation purposes.

Example 17-15 *OSPFv2 Redistribution Options*

```
R1(config)# router ospf 1
R1(config-router)# redistribute eigrp 100 ?
  metric       Metric for redistributed routes
  metric-type  OSPF/IS-IS exterior metric type for redistributed routes
  nssa-only    Limit redistributed routes to NSSA areas
  route-map    Route map reference
  subnets      Consider subnets for redistribution into OSPF
  tag          Set tag for routes redistributed into OSPF
  <cr>
```

Look closely at Example 17-16, which displays the options available when redistributing into OSPFv3. What has been added and what is missing compared to using OSPFv2? The **include-connected** keyword has been added. By default, with OSPFv2, the networks associated with the local interfaces that are participating in the routing process that is being redistributed are redistributed as well. However, with OSPFv3, they are not. Therefore, if you want to include the networks associated with the interfaces participating in the routing protocol that is being redistributed on the ASBR, you need to use the **include-connected** keyword.

The **subnets** keyword is not an option with OSPFv3 because the concepts of classful and classless do not exist with IPv6.

Example 17-16 *OSPFv3 Redistribution Options*

```
R1(config)# ipv6 router ospf 1
R1(config-rtr)# redistribute eigrp 100 ?
 include-connected  Include connected
 metric             Metric for redistributed routes
 metric-type        OSPF/IS-IS exterior metric type for redistributed routes
 nssa-only          Limit redistributed routes to NSSA areas
 route-map          Route map reference
 tag                Set tag for routes redistributed into OSPF
 <cr>
```

The **show ip protocols** command enables you to verify which routing protocols are being redistributed into the OSPFv2 process. In Example 17-17, you can see that EIGRP 100 routes, including subnets, are being redistributed into the OSPFv2 process.

Example 17-17 *Verifying Protocols Being Redistributed into OSPFv2*

```
R2# show ip protocols
...output omitted...
Routing Protocol is "ospf 1"
  Outgoing update filter list for all interfaces is not set
  Incoming update filter list for all interfaces is not set
  Router ID 203.0.113.1
  It is an autonomous system boundary router
  Redistributing External Routes from,
    eigrp 100, includes subnets in redistribution
  Number of areas in this router is 1. 1 normal 0 stub 0 nssa
  Maximum path: 4
  Routing for Networks:
    10.1.12.2 0.0.0.0 area 0
  Routing Information Sources:
    Gateway         Distance      Last Update
    10.1.14.1       110           00:19:48
  Distance: (default is 110)
```

Routes redistributed into an OSPFv2 normal area are advertised within a Type 5 LSA. Routes redistributed into an OSPFv2 NSSA or totally NSSA area are advertised within a Type 7

LSA and then converted to a Type 5 LSA at an area border router (ABR). You can view the redistributed routes that are injected into the OSPFv2 LSDB with the **show ip ospf database** command, as shown in Example 17-18. In this example, the 10.1.3.0 and 10.1.23.0 networks have been redistributed into the OSPFv2 routing process.

Example 17-18 *Verifying Redistributed Routes in the OSPFv2 LSDB*

```
R2# show ip ospf database

              OSPF Router with ID (203.0.113.1) (Process ID 1)


              Router Link States (Area 0)

Link ID          ADV Router       Age     Seq#       Checksum      Link count
10.1.14.1        10.1.14.1        738     0x80000003 0x009AEA      3
203.0.113.1      203.0.113.1      596     0x80000003 0x005829      1


              Net Link States (Area 0)

Link ID          ADV Router       Age     Seq#       Checksum
10.1.12.1        10.1.14.1        738     0x80000002 0x001F8F


              Type-5 AS External Link States

Link ID          ADV Router       Age     Seq#       Checksum   Tag
10.1.3.0         203.0.113.1      596     0x80000002 0x00EB67   0
10.1.23.0        203.0.113.1      596     0x80000002 0x000F30   0
```

When examining a redistributed route in the routing table on the boundary router (the ASBR), as shown in Example 17-19, with the **show ip route** *ip_address* command, the output indicates how the route is known, how it is being redistributed, and how it is being advertised. In this case, the route is known through EIGRP 100 and is being redistributed into the OSPF 1 process with the **subnets** keyword.

Example 17-19 *Verifying Redistributed Routes in the ASBR's Routing Table*

```
R2# show ip route 10.1.3.0
Routing entry for 10.1.3.0/24
  Known via "eigrp 100", distance 90, metric 3072, type internal
  Redistributing via eigrp 100, ospf 1
  Advertised by ospf 1 subnets
  Last update from 10.1.23.3 on GigabitEthernet1/0, 00:50:19 ago
  Routing Descriptor Blocks:
  * 10.1.23.3, from 10.1.23.3, 00:50:19 ago, via GigabitEthernet1/0
      Route metric is 3072, traffic share count is 1
      Total delay is 20 microseconds, minimum bandwidth is 1000000 Kbit
      Reliability 255/255, minimum MTU 1500 bytes
      Loading 1/255, Hops 1
```

When examining the routing table on other routers (not the ASBR) in the OSPFv2 domain, by default the redistributed routes have an AD of 110 and the code O E2, as shown in Example 17-20. If you change the metric type to E1, the routes appear with the code E1. Within an NSSA or a totally NSSA, the routes will appear as O N1 or O N2.

Example 17-20 *Examining OSPFv2 Redistributed Routes in a Routing Table*

```
R1# show ip route
Codes: L - local, C - connected, S - static, R - RIP, M - mobile, B - BGP
       D - EIGRP, EX - EIGRP external, O - OSPF, IA - OSPF inter area
       N1 - OSPF NSSA external type 1, N2 - OSPF NSSA external type 2
       E1 - OSPF external type 1, E2 - OSPF external type 2
       i - IS-IS, su - IS-IS summary, L1 - IS-IS level-1, L2 - IS-IS level-2
       ia - IS-IS inter area, * - candidate default, U - per-user static route
       o - ODR, P - periodic downloaded static route, H - NHRP, l - LISP
       + - replicated route, % - next hop override

Gateway of last resort is not set

      10.0.0.0/8 is variably subnetted, 8 subnets, 2 masks
C        10.1.1.0/24 is directly connected, GigabitEthernet0/0
L        10.1.1.1/32 is directly connected, GigabitEthernet0/0
O E2     10.1.3.0/24 [110/20] via 10.1.12.2, 00:49:11, GigabitEthernet1/0
C        10.1.12.0/24 is directly connected, GigabitEthernet1/0
L        10.1.12.1/32 is directly connected, GigabitEthernet1/0
C        10.1.14.0/24 is directly connected, FastEthernet3/0
L        10.1.14.1/32 is directly connected, FastEthernet3/0
O E2     10.1.23.0/24 [110/20] via 10.1.12.2, 00:49:11, GigabitEthernet1/0
```

For OSPFv3, the **show ipv6 protocols** output is shown in Example 17-21. Notice that it states the protocol, the seed metric, and whether connected networks are included.

Example 17-21 *Verifying OSPFv3 Redistribution with show ipv6 protocols*

```
R2# show ipv6 protocols
...output omitted...
IPv6 Routing Protocol is "ospf 1"
  Router ID 2.2.2.2
  Autonomous system boundary router
  Number of areas: 1 normal, 0 stub, 0 nssa
  Interfaces (Area 0):
    GigabitEthernet0/0
  Redistribution:
    Redistributing protocol eigrp 100 with metric 10 include-connected
```

The output of **show ipv6 ospf database** on the ASBR identifies the external Type 5 routes just as OSPFv2 does, as shown in Example 17-22.

Example 17-22 *Verifying OSPFv3 Redistribution with* **show ipv6 ospf database**

```
R2# show ipv6 ospf database

              OSPFv3 Router with ID (2.2.2.2) (Process ID 1)

              Router Link States (Area 0)

ADV Router       Age         Seq#         Fragment ID   Link count Bits
   1.1.1.1       1429        0x80000004   0                    1        B
   2.2.2.2       1446        0x80000003   0                    1        E

              Net Link States (Area 0)

ADV Router       Age         Seq#         Link ID      Rtr count
   1.1.1.1       1429        0x80000002   4                 2

              Inter Area Prefix Link States (Area 0)

ADV Router       Age         Seq#         Prefix
   1.1.1.1       1693        0x80000002   2001:DB8:0:14::/64

              Link (Type-8) Link States (Area 0)

ADV Router       Age         Seq#         Link ID   Interface
   1.1.1.1       1693        0x80000002   4         Gi0/0
   2.2.2.2       1446        0x80000002   3         Gi0/0

              Intra Area Prefix Link States (Area 0)

ADV Router       Age         Seq#         Link ID Ref-lstype Ref-LSID
   1.1.1.1       1429        0x80000006   0         0x2001     0
   1.1.1.1       1429        0x80000002   4096      0x2002     4

              Type-5 AS External Link States

ADV Router       Age         Seq#         Prefix
   2.2.2.2       46          0x80000003   2001:DB8:0:3::/64
   2.2.2.2       46          0x80000003   2001:DB8:0:23::/64
```

When examining the routing table on other routers (not the ASBR) in the OSPFv3 domain, by default the redistributed routes have an administrative distance of 110 and the code OE2, as shown in Example 17-23. If the metric type is changed to Type 1, the code is OE1. In an NSSA or a totally NSSA, the redistributed routes are listed as ON1 or ON2.

Example 17-23 *Verifying OSPFv3 Redistributed Routes*

```
R1# show ipv6 route
IPv6 Routing Table - default - 9 entries
Codes: C - Connected, L - Local, S - Static, U - Per-user Static route
 B - BGP, R - RIP, H - NHRP, I1 - ISIS L1
 I2 - ISIS L2, IA - ISIS interarea, IS - ISIS summary, D - EIGRP
 EX - EIGRP external, ND - ND Default, NDp - ND Prefix, DCE - Destination
 NDr - Redirect, O - OSPF Intra, OI - OSPF Inter, OE1 - OSPF ext 1
 OE2 - OSPF ext 2, ON1 - OSPF NSSA ext 1, ON2 - OSPF NSSA ext 2, l - LISP
C    2001:DB8:0:1::/64 [0/0]
     via GigabitEthernet0/0, directly connected
L    2001:DB8:0:1::1/128 [0/0]
     via GigabitEthernet0/0, receive
OE2 2001:DB8:0:3::/64 [110/10]
       via FE80::C802:AFF:FE88:8, GigabitEthernet1/0
C    2001:DB8:0:12::/64 [0/0]
     via GigabitEthernet1/0, directly connected
L    2001:DB8:0:12::1/128 [0/0]
     via GigabitEthernet1/0, receive
C    2001:DB8:0:14::/64 [0/0]
     via FastEthernet3/0, directly connected
L    2001:DB8:0:14::1/128 [0/0]
     via FastEthernet3/0, receive
OE2 2001:DB8:0:23::/64 [110/10]
       via FE80::C802:AFF:FE88:8, GigabitEthernet1/0
L    FF00::/8 [0/0]
     via Null0, receive
```

Note that if you are redistributing from BGP into OSPF, EIGRP, or RIP, only eBGP routes are redistributed by default. If you want iBGP routes to be redistributed, you must issue the **bgp redistribute-internal** command in router BGP configuration mode.

Troubleshooting Redistribution into BGP

When redistributing EIGRP into BGP for IPv4, you have the same options as when redistributing into EIGRP. You can apply a metric with the **metric** keyword or a route map with the **route-map** keyword. If you are redistributing OSPF into BGP, as shown in Example 17-24, you also have the option to specify the **match** option, which allows you to match just **internal** routes, just **external** routes, just **nssa-external** routes, or a combination of them. With BGP, only internal OSPF routes are redistributed by default. If you want external OSPF routes to be redistributed, you must indicate so during redistribution.

The **metric** keyword is not required because BGP uses the IGP metric by default. If the wrong route map is applied, or if there is an error in the route map, routes are not redistributed properly.

17

Example 17-24   *BGP for IPv4 Redistribution Options*

```
R1(config)# router bgp 65001
R1(config-router)# address-family ipv4 unicast
R1(config-router-af)# redistribute ospf 1 ?
 match        Redistribution of OSPF routes
 metric       Metric for redistributed routes
 route-map    Route map reference
 vrf          VPN Routing/Forwarding Instance
 <cr>
```

With BGP for IPv6, you have the same **match**, **metric**, and **route-map** keywords, as well as the **include-connected** keyword. By default, with BGP for IPv4, the networks of the local interfaces participating in the routing protocol that is being redistributed on the border router are redistributed as well. However, with BGP for IPv6, they are not. Therefore, if you want to redistribute the networks associated with the local interfaces participating in the routing process being redistributed into BGP for IPv6, you need to use the **include-connected** keyword, as shown in Example 17-25.

Example 17-25   *BGP for IPv6 Redistribution Options*

```
R1(config)# router bgp 65001
R1(config-router) # address-family ipv6 unicast
R1(config-router-af) # redistribute ospf 1 ?
 include-connected   Include connected
 match               Redistribution of OSPF routes
 metric              Metric for redistributed routes
 route-map           Route map reference
 <cr>
```

By using the commands **show ip protocols** and **show ipv6 protocols**, you can verify which protocols are being redistributed into the BGP routing process, as shown in Example 17-26.

Example 17-26   *Verifying Protocols Being Redistributed into BGP*

```
R2# show ip protocols
...output omitted...
Routing Protocol is "bgp 65500"
  Outgoing update filter list for all interfaces is not set
  Incoming update filter list for all interfaces is not set
  IGP synchronization is disabled
  Automatic route summarization is disabled
  Redistributing: ospf 1 (internal)

  Neighbor(s):
```

```
    Address      FiltIn FiltOut DistIn DistOut Weight RouteMap
    10.1.23.3
 Maximum path: 1
Routing Information Sources:
   Gateway         Distance      Last Update
 Distance: external 20 internal 200 local 200


R2# show ipv6 protocols
...output omitted...
IPv6 Routing Protocol is "bgp 65500"
  IGP synchronization is disabled
  Redistribution:
    Redistributing protocol ospf 1 (internal) include-connected
  Neighbor(s):
  Address FiltIn FiltOut Weight RoutemapIn RoutemapOut
    2001:DB8:0:23::3
```

In the BGP table, redistributed routes appear with a question mark (?) under the Path column, as shown in Example 17-27.

Example 17-27   *Verifying Redistributed Routes in the BGP Table*

```
R2# show bgp all
For address family: IPv4 Unicast


BGP table version is 4, local router ID is 203.0.113.1
Status codes: s suppressed, d damped, h history, * valid, > best, i - internal,
              r RIB-failure, S Stale, m multipath, b backup-path, f RT-Filter,
              x best-external, a additional-path, c RIB-compressed,
Origin codes: i - IGP, e - EGP, ? - incomplete
RPKI validation codes: V valid, I invalid, N Not found


   Network          Next Hop    Metric LocPrf  Weight  Path
 *> 10.1.1.0/24      10.1.12.1        2         32768  ?
 *> 10.1.12.0/24     0.0.0.0          0         32768  ?
 *> 10.1.14.0/24     10.1.12.1        2         32768  ?


For address family: IPv6 Unicast


BGP table version is 4, local router ID is 203.0.113.1
Status codes: s suppressed, d damped, h history, * valid, > best, i - internal,
              r RIB-failure, S Stale, m multipath, b backup-path, f RT-Filter,
              x best-external, a additional-path, c RIB-compressed,
```

17

```
Origin codes: i - IGP, e - EGP, ? - incomplete
RPKI validation codes: V valid, I invalid, N Not found


Network              Next Hop    Metric   LocPrf   Weight  Path
*> 2001:DB8:0:1::/64   ::              2             32768  ?
*> 2001:DB8:0:12::/64  ::              0             32768  ?
*> 2001:DB8:0:14::/64  ::              2             32768  ?


...output omitted...
```

Troubleshooting Redistribution with Route Maps

When applying a route map with the **redistribution** command, you have a few extra items to verify during the troubleshooting process:

- Is the correct route map applied?

- Is **permit** or **deny** specified for the sequence, and is it correct? A permit sequence indicates that what is matched is redistributed. A deny sequence indicates that what is matched is not redistributed.

- If there is an access list or a prefix list being used in the **match** statement, you need to verify that they are correct by using the **show** {**ip** | **ipv6**} **access-list** command or the **show** {**ip** | **ipv6**} **prefix-list** command.

- If there are **set** statements, you need to verify that the correct values have been specified to accomplish the desired goal.

- If a route does not match any of the **match** statements in any of the sequences, it falls into the implicit deny sequence at the end of the route map and is not redistributed.

- If a route map is attached to the **redistribution** command but that route map does not exist, none of the routes are redistributed.

> **NOTE** If you need to review route maps, see Chapter 15, "Route Maps and Conditional Forwarding."

Redistribution Trouble Tickets

This section presents various trouble tickets related to the topics discussed in this chapter. The purpose of these trouble tickets is to show a process that you can follow when troubleshooting in the real world or in an exam environment. All trouble tickets in this section are based on the topology shown in Figure 17-11.

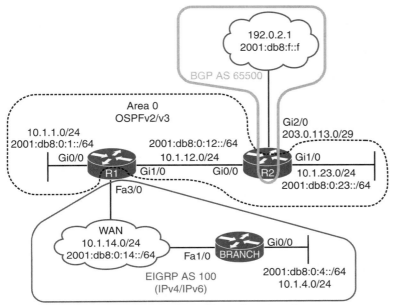

Figure 17-11 *Redistribution Trouble Tickets Topology*

Trouble Ticket 17-1

Problem: Users in the IPv4 Branch site indicate that they are not able to access any resources outside the Branch office.

On Branch, you first check the routing table to see which routes Branch knows; you do this by using the **show ip route** command, as shown in Example 17-28. The output indicates that Branch only knows about connected and local routes.

Example 17-28 *Verifying the Routing Table on Branch*

```
Branch# show ip route
...output omitted...
      10.0.0.0/8 is variably subnetted, 4 subnets, 2 masks
C        10.1.4.0/24 is directly connected, GigabitEthernet0/0
L        10.1.4.4/32 is directly connected, GigabitEthernet0/0
C        10.1.14.0/24 is directly connected, FastEthernet1/0
L        10.1.14.4/32 is directly connected, FastEthernet1/0
```

You decide that an EIGRP neighbor relationship might not have been formed with R1. Therefore, you issue the **show ip eigrp neighbors** command on Branch to confirm. As shown in Example 17-29, the device with IP address 10.1.14.1 has formed an adjacency with Branch. The **show cdp neighbors detail** command reveals that the IP address belongs to R1, as shown in the same example.

Example 17-29 *Verifying EIGRP Neighbors on Branch*

```
Branch# show ip eigrp neighbors
EIGRP-IPv4 VR(TSHOOT) Address-Family Neighbors for AS(100)
H   Address                  Interface        Hold Uptime    SRTT RTO   Q    Seq
                                              (sec)          (ms)       Cnt  Num

0   10.1.14.1                Fa1/0            12  01:40:12   62   372   0    6


Branch# show cdp neighbors detail
-----------------------
Device ID: R1
Entry address(es):
  IP address: 10.1.14.1
  IPv6 address: 2001:DB8:0:14::1 (global unicast)
  IPv6 address: FE80::C801:AFF:FE88:54 (link-local)
...output omitted...
```

Because R1 and Branch are neighbors, but Branch is not learning any routes from R1, you decide to check whether there are any incoming route filters configured on Branch by using the **show ip protocols** command. The output shown in Example 17-30 indicates that there are no route filters.

Example 17-30 *Verifying Route Filters on Branch*

```
Branch# show ip protocols
*** IP Routing is NSF aware ***

Routing Protocol is "eigrp 100"
  Outgoing update filter list for all interfaces is not set
  Incoming update filter list for all interfaces is not set
  Default networks flagged in outgoing updates
...output omitted...
```

Next, you decide to check for outbound route filters on R1 by using **show ip protocols**. As shown in Example 17-31, there are no route filters.

Example 17-31 *Verifying Route Filters on R1*

```
R1# show ip protocols
*** IP Routing is NSF aware ***

Routing Protocol is "eigrp 100"
  Outgoing update filter list for all interfaces is not set
  Incoming update filter list for all interfaces is not set
  Default networks flagged in outgoing updates
  Default networks accepted from incoming updates
```

```
 Redistributing: ospf 1
 EIGRP-IPv4 Protocol for AS(100)
 Metric weight K1=1, K2=0, K3=1, K4=0, K5=0
 NSF-aware route hold timer is 240
...output omitted...
```

Because Figure 17-11 shows that R1 is a boundary router performing redistribution, you shift your attention to R1's redistribution configuration to make sure the OSPF routes are being redistributed into EIGRP. In Example 17-32, the output of **show ip protocols** indicates that OSPF process 1 is being redistributed into EIGRP autonomous system 100. However, so far all your troubleshooting efforts are indicating that Branch is not learning any redistributed routes.

Example 17-32   *Verifying That OSPF Is Being Redistributed into EIGRP*

```
R1# show ip protocols
*** IP Routing is NSF aware ***

Routing Protocol is "eigrp 100"
  Outgoing update filter list for all interfaces is not set
  Incoming update filter list for all interfaces is not set
  Default networks flagged in outgoing updates
  Default networks accepted from incoming updates
  Redistributing: ospf 1
  EIGRP-IPv4 Protocol for AS(100)
    Metric weight K1=1, K2=0, K3=1, K4=0, K5=0
    NSF-aware route hold timer is 240
..output omitted...
```

You now issue the **show ip eigrp topology** command on R1 to determine whether routes are truly being redistributed from OSPF into EIGRP. As shown in Example 17-33, none of the OSPF routes are being redistributed into the EIGRP autonomous system.

Example 17-33   *Verifying That Redistributed Routes Are in the EIGRP Topology Table*

```
R1# show ip eigrp topology
EIGRP-IPv4 Topology Table for AS(100)/ID(10.1.14.1)
Codes: P - Passive, A - Active, U - Update, Q - Query, R - Reply,
       r - reply Status, s - sia Status

P 10.1.14.0/24, 1 successors, FD is 28160
        via Connected, FastEthernet3/0
P 10.1.4.0/24, 1 successors, FD is 28416
        via 10.1.14.4 (28416/2816), FastEthernet3/0
```

You recall that for routes to be redistributed, they have to be in the routing table. Therefore, you issue the **show ip route** command on R1, as shown in Example 17-34, and confirm that there are routes in the routing table that should be redistributed.

Example 17-34 *Verifying That Routes to Be Redistributed Are in the Routing Table*

```
R1# show ip route
...output omitted...
      10.0.0.0/8 is variably subnetted, 8 subnets, 2 masks
C        10.1.1.0/24 is directly connected, GigabitEthernet0/0
L        10.1.1.1/32 is directly connected, GigabitEthernet0/0
D        10.1.4.0/24 [90/28416] via 10.1.14.4, 02:05:59, FastEthernet3/0
C        10.1.12.0/24 is directly connected, GigabitEthernet1/0
L        10.1.12.1/32 is directly connected, GigabitEthernet1/0
C        10.1.14.0/24 is directly connected, FastEthernet3/0
L        10.1.14.1/32 is directly connected, FastEthernet3/0
O        10.1.23.0/24 [110/2] via 10.1.12.2, 02:02:11, GigabitEthernet1/0
      192.0.2.0/32 is subnetted, 1 subnets
O E2     192.0.2.1 [110/1] via 10.1.12.2, 01:03:22, GigabitEthernet1/0
```

Next, you review the **redistribute** command configured on R1 for the EIGRP process by using the **show run | section router eigrp** command, as shown in Example 17-35. You notice the command **redistribute ospf 1**; however, you quickly realize that the metric is missing. The metric is mandatory with EIGRP. If you fail to specify one with the **default-metric** command, with the **metric** command, or in a route map, the routes to be redistributed will be unreachable and not redistributed. You have located the issue.

Example 17-35 *Verifying the redistribute Command on R1*

```
R1# show run | section router eigrp
router eigrp 100
 network 10.1.14.1 0.0.0.0
 redistribute ospf 1
ipv6 router eigrp 100
 redistribute ospf 1 metric 100000 100 255 1 1500 include-connected
```

To solve the issue, you reissue the **redistribute ospf 1** command with the metric values **100000 100 255 1 1500**. You then issue the **show ip eigrp topology** command, as shown in Example 17-36, and confirm that routes are now redistributed.

Example 17-36 *Verifying That Routes to Be Redistributed Are in the R1 Topology Table*

```
R1# show ip eigrp topology
EIGRP-IPv4 Topology Table for AS(100)/ID(10.1.14.1)
Codes: P - Passive, A - Active, U - Update, Q - Query, R - Reply,
       r - reply Status, s - sia Status
```

```
P 10.1.12.0/24, 1 successors, FD is 51200
        via Redistributed (51200/0)
P 10.1.14.0/24, 1 successors, FD is 28160
        via Connected, FastEthernet3/0
P 10.1.23.0/24, 1 successors, FD is 51200
        via Redistributed (51200/0)
P 10.1.4.0/24, 1 successors, FD is 28416
        via 10.1.14.4 (28416/2816), FastEthernet3/0
P 192.0.2.1/32, 1 successors, FD is 51200
        via Redistributed (51200/0)
P 10.1.1.0/24, 1 successors, FD is 51200
        via Redistributed (51200/0)
```

Using the **show ip route** command on Branch, as shown in Example 17-37, allows you to conclude that the problem is solved because there are now external EIGRP routes learned by Branch, and users can successfully connect to resources outside the Branch office.

Example 17-37 *Verifying That Routes to Be Redistributed Are in the Branch Routing Table*

```
Branch# show ip route
Codes: L - local, C - connected, S - static, R - RIP, M - mobile, B - BGP
  D - EIGRP, EX - EIGRP external, O - OSPF, IA - OSPF inter area
  N1 - OSPF NSSA external type 1, N2 - OSPF NSSA external type 2
  E1 - OSPF external type 1, E2 - OSPF external type 2
  i - IS-IS, su - IS-IS summary, L1 - IS-IS level-1, L2 - IS-IS level-2
  ia - IS-IS inter area, * - candidate default, U - per-user static route
  o - ODR, P - periodic downloaded static route, H - NHRP, l - LISP
  + - replicated route, % - next hop override

Gateway of last resort is not set

      10.0.0.0/8 is variably subnetted, 7 subnets, 2 masks
D EX     10.1.1.0/24 [170/614400] via 10.1.14.1, 00:02:58, FastEthernet1/0
C        10.1.4.0/24 is directly connected, GigabitEthernet0/0
L        10.1.4.4/32 is directly connected, GigabitEthernet0/0

D EX     10.1.12.0/24 [170/614400] via 10.1.14.1, 00:02:58, FastEthernet1/0
C        10.1.14.0/24 is directly connected, FastEthernet1/0
L        10.1.14.4/32 is directly connected, FastEthernet1/0
D EX     10.1.23.0/24 [170/614400] via 10.1.14.1, 00:02:58, FastEthernet1/0
      192.0.2.0/32 is subnetted, 1 subnets
D EX      192.0.2.1 [170/614400] via 10.1.14.1, 00:02:58, FastEthernet1/0
```

Trouble Ticket 17-2

Problem: Users in the 10.1.23.0/24 network indicate that they are not able to access resources in the 10.1.4.0/24 network.

You begin troubleshooting by verifying the problem on R2. You issue a ping to 10.1.4.4 from 10.1.23.2, but it fails, as shown in Example 17-38. Because R2 is not able to ping the destination network, you confirm that the clients in 10.1.23.0/24 are not able to connect with resources in 10.1.4.0/24.

Example 17-38 *Verifying the Problem from R2*

```
R2# ping 10.1.4.4 source 10.1.23.2
Type escape sequence to abort.
Sending 5, 100-byte ICMP Echos to 10.1.4.4, timeout is 2 seconds:
Packet sent with a source address of 10.1.23.2
.....
Success rate is 0 percent (0/5)
```

On R2, you decide to issue a **traceroute** to help identify where the issue might be. The trace to 10.1.4.4 from 10.1.23.2, as shown in Example 17-39, is headed toward 203.0.113.2, which is out interface GigabitEthernet2/0, as confirmed in the output of **show ip interface brief** in Example 17-40.

Example 17-39 *Issuing a Trace to Identify Where the Issue Might Be*

```
R2# traceroute 10.1.4.4 source 10.1.23.2
Type escape sequence to abort.
Tracing the route to 10.1.4.4
VRF info: (vrf in name/id, vrf out name/id)
  1 203.0.113.2 28 msec 44 msec 32 msec
  2 * * *
...output omitted...
```

Example 17-40 *Verifying Interface IP Addresses*

```
R2# show ip interface brief
Interface            IP-Address      OK? Method Status                 Protocol
Ethernet0/0          unassigned      YES NVRAM  administratively down   down
GigabitEthernet0/0   10.1.12.2       YES NVRAM  up                      up
GigabitEthernet1/0   10.1.23.2       YES NVRAM  up                      up
GigabitEthernet2/0   203.0.113.1     YES NVRAM  up                      up
```

Next, you decide to issue the **show ip route 10.1.4.4** command on R2, and the result, as shown in Example 17-41, is that the subnet is not in the table.

Example 17-41 *Verifying the Route on R2*

```
R2# show ip route 10.1.4.4
% Subnet not in table
```

You shift your attention to R1 and issue the **show ip route 10.1.4.4** command, as shown in Example 17-42, and the result indicates that 10.1.4.4 is reachable using EIGRP out interface FastEthernet3/0. In addition, based on the topology, it should be redistributed into the OSPF process for the OSPF domain to have routes to it. Based on Example 17-42, it is being redistributed into OSPF process 1.

Example 17-42 *Verifying the Route on R1*

```
R1# show ip route 10.1.4.4
Routing entry for 10.1.4.0/24
  Known via "eigrp 100", distance 90, metric 28416, type internal
  Redistributing via eigrp 100, ospf 1
  Last update from 10.1.14.4 on FastEthernet3/0, 2d14h ago
  Routing Descriptor Blocks:
  * 10.1.14.4, from 10.1.14.4, 2d14h ago, via FastEthernet3/0
      Route metric is 28416, traffic share count is 1
      Total delay is 110 microseconds, minimum bandwidth is 100000 Kbit
      Reliability 255/255, minimum MTU 1500 bytes
      Loading 1/255, Hops 1
```

You double-check the OSPF database on R1, as shown in Example 17-43, and notice that 10.1.4.0 is not listed as an external Type 5 LSA. This means that it is not being successfully redistributed into the OSPF process.

Example 17-43 *Verifying the OSPF Database on R1*

```
R1# show ip ospf database

            OSPF Router with ID (10.1.14.1) (Process ID 1)

                Router Link States (Area 0)

Link ID        ADV Router      Age       Seq#         Checksum Link count
10.1.14.1      10.1.14.1       1698      0x8000007D   0x0064CD 2
203.0.113.1    203.0.113.1     1274      0x80000084   0x005972 2


                Net Link States (Area 0)

Link ID        ADV Router      Age       Seq#         Checksum
10.1.12.2      203.0.113.1     1274      0x8000007C   0x0010FE


                Type-5 AS External Link States

Link ID        ADV Router      Age       Seq#         Checksum Tag
192.0.2.1      203.0.113.1     1274      0x8000007C   0x00FD38 0
```

You issue the **show run | section router ospf** command on R1 to verify the OSPF configuration on R1. As shown in Example 17-44, the **redistribute eigrp 100** command is listed in the configuration. However, as you discovered earlier, the EIGRP routes are not being redistributed. You double-check to make sure the correct EIGRP autonomous system is being redistributed by issuing the **show run | section router eigrp** command, as shown in Example 17-45. This output confirms that the correct EIGRP autonomous system is being redistributed.

Example 17-44 *Verifying the OSPF Configuration on R1*

```
R1# show run | section router ospf
router ospf 1
 redistribute eigrp 100
 network 10.1.1.1 0.0.0.0 area 0
 network 10.1.12.1 0.0.0.0 area 0
ipv6 router ospf 1
 redistribute eigrp 100 include-connected
```

Example 17-45 *Verifying the EIGRP Configuration on R1*

```
R1# show run | section router eigrp
router eigrp 100
 network 10.1.14.1 0.0.0.0
 redistribute ospf 1 metric 100000 100 255 1 1500
ipv6 router eigrp 100
 redistribute ospf 1 metric 100000 100 255 1 1500 include-connected
```

After some thought, you realize that the 10.1.4.0/24 network is a classless network and that the current **redistribute eigrp 100** command redistributes only classful networks. You need to add the **subnets** keyword to the **redistribute** command, as shown in Example 17-46, to redistribute classless networks. By issuing the **show ip ospf database** command, as shown in Example 17-47, you confirm that the OSPF database is now learning the EIGRP route 10.1.4.0/24.

Example 17-46 *Adding the subnets Keyword to the redistribute Command*

```
R1# config t
Enter configuration commands, one per line. End with CNTL/Z.
R1(config)# router ospf 1
R1(config-router)# redistribute eigrp 100 subnets
```

Example 17-47 *Verifying That the 10.1.4.0 Route Is in the OSPF Database on R1*

```
R1# show ip ospf database

            OSPF Router with ID (10.1.14.1) (Process ID 1)

                Router Link States (Area 0)
```

```
Link ID           ADV Router        Age         Seq#          Checksum Link count
10.1.14.1         10.1.14.1         1698        0x8000007D    0x0064CD 2
203.0.113.1       203.0.113.1       1274        0x80000084    0x005972 2


                  Net Link States (Area 0)


Link ID           ADV Router        Age         Seq#          Checksum
10.1.12.2         203.0.113.1       1274        0x8000007C    0x0010FE


                  Type-5 AS External Link States


Link ID           ADV Router        Age         Seq#          Checksum Tag
10.1.4.0          10.1.14.1         17          0x80000001    0x006215 0
10.1.14.0         10.1.14.1         17          0x80000001    0x00F379 0
192.0.2.1         203.0.113.1       1923        0x8000007C    0x00FD38 0
```

Next, you visit R2 and issue the **show ip route 10.1.4.4** command and confirm that the route has been added, as shown in Example 17-48.

Example 17-48   *Verifying That R2 Now Knows About the 10.1.4.0 Network*

```
R2# show ip route 10.1.4.4
Routing entry for 10.1.4.0/24
 Known via "ospf 1", distance 110, metric 20, type extern 2, forward metric 1
 Redistributing via bgp 65500
 Advertised by bgp 65500 match internal external 1 & 2
 Last update from 10.1.12.1 on GigabitEthernet0/0, 00:04:52 ago
 Routing Descriptor Blocks:
 * 10.1.12.1, from 10.1.14.1, 00:04:52 ago, via GigabitEthernet0/0
     Route metric is 20, traffic share count is 1
```

Finally, you confirm that the problem is solved with a ping from 10.1.23.2 to 10.1.4.4, and it is successful, as shown in Example 17-49.

Example 17-49   *Successful Ping*

```
R2# ping 10.1.4.4 source 10.1.23.2
Type escape sequence to abort.
Sending 5, 100-byte ICMP Echos to 10.1.4.4, timeout is 2 seconds:
Packet sent with a source address of 10.1.23.2
!!!!!
Success rate is 100 percent (5/5), round-trip min/avg/max = 36/55/72 ms
```

Trouble Ticket 17-3

Problem: IPv6 users in the 2001:db8:0:4::/64 network report that they are not able to access resources in the 2001:db8:0:1::/64 network.

You begin troubleshooting by confirming the problem on Branch. As shown in Example 17-50, the ping from 2001:db8:0:4::4 to 2001:db8:0:1::1 fails.

Example 17-50   *Confirming the Problem with a Ping*

```
Branch# ping 2001:db8:0:1::1 source 2001:db8:0:4::4
Type escape sequence to abort.
Sending 5, 100-byte ICMP Echos to 2001:DB8:0:1::1, timeout is 2 seconds:
Packet sent with a source address of 2001:DB8:0:4::4
.....
Success rate is 0 percent (0/5)
```

While gathering further information, you decide to ping an IPv6 address in the 2001:db8:0:23::/64 network. As shown in Example 17-51, the ping is successful. Therefore, you conclude that only some of the routes in the IPv6 OSPF domain are being redistributed into the IPv6 EIGRP domain. You issue the **show ipv6 route** command on Branch, as shown in Example 17-52, and the output confirms that only two external routes are being learned by Branch: 2001:db8:0:23::/64 and 2001:db8:f::/64.

Example 17-51   *Gathering More Information with a Ping*

```
Branch# ping 2001:db8:0:23::2 source 2001:db8:0:4::4
Type escape sequence to abort.
Sending 5, 100-byte ICMP Echos to 2001:DB8:0:23::2, timeout is 2 seconds:
Packet sent with a source address of 2001:DB8:0:4::4
!!!!!
Success rate is 100 percent (5/5), round-trip min/avg/max = 8/47/120 ms
```

Example 17-52   *Verifying Routes on Branch*

```
Branch# show ipv6 route
...output omitted...
C   2001:DB8:0:4::/64 [0/0]
     via GigabitEthernet0/0, directly connected
L   2001:DB8:0:4::4/128 [0/0]
     via GigabitEthernet0/0, receive
C   2001:DB8:0:14::/64 [0/0]
     via FastEthernet1/0, directly connected
L   2001:DB8:0:14::4/128 [0/0]
     via FastEthernet1/0, receive
EX  2001:DB8:0:23::/64 [170/614400]
     via FE80::C801:AFF:FE88:54, FastEthernet1/0
EX  2001:DB8:F::/64 [170/614400]
     via FE80::C801:AFF:FE88:54, FastEthernet1/0
L   FF00::/8 [0/0]
     via Null0, receive
```

Based on the information you have gathered, you decide to check whether redistribution is being performed on R1. You issue the **show ipv6 protocols** command on R1, as shown in Example 17-53. In the output, you focus on the EIGRP section and review the redistribution information. It clearly indicates that redistribution from OSPF process 1 into EIGRP autonomous system 100 is occurring. In addition, the metric values have been applied (which is mandatory for redistribution into EIGRP), and internal and external routes are being redistributed. You think that a route map might be controlling the routes that are being redistributed. However, you notice that a route map is not listed under the *Redistribution* section of the **show ipv6 protocols** command. Therefore, that is not the issue.

Example 17-53   *Verifying IPv6 Redistribution on R1*

```
R1# show ipv6 protocols
IPv6 Routing Protocol is "connected"
IPv6 Routing Protocol is "ND"
IPv6 Routing Protocol is "eigrp 100"
EIGRP-IPv6 Protocol for AS(100)
  Metric weight K1=1, K2=0, K3=1, K4=0, K5=0
  NSF-aware route hold timer is 240
  Router-ID: 10.1.14.1
  Topology : 0 (base)
    Active Timer: 3 min
    Distance: internal 90 external 170
    Maximum path: 16
    Maximum hopcount 100
    Maximum metric variance 1
 Interfaces:
    FastEthernet3/0
  Redistribution:
    Redistributing protocol ospf 1 with metric 100000 100 255 1 1500 (internal,
external 1 & 2, nssa-external 1 & 2)
IPv6 Routing Protocol is "ospf 1"
  Router ID 10.1.14.1
  Autonomous system boundary router
  Number of areas: 1 normal, 0 stub, 0 nssa
  Interfaces (Area 0):
    GigabitEthernet1/0
    GigabitEthernet0/0
  Redistribution:
    Redistributing protocol eigrp 100 include-connected
```

On R1, you issue the **show ipv6 eigrp topology** command to confirm whether the routes are being redistributed into EIGRP from OSPF. As shown in Example 17-54, only the routes 2001:db8:0:23::/64 and 2001:db8:f::/64 are being redistributed.

Example 17-54 *Reviewing R1's EIGRP Topology*

```
R1# show ipv6 eigrp topology
EIGRP-IPv6 Topology Table for AS(100)/ID(10.1.14.1)
Codes: P - Passive, A - Active, U - Update, Q - Query, R - Reply,
       r - reply Status, s - sia Status


P 2001:DB8:0:4::/64, 1 successors, FD is 28416
        via FE80::C800:CFF:FEE4:1C (28416/2816), FastEthernet3/0
P 2001:DB8:F::/64, 1 successors, FD is 51200
        via Redistributed (51200/0)
P 2001:DB8:0:14::/64, 1 successors, FD is 28160
        via Connected, FastEthernet3/0
P 2001:DB8:0:23::/64, 1 successors, FD is 51200
        via Redistributed (51200/0)
```

You check the output of **show ipv6 route** on R1 and note that 2001:db8:0:1::/64 and 2001:db8:0:12::/64 are both in R1's routing table as connected routes, as shown in Example 17-55. Therefore, for them to be redistributed, they either have to be redistributed as connected routes or participating in the OSPF process because R1 is configured to redistribute OSPF into EIGRP. Therefore, on R1, you issue the **show ipv6 ospf interface brief** command, as shown in Example 17-56, and confirm that both Gig0/0 and Gig1/0 are participating in the OSPF process. However, based on your information gathering so far, you have determined that the routes are still not being redistributed.

Example 17-55 *Reviewing R1's IPv6 Routing Table*

```
R1# show ipv6 route
...output omitted...
C   2001:DB8:0:1::/64 [0/0]
     via GigabitEthernet0/0, directly connected
L   2001:DB8:0:1::1/128 [0/0]
     via GigabitEthernet0/0, receive
D   2001:DB8:0:4::/64 [90/28416]
     via FE80::C800:CFF:FEE4:1C, FastEthernet3/0
C   2001:DB8:0:12::/64 [0/0]
     via GigabitEthernet1/0, directly connected
L   2001:DB8:0:12::1/128 [0/0]
     via GigabitEthernet1/0, receive
C   2001:DB8:0:14::/64 [0/0]
     via FastEthernet3/0, directly connected
L   2001:DB8:0:14::1/128 [0/0]
     via FastEthernet3/0, receive
O   2001:DB8:0:23::/64 [110/2]
     via FE80::C802:AFF:FE88:8, GigabitEthernet1/0
OE2 2001:DB8:F::/64 [110/1]
     via FE80::C802:AFF:FE88:8, GigabitEthernet1/0
L   FF00::/8 [0/0]
     via Null0, receive
```

Example 17-56 *Reviewing R1's IPv6 OSPF Interfaces*

```
R1# show ipv6 ospf interface brief
Interface   PID     Area    Intf ID     Cost    State   Nbrs F/C
Gi1/0       1       0       4           1       BDR     1/1
Gi0/0       1       0       3           1       DR      0/0
```

At this point, you recall that IPv6 redistribution behaves differently from IPv4 redistribution with directly connected networks. IPv6 directly connected networks are not redistributed by default. You need to use the **include-connected** keyword to force the directly connected networks to be redistributed. By reviewing the *Redistribution* section in the **show ipv6 protocols** output of Example 17-53 again, you confirm that the **include-connected** keyword was not included in the command.

On R1, you issue the command **redistribute ospf 1 metric 100000 100 255 1 1500 include-connected** in IPv6 EIGRP configuration mode, as shown in Example 17-57, to fix the issue.

Example 17-57 *Modifying the redistribute Command*

```
R1# config t
Enter configuration commands, one per line. End with CNTL/Z.
R1(config)# ipv6 router eigrp 100
R1(config-rtr)# redistribute ospf 1 metric 100000 100 255 1 1500 include-connected
```

You reissue the **show ipv6 protocols** command and the **show ipv6 eigrp topology** command and confirm that the directly connected routes are now being redistributed, as shown in Example 17-58.

Example 17-58 *Verifying That Routes Are Redistributed After Changes*

```
R1# show ipv6 protocols
IPv6 Routing Protocol is "connected"
IPv6 Routing Protocol is "ND"
IPv6 Routing Protocol is "eigrp 100"
EIGRP-IPv6 Protocol for AS(100)
  Metric weight K1=1, K2=0, K3=1, K4=0, K5=0
...output omitted...
  Redistribution:
    Redistributing protocol ospf 1 with metric 100000 100 255 1 1500 (internal,
external 1 & 2, nssa-external 1 & 2) include-connected
...output omitted...

R1# show ipv6 eigrp topology
EIGRP-IPv6 Topology Table for AS(100)/ID(10.1.14.1)
Codes: P - Passive, A - Active, U - Update, Q - Query, R - Reply,
       r - reply Status, s - sia Status
```

17

```
P 2001:DB8:0:4::/64, 1 successors, FD is 28416
        via FE80::C800:CFF:FEE4:1C (28416/2816), FastEthernet3/0
P 2001:DB8:0:1::/64, 1 successors, FD is 51200
        via Redistributed (51200/0)
P 2001:DB8:F::/64, 1 successors, FD is 51200
        via Redistributed (51200/0)
P 2001:DB8:0:14::/64, 1 successors, FD is 28160
        via Connected, FastEthernet3/0
P 2001:DB8:0:12::/64, 1 successors, FD is 51200
        via Redistributed (51200/0)
P 2001:DB8:0:23::/64, 1 successors, FD is 51200
        via Redistributed (51200/0)
```

When you go back to Branch and issue the **show ipv6 route** command, you notice that there are entries in the routing table for 2001:db8:0:1::/64 and 2001:db8:0:12::/64 now, as shown in Example 17-59.

Example 17-59   *Verifying That Routes Are Learned by Branch*

```
Branch# show ipv6 route
IPv6 Routing Table - default - 9 entries
Codes: C - Connected, L - Local, S - Static, U - Per-user Static route
       B - BGP, R - RIP, H - NHRP, I1 - ISIS L1
       I2 - ISIS L2, IA - ISIS interarea, IS - ISIS summary, D - EIGRP
       EX - EIGRP external, ND - ND Default, NDp - ND Prefix, DCE - Destination
       NDr - Redirect, O - OSPF Intra, OI - OSPF Inter, OE1 - OSPF ext 1
       OE2 - OSPF ext 2, ON1 - OSPF NSSA ext 1, ON2 - OSPF NSSA ext 2, l - LISP
EX   2001:DB8:0:1::/64 [170/614400]
        via FE80::C801:AFF:FE88:54, FastEthernet1/0
C    2001:DB8:0:4::/64 [0/0]
        via GigabitEthernet0/0, directly connected
L    2001:DB8:0:4::4/128 [0/0]
        via GigabitEthernet0/0, receive
EX   2001:DB8:0:12::/64 [170/614400]
        via FE80::C801:AFF:FE88:54, FastEthernet1/0
C    2001:DB8:0:14::/64 [0/0]
        via FastEthernet1/0, directly connected
L    2001:DB8:0:14::4/128 [0/0]
        via FastEthernet1/0, receive
EX   2001:DB8:0:23::/64 [170/614400]
        via FE80::C801:AFF:FE88:54, FastEthernet1/0
EX   2001:DB8:F::/64 [170/614400]
        via FE80::C801:AFF:FE88:54, FastEthernet1/0
L    FF00::/8 [0/0]
        via Null0, receive
```

You verify that the problem is solved with a ping from Branch at 2001:db8:0:4::4 to 2001:db8:0:1::1, as shown in Example 17-60. The ping is successful, and the problem is solved.

Example 17-60   *Verifying That the Problem Is Solved with a Successful Ping*

```
Branch# ping 2001:db8:0:1::1 source 2001:db8:0:4::4
Type escape sequence to abort.
Sending 5, 100-byte ICMP Echos to 2001:DB8:0:1::1, timeout is 2 seconds:
Packet sent with a source address of 2001:DB8:0:4::4
!!!!!
Success rate is 100 percent (5/5), round-trip min/avg/max = 24/32/44 ms
```

Trouble Ticket 17-4

Problem: A junior administrator has approached you, asking for help. They claim that users in BGP autonomous system 65500 are unable to access IPv4 resources in the IPv4 EIGRP autonomous system 100. However, they can access resources in the OSPFv2 domain. Because access to routers in BGP autonomous system 65500 is limited to only R2, the junior administrator has asked you for help.

You start by reviewing Figure 17-11 to confirm which local router is running BGP. It is R2. You issue the **show bgp ipv4 unicast summary** command on R2 to confirm whether R2 has any BGP neighbors. As shown in Example 17-61, 203.0.113.2 is listed as a neighbor, and because the State/PfxRcd column has a number, it is an established neighborship. To further confirm, you issue the **show bgp ipv4 unicast neighbors | include BGP** command, as shown in Example 17-62, and the output indicates that 203.0.113.2 is an established neighbor.

Example 17-61   *Verifying BGP Neighbors*

```
R2# show bgp ipv4 unicast summary
BGP router identifier 203.0.113.1, local AS number 65500
BGP table version is 33, main routing table version 33
4 network entries using 576 bytes of memory
4 path entries using 320 bytes of memory
3/3 BGP path/bestpath attribute entries using 408 bytes of memory
0 BGP route-map cache entries using 0 bytes of memory
0 BGP filter-list cache entries using 0 bytes of memory
BGP using 1304 total bytes of memory
BGP activity 28/18 prefixes, 30/20 paths, scan interval 60 secs

Neighbor        V    AS   MsgRcvd MsgSent TblVer InQ OutQ Up/Down  State/PfxRcd
203.0.113.2     4  65500 496       500      33     0   0   07:26:42            1
```

Example 17-62   *Verifying an Established BGP Neighbor*

```
R2# show bgp ipv4 unicast neighbors | include BGP
BGP neighbor is 203.0.113.2, remote AS 65500, internal link
  BGP version 4, remote router ID 192.0.2.1
  BGP state = Established, up for 07:31:19
  BGP table version 33, neighbor version 33/0
  Last reset 07:31:29, due to BGP Notification received of session 1, header syn-
chronization problems
```

Next, you verify whether any routes are being advertised to the neighbor at 203.0.113.2 by issuing the **show bgp ipv4 unicast neighbors 203.0.113.2 advertised-routes** command. In Example 17-63, you can see that three routes are being advertised to 203.0.113.2 from R2. The routes are 10.1.1.0/24, 10.1.12.0/24, and 10.1.23.0/24. Figure 17-11 indicates that the EIGRP networks are 10.1.14.0/24 and 10.1.4.0/24 and that they are not listed as routes being advertised.

Example 17-63   *Verifying Advertised BGP Routes*

```
R2# show bgp ipv4 unicast neighbors 203.0.113.2 advertised-routes
BGP table version is 33, local router ID is 203.0.113.1
Status codes: s suppressed, d damped, h history, * valid, > best, i - internal,
              r RIB-failure, S Stale, m multipath, b backup-path, f RT-Filter,
              x best-external, a additional-path, c RIB-compressed,
Origin codes: i - IGP, e - EGP, ? - incomplete
RPKI validation codes: V valid, I invalid, N Not found

     Network          Next Hop      Metric    LocPrf    Weight    Path
 *>  10.1.1.0/24      10.1.12.1       2                           32768 ?
 *>  10.1.12.0/24     0.0.0.0         0                           32768 ?
 *>  10.1.23.0/24     0.0.0.0         0                           32768 ?

Total number of prefixes 3
```

You issue the **show ip protocols** command on R2, as shown in Example 17-64, to verify the BGP configuration. You notice that there are no filters, no distribute lists, and no route maps applied to neighbor 203.0.113.2 that could be preventing routes from being advertised. However, you notice that only OSPF internal routes are being redistributed in the output. You issue the **show ip route** command on R2, as shown in Example 17-65, and confirm that 10.1.4.0/24 and 10.1.14.0/24 are both external OSPF routes. You conclude that the problem is related to BGP not redistributing OSPF external routes.

Example 17-64   *Verifying BGP Configuration with show ip protocols*

```
R2# show ip protocols
*** IP Routing is NSF aware ***
...output omitted...
Routing Protocol is "bgp 65500"
```

```
    Outgoing update filter list for all interfaces is not set
    Incoming update filter list for all interfaces is not set
    IGP synchronization is disabled
    Automatic route summarization is disabled
    Redistributing: ospf 1 (internal)


    Neighbor(s):
      Address             FiltIn FiltOut DistIn DistOut Weight RouteMap
      203.0.113.2
    Maximum path: 1
    Routing Information Sources:
      Gateway         Distance      Last Update
      203.0.113.2     200           07:54:48
    Distance: external 20 internal 200 local 200
```

Example 17-65   *Verifying IPv4 Routes on R2*

```
R2# show ip route
Codes: L - local, C - connected, S - static, R - RIP, M - mobile, B - BGP
       D - EIGRP, EX - EIGRP external, O - OSPF, IA - OSPF inter area
       N1 - OSPF NSSA external type 1, N2 - OSPF NSSA external type 2
       E1 - OSPF external type 1, E2 - OSPF external type 2
       i - IS-IS, su - IS-IS summary, L1 - IS-IS level-1, L2 - IS-IS level-2
       ia - IS-IS inter area, * - candidate default, U - per-user static route
       o - ODR, P - periodic downloaded static route, H - NHRP, l - LISP
       + - replicated route, % - next hop override

Gateway of last resort is 203.0.113.2 to network 0.0.0.0

S*     0.0.0.0/0 [1/0] via 203.0.113.2
       10.0.0.0/8 is variably subnetted, 7 subnets, 2 masks
O        10.1.1.0/24 [110/2] via 10.1.12.1, 4d20h, GigabitEthernet0/0
O E2     10.1.4.0/24 [110/20] via 10.1.12.1, 1d23h, GigabitEthernet0/0
C        10.1.12.0/24 is directly connected, GigabitEthernet0/0
L        10.1.12.2/32 is directly connected, GigabitEthernet0/0
O E2     10.1.14.0/24 [110/20] via 10.1.12.1, 1d23h, GigabitEthernet0/0
C        10.1.23.0/24 is directly connected, GigabitEthernet1/0
L        10.1.23.2/32 is directly connected, GigabitEthernet1/0
       192.0.2.0/32 is subnetted, 1 subnets
B        192.0.2.1 [200/0] via 203.0.113.2, 08:00:48
       203.0.113.0/24 is variably subnetted, 2 subnets, 2 masks
C        203.0.113.0/29 is directly connected, GigabitEthernet2/0
L        203.0.113.1/32 is directly connected, GigabitEthernet2/0
```

On R2, you issue the **show run | section router bgp** command, as shown in Example 17-66, to verify the BGP configuration. Under the IPv4 address family, you notice that the **redistribute ospf 1** command has been issued. However, that command only redistributes internal OSPF routes. It does not redistribute OSPF external routes by default.

Example 17-66 *Verifying BGP Configuration on R2*

```
R2# show run | section router bgp
router bgp 65500
 bgp log-neighbor-changes
 neighbor 2001:DB8:0:A::A remote-as 65500
 neighbor 203.0.113.2 remote-as 65500
 !
 address-family ipv4
  bgp redistribute-internal
  redistribute ospf 1
  no neighbor 2001:DB8:0:A::A activate
  neighbor 203.0.113.2 activate
 exit-address-family
 !
 address-family ipv6
  redistribute ospf 1 match internal external 1 external 2 include-connected
  bgp redistribute-internal
  neighbor 2001:DB8:0:A::A activate
 exit-address-family
```

Because the routes are external Type 2 OSPF routes, you issue the command **redistribute ospf 1 match internal external 2** in IPv4 BGP address family configuration mode, as shown in Example 17-67. You then issue the command **show ip protocols** to verify that external Type 2 routes are now being redistributed as well. Example 17-68 shows that they are.

Example 17-67 *Modifying the **redistribute** Command in IPv4 Address Family Configuration Mode*

```
R2# config t
Enter configuration commands, one per line. End with CNTL/Z.
R2(config)# router bgp 65500
R2(config-router)# address-family ipv4 unicast
R2(config-router-af)# redistribute ospf 1 match internal external 2
```

Example 17-68 *Verifying the Types of OSPF Routes Being Advertised into BGP*

```
R2# show ip protocols
...output omitted...
Routing Protocol is "bgp 65500"
  Outgoing update filter list for all interfaces is not set
  Incoming update filter list for all interfaces is not set
```

```
IGP synchronization is disabled
Automatic route summarization is disabled
Redistributing: ospf 1 (internal, external 2)


Neighbor(s):
  Address            FiltIn FiltOut DistIn DistOut Weight RouteMap
  203.0.113.2
Maximum path: 1
Routing Information Sources:
  Gateway          Distance      Last Update
  203.0.113.2      200           1d07h
Distance: external 20 internal 200 local 200
```

You then reissue the **show bgp ipv4 unicast neighbors 203.0.113.2 advertised-routes** command to verify that 10.1.14.0/24 and 10.1.4.0/24 are being advertised in BGP autonomous system 65500. Example 17-69 shows that they are.

Example 17-69   *Verifying That OSPF Routes Are Advertised to the BGP Neighbor*

```
R2# show bgp ipv4 unicast neighbors 203.0.113.2 advertised-routes
BGP table version is 35, local router ID is 203.0.113.1
Status codes: s suppressed, d damped, h history, * valid, > best, i - internal,
              r RIB-failure, S Stale, m multipath, b backup-path, f RT-Filter,
              x best-external, a additional-path, c RIB-compressed,
Origin codes: i - IGP, e - EGP, ? - incomplete
RPKI validation codes: V valid, I invalid, N Not found

  Network          Next Hop          Metric LocPrf Weight Path
 *> 10.1.1.0/24     10.1.12.1              2            32768 ?
 *> 10.1.4.0/24     10.1.12.1             20            32768 ?
 *> 10.1.12.0/24    0.0.0.0 0                          32768 ?
 *> 10.1.14.0/24    10.1.12.1             20            32768 ?
 *> 10.1.23.0/24    0.0.0.0 0                          32768 ?

Total number of prefixes 5
```

Next, you pick up the phone and call the administrator of the other routers in BGP autonomous system 65500 and confirm that those users can access the resources in EIGRP autonomous system 100. The administrator states that they can; therefore, you have solved the issue.

Exam Preparation Tasks

As mentioned in the section "How to Use This Book" in the Introduction, you have a couple choices for exam preparation: the exercises here, Chapter 24, "Final Preparation," and the exam simulation questions in the Pearson Test Prep software.

Review All Key Topics

Review the most important topics in this chapter, noted with the Key Topic icon in the outer margin of the page. Table 17-3 lists these key topics and the page number on which each is found.

Table 17-3 Key Topics

Key Topic Element	Description	Page Number
Paragraph	Solving and preventing suboptimal routing caused by redistribution	678
List	Troubleshooting suboptimal routing issues caused by redistribution	679
Paragraphs	Routing loops with redistribution at multiple points	679
Paragraph	Routing table instability with redistribution at multiple points	681
Paragraph	How traffic might get blackholed with redistribution at multiple points	681
Paragraphs	Modifying the EIGRP administrative distance	682
Paragraphs	Modifying the OSPF administrative distance	683
Paragraphs	Modifying the BGP administrative distance	683
Example 17-3	Using a distribute list to control OSPF routes that are installed in the routing table	684
Example 17-4	Tagging routes as they are being redistributed	685
Example 17-5	Using route tags to prevent routes from being reinjected	686
Paragraph	The redistribution process	687
List	Three methods for configuring a seed metric	688
List	Prerequisites for redistributing a route	689
Table 17-2	Troubleshooting targets for route redistribution	689
Section	Troubleshooting redistribution into EIGRP	694
Section	Troubleshooting redistribution into OSPF	699
Section	Troubleshooting redistribution into BGP	702
List	Troubleshooting redistribution that uses route maps	722

Define Key Terms

Define the following key terms from this chapter and check your answers in the glossary:

redistribution, multipoint redistribution, seed metric, boundary router, metric, ASBR, administrative distance, Type 5 LSA, routing loop, route tag, **subnets** keyword,

Command Reference to Check Your Memory

The ENARSI 300-410 exam focuses on the practical, hands-on skills that networking professionals use. Therefore, you should be able to identify the commands needed to configure, verify, and troubleshoot the topics covered in this chapter.

This section includes the most important configuration and verification commands covered in this chapter. It might not be necessary to memorize the complete syntax of every command, but you should be able to remember the basic keywords that are needed.

To test your memory of the commands in Table 17-4, go to the companion website and download Appendix B, "Command Reference Exercises." Fill in the missing commands in the tables based on each command description. You can check your work by downloading Appendix C, "Command Reference Exercise Answer Key," from the companion website.

Table 17-4 Command Reference

Task	Command Syntax
Display the IPv4 sources of routing information that are being redistributed into the IPv4 routing protocols enabled on the device.	show ip protocols
Display the IPv6 sources of routing information that are being redistributed into the IPv6 routing protocols enabled on the device.	show ipv6 protocols
Show which IPv4 routes have been redistributed into the IPv4 EIGRP process on the boundary router.	show ip eigrp topology
Show which IPv6 routes have been redistributed into the IPv6 EIGRP process on the boundary router.	show ipv6 eigrp topology
Show which IPv4 routes have been redistributed into the OSPFv2 process; they are represented as Type 5 or Type 7 LSAs.	show ip ospf database
Show which IPv6 routes have been redistributed into the OSPFv3 process; they are represented as Type 5 or Type 7 LSAs.	show ipv6 ospf database
Display the IPv4 and IPv6 BGP learned routes; routes originally learned through redistribution have a question mark (?) in the Path column.	show bgp all
Display a router's BGP router ID, autonomous system number, information about the BGP's memory usage, and summary information about IPv4 unicast BGP neighbors.	show bgp ipv4 unicast summary
Display detailed information about all the IPv4 BGP neighbors of a router.	show bgp ipv4 unicast neighbors

17

CHAPTER 18

VRF, MPLS, and MPLS Layer 3 VPNs

This chapter covers the following topics:

- **Implementing and Verifying VRF-Lite:** This section introduces VRF and how to configure and verify a VRF-Lite implementation.

- **An Introduction to MPLS Operations:** This section introduces MPLS and explores the main MPLS topics, such as LSRs, LDP, LSP, and label switching.

- **An Introduction to MPLS Layer 3 VPNs:** This section introduces the concept of MPLS Layer 3 VPNs.

A virtual private network (VPN) connects private networks together over a public network. With VPNs, packets sent between private networks are encapsulated with new headers that are used to move the packets across the public network without exposing the private network's original packet headers. This allows the packets to be forwarded between the two endpoints without any intermediary routers extracting information from the original packet headers and data. Once packets reach the remote endpoints, the VPN headers are removed, and the original headers are used to make decisions. A VPN is a type of *overlay network* that exists on top of an existing network, known as the *underlay network*.

This chapter introduces you to virtual routing and forwarding (VRF), which is a fundamental component of MPLS (Multiprotocol Label Switching), and shows you how to configure and verify a VRF-Lite solution. It also introduces the fundamental concepts of MPLS operations and explores what label switching routers (LSRs) are, what Label Distribution Protocol (LDP) is used for, what a label switched path (LSP) is, and how label switching occurs. To wrap up, this chapter introduces you to MPLS Layer 3 VPNs.

"Do I Know This Already?" Quiz

The "Do I Know This Already?" quiz allows you to assess whether you should read this entire chapter thoroughly or jump to the "Exam Preparation Tasks" section. If you are in doubt about your answers to these questions or your own assessment of your knowledge of the topics, read the entire chapter. Table 18-1 lists the major headings in this chapter and their corresponding "Do I Know This Already?" quiz questions. You can find the answers in Appendix A, "Answers to the 'Do I Know This Already?' Quiz Questions."

Table 18-1 "Do I Know This Already?" Foundation Topics Section-to-Question Mapping

Foundation Topics Section	Questions
Implementing and Verifying VRF-Lite	1–4
An Introduction to MPLS Operations	5–11
An Introduction to MPLS Layer 3 VPNs	12–16

1. What does VRF allow you to do?
   a. Divide a single physical router into multiple virtual routers.
   b. Run Spanning Tree Protocol on a router.
   c. Use BGP on a router that does not support BGP.
   d. Use a server as a virtual router.

2. Which commands are used to associate an interface with VRF? (Choose two.)
   a. **ip vrf** *vrf-name*
   b. **vrf** *vrf-name*
   c. **ip vrf forwarding** *vrf-name*
   d. **vrf forwarding** *vrf-name*

3. You have created a VRF instance called RED and associated the required interfaces with it. Which command is used to verify the contents of the VRF routing table?
   a. **show ip cef**
   b. **show ip vrf**
   c. **show ip route vrf**
   d. **show ip route vrf RED**

4. You have received the following message while implementing VRF-Lite: `% Interface GigabitEthernet0/0 IPv4 disabled and address(es) removed due to enabling VRF GREEN`. What is the reason for this?
   a. You did not issue the **vrf GREEN** command in global configuration mode.
   b. You can't enable VRF-Lite on an IPv4 interface.
   c. You used the **vrf forwarding GREEN** command on the interface.
   d. You issued the **shutdown** command on GigabitEthernet0/0.

5. How are packets forwarded in an MPLS domain?
   a. Using the destination IP address of the packet
   b. Using the source IP address of the packet
   c. Using a number that has been specified in a label
   d. Using the MAC address of the frame

6. What type of router is responsible for adding MPLS labels to a packet?
   a. Ingress edge LSR
   b. Egress edge LSR

    c.   Intermediate LSR

    d.   P router

7. Which protocol do routers use to exchange labels?

    a.   LLDP

    b.   STP

    c.   LDP

    d.   CDP

8. To improve MPLS performance, how can labels be removed on the second-to-last LSR in the LSP instead of waiting until the last LSR to remove the label?

    a.   Use LLDP.

    b.   Use LDP.

    c.   Use PHP.

    d.   Use HTTP.

9. Which of the following best defines what FEC means in MPLS?

    a.   It is a protocol that is used for traffic engineering in MPLS.

    b.   It refers to packets that are grouped together and that will be forwarded in the same manner.

    c.   It is used to uniquely identify IP addresses from other identical IP addresses.

    d.   It is used to control the importing and exporting of routes.

    e.   It is used to inform the router that it should pop the label before forwarding the packet.

10. The output of **show mpls ldp bindings** includes entries with imp-null. What can you conclude from these entries?

    a.   It is a protocol that is used for traffic engineering in MPLS.

    b.   It refers to packets that are grouped together and that will be forwarded in the same manner.

    c.   It is used to uniquely identify IP addresses from other identical IP addresses.

    d.   It is used to control the importing and exporting of routes.

    e.   It is used to inform the router that it should pop the label before forwarding the packet.

11. Which protocol is used for MPLS-TE?

    a.   MP-BGP

    b.   RSVP

    c.   LDP

    d.   CDP

12. What types of labels are used for MPLS Layer 3 VPNs? (Choose two.)

    a.   LDP label

    b.   VPN label

    c.   802.1q label

    d.   MPLS label

13. Which dynamic routing protocol is used to form peerings between PE routers in MPLS Layer 3 VPNs?

   a. OSPF

   b. EIGRP

   c. IS-IS

   d. MP-BGP

14. How are customer routes isolated on PE routers in an MPLS Layer 3 VPN?

   a. By using VRF

   b. By using VDCs

   c. By using MP-BGP

   d. By using LDP

15. What is a route target?

   a. It is a protocol that is used for traffic engineering in MPLS.

   b. It refers to packets that are grouped together and that will be forwarded in the same manner.

   c. It is used to uniquely identify IP addresses from other identical IP addresses.

   d. It is used to control the importing and exporting of routes.

   e. It is used to inform the router that it should pop the label before forwarding the packet.

16. What is a route distinguisher?

   a. It is a protocol that is used for traffic engineering in MPLS.

   b. It refers to packets that are grouped together and that will be forwarded in the same manner.

   c. It is used to uniquely identify IP addresses from other identical IP addresses.

   d. It is used to control the importing and exporting of routes.

   e. It is used to inform the router that it should pop the label before forwarding the packet.

18

Foundation Topics

Implementing and Verifying VRF-Lite

Virtual routing and forwarding (VRF) is a technology for creating separate virtual routers on a single physical router. *VRF-Lite* provides VRF without MPLS. Router interfaces, routing tables, and forwarding tables are isolated on an instance-by-instance basis and therefore prevent traffic from one VRF instance from interfering with another VRF instance. VRF is an essential component of the MPLS L3VPN architecture and provides increased router functionality through segmentation in lieu of using multiple devices.

This section introduces you to VRF and demonstrates how you can configure and verify VRF-Lite on a Cisco IOS router.

VRF-Lite Overview

By default, all router interfaces, the routing table, and any forwarding tables are associated with the global VRF instance. So, what you've been calling your routing table is actually the routing table of the global VRF instance. If you need to divide your router up into multiple virtual routers, you can do so by creating additional VRF instances; by doing so, you also create additional routing and forwarding tables.

Why might you want to divide up your physical router into multiple virtual routers? Consider this scenario as a possible reason. Let's say that for security reasons, you need to build three different networks so that traffic in each network is isolated from traffic in the other networks. However, you only want to build a single physical network to accomplish this. You can do this by using VRF. Figure 18-1 shows a single physical topology that is divided into three different logically isolated networks. For the sake of simplicity, we can call them the RED, GREEN, and BLUE networks. The RED network is using the 10.0.0.0/8 addressing space, the GREEN network is using the 172.16.0.0/16 addressing space, and the BLUE network is using the 192.168.0.0/16 addressing space. With VRF-Lite, you can isolate the traffic within its respective virtual network and have multiple virtual routing tables on each router, each dedicated to its respective VRF instance.

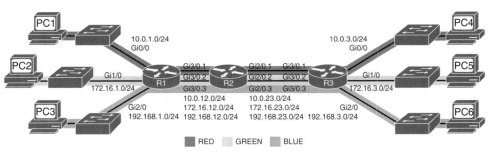

Figure 18-1   *An Example of Three VRF Instances (from top to bottom: RED, GREEN, and BLUE)*

Creating and Verifying VRF Instances

With Cisco IOS there are two different command sets to create and verify VRF instances. There is the classic command set, which supports only IPv4 addressing and networks, and there is the newer command set that supports both IPv4 and IPv6 addressing and networks. The ENARSI exam could test you on either of these command sets. Therefore, we cover both of them. In this chapter, the classic commands are identified with the word *classic*, and the newer commands are identified with the word *new*. If you do not see *classic* or *new* with a command, it means the command can be used for both new and classic configuration or verification.

To begin, let's create the RED, GREEN, and BLUE VRF instances on router R1. Example 18-1 shows how the classic **ip vrf** *vrf-name* command and the new **vrf definition** *vrf-name* command are used on the routers to create the VRF instances. For the new **vrf definition** *vrf-name* configuration, anything you configure at the root level of the VRF instance definition applies to both IPv4 and IPv6. However, you have to enable the VRF instance for IPv4 or IPv6 by using the **address-family [ipv4 | ipv6] [unicast | multicast]** command. In addition, any commands you enter in address family configuration mode will only affect the IPv4 or IPv6 address family you specified.

Example 18-1 *Configuring VRF Instances on R1 with the **ip vrf** Command*

```
Classic:
R1# configure terminal
R1(config)# ip vrf RED
R1(config-vrf)# exit
R1(config)# ip vrf GREEN
R1(config-vrf)# exit
R1(config)# ip vrf BLUE
New:
R1# configure terminal
R1(config)# vrf definition RED
R1(config-vrf)# ?
VPN Routing/Forwarding instance configuration commands:
  address-family  Enter Address Family command mode
  default         Set a command to its defaults
  description     VRF specific description
  exit            Exit from VRF configuration mode
  help            Description of the interactive help system
  ipv4            VRF IPv4 configuration
  no              Negate a command or set its defaults
  rd              Specify Route Distinguisher
  route-target    Specify Target VPN Extended Communities
  vnet            Virtual NETworking configuration
  vpn             Configure VPN ID as specified in rfc2685
R1(config-vrf)# address-family ?
  ipv4  Address Family
  ipv6  Address Family
R1(config-vrf)# address-family ipv4 unicast
R1(config-vrf-af)# exit
R1(config-vrf)# address-family ipv6 unicast
R1(config-vrf-af)# exit
R1(config-vrf)# exit
R1(config)# vrf definition Green
R1(config-vrf)# address-family ipv4 unicast
R1(config-vrf-af)# exit
R1(config-vrf)# address-family ipv6 unicast
R1(config-vrf-af)# exit
R1(config-vrf)# exit
R1(config)# vrf definition BLUE
R1(config-vrf)# address-family ipv4 unicast
R1(config-vrf-af)# exit
R1(config-vrf)# address-family ipv6 unicast
R1(config-vrf-af)# exit
R1(config-vrf)# exit
```

18

To verify that the VRF instances have been created, use the classic **show ip vrf** command or the new **show vrf** command as shown in Example 18-2 for R1. Notice that the Interfaces column is empty. You need to assign interfaces to each of the VRF instances to separate and isolate the traffic. Also notice that in the **show vrf** output, the protocols that are participating in the VRF instance are listed. If any of them are missing, it is because you did not use the **address-family** command to enable them in the VRF instance definition.

Example 18-2   *Verifying That the VRF Instances Are Configured on R1*

```
Classic:
R1# show ip vrf
  Name                          Default RD            Interfaces
  BLUE                          <not set>
  GREEN                         <not set>
  RED                           <not set>
New:
R1# show vrf
  Name                          Default RD            Protocols    Interfaces
  BLUE                          <not set>             ipv4,ipv6
  GREEN                         <not set>             ipv4,ipv6
  RED                           <not set>             ipv4,ipv6
```

To assign an interface to a VRF instance, use the classic **ip vrf forwarding** *vrf-name* command or the new **vrf forwarding** *vrf-name* command in interface configuration mode, as shown in in Example 18-3.

> **NOTE**   VRF instance names are case sensitive. Therefore, red is not the same as RED or Red or rED.

Example 18-3   *Assigning Interfaces to the VRF Instances with the **ip vrf forwarding** Command*

```
Classic:
R1# configure terminal
R1(config)# interface gigabitEthernet 0/0
R1(config-if)# ip vrf forwarding RED
R1(config-if)# interface gigabitEthernet 1/0
R1(config-if)# ip vrf forwarding GREEN
R1(config-if)# interface gigabitEthernet 2/0
R1(config-if)# ip vrf forwarding BLUE
R1(config-if)# end

New:
R1# configure terminal
```

```
R1(config)# interface gigabitEthernet 0/0
R1(config-if)# vrf forwarding RED
R1(config-if)# interface gigabitEthernet 1/0
R1(config-if)# vrf forwarding GREEN
R1(config-if)# interface gigabitEthernet 2/0
R1(config-if)# vrf forwarding BLUE
R1(config-if)# end
```

NOTE   When you add an interface to a VRF instance, you receive the following messages if there is already an IPv4 or IPv6 address on the interface:

```
% Interface GigabitEthernet0/0 IPv4 disabled and address(es)
removed due to enabling VRF GREEN

% Interface GigabitEthernet0/0 IPv6 disabled and address(es)
removed due to enabling VRF GREEN???This font is different than
the previous font. Should they be the same - Raymond
```

This is due to the fact that the interface has now been placed in a VRF instance, and the IP address it has does not belong to the VRF instance it is now in. So, no matter what, when you are configuring VRF instances, you have to configure IPv4 and IPv6 addresses on your interfaces after you have placed them in the VRF instances. So it is best to remember to put an interface in a VRF instance first and then configure the IP address. If you configure the IP address first and then put it in the VRF instance, you will have to configure the IP address again, which is a waste of time.

Using the classic **show ip vrf** command or the new **show vrf** command again, you can verify that each interface has been assigned to the correct VRF instance, as shown in Example 18-4.

Example 18-4   *Verifying That the Interfaces Are Assigned to the Correct VRF Instances*

```
Classic:
R1# show ip vrf
  Name                       Default RD            Interfaces
  BLUE                       <not set>             Gi2/0
  GREEN                      <not set>             Gi1/0
  RED                        <not set>             Gi0/0


New:
R1# show vrf
  Name                       Default RD            Protocols    Interfaces
  BLUE                       <not set>             ipv4,ipv6    Gi2/0
  GREEN                      <not set>             ipv4,ipv6    Gi1/0
  RED                        <not set>             ipv4,ipv6    Gi0/0
```

18

Refer to Figure 18-1. R1's interface Gi3/0 is a single physical link connecting to R2. Note that each interface can belong to only a single VRF instance. If a single physical interface needs to support multiple VRF instances, the physical interface needs to be broken into subinterfaces. Therefore, Gi3/0 needs to be broken into subinterfaces. Example 18-5 shows how to create the subinterfaces and assign them to the correct VRF instances. It also shows the use of **show ip vrf** and **show vrf** to verify that the interfaces are in the correct VRF instances.

Example 18-5 *Creating Subinterfaces on R1 and Assigning Them to the Correct VRF Instances*

```
Classic:
R1# configure terminal
R1(config)# interface gigabitEthernet 3/0.1
R1(config-subif)# ip vrf forwarding RED
R1(config-vrf)# interface gigabitEthernet 3/0.2
R1(config-subif)# ip vrf forwarding GREEN
R1(config-vrf)# interface gigabitEthernet 3/0.3
R1(config-subif)# ip vrf forwarding BLUE
R1(config-vrf)# end
R1# show ip vrf
  Name                      Default RD            Interfaces
  BLUE                      <not set>              Gi2/0
                                                   Gi3/0.3
  GREEN                     <not set>              Gi1/0
                                                   Gi3/0.2
  RED                       <not set>              Gi0/0
                                                   Gi3/0.1


New:
R1# configure terminal
R1(config)# interface gigabitEthernet 3/0.1
R1(config-subif)# vrf forwarding RED
R1(config-vrf)# interface gigabitEthernet 3/0.2
R1(config-subif)# vrf forwarding GREEN
R1(config-vrf)# interface gigabitEthernet 3/0.3
R1(config-subif)# vrf forwarding BLUE
R1(config-vrf)# end
R1# show vrf
  Name                      Default RD            Protocols    Interfaces
  BLUE                      <not set>             ipv4,ipv6    Gi2/0
                                                               Gi3/0.3
  GREEN                     <not set>             ipv4,ipv6    Gi1/0
                                                               Gi3/0.2
  RED                       <not set>             ipv4,ipv6    Gi0/0
                                                               Gi3/0.1
```

Next, you can configure network addressing on R1. Example 18-6 shows the IP addressing configuration of each of the interfaces on R1, based on Figure 18-1. Notice that the subinterfaces must be configured with dot1q encapsulation, or you can't assign an IP address to the interface. Also, note that when you configure R2's subinterfaces connecting to R1, they need to be configured with the same VLAN numbers.

Example 18-6 *Configuring R1's Interfaces and Subinterfaces with IPv4 and IPv6 Addresses*

```
R1# configure terminal
R1(config)# int gig 0/0
R1(config-if)# ip address 10.0.1.1 255.255.255.0
R1(config-if)# ipv6 address fc00::1/64
R1(config-if)# int gig 1/0
R1(config-if)# ip address 172.16.1.1 255.255.255.0
R1(config-if)# ipv6 address fc01::1/64
R1(config-if)# int gig 2/0
R1(config-if)# ip address 192.168.1.1 255.255.255.0
R1(config-if)# ipv6 address fc02::1/64
R1(config-if)# int gig 3/0.1
R1(config-subif)# encapsulation dot1Q 100
R1(config-subif)# ip address 10.0.12.1 255.255.255.0
R1(config-subif)# ipv6 address fc03::1/64
R1(config-subif)# int gig 3/0.2
R1(config-subif)# encapsulation dot1Q 200
R1(config-subif)# ip address 172.16.12.1 255.255.255.0
R1(config-subif)# ipv6 address fc04::1/64
R1(config-subif)# int gig 3/0.3
R1(config-subif)# encapsulation dot1Q 300
R1(config-subif)# ip address 192.168.12.1 255.255.255.0
R1(config-subif)# ipv6 address fc05::1/64
```

You can use the classic **show ip vrf interfaces** command and the new **show vrf ipv4 unicast interfaces** command to verify the IPv4 address assigned to the interface, the VRF instance the interface is in, and whether the interface is up or down, as shown in Example 18-7. You can use the new **show vrf ipv6 unicast interfaces** command to verify the IPv6 address assigned to the interface, the VRF instance the interface is in, and whether the interface is up or down, as shown in Example 18-7.

Example 18-7 *Verifying Interface IPv4 and IPv6 Address, VRF, and Protocol Configurations*

```
Classic:
R1# show ip vrf interfaces
Interface          IP-Address      VRF                         Protocol
Gi2/0              192.168.1.1     BLUE                        up
Gi3/0.3            192.168.12.1    BLUE                        up
```

```
Gi1/0                    172.16.1.1        GREEN                        up
Gi3/0.2                  172.16.12.1       GREEN                        up
Gi0/0                    10.0.1.1          RED                          up
Gi3/0.1                  10.0.12.1         RED                          up


New:
R1# show vrf ipv4 unicast interfaces
Interface                VRF           Protocol    Address
GigabitEthernet0/0       RED           up          10.0.1.1
GigabitEthernet1/0       GREEN         up          172.16.1.1
GigabitEthernet2/0       BLUE          up          192.168.1.1
GigabitEthernet3/0.1     RED           up          10.0.12.1
GigabitEthernet3/0.2     GREEN         up          172.16.12.1
GigabitEthernet3/0.3     BLUE          up          192.168.12.1


R1# show vrf ipv6 unicast interfaces
Interface                VRF           Protocol    Address
GigabitEthernet0/0       RED           up          FE80::6E41:6AFF:FE83:2228
                                                   FC00::1
GigabitEthernet1/0       GREEN         up          FE80::6E41:6AFF:FE83:2229
                                                   FC01::1
GigabitEthernet2/0       BLUE          up          FE80::6E41:6AFF:FE83:2230
                                                   FC02::1
GigabitEthernet3/0.1     RED           up          FE80::6E41:6AFF:FE83:2231
                                                   FC03::1
GigabitEthernet3/0.2     GREEN         up          FE80::6E41:6AFF:FE83:2232
                                                   FC04::1
GigabitEthernet3/0.3     BLUE          up          FE80::6E41:6AFF:FE83:2233
                                                   FC05::1
```

As mentioned earlier, when you create VRF instances, you are creating virtual networks. Each of these virtual networks needs to have its own routing table to ensure isolation. As soon as you created the VRF instance with the classic **ip vrf** *vrf-name* command or the new **vrf definition** *vrf-name* command, the virtual routing table was created for the network. You can use the **show ip route** command to display the IPv4 global routing table, as shown in Example 18-8, or the **show ipv6 route** command to display the IPv6 global routing table (which is not shown). Notice that there are no routes in the IPv4 global routing table, even though you created IPv4 addresses on interfaces. You should therefore have connected and local routes in the routing table. However, because the interfaces are in VRF instances, the networks are not listed in the global routing table but are listed in the VRF-specific routing table. Therefore, you need to view the routing table of each of the VRF instances. To view the routing table for a VRF instance, use the **show ip route vrf** *vrf-name* command. Example 18-9 shows the output of **show ip route vrf RED**, **show ip route vrf GREEN**, and **show ip route vrf BLUE**. For IPv6, it would be **show ipv6 route vrf RED**, **show ipv6 route vrf GREEN**, and **show ipv6 route vrf BLUE** (not shown).

Example 18-8 *Verifying the IPv4 Global Routing Table*

```
R1# show ip route
Codes: L - local, C - connected, S - static, R - RIP, M - mobile, B - BGP
       D - EIGRP, EX - EIGRP external, O - OSPF, IA - OSPF inter area
       N1 - OSPF NSSA external type 1, N2 - OSPF NSSA external type 2
       E1 - OSPF external type 1, E2 - OSPF external type 2
       i - IS-IS, su - IS-IS summary, L1 - IS-IS level-1, L2 - IS-IS level-2
       ia - IS-IS inter area, * - candidate default, U - per-user static route
       o - ODR, P - periodic downloaded static route, H - NHRP, l - LISP
       + - replicated route, % - next hop override


Gateway of last resort is not set
R1#
```

Example 18-9 *Verifying the IPv4 VRF Routing Tables*

Key Topic

```
R1# show ip route vrf RED

Routing Table: RED
...output omitted...
Gateway of last resort is not set


      10.0.0.0/8 is variably subnetted, 4 subnets, 2 masks
C        10.0.1.0/24 is directly connected, GigabitEthernet0/0
L        10.0.1.1/32 is directly connected, GigabitEthernet0/0
C        10.0.12.0/24 is directly connected, GigabitEthernet3/0.1
L        10.0.12.1/32 is directly connected, GigabitEthernet3/0.1


R1# show ip route vrf GREEN

Routing Table: GREEN
...output omitted...
Gateway of last resort is not set


      172.16.0.0/16 is variably subnetted, 4 subnets, 2 masks
C        172.16.1.0/24 is directly connected, GigabitEthernet1/0
L        172.16.1.1/32 is directly connected, GigabitEthernet1/0
C        172.16.12.0/24 is directly connected, GigabitEthernet3/0.2
L        172.16.12.1/32 is directly connected, GigabitEthernet3/0.2


R1# show ip route VRF BLUE

Routing Table: BLUE
```

18

```
...output omitted...
Gateway of last resort is not set


      192.168.1.0/24 is variably subnetted, 2 subnets, 2 masks
C        192.168.1.0/24 is directly connected, GigabitEthernet2/0
L        192.168.1.1/32 is directly connected, GigabitEthernet2/0
      192.168.12.0/24 is variably subnetted, 2 subnets, 2 masks
C        192.168.12.0/24 is directly connected, GigabitEthernet3/0.3
L        192.168.12.1/32 is directly connected, GigabitEthernet3/0.3
R1#
```

NOTE To finish our scenario, we focus on IPv4 on R2 and R3, using the new VRF instance definition configuration and verification commands. For IPv6, you would only have to enter the needed IPv6 values as we did in the examples for R1.

Now configure R2. Example 18-10 shows the configuration required on R2 using the new VRF instance definition commands

Example 18-10 *Configuring R2 VRF Instances, Assigning Subinterfaces to VRF Instances, and Configuring IP Addresses on Subinterfaces*

```
R2# config terminal
R2(config)# vrf definition RED
R2(config-vrf)# address-family ipv4 unicast
R2(config-vrf-af)# exit
R2(config)# vrf definition GREEN
R2(config-vrf)# address-family ipv4 unicast
R2(config-vrf-af)# exit
R2(config)# vrf definition BLUE
R2(config-vrf)# address-family ipv4 unicast
R2(config-vrf-af)# exit
R2(config-vrf)# int gig 3/0.1
R2(config-subif)# vrf forwarding RED
R2(config-subif)# encapsulation dot1Q 100
R2(config-subif)# ip address 10.0.12.2 255.255.255.0
R2(config-subif)# int gig 3/0.2
R2(config-subif)# vrf forwarding GREEN
R2(config-subif)# encapsulation dot1Q 200
R2(config-subif)# ip address 172.16.12.2 255.255.255.0
R2(config-subif)# int gig 3/0.3
R2(config-subif)# vrf forwarding BLUE
R2(config-subif)# encapsulation dot1Q 300
```

```
R2(config-subif)# ip address 192.168.12.2 255.255.255.0
R2(config-subif)# interface gigabitEthernet 2/0.1
R2(config-subif)# vrf forwarding RED
R2(config-subif)# encapsulation dot1Q 100
R2(config-subif)# ip address 10.0.23.2 255.255.255.0
R2(config-subif)# interface gigabitEthernet 2/0.2
R2(config-subif)# vrf forwarding GREEN
R2(config-subif)# encapsulation dot1Q 200
R2(config-subif)# ip address 172.16.23.2 255.255.255.0
R2(config-subif)# interface gigabitEthernet 2/0.3
R2(config-subif)# vrf forwarding BLUE
R2(config-subif)# encapsulation dot1Q 300
R2(config-subif)# ip address 192.168.23.2 255.255.255.0
```

Example 18-11 shows the output of the new **show vrf ipv4 unicast interfaces** command and the **show ip route vrf** *vrf_name* commands to verify that R2 has been configured correctly.

Example 18-11   *Verifying R2's Configuration with the show vrf ipv4 unicast interfaces Command and the show ip route vrf Command*

```
R2# show vrf ipv4 unicast interfaces
Interface                VRF      Protocol   Address
GigabitEthernet2/0.1     RED      up         10.0.23.2
GigabitEthernet2/0.2     GREEN    up         172.16.23.2
GigabitEthernet2/0.3     BLUE     up         192.168.23.2
GigabitEthernet3/0.1     RED      up         10.0.12.2
GigabitEthernet3/0.2     GREEN    up         172.16.12.2
GigabitEthernet3/0.3     BLUE     up         192.168.12.2


R2# show ip route vrf RED

Routing Table: RED
...output omitted...
Gateway of last resort is not set


      10.0.0.0/8 is variably subnetted, 4 subnets, 2 masks
C         10.0.12.0/24 is directly connected, GigabitEthernet3/0.1
L         10.0.12.2/32 is directly connected, GigabitEthernet3/0.1
C         10.0.23.0/24 is directly connected, GigabitEthernet2/0.1
L         10.0.23.2/32 is directly connected, GigabitEthernet2/0.1


R2# show ip route vrf GREEN

Routing Table: GREEN
...output omitted...
Gateway of last resort is not set
```

18

```
        172.16.0.0/16 is variably subnetted, 4 subnets, 2 masks
C       172.16.12.0/24 is directly connected, GigabitEthernet3/0.2
L       172.16.12.2/32 is directly connected, GigabitEthernet3/0.2
C       172.16.23.0/24 is directly connected, GigabitEthernet2/0.2
L       172.16.23.2/32 is directly connected, GigabitEthernet2/0.2

R2# show ip route vrf BLUE


Routing Table: BLUE
...output omitted...
Gateway of last resort is not set


        192.168.12.0/24 is variably subnetted, 2 subnets, 2 masks
C       192.168.12.0/24 is directly connected, GigabitEthernet3/0.3
L       192.168.12.2/32 is directly connected, GigabitEthernet3/0.3
        192.168.23.0/24 is variably subnetted, 2 subnets, 2 masks
C       192.168.23.0/24 is directly connected, GigabitEthernet2/0.3
L       192.168.23.2/32 is directly connected, GigabitEthernet2/0.3
R2#
```

Now you can configure R3. Example 18-12 shows the configuration required on R3 using the new VRF instance definition commands.

Example 18-12 *Configuring R3 VRF Instances, Assigning Interfaces to VRF Instances, and Configuring IP Addresses on Interfaces*

```
R3# configure terminal
R3(config)# vrf definition RED
R3(config-vrf)# address-family ipv4 unicast
R3(config-vrf-af)# exit
R3(config)# vrf definition GREEN
R3(config-vrf)# address-family ipv4 unicast
R3(config-vrf-af)# exit
R3(config)# vrf definition BLUE
R3(config-vrf)# address-family ipv4 unicast
R3(config-vrf-af)# exit
R3(config-vrf)# interface gigabitethernet 0/0
R3(config-if)# vrf forwarding RED
R3(config-if)# ip address 10.0.3.3 255.255.255.0
R3(config-if)# interface gigabitethernet 1/0
R3(config-if)# vrf forwarding GREEN
R3(config-if)# ip address 172.16.3.3 255.255.255.0
R3(config-if)# interface gigabitethernet 2/0
R3(config-if)# vrf forwarding BLUE
R3(config-if)# ip address 192.168.3.3 255.255.255.0
```

```
R3(config-if)# interface gigabitethernet 3/0.1
R3(config-subif)# vrf forwarding RED
R3(config-subif)# encapsulation dot1Q 100
R3(config-subif)# ip address 10.0.23.3 255.255.255.0
R3(config-subif)# interface gigabitethernet 3/0.2
R3(config-subif)# vrf forwarding GREEN
R3(config-subif)# encapsulation dot1Q 200
R3(config-subif)# ip address 172.16.23.3 255.255.255.0
R3(config-subif)# interface gigabitethernet 3/0.3
R3(config-subif)# vrf forwarding BLUE
R3(config-subif)# encapsulation dot1Q 300
R3(config-subif)# ip address 192.168.23.3 255.255.255.0
```

Example 18-13 shows the output of the **show vrf ipv4 unicast interfaces** command and the **show ip route vrf** command to verify that R3 has been configured correctly.

Example 18-13 *Verifying R3's Configuration with the show vrf ipv4 unicast interfaces Command and the show ip route vrf Command*

```
R3# show vrf ipv4 unicast interfaces
Interface               VRF         Protocol    Address
GigabitEthernet0/0      RED         up          10.0.3.3
GigabitEthernet1/0      GREEN       up          172.16.3.3
GigabitEthernet2/0      BLUE        up          192.168.3.3
GigabitEthernet3/0.1    RED         up          10.0.23.3
GigabitEthernet3/0.2    GREEN       up          172.16.23.3
GigabitEthernet3/0.3    BLUE        up          192.168.23.3


R3# show ip route VRF RED


Routing Table: RED
...output omitted...
Gateway of last resort is not set


      10.0.0.0/8 is variably subnetted, 4 subnets, 2 masks
C         10.0.3.0/24 is directly connected, GigabitEthernet0/0
L         10.0.3.3/32 is directly connected, GigabitEthernet0/0
C         10.0.23.0/24 is directly connected, GigabitEthernet3/0.1
L         10.0.23.3/32 is directly connected, GigabitEthernet3/0.1


R3# show ip route VRF GREEN


Routing Table: GREEN
...output omitted...
Gateway of last resort is not set
```

18

```
          172.16.0.0/16 is variably subnetted, 4 subnets, 2 masks
C         172.16.3.0/24 is directly connected, GigabitEthernet1/0
L         172.16.3.3/32 is directly connected, GigabitEthernet1/0
C         172.16.23.0/24 is directly connected, GigabitEthernet3/0.2
L         172.16.23.3/32 is directly connected, GigabitEthernet3/0.2


R3# show ip route VRF BLUE


Routing Table: BLUE
...output omitted...
Gateway of last resort is not set


          192.168.3.0/24 is variably subnetted, 2 subnets, 2 masks
C         192.168.3.0/24 is directly connected, GigabitEthernet2/0
L         192.168.3.3/32 is directly connected, GigabitEthernet2/0
          192.168.23.0/24 is variably subnetted, 2 subnets, 2 masks
C         192.168.23.0/24 is directly connected, GigabitEthernet3/0.3
L         192.168.23.3/32 is directly connected, GigabitEthernet3/0.3
```

To verify connectivity when using VRF instances, you must specify the VRF instance with the **ping** command. If you do not, the global routing table is used instead of the VRF routing table. Example 18-14 shows a series of pings from R1 to R2. The first ping, with a destination of 10.0.12.2, fails as the global routing table is being used because the VRF instance was not specified. The second ping specifies the GREEN VRF but is using an IP address in the RED VRF instance; therefore, the ping fails. The last ping uses the correct VRF instance (RED) and an IP address in the RED VRF instance (10.0.12.2); therefore, the ping is successful. This is a great example of how VRF instances provide isolation.

Example 18-14 *Verifying Connections with the **ping** Command*

```
R1# ping 10.0.12.2
Type escape sequence to abort.
Sending 5, 100-byte ICMP Echos to 10.0.12.2, timeout is 2 seconds:
.....
Success rate is 0 percent (0/5)
R1# ping vrf GREEN 10.0.12.2
Type escape sequence to abort.
Sending 5, 100-byte ICMP Echos to 10.0.12.2, timeout is 2 seconds:
.....
Success rate is 0 percent (0/5)
R1# ping vrf RED 10.0.12.2
Type escape sequence to abort.
Sending 5, 100-byte ICMP Echos to 10.0.12.2, timeout is 2 seconds:
!!!!!
Success rate is 100 percent (5/5), round-trip min/avg/max = 44/49/60 ms
```

Example 18-15 shows the output of the RED VRF instance routing table. At this point, you have only directly connected and local routes. For all the routers to learn about all the other networks, you can use static or dynamic routing. The following examples use EIGRP as the dynamic routing protocol to provide full connectivity for each of the VRF instances, but you could use any other dynamic routing protocol, such as OSPF or BGP.

Example 18-15 *Using the* **show ip route vrf RED** *Command to Verify the Contents of the RED VRF Routing Table*

```
R1# show ip route vrf RED


Routing Table: RED
...output omitted...
Gateway of last resort is not set


      10.0.0.0/8 is variably subnetted, 4 subnets, 2 masks
C        10.0.1.0/24 is directly connected, GigabitEthernet0/0
L        10.0.1.1/32 is directly connected, GigabitEthernet0/0
C        10.0.12.0/24 is directly connected, GigabitEthernet3/0.1
L        10.0.12.1/32 is directly connected, GigabitEthernet3/0.1
```

To configure EIGRP for multiple VRF instances, you use EIGRP named configuration mode as it permits you to create multiple address families, as shown in Example 18-16. You enter EIGRP named configuration mode by using the **router eigrp** *name* command in global configuration mode. Next, you need to create an address family for each of the VRF instances. You accomplish this with the **address-family ipv4 vrf** *vrf-name* **autonomous-system** *as-number* command. You then specify any EIGRP configuration commands that are needed for your scenario. In this case, you are enabling the routing process on only certain interfaces (see Example 18-16).

Example 18-16 *Configuring EIGRP for Multiple VRF Instances*

```
R1# configure terminal
R1(config)# router eigrp VRFEXAMPLE
R1(config-router)# address-family ipv4 vrf RED autonomous-system 10
R1(config-router-af)# network 10.0.1.1 0.0.0.0
R1(config-router-af)# network 10.0.12.1 0.0.0.0
R1(config-router)# address-family ipv4 vrf GREEN autonomous-system 172
R1(config-router-af)# network 172.16.1.1 0.0.0.0
R1(config-router-af)# network 172.16.12.1 0.0.0.0
R1(config-router)# address-family ipv4 vrf BLUE autonomous-system 192
R1(config-router-af)# network 192.168.1.1 0.0.0.0
R1(config-router-af)# network 192.168.12.1 0.0.0.0
R1(config-router-af)# end
```

To verify that the interfaces are participating in the EIGRP process for the correct VRF instance, use the **show ip eigrp vrf** *vrf-name* **interfaces** command, as shown in

Example 18-17. Notice that each EIGRP AS contains only the interfaces that have been enabled for the EIGRP routing process in the respective VRF.

Example 18-17 *Verifying That the Interfaces Are Participating in the EIGRP Process for Each VRF*

```
R1# show ip eigrp vrf RED interfaces
EIGRP-IPv4 VR(VRFEXAMPLE) Address-Family Interfaces for AS(10)
          VRF(RED)
                    Xmit Queue   PeerQ        Mean  Pacing Time  Multicast   Pending
Interface  Peers  Un/Reliable  Un/Reliable  SRTT  Un/Reliable  Flow Timer  Routes
Gi0/0        0      0/0          0/0          0     0/0          0           0
Gi3/0.1      0      0/0          0/0          0     0/0          0           0
R1# show ip eigrp vrf GREEN interfaces
EIGRP-IPv4 VR(VRFEXAMPLE) Address-Family Interfaces for AS(172)
          VRF(GREEN)
                    Xmit Queue   PeerQ        Mean  Pacing Time  Multicast   Pending
Interface  Peers  Un/Reliable  Un/Reliable  SRTT  Un/Reliable  Flow Timer  Routes
Gi1/0        0      0/0          0/0          0     0/0          0           0
Gi3/0.2      0      0/0          0/0          0     0/0          0           0
R1# show ip eigrp vrf BLUE interfaces
EIGRP-IPv4 VR(VRFEXAMPLE) Address-Family Interfaces for AS(192)
          VRF(BLUE)
                    Xmit Queue   PeerQ        Mean  Pacing Time  Multicast   Pending
Interface  Peers  Un/Reliable  Un/Reliable  SRTT  Un/Reliable  Flow Timer  Routes
Gi2/0        0      0/0          0/0          0     0/0          0           0
Gi3/0.3      0      0/0          0/0          0     0/0          0           0
```

When all the other routers have been configured for EIGRP, you can verify neighbor adjacencies by using the **show ip eigrp vrf** *vrf-name* **neighbors** command. As before, because you are dealing with multiple VRF instances, you will notice that each **show** command in Example 18-18 displays only the neighbors that are within that VRF instance.

Example 18-18 *Verifying EIGRP Neighbors for Each VRF Instance with the show ip eigrp vrf vrf-name neighbors Command*

```
R1# show ip eigrp vrf RED neighbors
EIGRP-IPv4 VR(VRFEXAMPLE) Address-Family Neighbors for AS(10)
          VRF(RED)
H   Address          Interface        Hold Uptime   SRTT   RTO   Q    Seq
                                       (sec)         (ms)        Cnt  Num
0   10.0.12.2        Gi3/0.1          13  00:02:31   48     288   0    7
```

```
R1# show ip eigrp vrf GREEN neighbors
EIGRP-IPv4 VR(VRFEXAMPLE) Address-Family Neighbors for AS(172)
          VRF(GREEN)
H   Address              Interface        Hold Uptime   SRTT   RTO  Q   Seq
                                          (sec)         (ms)        Cnt Num
0   172.16.12.2          Gi3/0.2          12 00:02:09   64     384  0   7
R1# show ip eigrp vrf BLUE neighbors
EIGRP-IPv4 VR(VRFEXAMPLE) Address-Family Neighbors for AS(192)
          VRF(BLUE)
H   Address              Interface        Hold Uptime   SRTT   RTO  Q   Seq
                                          (sec)         (ms)        Cnt Num
0   192.168.12.2         Gi3/0.3          12 00:01:53   49     294  0   7
```

Once each VRF network converges, you can verify that routing tables contain the EIGRP learned routes by using the **show ip route vrf** *vrf-name* command. Example 18-19 uses the **show ip route vrf** *vrf-name* **eigrp** command to limit the output to just EIGRP learned routes.

Example 18-19 *Verifying EIGRP Routes in the VRF Routing Table with the* **show ip route vrf** *vrf-name* **eigrp** *Command*

```
R1# show ip route vrf RED eigrp

Routing Table: RED
...output omitted...
Gateway of last resort is not set

     10.0.0.0/8 is variably subnetted, 6 subnets, 2 masks
D       10.0.3.0/24 [90/20480] via 10.0.12.2, 00:02:17, GigabitEthernet3/0.1
D       10.0.23.0/24 [90/15360] via 10.0.12.2, 00:03:51, GigabitEthernet3/0.1
R1# show ip route vrf GREEN eigrp

Routing Table: GREEN
...output omitted...
Gateway of last resort is not set

     172.16.0.0/16 is variably subnetted, 6 subnets, 2 masks
D       172.16.3.0/24
           [90/20480] via 172.16.12.2, 00:01:55, GigabitEthernet3/0.2
D       172.16.23.0/24
           [90/15360] via 172.16.12.2, 00:03:28, GigabitEthernet3/0.2
R1# show ip route vrf BLUE eigrp

Routing Table: BLUE
...output omitted...
```

18

```
Gateway of last resort is not set

D     192.168.3.0/24
              [90/20480] via 192.168.12.2, 00:01:41, GigabitEthernet3/0.3
D     192.168.23.0/24
              [90/15360] via 192.168.12.2, 00:03:06, GigabitEthernet3/0.3
R1#
```

By using the **ping vrf** *vrf-name ipv4-address* command, as shown in Example 18-20, you can verify that connectivity exists from R1 to R3.

Example 18-20   *Verifying VRF Connectivity from R1 to R3*

```
R1# ping vrf RED 10.0.3.3
Type escape sequence to abort.
Sending 5, 100-byte ICMP Echos to 10.0.3.3, timeout is 2 seconds:
!!!!!
Success rate is 100 percent (5/5), round-trip min/avg/max = 68/91/112 ms
R1# ping vrf GREEN 172.16.3.3
Type escape sequence to abort.
Sending 5, 100-byte ICMP Echos to 172.16.3.3, timeout is 2 seconds:
!!!!!
Success rate is 100 percent (5/5), round-trip min/avg/max = 64/71/80 ms
R1# ping vrf BLUE 192.168.3.3
Type escape sequence to abort.
Sending 5, 100-byte ICMP Echos to 192.168.3.3, timeout is 2 seconds:
!!!!!
Success rate is 100 percent (5/5), round-trip min/avg/max = 64/68/72 ms
R1#
```

Example 18-21 shows the output of a few different pings from R1 to different destinations to show how communication is isolated to the VRF instance. In the first ping, PC1 pings PC4, and because they are in the same VRF instance, the ping is successful. In the second ping, PC1 pings PC5, and because they are in different VRF instances, the ping fails. In the third ping, PC1 pings PC6, and because they are in different VRF instances, the ping fails. For the fourth ping, PC2 is pinging PC5, and because they are in the same VRF instance, it is a success. In the last ping, PC3 is pinging PC6, and because they are in the same VRF instance, it is a success.

Example 18-21   *Verifying VRF Connectivity Between PCs*

```
PC-1> ping 10.0.3.10
84 bytes from 10.0.3.10 icmp_seq=1 ttl=61 time=71.777 ms
84 bytes from 10.0.3.10 icmp_seq=2 ttl=61 time=62.830 ms
84 bytes from 10.0.3.10 icmp_seq=3 ttl=61 time=55.874 ms
84 bytes from 10.0.3.10 icmp_seq=4 ttl=61 time=59.833 ms
```

```
PC-1> ping 172.16.3.10
*10.0.1.1 icmp_seq=1 ttl=255 time=7.773 ms (ICMP type:3, code:1, Destination host
unreachable)
*10.0.1.1 icmp_seq=2 ttl=255 time=11.936 ms (ICMP type:3, code:1, Destination host
unreachable)
*10.0.1.1 icmp_seq=3 ttl=255 time=4.985 ms (ICMP type:3, code:1, Destination host
unreachable)
*10.0.1.1 icmp_seq=4 ttl=255 time=5.986 ms (ICMP type:3, code:1, Destination host
unreachable)
PC-1> ping 192.168.3.10
*10.0.1.1 icmp_seq=1 ttl=255 time=9.973 ms (ICMP type:3, code:1, Destination host
unreachable)
*10.0.1.1 icmp_seq=2 ttl=255 time=7.980 ms (ICMP type:3, code:1, Destination host
unreachable)
*10.0.1.1 icmp_seq=3 ttl=255 time=3.990 ms (ICMP type:3, code:1, Destination host
unreachable)
*10.0.1.1 icmp_seq=4 ttl=255 time=12.068 ms (ICMP type:3, code:1, Destination host
unreachable)

PC-2> ping 172.16.3.10
84 bytes from 172.16.3.10 icmp_seq=1 ttl=61 time=72.805 ms
84 bytes from 172.16.3.10 icmp_seq=2 ttl=61 time=55.850 ms
84 bytes from 172.16.3.10 icmp_seq=3 ttl=61 time=56.875 ms
84 bytes from 172.16.3.10 icmp_seq=4 ttl=61 time=56.840 ms

PC-3> ping 192.168.3.10
84 bytes from 192.168.3.10 icmp_seq=1 ttl=61 time=71.835 ms
84 bytes from 192.168.3.10 icmp_seq=2 ttl=61 time=65.802 ms
84 bytes from 192.168.3.10 icmp_seq=3 ttl=61 time=58.842 ms
84 bytes from 192.168.3.10 icmp_seq=4 ttl=61 time=52.831 ms
```

If you were to use OSPFv2 for routing, you could create different processes. For example, you could use **router ospf 1 vrf BLUE, router ospf 2 vrf GREEN**, and **router ospf 3 vrf RED** and then configure the respective interfaces in the correct OSPFv2 process.

If you were using OSPFv3 address families, you could create a different address family for each VRF instance, as shown in Example 18-22, and then configure the respective interfaces to participate in the OSPFv3 process. Since the interface is configured for RED VRF instance in this example, when you use the **ospfv3** *process-id* **ipv4 area** *area-id* command, it automatically places the interface in the RED OSPFv3 address family, which you can see in the **show ospfv3 vrf RED interface brief** output in this example.

Example 18-22 *Configuring OSPFv3 Address Families for Multiple VRF Instances*

```
R1(config)# router ospfv3 1
R1(config-router)# address-family ipv4 vrf RED
R1(config-router-af)# exit
R1(config-router)# address-family ipv4 vrf GREEN
R1(config-router-af)# exit
R1(config-router)# address-family ipv4 vrf BLUE
R1(config-router-af)# exit
R1(config-router)# interface gigabitethernet 0/0
R1(config-if)# vrf forwarding RED
R1(config-if)# ip address 10.0.0.1 255.255.255.0
R1(config-if)# ipv6 enable
R1(config-if)# ospfv3 1 ipv4 area 0


R1# show ospfv3 vrf RED interface brief
Interface    PID   Area            AF        Cost  State Nbrs F/C
Gi0/0        1     0               ipv4      1     DR    0/0
```

When configuring BGP for VRF-Lite, you use a different VRF address family for each and every VRF instance, as shown in Example 18-23. Once you have created each VRF instance, in router BGP configuration mode, you can create a VRF address family by using the **address-family [ipv4 | ipv6] vrf** *vrf-name* command. After you execute the command, the VRF address family is created, and you use the address family configuration mode for that VRF instance. In VRF address family configuration mode, you can use the **neighbo0r** command to set up BGP neighbor adjacencies as well as other BGP commands that you need to configure for that specific VRF address family.

Example 18-23 *Configuring MP-BGPv4 Address Families for Multiple VRF Instances*

```
R3(config)# router bgp 65000
R3(config-router)# address-family ipv4 vrf RED
R3(config-router-af)# neighbor 203.0.113.89 remote-as 65001
R3(config-router-af)# exit
R3(config-router)# address-family ipv4 vrf GREEN
R3(config-router-af)# neighbor 192.0.2.54 remote-as 65021
R3(config-router-af)# exit
R3(config-router)# address-family ipv4 vrf BLUE
R3(config-router-af)# neighbor 198.51.100.88 remote-as 65229
R3(config-router-af)# exit
R3(config-router)#
```

A *route distinguisher* (RD) is not a requirement with VRF-Lite (except when using MP-BGP) and is a requirement with MPLS L3 VPNs, as discussed later, because they use MP-BGP as the dynamic routing protocol. However, a RD can be used with VRF-Lite to expand an IP prefix so that it includes a unique value (the RD) that distinguishes the IP address from other identical IP addresses in different VRF instances. So the RD is a tool that is used to ensure uniqueness of IP addresses in VRF instances if there are any overlapping or identical addresses being used in different VRF instances. (See Figure 18-14, later in this chapter, for a depiction of an RD.) To configure a route distinguisher, you use the **rd** *number:number* command in VRF configuration mode.

Route targets are another VRF feature that are not a requirement with VRF-Lite. They are more commonly used with MPLS L3 VPNs, as discussed later in this chapter. A route target is used to control the importing and exporting of routes for a VRF instance. So for your VRF instance, you can configure a route target with the VRF configuration mode command **route-target import** *route-target* for importing routes and the VRF configuration mode command **route-target export** *route-target* for exporting routes (for example, **route-target import 1:1** and **route-target export 1:1**). Note that the **route-target** value on your router for importing and exporting do not have to be the same as above; they can be different values. However, what is important is that the router that is importing matches the router that is exporting. If you are exporting with a route target of 1:5 on one router, then the other router needs to be importing with the route target 1:5. If not, the export and import process will fail.

To wrap up our VRF-Lite discussion, consider what happens if you connect a router using VRF with a router that is not using VRF. First, is this even possible? Yes, it is. You would see this in an MPLS environment, for example. The service provider has a router connected to multiple customers, as you'll see later in the chapter, in Figure 18-11. In that figure, the PE-R1 router is connected to two different customers. Therefore, the PE-R1 router would be configured with VRF instances. But the CE-R1 and CE-RA routers each belong to a single enterprise and do not need VRF instances. So, when the administrators of CE-R1 and CE-RA configure their routers, they do not have to worry about VRF instances, but when the ISP configures their PE-R1 router, they have to be concerned about implementing VRF instances that connect to each of the customer routers.

An Introduction to MPLS Operations

Multiprotocol Label Switching (MPLS) is a packet-forwarding method that makes forwarding decisions based on *labels* instead of based on the Layer 3 destination of the packet. MPLS was designed to support many different Layer 3 protocols, but in this section, we focus on IP only. Therefore, in our scenarios, we analyze how labels—instead of the destination IPv4 address—can be used to forward IP packets. Before we dive into MPLS, let's be clear that with today's routers, MPLS is not much faster than traditional IP routing. So why would you even consider MPLS? Well, MPLS decreases forwarding overhead on core routers, making them more efficient. In addition, MPLS can forward other Layer 3 protocols besides IPv4, and MPLS supports multiple services, such as unicast routing, multicast routing, VPNs, Traffic Engineering (TE), QoS, and Any Transport over MPLS (AToM). Therefore, MPLS is very efficient and flexible.

This section examines the Label Information Base (LIB), the Label Forwarding Information Base (LFIB), Label Distribution Protocol (LDP), the label-switched path (LSP), label switching routers (LSRs), Forward Equivalence Class (FEC), Resource Reservation Protocol (RSVP), and various LDP Features.

18

MPLS LIB and LFIB

In Figure 18-2, notice that the control plane of the MPLS-enabled router is responsible for exchanging labels with other MPLS-enabled routers, using a label distribution protocol, in addition to exchanging routing information using routing protocols to populate the IP routing table (*RIB*). Once labels have been exchanged, the label information is used to populate the *LIB*, and then the best label information can be used to populate the Forwarding Information Base (*FIB*) (so unlabeled packets can be labeled) and the *LFIB* (so labeled packets can be forwarded or labels can be removed when packets need to be forwarded by the FIB).

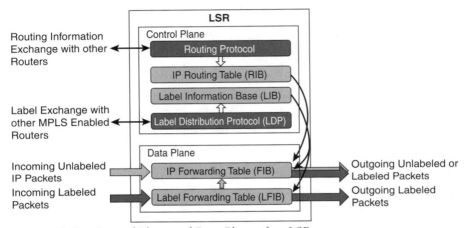

Figure 18-2 *Control Plane and Data Plane of an LSR*

Let's say an unlabeled IP packet arrives with a destination of 10.0.0.5. Because it is unlabeled, the FIB is used to make a forwarding decision. If the FIB indicates that the outgoing interface is not an MPLS-enabled interface, the packet is forwarded unlabeled. If the FIB indicates that the outgoing interface is an MPLS-enabled interface, a label is added to the packet, and the labeled packet is forwarded, labeled, out the MPLS interface.

Let's say a labeled packet arrives on an MPLS-enabled interface. Because it is labeled, the LFIB is used to make a forwarding decision. If the LFIB indicates that the outgoing interface is an MPLS-enabled interface, the label is removed, a new label is added, and the labeled packet is forwarded out the MPLS interface, labeled. If the LFIB indicates that the outgoing interface is not an MPLS-enabled interface, the label is removed, and the unlabeled packet is forwarded, unlabeled, using the information in the FIB.

Label Switching Routers

Examine Figure 18-3. Routers R1 through R5 are part of the MPLS domain. They are known as label switching routers (*LSRs*) because they support MPLS. They understand MPLS labels and can receive and transmit labeled packets on their interfaces. In this case, R1 and R5 are considered *edge LSRs*, and R2, R3, and R4 are considered intermediate LSRs. An edge LSR sits at the edge of the MPLS domain and adds labels to packets that are entering the MPLS domain (known as an *ingress LSR*), removes labels from packets that will be leaving the MPLS domain (known as an *egress LSR*), and even forwards packets as needed based on labels or the lack of a label. An *intermediate LSR* sits within the MPLS domain and primarily forwards packets using label information.

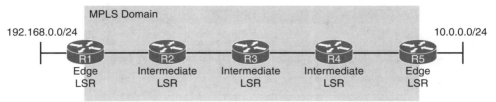

Figure 18-3   *Label Switching Routers in an MPLS Domain*

Forwarding Equivalence Class (FEC)

MPLS is a forwarding technology that is based on classification. Behind the scenes, MPLS groups together packets that will be forwarded in the same manner into a class called the FEC. Therefore, any packets that are part of the same FEC will be handled in exactly the same way. Classification can be based on any of the following:

- Source address

- Destination address

- Source port

- Destination port

- Protocol type

- VPN

For example, with traditional IP forwarding, decisions are based on destination addresses. Therefore, every packet going to the same destination is part of exactly the same FEC, and they will all be handled in exactly the same way by receiving the same label and following the same label-switched path (LSP).

Label-Switched Path

The label-switched path (*LSP*) is the cumulative labeled path (sequence of routers) that labeled packets of the same (FEC) take through the MPLS domain. It is a unidirectional path, as shown in Figure 18-4; therefore, in a complex network with multiple potential paths between source and destination, it is possible that the LSP from source to destination could be different from the LSP that is used for the return traffic. However, typically the same path in reverse is used for the return traffic because of the underlying dynamic routing protocols, such as OSPF and EIGRP, that are used to build the symmetrical network and its forwarding paths. In this case, the LSP from R1 to 10.0.0.0/24 uses labels 87, 11, 65, and 23. Along the path, each router examines the label to make a forwarding decision, removes the label, adds a new label if required, and then forwards the packet.

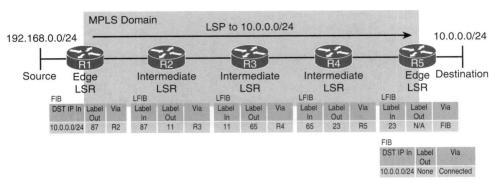

Figure 18-4   *The Label-Switched Path in an MPLS Domain*

Labels

For MPLS to work, a label needs to be added to a packet. The label is added as a shim header between the Layer 2 frame header and the Layer 3 packet header. Figure 18-5 shows the placement of the MPLS label shim header. The label is 4 bytes (32 bits) in size and contains four different fields, as shown in Figure 18-6. The first 20 bits (label) define the label number, the next 3 bits (TC) are used for quality of service (QoS), the 1 bit (S) field is used to define whether the label is the last label in the stack when more than one label is used in the packet (for example, with MPLS VPNs), and the final 8 bits (TTL [time to live]) are used just like IP's TTL so that MPLS frames are discarded if they have not reached the destination by the time the TTL reaches 0.

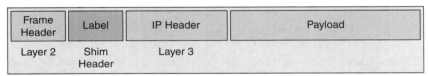

Figure 18-5   *Placement of the MPLS Label*

Figure 18-6   *Format of the MPLS Label*

MPLS-enabled routers automatically assign labels to every network that they know about. How does a router know about a network? It can be locally configured by configuring an IP address on a router interface and issuing the **no shutdown** command on the interface or through the propagation of routing information with dynamic routing protocols such as OSPF and EIGRP. For example, in Figure 18-7, R5 gave a label of 23 to network 10.0.0.0/24, R4 gave a label of 65 to network 10.0.0.0/24, R3 gave a label of 11 to network 10.0.0.0/24, R2 gave a label of 87 to network 10.0.0.0/24, and R1 gave a label of 19 to network 10.0.0.0/24. What you should notice from this is the local significance of labels. Each router, regardless of whether it is locally connected to the network 10.0.0.0/24, like R5, or not locally connected, like the other routers, generates a local label for the network it knows about, regardless of how it learned about it. The process of adding a label to a destination prefix is known as *LDP label binding*.

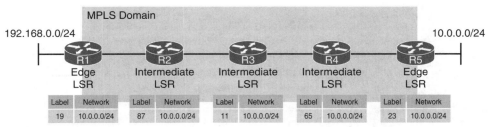

Figure 18-7   *Routers Associating a Label with the 10.0.0.0/24 Network*

Label Distribution Protocol

In order to build the LSP, labels need to be shared/distributed with directly connected LSRs. This is done using a label distribution protocol such as Label Distribution Protocol (*LDP*), which is the most common control plane protocol in use when sharing/distributing labels for IPv4 prefixes. It is an industry-standard method for hop-by-hop, dynamic label distribution in an MPLS network.

Once MPLS has been enabled on an interface, LDP hello packets are sent out the interface to the destination multicast address 224.0.0.2 (the all routers multicast address), using UDP port 646. This is known as basic discovery and is symmetrical. Any device on that same link that is also enabled for MPLS and that receives the hello packet forms an LDP TCP session using port 646 with the neighboring device so that label information can be exchanged. Within the hello packet is an LDP ID that is used to uniquely identify the neighbor and the label space, which will either be per platform (same label used out all interfaces for a single destination) or per interface (different label used out each interface for a single network). When establishing the LDP TCP session between two LSRs, one of the routers needs to be the active router. The active router is responsible for setting up the TCP session. The router with the higher LDP ID is selected as the active router and sets up the TCP session between the two routers.

In the preceding discussion and all the examples going forward, our LDP neighbors are directly connected to each other at the link level. Therefore, basic discovery is used. However, is it possible to have two routers form an LDP session with each other even if they are not directly connected? The answer is yes, and this would be needed with AToM (Any Transport over MPLS) networks and TE tunnels using L2VPNs. When you need to have LDP neighbors that are not directly connected, you need to target your Hellos to a specific address instead of to the 224.0.0.2 multicast address. You accomplish this by setting up a targeted session using the command **mpls ldp neighbor** *ip-addr* **targeted ldp** on each router. This is known as extended discovery. Unlike basic discovery, which is symmetrical, extended discovery is asymmetrical.

Figure 18-8 shows how R1 distributes its label of 19 for network 10.0.0.0/24 out all MPLS-enabled interfaces, R2 distributes its label of 87 for network 10.0.0.0/24 out all MPLS-enabled interfaces, R3 distributes its label of 11 for network 10.0.0.0/24 out all MPLS-enabled interfaces, R4 distributes its label of 65 for network 10.0.0.0/24 out all MPLS-enabled interfaces, and R5 distributes its label of 23 for network 10.0.0.0/24 out all MPLS-enabled interfaces after the TCP sessions have been established.

18

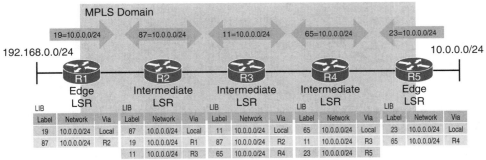

Figure 18-8 *LSRs Using LDP to Distribute Labels Out All MPLS-Enabled Interfaces*

Each router takes the labels it has learned from the LDP neighbors and populates its LIB. At first, this does not look right because if you focus on R3, you see that there are three entries for 10.0.0.0/24. What does each one mean? The entry with label 11 is the locally significant label. It is the label R3 advertises to other routers, so they know which label to place in a packet when they send to R3 a packet that is destined to 10.0.0.0/24. The entry with the label 87 is from R2, and it is the label that R2 wants R3 to use when R3 sends to R2 packets that are destined to 10.0.0.0/24. The entry with the label 65 is from R4, and it is the label that R4 wants R3 to use when R3 sends to R4 packets that are destined to 10.0.0.0/24. What we are examining is the LIB, which contains all the labels that the router knows about for all the different destination networks it knows about. It then takes the best labels/networks and populates the LFIB, which is used to make forwarding decisions.

For LDP to work properly, each router needs to have a unique identifier known as a router ID, which will be part of the LDP ID mentioned earlier. The router ID can be a manually configured value, or it can be dynamically chosen by the router when MPLS is being set up. The router ID is a 32-bit value in dotted-decimal notation. Therefore, it looks like an IPv4 address, but it is important to remember that it is a router ID and not an IPv4 address.

To manually configure the router ID, you use the command **mpls ldp router-id** *router-id*.

If you have not manually configured the router ID, because the router ID is a 32-bit value in dotted-decimal notation, the router can use any IP addresses configured on the router as the router ID. To accomplish this, the router looks for any loopback interfaces that have IP addresses on the router. If there are any loopback interfaces, the router finds the highest IP address of all the loopback interfaces and uses it as the router ID. If there are no loopback interfaces, the router examines the rest of the interfaces on the router and chooses the highest IP address of the remaining interfaces as the router ID.

Label Switching

Based on information found in the IP routing table and the LIB, the routers in Figure 18-9 have populated their LFIB and FIB as shown. Now, when R1 receives a packet with the label 19, it examines the LFIB and notices that it must forward it with the label 87 to R2. However, in this case, if the packet is coming in the interface that is connected to the 192.168.0.0/24 network, it does not have a label as there are no routers imposing labels on packets out that interface. Therefore, when the packet arrives on the interface connected to the 192.168.0.0/24 network of R1 with a destination IP address in the packet for 10.0.0.0/24, the FIB indicates that label 87 has to be added, and the packet needs to be forwarded with R2 as the next-hop address. When R2 receives the packet with the label 87, it examines the LFIB and notices that it must forward it with the label 11 and R3 as the next-hop address. When R3 receives the packet with the label 11, it examines the LFIB and notices that it must forward it with the label 65 and R4 as the next-hop address. When R4 receives the packet with the label 65, it examines the LFIB and notices that it must forward it with the label 23 and R5 as the next-hop address. When R5 receives the packet with the label 23, it examines the LFIB and notices that there is no outgoing label, which means it is the end of the LSP, and therefore the label must be removed, and normal routing has to occur with the IP routing table (FIB).

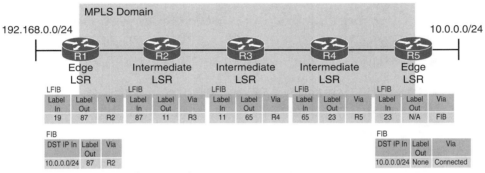

Figure 18-9 *Populated FIBs and LFIBs*

Penultimate-Hop Popping

Review Figure 18-9 and pay close attention to R5. R5 must do two lookups when it receives a labeled packet destined to 10.0.0.0/24. First, it must look in the LFIB because it received a labeled frame. In this case, there is no label out. Therefore, it must remove the label and make a forwarding decision based on a second lookup, using the FIB to forward the packet. This is not efficient. The solution to this inefficiency is penultimate-hop popping (*PHP*). With PHP, R4 pops the label before sending the packet to R5. So, instead of R5 advertising a label of 23 to R4 for 10.0.0.0/24, as in the previous scenarios, it advertises a "pop." Essentially, R5 tells R4 that it is the end of the LSP for the 10.0.0.0/24 network and that R4 should remove any label and forward the packet, unlabeled, to R5. Therefore, R5 receives an unlabeled packet and can do a single lookup using the FIB to forward the packet. In Figure 18-10, R5 has advertised the label pop to R4, and R4 has populated its LFIB accordingly. Notice the pop in the Label Out column of R4's LFIB. Now, when R4 receives a packet with the label 65, it pops the label and forwards it through R5. R5 receives the unlabeled packet and uses the FIB to forward the packet to the destination IP address in network 10.0.0.0/24. Example 18-24 shows that in the output of **show mpls ldp bindings**, which displays the LDP Label Information Base (LIB), a pop appears as imp-null. If you see *imp-null*, it means to pop the label before sending the packet to the next-hop router.

18

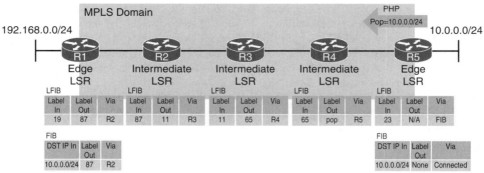

Figure 18-10 *PHP: R5 Indicating to R4 to Pop the Label*

Example 18-24 *Verifying PHP with the show mpls ldp bindings Command*

```
R4# show mpls ldp bindings
   ...output omitted...
lib entry: 10.0.0.0/24, rev 8
      local binding:  label: 65
      remote binding: lsr: 5.5.5.5:0, label: imp-null
      remote binding: lsr: 3.3.3.3:0, label: 11
lib entry: 192.168.0.0/24, rev 12
      local binding:  label: 33
      remote binding: lsr: 2.2.2.2:0, label: 17
      remote binding: lsr: 5.5.5.5:0, label: 20
... output omitted...
```

MPLS LDP Features

For the ENARSI exam you need to have a very basic understanding of some additional LDP features:

- **Inbound label binding filtering:** This is used to control the label bindings that an LSR accepts from other peered LSRs. It involves using access control lists (ACLs) to identify what will and will not be accepted from peers. You would use this, for example, when you need to control the amount of memory used to store LDP label bindings advertised by other devices.

- **Entropy label:** This is used for load balancing. Without it, at each MPLS hop, deep packet inspection (DPI) occurs to determine what should be done about load balancing. With it, DPI is done once at the ingress router (edge LSR) to create an entropy label, which is then used by all the other MPLS routers to make load balancing decisions.

- **Implicit NULL label:** This is a reserved label that has a value of 3 in the MPLS header. The value 3 indicates that it is an implicit NULL label. This is what is used for PHP, which we discussed earlier. When an LSR receives a label with the value 3 in the MPLS header, it knows that it will have to pop the label before it forwards the packet to the next MPLS device.

■ **Explicit NULL label:** This is a reserved label that has a value of 0 in the MPLS header, which indicates that it is an explicit NULL label. This particular label can be used to preserve the QoS EXP bits that are used in the MPLS environment and copy them into the QoS IP precedence or DiffServ bits that are needed in the packet after PHP occurs.

■ **MPLS LDP autoconfiguration feature:** This feature helps simplify MPLS configuration. When used, it enables LDP on every interface associated with a specified Interior Gateway Protocol (IGP) so you don't have to manually configure MPLS on an interface-by-interface basis. The only supported IGPs are Open Shortest Path Fist (OSPF) and Intermediate System-to-Intermediate System (IS-IS).

MPLS Traffic Engineering

MPLS Traffic Engineering (TE) is all about manipulating traffic as it flows through the MPLS environment so that it conforms to a particular need. TE is important when the MPLS environment is used by many different organizations. Take, for example, a service provider that has a multitude of customers that it is trying to provide connectivity for through the MPLS environment. Jump ahead to Figure 18-11 for an example of an MPLS environment that is servicing multiple customers (Customer A and Customer B). Each of those customers will have very specific requirements when it comes to bandwidth, delay, jitter, reliability, and more. The service provider needs to meet the needs (service-level agreements [SLAs]) of each customer. There is no one-size-fits-all in this case.

TE enables the service provider to accommodate the needs (SLAs) of their different customers. It is essentially quality of service (QoS) for the MPLS environment. The control plane protocol that is used for MPLS-TE is *Resource Reservation Protocol (RSVP)*.

RSVP is actually a signaling protocol used between systems that enables those systems to request resource reservations from the network. RSVP has the ability to generate protocol message requests and process protocol request messages that it has received from other systems and local clients. Therefore, RSVP ensures that resources are reserved for data flows from a source to a destination in the form of an LSP that the traffic will flow along.

An Introduction to MPLS Layer 3 VPNs

MPLS Layer 3 VPNs provide peer-to-peer connectivity between private customer sites across a shared network. Figure 18-11 shows a provider (such as an ISP) MPLS domain, with Customer A and Customer B both using the same MPLS domain to connect their own private sites together. The MPLS domain is referred to as the *P-network*, and the customer sites are referred to as the *C-network*.

This section explores how you can use MPLS Layer 3 VPNs to connect your private networks over your provider's public network.

18

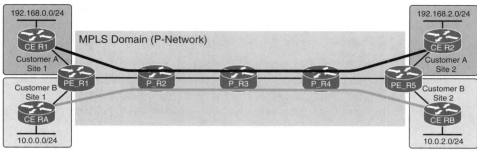

Figure 18-11   *A Sample MPLS Domain Connecting Customer Sites Together*

MPLS Layer 3 VPNs

In an MPLS Layer 3 VPN architecture, customer routers are known as CE (customer edge) routers, and they do not run MPLS. In fact, they have no knowledge of MPLS, labels, or even VRF instances, which makes it easier for the customer to take advantage of the benefits provided by a provider's MPLS domain. The *CE routers* connect to the PE (provider edge) routers of the MPLS domain. The *PE routers*, such as PE_R1 and PE_R5 in Figure 18-11, are the ingress and egress LSRs for the MPLS domain. The P (provider) routers, such as P_R2, P_R3, and P_R4 in Figure 18-11, are the intermediate LSRs of the MPLS domain. The goal is to have Customer A Site 1 and Customer A Site 2 exchange their local routing information over the MPLS domain and then forward traffic as needed from Site 1 and Site 2 over the MPLS domain. The same would be true for Customer B Site 1 and Customer B Site 2. Due to the nature of the MPLS Layer 3 VPN, overlapping address spaces between customers is of no concern. Therefore, Customer A and Customer B can be using the same private IP address space. We will discuss this further later in the chapter.

In order to support multiple customers, the PE routers need to use VRF instances, as shown in Figure 18-12, to isolate customer information and traffic from other customers. A different VRF instance needs to be created on the PE routers for each customer, and the interface that connects to the customer's CE router needs to be associated with the correct VRF. The CE router and the PE router exchange IPv4 routes using a routing protocol such as RIP (Routing Information Protocol), EIGRP (Enhanced Interior Gateway Routing Protocol), OSPF (Open Shortest Path First), or BGP (Border Gateway Protocol), and the routes are placed in the customer-specific VRF table on the PE router. Therefore, from the customer's perspective, the PE router is simply another router in the customer's network, but it is under the control of the provider. However, note that all P routers are hidden from the customer.

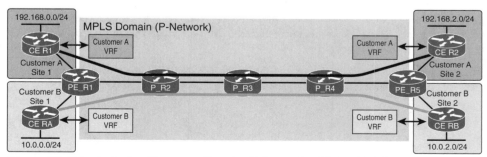

Figure 18-12   *Isolating Customer Routing Information Using VRF Instances*

Once the PE routers learn routes from the CE routers, the PE routers redistribute the routes into MP-BGP so they can be exchanged with other PE routers. When another PE router receives the routes, they are placed in the correct customer VRF instance so they can be redistributed (if needed) and exchanged with the CE router, as shown in Figure 18-13.

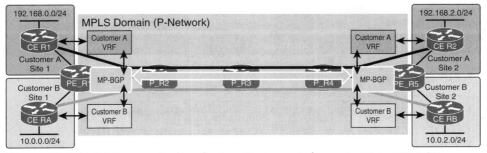

Figure 18-13 *PE Routers Redistributing Customer Information into MP-BGP*

An important point to consider is that the P routers are not participating in BGP. Only the PE routers are. They are forming an MP-IBGP (Multiprotocol-Interior Border Gateway Protocol) neighborship with each other and exchanging the routes using the underlying network that is built with an IGP such as OSPF or IS-IS. So the PE routers and the P routers are using a dynamic routing protocol to learn about all the destinations in the P network, and only the PE routers are using MP-IBGP on top of that to exchange the customer routes.

Since MP-IBGP is being used between the PE routers, you should consider taking advantage of BGP MD5 authentication between them for added security. You don't want to have a cybercriminal hijacking your BGP routers and sessions and introducing bogus routes or routers.

Note that Figure 18-13 has only a single path between the MP-IBGP routers. However, most deployments have a multitude of paths that can be taken due to the need for resiliency. When you have multiple paths, you may want to consider taking advantage of load balancing between the MP-IBGP peers by configuring the **maximum-paths ibgp** *number* command in router BGP configuration mode.

MPLS Layer 3 VPNv4 Addresses, RDs, and RTs

Let's now consider what happens with overlapping IPv4 address spaces. If all customer routes are being redistributed into MP-BGP, how does BGP handle identical network prefixes that belong to different customers? It uses a route distinguisher (RD) to expand the customer's IP prefix so that it includes a unique value that distinguishes it from the other identical prefixes. The RD is generated and used by the PE routers on a per-customer VRF instance basis, and to keep things simple, the RD is used regardless of whether there are overlapping address spaces. So, the RD is used all the time.

The unique 64-bit RD is prepended to the 32-bit customer prefix (IPv4 route) to create a 96-bit unique prefix called a VPNv4 address, as shown in Figure 18-14. This VPNv4 address is exchanged by the MP-IBGP neighboring routers.

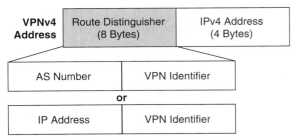

Figure 18-14 *Format of a VPNv4 Address*

In Figure 18-15, the Customer A VRF instance is using an RD of 1:100, and the Customer B VRF instance is using an RD of 1:110. RDs are configured using the **rd** *rd-value* command in VRF configuration mode for the respective customer VRF. For example, for Customer A, the command **rd 1:100** would have been used in this case. When these RDs are prepended to the IPv4 prefixes, the results are a VPNv4 route of 1:100:192.168.0.0/24 and a VPNv4 route of 1:110:10.0.0.0/24. Now let's say Customer A also chooses to use the 10.0.0.0/24 network and advertise it over to its other site. This is where the RDs keep everything unique. Customer A would have a VPNv4 route of 1:100:10.0.0.0/24, and Customer B would have the route 1:110:10.0.0.0/24.

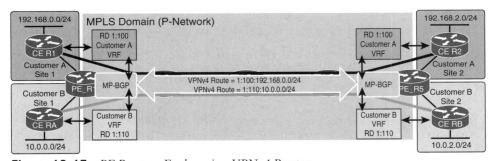

Figure 18-15 *PE Routers Exchanging VPNv4 Routes*

The following steps occur:

Step 1. The CE router and PE router exchange routes using a dynamic routing protocol such as OSPF, EIGRP, or BGP.

Step 2. The PE router places the customer-specific routes in the customer-specific VRF table.

Step 3. The routes in the customer's VRF table are redistributed (if IGPs are used between the provider and customer) into MP-BGP as VPNv4 routes. If BGP was used between the provider and customer, then redistribution is not needed to place the routes in the VRF table as MP-BGP VPNv4 routes since they are already BGP routes.

Step 4. The PE routers exchange VPNv4 routes over their MP-IBGP peering.

Step 5. The receiving PE router redistributes (if IGPs are used between the provider and customer) the VPNv4 routes as OSPF or EIGRP into the customer-specific VRF table. If BGP is used between the provider and the customer, then the routes can be placed into the customer-specific VRF table without redistribution.

Step 6.   The PE router and CE router exchange routes using a dynamic routing protocol such as OSPF, EIGRP, or BGP.

Now, revisit Figure 18-15. Take a moment to consider this: How does the provider ensure that what has been exported from a customer VRF instance on a PE router is sent across the MPLS environment and successfully imported into the correct customer VRF instance on another PE router? The answer: route target (RTs).

RTs are used to control the import and export process for customer VRF instance routes. An RT, like an RD, is configured in the VRF configuration for the customer VRF instance. For example, on PE_R5, you might configure an export RT of 653:27 with the command **route-target export** *route-target-number* and an import RT of 123:123 with the command **route-target import** *route-target-number* for the Customer A VRF instance. On PE_R1, you would then have to do the reverse and configure an export RT of 123:123 and an import RT of 653:27 for the Customer A VRF instance. Then, when PE_R1 exports the customer VRF routes, it attaches the RT 123:123 so that when PE_R5 receives the routes, it knows they belong to the Customer A VRF instance because you configured it with the import RT 123:123, and it therefore places the routes in the Customer A VRF table. In the other direction, when PE_R5 exports Customer A routes, it attaches the RT 653:27 so that when PE_R1 receives the routes, it knows to import them into the Customer A VRF instance because it has been configured with the import RT 653:27.

We can take this concept further. Consider other VRF instances, like Customer B VRF instances. The provider would configure unique RTs for Customer B VRF instances so that the routes for Customer B can be successfully exported and imported correctly; this ensures that the routes do not end up in the wrong VRF instance. Therefore, RTs must be unique within the MPLS environment.

MPLS Layer 3 VPN Label Stack

For the MPLS domain to forward traffic, a *label stack* is required. Specifically, two labels are required for traffic to be successfully forwarded through the MPLS domain. The first label that is attached to the packet is a *VPN label*, and the second label that is attached is the *LDP label*, as shown in Figure 18-16. When the IP packet arrives at the ingress PE router, the PE router attaches both labels. The egress router uses the VPN label to determine customer specifics about the packet and what should be done with it. The LDP label is used for label switching from PE to PE in the MPLS domain. VPN labels are learned from PE routers over the MP-IBGP peering, and the LDP labels are learned using the methods we explored in the "An Introduction to MPLS Operations" section of this chapter.

Figure 18-16   *Sample Label Stack for MPLS L3 VPNs*

Refer to Figure 18-17. Let's say that when PE_R5 learns of 10.0.2.0/24 from CE_RB, it places it in the Customer B VRF instance. It then redistributes it into MP-BGP and thus creates the VPNv4 route 1:110:10.0.2.0/24. This VPNv4 route needs a VPN label created for it so

that forwarding will be successful. In this case, PE_R5 assigns it the label 35. This label is
shared with PE_R1 over the MP-IBGP peering they have. Now, any time PE_R1 receives an
IP packet that is destined for 10.0.2.0/24, it knows to attach the label 35 so the packet can
be forwarded. However, this label is known only by the PE routers. Therefore, if PE_R1 forwards this VPN packet to P_R2, it will be dropped because P_R2 has no idea what the VPN
label 35 means. Therefore, the LDP label is needed to forward the packet from PE_R1 and
PE_R5.

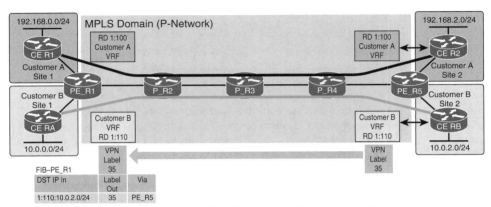

Figure 18-17 *VPN Label Assigned by PE_R5 and Shared with PE_R1*

Figure 18-18 shows how LDP is used to exchange labels that have been generated by the PE
routers (ingress and egress LSRs) and the P routers (intermediate LSRs). PE_R5 tells P_R4 to
pop the label. P_R4 tells P_R3 to use the label 52. P_R3 tells P_R2 to use the label 10. P_R2
tells PE_R1 to use the label 99. This is exactly as described earlier in this chapter.

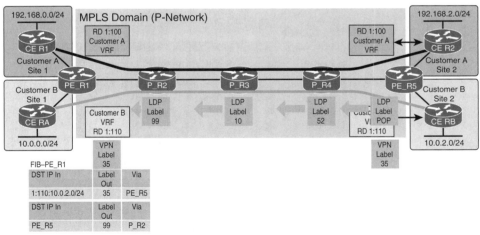

Figure 18-18 *LDP Label Assignment*

In Figure 18-19, the complete LSP is now ready to label switch the VPN packet from PE_R1
to PE_R5.

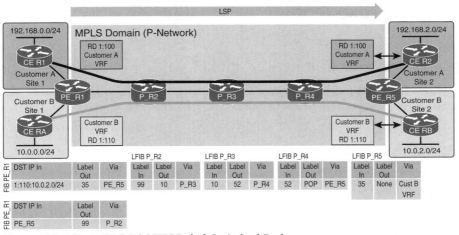

Figure 18-19 *MPLS L3 VPN Label-Switched Path*

Take a look at Figure 18-20. Now when an IP packet destined to 10.0.2.0/24 arrives at PE_R1 from CE_RA, PE_R1 determines that the packet needs a VPN label of 35 so PE_R5 will know what to do with the VPN packet and an LDP label of 99 so that the VPN packet can be label switched through the MPLS domain. Once the label stack is complete, PE_R1 sends the label-stacked packet to P_R2. When P_R2 receives it, it only examines the LDP label. Based on the LFIB, it states that the label 99 needs to be swapped to 10 and forwarded to P_R3. So, it does so. When P_R3 receives it, it only examines the LDP label. Based on the LFIB, it states that the label 10 needs to be swapped to 52 and forwarded to P_R4. So, it does so. When P_R4 receives it, it only examines the LDP label. Based on the LFIB, it states that the label 52 needs to be popped and forwarded to P_R5. So, it makes this happen. Now PE_R5 only needs to read the VPN label, which is 35. Based on the scenario, the label is removed, and the VRF instance for Customer B is used to forward the IP packet to the CE_RB router.

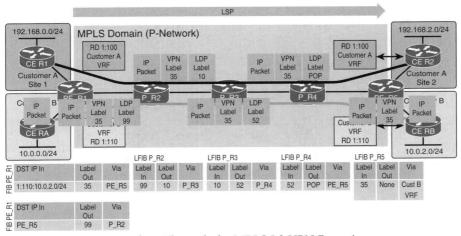

Figure 18-20 *Forwarding Through the MPLS L3 VPN Domain*

Reference in This Chapter

Moy, John, *MPLS: Implementing Cisco MPLS Student Guide*, Version 3.0.1, Cisco, 2018.

Exam Preparation Tasks

As mentioned in the section "How to Use This Book" in the Introduction, you have a couple choices for exam preparation: the exercises here, Chapter 24, "Final Preparation," and the exam simulation questions in the Pearson Test Prep software.

Review All Key Topics

Review the most important topics in this chapter, noted with the Key Topic icon in the outer margin of the page. Table 18-2 lists these key topics and the page number on which each is found.

Table 18-2   Key Topics

Key Topic Element	Description	Page Number
Paragraph	The purpose of VRF	728
Example 18-1	Configuring VRF on R1 with the **ip vrf** command	729
Example 18-3	Assigning interfaces to the VRF instances with the **ip vrf forwarding** command	730
Example 18-5	Creating subinterfaces on R1 and assigning them to the correct VRF instances	732
Example 18-7	Verifying the interface IP address, VRF, and protocol configurations	733
Example 18-9	Verifying the VRF routing tables	735
Section	MPLS LIB and LFIB	748
Section	Label-switching routers	748
Section	Forwarding Equivalence Class (FEC)	749
Section	Labels	750
Section	Label Distribution Protocol	751
Paragraph	The benefit of PHP	753
Section	MPLS Layer 3 VPNs	754
Section	MPLS LDP Features	755
Section	MPLS Traffic Engineering (TE)	756
Paragraph	MPLS Layer 3 VPNv4 Addresses, RDs, and RTs	757
Steps	How routes are learned by CE routers over an MPLS Layer 3 VPN	758
Section	MPLS Layer 3 VPN label stack	759

Define Key Terms

Define the following key terms from this chapter and check your answers in the glossary:

virtual routing and forwarding (VRF), VRF-Lite, Multiprotocol Label Switching (MPLS), label, RIB, LIB, FIB, LFIB, LSR, edge LSR, ingress LSR, egress LSR, intermediate LSR, LSP, LDP, PHP, Resource Reservation Protocol (RSVP), route distinguisher, route target, imp-null, push, pop, MPLS Layer 3 VPN, P-network, C-network, CE router, PE router, P router, VPNv4 address, label stack, LDP label, VPN label

Use the Command Reference to Check Your Memory

The ENARSI 300-410 exam focuses on the practical, hands-on skills that networking professionals use. Therefore, you should be able to identify the commands needed to configure, verify, and troubleshoot the topics covered in this chapter.

This section includes the most important configuration and verification commands covered in this chapter. It might not be necessary to memorize the complete syntax of every command, but you should be able to remember the basic keywords that are needed.

To test your memory of the commands in Table 18-3, go to the companion website and download Appendix B, "Command Reference Exercises." Fill in the missing commands in the tables based on each command description. You can check your work by downloading Appendix C, "Command Reference Exercise Answer Key," from the companion website.

Table 18-3 Command Reference

Task	Command Syntax
Define a VRF instance and enter VRF configuration mode for the instance (in global configuration mode) by using a classic command.	**ip vrf** *vrf-name*
Define a VRF instance and enter VRF configuration mode for the instance (in global configuration mode) by using a newer command that supports IPv4 and IPv6 networks.	**vrf definition** *vrf-name*
Associate an interface or a subinterface with a VRF instance (in interface configuration mode) by using a classic command.	**ip vrf forwarding** *vrf-name*
Associate an interface or a subinterface with a VRF instance (in interface configuration mode) by using a newer command that supports IPv4 and IPv6 networks.	**vrf forwarding** *vrf-name*
Display configured VRF instances and associated router interfaces.	**show ip vrf**
Display the routes in the global routing table.	**show ip route**
Display the routes in the routing table for the VRF specified in the command.	**show ip route vrf** *vrf-name*

18

Task	Command Syntax
Display all VRF-enabled interfaces on the router, including their IP addresses and whether the protocol is up or down, by using a classic command.	show ip vrf interfaces
Display all IPv4 VRF-enabled interfaces on the router, including their IP addresses and whether the protocol is up or down, by using a newer command.	show vrf ipv4 unicast interfaces
Display all IPv6 VRF-enabled interfaces on the router, including their IP addresses and whether the protocol is up or down, by using a newer command.	show vrf ipv6 unicast interfaces
Test IP connectivity for a specific VRF instance.	ping vrf *vrf-name ipv4-address*

DMVPN Tunnels

This chapter covers the following topics:

- **Generic Routing Encapsulation (GRE) Tunnels:** This section explains how GRE tunnels operate and explains the configuration of GRE tunnels.

- **Next Hop Resolution Protocol (NHRP):** This section describes NHRP and how it dynamically maps underlay IP addresses to overlay tunnel IP addresses.

- **Dynamic Multipoint VPN (DMVPN):** This section explains the three DMVPN phases and the technologies involved with DMVPN tunnels.

- **DMVPN Configuration:** This section explains the configuration of DMVPN tunnels.

- **Spoke-to-Spoke Communication:** This section explains how spoke-to-spoke DMVPN tunnels form.

- **Problems with Overlay Networks:** This section describes common issues with overlay networks and optimal design concepts to prevent those issues.

- **DMVPN Failure Detection and High Availability:** This section explains the DMVPN mechanisms to detect failure and methods for providing a resilient DMVPN network.

- **IPv6 DMVPN Configuration:** This section explains how DMVPN tunnels can use an IPv6 network as an underlay or overlay network.

Dynamic Multipoint Virtual Private Network (DMVPN) is a Cisco solution that provides a scalable VPN architecture. DMVPN uses *Generic Routing Encapsulation (GRE)* for tunneling, *Next Hop Resolution Protocol (NHRP)* for on-demand forwarding and mapping information, and IPsec to provide a secure overlay network to address the deficiencies of site-to-site VPN tunnels while providing full-mesh connectivity. This chapter explains the underlying technologies and components involved in deploying DMVPN.

"Do I Know This Already?" Quiz

The "Do I Know This Already?" quiz allows you to assess whether you should read this entire chapter thoroughly or jump to the "Exam Preparation Tasks" section. If you are in doubt about your answers to these questions or your own assessment of your knowledge of the topics, read the entire chapter. Table 19-1 lists the major headings in this chapter and their corresponding "Do I Know This Already?" quiz questions. You can find the answers in Appendix A, "Answers to the 'Do I Know This Already?' Quiz Questions."

Table 19-1 "Do I Know This Already?" Foundation Topics Section-to-Question Mapping

Foundation Topics Section	Questions
Generic Routing Encapsulation (GRE) Tunnels	1
Next Hop Resolution Protocol (NHRP)	2
Dynamic Multipoint VPN (DMVPN)	3–7
Spoke-to-Spoke Communication	8
Problems with Overlay Networks	9
DMVPN Failure Detection and High Availability	10
IPv6 DMVPN Configuration	11

CAUTION   The goal of self-assessment is to gauge your mastery of the topics in this chapter. If you do not know the answer to a question or are only partially sure of the answer, you should mark that question as wrong for purposes of self-assessment. Giving yourself credit for an answer that you correctly guess skews your self-assessment results and might provide you with a false sense of security.

1. Which of the following protocols do Generic Routing Encapsulation (GRE) tunnels support? (Choose all that apply.)

    a. DECnet

    b. Systems Network Architecture (SNA)

    c. IPv4

    d. IPv6

    e. MPLS

2. True or false: NHRP is a Cisco-proprietary protocol developed for DMVPN.

    a. True

    b. False

3. Which DMVPN phase does not work well with route summarization of spoke prefixes?

    a. DMVPN Phase 1

    b. DMVPN Phase 2

    c. DMVPN Phase 3

    d. DMVPN Phase 4

4. Which DMVPN phase introduced hierarchical tunnel structures?

    a. DMVPN Phase 1

    b. DMVPN Phase 2

    c. DMVPN Phase 3

    d. DMVPN Phase 4

5. True or false: DMVPN supports multicast.
   a. True
   b. False

6. What is the configuration difference between DMVPN Phase 1 and DMVPN Phase 2 on the hub router?
   a. The use of the command **ip nhrp shortcut**
   b. The use of the command **ip nhrp redirect**
   c. The use of the command **ip nhrp version 2**
   d. There is no difference in configuration.

7. What is the configuration difference between DMVPN Phase 2 and DMVPN Phase 3 on the spoke router?
   a. The use of the command **ip nhrp shortcut**
   b. The use of the command **ip nhrp redirect**
   c. The use of the command **ip nhrp version 3**
   d. There is no difference in configuration.

8. True or false: After a spoke router registers with the hub router, the hub router sends communication to the spoke router to establish a full mesh of tunnels with other spoke routers.
   a. True
   b. False

9. What does the syslog message "Midchain parent maintenance for IP midchain out" indicate?
   a. There is a problem with the PKI certificate infrastructure.
   b. There is a recursive routing loop on the tunnel.
   c. The remote peer has placed its tunnel in maintenance mode.
   d. The encapsulating interface has been shut down.

10. How long is the default NHRP cache timer?
    a. 2 hours
    b. 1 hour
    c. 30 minutes
    d. 15 minutes

11. Which of the following issues do network engineers commonly overlook when using IPv6 DMVPN tunnels?
    a. Changing the MTU on the tunnel interface to accommodate the larger packet header
    b. Configuring a link-local IP address on the tunnel interface
    c. Placing the tunnel into IPv6 GRE multipoint mode
    d. Configuring the NBMA address in CIDR notation (for example, 2001:12:14::1/64)

Foundation Topics

Generic Routing Encapsulation (GRE) Tunnels

A *GRE tunnel* provides connectivity to a wide variety of network layer protocols by encapsulating and forwarding those packets over an IP-based network. The original use of GRE tunnels was to provide a transport mechanism for nonroutable legacy protocols such as DECnet, Systems Network Architecture (SNA), and IPX.

DMVPN uses *Multipoint GRE (mGRE)* encapsulation and supports dynamic routing protocols, which eliminates many of the support issues associated with other VPN technologies. GRE tunnels are classified as an *overlay network* because a GRE tunnel is built on top of an existing transport network, also known as an *underlay network.*

Additional header information is added to a packet when the router encapsulates the packet for the GRE tunnel. The new header information contains the remote endpoint IP address as the destination. The new IP headers allow the packet to be routed between the two tunnel endpoints without inspection of the packet's payload. After the packet reaches the remote endpoint, the GRE headers are removed, and the original packet is forwarded out the remote router.

> **NOTE**   GRE tunnels support IPv4 or IPv6 addresses as an overlay or transport network.

GRE Tunnel Configuration

This section explains the fundamentals of a GRE tunnel and then explains mGRE tunnels, which are a component of DMVPN. GRE and mGRE tunnels do not use encryption by default and require additional configuration, as explained in Chapter 20, "Securing DMVPN Tunnels." The process for configuring a GRE tunnel is described in the following sections.

Figure 19-1 illustrates the configuration of a GRE tunnel. The 172.16.0.0/16 network range is the transport (underlay) network, and 192.168.100.0/24 is used for the GRE tunnel (overlay network).

In this topology, R11, R31, and the SP router have enabled Routing Information Protocol (RIP) on all the 10.0.0.0/8 and 172.16.0.0/16 network interfaces. This allows R11 and R31 to locate the remote router's encapsulating interface. R11 uses the SP router as a next hop to reach the 172.16.31.0/30 network, and R31 uses the SP router as a next hop toward the 172.16.11.0/30 network.

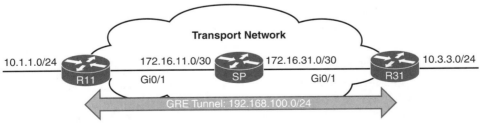

Figure 19-1   *GRE Tunnel Topology*

19

> **NOTE** The RIP configuration does not include the 192.168.0.0/16 network range.

Example 19-1 shows the routing table of R11 before the GRE tunnel is created. Notice that the 10.3.3.0/24 network is reachable by RIP and is two hops away.

Example 19-1 *R11 Routing Table Without the GRE Tunnel*

```
R11# show ip route
! Output omitted for brevity
Codes: L - local,    C - connected, S - static, R - RIP,    M - mobile, B - BGP
       D - EIGRP, EX - EIGRP external, O - OSPF, IA - OSPF inter area


Gateway of last resort is not set

     10.0.0.0/8 is variably subnetted, 3 subnets, 2 masks
C       10.1.1.0/24 is directly connected, GigabitEthernet0/2
R       10.3.3.0/24 [120/2] via 172.16.11.2, 00:00:01, GigabitEthernet0/1
     172.16.0.0/16 is variably subnetted, 3 subnets, 2 masks
C       172.16.11.0/30 is directly connected, GigabitEthernet0/1
R       172.16.31.0/30 [120/1] via 172.16.11.2, 00:00:10, GigabitEthernet0/1
R11# trace 10.3.3.3 source 10.1.1.1
Tracing the route to 10.3.3.3
   1 172.16.11.2 0 msec 0 msec 1 msec
   2 172.16.31.1 0 msec
```

The steps for configuring GRE tunnels are as follows:

Step 1. Create the tunnel interface by using the global configuration command **interface tunnel** *tunnel-number*.

Step 2. Identify the local source of the tunnel by using the interface parameter command **tunnel source** {*ip-address* | *interface-id*}. The tunnel source interface indicates the interface that will be used for encapsulation and decapsulation of the GRE tunnel. The tunnel source can be a physical interface or a loopback interface. A loopback interface can provide reachability if one of the transport interfaces fails.

Step 3. Identify the tunnel destination by using the interface parameter command **tunnel destination** *ip-address*. The tunnel destination is the remote router's underlay IP address toward which the local router sends GRE packets.

Step 4. Allocate an IP address to the tunnel interface by using the command **ip address** *ip-address subnet-mask*.

Step 5. Optionally define the tunnel bandwidth, measured in kilobits per second, by using the interface parameter command **bandwidth** [*1-10000000*]. Virtual interfaces do not have the concept of latency and need to have a reference bandwidth configured so that routing protocols that use bandwidth for best-path calculation can make intelligent decisions. Bandwidth is also used for quality of service (QoS) configuration on the interface.

Step 6. Optionally specify a GRE tunnel keepalive by using the interface parameter command **keepalive** [*seconds* [*retries*]]. The default timer is 10 seconds and three retries. Tunnel interfaces are GRE *point-to-point* (*P2P*) by default, and the line protocol enters an *up* state when the router detects that a route to the tunnel destination exists in the routing table. If the tunnel destination is not in the routing table, the tunnel interface (line protocol) enters a *down* state. Tunnel keepalives ensure that bidirectional communication exists between tunnel endpoints to keep the line protocol up. Otherwise, the router must rely on routing protocol timers to detect a dead remote endpoint.

Step 7. Optionally define the IP maximum transmission unit (MTU) for the tunnel interface by using the interface parameter command **ip mtu** *mtu*. The GRE tunnel adds a minimum of 24 bytes to the packet size to accommodate the headers that are added to the packet. Specifying the IP MTU on the tunnel interface has the router perform the fragmentation in advance of the host having to detect and specify the packet MTU.

Table 19-2 shows the amount of encapsulation overhead for various tunnel techniques. The header size may change based on the configuration options used. For all the examples in this chapter, the IP MTU is set to 1400.

Table 19-2 Encapsulation Overhead for Tunnels

Tunnel Type	Tunnel Header Size
GRE without IPsec	24 bytes
DES/3DES IPsec (transport mode)	18–25 bytes
DES/3DES IPsec (tunnel mode)	38–45 bytes
GRE/DMVPN + DES/3DES	42–49 bytes
GRE/DMVPN + AES + SHA-1	62–77 bytes

19

GRE Sample Configuration

Example 19-2 provides the GRE tunnel configuration for R11 and R31. EIGRP is enabled on the LAN (10.0.0.0/8) and GRE tunnel (192.168.100.0/24) networks. RIP is enabled on the LAN (10.0.0.0/8) and transport (172.16.0.0/16) networks but is not enabled on the GRE tunnel. R11 and R31 become direct EIGRP peers on the GRE tunnel because all the network traffic is encapsulated between them.

EIGRP has a lower administrative distance (AD), 90, and the routers use the route learned from the EIGRP connection (using the GRE tunnel) rather than the route learned from RIP (120) that came from the transport network. Notice that the EIGRP configuration uses named mode. *EIGRP named mode* provides clarity and keeps the entire EIGRP configuration in one centralized location. EIGRP named mode is the only method of EIGRP configuration that supports some of the newer features, such as stub sites.

Example 19-2 *GRE Configuration*

```
R11
interface Tunnel100
 bandwidth 4000
 ip address 192.168.100.11 255.255.255.0
 ip mtu 1400
 keepalive 5 3
 tunnel source GigabitEthernet0/1
tunnel destination 172.16.31.1
 !
router eigrp GRE-OVERLAY
 address-family ipv4 unicast autonomous-system 100
  topology base
  exit-af-topology
  network 10.0.0.0
  network 192.168.100.0
 exit-address-family
 !
router rip
 version 2
 network 10.0.0.0
 network 172.16.0.0
 no auto-summary
```

```
R31
interface Tunnel100
 bandwidth 4000
 ip address 192.168.100.31 255.255.255.0
 ip mtu 1400
 keepalive 5 3
 tunnel source GigabitEthernet0/1
 tunnel destination 172.16.11.1
 !
router eigrp GRE-OVERLAY
 address-family ipv4 unicast autonomous-system 100
  topology base
  exit-af-topology
  network 10.0.0.0
  network 192.168.100.0
 exit-address-family
 !
router rip
 version 2
 network 10.0.0.0
 network 172.16.0.0
 no auto-summary
```

When the GRE tunnel is configured, the state of the tunnel can be verified with the command **show interface tunnel** *number*. Example 19-3 displays output from this command. Notice that the output includes the tunnel source and destination addresses, keepalive values (if any), and the tunnel line protocol state; it also indicates that the tunnel is a GRE/IP tunnel.

Example 19-3 *Displaying GRE Tunnel Parameters*

```
R11# show interface tunnel 100
! Output omitted for brevity
Tunnel100 is up, line protocol is up
  Hardware is Tunnel
  Internet address is 192.168.100.1/24
  MTU 17916 bytes, BW 400 Kbit/sec, DLY 50000 usec,
    reliability 255/255, txload 1/255, rxload 1/255
  Encapsulation TUNNEL, loopback not set
  Keepalive set (5 sec), retries 3
  Tunnel source 172.16.11.1 (GigabitEthernet0/1), destination 172.16.31.1
  Tunnel Subblocks:
    src-track:
       Tunnel100 source tracking subblock associated with GigabitEthernet0/1
       Set of tunnels with source GigabitEthernet0/1, 1 member (includes
       iterators), on interface <OK>
  Tunnel protocol/transport GRE/IP
    Key disabled, sequencing disabled
    Checksumming of packets disabled
  Tunnel TTL 255, Fast tunneling enabled
  Tunnel transport MTU 1476 bytes
  Tunnel transmit bandwidth 8000 (kbps)
  Tunnel receive bandwidth 8000 (kbps)
  Last input 00:00:02, output 00:00:02, output hang never
```

Example 19-4 shows the routing table of R11 after it has become an EIGRP neighbor with R31. Notice that R11 learns the 10.3.3.0/24 network directly from R31 through tunnel 100.

Example 19-4 *R11 Routing Table with GRE Tunnel*

```
R11# show ip route
! Output omitted for brevity
Codes: L - local,    C - connected, S - static, R - RIP, M - mobile, B - BGP
       D - EIGRP, EX - EIGRP external, O - OSPF, IA - OSPF inter area

Gateway of last resort is not set
     10.0.0.0/8 is variably subnetted, 3 subnets, 2 masks
C       10.1.1.0/24 is directly connected, GigabitEthernet0/2
D       10.3.3.0/24 [90/38912000] via 192.168.100.31, 00:03:35, Tunnel100
```

19

```
      172.16.0.0/16 is variably subnetted, 3 subnets, 2 masks
C        172.16.11.0/30 is directly connected, GigabitEthernet0/1
R        172.16.31.0/30 [120/1] via 172.16.11.2, 00:00:03, GigabitEthernet0/1
      192.168.100.0/24 is variably subnetted, 2 subnets, 2 masks
C        192.168.100.0/24 is directly connected, Tunnel100
```

Example 19-5 shows how to verify that traffic from 10.1.1.1 takes tunnel 100 (192.168.100.0/24) to reach the 10.3.3.3 network.

Example 19-5   *Verifying the Path from R11 to R31*

```
R11# traceroute 10.3.3.3 source 10.1.1.1
Tracing the route to 10.3.3.3
  1 192.168.100.31 1 msec * 0 msec
```

> **NOTE**   Notice that from R11's perspective, the network is only one hop away. The traceroute does not display all the hops in the underlay. In the same fashion, the packet's *time to live (TTL)* is encapsulated as part of the payload. The original TTL decreases by only one for the GRE tunnel, regardless of the number of hops in the transport network.

Next Hop Resolution Protocol (NHRP)

Next Hop Resolution Protocol (NHRP) is defined in RFC 2332 as a method to provide address resolution for hosts or networks (with ARP-like capability) for nonbroadcast multi-access (NBMA) networks such as Frame Relay and ATM networks. NHRP provides a method for devices to learn the protocol and NBMA network, thereby allowing them to directly communicate with each other.

NHRP is a client/server protocol that allows devices to register themselves over directly connected or disparate networks. NHRP *next-hop servers (NHSs)* are responsible for registering addresses or networks, maintaining an NHRP repository, and replying to any queries received by next-hop clients (NHCs). The NHC and NHS are transactional in nature.

DMVPN uses mGRE tunnels and therefore requires a method of mapping tunnel IP addresses to the transport (underlay) IP address. NHRP provides the technology for mapping those IP addresses. DMVPN spokes (NHCs) are *statically* configured with the IP addresses of the hubs (NHSs) so that they can register their tunnel and NBMA (transport) IP addresses with the hubs. When a spoke-to-spoke tunnel is established, NHRP messages provide the necessary information for the spokes to locate each other so that they can build a spoke-to-spoke DMVPN tunnel. The NHRP messages also allow a spoke to locate a remote network. Cisco has added additional NHRP message types to those defined in RFC 2332 to provide some of the recent enhancements in DMVPN.

All NHRP packets must include the *source NBMA address*, *source protocol address*, *destination protocol address*, and NHRP message type. The NHRP message types are explained in Table 19-3.

NOTE The NBMA address refers to the transport network, and the protocol address refers to the IP address assigned to the overlay network (tunnel IP address or a network/host address).

Table 19-3 NHRP Message Types

Message Type	Description
Registration	Registration messages are sent by the NHC (DMVPN spoke) toward the NHS (DMVPN hub). Registration allows the hubs to know a spoke's NBMA information. The NHC also specifies the amount of time that the registration should be maintained by the NHS, along with other attributes.
Resolution	Resolution messages are NHRP messages to locate and provide the address resolution information of the egress router toward the destination. A resolution request is sent during the actual query, and a resolution reply provides the tunnel IP address and the NBMA IP address of the remote spoke.
Redirect	Redirect messages are an essential component of DMVPN Phase 3. They allow an intermediate router to notify the encapsulator (a router) that a specific network can be reached by using a more optimal path (spoke-to-spoke tunnel). The encapsulator may send a redirect suppress message to suppress redirect requests for a specified period of time. This is typically done if a more optimal path is not feasible or if the policy does not allow it.
Purge	Purge messages are sent to remove a cached NHRP entry. Purge messages notify routers of the loss of a route used by NHRP. A purge is typically sent by an NHS to an NHC (which it answered) to indicate that the mapping for an address/network that it answered is not valid anymore (for example, if the network is unreachable from the original station or has moved). Purge messages take the most direct path (spoke-to-spoke tunnel), if feasible. If a spoke-to-spoke tunnel is not established, purge messages are forwarded through the hub.
Error	Error messages are used to notify the sender of an NHRP packet that an error has occurred.

NHRP messages can contain additional information that is included in the extension part of a message. Table 19-4 lists the common NHRP message extensions.

Table 19-4 NHRP Message Extensions

NHRP Extension	Description
Responder address	This is used to determine the address of the responding node for reply messages.
Forward transit NHS record	This contains a list of NHSs that the NHRP request packet may have traversed.
Reverse transit NHS record	This contains a list of NHSs that the NHRP reply packet may have traversed.

NHRP Extension	Description
Authentication	This conveys authentication information between NHRP speakers. Authentication is done pairwise on a hop-by-hop basis. This field is transmitted in plaintext.
Vendor private	This conveys vendor private information between NHRP speakers.
Network Address Translation (NAT)	DMVPN works when a hub or spoke resides behind a device that performs NAT and when the tunnel is encapsulated in IPsec. This NHRP extension is able to detect the *claimed NBMA address* (that is, the inside local address) using the source protocol address of the NHRP packet and the inside global IP address from the IP headers of the NHRP packet.

Dynamic Multipoint VPN (DMVPN)

DMVPN provides the following benefits to network administrators:

- **Zero-touch provisioning:** DMVPN hubs do not require additional configuration when additional spokes are added. DMVPN spokes can use a templated tunnel configuration.

- **Scalable deployment:** Minimal peering and minimal permanent state on spoke routers allow for massive scale. Network scale is not limited by device (physical, virtual, or logical).

- **Spoke-to-spoke tunnels:** DMVPN provides full-mesh connectivity while requiring configuration of only the initial spoke-to-hub tunnel. Dynamic spoke-to-spoke tunnels are created as needed and torn down when no longer needed. There is no packet loss while building dynamic on-demand spoke-to-spoke tunnels after the initial spoke-to-hub tunnels are established. A spoke maintains forwarding states only for spokes with which it is communicating.

- **Flexible network topologies:** DMVPN operation does not make any rigid assumptions about either the control plane or data plane overlay topologies. The DMVPN control plane can be used in a highly distributed and resilient model that allows massive scale and avoids a single point of failure or congestion. At the other extreme, it can also be used in a centralized model for a single point of control.

- **Multiprotocol support:** DMVPN can use IPv4, IPv6, and MPLS as the overlay or transport network protocol.

- **Multicast support:** DMVPN allows multicast traffic to flow on the tunnel interfaces.

- **Adaptable connectivity:** DMVPN routers can establish connectivity behind Network Address Translation (NAT). Spoke routers can use dynamic IP addressing such as Dynamic Host Configuration Protocol (DHCP).

- **Standardized building blocks:** DMVPN uses industry-standardized technologies (NHRP, GRE, and IPsec) to build an overlay network. This propagates familiarity while minimizing the learning curve and easing troubleshooting.

DMVPN provides complete connectivity while simplifying configuration as new sites are deployed. It is considered a zero-touch technology because no configuration is needed on the DMVPN hub routers as new spokes are added to the DMVPN network. This facilitates consistent configuration, where all spokes can use identical tunnel configuration (that is, can be templatized) to simplify support and deployment with network provisioning systems like Cisco Prime Infrastructure.

A spoke site initiates a persistent VPN connection to the hub router. Network traffic between spoke sites does not have to travel through the hubs. DMVPN dynamically builds a VPN tunnel between spoke sites on an as-needed basis. This allows network traffic, such as voice over IP (VoIP), to take a direct path, which reduces delay and jitter without consuming bandwidth at the hub site.

DMVPN was released in three phases, each phase built on the previous one with additional functions. All three phases of DMVPN need only one tunnel interface on a router, and the DMVPN network size should accommodate all the endpoints associated with that tunnel network. DMVPN spokes can use DHCP or static addressing for the transport and overlay networks. They locate the other spokes' IP addresses (protocols and NBMA) through NHRP.

Phase 1: Spoke-to-Hub

DMVPN Phase 1, the first DMVPN implementation, provides a zero-touch deployment for VPN sites. VPN tunnels are created only between spoke and hub sites. Traffic between spokes must traverse the hub to reach any other spoke.

Phase 2: Spoke-to-Spoke

DMVPN Phase 2 provides additional capability beyond DMVPN Phase 1 and allows spoke-to-spoke communication on a dynamic basis by creating an on-demand VPN tunnel between the spoke devices. DMVPN Phase 2 does not allow summarization (next-hop preservation). As a result, it also does not support spoke-to-spoke communication between different DMVPN networks (multilevel hierarchical DMVPN).

Phase 3: Hierarchical Tree Spoke-to-Spoke

DMVPN Phase 3 refines spoke-to-spoke connectivity by enhancing the NHRP messaging and interacting with the routing table. With DMVPN Phase 3, the hub sends an NHRP redirect message to the spoke that originated the packet flow. The *NHRP redirect* message provides the necessary information so that the originator spoke can initiate a resolution of the destination host/network.

In DMVPN Phase 3, NHRP installs paths in the routing table for the shortcuts it creates. *NHRP shortcuts* modify the next-hop entry for existing routes or add a more explicit route entry to the routing table. Because NHRP shortcuts install more explicit routes in the routing table, DMVPN Phase 3 supports summarization of networks at the hub while providing optimal routing between spoke routers. NHRP shortcuts allow a hierarchical tree topology so that a regional hub is responsible for managing NHRP traffic and subnets within that region, but spoke-to-spoke tunnels can be established outside that region.

DMVPN Phase Comparison

Figure 19-2 illustrates the differences in traffic patterns for the three DMVPN phases. All three models support direct spoke-to-hub communication, as shown by R1 and R2.

19

Spoke-to-spoke packet flow in DMVPN Phase 1 is different from the packet flow in DMVPN Phases 2 and 3. Traffic between R3 and R4 must traverse the hub for Phase 1 DMVPN, whereas a dynamic spoke-to-spoke tunnel is created for DMVPN Phase 2 and Phase 3 that allows direct communication.

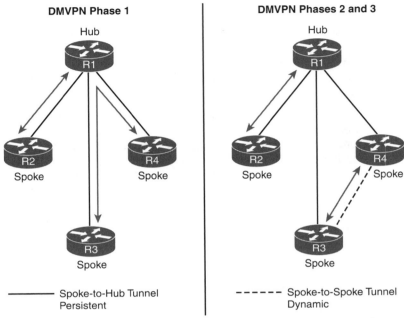

Figure 19-2 *DMVPN Traffic Patterns in the Different DMVPN Phases*

Figure 19-3 illustrates the difference in traffic patterns between Phase 2 and Phase 3 DMVPN with hierarchical topologies (multilevel). In this two-tier hierarchical design, R2 is the hub for DMVPN tunnel 20, and R3 is the hub for DMVPN tunnel 30. Connectivity between DMVPN tunnels 20 and 30 is established by DMVPN tunnel 10. All three DMVPN tunnels use the same DMVPN tunnel ID, even though they use different tunnel interfaces. For Phase 2 DMVPN tunnels, traffic from R5 must flow to the hub R2, where it is sent to R3 and then back down to R6. For Phase 3 DMVPN tunnels, a spoke-to-spoke tunnel is established between R5 and R6, and the two routers can communicate directly.

> **NOTE**   Each DMVPN phase has its own specific configuration. Intermixing DMVPN phases on the same tunnel network is not recommended. If you need to support multiple DMVPN phases for a migration, a second DMVPN network (subnet and tunnel interface) should be used.

This chapter explains the DMVPN fundamentals with DMVPN Phase 1 and then explains DMVPN Phase 3. It does not cover DMVPN Phase 2.

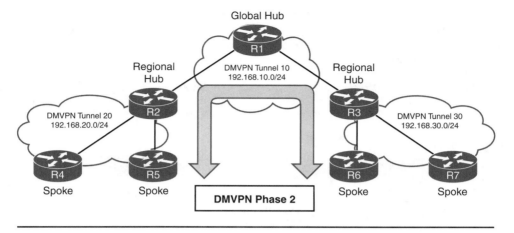

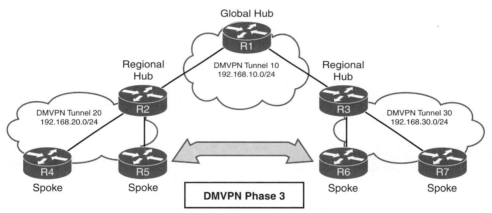

Figure 19-3 *Comparison of DMVPN Phase 2 and Phase 3*

DMVPN Configuration

There are two types of DMVPN configurations, hub and spoke, and which one is used depends on a router's role. The DMVPN hub is the NHRP NHS, and the DMVPN spoke is the NHRP NHC. The spokes should be preconfigured with the hub's static IP address, but a spoke's NBMA IP address can be static or can be assigned via DHCP.

> **NOTE**   In this book, the terms *spoke router* and *branch router* are used interchangeably, as are the terms *hub router* and *headquarters/data center router*.

Figure 19-4 shows the first topology used to explain DMVPN configuration and functions. R11 acts as the DMVPN hub, and R31 and R41 are the DMVPN spokes. All three routers use a static default route to the SP router that provides connectivity for the NBMA (transport) networks in the 172.16.0.0/16 network range. EIGRP has been configured to operate on the DMVPN tunnel and to advertise the local LAN networks with care to prevent recursive routing. Recursive routing is explained later in this chapter, in the section "Problems with Overlay Networks."

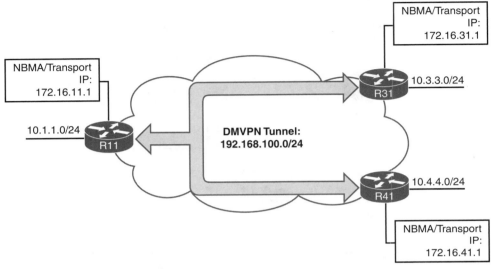

Figure 19-4 *Simple DMVPN Topology*

DMVPN Hub Configuration

The steps for configuring DMVPN on a hub router are as follows:

Step 1. Create the tunnel interface by using the global configuration command **interface tunnel** *tunnel-number*.

Step 2. Identify the local source of the tunnel by using the interface parameter command **tunnel source** {*ip-address* | *interface-id*}. The tunnel source depends on the transport type. The *encapsulating interface* can be a logical interface such as a loopback or a subinterface.

> **NOTE** QoS problems can occur with the use of loopback interfaces when there are multiple paths in the forwarding table to the decapsulating router. The same problems occur automatically with port channels, which are not recommended at the time of this writing.

Step 3. Configure the DMVPN tunnel as an mGRE tunnel by using the interface parameter command **tunnel mode gre multipoint**.

Step 4. Allocate an IP address for the DMVPN network (tunnel) by using the command **ip address** *ip-address subnet-mask*.

NOTE The subnet mask or size of the network should accommodate the total number of routers that are participating in the DMVPN tunnel. All the DMVPN tunnels in this book use /24, which accommodates 254 routers. Depending on the hardware used, the DMVPN network can scale much larger, to 2000 or more devices.

Step 5. Enable NHRP on the tunnel interface and uniquely identify the DMVPN tunnel for the virtual interface by using the interface parameter command **ip nhrp network-id** *1-4294967295*. The NHRP network ID is locally significant and is used to identify a DMVPN cloud on a router because multiple tunnel interfaces can belong to the same DMVPN cloud. It is recommended that the NHRP network ID match on all routers participating in the same DMVPN network.

Step 6. Optionally define the tunnel key, which helps identify the DMVPN virtual tunnel interface if multiple tunnel interfaces use the same tunnel source interfaces as defined in step 3. Tunnel keys, if configured, must match for a DMVPN tunnel to be established between two routers. The tunnel key adds 4 bytes to the DMVPN header. The tunnel key is configured with the command **tunnel key** *0-4294967295*.

NOTE There is no technical correlation between the NHRP network ID and the tunnel interface number; however, keeping them the same helps from an operational support standpoint.

Step 7. Optionally enable multicast support for NHRP. NHRP provides a mapping service of the protocol (tunnel IP) address to the NBMA (transport) address for multicast packets, too. To support multicast or routing protocols that use multicast, enable this on DMVPN hub routers by using the tunnel command **ip nhrp map multicast dynamic**.

Step 8. For Phase 3, enable NHRP redirect functions by using the command **ip nhrp redirect**.

Step 9. Optionally define the tunnel bandwidth, measured in kilobits per second, by using the interface parameter command **bandwidth** [*1-10000000*]. Virtual interfaces do not have the concept of latency and need to have a reference bandwidth configured so that routing protocols that use bandwidth for best-path calculation can make intelligent decisions. Bandwidth is also used for QoS configuration on the interface.

Step 10. Optionally configure the IP MTU for the tunnel interface by using the interface parameter command **ip mtu** *mtu*. Typically, an MTU of 1400 is used for DMVPN tunnels to account for the additional encapsulation overhead.

Step 11. Optionally define the TCP maximum segment size (MSS) by using the command **ip tcp adjust-mss** *mss-size*. The TCP Adjust MSS feature ensures that the router will edit the payload of a TCP three-way handshake if the MSS exceeds the configured value. Typically, DMVPN interfaces use a value of 1360 to accommodate IP, GRE, and IPsec headers.

19

> **NOTE** mGRE tunnels do not support the option for using a keepalive.

DMVPN Spoke Configuration for DMVPN Phase 1 (Point-to-Point)

The configuration of DMVPN Phase 1 spokes is similar to the configuration for a hub router except in two ways:

- You do not use an mGRE tunnel. Instead, you specify the tunnel destination.

- The NHRP mapping points to at least one active NHS.

The process for configuring a DMVPN Phase 1 spoke router is as follows:

Step 1. Create the tunnel interface by using the global configuration command **interface tunnel** *tunnel-number*.

Step 2. Identify the local source of the tunnel by using the interface parameter command **tunnel source** {*ip-address* | *interface-id*}.

Step 3. Identify the tunnel destination by using the interface parameter command **tunnel destination** *ip-address*. The tunnel destination is the DMVPN hub IP (NBMA) address that the local router uses to establish the DMVPN tunnel.

Step 4. Allocate an IP address for the DMVPN network (tunnel) by using the command **ip address** {*ip-address subnet-mask* | **dhcp**} or the command **ipv6 address** *ipv6-address/prefix-length*. At the time of this writing, DHCP is not supported for tunnel IPv6 address allocation.

Step 5. Enable NHRP on the tunnel interface and uniquely identify the DMVPN tunnel for the virtual interface by using the interface parameter command **ip nhrp network-id** *1-4294967295*.

Step 6. Optionally define the NHRP tunnel key, which helps identify the DMVPN virtual tunnel interface if multiple tunnels terminate on the same interface as defined in step 3. Tunnel keys must match for a DMVPN tunnel to establish between two routers. The tunnel key adds 4 bytes to the DMVPN header. Configure the tunnel by using the command **tunnel key** *0-4294967295*.

> **NOTE** If the tunnel key is defined on the hub router, it must be defined on all the spoke routers.

Step 7. Specify the address of one or more NHRP NHSs by using the command **ip nhrp nhs** *nbs-address* **nbma** *nbma-address* [**multicast**]. The **multicast** keyword provides multicast mapping functions in NHRP and is required to support the following routing protocols: RIP, EIGRP, and Open Shortest Path First (OSPF). Using this command is the simplest method of defining the NHRP configuration. Table 19-5 lists the alternative NHRP mapping commands, which are needed only in cases where a static unicast or multicast map is needed for a node that is not an NHS.

Table 19-5   Alternative NHRP Mapping Commands

Command	Function
ip nhrp nhs *nhs-address*	Creates an NHS entry and assigns it to the tunnel IP address.
ip nhrp map *ip-address nbma-address*	Maps the NBMA address to the tunnel IP address.
ip nhrp map multicast [*nbma-address* | dynamic]	Maps NBMA addresses used as destinations for broadcast or multicast packets to be sent across the network.

NOTE   Remember that the NBMA address is the transport IP address, and the NHS address is the protocol address for the DMVPN hub. This is the hardest concept for most network engineers to remember.

Step 8.   Optionally define the tunnel bandwidth, measured in kilobits per second, by using the interface parameter command **bandwidth** [*1-10000000*]. Virtual interfaces do not have the concept of latency and need to have a reference bandwidth configured so that routing protocols that use bandwidth for best-path calculation can make intelligent decisions. Bandwidth is also used for QoS configuration on the interface.

Step 9.   Optionally define the IP MTU for the tunnel interface by using the interface parameter command **ip mtu** *mtu*. Typically an MTU of 1400 is used for DMVPN tunnels to account for the additional encapsulation overhead.

Step 10.   Optionally define the TCP MSS by using the command **ip tcp adjust-mss** *mss-size*. The TCP Adjust MSS feature ensures that the router will edit the payload of a TCP three-way handshake if the MSS exceeds the configured value. Typically DMVPN interfaces use a value of 1360 to accommodate IP, GRE, and IPsec headers.

Example 19-6 provides a sample configuration for R11 (hub), R31 (spoke), and R41 (spoke). Notice that R11 uses the **tunnel mode gre multipoint** configuration, whereas R31 and R41 use **tunnel destination 172.16.11.1** (R11's transport endpoint IP address). All three routers have the appropriate MTU, bandwidth, and TCP maximum segment size (MSS) values set.

NOTE   R31's NHRP settings are configured with a single multi-value NHRP command, whereas R41's configuration uses three NHRP commands to provide identical functions. This configuration is highlighted in Example 19-6, which demonstrates the complexity the configuration may add for typical uses.

19

Example 19-6   *Phase 1 DMVPN Configuration*

```
R11-Hub
interface Tunnel100
 bandwidth 4000
 ip address 192.168.100.11 255.255.255.0
 ip mtu 1400
 ip nhrp map multicast dynamic
 ip nhrp network-id 100
 ip tcp adjust-mss 1360
 tunnel source GigabitEthernet0/1
 tunnel mode gre multipoint
 tunnel key 100
```

```
R31-Spoke (Single Command NHRP Configuration)
interface Tunnel100
 bandwidth 4000
 ip address 192.168.100.31 255.255.255.0
 ip mtu 1400
 ip nhrp network-id 100
 ip nhrp nhs 192.168.100.11 nbma 172.16.11.1 multicast
 ip tcp adjust-mss 1360
 tunnel source GigabitEthernet0/1
 tunnel destination 172.16.11.1
 tunnel key 100
```

```
R41-Spoke (Multi-Command NHRP Configuration)
interface Tunnel100
 bandwidth 4000
 ip address 192.168.100.41 255.255.255.0
 ip mtu 1400
 ip nhrp map 192.168.100.11 172.16.11.1
 ip nhrp map multicast 172.16.11.1
 ip nhrp network-id 100
 ip nhrp nhs 192.168.100.11
 ip tcp adjust-mss 1360
 tunnel source GigabitEthernet0/1
 tunnel destination 172.16.11.1
 tunnel key 100
```

Viewing DMVPN Tunnel Status

After configuring a DMVPN network, it is a good practice to verify that the tunnels have been established and that NHRP is functioning properly.

The command **show dmvpn [detail]** provides the tunnel interface, tunnel role, tunnel state, and tunnel peers with uptime. When the DMVPN tunnel interface is administratively shut down, there are no entries associated with that tunnel interface. These are the tunnel states, in order of establishment:

- **INTF:** The line protocol of the DMVPN tunnel is down.

- **IKE:** DMVPN tunnels configured with IPsec have not yet successfully established an Internet Key Exchange (IKE) session.

- **Ipsec:** An IKE session has been established, but an Ipsec security association (SA) has not yet been established.

- **NHRP:** The DMVPN spoke router has not yet successfully registered.

- **Up:** The DMVPN spoke router has registered with the DMVPN hub and received an ACK (positive registration reply) from the hub.

Example 19-7 provides sample output of the command **show dmvpn**. The output indicates that R31 and R41 have defined one tunnel with one NHS (R11). This entry is in a static state because of the static NHRP mappings in the tunnel interface. R11 has two tunnels that were learned dynamically when R31 and R41 registered and established a tunnel to R11.

Example 19-7   *Viewing the DMVPN Tunnel Status for DMVPN Phase 1*

```
R11-Hub# show dmvpn
Legend: Attrb ◊-S - Static,-D - Dynamic,-I - Incomplete
          -N - NATed,-L - Local,-X - No Socket
           -1 - Route Installed, -2 - Nexthop-override
          -C - CTS Capable
           # Ent --> Number of NHRP entries with same NBMA peer
           NHS Status: E --> Expecting Replies, R --> Responding, W --> Waiting
           UpDn Time --> Up or Down Time for a Tunn==


Interface: Tunnel100, IPv4 NHRP Details
Type:Hub, NHRP Peers:2,


 # Ent  Peer NBMA Addr Peer Tunnel Add State  UpDn Tm Attrb
 -----  -------------- --------------- ----- -------- -----
     1 172.16.31.1      192.168.100.31   UP 00:05:26      D
     1 172.16.41.1      192.168.100.41   UP 00:05:26      D

R31-Spoke# show dmvpn
! Output omitted for brevity
Interface: Tunnel100, IPv4 NHRP Details
Type:Spoke, NHRP Peers:1,
```

```
# Ent   Peer NBMA Addr Peer Tunnel Add State   UpDn Tm Attrb
----- --------------- --------------- ----- -------- -----
    1 172.16.11.1      192.168.100.11     UP 00:05:26       S
```

```
R41-Spoke# show dmvpn
! Output omitted for brevity
Interface: Tunnel100, IPv4 NHRP Details
Type:Spoke, NHRP Peers:1,

# Ent   Peer NBMA Addr Peer Tunnel Add State   UpDn Tm Attrb
----- --------------- --------------- ----- -------- -----
    1 172.16.11.1      192.168.100.11    UP  00:05:26       S
```

NOTE   Both routers must maintain an up NHRP state with each other for data traffic to flow successfully between them.

Example 19-8 provides output of the command **show dmvpn detail**. Notice that the **detail** keyword provides the local tunnel and NBMA IP addresses, tunnel health monitoring, and VRF contexts. In addition, IPsec crypto information (if configured) is displayed.

Example 19-8   *Viewing the DMVPN Tunnel Status for Phase 1 DMVPN*

```
R11-Hub# show dmvpn detail
Legend: Attrb --> S - Static, D - Dynamic, I - Incomplete
            N - NATed, L - Local, X - No Socket
            T1 - Route Installed, T2 - Nexthop-override
            C - CTS Capable
            # Ent --> Number of NHRP entries with same NBMA peer
            NHS Status: E --> Expecting Replies, R --> Responding, W --> Waiting
            UpDn Time --> Up or Down Time for a Tunnel
==========================================================================

Interface Tunnel100 is up/up, Addr. is 192.168.100.11, VRF ""
    Tunnel Src./Dest. addr: 172.16.11.1/MGRE, Tunnel VRF ""
    Protocol/Transport: "multi-GRE/IP"", Protect ""
    Interface State Control: Disabled
    nhrp event-publisher : Disabled
Type:Hub, Total NBMA Peers (v4/v6): 2

# Ent   Peer NBMA Addr Peer Tunnel Add State   UpDn Tm Attrb    Target Network
----- --------------- --------------- ----- -------- ----- -----------------
```

```
      1 172.16.31.1          192.168.100.31      UP 00:01:05      D   192.168.100.31/32
      1 172.16.41.1          192.168.100.41      UP 00:01:06      D   192.168.100.41/32
```

```
R31-Spoke# show dmvpn detail
! Output omitted for brevity


Interface Tunnel100 is up/up, Addr. is 192.168.100.31, VRF ""
   Tunnel Src./Dest. addr: 172.16.31.1/172.16.11.1, Tunnel VRF ""
   Protocol/Transport: "GRE/IP", Protect ""
   Interface State Control: Disabled
   nhrp event-publisher : Disabled
IPv4 NHS:
192.168.100.11 RE NBMA Address: 172.16.11.1 priority = 0 cluster = 0
Type:Spoke, Total NBMA Peers (v4/v6): 1


# Ent   Peer NBMA Addr Peer Tunnel Add State  UpDn Tm Attrb    Target Ne
----- --------------- --------------- ----- -------- ----- ------------
      1 172.16.11.1          192.168.100.11      UP 00:00:28      S   192.168.100
```

```
R41-Spoke# show dmvpn detail
! Output omitted for brevity


Interface Tunnel100 is up/up, Addr. is 192.168.100.41, VRF ""
   Tunnel Src./Dest. addr: 172.16.41.1/172.16.11.1, Tunnel VRF " "
   Protocol/Transport: "GRE/IP", Protect ""
   Interface State Control: Disabled
   nhrp event-publisher : Disabled


IPv4 NHS:
192.168.100.11 RE NBMA Address: 172.16.11.1 priority = 0 cluster = 0
Type:Spoke, Total NBMA Peers (v4/v6): 1


# Ent   Peer NBMA Addr Peer Tunnel Add State  UpDn Tm Attrb    Target Network
----- --------------- --------------- ----- -------- ----- ----------------
      1 172.16.11.1          192.168.100.11      UP 00:02:00      S   192.168.100.11/32
```

Viewing the NHRP Cache

The information that NHRP provides is a vital component of the operation of DMVPN. Every router maintains a cache of requests that it receives or is processing. The command **show ip nhrp [brief]** displays the local NHRP cache on a router. The NHRP cache contains the following fields:

- Network entry for hosts (IPv4: /32 or IPv6: /128) or for a *network*/xx and the tunnel IP address to NBMA (transport) IP address.

- The interface number, duration of existence, and when it will expire (*hours:minutes:seconds*). Only dynamic entries expire.

- The NHRP mapping entry type. Table 19-6 provides a list of NHRP mapping entries in the local cache.

Table 19-6   NHRP Mapping Entries

NHRP Mapping Entry	Description
static	An entry created statically on a DMVPN interface.
dynamic	An entry created dynamically. In DMVPN Phase 1, it is an entry created from a spoke that registered with an NHS with an NHRP registration request.
incomplete	A temporary entry placed locally while an NHRP resolution request is processing. An incomplete entry prevents repetitive NHRP requests for the same entry, avoiding unnecessary consumption of router resources. Eventually this will time out and permit another NHRP resolution request for the same network.
local	Local mapping information. One typical entry represents a local network that was advertised for an NHRP resolution reply. This entry records which nodes received this local network mapping through an NHRP resolution reply.
(no-socket)	Mapping entries that do not have associated IPsec sockets and where encryption is not triggered.
NBMA address	Nonbroadcast multi-access address, or the transport IP address where the entry was received.

NHRP message flags specify attributes of an NHRP cache entry or of the peer for which the entry was created. Table 19-7 provides a list of the NHRP message flags and their meanings.

Table 19-7   NHRP Message Flags

NHRP Message Flag	Description
used	Indicates that this NHRP mapping entry was used to forward data packets within the past 60 seconds.
implicit	Indicates that the NHRP mapping entry was learned implicitly. Examples of such entries are the source mapping information gleaned from an NHRP resolution request received by the local router or from an NHRP resolution packet forwarded through the router.
unique	Indicates that this NHRP mapping entry must be unique and that it cannot be overwritten with a mapping entry that has the same tunnel IP address but a different NBMA address.
router	Indicates that this NHRP mapping entry is from a remote router that provides access to a network or host behind the remote router.
rib	Indicates that this NHRP mapping entry has a corresponding routing entry in the routing table. This entry has an associated *H* route.

NHRP Message Flag	Description
nho	Indicates that this NHRP mapping entry has a corresponding path that overrides the next hop for a remote network, as installed by another routing protocol.
nhop	Indicates an NHRP mapping entry for a remote next-hop address (for example, a remote tunnel interface) and its associated NBMA address.

The command **show ip nhrp [brief | detail]** displays the local NHRP cache on a router. Example 19-9 shows the local NHRP cache for the various routers in the sample topology. R11 contains only dynamic registrations for R31 and R41. In the event that R31 and R41 cannot maintain connectivity to R11's transport IP address, eventually the tunnel mapping is removed on R11. The NHRP message flags on R11 indicate that R31 and R41 successfully registered with the unique registration to R11 and that traffic has recently been forwarded to both routers.

Example 19-9 *Local NHRP Cache for DMVPN Phase 1*

```
R11-Hub# show ip nhrp
192.168.100.31/32 via 192.168.100.31
  Tunnel100 created 23:04:04, expire 01:37:26
  Type: dynamic, Flags: unique registered used nhop
  NBMA address: 172.16.31.1
192.168.100.41/32 via 192.168.100.41
  Tunnel100 created 23:04:00, expire 01:37:42
  Type: dynamic, Flags: unique registered used nhop
  NBMA address: 172.16.41.1

R31-Spoke# show ip nhrp
192.168.100.11/32 via 192.168.100.11
  Tunnel100 created 23:02:53, never expire
  Type: static, Flags:
  NBMA address: 172.16.11.1

R41-Spoke# show ip nhrp
192.168.100.11/32 via 192.168.100.11
  Tunnel100 created 23:02:53, never expire
  Type: static, Flags:
  NBMA address: 172.16.11.1
```

19

NOTE The optional **detail** keyword provides a list of routers that submitted NHRP resolution requests and their request IDs.

Example 19-10 shows the output of the **show ip nhrp brief** command. With the **brief** keyword, some information—such as the *used* and *nhop* NHRP message flags—is not shown.

Example 19-10   *Sample Output from the show ip nhrp brief Command*

```
R11-Hub# show ip nhrp brief
******************************************************************************
    NOTE: Link-Local, No-socket and Incomplete entries are not displayed
******************************************************************************
Legend: Type --> S - Static, D - Dynamic
        Flags --> u - unique, r - registered, e - temporary, c - claimed
        a - authoritative, t - route
==============================================================================
Intf      NextHop Address                              NBMA Address
          Target Network                    T/Flag
--------- ----------------------------------------- ------ ----------------

Tu100     192.168.100.31                               172.16.31.1
          192.168.100.31/32                 D/ur
Tu100     192.168.100.41                               172.16.41.1
          192.168.100.41/32                 D/ur
```

```
R31-Spoke# show ip nhrp brief
! Output omitted for brevity
Intf      NextHop Address                              NBMA Address
          Target Network                    T/Flag
--------- ----------------------------------------- ------ ----------------

Tu100     192.168.100.11                               172.16.11.1
          192.168.100.11/32                 S/
```

```
R41-Spoke# show ip nhrp brief
! Output omitted for brevity
Intf      NextHop Address                              NBMA Address
          Target Network                    T/Flag
--------- ----------------------------------------- ------ ----------------

Tu100     192.168.100.11                               172.16.11.1
          192.168.100.11/32                 S/
```

Example 19-11 shows the routing tables for R11, R31, and R41. All three routers maintain connectivity to the LAN networks 10.1.1.0/24, 10.3.3.0/24, and 10.4.4.0/24 for each of the routers. Notice that the next-hop address between spoke routers is 192.168.100.11 (R11).

Example 19-11   *DMVPN Phase 1 Routing Table*

```
R11-Hub# show ip route
! Output omitted for brevity
Codes: L - local,   C - connected, S - static, R - RIP, M - mobile, B - BGP
       D - EIGRP, EX - EIGRP external, O - OSPF, IA - OSPF inter area
```

```
Gateway of last resort is 172.16.11.2 to network 0.0.0.0


S*      0.0.0.0/0 [1/0] via 172.16.11.2
        10.0.0.0/8 is variably subnetted, 4 subnets, 2 masks
C          10.1.1.0/24 is directly connected, GigabitEthernet0/2
D          10.3.3.0/24 [90/27392000] via 192.168.100.31, 23:03:53, Tunnel100
D          10.4.4.0/24 [90/27392000] via 192.168.100.41, 23:03:28, Tunnel100
        172.16.0.0/16 is variably subnetted, 2 subnets, 2 masks
C          172.16.11.0/30 is directly connected, GigabitEthernet0/1
        192.168.100.0/24 is variably subnetted, 2 subnets, 2 masks
C          192.168.100.0/24 is directly connected, Tunnel100
```

```
R31-Spoke# show ip route
! Output omitted for brevity
Gateway of last resort is 172.16.31.2 to network 0.0.0.0
S*      0.0.0.0/0 [1/0] via 172.16.31.2
        10.0.0.0/8 is variably subnetted, 4 subnets, 2 masks
D          10.1.1.0/24 [90/26885120] via 192.168.100.11, 23:04:48, Tunnel100
C          10.3.3.0/24 is directly connected, GigabitEthernet0/2
D          10.4.4.0/24 [90/52992000] via 192.168.100.11, 23:04:23, Tunnel100
        172.16.0.0/16 is variably subnetted, 2 subnets, 2 masks
C          172.16.31.0/30 is directly connected, GigabitEthernet0/1
        192.168.100.0/24 is variably subnetted, 2 subnets, 2 masks
C          192.168.100.0/24 is directly connected, Tunnel100
```

```
R41-Spoke# show ip route
! Output omitted for brevity
Gateway of last resort is 172.16.41.2 to network 0.0.0.0


S*      0.0.0.0/0 [1/0] via 172.16.41.2
        10.0.0.0/8 is variably subnetted, 4 subnets, 2 masks
D          10.1.1.0/24 [90/26885120] via 192.168.100.11, 23:05:01, Tunnel100
D          10.3.3.0/24 [90/52992000] via 192.168.100.11, 23:05:01, Tunnel100
C          10.4.4.0/24 is directly connected, GigabitEthernet0/2
        172.16.0.0/16 is variably subnetted, 2 subnets, 2 masks
C          172.16.41.0/24 is directly connected, GigabitEthernet0/1
        192.168.100.0/24 is variably subnetted, 2 subnets, 2 masks
C          192.168.100.0/24 is directly connected, Tunnel100
```

The traceroute shown in Example 19-12 verifies that R31 can connect to R41, but network traffic must still pass through R11.

Example 19-12 *Phase 1 DMVPN Traceroute from R31 to R41*

```
R31-Spoke# traceroute 10.4.4.1 source 10.3.3.1
Tracing the route to 10.4.4.1
  1 192.168.100.11 0 msec 0 msec 1 msec
  2 192.168.100.41 1 msec * 1 msec
```

DMVPN Configuration for Phase 3 DMVPN (Multipoint)

The Phase 3 DMVPN configuration for the hub router adds the interface parameter command **ip nhrp redirect** on the hub router. This command checks the flow of packets on the tunnel interface and sends a redirect message to the source spoke router when it detects packets hairpinning out of the DMVPN cloud. *Hairpinning* means that traffic is received and sent out an interface in the same cloud (identified by the NHRP network ID). For instance, hairpinning occurs when packets come in and go out the same tunnel interface.

The Phase 3 DMVPN configuration for spoke routers uses the mGRE tunnel interface and uses the command **ip nhrp shortcut** on the tunnel interface.

> **NOTE**   There are no negative effects of placing **ip nhrp shortcut** and **ip nhrp redirect** on the same DMVPN tunnel interface.

The process for configuring a DMVPN Phase 3 spoke router is as follows:

Step 1.   Create the tunnel interface by using the global configuration command **interface tunnel** *tunnel-number*.

Step 2.   Identify the local source of the tunnel by using the interface parameter command **tunnel source** {*ip-address* | *interface-id*}.

Step 3.   Configure the DMVPN tunnel as a GRE multipoint tunnel by using the interface parameter command **tunnel mode gre multipoint**.

Step 4.   Allocate an IP address for the DMVPN network (tunnel) by using the command **ip address** *ip-address subnet-mask*.

Step 5.   Enable NHRP and uniquely identify the DMVPN tunnel for the virtual interface by using the interface parameter command **ip nhrp network-id** *1-4294967295*.

Step 6.   Optionally configure the tunnel key by using the command **tunnel key** *0-4294967295*. Tunnel keys must match for a DMVPN tunnel to be established between two routers.

Step 7.   Enable the NHRP shortcut function by using the command **ip nhrp shortcut**.

Step 8.   Specify the address of one or more NHRP NHSs by using the command **ip nhrp nhs** *nhs-address* **nbma** *nbma-address* [**multicast**].

Step 9.   Optionally define the IP MTU for the tunnel interface by using the interface parameter command **ip mtu** *mtu*. Typically, an MTU of 1400 is used for DMVPN tunnels.

Step 10.   Optionally define the TCP MSS feature, which ensures that the router will edit the payload of a TCP three-way handshake if the MSS exceeds the configured value. The command is **ip tcp adjust-mss** *mss-size*. Typically, DMVPN interfaces use a value of 1360 to accommodate IP, GRE, and IPsec headers.

Example 19-13 provides a sample configuration for R11 (hub), R21 (spoke), and R31 (spoke) configured with Phase 3 DMVPN. Notice that all three routers have **tunnel mode gre**

multipoint and have the appropriate MTU, bandwidth, and TCP MSS values set. For R11 you use the command **ip nhrp redirect**, and for R31 and R41 you use the command **ip nhrp shortcut**.

Example 19-13   *DMVPN Phase 3 Configuration for Spokes*

```
R11-Hub
interface Tunnel100
 bandwidth 4000
 ip address 192.168.100.11 255.255.255.0
 ip mtu 1400
 ip nhrp map multicast dynamic
 ip nhrp network-id 100
 ip nhrp redirect
 ip tcp adjust-mss 1360
 tunnel source GigabitEthernet0/1
 tunnel mode gre multipoint
 tunnel key 100
```

```
R31-Spoke
interface Tunnel100
 bandwidth 4000
 ip address 192.168.100.31 255.255.255.0
 ip mtu 1400
 ip nhrp network-id 100
 ip nhrp nhs 192.168.100.11 nbma 172.16.11.1 multicast
 ip nhrp shortcut
 ip tcp adjust-mss 1360
 tunnel source GigabitEthernet0/1
 tunnel mode gre multipoint
 tunnel key 100
```

```
R41-Spoke
interface Tunnel100
 bandwidth 4000
 ip address 192.168.100.41 255.255.255.0
 ip mtu 1400
 ip nhrp network-id 100
 ip nhrp nhs 192.168.100.11 nbma 172.16.11.1 multicast
 ip nhrp shortcut
 ip tcp adjust-mss 1360
 tunnel source GigabitEthernet0/1
 tunnel mode gre multipoint
 tunnel key 100
```

19

IP NHRP Authentication

NHRP includes an authentication capability, but this authentication is weak because the password is stored in plaintext. Most network administrators use NHRP authentication as a method to ensure that two different tunnels do not accidentally form. You enable NHRP authentication by using the interface parameter command **ip nhrp authentication** *password*.

Unique IP NHRP Registration

When an NHC registers with an NHS, it provides the protocol (tunnel IP) address and the NBMA (transport IP) address. By default, an NHC requests that the NHS keep the NBMA address assigned to the protocol address unique so that the NBMA address cannot be over-written with a different IP address. The NHS maintains a local cache of these settings. This capability is indicated by the NHRP message flag *unique* on the NHS, as shown in Example 19-14.

Example 19-14   *Unique NHRP Registration*

```
R11-Hub# show ip nhrp 192.168.100.31
192.168.100.31/32 via 192.168.100.31
    Tunnel100 created 00:11:24, expire 01:48:35
    Type: dynamic, Flags: unique registered used nhop
    NBMA address: 172.16.31.1
```

If an NHC client attempts to register with the NHS using a different NBMA address, the registration process fails. Example 19-15 demonstrates this concept by disabling the DMVPN tunnel interface, changing the IP address on the transport interface, and reenabling the DMVPN tunnel interface. Notice that the DMVPN hub denies the NHRP registration because the protocol address is registered to a different NBMA address.

Example 19-15   *Failure to Connect Because of Unique Registration*

```
R31-Spoke(config)# interface tunnel 100
R31-Spoke(config-if)# shutdown
00:17:48.910: %DUAL-5-NBRCHANGE: EIGRP-IPv4 100: Neighbor 192.168.100.11
        (Tunnel100) is down: interface down
00:17:50.910: %LINEPROTO-5-UPDOWN: Line protocol on Interface Tunnel100,
    changed state to down
00:17:50.910: %LINK-5-CHANGED: Interface Tunnel100, changed state to
    administratively down
R31-Spoke(config-if)# interface GigabitEthernet0/1
R31-Spoke(config-if)# ip address 172.16.31.31 255.255.255.0
R31-Spoke(config-if)# interface tunnel 100
R31-Spoke(config-if)# no shutdown
00:18:21.011: %NHRP-3-PAKREPLY: Receive Registration Reply packet with error -
    unique address registered already(14)
00:18:22.010: %LINEPROTO-5-UPDOWN: Line protocol on Interface Tunnel100, changed
    state to up
```

This can cause problems for sites with transport interfaces that connect using DHCP, where they could be assigned different IP addresses before the NHRP cache times out. If a router loses connectivity and is assigned a different IP address, because of its age, it cannot register with the NHS router until that router's entry is flushed from the NHRP cache.

The interface parameter command **ip nhrp registration no-unique** stops routers from placing the *unique* NHRP message flag in registration request packets sent to the NHS. This allows clients to reconnect to the NHS even if the NBMA address changes. This should be enabled on all DHCP-enabled spoke interfaces. However, placing this on all spoke tunnel interfaces keeps the configuration consistent for all tunnel interfaces and simplifies verification of settings from an operational perspective.

> **NOTE** The NHC (spoke) has to register for this change to take effect on the NHS. This happens during the normal NHRP expiration timers or can be accelerated by resetting the tunnel interface on the spoke router before its transport IP address changes.

Spoke-to-Spoke Communication

After the configuration on R11, R31, and R41 has been modified to support DMVPN Phase 3, the tunnels are established. All the DMVPN, NHRP, and routing tables look exactly as they did in Examples 19-7 through 19-11. Note that no traffic is exchanged between R31 and R41 at this time.

This section focuses on the underlying mechanisms used to establish spoke-to-spoke communication. In DMVPN Phase 1, the spoke devices rely on the configured tunnel destination to identify where to send the encapsulated packets. Phase 3 DMVPN uses mGRE tunnels and thereby relies on NHRP redirect and resolution request messages to identify the NBMA addresses for any destination networks.

Packets flow through the hub in a traditional hub-and-spoke manner until the spoke-to-spoke tunnel has been established in both directions. As packets flow across the hub, the hub engages NHRP redirection to start the process of finding a more optimal path with spoke-to-spoke tunnels.

In Example 19-16, R31 initiates a traceroute to R41. Notice that the first packet travels across R11 (hub), but by the time a second stream of packets is sent, the spoke-to-spoke tunnel has been initialized so that traffic flows directly between R31 and R41 on the transport and overlay networks.

Example 19-16 *Initiation of Traffic Between Spoke Routers*

```
! Initial Packet Flow
R31-Spoke# traceroute 10.4.4.1 source 10.3.3.1
Tracing the route to 10.4.4.1
  1 192.168.100.11 5 msec 1 msec 0 msec <- This is the Hub Router (R11-Hub)
  2 192.168.100.41 5 msec * 1 msec

! Packetflow after Spoke-to-Spoke Tunnel is Established
R31-Spoke# traceroute 10.4.4.1 source 10.3.3.1
Tracing the route to 10.4.4.1
  1 192.168.100.41 1 msec * 0 msec
```

19

Forming Spoke-to-Spoke Tunnels

This section explains in detail how a spoke-to-spoke DMVPN tunnel is formed. Figure 19-5 illustrates the packet flow among all three devices—R11, R31, and R41—to establish a bidirectional spoke-to-spoke DMVPN tunnel.

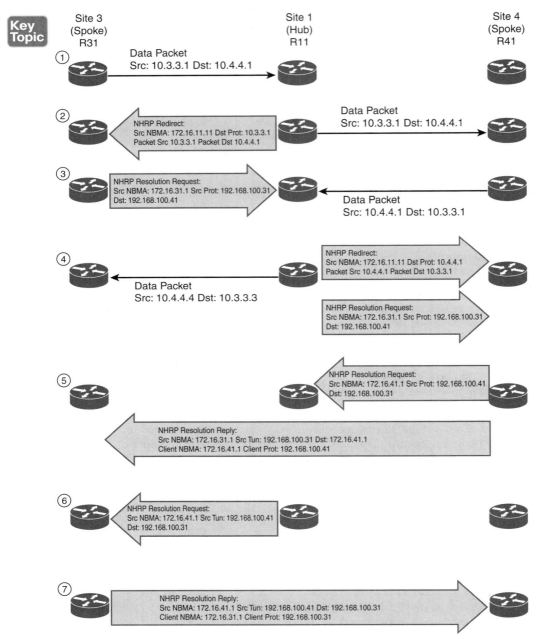

Figure 19-5   *Phase 3 DMVPN Spoke-to-Spoke Traffic Flow and Tunnel Creation*

The numbers in Figure 19-5 correspond to the steps in the following list:

Step 1.   R31 performs a route lookup for 10.4.4.1 and finds the entry 10.4.4.0/24 with the next-hop IP address 192.168.100.11. R31 encapsulates the packet destined for 10.4.4.1 and forwards it to R11 out the tunnel 100 interface.

Step 2.   R11 receives the packet from R31 and performs a route lookup for the packet destined for 10.4.4.1. R11 locates the 10.4.4.0/24 network with the next-hop IP address 192.168.100.41. R11 checks the NHRP cache and locates the entry for the 192.168.100.41/32 address. R11 forwards the packet to R41, using the NBMA IP address 172.16.41.1, found in the NHRP cache. The packet is then forwarded out the same tunnel interface.

R11 has **ip nhrp redirect** configured on the tunnel interface and recognizes that the packet received from R31 hairpinned out of the tunnel interface. R11 sends an NHRP redirect to R31, indicating the packet source 10.3.3.1 and destination 10.4.4.1. The NHRP redirect indicates to R31 that the traffic is using a suboptimal path.

Step 3.   R31 receives the NHRP redirect and sends an NHRP resolution request to R11 for the 10.4.4.1 address. Inside the NHRP resolution request, R31 provides its protocol (tunnel IP) address, 192.168.100.31, and source NBMA address, 172.16.31.1. R41 performs a route lookup for 10.3.3.1 and finds the entry 10.3.3.0/24 with the next-hop IP address 192.168.100.11. R41 encapsulates the packet destined for 10.4.4.1 and forwards it to R11 out the tunnel 100 interface.

Step 4.   R11 receives the packet from R41 and performs a route lookup for the packet destined for 10.3.3.1. R11 locates the 10.3.3.0/24 network with the next-hop IP address 192.168.100.31. R11 checks the NHRP cache and locates an entry for 192.168.100.31/32. R11 forwards the packet to R31, using the NBMA IP address 172.16.31.1, found in the NHRP cache. The packet is then forwarded out the same tunnel interface. R11 has **ip nhrp redirect** configured on the tunnel interface and recognizes that the packet received from R41 hairpinned out the tunnel interface. R11 sends an NHRP redirect to R41, indicating the packet source 10.4.4.1 and destination 10.3.3.1 The NHRP redirect indicates to R41 that the traffic is using a suboptimal path. R11 forwards R31's NHRP resolution requests for the 10.4.4.1 address.

Step 5.   R41 sends an NHRP resolution request to R11 for the 10.3.3.1 address and provides its protocol (tunnel IP) address, 192.168.100.41, and source NBMA address, 172.16.41.1. R41 sends an NHRP resolution reply directly to R31, using the source information from R31's NHRP resolution request. The NHRP resolution reply contains the original source information in R31's NHRP resolution request as a method of verification and contains the client protocol address of 192.168.100.41 and the client NBMA address 172.16.41.1. (If IPsec protection is configured, the IPsec tunnel is set up before the NHRP reply is sent.)

19

NOTE   The NHRP reply is for the entire subnet rather than the specified host address.

Step 6.   R11 forwards R41's NHRP resolution requests for the 192.168.100.31 and 10.4.4.1 entries.

Step 7.   R31 sends an NHRP resolution reply directly to R41, using the source information from R41's NHRP resolution request. The NHRP resolution reply contains the original source information in R41's NHRP resolution request as a method of verification and contains the client protocol address 192.168.100.31 and the client NBMA address 172.16.31.1. (Again, if IPsec protection is configured, the tunnel is set up before the NHRP reply is sent back in the other direction.)

A spoke-to-spoke DMVPN tunnel is established in both directions after step 7 is complete. This allows traffic to flow across the spoke-to-spoke tunnel instead of traversing the hub router.

Example 19-17 shows the status of DMVPN tunnels on R31 and R41, where there are two new spoke-to-spoke tunnels (highlighted). The *DLX* entries represent the local (no-socket) routes. The original tunnel to R11 remains a static tunnel.

Example 19-17   *Detailed NHRP Mapping with Spoke-to-Hub Traffic*

```
R31-Spoke# show dmvpn detail
Legend: Attrb --> S - Static, D - Dynamic, I - Incomplete
          N - NATed, L - Local, X - No Socket
          T1 - Route Installed, T2 - Nexthop-override
          C - CTS Capable
          # Ent --> Number of NHRP entries with same NBMA peer
          NHS Status: E --> Expecting Replies, R --> Responding, W --> Waiting
          UpDn Time --> Up or Down Time for a Tunnel
==============================================================================
Interface Tunnel100 is up/up, Addr. is 192.168.100.31, VRF ""
      Src./Dest. addr: 172.16.31.1/MGRE, Tunnel VRF ""
      Protocol/Transport: "multi-GRE/IP", Protect ""
      Interface State Control: Disabled
      nhrp event-publisher : Disabled


IPv4 NHS:
192.168.100.11 RE NBMA Address: 172.16.11.1 priority = 0 cluster = 0
Type:Spoke, Total NBMA Peers (v4/v6): 3


# Ent  Peer NBMA Addr Peer Tunnel Add State  UpDn Tm Attrb   Target Network
----- --------------- --------------- ----- -------- ----- ----------------
    1 172.16.31.1     192.168.100.31  UP 00:00:10   DLX      10.3.3.0/24
    2 172.16.41.1     192.168.100.41  UP 00:00:10   DT2    10.4.4.0/24
      172.16.41.1     192.168.100.41  UP 00:00:10   DT1    192.168.100.41/32
    1 172.16.11.1     192.168.100.11  UP 00:00:51     S    192.168.100.11/32
R41-Spoke# show dmvpn detail
! Output omitted for brevity
```

```
IPv4 NHS:
192.168.100.11 RE NBMA Address: 172.16.11.1 priority = 0 cluster = 0
Type:Spoke, Total NBMA Peers (v4/v6): 3


# Ent   Peer NBMA Addr Peer Tunnel Add State  UpDn Tm Attrb   Target Network
-----   -------------- --------------- -----  -------- -----   ----------------
    2 172.16.31.1      192.168.100.31  UP 00:00:34  DT2       10.3.3.0/24
      172.16.31.1      192.168.100.31  UP 00:00:34  DT1    192.168.100.31/32
    1 172.16.41.1      192.168.100.41  UP 00:00:34  DLX       10.4.4.0/24
    1 172.16.11.1      192.168.100.11  UP 00:01:15   S     192.168.100.11/32
```

Example 19-18 shows the NHRP cache for R31 and R41. Notice the NHRP mappings *router*, *rib*, *nho*, and *nhop*. The flag *rib nho* indicates that the router has found an identical route in the routing table that belongs to a different protocol. NHRP has overridden the other protocol's next-hop entry for the network by installing a *next-hop shortcut* in the routing table. The flag *rib nhop* indicates that the router has an explicit method to reach the tunnel IP address using an NBMA address and has an associated route installed in the routing table.

Example 19-18 *NHRP Mapping with Spoke-to-Hub Traffic*

```
R31-Spoke# show ip nhrp detail
10.3.3.0/24 via 192.168.100.31
    Tunnel100 created 00:01:44, expire 01:58:15
    Type: dynamic, Flags: router unique local
    NBMA address: 172.16.31.1
    Preference: 255
    (no-socket)
    Requester: 192.168.100.41 Request ID: 3
10.4.4.0/24 via 192.168.100.41
    Tunnel100 created 00:01:44, expire 01:58:15
    Type: dynamic, Flags: router rib nho
    NBMA address: 172.16.41.1
    Preference: 255
192.168.100.11/32 via 192.168.100.11
    Tunnel100 created 10:43:18, never expire
    Type: static, Flags: used
    NBMA address: 172.16.11.1
    Preference: 255
192.168.100.41/32 via 192.168.100.41
    Tunnel100 created 00:01:45, expire 01:58:15
    Type: dynamic, Flags: router used nhop rib
    NBMA address: 172.16.41.1
    Preference: 255

R41-Spoke# show ip nhrp detail
10.3.3.0/24 via 192.168.100.31
```

19

```
    Tunnel100 created 00:02:04, expire 01:57:55
    Type: dynamic, Flags: router rib nho
    NBMA address: 172.16.31.1
    Preference: 255
10.4.4.0/24 via 192.168.100.41
    Tunnel100 created 00:02:04, expire 01:57:55
    Type: dynamic, Flags: router unique local
    NBMA address: 172.16.41.1
    Preference: 255
      (no-socket)
    Requester: 192.168.100.31 Request ID: 3
192.168.100.11/32 via 192.168.100.11
    Tunnel100 created 10:43:42, never expire
    Type: static, Flags: used
    NBMA address: 172.16.11.1
    Preference: 255
192.168.100.31/32 via 192.168.100.31
    Tunnel100 created 00:02:04, expire 01:57:55
    Type: dynamic, Flags: router used nhop rib
    NBMA address: 172.16.31.1 Preference: 255
```

NOTE   Example 19-18 uses the optional **detail** keyword for viewing the NHRP cache information. The 10.3.3.0/24 entry on R31 and the 10.4.4.0/24 entry on R41 display a list of devices to which the router responded to resolution request packets and the request ID that they received.

NHRP Routing Table Manipulation

NHRP tightly interacts with the routing/forwarding tables and installs or modifies routes in the *Routing Information Base* (*RIB*), also known as the routing table, as necessary. In the event that an entry exists with an exact match for the network and prefix length, NHRP overrides the existing next hop with a shortcut. The original protocol is still responsible for the prefix, but overwritten next-hop addresses are indicated in the routing table by the percent sign (%).

Example 19-19 provides the routing tables for R31 and R41. The next-hop IP address for the EIGRP remote network (highlighted) still shows 192.168.100.11 as the next-hop address but includes a percent sign (%) to indicate a next-hop override. Notice that R31 installs the NHRP route to 192.168.10.41/32 and that R41 installs the NHRP route to 192.168.100.31/32 into the routing table as well.

Example 19-19   *NHRP Routing Table Manipulation*

```
R31-Spoke# show ip route
! Output omitted for brevity
Codes: L - local, C - connected, S - static, R - RIP, M - mobile, B - BGP
       D - EIGRP, EX - EIGRP external, O - OSPF, IA - OSPF inter area
       o - ODR, P - periodic downloaded static route, H - NHRP, l - LISP
       + - replicated route, % - next hop override, p - overrides from PfR


Gateway of last resort is 172.16.31.2 to network 0.0.0.0

S*     0.0.0.0/0 [1/0] via 172.16.31.2
       10.0.0.0/8 is variably subnetted, 4 subnets, 2 masks
D         10.1.1.0/24 [90/26885120] via 192.168.100.11, 10:44:45, Tunnel100
C         10.3.3.0/24 is directly connected, GigabitEthernet0/2
D %       10.4.4.0/24 [90/52992000] via 192.168.100.11, 10:44:45, Tunnel100
       172.16.0.0/16 is variably subnetted, 2 subnets, 2 masks
C         172.16.31.0/30 is directly connected, GigabitEthernet0/1
       192.168.100.0/24 is variably subnetted, 3 subnets, 2 masks
C         192.168.100.0/24 is directly connected, Tunnel100
H         192.168.100.41/32 is directly connected, 00:03:21, Tunnel100
```

```
R41-Spoke# show ip route
! Output omitted for brevity
Gateway of last resort is 172.16.41.2 to network 0.0.0.0
S*     0.0.0.0/0 [1/0] via 172.16.41.2
       10.0.0.0/8 is variably subnetted, 4 subnets, 2 masks
D         10.1.1.0/24 [90/26885120] via 192.168.100.11, 10:44:34, Tunnel100
D %       10.3.3.0/24 [90/52992000] via 192.168.100.11, 10:44:34, Tunnel100
C         10.4.4.0/24 is directly connected, GigabitEthernet0/2
       172.16.0.0/16 is variably subnetted, 2 subnets, 2 masks
C         172.16.41.0/24 is directly connected, GigabitEthernet0/1
       192.168.100.0/24 is variably subnetted, 3 subnets, 2 masks
C         192.168.100.0/24 is directly connected, Tunnel100
H         192.168.100.31/32 is directly connected, 00:03:10, Tunnel100
```

The command **show ip route next-hop-override** displays the routing table with the explicit NHRP shortcuts that were added. Example 19-20 shows the command's output for the sample topology. Notice that the NHRP shortcut is indicated by the *NHO* marking and shown underneath the original entry with the correct next-hop IP address.

Example 19-20   *Next-Hop Override Routing Table*

```
R31-Spoke# show ip route next-hop-override
! Output omitted for brevity
Codes: L - local, C - connected, S - static, R - RIP, M - mobile, B - BGP
       D - EIGRP, EX - EIGRP external, O - OSPF, IA - OSPF inter area
```

19

```
        + - replicated route, % - next hop override


Gateway of last resort is 172.16.31.2 to network 0.0.0.0


S*     0.0.0.0/0 [1/0] via 172.16.31.2
       10.0.0.0/8 is variably subnetted, 4 subnets, 2 masks
D        10.1.1.0/24 [90/26885120] via 192.168.100.11, 10:46:38, Tunnel100
C        10.3.3.0/24 is directly connected, GigabitEthernet0/2
D %      10.4.4.0/24 [90/52992000] via 192.168.100.11, 10:46:38, Tunnel100
                [NHO][90/255] via 192.168.100.41, 00:05:14, Tunnel100
       172.16.0.0/16 is variably subnetted, 2 subnets, 2 masks
C        172.16.31.0/30 is directly connected, GigabitEthernet0/1
       192.168.100.0/24 is variably subnetted, 3 subnets, 2 masks
C        192.168.100.0/24 is directly connected, Tunnel100
H        192.168.100.41/32 is directly connected, 00:05:14, Tunnel100
```

```
R41-Spoke# show ip route next-hop-override
! Output omitted for brevity
Gateway of last resort is 172.16.41.2 to network 0.0.0.0


S*     0.0.0.0/0 [1/0] via 172.16.41.2
       10.0.0.0/8 is variably subnetted, 4 subnets, 2 masks
D        10.1.1.0/24 [90/26885120] via 192.168.100.11, 10:45:44, Tunnel100
D %      10.3.3.0/24 [90/52992000] via 192.168.100.11, 10:45:44, Tunnel100
                [NHO][90/255] via 192.168.100.31, 00:04:20, Tunnel100
C        10.4.4.0/24 is directly connected, GigabitEthernet0/2
       172.16.0.0/16 is variably subnetted, 2 subnets, 2 masks
C        172.16.41.0/24 is directly connected, GigabitEthernet0/1
       192.168.100.0/24 is variably subnetted, 3 subnets, 2 masks
C        192.168.100.0/24 is directly connected, Tunnel100
H        192.168.100.31/32 is directly connected, 00:04:20, Tunnel100
```

> **NOTE**   Review the output in Example 19-17 again. Notice that the *DT2* entries represent
> the networks that have had the next-hop IP address overwritten.

NHRP Routing Table Manipulation with Summarization

Summarizing routes on WAN links provides stability by hiding network convergence and
thereby adding scalability. This section demonstrates NHRP's interaction on the routing
table when the exact route does not exist there. R11's EIGRP configuration now advertises
the 10.0.0.0/8 summary prefix out tunnel 100. The spoke routers use the summary route for
forwarding traffic until the NHRP establishes the spoke-to-spoke tunnel. The more explicit
entries from NHRP are installed into the routing table after the spoke-to-spoke tunnels have
been initialized.

Example 19-21 shows the change to R11's EIGRP configuration for summarizing the 10.0.0.0/8 networks out the tunnel 100 interface.

Example 19-21 *R11's Summarization Configuration*

```
R11-Hub
router eigrp GRE-OVERLAY
 address-family ipv4 unicast autonomous-system 100
 af-interface Tunnel100
  summary-address 10.0.0.0 255.0.0.0
  hello-interval 20
  hold-time 60
  no split-horizon
 exit-af-interface
 !
 topology base
 exit-af-topology
 network 10.0.0.0
 network 192.168.100.0
 exit-address-family
```

You can clear the NHRP cache on all routers by using the command **clear ip nhrp**, which removes any NHRP entries. Example 19-22 shows the routing tables for R11, R31, and R41. Notice that only the 10.0.0.0/8 summary route provides initial connectivity among all three routers.

Example 19-22 *Routing Table with Summarization*

```
R11-Hub# show ip route
! Output omitted for brevity
Gateway of last resort is 172.16.11.2 to network 0.0.0.0

S*    0.0.0.0/0 [1/0] via 172.16.11.2
      10.0.0.0/8 is variably subnetted, 5 subnets, 3 masks
D        10.0.0.0/8 is a summary, 00:28:44, Null0
C        10.1.1.0/24 is directly connected, GigabitEthernet0/2
D        10.3.3.0/24 [90/27392000] via 192.168.100.31, 11:18:13, Tunnel100
D        10.4.4.0/24 [90/27392000] via 192.168.100.41, 11:18:13, Tunnel100
      172.16.0.0/16 is variably subnetted, 2 subnets, 2 masks
C        172.16.11.0/30 is directly connected, GigabitEthernet0/1
      192.168.100.0/24 is variably subnetted, 2 subnets, 2 masks
C        192.168.100.0/24 is directly connected, Tunnel100

R31-Spoke# show ip route
! Output omitted for brevity
Gateway of last resort is 172.16.31.2 to network 0.0.0.0
```

```
S*       0.0.0.0/0 [1/0] via 172.16.31.2
         10.0.0.0/8 is variably subnetted, 3 subnets, 3 masks
D        10.0.0.0/8 [90/26885120] via 192.168.100.11, 00:29:28, Tunnel100
C        10.3.3.0/24 is directly connected, GigabitEthernet0/2
         172.16.0.0/16 is variably subnetted, 2 subnets, 2 masks
C        172.16.31.0/30 is directly connected, GigabitEthernet0/1
         192.168.100.0/24 is variably subnetted, 2 subnets, 2 masks
C        192.168.100.0/24 is directly connected, Tunnel100
```

```
R41-Spoke# show ip route
! Output omitted for brevity
Gateway of last resort is 172.16.41.2 to network 0.0.0.0

S*       0.0.0.0/0 [1/0] via 172.16.41.2
         10.0.0.0/8 is variably subnetted, 3 subnets, 3 masks
D        10.0.0.0/8 [90/26885120] via 192.168.100.11, 00:29:54, Tunnel100
C        10.4.4.0/24 is directly connected, GigabitEthernet0/2
         172.16.0.0/16 is variably subnetted, 2 subnets, 2 masks
C        172.16.41.0/24 is directly connected, GigabitEthernet0/1
         192.168.100.0/24 is variably subnetted, 2 subnets, 2 masks
C        192.168.100.0/24 is directly connected, Tunnel100
```

Traffic was re-initiated from 10.3.3.1 to 10.4.4.1 to initialize the spoke-to-spoke tunnels. R11 still sends the NHRP redirect for hairpinned traffic, and the pattern would complete as shown earlier except that NHRP would install a more specific route into the routing table on R31 (10.4.4.0/24) and R41 (10.3.3.0/24). The NHRP injected route is indicated by the *H* entry, as shown in Example 19-23.

Example 19-23 *Routing Table with Summarization and Spoke-to-Spoke Traffic*

```
R31-Spoke# show ip route
! Output omitted for brevity
Codes: L - local, C - connected, S - static, R - RIP, M - mobile, B - BGP
       D - EIGRP, EX - EIGRP external, O - OSPF, IA - OSPF inter area
       o - ODR, P - periodic downloaded static route, H - NHRP, l - LISP


Gateway of last resort is 172.16.31.2 to network 0.0.0.0


S*       0.0.0.0/0 [1/0] via 172.16.31.2
         10.0.0.0/8 is variably subnetted, 4 subnets, 3 masks
D        10.0.0.0/8 [90/26885120] via 192.168.100.11, 00:31:06, Tunnel100
C        10.3.3.0/24 is directly connected, GigabitEthernet0/2
H        10.4.4.0/24 [250/255] via 192.168.100.41, 00:00:22, Tunnel100
         172.16.0.0/16 is variably subnetted, 2 subnets, 2 masks
C        172.16.31.0/30 is directly connected, GigabitEthernet0/1
         192.168.100.0/24 is variably subnetted, 3 subnets, 2 masks
```

```
C        192.168.100.0/24 is directly connected, Tunnel100
H        192.168.100.41/32 is directly connected, 00:00:22, Tunnel100
```

```
R41-Spoke# show ip route
! Output omitted for brevity
Gateway of last resort is 172.16.41.2 to network 0.0.0.0

S*    0.0.0.0/0 [1/0] via 172.16.41.2
         10.0.0.0/8 is variably subnetted, 4 subnets, 3 masks
D        10.0.0.0/8 [90/26885120] via 192.168.100.11, 00:31:24, Tunnel100
H        10.3.3.0/24 [250/255] via 192.168.100.31, 00:00:40, Tunnel100
C        10.4.4.0/24 is directly connected, GigabitEthernet0/2
         172.16.0.0/16 is variably subnetted, 2 subnets, 2 masks
C        172.16.41.0/24 is directly connected, GigabitEthernet0/1
         192.168.100.0/24 is variably subnetted, 3 subnets, 2 masks
C        192.168.100.0/24 is directly connected, Tunnel100
H        192.168.100.31/32 is directly connected, 00:00:40, Tunnel100
```

Example 19-24 shows the DMVPN tunnels after R31 and R41 have initialized the spoke-to-spoke tunnel with summarization on R11. Notice that both of the new spoke-to-spoke tunnel entries are *DT1* because they are new routes in the RIB. If the routes had been more explicit (as shown in Example 19-19), NHRP would have overridden the next-hop address and used a *DT2* entry.

Example 19-24   *Detailed DMVPN Tunnel Output*

```
R31-Spoke# show dmvpn detail
! Output omitted for brevity
Legend: Attrb --> S - Static, D - Dynamic, I - Incomplete
         N - NATed, L - Local, X - No Socket
         T1 - Route Installed, T2 - Nexthop-override
         C - CTS Capable
         # Ent --> Number of NHRP entries with same NBMA peer
         NHS Status: E --> Expecting Replies, R --> Responding, W --> Waiting
         UpDn Time --> Up or Down Time for a Tunnel
==========================================================================
IPv4 NHS:
192.168.100.11 RE NBMA Address: 172.16.11.1 priority = 0 cluster = 0
Type:Spoke, Total NBMA Peers (v4/v6): 3

# Ent  Peer NBMA Addr Peer Tunnel Add State  UpDn Tm Attrb   Target Network
-----  -------------- --------------- ----- -------- -----   ----------------
    1 172.16.31.1     192.168.100.31  UP 00:01:17  DLX       10.3.3.0/24
    2 172.16.41.1     192.168.100.41  UP 00:01:17  DT1       10.4.4.0/24
```

```
      172.16.41.1      192.168.100.41    UP 00:01:17   DT1  192.168.100.41/32
   1  172.16.11.1      192.168.100.11    UP  11:21:33   S   192.168.100.11/32

R41-Spoke# show dmvpn detail
! Output omitted for brevity
IPv4 NHS:
192.168.100.11 RE NBMA Address: 172.16.11.1 priority = 0 cluster = 0
Type:Spoke, Total NBMA Peers (v4/v6): 3
# Ent  Peer NBMA Addr Peer Tunnel Add State  UpDn Tm Attrb    Target Network
-----  -------------- --------------- ----- -------- -----  -----------------
    2  172.16.31.1      192.168.100.31    UP 00:01:56   DT1      10.3.3.0/24
       172.16.31.1      192.168.100.31    UP 00:01:56   DT1  192.168.100.31/32
    1  172.16.41.1      192.168.100.41    UP 00:01:56   DLX      10.4.4.0/24
    1  172.16.11.1      192.168.100.11    UP 11:22:09    S   192.168.100.11/32
```

In this section you have seen the process for establishing spoke-to-spoke DMVPN tunnels and the methods by which NHRP interacts with the routing table. Phase 3 DMVPN fully supports summarization, which should be used to minimize the number of prefixes advertised across the WAN.

Problems with Overlay Networks

Two problems are frequently found with tunnel or overlay networks: recursive routing and outbound interface selection. The following sections explain these problems and describe solutions.

Recursive Routing Problems

It's important to be careful when using a routing protocol on a network tunnel. If a router tries to reach the remote router's encapsulating interface (transport IP address) through the tunnel (overlay network), problems will occur. This is a common issue when a transport network is advertised into the same routing protocol that runs on the overlay network.

Figure 19-6 demonstrates a simple GRE tunnel between R11 and R31. R11, R31, and the SP routers are running OSPF on the 100.64.0.0/16 transport networks. R11 and R31 are running EIGRP on the 10.0.0.0/8 LAN and 192.168.100.0/24 tunnel network.

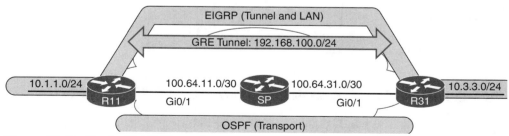

Figure 19-6 *Typical LAN Network*

Example 19-25 shows R11's routing table, with everything working properly.

Example 19-25 *R11 Routing Table with GRE Tunnel*

```
R11# show ip route
! Output omitted for brevity
      10.0.0.0/8 is variably subnetted, 3 subnets, 2 masks
C        10.1.1.0/24 is directly connected, GigabitEthernet0/2
D        10.3.3.0/24 [90/25610240] via 192.168.100.31, 00:02:35, Tunnel0
      100.0.0.0/8 is variably subnetted, 3 subnets, 2 masks
C        100.64.11.0/24 is directly connected, GigabitEthernet0/1
O        100.64.31.0/24 [110/2] via 100.64.11.2, 00:03:11, GigabitEthernet0/1
      192.168.100.0/24 is variably subnetted, 2 subnets, 2 masks
C        192.168.100.0/24 is directly connected, Tunnel100
```

Say that a junior network administrator has accidentally added the 100.64.0.0/16 network
interfaces to EIGRP on R11 and R31. The SP router is not running EIGRP, so an adjacency
does not form, but R11 and R31 add the transport network to EIGRP, which has a lower
AD than OSPF. The routers then try to use the tunnel to reach the tunnel endpoint address,
which is not possible. This scenario is known as *recursive routing*.

The router detects recursive routing and provides an appropriate syslog message, as shown
in Example 19-26. The tunnel is brought down, which terminates the EIGRP neighbors, and
then R11 and R31 find each other again by using OSPF. The tunnel is reestablished, EIGRP
forms a relationship, and the problem repeats over and over again.

Example 19-26 *Recursive Routing Syslog Messages on R11 for GRE Tunnels*

```
00:49:52: %DUAL-5-NBRCHANGE: EIGRP-IPv4 100: Neighbor 192.168.100.31 (Tunnel100)
          is up: new adjacency
00:49:52: %ADJ-5-PARENT: Midchain parent maintenance for IP midchain out of
          Tunnel100 - looped chain attempting to stack
00:49:57: %TUN-5-RECURDOWN: Tunnel100 temporarily disabled due recursive routing
00:49:57: %LINEPROTO-5-UPDOWN: Line protocol on Interface Tunnel100, changed
          state to down
00:49:57: %DUAL-5-NBRCHANGE: EIGRP-IPv4 100: Neighbor 192.168.30.3 (Tunnel100) is
          down: interface down
00:50:12: %LINEPROTO-5-UPDOWN: Line protocol on Interface Tunnel100, changed
          state to up
00:50:15: %DUAL-5-NBRCHANGE: EIGRP-IPv4 100: Neighbor 192.168.100.31 (Tunnel100)
          is up: new adjacency
```

NOTE   Only point-to-point GRE tunnels provide the syslog message "temporarily disabled
due to recursive routing." Both DMVPN and GRE tunnels use the message "looped chained
attempting to stack."

You can remediate recursive routing problems by preventing the tunnel endpoint address
from being advertised across the tunnel network. You can remove EIGRP on the transport
network to stabilize this topology.

Outbound Interface Selection

In certain scenarios, it is difficult for a router to properly identify the outbound interface for encapsulating packets for a tunnel. Typically, a branch site uses multiple transports (one DMVPN tunnel per transport) for network resiliency. Imagine that R31 is connected to two different Internet service providers that receive their IP addresses from DHCP. R31 would have only two default routes for providing connectivity to the transport networks, as shown in Example 19-27.

How would R31 know which interface to use to send packets for tunnel 100? How does the decision process change when R31 sends packets for tunnel 200? If the router picks the correct interface, the tunnel comes up; if it picks the wrong interface, the tunnel never comes up.

Example 19-27 *Two Default Routes and Path Selection*

```
R31-Spoke# show ip route
! Output omitted for brevity
Gateway of last resort is 172.16.31.2 to network 0.0.0.0

S*    0.0.0.0/0 [254/0] via 172.16.31.2
                [254/0] via 100.64.31.2
C     100.64.31.0/30 is directly connected, GigabitEthernet0/2
C     172.16.31.0/30 is directly connected, GigabitEthernet0/1
```

NOTE   The problem can be further exacerbated if the hub routers need to advertise a default route across the DMVPN tunnel.

Front Door Virtual Routing and Forwarding (FVRF)

Virtual routing and forwarding (VRF) contexts create unique logical routers on a physical router so that router interfaces, routing tables, and forwarding tables are completely isolated from other VRF instances. This means that the routing table of one transport network is isolated from the routing table of the other transport network and that the routing table of the LAN interfaces is separate from those of all the transport networks.

DMVPN tunnels are VRF aware in the sense that the tunnel source or destination can be associated to a different VRF instance from the DMVPN tunnel itself. This means that the interface associated with the transport network can be associated with a transport VRF instance, while the DMVPN tunnel is associated with a different VRF instance. The VRF instance associated with the transport network is known as a *front door VRF (FVRF)* instance.

Using an FVRF instance for every DMVPN tunnel prevents route recursion because the transport and overlay networks remain in separate routing tables. Using a unique FVRF instance for each transport and associating it to the correlating DMVPN tunnel ensures that packets will always use the correct interface.

NOTE   VRF instances are locally significant, but the configuration/naming should be consistent to simplify the operational aspects.

Configuring Front Door VRF (FVRF)

The following steps are required to create an FVRF instance, assign it to the transport interface, and make the DMVPN tunnel aware of the FRF instance:

Step 1.   Create the FVRF instance by using the command **vrf definition** *vrf-name*.

Step 2.   Initialize the appropriate address family for the transport network by using the command **address-family** {**ipv4** | **ipv6**}. The address family can be IPv4, IPv6, or both.

Step 3.   Enter interface configuration submode and specify the interface to be associated with the VRF instance by using the command **interface** *interface-id*. The VRF instance is linked to the interface with the interface parameter command **vrf forwarding** *vrf-name*.

NOTE   If an IP address is already configured on the interface, when the VRF instance is linked to the interface, the IP address is removed from that interface.

Step 4.   Configure an IPv4 address by using the command **ip address** *ip-address subnet-mask* or an IPv6 address by using the command **ipv6 address** *ipv6-address/prefix-length*.

Step 5.   Associate the FVRF instance with the DMVPN tunnel by using the interface parameter command **tunnel vrf** *vrf-name* on the DMVPN tunnel.

NOTE   DMVPN tunnels can be associated with a VRF instance while using an FVRF instance. Both of the commands **vrf forwarding** *vrf-name* and **tunnel vrf** *vrf-name* are used on the tunnel interface. Different VRF names need to be selected for this to be effective.

Example 19-28 shows how the FVRF instances named INET01 and INET02 are created on R31. Notice that when the FVRF instances are associated, the IP addresses are removed from the interfaces. The IP addresses are reconfigured and the FVRF instances are associated with the DMVPN tunnels.

Example 19-28   *FVRF Configuration Example*

```
R31-Spoke(config)# vrf definition INET01
R31-Spoke(config-vrf)# address-family ipv4
R31-Spoke(config-vrf-af)# vrf definition INET02
R31-Spoke(config-vrf)# address-family ipv4
R31-Spoke(config-vrf-af)# interface GigabitEthernet0/1
R31-Spoke(config-if)# vrf forwarding INET01
```

19

```
% Interface GigabitEthernet0/1 IPv4 disabled and address(es) removed due to
     enabling VRF INET01
R31-Spoke(config-if)# ip address 172.16.31.1 255.255.255.252
R31-Spoke(config-if)# interface GigabitEthernet0/2
R31-Spoke(config-if)# vrf forwarding INET02
% Interface GigabitEthernet0/2 IPv4 disabled and address(es) removed due to
     enabling VRF INET02
R31-Spoke(config-if)# ip address dhcp
R31-Spoke(config-if)# interface tunnel 100
R31-Spoke(config-if)# tunnel vrf INET01
R31-Spoke(config-if)# interface tunnel 200
R31-Spoke(config-if)# tunnel vrf INET02
```

FVRF Static Routes

FVRF interfaces that are assigned an IP address by DHCP automatically install a default route with an AD of 254. FVRF interfaces with static IP addressing require only a static default route in the FVRF context. This is accomplished with the command **ip route vrf** *vrf-name* **0.0.0.0 0.0.0.0** *next-hop-ip*. Example 19-29 shows the configuration for R31 for the INET01 FVRF instance. The INET02 FVRF instance does not need a static default route because it gets the route from the DHCP server.

Example 19-29 *FVRF Static Default Route Configuration*

```
R31-Spoke
ip route vrf INET01 0.0.0.0 0.0.0.0 172.16.31.2
```

DMVPN Failure Detection and High Availability

An NHRP mapping entry stays in the NHRP cache for a finite amount of time. The entry is valid based on the *NHRP holdtime* period, which defaults to 7200 seconds (2 hours). The NHRP holdtime can be modified with the interface parameter command **ip nhrp holdtime** *1-65535* and should be changed to the recommended value of 600 seconds.

A secondary function of the NHRP registration packets is to verify that connectivity is maintained to the NHSs (hubs). NHRP registration messages are sent every *NHRP timeout* period, and if the NHRP registration reply is not received for a request, the NHRP registration request is sent again with the first packet delayed for 1 second, the second packet delayed for 2 seconds, and the third packet delayed for 4 seconds. The NHS is declared *down* if the NHRP registration reply has not been received after the third retry attempt.

NOTE To further clarify, the spoke-to-hub registration is taken down and displays as *NHRP* for the tunnel state when examined with the **show dmvpn** command. The actual tunnel interface still has a line protocol state of *up*.

During normal operation of the spoke-to-hub tunnels, the spoke continues to send periodic NHRP registration requests, refreshing the NHRP timeout entry and keeping the spoke-to-hub tunnel up. However, in spoke-to-spoke tunnels, if a tunnel is still being used within 2 minutes of the expiration time, an NHRP request refreshes the NHRP timeout entry and keeps the tunnel. If the tunnel is not being used, it is torn down.

The NHRP timeout period defaults to one-third of the NHRP holdtime, which equates to 2400 seconds (40 minutes). The NHRP timeout period can be modified using the interface parameter command **ip nhrp registration timeout** *1-65535*.

> **NOTE** When an NHS is declared down, NHCs still attempt to register with the down NHS. This is known as the *probe state*. The delay between retry packets increments between iterations and uses the following delay pattern: 1, 2, 4, 8, 16, 32, and 64 seconds. The delay never exceeds 64 seconds, and after a registration reply is received, the NHS (hub) is declared *up* again.

DMVPN Hub Redundancy

Connectivity from a DMVPN spoke to a hub is essential to maintain connectivity. If the hub fails, or if a spoke loses connectivity to a hub, that DMVPN tunnel loses its ability to transport packets. Deploying multiple DMVPN hubs for the same DMVPN tunnel provides redundancy and eliminates a single point of failure.

Additional DMVPN hubs are added simply by adding NHRP mapping commands to the tunnel interface. All active DMVPN hubs participate in the routing domain for exchanging routes. DMVPN spoke routers maintain multiple NHRP entries (one per DMVPN hub). No additional configuration is required on the hubs.

IPv6 DMVPN Configuration

DMVPN uses GRE tunnels and is capable of tunneling multiple protocols. Enhancements to NHRP added support for IPv6 so that mGRE tunnels can find the appropriate IPv6 addresses. This means that DMVPN supports the use of IPv4 and IPv6 as the tunnel protocol or the transport protocol in the combination required.

For all the commands explained earlier for IPv4, there are equivalent commands to support IPv6. Table 19-8 provides a list of the tunneled protocol commands for IPv4 and the equivalent commands for IPv6.

Table 19-8 Correlation of IPv4-to-IPv6 Tunneled Protocol Commands

IPv4 Command	IPv6 Command
ip mtu *mtu*	**ipv6 mtu** *mtu*
ip tcp adjust-mss *mss-size*	**ipv6 tcp adjust-mss** *mss-size*
ip nhrp network-id *1-4294967295*	**ipv6 nhrp network-id** *1-4294967295*
ip nhrp nhs *nhs-address* **nbma** *nbma-address* [**multicast**] [**priority** *0-255*]	**ipv6 nhrp nhs** *nhs-address* **nbma** *nbma-address* [**multicast**] [**priority** *0-255*]
ip nrhp redirect	**ipv6 nhrp redirect**
ip nhrp shortcut	**ipv6 nhrp shortcut**

IPv4 Command	IPv6 Command
ip nhrp authentication *password*	ipv6 nhrp authentication *password*
ip nhrp registration no-unique	ipv6 nhrp registration no-unique
ip nhrp holdtime *1-65535*	ipv6 nhrp holdtime *1-65535*
ip nhrp registration timeout *1-65535*	ipv6 nhrp registration timeout *1-65535*

Table 19-9 provides a list of the configuration commands that are needed to support an IPv6 transport network. Any tunnel commands not listed in Table 19-9 are transport agnostic and are used regardless of the transport IP protocol version.

Table 19-9   Correlation of IPv4-to-IPv6 Transport Protocol Commands

IPv4 Command	IPv6 Command
tunnel mode gre multipoint	tunnel mode gre multipoint ipv6
ip route vrf *vrf-name* 0.0.0.0 0.0.0.0 *next-hop-ip*	ipv6 route vrf *vrf-name* 0.0.0.0 0.0.0.0 *next-hop-ip*

IPv6 over DMVPN can be interpreted differently depending on the perspective. There are three possible interpretations:

- **IPv4 over IPv6:** IPv4 is the tunneled protocol over an IPv6 transport network.

- **IPv6 over IPv6:** IPv6 is the tunneled protocol over an IPv6 transport network.

- **IPv6 over IPv4:** IPv6 is the tunneled protocol over an IPv4 transport network.

Regardless of the interpretation, DMVPN supports the IPv4 or IPv6 protocol as the tunneled protocol or the transport, but choosing the correct set of command groups is vital and should be based on the tunneling technique selected. Table 19-10 provides a matrix to help you select the appropriate commands from Table 19-8 and Table 19-9. It is important to note that *nhs-address* and *NBMA-address* in Table 19-8 can be IPv4 or IPv6 addresses.

Table 19-10   Matrix of DMVPN Tunnel Technique to Configuration Commands

Tunnel Mode	Tunnel Protocol Commands	Transport Commands
IPv4 over IPv4	IPv4	IPv4
IPv4 over IPv6	IPv4	IPv6
IPv6 over IPv4	IPv6	IPv4
IPv6 over IPv6	IPv6	IPv6

NOTE   It is vital that a unique IPv6 link-local IP address be assigned to the tunnel interface when the tunneling protocol is IPv6. IPv6 routing protocols use link-local addresses to discover each other and for installation into the routing table.

Table 19-11 provides a list of IPv4 display commands correlated to the IPv6 equivalents.

Table 19-11 Display Commands for IPv6 DMVPN

IPv4 Command	IPv6 Command
show ip nhrp [brief | detail]	show ipv6 nhrp [brief | detail]
show dmvpn [ipv4][detail]	show dmvpn [ipv6][detail]
show ip nhrp traffic	show ipv6 nhrp traffic
show ip nhrp nhs [detail]	show ipv6 nhrp nhs [detail]

IPv6-over-IPv6 Sample Configuration

To fully understand an IPv6 DMVPN configuration, this section provides a sample configuration using the topology from Figure 19-4 for the IPv6-over-IPv6 topology. To simplify the IPv6 addressing scheme, the first two hextets of the book's IPv6 addresses use 2001:db8 (the RFC-defined address space for IPv6 documentation). After the first two hextets, an IPv4 octet number is copied into an IPv6 hextet, so the IPv6 addresses should look familiar. Table 19-12 provides an example of how the book converts existing IPv4 addresses and networks to IPv6 format.

Table 19-12 IPv6 Addressing Scheme

IPv4 Address	IPv4 Network	IPv6 Address	Network
10.1.1.11	10.1.1.0/24	2001:db8:10:1:1::11	2001:db8:10:1:1::/80
172.16.11.1	172.16.11.0/30	2001:db8:172:16:11::1	2001:db8:172:16:11::/126
10.1.0.11	10.1.0.11/32	2001:db8:10:1:0::11	2001:db8:10.1.:11/128

Example 19-30 provides the IPv6-over-IPv6 DMVPN configuration for hub router R11. The VRF definition uses the **address-family ipv6** command, and the GRE tunnel is defined with the command **tunnel mode gre multipoint ipv6**. Notice that the tunnel interface has a regular IPv6 address configured as well as a link-local IPv6 address. The tunnel number is integrated into the link-local IP addressing.

Example 19-30 *IPv6 DMVPN Hub Configuration on R11*

```
R11-Hub
vrf definition INET01
 address-family ipv6
 exit-address-family
 !
interface Tunnel100
 description DMVPN-INET
 bandwidth 4000
 ipv6 tcp adjust-mss 1360
 ipv6 address FE80:100::11 link-local
 ipv6 address 2001:DB8:192:168:100::11/80
 ipv6 mtu 1380
 ipv6 nhrp authentication CISCO
```

19

```
 ipv6 nhrp map multicast dynamic
 ipv6 nhrp network-id 100
 ipv6 nhrp holdtime 600
 ipv6 nhrp redirect
 tunnel source GigabitEthernet0/1
 tunnel mode gre multipoint ipv6
 tunnel key 100
 tunnel vrf INET01
!
interface GigabitEthernet0/1
 description INET01-TRANSPORT
 vrf forwarding INET01
 ipv6 address 2001:DB8:172:16:11::1/126
interface GigabitEthernet1/0
 description LAN
 ipv6 address 2001:DB8:10:1:111::11/80
!
ipv6 route vrf INET01 ::/0 GigabitEthernet0/1 2001:DB8:172:16:11::2
```

Example 19-31 provides the IPv6 DMVPN configuration for spoke routers R31 and R41.

Example 19-31 *IPv6 DMVPN Configuration for R31 and R41*

```
R31-Spoke
vrf definition INET01
 address-family ipv6
 exit-address-family
!
interface Tunnel100
 description DMVPN-INET01
 bandwidth 4000
 ipv6 tcp adjust-mss 1360
 ipv6 address FE80:100::31 link-local
 ipv6 address 2001:DB8:192:168:100::31/80
 ipv6 mtu 1380
 ipv6 nhrp authentication CISCO
 ipv6 nhrp map multicast dynamic
 ipv6 nhrp network-id 100
 ipv6 nhrp holdtime 600
 ipv6 nhrp nhs 2001:DB8:192:168:100::11 nbma 2001:DB8:172:16:11::1 multicast
 ipv6 nhrp shortcut
 if-state nhrp
 tunnel source GigabitEthernet0/1
 tunnel mode gre multipoint ipv6
```

```
  tunnel key 100
  tunnel vrf INET01
 !
interface GigabitEthernet0/1
 description INET01-TRANSPORT
 vrf forwarding INET01
 ipv6 address 2001:DB8:172:16:31::1/126
interface GigabitEthernet1/0
 description SiteB-Local-LAN
 ipv6 address 2001:DB8:10:3:3::31/80
 !
ipv6 route vrf INET01 ::/0 GigabitEthernet0/1 2001:DB8:172:16:31::2
```

```
R41-Spoke
vrf definition INET01
 address-family ipv6
 exit-address-family
 !
interface Tunnel100
 description DMVPN-INET
 bandwidth 4000
ipv6 tcp adjust-mss 1360
 ipv6 address FE80:100::41 link-local
 ipv6 address 2001:DB8:192:168:100::41/80
 ipv6 mtu 1380
 ipv6 nhrp authentication CISCO
 ipv6 nhrp map multicast dynamic
 ipv6 nhrp network-id 100
 ipv6 nhrp holdtime 600
 ipv6 nhrp nhs 2001:DB8:192:168:100::11 nbma 2001:DB8:172:16:11::1 multicast
 ipv6 nhrp shortcut
 if-state nhrp
 tunnel source GigabitEthernet0/1
 tunnel mode gre multipoint ipv6
 tunnel key 100
 tunnel vrf INET01
 !
interface GigabitEthernet0/1
 description INET01-TRANSPORT
 vrf forwarding INET01
 ipv6 address 2001:DB8:172:16:41::1/126
interface GigabitEthernet1/0
 description Site4-Local-LAN
 ipv6 address 2001:DB8:10:4:4::41/80
 !
ipv6 route vrf INET01 ::/0 GigabitEthernet0/1 2001:DB8:172:16:41::2
```

19

IPv6 DMVPN Verification

The **show dmvpn [detail]** command can be used for viewing any DMVPN tunnel, regardless of the tunnel or transport protocol. The data is structured slightly differently because of the IPv6 address format, but it still provides the same information as before.

Example 19-32 shows the DMVPN tunnel state from R31 after it has established its static tunnels to the DMVPN hubs. Notice that the protocol transport now shows IPv6, and the NHS devices are using IPv6 addresses.

Example 19-32   *Verifying IPv6 DMVPN*

```
R31-Spoke# show dmvpn detail
Legend: Attrb --> S - Static, D - Dynamic, I - Incomplete
        N - NATed, L - Local, X - No Socket
        T1 - Route Installed, T2 - Nexthop-override
        C - CTS Capable
        # Ent --> Number of NHRP entries with same NBMA peer
        NHS Status: E --> Expecting Replies, R --> Responding, W --> Waiting
        UpDn Time --> Up or Down Time for a Tunnel
==========================================================================


Interface Tunnel100 is up/up, Addr. is 2001:DB8:192:168:100::31, VRF ""
   Tunnel Src./Dest. addr: 2001:DB8:172:16:31::1/MGRE, Tunnel VRF "INET01"
   Protocol/Transport: "multi-GRE/IPv6", Protect ""
   Interface State Control: Enabled
   nhrp event-publisher : Disabled


IPv6 NHS:
2001:DB8:192:168:100::11  RE NBMA Address: 2001:DB8:172:16:11::1 priority = 0
cluster = 0
Type:Spoke, Total NBMA Peers (v4/v6): 2
   1.Peer NBMA Address: 2001:DB8:172:16:11::1
       Tunnel IPv6 Address: 2001:DB8:192:168:100::11
       IPv6 Target Network: 2001:DB8:192:168:100::11/128
       # Ent: 2, Status: UP, UpDn Time: 00:00:53, Cache Attrib: S
! Following entry is shown in the detailed view and uses link-local addresses
   2.Peer NBMA Address: 2001:DB8:172:16:11::1
       Tunnel IPv6 Address: FE80:100::11
       IPv6 Target Network: FE80:100::11/128
       # Ent: 0, Status: NHRP, UpDn Time: never, Cache Attrib: SC
```

Example 19-33 demonstrates the connectivity between R31 and R41 before and after the spoke-to-spoke DMVPN tunnel is established.

Example 19-33 *IPv6 Connectivity Between R31 and R41*

```
! Initial packet flow
R31-Spoke# traceroute 2001:db8:10:4:4::41
Tracing the route to 2001:DB8:10:4:4::41

  1 2001:DB8:192:168:100::11 2 msec
  2 2001:DB8:192:168:100::41 5 msec 4 msec 5 msec

! Packet flow after spoke-to-spoke tunnel is established
R31-Spoke# traceroute 2001:db8:10:4:4::41
Tracing the route to 2001:DB8:10:4:4::41

  1 2001:DB8:192:168
```

References in This Chapter

Cisco, "IPv6 over DMVPN," www.cisco.com.

Sullenberger, Mike, "Advanced Concepts of DMVPN (Dynamic Multipoint VPN)," Presented at Cisco Live, San Diego, 2015.

Informational RFC, *Flexible Dynamic Mesh VPN*, F. Detienne, M. Kumar, and M. Sullenberger, http://tools.ietf.org/html/draft-detienne-dmvpn-01, December 2013.

RFC 1702, *Generic Routing Encapsulation over IPv4 Networks*, S. Hanks, T. Lee, D. Farianacci, and P. Traina, http://tools.ietf.org/html/rfc1702, October 2004.

RFC 2332, *NBMA Next Hop Resolution Protocol (NHRP)*, J. Luciani, D. Katz, D. Piscitello, B. Cole, and N. Doraswamy, http://tools.ietf.org/html/rfc2332, April 1998.

Exam Preparation Tasks

As mentioned in the section "How to Use This Book" in the Introduction, you have a couple choices for exam preparation: the exercises here, Chapter 24, "Final Preparation," and the exam simulation questions in the Pearson Test Prep software.

Review All Key Topics

Review the most important topics in this chapter, noted with the Key Topic icon in the outer margin of the page. Table 19-13 lists these key topics and the page number on which each is found.

Table 19-13 Key Topics

Key Topic Element	Description	Page Number
Paragraph	Generic Routing Encapsulation (GRE) tunnels	769
Paragraph	GRE tunnel configuration	770
Paragraph	Next Hop Resolution Protocol (NHRP)	774
Table 19-3	NHRP message types	775
Paragraph	Dynamic Multipoint VPN (DMVPN)	776
Paragraph	Phase 1 DMVPN	777
Paragraph	Phase 3 DMVPN	777

Key Topic Element	Description	Page Number
Paragraph	DMVPN hub configuration	780
Paragraph	Phase 1 DMVPN spoke configuration	782
Table 19-5	Alternative NHRP mapping commands	783
Paragraph	Viewing DMVPN tunnel status	784
Paragraph	Phase 3 DMVPN spoke configuration	792
Paragraph	IP NHRP authentication	794
Paragraph	Unique IP NHRP registration	794
Figure 19-5	Forming spoke-to-spoke DMVPN tunnels	796
Paragraph	NHRP routing table manipulation	800
Paragraph	NHRP route table manipulation with summarization	802
Paragraph	Recursive routing problems	806
Paragraph	Outbound interface selection	808
Paragraph	Front door virtual routing and forwarding (FVRF)	808
Paragraph	DMVPN failure detection and high availability	810
Paragraph	DMVPN hub redundancy	811
Paragraph	IPv6 DMVPN configuration	811

Define Key Terms

Define the following key terms from this chapter and check your answers in the glossary:

Dynamic Multipoint Virtual Private Network (DMVPN), GRE tunnel, Next Hop Resolution Protocol (NHRP), NHRP redirect, NHRP shortcut, next-hop server (NHS), DMVPN Phase 1, DMVPN Phase 3, encapsulating interface, recursive routing, front door VRF

Use the Command Reference to Check Your Memory

The ENARSI 300-410 exam focuses on the practical, hands-on skills that networking professionals use. Therefore, you should be able to identify the commands needed to configure, verify, and troubleshoot the topics covered in this chapter.

This section includes the most important configuration and verification commands covered in this chapter. It might not be necessary to memorize the complete syntax of every command, but you should be able to remember the basic keywords that are needed.

To test your memory of the commands in Table 19-14, go to the companion website and download Appendix B, "Command Reference Exercises." Fill in the missing commands in the tables based on each command description. You can check your work by downloading Appendix C, "Command Reference Exercise Answer Key," from the companion website.

Table 19-14   Command Reference

Task	Command Syntax
Specify the source IP address or interface used for encapsulating packets for a tunnel.	**tunnel source** {*ip-address* | *interface-id*}
Specify the destination IP address for establishing a tunnel.	**tunnel destination ip-address**
Convert a GRE tunnel into an mGRE tunnel.	**tunnel mode gre multipoint**
Enable NRHP and uniquely identify a DMVPN tunnel locally.	**ip nhrp network-id** *1-4294967295*
Define a tunnel key globally on a DMVPN tunnel interface to allow routers to identify when multiple tunnels use the same encapsulating interface.	**tunnel key 0-4294967295**
Enable plaintext NHRP authentication.	**ip nhrp authentication** password
Associate a front door VRF instance to a DMVPN tunnel interface.	**tunnel vrf** *vrf-name*
Allow for an NHRP client to register with a different IP address before timing out at the hub.	**ip nhrp registration no-unique**
Enable the NHRP redirect function on a DMVPN hub tunnel interface.	**ip nhrp redirect**
Enable the ability to install NHRP shortcuts into a spoke router's RIB.	**ip nhrp shortcut**
Enable the mapping of multicast on a DMVPN hub tunnel interface.	**ip nhrp map multicast dynamic**
Specify the NHRP NHS, NBMA address, and multicast mapping on a spoke.	**ip nhrp nhs** *nhs-address* **nbma** *nbma-address* [**multicast**] or **ip nhrp nhs** *nhs-address* **ip nhrp map** *ip-address nbma-address* **ip nhrp map multicast** [*nbma-address* | **dynamic**]
Display the tunnel interface state and statistics.	**show interface tunnel** *number*
Display DMVPN tunnel interface association, NHRP mappings, and IPsec session details.	**show dmvpn** [detail]
Display the NHRP cache for a router.	**show ip nhrp** [brief]
Display the NHRP shortcut that is installed for an overridden route.	**show ip route next-hop-override**

19

## CHAPTER 20

Securing DMVPN Tunnels

This chapter covers the following topics:

- **Elements of Secure Transport:** This section explains the need for data integrity, data confidentiality, and data availability.

- **IPsec Fundamentals:** This section explains the core concepts involved with IP security encryption.

- **IPsec Tunnel Protection:** This section explains how IPsec protection integrates with DMVPN tunnels.

This chapter focuses on the security components of a WAN network that provide data integrity, data confidentiality, and data availability. A certain level of trust is placed in the SP network to maintain data integrity and confidentiality, but when IPsec protection is enabled on the Dynamic Multipoint Virtual Private Network (DMVPN) tunnels, the trust boundary is moved from the SP to your own organization's control. DMVPN IPsec tunnel protection can be deployed on any transport by using Pre-Shared Key or public key infrastructure (PKI). This chapter focuses on protecting the data transmitted on a DMVPN network between routers.

"Do I Know This Already?" Quiz

The "Do I Know This Already?" quiz allows you to assess whether you should read this entire chapter thoroughly or jump to the "Exam Preparation Tasks" section. If you are in doubt about your answers to these questions or your own assessment of your knowledge of the topics, read the entire chapter. Table 20-1 lists the major headings in this chapter and their corresponding "Do I Know This Already?" quiz questions. You can find the answers in Appendix A, "Answers to the 'Do I Know This Already?' Quiz Questions."

Table 20-1 Do I Know This Already?" Foundation Topics Section-to-Question Mapping

Foundation Topics Section	Questions
Elements of Secure Transport	1, 2
IPsec Fundamentals	3–5
IPsec Tunnel Protection	6

CAUTION The goal of self-assessment is to gauge your mastery of the topics in this chapter. If you do not know the answer to a question or are only partially sure of the answer, you should mark that question as wrong for purposes of self-assessment. Giving yourself credit for an answer that you correctly guess skews your self-assessment results and might provide you with a false sense of security.

1. In an MPLS Layer 3 VPN WAN model, which of the following is true?

   a. Data confidentiality is protected because MPLS Layer 3 VPNs include encryption on the SP network.

   b. Data integrity is maintained because MPLS Layer 3 VPNs include checksums on the SP network.

   c. Data integrity is not protected on the SP network.

   d. Data confidentiality is dependent on the SP's processes.

2. Which IPsec security mechanism ensures that a hacker who gains access to a session key cannot maintain access to that session indefinitely?

   a. Replay detection

   b. Periodic rekey

   c. Perfect forward secrecy

   d. Encapsulating Security Payload

3. True or false: The IKEv2 keyring functionality allows for pre-shared keys to be set on a neighbor-by-neighbor basis.

   a. True

   b. False

4. True or false: Enabling IPsec tunnel encryption involves the configuration of the IKEv2 profile and its association to a tunnel interface.

   a. True

   b. False

5. Which command enables IPsec encryption on a tunnel interface?

   a. **tunnel protection ipsec profile** *profile-name*

   b. **ipsec protection profile** *profile-name*

   c. **crypto map** map-name **ipsec-isakmp interface** interface-id

   d. **crypto map** *map-name* **tunnel** *tunnel-id* **ipsec-isakmp**

6. A router has just been configured with IPsec DMVPN tunnel protection and needs to have the IPsec packet replay feature set the number of packets to 64. Which command should be used?

   a. **crypto ipsec security-association replay window-size 64**

   b. **ipsec security-replay window-size 64**

   c. **ipsec window-size 64**

   d. None. The command is not needed.

Foundation Topics

Elements of Secure Transport

When employees think about the data that is transmitted on their network, they associate a certain level of sensitivity with it. For example, bank statements, credit card numbers, and product designs are considered highly sensitive. If such information is made available to the wrong party, there could be repercussions for the company or for a specific user. Employees assume that their data is secure because their company owns all the infrastructure, but this is not necessarily the case when a WAN is involved. A properly designed network provides data confidentiality, integrity, and availability. Without these components, a business might lose potential customers who do not think that their information is secure.

The following list defines the terms data confidentiality, data integrity, and data availability and describes the function of each:

- *Data confidentiality*: Ensuring that data is viewable only by authorized users. Data confidentiality is maintained through encryption.

- *Data integrity*: Ensuring that data is modified only by authorized users. Information is valuable only if it is accurate. Inaccurate data can result in an unanticipated cost, for example, if a product design is modified and the product therefore does not work. When the product breaks, the time it takes to identify and correct the issue has a cost associated with it. Data integrity is maintained by using an encrypted digital signature, which is typically a checksum.

- *Data availability*: Ensuring that the network is always available allows for the secure transport of the data. Redundancy and proper design ensure data availability.

WAN network designs are based on the concept of trusted service provider (SP) connections. Original network circuits were point-to-point connections and placed trust in the SP's ability to control access to the infrastructure and assurances of privacy. Even though SPs use peer-to-peer networks, technologies such as MPLS VPNs have provided a layer of logical segmentation.

A certain level of data confidentiality on a WAN is based on the type of transport and the limited access to the network by the SP's employees. Information security and network engineers assume that the SP network is secure and does not require encryption on the SP WAN circuits.

Figure 20-1 shows the traditional approach to securing data on a network. The entire controlled infrastructure (enterprise and SP) is assumed to be safe. Traffic is encrypted only when exposed to the public Internet.

Also, the Internet edge is the only identified intrusion point for a network. The Internet edge is protected by a firewall such as a Cisco Adaptive Security Appliance (ASA), which prevents outside users from accessing the network and servers in the data center (DC) that hosts e-commerce applications.

In Figure 20-2, the Internet is used as the transport for the WAN. The Internet does not provide controlled access and cannot guarantee data integrity or data confidentiality. Hackers, eavesdroppers, and man-in-the-middle intrusions are common threats on public transports like the Internet. In addition, the branch WAN, corporate WAN, and Internet edge become intrusion points for the network.

Data confidentiality and integrity are maintained by adding IPsec encryption to the DMVPN tunnel that uses the Internet as a transport. IPsec is a set of industry standards defined in RFC 2401 to secure IP-based network traffic.

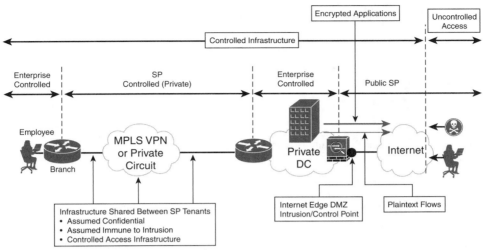

Figure 20-1 *Typical WAN Network*

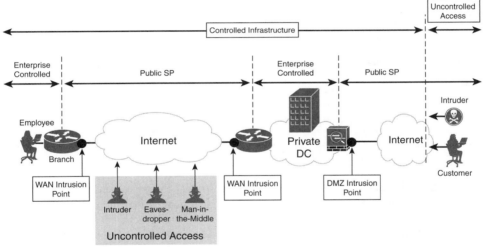

Figure 20-2 *Internet as a WAN Transport*

In the traditional private WAN model, trust is placed in the SP and its ability to control access to a company's network. Provisioning systems occasionally fail, and data may be leaked into another customer's networks. Other times, more blatant attempts to compromise data confidentiality or integrity may occur in other geographic regions. Some organizations that are subject to stringent privacy regulations (such as healthcare, government, and financial regulations) often require all traffic to be encrypted across all WAN links, regardless of the transport used. Adding IPsec tunnel protection is a straightforward process and avoids the headaches associated with IPsec point-to-point tunnels.

IPsec Fundamentals

DMVPN tunnels are not encrypted by default, but they can be encrypted by using IPsec. IPsec provides encryption through cryptographically based security and was designed with interoperability in mind. When IPsec is integrated with DMVPN tunnels, the encrypted DMVPN tunnels provide a secure overlay network over any transport with the following functions:

- *Origin authentication*: Authentication of origin is accomplished by Pre-Shared Key (static) or through certificate-based authentication (dynamic).

- **Data confidentiality:** A variety of encryption algorithms are used to preserve confidentiality.

- **Data integrity:** Hashing algorithms ensure that packets are not modified in transit.

- *Replay detection*: IPsec provides protection against hackers trying to capture and insert network traffic.

- *Periodic rekey*: New security keys are created between endpoints every specified time interval or within a specific volume of traffic.

- **Perfect forward secrecy:** Each session key is derived independently of the previous key. A compromise of one key does not mean compromise of future keys.

The IPsec security architecture is composed of the following independent components:

- Security protocols
- Security associations
- Key management

Security Protocols

IPsec uses two protocols to provide data integrity and confidentiality. The protocols can be applied individually or combined based on need. Both protocols are explained further in the following sections.

Authentication Header

The *IP authentication header* provides data integrity, authentication, and protection from hackers replaying packets. The *authentication header protocol* ensures that the original data packet (before encapsulation/encryption) has not been modified during transport on the public network. It creates a digital signature similar to a checksum to ensure that the packet has not been modified, using protocol number 51 located in the IP header.

Encapsulating Security Payload (ESP)

The *Encapsulating Security Payload (ESP)* provides data confidentiality, authentication, and protection from hackers replaying packets. Typically, *payload* refers to the actual data minus any headers, but in the context of ESP, the payload is the portion of the original packet that is encapsulated in the IPsec headers. ESP ensures that the original payload (before encapsulation) maintains data confidentiality by encrypting the payload and adding a new set of headers during transport across a public network. ESP uses the protocol number 50 located in the IP header.

Key Management

A critical component of secure encryption is the communication of the keys used to encrypt and decrypt the traffic being transported over the insecure network. The process of generating, distributing, and storing these keys is called *key management*. IPsec uses the *Internet Key Exchange (IKE)* protocol by default.

RFC 4306 defines the second iteration of IKE, called IKEv2, which provides mutual authentication of the parties. IKEv2 introduced support of Extensible Authentication Protocol (EAP) (certificate-based authentication), reduction of bandwidth consumption, Network Address Translation (NAT) traversal, and the ability to detect whether a tunnel is still alive.

Security Associations

Security associations (SAs), which are a vital component of IPsec architecture, contain the security parameters that were agreed upon between the two endpoint devices. There are two types of SAs:

- **IKE SA:** Used for control plane functions like IPsec key management and management of IPsec SAs.

- **IPsec SA:** Used for data plane functions to secure data transmitted between two different sites.

There is only one IKE SA between endpoint devices, but multiple IPsec SAs can be established between the same two endpoint devices.

> **NOTE** IPsec SAs are unidirectional, and at least two IPsec SAs (one for inbound, one for outbound) are required to exchange network traffic between two sites.

ESP Modes

Traditional IPsec provides two ESP modes of packet protection:

- **Tunnel mode:** Encrypts the entire original packet and adds a new set of IPsec headers. These new headers are used to route the packet and also provide overlay functions.

- **Transport mode:** Encrypts and authenticates only the packet payload. This mode does not provide overlay functions and routes based on the original IP headers.

Figure 20-3 shows an original packet, an IPsec packet in transport mode, and an IPsec packet in tunnel mode. The following section expands on these concepts by explaining the structure of various DMVPN packets. The DMVPN packet structure can be compared to that of a regular packet as well.

20

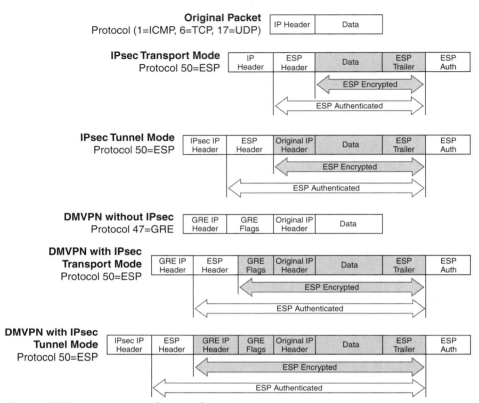

Figure 20-3 *DMVPN Packet Headers*

DMVPN Without IPsec

In unencrypted DMVPN packets, the original packets have Generic Routing Encapsulation (GRE) flags added to them, and then the new GRE IP header is added for routing the packets on the transport (underlay) network. The GRE IP header adds an extra 20 bytes of overhead, and the GRE flags add an extra 4 bytes of overhead. These packets use the protocol field GRE (47).

> **NOTE** If a tunnel key is specified, an additional 4 bytes are added to every packet, regardless of whether the encryption type (if any) is selected.

DMVPN with IPsec in Transport Mode

For encrypted DMVPN packets that use ESP transport mode, the original packets have the GRE flags added to them, and then that portion of the packets is encrypted. A signature for the encrypted payload is added, and then the GRE IP header is added for routing the packets on the transport (underlay) network.

The GRE IP header adds an extra 20 bytes of overhead, the GRE flags add an extra 4 bytes of overhead, and depending on the encryption mechanism, a varying number of additional bytes(s) are added for the encrypted signature. These packets use the protocol field ESP (50).

DMVPN with IPsec in Tunnel Mode

For encrypted DMVPN packets that use ESP tunnel mode, the original packets have the GRE flags added to them, and then the new GRE IP header is added for routing the packets on the transport (underlay) network. That portion of the packets is encrypted, a signature for the encrypted payload is added, and then a new IPsec IP header is added for routing the packets on the transport (underlay) network.

The GRE IP header adds an extra 20 bytes of overhead, the GRE flags add an extra 4 bytes of overhead, the IPsec IP header adds an extra 20 bytes of overhead, and depending on the encryption mechanism, a varying number of additional bytes are added for the encrypted signature. These packets use the IP protocol field ESP (50).

It is important to note that the use of IPsec tunnel mode for DMVPN networks does not add any perceived value and adds 20 bytes of overhead. Transport mode should be used for encrypted DMVPN tunnels.

IPsec Tunnel Protection

Enabling IPsec protection on a DMVPN network requires that all devices have IPsec protection enabled. If some routers have IPsec enabled and others do not, devices with mismatched settings will not be able to establish connections on the tunnel interfaces.

Pre-Shared Key Authentication

The first scenario for deploying IPsec tunnel protection is with the use of static Pre-Shared Key, which involves the creation of the following:

- IKEv2 keyring
- IKEv2 profile
- IPsec transform set
- IPsec profile

In this section, emphasis is on the DMVPN routers that are attached to the Internet, as shown in Figure 20-4. The following sections explain how to configure IPsec tunnel protection on the DMVPN tunnel 200.

20

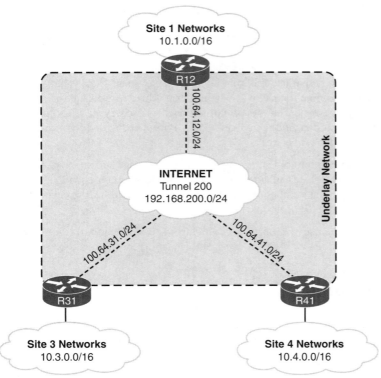

Figure 20-4   *Sample DMVPN Network*

IKEv2 Keyring

The IKEv2 keyring is a repository of the pre-shared keys. In a keyring, it is possible to define which keys apply to which hosts. Identification of the password is based on the IP address of the remote router. The IKEv2 keyring is created with the following steps:

Step 1.   Create the IKEv2 keyring by using the command **crypto ikev2 keyring** *keyring-name*.

Step 2.   Create the peer by using the command **peer** *peer-name*. In this case, for simplicity, create only one peer, called *ANY*. However, multiple peers can exist in a keyring. Each peer has a matching qualifier and can use a different password.

Step 3.   Identify the IP address so that the appropriate peer configuration is used, based on the remote device's IP address. The command **address** *network subnet-mask* defines the IP address range. For simplicity, the value of 0.0.0.0 0.0.0.0 is used to allow a match against any peer. IPv6 transport can use the value ::/0 for any IPv6 peer.

Step 4.   Define the pre-shared key with the command **pre-shared-key** *secure-key*. Generally, a long alphanumeric password is used for increased security.

Example 20-1 demonstrates a simple keyring that is used to secure the DMVPN routers on the Internet.

Example 20-1 *IKEv2 Keyring*

```
crypto ikev2 keyring DMVPN-KEYRING-INET
peer ANY
address 0.0.0.0 0.0.0.0
pre-shared-key CISCO456
```

IKEv2 Profile

The IKEv2 profile is a collection of nonnegotiable security parameters used during the IKE security association. The IKEv2 profile is later associated with the IPsec profile. Within the IKEv2 profile, local and remote authentication methods must be defined, as well as a match statement (identity, certificate, and so on).

The basic steps for creating an IKEv2 profile are as follows:

Step 1. Define the IKEv2 profile by using the command **crypto ikev2 profile** *ike-profile-name.*

Step 2. Define the peer IP address by using the command **match identity remote address** *ip-address.* For simplicity, the value 0.0.0.0 is used to allow a match against any peer. IPv6 transport can use the value ::/0 for any IPv6 peer.

Step 3. Optionally set the local router's identity based on an IP address by using the command **identity local address** *ip-address.* This command is not needed for Pre-Shared Key authentication but is very helpful with the deployment of public key infrastructure (PKI) authentication. The IP address specified should match the IP address used when registering the certificate (the recommended Loopback 0 IP address).

Step 4. If Front Door VRF (FVRF) is used on the DMVPN tunnel, associate the FVRF instance with the IKEv2 profile with the command **match fvrf** {*vrf-name* | **any**}. Using the **any** keyword allows either FVRF instance to be selected.

Step 5. Define the authentication method for connection requests that are received by remote peers. The command **authentication local** {**pre-share** | **rsa-sig**} defines the local authentication. Only one local authentication can be selected. The **pre-share** keyword is used for pre-shared static keys, and **rsa-sig** is used for certificate-based authentication.

Step 6. Define the authentication method for connection requests that are sent to remote peers. The command **authentication remote** {**pre-share** | **rsa-sig**} defines the remote authentication. Multiple remote authentication methods can be defined by repeating the command. The **pre-share** keyword is used for pre-shared static keys, and **rsa-sig** is used for certificate-based authentication.

Step 7. For pre-shared authentication, associate the IKEv2 keyring with the IKEv2 profile by using the command **keyring local** *keyring-name.*

20

Example 20-2 provides a sample IKEv2 profile that uses Pre-Shared Key authentication.

Example 20-2 *Sample IKEv2 Profile*

```
crypto ikev2 profile DMVPN-IKE-PROFILE-INET
 match fvrf INET01
 match identity remote address 0.0.0.0
 authentication remote pre-share
 authentication local pre-share
 keyring local DMVPN-KEYRING-INET
```

The IKEv2 profile settings are displayed with the command **show crypto ikev2 profile**, as shown in Example 20-3. Notice that the authentication, FVRF, IKE keyring, and identity IP address are displayed along with the IKE lifetime.

Example 20-3 *Display of IKEv2 Profile Settings*

```
R12-DC1-Hub2# show crypto ikev2 profile
IKEv2 profile: DMVPN-IKE-PROFILE-INET
 Ref Count: 1
 Match criteria:
  Fvrf: INET01
  Local address/interface: none
  Identities:
   address 0.0.0.0
  Certificate maps: none
 Local identity: none
 Remote identity: none
 Local authentication method: pre-share
 Remote authentication method(s): pre-share
 EAP options: none
 Keyring: DMVPN-KEYRING-INET
 Trustpoint(s): none
 Lifetime: 86400 seconds
 DPD: disabled
 NAT-keepalive: disabled
 Ivrf: none
 Virtual-template: none
 mode auto: none
 AAA AnyConnect EAP authentication mlist: none
 AAA EAP authentication mlist: none
 AAA Accounting: none
 AAA group authorization: none
 AAA user authorization: none
```

IPsec Transform Set

The transform set identifies the security protocols (such as ESP) for encrypting traffic. It specifies the protocol ESP or authentication header that is used to authenticate the data.

Table 20-2 provides a matrix of common IPsec transforms that can be inserted into a transform set. Following are some guidelines:

- Select an ESP encryption transform for data confidentiality.

- Select an authentication header or ESP authentication transform for data confidentiality.

Table 20-2 IPsec Transform Matrix

Transform Type	Transform	Description
ESP encryption	esp-aes 128	ESP with the 128-bit Advanced Encryption Standard (AES) encryption algorithm
	esp-aes 192	ESP with the 192-bit AES encryption algorithm
	esp-aes 256	ESP with the 256-bit AES encryption algorithm
	esp-gcm 128	ESP transform using the Galois Counter Mode (GCM) 128-bit cipher
	esp-gcm 192	ESP transform using the GCM 192-bit cipher
	esp-gcm 256	ESP transform using the GCM 256-bit cipher (next-generation encryption)
ESP authentication	esp-sha-hmac	ESP with the Secure Hash Algorithm (SHA) (HMAC variant) authentication algorithm
	esp-sha256-hmac	ESP with the 256-bit SHA2 (HMAC variant) authentication algorithm
	esp-sha384-hmac	ESP with the 384-bit SHA2 (HMAC variant) authentication algorithm
	esp-sha512-hmac	ESP with the 512-bit SHA2 (HMAC variant) authentication algorithm
Authentication header authentication	ah-md5-hmac	Authentication header with the MD5 (Message Digest 5) authentication algorithm
	ah-sha-hmac	Authentication header with the SHA authentication algorithm

The transform set is created using the following steps:

Step 1.   Create the transform set and identify the transforms by using the command **crypto ipsec transform-set** *transform-set-name* [*esp-encryption-name*] [*esp-authentication-name*] [*ah-authentication-name*]. The transform set and identification of transforms are accomplished with this one command. Only one transform set can be selected for ESP encryption, ESP authentication, and authentication header authentication. The following are suggested transform set combinations:

```
esp-aes 256 and esp-sha-hmac
esp-aes and esp-sha-hmac
```

Step 2. Configure the ESP mode by using the command **mode {transport | tunnel}**. The ESP tunnel mode is the default mode and does not provide any benefits, but it does add 20 bytes of overhead per packet. Use the ESP mode of transport.

Example 20-4 provides a sample IPsec transform set.

Example 20-4 *Sample IPsec Transform Set*

```
crypto ipsec transform-set AES256/SHA/TRANSPORT esp-aes 256 esp-sha-hmac
 mode transport
```

The transform set can be verified with the command **show crypto ipsec transform-set**, as shown in Example 20-5.

Example 20-5 *Verifying the IPsec Transform Set*

```
R12-DC1-Hub2# show crypto ipsec transform-set
! Output omitted for brevity
Transform set AES256/SHA/TRANSPORT: { esp-256-aes esp-sha-hmac }
 will negotiate = { Transport, },
```

IPsec Profile

The IPsec profile combines the IPsec transform set and the IKEv2 profile. The IPsec profile is created using the following steps:

Step 1. Create the IPsec profile by using the command **crypto ipsec profile** *profile-name*. The configuration context is then placed in IPsec profile configuration submode.

Step 2. Specify the transform set by using the command **set transform-set** *transform-set-name*.

Step 3. Specify the IKEv2 profile by using the command **set ikev2-profile** *ike-profile-name*.

Example 20-6 provides a sample IPsec profile configuration.

Example 20-6 *Sample IPsec Profile*

```
crypto ipsec profile DMVPN-IPSEC-PROFILE-INET
 set transform-set AES256/SHA/TRANSPORT
 set ikev2-profile DMVPN-IKE-PROFILE-INET
```

The command **show crypto ipsec profile** displays the components of the IPsec profile, as shown in Example 20-7.

Example 20-7   *Verifying the IPsec Profile*

```
R12-DC1-Hub2# show crypto ipsec profile
! Output omitted for brevity
IPSEC profile DMVPN-IPSEC-PROFILE-INET
        IKEv2 Profile: DMVPN-IKE-PROFILE-INET
        Security association lifetime: 4608000 kilobytes/3600 seconds
        Responder-Only (Y/N): N
        PFS (Y/N): N
        Mixed-mode : Disabled
        Transform sets={
                AES256/SHA/TRANSPORT: { esp-256-aes esp-sha-hmac } ,
```

Encrypting the Tunnel Interface

When all the required IPsec components have been configured, the IPsec profile is associated to the DMVPN tunnel interface with the command **tunnel protection ipsec profile** profile-name [**shared**]. The **shared** keyword is required for routers that terminate multiple encrypted DMVPN tunnels on the same transport interface. The command shares the IPsec *security association database* (*SADB*) among multiple DMVPN tunnels. Because the SADB is shared, a unique tunnel key must be defined on each DMVPN tunnel interface to ensure that the encrypted/decrypted traffic aligns to the proper DMVPN tunnel.

> **NOTE**   The topology in this book does not terminate multiple DMVPN tunnels on the same transport interface. The **shared** keyword is not required, nor is the tunnel key.

Example 20-8 provides a sample configuration for encrypting a DMVPN tunnel interface. After the configuration in this section is applied to R12, R31, and R41, the DMVPN tunnels are protected with IPsec.

Example 20-8   *Enabling IPsec Tunnel Protection*

```
interface Tunnel200
 tunnel protection ipsec profile DMVPN-IPSEC-PROFILE-INET
```

IPsec Packet Replay Protection

The Cisco IPsec implementation includes an anti-replay mechanism that prevents intruders from duplicating encrypted packets by assigning a unique sequence number to each encrypted packet. When a router decrypts the IPsec packets, it keeps track of the packets it has received. The IPsec anti-replay service rejects (discards) duplicate packets or old packets.

The router identifies acceptable packet age according to the following logic. The router maintains a sequence number window size (with a default of 64 packets). The minimum sequence number is defined as the highest sequence number for a packet minus the window size. A packet is considered of age when the sequence number is between the minimum sequence number and the highest sequence number.

At times, the default 64-packet window size is not adequate. The sequence number is set during encryption, and this happens before any quality-of-service (QoS) policies are

20

processed. Packets can be delayed because of QoS priorities, resulting in out-of-order packets (where low-priority packets are queued, and high-priority packets are immediately forwarded). The sequence number increases on the receiving router because the high-priority packets shift the window ahead, and when the lower-priority packets arrive later, they are discarded.

Increasing the anti-replay window size has no impact on throughput or security. An additional 128 bytes per incoming IPsec SA are needed to store the sequence number on the decryptor. The window size is increased globally with the command **crypto ipsec security-association replay window-size** *window-size*. Cisco recommends using the largest window size possible for the platform, which is 1024.

Dead Peer Detection

When two routers establish an IPsec VPN tunnel between them, it is possible for connectivity between the two routers to be lost for some reason. In most scenarios, IKE and IPsec do not natively detect a loss of peer connectivity, which results in network traffic being blackholed until the SA lifetime expires.

The use of *Dead Peer Detection (DPD)* helps detect the loss of connectivity to a remote IPsec peer. When DPD is enabled in on-demand mode, the two routers check for connectivity only when traffic needs to be sent to the IPsec peer and the peer's liveliness is questionable. In such scenarios, the router sends a DPD R-U-THERE request to query the status of the remote peer. If the remote router does not respond to the R-U-THERE request, the requesting router starts to transmit additional R-U-THERE messages every retry interval for a maximum of five retries. After that, the peer is declared dead.

DPD is configured with the command **crypto ikev2 dpd** [*interval-time*] [*retry-time*] **on-demand** in the IKEv2 profile. As a general rule, the interval time is set to twice that of the routing protocol timer (2×20), and the retry interval is set to 5 seconds. In essence, the total time is $(2 \times 20(routing\text{-}protocol)) + (5 \times 5(retry\text{-}count)) = 65$ seconds. This exceeds the hold time of the routing protocol and engages only when the routing protocol is not operating properly.

DPD is configured on the spoke routers and not on the hubs because of the CPU processing that is required to maintain state for all the branch routers.

NAT Keepalives

Network Address Translation (NAT) keepalives are enabled to keep the dynamic NAT mapping alive during a connection between two peers. A NAT keepalive is a UDP (User Datagram Protocol) packet that contains an unencrypted payload of 1 byte. When DPD is used to detect peer status, NAT keepalives are sent if the IPsec entity has not transmitted or received a packet within a specified time period. NAT keepalives are enabled with the command **crypto isakmp nat keepalive** *seconds*.

NOTE The command **crypto isakmp nat keepalive** *seconds* is placed on the DMVPN spokes because the routing protocol between the spoke and the hub keeps the NAT state, whereas spoke-to-spoke tunnels do not maintain a routing protocol relationship, so NAT state is not maintained.

Complete IPsec DMVPN Configuration with Pre-Shared Authentication

Example 20-9 displays the complete configuration to enable IPsec protection on the Internet DMVPN tunnel on R12, R31, and R41 with all the settings from this section.

Example 20-9 *Complete IPsec DMVPN Configuration with Pre-Shared Authentication*

```
R12
crypto ikev2 keyring DMVPN-KEYRING-INET
 peer ANY
   address 0.0.0.0 0.0.0.0
   pre-shared-key CISCO456
!
crypto ikev2 profile DMVPN-IKE-PROFILE-INET
 match fvrf INET01
 match identity remote address 0.0.0.0
 authentication remote pre-share
 authentication local pre-share
 keyring local DMVPN-KEYRING-INET
!
crypto ipsec transform-set AES256/SHA/TRANSPORT esp-aes 256 esp-sha-hmac
 mode transport
!
crypto ipsec profile DMVPN-IPSEC-PROFILE-INET
 set transform-set AES256/SHA/TRANSPORT
 set ikev2-profile DMVPN-IKE-PROFILE-INET
!
interface Tunnel200
 tunnel protection ipsec profile DMVPN-IPSEC-PROFILE-INET
!
crypto ipsec security-association replay window-size 1024

R31 and R41
crypto ikev2 keyring DMVPN-KEYRING-INET
 peer ANY
  address 0.0.0.0 0.0.0.0
  pre-shared-key CISCO456
!
crypto ikev2 profile DMVPN-IKE-PROFILE-INET
 match fvrf INET01
 match identity remote address 0.0.0.0
 authentication remote pre-share
 authentication local pre-share
 keyring local DMVPN-KEYRING-INET
 dpd 40 5 on-demand
!
crypto ipsec transform-set AES256/SHA/TRANSPORT esp-aes 256 esp-sha-hmac
 mode transport
```

20

```
!
crypto ipsec profile DMVPN-IPSEC-PROFILE-INET
 set transform-set AES256/SHA/TRANSPORT
 set ikev2-profile DMVPN-IKE-PROFILE-INET
!
interface Tunnel200
 tunnel protection ipsec profile DMVPN-IPSEC-PROFILE-INET
!
crypto ipsec security-association replay window-size 1024
!
crypto isakmp nat keepalive 20
```

Verifying Encryption on DMVPN Tunnels

After the DMVPN tunnels have been configured for IPsec protection, the status should be verified. The command **show dmvpn detail** provides the relevant IPsec information.

Example 20-10 demonstrates the command on R31. The output lists the status of the DMVPN tunnel, the underlay IP addresses, and packet counts. Examining the packet counts in this output is one of the steps that can be taken to verify that network traffic is being transmitted out of a DMVPN tunnel or received on a DMVPN tunnel.

Example 20-10   *Verifying IPsec DMVPN Tunnel Protection*

```
R31-Spoke# show dmvpn detail
! Output omitted for brevity
# Ent Peer NBMA Addr  Peer Tunnel Add State UpDn Tm Attrb Target Network
----- --------------- --------------- ----- -------- ----- -------
    1  100.64.12.1      192.168.200.12     UP    00:03:39    S   192.168.200.12/32


Crypto Session Details:
-----------------------------------------------------------
Interface: Tunnel200
Session: [0xE7192900]
 Session ID: 1
 IKEv2 SA: local 100.64.31.1/500 remote 100.64.12.1/500 Active
 Capabilities:(none) connid:1 lifetime:23:56:20
 Crypto Session Status: UP-ACTIVE
 fvrf: INET01, Phase1_id: 100.64.12.1
 IPSEC FLOW: permit 47 host 100.64.31.1 host 100.64.12.1
       Active SAs: 2, origin: crypto map
       Inbound: #pkts dec'ed 22 drop 0 life (KB/Sec) 4280994/3380
       Outbound: #pkts enc'ed 20 drop 0 life (KB/Sec) 4280994/3380
 Outbound SPI : 0x35CF62F4, transform : esp-256-aes esp-sha-hmac
   Socket State: Open

Pending DMVPN Sessions:
```

The command **show crypto ipsec sa** provides additional information that is not included in the output of the command **show dmvpn detail**. Example 20-11 displays explicit information about all the security associations. Examine the path MTU, tunnel mode, and replay detection.

Example 20-11 *Verifying IPsec Security Association*

```
R31-Spoke# show crypto ipsec sa

interface: Tunnel200
   Crypto map tag: Tunnel200-head-0, local addr 100.64.31.1

   protected vrf: (none)
   local ident (addr/mask/prot/port): (100.64.31.1/255.255.255.255/47/0)
   remote ident (addr/mask/prot/port): (100.64.12.1/255.255.255.255/47/0)
   current_peer 100.64.12.1 port 500
    PERMIT, flags={origin_is_acl,}
   #pkts encaps: 16, #pkts encrypt: 16, #pkts digest: 16
   #pkts decaps: 18, #pkts decrypt: 18, #pkts verify: 18
   #pkts compressed: 0, #pkts decompressed: 0
   #pkts not compressed: 0, #pkts compr. failed: 0
   #pkts not decompressed: 0, #pkts decompress failed: 0
   #send errors 0, #recv errors 0

    local crypto endpt.: 100.64.31.1, remote crypto endpt.: 100.64.12.1
    plaintext mtu 1362, path mtu 1400, ip mtu 1400, ip mtu idb Tunnel200
    current outbound spi: 0x366F5BFF(913267711)
    PFS (Y/N): N, DH group: none

    inbound esp sas:
     spi: 0x66DD2026(1725767718)
       transform: esp-256-aes esp-sha-hmac ,
       in use settings ={Transport, }
       conn id: 4, flow_id: SW:4, sibling_flags 80000000, crypto map: Tunnel200-head-0
       sa timing: remaining key lifetime (k/sec): (4306710/3416)
       IV size: 16 bytes
       replay detection support: Y
       Status: ACTIVE(ACTIVE)

    inbound ah sas:
    inbound pcp sas:
    outbound esp sas:
     spi: 0x366F5BFF(913267711)
       transform: esp-256-aes esp-sha-hmac ,
```

```
     in use settings ={Transport, }
      conn id: 3, flow_id: SW:3, sibling_flags 80000000, crypto map: Tunnel200-head-0
      sa timing: remaining key lifetime (k/sec): (4306711/3416)
     IV size: 16 bytes
     replay detection support: Y
     Status: ACTIVE(ACTIVE)

   outbound ah sas:
   outbound pcp sas:
```

NOTE Using encryption over all transports allows for ease of deployment and trouble-shooting workflows because any and all transports are configured exactly the same. No special review or concern for traffic is needed because all paths are configured the same.

IKEv2 Protection

Protecting routers from various IKE intrusion methods was the key reason for the development of IKEv2, based on prior known IKEv1 limitations. The first key concept is limiting the number of packets required to process IKE establishment. CPU utilization increases for every SA state the CPU maintains, along with the negotiation of a session. During high CPU utilization, a session that has started may not complete because other sessions are consuming limited CPU resources. Problems can occur when the number of expected sessions is different from the number of sessions that can be established. Limiting the number of sessions that can be in negotiation minimizes the CPU resources needed so that the expected number of established sessions can be obtained.

The command **crypto ikev2 limit** {**max-in-negotiation-sa** *limit* | **max-sa** *limit*} [**outgoing**] limits the number of sessions being established or that are allowed to be established:

- The **max-sa** keyword limits the total count of SAs that a router can establish under normal conditions. You set the value to double the number of ongoing sessions in order to achieve renegotiation.

- To limit the number of SAs being negotiated at one time, you can use the **max-in-negotiation-sa** keyword.

- To protect IKE from half-open sessions, a cookie can be used to validate that sessions are valid IKEv2 sessions and not denial-of-service intrusions. The command **crypto ikev2 cookie-challenge** *challenge-number* defines the threshold of half-open SAs before issuing an IKEv2 cookie challenge.

In Example 20-12, R41 limits the number of SAs to 10, limits the number in negotiation to 6, and sets an IKEv2 cookie challenge for sessions above 4. R41 has 1 static session to the hub router (R11) and is limited to 9 additional sessions that all use the IKEv2 cookie challenge.

The command **show crypto ikev2 stats** displays the SA restrictions and shows that the four sessions are currently established to the four DMVPN hub routers.

Example 20-12   *Crypto IKEv2 Limit Configuration*

```
R41-Spoke(config)# crypto ikev2 limit max-sa 10
R41-Spoke(config)# crypto ikev2 limit max-in-negotiation-sa 6 outgoing
R41-Spoke(config)# crypto ikev2 limit max-in-negotiation-sa 6
R41-Spoke(config)# crypto ikev2 cookie-challenge 4
R41-Spoke(config)# end

R41-Spoke# show crypto ikev2 stats
----------------------------------------------------------------------------
              Crypto IKEv2 SA Statistics
----------------------------------------------------------------------------
System Resource Limit:    0     Max  IKEv2 SAs: 10  Max in nego(in/out): 6/6
Total incoming IKEv2 SA Count: 0          active :   0    negotiating: 0
Total outgoing IKEv2 SA Count: 4          active:    4    negotiating: 0
Incoming IKEv2 Requests: 1      accepted:    1       rejected:     0
Outgoing IKEv2 Requests: 4      accepted:    4       rejected:     0
Rejected IKEv2 Requests: 0    rsrc low:     0       SA limit:     0
IKEv2 packets dropped at dispatch: 0
Incoming IKEV2 Cookie Challenged Requests: 0
             accepted: 0         rejected: 0        rejected no cookie: 0
Total Deleted sessions of Cert Revoked Peers: 0
conformed 0000 bps, exceeded 0000 bps, violated 0000 bps
```

By using all the techniques described in this chapter, you can secure a router and its transports so that the router provides data integrity, data confidentiality, and data availability to the network.

References in This Chapter

Bolapragada, Vijay, Khalid, Mohamed, and Wainner, Scott, *IPsec VPN Design*, Cisco Press, 2005.

RFC 2401, *Security Architecture for the Internet Protocol*, S. Kent and R. Atkinson, http://tools.ietf.org/html/rfc2401, November 1998.

RFC 3706, *A Traffic-Based Method of Detecting Dead Internet Key Exchange (IKE) Peers*, G. Huang, S. Beaulieu, and D. Rochefort, http://tools.ietf.org/html/rfc3706, February 2004.

RFC 4301, *Security Architecture for the Internet Protocol*, S. Kent and K. Seo, http://tools.ietf.org/html/rfc4301, December 2005.

RFC 5996, *Internet Key Exchange Protocol Version 2 (IKEv2)*, C. Kaufman, P. Hoffman, Y. Nir, and P. Eronen, http://tools.ietf.org/html/rfc5996, September 2010.

20

Exam Preparation Tasks

As mentioned in the section "How to Use This Book" in the Introduction, you have a couple choices for exam preparation: the exercises here, Chapter 24, "Final Preparation," and the exam simulation questions in the Pearson Test Prep software.

Review All Key Topics

Review the most important topics in this chapter, noted with the Key Topic icon in the outer margin of the page. Table 20-3 lists these key topics and the page number on which each is found.

Table 20-3   Key Topics

Key Topic Element	Description	Page Number
Paragraph	Data security terms	822
Paragraph	Security associations	825
Paragraph	ESP modes	825
Paragraph	IKEv2 keyring	828
Paragraph	IKEv2 profile	829
Paragraph	IPsec transform set	831
Paragraph	Encrypting the tunnel interface	833
Paragraph	IPsec packet replay protection	833
Paragraph	Verifying encryption on DMVPN tunnels	836
Paragraph	IKEv2 protection	838

Define Key Terms

Define the following key terms from this chapter and check your answers in the glossary:

authentication header protocol, Encapsulating Security Payload (ESP), data confidentiality, data integrity, data availability, origin authentication, replay detection, periodic rekey, security association (SA)

Use the Command Reference to Check Your Memory

The ENARSI 300-410 exam focuses on the practical, hands-on skills that networking professionals use. Therefore, you should be able to identify the commands needed to configure, verify, and troubleshoot the topics covered in this chapter.

This section includes the most important configuration and verification commands covered in this chapter. It might not be necessary to memorize the complete syntax of every command, but you should be able to remember the basic keywords that are needed.

To test your memory of the commands in Table 20-4, go to the companion website and download Appendix B, "Command Reference Exercises." Fill in the missing commands in the tables based on each command description. You can check your work by downloading Appendix C, "Command Reference Exercise Answer Key," from the companion website.

Table 20-4 Command Reference

Task	Command Syntax
Configure an IKEv2 keyring.	crypto ikev2 keyring *keyring-name* peer *peer-name* address *network subnet-mask* pre-shared-key *secure-key*
Configure an IKEv2 profile.	crypto ikev2 profile *ike-profile-name* match identity remote address *ip-address* identity local address *ip-address* match fvrf {*vrf-name* | any} authentication local pre-share authentication remote pre-share keyring local keyring-name
Configure an IPsec transform set.	crypto ipsec transform-set *transform-set-name* [*esp-encryption-name*] [*esp-authentication-name*] [*ah-authentication-name*] mode {transport | tunnel}
Configure an IPsec profile.	crypto ipsec profile *profile-name* set transform-set transform-set-name set ikev2-profile *ike-profile-name*
Encrypt the DMVPN tunnel interface.	tunnel protection ipsec profile profile-name [shared]
Modify the default IPsec replay window size.	crypto ipsec security-association replay window-size *window-size*
Enable IPsec NAT keepalives.	crypto isakmp nat keepalive *seconds*
Display the IKEv2 profile.	show crypto ikev2 profile
Display the IPsec profile.	show crypto ipsec profile

20

## CHAPTER 21

Troubleshooting ACLs and Prefix Lists

This chapter covers the following topics:

- **Troubleshooting IPv4 ACLs:** This section examines how to read IPv4 ACLs so that you are more efficient at troubleshooting IPv4 ACL-related issues. It also shows the commands and processes you use for troubleshooting IPv4 packet filtering with standard, extended, and time-based IPv4 ACLs.

- **Troubleshooting IPv6 ACLs:** This section examines how to read IPv6 ACLs so that you are more efficient at troubleshooting IPv6 ACL-related issues. It also shows the commands and processes that you can use for troubleshooting IPv6 packet filtering.

- **Troubleshooting Prefix Lists:** This section reviews how to efficiently examine a prefix list for troubleshooting purposes so that when you are dealing with an issue that has a prefix list associated with it, you can determine whether the prefix list is or is not the problem.

- **Trouble Tickets:** This section provides trouble tickets that demonstrate how to use a structured troubleshooting process to solve a reported problem.

Access control lists (ACLs) and prefix lists are powerful tools that you need to be comfortable with for troubleshooting. They enable you to classify traffic or routes and then, depending on how you apply them, take specific actions. One slight error in an ACL or a prefix list can change the meaning of the ACL or prefix list and, as a result, how a service or feature that relies on it handles the route or traffic.

Therefore, you need to be able to read ACLs and prefix lists efficiently. You need a solid understanding of the way they are processed and how the devices using them make decisions based on the entries. Without this knowledge, you cannot successfully eliminate or prove that an ACL or a prefix list is the problem.

This chapter covers the ins and outs of ACLs and prefix lists. You will explore how they are processed, how they are read, and how to identify issues related to them. In addition, this chapter explains how to use ACLs for traffic filtering and how to use a prefix list for route filtering.

"Do I Know This Already?" Quiz

The "Do I Know This Already?" quiz allows you to assess whether you should read this entire chapter thoroughly or jump to the "Exam Preparation Tasks" section. If you are in doubt about your answers to these questions or your own assessment of your knowledge of the topics, read the entire chapter. Table 21-1 lists the major headings in this chapter and their corresponding "Do I Know This Already?" quiz questions. You can find the answers in Appendix A, "Answers to the 'Do I Know This Already?' Quiz Questions."

Table 21-1 "Do I Know This Already?" Foundation Topics Section-to-Question Mapping

Foundation Topics Section	Questions
Troubleshooting IPv4 ACLs	1–8
Troubleshooting IPv6 ACLs	9–11
Troubleshooting Prefix Lists	12–14

CAUTION The goal of self-assessment is to gauge your mastery of the topics in this chapter. If you do not know the answer to a question or are only partially sure of the answer, you should mark that question as wrong for purposes of self-assessment. Giving yourself credit for an answer that you correctly guess skews your self-assessment results and might provide you with a false sense of security.

1. What is the correct order of operations for an IPv4 ACL?

   a. Top-down processing, execute upon the longest match, implicit deny all

   b. Execute upon the longest match, top-down processing, implicit deny all

   c. Implicit deny all, immediate execution upon a match, top-down processing

   d. Top-down processing, immediate execution upon a match, implicit deny all

2. What occurs to a packet when an ACL is applied to an interface but the packet does not match any of the entries in the ACL?

   a. It is forwarded.

   b. It is flooded.

   c. It is dropped.

   d. It is buffered.

3. What does the following ACL entry accomplish when applied to an interface: **20 permit tcp 10.1.1.0 0.0.0.63 host 192.0.2.1 eq 23?**

   a. Permits Telnet traffic from the device with IP address 192.0.2.1 going to any device with an IP address from 10.1.1.0 to 10.1.1.63.

   b. Permits Telnet traffic from any device with IP address from 10.1.1.0 to 10.1.1.63 going to the device with IP address 192.0.2.1.

   c. Permits SSH traffic from any device with IP address from 10.1.1.0 to 10.1.1.63 going to the device with IP address 192.0.2.1.

   d. Permits SSH traffic from the device with IP address 192.0.2.1 going to any device with IP address from 10.1.1.0 to 10.1.1.63.

4. Which command successfully filters ingress traffic using ACL 100 on an interface?

   a. access-group 100 in

   b. access-class 100 in

   c. ip access-group 100 in

   d. ip traffic-filter 100 in

5. Which of the following uses the default port number 443?

    a. SSH

    b. HTTP

    c. Telnet

    d. HTTPs

6. Which of the following uses the default port number 22?

    a. SSH

    b. HTTP

    c. Telnet

    d. HTTPs

7. Which port and protocol do SNMP use?

    a. TCP/161

    b. UDP/161

    c. TCP/520

    d. UDP/520

    e. TCP/514

    f. UDP/514

8. Which port numbers does DHCP use? (Choose two.)

    a. 88

    b. 25

    c. 68

    d. 69

    e. 67

    f. 53

9. What is the correct order of operations for an IPv6 ACL?

    a. Immediate execution upon a match, implicit permit icmp nd, implicit deny all, top-down processing

    b. Top-down processing, immediate execution upon a match, implicit permit icmp nd, implicit deny all

    c. Top-down processing, implicit permit icmp nd, immediate execution upon a match, implicit deny all

    d. Implicit permit icmp nd, top-down processing, immediate execution upon a match, implicit deny all

10. What happens if you add the following entry to the end of an IPv6 ACL: **deny ipv6 any any log?** (Choose two.)

    a. All traffic is denied and logged.

    b. All traffic that does not match an entry in the ACL is denied and logged.

    c. ICMP Neighbor Discovery messages are implicitly permitted.

    d. ICMP Neighbor Discovery messages are denied.

11. Which command successfully filters egress traffic using an IPv6 ACL named ENARSI on an interface?

    a. access-group ENARSI out

    b. access-class ENARSI out

    c. ipv6 access-group ENARSI out

    d. ipv6 traffic-filter ENARSI out

12. Which IP prefix list entry matches only the default route?

    a. ip prefix-list ENARSI permit 0.0.0.0/0 le 32

    b. ip prefix-list ENARSI permit 0.0.0.0/0 ge 32

    c. ip prefix-list ENARSI permit 0.0.0.0/0 ge 1

    d. ip prefix-list ENARSI permit 0.0.0.0/0

13. Which IP prefix list matches all routes?

    a. ip prefix-list ENARSI permit 0.0.0.0/0 le 32

    b. ip prefix-list ENARSI permit 0.0.0.0/0 ge 32

    c. ip prefix-list ENARSI permit 0.0.0.0/0 ge 1

    d. ip prefix-list ENARSI permit 0.0.0.0/0

14. What routes match the prefix list **ip prefix-list ENARSI seq 35 deny 192.168.0.0/20 ge 24 le 28?**

    a. Routes with an address from 192.168.0.0 to 192.168.15.255 with a subnet mask of 24 to 28

    b. Routes within the 192.168.0.0/20 subnet with a subnet mask greater than 24 and less than 28

    c. Routes with the subnet ID and mask 192.168.0.0/20

    d. Routes with an address from 192.168.0.0 to 192.168.15.255 with a subnet mask of 24 or 28

Foundation Topics

Troubleshooting IPv4 ACLs

The purpose of an access control list (ACL) is to identify traffic based on different criteria, such as source or destination IP address, source or destination port number, transport layer protocol, and quality of service (QoS) markings. An ACL that has been created does nothing unless it is applied to a service, a feature, or an interface. For example, it can be used to identify the private IP addresses that will be translated to a public address with Network Address Translation (NAT) and Port Address Translation (PAT). It can also be used to control which routes will be redistributed, which packets will be subject to policy-based routing, and which packets will be permitted or denied through the router. Therefore, it is imperative that you be able to read an ACL to determine whether it was created correctly; otherwise, the services you are applying it to will fail to produce the results you want.

This section explains how to troubleshoot an IPv4 ACL to make sure it is correctly created for the purpose it is intended for. The section also provides examples related to packet filtering. Other examples related to distribute lists, route maps, and policy-based routing (PBR) are covered in other chapters related to those features.

21

Reading an IPv4 ACL

Being able to read an ACL and understand what it's created for is important for troubleshooting. However, understanding how an ACL functions is even more important as you troubleshoot because you need to identify why you are experiencing the issues that are occurring. Following is a list of steps that IPv4 ACLs use. These steps can help you identify why an IPv4 ACL is behaving the way it is:

Step 1.   **Top-down processing:** An ACL is made up of various entries; these entries are processed from the top of the ACL to the bottom of the ACL, in order.

Step 2.   **Immediate execution upon a match:** The very first entry that matches the values in the packet that are being compared is the entry that is used. This may be a permit entry or a deny entry, and it dictates how the packet is treated based on the ACL implementation. It doesn't matter if there is another entry later in the ACL that matches; only the first entry that matches matters.

Step 3.   **Implicit deny any:** If there is no matching entry for the packet, the packet is automatically denied based on the invisible implicit deny any entry at the end of an ACL. (Because of this, you need at least one permit entry in an ACL, or everything will be denied automatically.)

Example 21-1 shows a sample ACL with standard numbering that uses only source IPv4 addresses. In this example, the ACL is numbered 1 and has four entries. The entries are listed from most specific to least specific. With earlier IOS versions, if you did not create *standard ACL* entries from most specific to least specific, you ended up with generic entries earlier in the ACL that would cause issues by dropping or permitting traffic that should not be dropped or permitted. In newer IOS versions, if you attempt to create a standard ACL entry that is more specific than an entry that already exists, the router prevents the entry from being created and gives an error message.

Notice how traffic sourced from 10.1.1.5 is denied in sequence 5. Even though the very next sequence, 10, permits 10.1.1.5, 10.1.1.5 will be denied because of top-down processing and then immediate execution upon a match. Likewise, even though sequence 30 permits all addresses from 10.1.1.0 through 10.1.1.255, 10.1.1.5 is denied by sequence 5, and 10.1.1.64 through 10.1.1.127 are denied by sequence 20. What about all other source IP addresses that do not match an entry in the ACL (for example, 192.168.2.1)? They are all denied because of the *implicit deny* entry (which you cannot see) at the end of the ACL.

Example 21-1   *Sample Standard Numbered ACL*

```
Router# show access-lists
Standard IP access list 1
 5 deny 10.1.1.5
 10 permit 10.1.1.0, wildcard bits 0.0.0.63 (1 match)
 20 deny 10.1.1.64, wildcard bits 0.0.0.63
 30 permit 10.1.1.0, wildcard bits 0.0.0.255
```

Extended ACLs are a little more complicated to read and troubleshoot than standard ACLs because they contain more parameters. Example 21-1 shows a standard ACL that only allows a source address to be specified. An extended ACL can take source and destination addresses, source and destination port numbers, protocols, and other parameters that give you granular control over what you are trying to match. Also remember that standard and extended IPv4 ACLs can be named instead of numbered.

Key Topic

Example 21-2 provides a sample extended numbered ACL. In this example, it is numbered 100. It has four entries, listed from most specific to least specific. Notice in sequence 10 that 10.1.1.5 is denied from accessing TCP services using port 80 on 192.0.2.1. At the same time, under sequence 20, 10.1.1.5 would be permitted to Telnet to 192.0.2.1, and in sequence 40, it would be permitted to any destination on any port using any protocol. Therefore, you have much more granular control over how the traffic will be matched in an extended ACL. Revisit sequence 10 and focus on the log-input option. This will generate syslog messages indicating that host 10.1.1.5 was denied when this ACL entry is a match. It will also indicate the interface this happened on because of the input part of the option.

Example 21-2 *Sample Extended Numbered ACL*

```
R1# show access-lists 100
Extended IP access list 100
 10 deny tcp host 10.1.1.5 host 192.0.2.1 eq www log-input
 20 permit tcp 10.1.1.0 0.0.0.63 host 192.0.2.1 eq telnet
 30 deny ip 10.1.1.64 0.0.0.63 host 192.0.2.1
 40 permit ip 10.1.1.0 0.0.0.255 any
```

Before you sit for the ENARSI exam, it is important to ensure that you are comfortable with different applications/services, protocols, and port numbers as you are likely to see them referenced in a multitude of questions. Table 21-2 provides a few that you should be aware of.

Table 21-2 Port Numbers and Protocols Associated with Various Applications

Application/Service	Protocols	Port Numbers
HTTP	TCP	80
HTTPS	TCP	443
Telnet	TCP	23
SSH	TCP	22
FTP	TCP	20/21
DNS	TCP/UDP	53
BGP	TCP	179
NTP	UDP	123
SNMP	UDP	161/162
SMTP	TCP	25
Syslog	UDP/TCP	514/6514
RIP	UDP	520
TFTP	UDP	69
PING	ICMP	Various
TRACE ROUTE	ICMP or UDP	Various
BootP (DHCP) Client	UDP	68
BootP (DHCP) Server	UDP	67
EIGRP	88	N/A
OSPF	89	N/A

21

Using an IPv4 ACL for Filtering

To use an ACL for packet filtering, you must apply the ACL to an interface. You accomplish this with the **ip access-group** {*acl_number* | *acl_name*} {**in** | **out**} command in interface configuration mode, as shown in Example 21-3.

The direction in which you apply the ACL on an interface is significant. You need to consider this while you are creating the ACL. If you apply it to the wrong interface or in the wrong direction, you will not get the desired result. You can verify what ACLs are applied to an interface by using the **show ip interface** *interface_type interface_number* command. Example 21-3 shows how access list 1 is applied inbound on GigabitEthernet0/0 and access list 100 is applied outbound on Gig0/0.

To apply an IPv4 ACL to a vty line, use the command **access-class** *acl_name* {**in** | **out**}.

Example 21-3 *Verifying Access Lists Applied to Interfaces*

```
R1(config)# interface gigabitEthernet 0/0
R1(config-if)# ip access-group 100 out
R1(config-if)# ip access-group 1 in
R1(config-if)# end
R1# show ip interface gigabitEthernet 0/0
GigabitEthernet0/0 is up, line protocol is up
 Internet address is 10.1.1.1/24
 Broadcast address is 255.255.255.255
 Address determined by non-volatile memory
 MTU is 1500 bytes
 Helper address is 172.16.1.10
 Directed broadcast forwarding is disabled
 Multicast reserved groups joined: 224.0.0.5 224.0.0.6
 Outgoing access list is 100
 Inbound access list is 1
 Proxy ARP is enabled
 Local Proxy ARP is disabled
```

NOTE ACLs applied to a router interface in the outbound direction do not affect locally generated traffic from the router that is leaving that interface. For example, if you apply an ACL outbound that denies ICMP messages or OSPF messages out the router interface, ICMP and OSPF messages generated by the router and sent out the interface will still be permitted.

Using a Time-Based IPv4 ACL

By default, an ACL you apply is active the entire time it is applied. However, that might not be your goal. For example, perhaps you want to prevent traffic from going to the Internet after hours but allow it during open hours. Or you might want to give a certain service or user the ability to back up files to a server from 9 p.m. to 1 a.m. Monday to Friday and prevent them from doing it any other time.

To accomplish these goals, you need to use *time-based ACLs*. Example 21-4 provides a sample time-based ACL. Notice that the ACL entry with sequence number 10 has the time-range option. The time range is based on values configured in the AFTERHOURS time range. It also states that it is active, meaning that the current entry will be denying web traffic from host 10.1.1.5 to 192.0.2.1. Because the ACL entry is attached to a time range, when troubleshooting time-based ACLs, you also have to review the configuration of the time range itself. Example 21-5 shows the AFTERHOURS time range with the **show time-range AFTERHOURS** command. It has two *weekdays* entries, one from 5 p.m. to midnight and the other from midnight to 9 a.m. It also has a *weekend* entry that covers all day and all night. It also states that it is active and used in an ACL. When the access control entry is outside the time range, it displays inactive.

Example 21-4 *Sample Time-Based ACL*

```
R1# show access-lists 100
Extended IP access list 100
 10 deny tcp host 10.1.1.5 host 192.0.2.1 eq www time-range AFTERHOURS (active)
 20 permit tcp 10.1.1.0 0.0.0.63 host 192.0.2.1 eq telnet
 30 deny ip 10.1.1.64 0.0.0.63 host 192.0.2.1
 40 permit ip 10.1.1.0 0.0.0.255 any
```

Example 21-5 *Sample Time Range Configured on R1*

```
R1# show time-range AFTERHOURS
time-range entry: AFTERHOURS (active)
 periodic weekdays 17:00 to 23:59
 periodic weekdays 0:00 to 8:59
 periodic weekend 0:00 to 23:59
 used in: IP ACL entry
```

So far, you have seen that you have to troubleshoot an ACL and the time range when dealing with issues related to time-based ACLs. However, there is one more item of troubleshooting: time. A time-based ACL is based on the device's clock. If the clock is not correct, the time-based ACL may be active or inactive at the wrong time. Example 21-6 shows how you can verify the current time on a router by using the **show clock** command. Notice that the output says it's Sunday May 25, 2019, at 10:53 a.m. Therefore, the time-based ACL entry should be active because it is AFTERHOURS. In this case, you only want to permit web traffic Monday to Friday 9 a.m. to 5 p.m. and deny it at all other times.

Example 21-6 *Viewing the Time on a Cisco Router*

```
R1# show clock
*10:53:50.067 UTC Sun May 25 2019
```

21

But wait, are you sure this is the right time? Are you using manually set clocks, and have they changed? Or are you using a Network Time Protocol (NTP) server? You will want to verify with another time source that this is in fact the right time. In addition, if you are using NTP (as you should be), you need to check your NTP settings to make sure the clocks are synchronized and that the time is right. Are you using UTC time or local time? Depending on that answer, you might have to consider daylight saving time.

Troubleshooting IPv6 ACLs

IPv6 ACLs play an important role in IPv6 networks. They allow you to classify traffic for many different reasons. For example, you might need to classify traffic that will be subject to policy-based routing, or you might need to classify the traffic that will be filtered as it passes through the router.

IPv6 traffic filtering can be done on an interface-by-interface basis with IPv6 access lists. This section explains how to read IPv6 access lists so that you can troubleshoot them efficiently and identify whether they have been correctly applied to an interface for filtering purposes.

Reading an IPv6 ACL

Being able to read an IPv6 ACL and understand what it was created for is important for troubleshooting. However, understanding how an IPv6 ACL functions is even more important as you troubleshoot because you need to identify why you are experiencing the issues that are occurring. Following is a list of steps that IPv6 ACLs use; most of them are the same as the steps for IPv4 ACLs. Being familiar with these steps will help you identify why an IPv6 ACL is behaving the way it is:

Step 1.   **Top-down processing:** An ACL is made up of various entries; these entries are processed from the top of the ACL to the bottom of the ACL, in order.

Step 2.   **Immediate execution upon a match:** The very first entry that matches the values in the packet that are being compared is the entry that is used. This may be a permit entry or a deny entry, and it dictates how the packet is treated based on the ACL implementation. It doesn't matter if there is another entry later in the ACL that matches; only the first entry that matches matters.

Step 3.   **Implicit permit icmp nd:** If the packet is an NA or NS message, permit it.

Step 4.   **Implicit deny any:** If there is no matching entry for the packet, the packet is automatically denied based on the invisible implicit deny any entry at the end of an ACL.

Pause here for a moment. Did you notice the steps differ a little from IPv4? There is an added step before the implicit deny any. Recall that IPv6 relies on the Neighbor Discovery Protocol (NDP) NA (neighbor advertisement) and NS (neighbor solicitation) messages to determine the MAC address associated with an IPv6 address. Therefore, the *implicit permit icmp nd* entries for NA and NS messages have been added before the implicit deny any, so they are not denied:

```
permit icmp any any nd-na

permit icmp any any nd-ns
```

However, because these are implicit permit statements, all statically entered commands come before them. Therefore, if you issue the **deny ipv6 any any log** command at the end of an

IPv6 ACL, as you might be accustomed to doing in IPv4, you will break the NDP process because NA and NS messages will be denied. Therefore, when troubleshooting NDP, keep in mind that an ACL might be the reason it is not working.

With IPv4 ACLs, a clear separation exists between standard and extended IPv4 ACLs. However, with IPv6, you have just one type, which is similar to an IPv4 extended ACL. Therefore, within an IPv6 ACL entry, you can provide source and destination IPv6 addresses, protocol, source and destination port numbers, QoS markings, and more. You can provide as little or as much information as you need to accomplish your goal.

Example 21-7 shows a sample IPv6 ACL that was created on R1. The IPv6 access list is named ENARSI, and you read it exactly as you read an IPv4 ACL. For example, sequence 20 states that TCP (Transmission Control Protocol) traffic related to Telnet will be denied from any device going to 2001:DB8:A:B::7/128. Sequence 30 states that TCP traffic related to WWW from 2001:DB8:A:A::20/128 to 2001:DB8:D::1/128 will be permitted.

Key Topic

Example 21-7 *Sample IPv6 ACL*

```
R1# show ipv6 access-list
IPv6 access list ENARSI
 permit tcp host 2001:DB8:A:A::20 host 2001:DB8:A:B::7 eq telnet sequence 10
 deny tcp any host 2001:DB8:A:B::7 eq telnet sequence 20
 permit tcp host 2001:DB8:A:A::20 host 2001:DB8:D::1 eq www sequence 30
 deny ipv6 2001:DB8:A:A::/80 any sequence 40
 permit ipv6 2001:DB8:A:A::/64 any sequence 50
```

Notice that there are no wildcard masks with IPv6. Instead, you specify a prefix, as shown in sequences 40 and 50 in Example 21-7, which accomplishes the same goal as the wildcard mask (defining a range of addresses). For example, the prefix /128 is like having the all 0s wildcard mask, which means matching exactly this address or host (that is, all bits in the address). A /0 prefix is like having the all 255s wildcard mask (that is, not matching any bits in the address). A /64 prefix indicates that the first 64 bits must match and that the last 64 bits do not have to match. As a result, this prefix would include all interface IDs within a /64 network. What if the prefix is /80? This means the first 80 bits must match, and the last 48 bits do not have to match. As a result, the prefix is defining which bits of the IPv6 address must match.

Using an IPv6 ACL for Filtering

To use an IPv6 ACL for packet filtering, you need to apply the IPv6 ACL to an interface. You can accomplish this with the **ipv6 traffic-filter** *acl_name* {**in** | **out**} command in interface configuration mode, as shown in Example 21-8. The direction in which you apply the IPv6 ACL on an interface is significant. You need to consider this while you are creating the ACL. If you apply it to the wrong interface or in the wrong direction, you will not get the desired result. You can verify the IPv6 ACLs that are applied to an interface by using the **show ipv6 interface** *interface_type interface_number* command. Example 21-8 shows the IPv6 access list ENARSI applied inbound on interface Gig0/0.

To apply an IPv6 ACL to a vty line, use the command **ipv6 access-class** *acl_name* {**in** | **out**}.

21

Example 21-8   *Verifying IPv6 Access Lists Applied to Interfaces*

```
R1(config)# interface gigabitEthernet 0/0
R1(config-if)# ipv6 traffic-filter ENARSI in
R1(config-if)# end
R1# show ipv6 interface gigabitEthernet 0/0
GigabitEthernet0/0 is up, line protocol is up
 IPv6 is enabled, link-local address is FE80::C808:3FF:FE78:8
 No Virtual link-local address(es):
 Global unicast address(es):
 2001:DB8:A:A::1, subnet is 2001:DB8:A:A::/64
 Joined group address(es):
 FF02::1
 FF02::2
 FF02::1:2
 FF02::1:FF00:1
 FF02::1:FF78:8
 MTU is 1500 bytes
 ICMP error messages limited to one every 100 milliseconds
 ICMP redirects are enabled
 ICMP unreachables are sent
 Input features: Access List
 Inbound access list ENARSI
 ND DAD is enabled, number of DAD attempts: 1
 ND reachable time is 30000 milliseconds (using 30000)
 ND advertised reachable time is 0 (unspecified)
 ND advertised retransmit interval is 0 (unspecified)
 ND router advertisements are sent every 200 seconds
 ND router advertisements live for 1800 seconds
 ND advertised default router preference is Medium
 Hosts use stateless autoconfig for addresses.
 Hosts use DHCP to obtain other configuration.
```

Troubleshooting Prefix Lists

Although an ACL can give you extremely granular control of the traffic you want to match, it does not help you identify routes based on a subnet mask. Therefore, ACLs do not give you granular control when matching routes for route filtering. This is why *prefix lists* exist. They allow you to define the route and prefix that you want to match. This section explains how to read a prefix list so that when you are troubleshooting features that call upon a prefix list, you will have the ability to eliminate the prefix list as the cause of the issue or prove that the prefix list is the cause of the issue.

> **NOTE**   This discussion applies to both IPv4 prefix lists and IPv6 prefix lists. The only difference is that in an IPv4 prefix list, you have IPv4 addresses and masks, and in an IPv6 prefix list, you have IPv6 addresses and masks. However, the same principles and concepts apply. As a result, all the examples in this section are based on IPv4.

Reading a Prefix List

Example 21-9 shows the commands used to create a sample prefix list called ENARSI and the output of **show ip prefix-list**, which you can use to verify the IPv4 prefix lists configured on a router. To verify IPv6 prefix lists, you use the command **show ipv6 prefix-list**.

Example 21-9 *Sample IPv4 Prefix List*

```
R1# config t
Enter configuration commands, one per line. End with CNTL/Z.
R1(config)# ip prefix-list ENARSI seq 10 deny 10.1.1.0/26
R1(config)# ip prefix-list ENARSI seq 20 permit 10.1.1.0/24 le 32
R1(config)# ip prefix-list ENARSI seq 30 permit 0.0.0.0/0
R1(config)# ip prefix-list ENARSI seq 35 deny 192.168.0.0/20 ge 24 le 28
R1(config)# end
R1# show ip prefix-list
ip prefix-list ENARSI: 4 entries
 seq 10 deny 10.1.1.0/26
 seq 20 permit 10.1.1.0/24 le 32
 seq 30 permit 0.0.0.0/0
 seq 35 deny 192.168.0.0/20 ge 24 le 28
```

There are two different ways to read a prefix list entry, depending on whether *le* (less than or equal to) or *ge* (greater than or equal to) appears at the end of the prefix list entry:

- **There is no ge or le:** If the entry does not contain ge or le, the prefix is treated as an address and a subnet mask. Refer to the entry with sequence number 10 in Example 21-9. There is no ge or le; therefore, the network 10.1.1.0/26 is matched exactly. For example, if you are using the prefix list to filter EIGRP routing updates, the 10.1.1.0/26 network will be denied (meaning that it will be filtered and not sent to or received from the neighbor).

- **There is a ge or le:** If the entry does contain ge or le, the prefix is treated as an address and a wildcard mask. Refer to the entry with sequence number 20 in Example 21-9. Because there is ge or le, the entry is defining a range of values. 10.1.1.0/24 really means 10.1.1.0 0.0.0.255 (where 0.0.0.255 is the inverse of the subnet mask), which indicates a range of addresses from 10.1.1.0 through 10.1.1.255 (just as with an ACL). The le at the end means less than or equal to, and the 32 refers to a subnet mask. Therefore, this entry is permitting any address from 10.1.1.0 through 10.1.1.255 with a subnet mask less than or equal to 32 (0 to 32). For example, if you are using the prefix list to filter routing updates, the 10.1.1.0/24, 10.1.1.64/26, and 10.1.1.128/30 networks would all be permitted because they fall within the prefix range and subnet mask range.

Refer to sequence 30 in Example 21-9. Because there is no ge or le, it will be an exact match to the address and mask listed. In this case, the address and mask are 0.0.0.0/0, which is the default route. Therefore, if this prefix list is being used to filter routing updates, the filter would permit the default route.

21

Refer to sequence 35 in Example 21-9. Because there is ge or le, the address and mask are treated as an address and wildcard mask to define a range. Therefore, 192.168.0.0/20 is 192.168.0.0 0.0.15.255, which defines a range of 192.168.0.0 through 192.168.15.255. The ge 24 le 28 values specify a subnet mask range from 24 to 28. Therefore, if this prefix entry is used to filter routes, all routes with an address from 192.168.0.0 to 192.168.15.255 with a subnet mask of 24 to 28 are denied.

Now it is your turn. Which routes will match the following prefix list?

```
ip prefix-list EXAMPLE permit 10.1.1.0/24 ge 26
```

Before you read any further, try to determine the answer on your own.

Because there is ge, the /24 is treated as a wildcard mask of 0.0.0.255. Therefore, the range of routes is from 10.1.1.0 to 10.1.1.255. (The first 24 bits must match.) However, the ge 26 indicates that the routes also must have a subnet mask from 26 to 32. So, to sum up the prefix list, any route from 10.1.1.0 to 10.1.1.255 with a subnet mask from 26 to 32 will match this prefix list.

Prefix List Processing

Following is a list of steps that prefix lists use. These steps can help you identify why a prefix list is behaving the way it is:

Step 1.   **Top-down processing:** A prefix list is made up of various sequences; these sequences are processed from the top of the prefix list to the bottom of the prefix list, in order of sequence number. In Example 21-9, sequence 10 is processed first, then 20, 30, and 40.

Step 2.   **Immediate execution upon a match:** The very first sequence that matches is the sequence that is used. This may be a permit sequence or a deny sequence, and it dictates how the information is treated. It doesn't matter if there is another sequence later in the prefix list that matches. Only the first sequence that matches matters. For example, even though in Example 21-9 the 10.1.1.0/26 network falls within the range defined in sequence 20, which would permit it, it is denied in sequence 10, which is processed first. Therefore, 10.1.1.0/26 is denied.

Step 3.   **Implicit deny any:** If there is no matching sequence, the information is automatically denied based on the invisible implicit deny any entry at the end of a prefix list. For example, if the prefix list in Example 21-9 is used to filter routing updates, and an update is received for 172.16.32.0/29, it is denied because it does not match sequence 10, 20, 30, or 40.

Because there is an implicit deny any at the end of a prefix list, you need at least one permit sequence in a prefix list, or everything will be denied. For example, if you are creating a prefix list to deny a specific route or two (for example, 10.1.1.0/24 and 10.1.2.0/24), you can create the following entries:

```
ip prefix-list NAME seq 10 deny 10.1.1.0/24

ip prefix-list NAME seq 20 deny 10.1.2.0/24
```

Although this denies both prefixes, it also denies every other prefix because of the implicit deny any at the end. Therefore, to permit everything else, you need to include an entry that does so. The following entry would do just that:

```
ip prefix-list NAME seq 30 permit 0.0.0.0/0 le 32
```

Do not confuse this with the default route entry (seq 30) from Example 21-9. That does not have le or ge, and this example does. Let's review it. The le indicates an address and a wildcard mask. So, 0.0.0.0/0 is really 0.0.0.0 255.255.255.255. Therefore, the range is all/any addresses. The subnet mask is le 32, which is 0 to 32. Therefore, this entry permits all routes. For IPv6, the equivalent permit all is as follows:

```
ipv6 prefix-list NAME seq 30 permit ::/0 le 128
```

Trouble Tickets

This section presents various trouble tickets related to the topics discussed in this chapter. The purpose of these trouble tickets is to show a process that you can follow when troubleshooting in the real world or in an exam environment.

Trouble Ticket 21-1: IPv4 ACL Trouble Ticket

Problem: A user at PC1 (see Figure 21-1) has indicated that he cannot Telnet to 192.0.2.1, and he needs to. However, he can ping 192.0.2.1 and access web-enabled resources.

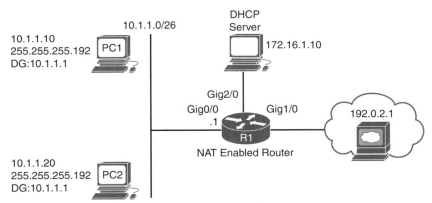

Figure 21-1 *IPv4 ACL Trouble Ticket Topology*

You start by verifying the problem. On PC1, you attempt to Telnet to 192.0.2.1, but it fails, as shown in Example 21-10. You then ping 192.0.2.1, and it is successful, as also shown in Example 21-10.

Example 21-10 *Failed Telnet and Successful Ping from PC1 to 192.0.2.1*

21

```
C:\PC1>telnet 192.0.2.1
Connecting To 192.0.2.1...Could not open connection to the host, on port 23: Connect
failed

C:\PC1>ping 192.0.2.1
Reply from 192.0.2.1: bytes=32 time 1ms TTL=128
```

```
Reply from 192.0.2.1: bytes=32 time 1ms TTL=128
Reply from 192.0.2.1: bytes=32 time 1ms TTL=128
Reply from 192.0.2.1: bytes=32 time 1ms TTL=128


Ping statistics for 192.0.2.1:
 Packets: Sent = 4, Received = 4, Lost = 0 (0% loss),
Approximate round trip times in milli-seconds:
 Minimum = 0ms, Maximum = 0ms, Average = 0ms
```

At this point, you should be thinking that the issue is related to either the Telnet service being disabled on 192.0.2.1 or an ACL. Why an ACL? Certain types of traffic are allowed through, but others are not, and this is accomplished with filtering.

First, you need to verify whether there are any ACLs configured on R1 that might filter Telnet-related traffic. In Example 21-11, the **show ip access-lists** command is used to verify whether any ACLs are configured on R1. In this example, there is one extended IPv4 ACL identified as number 100. You can see that there are two entries related to Telnet. One is a permit entry with sequence number 10, and the other is a deny entry with sequence number 20. Notice that the deny entry has nine matches, and the permit entry has no matches. Read sequence 10 out loud:

Sequence 10 will permit tcp traffic related to telnet from 192.0.2.1 to 10.1.1.10.

Read it again and think about how the traffic is flowing based on this entry:

FROM 192.0.2.1 TO 10.1.1.10

PC1 is trying to establish a Telnet session to 192.0.2.1 (not the other way around). Therefore, sequence 10 does not match Telnet traffic from PC1 to 192.0.2.1. It matches Telnet traffic from 192.0.2.1 to PC1.

Sequence 20 states that TCP traffic related to Telnet from the 10.1.1.0/26 network to any destination will be denied. Therefore, using top-down processing and immediate execution upon a match flow, sequence 20 matches the Telnet traffic from PC1 to 192.0.2.1, and as a result, the traffic is denied.

Example 21-11 *Verifying ACLs Configured on R1*

```
R1# show ip access-lists
Extended IP access list 100
 10 permit tcp host 192.0.2.1 host 10.1.1.10 eq telnet
 20 deny tcp 10.1.1.0 0.0.0.63 any eq telnet (9 matches)
 30 deny tcp 10.1.1.0 0.0.0.63 any eq ftp
 40 permit tcp 10.1.1.0 0.0.0.63 any eq 22
 50 deny tcp 10.1.1.0 0.0.0.63 any eq smtp
 60 permit ip any any (2 matches)
```

The best way to fix this is to remove sequence 10 and replace it with the correct entry. You can use *named ACL* configuration mode to accomplish this. Example 21-12 shows how you can use named ACL configuration mode to edit a numbered ACL and the output of **show ip access-lists**, which verifies that the changes were made.

Example 21-12   *Using Named ACL Configuration Mode to Modify a Numbered ACL*

```
R1# config t
Enter configuration commands, one per line. End with CNTL/Z.
R1(config)# ip access-list extended 100
R1(config-ext-nacl)# no 10
R1(config-ext-nacl)# 10 permit tcp host 10.1.1.10 host 192.0.2.1 eq 23
R1(config-ext-nacl)# end
R1#
R1# show access-lists
Extended IP access list 100
 10 permit tcp host 10.1.1.10 host 192.0.2.1 eq telnet
 20 deny tcp 10.1.1.0 0.0.0.63 any eq telnet (9 matches)
 30 deny tcp 10.1.1.0 0.0.0.63 any eq ftp
 40 permit tcp 10.1.1.0 0.0.0.63 any eq 22
 50 deny tcp 10.1.1.0 0.0.0.63 any eq smtp
 60 permit ip any any (4 matches)
```

Example 21-13 shows the **telnet 192.0.2.1** command being issued from PC1 for a successful connection.

Example 21-13   *Successful Telnet Connection from PC1 to 192.0.2.1*

```
C:\PC1>telnet 192.0.2.1
User Access Verification
Password:
```

The output of **show ip access-lists** on R1, as shown in Example 21-14, reveals the matches associated with sequence 10.

Example 21-14   *Verifying Packet Matches for an ACL Entry*

```
R1# show ip access-lists
Extended IP access list 100
 10 permit tcp host 10.1.1.10 host 192.0.2.1 eq telnet (25 matches)
 20 deny tcp 10.1.1.0 0.0.0.63 any eq telnet (9 matches)
 30 deny tcp 10.1.1.0 0.0.0.63 any eq ftp
 40 permit tcp 10.1.1.0 0.0.0.63 any eq 22
 50 deny tcp 10.1.1.0 0.0.0.63 any eq smtp
 60 permit ip any any (5 matches)
```

21

Trouble Ticket 21-2: IPv6 ACL Trouble Ticket

Problem: A user at PC2 (see Figure 21-2) has indicated that she is not able to Telnet to 2001:db8:a:b::7, and she needs to. However, she can ping 2001:db8:a:b::7 and receive DHCP-related information from the DHCP server.

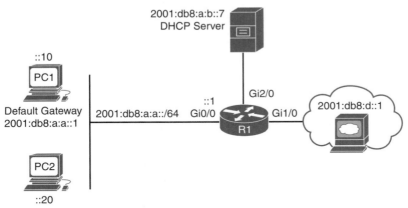

Figure 21-2   *IPv6 ACL Trouble Ticket Topology*

You start by verifying the problem. On PC2, you attempt to Telnet to 2001:db8:a:b::7, but it fails, as shown in Example 21-15. You then ping 2001:db8:a:b::7, and it is successful, as also show in Example 21-15.

Example 21-15   *Failed Telnet and Successful Ping from PC2 to 2001:db8:a:b::7*

```
C:\PC2>telnet 2001:db8:a:b::7
Connecting To 2001:db8:a:B::7...Could not open connection to the host, on port 23:
Connect failed

C:\PC2>ping 2001:db8:a:b::7

Pinging 2001:db8:a:b::7 with 32 bytes of data:
Reply from 2001:db8:a:b::7: time=46ms
Reply from 2001:db8:a:b::7: time=40ms
Reply from 2001:db8:a:b::7: time=40ms
Reply from 2001:db8:a:b::7: time=40ms

Ping statistics for 2001:db8:a:b::7:
 Packets: Sent = 4, Received = 4, Lost = 0 (0% loss),
Approximate round trip times in milli-seconds:
 Minimum = 40ms, Maximum = 46ms, Average = 41ms
```

What could allow pings yet deny Telnet? At this point, you should be thinking that the issue is related to either the Telnet service being disabled on 2001:db8:a:b::7 or an IPv6 ACL filtering traffic into or out of an interface. This is because certain traffic is allowed while other traffic is denied. Most times, this is because of traffic filtering.

First, you verify whether the Telnet service is running by using Telnet from R1 to 2001:db8:a:b::7. As shown in Example 21-16, it is successful. If it were not successful, you could then access the server or contact the users responsible for the server to see whether Telnet is enabled.

Example 21-16   *Successful Telnet from R1 to 2001:db8:a:b::7*

```
R1# telnet 2001:db8:a:b::7
Trying 2001:DB8:A:B::7 ... Open


User Access Verification


Password:
```

Next, you check whether there are any ACLs associated with interface Gi2/0 on R1 by using the command **show ipv6 interface gigabitEthernet2/0**. As shown in Example 21-17, there are no IPv6 ACLs.

Example 21-17   *Verifying ACLs on Gig2/0 of R1*

```
R1# show ipv6 interface gigabitEthernet 2/0
GigabitEthernet2/0 is up, line protocol is up
 IPv6 is enabled, link-local address is FE80::C808:3FF:FE78:38
 No Virtual link-local address(es):
 Global unicast address(es):
 2001:DB8:A:B::1, subnet is 2001:DB8:A:B::/64
 Joined group address(es):
 FF02::1
 FF02::2
 FF02::1:FF00:1
 FF02::1:FF78:38
 MTU is 1500 bytes
 ICMP error messages limited to one every 100 milliseconds
 ICMP redirects are enabled
 ICMP unreachables are sent
 ND DAD is enabled, number of DAD attempts: 1
 ND reachable time is 30000 milliseconds (using 30000)
 ND advertised reachable time is 0 (unspecified)
 ND advertised retransmit interval is 0 (unspecified)
 ND router advertisements are sent every 200 seconds
 ND router advertisements live for 1800 seconds
 ND advertised default router preference is Medium
Hosts use stateless autoconfig for addresses.
```

Next, you check whether there are any ACLs associated with interface Gi0/0 on R1 by using the command **show ipv6 interface gigabitEthernet0/0**. As shown in Example 21-18, there is an inbound IPv6 ACL named ENARSI attached to the interface.

21

Example 21-18 *Verifying ACLs on Gig0/0 of R1*

```
R1# show ipv6 interface gigabitEthernet 0/0
GigabitEthernet0/0 is up, line protocol is up
 IPv6 is enabled, link-local address is FE80::C808:3FF:FE78:8
 No Virtual link-local address(es):
 Global unicast address(es):
 2001:DB8:A:A::1, subnet is 2001:DB8:A:A::/64
 Joined group address(es):
 FF02::1
 FF02::2
 FF02::1:2
 FF02::1:FF00:1
 FF02::1:FF78:8
 MTU is 1500 bytes
 ICMP error messages limited to one every 100 milliseconds
 ICMP redirects are enabled
 ICMP unreachables are sent
 Input features: Access List
 Inbound access list ENARSI
 ND DAD is enabled, number of DAD attempts: 1
 ND reachable time is 30000 milliseconds (using 30000)
 ND RAs are suppressed (all)
 Hosts use stateless autoconfig for addresses.
 Hosts use DHCP to obtain other configuration.
```

Now you need to verify the IPv6 ACL named ENARSI by using the **show ipv6 access-list ENARSI** command. Example 21-19 shows this output. Notice sequence 20. It is a permit statement that allows PC2 to Telnet to 2001:db8:a:b::7. However, notice sequence 10. It is a deny statement that is preventing all devices from using Telnet to 2001:db8:a:b::7. Remember that IPv6 ACLs are processed from the top down, and then when a match is found, it is immediately executed on. That is what is happening here. Sequence 10 matches PC2's Telnet and denies it.

Notice that for IPv6, the router allows a more specific entry to be placed after a more general entry. This differs from the behavior shown earlier with IPv4 ACLs.

Example 21-19 *ENARSI IPv6 ACL on R1*

```
R1# show ipv6 access-list ENARSI
IPv6 access list ENARSI
 deny tcp any host 2001:DB8:A:B::7 eq telnet (6 matches) sequence 10
 permit tcp host 2001:DB8:A:A::20 host 2001:DB8:A:B::7 eq telnet sequence 20
 permit tcp host 2001:DB8:A:A::20 host 2001:DB8:D::1 eq www sequence 30
 permit ipv6 2001:DB8:A:A::/64 any (67 matches) sequence 40
```

To solve this issue, you connect to R1, enter IPv6 ACL configuration mode for the ACL named ENARSI, and then remove sequence 20 and add the same entry with sequence number 5 so that it is before sequence 10, as shown in Example 21-20. In addition, you verify the changes by using the **show ipv6 access-list ENARSI** command.

Example 21-20 *Modifying the ENARSI IPv6 ACL on R1*

```
R1# config t
Enter configuration commands, one per line. End with CNTL/Z.
R1(config)# ipv6 access-list ENARSI
R1(config-ipv6-acl)# no sequence 20
R1(config-ipv6-acl)# seq 5 permit tcp host 2001:DB8:A:A::20 host 2001:DB8:A:B::7 eq
telnet

R1# show ipv6 access-list ENARSI
IPv6 access list ENARSI
 permit tcp host 2001:DB8:A:A::20 host 2001:DB8:A:B::7 eq telnet sequence 5
 deny tcp any host 2001:DB8:A:B::7 eq telnet (6 matches) sequence 10
 permit tcp host 2001:DB8:A:A::20 host 2001:DB8:D::1 eq www sequence 30
 permit ipv6 2001:DB8:A:A::/64 any (67 matches) sequence 40
```

Now you go back to PC2 and attempt to Telnet to 2001:db8:a:b::7. As shown in Example 21-21, it is successful.

Example 21-21 *Successful Telnet from PC2 to 2001:db8:a:b::7*

```
C:\PC2>telnet 2001:db8:a:b::7

User Access Verification

Password:
```

Trouble Ticket 21-3: Prefix List Trouble Ticket

Problem: Your junior admin has contacted you and said that R1 (see Figure 21-3) is not learning any routes from Enhanced Interior Gateway Routing Protocol (EIGRP), as shown in Example 21-22. The admin has confirmed that neighbor relationships are being formed, interfaces are participating in the routing process, and other routers are learning about the routes. The admin has come to you for help. You have extensive knowledge, and you ask your junior admin if he checked for any route filters. He says no.

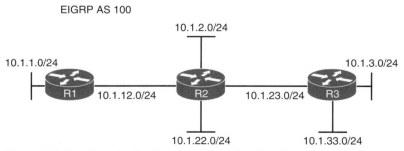

Figure 21-3 *IPv4 Prefix List Trouble Ticket Topology*

Example 21-22   *Verifying Routes in R1's Routing Table*

```
R1# show ip route
...output omitted...
Gateway of last resort is not set


 10.0.0.0/8 is variably subnetted, 4 subnets, 2 masks
C 10.1.1.0/24 is directly connected, GigabitEthernet0/0
L 10.1.1.1/32 is directly connected, GigabitEthernet0/0
C 10.1.12.0/24 is directly connected, GigabitEthernet1/0
L 10.1.12.1/32 is directly connected, GigabitEthernet1/0
```

You execute the **show ip protocols** command on R1, as shown in Example 21-23. The output indicates that there is an inbound route filter, using a prefix list called FILTER_10.1.3.0.

Example 21-23   *Verifying Whether There Are Any Route Filters on R1*

```
R1# show ip protocols
*** IP Routing is NSF aware ***


Routing Protocol is "eigrp 100"
 Outgoing update filter list for all interfaces is not set
 Incoming update filter list for all interfaces is (prefix-list) FILTER_10.1.3.0
 Default networks flagged in outgoing updates
 Default networks accepted from incoming updates
...output omitted...
```

Next, you issue the **show ip prefix-list** command on R1 to review the prefix list called FILTER_10.1.3.0, as shown in Example 21-24. In this output, you can see that the 10.1.3.0/24 prefix is being denied. Your junior admin states that this is not the problem because 10.1.3.0/24 is supposed to be denied based on the documentation, while all others are permitted. You respond by saying that you are very sure that it is the problem. You remind your junior admin about how prefix lists are processed: (1) top down, (2) immediate execution upon a match, (3) implicit deny any at the end. Therefore, due to the implicit deny any, this prefix list denies all prefixes—not just 10.1.3.0/24.

Example 21-24   *Reviewing the Prefix List on R1*

```
R1# show ip prefix-list
ip prefix-list FILTER_10.1.3.0: 1 entries
 seq 5 deny 10.1.3.0/24
```

To fix this problem, you create another entry for the FILTER_10.1.3.0 prefix list that permits all other routes, as follows:

```
ip prefix-list FILTER_10.1.3.0 seq 10 permit 0.0.0.0/0 le 32
```

Example 21-25 shows the updated prefix list on R1, and Example 21-26 shows the updated routing table, which has all the routes except for 10.1.3.0/24, which is denied by sequence 5.

Example 21-25 *Reviewing the Updated Prefix List on R1*

```
R1# show ip prefix-list
ip prefix-list FILTER_10.1.3.0: 2 entries
  seq 5 deny 10.1.3.0/24
  seq 10 permit 0.0.0.0/0 le 32
```

Example 21-26 *Verifying Updated Routes in R1's Routing Table*

```
R1# show ip route
...output omitted...
Gateway of last resort is not set


 10.0.0.0/8 is variably subnetted, 8 subnets, 2 masks
C 10.1.1.0/24 is directly connected, GigabitEthernet0/0
L 10.1.1.1/32 is directly connected, GigabitEthernet0/0
D 10.1.2.0/24 [90/130816] via 10.1.12.2, 00:01:32, GigabitEthernet1/0
C 10.1.12.0/24 is directly connected, GigabitEthernet1/0
L 10.1.12.1/32 is directly connected, GigabitEthernet1/0
D 10.1.22.0/24 [90/130816] via 10.1.12.2, 00:01:32, GigabitEthernet1/0
D 10.1.23.0/24 [90/3072] via 10.1.12.2, 00:01:32, GigabitEthernet1/0
D 10.1.33.0/24 [90/131072] via 10.1.12.2, 00:01:32, GigabitEthernet1/0
```

Exam Preparation Tasks

As mentioned in the section "How to Use This Book" in the Introduction, you have a couple choices for exam preparation: the exercises here, Chapter 24, "Final Preparation," and the exam simulation questions in the Pearson Test Prep software.

Review All Key Topics

Review the most important topics in this chapter, noted with the Key Topic icon in the outer margin of the page. Table 21-3 lists these key topics and the page number on which each is found.

Table 21-3 Key Topics

Key Topic Element	Description	Page Number
List	The IPv4 ACL order of operations	846
Paragraph	Reading an IPv4 standard ACL	846
Paragraph	Reading an IPv4 extended ACL	847
Example 21-3	Verifying access lists applied to interfaces	848
Example 21-4	Sample time-based ACL	849
Step list	The IPv6 ACL order of operations	850
Example 21-7	Sample IPv6 ACL	851
Example 21-8	Verifying IPv6 access lists applied to interfaces	852
Paragraphs	Reading a prefix list	853
Step list	The prefix list order of operations	854
Paragraph	Reading an IPv4 standard ACL	855

21

Define Key Terms

Define the following key terms from this chapter and check your answers in the glossary:

standard ACL, implicit deny, extended ACL, time-based ACL, IPv6 ACL, implicit permit, prefix list, ge, le, named ACL

Use the Command Reference to Check Your Memory

The ENARSI 300-410 exam focuses on the practical, hands-on skills that networking professionals use. Therefore, you should be able to identify the commands needed to configure, verify, and troubleshoot the topics covered in this chapter.

This section includes the most important configuration and verification commands covered in this chapter. It might not be necessary to memorize the complete syntax of every command, but you should be able to remember the basic keywords that are needed.

To test your memory of the commands in Table 21-4, go to the companion website and download Appendix B, "Command Reference Exercises." Fill in the missing commands in the tables based on each command description. You can check your work by downloading Appendix C, "Command Reference Exercise Answer Key," from the companion website.

Table 21-4   Command Reference

Task	Command Syntax
Display all the access lists configured on the device.	show access-lists
Display all the IPv4 access lists configured on the device.	show ip access-lists
Display all the IPv6 access lists configured on the device.	show ipv6 access-list
Display the inbound and outbound IPv4 access lists applied to an interface.	show ip interface *interface_type interface_number*
Display the inbound and outbound IPv6 access lists applied to an interface.	show ipv6 interface *interface_type interface_number*
Display any time ranges that have been configured on the device.	show time-range
Display the date and time on the device.	show clock

## CHAPTER 22

Infrastructure Security

This chapter covers the following topics:

- **Cisco IOS AAA Troubleshooting:** This section explains how to identify and troubleshoot issues related to AAA using the local database, a RADIUS server, and a TACACS+ server.

- **Troubleshooting Unicast Reverse Path Forwarding (uRPF):** This section explores what to look for in troubleshooting issues with uRPF.???I don't like "in"… can we use when troubleshooting? - Raymond

- **Troubleshooting Control Plane Policing (CoPP):** This section examines CoPP and what you should consider when troubleshooting issues related to CoPP.

- **IPv6 First-Hop Security:** This section describes the IPv6 First-Hop Security features, such as the Binding Table, IPv6 Snooping, Router Advertisement Guard, DHCPv6 Guard, Source Guard, Destination Guard, and Prefix Guard.

AAA is a framework that enhances authentication, authorization, and accounting services using either a local username and password database or a AAA server such as a RADIUS or TACACS+ server. AAA can be used with many different services and features. For ENARSI, the focus is on management access (that is, using it for console and vty access). Being able to troubleshoot issues related to AAA in this case is important as you will not be able to access your devices for management reasons if AAA is not working. This chapter examines these issues.

uRPF is a security feature that helps limit or even eliminate spoofed IP packets on a network. If it is implemented incorrectly, you could end up dropping legitimate packets. This chapter examines what to look out for with uRPF to troubleshoot uRPF in the real world.

For CoPP, a lot of parts need to be configured correctly, such as access control lists (ACLs), class maps, and policy maps. Knowing the various parts and what to look out for will help you become a successful troubleshooter in the real world. This chapter provides a list of items to check off as you troubleshoot CoPP.

Finally, IPv6 is the future of IP communication, and you need to be able to secure it. This chapter introduces various IPv6 First-Hop Security features to help you identify them and describe them for the ENARSI certification exam.

"Do I Know This Already?" Quiz

The "Do I Know This Already?" quiz allows you to assess whether you should read this entire chapter thoroughly or jump to the "Exam Preparation Tasks" section. If you are in doubt about your answers to these questions or your own assessment of your knowledge of the topics, read the entire chapter. Table 22-1 lists the major headings in this chapter and their corresponding "Do I Know This Already?" quiz questions. You can find the answers in Appendix A, "Answers to the 'Do I Know This Already?' Quiz Questions."

Table 22-1 "Do I Know This Already?" Foundation Topics Section-to-Question Mapping

Foundation Topics Section	Questions
Cisco IOS AAA Troubleshooting	1–4
Troubleshooting Unicast Reverse Path Forwarding (uRPF)	5, 6
Troubleshooting Control Plane Policing (CoPP)	7–9
IPv6 First-Hop Security	10–12

CAUTION The goal of self-assessment is to gauge your mastery of the topics in this chapter. If you do not know the answer to a question or are only partially sure of the answer, you should mark that question as wrong for purposes of self-assessment. Giving yourself credit for an answer that you correctly guess skews your self-assessment results and might provide you with a false sense of security.

1. Which command successfully configures a user-defined method list on a Cisco IOS device that uses the database on the device if the external server is not available for authentication?

   a. aaa authentication login default local group radius

   b. aaa authentication login default group radius local

   c. aaa authentication login REMOTE_ACCESS local group radius

   d. aaa authentication login MANAGEMENT_ACCESS group radius local

2. Your Cisco router is configured with the following command:

   ```
   aaa authentication login default group radius local
   ```

   What will occur during login if the local database does not contain any username and password when it is checked?

   a. The RADIUS server will be used for authentication.

   b. Authentication will fail.

   c. The user will be granted access.

   d. The line password will be used.

3. Your router is configured as follows:

   ```
   R1# show run | i aaa|username
   aaa new-model
   username ENARSI password 0 EXAM
   R1# show run | s vty
   line vty 0 4
    password cisco
    transport input all
   R1#
   ```

Based on this configuration, what will occur when someone uses Telnet to reach the router?

   a. Authentication will fail because there is no AAA method list.

   b. The user will be required to use the line password cisco.

   c. The user will be required to use the username ENARSI with the password EXAM.

   d. The user will be granted access either with the username ENARSI with the password EXAM or with the line password cisco.

4. Your router console is displaying the following message:

```
Invalid AUTHEN packet (check keys).
```

What does this mean?

   a. The user supplied the wrong password when connecting via SSH.

   b. The router and server are not using the same encryption algorithm.

   c. The router or server is configured with the wrong pre-shared key.

   d. The **transport input ssh** command is missing.

5. Which of the following commands would you use if you needed uRPF to match the return interface with the incoming interface and a default route?

   a. **ip verify unicast source reachable-via rx allow-default**

   b. **ip verify unicast source reachable-via any allow-default**

   c. **ip verify unicast source reachable-via any allow-default 111**

   d. **ip verify unicast source reachable-via rx allow-self-ping**

6. Which of the following commands would you use for uRPF if the traffic flow were asynchronous?

   a. **ip verify unicast source reachable-via rx allow-default**

   b. **ip verify unicast source reachable-via rx**

   c. **ip verify unicast source reachable-via any**

   d. **ip verify unicast source reachable-via rx allow-self-ping**

7. Which of the following commands would you use to verify the number of packets that have conformed to a specific class map that you are using for CoPP?

   a. **show access-list**

   b. **show class-map**

   c. **show policy-map**

   d. **show policy-map control-plane**

8. How is a policy map processed?

   a. All at once, matching the best class map.

   b. From the top down, matching the first class map that applies.

   c. From the bottom up, matching the first class map that applies.

   d. It is not processed; the class map is processed.

9. What happens when traffic does not match any of the user-defined class maps specified in the policy map?

   a. It is ignored.

   b. It is dropped.

   c. It is transmitted.

   d. It is subject to the policy defined in the default class.

10. Which IPv6 First-Hop Security feature is used to block unwanted RA messages?

    a. RA Guard

    b. DHCPv6 Guard

    c. IPv6 ND inspection/snooping

    d. Source Guard

11. Which IPv6 First-Hop Security feature is able to validate the source of IPv6 traffic and, if the source is not valid, block it?

    a. RA Guard

    b. DHCPv6 Guard

    c. IPv6 ND inspection/snooping

    d. Source Guard

12. Which of the following is true about RA Guard? (Choose two.)

    a. You configure it inbound on an interface.

    b. It is supported on EtherChannel bundles.

    c. It protects tunneled IPv6 traffic.

    d. It supports host mode and router mode.

Foundation Topics

Cisco IOS AAA Troubleshooting

AAA is a framework that provides authentication, authorization, and accounting when securing the management plane. The first A in AAA stands for *authentication*, which is about identifying and verifying the user based on something she knows, something she has, or something she is. The second A in AAA stands for *authorization*, which is about determining and controlling what the authenticated user is permitted to do. The final A in AAA stands for *accounting*, which is about collecting information to be used for billing, auditing, and reporting.

This section examines AAA, using the local database, a *RADIUS* server, and a *TACACS+* server. Cisco Identity Services Engine (ISE) is an example of a RADIUS or TACACS+ server. In addition, this examines a few authorization options.

Example 22-1 provides a sample Cisco IOS AAA configuration for management access to the vty lines and the console port. The **aaa new-model** command is used to enable AAA services on the router. By default, AAA is disabled. AAA commands are not available on Cisco IOS products until you enable AAA.

The **username admin password 0 letmein** command is used in this case to create the username admin and the password letmein, which will be stored in the local username and password database. As you will see shortly, these credentials will be used for fallback authentication if the AAA servers are not available.

> **NOTE**   admin is a bad username, and letmein is a bad password. They are used here only for demonstration purposes, and you should never use such weak credentials.

The **tacacs server TACSRV1** command is used to provide the settings needed to connect to a TACACS+ server. In this case, the server is at 10.0.10.51, and it is using the pre-shared key TACACSPASSWORD.

The **radius server RADSRV1** command is used to provide the settings needed to connect to a RADIUS server. In this case, the server is at 10.0.10.51, and it is using authentication port 1812, acct-pot 1813, and the pre-shared key RADIUSPASSWORD.

The **aaa group server radius RADIUSMETHOD** command is used to group one or more RADIUS servers that will be used together within a distinct list or method and to specify any common settings that will be used. In this case, RADSRV1 will be in this group due to the **server name RADSRV1** command, and all packets sourced by the router going to the RADIUS server will be sourced from the IP address of Loopback 1, as indicated in the command **ip radius source-interface Loopback1**. In this case, the **server** command allows the server to be used with other groups. However, if you wanted your server to only be used with this group, you would use the **server-private name** *srv-name* command instead. In addition, if this server group and server were for a specific virtual routing and forwarding (VRF) instance, you would need to use the command **ip vrf forwarding** *vry-name* in the group to specify the VRF instance the group belongs to.

The **aaa group server tacacs+ TACACSMETHOD** command is used to group one or more TACACS+ servers that will be used together within a distinct list or method and to specify any common settings that will be used. In this case, TACSRV1 will be in this group due to the **server name TACSRV1** command, and all packets sourced by the router going to the RADIUS server will be sourced from the IP address of Loopback 1, as indicated in the command **ip tacacs source-interface Loopback1**. In this case, the **server** command allows the server to be used with other groups. However, if you wanted your server to only be used with this group, you would use the **server-private name** *srv-name* command instead. In addition, if this server group and server were for a specific VRF instance, you would need to use the command **ip vrf forwarding** *vry-name* in the group to specify the VRF instance the group belongs to.

The **aaa authentication login VTY_ACCESS group RADIUSMETHOD local** command creates a AAA *method list* called VTY_ACCESS for login authentication. The first method that will be used is the group of servers in the RADIUSMETHOD group, and if the RADIUS servers are not available, the second method that will be used is the local username and password database.

The **aaa authentication login CONSOLE_ACCESS group TACACSMETHOD local** command creates a AAA method list called CONSOLE_ACCESS for login authentication. The first method that will be used is TACACSMETHOD, and if the TACACS+ servers are not available, the second method that will be used is the local username and password database.

The command **login authentication CONSOLE_ACCESS** in line con 0 configuration mode configures the console port to use the AAA method list called CONSOLE_ACCESS for authenticating to the console port.

The command **login authentication VTY_ACCESS** in line vty 0 4 configuration mode configures the vty lines to use the AAA method list called VTY_ACCESS for authenticating vty access, such as Telnet and SSH connections.

Example 22-1   *Verifying Cisco IOS AAA Configuration*

```
R1# show run | section username|aaa|line|radius|tacacs
aaa new-model
username admin password 0 letmein
tacacs server TACSRV1
 address ipv4 10.0.10.51
 key TACACSPASSWORD
radius server RADSRV1
 address ipv4 10.0.10.51 auth-port 1812 acct-port 1813
 key RADIUSPASSWORD
aaa group server radius RADIUSMETHOD
 server name RADSRV1
 ip radius source-interface Loopback1
aaa group server tacacs+ TACACSMETHOD
 server name TACSRV1
 ip tacacs source-interface Loopback1
aaa authentication login VTY_ACCESS group RADIUSMETHOD local
aaa authentication login CONSOLE_ACCESS group TACACSMETHOD local
line con 0
 logging synchronous
 login authentication CONSOLE_ACCESS
line vty 0 4
 login authentication VTY_ACCESS
 transport input all
```

Using Example 22-1, consider the following when troubleshooting Cisco IOS AAA authentication:

- **AAA needs to be enabled:** AAA is disabled by default on Cisco routers and switches. To enable AAA, use the **aaa new-model** command. Local authentication is immediately applied to all lines except the console line. Therefore, you will not be able to access the device remotely if the local database does not contain at least one username and password. However, the Console can still be accessed with no username or password by default.

- **AAA relies on the local username and password database or a AAA server such as RADIUS or TACACS+:** By default, AAA uses the local username and password database for authentication. If no username and password exist that can be used for remote access, authentication fails. Therefore, if you are using local authentication, a

22

username and password needs to exist on the local device. However, if you are using a AAA server, you should still configure at least one username and password in the local database that can be used for fallback purposes in the event that the AAA server is not available. In Example 22-1, the username admin with the password letmein can be used for AAA authentication.

- **A method list defines the authentication methods:** When no method list exists, the vty lines use the local username and password database by default. However, with the method list, you can define what methods of authentication will be used and in what order. In Example 22-1, a user-defined method list for login authentication called VTY_ACCESS will use the servers in the RADIUS group RADIUSMETHOD, and if the servers are not accessible, local authentication will be used as the fallback method. Please note that if the database has no username or password, authentication fails because the servers are not available.

- **Method list service is incorrect:** When you create a method list, you specify the service that method list is for. For example, the AAA authentication login method list is for authenticating the console and vty lines. The AAA authentication PPP method list is for authenticating PPP sessions. The AAA authentication dot1x method list is for authenticating users connecting to a dot1x-enabled interface. Therefore, if you create a method list for login and then apply it to your PPP interfaces, it will not work. If you create a method list for dot1x and then apply it to the vty lines, it will not work. The method list service must match the service for which you are creating the list.

- **AAA method lists are applied to the lines:** The method list that will be used to define how authentication will occur for the vty lines or console line needs to be applied with the **login authentication** {**default** | *list_name*} command. In Example 22-1, the VTY_ACCESS method list is attached to the vty lines, and the CONSOLE_ACCESS method list is attached to the console line.

- **The router needs to be able to reach the AAA server:** Use the **test aaa** command on the router or use Telnet to reach the authentication port number of the AAA server to verify connectivity.

- **The router needs to be configured with the correct pre-shared key:** Ensure that the router and the AAA server are configured with the same pre-shared key. In this case, the pre-shared key for the RADIUS server is RADIUSPASSWORD, and the pre-shared key for the TACACS+ server is TACACSPASSWORD. If the correct pre-shared key is not configured on the client (router) or the server, you will receive the message "Invalid AUTHEN packet (check keys)." in the debug output.

- **The correct authenticating and accounting ports need to be configured:** RADIUS uses ports 1812 or 1645 (Cisco default) for authentication and 1813 or 1646 (Cisco default) for accounting. So, if your RADIUS server is using ports 1812 and 1813, you have to configure the port numbers on your Cisco devices as they use 1645 and 1646 by default. TACACS+ uses port 49.

- **Usernames and passwords need to be configured on the AAA server:** Double-check to make sure the correct usernames and passwords are configured on the AAA server.

- **The AAA server group needs to have the correct AAA server IP addresses:** Ensure that the IP addresses of the servers in the AAA server group are correct.

- **A user can authenticate but can't execute any commands:** Make sure the user has been authorized on the server to execute the commands he or she needs to execute.

- **The IP address of the client must be configured on the AAA server:** When configuring a AAA server, you must specify the client IP address, which would be the router in this case. Remember that when a router sources packets, it uses the exit interface as the source of a packet. If the exit interface is not configured with the IP address that the AAA server is expecting, the client cannot use the AAA server and its services. It is recommended that the IP address of a loopback interface be used for the source of packets and as the client IP address that is configured on the AAA server. Therefore, you must configure the router with the **ip radius source-interface** *interface_type interface_number* command or the **ip tacacs source-interface** *interface_type interface_number* command so that it sources RADIUS and TACACS packets with the correct IP address every time.

You can use the **debug aaa authentication** command to verify the AAA authentication process in real time.

You can use the **debug radius authentication** command to view the RADIUS authentication processes in real time.

You can use the **debug tacacs authentication** command to view the TACACS authentication processes in real time.

You can use the **debug aaa protocol local** command to view local authentication processes in real time.

Now let's shift our focus to AAA authorization.

You use the global configuration command **aaa authorization exec** to create a method list to control whether the user will be placed in the exec shell (privileged exec mode) after successfully authenticating. Just as with authentication method lists, you can use the default name, which is default, or you can create your own custom user-defined named. (For example, the command **aaa authorization exec default** would be used to create a method list using the name default.) Next, you specify the methods that are used to determine authorization. For example, you could use a RADIUS or TACACS+ group by using the **group** option, or you could use no authorization by using the **none** option, or you could even use the local username and password database by using the **local** option.

So, let's say that you have the following local user in your local username and password database:

```
username raymond privilege 15 password cisco
```

By default, with AAA, the privilege 15 will be ignored. Therefore, when Raymond logs in, he will be placed in user -exec mode, not in privileged exec mode. To invoke the privilege level, you would need to type the following in global configuration mode:

```
aaa authorization exec default local
```

22

In this case, default is the name of the authorization method list, and local is the only method that has been specified for this list. In addition, you would need to go to your line—for example, **line vty 0 4**—and use the command **authorization exec default**, as shown in the following code snippet, to enforce the AAA authorization using the default authorization method list you created earlier:

```
line vty 0 4
    authorization exec default
```

Now when Raymond logs in using Telnet or SSH, he will be immediately placed into privileged exec mode.

For the console port, you need one additional command that is not needed for the vty lines: **aaa authorization console** in global configuration mode. Without this command, when you connect to the console port, the authorization commands will be ignored.

Troubleshooting Unicast Reverse Path Forwarding (uRPF)

uRPF is a security feature that helps limit or even eliminate spoofed IP packets on a network. This is accomplished by examining the source IP address of an ingress packet and determining whether it is valid. If it is valid, the packet will be forwarded. If it is not valid, the packet will be discarded. Note that CEF (Cisco Express Forwarding) must be enabled on the IOS device for uRPF to work.

uRPF can operate in three different modes: strict, loose, and VRF. The mode you choose determines how the packet is identified as being valid or not valid:

- **Strict:** With strict mode, the router reviews the source IP address of the packet and notes the ingress interface. It then looks at the routing table to identify the interface (other than a default route) that would be used to reach the source IP address of the packet. If the interface is exactly the same interface on which the packet was received, and it is not the default route, the packet is valid and is forwarded. If the interface is a different interface, the packet is discarded.

- **Loose:** With loose mode, the router reviews only the source IP address of the packet. It then looks in the routing table to identify whether there is any interface (other than a default route) that can be used to reach the source IP address listed in the packet. If there is and it is not the default route, the packet is valid and is forwarded. If not, the packet is discarded.

- **VRF:** VRF mode is the same as loose mode; however, it only examines interfaces that are in the same VRF as the interface on which the packet was received.

> **NOTE** Modes may not be supported by all devices. Please reference Cisco product documentation to verify whether a specific mode is supported on your product.

Since uRPF is configured on an interface-by-interface basis with the command **ip verify unicast source reachable-via** {**rx** | **any**} [**allow-default**] [**allow-self-ping**] [*list*], choosing the correct mode is important. (**rx** is for strict mode, and **any** is for loose mode.) If you choose the wrong mode, you may end up dropping valid packets because of symmetric versus asymmetric routing. With symmetric routing, the same path is used for the source traffic and the return traffic. With asymmetric routing, a different path ends up being used for return traffic. As a result, if you use strict mode when asymmetric routing occurs, the legitimate traffic is dropped. Therefore, in your enterprise network, you will use a combination of loose and strict. Where asymmetric routing might occur, you use loose, and where symmetric routing is guaranteed to occur, you could use strict. For example, on router interfaces that connect to subnets with end stations, you typically use strict, and on uplinks, you typically use loose.

You use the **allow-default** option when the return path is associated with an interface that is chosen based on a default route. By default, it is discarded. However, in cases where you need to override this behavior, you use the **allow-default** option in the command.

Another consideration is the *list* option, which allows you to attach an ACL that identifies which packets are subject to a uRPF check and which ones are not. So, if you are troubleshooting a scenario in which packets are not being checked, it might be because of the ACL.

With uRPF, by default the router is not able to ping its own interface. Any packets generated by the router and destined to the router are discarded. If you need to self-ping, you use the **allow-self-ping** option. However, use caution as this could allow for a DoS attack to be performed.

To verify that uRPF and CEF are enabled on an interface, you use the **show cef interface** *interface_name interface number* command in privileged exec mode. If CEF is enabled, the output shows "IP CEF switching enabled." If uRPF is enabled, the output shows "IP unicast RPF check is enabled."

> **NOTE**   You may come across an older version of the uRPF configuration command in older versions of Cisco IOS: **ip verify unicast reverse-path** [**allow-self-ping**] *access-list-number*. This command does not have a strict or loose option.

You can enable SNMP traps for uRPF with the command **snmp trap ip verify drop-rate** in interface configuration mode. In interface configuration mode, you can use the command **ip verify notification threshold <0-4294967295>** to specify the drop rate, in packets per second (pps), that will trigger the notification.

Troubleshooting Control Plane Policing (CoPP)

CoPP varies by IOS version and platform version. This section covers the general elements that apply to all versions; for specific details, refer to the specific configuration guides for the IOS version and platforms you are working with at www.cisco.com.

When configuring CoPP, you need to do the following:

- Create ACLs to identify the traffic you want to police.
- Create class maps to define a traffic class.
- Create policy maps to define a service policy.
- Apply the service policy to the control plane.

22

When troubleshooting, you need to be on the lookout for issues in the ACLs, the class maps, the policy maps, and the application of the service policy.

Creating ACLs to Identify the Traffic

Access control lists (ACLs) are used with CoPP for identifying traffic. Once the traffic is matched, it becomes the object of the policy action. So, defining the ACLs is the most critical step of the CoPP process as it is the foundation or primary building block of CoPP. If the ACL is not created correctly, the traffic will not be matched, and therefore the policies will not be correctly applied. The ENARSI exam objectives state that you need to be able to "troubleshoot control plane policing (CoPP) (Telnet, SSH, HTTP(S), SNMP, EIGRP, OSPF, BGP)." In all of these cases, it is the ACL that makes the difference. So, being able to read an ACL is one of the most important parts of being able to answer the CoPP questions correctly.

Example 22-2 shows three ACLs defined. Each ACL was created with a specific purpose in mind. (Note that this is not a perfect example and may not contain every possible element that is necessary to get it to work in the real world. It is only being used for demonstration purposes.)

Example 22-2   *A Sample ACL Configuration for CoPP*

```
R1# config terminal
Enter configuration commands, one per line.  End with CNTL/Z.
R1(config)# ip access-list extended COPP-ICMP-ACL-EXAMPLE
R1(config-ext-nacl)# permit udp any any range 33434 33463 ttl eq 1
R1(config-ext-nacl)# permit icmp any any unreachable
R1(config-ext-nacl)# permit icmp any any echo
R1(config-ext-nacl)# permit icmp any any echo-reply
R1(config-ext-nacl)# permit icmp any any ttl-exceeded
R1(config-ext-nacl)# exit
R1(config)# ip access-list extended COPP-MGMT-TRAFFIC-ACL-EXAMPLE
R1(config-ext-nacl)# permit udp any eq ntp any
R1(config-ext-nacl)# permit udp any any eq snmp
R1(config-ext-nacl)# permit tcp any any eq 22
R1(config-ext-nacl)# permit tcp any eq 22 any established
R1(config-ext-nacl)# permit tcp any any eq 23
R1(config-ext-nacl)# exit
R1(config)# ip access-list extended COPP-ROUTING-PROTOCOLS-ACL-EXAMPLE
R1(config-ext-nacl)# permit tcp any eq bgp any established
R1(config-ext-nacl)# permit eigrp any host 224.0.0.10
R1(config-ext-nacl)# permit ospf any host 224.0.0.5
R1(config-ext-nacl)# permit ospf any host 224.0.0.6
R1(config-ext-nacl)# permit pim any host 224.0.0.13
R1(config-ext-nacl)# permit igmp any any
R1(config-ext-nacl)# end
R1#
```

When troubleshooting ACLs for CoPP, you need to focus on the following:

- **Grouping:** When grouping traffic types together, ensure that they are grouped based on function within the network. For example, routing protocols (BGP, OSPF, and EIGRP) may be grouped together, and management protocols (SSH, Telnet, HTTP(s), TFTP, SNMP, NTP, and DNS) may be grouped together. If you mix and match various protocols, the policies you apply later may not work for the type of traffic in question. Initially, you may not want to do any groupings and instead create a different ACL for each individual traffic flow to verify what the end results are and then do some grouping after the fact.

- **Action:** With ACLs, you can specify a permit or deny action. For CoPP, permit means to match the traffic and apply the policy. Deny means to exclude that traffic from the class and move on to the next entry. So, if you are troubleshooting a CoPP scenario and there is traffic for a class that is not being applied but should be or for a class that is being applied that should not be, check to see if the ACL is a permit or deny. If it is a deny, that traffic would be ignored; if it is a permit, that traffic would be matched. Make any adjustments needed to the ACL to get your desired results.

- **Protocol:** In an ACL, you can define a protocol that you want to match. If the wrong protocol is specified in the ACL, then the wrong type of traffic will be matched in the class. So, when troubleshooting, verify that the correct protocol is being specified in the ACL (for example, OSPF or protocol 89 for OSPF; EIGRP or protocol 88 for EIGRP, TCP for SSH, Telnet, FTP, HTTP, or HTTPS; or UDP for RIP, SNMP, TFTP, or NTP).

- **Source and destination:** Because ACLs allow you to specify source and destination addresses, you can be granular with your CoPP policies and match only if the traffic is from a specific source or destination. Therefore, it is imperative that the ACLs have the correct source and destination IP addresses applied, or the traffic will not be matched when it should be. When troubleshooting scenarios where specific source and destination IP addresses are used in the ACL, it is recommended that you change the IP addresses in the ACL to **any / any**. If the match is successful, then there is an issue with the original IP addresses. If not, the IP addresses were likely not the problem.

- **Operators and ports:** Protocols, applications, and services all have port numbers associated with them. ACLs allow you to define operators such as greater-than, less-than, and equal-to and port numbers such as 179 for BGP, 20 and 21 for FTP, 22 for SSH, 23 for Telnet, 80 for HTTP, and 443 for HTTPS, 161 and 162 for SNMP, and 123 for NTP. Ensuring that you have the correct operator and port numbers defined in your ACLs is paramount for CoPP success.

NOTE   You should never use the **log** or **log-input** keywords in ACLs that are used for CoPP. These keywords have been known to cause unexpected results with CoPP functionality, and it is best to avoid them.

22

You can verify ACLs by using the **show access-lists** command, as shown in Example 22-3.

Example 22-3 *Verifying ACLs with the **show access-lists** Command*

```
R1# show access-lists
Extended IP access list COPP-ICMP-ACL-EXAMPLE
     10 permit udp any any range 33434 33463 ttl eq 1
     20 permit icmp any any unreachable
     30 permit icmp any any echo (28641 matches)
     40 permit icmp any any echo-reply
     50 permit icmp any any ttl-exceeded
Extended IP access list COPP-MGMT-TRAFFIC-ACL-EXAMPLE
     10 permit udp any eq ntp any
     20 permit udp any any eq snmp
     30 permit tcp any any eq 22
     40 permit tcp any eq 22 any established
     50 permit tcp any any eq telnet (73 matches)
Extended IP access list COPP-ROUTING-PROTOCOLS-ACL-EXAMPLE
     10 permit tcp any eq bgp any established
     20 permit eigrp any host 224.0.0.10 (2499 matches)
     30 permit ospf any host 224.0.0.5 (349 matches)
     40 permit ospf any host 224.0.0.6
     50 permit pim any host 224.0.0.13
     60 permit igmp any any
R1#
```

Creating Class Maps to Define a Traffic Class

Class maps are used to define a traffic class that is composed of three different elements. First, there is a name; second, one or more **match** commands are used to identify the packets that are part of the class; and third, there are instructions on how the **match** commands will be evaluated. In Example 22-4, the name of the first class map listed is COPP-ICMP-CLASSMAP-EXAMPLE, with the instructions to match all. There is only one match condition, and it is to match the ACL named COPP-ICMP-ACL-EXAMPLE. (Note that this is not a perfect example and may not contain every possible element that is necessary to get it to work in the real world. It is only being used for demonstration purposes.)

Example 22-4 *A Sample Class Map Configuration for CoPP*

```
R1# configure terminal
Enter configuration commands, one per line.  End with CNTL/Z.
R1(config)# class-map match-all COPP-ICMP-CLASSMAP-EXAMPLE
R1(config-cmap)# match access-group name COPP-ICMP-ACL-EXAMPLE
R1(config-cmap)# exit
R1(config)# class-map match-all COPP-MGMT-TRAFFIC-CLASSMAP-EXAMPLE
R1(config-cmap)# match access-group name COPP-MGMT-TRAFFIC-ACL-EXAMPLE
R1(config-cmap)# exit
R1(config)# class-map match-all COPP-ROUTING-PROTOCOLS-CLASSMAP-EXAMPLE
R1(config-cmap)# match access-group name COPP-ROUTING-PROTOCOLS-ACL-EXAMPLE
R1(config-cmap)# end
R1#
```

The syntax of a class map is as follows:

```
router(config)# class-map [match-any | match-all] class-name
router(config-cmap)# match [access-group | protocol | ip prec |
ip dscp]
```

When troubleshooting class maps, you need to focus on the following:

- **Access group:** Is the correct ACL being used in the **match** command? The ACL in the class map is responsible for defining the interesting traffic (packets) that must be matched. If matched, the packets are classified as being members of the class, and the correct service policy applies. If the wrong ACL is applied, the desired results are not achieved. In addition, the ACL may not contain the correct protocol, or address, or operator, or port, or action, and therefore the traffic is not matched by the class map. If that is the case, you have to troubleshoot the ACL.

- **Instruction:** A class map may contain one of two instructions: **match-any** or **match-all**. Using the correct instruction is important only if you have multiple **match** commands in the class map. If you have only one **match** command in the class map, the instruction does not matter. Let's say you do have multiple **match** commands in a single class map. If you use **match-any**, it means the traffic must match one of the **match** commands to be classified as part of the traffic class. If you use **match-all**, the traffic must match all the **match** commands to be part of the traffic class. This is where people get caught when troubleshooting. In Example 22-5, notice that the class map is using the **match-all** instruction. Based on the **match** commands and the ACLs, does this make sense? If you are not sure, think about whether it is possible for a packet to be ICMP (Internet Control Message Protocol), BGP (Border Gateway Protocol), and EIGRP (Enhanced Interior Gateway Routing Protocol) at the same time. Of course it's not. So, the traffic would never match the CoPP-CLASS class map and therefore would never be subject to the implicit default class. In this case, the correct option would be the **match-any** instruction instead of the **match-all** instruction.

- **Protocol:** If you choose not to use an ACL for matching, you can use the built-in protocol options of the **match** command. When using the **protocol** option, you must ensure that the correct protocol has been specified. For example, if you want to match ARP (Address Resolution Protocol) packets, you use the **match protocol arp** command.

- **IP PREC/IP DSCP:** If you only need to match based on IP precedence or IP DSCP (Differentiated Services Code Point) values, you can use the **ip prec** or **ip dscp** options of the **match** command. Based on the traffic you want to match, make sure the correct one has been chosen and ensure that the correct values have been specified.

- **Case:** ACL names are case sensitive. When specifying an ACL in a class map, double-check to make sure the name matches exactly.

22

Example 22-5   *A CoPP **match-all** Versus **match-any** Example*

```
ip access-list extended CoPP-ICMP
 permit icmp any any echo
!
ip access-list extended CoPP-BGP
 permit tcp any eq bgp any established
!
ip access-list extended CoPP-EIGRP
 permit eigrp any host 224.0.0.10
!
class-map match-all CoPP-CLASS
 match access-group name CoPP-ICMP
 match access-group name CoPP-BGP
 match access-group name CoPP-EIGRP
!
```

To verify all configured class maps, use the **show class-map** command, as shown in Example 22-6.

Remember that if the traffic does not match any of the class maps, the traffic is classified as a member of the default class and has the default policy map applied.

Example 22-6   *Verifying Class Maps with the **show class-map** Command*

```
R1# show class-map
 Class Map match-all COPP-MGMT-TRAFFIC-CLASSMAP-EXAMPLE (id 2)
   Match access-group name COPP-MGMT-TRAFFIC-ACL-EXAMPLE

 Class Map match-any class-default (id 0)
   Match any

 Class Map match-all COPP-ROUTING-PROTOCOLS-CLASSMAP-EXAMPLE (id 3)
   Match access-group name COPP-ROUTING-PROTOCOLS-ACL-EXAMPLE

 Class Map match-all COPP-ICMP-CLASSMAP-EXAMPLE (id 1)
   Match access-group name COPP-ICMP-ACL-EXAMPLE
R1#
```

Creating Policy Maps to Define a Service Policy

Policy maps are used with CoPP to associate the traffic class (as defined by the class map) with one or more policies, resulting in a service policy. The three elements are a name, a traffic class, and a policy. In Example 22-7, there is a policy map named COPP-POLICYMAP-EXAMPLE that identifies multiple classes and the policy that is applied if the traffic matches. (Note that this is not a perfect example and may not contain every possible element that is necessary to get it to work in the real world. It is only being used for demonstration purposes.)

Example 22-7 *A Sample Policy Map Configuration for CoPP*

```
R1# configure terminal
Enter configuration commands, one per line.  End with CNTL/Z.
R1(config)# policy-map COPP-POLICYMAP-EXAMPLE
R1(config-pmap)# class COPP-MGMT-TRAFFIC-CLASSMAP-EXAMPLE
R1(config-pmap-c)# police 32000 conform-action transmit exceed-action transmit
R1(config-pmap-c-police)# violate-action transmit
R1(config-pmap-c-police)# exit
R1(config-pmap-c)# exit
R1(config-pmap)# class COPP-ROUTING-PROTOCOLS-CLASSMAP-EXAMPLE
R1(config-pmap-c)# police 34000 conform-action transmit exceed-action transmit
R1(config-pmap-c-police)# violate-action transmit
R1(config-pmap-c-police)# exit
R1(config-pmap-c)# exit
R1(config-pmap)# class COPP-ICMP-CLASSMAP-EXAMPLE
R1(config-pmap-c)# police 8000 conform-action transmit exceed-action transmit
R1(config-pmap-c-police)# violate-action drop
R1(config-pmap-c-police)# end
R1#
```

The syntax used when creating a policy map for CoPP is as follows:

```
router(config)# policy-map service_policy_name

router(config-pmap)# class traffic_class_name

router(config-pmap-c)# police [cir | rate] conform-action
[transmit | drop] exceed-action [transmit | drop]
```

When troubleshooting policy maps, you need to consider the following:

- **Order of operations:** Policy maps are processed from the top down. Therefore, if there is more than one class specified, the first class listed is evaluated first, then the second, then the third, and so on down the list until you reach the default class at the end. If at any point the traffic matches any of the classes from the top down, the evaluation stops (no further processing is performed), and the policy along with its actions is applied to the traffic. This is important because if you have a policy map with seven classes, and a packet ends up matching the third and fifth class listed, only the third class is matched and applied as it is the first one in the list from the top down. Therefore, if you are expecting the fifth class in the list to be matched but you are not getting the expected results, check to see if an earlier class is being applied instead.

- **Class map:** Has the correct class map been defined in the policy map? If it has, you still need to check that the class map has been constructed properly based on the class map discussion earlier in this chapter. You also need to ensure that the ACLs are being crafted correctly for the desired outcome, as discussed earlier.

- **Policy:** In the policy, make sure the correct CIR (in bits per second) has been applied or the correct RATE (in packets per second) has been applied. If the value is too low,

22

you may be dropping packets you don't want, but if it is too high, you may be allowing more packets than you want. For example, a value that is too low for CoPP with BGP or OSPF would cause neighbor flapping and destabilize your routing architecture. But a value that is too high for something like SNMP or a ping could cause the router CPU to become overwhelmed and unresponsive. Determining the correct value will only be possible with time and testing to determine the perfect fit. For conformaction, you can either transmit or drop, and you need to ensure that the correct one is applied for the desired results; for exceed-action, you can either transmit or drop, and you need to ensure that the correct one is applied for the desired results. Note that in some versions of IOS, if your plan is to drop all the traffic that matches the class, you can replace the **police** command with just the keyword **drop**. So maybe you have the desire to prohibit all BGP neighborships or neighborships from specific IP addresses for security reasons. In this case, you could match BGP in the ACL and then match the ACL in a class map, and once you get to the policy map, you can replace the police option for the class map with drop to prevent that traffic from being punted to the CPU and, therefore, prevent the neighborships from being formed.

- **Default class:** Remember that if a packet does not match any of the defined classes, it is subject to the conditions laid out in the default class. Therefore, if traffic is falling into the default class (which is likely to occur), you need to ensure that the default class is handling the traffic as intended.

- **Case:** Class map names are case sensitive. When specifying the class map in the policy map, double-check to make sure the name matches exactly.

To verify all configured policy maps, use the command **show policy-map**, as shown in Example 22-8.

Example 22-8   *Verifying Policy Maps with the **show policy-map** Command*

```
R1# show policy-map
  Policy Map COPP-POLICYMAP-EXAMPLE
    Class COPP-MGMT-TRAFFIC-CLASSMAP-EXAMPLE
     police cir 32000 bc 1500 be 1500
       conform-action transmit
       exceed-action transmit
       violate-action transmit
    Class COPP-ROUTING-PROTOCOLS-CLASSMAP-EXAMPLE
     police cir 34000 bc 1500 be 1500
       conform-action transmit
       exceed-action transmit
       violate-action transmit
    Class COPP-ICMP-CLASSMAP-EXAMPLE
     police cir 8000 bc 1500 be 1500
       conform-action transmit
       exceed-action transmit
       violate-action drop

  R1#
```

Applying the Service Policy to the Control Plane

The service policy (as specified in the policy map) needs to be attached to the correct interface (see Example 22-9).

Example 22-9   *Applying the Policy to the Control Plane Interface*

```
R1# configure terminal
Enter configuration commands, one per line.  End with CNTL/Z.
R1(config)# control-plane
R1(config-cp)# service-policy input COPP-POLICYMAP-EXAMPLE
*Sep 20 22:24:58.939: %CP-5-FEATURE: Control-plane Policing feature enabled on
Control plane aggregate path
R1(config-cp)# end
R1#
```

When troubleshooting the application of the service policy, you need to consider the following:

- **The correct interface:** There is only one interface to which you can apply CoPP—the control plane interface—so this one is easy to troubleshoot: It is either applied or not applied. You can verify this with the **show policy-map control-plane** [**input** | **output**] command, as shown in Example 22-10.

- **Direction:** CoPP can be applied to packets entering or leaving the control plane interface. Therefore, the correct direction needs to be specified. For incoming packets, you specify **input**, and for outgoing packets you specify **output**. Direction can be verified with the output of **show policy-map control-plane** as well. Note that not all Cisco IOS versions support output CoPP, and for the ones that do, you need to ensure that the correct traffic is being classified in the ACLs and the class maps. For example, when it comes to BGP, OSPF (Open Shortest Path First), and EIGRP, you typically use output CoPP for the replies that are being sent because of an already received packet. For ICMP, it would be error and informational reply messages. For Telnet, SSH, HTTP, or SNMP, you would be dealing with replies or traps. If the ACL and class map are not configured appropriately for the replies, the desired result will not be achieved.

- **Case:** Policy map names are case sensitive. When attaching a policy map to the control plane interface, double-check to make sure the names match exactly.

In addition, the output of **show policy-map control-plane** provides a large amount of information in one section that can assist you with your troubleshooting efforts. You can verify the applied policy map, the class maps in the order they will be applied, the match conditions of the class maps, and the policies that are applied to the traffic that is matched. In addition, you can verify the values for cir, bc, and be, as well as the number of conformed, exceeded, and violated packets.

22

Example 22-10 *Output of the show policy-map control-plane Command*

```
R1# show policy-map control-plane
Control Plane

  Service-policy input: COPP-POLICYMAP-EXAMPLE

    Class-map: COPP-MGMT-TRAFFIC-CLASSMAP-EXAMPLE (match-all)
        73 packets, 4386 bytes
        5 minute offered rate 0000 bps, drop rate 0000 bps
        Match: access-group name COPP-MGMT-TRAFFIC-ACL-EXAMPLE
        police:
            cir 32000 bps, bc 1500 bytes, be 1500 bytes
          conformed 73 packets, 4386 bytes; actions:
            transmit
          exceeded 0 packets, 0 bytes; actions:
            transmit
          violated 0 packets, 0 bytes; actions:
            transmit
          conformed 0000 bps, exceeded 0000 bps, violated 0000 bps

    Class-map: COPP-ROUTING-PROTOCOLS-CLASSMAP-EXAMPLE (match-all)
        2765 packets, 211446 bytes
        5 minute offered rate 0000 bps, drop rate 0000 bps
        Match: access-group name COPP-ROUTING-PROTOCOLS-ACL-EXAMPLE
        police:
            cir 34000 bps, bc 1500 bytes, be 1500 bytes
          conformed 2765 packets, 211446 bytes; actions:
            transmit
          exceeded 0 packets, 0 bytes; actions:
            transmit
          violated 0 packets, 0 bytes; actions:
            transmit
          conformed 0000 bps, exceeded 0000 bps, violated 0000 bps

    Class-map: COPP-ICMP-CLASSMAP-EXAMPLE (match-all)
        28641 packets, 3265074 bytes
        5 minute offered rate 0000 bps, drop rate 0000 bps
        Match: access-group name COPP-ICMP-ACL-EXAMPLE
        police:
            cir 8000 bps, bc 1500 bytes, be 1500 bytes
          conformed 22436 packets, 2557704 bytes; actions:
            transmit
          exceeded 5157 packets, 587898 bytes; actions:
            transmit
```

```
        violated 1048 packets, 119472 bytes; actions:
          drop
        conformed 0000 bps, exceeded 0000 bps, violated 0000 bps

    Class-map: class-default (match-any)
      675 packets, 101548 bytes
      5 minute offered rate 0000 bps, drop rate 0000 bps
      Match: any
  R1#
```

CoPP Summary

So, putting it all together, when troubleshooting CoPP, consider the following steps:

Step 1.   Verify that the service policy is applied and in the correct direction by using the **show policy-map control-plane** command. If it is not, fix the issue. If it is, move on to step 2.

Step 2.   Verify that the policy map is configured correctly with either the **show policy-map control-plane** command or the **show policy-map** command. Check that the correct class-map, rate/cir, conform-action, and exceed-action options have been applied. Also ensure that the classes are defined in the correct order, based on top-down processing. If not, fix the issues. If everything is correct, move on to step 3.

Step 3.   Verify that the class map is configured correctly by using the **show class-map** command. Verify that the correct instructions (**match-any, match-all**) are applied, along with the correct ACL, protocol, IP precedence, or IP DSCP values. If not, fix the issues. If everything is correct, move on to step 4.

Step 4.   Verify that the ACLs have been configured correctly for the types of traffic you want to match by using the **show access-list** command. This requires you to verify the action (permit, deny), protocol, addresses, operators, port numbers, and anything else you can use to identify interesting traffic. If you find any issues, fix them.

At this point, everything should be working as intended. If not, go back and verify everything again because you missed something.

IPv6 First-Hop Security

The ENARSI certification exam objectives require you to describe IPv6 First-Hop Security features. This section provides information that will assist you in describing the Binding Table, IPv6 Snooping, Router Advertisement Guard, DHCPv6 Guard, Source Guard, Destination Guard, and Prefix Guard.

Binding Table

The L2 binding table is a database that lists IPv6 neighbors that are connected to a device. It contains information such as the link-layer address and the prefix binding. Other IPv6

22

First-Hop Security features use the information in this table to prevent snooping and redirect attacks.

IPv6 Snooping

IPv6 snooping is a feature that is used to capture IPv6 traffic so the IPv6 addresses in the packets can be used to populate the binding table. It accomplishes this by analyzing *IPv6 neighbor discovery* messages (IPv6 neighbor discovery inspection) as well as DHCPv6 messages. Depending on the security level, it can block unwanted messages such as router advertisements (RAs) or DHCP replies. This feature is a prerequisite for all the other features covered in the section.

Router Advertisement (RA) Guard

RA Guard is a feature that analyzes RAs and can filter out unwanted RAs from unauthorized devices. You may recall from earlier IPv6 studies that routers use RAs to announce themselves on the link. It is possible that some RAs will be unwanted, or "rogue"; you wouldn't want them on the network. You can use RA Guard to block or reject these unwanted RA messages. RA Guard requires a policy to be configured in RA Guard policy configuration mode, and RA Guard is enabled on an interface-by-interface basis by applying the policy to the interface with the **ipv6 nd raguard attach-policy** [*policy-name* [**vlan** {**add** | **except** | **none** | **remove** | **all**} *vlan* [*vlan1, vlan2, vlan3*...]]] command.

Note the following about RA Guard:

- It is configured inbound on an interface.

- Two modes are available: host mode and router mode.

- It does not offer any protection when IPv6 traffic is tunneled.

- It is only supported in hardware when the Ternary Content Addressable Memory (TCAM) is programmed.

- It is not supported on EtherChannel members or trunk ports with merge mode.

DHCPv6 Guard

DHCPv6 Guard is a feature that is very similar to DHCP (Dynamic Host Configuration Protocol) snooping for IPv4. It is designed to ensure that rogue DHCPv6 servers are not able to hand out IPv6 addressing information to IPv6 clients, redirect client traffic, or starve out the DHCPv6 server and cause a DoS attack. For IPv6, DHCPv6 Guard can block reply and advertisement messages that come from unauthorized DHCPv6 servers and relay agents. It determines if it should switch or block the DHCP messages based on information found in a message as well as the device role configuration. It classifies messages into one of three DHCP types: client, server, and relay. All client messages are switched, regardless of the device role, and the DHCP server messages are processed further only if the device role is set to server. DHCPv6 Guard requires a policy to be configured in DHCP Guard configuration mode, and DHCPv6 Guard is enabled on an interface-by-interface basis by applying the policy to the interface with the **ipv6 dhcp guard attach-policy** [*policy-name* [**vlan** {**add** | **except** | **none** | **remove** | **all**} *vlan* [*vlan1, vlan2, vlan3*...]]] command.

Source Guard

IPv6 *Source Guard* is a Layer 2 snooping interface feature for validating the source of IPv6 traffic. If the traffic arriving on an interface is from an unknown source (that is not in the binding table), IPv6 Source Guard can block it and drop it. For traffic to be from a known source and allowed, the source must be in the binding table. The source is either learned using ND inspection or IPv6 address gleaning and therefore relies on IPv6 snooping being configured first on Layer 2 access or trunk ports and VLANs. In addition, Source Guard requires validate prefix to be enabled (which it is by default) in the Source Guard policy.

Destination Guard

IPv6 Destination Guard is a feature that can be used to filter IPv6 traffic based on the destination address. It performs address resolution only for addresses that are active on a link, and it therefore requires the binding table to be populated using the IPv6 snooping feature. In addition, it can block NDP resolution for destination addresses that are not found in the binding table. By default, Destination Guard blocks and drops traffic coming for an unknown destination. As such, Destination Guard can help minimize DoS attacks.

Prefix Guard

IPv6 Prefix Guard is used on ingress interfaces to deny access to traffic that has a correct address but that is not topologically correct. The feature discovers ranges of addresses that have been assigned to a link and blocks any traffic sourced with an address outside that range, ensuring that traffic is sourced from its assigned location.

Exam Preparation Tasks

As mentioned in the section "How to Use This Book" in the Introduction, you have a couple choices for exam preparation: the exercises here, Chapter 24, "Final Preparation," and the exam simulation questions in the Pearson Test Prep software.

Review All Key Topics

Review the most important topics in this chapter, noted with the Key Topic icon in the outer margin of the page. Table 22-2 lists these key topics and the page number on which each is found.

Table 22-2   Key Topics

Key Topic Element	Description	Page Number
List	Troubleshooting AAA issues	871
Paragraph	Using uRPF strict versus loose mode to avoid issues	874
Paragraph	Using the **allow-default** option with uRPF	875
List	Troubleshooting ACL issues related to CoPP	877
List	Troubleshooting class map issues related to CoPP	879
List	Troubleshooting policy map issues related to CoPP	881
Example 22-10	Output of the **show policy-map control-plane** command	884
Section	IPv6 First-Hop Security	885

22

Define Key Terms

Define the following key terms from this chapter and check your answers in the glossary:

AAA, method list, RADIUS, TACACS+, uRPF, CoPP, class map, policy map, access control list (ACL), IPv6 snooping, IPv6 neighbor discovery, RA Guard, DHCPv6 Guard, Source Guard

Use the Command Reference to Check Your Memory

The ENARSI 300-410 exam focuses on the practical, hands-on skills that networking professionals use. Therefore, you should be able to identify the commands needed to configure, verify, and troubleshoot the topics covered in this chapter.

This section includes the most important configuration and verification commands covered in this chapter. It might not be necessary to memorize the complete syntax of every command, but you should be able to remember the basic keywords that are needed.

To test your memory of the commands in Table 22-3, go to the companion website and download Appendix B, "Command Reference Exercises." Fill in the missing commands in the tables based on each command description. You can check your work by downloading Appendix C, "Command Reference Exercise Answer Key," from the companion website.

Table 22-3 Command Reference

Task	Command Syntax
Display the configuration of the local usernames and passwords on the device, the AAA commands that have been configured, and the vty line configuration.	**show run	section usernamelaaalline vty**
Display the authentication process in real time.	**debug aaa authentication**
Display the RADIUS authentication process in real time.	**debug radius authentication**
Display the local authentication process in real time.	**debug aaa protocol local**
Enable AAA services on the router.	**aaa new-model**
Create a username and password in the local username and password database.	**username** *name* **password** *password*
Create a method list for AAA login purposes using a group of AAA servers for authentication with fallback to the local username and password database if the servers are not reachable.	**aaa authentication login** *method-list-name* **group** *server-group* **local**
Apply a AAA method list to a vty or console line in line configuration mode.	**login authentication** *method-list-name*
Configure uRPF on an interface in interface configuration mode.	**ip verify unicast source reachable-via {rx	any} [allow-default] [allow-self-ping]** [*list*]
Display all configured ACLs on the router.	**show access-lists**
Display all configured class maps on the router.	**show class-map**
Display all configured policy maps on the router.	**show policy-map**
Verify the applied policy map, the class maps in the order in which they will be applied, the match conditions of the class maps, and the policies that are applied to the traffic that is matched.	**show policy-map control-plane**

Use the IPv6 Features Table to Check Your Memory

Table 22-4 lists of all the IPv6 features and the reasons you would use them. To test your memory, cover the right or left side of Table 22-4 with a piece of paper and see how many of the features you can remember.

The ENARSI 300-410 exam will test you on your ability to describe IPv6 First-Hop Security features, so it is imperative that you know this table.

Table 22-4   IPv6 Features

IPv6 Feature	Definition
Binding table	A database that lists IPv6 neighbors that are connected to a device
IPv6 snooping	A feature that is used to capture IPv6 traffic so the IPv6 addresses in the packets can be used to populate the binding table
RA Guard	A feature that analyzes RAs and can filter out unwanted RAs from unauthorized devices
DHCPv6 Guard	A feature that is designed to ensure that rogue DHCPv6 servers are not able to hand out IPv6 addressing information to IPv6 clients, redirect client traffic, or starve out the DHCPv6 server and cause a DoS attack
Source Guard	A Layer 2 snooping interface feature for validating the source of IPv6 traffic
Destination Guard	A feature that can be used to filter IPv6 traffic based on the destination address
Prefix Guard	A feature used on ingress interfaces to deny access to traffic that has the correct address but that is not topologically correct

22

## CHAPTER 23

Device Management and Management Tools Troubleshooting

This chapter covers the following topics:

- **Device Management Troubleshooting:** This section explains how to identify and troubleshoot issues related to console and vty access, as well as remote transfer tools. Various protocols are covered, including Telnet, SSH, TFTP, HTTP, HTTPS, and SCP.

- **Management Tools Troubleshooting:** This section examines how to use and troubleshoot various management tools, including syslog, SNMP, Cisco IP SLA, Object Tracking, NetFlow, and Flexible NetFlow. In addition, it examines Bidirectional Forwarding Detection (BFD) and Cisco DNA Center Assurance.

To troubleshoot issues with Cisco routers, you need access to them. You can access them physically by using the console port or remotely by using vty lines. If you attempt to access a device for management purposes and access fails, you need to troubleshoot why the failure is occurring before you can troubleshoot the other issues.

From time to time, you will need to copy files and IOS images to and from your routers. To do this, you need protocols that were designed for remote transfers. If for some reason a transfer is failing, you need to be able to troubleshoot why the failure is occurring, based on the protocol in question.

Tools are like your best friend. When you are in trouble or just need a shoulder to lean on, tools are there to help. Tools such as syslog, SNMP (Simple Network Management Protocol), Cisco IP SLA, Object Tracking, NetFlow, Flexible NetFlow, and Cisco DNA Center Assurance help you ensure that things are okay.

This chapter focuses on the different reasons device management and management tools may not be working. It examines console/vty access, remote transfer tools such as TFTP (Trivial File Transfer Protocol), HTTP (Hypertext Transfer Protocol), HTTPS (Hypertext Transfer Protocol over Secure Sockets Layer), and SCP (Secure Copy Protocol), as well as network management tools, including syslog, SNMP, Cisco IP SLA, Object Tracking, NetFlow, and Flexible NetFlow. The chapter also covers BFD (Bidirectional Forwarding Detection) and discusses how you can troubleshoot network problems by using Cisco DNA Center Assurance.

"Do I Know This Already?" Quiz

The "Do I Know This Already?" quiz allows you to assess whether you should read this entire chapter thoroughly or jump to the "Exam Preparation Tasks" section. If you are in doubt about your answers to these questions or your own assessment of your knowledge of the topics, read the entire chapter. Table 23-1 lists the major headings in this chapter and their corresponding "Do I Know This Already?" quiz questions. You can find the answers in Appendix A, "Answers to the 'Do I Know This Already?' Quiz Questions."

Table 23-1 "Do I Know This Already?" Foundation Topics Section-to-Question Mapping

Foundation Topics Section	Questions
Device Management Troubleshooting	1–4
Management Tools Troubleshooting	5–11

CAUTION   The goal of self-assessment is to gauge your mastery of the topics in this chapter. If you do not know the answer to a question or are only partially sure of the answer, you should mark that question as wrong for purposes of self-assessment. Giving yourself credit for an answer that you correctly guess skews your self-assessment results and might provide you with a false sense of security.

1. Which of the following are the default serial terminal settings for a Cisco router or switch? (Choose two.)

   a. 9600 baud

   b. 16 data bits

   c. 1 stop bit

   d. Parity

2. Which command enables you to define which protocols will be used for remote access to a Cisco device using vty lines?

   a. transport input

   b. login

   c. login local

   d. exec

3. Which command enables you to specify that SSH access will be authenticated using the local database?

   a. login

   b. login local

   c. login authentication default

   d. transport input ssh

4. The following command has been typed on a Cisco IOS router:

   ```
   copy http://10.0.3.8/cisco_ios_files/c3900-universalk9-mz.
   SPA.156-3.M6a.bin flash:c3900-universalk9-mz.SPA.156-3.M6a.bin
   ```

   What will this accomplish?

   a. A configuration file will be copied from a web server to the router.

   b. An IOS image will be copied from the router to the web server.

   c. An IOS image will be copied from the web server to the router.

   d. A configuration file will be copied from a router to a web server.

5. Timestamps are not appearing with syslog messages on your router. What is most likely the reason for this?

    a. NTP is not configured correctly.

    b. The router has the wrong time set, according to the output of the **show clock** command.

    c. The **no service timestamps** command was executed on the router.

    d. You have not used the **terminal monitor** command.

6. Your router clock displays the following time:

```
R3#show clock
*20:10:43.023 EST Mon Mar 20 2023
```

However, your syslog messages display the time as follows:

```
R3#
*Mar 21 01:10:50.371: BGP: topo global:IPv4 Unicast:base
Scanning...
*Mar 21 01:10:50.375: BGP: topo global:VPNv4 Unicast:base
Scanning...
*Mar 21 01:10:50.375: BGP: topo RED:VPNv4 Unicast:base
Scanning...
*Mar 21 01:10:50.379: BGP: topo GREEN:VPNv4 Unicast:base
Scanning...
```

What is the most likely reason for this?

    a. Your syslog messages are being generated by a router in a different time zone.

    b. The router has the wrong local time set.

    c. The **localtime** option was not used with the **service timestamps** command.

    d. NTP has not been configured correctly.

    e. You used the **summer-time** option with the **clock** command .

7. Which of the following is a valid SNMP security level that provides authentication using a hashing algorithm such as SHA and encryption using an encryption algorithm such as AES?

    a. noAUTHnoPRIV

    b. AUTHnoPRIV

    c. AUTHPRIV

    d. PRIV

8. In which of the following situations would you require an IP SLA responder?

    a. Testing one-way delay for voice packets

    b. Testing connectivity for a floating static route

    c. Testing connectivity for First-Hop Resiliency Protocol

    d. Testing round-trip time with an ICMP echo

9. Which command is used to verify the version of NetFlow that has been configured on a router?

   a. show ip flow export

   b. show ip flow Interface

   c. show ip flow cache

   d. show flow record

10. Which command is used to verify the flow exporter that has been assigned to a flow monitor?

    a. show flow Interface

    b. show flow exporter

    c. show flow monitor

    d. show flow record

11. Which Cisco DNA Center Assurance tool graphically shows the path that applications and services running on a client take through all the devices on the network to reach the destination?

    a. Application Experience

    b. Device 360

    c. Client 360

    d. Path Trace

Foundation Topics

Device Management Troubleshooting

You can access a Cisco IOS router for management purposes in various ways. The console line is used when you have physical access to the device or when you are using an access server. In addition, vty lines provide remote connectivity using *Telnet* or Secure Shell (*SSH*), so device management can be accomplished from a remote location. Regardless of the method you use for management purposes, at some point you will likely end up having to troubleshoot problems connecting to a device so that you can troubleshoot another issue that has been presented to you. Therefore, you might need to solve one issue to get to the next issue. In addition, at some point you will have to transfer configuration files or IOS images while you are solving a troubleshooting issue. Therefore, you need to be able to troubleshoot issues related to your remote transfers using protocols such as TFTP, HTTP(S), and SCP.

This section explains why management access to a Cisco IOS router may fail, how you can determine why the problem is occurring, and how you can fix it. This section also discusses what to look out for when troubleshooting remote transfers.

Console Access Troubleshooting

The default out-of-the-box method of accessing Cisco routers and switches is by using the console port. Here are some things you should look out for when troubleshooting console access:

- **Has the correct COM port been selected in the terminal program?** Most times, multiple COM (communication) ports are displayed in the terminal program; however, knowing which one to use is not always easy. It is really a trial-and-error process. If you are unsure which one to use, you need to determine the COM port numbers of the operating system you are using to run the terminal program. For example, with Windows 10 you can identify COM port numbers in Device Manager.

- **Are the terminal program's settings configured correctly?** Cisco devices use the following default values: 9600 baud, 8 data bits, 1 stop bit, and no parity.

- **Is a *line* password used to authenticate to the console?** If a line password is being used, the *login* command needs to be configured as well. The **login** command and a line password are not configured by default, therefore, no authentication is required.

- **Are a local username and password used to authenticate to the console?** If local authentication is being used, a username and password must exist in the local database, and the *login local* command is required on the line.

- **Is an AAA (authentication, authorization, and accounting) server used to authenticate to the console?** If *AAA* authentication is being used, a method list needs to be defined with the **login authentication** {default | *list_name*} command in line console configuration mode.

- **Are the correct cable and drivers being used to connect to the console port?** Check your device's documentation to see what is needed. Newer devices use a mini-USB port as the console port (with drivers required on a PC), and older devices use the serial-to-RJ45 console (rollover) cable; if a device does not have a serial port, you need a USB-to-serial cable to connect to the console cable and the correct drivers on your PC to use it. Recently Cisco has started to provide USB console cable drivers for various operating systems. So it is recommended that you grab the verified drivers from Cisco.

- **Is the line enabled?** Note that EXEC and EXEC-TIMEOUT accomplish very different things for the console and vty lines. EXEC is used to enable or disable the line. For example, typing the **exec** command in line configuration mode enables the line, but typing **no exec** in line configuration mode disables the line. EXEC-TIMEOUT is used to control the inactivity timer. For example, if you type **exec-timeout 5 0** in line configuration mode, you configure the device to log you out automatically after 5 minutes of inactivity. I mention this because if you accidently type in **no exec** and hit Enter when you really wanted to type in **no exec-timeout**, you have accidently disabled the line, which results in the console no longer responding when you connect to it.

- **Are you being overwhelmed by syslog messages on the screen and unable to see commands properly as you type them in?** Make sure you have enabled logging synchronous on the console line with the **logging synchronous** command.

vty Access Troubleshooting

Most devices are administered remotely via the vty lines, which support protocols such as Telnet and SSH for remote access. Telnet is not recommended because it uses plaintext for all traffic between the management station and the router/switch. If a malicious user can capture the packets, that user will be able to see all the data being transmitted back and forth. If you use SSH, the packets will be encrypted, ensuring that if they are captured, they will not be readable.

Telnet

Consider the following when troubleshooting Telnet access to a device:

- **Is the IP address of the remote router/switch reachable?** You can test this with the **ping** command.

- **Are the correct transport protocols defined for the line?** By default, with IOS 15.0 and later, Telnet and SSH are allowed, and if other protocols are supported, they are typically allowed as well; however, with the **transport input** command, you can change which transport protocols are allowed. You can verify the allowed protocols with the command **show line vty** *line_number* | **include Allowed**, as shown in Example 23-1. In this example, Telnet and SSH are allowed for inbound and outbound connections.

- **Is the line configured to ask the user for credentials?** By default, it is. The **login** command tells the line to prompt the user for the line password, as shown in Example 23-2. However, if you need to authenticate the user through the local database, the **login local** command is required, and if you need to authenticate the user through AAA, the **login authentication** {**default** | *list_name*} command is required.

- **Is a password specified?** Because the **login** command is enabled by default, a password is required. If the password is not set, the error message "Password required, but none set" appears. If you are using the **login local** command or AAA, you are prompted for a username and password. However, if the username and password are not stored in the database, your login is invalid and fails.

- **Is there an ACL (access control list) defining which management stations, based on IP address, can access the router/switch?** Example 23-3 shows ACL 1 applied to the vty lines. It only allows access from the IP address 192.168.1.11. Notice the explicit deny that was added to keep track of the number of denied remote access attempts that have occurred (seven in this case). To receive a log message indicating which IP address was denied, you need to add the **log** keyword to the end of the explicit deny entry in the ACL. The following log message appears if the **log** keyword is added:

  ```
  %SEC-6-IPACCESSLOGS: list 1 denied 10.1.12.2 1 packet.
  ```

- **Are all vty lines busy?** By default, there are five vty lines on Cisco routers and switches, numbered 0 to 4. Some devices have more. However, regardless of the number, if all the lines have established connections, a new connection will not be made, as shown in Example 23-4. In this case, the **show users** command on SW1 indicates that there is one console connection, and there are five vty connections on lines 0 to 4. The next device that tries to use Telnet will be refused and will receive the message "Password required, but none set," even though that is not technically the issue. If you need to manually clear the lines, use the **clear line** command followed by the line number specified before vty, as shown in Example 23-4, rather than the actual vty number listed after vty.

- **Are you allowing EXEC access to the line?** By default, EXEC access is allowed. But if you configured the command **no exec** on the line, then remote connections are not allowed, and when someone tries to make a connection, they receive the following message displayed in the IOS output:

```
R2#telnet 10.0.123.1
Trying 10.0.123.1 ... Open
[Connection to 10.0.123.1 closed by foreign host]
```

- **Are you unable to see syslog messages when you are remotely connected to device?** Type the **terminal monitor** command in privileged exec mode. When you need to disable it, enter **terminal no monitor.**

- **Are you being overwhelmed by syslog messages on the screen and unable to see commands properly as you type them in?** Make sure you have enabled logging synchronous on the console line with the **logging synchronous** command.

- **Is there an ACL in the path between the client and the device blocking port 23?** Telnet uses TCP *port 23*. If an ACL configured on a router or firewall is blocking port 23, you will be unable to make a successful Telnet connection.

- **Do you receive the following error messages when trying to make outbound Telnet connections:** `% Telnet connections not permitted from this terminal.`? You need to enable the line to initiate outbound Telnet sessions with the **transport output telnet** line configuration mode command.

Example 23-1 *Verifying Transport Protocols for a Line*

```
SW1# show line vty 0 | include Allowed
Allowed input transports are telnet ssh.
Allowed output transports are telnet ssh.
```

Example 23-2 *Verifying the vty login Command*

```
SW1# show run | section line vty
line vty 0 4
 login
```

Example 23-3 *Verifying ACLs Used to Secure Management Access*

```
SW1# show run | section line vty
line vty 0 4
 access-class 1 in
 password cisco
 login
DSW1# show ip access-lists 1
Standard IP access list 1
 10 permit 192.168.1.11 (4 matches)
 20 deny any (7 matches)
```

Example 23-4   *Verifying Which Lines Are Being Used*

```
SW1# show users
 Line User Host(s) Idle Location
* 0 con 0 idle 00:00:00
 1 vty 0 idle 00:00:42 10.1.1.2
 2 vty 1 idle 00:00:48 10.1.10.1
 3 vty 2 idle 00:00:55 10.1.20.1
 4 vty 3 idle 00:00:47 10.1.23.3
 5 vty 4 idle 00:00:41 10.1.43.4
```

SSH

Recall from your CCNA or ENCOR studies that to configure Secure Shell (SSH) using local cryptographic keys, you need to make sure you are using a K9 IOS image, which you can verify with the **show version** command. You need to specify a hostname and a domain name with the **hostname** *hostname* and **ip domain-name** *domain-name* command, you need to generate the local cryptographic keys with the **crypto key generate rsa modulus** *key-size* command, you need to have at least one local username and password configured, and you need to allow inbound SSH connections to the device with the **transport input ssh** command. If any of these are missing, the SSH connection will fail.

With SSH, you may experience the same issues as described with Telnet, in addition to several others. Consider the following additional issues when troubleshooting SSH access to a device:

- **Is the correct version of SSH specified?** By default, both versions 1 and 2 are enabled. However, with the **ip ssh version** {1 | 2} command, you can change the version to just 1 or 2. If clients are connecting with version 2 and the device is configured for version 1, the SSH connection will fail; the same is true if clients are using version 1 and the devices are configured for version 2. To check the version of SSH that is running, use the **show ip ssh** command, as shown in Example 23-5. If it states version 1.99, it means versions 1 and 2 are running. If it states version 1.5, then SSHv1 is running, and if it states version 2, then SSHv2 is running. Also, notice that it displays the cryptographic key. If a key is missing and it says **None**, this means you have not imported or generated a key, and you need to do so.

- **Has the correct login command been specified?** SSH uses a username and password for authentication. Therefore, the **login** command does not work in this case because it only requests a password. If you accidentally use **login**, you will only be asked for a password, and once you enter it, the SSH authentication and connection will fail. You need to use the **login local** command to authenticate with the local database or the **login authentication** {default | *list_name*} command to authenticate with an AAA server. Example 23-6 shows the **login local** command specified.

- **Has the correct key size been specified?** SSHv2 uses an RSA key size of 768 or greater. If you were using a smaller key size with SSHv1 and then switched to SSHv2, you would need to create a new key with the correct size; otherwise, SSHv2 would not work. If you are using SSHv2 but accidentally specify a key size less than 768, SSHv2 connections are not allowed.

■ **Is there an ACL in the path between the client and the device blocking port 22?**
SSH uses TCP (Transmission Control Protocol) *port 22*. If an ACL blocking port 22
is configured on a router or firewall, you will be unable to make a successful SSH
connection.

■ **Do you receive the following error messages when trying to make outbound
SSH connections:** % SSH connections not permitted from this
terminal.**? You need to enable the line to initiate outbound SSH sessions with the
transport output ssh line configuration mode command.

Example 23-5   *Verifying the SSH Version*

```
SW1# show ip ssh
SSH Enabled - version 1.99
Authentication timeout: 120 secs; Authentication retries: 3
Minimum expected Diffie Hellman key size : 1024 bits
IOS Keys in SECSH format(ssh-rsa, base64 encoded):
ssh-rsa AAAAB3NzaC1yc2EAAAADAQABAAAAgQDtRqwdcEI+aGEXYmklh4G6pSJW1th6/Ivg4BCp19tO
BmdoW6NZahL2SxdzjKW8VIBjO1lVeaMfdmvKlpLjUlx7JDAkPs4Q39kzdPHY74MzD1/u+Fwvir8O5AQO
rUMkc5vuVEHFVc4WxQsxH4Q4Df10a6Q3UAOtnL4E0a7ez/imHw==
```

Example 23-6   *Verifying the vty Line Configuration*

```
SW1# show run | s line vty
line vty 0 4
 password cisco
 login local
```

When establishing an SSH connection from a Cisco IOS device, you need to specify the
username in the **ssh** command (for example, **R2#ssh -l raymond 10.0.123.1**). If you omit the
username, you will receive the following error message:

% No user specified nor available for SSH client

To verify the current SSH connections, use the **show ssh** command. Example 23-7 shows
SSHv2 inbound and outbound connections with the username cisco. The session is using
aes128-cbc encryption and the hashed message authentication code (HMAC) hmac-sha1.

Example 23-7   *Verifying SSH Connections*

```
SW1# show ssh
Connection Version  Mode  Encryption  Hmac       State             Username
0           2.0     IN    aes128-cbc  hmac-sha1  Session started   cisco
0           2.0     OUT   aes128-cbc  hmac-sha1  Session started   cisco
%No SSHv1 server connections running.
```

Password Encryption Levels

By default, all passwords are stored in plaintext within the IOS configuration. It is
recommended that passwords either be encrypted or hashed in the configuration for
security reasons. Example 23-8 shows sample output of the passwords stored in the running

configuration. The level 0 indicates no encryption. The *level 8* indicates that SHA-256 was used. The *level 5* indicates that Message Digest 5 (MD5) was used. The *level 7* indicates that Type 7 encryption was used. The levels from strongest to weakest are 8, 5, 7, and then 0. To implement Type 7 encryption, you issue the **service password-encryption** command. In most IOS versions, the default is level 5 when you use the **secret** option in a password, which uses the MD5 hashing algorithm. For example, by typing **username Raymond secret cisco**, you automatically use MD5, as shown the Example 23-8. To implement level 8, you need to specify the **algorithm-type** as **sha256** with the **secret** option when creating the username and password—for example, **username cisco algorithm-type sha256 secret cisco**. In Example 23-8, the result is shown as secret 8 followed by the hash.

Let's go back to **service password-encryption** for a moment. This is a command that, once executed, encrypts all current plaintext passwords and all future plaintext passwords you create. So, for example, if you type in **username administrator password cisco** and **service password-encryption** has been enabled, the password cisco will be encrypted as level 7, as shown in Example 23-8. If you want to create an already encrypted password using level 7, you can use the command **username administrator password 7** *password*. Notice the **7** in the command. If you use this, you must also specify an encrypted password. So, for example, if your password is cisco, you would not be able to type **cisco** as that would not meet the requirements of an encrypted password, and the IOS would return the error message Invalid Encrypted Password. In this case, you would have to type in the level 7 encrypted version of cisco—for example, **username administrator password 7 082D495A041C0C19**.

Example 23-8 *Verifying Password Security Levels*

```
SW1# show run | section username
username admin password 0 letmein
username administrator password 7 082D495A041C0C19
username cisco secret 8 $8$II/KfXazLA0MCF$5T4HGPiT8CWOiQQARmithsrhbNu6eZfKvkc1WLawTfw
username Raymond secret 5 $1$sHu.$sIjLazYcNOkRrgAjhyhxn0
```

Remote Transfer Troubleshooting

Although Cisco devices come preloaded with IOS and other files, it's highly probable that at some point you will want to upgrade the IOS image or any of the other files that are stored on the device. There are many different protocols you can use to accomplish this. This section focuses on TFTP, SCP, HTTP, and HTTPS.

TFTP

TFTP is an unsecure file transfer protocol that can be used to transfer files to and from a Cisco device using a TFTP server. TFTP uses UDP port 69. Therefore, it is classified as an unreliable protocol. If you require reliable transport from source to destination, use a TCP-based protocol. Consider the following when troubleshooting TFTP issues:

- When copying to a TFTP server, make sure the TFTP server has enough storage space.

- When copying from a TFTP server, make sure the storage location on the Cisco device has enough storage space. Use the **show flash** command to verify the amount of free space available and compare it to the size of the file you want to copy. If you copy a file that is larger than the available space, it will be partially copied, and you will get the failure message "buffer overflow - xxxx /xxxx". The first four x's identify the number of bytes read from the source file, and the second four x's identify the number of bytes available on the destination.

- Ensure that the TFTP server is reachable from the Cisco device.

- Check along the path from source to destination for access lists that might be blocking TFTP traffic.

- If you are using a management interface for TFTP traffic, use the **ip tftp source-interface** *interface_type interface_number* command to specify what management interface will be used for sourcing TFTP traffic.

- Ensure that you are using the **copy** command correctly. Remember that it is always **copy** *source destination*. This example copies from the TFTP server to the flash on the IOS device:

```
copy tftp://10.0.3.8/cisco_ios_files/c3900-universalk9-mz.
SPA.156-3.M6a.bin flash:c3900-universalk9-mz.SPA.156-3.M6a.bin
```

This example copies from the flash on the IOS device to a TFTP server:

```
copy flash:c3900-universalk9-mz.SPA.156-3.M6a.bin tftp://
10.0.3.8/cisco_ios_files/c3900-universalk9-mz.SPA.156-3.M6a.bin
```

- When copying to flash, make sure the filename is not longer than 63 characters. There is a 63-character limit on filenames in flash memory.

HTTP(S)

You can use HTTP, an unsecure protocol that uses TCP port 80, or its more secure version HTTPS, which uses TCP port 443, to copy Cisco IOS image files, core files, configuration files, log files, scripts, and more to or from a remote web server. Consider the following when troubleshooting HTTP(S) access for a device:

- Make sure your Cisco device supports the HTTP client. You can do this with the **show ip http client all** command. If the command works, the client is supported.

- Check that your router can connect to the web server. To do so, use the **ping** command on the Cisco device and ping the URL of the web server or its IP address.

- Ensure that the correct URL or IP address of the web server has been specified in the **copy** command. The **copy** command requires you to specify a source and destination, in that order. As an example, when copying from a web server to flash, the source would be the web server, as shown here with the IP address 10.0.3.8:

```
copy http://10.0.3.8/cisco_ios_files/c3900-universalk9-mz.
SPA.156-3.M6a.bin flash:c3900-universalk9-mz.SPA.156-3.M6a.bin
```

- When copying to a web server from flash, the destination would be the web server, as seen here with the IP address 10.0.3.8:

```
copy flash:c3900-universalk9-mz.SPA.156-3.M6a.bin
http://10.0.3.8/cisco_ios_files/c3900-universalk9-mz.
SPA.156-3.M6a.bin
```

- Ensure that the correct filename is specified with the **copy** command.

- Make sure the correct username and password are specified with the **copy** command. In this case, the username is user1, and the password is mypassword:

```
copy http://user1:mypasswrod@10.0.3.8/cisco_ios_files/c3900-
universalk9-mz.SPA.156-3.M6a.bin flash:c3900-universalk9-mz.
SPA.156-3.M6a.bin
```

  You can also specify the authentication credentials with the **ip http client username** *username* command and the **ip http client password** *password* command. Note that the username and password used with the **copy** command override the ones in these other commands.

- Check that the correct port is specified in the **copy** command. By default, HTTP uses port 80, and HTTPS uses port 443, but you can configure your web server to use whatever you want. In this example, the port number being specified is 8080:

```
copy http://user1:mypasswrod@10.0.3.8:8080/cisco_ios_files/
c3900-universalk9-mz.SPA.156-3.M6a.bin flash: c3900-
universalk9-mz.SPA.156-3.M6a.bin
```

- Check that packets to the web server from the Cisco device are being sourced from the correct IP address. If not, it is possible that an ACL along the path might be dropping the packets. You can configure the source IP address by using the **ip http client source-interface** *interface-id* command.

- Make sure you specified the correct protocol: HTTP or HTTPS. If you are connecting to an HTTP server, your URL should begin with http. If you are connecting to an HTTPS server, your URL should begin with HTTPS.

- For additional help with troubleshooting HTTP and HTTPS copy issues, use the **debug ip http client all** command.

FTP

You can use FTP, an unsecure protocol that uses TCP port 20 and port 21, to copy Cisco IOS image files, core files, configuration files, log files, scripts, and more to or from a remote FTP server. Consider the following when troubleshooting FTP access for a device:

- Verify that your router can connect to the FTP server. To do so, use the **ping** command on the Cisco device and ping the IP address of the FTP server.

- Ensure that the correct IP address of the FTP server has been specified with the **copy** command. The **copy** command requires you to specify a source and destination, in that order. As an example, when copying from an FTP server to flash, the source would be the FTP server, as shown here with the IP address 10.0.3.8:

```
copy ftp://10.0.3.8/cisco_ios_files/c3900-universalk9-mz.
SPA.156-3.M6a.bin flash:c3900-universalk9-mz.SPA.156-3.M6a.bin
```

- When copying to an FTP server from flash, the destination would be the FTP server, as shown here with the IP address 10.0.3.8:

```
copy flash:c3900-universalk9-mz.SPA.156-3.M6a.bin
ftp://10.0.3.8/cisco_ios_files/c3900-universalk9-mz.SPA.156-3.
M6a.bin
```

- Ensure that the correct filename is specified in the **copy** command.

- Make sure the correct username and password are specified in the **copy** command if you have set up FTP authentication on the FTP server. In this case, the username is user1, and the password is mypassword:

```
copy ftp://user1:mypasswrod@10.0.3.8/cisco_ios_files/c3900-
universalk9-mz.SPA.156-3.M6a.bin flash:c3900-universalk9-mz.
SPA.156-3.M6a.bin
```

You can also specify the authentication credentials with the **ip ftp client username** *username* command and the **ip ftp client password** *password* command. Note that the username and password used with the **copy** command override the ones in these other commands.

- Check that packets to the FTP server from the Cisco device are being sourced from the correct IP address. If not, it is possible that an ACL along the path might be dropping the packets or a filter on the FTP server may be dropping the packets. You can configure the source IP address by using the **ip ftp source-interface** *interface-id* command.

SCP

Secure Copy Protocol (SCP) is another option you have for copying files from a storage location to a Cisco device. It relies on Secure Shell (SSH) to provide a secure and authenticated method of transferring files. In addition, it requires AAA to be enabled so that the router is able to determine if the user is authorized to copy. Example 23-9 provides a sample SCP configuration on a Cisco IOS router.

Example 23-9 *SCP Configuration on a Cisco Router*

```
R1# config terminal
Enter configuration commands, one per line.  End with CNTL/Z.
R1(config)# aaa new-model
R1(config)# aaa authentication login default local
R1(config)# aaa authorization exec default local
R1(config)# username ENARSI privilege 15 password EXAM
R1(config)# ip domain-name ENARSI.LOCAL
R1(config)# crypto key generate rsa modulus 1024
The name for the keys will be: R1.ENARSI.LOCAL
% The key modulus size is 1024 bits
% Generating 1024 bit RSA keys, keys will be non-exportable...
[OK] (elapsed time was 7 seconds)
```

23

```
R1(config)#
*Sep 21 02:04:36.546: %SSH-5-ENABLED: SSH 1.99 has been enabled
R1(config)#ip ssh version 2
R1(config)#ip scp server enable
R1(config)#end
R1#
```

Consider the following when troubleshooting SCP issues:

- Ensure that SSH, authentication, and authorization have been configured correctly on the device.

- Ensure that an RSA (Rivest–Shamir–Adleman) key is available and can be used for encryption.

- Ensure that AAA is configured correctly and is functioning.

- Ensure that SCP is enabled on the Cisco device. If it isn't, use the **ip scp server enable** command to enable it.

- Ensure that the **copy** command is being used correctly.

- Verify that the correct username and password are being used for copying. If you are using an external authentication server, verify the credentials on the server.

- For additional help troubleshooting SCP issues, use the **debug ip scp** command.

Example 23-10 shows a successful copy from flash on the router to the SCP server at 10.0.3.8, using the username ENARSI. Note that if you do not specify the password in the **copy** command, the CLI (command-line interface) prompts you for a password, as shown in this example.

Example 23-10 *SCP copy Command on a Cisco Router*

```
copy flash:c3900-universalk9-mz.SPA.156-3.M6a.bin scp://ENARSI@10.0.3.8/
Address or name of remote host [10.0.3.8]?
Destination username [ENARSI]?
Destination filename [c3900-universalk9-mz.SPA.156-3.M6a.bin]?
Writing c3900-universalk9-mz.SPA.156-3.M6a.bin
Password:
!!!!!!!!!!!!!!!!!!!!!!!!!!!!!!!!!!!!!!!!!!!!!!!!!!!!!!!!!!!!!!!!!!!!!!!!!!!!!!!!!!!!!
```

Management Tools Troubleshooting

The health and well-being of your network and the clients on your network are critical for success. Being able to monitor your network using various tools will help you stay on top of any issues that show up. However, when the tools break or don't provide the results you need, you have to troubleshoot the tools that help you troubleshoot. This section examines how to troubleshoot issues with tools such as syslog, SNMP, IP SLA (Internet Protocol Service Level Agreement), Object Tracking, NetFlow, and Flexible NetFlow. In addition, it explores the benefits of using BFD (Bidirectional Forwarding Detection) and examines how Cisco DNA Center Assurance can assist you with your troubleshooting efforts.

Syslog Troubleshooting

To verify your *syslog* configuration, confirm that logging is enabled, and view the syslog messages stored in the buffer, you use the command **show logging**, as shown in Example 23-11. When troubleshooting, you need syslog to generate the right type of messages at the right time. By default, console, monitor, and buffer logging display messages with severity levels of debugging (7) and lower. Logging to a server is disabled by default, but when it is enabled, all severity levels are sent to the server. Therefore, in all cases, if you are not receiving the syslog messages you expect, verify that the correct level is configured. In Example 23-11, the console and monitor are configured with the level informational (which means informational and all lower levels), the buffer is configured with the level debugging (which means all levels), and the trap logging (server) is configured with the level warnings (which means warnings and all lower levels).

When logging to a server, the correct server IP address needs to be specified, and the server needs to be reachable. In addition, because syslog uses UDP (User Datagram Protocol) port 514, it is important to make sure that no ACLs are blocking traffic destined to UDP port 514.The buffer has a default size of 8192 bytes. When the buffer fills up, the older entries are overwritten. Therefore, if you are using the buffer and experiencing a loss of syslog messages, consider increasing the size of the buffer with the **logging buffered** *size* global configuration command or sending the messages to a syslog server instead.

Finally, if you have remotely connected to a device by using Telnet or SSH, and no syslog messages are appearing, it is because the **terminal monitor** command has not been issued.

Example 23-11   *Verifying Syslog Configuration*

```
R4# show logging
Syslog logging: enabled (0 messages dropped, 0 messages rate-limited, 0 flushes, 0
overruns, xml disabled, filtering disabled)


No Active Message Discriminator.


Inactive Message Discriminator:
OSPF severity group drops 4


        Console logging: level informational, 116 messages logged, xml disabled,
                         filtering disabled
        Monitor logging: level informational, 0 messages logged, xml disabled,
                         filtering disabled
        Buffer logging: level debugging, 175 messages logged, xml disabled,
                         filtering disabled
        Exception Logging: size (8192 bytes)
        Count and timestamp logging messages: disabled
        Persistent logging: disabled
No active filter modules.


        Trap logging: level warnings, 108 message lines logged
```

23

```
        Logging to 10.1.100.100 (udp port 514, audit disabled,
                link up),
                2 message lines logged,
                0 message lines rate-limited,
                0 message lines dropped-by-MD,
                xml disabled, sequence number disabled
                filtering disabled
        Logging Source-Interface: VRF Name:


Log Buffer (8192 bytes):
Jul 24 21:54:50.422: %SYS-5-CONFIG_I: Configured from console by console
Jul 24 21:57:16.070: %OSPFv3-4-ERRRCV: OSPFv3-10-IPv6 Received invalid packet: Bad
Checksum from FE80::C829:FFF:FE50:54, GigabitEthernet2/0
Jul 24 21:58:20.014: NTP message received from 192.168.1.10 on interface
'GigabitEthernet2/0' (10.1.34.4).
Jul 24 21:58:20.018: NTP Core(DEBUG): ntp_receive: message received
Jul 24 21:58:20.022: NTP Core(DEBUG): ntp_receive: peer is 0x00000000, next action is 3.
Jul 24 21:58:20.030: NTP message sent to 192.168.1.10, from interface
'GigabitEthernet2/0' (10.1.34.4).
Jul 24 21:59:25.014: NTP message received from 192.168.1.10 on interface
'GigabitEthernet2/0' (10.1.34.4).
Jul 24 21:59:25.018: NTP Core(DEBUG): ntp_receive: message received
Jul 24 21:59:25.022: NTP Core(DEBUG): ntp_receive: peer is 0x00000000, next action is 3.
Jul 24 21:59:25.026: NTP message sent to 192.168.1.10, from interface
'GigabitEthernet2/0' (10.1.34.4).
```

Having log messages and debug messages timestamped is critical for troubleshooting. If no timestamps are included with either log messages or debug messages, it is because the **no service timestamps** command has been executed. To configure timestamps, use the **service timestamps** [**debug** | **log**] [**datetime** | **uptime**] command. The **datetime** option includes the date and time the log or debug message occurred. Therefore, it is important to have an accurate calendar and time set. Use NTP (Network Time Protocol) for this. The **uptime** option provides a timestamp based on the amount of time that has passed since the last reboot.

Note that syslog messages are by default displayed in UTC time. Therefore, if your system clock is set to display time in your local time zone and not UTC time, the syslog messages will not display the same time that is shown on the clock. For example, you might issue the command **show clock** and get the result 13:35:00, but a recent syslog message might display 17:35:00. If this is not the result you desire and you want the syslog messages to be displayed using the same time as the output of **show clock**, you need to include the **localtime** option in the **service timestamps** command, as shown in this snippet:

```
R2(config)#service timestamps log datetime localtime
```

NOTE   When you have devices in different time zones, it is best to keep your messages in UTC time for troubleshooting purposes.

debug commands are fantastic troubleshooting tools if you use them properly. Every single Cisco IOS service and feature has **debug** commands associated with it to provide real-time information about what is happening with that protocol or service; **show** commands, in contrast, only provide snapshots in time for a protocol or service. However, it is important to be careful when using **debug** commands. If you use a **debug** command at the wrong time, you could overload the CPU on your router and cause it to become unstable and crash. A physical reboot would be your only option at that point. For example, with NAT (Network Address Translation), **show ip nat translations** gives you a snapshot in time of the translations that have occurred as of the time you typed in the command. The command **debug ip nat translations** shows you, in real time, all the translations that are occurring. In a very busy environment, this could crash your router as the number of translations occurring could overwhelm your router. So, using this **debug** command at the wrong time would be disastrous. As an example, the **debug eigrp packet** command debugs every EIGRP (Enhanced Interior Gateway Routing Protocol) packet, but if you only want to debug the hello packets, it would be better to use the **debug eigrp packet hello** command. So, when troubleshooting, it is important to use the best **debug** command to get exactly the information you need—no more, no less—so you don't jeopardize the performance of your router.

Conditional **debug** commands are a little misleading. Most people think the term *conditional* **debug** command refers to specifying conditions within a debug command to limit the output. For example, think about **debug eigrp packet** and **debug eigrp packet hello**. At first, you might think the second command is a conditional **debug** command, but it is not. It is just a more granular **debug** command. For the sake of the ENRASI exam and the real world, you need to understand that conditional debugging allows you to specify conditions that limit the output of a **debug** command to a specific interface, IP address, MAC address, VLAN, username, and so on. For example, if you wanted to limit the output of the command **debug eigrp packet hello** to show only the packets that arrive on interface GigabitEthernet 0/0, you could create this condition in privileged exec mode:

```
debug condition interface gigabitethernet 0/0
```

When you issue any **debug** command after that or if any **debug** commands are already running, the output will only display the **debug** commands that are associated with interface GigabitEthernet 0/0, and the condition will apply until you disable it or reboot the device. You can also stack conditional **debug** commands by simply specifying multiple conditions, as follows:

```
debug condition interface gigabitethernet 0/0

debug condition ip 10.0.1.1
```

Now debugs will only be displayed if they match both conditions.

To verify if you have any conditions currently specified, use the **show debug condition** command.

SNMP Troubleshooting

Regardless of whether you are using *SNMPv2c* or *SNMPv3*, you need to be able to ping the server from the agent. If Layer 3 connectivity does not exist, the SNMP (Simple Network Management Protocol) network management server (NMS) cannot access the information in the Management Information Base (MIB) on the agent. In addition, SNMP uses UDP port

161 for general messages and UDP port 162 for unreliable traps and reliable informs. Therefore, if an ACL is denying these ports, SNMP communication does not occur between the NMS and the agent.

Keep the following in mind as you troubleshoot SNMPv2c:

■ **Ensure that community strings match:** For the NMS to read from or write to the agent, the read community string or the read/write community string must match between the NMS and the agent. In Example 23-12, the read-only community string specified is CISCO.

■ **Ensure that ACLs classifying servers are correct:** If you are using ACLs to define which NMS (based on IP address) is allowed to retrieve objects from the MIB, the ACL has to accurately define the server addresses. In Example 23-12, ACL 10 is only permitting the NMS with the IP address 10.1.100.100 to read from the MIB using the read-only community string CISCO.

■ **Ensure the correct configuration for notifications:** If your agent is configured to send traps or informs, you should verify the following:

  ■ Ensure that traps are enabled.

  ■ Ensure that the correct host (NMS) IP address is specified.

  ■ Ensure that the correct SNMP version is specified.

  ■ Ensure that the correct community string is specified.

  If you do not want all traps to be sent, it is imperative that you specify the correct ones to send. In Example 23-12, the **snmp-server host** command indicates that SNMPv2c informs will be sent to the NMS at 10.1.100.100 with the community string CISCO.

■ **Prevent indexes from shuffling:** To prevent index shuffling and guarantee index persistence during reboots or minor software upgrades, use the **snmp-server ifindex persist** command, which shows up as **snmp ifmib ifindex persist** in the running configuration.

Example 23-12 *SNMPv2c Configuration Example*

```
R4# show run | section snmp
snmp-server community CISCO RO 10
snmp-server enable traps cpu threshold
snmp-server host 10.1.100.100 informs version 2c CISCO
snmp ifmib ifindex persist
R4# show ip access-lists
Standard IP access list 10
 10 permit 10.1.100.100
```

SNMPv3 offers major improvements over SNMPv2c when it comes to security. It offers improved authentication and encryption. Keep the following in mind as you troubleshoot SNMPv3:

- **Nesting of users, views, and groups:** With SNMPv3, you create users with authentication and encryption parameters that are nested into groups that define the servers that are allowed to read from or write to the objects within the MIB on the agent. If you fail to nest the users, views, and groups, SNMPv3 will not function as expected. In Example 23-13, the user NMSERVER is nested into the group NMSREADONLY, which allows read-only access to the object identifiers (OIDs) listed in the view MIBACCESS to the NMS with the IP address 10.1.100.100.

- **Wrong security level specified:** SNMPv3 supports three security levels: noAuth, auth, and priv. Remember that noAuth uses a plaintext username to authenticate and passes all messages in plaintext, auth uses hashing algorithms for authentication and integrity checking but still passes all messages in plaintext, and priv uses hashing algorithms for authentication and integrity checking and encryption algorithms to encrypt the messages in transit. The security levels specified for the group, for the users, and for the sending of traps must match what is used on the server. In Example 23-13, authPriv is being used extensively (with the priv parameter in the commands), which means that authentication and encryption will be used.

- **Wrong hashing algorithm, encryption algorithm, or passwords defined:** When authenticating, the hashing algorithm must match, along with the password; otherwise, authentication will fail. When performing encryption, the encryption algorithm and password must match; otherwise, the NMS will not be able to decrypt the data it receives. In Example 23-13, SHA is being used as the hashing algorithm, AES-256 as the encryption algorithm, and MYPASSWORD as the password.

- **Wrong OIDs specified in the view:** The views identify the objects within the MIB that the NMS will be able to access. If the wrong objects are defined, SNMPv3 will not produce the desired results. In Example 23-13, the objects sysUpTime, ifAdminStatus, and ifOperStatus are defined in the MIBACCESS view.

- **ACLs classifying servers:** If you are using ACLs to define which NMS (based on IP address) is allowed to retrieve objects from the MIB, the ACL has to accurately define the server addresses. In Example 23-13, ACL 99 is only permitting the NMS with the IP address 10.1.100.100.

- **Notification configuration:** If your agent is configured to send traps or informs, you should verify that traps are enabled, the correct host (NMS) IP address is specified, the correct SNMP version is specified, and the correct security level is specified, and you should make sure you have specified traps or informs (default is traps). If you do not want all traps to be sent, it is imperative that you specify the correct ones. You also need to specify the correct SNMPv3 username for the authentication/encryption process. In Example 23-13, the **snmp-server host** command indicates that SNMPv3 will send traps related to the CPU to the NMS at 10.1.100.100, with authentication and encryption provided by the username NMSERVER.

■ **Shuffling indexes:** To prevent index shuffling and guarantee index persistence during reboots or minor software upgrades, use the **snmp-server ifindex persist** command, which shows up as **snmp ifmib ifindex persist** in the running configuration. You can verify the index numbers and whether persistence is enabled for the interfaces by using the **show snmp mib ifmib ifindex detail** command, as shown in Example 23-13.

Example 23-13   *SNMPv3 Configuration Example*

```
R2# show run | section snmp
snmp-server group NMSREADONLY v3 priv read MIBACCESS access 99
snmp-server view MIBACCESS sysUpTime included
snmp-server view MIBACCESS ifAdminStatus included
snmp-server view MIBACCESS ifOperStatus included
snmp-server user NMSERVER NMSREADONLY v3 auth sha MYPASSWORD priv aes 256 MYPASSWORD
snmp-server host 10.1.100.100 version 3 priv NMSERVER cpu
snmp ifmib ifindex persist


R2# show ip access-lists
Standard IP access list 99
 10 permit 10.1.100.100
R2# show snmp mib ifmib ifindex detail
Description          ifIndex  Active  Persistent  Saved  TrapStatus
GigabitEthernet2/0      4       yes     enabled     no     enabled
GigabitEthernet3/0      5       yes     enabled     no     enabled
Ethernet0/0             1       yes     enabled     no     enabled
GigabitEthernet0/0      2       yes     enabled     no     enabled
GigabitEthernet1/0      3       yes     enabled     no     enabled
```

You can verify the configured SNMP groups by using the **show snmp group** command. In Example 23-14 the group is NMSREADONLY, the security model is v3 priv (authPriv), the associated read-only view is MIBACCESS, and only servers in access list 99 are permitted to read the OIDs in the view.

Example 23-14   *Verifying SNMP Groups*

```
R2# show snmp group
groupname: NMSREADONLY                              security model:v3 priv
contextname: <no context specified>                storage-type:
nonvolatile
readview : MIBACCESS                                writeview: <no
writeview specified>
notifyview: *tv.00000000.00000000.10000000.0
row status: active              access-list: 99
```

You can verify the configured SNMP users by using the **show snmp user** command. Example 23-15 shows a user named NMSERVER that is using the SHA authentication protocol and the AES-256 privacy (encryption) protocol. The user is also associated with the group NMSREADONLY.

Example 23-15 *Verifying SNMP Users*

```
SW2# show snmp user

User name: NMSERVER
Engine ID: 800000090300001C57FEF601
storage-type: nonvolatile active
Authentication Protocol: SHA
Privacy Protocol: AES256
Group-name: NMSREADONLY
```

To verify where traps or informs (notifications) are being sent, use the **show snmp host** command. In Example 23-16, the notifications are being sent to the NMS at 10.1.100.100, using UDP port 162. The specific notifications are traps, and the username to be used for authentication and encryption is NMSERVER, with the security model v3 priv.

Example 23-16 *Verifying SNMP Hosts*

```
SW2# show snmp host
Notification host: 10.1.100.100    udp-port: 162      type: trap
user: NMSERVER      security model: v3 priv
```

You can use the **show snmp view** command to view the OIDs that are included in each of the views. In Example 23-17, the MIBACCESS view has the OIDs sysUpTime, ifAdminStatus, and ifOperStatus included.

Example 23-17 *Verifying SNMP Views*

```
SW2# show snmp view
...output omitted...
cac_view lifEntry.20 - included read-only active
cac_view cciDescriptionEntry.1 - included read-only active
MIBACCESS sysUpTime - included nonvolatile active
MIBACCESS ifAdminStatus - included nonvolatile active
MIBACCESS ifOperStatus - included nonvolatile active
v1default iso - included permanent active
v1default internet - included permanent active
...output omitted...
```

Cisco IOS IP SLA Troubleshooting

Cisco IOS *IP SLA* enables you to measure network performance and test network availability by generating a continuous, reliable probe (simulated traffic) in a predictable manner. The data you can collect varies greatly, depending on how you set up the probe. You can collect information about packet loss, one-way latency, response times, jitter, network resource availability, application performance, server response times, and even voice quality.

IP SLA consists of an IP SLA source (which sends the probes) and IP SLA responder (which replies to the probes). However, both are not needed in all cases. Only the IP SLA source is required all the time. The IP SLA responder is needed only when gathering highly accurate statistics for services that are not offered by any specific destination device. The responder has the ability to respond to the source with accurate measurements, taking into account its own processing time of the probe. Figure 23-1 shows a scenario with just the IP SLA source sending a ping to test connectivity. Figure 23-2 shows a scenario with an IP SLA source and an IP SLA responder measuring jitter (interpacket delay variance).

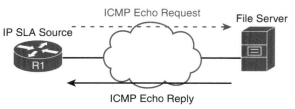

Figure 23-1   *IP SLA Source Topology*

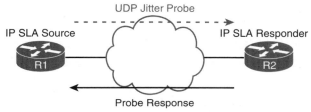

Figure 23-2   *IP SLA Source and Responder Topology*

Example 23-18 shows a sample configuration based on Figure 23-1. In this example, R1 is configured as an IP SLA source. The probe it's sending is an Internet Control Message Protocol (ICMP) echo (ping) to 10.1.100.100, using the local source address 192.168.1.11. (Specifying the source address is especially important when you have multiple paths to reach the destination because it helps control which interface the probe is sent from.) This probe is being sent every 15 seconds, it is scheduled to start now, and it will never expire.

Example 23-18   *IP SLA icmp-echo Probe Configuration Example*

```
R1# show run | section sla
ip sla 2
 icmp-echo 10.1.100.100 source-ip 192.168.1.11
 frequency 15
ip sla schedule 2 life forever start-time now
```

Example 23-19 shows a sample configuration based on Figure 23-2. In this example, R1 is configured as an IP SLA source. The probe it's sending is testing UDP jitter from the source address 192.168.1.11 to 10.1.34.4, using port 65051. It will send 20 probe packets for each test with a size of 160 bytes each, and it will repeat every 30 seconds. The probe is started and will never expire. To get measurements related to jitter, you need to have a device that can process the probes and respond accordingly. Therefore, the destination device needs to be able to support Cisco IOS IP SLA and must be configured as a responder. R2 is configured as the IP SLA responder with the **ip sla responder** command. You can be more granular with the **ip sla responder** command and specify the operation, such as **udp echo** or **tcp connect**, the IP address to respond to, and the port number to use (for example, **ip sla responder udp-echo ipaddress 10.0.52.4 port 1967**).

Example 23-19 *IP SLA UDP-JITTER Probe Configuration Example*

```
R1# show run | section sla
ip sla 1
 udp-jitter 10.1.34.4 65051 source-ip 192.168.1.11 num-packets 20
 request-data-size 160
 frequency 30
ip sla schedule 1 life forever start-time now


R2# show run | section sla
ip sla responder
```

When troubleshooting Cisco IOS IP SLA, consider the following:

- The correct operation needs to be chosen for the metrics you intend to measure.

- The destination IP address needs to be reachable and correctly defined.

- The source IP address needs to be reachable from the destination and correctly defined.

- Any necessary port numbers need to be correctly identified.

- The SLA instance needs to be started.

- If the operation needs an IP SLA responder, one must be configured and reachable.

To verify which operations are supported on the platform in addition to how many operations are configured and how many are currently active, use the **show ip sla application** command, as shown in Example 23-20.

Example 23-20 *Output of show ip sla application*

```
R1# show ip sla application
        IP Service Level Agreements
Version: Round Trip Time MIB 2.2.0, Infrastructure Engine-III
Supported Operation Types:
        icmpEcho, path-echo, path-jitter, udpEcho, tcpConnect, http
        dns, udpJitter, dhcp, ftp, lsp Group, lspPing, lspTrace
        802.1agEcho VLAN, EVC, Port, 802.1agJitter VLAN, EVC, Port
        pseudowirePing, udpApp, wspApp

Supported Features:
        IPSLAs Event Publisher

IP SLAs low memory water mark: 30919230
Estimated system max number of entries: 22645
```

```
Estimated number of configurable operations: 22643
Number of Entries configured  : 2
Number of active Entries      : 2
Number of pending Entries     : 0
Number of inactive Entries    : 0
Time of last change in whole IP SLAs: 09:29:04.789 UTC Sat Jul 26 2014
```

To verify the configuration values for each IP SLA instance as well as the default values that you did not modify, use the **show ip sla configuration** command, as shown in Example 23-21. In this example, there are two entries (instances): number 1 and number 2. You can verify for each entry the type of operation that is being performed, the operation timeout, the source and destination addresses, the source and destination ports, the type of service values, the packet size, the packet interval (if the operation supports it), and the schedule that has been configured for the operation. In this case, both entry 1 and entry 2 are started, and they will never expire.

Example 23-21 *Output of show ip sla configuration*

```
R1# show ip sla configuration
IP SLAs Infrastructure Engine-III
Entry number: 1
Owner:
Tag:
Operation timeout (milliseconds): 5000
Type of operation to perform: udp-jitter
Target address/Source address: 10.1.34.4/192.168.1.11
Target port/Source port: 65051/0
Type Of Service parameter: 0x0
Request size (ARR data portion): 160
Packet Interval (milliseconds)/Number of packets: 20/20
Verify data: No
Vrf Name:
Control Packets: enabled
Schedule:
   Operation frequency (seconds): 30 (not considered if randomly scheduled)
   Next Scheduled Start Time: Start Time already passed
   Group Scheduled : FALSE
   Randomly Scheduled : FALSE
   Life (seconds): Forever
   Entry Ageout (seconds): never
   Recurring (Starting Everyday): FALSE
   Status of entry (SNMP RowStatus): Active
Threshold (milliseconds): 5000
Distribution Statistics:
   Number of statistic hours kept: 2
   Number of statistic distribution buckets kept: 1
   Statistic distribution interval (milliseconds): 20
Enhanced History:
```

```
Entry number: 2
Owner:
Tag:
Operation timeout (milliseconds): 5000
Type of operation to perform: icmp-echo
Target address/Source address: 10.1.100.100/192.168.1.11
Type Of Service parameter: 0x0
Request size (ARR data portion): 28
Verify data: No
Vrf Name:
Schedule:
   Operation frequency (seconds): 15 (not considered if randomly scheduled)
   Next Scheduled Start Time: Start Time already passed
   Group Scheduled : FALSE
   Randomly Scheduled : FALSE
   Life (seconds): Forever
   Entry Ageout (seconds): never
   Recurring (Starting Everyday): FALSE
   Status of entry (SNMP RowStatus): Active
Threshold (milliseconds): 5000
Distribution Statistics:
   Number of statistic hours kept: 2
   Number of statistic distribution buckets kept: 1
   Statistic distribution interval (milliseconds): 20
Enhanced History:
History Statistics:
   Number of history Lives kept: 0
   Number of history Buckets kept: 15
   History Filter Type: None
```

To display the results of the IP SLA operations and the statistics collected, use the **show ip sla statistics** command, as shown in Example 23-22. In this output, you can verify the type of operation, when it last started, the latest return code, the values returned (depending on the operation), and the number of successes and failures.

Example 23-22 *Output of show ip sla statistics*

```
R1# show ip sla statistics
IPSLAs Latest Operation Statistics

IPSLA operation id: 1
Type of operation: udp-jitter
        Latest RTT: 53 milliseconds
Latest operation start time: 09:52:23 UTC Sat Jul 26 2014
Latest operation return code: OK
```

```
RTT Values:
        Number Of RTT: 17    RTT Min/Avg/Max: 46/53/66 milliseconds
Latency one-way time:
        Number of Latency one-way Samples: 0
        Source to Destination Latency one way Min/Avg/Max: 0/0/0 milliseconds
        Destination to Source Latency one way Min/Avg/Max: 0/0/0 milliseconds
Jitter Time:
        Number of SD Jitter Samples: 14
        Number of DS Jitter Samples: 14
        Source to Destination Jitter Min/Avg/Max: 1/7/13 milliseconds
        Destination to Source Jitter Min/Avg/Max: 1/6/13 milliseconds
Packet Loss Values:
        Loss Source to Destination: 0
        Source to Destination Loss Periods Number: 0
        Source to Destination Loss Period Length Min/Max: 0/0
        Source to Destination Inter Loss Period Length Min/Max: 0/0
        Loss Destination to Source: 3
        Destination to Source Loss Periods Number: 2
        Destination to Source Loss Period Length Min/Max: 1/2
        Destination to Source Inter Loss Period Length Min/Max: 1/9
        Out Of Sequence: 0 Tail Drop: 0
        Packet Late Arrival: 0 Packet Skipped: 0
Voice Score Values:
        Calculated Planning Impairment Factor (ICPIF): 0
        Mean Opinion Score (MOS): 0
Number of successes: 61
Number of failures: 0
Operation time to live: Forever



IPSLA operation id: 2
        Latest RTT: 1 milliseconds
Latest operation start time: 09:52:49 UTC Sat Jul 26 2014
Latest operation return code: OK
Number of successes: 95
Number of failures: 1
Operation time to live: Forever
```

To verify the operation of the IP SLA responder, use the command **show ip sla responder**, as shown in Example 23-23, on the Cisco IOS device acting as the responder. You can verify the general control port number, the total number of probes received, the number of errors, and the recent sources of IP SLA probes.

Example 23-23 *Output of show ip sla responder*

```
R2# show ip sla responder
        General IP SLA Responder on Control port 1967
General IP SLA Responder is: Enabled
Number of control message received: 2333 Number of errors: 0
Recent sources:
        192.168.1.11 [09:53:52.001 UTC Sat Jul 26 2014]
        192.168.1.11 [09:53:22.033 UTC Sat Jul 26 2014]
        192.168.1.11 [09:52:52.029 UTC Sat Jul 26 2014]
        192.168.1.11 [09:52:22.049 UTC Sat Jul 26 2014]
        192.168.1.11 [09:51:52.029 UTC Sat Jul 26 2014]
Recent error sources:


        Permanent Port IP SLA Responder
Permanent Port IP SLA Responder is: Disabled


udpEcho Responder:
  IP Address            Port
```

Example 23-24 shows real-time output of an SLA operation with the **debug ip sla trace 2** command. The output shows a successful trace of the IP SLA instance 2. The operation is waking up, starting, sending the probe, and receiving a response and then the statistics are updated accordingly.

Example 23-24 *debug Command Output Showing a Successful IP SLA Operation*

```
R1# debug ip sla trace 2
IPSLA-INFRA_TRACE:OPER:2 slaSchedulerEventWakeup
IPSLA-INFRA_TRACE:OPER:2 Starting an operation
IPSLA-OPER_TRACE:OPER:2 source IP:192.168.1.11
IPSLA-OPER_TRACE:OPER:2 Starting icmpecho operation - destAddr=10.1.100.100,
sAddr=192.168.1.11
IPSLA-OPER_TRACE:OPER:2 Sending ID: 113
IPSLA-OPER_TRACE:OPER:2 ID:113, RTT=1
IPSLA-INFRA_TRACE:OPER:2 Updating result
```

Example 23-25 shows real-time output of an SLA operation with the **debug ip sla trace 2** command. The output shows an unsuccessful trace of the IP SLA instance 2. You can see that the operation timed out between the source IP address 192.168.1.11 and the destination IP address 10.1.100.100. The results were then updated accordingly in the SLA statistics. This output confirms that the IP SLA operation was not successful.

Example 23-25 *debug Command Output Showing an Unsuccessful IP SLA Operation*

```
R1# debug ip sla trace 2
IPSLA-INFRA_TRACE:OPER:2 slaSchedulerEventWakeup
IPSLA-INFRA_TRACE:OPER:2 Starting an operation
IPSLA-OPER_TRACE:OPER:2 source IP:192.168.1.11
```

```
IPSLA-OPER_TRACE:OPER:2 Starting icmpecho operation - destAddr=10.1.100.100,
sAddr=192.168.1.11
IPSLA-OPER_TRACE:OPER:2 Sending ID: 205
IPSLA-OPER_TRACE:OPER:2 Timeout - destAddr=10.1.100.100, sAddr=192.168.1.11
IPSLA-INFRA_TRACE:OPER:2 Updating result
```

Object Tracking Troubleshooting

Object Tracking enables you to dynamically control what occurs if the result of a tracking object is up or down. For example, you can attach an object to a static route; if the object is up, the route is installed in the routing table. If the object is down, the route is not installed in the routing table. With First-Hop Redundancy Protocol (FHRP), you can decrement or increment the priority based on the status of the object. For example, if the status of the tracking object is down, the FHRP priority is decremented.

With Object Tracking, you can track IP routes, IP SLA instances, interfaces, and groups of objects. For example, you can track an IP SLA instance that is using ICMP echoes. If an echo fails, the IP SLA instances fails, which brings down the tracking object. If the tracking object is tied to FHRP, the priority is decremented; if the tracking object is tied to a static route, the static route is removed from the routing table.

To verify the configuration of a tracking object and the status of the tracking object, use the **show track** command. In Example 23-26, tracking object 1 exists on SW1. It is tracking the reachability of an IP route, 10.1.43.0/24. If the route is in the routing table, the object is up. If the route is not in the routing table, the object is down. The object is attached to HSRP Group 10, as shown after Tracked by: in the output.

Example 23-26 *Verifying the Configuration and Status of a Tracking Object (Up)*

```
SW1# show track
Track 1
  IP route 10.1.43.0 255.255.255.0 reachability
  Reachability is Up (EIGRP)
    1 change, last change 00:01:55
  First-hop interface is GigabitEthernet1/0/10
  Tracked by:
    HSRP Vlan10 10
```

In Example 23-27, the tracking object is down because the route to 10.1.43.0/24 is no longer in the routing table. Because it is attached to HSRP Group 10, an action based on the configuration of HSRP Group 10 would occur, such as decrementing the local HSRP priority.

Example 23-27 *Verifying the Configuration and Status of a Tracking Object (Down)*

```
SW1#
%TRACKING-5-STATE: 1 ip route 10.1.43.0/24 reachability Up->Down
SW1# show track
Track 1
   IP route 10.1.43.0 255.255.255.0 reachability
```

```
Reachability is Down (no route)
    2 changes, last change 00:00:04
First-hop interface is unknown
Tracked by:
    HSRP Vlan10 10
```

Now we will explore how we can combine IP SLA with Object Tracking and floating static routes. Refer to Figure 23-3 as you explore Example 23-28.

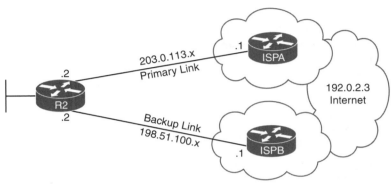

Figure 23-3 *IP SLA Source and Responder Topology*

In Figure 23-3, R2 is configured with two static default routes: **ip route 0.0.0.0 0.0.0.0 203.0.113.1 track 22** and **ip route 0.0.0.0 0.0.0.0 198.51.100.1 4**. Recognize that the first one points to the next hop of ISPA, and there is a tracking object (numbered 22) tied to it. The tracking object is designed to control whether the static route should be installed in the routing table or not. So, the tracking object **track 22 ip sla 1 reachability** is up if the IP SLA 1 probe is reachable (successful) and down if the IP SLA 1 probe is not reachable (not successful). Therefore, when the tracking object is up, the static route is installed in the routing table. When the tracking object is down, the static route is removed from the routing table. Now focus on the IP SLA 1 configuration. The probe is an icmp-echo to 192.0.2.3 from 203.0.113.2 of R2, and it has been scheduled to start now and last forever. As a result, if the icmp-echo is successful, the tracking object is up, and the static route to ISPA is installed in the routing table. If the icmp-echo fails, the tracking object is down, and the static route to ISPA is removed from the routing table.

One final part to this is the other static route, **ip route 0.0.0.0 0.0.0.0 198.51.100.1 4**, which points to ISPB. It is not installed by default in the routing table because of the higher administrative distance that has been assigned to it (4). The static route to ISPA has a default administrative distance of 1 since we did not configure the administrative distance in the command as we did with the route to ISPB. Therefore, the ISPA path has priority over the ISPB path, and this is the reason A is installed and B is not in the routing table.

So, to put it all together now, when the route to ISPA is valid, it has priority over the route to ISPB because of the higher administrative distance. But if the icmp-echo fails, then the IP SLA 1 probe has failed, which means the tracking object is down, so the path to ISPA is removed from the routing table and the path to ISPB is added to the routing table. When the icmp-echo is successful, the IP SLA probe is a success, which means the tracking object is up, so the route through ISPA is installed in the routing table instead of the route through ISPB.

Example 23-28   *IP SLA with Object Tracking and a Floating Static Route*

```
R2# show run | i ip route|track
track 22 ip sla 1 reachability
ip route 0.0.0.0 0.0.0.0 203.0.113.1 track 22
ip route 0.0.0.0 0.0.0.0 198.51.100.1 4


R2# show run | s ip sla
ip sla 1
 icmp-echo 192.0.2.3 source-ip 203.0.113.2
 frequency 5
ip sla schedule 1 life forever start-time now
```

NetFlow and Flexible NetFlow Troubleshooting

Cisco IOS *NetFlow* can provide you with tremendous insight into your network traffic patterns. Several companies market NetFlow collectors, which are software applications that can take the NetFlow information that is stored in a local device's cache and convert that raw data into useful graphs, charts, and tables reflecting traffic patterns.

NetFlow can distinguish between different traffic flows. A *flow* is a series of packets, all of which have shared header information, such as source and destination IP addresses, protocol numbers, port numbers, and type of service (TOS) field information. In addition, the packets are entering the same interface on the device. NetFlow can keep track of the number of packets and bytes observed in each flow. This information is stored in a *flow cache* in the router's memory.

You can use the NetFlow feature as a standalone feature on an individual router and view flow cache information in the CLI. Such a standalone configuration might be useful for troubleshooting because you can observe flows being created as packets enter a router. However, rather than use just a standalone implementation of NetFlow, you can export the entries in a router's flow cache to a *NetFlow collector*, which is a software application running on a computer/server in the network. After the NetFlow collector has received flow information over a period, analysis software running on the NetFlow collector can produce reports detailing traffic statistics.

Example 23-29 provides a sample NetFlow configuration on a router. Notice that the **ip flow ingress** command is issued for Fast Ethernet 0/0, and **ip flow egress** is configured on Fast Ethernet 0/1. You configure **ingress** when you want to capture traffic arriving inbound on an interface, and you use the **egress** command when you want to capture traffic exiting an interface. If you want to capture traffic in both directions, you can configure both **ingress** and **egress** on an interface.

Although not required, router R4 is configured to export its flow cache information to a NetFlow collector. The **ip flow-export source lo 0** command indicates that all communication between router R4 and the NetFlow collector will occur through the Loopback 0 interface. NetFlow version 5 is specified, and this version needs to match the NetFlow collector. You should check the documentation of your NetFlow collector software to confirm which version to configure.

Finally, the **ip flow-export destination 192.168.1.50 5000** command is issued to specify that the NetFlow collector's IP address is 192.168.1.50, and communication to the NetFlow collector should be done over UDP port 5000. NetFlow does not have a standardized port number, so check your NetFlow collector's documentation when selecting a port.

Example 23-29   *NetFlow Sample Configuration*

```
R4# configure terminal
R4(config)# int fa 0/0
R4(config-if)# ip flow ingress
R4(config-if)# exit
R4(config)# int fa 0/1
R4(config-if)# ip flow egress
R4(config-if)# exit
R4(config)# ip flow-export source lo 0
R4(config)# ip flow-export version 5
R4(config)# ip flow-export destination 192.168.1.50 5000
R4(config)# end
```

Although an external NetFlow collector is valuable for longer-term flow analysis and can provide detailed graphs and charts, you can issue the **show ip cache flow** command at a router's CLI prompt to produce a summary of flow information, as shown in Example 23-30. A troubleshooter can look at the output displayed in Example 23-30 and confirm, for example, that traffic is flowing between IP addresses 10.8.8.6 and 192.168.0.228.

Example 23-30   *Viewing NetFlow Information with show ip cache flow*

```
R4# show ip cache flow
...OUTPUT OMITTED...
Protocol    Total    Flows   Packets  Bytes   Packets  Active(Sec)   Idle(Sec)
----------  Flows    /Sec    /Flow    /Pkt    /Sec     /Flow         /Flow
TCP-Telnet  12       0.0     50       40      0.1      15.7          14.2
TCP-WWW     12       0.0     40       785     0.1      7.1           6.2
TCP-other   536      0.1     1        55      0.2      0.3           10.5
UDP-TFTP    225      0.0     4        59      0.1      11.9          15.4
UDP-other   122      0.0     114      284     3.0      15.9          15.4
ICMP        41       0.0     13       91      0.1      49.9          15.6
IP-other    1        0.0     389      60      0.0      1797.1        3.4
Total:      949      0.2     18       255     3.8      9.4           12.5


SrcIf     SrcIPaddress    DstIf    DstIPaddress    Pr  SrcP   DstP   Pkts
Fa0/0     10.3.3.1        Null     224.0.0.10      58  0000   0000   62
Fa0/1     10.8.8.6        Fa0/0    192.168.0.228   06  C2DB   07D0   2
Fa0/0     192.168.0.228   Fa0/1    10.8.8.6        06  07D0   C2DB   1
Fa0/0     192.168.1.50    Fa0/1    10.8.8.6        11  6002   6BD2   9166
Fa0/1     10.8.8.6        Fa0/0    192.168.1.50    11  6BD2   6002   9166
Fa0/0     10.1.1.2        Local    10.3.3.2        06  38F2   0017   438
```

When troubleshooting NetFlow, consider the following:

- **Traffic direction:** NetFlow collection is enabled on an interface-by-interface basis, and it is unidirectional. This means you can enable it to capture traffic inbound on an interface with the **ip flow ingress** command or outbound on an interface with the **ip flow egress** command. Understanding the traffic flow is important to ensure that you are collecting the information you require. Also, because the traffic is unidirectional, if you want to capture the traffic in both directions, you need to enable ingress and egress on the same interface. To verify the direction on an interface, use the **show ip flow interface** command, as shown in Example 23-31.

- **Interface:** Because NetFlow collection is enabled on an interface-by-interface basis, choosing the right interface along with the correct direction is critical. For example, if you have a router with three interfaces, collecting ingress on one interface only captures the traffic that arrives on that interface, whereas collecting egress on an interface would collect all traffic leaving the interface, regardless of the interface it arrived on. So, knowing how traffic flows and what it is you want to capture will help you choose the right interface and the correct direction. To verify the NetFlow-enabled interfaces and the direction in which traffic is being captured, use the **show ip flow interface** command, as shown in Example 23-31.

- **Export destination:** By default, NetFlow collection is local. To export collected information from the flow cache, you need to have a NetFlow collector configured. You can configure your router to export NetFlow data to the collector with the **ip flow-export destination** {*ip address* | *hostname*} *udp-port* command. Ensure that the correct IP address or hostname has been specified, along with the UDP port number of the NetFlow collector. You can verify the export source and destination details by using the **show ip flow export** command, as shown in Example 23-32.

- **Export source:** If your NetFlow collector is configured to receive NetFlow information from your device based on a specific IP address, you need to configure your device to use that IP address as the source of NetFlow export packets. You can accomplish this with the **ip flow-export source** *interface-type interface number* command. You can verify the export source and destination details with the **show ip flow export** command, as shown in Example 23-32.

- **Version:** The NetFlow collector can support different versions. The most common versions are 5 and 9, with 9 now being the more popular choice. The version dictates how the information will be formatted when sent to the collector. If you are using 5 on your device and the collector is using 9, the formats are not the same. If you are using 9 and the server is using 5, again, the formats are not the same. In both of these cases, collection will not be successful. To ensure that your device is exporting the collected information to the NetFlow collector in the correct format, use the **ip flow-export version** [5 | 9] command. You can verify the version of NetFlow that is being used for export by using the **show ip flow export** command, as shown in Example 23-32.

Example 23-31 *Viewing NetFlow Information with show ip flow interface*

```
R3# show ip flow interface
GigabitEthernet2/0
  ip flow ingress
  ip flow egress
R3#
```

Example 23-32 *Viewing NetFlow Information with show ip flow export*

```
R3# show ip flow export
Flow export v5 is enabled for main cache
  Export source and destination details :
  VRF ID : Default
    Source(1)       192.168.23.1 (Loopback0)
    Destination(1)  192.168.1.50 (5000)
  Version 5 flow records
  0 flows exported in 0 udp datagrams
  0 flows failed due to lack of export packet
  0 export packets were sent up to process level
  0 export packets were dropped due to no fib
  0 export packets were dropped due to adjacency issues
  0 export packets were dropped due to fragmentation failures
  0 export packets were dropped due to encapsulation fixup failures
R3#
```

It is important to note that flows are temporary on the local Cisco device. If they are not exported to a NetFlow collector, the flows will be removed from the cache at some point to free up resources. Flows are exported to the NetFlow collector only if you set up the device to export the flows and only after the flows expire in the flow cache on the local device. A flow expires and is exported under the following scenarios:

- When the flow has been idle or inactive (for 15 seconds by default), it can be removed from the cache and exported.

- When the flow's max age has been reached (30 minutes by default), known as the active timer, the flow can be removed from the cache and exported.

- When the cache is full, heuristics are applied to age out older flows immediately, and they are exported.

- When the TCP connection has been closed (that is, the FIN byte has been seen) or reset (that is, the RST byte has been seen), the flow can be removed from the cache and exported.

If needed, you can modify the expiration settings. Use the **ip flow-cache entries** *number* command to change the size of the cache if it is filling up too often. Use the **ip flow-cache timeout active** *minutes* command to modify the max age of a flow (active timer). Use the

ip flow-cache timeout inactive *seconds* command to modify the idle (inactive) timer. You can verify the configured timers by using the **show ip cache flow** command, as shown in Example 23-33.

If you ever need to clear the NetFlow statistics from the router, issue the **clear ip flow stats** command. You can verify when the statistics were last cleared by using the **show ip cache flow** command, as shown in Example 23-33.

Example 23-33 *Viewing NetFlow Timers with show ip cache flow*

```
R3# show ip cache flow
IP packet size distribution (97 total packets):
   1-32   64   96   128   160   192   224   256   288   320   352   384   416   448   480
   .000 .000 1.00 .000 .000 .000 .000 .000 .000 .000 .000 .000 .000 .000 .000


   512   544   576  1024  1536  2048  2560  3072  3584  4096  4608
   .000 .000 .000 .000 .000 .000 .000 .000 .000 .000 .000

IP Flow Switching Cache, 4456704 bytes
  2 active, 65534 inactive, 3 added
  1239 ager polls, 0 flow alloc failures
  Active flows timeout in 30 minutes
  Inactive flows timeout in 15 seconds
IP Sub Flow Cache, 533256 bytes
  1 active, 16383 inactive, 1 added, 1 added to flow
  0 alloc failures, 0 force free
  1 chunk, 1 chunk added
  last clearing of statistics never
...output omitted...
```

Flexible NetFlow takes NetFlow to the next level, allowing you to customize the traffic analysis parameters for your specific requirements. With NetFlow, flows are defined based on source and destination IP addresses, source and destination ports, protocols, QoS, and ingress interface. Flexible NetFlow enables you to define a flow by using those values and more. When troubleshooting Flexible NetFlow, you need to be able to verify the flow records, flow monitors, flow exports, and interface configurations.

Flow records define what will be captured. You can use predefined records (created by Cisco) or user-defined records (created by you). Regardless of whether you use predefined or user-defined records, you need to be able to verify that they are configured to capture what you intend to have captured. With predefined records, you need to use Cisco documentation to identify what they capture as the list will evolve over time. When using user-defined records, you can use the **show flow record** command to verify that the correct match and collection conditions were specified in the flow record, or you can use the **show running-config flow record** command, as shown in Example 23-34. Note that if you are using a predefined flow record, you can use the **show flow monitor** command to verify which one is being used.

Example 23-34   *Viewing Flexible NetFlow Flow Records*

```
R3# show flow record
flow record ENARSI-FLOWRECORD:
  Description:         User defined
  No. of users:        1
  Total field space  16 bytes
  Fields:
     match ipv4 source address
     match ipv4 destination address
     match application name
     collect interface input

R3# show running-config flow record
Current configuration:
!
flow record ENARSI-FLOWRECORD
 match ipv4 source address
 match ipv4 destination address
 match application name
 collect interface input
!
R3#
```

A *flow monitor* is a Flexible NetFlow component that is applied to an interface. The flow monitor contains the flow record (predefined or user defined) that identifies what is matched and collected. The collected flows can then be added to the flow monitor cache. The **show flow monitor** command, as shown in Example 23-35, displays the applied flow record, the applied *flow exporter*, the cache type, the cache size, and the timers that have been set for the flow monitor. The **show flow monitor name** *monitor-name* **cache format record** command displays the status, statistics, and flow data in the cache for a flow monitor, as shown in Example 23-36.

A flow monitor cache can be set to Normal, Immediate, or Permanent. A Normal cache expires flows and exports them based on inactive and active timers, when the cache is full, or when TCP connections are closed or reset, as discussed earlier. An Immediate cache expires as soon as the packet arrives. Therefore, it is exported right away, one packet at a time. In this case, the timers do not matter, and if there are a lot of packets collected and exported, they could overwhelm the network links and overload the NetFlow collector. Therefore, you should use an Immediate cache with caution. A Permanent cache never deletes the information locally; however, the information is still sent to the collector, based on the "timeout update." This is useful if you need to keep the information locally on the device as well. However, be mindful that if the cache becomes full, no new flows are monitored, and you receive a "Flows not added" message in the cache statistics. Therefore, you should use a Permanent cache with caution.

Example 23-35   *Viewing Flexible NetFlow Flow Monitors*

```
R3# show flow monitor
Flow Monitor ENARSI-FLOWMONITOR:
  Description:          User defined
  Flow Record:         ENARSI-FLOWRECORD
  Flow Exporter:       ENARSI-FLOWEXPORTER
  Cache:
    Type:              normal
    Status:            allocated
    Size:                  4096 entries / 213008 bytes
    Inactive Timeout:  15 secs
    Active Timeout:    1800 secs
    Update Timeout:    1800 secs

R3#
```

Example 23-36   *Viewing Flexible NetFlow Flow Monitor Cache Format Records*

```
R3# show flow monitor name ENARSI-FLOWMONITOR cache format record
  Cache type:                          Normal
  Cache size:                          4096
  Current entries:                     3
  High Watermark:                      3

  Flows added:                         57
  Flows aged:                          54
    - Active timeout      (  1800 secs)    24
    - Inactive timeout    (    15 secs)    30
    - Event aged                         0
    - Watermark aged                     0
    - Emergency aged                     0

IPV4 SOURCE ADDRESS:       10.0.123.1
IPV4 DESTINATION ADDRESS:  224.0.0.5
APPLICATION NAME:          cisco unclassified
interface input:          Gi2/0

IPV4 SOURCE ADDRESS:       10.0.123.2
IPV4 DESTINATION ADDRESS:  224.0.0.5
APPLICATION NAME:          cisco unclassified
interface input:          Gi2/0

IPV4 SOURCE ADDRESS:       10.0.123.1
IPV4 DESTINATION ADDRESS:  192.168.4.4
APPLICATION NAME:          prot icmp
interface input:          Gi2/0

R3#
```

Flexible NetFlow collects data only when it's enabled on an interface. You enable Flexible NetFlow on an interface by using the {ip | ipv6 } flow monitor *monitor-name* {input | output} command. You can display the status of Flexible NetFlow and verify whether it is enabled or disabled on the specified interface by using the **show flow interface** command, as shown in Example 23-37.

Example 23-37   *Viewing Flexible NetFlow–Enabled Interfaces*

```
R3# show flow interface
Interface GigabitEthernet2/0
  FNF:  monitor:           ENARSI-FLOWMONITOR
        direction:         Input
        traffic(ip):       on
R3#
```

In almost all cases, you export the data collected and stored in the flow monitor cache to a NetFlow collector. To do so, you need to configure a flow exporter. When configuring a flow exporter, you need to specify the hostname or IP address of the NetFlow collector, the version (v5 or v9) of NetFlow so your Cisco device formats the data correctly before sending, the UDP port number that the NetFlow collector is using, and which flow monitor it is assigned to. When troubleshooting flow exporter issues, you use the **show flow exporter** command, as shown in Example 23-38, to verify that the correct parameters have been specified, and you use the **show flow monitor** command to verify that the correct exporter is assigned to the correct monitor, as shown earlier, in Example 23-35.

Example 23-38   *Viewing Flexible NetFlow Exporter Information*

```
R3# show flow exporter
Flow Exporter ENARSI-FLOWEXPORTER:
  Description:             User defined
  Export protocol:        NetFlow Version 9
  Transport Configuration:
    Destination IP address: 10.0.3.15
    Source IP address:      10.0.1.1
    Source Interface:       Loopback0
    Transport Protocol:     UDP
    Destination Port:       5000
    Source Port:            63006
    DSCP:                   0x0
    TTL:                    255
    Output Features:        Not Used
R3#
```

NOTE   Flexible NetFlow requires CEF (Cisco Express Forwarding) to be enabled for IPv4 and IPv6. So, if you are using NetFlow for IPv4, the command **ip cef** is required, and if you are using NetFlow for IPv6, the command **ipv6 cef** is required. Use the commands **show ip cef** and **show ipv6 cef** to verify whether NetFlow for IPv4 and IPv6 are running. If they are running, you see the CEF table, but if they are not running, you receive the following messages:

```
For IPv4: %IPv4 CEF not running
For IPv6: %IPv6 CEF not running
```

Bidirectional Forwarding Detection (BFD)

In some environments, no carrier detect signaling mechanism is available to quickly detect whether the link between routers is down. Figure 23-4 illustrates three types of environments where a link failure may not occur on the directly connected interface. When the link failure is not directly connected, the router needs to rely on the routing protocol keepalive messages to determine remote-end neighbor reachability. This can take an unacceptably long amount of time by today's standards. For example, OSPF by default waits 40 seconds to declare a neighbor down.

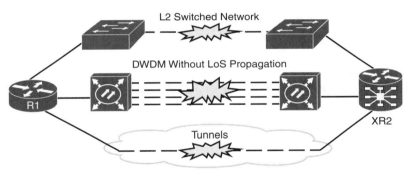

Figure 23-4   *Loss of Signal Detection Challenges*

One option for quickly identifying routing protocol neighbor reachability loss is to set the hello and keepalive timers on the routing protocol to a very short interval. However, introducing fast hellos does not always reduce the failure detection interval to a level where the network can route around the problem before time-sensitive applications notice the communication failure. In addition, fast hellos can tax the router's CPU and do not scale well as the number of neighbor sessions increases.

BFD to the rescue. *BFD* is a "detection" protocol that works with all media types, routing protocols, topologies, and encapsulations. It is used to quickly detect reachability failures between two routers in the same Layer 3 network so that network issues can be identified as soon as possible, and convergence can occur at a far faster rate. BFD is a lightweight protocol (that is, it has small fixed-length packets), which means it is less CPU intensive than fast routing protocol hellos. BFD can provide failure detection in milliseconds, with minimal to no overhead.

For example, if you wanted EIGRP to discover neighbor issues quickly, you could set the EIGRP hello and hold timers to 1 and 3, respectively. This would allow any EIGRP neighbor issues to be detected within 3 seconds, and convergence would occur. However, this might not be quick enough, and the additional CPU processing that will be required to handle all the additional EIGRP hello packets might not be acceptable. If instead you used BFD between the routers, you could leave the hello interval at 5 and hold time at 15 and use the lightweight BFD packets to keep track of the connection between the two routers. In this case, if anything happened to the connection between the two routers, BFD would notify its client (EIGRP in this case) so that EIGRP could converge as needed without waiting for the EIGRP hold timer to expire. This is less CPU intensive because the BFD packets are smaller and quicker to process than the EIGRP packets, and on distributed routing platforms, it is even more efficient because the line cards process the BFD packet instead of punting it to the CPU. BFD timers can be set to subsecond values, which makes it possible to detect failures far faster than any routing protocol is capable of.

In Figure 23-5, R1 and R2 are using BFD to keep track of reachability: BFD packets are being sent every 100 msec, and if three consecutive packets are missed, BFD triggers a session failure and notifies EIGRP. The EIGRP timers are set to their defaults of 5 and 15. You enable BFD on the interfaces participating in EIGRP by using the command **bfd interface** *interface-type interface-number* in router EIGRP configuration mode. You set BFD timers on an interface-by-interface basis by using the **bfd interval** [*50-999*] **min_rx** [*1-999*] **multiplier** [*3-50*] interface command. The **interval** value identifies, in milliseconds, how often to send a BFD packet, and the **min_rx** value identifies, in milliseconds, how long to wait to receive a BFD packet. The **multiplier** value specifies how many consecutive packets not received will trigger a failure. For example, if the **min-rx** value is set to 200 and the **multiplier** value is set to 3, BFD will only trigger a failure notification after 600 ms (200 ms × 3).

Official Cisco documentation indicates that you need to keep in mind a few things for BFD:

- CEF and IP routing must be enabled on all participating routers.

- The IP routing protocols supported by BFD must be configured on the routers before BFD is deployed.

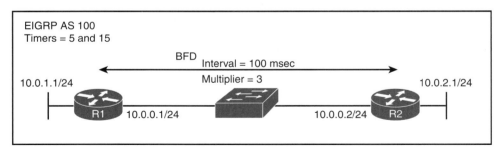

Figure 23-5 *BFD Configured Between Two EIGRP Neighbors*

NOTE The ENARSI exam objectives require you to describe BFD; therefore, that is the extent of BFD coverage in this book. If you require more details about BFD, visit www.cisco.com.

Cisco DNA Center Assurance

The health of a network is paramount to its ongoing success. Your network may include thousands of devices, including routers, switches, wireless LAN controllers, and wireless access points. Troubleshooting the old-fashioned way does not provide the insights you need to keep up with today's network demands. It is important to have the ability to see the health of the network in its entirety and identify any potential issues that must be addressed.

Cisco DNA Center is the command and control center for Cisco DNA. With Cisco DNA Center, you can configure and provision your devices in minutes; proactively monitor, troubleshoot, and optimize your network using artificial intelligence (AI) and machine learning (ML); and improve your operational processes by integrating third-party systems.

Cisco DNA Center Assurance is just one component of Cisco DNA Center. With Cisco DNA Center Assurance, you can predict problems more quickly, thanks to proactive monitoring, and get insights from network devices, network applications, network services, and clients. As a result, you will be able to ensure that implemented polices as well as configuration changes achieve the desired business results, provide users with the experience they want, and spend less time troubleshooting and more time innovating.

Cisco DNA Center is a massive topic that is beyond the scope of the ENARSI exam. The official exam objectives for ENARSI state that you should be able to "troubleshoot network problems using Cisco DNA Center Assurance (connectivity, monitoring, device health, network health)." Therefore, this section remains focused on this objective.

To access Cisco DNA Center Assurance, you select the menu option in the upper-right corner of DNA Center to reveal the menu shown in Figure 23-6. In this menu, you can then select Assurance and choose the dashboard, AI network analytics, or settings you wish to access.

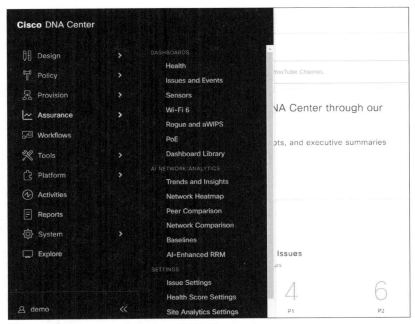

Figure 23-6 *Accessing Cisco DNA Center Assurance*

Your first valuable troubleshooting tool is the Overall Health page, shown in Figure 23-7. You can reach this page by clicking on Assurance and then Health from the menu shown in Figure 23-6. This page provides an overview of the overall health of the network devices and clients in the environment, which can be displayed based on information gathered from the most recent 3 hours, 24 hours, or 7 days. In the Network Devices area as well as the Client area, you can get an overall network/client score based on the health of the network devices as well as the wired and wireless clients. An overview of site analytics is also available, and if you click on any of the sites, you will be taken to the AI Analytics page for that site. The health of network services is also provided. For example, AAA server successes and failures as well as DHCP server successes and failures are shown in Figure 23-7, and you can access their related dashboard by clicking on View AAA Dashboard or View DHCP Dashboard for more detailed information. The Top 10 Issues area at the bottom of the page displays the issues that should be addressed. When you click on them, you are presented with the issue details, including the impact of the issue, as well as suggested actions to fix the issue, as shown in Figure 23-8 and Figure 23-9.

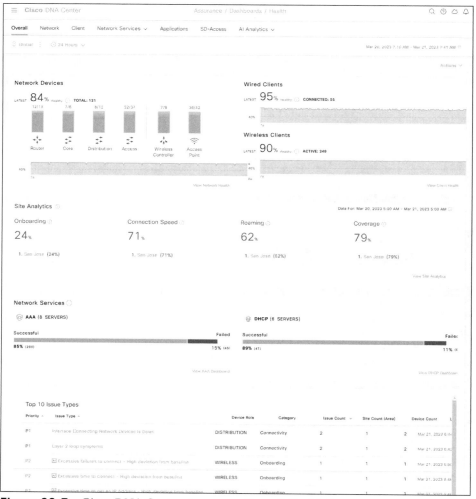

Figure 23-7   *Cisco DNA Center Assurance Overall Health Page*

Figure 23-8 *Example of Cisco DNA Center Assurance Issues*

Figure 23-9 *Example of Cisco DNA Center Assurance Issue Details*

Another valuable troubleshooting tool is the Network Health page, shown in Figure 23-10, which you can access in Cisco DNA Center Assurance by selecting Network in the Health dashboard. In addition, you can access the Client Health page, shown in Figure 23-11, in Cisco DNA Center Assurance by selecting Client in the Health dashboard. These pages provide an overview of the operational status of the network and client devices that are part of the network. If the devices have any issues, they are highlighted, and possible remediations are suggested.

You can use the Network Health page to get a sense of the health of the network and the devices in it. You can view the percentage of healthy devices in your overall network based on categories such as access, core, distribution, router, and wireless. Information can be displayed in 5-minute intervals over the past 24 hours.

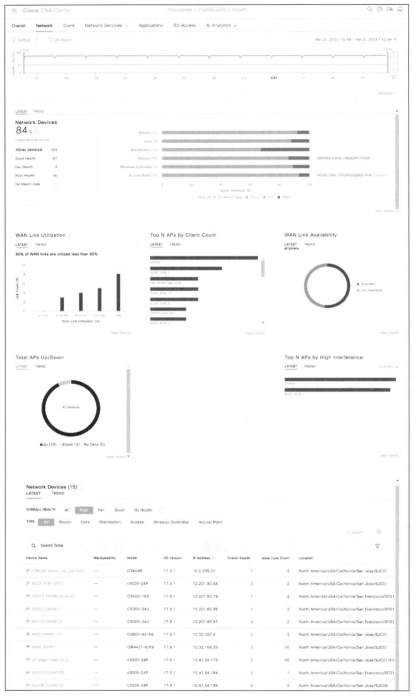

Figure 23-10 *Cisco DNA Center Assurance Network Health Page*

The Network Devices section at the bottom lists all the devices on an individual basis and provides information such as the device type, address, OS version, reachability, issue count, and location. In addition, it provides an overall health score. Anything with a health score from 1 to 3 is a critical issue and is displayed in red. Anything with a health score from 4 to 7 is a warning and is displayed in orange/amber. Anything with a health score from 8 to 10 signifies no errors or warnings and is displayed in green. A health score of 0 indicates that no data is available, and it is displayed in gray. You can click on the device to get further details about a device in Device 360, as discussed later in this chapter.

The Client Health page shows the health of wired and wireless clients. You can see the percentage of clients connected to the network that are healthy and unhealthy. A score is provided as a percentage so you can quickly see the health of all the clients on the network.

The Client Devices section of the Client Health page, shown in Figure 23-11, lists all the clients individually and provides information such as the identifier, address, type, when it was last seen, the switch or AP it is connected to, and location. In addition, it provides an overall health score. Anything with a health score from 1 to 3 is a critical issue and is displayed in red. Anything with a health score from 4 to 7 is a warning and is displayed in orange/amber. Anything with a health score from 8 to 10 signifies no errors or warnings and is displayed in green. A health score of 0 indicates that no data is available, and it is displayed in gray. You can click on the device to get further details about a device in Client 360, as discussed later in this chapter.

The next valuable troubleshooting tools are *Device 360* and *Client 360*. These features can be accessed by clicking on any of the devices or clients shown in Figure 23-10 and Figure 23-11. These features drill down into the device or client and display information about the topology, throughput, and latency from various times and applications so you can get a detailed view on the performance of the specific device or client over a specified period. With these tools, you have granular troubleshooting at your fingertips in seconds. Figure 23-12 shows the Client 360 dashboard for an Apple iPad with the IP address 10.30.100.41 that belongs to Gordon.Thomson. Notice that the client is experiencing application and onboarding issues. If you click on any of the issues, you will see further details about the issue and how you can go about troubleshooting based on possible suggestions.

Figure 23-13 shows the Device 360 page for a switch named p1.edge1-sda1.local with IP address 10.41.54.172. Notice in the image that there are multiple issues. If you click on any of the issues, you get a description of the issue and possibly suggested actions you could take to resolve it, as shown in Figure 23-14.

Figure 23-11   *Cisco DNA Center Assurance Client Health Page*

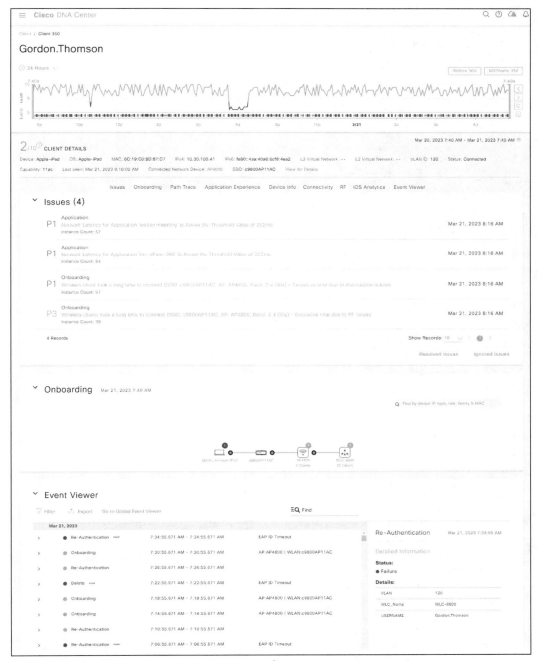

Figure 23-12   *Cisco DNA Center Assurance Client 360 Page*

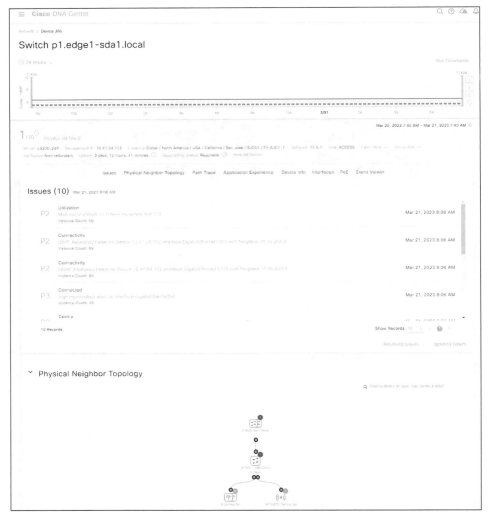

Figure 23-13   *Cisco DNA Center Assurance Device 360 Page*

The next troubleshooting feature in DNA Center Assurance that will make your life easier is *Path Trace*. This feature is basically the ping and traceroute you have always dreamed of. With Path Trace, you can graphically see the path that applications and services running on a client will take through all the devices on the network to reach the destination (a server, for example). With a few clicks, you can use this tool to do multiple troubleshooting tasks that would take you 5 to 10 minutes at the command line. Figure 23-15 shows an example of using Path Trace between two devices. Path Trace can be accessed within Client 360 or Device 360. Take a moment to absorb Figure 23-15 and notice all the details, such as the CAPWAP tunnel and the ACL.

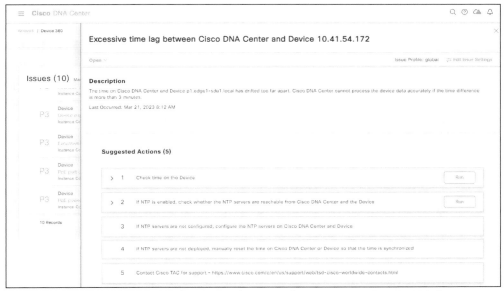

Figure 23-14 *Description and Suggested Actions for an Issue in Cisco DNA Center Assurance*

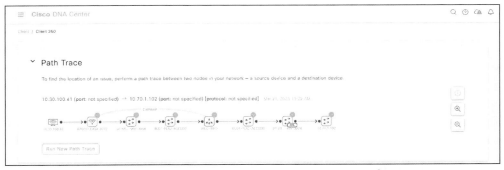

Figure 23-15 *Using Path Trace from the DNA Center Assurance Client 360 Page*

Another great tool for troubleshooting in Cisco DNA Center Assurance is Network Time Travel. This tool allows you to hop into a time machine and see the cause of a network issue instead of trying to reproduce the issue. Refer to Figure 23-13, which shows an example of a timeline view for a client in Client 360. Timeline views exist in many different areas of DNA Center. You can get timeline views for overall network health, for the health of network devices, for the health of client devices, and for the health of individual devices and clients in Device 360 and Client 360.

Monitoring your network has never been easier than it is with Cisco DNA Center Assurance. The AI Analytics feature performs assurance and analytics on Cisco switches, routers, and wireless controllers. With this feature, whenever critical metrics are identified, they can be immediately acted on before an incident occurs. ITIL describes an incident as any disruption of a service or the reduction in the quality of a service. Through KPIs (key performance indicators) that are linked to the overall business goals and objectives, you can ensure that disruptions and reductions never see the light of day.

With Cisco AI network analytics, AI and ML can enhance the performance and remediation capabilities of Cisco DNA Center Assurance. Performance is enhanced with customized baselines that allow AI and ML to pinpoint core performance improvements while enhancing remediation capabilities through automation for improved resolution times.

Finally, if you need to view all the issues and events that Cisco DNA Center Assurance has identified, you can do so in one place by selecting the Issues and Events dashboard from the Assurance menu. The Issues and Events page is shown in Figure 23-16. On this page, you can see any open, resolved, or ignored issues.

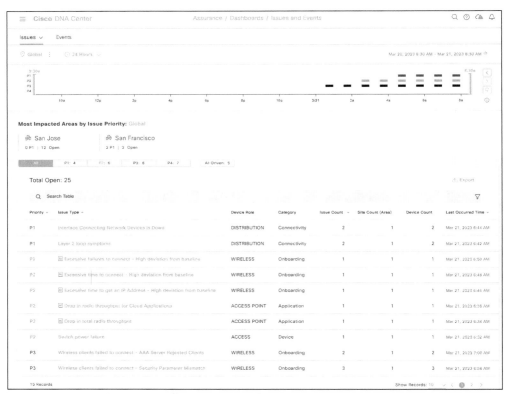

Figure 23-16 *The Issues and Events Page of Cisco DNA Center Assurance*

Command Runner is a tool that allows you to send diagnostic CLI commands to your devices. Currently, **show** and various other read-only commands are permitted. You can access Command Runner from the DNA Center menu by choosing Tools and then Command Runner (see Figure 23-17).

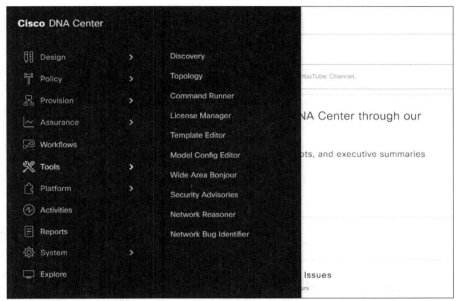

Figure 23-17   *How to Access Command Runner in Cisco DNA Center Assurance*

In the Search field, you can then search for your devices by IP address or name and then choose which ones you want to run your diagnostic commands on. You can select up to 20 devices. You can then enter your commands in the Select/Enter commands field and Click Run Command(s), as shown in Figure 23-18.

Figure 23-18   *Example of Using Command Runner*

If the diagnostic commands are successful, a "Command(s) executed successfully" message appears, and you can view the output by selecting the device and then the command underneath the device to have the output displayed on the right of the page, as shown in Figure 23-19.

Figure 23-19 *Using Command Runner*

Exam Preparation Tasks

As mentioned in the section "How to Use This Book" in the Introduction, you have a couple choices for exam preparation: the exercises here, Chapter 24, "Final Preparation," and the exam simulation questions in the Pearson Test Prep software.

Review All Key Topics

Review the most important topics in this chapter, noted with the Key Topic icon in the outer margin of the page. Table 23-2 lists these key topics and the page number on which each is found.

Table 23-2 Key Topics

Key Topic Element	Description	Page Number
List	Considerations when troubleshooting issues related to console port access	893
List	Considerations when troubleshooting issues related to Telnet	895
List	Considerations when troubleshooting issues related to SSH	897
Section	Password encryption levels	898
List	Considerations when troubleshooting issues related to remote transfers with TFTP	899
List	Considerations when troubleshooting issues related to remote transfers with HTTP(S)	900
List	Considerations when troubleshooting issues related to remote transfers with FTP	901
List	Considerations when troubleshooting issues related to remote transfers with SCP	903

Key Topic Element	Description	Page Number
Example 23-11	Verifying syslog configuration	904
List	Considerations when troubleshooting issues related to SNMPv2c	907
List	Considerations when troubleshooting issues related to SNMPv3	908
List	Considerations when troubleshooting issues related to IP SLA	912
Paragraphs	Configuring IPSLA and Object Tracking for Floating Static Routes	918
List	Considerations when troubleshooting issues related to NetFlow	921
Example 23-34	Viewing Flexible NetFlow flow records	924
Example 23-35	Viewing Flexible NetFlow flow monitors	925
Example 23-36	Viewing Flexible NetFlow flow monitor cache format records	925
Example 23-37	Viewing Flexible NetFlow–enabled interfaces	926
Example 23-38	Viewing Flexible NetFlow flow exporter information	926
List	BFD Considerations	928
Paragraphs	Path Trace in Cisco DNA Center Assurance	935
Paragraphs	The Cisco DNA Center Assurance Issues and Events dashboard	937
Paragraphs	Command Runner in Cisco DNA Center Assurance	938

Define Key Terms

Define the following key terms from this chapter and check your answers in the glossary:

Telnet, SSH, line, **login**, **login local**, AAA, port 23, port 22, level 8 encryption, level 5 encryption, level 7 encryption, syslog, SNMPv2c, SNMPv3, IP SLA, Object Tracking, NetFlow, flow cache, Flexible NetFlow, flow record, flow exporter, flow monitor, BFD, Cisco DNA Center Assurance, Client 360, Device 360, Path Trace, Command Runner

Use the Command Reference to Check Your Memory

The ENARSI 300-410 exam focuses on the practical, hands-on skills that networking professionals use. Therefore, you should be able to identify the commands needed to configure, verify, and troubleshoot the topics covered in this chapter.

This section includes the most important configuration and verification commands covered in this chapter. It might not be necessary to memorize the complete syntax of every command, but you should be able to remember the basic keywords that are needed.

To test your memory of the commands in Table 23-3, go to the companion website and download Appendix B, "Command Reference Exercises." Fill in the missing commands in the tables based on each command description. You can check your work by downloading Appendix C, "Command Reference Exercise Answer Key," from the companion website.

Table 23-3   Command Reference

Task	Command Syntax
Display the ingress and egress allowed transport protocols on a vty line.	show line vty *line_number* | include Allowed
Display only the ingress allowed transport protocols on a vty line.	show line vty *line_number* | include Allowed input transports
Display the vty line configuration in the running configuration.	show run | section line vty
Display the lines that are currently being used for management connectivity.	show users
Display whether SSH is enabled or disabled, the version of SSH enabled, and the SSH RSA key.	show ip ssh
Display the SSHv1 and SSHv2 connections to the local device.	show ssh
Display information related to syslog, including level settings and messages logged for console, monitor, buffer, and traps logging; verify the buffer size and its contents for buffer logging and the IP address/port number of the syslog server.	show logging
Display the conditional **debug** commands that have been configured on the router.	show debug condition
Display SNMP group information, including the group name, the security mode, the read and write views, and any applied ACLs.	show snmp group
Display any configured SNMP users; output includes the username, the authentication protocol used, the encryption protocol used, and the group the user is applied to.	show snmp user
Display the local configuration of the SNMP server, including the IP address, UDP port, type, attached user, and security model being used.	show snmp host
Display the SNMP views configured on the local device.	show snmp view
Display which IP SLA operations are supported on the platform, how many operations are configured, and how many operations are currently active.	show ip sla application
Display the IP SLA configuration values for the IP SLA instances.	show ip sla configuration
Display the IP SLA operational results of IP SLA instances.	show ip sla statistics
Display the operational results of the IP SLA responder.	show ip sla responder

Task	Command Syntax
Display the configured tracking objects on the local device, including the current state and the service or feature it is attached to.	**show track**
Display the local NetFlow flow cache as well as the configured timers.	**show ip cache flow**
Display the interfaces enabled for NetFlow and the direction in which they are capturing information.	**show ip flow interface**
Display the NetFlow exporter configuration, including the source and destination addresses, port number, and version of NetFlow.	**show ip flow export**
Display all user-defined Flexible NetFlow flow records that are configured on the local device.	**show flow record**
Display the locally configured Flexible NetFlow flow monitors; verify the attached flow record and flow exporter as well as the configured timers.	**show flow monitor**
Display the interfaces enabled for Flexible NetFlow and the direction in which they are capturing information.	**show flow interface**
Display the Flexible NetFlow exporter configuration, including the source and destination addresses, port number, and version of NetFlow.	**show flow exporter**

23

## CHAPTER 24

Final Preparation

Congratulations! You've made it through the book, and now it's time to finish getting ready for the exam. This chapter helps you get ready to take and pass the exam in two ways.

This chapter begins by talking about the exam itself. You know the content and topics. Now you need to think about what happens during the exam and what you need to do in these last few weeks before taking the exam. At this point, your focus should be on getting ready to pass so that you can finish up this hefty task.

The second section of this chapter gives you some exam review tasks as your final preparation for your ENARSI 300-410 exam.

Advice About the Exam Event

Now that you have finished the bulk of this book, you could just register for your ENARSI 300-410 exam, show up, and take the exam. However, if you spend a little time thinking about the exam event itself, learning more about the user interface of the real Cisco exams, and getting to know the environment at the Vue testing centers, you will be better prepared. This is particularly important if this is your first Cisco exam.

> **NOTE** Typically, ENARSI would not be your first Cisco exam, as you would usually take CCNA or CCNP ENCOR first; however, since Cisco has removed all prerequisites, there is nothing stopping you from making this your first exam.

The following sections give some advice about the Cisco exams and the exam event itself.

Think About Your Time Budget Versus Numbers of Questions

On exam day, you need to keep an eye on your speed. Going too slowly hurts you because you might not have time to answer all the questions. Going too fast can also hurt you if it means you are rushing and not taking the time to fully understand the questions. So, you need to be able to somehow know whether you are moving quickly enough to answer all the questions while not rushing.

The exam user interface shows some useful information, including a countdown timer and a question counter. The question counter shows a question number for the question you are answering, and it shows the total number of questions on the exam.

Unfortunately, some questions require a lot more time than others, and for this and other reasons, estimating time can be challenging.

Before you show up to take the exam, you only know a range of the number of questions for the exam. For example, the Cisco website might list the ENARSI exam as having 55 to 65 questions. But you do not know exactly how many questions are on your exam until the exam begins, when you go through the screens that lead up to the point where you click Start Exam, which starts your timed exam.

Some questions (which some people call *time burners*) clearly take a lot more time to answer than others:

- **Normal-time questions:** Multichoice and drag-and-drop, approximately 1 minute each

- **Time burners:** Sims, Simlets, and Testlets, approximately 6–8 minutes each

Finally, in the count of 55–65 questions on a single exam, even though Testlet and Simlet questions contain several multichoice questions, the exam software counts each Testlet and Simlet question as one question in the question counter. For example, if a Testlet question has four embedded multiple-choice questions, in the exam software's question counter, that counts as 1 question. So when you start the exam, you might see that you have 55 questions, but you don't know how many of those are time burners.

> **NOTE** While Cisco does not tell us why you might get 55 questions, while someone else taking the same exam might get 65 questions, it seems reasonable to think that the person with 55 questions might have a few more of the time burners, making the two exams equivalent.

You need a plan for how you will check your time, and that plan should not distract you from the exam. You can ponder the facts listed above and come up with your own plan. If you want a little more guidance, read on as the next section shows one way to check your time by using some simple math.

A Suggested Time-Check Method

You can use some simple math to do your time check in a way that weights your time based on time-burner questions. You do not have to use this method. But this math uses only addition of whole numbers to keep things simple. It gives you a pretty close time estimate, in our opinion.

The concept is simple: Just do a simple calculation that estimates the time you should have used so far. Here's the math:

Number of Questions Answered So Far + 7 per Time Burner Answered So Far

Then, you check the timer to figure out how much time you have spent:

- If you have used exactly that much time or a little more time, your timing is perfect.

- If you have used less time, you are ahead of schedule.

- If you have used considerably more time, you are behind schedule.

For example, if you have already finished 17 questions, 2 of which were time burners, your time estimate is 17 + 7 + 7 = 31 minutes. If your actual time is also 31 minutes, or maybe 32 or 33 minutes, you are right on schedule. If you have spent less than 31 minutes, you are ahead of schedule.

So, the math is pretty easy: Questions answered, plus 7 per time burner, is the guesstimate of how long you should have taken so far if you are right on time.

> **NOTE** This math is an estimate; we make no guarantees that the math will be an accurate predictor on every exam.

Miscellaneous Pre-Exam Suggestions

Here are a few more suggestions for things to think about before exam day arrives:

- Get some earplugs. Testing centers often have some, but if you do not want to chance it, come prepared with your own. (They will not let you bring your own noise-canceling headphones into the room if they follow the rules disallowing any user electronic devices in the room, so think low tech.) The testing center is typically a room inside the space of a company that does something else as well, oftentimes a training center, and almost certainly you will share the room with other test takers coming and going. So, there are likely to be people talking in nearby rooms and other office noises. Earplugs can help.

- Some people like to spend the first minute of the exam writing down some notes for reference before actually starting the exam. For example, maybe you want to write down the table of magic numbers for finding IPv4 subnet IDs. If you plan to do that, practice making those notes. Before each practice exam, transcribe those lists, just as you expect to do at the real exam.

- Plan your travel to the testing center to allow enough time so that you will not be rushing to make it just in time.

- If you tend to be nervous before exams, practice your favorite relaxation techniques for a few minutes before each practice exam so you are ready to use them before and during the actual exam.

Exam-Day Advice

I hope the exam goes well for you. Certainly, the better prepared you are, the more likely you are to do well on the exam. These small tips can help you do your best on exam day:

- Rest the night before the exam rather than staying up late to study. Clarity of thought is more important than one extra fact, especially because the exam requires a lot of analysis and thinking rather than just remembering facts.

- If you did not bring earplugs, ask the testing center for some, even if you cannot imagine that you will use them. You never know whether they might help.

- You can bring personal effects into the building and testing company's space but not into the room in which you actually take the exam. So, save a little stress and bring as little extra stuff with you as possible. If you have a safe place to leave briefcases, purses, electronics, and so on, leave them there. However, the testing center should have a place to store your things as well. Simply put, the less you bring, the less you have to worry about storing. (For example, you may even be asked to remove your analog wristwatch.)

- The exam center will give you a laminated sheet and a dry erase marker for taking notes. (Test center personnel typically do not let you bring paper and pen into the room, even if supplied by the testing center.) You can also ask for an additional pen and laminated sheet.

- If available, grab a few tissues from the box in the room, for two reasons: (1) to avoid having to get up in the middle of the exam and (2) if you need to erase your laminated sheet, doing that with a tissue helps prevent the oil from your hand from affecting the pen. (Yes, that's often why pens seem to not work and then later work on dry erase boards!)

- Leave for the testing center with extra time so you do not have to rush.

- Plan on finding a restroom before going into the testing center. If you cannot find one, of course you can use one in the testing center, and test personnel will direct you and give you time before your exam starts.

- Do not drink a 64-ounce caffeinated drink on the trip to the testing center. After the exam starts, the exam timer will not stop while you go to the restroom.

- On exam day, use any relaxation techniques that you have practiced to help get your mind focused while you wait for the exam.

Reserve the Hour After the Exam in Case You Fail

Some people pass these exams on the first attempt, and some do not. The exams are not easy. If you fail to pass the exam that day, you will likely be disappointed. And that is understandable. But it is not a reason to give up. In fact, we added this short topic to give you a big advantage in case you do fail.

The most important study hour for your next exam attempt is the hour just after your failed attempt.

Prepare to fail before you take the exam. That is, prepare your schedule to give yourself an hour, or at least a half hour, immediately after the exam attempt, in case you fail. Then follow these suggestions:

- Bring pen and paper or a notebook you can write in if you have to write standing up or sitting somewhere inconvenient.

- Make sure you know where your pen and paper are so that you can take notes immediately after the exam. Keep them in your backpack if using the train or bus or on the car seat in the car.

- Install and practice with an audio recording app on your phone and be prepared to start talking into your app when you leave the testing center.

- Before the exam, scout the testing center and plan the place where you will sit and take your notes, preferably somewhere quiet.

- Write down anything in particular that you can recall from any question.

- Write down details of questions you know you got right as well because doing so may help trigger a memory of another question.

- Draw the figures that you can remember.

- Write down any tidbit that might have confused you: terms, configuration commands, **show** commands, scenarios, topology drawings, anything.

- Take at least three passes at remembering. You will hit a wall where you do not remember more. So, start on your way back to the next place and then find a place to pause and take more notes. And do it again.

- When you have sucked your memory dry, take one more pass while thinking of the major topics in the book to see if that triggers any other memory of a question.

Once you have collected this information, *you cannot share it with anyone* because doing so would violate Cisco's nondisclosure agreement (NDA). Cisco is serious about cheating and would consider it cheating to share such info publicly. But you can use your information to study for your next attempt. Remember, anything that uncovers what you do not know related to the exam is valuable, so your notes will be very valuable to you. See the section "Study Suggestions After Failing to Pass" for the rest of the story.

Take Practice Exams

One day soon, you need to pass a real Cisco exam at a Vue testing center. It's a good idea to practice for the real event as much as possible.

A practice exam using the Pearson IT Certification Practice Test (PCPT) exam software lets you experience many of the same issues you'll face when you take a real Cisco exam. The software gives you a number of questions and shows a countdown timer. After you answer a question, you cannot go back to it (which is also true on Cisco exams). If you run out of time, the questions you did not answer count as incorrect.

The process of taking the timed practice exams helps you prepare in three key ways:

- To practice for the exam event, including time pressure, reading carefully, and concentrating for long periods

- To build your analysis and critical thinking skills when examining the network scenarios that are built into many questions

- To discover the gaps in your networking knowledge so that you can study those topics before the real exam

As much as possible, treat the practice exam events as if you were taking the real Cisco exam at a Vue testing center. The following list gives some advice on how to make your practice exam more meaningful rather than just one more thing to do before exam day rolls around:

- Set aside 2 hours for taking the 90-minute timed practice exam.

- Make a list of what you expect to do for the 10 minutes before the real exam event. Then visualize yourself doing those things. Before taking each practice exam, practice those final 10 minutes before your exam timer starts. (The earlier section "Exam-Day Advice" lists some suggestions about what to do in those final few minutes.)

■ You cannot bring anything with you into the Vue exam room, so remove all notes and help materials from your work area before taking a practice exam. You can use blank paper, a pen, and your brain only. Do not use calculators, notes, web browsers, or any other app on your computer.

■ Real life can get in the way, but if at all possible, ask anyone around you to leave you alone for the time you will practice. If you must do your practice exam in a distracting environment, wear headphones or earplugs to reduce distractions.

■ Do not guess, hoping to improve your score. Answer only when you have confidence in the answer. Then, if you get the question wrong, you can go back and think more about the question in a later study session.

Advice on How to Answer Exam Questions

Open a web browser. Yes, take a break and open a web browser on any device. Do a quick search on a fun topic. Then, before you click a link, get ready to think where your eyes go for the first 5–10 seconds after you click the link. Now, click a link and look at the page. Where did your eyes go?

Interestingly, web browsers, and the content on those web pages, have trained us all to scan. Web page designers actually design content expecting certain scan patterns. Regardless of the pattern, when reading a web page, almost no one reads sequentially, and no one reads entire sentences. They scan for the interesting graphics and the big words and then scan the space around those noticeable items.

Other parts of our electronic culture have also changed how the average person reads. For example, many of you grew up using texting and social media, sifting through hundreds or thousands of messages—but each message barely fills an entire sentence.

Those everyday habits have changed how we all read and think in front of a screen. Unfortunately, those same habits often hurt our scores when we take computer-based exams.

If you scan exam questions the way you read web pages, texts, and tweets, you will probably make some mistakes because you will miss key facts in the questions, answers, or exhibits. It helps to start at the beginning and read all the words—a process that is amazingly unnatural for many people today.

> **NOTE** We have talked to many college professors, in multiple disciplines, as well as Cisco Networking Academy instructors, and they consistently tell us that the number-one test-taking issue today is that people do not read questions well enough to understand the details.

Let us make two suggestions related to taking the practice exams and answering individual questions. First, before the practice exam, think about your own personal strategy for how you will read a question. Consciously choose an approach to multiple-choice questions in particular. Second, when reading an exam question, use the following strategy:

Step 1.   Read the question thoroughly, from start to finish.

Step 2.   Scan any exhibit (usually command output) or figure.

Step 3.   Scan the answers to look for the types of information. (Numeric? Terms? Single words? Phrases?)

Step 4.   Reread the question thoroughly, from start to finish, to make sure you understand it.

Step 5.   Read each answer thoroughly and refer to the figure/exhibit as needed. After reading each answer, before reading the next answer:

A.   If correct, select as correct.

B.   If for sure it is incorrect, mentally rule it out.

C.   If unsure, mentally note it as a possible correct answer.

NOTE   Cisco exams tell you the number of correct answers. The exam software also helps you finish the question with the right number of answers noted. For example, the software prevents you from selecting too many answers. Also, if you try to move on to the next question but have too few answers noted, the exam software asks if you truly want to move on. Make an educated guess when unsure; there is no penalty for guessing, and you can't move on to the next question until you pick an answer. So don't waste time if you don't know the answer. Guess and move on.

Use the practice exams to practice your approach to reading. Every time you click to the next question, try to follow your approach to reading the question. If you are feeling time pressure, that is the perfect time to keep practicing your approach to reduce and eliminate questions you miss because you scan the question instead of reading thoroughly.

Assessing Whether You Are Ready to Pass (and the Fallacy of Exam Scores)

When you take a practice exam with the PCPT software, it gives you a score on a scale from 300 to 1000. Why? Cisco tells us it gives a score of between 300 and 1000 as well. But the similarities end there.

With PCPT, the score is a basic percentage, although it is expressed as a number from 0 to 1000. For example, answer 80% correct, and the score is 800; get 90% correct, and the score is 900. If you start a practice exam and click through it without answering a single question, you get a 0.

However, Cisco does not score exams in the same way. This is what we do know about Cisco exam scoring:

- Cisco uses a scoring scale from 300 to 1000.

- Cisco tell us that it gives partial credit, but with no further details.

So, what does an 800 or a 900 mean? Many people think those scores mean 80% or 90%, but we do not know. Cisco does not reveal the details of scoring to us. It does not reveal the details of partial credit. It seems reasonable to expect a Sim question to be worth more points than a multiple-choice single-answer question, but we do not know.

The bottom line: Do not rely too much on your PCPT practice exam scores to assess whether you are ready to pass the real Cisco exam. Those scores are general indicators, in that if you make a 700 one time, and a 900 a week later, you are probably now better prepared. But your 900 on a PCPT practice exam does not mean you will likely make a 900 on the actual exam. Remember that we do not know how Cisco scores the exam.

So, how can you assess whether you are ready to pass the exam? Unfortunately, the answer requires some extra effort, and the answer will not be some nice convenient number that looks like an exam score. But you can self-assess your skills as follows:

■ When you take an exam with PCPT, you should understand the terms used in the questions and answers.

■ You should be able to look at the list of key topics in each chapter of this book and explain each topic to a friend in a sentence or two.

■ For chapters of this book that include **show** commands, you should understand the fields highlighted in gray in the examples spread about the book, and when looking at those examples, you should know which values show configuration settings and which show status information.

■ When you review the lists of key topics in this book, you should remember and understand the concept behind each item in a list without needing to look further at the chapter.

Study Suggestions After Failing to Pass

None of us wants to take and fail any exam. However, you cannot think about Cisco exams the same way you think of exams in school. Lots of people take and fail Cisco exams. We have studied hard for some Cisco exams and have failed multiple times. We want you to pass, but you also need to be ready to complete the task if you do fail.

When you fail, you can keep studying exactly the same way, but you can also benefit from some small changes in tactics. This short section provides a summary of the kinds of advice we've given for years to people who reach out in frustration after failing.

First, study the notes you took about your failed attempt. (See the earlier section "Reserve the Hour After Your Exam in Case You Fail.") Do not share that information with others but use it to study. You should be able to answer every actual exam question you can remember, or at least understand everything you remember that confused you, before showing up for the next attempt. Even if you never see exactly the same question again, you will get a good return for your effort.

Second, spend more time on activities that uncover your weaknesses. To do that, you have to slow down and be more self-aware. For instance, answer practice questions in study mode and do not guess. Do not click on to the next question but pause and ask yourself if you are really sure about both the incorrect and correct answers. If you're unsure, fantastic! You just discovered a topic to go back and dig into to learn it more deeply. Or when you do a lab, you may refer to your notes without thinking—so now think about it. That might be a signal that you have not mastered those commands yet.

Third, think about your time spent on the exam. Did you run out of time? Go too quickly? Too slowly? If you went too slowly, were you slow on subnetting, or Sims, or something else? Make a written plan for how you will approach time on the next attempt and how you will track time use. If you ran out of time on your failed exam attempt, practice for the things that slowed you down.

Finally, change your mindset. Cisco exams are not like high school or college exams, where your failing grade matters. Instead, a Cisco exam is more like a major event on the road to completing an impressive major accomplishment—one that most people have to try a few times to achieve.

For instance, preparing for a Cisco exam is like training to run a marathon in under 4 hours. The first time running a marathon, you might not even finish, or you might finish at 4:15 rather than under 4:00. But finishing a marathon in 4:15 is not a failure by any means. Or maybe it is more like training to complete an obstacle course (any *American Ninja Warrior* fans out there?). Maybe you got past the first three obstacles today, but you couldn't climb over the 14-foot-high warped wall. That just means you need to practice on that wall a little more.

So change your mindset. You're a marathon runner looking to improve your time, or a Ninja warrior looking to complete the obstacle course. And you are getting better skills every time you study, which helps you compete in the market.

Other Study Tasks

In case you feel the need to prepare some more, this last topic gives you suggestions.

First, at the end of each chapter in this book, you'll find some useful study tasks. Complete them.

Second, use more exam questions from other sources. You can always get more questions in the Cisco Press Premium Edition eBook and Practice Test products, which include an eBook copy of this book plus additional questions in additional PCPT exam banks. In addition, you can search the Internet for questions from many sources and review those questions as well.

NOTE   Some vendors claim to sell practice exams that contain the exam questions from the actual exam. These exams, called "brain dumps," are against the Cisco testing policies. Cisco strongly discourages using any such tools for study.

Third, reading is not enough. Any network engineer will tell you that to fully understand a technology, you have to implement it. You are encouraged to re-create the topologies and technologies and follow the examples in this book.

A variety of resources are available for practicing the concepts presented in this book. Look online for the following:

- Cisco VIRL (Virtual Internet Routing Lab) provides a scalable, extensible network design and simulation environment. For more information about VIRL, see https://learningnetwork.cisco.com/s/virl.

- Cisco dCloud provides a huge catalog of demos, training, and sandboxes for every Cisco architecture. It operates with customizable environments and is free. For more information, see https://dcloud.cisco.com/.

- Cisco Devnet provides a number of resources on programming and programmability with free labs. For more information, see http://developer.cisco.com.

■ Join the discussions on the Cisco Learning Network, at https://learningnetwork. cisco.com/welcome. Try to answer questions asked by other learners; the process of answering makes you think much harder about the topic. When someone posts an answer with which you disagree, think about why and talk about it online. This is a great way to both learn more and build confidence.

24

Final Thoughts

You have studied quite a bit, worked hard, and sacrificed time and money to be ready for the exam. We hope your exam goes well and that you pass, and we hope that you pass because you really know your stuff and will do well in your IT and networking career.

We encourage you to celebrate when you pass and ask advice when you do not. The Cisco Learning Network is a great place to make posts to celebrate and to ask advice for the next time around. We wish you well, great success, and congratulations for working through the entire book!

## CHAPTER 25

ENARSI 300-410 Exam Updates

The Purpose of This Chapter

For all the other chapters of this book, the content should remain unchanged throughout this edition. However, this chapter will change over time, and an updated PDF will be posted online periodically so you can see the latest version of the chapter even after you purchase this book.

Why do we need a chapter that updates over time? For two reasons:

- To add more technical content to the book before it is time to replace the current edition with the next edition. This chapter will include additional technical content and possibly additional PDFs containing more content.

- To communicate details about the next version of the exam, to tell you about our publishing plans for that version, and to help you understand what the changes mean for you.

After the initial publication of this book, Cisco Press will provide supplemental updates as digital downloads for minor exam updates. If an exam has major changes or accumulates enough minor changes, we will then announce a new edition. We will do our best to provide any updates to you free of charge before we release a new edition. However, if the updates are significant enough in between editions, we may release the updates as a low-priced standalone eBook.

If we do produce a free updated version of this chapter, you can access it on the book's companion website. Simply go to the companion website page and go to the "Exam Updates Chapter" section of the page.

If you have not yet accessed the companion website, follow this process:

Step 1. Browse to **www.ciscopress.com/register**.

Step 2. Enter the print book ISBN (even if you are using an eBook): **9780138217525**.

Step 3. After registering the book, go to your account page and select the **Registered Products** tab.

Step 4. Click on the **Access Bonus Content** link to access the companion website. Select the **Exam Updates Chapter** link or scroll down to that section to check for updates.

About Possible Exam Updates

Cisco introduced the CCNA and CCNP certifications in 1998. For the first 25 years of those certification tracks, Cisco typically updated the exams every 3 or 4 years. However, Cisco did not pre-announce the exam changes, and they felt very sudden. Usually, a new exam would be announced, with new exam topics, and you would have 3 to 6 months before your only option was to take the new exam. As a result, you could be studying with no idea about Cisco's plans, and the next day, you had a 3- to 6-month timeline to either pass the old exam or pivot and prepare for the new exam.

Thankfully, Cisco changed its exam release approach in 2023. The new approach, called the Cisco Certification Roadmap (https://cisco.com/go/certroadmap), includes these features:

- Cisco considers changes to all exam tracks (CCNA, CCNP Enterprise, CCNP Security, and so on) annually.

- Cisco uses a predefined annual schedule for each track, so even before any announcements, you know the timing of possible changes to the exam you are studying for.

- The schedule moves in a quarterly sequence:

    a. Privately review the exam to consider what to change.
    b. Publicly announce if an exam is changing, and if so, announce details like exam topics and release date.
    c. Release the new exam.

- Exam changes might not occur each year. If changes occur, Cisco characterizes them as minor (less than 20% change) or major (more than 20% change).

The specific dates for a given certification track can be confusing because Cisco organizes the work by fiscal year quarter. Figure 25-1 show an example of the quarters for the 2024 fiscal year. Cisco's fiscal year begins in August, so, for example, the first quarter (Q1) of fiscal year (FY) 2024 begins in August 2023.

| August 2023 – October 2023 **Q1FY24** | November 2023 – January 2024 **Q2FY24** | February 2024 – April 2024 **Q3FY24** | May 2024 – July 2024 **Q4FY24** |

Figure 25-1 *Cisco Fiscal Year and Months Example (Fiscal Year 2024)*

Over time, Cisco may make no changes in some years and minor changes in others.

Impact on You and Your Study Plan

Cisco's new policy helps you plan, but it also means that the exam might change before you pass the current exam. That impacts you and affects how we deliver this book to you. This chapter gives us a way to communicate in detail about changes as they occur. But you should watch other spaces as well. Bookmark and check these sites for news:

- **Cisco:** Check the Certification Roadmaps page, at https://cisco.com/go/certroadmap. Make sure to sign up for automatic notifications from Cisco on that page.

- **Publisher:** For information on new certification products, offers, discounts, and free downloads related to exam updates, visit https://www.ciscopress.com/newcert.

- **Cisco Learning Network:** Subscribe to the CCNA Community at http://cs.co/9780138217525, where you can expect to find ongoing discussions about exam changes over time. If you have questions, search for "roadmap" in the CCNA community, and if you do not find an answer, ask a new one!

As changes arise, we will update this chapter with more details about exam and book content. We will periodically publish updated versions of this chapter, listing our content plans. That details will likely include the following:

- Content removed, so if you plan to take the new exam version, you can ignore that content when studying

- New content planned for new exam topics, so you know what's coming

The remainder of this chapter shows the new content that may change over time.

News About the Next Exam Release

This statement was last updated in June 2023, before the publication of the *CCNP Enterprise Advanced Routing ENARSI 300-410 Official Cert Guide*, 2nd edition.

This version of this chapter has no news to share about the next exam release.

When the most recent version this chapter was published, the ENARSI 300-410 exam version number was Version 1.1.

Updated Technical Content

The current version of this chapter has no additional technical content.

Answers to the "Do I Know This Already?" Quiz Questions

Chapter 1

1. **b and d.** When two PCs are in the same subnet and communicate with each other, frames are sent directly to the destination PC, and ARP is used to get the MAC address of the destination PC.

2. **a and c.** When two PCs are in different subnets and communicate with each other, frames are sent to a default gateway, and ARP is used to get the MAC address of the default gateway.

3. **b.** You can verify the IP address configured on a router interface by using the **show ip interface** command.

4. **d.** The correct order is discover, offer, request, acknowledge (DORA).

5. **b.** To forward DHCP discover messages to a DHCP server in a different subnet, you use the **ip helper-address** command.

6. **c.** The **ip address dhcp** command is used to enable a router interface to obtain an IP address from a DHCP server.

7. **c.** Neighbor Discovery Protocol is used with IPv6 to determine the MAC address of a device in the same local area network.

8. **b and c.** With EUI-64, the interface MAC address is used with FFFE added to the middle, and the seventh bit from the left in the MAC address is flipped.

9. **a.** To enable SLAAC, you use the **ipv6 address autoconfig** command.

10. **a, b, and c.** SLAAC requires the prefix to be /64, the router must be sending RA messages, and IPv6 unicast routing must be enabled.

11. **d.** The **ipv6 nd other-config-flag** command is used to enable a router to inform clients that they need to get additional configuration information from a DHCPv6 server.

12. **c.** The **ipv6 dhcp relay destination** command enables you to configure a router interface as a DHCPv6 relay agent.

13. **c and d.** The router's data plane includes the Forwarding Information Base and the adjacency table.

14. **c.** The **show ip cef** command enables you to verify routes in the FIB.

15. **a, b, and c.** Updates from a neighbor, redistributed routes, and interfaces enabled for the routing process all populate a routing protocol's data structure.

16. **d.** eBGP has an AD of 20, OSPF 110, EIGRP internal 90, and RIP 120.

17. **b.** OSPF has a default AD of 110.

18. **a.** EIGRP has the lowest AD of the sources listed, and it is an AD of 90.

19. **d.** When multiple sources of information exist for the same prefix, you can manipulate the source that is used by adjusting the AD. Of the options listed, the best is to lower the IS-IS route to 80 so that IS-IS has the lowest AD.

20. **c.** You can create a floating static route by providing the static route with an AD higher than the preferred source of the route.

21. **d.** The router uses ARP to get the MAC address of the IP address in the destination of the packet when you create an IPv4 static route with an Ethernet interface designated instead of a next-hop IP address.

Chapter 2

1. **b.** EIGRP uses protocol number 88 for inter-router communication.

2. **c.** EIGRP uses the hello, request, reply, update, and query packet types.

3. **c.** The hello and hold timers can vary from neighbor to neighbor, as long as the hello packets are advertised before the hold timer expires.

4. **a.** An EIGRP successor is the next-hop router for the successor route (which is the loop-free route with the lowest path metric).

5. **a, b, c, and e.** The EIGRP topology table contains the destination network prefix, path attributes (hop count, minimum path bandwidth, total path delay), and a list of nearby EIGRP neighbors.

6. **b and d.** EIGRP uses multicast IP address 224.0.0.10 or MAC address 01:005E:00:00:0A when feasible.

7. **b and c.** The EIGRP process is initialized with the global configuration command **router eigrp** *as-number* (classic configuration) or **router eigrp** *process-name* (named mode configuration).

8. **b.** The EIGRP RID dynamically selects an IPv4 address as the RID.

9. **b.** The key-chain sequence number is a component of the hash that is built with the password.

10. **c.** The interface delay can be modified to change EIGRP path calculations without the path calculations of OSPF.

Chapter 3

1. **b.** EIGRP uses a default hello timer of 5 seconds for high-speed interfaces.

2. **f.** EIGRP uses a default hello timer of 60 seconds for low-speed interfaces.

3. **a.** EIGRP considers stable paths to be passive.

4. **c.** EIGRP sends out a query packet with the delay set to infinity to indicate that a route has gone active.

5. **b.** Summarization of prefixes involves using the interface command **ip summary-address** *eigrp as-number network subnet-mask* for classic EIGRP configuration.

6. **b.** Current IOS XE releases have automatic summarization disabled by default.

7. **a.** The EIGRP stub site function removes the limitations of a classic EIGRP stub router by allowing for routes from downstream routers to be advertised outside WAN interfaces.

8. **d.** EIGRP adds to the total path metric by adding delay to the path calculations. It never adds a raw number to the total path metric.

Chapter 4

1. **b.** The command **show ip eigrp neighbors** enables you to verify the routers that have formed EIGRP adjacencies with the local router, how long they have been neighbors, and the current sequence numbers of EIGRP packets.

2. **a, b, and d.** EIGRP neighbor relationships will not form if the neighbors have different AS numbers, K values, or authentication parameters.

3. **a.** Use the **show ip protocols** command to verify EIGRP K values.

4. **c.** Verify EIGRP authentication, split horizon, and configured EIGRP timers with the command **show ip eigrp interface detail**.

5. **a, b, and c.** Routes might be missing in an EIGRP autonomous system because an interface is not participating in the EIGRP process, a filter is filtering it, or there is an incorrect stub configuration.

6. **c.** The command **show ip protocols** enables you to verify whether any route filters have been applied to an EIGRP-enabled interface.

7. **a.** The command **show ip protocols** enables you to verify the maximum paths configured for load balancing and whether unequal-path load balancing has been enabled

8. **b.** When split horizon is enabled on the hub's mGRE interface, the spokes will not learn the routes of the other spokes

9. **a, b, and c.** When an EIGRP summary route is not showing up on the expected routers in the AS, you need to determine if you enabled route summarization on the correct interface, if you associated the summary route with the correct EIGRP autonomous system, and if you created the appropriate summary route.

10. **a.** When you have a discontiguous IP addressing scheme for your EIGRP AS, you need to disable autosummarization with the **no auto-summary** command.

Chapter 5

1. **e.** EIGRPv6 uses link-local addresses for a majority of communication, but it uses the destination IPv6 address FF02::A for hello, query, and update packets.

2. **c.** EIGRPv6 classic configuration requires identification with the command **ipv6 eigrp** *as-number* under the router.

3. **d.** All EIGRPv6 interfaces become active when the IPv6 address family has been identified under the process.

4. **a.** The command **show ipv6 protocols** can be used to verify whether any interfaces have been configured as passive interfaces.

5. **a.** Use the command **show ipv6 eigrp interfaces detail** to verify whether the local router is a stub router.

6. c. Use the **show ipv6 eigrp neighbors detail** command to verify whether a neighboring router is a stub router.

7. a and b. To verify which interfaces are participating in the named EIGRP IPv4 address family, use the commands **show ip eigrp interfaces** and **show eigrp address-family ipv4 interfaces**.

8. b and d. To form an EIGRPv6 neighborship, the AS numbers must match, and the K values must match.

9. a and c. The link-local address of the neighboring device and the FF02::A multicast address must be permitted within an IPv6 ACL for an EIGRPv6 neighbor adjacency to be formed.

10. a and c. If your router is only receiving connected routes and summary routes for a neighboring EIGRP router, it is possible that a distribute list has been applied to an interface or the **eigrp stub** command was configured on the router.

11. b. The EIGRP split-horizon rule will prevent the hub from advertising routes learned from the spokes to all the other spokes. Therefore, you would need to disable the split-horizon rule on the hub router.

Chapter 6

1. c. OSPF uses protocol number 89.

2. c. OSPFv2 uses five packet types for communication: hello, database description, link-state request, link-state update, and link-state acknowledgment.

3. a and d. OSPF uses the multicast IP address 224.0.0.5 or MAC address 01:00:5e:00:00:05 for the AllSPFRouters group.

4. b. A router needs to have an interface in Area 0 so that it can be an ABR.

5. b. An OSPF member router contains only a copy of the LSDB for the areas it participates in.

6. d. OSPF maintains eight states when dealing with a neighbor adjacency: Down, Attempt, Init, Two-way, ExStart, Exchange, Loading, and Full.

7. b. The OSPF process ID is locally significant and is not required to match for neighbor adjacency.

8. b. OSPF can be enabled with the interface parameter command **ip ospf** *process-id* **area** *area-id*.

9. b. An OSPF advertised default route always appears as an external route. The exception is when OSPF stub areas are used.

10. b. Serial point-to-point links are automatically set as the OSPF point-to-point network type, which does not have a designated router.

11. a. Setting the interface priority to 0 removes that interface from the DR election process.

12. c. The loopback address is classified as an OSPF loopback interface type, which is always advertised as a /32 address, regardless of the subnet mask.

13. c. The OSPF dead interval defaults to four times the hello interval.

14. a. You can enable OSPF authentication on all interfaces for an area by configuring the area authentication in the OSPF process and then configuring the password for an interface under each member interface.

Chapter 7

1.   d. OSPF uses six OSPF types for routing IPv4 packets (Types 1, 2, 3, 4, 5, and 7). Additional LSAs exist for IPv6 and MPLS.

2.   d. LSAs are deemed invalid when they reach 3600 seconds, at which point they are purged from the LSDB.

3.   c. A router LSA (Type 1) is associated with every OSPF-enabled interface.

4.   b. Network LSAs (Type 2) are not advertised outside the originating area. They are used with router LSAs (Type 1) to build summary LSAs (Type 3).

5.   c and d. An OSPF area blocks the injection of Type 5 LSAs into an area and inserts a default route instead. Because Type 5 LSAs are blocked, there is not a need for a Type 4 LSA, so those are blocked as well.

6.   b. A default route is considered optional in the OSPF NSSA configuration.

7.   a. IOS XE uses a reference bandwidth of 100 Mbps for dynamic metric assignment to an interface.

8.   b. OSPF inserts an additional check for the forwarding cost (which consists of the path metric to reach the ASBR). If the forwarding cost is the same, then both paths are installed. If the costs are different, then the path with the lowest forwarding metric is installed.

9.   a. While the number of network prefixes might remain the same, the numbers of Type 1 and Type 2 LSAs are reduced.

10.   b. You configure OSPF route summarization on the ASBR with the OSPF process configuration command **summary-address** *network subnet-mask*.

11.   b. Type 3 LSAs received from a nonbackbone area are inserted into the LSDB only for the source area. ABRs do not create Type 3 LSAs for the other areas.

12.   b. A virtual link is an OSPF mechanism that connects an ABR and another multi-area router to extend the backbone and enable proper LSA propagation.

Chapter 8

1.   a, b, and c. Mismatched timers, mismatched area numbers, and duplicate router IDs can prevent OSPF neighborships from forming.

2.   c and d. If your neighbors are stuck in the ExStart or Exchange state, you likely have an MTU mismatch.

3.   b. Use the command **show ip ospf interface** to verify the hello interval and the dead interval.

4.   b. You can use the command **debug ip ospf adj** to verify whether area numbers are mismatched.

5.   a. The broadcast OSPF network type is the default on LAN interfaces.

6. **c.** Type 3 LSAs describe routes outside the area but still within the OSPF routing domain (that is, inter-area routes).

7. **c.** An inbound ACL can prevent an OSPF neighborship from being formed.

8. **b and d.** Duplicate router IDs in the routing domain and a spoke being the DR in a hub-and-spoke topology are reasons any router may be missing routes in the local LSDB or the local routing table.

9. **c.** The command **default-information originate** is used to redistribute a static default route into OSPF.

10. **a and b.** A virtual link may not form if the router's interface IP address is being used in the **virtual-link** command or the local area ID is being used in the **virtual-link** command.

Chapter 9

1. **c.** The IANA has reserved protocol 89 for OSPF.

2. **c.** OSPFv2 and OSPFv3 use five packet types for communication: hello, database description, link-state request, link-state update, and link-state acknowledgement.

3. **c.** The command **ospfv3** *process-id* **ipv6 area** *area-id* needs to be placed under the interface.

4. **b.** Without an IPv4 address, the router ID is set to 0.0.0.0, and the router needs to be statically set to form an adjacency with another OSPFv3 router.

5. **b.** OSPFv3 requires an IPv6 link-local address in order to establish an adjacency to exchange IPv4 or IPv6 routers.

6. **a.** The link-local scope is limited to the flooding of LSAs between two routers sharing the same link.

Chapter 10

1. **a and c.** With **show ipv6 protocols**, you can verify the router ID as well as which interfaces are participating in the routing process.

2. **a and c.** You can verify the cost of the interface and the area the interface is participating in with the command **show ipv6 ospf interface brief**.

3. **b.** You can verify the configured hello and dead interval with the command **show ipv6 ospf interface**.

4. **c and d.** FF02::5 and FF02::6 are OSPFv3 multicast addresses.

5. **c.** Inter-area prefix link states describe prefixes outside an area but that are still within the OSPF routing domain.

6. **b.** Type 9 LSAs are only flooded on the local link and are not reflooded by other OSPF routers.

7. **b.** The command **show ipv6 ospf** enables you to verify whether an area is a stub area, a totally stubby area, an NSSA, or a totally NSSA.

8. **d.** The **show ipv6 ospf neighbor** command enables you to verify which routers the local router has formed neighbor adjacencies with.

9. **b and c.** You can verify which OSPFv3 address family an interface is participating in with the commands **show ospfv3 interface brief** and **show ospfv3 neighbor**.

10. **a.** Use the **debug ospfv3 hello** command to determine whether there is a mismatched stub area configuration.

Chapter 11

1. **a and c.** ASNs 64,512 through 65,535 are private ASNs within the 16-bit ASN range, and 4,200,000,000 through 4,294,967,294 are private ASNs within the extended 32-bit range.

2. **a.** Well-known mandatory attributes must be recognized by all BGP implementations and included with every prefix advertisement.

3. **b.** BGP neighbors are statically defined. There is a feature that supports dynamic discovery by one peer (which is beyond the scope of this book), but the other router must still statically configure the remote BGP peer.

4. **b.** BGP supports multi-hop neighbor adjacency.

5. **b.** The IPv4 address family is automatically initialized by default on IOS-based devices.

6. **b.** The command **show bgp** *afi safi* **neighbors** displays all the neighbors, their capabilities, session timers, and other useful troubleshooting information.

7. **c.** BGP uses three tables for storing BGP prefixes: Adj-RIB-in, Loc-RIB, and Adj-RIB-out.

8. **a.** A route learned from an eBGP peer is advertised to an iBGP peer.

9. **b.** A route learned from an iBGP peer is not advertised to an iBGP peer. This is a loop-prevention mechanism as the AS_Path is not prepended by an iBGP advertisement.

10. **a and c.** BGP route reflectors and confederations provide a method of scaling iBGP without requiring full-mesh connectivity within an AS.

11. **a.** The IPv6 address family does not exist by default on IOS-based devices.

12. **b.** BGP is considered a routing application and can exchange network prefixes (such as IPv6 prefixes) with a different session protocol (such as IPv4.)

Chapter 12

1. **b.** The command **aggregate-address** *network subnet-mask* **summary-only** creates a BGP aggregate and suppresses the component routes.

2. **b.** The BGP atomic aggregate is a path attribute that indicates a loss of path attributes when a prefix is summarized.

3. **a.** The correct source fields match against the 172.16.0.0 network range, and the destination fields match against any mask between /24 and /32.

4. **c.** Please refer to Example 12-33.

5. **a.** A distribution list and a prefix list cannot be used at the same time for a neighbor. All other filtering techniques can be combined.

6. **d.** The other communities listed here—No_Advertise, Internet, and No_Export—are common global communities.

7. c. When a peer advertises more routes than the maximum prefix count, the peer shuts down the BGP session with the status PfxCt.

8. a. BGP peer groups require all of the routers to have the same outbound routing policy. A BGP peer template allows for routers to have different outbound routing policies.

Chapter 13

1. a. Summarizing prefixes can shorten the prefix length, making a path less desirable compared to a longer prefix length.

2. b. BGP advertises only the path that the local router deems the best path.

3. b. Local preference is the second selection criterion for the BGP best path.

4. b. A router deletes paths from the Loc-RIB table for a network prefix only after the route (path) has been withdrawn by the advertising neighbor. A router withdraws a path for a prefix if it is no longer available or if it needs to advertise a different best path for that network prefix.

5. c. BGP uses AIGP after network origination.

6. a. BGP weight is locally significant to the local router and does not impact other routers in an organization as it is not advertised to other routers.

7. b. By default, MED can only be compared between paths that are advertised from the same AS. Other configuration options, such as **always-compare med**, can change this behavior.

8. b. BGP selects only one best path, even with multipathing enabled. BGP can present multiple paths to the RIB for installation.

Chapter 14

1. c and d. The commands **show bgp ipv4 unicast summary** and **show bgp ipv4 unicast neighbors** enable you to identify the IPv4 unicast BGP neighbor adjacencies that have been formed.

2. c. When the State/PfxRcd column has a number in it, you can conclude that a neighborship has been successful, and routes have been exchanged.

3. b and c. A BGP neighbor relationship will not form if packets are sourced from the wrong IP address. In addition, the neighbor must be reachable from a route in the routing table other than the default route.

4. c. BGP uses TCP port 179.

5. b. If a TCP session cannot be formed, the BGP state will be Idle.

6. b, c, and d. The split-horizon rule, a missing **network mask** command, or route filtering could prevent a route from being advertised to another BGP router.

7. b. You can verify the IPv4 BGP routes that have been learned from all BGP neighbors by using the command **show ip route bgp**.

8. c. When the next hop of a BGP-learned route is not reachable, the route is placed in the BGP table and not marked as valid.

9. **a.** The BGP split-horizon rule states that a BGP router that receives a BGP route from an iBGP peering shall not advertise that route to another router that is an iBGP peer.

10. **a and d.** eBGP has an AD of 20, and iBGP has an AD of 200.

11. **a.** The correct order for the BGP best-path process is weight, local preference, route origin, AS_Path, origin code, MED.

12. **a and c.** When using MP-BGP, you need to activate the IPv6 neighbors in address family configuration mode and define the IPv6 neighbors in router configuration mode.

13. **a.** You can verify the IPv6 unicast BGP routes that have been learned by using the command **show bgp ipv6 unicast**.

Chapter 15

1. **a.** IGPs use the destination field to select the smallest prefix length, whereas BGP uses the destination field to match the subnet mask for a route.

2. **b and c.** Please see Figure 15-3 for an explanation.

3. **a.** Any remaining routes are discarded, and routes that were processed earlier remain.

4. **a.** Because the route does not match the prefix list, sequence 10 does not apply, and the route moves on to sequence 20, which sets the metric to 200. It is implied that the route proceeds because it was modified.

5. **a.** Only one conditional match of the same type must occur in a route map. If there are multiple different conditional match types, then all the attributes must match to apply for that route map sequence.

6. **b.** Policy-based routing occurs for traffic that is received on a specific interface and is then conditionally forwarded. The routing table is used for forwarding all traffic, regardless of which interface the packet is received on.

Chapter 16

1. **b.** Route redistribution is not transitive on a single router.

2. **c.** The AD for external EIGRP routes is 170.

3. **a.** The default seed metric for OSPF is 20.

4. **a.** Sequential redistribution is allowed.

5. **b.** The AD for external OSPF routes is 110, which is the same as the AD for internal OSPF routes.

6. **d.** The default seed metric for EIGRP is infinity.

7. **d.** External OSPF routes redistribute into EIGRP with the basic redistribution command.

8. **b.** External OSPF routes are not redistributed into BGP with the basic redistribution command; the command **match external** must also be used.

Chapter 17

1. **a, b, and c.** You can solve multipoint redistribution issues by modifying the seed metrics of the redistributed routes, modifying the administrative distances of redistributed routes, and tagging routes as they are redistributed and then denying them from being redistributed back into the originating routing source.

2. **a.** You can solve suboptimal routing issues caused by redistribution by modifying the seed metrics of the redistributed routes.

3. **c.** The EIGRP command **distance 165 10.1.1.1 0.0.0.0** changes the AD to 165 for internal EIGRP routes learned from neighbor 10.1.1.1.

4. **a.** When redistributing into EIGRP, routes get an AD of 170 and a code of D EX.

5. **d.** When you redistribute in OSPF, by default the AD will be 110, and the code will be O E2.

6. **c.** For a route from one routing source to be redistributed into a different routing source, the route must be in the routing table on the router performing redistribution.

7. **a and b.** RIP and EIGRP have a default seed metric of unreachable.

8. **d.** OSPFv3 has a default seed metric of 20.

9. **d.** Route maps attached to the **redistribute** command are preferred over all the other options.

10. **a.** When redistributing OSPF into EIGRP, it is mandatory to specify a metric.

11. **c.** When redistributing classless networks into OSPFv2, you need to use the **subnets** keyword.

12. **c.** A directly connected route participating in the routing process is not included when redistributing from one IPv6 routing protocol into another IPv6 routing protocol.

13. **d.** A route will not be redistributed if it matches a deny entry in a route map.

14. **c.** The most likely reason of those listed is that the **subnets** keyword was not provided because when redistributing classless networks into OSPFv2, you need to use the **subnets** keyword.

Chapter 18

1. **a.** VRF instances divide a single physical router into multiple virtual routers.

2. **c and d.** You can associate an interface with a VRF instance by using the **ip vrf forwarding** *vrf-name* command or the **vrf forwarding** *vrf-name* command.

3. **d.** To verify the contents of a VRF instance routing table, you use the **show ip route vrf** *vrf-name* command.

4. **c.** When you associate an interface with a VRF instance, you receive a syslog message indicating that IPv4 has been disabled on an interface and any IPv4 addresses have been removed. Therefore, you need to configure IPv4 addressing on the interface.

5. **c.** Packets are forwarded in an MPLS domain using numbers that have been specified in a label.

6. **a.** An ingress edge LSR is responsible for adding MPLS labels to a packet.

7. **c.** Labels are exchanged with the Label Distribution Protocol (LDP).

8. **c.** PHP is used to improve the performance of MPLS by popping labels on the second-to-last router.

9. **b.** FEC refers to packets that are grouped together that will be forwarded in the same manner.

10. **e. imp-null** is used to inform the router that it should pop the label before forwarding the packet.

11. **b.** MPLS-TE uses RSVP.

12. **a and b.** LDP and VPN labels are used for MPLS Layer 3 VPNs.

13. **d.** Peerings between PE routers in MPLS Layer 3 VPNs use MP-BGP.

14. **a.** Customer routes are isolated on PE routers using VRF instances.

15. **d.** A route target is used to control the importing and exporting of routes.

16. **c.** A route distinguisher is used to uniquely identify IP addresses from other identical IP addresses.

Chapter 19

1. **a, b, c, d, and e.** GRE tunnels support the encapsulation of all the listed protocols.

2. **b.** NHRP, which is defined in standard RFC 2332, is used to map IP addresses to Frame Relay and ATM addresses.

3. **b.** DMVPN Phase 2 does not work well with summarized spoke addresses because of the lack of next-hop preservation.

4. **c.** DMVPN Phase 3 provides a hierarchical tunnel structure.

5. **a.** DMVPN supports multicast traffic across the tunnel interfaces.

6. **d.** There is no difference in the configuration on the hub router with DMVPN Phase 1 and DMVPN Phase 2.

7. **a.** In DMVPN Phase 3, the NHRP shortcut must be enabled on the spoke router's tunnel interface.

8. **b.** Spoke-to-spoke tunnels are formed only after the traffic between the spokes has started.

9. **b.** The message "Midchain parent maintenance for IP midchain out" indicates a recursive routing loop with a tunnel.

10. **a.** The default NHRP cache defaults to 2 hours (7200 seconds).

11. **b.** Network engineers commonly overlook the configuration of an IPv6 link-local address for the routing protocol.

Chapter 20

1. **d.** MPLS Layer 3 VPNs do not add encryption or checksums as part of their server. Data confidentiality is dependent on the SP's processes to ensure that data does not leak from one customer to a different one.

2. **c.** Perfect forward secrecy ensures that new session keys are derived independently of a previous key to ensure that the compromise of one key does not mean compromise of future keys.

3. **a.** There can be multiple peers and associated IP addresses in the IKEv2 keyring.

4. **b.** IPsec tunnel encryption involves the association of an IPsec profile to an tunnel interface. The IPsec profile consists of an IKEv2 profile and a transform set.

5. **a.** The command **tunnel protection ipsec profile** *profile-name* [**shared**] associates an IPsec profile to an interface.

6. **d.** The default tunnel replay window is set to 64 packets.

Chapter 21

1. **d.** The correct order of operations for an IPv4 ACL is top-down processing, immediate execution upon a match, implicit deny all.

2. **c.** Traffic is dropped when an ACL is applied to an interface but the packet does not match any of the entries in the ACL.

3. **b.** The ACL entry instance **20 permit tcp 10.1.1.0 0.0.0.63 host 192.0.2.1 eq 23**, when applied to an interface, permits Telnet traffic from any device with an IP address from 10.1.1.0 to 10.1.1.63 going to the device with IP address 192.0.2.1.

4. **c.** The command **ip access-group 100 in** filters ingress traffic using ACL 100 on an interface.

5. **d.** HTTPS uses a default port number of 443.

6. **a.** SSH uses a default port number of 22.

7. **b.** SNMP uses UDP port 161 by default.

8. **c.** DHCP uses UDP port numbers 67 and 68.

9. **b.** The correct order of operations for an IPv6 ACL is top-down processing, immediate execution upon a match, implicit permit ICMP, and implicit deny all.

10. **b and d.** The entry **deny ipv6 any any log** will deny and log all traffic that does not match an entry in the ACL, and ICMP Neighbor Discovery messages will also be denied.

11. **d.** The command **ipv6 traffic-filter ENARSI out** successfully filters egress traffic using an IPv6 ACL named ENARSI on an interface.

12. **d.** IP prefix list entry **ip prefix-list ENARSI permit 0.0.0.0/0** matches only the default route.

13. **a.** IP prefix list entry **ip prefix-list ENARSI permit 0.0.0.0/0 le 32** matches all routes.

14. **a.** Routes with an address from 192.168.0.0 to 192.168.15.255 with a subnet mask of 24 to 28 will match the prefix list **ip prefix-list ENARSI seq 35 deny 192.168.0.0/20 ge 24 le 28**.

Chapter 22

1. **d.** The command **aaa authentication login MANAGEMENT_ACCESS group radius local** configures a user-defined method list on a Cisco IOS device that uses the database on the device if the external server is not available for authentication.

2. **b.** The **local** keyword invokes the use of the local username and password database, so if it is checked and there is no username and password in the local database, authentication will fail.

3. c. Based on the scenario, the user will be required to use the username ENARSI with the password EXAM.

4. c. When you receive the error "Invalid AUTHEN packet (check keys)," the router or server is configured with the wrong pre-shared key.

5. a. If you need uRPF to match the return interface with the incoming interface and a default route, use the command **ip verify unicast source reachable-via rx allow-default.**

6. c. You use the **ip verify unicast source reachable-via any** command for uRPF if the traffic flow is asymmetric.

7. d. The command **show policy-map control-plane** is used to verify the number of packets that have conformed to a specific class map that you are using for CoPP.

8. b. A policy map is processed from top down, matching the first class map that applies.

9. d. When traffic does not match any of the user-defined class maps specified in the policy map, it is subject to the policy defined in the default class.

10. a. RA Guard is an IPv6 First-Hop Security feature that is used to block unwanted RA messages.

11. d. Source Guard is an IPv6 First-Hop Security feature that validates the source of IPv6 traffic and, if the source is not valid, blocks it.

12. d. RA Guard is configured inbound on an interface and supports host mode and router mode.

Chapter 23

1. a and c. 9600 baud and 1 stop bit are default serial terminal settings.

2. a. The command **transport input** enables you to define which protocols will be used for remote access to a Cisco device using vty lines.

3. b. The command **login local** enables you to specify that SSH access will be authenticated using the local database.

4. c. This command will copy an IOS image from the web server to the router.

5. c. The **no service timestamps** command will prevent timestamps from being displayed in syslog messages.

6. c. The **localtime** option is needed to display syslog messages using the local time instead of UTC time.

7. c. AUTHPRIV is a valid SNMP security level that provides authentication using a hashing algorithm such as SHA and encryption using an encryption algorithm such as AES.

8. a. To test one-way delay for voice packets, you need an IP SLA responder.

9. a. The command **show ip flow export** is used to verify the version of NetFlow that has been configured on a router.

10. c. The command **show flow monitor** is used to verify the flow exporter that has been assigned to a flow monitor.

11. d. Path Trace is a Cisco DNA Center Assurance tool that graphically shows the path that applications and services running on a client take through all the devices on the network to reach the destination.

GLOSSARY

NUMERICS

224.0.0.10 The multicast IPv4 address that EIGRP routers use to form neighbor adjacencies.

224.0.0.5 The All OSPF Routers multicast IPv4 address, listened for by all OSPF routers.

224.0.0.6 The All OSPF DR Routers multicast IPv4 address, listened to by DR and BDR routers.

A

AAA A framework that provides authentication, authorization, and accounting when securing the management plane.

access control list (ACL) A list that contains entries configured on a router or switch that can be used to identify traffic that will have a particular action applied to it, based on the service or feature that is using the list.

address family (named EIGRP/OSPFv3/MP-BGP) A method of configuring IPv4 and IPv6 routing services under the same routing process. IPv4 address families are used for IPv4 routing, and IPv6 address families are used for IPv6 routing.

Address Resolution Protocol (ARP) Defined in RFC 826, a protocol used on an Ethernet LAN by devices to determine the Layer 2 MAC address of a known Layer 3 IP address.

adjacency table A table used by CEF that stores the Layer 2 addressing for all FIB entries of next-hop devices.

administrative distance (AD) In Cisco routers, a means for one router to choose between multiple routes to reach the same subnet when those routes are learned by different routing protocols. The lower the administrative distance, the more preferred the source of the routing information.

ADVERTISE message The unicast message DHCPv6 servers send to respond to SOLICIT messages to offer addressing information to the DHCPv6 client.

APIPA *See* Automatic Private IP Addressing.

area border router (ABR) A router that connects an OSPF area to Area 0 (that is, the backbone area).

ARP *See* Address Resolution Protocol (ARP).

ARP cache A table that Ethernet-enabled devices use to maintain the IPv4-to-MAC address mappings.

AS_Path A BGP attribute used to track the autonomous systems a network has been advertised through as a loop prevention mechanism.

AS_Path ACL   An ACL based on regex for identifying BGP routes based on the AS_Path and used for direct filtering or conditional matching in a route map.

ASBR   *See* autonomous system boundary router (ASBR).

ASBR summary LSA   A Type 4 LSA that allows routers to locate an ASBR that is in a different OSPF area.

atomic aggregate   A BGP path attribute that indicates that a prefix has been summarized and the path information from component routes was not all included in the aggregate.

Authentication Header (AH)   A protocol that uses a digital signature similar to a checksum to ensure that the original data packet (before encapsulation/encryption) has not been modified.

Automatic Private IP Addressing (APIPA)   An IPv4 addressing method used by DHCPv4 clients when the DHCPv4 server is not available. The clients automatically assign themselves an IPv4 address in the 169.254.0.0/16 network.

autonomous system (AS)   A set of routers running the same routing protocol under a single realm of control and authority.

autonomous system boundary router (ASBR)   A router that redistributes external routes into an OSPF routing domain.

autonomous system number (ASN)   A number between 1 and 64,511 (public) and 64,512 and 65,535 (private) assigned to an autonomous system for the purpose of proper BGP operation.

autonomous system path   In BGP, a path through all the autonomous systems taken to reach a network on the Internet.

autosummarization   A routing protocol feature in which a router that connects to more than one classful network advertises summarized routes for each entire classful network when sending updates out interfaces connected to other classful networks.

B

backbone area   The OSPF Area 0 that connects to all other OSPF areas. The backbone area is the only area that should provide connectivity between all other OSPF areas.

backup designated router (BDR)   A backup pseudonode that maintains the network segment's state to replace the DR in the event of its failure.

BGP   *See* Border Gateway Protocol (BGP).

BGP community   A well-known BGP attribute that allows for identification of routes for later actions such as identification of source or route filtering/modification.

BGP confederation   A grouping of ASs that appear as a larger AS. A BGP confederation allows for scalability in an iBGP deployment.

BGP multihoming   The method of providing redundancy and optimal routing by adding multiple links to external autonomous systems.

BGP multipathing The presentation of multiple paths to the RIB so that traffic can be load balanced.

Bidirectional Forwarding Detection (BFD) A detection protocol that works with all media types, routing protocols, topologies, and encapsulations. It is used to quickly detect reachability failures between two routers in the same Layer 3 network so that network issues can be identified as soon as possible and so convergence can occur at a far faster rate.

Border Gateway Protocol (BGP) An exterior routing protocol designed to exchange prefix information between different autonomous systems. The information includes a rich set of characteristics called path attributes, which allows for great flexibility regarding routing choices.

boundary router A router that sits at the boundary of the routing domains and performs redistribution.

C

CE router The customer's router, which is connected to the PE router of the MPLS domain.

Cisco DNA Center Assurance A component of Cisco DNA Center that enables you to predict problems faster through proactive monitoring and receive insights from network devices, network applications, network services, and clients.

Cisco Express Forwarding (CEF) An optimized Layer 3 forwarding path through a router or switch. CEF optimizes routing table lookups by creating a special, easily searched tree structure based on the contents of the IP routing table. The forwarding information is called the Forwarding Information Base (FIB), and the cached adjacency information is called the adjacency table.

classful A convention for discussing and thinking about IP addresses by which Class A, B, and C default network prefixes (of 8, 16, and 24 bits, respectively) are considered.

classless A convention for IP addresses in which Class A, B, and C default network prefixes (of 8, 16, and 24 bits, respectively) are ignored and subnetting is performed.

class map A construct used with CoPP and QoS to define a traffic class.

Client 360 A dashboard within Cisco DNA Center Assurance that displays details about client devices.

C-network The customer's network connected to an MPLS domain.

Command Runner A Cisco DNA Center tool that allows you to send diagnostic CLI commands to your devices.

control plane The plane of operation that encompasses protocols used between routers and switches. These protocols include, for example, routing protocols and Spanning Tree Protocol (STP). Also, a router's or switch's processor and memory reside in the control plane.

Control Plane Policing (CoPP) A policy applied to traffic destined to or sourced by the router's control plane CPU to limit known traffic to a given rate while protecting the CPU from unexpected extreme rates of traffic that could impact the stability of the router.

D

data availability   The protection of a network that allows for the secure transport of data.

data confidentiality   The protection of data so that it is viewable only by authorized users.

data integrity   The protection of data so that it can be modified only by authorized users.

data plane   In IP routing, a set of processes that forward packets through a router or a multi-layer switch.

dead interval   The amount of time required for a hello packet to be received for the neighbor to be deemed healthy. Upon receipt, the value resets and decrements toward zero.

designated router (DR)   A pseudonode to manage the adjacency state with other routers on the broadcast network segment.

destination protocol   A routing protocol and process that receives network prefixes from the routing protocol sending the network prefixes.

Device 360   A dashboard within Cisco DNA Center Assurance that displays details about network devices.

DHCP   *See* Dynamic Host Configuration Protocol (DHCP).

DHCPACK   A DHCPv4 unicast message used by a DHCPv4 server to acknowledge that the addressing information is reserved for the client.

DHCPDISCOVER   A DHCPv4 broadcast message used by a client to locate a DHCPv4 server.

DHCPOFFER   A DHCPv4 unicast message used by a DHCPv4 server to provide a client with addressing information.

DHCPREQUEST   A DHCPv4 broadcast message used by a client to request the addressing information that was provided in the offer.

DHCPv4 relay agent   A device such as a router or multilayer switch that is able to relay DHCPv4 DISCOVER messages to a DHCPv4 server in a different IPv4 network.

DHCPv6 Guard   A security feature designed to ensure that rogue DHCPv6 servers are not able to hand out addresses to clients, redirect client traffic, or starve out the DHCPv6 server and cause a DoS attack.

DHCPv6 relay agent   A device such as a router or multilayer switch that is able to relay DHCPv6 SOLICIT messages to a DHCPv6 server in a different IPv6 network.

Dijkstra's shortest path first (SPF) algorithm   The algorithm used by link-state routing protocols.

discontiguous network   In IPv4, an internetwork design in which packets forwarded between two subnets of a single classful network must pass through the subnets of another classful network. In OSPF, a network where Area 0 is not contiguous, which generally results in routes not being advertised pervasively through the OSPF routing domain.

distribute list   A list used for filtering routes with an ACL for a specific BGP neighbor.

DMVPN Phase 1   A DMVPN topology in which the spokes only establish tunnels with the DMVPN hubs.

DMVPN Phase 3   A DMVPN topology in which the spokes can establish dynamic spoke-to-spoke tunnels between sites as needed.

DORA   The DHCP process a client and server use to determine the appropriate IPv4 addressing information the client needs. Stands for Discover, Offer, Request, Ack.

Dynamic Host Configuration Protocol (DHCP)   A standard (RFC 2131) protocol by which a host can dynamically broadcast a request for a server to assign to it an IP address, along with other configuration settings, including a subnet mask and default gateway IP address.

Dynamic Multipoint VPN (DMVPN)   A VPN architecture that combines multipoint GRE tunnels, IPsec, and NHRP for dynamic VPN tunnel creation and registration.

E

eBGP session   A BGP session maintained with BGP peers from a different autonomous system.

edge LSR   A router that sits at the edge of the MPLS domain and adds labels to packets that are entering the MPLS domain (known as an ingress LSR), removes labels from packets that will be leaving the MPLS domain (known as an egress LSR), and forwards packets as needed based on labels or the lack of labels.

egress LSR   A router at the edge of the MPLS domain that removes labels from packets that are leaving the MPLS domain.

EIGRP classic configuration   An EIGRP configuration mode in which most of the configuration resides under the EIGRP process, but some settings are configured under the interface configuration submode.

EIGRP named mode configuration   An EIGRP configuration mode that provides a hierarchical configuration and stores settings in three subsections: address family, interface, and topology.

EIGRP stub router   An EIGRP feature by which a router advertises to all other neighbors that it is isolated and should not be queried when routes go active.

EIGRP stub-site router   An EIGRP router that advertises to all other upstream neighbors that it is isolated but provides a mechanism to prevents transit routing through its WAN interfaces while still allowing connectivity to local downstream neighbors.

encapsulating interface   The interface that receives tunneled traffic from the underlay network and removes the outer IP headers, or the interface that receives traffic and adds outer IP headers for the underlay network.

Encapsulating Security Payload (ESP)   A protocol that ensures that the original payload (before encapsulation) maintains data confidentiality by encrypting the payload and adding a new set of headers during transport across a public network.

EUI-64   A specification for the 64-bit interface ID in an IPv6 address, composed of the first half of a MAC address (with the seventh bit flipped), the added hex values FFFE, and by the last half of the MAC address.

extended ACL   An ACL that is able to match packets based on multiple criteria, such as source and destination IP address, source and destination port numbers, protocols, and QoS parameters.

Exterior Gateway Protocol (EGP)   A routing protocol that was designed to exchange routing information between different autonomous systems. EGP has been replaced by BGP and is no longer supported in Cisco IOS.

external BGP (eBGP)   A term that refers to how a router views a BGP peer relationship, in which the peer is in another AS.

external LSA   A Type 5 LSA that advertises an external route into a routing domain and indicates the router acting as the ASBR for that route.

external OSPF route   A route that is injected into the OSPF routing domain that is learned from outside the native OSPF process.

F

feasibility condition   The condition which says that for a route to be considered a backup route, the reported distance received for that route must be less than the feasible distance calculated locally. This logic guarantees a loop-free path.

feasible distance   The metric value for the lowest-metric path to reach a destination.

feasible successor   A route that satisfies the feasibility condition that is maintained as a backup route.

FF02::A   The multicast IPv6 address that EIGRP routers use to form neighbor adjacencies.

FIB   *See* Forwarding Information Base (FIB).

Flexible NetFlow   A version of NetFlow that allows you to customize traffic analysis parameters for your specific requirements.

flow cache   A temporary storage location for captured flows.

flow exporter   A component of Flexible NetFlow that identifies where captured flows will be exported to.

flow monitor   A component of Flexible NetFlow that is applied to an interface to identify the applied flow record and flow exporter.

flow record   A record that defines what will be captured when using Flexible NetFlow. Cisco IOS supports predefined records as well as user-defined records.

Forwarding Information Base (FIB)   A CEF database that contains Layer 3 information, similar to the information found in an IP routing table. In addition, an FIB contains information about multicast routes and directly connected hosts.

front-door VRF   A VRF that is used to isolate the encapsulating interface to prevent issues with recursive routing or identifying the outbound interface.

G

ge (prefix list)   An indicator that the mask of a network must be greater than or equal to the specified value in order to be a match to the prefix list.

global unicast address   A type of unicast IPv6 address that has been allocated from a range of public globally unique IP addresses, as registered through ICANN, its member agencies, and other registries or ISPs.

GRE tunnel   A tunnel that supports a variety of protocols (IPv4, IPv6, DECnet, MPLS) over an IP-based network.

H

hello interval   The frequency at which hello packets are advertised out an interface.

hello packet   A packet that is sent out to detect neighbors for establishing adjacency and ensuring that neighbors are still available.

hello timer   The amount of time between hello packets being advertised out an interface.

hold timer   The amount of time required for a hello packet to be received for the neighbor to be deemed healthy. Upon receipt, the value resets and decrements toward zero.

I

iBGP session   A BGP session maintained with BGP peers from the same autonomous system.

implicit deny   An invisible entry at the end of an ACL, a prefix list, a route map, or a VACL that automatically prevents all traffic or routes that do not match any of the earlier entries.

implicit permit   An invisible permanent statement in an IPv6 ACL that comes before the implicit deny to allow ND traffic. The implicit permit statements are **permit icmp any any nd-na** and **permit icmp any any nd-na**.

imp-null   A value in the MPLS LDP binding table which indicates that the label should be popped (removed) before the packet is forwarded.

ingress LSR   A router at the edge of the MPLS domain that adds labels to packets that are entering the MPLS domain.

inter-area route   An OSPF route learned from an ABR from another area. Such routes are built based on Type 3 LSAs.

interface priority   The reference value for an interface to deem preference for being elected as the designated router.

intermediate LSR   A router that sits within the MPLS domain that primarily forwards packets using label information.

Internet service provider (ISP)   An organization that provides Internet services to its customers.

intra-area route   An OSPF route learned from routers within the same area. Such routes are built based on Type 1 and Type 2 LSAs.

IP SLA   An IOS tool that you can use to test network connectivity and measure network performance.

IPv6 ACL   An ACL that is used to identify IPv6 traffic based on multiple criteria, such as source and destination IP addresses, source and destination port numbers, protocols, and QoS parameters and either allow or prevent the traffic.

IPv6 neighbor discovery inspection/IPv6 snooping   A security feature that learns and populates a binding table for stateless autoconfiguration addresses. It analyzes ND messages and places valid bindings in the binding table and drops all messages that do not have valid bindings. A valid ND message is one where the IPv6-to-MAC mapping can be verified.

K

K values   A set of values that EIGRP uses to calculate the best path.

keychain   A collection of one or more keys (that is, passwords) used for authentication, where each key has an associated key ID and key string.

key ID (keychain)   The numeric value that identifies the key used for authentication.

key string (keychain)   The alphanumeric string of characters that is being used for authentication. This is not to be confused with the name of the keychain.

L

label   A 4-byte shim header added between the packet and frame headers that is used for forwarding the packet from router to router through the MPLS domain.

Label Distribution Protocol (LDP)   A protocol used between MPLS-enabled routers to generate and exchange labels that will be used to forward packets in the MPLS domain.

Label Forwarding Information Base (LFIB)   A data plane table that is used to forward labeled packets.

Label Information Base (LIB)   A control plane table that stores label information.

label stack   Two labels (VPN label and LDP label) added to a packet to forward the packet through the MPLS Layer 3 VPN.

label-switched path (LSP)   The cumulative labeled path (sequence of routers) that a labeled packet takes through the MPLS domain.

label switching router (LSR)   A router in an MPLS domain that forwards packets using label information.

LDP label   *See* label.

le (prefix list)   An indicator that the mask of a network must be less than or equal to the specified value in order to be a match to a prefix list.

level 5 encryption   On Cisco IOS devices, a type of encryption in which passwords are hashed using MD5.

level 7 encryption   On Cisco IOS devices, a type of encryption in which passwords are encrypted using a weak Type 7 encryption.

level 8 encryption   On Cisco IOS devices, a type of encryption in which passwords are hashed using SHA 256.

line   A configuration mode that can be used to manage a Cisco IOS device (for example, a console line or a vty line).

link-local address   A type of unicast IPv6 address that represents an interface on a single data link. Packets sent to a link-local address cross only that particular link and are never forwarded to other subnets by a router. Used for communications, such as neighbor discovery, that do not need to leave the local link.

link-state advertisement (LSA)   A class of OSPF data structures that hold topology information. LSAs are held in memory in the LSDB and communicated over the network in LSU messages.

local AS community   A BGP community that does not allow for network prefixes to be advertised to eBGP peers or another member AS.

LOCAL_PREF   A BGP path attribute that is communicated throughout a single AS to signify which route of multiple possible routes is the best route to be taken when leaving that AS. A larger value is considered to be better.

Loc-RIB   The main BGP table that contains all of the active BGP prefixes and path attributes that is used to select the best path and install routes into the RIB.

login   A Cisco IOS command used on lines to define that authentication is required, using a line password, to access the line for management purposes.

login local   A Cisco IOS command used on lines to define that authentication is required, using the local username and password database, to access the line for management purposes.

LSP   *See* label-switched path (LSP).

LSR   *See* label switching router (LSR).

M

maximum paths   The number of paths that a router can use to load balance traffic.

method list   In AAA authentication, a list of methods, such as a RADIUS server, the type of authentication, the local database, and the line passwords, that can be used to successfully authenticate. Typically listed in the sequence in which they will be performed.

metric   With routing protocols, a measurement of favorability that determines which entry will be installed in a routing table if more than one router is advertising that exact network and mask with one routing protocol.

MPLS Layer 3 VPN   A VPN that provides peer-to-peer connectivity between private customer sites across a shared network such as an ISP.

MULTI_EXIT_DISC (MED)   A BGP path attribute that allows routers in one autonomous system to set a value and advertise it into a neighboring AS, impacting the decision process in that neighboring autonomous system. A smaller value is considered better. Also called the BGP metric or multi-exit discriminator (MED).

multipoint redistribution   A process in which redistribution occurs at multiple points between two different routing protocols.

Multiprotocol BGP (MP-BGP)   An updated version of BGPv4 that includes components supporting the routing of both IPv4 and IPv6 networks.

Multiprotocol Label Switching (MPLS)   A switching method that uses labels to forward packets instead of the packets' destination IP addresses.

mutual redistribution   A process in which two routing protocols redistribute into each other in both directions on the same router.

N

named ACL   An access list that identifies the various statements/entries in the ACL based on a name rather than a number.

named EIGRP   An EIGRP configuration approach that allows you to configure all EIGRP commands under a single hierarchical configuration.

Neighbor Discovery (ND)   A protocol used in IPv6 for many functions, including address autoconfiguration; duplicate address detection; router, neighbor, and prefix discovery; neighbor address resolution; and parameter discovery.

NetFlow   A Cisco IOS feature that collects detailed information about traffic flows on routers and high-end switches. Collected information can optionally be sent to a NetFlow collector (flow exporter), which can produce reports about the traffic flows.

network command   A command used to enable the RIPv2, EIGRP for IPv4, and OSPFv2 routing processes on an interface.

network LSA   A Type 2 LSA that advertises the routers connected to the DR pseudonode. Type 2 LSA remains within the OSPF area of origination.

Next Hop Resolution Protocol (NHRP)   A protocol that provides address resolution for hosts on nonbroadcast multi-access (NBMA) networks.

next-hop server (NHS)   A server that is responsible for registering addresses and responding to any queries.

NHRP redirect   An NHRP message that is sent toward the source spoke upon detecting the hairpinning network traffic out of the DMVPN tunnel interface.

NHRP shortcut   The method of installing an NHRP learned route into the router's global RIB.

No_Advertise   A BGP community that does not allow for the network prefix to be advertised to any BGP peer (eBGP or iBGP).

No_Export community   A BGP community that does not allow for the network prefix to be advertised to an eBGP peer. Prefix advertisement to another Member_AS is acceptable.

NSSA   *See* OSPF not-so-stubby area (NSSA).

NSSA external LSA   A Type 7 LSA that allows for an external route to exist in an OSPF totally NSSA or NSSA.

O

Object Tracking   An IOS feature in which IOS repeatedly checks the current state of some item so that other items can then react to a change in that state. For example, Object Tracking can track the state of IP SLA operations, with static routes and policy routes reacting to a change in the Object Tracking feature.

offset list   A list used for increasing the delay for received or advertised EIGRP routes.

optional nontransitive   BGP path attributes that might be recognized by a BGP implementation and are not advertised between autonomous systems.

optional transitive   BGP path attributes that might be recognized by a BGP implementation and are advertised between autonomous systems.

origin authentication   Authentication that is accomplished through Pre-Shared Key (static) or certificate-based authentication (dynamic).

OSPF ABR   *See* area border router (ABR).

OSPF area   A group of routers and links, identified by a 32-bit area number, whose detailed topology information OSPF shares among all routers in the group. Routers inside an area learn full detailed topology information about the area; this detailed information is not advertised outside the area.

OSPF ASBR   *See* autonomous system boundary router (ASBR).

OSPF interface table   *See* interface table.

OSPF link-state database   *See* link-state database.

OSPF neighbor table   *See* neighbor table.

OSPF not-so-stubby area (NSSA)   An OSPF area that does not allow external routes (Type 4 or Type 5 LSAs) in it. This area allows for routes to be redistributed into it.

OSPF stub area   An OSPF area that does not allow for external routes (Type 4 or Type 5 LSAs) in it. A default route is advertised by the ABR in lieu of the blocked prefixes.

OSPF totally NSSA   An OSPF area that does not allow for inter-area or external routes (Type 3, Type 4, or Type 5 LSAs) in it. A default route is advertised by the ABR in lieu of the blocked prefixes. This area allows for routes to be redistributed into this area.

OSPF totally stubby area   An OSPF area that does not allow for inter-area or external routes (Type 3, Type 4, or Type 5 LSAs) in. A default route is advertised by the ABR in lieu of the block prefixes.

OSPFv3   The version of OSPF that supports IPv6 routing.

OSPFv3 ABR   *See* area border router (ABR).

OSPFv3 address family   *See* address family.

OSPFv3 area   *See* OSPF area.

OSPFv3 ASBR   *See* autonomous system boundary router (ASBR).

OSPFv3 interface table   A table that lists all the interfaces participating in an OSPFv3 routing process.

OSPFv3 link-state database   A table that lists all the LSAs that an OSPFv3 router is aware of.

OSPFv3 neighbor table   A table that lists all the OSPFv3 neighbors that have been formed.

P

P router   The provider's routers inside an MPLS domain.

packet forwarding   The process of forwarding packets through a router. Also called IP routing.

passive interface   An interface that has been enabled with a routing protocol to advertise its associated interfaces into its RIB but that does not establish neighborship with other routers associated to that interface.

Path Trace   A Cisco DNA Center tool that graphically traces the path that applications and services running on a client take through all the devices on the network to reach the destination.

path vector routing protocol   A routing protocol that selects the best path based on path attributes.

PE router   A provider's router connected to the CE router of the customer's network.

peer group   A feature that allows for the grouping of BGP peers based on similar BGP session information and outbound routing policy.

peer templates   A feature that allows for the modular reuse of BGP settings between iBGP or eBGP peers.

Penultimate Hop Popping (PHP)   An MPLS efficiency feature that allows the next-to-last router in the LSP to remove the label so the last router in the LSP does not have to.

periodic rekey   The process of issuing new security keys between endpoints every specified time interval or within a specific volume of traffic.

P-network   The provider's network in an MPLS domain.

Policy-based routing   A method of forwarding packets down a different path, based on the characteristics of the traffic.

policy map   A construct used with CoPP to associate the traffic class (as defined by the class map) with one or more policies resulting in a service policy.

pop   To remove an MPLS label from a packet.

port 22   The well-known port number used by SSH.

port 23   The well-known port number used by Telnet.

prefix list   A list used to select routes based on binary patterns, specifically the high-order bit pattern, high-order bit count, and an optional prefix-length parameter.

proxy ARP   A router feature used when a router sees an ARP request searching for an IP host's MAC address when the router believes the IP host could not be on that LAN because the host is in another subnet. If the router has a route to reach the subnet where the ARP-determined host resides, the router replies to the ARP request with the router's MAC address.

push   To add an MPLS label to a packet.

R

RA   *See* router advertisement (RA).

RA Guard   A feature that analyzes RAs and can filter out unwanted RAs from unauthorized devices.

RADIUS   A standards-based protocol used to communicate with AAA servers.

recursive routing   A routing loop for encapsulated interfaces in which the preferred path of the router is to take the tunnel rather than the underlay network. This then brings down the tunnel interface.

redistribution   The process on a router of taking the routes from the IP routing table, as learned by one routing protocol, and injecting routes for those same subnets into another routing protocol.

regular expression (regex)   A method of parsing and matching with search patterns using special key characters.

replay detection   A method of sending sequence numbers to protect against hackers trying to capture and insert network traffic.

REPLY message   A message that a DHCPv6 server sends to finalize the DHCPv6 addressing process.

reported distance   The distance reported by a router to reach a prefix. The reported distance value is the feasible distance for the advertising router.

REQUEST message   A message that a DHCPv6 client sends to a DHCPv6 server to confirm the addresses provided and any other parameters.

Resource Reservation Protocol (RSVP)   A control plane signaling protocol used between systems for MPLS-TE (Traffic Engineering) that enables the systems to request resource reservations from the network.

RIB   *See* Routing Information Base (RIB).

route distinguisher   A unique value used with MPLS and VRF that is appended to IPv4 and IPv6 addresses to ensure uniqueness if there are overlapping customer address spaces.

route map   A feature used in BGP (and other IGP components) that allows for filtering or modification of routes using a variety of conditional matching.

route reflector   A router that is configured to advertise routes learned from an iBGP peer to another iBGP peer.

route reflector client   A router that receives routes that are advertised from a route reflector.

route tag   A field in a route entry in a routing update that is used to associate a generic number with a route. It is used when passing routes between routing protocols, allowing an intermediate routing protocol to pass information about a route that is not natively defined to that intermediate routing protocol. Often used for identifying certain routes for filtering by a downstream routing process.

route target   A unique value used with MPLS to control the import and export process for customer VRF routes. It ensures that what has been exported from a customer VRF instance on a PE router and sent across the MPLS environment is successfully imported into the correct customer VRF instance on another PE router.

router advertisement (RA)   In IPv6, a message that an IPv6 router uses to send information about itself to nodes and other routers connected to that router.

router ID (RID)   A 32-bit number that uniquely identifies the router in a routing domain.

router LSAs   A Type 1 LSA that is a fundamental building block and represents all OSPF-enabled interface. Type 1 LSAs remain within the OSPF area of origination.

router solicitation (RS)   An IPv6 message, part of the Neighbor Discovery Protocol (NDP), used by a host to request that the routers on the same data link announce their presence, IPv6 addresses, and all prefix/length combinations using an RA message.

Routing Information Base (RIB)   The IP routing table.

routing loop   A situation in which traffic is routed back in the direction that it came from or in a circular pattern through the network so that it never reaches the intended destination.

routing table   The table a router uses to determine the most appropriate way to forward a packet.

S

Secure Shell (SSH)   A secure protocol that can be used to remotely manage a Cisco IOS device.

security association (SA)   A component of IPsec architecture that contains the security parameters agreed upon between the two endpoint devices.

seed metric   A baseline value used by the destination protocol to allow for the calculation of a best path for that network prefix.

sequential protocol redistribution   A method of redistribution of network prefixes between multiple routing protocols over a series of routers.

shortest path first tree (SPT)   A router's view of the topology to reach all destinations in the topology, where the local router is the top of the tree, and all the destinations are the branches of the tree.

single-point redistribution   A situation in which redistribution occurs at a single point between two different routing protocols.

SNMPv2c   A version of SNMP that uses community strings.

SNMPv3   A version of SNMP that can use hashing algorithms and encryption algorithms to enhance SNMP security.

SOLICIT message   A message that a DHCPv6 client sends to locate DHCPv6 servers using the multicast address FF02::1:,2 which is the all DHCPv6 servers multicast address.

Source Guard   A Layer 2 snooping interface feature for validating the source of IPv6 traffic.

source protocol   A routing protocol and process to provide network prefixes to the routing protocol receiving the network prefixes.

split horizon   A routing loop-prevention mechanism that prevents a route from being advertised out of the same interface on which it was learned.

split-horizon rule   A loop-prevention mechanism that keeps iBGP routers from advertising BGP learned routes to other iBGP neighbors.

SSH   *See* Secure Shell (SSH).

standard ACL   A list of IOS global configuration commands that can match only a packet's source IP address for the purpose of deciding which packets to discard and which ones to allow.

stateful DHCPv6   A term used in IPv6 to contrast with stateless DHCP. Stateful DHCP keeps track of which clients have been assigned which IPv6 addresses (state information).

stateless address autoconfiguration (SLAAC)   A method used by an IPv6 host to determine its own IP address, without DHCPv6, by using NDP and the modified EUI-64 address format.

stateless DHCPv6   A term used in IPv6 to contrast with stateful DHCP. Stateless DHCP servers don't lease IPv6 addresses to clients. Instead, they supply other useful information, such as DNS server IP addresses, but with no need to track information about the clients (state information).

static route   A route manually configured by an administrator using the **ip route** or **ipv6 route** command.

stub   *See* stub router.

stub area   An OSPF area into which external (Type 5) LSAs are not introduced by its ABRs; instead, the ABRs originate and inject default routes into the area.

stub router   A router running EIGRP that limits EIGRP DUAL algorithm computations and reduces the EIGRP query scope.

stuck in active (SIA)   An event that occurs when an EIGRP query is sent to downstream neighbors and the router doesn't receives a reply within 90 seconds.

subnets keyword   A keyword used with OSPF so that classful and classless networks are redistributed.

successor   The first next-hop router for the successor route.

successor route   The route with the lowest-path metric to reach a destination.

summarization   A method of reducing the routing table by advertising a less specific network prefix rather than multiple more specific network prefixes.

summary LSA   A Type 3 LSA that contains the routes learned from another area. Type 3 LSAs are generated on ABRs.

syslog   A system message log that is generated by a switch and can be collected locally or sent to and collected on a remote server.

T

TACACS+   A Cisco-proprietary protocol used to communicate with AAA servers.

Telnet   An unsecure protocol that sends data in plaintext and that can be used to remotely manage a Cisco IOS device.

time-based ACL   An access control list that can permit or deny defined traffic based on time of day and day of week.

time-to-live (TTL)   A field in an IP header that is decremented at each pass through a Layer 3 forwarding device.

topology table   A table used by EIGRP that maintains all network prefixes, advertising EIGRP neighbors for that prefix and path metrics for calculating the best path.

totally not-so-stubby (NSSA) area   A type of OSPF NSSA area for which neither external (Type 5) LSAs nor Type 3 summary LSAs are introduced; instead, the ABRs originate and inject default routes into the area. External routes can be injected into a totally NSSA area.

totally stubby area   A type of OSPF stub area for which neither external (Type 5) LSAs nor Type 3 Summary LSAs are introduced; instead, the ABRs originate and inject default routes into the area. External routes cannot be injected into a totally stubby area.

transit routing   Routing in which traffic is allowed to flow from one external autonomous system through your autonomous system to reach a different external autonomous system.

time-to-live (TTL)   In BGP, a value that identifies the lifetime of a BGP message in router hops. For eBGP peers, it is set to 1 by default, and for iBGP peers, it is set to 255 by default.

Type 5 LSA   *See* external LSA.

U

Unicast Reverse Path Forwarding (uRPF)   A security feature that helps limit or even eliminate spoofed IP packets on a network. This is accomplished by examining the source IP address of an ingress packet and determining whether it is valid. If it is valid, the packet is forwarded. If it is not valid, the packet is discarded.

V

variance value   With EIGRP, the feasible distance (FD) for a route multiplied by the EIGRP variance multiplier. Any feasible successor's FD with a metric below the EIGRP variance value is installed into the RIB.

virtual link   A virtual tunnel that allows Area 0 to be extended further into the network and that is often used to resolve discontiguous networks.

virtual routing and forwarding (VRF)   A router virtualization technology that allows you to create multiple routing tables on a single router and isolate them from each other.

VPN label   A label used in an MPLS Layer 3 VPN to forward packets from one PE router to another PE router.

VPNv4 address   An address made up of a route distinguisher (RD) and an IP address that is used in MPLS Layer 3 VPNs to ensure that customer information is unique within the MPLS domain.

VRF-Lite   A method for creating multiple routing domains on the same routers in a network by using VRF.

W

weight   A local Cisco-proprietary BGP attribute that is not advertised to any peers. A larger value is considered to be better.

well-known discretionary   BGP path attributes recognized by all BGP implementations that may or may not be advertised to other peers.

well-known mandatory   BGP path attributes recognized by all BGP implementations that must be advertised to other peers.

wide metrics   A method of advertising and identifying interface speeds and delay that accounts for higher-bandwidth interfaces (20 Gbps and higher).

Index

B

I

J-K

M

O

R

S

W

Register your product at **ciscopress.com/register** to unlock additional benefits:

- Save 35%* on your next purchase with an exclusive discount code
- Find companion files, errata, and product updates if available
- Sign up to receive special offers on new editions and related titles

Get more when you shop at **ciscopress.com**:

- Everyday discounts on books, eBooks, video courses, and more
- Free U.S. shipping on all orders
- Multi-format eBooks to read on your preferred device
- Print and eBook Best Value Packs

Cisco Press